CHESHIRE AND BURN'S
MODERN LAW OF REAL PROPERTY

First Edition	September	1925
Second Edition	September	1927
Third Edition	February	1933
Fourth Edition	July	1944
Second Impression	August	1945
Third Impression	January	1947
Fourth Impression	December	1947
Sixth Edition	September	1949
Second Impression	July	1952
Seventh Edition	September	1954
Second Impression	September	1956
Eighth Edition	March	1958
Second Impression	January	1961
Ninth Edition	March	1962
Second Impression	February	1964
Third Impression	August	1966
Tenth Edition	May	1967
Second Impression	April	1970
Eleventh Edition	April	1972
Second Impression	May	1974
Twelfth Edition	May	1976
Thirteenth Edition	August	1982
Second Impression	August	1983
Third Impression	January	1987
Fourteenth Edition	June	1988
Fifteenth Edition	July	1994
Sixteenth Edition	September	2000
Seventeenth Edition	August	2006

CHESHIRE AND BURN'S

MODERN LAW OF REAL PROPERTY

Seventeenth Edition

E H BURN BCL, MA

Barrister and Honorary Bencher of Lincoln's Inn

Professor of Law, The City University

Emeritus Student of Christ Church, Oxford

J CARTWRIGHT BCL, MA

Solicitor

Reader, Oxford University

Student and Tutor in Law, Christ Church, Oxford

OXFORD
UNIVERSITY PRESS

OXFORD
UNIVERSITY PRESS

Great Clarendon Street, Oxford OX2 6DP

Oxford University Press is a department of the University of Oxford.
It furthers the University's objective of excellence in research, scholarship,
and education by publishing worldwide in

Oxford New York

Auckland Cape Town Dar es Salaam Hong Kong Karachi
Kuala Lumpur Madrid Melbourne Mexico City Nairobi
New Delhi Shanghai Taipei Toronto

With offices in

Argentina Austria Brazil Chile Czech Republic France Greece
Guatemala Hungary Italy Japan Poland Portugal Singapore
South Korea Switzerland Thailand Turkey Ukraine Vietnam

Oxford is a registered trade mark of Oxford University Press
in the UK and in certain other countries

Published in the United States
by Oxford University Press Inc., New York

© Oxford University Press 2006

The moral rights of the authors have been asserted
Database right Oxford University Press (maker)

Seventeenth edition 2006

Crown copyright material is reproduced under Class Licence Number
C01P0000148 with the permission of OPSI and the Queen's Printed for
Scotland

All rights reserved. No part of this publication may be reproduced,
stored in a retrieval system, or transmitted, in any form or by any means,
without the prior permission in writing of Oxford University Press,
or as expressly permitted by law, or under terms agreed with the appropriate
reprographics rights organization. Enquiries concerning reproduction
outside the scope of the above should be sent to the Rights Department,
Oxford University Press, at the address above

You must not circulate this book in any other binding or cover
and you must impose the same condition on any acquirer

British Library Cataloguing in Publication Data

Data available

Library of Congress Cataloging in Publication Data

Data available

Typeset by Newgen Imaging Systems (P) Ltd., Chennai, India
Printed in Great Britain
on acid-free paper by
Ashford Colour Press Ltd., Gosport, Hampshire

ISBN 978–0–19–928533–4

3 5 7 9 10 8 6 4 2

CONTENTS

PART I INTRODUCTION TO THE MODERN LAW

PART II ESTATES AND INTERESTS IN LAND

PART III THE CREATION, TRANSFER AND EXTINCTION OF ESTATES AND INTERESTS IN LAND

PART IV PUBLIC CONTROL OVER THE USE OF LAND

PREFACE

Geoffrey Cheshire published the first edition of *Modern Law of Real Property* in 1925, and then handed it to me to edit the eleventh edition of 1972. The time has now come for me to hand on in my turn. Fortunately I have been able to persuade John Cartwright, Student of Christ Church and Reader in the University of Oxford, to take on this seventeenth edition. He is a long-standing friend of mine, my old pupil and successor as law tutor at Christ Church. We have worked together over this edition, but it has been John Cartwright who has masterminded it all. We have made use of the eighth edition of *Maudsley and Burn's Land Law Cases and Materials*, and have referred to it throughout.

E.H.B.

In spite of significant changes in structure and detail in this new edition, we have nevertheless maintained the approach of Cheshire to the presentation of land law. He took the view that changes in land law could best be understood and explained in the light of the law which had preceded those changes. The title to this book, "Modern", now has a new connotation. In the first edition it meant the land law which had evolved in the 1925 legislation, itself a consolidation of the Law of Property Act 1922 and other statutes, which came into force on 1 January 1926. For this seventeenth edition modernity connotes the law as restructured by the Land Registration Act 2002 and the Land Registration Rules 2003, which came into force on 13 October 2003.

Holdsworth, in his *Historical Introduction to the Land Law*, explained the evolutionary nature of English land law:

Some five centuries of law makers and law reformers have contributed to the Property Acts. Revolutionary as the new Acts may at first sight appear, they are historically the product of the efforts of a long series of judges, conveyancers, and legislators; and their provisions are a striking illustration of the continuity of the history of the land law. They are, as Sir Leslie Scott has said, "not revolution, but evolution". Like the other great reforms of the past, they will, no doubt, become the foundation upon which the judges and conveyancers will build up a new fabric of property law, related to the old in somewhat the same way as the modern law of real property, constructed on the basis of the statutes of Uses and Wills, was related to the medieval land law.

In spite of the revolutionary subtitle of the Law Commission's admirable Consultative Paper on *Land Registration in the Twenty-First Century*, the new registration provisions are in fact evolutionary. The mechanics of creation and transfer involve the use of modern technology in a dramatic way. From the days of parchment and the quill pen, via the typewriter and sheets of paper, a new system of paperless creation and transfer by electronic means has emerged. The details and consequences of this are now to be worked out in the first decade of this century.

The main substantive changes in this edition are statutory. The new Land Registration Act and Rules follow the two major statutes which were incorporated into the last edition: the Landlord and Tenant (Covenants) Act 1995 and the Trusts of Land and Appointment of Trustees Act 1996. Other statutes which have been incorporated into the text are the Countryside and Rights of Way Act 2000 (suitably abbreviated as CROW 2000); the

Commonhold and Leasehold Reform Act 2002; the Housing Act 2004; and the Planning and Compulsory Purchase Act 2004. Two further Bills currently before Parliament, the Commons Bill and the Consumer Credit Bill, are expected to be enacted during 2006.

The Law Commission promises us further major changes. Already we have two Final Reports on Towards a Compulsory Purchase Code; and Consultation Papers on Renting Homes and the Termination of Tenancies for Tenant Default. And we have promises before the end of 2006 of the final Reports on Renting Homes, and Termination of Tenancies; and Consultation Papers on Cohabitation; Housing: Proportionate Dispute Resolution; Ensuring Responsible Renting; and Land Obligations, which is designed to create a coherent scheme of easements, analogous rights and covenants; and also (but in the slightly longer term) on Feudal Land Law to eliminate residual but significant elements dating from 1066.

New players have made their entrances onto the legal stage: from statute, the civil partner, the limited partner and the anti-social behaviourist (the demoted tenant); and from the judges, the tolerated trespasser.

There have been significant developments in judge-made law. The House of Lords has refined in detail the rule in *Barclays Bank plc v O'Brien* in mortgages, and the criteria for adverse possession in limitation of actions; settled the question of the appropriate limitation period for mortgagees seeking to recover a shortfall after exercising the power of sale; held that a profit appurtenant of grazing can be severed so as to become a profit in gross (a decision that will be reversed by the Commons Bill), and that a private right of way can be acquired over common land by prescription, in spite of the exercise of such a right without permission being illegal (a decision that renders a provision in CROW 2000 otiose); and interpreted the anti-avoidance provisions under the Landlord and Tenant (Covenants) Act 1995.

The Court of Appeal, in examining the elements of proprietary estoppel, has construed them in the round; it has also compared proprietary estoppel with constructive trusts, and rediscovered a remedial discretion in both; and has twice affirmed the way in which it may remedy the failure to satisfy the formality requirements of section 2 of the Law of Property (Miscellaneous Provisions) Act 1989. The Court of Appeal has also applied *Re Ellenborough Park* where a similar easement was created by prescription; distinguished *Phipps v Pears* where the adjacent tenements were bonded together; cast doubt on the relevance of diversity of occupation in the creation of an easement by implied grant under section 62 of the Law of Property Act 1925; continued the disapproval, begun by Sir Frederick Pollock in 1903, of the doctrine of the clog on the equity of redemption; reviewed in detail the interpretation of sections 78 and 79 in the context of restrictive covenants; and rejected the reasoning in *Scala House and District Property Co Ltd v Forbes* on the meaning of capability of remedy in section 146(1) of the Law of Property Act 1925.

There have also been important decisions at first instance on the rare creation of an easement by reservation based on the common intention of the parties; on the effect of an increase in user of an easement of drainage created by prescription; and on the duties of a mortgagee and a receiver on the sale of mortgaged property.

The courts at all levels have also had to consider the impact of the European Convention on Human Rights (via the Human Rights Act 1998) on many areas of land law—not always taking quite the same view as the European Court of Human Rights in Strasbourg.

We would particularly like to thank Marilyn Kennedy-McGregor, Barrister of Gray's Inn and Lincoln's Inn, for her valuable comments and advice; and Keith Davies, Emeritus

Professor of Law in the University of Reading for revising Planning Law. We would also like to thank our new publishers for undertaking the compilation of the various Tables and for their ready and expert help at all times.

This edition purports to state the law as it was on 1 January 2006, but more recent developments have been incorporated where space permitted.

E.H.B.

J.C.

29 March
2006

PREFACE TO THE FIRST EDITION

My classical friends assure me that the principles which every author should observe were laid down for all time by Horace. Compose, submit the result line by line to Maecius, consult the judgment of two friends, and preserve to yourself a *locus poenitentiae* by withholding publication for nine years. Such rules are no doubt of inestimable value, but unfortunately the real property legislation of the last few years has been too rapid to permit of an author profiting by the wisdom of Horace in the particular matter of delay. Despite his awful warning,

nescit vox missa reverti,

which never seemed so impressive to me as it does now on the eve of publication, I felt, in view of the representations of colleagues and pupils, that some attempt should be made to publish with as little delay as possible an account of the new system of real property law.

As the lack of adequate time is the only excuse that I can offer for the shortcomings of this book, it may be in point to indicate why I have thought it advisable to publish as soon as possible. The old system of real property law was described with such lucidity and fullness in several works of repute that it would have been presumptuous to offer another book had the law remained unaltered. It is, however, to be profoundly modified on 1 January 1926. The process of modification was begun by the Law of Property Act 1922. This was originally designed to come into operation on 1 January 1925, but a closer examination of the Act showed that it would not lead to a simplification of the law, especially in the matter of accessibility, unless it were cast into a different form. Its greatest defect was that while it introduced a number of new rules and brought about a number of abolitions, both in the existing common law and the existing statutes, it did not repeal and re-enact the latter in a manner calculated to render the search for the law the simple task it should be. To avoid, therefore, what might have been chaos, the legislature set to work in 1924 to consolidate a great part of the statute law bearing on real property, and to incorporate the principles and alteration of the Act of 1922 in the consolidating statutes. Such of the provisions of the Act of 1922 as were not of a merely transitional character were repealed and re-enacted in the consolidating statutes, while the date at which the transitional provisions were to come into operation was postponed to 1 January 1926. Six consolidating bills were drafted and appeared in print during the late summer of 1924, but it was not until April 1925, that they were passed by Parliament.

The position was, then that only in April 1925, did the new legal rules which, for the moment at any rate, are destined to regulate rights of property in the land, become known, and though they were postponed from coming into operation until 1 January 1926, the result was that a student had but eight months within which to master the new system. Examinations wait for no man, and when it is remembered that the King's Printer's copies of the new Acts cover more than six hundred pages, it will be realised that the prospect with which a student was faced was not a happy one.

When it was known in January 1924, what the intentions of the legislature were, I therefore felt justified in attempting to prepare a book which would not merely record the changes, but would present the law as a composite whole. Despite the short time available, I felt that something was required, before the new era dawned in January 1926, to enable students to envisage a legal system which is, in many respects, widely different from that described in existing books. The present book represents an attempt to supply the want. It has many defects, but it is hoped that they are defects which can be readily eradicated should sufficient support be forthcoming to justify the publication of a second edition.

One of these defects is a somewhat excessive length, though something may be said in palliation of what, to a student, is perhaps the worst vice known to the law. In the first place the number of pages has been greatly increased owing to the manner in which the text has been set out. The subject is complicated, and the design has been to space the text out and to add numerous headings and indentations, so that the subject matter may easily catch the eye of a reader. Secondly, the book contains a number of repetitions which are due partly to the speed at which it has been written and partly to the intervals which, owing to other calls upon my time, have separated the composition of its various parts. Thirdly, it must be admitted that the bulk of real property law is greater now than it formerly was. At the beginning of my labours I was imbued with the idea that the task of a student has been lightened. So much has disappeared. The old rules relating to remainders, the old canons of descent, the rule in Shelley's Case, copyholds, gavelkind—they were all gone, and one's first impression was that the amount of law which a book on real property need deal with has been diminished. This will be true in twenty or thirty years' time, but unfortunately it is far from the truth at the present moment. Quite apart from the fact that a knowledge of the old law remains necessary for the purpose of investigating title, it is also a fact that a great many of the new rules can neither be understood nor explained unless the former rules are known. The Administration of Estates Act 1925, for instance, abolishes curtesy, but the Law of Property Act 1925 retains it in the case of entailed interests.

So much may be said by way of excuse. The Horatian requirement of time has been lacking, but not the other essentials. The role of Maecius has been filled by Mr. T. K. Brighouse MA, a former colleague of mine in the University College of Wales, Aberystwyth, who, though not a lawyer, has been an experienced and valuable critic on the literary side. Despite what must be a distinctly repellent subject to a layman, he has read every word of this book at least twice, and has not only saved me from some of the worst mistakes of a naturally defective style, but has advised and procured alterations in many passages where my proposed treatment would have obscured the lucidity of statement. The extent of my obligation to him is immeasurable.

On the legal side, the help I have received has been equally considerable. The main task has fallen on Mr. P. H. L. Brough of the Equity Bar, who has sacrificed a great deal of his time to reading and advising on the manuscript before it has been submitted to others. Moreover, he has given me the benefit of his practical experience in the initial stages of the book by helping to arrange the form in which some of the more difficult parts of the new legislation might be set out. His clearness of vision and his natural aptitude for realising the object of an obscure enactment have been of inestimable value to me.

I owe a debt of deep gratitude to Sir John Miles BCL, MA, Fellow and Tutor of Merton College, Oxford, who besides encouraging me to begin the preparation of this book, has always been anxious at the sacrifice of his own time to afford me the benefit of his mature knowledge and sound advice.

To Professor J. D. I. Hughes BCL, MA, of Leeds University, to Mr. Ernest A. Steele LLB, of Halifax, and to Mr. L. E. Salt MA, Fellow and Bursar of Pembroke College, Oxford, I am under a deep obligation. They have each done me the honour of reading the whole of the book in proof form, and when I recall the number of their suggestions and criticisms to which I have paid heed, I realise the extent of my indebtedness to them. Their unselfish labours have prevented the appearance of innumerable sins, both of omission and commission, and their judgment has frequently kept me from straying into an unwise method of treatment.

Mr. Harold Potter LLB, of Birmingham University, and Mr. John Snow MA, of New College, Oxford, have very kindly read the chapter on conveyancing and have suggested several practical improvements which have been of the utmost value to me. It is, however, only fair to Mr. Potter to say that he would have elaborated the introductory note to Book III in a manner which would have greatly increased its usefulness and value, had not his proposals unfortunately reached me too late to permit of their inclusion.

The above is an inadequate acknowledgment of the services which have been rendered to me, but at the same time it must be recorded that none of the gentlemen who have so willingly extended me their aid is responsible in the slightest degree for the mistakes and failings which no doubt will be found to characterise this book. For these I am wholly responsible, while only partially responsible for anything which may be worthy of approval.

Lastly, I must acknowledge the help, of a different character, but no less valuable, which I have received from my wife. From the moment when this book was begun she abandoned a great part of her leisure and, having mastered for the occasion the unattractive art of typing, converted an almost illegible manuscript into a form which made the task of all those who had to deal with it a task of ease instead of a burden.

G. C. C.

OXFORD
September 1925

TABLE OF STATUTES

TABLE OF STATUTORY INSTRUMENTS

TABLE OF CASES

ABBREVIATIONS

Statutes and Rules

AEA	Administration of Estates Act
AJA	Administration of Justice Act
CA	Conveyancing Act
CCA	Consumer Credit Act
CLRA	Commonhold and Leasehold Reform Act
C(LR)R	Commonhold (Land Registration) Rules
CPA	Compulsory Purchase Act
CPR	Civil Procedure Rules
CROW	Countryside and Rights of Way Act
ECHR	Convention for the Protection of Human Rights and Fundamental Freedoms (the European Convention on Human Rights)
FA	Finance Act
GDPO	Town and Country Planning (General Development Procedure) Order
GPDO	Town and Country Planning (General Permitted Development) Order
HA	Housing Act
HRA	Human Rights Act
IEA	Intestates' Estates Act
ITA	Inheritance Tax Act
LA	Limitation Act
LCA	Land Charges Act
LLCA	Local Land Charges Act
LLCR	Local Land Charges Rules
LPA	Law of Property Act
LP(A)A	Law of Property (Amendment) Act
LP(MP)A	Law of Property (Miscellaneous Provisions) Act
LRA	Land Registration Act
LR(A)R	Land Registration (Amendment) Rules
LRR	Land Registration Rules
LTA	Landlord and Tenant Act
LT(C)A	Landlord and Tenant (Covenants) Act
PAA	Perpetuities and Accumulations Act
PCPA	Planning and Compulsory Purchase Act
RSC	Rules of the Supreme Court
SCA	Supreme Court Act (or, after the coming into force of the Constitutional Reform Act 2005, Senior Courts Act)
SI	Statutory Instrument
SLA	Settled Land Act
TA	Trustee Act
TCPA	Town and Country Planning Act
TLATA	Trusts of Land and Appointment of Trustees Act

Reports and Periodicals

All ER Rev	All England Law Reports Annual Review
Anglo-Am	Anglo-American Law Review
CLJ	Cambridge Law Journal
CLP	Current Legal Problems
CLY	Current Law Yearbook
Conv (NS)	Conveyancer (New Series)
Conv Prec	Precedents for the Conveyancer
EG	Estates Gazette
EGLR	Estates Gazette Law Reports
EHR	Economic History Review
Harv L Rev	Harvard Law Review
HLR	Housing Law Reports
JPL	Journal of Planning and Environment Law (until 1972, Journal of Planning and Property Law)
Jurid Soc	Juridical Society's Papers
L & TR	Landlord and Tenant Reports
LJ News	Law Journal Newspaper
LQR	Law Quarterly Review
LS	Legal Studies
LSG	Law Society's Gazette
LT	Law Times
L & T Rev	Landlord and Tenant Review
MLR	Modern Law Review
NILQ	Northern Ireland Legal Quarterly
NLJ	New Law Journal
NPC	New Property Cases
OJLS	Oxford Journal of Legal Studies
P & CR	Property, Planning and Compensation Reports
RLR	Restitution Law Review
SJ	Solicitors' Journal
Yale LJ	Yale Law Journal

Books

(See detailed bibliography)

Aldridge	*Leasehold Law*
Emmet	Emmet and Farrand on Title
Gale	*Gale on Easements* (17th edn)
H & B	Harpum and Bignell, *Registered Land: Law and Practice under the Land Registration Act 2002*
H & M	Hanbury and Martin
M & B	Maudsley & Burn's *Land Law: Cases and Materials*
M & W	Megarry and Wade
R & R	Ruoff and Roper (2003 looseleaf edn)
W & C	Wolstenholme and Cherry
W & H	Whitehouse and Hassall

Miscellaneous

CML	Council of Mortgage Lenders
DCA	Department for Constitutional Affairs
Defra	Department for Environment, Food and Rural Affairs
FSA	Financial Services Authority
LCD	Lord Chancellor's Department
ODPM	Office of the Deputy Prime Minister

PART I

INTRODUCTION TO THE MODERN LAW

The modern law of real property in England can be understood only by reference to its history. The land law of the twenty-first century contains structures, concepts and language which date back to the middle ages. There has never been a codification of the law in England similar to the great civil codes on the Continent.[1] The nearest we have come to a codification of the land law is in the great reforms of 1925—which, however, did not constitute a complete code, breaking with the past and laying down a new, self-contained set of legal rules and principles for land ownership and transactions relating to land. Instead, the 1925 legislation, which is still the basis of the modern land law in England, itself reformed and developed the law as it then stood.

In this Part, we explain the origins of the modern law through the historical developments from the Conquest up to 1925. We then consider in outline the reforms made by the 1925 legislation, and more recent changes in 1996 (the trust of land) and 2002 (land registration), as well as some key features of the contemporary law. In Part II we shall move on to consider in more detail the estates and interests, legal and equitable, that are recognised in English land law today; in Part III we shall see how those estates and interests are created, transferred and extinguished.

---

[1] Pre-eminent amongst the codes are the French *Code civil* of 1804, and the German *Bürgeliches Gesetzbuch* ("BGB") which came into force on 1 January 1900. But there are systematic civil codes throughout continental Europe—with the exception of the Scandinavian countries.

PART I

INTRODUCTION TO

THE MODERN LAW

A. Origins of the Modern Law

SUMMARY

1

THE PATTERN OF DEVELOPMENT

SUMMARY

I Origin of Modern Land Law

Modern English[1] land law is based on the reforms enacted in a series of statutes which were passed in 1925 and came into force on 1 January 1926. These were:

Settled Land Act;

Trustee Act;

Law of Property Act;

Land Registration Act;

Land Charges Act;

Administration of Estates Act.

Since 1925 there has been continuous legislative activity, especially in the fields of landlord and tenant and the public control of the use of land; and the system of registration of title to land has in large part superseded earlier methods of conveyancing. But the principles of modern land law are contained in the 1925 legislation. An understanding of those principles is essential to the understanding of the modern law; at the same time, some understanding of the land law as it developed from medieval times to 1926 is essential to the understanding of the 1925 legislation.

---

[1] This includes Wales, but not Scotland or Northern Ireland. For the inter-relation between English and Irish land law, see Wylie, *Irish Land Law*, chap. 1.

A Feudal Basis

In this development over a period of nearly a thousand years, the land law is a mirror of one aspect of English life; it is a body of law which, while based on a feudal system imposed by the Norman Conquest, has adapted itself to a succession of political and social upheavals, culminating in the welfare state of the twentieth century. It was the public importance of the land law in the feudal society of its origin which eventually brought its troubles. When the country settled down after the upheaval of the Norman Conquest, the social bond which, both on the public and on the private side of life, united men together in a political whole was the land. Broadly speaking, land constituted the sole form of wealth, and it was through its agency that the everyday needs of the governing and the governed classes were satisfied. The result of this was that from an early date a complicated system of law, founded on custom and developed by the decisions of the courts, began to grow up, and we may call it for convenience the common law system.

B Legislative Reforms of Early Nineteenth Century

In its origin this system was eminently suitable for a society that was based and centred on the land, and appropriate to the simple notions prevailing in a feudal population, but in several respects it gradually came to outlive the reason for its existence. It tended to become static. Rules that were in harmony with their early environment lived on long after they had become anachronisms. Law will wither unless it expands to keep pace with the progressive ideas of an advancing community, but in this particular context the rigidity and formalism of the common lawyers retarded the process, and, though equity intervened to great effect in several directions, the few reforms attempted by the legislation before the first quarter of the nineteenth century served to complicate rather than to simplify the law. Statutory reform, however, began in earnest after the report of the Real Property Commissioners in 1829. Although the commissioners began their report by saying that this department of English law "appears to come almost as near to perfection as can be expected in any human institutions", [2] they nevertheless went on to express their opinion that the modes by which interests in land were created, transferred and secured had become unnecessarily defective and that they demanded substantial alteration. The result of this view was that on their recommendation a number of statutes were passed between 1832 and 1837 which swept away many impediments to the smooth operation of the law. The chief of these were:

Prescription Act 1832;

Fines and Recoveries Act 1833;

Real Property Limitation Act 1833;

Dower Act 1833;

Inheritance Act 1833;

Wills Act 1837.

---

[2] Real Property Commissioners' First Report, p. 6.

II Legislation of 1925

A Main Object

Between 1837 and 1922 the legislature became more and more active in the sphere of real property law, but most of the enactments were directed towards the simplification of conveyancing and the extension of the landowner's powers of enjoyment. No comprehensive effort was made to smooth the path by abolishing the substantive defects that had settled on the main body of the law like barnacles on the hull of a ship. Then came the war of 1914–1918, and with it a general desire to set the social life of the nation in order. One of the results of this desire was to give an impetus to land legislation, and it will be as well to state at the outset the main idea which lay at the back of the legislation that resulted. It was nothing more than a desire to render the sale of land as rapid and simple a matter as is the sale of goods or of stocks and shares.[3] A layman knows that if he desires to transfer to another the ownership of a chattel, such as a motor car or a picture, the normal requirement is the making of a contract which names the parties, records their intention, describes the article to be sold and states the price to be paid. The moment that such a contract is concluded, the property in the article, in the absence of a contrary intention, passes to the buyer. At first sight it is difficult to appreciate why the same simple expedient cannot be adopted in the case of land, and not unnaturally a layman grows impatient of the long and expensive investigation attendant upon the conveyance of a piece of land.

But the difference is inevitable, and the reason is that in the great majority of cases the possessor of personal goods is their absolute owner, and therefore able to pass a title which will confer upon their deliveree an equally full and unincumbered ownership. If A is in possession of a piano, it is probable that he is its owner, and in most cases a buyer is safe in paying its value and taking delivery of possession. A seller cannot generally transfer a title greater than his own—*nemo dat quod non habet*—and if it should happen that A, instead of being the owner, is a thief or is merely holding the piano under a hire purchase agreement, then a buyer from him will not acquire ownership. But the fact remains that despite risks of this nature a buyer is generally justified in assuming that the possessor of goods is also the owner, and as a rule there is no need to go to trouble and expense in order to ascertain whether some person other than the possessor has any interest in them. It is a legitimate risk to take. But for a purchaser of land to be content with the word of the vendor and with the appearance of ownership that flows from his possession would be an act of sheer folly.

Land and goods are and must ever be on a different plane. Land is fixed, permanent and vital to the needs of society, and a subject-matter in which rights may be granted to persons other than the ostensible owner. A is in possession of land and is obviously exercising all the powers of enjoyment and management which amount to the popular idea of ownership, but none the less it is by no means certain that he is in fact entitled to dispose of the interest that he may have agreed to sell. He may be in possession under a lease for any period from one to 999 years or more, or he may have a life interest under a family settlement; and even if he

---

[3] See Birkenhead, *Points of View*, vol. ii. p. 34, discussing LPA 1922. As Lord Chancellor, he was responsible for the passage of this Act and, subsequently, the whole of the 1925 legislation through the House of Lords.

holds the fee simple—the largest interest known to the law and one that approximates to the absolute ownership of goods—it is likely that he or his predecessors have granted to third parties rights, such as mortgages, restrictive covenants and rights of way, which continue to be enforceable against the land regardless of any transfer to which it may have been subjected. So long as third parties can in this way have enforceable rights against land which outwardly appears to belong absolutely to the possessor, it is difficult, in the absence of a complete register of title, to devise a system under which conveyances of land can be conducted with the facility of sales of goods; and even then it will always be necessary for a purchaser to make careful searches and inquiries in order to see that there are no third-party rights which will bind the land after it has been transferred to him.

We may start, then, with the assumption that no effort of legislative genius can, from the point of view of simplicity and rapidity, put conveyances of land on an equal footing with sales of goods. But when the question of reforming the law came before Parliament in 1922, the result of nearly a thousand years of development from a feudal origin was that the law of real property contained so many antiquated rules and useless technicalities that additional and unnecessary impediments had arisen to hinder the transfer of land. The real property law as it existed in 1922 might justly be described as an archaic feudalistic system which, though originally evolved to satisfy the needs of a society based and centred on the land, had by considerable ingenuity been twisted and distorted into a shape more or less suitable to a commercial society dominated by money. The movement of progressive societies has been from land to money, or rather to trade, and a legal system which acquired its main features at a time when land constituted the major part of the country's wealth can scarcely be described as suitable to an industrial community. To borrow the words of Bagehot directed to a different subject, the 1922 real property law might be likened to "an old man who still wears with attached fondness clothes in the fashion of his youth; what you see of him is the same; what you do not see is wholly altered".

To take any structure, whether it be a system of law, a constitution or a house, and for a period of some thousand years to patch it here and there in order to adapt it to new conditions, cannot fail to lead to complications of a bewildering character.

B Law of Property Act 1922. Assimilation of Real and Personal Property

Confirmed in the views just mentioned, the legislature began in 1922 to reform the law on a far more ambitious scale than had been attempted in the earlier legislative changes, for, though the main purpose was to simplify conveyancing, yet this was pursued not merely by a simplification of the machinery of land transfer, but also by a free use of the pruning knife. In the official view, reforms were needed as a prelude to the simplification and extension of the system of registration of title.[4]

The first Act to be passed was the Law of Property Act 1922, which was described in its preamble as:

---

[4] Wolstenholme and Cherry, *Conveyancing Statutes* (12th edn), vol. i. p. clxvi. See the speech of Sir Leslie Scott, who was Solicitor-General, introducing the Bill into the House of Commons (1922) 154 HC Debates (5th Series) 90; reproduced with annotations by B. B. Benas in Scott, *The New Law of Property Explained*; and the

An Act to assimilate and amend the law of Real and Personal Estate, to abolish copyhold and other special tenures, to amend the law relating to commonable lands and of intestacy, and to amend the Wills Act, 1837, the Settled Land Acts, 1882 to 1890, the Conveyancing Acts, 1881 to 1911, the Trustee Act, 1893 and the Land Transfer Acts, 1875 and 1897.

The all-important fact that emerges from this descriptive title is that one main object was to "assimilate . . . the law of real and personal estate".

We shall see as we proceed that a comparison of the law relating to real and personal property respectively is, from the point of view of convenience and reason, very much to the advantage of the latter. Part I of the Act put the two forms of property as nearly as possible upon the same footing, a result which was obtained partly by abolishing the chief differences that formerly existed between the two, and partly by eliminating many of the technical anachronisms that had grown up in the land laws. In addition, the law of personal property, which thus became the dominating system, was itself amended in several particulars.

C Legislation of 1925. Consolidating Acts

The date at which the Act of 1922 was appointed to come into operation, however, was postponed, for the changes it made were sufficiently drastic to necessitate the re-drafting and consolidation of the real property statute law from the year 1285. The Law of Property (Amendment) Act 1924 was therefore passed to facilitate the task of consolidation, and then all but the transitional provisions of this Act and of the Act of 1922 were absorbed into the six statutes, passed in 1925, which are set out at the beginning of this chapter.[5]

These statutes are all consolidating Acts. Where the Acts of 1922 and 1924 make no change in the old law, there is a presumption that the Acts of 1925 did not change it. But where the Acts of 1922 and 1924 do make some change, there is only a presumption that the Acts of 1925 did not change the changes made by those two Acts.[6]

III Further Developments in 1996 and 2002

The reform of the land law by the legislator did not stop in 1925. Throughout the twentieth century, and now already in the twenty-first century, there has been further legislative activity in many areas. Most has not changed the fundamental principles of the modern law set out in the 1925 legislation, but two particular developments should be noted which have changed the significance of those statutes.

valuable six *Lectures* by Sir Benjamin Cherry on *The New Property Acts*, and especially his series of Questions and Answers at pp. 104 et seq. See also Anderson, *Lawyers and the Making of English Land Law 1832–1940*.

[5] For a detailed commentary on the 1925 legislation, see the six volumes of Wolstenholme and Cherry, *Conveyancing Statutes* (13th edn 1972, edited by J. T. Farrand). Previous editions are valuable, as these contain the commentaries of Wolstenholme (who was responsible for drafting CA 1881 and SLA 1882) and Cherry (the property statutes of 1922 and 1925). On the 1922 Act, see Underhill, *A Concise Explanation of Lord Birkenhead's Act (the Law of Property Act 1922) in Plain Language*.

[6] *Beswick v Beswick* [1968] AC 58; cf *Maunsell v Olins* [1975] AC 373 at 392–3; *Farrell v Alexander* [1977] AC 59 at 72, 82, 96; *Johnson v Moreton* [1980] AC 37 at 56. See also *Grey v IRC* [1960] AC 1; *Lloyds Bank Ltd v Marcan* [1973] 1 WLR 339 at 344; affd [1973] 1 WLR 1387; *Re Dodwell & Co Ltd's Trust* [1979] Ch 301 at 308; *R v Heron* [1982] 1 WLR 451 at 459; Wolstenholme and Cherry, vol. 1, p. 31; (1959) 75 LQR 307 (R.E.M.).

In the first, the Trusts of Land and Appointment of Trustees Act 1996, legislation intervened to make significant changes to the principles by which beneficial interests can be held in land. We shall see the detail later. But for the present purposes we should notice that the effect of the 1996 Act was to prevent the future creation of strict settlements—which had been part of the historical structure of family land ownership in English law. The significance of the Settled Land Act 1925 was thereby considerably reduced.

Most recently, the Land Registration Act 1925 was repealed and replaced by the Land Registration Act 2002. This was not just a cosmetic change, nor simply designed to bring the former statute up to date.[7] It constitutes a revision of the principles of registered conveyancing, designed to lead within the next decade to a complete register of title to every parcel of land in England and Wales, and to the introduction of electronic conveyancing.

IV Tripartite Historical Division

Real property law, like most of the other branches of our law, falls into three divisions, which are due to the order of its historical development:

First of all we get the purely common law system, which was designed to meet the needs of a feudal society.

Secondly in order of time we have the equitable system which, though not comprehensive, was gradually evolved in certain directions with a view to adapting the common law rules to a society moved by different ideals and possessing a more commercial outlook on life.

And finally we come to the various legislative enactments by which the judge-made law of land was rendered more adequate to the needs of society.

We will now sketch in its barest outline the common law system, then describe at somewhat greater length certain conceptions that were introduced into the law by the Chancellor in the exercise of his equitable jurisdiction, and finally discuss the legislative changes of 1925, 1996 and 2002.

---

[7] The Land Charges Act 1925 was repealed and replaced by the Land Charges Act 1972, although without fundamental changes of substance. The other statutes of 1925, listed on page 5, remain in force, although all have been amended from time to time.

2

THE COMMON LAW SYSTEM

SUMMARY

We begin by exploring the system of land law devised by the common law. It has been substantially modified, first by equity, and then by statute, as we shall see in the following chapters. But the modern structure of land law cannot be understood without first having an understanding of the feudal origins of the common law system of land tenure, and the common law doctrine of the *estate*.

I The Doctrine of Tenure[1]

A *Feudalism in Europe*

(1) Development of Continental Feudalism

The outstanding feature of the English land law and one that explains many of its peculiarities is that, at least from the time of the Norman Conquest, it fell into line with the continental systems and became and remained for several centuries intensely feudalistic. *Feudalism* itself is a word of some vagueness and ambiguity, and one that was certainly unknown to the peoples to whom it is applied. It is often thought to represent the history of Western Europe from the eighth to the fourteenth century,[2] and, like the modern use of

---

[1] For the history of this doctrine, see Simpson, *A History of the Land Law*, pp. 1 et seq; Bean, *The Decline of English Feudalism*, esp. chap. 1; Baker, *Introduction to English Legal History*, chap. 13.

[2] Pollock and Maitland, *History of English Law*, vol. i. p. 67.

the word *capitalism*, to describe the social characteristics of the period.[3] To a lawyer, however, it represents:

A state of society in which the main social bond is the relation between lord and man, a relation implying on the lord's part protection and defence; on the man's part protection, service and reverence, the service including service in arms. This personal relation is inseparably involved in a proprietary relation, the tenure of land—the man holds of the lord, the man's service is a burden on the land, the lord has important rights in the land.[4]

Thus it is the negation of independence. It implies subordination; it means that one man is deliberately made inferior to another.

In pre-feudal days the land of Europe was owned absolutely, though subject to custom, by persons who were grouped together in village communities and it therefore becomes a matter of interest to discover why it was that a great part of the world lapsed from a state of comparative freedom into one of servility, why landownership disappeared and land tenure took its place. The change represented a retrogressive step in the history of man, but in Europe it was one of the necessary consequences of the disruption of the Roman Empire by the Barbarian invaders. The overthrow of that Empire caused chaos and disorganisation in Europe and produced conditions in which it was necessary for private persons to procure for themselves a higher degree of protection than could be furnished by their own unaided efforts. In those days interference with personal freedom or with the ownership of property might come from several different quarters, such as a revolt of peasants, the arrogance of a powerful neighbour, the extortion of a government or the hostility of some tribe. The only method of obtaining security was mutual support, and so men deliberately subordinated themselves to the strong hand of some magnate versed in the arts of war, and were compensated for the diminution of personal independence and the loss of landownership by acquiring the protection afforded by the forces of which he disposed. This process involved both a personal and a proprietary subordination, but it is only on the latter that we need dwell.

One of the effects of the feudalisation of Europe was that from a legal aspect land became the exclusive bond of union between men. Individual or communal landownership was destroyed. The ownership of the whole of the land in any given district was vested in the overlord, and the persons who had formerly owned it in their own right now held it from the overlord. In return for the land which they held they were bound to render services, chiefly of a military nature, to the overlord, while the latter in his turn was bound to protect his tenants. Feudalism implied a reciprocity of rights and duties. The lord gained in dignity and became entitled to personal services, while the tenant obtained security.

This conversion from ownership to tenure began in the lower ranks of society, but quickly spread upwards until it finally embraced the greater part of the land of Western Europe. Various reasons contributed to this extension. The general anarchy of the times, the lack of a central government sufficiently strong to ensure a well-ordered and peaceful existence, and the natural ambition of magnates to increase the extent of their possessions induced even the large landowners to put themselves and their land under the protection of someone greater than themselves.

This development took place under the Franks, and in the time of the Carolingians a still further impetus was given to the movement, for the government itself—if such a term

---

[3] Plucknett, *Concise History of the Common Law*, p. 506.
[4] Maitland, *Constitutional History of England*, p. 143.

can be applied to those times—was obliged to resort to the principle of feudalism. Administration had to be carried on somehow and taxes were difficult to collect. The solution was to farm out Crown lands to great men who paid a sum of money to the government and who in return became lords of the lands (which were called benefices) and of the persons who dwelt thereon. A little later, when military pressure from the east and the south made it imperative that society should be organised on a basis that would afford protection to the State, the device of granting benefices in return for military services, a device that was gradually failing owing to the scarcity of Crown lands, was widened in scope by an act of confiscation.

The Church had become the greatest landowner in Europe. Charles Martel, who was Mayor of the Frankish Empire in the first part of the eighth century, deliberately carried out wholesale seizures of Church property, but in AD 751 some sort of amicable arrangement was made whereby vast tracts of Church lands were granted by the ecclesiastical corporations to laymen at the request of the King. The Church ownership of the lands was recognised by the payment of an uneconomic rent to the corporations, while the tenants—and this was the significance of the transaction—became liable by virtue of their holdings to render services to the King.[5] Thus the net of feudalism spread everywhere. In this way life and government were made to depend upon the land.[6]

(2) The Manor

This can be seen by an examination of that unit of society which is called the manor. The grant of benefices led to the creation of great estates or manors vested in the grantees from the Crown. Topographically a manor denoted a certain area of land consisting of a number of houses, strips of arable and pasture land and waste lands, all of which were within the domain of the lord of the manor. The waste, in proportion to the cultivated land, formed by far the greater part of the manor, a fact which serves to explain the inclosures of later centuries. But we shall miss the significance of this system unless we realise that the manor was both a social and an administrative unit through the agency of which a whole country was governed. Each manor was, as it were, a small government in itself.

The central government required soldiers and money, but instead of approaching its subjects directly it looked no further than the lord of the manor. His obligation vis-à-vis the government was to supply a fully equipped fighting force, and the right which he obtained in return was that of holding his manor or group of manors immune from the legal and administrative control of the government. Thus, when the power of a central government was on the wane, it became customary to grant immunities to powerful men, which meant nothing more nor less than that the functions of government were handed over to feudal lords. As Vinogradoff has said:[7]

As in the later Empire, the government is obliged to have recourse to great landlords in order to carry out its functions of police, justice, military and fiscal authority. Great estates had become extra-territorial already under Roman rule in the fourth and fifth centuries, and it would be superfluous to point out how much more the governments of the barbarians stood in need of the help of great landowners.

[5] Vinogradoff, *Cambridge Medieval History*, vol. ii. p. 646.
[6] See generally, *Encyclopaedia Britannica*, under the title *Feudalism*.
[7] Vinogradoff, *Cambridge Medieval History*, p. 651.

One of the most important features of the administrative side of a Continental manor was the lord's right of jurisdiction. As the royal writ did not run within the territorial limits of a manor, the lord set up local courts of his own, and it was only in the manorial court of the defendant that a plaintiff was entitled to sue. Thus, to use the expressive language of Stubbs,[8] there was "a graduated system of jurisdiction based on land tenure, in which every lord judged, taxed, and commanded the class next below him, . . . in which private war, private coinage, private prisons took the place of the imperial institutions of government."

(3) Characteristics of Feudalism

By way of summary we may say that the characteristics of feudalism are the relation of lord and vassal; the principle that every person interested in land is a mere holder of it, a tenant and not an owner; the condition that this tenure shall continue to exist only so long as the tenant performs the particular services imposed upon him at the beginning of the tenure; and lastly, the recognition of a reciprocity of rights and duties. The foundation of the whole system is the fief—that is to say, the land which the inferior holds as tenant of the superior. The word *fief* becomes *feudum* in Latin, and *feud*, and later *fee* in English.

B Feudalism in England

(1) Development of English Feudalism

We now come to consider the effect which this Continental feudalism had upon the land law of England. As the scope of this book makes it undesirable to elaborate particular questions of legal history, it is not proposed to discuss the extent to which feudalism existed in England prior to the Conquest. That a system was in vogue which bore similarities to Continental feudalism cannot be doubted, but the only fact that we need notice here is that the Normans applied their own ideas to the conditions prevalent in this country, and succeeded in establishing an English variety of feudalism which, though differing in many respects from that of the Continent, became a striking and universal feature of the land law. The policy of William the Conqueror left England, whatever it may have been before, a highly feudalised state. He took the line that, since the English landowners had denied his right to the Crown of England and had compelled him to assert it by force, their landed possessions became his to dispose of as he chose.[9] What he did was not so much to seize land and parcel it out among his Norman followers, as to allow all Englishmen who recognised him as King to redeem by money payments the estates which by right of conquest had momentarily passed to him.

This process of confiscation and redistribution flowed on evenly, and though it cannot be said that the redistributions amounted to direct feudal grants, there is no doubt that they came to be regarded as such when the idea of Norman feudalism took hold of men's minds. As Stubbs says:[10]

After each effort the royal hand was laid on more heavily; more and more land changed owners, and with the change of owners the title changed. The complicated and unintelligible irregularities of the Anglo-Saxon tenures were exchanged for the simple and uniform feudal theory. The 1500 tenants in

---

[8] Stubbs, *Constitutional History*, vol. i. p. 292.   [9] Stenton, *William the Conqueror*, pp. 494–5.
[10] Stubbs, *Constitutional History*, vol. i. pp. 296–7.

chief of Domesday take the place of the countless landowners of King Edward's day . . . It is enough for our purpose to ascertain that a universal assimilation of title followed the general changes of ownership. The King of Domesday is the supreme landlord; all the land of the nation, the old folkland, has become the King's, and all private land is held mediately or immediately of him; all holders are bound to their lords by homage and fealty, either actually demanded or understood to be demandable, in every case of transfer by inheritance or otherwise.

This English feudalism differed from the Continental variety in that all freemen were bound by the Salisbury Oath of 1086 to swear allegiance directly to the King instead of to the immediate lord from whom they held their lands; and again in the fact that William, instead of setting up great territorial jurisdictions, organised administration in such a way that he governed the country through sheriffs who were directly responsible to him. Though the Frankish system of tenure displaced the Anglo-Saxon system, the establishment of a feudal mode of government was deliberately avoided. But in respect of tenure the result was much the same as on the Continent. By a certain date, which we need not attempt to define, the doctrine of land tenure became universal in England.

(2) Land Tenure

Every acre of land in the country was held of the King. As Pollock and Maitland have said:[11] "The person whom we may call the owner, the person who has the right to use and abuse the land, to cultivate it or leave it uncultivated, to keep all others off it, holds the land of the King either immediately or mediately."

(a) Seignories

If a tenant held immediately of the King, he was said to hold of him in chief or *in capite*. But the position might be less simple. Instead of a tenant holding directly of the King he might hold mediately, as for instance where C held of B who held of A who held of the King. C, who stood at the bottom of the scale, and who to a layman would look more like an owner than anybody else, was called the *tenant in demesne—tenet terram in dominico suo*. The persons between him and the King were called *mesne lords*, and their lordships were called *seignories*. A held the land, not in *demesne* but in service, since he was entitled to the services of B, and B was in a similar position, since he was entitled to the services of C. The services due from these tenants would not necessarily be of the same nature, for A might hold of the King by military service, B of A in return for a money rent, and C of B in return for some personal service. In such a case each grantee owed to his immediate grantor the service that he had agreed to render, and from this point of view the service was called *intrinsec*. Services were not merely personal, but charged on the tenement, so that if A failed in the performance of his military duties the King could distrain upon the land in the hands of C, as could A if B fell into arrears with the rent. B could agree to perform the military service in place of A, but no private arrangement of this kind could free the land from the burden. From this point of view the service was called *forinsec*, that is, foreign to any bargain between other parties.[12] Of course, if, for example, A failed to perform his military service and the King proceeded against the land in C's occupation, the latter had a remedy against A, called the writ of *mesne*. A tenant came under an obligation, confirmed by the oath of fealty, to serve his lord

---

[11] Pollock and Maitland, *History of English Law*, vol. ii. p. 232.
[12] Pollock and Maitland, *History of English Law*, vol. i. p. 237.

faithfully, and the price of infidelity in this respect was the forfeiture of his fief. In particular, forfeiture ensued if he did anything to the disinherison of his lord, as, for example, if he deliberately failed to defend an action for the recovery of land brought against him by a third party.[13]

Perhaps the most striking fact about English feudalism was the universality of this doctrine of land tenure. On the Continent tenure applied only to those who held lands in return for military services,[14] but in England it applied to every holder whatever the nature of the duties that he had agreed to perform might be. Moreover a movement began by which the number of mesne lordships was increased to a bewildering extent. As each year passed, more and more sub-tenancies were created. A, who held of the King, would transfer his land or part of it to B, and B to C, and so on, but each transfer, instead of being an out and out grant by which the transferor got rid of his entire interest, would operate as a grant of land to be held by each transferee as tenant of his immediate transferor. As a result "innumerable petty lords sprang up between the great barons and the immediate tenant of the soil".[15]

(b) Subinfeudation

This process, which was termed subinfeudation, was carried to such lengths that Maitland was able to discover a case where there were as many as eight sub-tenancies in the same piece of land. One explanation of this reluctance to part with one's entire interest was the economic significance of land in the centuries immediately succeeding the Conquest. Apart from cattle, land was practically the only form of wealth. Money was scarce, and something had to take its place as a medium of exchange. This can be illustrated by the recompense usually given for services rendered.

Domestic servants in a manor were paid by a crude method of profit-sharing. As Vinogradoff has stated:[16]

The swine-herd of Glastonbury Abbey, for instance, received one sucking-pig a year, the interior parts of the best pig and the tails of all the others which were slaughtered in the abbey. The chief scullion had a right to all remnants of viands—but not of game—to the feathers and the bowels of geese.

But the form which payment took in the case of labourers on the manorial estate, and also in the case of servants who rendered non-domestic services for a great lord, was a grant of land to be held only so long as the services were properly performed. Thus it was through one of the forms of tenure, known as tenure by sergeanty, that most of the wants of men were satisfied. The persons who severally acted as president of a lord's court, carried his letters, fed his hounds, cared for his horses and found him in bows and arrows, generally held land as tenants in sergeanty of the lord.[17] They would continue to hold the land as long as they served faithfully, and no longer.

(c) Statute Quia Emptores 1290

In other words, the importance of land as a means of payment made it advisable for tenants to keep as tenacious a hold upon it as possible, and, when a transfer was contemplated, to subinfeudate rather than dispose of it outright. But, for reasons into which we need not

---

[13] For a discussion of this defunct principle, see the judgment of Denning LJ in *Warner v Sampson* [1959] 1 QB 297 at 312–16.   [14] Holdsworth, *History of English Law*, vol. ii. p. 199.

[15] Hayes, *Introduction to Conveyancing*, vol. i. p. 9.   [16] Vinogradoff, *Villainage in England*, pp. 321–2.

[17] Pollock and Maitland, *History of English Law*, vol. i. p. 285.

enter,[18] the practice of subinfeudation was obnoxious to the great lords, and was finally prohibited in 1290 by the Statute *Quia Emptores.*[19]

(1) EFFECT

This important statute altered the law in two respects:

First, it set at rest a controversy by enacting that every free man should be at liberty to alienate the whole or part of his land without the consent of his lord. If part only were conveyed, the services were to be apportioned.

Secondly, it enacted that every alienee should hold the land of the same lord of whom the alienor previously held. The effect of this was to prevent the creation of new tenancies. The alienor dropped out, the alienee stepped into his shoes for all purposes, and thus instead of a new sub-tenancy there was the substitution of one tenant for another. If, therefore, the existence of a mesne lordship is proved at the present day, it follows that it must have been created before 1290, or created by the Crown thereafter.

(2) LIMITS

The statute, however, extended only to land held for a fee simple estate, the largest interest known to the law,[20] and it never prevented the creation of a new tenure by the grant of a lesser estate, such as a fee tail or a life interest.

The statute did not bind the Crown. This had two consequences.

In the first place, the privilege of unrestricted alienation did not avail tenants in chief. In their case the consent of the Crown remained necessary and in practice this was given only on the payment of a fine.[21]

Secondly, the Crown was unaffected by the abolition of subinfeudation and was therefore still able to create new tenancies in respect of the fee simple.

(3) IMPORTANCE

Quia Emptores was indeed a landmark in the history of real property. Its chief virtue was that it led to the gradual disappearance of the numerous petty lordships that had arisen between the Crown and the tenant in demesne. Blackacre might no doubt have been held before 1290 by B of A, but if in course of time it passed into the hands of a succession of alienees, each one being substituted for his predecessor, it would ultimately become extremely difficult to prove the existence of A's original lordship. Thus, there was a constant tendency for seignories to become vested in the Crown, and to this extent the law was simplified.

C Forms of Tenure

A feature of English feudalism, and one that complicated the law of land, was that there was not one common kind of tenure. We have seen how in early days, if a man wanted work of a regular nature done for him, he would generally get it done in exchange for land granted by him to the workman. Considering the diversity of personal needs which require to be satisfied, it is obvious that the services due from tenants would vary considerably in nature,

---

[18] See Challis, *Law of Real Property*, pp. 18–19. [19] Holdsworth, *History of English Law*, vol. iii. p. 79.
[20] The meaning of "fee simple" will appear later; pp. 32–3, 167.
[21] Challis, pp. 14, 15. Such fines were abolished by the Tenures Abolition Act 1660.

importance and dignity. One tenant had to fight; another to look after a household, or to provide arms, or to pray for the soul of his overlord, or to do such agricultural work as might be demanded of him. There were vast differences between the possible services. It was considered an honourable thing to fight, but not to plough, and thus there gradually arose different forms of tenure based upon the differences in the nature of the services. The following table shows the state of affairs in the time of Edward I, when the tenures had become stabilised.

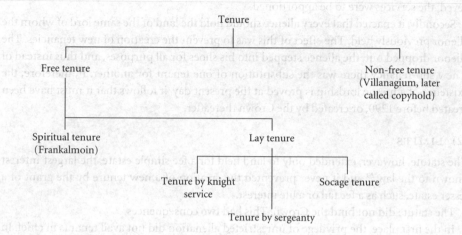

(1) Knight Service[22]

(a) Nature of knight service

The most important of the regular tenures in early days was knight service, or the tenure by which a man was obliged to render military services in return for the land that he held. Soon after the Conquest a process set in whereby the military needs of the country were satisfied in this manner. All the land of the country was held directly of the King, and it was a practically universal rule that the tenants in chief—that is, those men who held directly of the King as distinct from sub-tenants who owed their position to the practice of subinfeudation—held by knight service. Each tenant in chief had to produce for forty days in each year a definite number of fully armed horsemen. The number required in any particular case did not depend upon the extent of the tenant's land, but was arbitrarily fixed when the grant of the land was made, and, as the unit of the feudal host was a constabularia consisting of ten knights, it appears always to have been some multiple of five or ten.[23] For about a hundred years after the Conquest the army—to the strength of about five thousand knights—was actually raised in this way, but it was soon discovered that such a short service as forty days scarcely promoted the success of military operations, and the King began in about 1166 to exact money payments called scutage from the tenants in chief instead of requiring the production of the fixed quota of knights. But by the time of Edward I even scutage had become useless as a means of providing an army, and it can be said that thenceforth the tenure ceased to be military in the sense that it no longer served to supply forces for the defence of the realm.[24]

---

[22] See Holdsworth, *History of English Law*, vol. iii. pp. 37–46.
[23] Round, *Feudal England*, pp. 259–60.
[24] Pollock and Maitland, *History of English Law*, vol. i. p. 252.

What at first sight seems remarkable is that knight service, instead of falling into oblivion after it had ceased to fulfil its original function, continued to develop, and ended by hardening into a legal system far stricter and more onerous than it had hitherto been. The explanation of this inopportune survival was that, quite apart from the duty of military service, the tenure carried with it certain feudal incidents which had such a high financial value for the lords of whom the lands were held that to foster and develop it became a matter of great personal interest. Subinfeudation led to the extension of knight service, and though the military sub-tenant had neither to fight nor to pay scutage, yet, being a military tenant, he was subject to a number of onerous claims from which he would have been free had his tenure been one of the other forms. As the matter is now merely of antiquarian interest, we must confine ourselves to the barest statement of the most valuable of the rights enforceable against a military tenant, namely:

(b) Incidents of knight service

(1) RELIEF

The lord was entitled to the payment of a certain sum, called a relief, when a new tenant succeeded to the land on the death of the old tenant. Payment of the relief entitled the heir to immediate possession, but this was not so where the land was held of the King. In this case the official escheator took possession and held an inquest as to who was next heir. It was only when the heir had done homage and paid the relief that he was entitled to enter the land. This royal privilege of first possession was called primer seisin.[25]

(2) AIDS

The lord was entitled to demand in three special cases that his tenants should pay him a certain sum of money called an aid. The three cases arose when the lord was imprisoned and required a ransom; when he desired to make his eldest son a knight; and when he was obliged to supply his eldest daughter with a dowry on her marriage.

(3) ESCHEAT *PROPTER DELICTUM TENENTIS*

The commission by the tenant of a felony caused the land to escheat, that is to pass to the lord of whom it held. Felony originally meant a breach of that faith and trust which ought to exist between lord and vassal, for example, where the tenant laid violent hands on his lord. At an early date, however, felony lost its exclusively feudal signification and came to mean in effect any serious crime such as murder. The result of this was to benefit the lords, and though it would seem incompatible with the interests of the Crown as custodian of the public peace that the land of a murderer or a thief should pass to a subject, the right of escheat was expressly confirmed by Magna Carta in 1215, subject to the proviso that the land should be held by the Crown for a year and a day. Forfeiture of the land was now said to occur because the felon's blood was attainted or corrupted.[26]

(4) ESCHEAT *PROPTER DEFECTUM SANGUINIS*

This type of escheat was the right of the lord to take the land of his tenant who died intestate without leaving heirs.

[25] Ibid., vol. i. p. 311.

[26] Ibid., p. 303; Digby, *History of the Law of Real Property*, p. 132; Holdsworth, *History of English Law*, vol. iii. p. 67.

(5) WARDSHIP

The most profitable right of the lord was that of wardship. If an existing tenant died leaving as his heir a male under twenty-one or a female under fourteen, the lord was entitled to the wardship of the heir, and as a consequence was free to make what use he liked of the lands during the minority without any obligation to render an account of his stewardship. Upon reaching the prescribed age the ward might sue for *livery* or *ousterlemain*, that is, might enforce delivery of the land. For this privilege half a year's profits had to be paid, though relief was not exigible.

(6) MARRIAGE

Another privilege which the lord enjoyed in respect of infant tenants was the right of marriage. As Blackstone has said:[27]

While the infant was in ward, the guardian had the power of tendering him or her a suitable match, without disparagement or inequality; which if the infants refused, they forfeited the value of the marriage, *valorem maritagii*, to their guardian; that is, so much as a jury would assess, or anyone would bona fide give to the guardian for such an alliance; and if the infants married themselves without the guardian's consent, they forfeited double the value, *duplicem valorem maritagii*.

(2) Tenure by Sergeanty[28]

Tenure by sergeanty was in early times, and from an economic point of view, of considerable importance, but it soon ceased to be anything more than a peculiarly dignified method of holding land. All tenures imply service of one kind or another, but the characteristic of sergeanty was that it required the tenant to perform services of an essentially personal nature. It was that particular form of landholding which was designed to supply the necessities of life. In the first place the great officials of the realm were sergeants, and as such might be required:[29]

to carry the banner of the king, or his lance, or to lead his army, or to be his marshall, or to carry his sword before him at his coronation, or to be his sewer at his coronation or his carver or his butler, or to be one of his chamberlains at the receipt of his exchequer or to do other like services.

Duties of this nature came to be regarded as conferring honour and dignity, and for this reason outlasted the tenure itself, but they did not exhaust the forms of personal services that might be demanded from sergeants. A great lord would require that his accounts should be kept, his letters carried, his estates managed, armour provided, his food cooked, and so on, and he would in most cases grant lands to various sergeants to be held by them so long as the duties were faithfully performed. However, as time went on, it was realised that this was scarcely a convenient method of supplying the needs of life, and tenure by sergeanty began to decay as early as the fourteenth century. It died out altogether except in the case of those great men who performed honourable services for the King, or of humbler persons whose duty it might be to perform some small military duty, such as to supply transport. Moreover, the idea took root, and was fixed law by Littleton's day, that the tenure could exist only between the King and his immediate tenants in chief. The tenure of the great men who

---

27 Blackstone, vol. ii. p. 70.   28 Holdsworth, *History of English Law*, vol. iii. pp. 46 et seq.
29 Litt, s. 153.

performed what were regarded as honourable services came to be called *grand sergeanty*, while that of the lesser military tenants was termed *petit sergeanty*. Grand sergeanty came to be similar to knight service, while petit sergeanty, after the time of Littleton, was practically equivalent to socage.[30]

(3) Frankalmoin

Frankalmoin was the tenure by which a man made provision for the repose of his soul, and it arose where lands were granted to an ecclesiastical body on the understanding that as tenant it would say prayers and masses for the souls of the grantor and his heirs. For various reasons the tenure fell into desuetude.[31]

(4) Tenures Abolition Act 1660

It is not necessary to describe these tenures further because, in 1660, a considerable simpli-fication of the forms of landholding was effected by the legislature. The Tenures Abolition Act, which was passed in that year, destroyed practically all the *free* lay tenures except socage. Tenure by knight service was destroyed altogether, and sergeanty was allowed to continue only in a limited form. Formerly it had rendered the tenant liable to onerous duties similar to those that might be exacted from a knight service tenant, but the effect of the Act was to abolish it as a separate tenure, and, where it existed, only to leave the privilege of perform-ing those honorary services which, as we have seen, were peculiar to the higher ranks of sergeants. In other words, sergeanty was converted into socage,[32] the exceptional feature of the converted land being that the tenant might in some cases substantiate his right to perform certain honorary and dignified services.

Although frankalmoin was not formally abolished by the Act of 1660, it was seldom encountered in practice.

The Act of 1660 was, then, a move in the right direction, since it simplified the system of landholding by practically reducing the former tenures to two, that is to say, to socage and copyhold, though the simplification was not quite so complete as this, owing to the retention of divergent customary methods of holding land known as gavelkind, ancient demesne and borough-English.[33] Yet, even apart from these peculiar cases it is obvious that the existence from 1660 to 1925 of two separate and quite different methods by which a man might hold land, tended to increase the complexities of conveyancing and to render real property law unnecessarily difficult.

We must now briefly describe the two tenures of socage and copyhold which held the field until the legislation of 1925 abolished the latter.

(5) Socage[34]

As distinguished from knight service, socage was that species of tenure which represented the new aspect that the economic life of the country gradually assumed. It was essentially

---

[30] Holdsworth, *History of English Law*, vol. iii. p. 51.

[31] The chief reason for the decline of frankalmoin tenure was that upon alienation of the land, even to another ecclesiastical body, or upon escheat of the lordship to a superior lord, the tenure was converted into socage. Moreover, no fresh grant in frankalmoin, except by the Crown, has been possible since *Quia Emptores*; Challis, *Law of Real Property*, p. 11. Ecclesiastical bodies more frequently held land by one of the other tenures: Maitland, *Constitutional History of England*, p. 25.   [32] Challis, *Law of Real Property*, p. 9.

[33] P. 26, post.   [34] Holdsworth, *History of English Law*, vol. iii. pp. 51 et seq.

non-military and free from the worst features of knight service. At first it could not be defined in positive terms, but was described negatively as being that form of tenure which was neither spiritual, military, sergeanty nor villeinage.

(a) Origin

In early days the services due in respect of the land varied considerably. The tenant might pay a nominal rent sufficient to record the fact that the lands were held of the lord, or a substantial rent equal to the economic value of the land, while sometimes his obligation would extend to the performance of agricultural services. Originally, no doubt, the *socmanni*, as they were called, belonged to the lower orders of society, but the tendency was for this mode of landholding to extend upwards, since it was free from the worst of the feudal burdens incidental to knight service and, to escape those, even the greater landowners were willing to sacrifice something of their dignity.

(b) Commutation of services

The next step was that it became usual to commute services, whatever these might have been, into money payments, and though these, when they were originally fixed, no doubt represented the economic value of the land, yet with the gradual fall in the value of money they became in course of time so insignificant in amount as scarcely to merit the trouble of collection.[35] Thus by 1925 it had become practically impossible to prove that A held of B in socage tenure, for the payment of rent which would have revealed the existence of the tenure had in most cases not been made for centuries. B does not lose much, for the rent is generally of little pecuniary value, and the only other event which might have benefited him before the doctrine of escheat was abolished as from 1 January 1926—namely, the death of the tenant intestate and without heirs, whereby the land would pass to B by escheat—is normally of rare occurrence. Of course the land must be held of somebody, and the rule is that, where no private person can prove his lordship, it is deemed to be held of the Crown.

So socage became the great residuary tenure. It included every tenure which was not knight service, sergeanty, frankalmoin or villeinage, and its outstanding characteristic came to be that it involved some service which was absolutely certain and fixed, and which in the vast majority of cases took the form of a money payment.[36] Though subject to aids and to relief, it was free from the onerous rights of wardship and marriage that characterised knight service. The guardian of an infant socage tenant was the nearest relative who was incapable of inheriting the land. It was enacted by the Statute of Marlborough 1267 that a guardian in socage must account for the profits of the land at the end of his stewardship, and must not give or sell the ward in marriage.

(6) Copyhold[37]

The other tenure to which as late as 1925 English land might be subject was copyhold, the modern name for the old villeinage. Although this tenure was abolished as from 1 January 1926, something must be said about its origin and peculiar characteristics.

---

[35] Pollock and Maitland, *History of English Law*, vol. i. p. 291.   [36] Litt, s. 117.

[37] Holdsworth, *History of English Law*, vol. iii. pp. 491 et seq; vol. vii. pp. 296 et seq; Simpson, *A History of the Land Law*, pp. 155 et seq; Scriven, *Law of Copyholds*; Gray, *Copyhold, Equity and the Common Law*.

(a) Origin

We see in this tenure a system of land holding which represented in modern times customs far older than feudalism, and which dated back to the primitive method of agriculture called the open field system. In remote days the actual tillers of the English soil were almost certainly members of free village communities who owned in common the land that they farmed; but after the Conquest, although they still continued to follow those precepts and habits of agriculture that had been customary for generations, they were gradually absorbed into the feudal system. An overlord had appeared, a new concept in the shape of the manor had been established, and by imperceptible degrees the humble tillers found themselves part of the manorial organisation; no longer free owners, but instead subservient to an overlord upon whose will, according to the strict letter of the law, they were absolutely dependent. Blackstone thought that the modern copyholders were merely serfs who by continual encroachments on their superiors had gradually established a customary right to estates which, strictly speaking, had always been held at the will of the lords.[38] In fact, however, the truth is the exact reverse, for the lords had gradually induced the belief that only by their will were these ancient owners permitted to enjoy their customary rights and estates.[39]

(b) The manor

To understand the character of copyhold tenure we must refer once more to the feudal manor which was the unit of society in mediaeval England.

A typical manor consisted of:

(1) the land belonging to the lord, which was called his demesne;

(2) the land held of the lord by free tenants whether in socage or knight service;

(3) the land held of the lord by persons called villein tenants;

(4) rights of jurisdiction exercisable by the lord over the free tenants in the Court Baron, and over the villeins in the Court Customary;

(5) waste land on which the tenants were entitled to pasture their cattle.

(1) FARM SYSTEM

The first point that emerges about the villeins is that it was they who cultivated the lord's demesne, a practice which originated in what has been termed the farm system. "Farm" in Anglo-Saxon times meant food, and the system in vogue was for the tenant, in return for his holding, to produce a farm—that is, enough food to sustain his lord for some given period, say a night, a week or a fortnight.[40]

(2) LABOUR SERVICE SYSTEM

In the thirteenth century this primitive system gave way to the labour service system,[41] which meant that the villein tenant came under an obligation, often specified in the greatest detail,[42] to cultivate by his own labour his lord's demesne. But the mere obligation to perform agricultural services does not alone suffice to distinguish a villein from a socage

---

[38] Blackstone, vol. ii. p. 95.   [39] See Pollock, *The Land Laws*, pp. 43–52, 208–9.
[40] Vinogradoff, *Villainage in England*, pp. 301–2.   [41] Ibid., p. 304.
[42] See, for example, Pollock and Maitland, *History of English Law*, vol. i. p. 366.

tenant, since it was by no means impossible for a socage tenant to be subject to the same liability. What, then, was the test of villein tenure?

(c) Test of villein tenure

One fact which might be thought at first sight to provide this test is that the villeins received no protection in the King's courts. If they were unjustifiably ejected by the lord, they could recover neither possession nor damages in the royal courts, for in the view of the latter they were nothing more than tenants at the will of the lord.[43] But, though superficially the tenure seemed precarious to the last degree, it was saved from being so in actual fact because the tenants were entitled to protection from the lord's manorial court, where those rules which had been hallowed by immemorial custom within the manor were recognised and enforced. These manorial customs gradually grew into legal systems under which the rights and the duties of the tenants were defined, and the everyday events of marriage, succession, alienation and the like were regulated.[44] But the lack of a remedy in the royal courts was not a sufficient test of villeinage or no villeinage since it also affected an ordinary tenant for years.

That test is to be found, however, in the nature of the services rendered by a tenant. If a man was bound to perform agricultural services it could not be said that he was necessarily a villein tenant, but if he did not know from day to day *what* kind of work would be assigned to him, then he was looked upon as a villein tenant. In other words, the test was the uncertainty of the nature of the work. As Pollock and Maitland have said:[45]

When they go to bed on Sunday night they do not know what Monday's work will be; it may be threshing, ditching, carrying; they cannot tell. This seems the point that is seized by law and that general opinion of which law is the exponent: any considerable uncertainty as to the amount or the kind of the agricultural services makes the tenure unfree. The tenure is unfree, not because the tenant holds at the will of the lord, in the sense of being removable at a moment's notice, but because his services, though in many respects minutely defined by custom, cannot be altogether defined without frequent reference to the lord's will.

So, then, in the thirteenth century villeinage was that tenure in which the return made by the tenant for his holding was the performance on his lord's demesne of agricultural services uncertain in nature.

(d) Money payment system

In the fourteenth and fifteenth centuries this labour service system gave way to a money payment system under which the tenant in villeinage paid a rent to his lord instead of giving personal services, and the lord cultivated his demesne by hired labour.[46] This was an example of the general movement from natural husbandry to the money system, which was fostered in England by several causes, such as the growth of the woollen trade with Flanders and the great increase of trade with the Continent as a result of the English occupation of Normandy and Aquitaine.[47]

---

[43] Pollock and Maitland, *History of English Law*, vol. i. p. 360.
[44] Vinogradoff, *Villainage in England*, p. 172.
[45] Pollock and Maitland, *History of English Law*, vol. i. p. 371.
[46] Holdsworth, *History of English Law*, vol. iii. p. 204.
[47] Vinogradoff, *Villainage in England*, p. 180.

(e) Villein tenure becomes copyhold

The result of the change as regards villeinage was to benefit the tenant, because the rents remained stabilised despite the gradual fall in monetary values. This transition from labour services to money payments corresponded with the transition in nomenclature from villeinage to copyhold tenure. "With the completion of the transition from praedial services to money rents, tenure in villeinage may be said to have come to an end . . . The essence of villein tenure had consisted in the uncertainty of the tenant's services, and when the old agricultural services were commuted for a fixed money payment, this uncertainty passed away."[48]

The derivation of the word "copyhold" is this: the copyhold tenant, like his predecessor the villein, held at the will of the lord; but at the same time he held on the conditions which had become fixed by the customs of his particular manor. The lord's will could not be exercised capriciously, but only in conformity with custom. He still held a court, and that court kept records of all transactions affecting the lands. These records were called the rolls of the court. When, for instance, a tenant sold his interest to a third party, the circumstances of the sale would be recorded, and the buyer would receive a copy of the court rolls in so far as they affected his holding.[49] Inasmuch as he held his estate by copy of court roll, he came to be called a copyholder.

The change from villeinage to copyhold was of far-reaching importance to the tenant. He was rid of all traces of servility; he acquired an interest which in essentials was on all-fours with interests in land held by socage tenure, and above all he obtained recognition and protection from the King's courts. This protection was assured by the end of the fifteenth century. COKE summed up the position in expressive language:[50]

But now copyholders stand upon a sure ground, now they weigh not their lord's displeasure, they shake not at every sudden blast of wind, they eat, drink and sleep securely; only having a special care of the main chance, viz., to perform carefully what duties and services soever their tenure doth exact, and custom doth require: then let lord frown, the copyholder cares not, knowing himself safe, and not within any danger. For if the lord's anger grow to expulsion, the law hath provided several weapons of remedy; for it is at his election, either to sue a *subpoena* or an action of trespass against the lord. Time hath dealt very favourably with copyholders in divers respects.

(f) Defects of copyhold tenure

Despite the possibility of enfranchisement, a process by which copyhold might be converted into socage tenure, a great proportion of English land, even in 1925, was still copyhold. The tenure was distinguished by several defects. For instance, the customs, which represented the local law governing land of this tenure, varied considerably from manor to manor, so that it was impossible to determine the law applicable to a disputed matter without an examination of the manorial records; the form of conveyance was far different from that required in the case of socage; copyhold and socage lands were often intermixed in so confusing a fashion as to make it difficult to discriminate between them, a dilemma from which the only escape in the event of a sale was the execution of two conveyances, one appropriate for copyhold, the other for a socage holding; certain rights of the land were so burdensome to the tenant that they caused strife and ill-will; and finally, it was impossible

[48] Page, *The End of Villeinage*, p. 83, cited Holdsworth, vol. iii. p. 206.
[49] A system of registration of title thus existed long before LRA 1925. But, as we shall see, this system lapsed with the abolition of copyhold.   [50] Coke, *Compleat Copyholder*, s. 9.

for either the lord or the tenant, without the assent of the other, to exploit the minerals under the land.

This bare summary of the history of copyhold tenure should be enough to show that from about the beginning of the seventeenth century it was nothing more nor less than an outmoded and exceedingly inconvenient form of ordinary tenure. It served no particular social need and it certainly impeded a simplified system of conveyancing because of its frequent diversity from socage tenure. It has been rightly described as "an anachronism and a nuisance".[51]

(7) Customary Methods of Landholding

In addition to these regular tenures there also existed in certain districts a few customary methods of landholding under which land was subject in various respects to a number of abnormal incidents. Instances are gavelkind, borough-English and ancient demesne.

(a) Gavelkind

Gavelkind is a word which denotes the customs that have applied since the Conquest to socage land situated in Kent.[52] Such land was in certain particulars subject to different legal rules from those obtaining in other parts of the country. Thus,

   (i)   the land descended upon intestacy to all the sons equally;

   (ii)   a husband who survived his wife was entitled until his re-marriage to a life estate in one-half of her land although issue of the marriage might not have been born;[53]

   (iii)   a widow was entitled until her re-marriage to dower in one-half of her husband's land;

   (iv)   an infant could alienate his land by the form of conveyance known as a feoffment when he reached fifteen years of age; and

   (v)   the land was devisable.

(b) Borough-English

Borough-English was a custom, found in certain parts of the country, under which the land descended to the youngest son to the exclusion of all the other children.[54]

(c) Ancient demesne

Ancient demesne land was land held by freehold tenants in any manor which had belonged to the Crown in the time of Edward the Confessor or William the Conqueror.[55] The tenants in ancient demesne were subject to certain restraints and entitled to certain immunities.[56]

---

[51] Underhill, *Century of Law Reform*, p. 310.

[52] Pollock and Maitland, *History of English Law*, vol. ii. pp. 271 et seq; Blackstone, vol. ii. p. 84; Challis, *Law of Real Property*, p. 14.   [53] *Re Howlett* [1949] Ch 767.

[54] Litt, ss. 165, 211; Blackstone, vol. ii. p. 83.

[55] Co. Fourth Inst. 269; Blackstone, vol. ii. p. 99; Holdsworth, *History of English Law*, vol. iii. pp. 263–9; Challis, *Law of Real Property*, p. 29; *Merttens v Hill* [1901] 1 Ch 842.

[56] Real Property Commissioners, Third Report, pp. 12 et seq; *Merttens v Hill*, supra; *Iveagh v Martin* [1961] 1 QB 232.

(8) Summary of Tenures in 1925

If we now take stock of the feudal tenures as they existed in 1925 we shall find the position to have been as follows: the greater part of English land was held by socage tenure, a considerable part was subject to copyhold tenure, while the remainder was held either in grand sergeanty or in frankalmoin, or was affected by the peculiar customs of gavelkind, borough-English or ancient demesne. Here was room for at least one form of simplification, and we shall see later[57] that the Law of Property Acts 1922 and 1925 seized the opportunity. They converted copyhold and ancient demesne into socage tenure; they abolished gavelkind, borough-English, and all other customary modes of descent; and they purported to abolish frankalmoin.[58] The honorary services incident to sergeanty were retained. Escheat *propter defectum sanguinis*, which was the right of a lord to take the land of his tenant who had died intestate without leaving heirs, was abolished and replaced by a right in the Crown to take the land as *bona vacantia* in the same way that it takes goods.

The result is that though the general theory of tenure is still a part of English law in the sense that all land is held of a superior and is incapable of absolute ownership, yet the law of tenure is both simpler and of less significance than it was before 1926. It is simpler because there is now only one form of tenure—namely, socage. It is of less significance because all the tenurial incidents (including escheat) which might in exceptional cases have brought profit to a mesne lord have been abolished, so that there is no inducement for a private person to prove that he is the lord of land. We can, in fact, now describe the theory of tenure, despite the great part that it has played in the history of English law, as a conception of merely academic interest. It no longer restricts the tenant in his free enjoyment of the land.

II The Doctrine of the Estate[59]

A Seisin. Possession not Ownership

Tenure signifies the relation between lord and tenant, and what it implies is that the person whom we should naturally call the owner does not own the land, but merely holds it as tenant of the Crown or of some other feudal superior. But if he is not owner of the land, what is the nature of the interest that he holds? In statutes, in judicial decisions and in common speech he is always described as a "landowner", but we may well ask what it is that he owns.

It may be said at once that the doctrine of tenure as developed in England made it difficult, if not impossible, to regard either him or his lord as the owner of the land itself. The land could not be owned by the tenant, since it was recoverable by the lord if the tenurial services were not faithfully performed; it could not be owned by the lord, since he had no claim to it as long as the tenant fulfilled his duties.[60]

---

[57] P. 82, post.   [58] As to frankalmoin, see p. 83, post.
[59] Holdsworth, *History of English Law*, vol. iii. pp. 101–37; Pollock and Maitland, *History of English Law*, vol. ii. pp. 2–29; Hargreaves, *Introduction to Land Law*, pp. 19–25, 42–54; Simpson, *A History of the Land Law*, pp. 47 et seq.   [60] Hargreaves, p. 44.

Quite apart from this practical difficulty, however, the truth is that English law has never applied the conception of ownership to land. "Ownership" is a word of many meanings, but in the present context we can take it to signify a title to a subject-matter, whether movable or immovable, that is good against the whole world. The holder of the title, such as the owner of a motor car, has a real as opposed to a personal right—he is the absolute owner. This position is illustrated by the Roman doctrine of *dominium*, under which the *dominus* was entitled to the absolute and exclusive right of property in the land. Nothing less in the way of ownership was recognised. A man had either absolute ownership or no ownership at all. Possession was regarded as fundamentally different—*nihil commune habet proprietas cum possessione*[61]—and, though it was adequately protected, the remedies available were personal, not real.

In sharp contrast to this attitude, English law, in analysing the relation of the tenant to the land, has directed its attention not to ownership, but to possession, or, as it is called in the case of land, *seisin*. All titles to land are ultimately based upon possession in the sense that the title of the man seised prevails against all who can show no better right to seisin. Seisin is a root of title.

... "Seisin" ... is an enjoyment of property based upon title, and is not essentially distinguishable from right. In other words, the sharp distinction between property and possession made in Roman law did not obtain in English law; seisin is not the Roman possession and right is not the Roman owner-ship. Both of these conceptions are represented in English law only by seisin, and it was the essence of the conception of seisin that some seisins might be better than others.[62]

This unfailing emphasis upon the concrete and obvious fact of possession will be apparent if we consider for a moment the following three topics: the remedies that lay at common law for the recovery of land, the position of a tenant who was wrongfully dispossessed, and the long-established mechanism of conveyancing.

(1) Possessory Nature of Early Actions for Recovery of Land

The English actions for the recovery of land, called in early days *real actions*, have consis-tently and continuously turned upon the right to possession. Moreover, their object throughout has been not to inquire whether the title to possession set up by the defendant is an absolute title good against all persons, but whether it is relatively better than any title that the plaintiff can establish. English land law from the earliest days was committed to the doctrine of relative titles to possession. Thus, the issue raised in the most ancient and solemn remedy, the *writ of right*, was not whether the demandant (claimant) could prove an absolute title good against third parties, but whether he or the tenant (defendant) could establish the earlier and therefore the better seisin.[63] Similarly, the possessory assizes, sim-pler remedies introduced by Henry II to supplement the writ of right and to rectify a recent invasion of possession, merely considered the specific question whether the demandant or his ancestor had been unjustly diseised of his free tenement by the defendant. The assize of *novel disseisin*, in other words, recent dispossession, enabled A to recover land from B on proof that he had been ejected by B. The assize of *mort d'ancestor* availed him if he could

---

61 Ownership has nothing in common with possession: Digest of Justinian, 41.2.12.1.

62 Plucknett, *Concise History of the Common Law*, p. 358.

63 Lightwood, *Possession of Land*, pp. 73–4; Plucknett, *Concise History of the Common Law*, p. 358; Simpson, *A History of the Land Law*, pp. 37 et seq.

show that X, his ancestor, had died seised of his land, and that the defendant had entered upon the land on X's death.[64] The sole question in these actions was one of fact relating to seisin. Did B disseise A? Did B take the seisin held by A's ancestor?[65] If so, the court ordered restoration of the seisin, but it did not adjudge that A held an absolute title good against all adversaries. If the defendant wished to litigate the question of title further, he would be driven to issue a writ of right.[66]

At a later date the various *writs of entry* met the case where the disseisin of which the demandant complained was not so immediate, as, for example, where B, after disseising the demandant, had granted the land to Y, who had granted it to the defendant. These actions, no less than the possessory assizes, merely decided whether the better right to seisin lay in the demandant or in the defendant.

Finally, it must be observed that this mediaeval principle of relativity of titles dominated the later action of ejectment. All that the plaintiff needed to do was to prove that he had a better right to possession than the defendant, not that he had a better right than anybody else. If, for instance, he was ejected by the defendant, he would recover by virtue of his prior possession, notwithstanding that a still better right might reside in some third person.[67]

(2) Effect of Loss of Seisin on Proprietary Rights

The effects that flow from a disseisin of the tenant afford a further illustration of the crucial part played by possession in English law. It was established at an early date that the seisin wrongfully taken by the disseisor was the commencement of a fresh title and that it gave him a real, though tortious, interest, valid against all but the disseisee and his successors in title. "Possession being once admitted to be a root of title, every possession must create a title which, as against all subsequent intruders, has all the incidents and advantages of a true title."[68]

In the view of the common law, from the first day of his possession the disseisor had full beneficial rights over the land, holding a fee simple estate which was transmissible either *inter vivos* or by will.[69] Moreover, although the disseisee had a right of action to recover the land, for a long period in our legal history his lack of possession confronted him with serious and ever-increasing difficulties as against the disseisor and his successors in title. In mediaeval days and for long afterwards, the effect of the disseisin was to deprive him of most of his beneficial rights over the land until he had vindicated his claim to seisin in the appropriate real action. His former rights were reduced to a right of entry, a reduction that entailed certain important consequences.

Thus, the disseisee lost the power of alienation, for, being dispossessed, he was unable to make the delivery of seisin essential for a conveyance of land, and a right of entry could neither be devised until 1837,[70] nor be conveyed *inter vivos* until 1845.[71]

---

[64] Sutherland, *The Assize of Novel Disseisin.*

[65] Holdsworth, *History of English Law*, vol. iii. p. 90; Maitland, *Forms of Action*, p. 28.

[66] Plucknett, *Concise History of the Common Law*, p. 359.

[67] *Asher v Whitlock* (1865) LR 1 QB 1, M & B p. 233.

[68] Pollock and Wright, *Possession in the Common Law*, p. 95.

[69] It was only in LRA 2002 that English land law abandoned (for registered land) the common law principle of title based on possession, and the consequential principle that the title of a disseisor could no longer be defeated by the disseisee after the period prescribed by the Limitation Acts; pp. 145 et seq, post.

[70] Wills Act 1837, s. 3.   [71] Real Property Act 1845, s. 6.

Circumstances might well occur which would deprive him of his right of entry and leave him with a mere right of action—a *chose in action* that was equally inalienable, though it would descend to his heirs.[72] For instance, where the disseisor died while still in possession, the land passed to his heir by operation of law with the result that the interest held by him was no longer regarded as tortious. The right of entry was said to be "tolled", taken away, by descent cast.[73]

Again, if the disseisee failed to recover seisin, his widow had no right to dower;[74] if he died heirless, the land did not in all cases escheat to his lord;[75] and if he died leaving an infant heir, his lord was not entitled to wardship.[76]

The position may be summarised in the words of Holdsworth:

The person seised has all the rights of an owner; the person disseised has the right to get seisin by entry or action; but, till he has got it, he has none of the rights as an owner. In other words, the common law recognizes, not *dominium* and *possessio*, but seisin only.[77]

(3) Possession Root of Title for Conveyancing Purposes

The third illustration of the emphasis laid by English land law upon possession, not upon ownership, is afforded by the practice of conveyancers in unregistered land.[78] A vendor must prove to the satisfaction of the purchaser, not only that he is entitled to the land which he has agreed to sell, but also that his title is not subject to adverse claims vested in third parties. He can scarcely be expected to prove that he has a title good against the whole world, for, since land is permanent and indestructible, it may well be that there exists a competing and better title created many years ago and still existing.

English land law has no doctrine akin to that of Roman law by which possession for a definite but short period had the positive effect of investing the possessor with *dominium*. As one writer has observed, the absolute ownership of a perishable chattel, such as a motor car, is a comparatively easy matter to prove, but "if we were to insist upon the same fulness of ownership with regard to land we should have to trace back our title to the original grant of Paradise to Adam".[79] What the vendor can do, however, and what he does do in practice, is to rely upon the fundamental principle that seisin is evidence of his title to the land.

With very few exceptions, there is only one way in which an apparent owner of English land who is minded to deal with it can show his right so to do; and that way is to show that he and those through whom he claims have possessed the land for a time sufficient to exclude any reasonable probability of a superior adverse claim.[80]

What, then, emerges so far is that land cannot be the subject-matter of ownership, though the person in whom its seisin is vested is entitled to exercise proprietary rights in respect of it. But again the question recurs—what is the nature of the interest held by the person seised? Is there nothing that he can be said to own? The answer made by English law is unique. The person entitled to seisin owns an abstract entity, called an *estate*, which

---

[72] Hayes, *Introduction to Conveyancing*, vol. i. p. 231.

[73] The doctrine of descent cast was abolished by the Real Property Limitation Act 1833, s. 39.

[74] Maitland, *Collected Papers*, vol. i. p. 366.   [75] Ibid., pp. 368–9.

[76] Ibid., p. 369. On the subject generally, see Holdsworth, *History of English Law*, vol. iii. pp. 91–2.

[77] Holdsworth, *History of English Law*, vol. iii. p. 95.

[78] For the distinction between registered and unregistered land, see pp. 91 et seq, post.

[79] Hargreaves, *Introduction to Land Law*, p. 42.

[80] Pollock and Wright, *Possession in the Common Law*, pp. 94–5.

is interposed between him and the land.[81] "The English lawyer . . . first detaches the ownership from the land itself, and then attaches it to an imaginary thing which he calls an estate."[82]

B Features of Doctrine of Estate

The estate represents the extent of the right to seisin. Thus the correct description of a tenant entitled to immediate seisin for his life is that he is *seised of Blackacre for an estate for life*. This estate entitles its owner to exercise proprietary rights over the land for the prescribed period, subject to observance of the tenurial duties, and it may be disposed of as freely as any other subject-matter of ownership. This doctrine, as will be explained later,[83] is not confined to the case where a man is entitled to immediate seisin. If he is definitely entitled to it at some future time, he is equally the owner of an estate.

Two phenomena of great significance emerged during the development of this doctrine by the common law.

First, estates vary in size according to the time for which they are to endure. On this basis they are classified as estates of freehold and estates less than freehold.

Secondly, several different persons may simultaneously own distinct and separate estates in the same piece of land.

These matters will now be discussed in more detail.

(1) Estates Classified According to Duration

The main classification of estates depends upon their quantification and their quantification depends upon their duration. The estate will vary in size according to the time for which it is to continue. "Proprietary rights in land are, we may say, projected upon the plane of time."[84] Thus a person may be entitled to seisin for ever or for a lesser period.

(a) Meaning of freehold estate

Estates are sub-classified into those of freehold and those of less than freehold. Into which of these categories they fell depended in the earliest days upon the quality of the tenure by which the estate owner held his land. A tenant in knight service, sergeanty, socage or frankalmoin was called a "freeholder", since the services due from him were free from servile incidents. He was said to have a frank tenement or freehold estate to distinguish him from a villein tenant.[85] Such was the original meaning of the expression "freehold estate".

But one of the characteristics of these free tenants was that the time for which they were entitled to hold the land was not fixed and certain. They invariably held either for life or for some other space of time dependent upon an event that might not happen within a lifetime, and it was this uncertainty of duration, not the quality of the services to be rendered, that

---

[81] Lawson, *Rational Strength of English Law*, p. 87.   [82] Markby, *Elements of Law*, s. 330.
[83] P. 34, post.
[84] Pollock and Maitland, *History of English Law*, vol. ii. p. 10. Compare the language used in the course of argument in *Walsingham's Case* (1579) 2 Plowd 547 at 555: "The land itself is one thing, and the estate in the land is another thing, for an estate in the land is a time in the land, or land for a time, and there are diversities of estates, which are no more than diversities of time, for he who has a fee simple in land has a time in the land without end or the land for time without end."
[85] Ibid., vol. ii. p. 78; Holdsworth, *History of English Law*, vol. ii. p. 351.

gradually came to be regarded as the essential feature of a freehold estate.[86] Thus, even at the present day, an estate is freehold if its duration is uncertain; it is less than freehold if the time of its termination is fixed or capable of being fixed. The life tenant is a freeholder, but not so the tenant holding under a lease for a definite period, even though he holds for as long a period as 999 years.[87]

(b) Freeholds and non-freeholds distinguished in respect of seisin

Freehold and non-freehold estates were further distinguished in respect of seisin. At first the word "seisin" was used to denote possession both of land and of chattels, but this usage did not last long and by the fifteenth century a man was said to be seised of land, but possessed of chattels. Later the subject-matter of seisin became even further restricted. The real actions that lay for the recovery of land, the possessory assizes and the writs of entry, were available only to freeholders, that is, to tenants in fee simple, in tail and for life. These actions, as we have seen, were based entirely upon seisin and since they availed only freeholders it is not unnatural that the word "seisin" was reserved exclusively to describe the possession of a freehold estate. Since mediaeval days it has been correct, for instance, to describe a tenant for life as seised, but a tenant for years as possessed, of the land.

(c) Tabular illustration

On the basis of duration the common law classified estates in the manner set out in the following table.

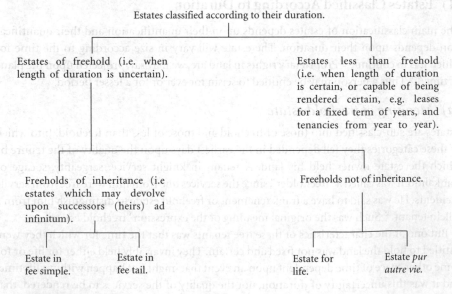

Estates classified according to their duration.

Estates of freehold (i.e. when length of duration is uncertain).

Estates less than freehold (i.e. when length of duration is certain, or capable of being rendered certain, e.g. leases for a fixed term of years, and tenancies from year to year).

Freeholds of inheritance (i.e estates which may devolve upon successors (heirs) ad infinitum).

Freeholds not of inheritance.

Estate in fee simple.

Estate in fee tail.

Estate for life.

Estate *pur autre vie*.

(d) Freehold estates

As regards duration, the three freehold estates may be distinguished as follows:

(1) FEE SIMPLE

The fee simple[88] is the largest estate in point of duration, for, being one that is granted to a man and his heirs, it will last as long as the person entitled to it for the time being dies leaving

---

[86] Co Litt 43b.   [87] See, generally, *Preston on Estates*, vol. i. c. 1.   [88] See chap. 8, post.

an heir, and therefore it may last for ever in the sense that it may never pass to the Crown so long as there is an heir. The word fee denotes its inheritability, and the word simple indicates that it is inheritable by the general heirs of the owner for the time being whether they be ascendants, descendants or collateral.

(2) FEE TAIL

The fee tail,[89] which is the only other estate of inheritance, is less in quantum than the fee simple since it is inheritable only by the specified descendants of the original grantee and never by his ascendants, and also because it is descendible only to his lineal issue and not to his collateral relatives. Thus it is inferior to the fee simple in the sense that it has not as great a capacity for perpetual existence. The classic formula for its creation was "to A and the *heirs of his body*".

(3) LIFE ESTATE

The life estate[90] includes an estate which A holds for his own life and also one that he holds during the lifetime of B, this second species being called an estate *pur autre vie*.

(2) Apportionment of Fee Simple

The second phenomenon mentioned above is that the fee simple, which entitles the tenant to use the land for an infinite time, is regarded by English law as an aggregate out of which any number of smaller *and simultaneous* estates may be carved.[91] The entire subject-matter of enjoyment is apportionable among a number of persons, each of whom is the present owner of his individual portion.

By way of illustration let us suppose that a fee simple owner desires that A shall enjoy Blackacre for life, that on A's death the right of enjoyment shall pass to B for life and that subject to these life interests the fee simple shall be vested in C.

(a) Civil law doctrine

Every legal system that permits dispositions of this kind must necessarily particularise the legal nature of the rights, if any, vested in the successive beneficiaries, and the solution reached must depend upon whether or not the land itself is capable of ownership. It is obvious that any system of law which admits this capacity cannot regard A, B and C as simultaneous owners, for, in so far as ownership imports the right of immediate user, B and C cannot use the land at the same time as A, unless, of course, they are made joint, not as in our example successive, owners. The jurisprudential solution, therefore, if the land itself is the subject of ownership, is to insist that it can be the subject only of absolute ownership, and that where, as in the above example, there is a limitation to a succession of persons the entire and absolute ownership shall pass from one beneficiary to another upon the happening of the prescribed events. This is what is called *substitution*. Under this doctrine, if land is limited to A, then to B and then to C, the legal result is that these persons in their turn become owners of the property, each taking by substitution for the one who preceded him; each in his turn being complete owner; but each taking nothing until his turn comes.[92]

---

[89] See chap. 14, post.   [90] See chap. 15, post.
[91] Digby, *History of the Law of Real Property*, p. 270.   [92] See Markby, *Elements of Law*, s. 330.

B, for instance, is not even a limited owner of the land during the life of A, but on the death of the latter he becomes the absolute owner of the land for a limited time. Until his turn comes he has no proprietary interest that he can alienate or otherwise dispose of.

This is the solution of Roman law and of certain modern legal systems[93] which regard dominium as the exclusive and unlimited right to the land itself, not merely to its user.

By Roman law, A, the owner, might indeed let the land to X by *locatio conductio* or grant it to him for life by way of *usufruct*, but his ownership was affected by neither transaction. In the former case, X, if evicted, had merely a contractual right enforceable against A alone; in the latter, he acquired only a *jus in re aliena*, that is, a right to use for his life land the owner-ship of which remained vested in A.

(b)　English law doctrine

English law, however, having divorced ownership from the land itself and attached it to an imaginary thing called an *estate*, which entitles the owner to use the land for a longer or a shorter period of time, has been able to take a bolder course. Having decided that estates may vary in size according to their duration, it goes a step further and concedes that any estate, whether its duration is long or short, and whether it confers a right to immediate or to future seisin, is capable of a present existing ownership.

(c)　Consequences of English law doctrine

Two results flow from this view.

(1)　DIFFERENT DEGREES OF ESTATE OWNERSHIP

First, there may be different degrees or gradations of estate ownership. The tenant in tail and the tenant for life, no less than the tenant in fee simple, are owners of their estates. As com-pared with the tenant in fee simple, they must, indeed, be described as *limited* owners, since their estates have not the same capacity of infinite duration. None the less they are owners, and their ownership differs from that of the tenant in fee simply only in degree—in quantity. There is no difference in kind or quality.[94]

The same remedies for the recovery of the land and the same powers of dealing with the estate by way of alienation are available, irrespective of the size of the estate. The different freehold estates, in other words, represent various grades in the hierarchy of ownership.

(2)　FUTURITY OF RIGHT TO SEISIN NOT INCOMPATIBLE WITH PRESENT OWNERSHIP

The second result of the English doctrine is that an estate may be the subject of a present existing ownership, even though the right of the owner to seisin is postponed to a future time. This is explicable in elementary terms.

An estate is the right to possess and use the land for the period of time for which it has been granted. In the case of the fee simple the period is infinite, since the estate is capable of

---

[93]　Typically, modern European civil systems follow the Roman model. See, e.g., Bell, Boyron and Whittaker, *Principles of French Law*, p. 277; *International Encyclopedia of Comparative Law*, vol. VI, *Property and Trust*, chap. 2 (J. H. Beekhuis), giving a general account of the law of property in civil law jurisdictions.

[94]　Pollock and Maitland, *History of English Law*, vol. ii. p. 7. As we shall see in the following chapters (a) equity recognised the equivalent estates—and so there could be an equitable fee simple, estate tail or life estate; and (b) in 1925 the *legal* estates were limited to the fee simple absolute in possession and the term of years

perpetual existence. The entire ownership, in other words, resides in the person holding the fee simple, since he and his successors are entitled to use the land for ever. But time is divisible, and this right of perpetual user may be divided into successive periods of limited duration or, as one writer put it, into successive intervals of time.[95] One slice of the perpetual time, one slice of the entire ownership, may be given to A, another to B, and so on. Therefore, if the fee simple owner makes a grant

to A for life, then to B for life and then to C in tail,

each grantee receives at once a portion of the one uniform subject-matter, namely the right to use the land. A, B and C each hold a distinct and separate share of the identical thing. The only difference between them lies in the periods for which the user is to be enjoyed. Moreover, there is no futurity about the *ownership* of B and C. Upon the execution of the grant they become the immediate and absolute owners of an estate. It is not the right of ownership, but the right to actual seisin of the land that is future. Indeed, by virtue of their power of disposition they may exchange their property for money and so make it immediately available.[96]

(d) Advantages of English law doctrine

In conclusion, it may be said that this doctrine of the estate has given an elasticity to the English law of land that is not found in countries outside the area of the common law.[97] This is particularly true in respect of settlements, that is, dispositions of property designed to provide for a succession of persons, such as the present and future members of a family. The desire to do this has dominated English real property law throughout its long history; for land, with its virtue of permanency, is an ideal source of endowment and its use for this purpose has been favoured by the courts. The aims of a settlor will be more effectively attained if he is permitted to vest a definite right of ownership in certain persons upon the occurrence of certain prescribed events in the future, as for example by directing that if a son is born to the present tenant of Blackacre, he shall, on reaching his majority, immediately acquire a definite proprietary interest, even though the present tenant is still alive. If the land itself is the subject-matter of ownership, the simultaneous existence of two or more owners, unless they are to take jointly, is, as we have seen, impossible, and therefore in countries where that concept of ownership prevails the power to create successive interests stretching into the future is necessarily restricted. But once admit that what is owned is an imaginary thing called an estate, then it immediately becomes possible to frame elaborate and subtle schemes for the passing of the beneficial enjoyment of the land to one person after another in certain prescribed eventualities. There is room "to deal with ownership in a more fanciful way than if it were attached to the soil".[98]

---

absolute. So in the modern law there are differences of kind or quality between a fee simple, an entail and a life interest, as regards their recognition by, respectively, the common law and equity. But the first stage in the development of the law of real property, described in the present chapter, was the recognition *by the common law* of these several estates.

[95] (1857) 1 Jurid Soc p. 537 (S. M. Leake).   [96] Ibid., p. 538.

[97] It has been described by a distinguished writer as "one of the most brilliant feats of the English mind": Lawson, *Rational Strength of English Law*, p. 97.   [98] Markby, *Elements of Law*, s. 330.

C Leasehold Interest. Term of Years[99]

We will now conclude with a short description of the leasehold interest or term of years which, quantitatively considered, is the smallest proprietary interest recognised by English law.

(1) Not a Freehold Estate

This interest, generally referred to as a term of years, arises where land has been demised, that is, leased, for a definite number of years. It thus lacks the requirement of an uncertain duration, and though the period for which it is to last may be very great, as for instance 999 years, yet it is not a freehold estate, and in the eye of the law is a smaller interest than a life estate.

(2) Not Real Property

Moreover it is not even real property. At an early period English law arrived at the general principle that, while land could be recovered specifically by a dispossessed tenant from a man who had ejected him, yet a person who was deprived of personal chattels could not enforce their actual recovery, but had to content himself with compensation in the shape of pecuniary damages. Broadly speaking, actions fell into two classes. The real actions lay for the restitution of some object, and the personal actions for the recovery of damages. As land was the only object of which restitution in specie could be enforced, it followed that it formed the only subject matter of a real action, and it is not surprising to find the ancient lawyers seizing upon this fact and defining land as real property. Property which could be recovered in a real action was itself called real property, and thus it resulted that real property consisted solely of interests in land.

But not every interest in land could be specifically recovered, for, as we have seen, the real actions were available only to freeholders, that is, only to tenants who were seised of the land. A tenant for years was possessed, not seised, and if dispossessed he could originally bring only a personal action for the recovery of damages against the grantor of his term. It is true that by the close of the Middle Ages a remedy had been introduced whereby he might recover the term itself, but nevertheless he was still regarded, and has ever since been regarded, as a non-freeholder. The doctrine of seisin was never extended to his interest, and the *possessory assizes* and the *writ of right*, which were the real actions properly so called, were never made available to him. He continued to hold merely personal property because originally his sole remedy was to bring a personal action.

At first sight this refusal of the law to regard a leaseholder's interest as real property is curious. It was not due to the unimportance or insignificance of terms of years. Such interests were on the contrary exceedingly valuable. The cause of their segregation, the reason why they were dissociated from the real actions and from feudal doctrine, was probably none other than economic pressure.[100]

At a time when investments in the modern sense of the term were unknown, one of the few methods by which a man might increase his income was to purchase a beneficial lease

---

[99] Holdsworth, *History of English Law*, vol. iii. pp. 213–17; vol. vii. pp. 238–96; Simpson, *A History of the Land Law*, pp. 71–7, 92–5, 247–56.

[100] Pollock and Maitland, *History of English Law*, vol. ii. pp. 113 et seq; Plucknett, *Concise History of the Common Law*, pp. 571–3.

and take the profits of the land as interest on the money expended. Again, one of the ordinary methods of exacting security for a debt was for the debtor to lease his lands at a nominal rent to the creditor, so that the latter could obtain interest at the agreed rate out of the profits of the land without coming into conflict with the usury laws.[101] Another familiar form of investment was to purchase a wardship, which was the right to administer for one's own benefit the lands of an infant tenant in knight service. But if terms of years and wardships were to be effective investments, it was necessary that they should not be regarded as freehold estates in land carrying seisin, or, in more general terms, it was convenient to exclude them from the domain of strict real property law. There were several considerations that made this line of action advisable, but none was more potent than the fact that freehold estates as distinct from chattels could not be left by will. It may have been a matter of sound policy that an estate in lands should inevitably descend to the heir of the deceased tenant, but it would be poor comfort to tell a man who had invested his money in the purchase of a term of years that he had lost the right of bequeathing his money because he had converted it into land. After showing that as early as 1200 there was a large speculative traffic in wardships, Pollock and Maitland say: "And then as to the term of years, we believe that in the twelfth century and later, this stands often, if not generally, in the same economic category. It is a beneficial lease bought for a sum of ready money; it is an investment of capital, and therefore for testamentary purposes it is *quasi catallum*."[102]

D Classification of Property

(1) Real and Personal Property

The position reached by the common law was that estates of freehold represented real property law in the strict sense of that term, and as such were subject to all the consequences of feudal tenure; while on the other hand leaseholds (together with some other rights in land) were personal property and not so subject, and for this reason were neither affected by the incidents of feudalism, nor governed by the same legal rules as freeholds.

(2) Chattels Real and Personal

This position soon gave rise to a difficulty, for a term of years, no matter how it might be treated by the technique of the law, was obviously a valuable interest in land, and one which it was appropriate to bring within the province of the land laws. To sever its connection with the law of land merely because it was outside the scope of the real actions would have been absurd, and so the law was obliged to surmount the difficulty by the invention of a new terminology.

It was already a commonplace that the subject-matter of proprietary interests was either real property or chattels. Chattels were personal property, since they were not specifically recoverable in a real action. Leaseholds were thus subject to the law of chattels, but since they lacked the attribute of movability the obvious solution was to regard them as a *tertium*

---

[101] Holdsworth, *History of English Law*, vol. iii. pp. 128, 215. For the significance of the usury laws in the modern law, see p. 741, post.

[102] Pollock and Maitland, *History of English Law*, vol. ii. p. 117. "Catallum" is the mediaeval Latin word for cattle, chattels or, generally, movable goods.

quid—interests partly real and partly personal. Thus it was that personal property was sub-divided into chattels real and chattels personal.

Chattels real, saith Sir Edward Coke, are such as concern or savour of the realty; as terms for years of land, wardships in chivalry, . . . the next presentation to a church, estates by statute merchant, statute staple,[103] *elegit*[104] or the like. And these are called real chattels, as being interests issuing out of or annexed to real estates; of which they have one quality, viz. immobility, which denominates them *real*, but want the other, viz. a sufficient legal indeterminate duration, and this want it is that constitutes them *chattels*.[105]

Thus there are two classes of chattels known to English law—chattels real as described by Coke, and chattels personal, which originally were confined to movable things, but which are now taken to comprise many forms of wealth, such as negotiable instruments, copyright, patents, trade marks, shares in a company and so on.

(3) Summary

We see, therefore, that the Law of Property as a whole falls into the following three divisions:

The *law of property* strictly so called, i.e. the rules that govern freehold interests in land—the fee simple, the entailed interest and the life interest;

The law of chattels real, i.e. the rules that govern leaseholds;

The law of pure personalty.

Of these three departments of law the first and the last stand furthest apart, for the law of real property has been constructed on feudal principles, while the law of pure personalty has drawn its inspiration from a variety of non-feudal sources, such as Roman and Canon law and the customs of merchants. Midway between the two comes the law of chattels real, which Blackstone describes as having a "mongrel amphibious nature", since it has derived its rules partly from real property law and partly from the law of pure personalty. The tendency, however, for several centuries has been to bring freeholds into conformity with chattels real, and the process of assimilation has been carried to such lengths, especially by the legislation of 1925, that we now have substantially a common and uniform system of law for real property and chattels real.[106] But, as we shall see, in spite of this assimilation, leaseholds today still remain personal as opposed to real property.[107]

---

[103] A tenancy by statute merchant or statute staple arose when a merchant creditor by taking advantage of the Statutes Merchant and Staple (Edward I and III) obtained seisin of his debtor's lands; see Digby, *History of the Law of Real Property*, p. 282.

[104] A writ of execution by which a judgment creditor might obtain seisin of his debtor's lands. It was abolished by SCA 1981, s. 141.

[105] Blackstone, vol. ii. p. 386.   [106] Pp. 86 et seq, post.   [107] P. 192, post.

3

MODIFICATION OF THE COMMON LAW BY EQUITY

SUMMARY

Our task is to show how equity modified and tempered the feudal principles of the common law by its introduction of the "use" and the consequent establishment of the trust concept, which is probably the most outstanding characteristic of English law. It is this concept that has produced the peculiarly English distinction between the legal and the equitable estate that forms the basis of modern conveyancing.

I Disadvantages Incidental to the Common Law Tenures

To understand the origin of uses it is necessary to examine the position of a tenant of land under the common law. That his position was not without its troubles can be realised by a glance at some of the disabilities and burdens which weighed upon him, several of which were due to the important part played by seisin in the feudal system. The feature of that system was its immaturity, as regards both the interests which might be created in land and the methods by which the interests could be dealt with. Possession is an obvious fact, and in early days it was the dominating fact upon which most of the repressive rules that came into being were founded.

Two fundamental principles which in themselves were sufficient to establish the importance of seisin were that the feudal services which in the early history of tenure were of such consequence to the lord were enforceable against the person seised and only against him; and again that it was only against the same person that an action for the recovery of land could be brought. It was necessary that there should always be some person capable of meeting adverse claims and preserving the seisin for successors.[1] The effect of not knowing who was actually seised of land would be the loss of public and private rights therein,[2] and therefore two inviolable rules that became established were that there must never be an abeyance of seisin, or in other words that there must be an uninterrupted tenancy of the freehold; and that every transfer of a freehold estate must be effected by an open and public delivery of seisin. Any disposition that would cloud the title to the seisin was forbidden at common law.

The following were some of the fetters laid on the free enjoyment of a freehold estate at common law:

A Conveyances were Required to be Public and Formal

In a feudal society it was imperative that there should be no uncertainty as to the identity of the freehold tenant of any piece of land. A question might arise regarding the title to the land or the right of a lord to enforce the feudal dues to which he was entitled, and as both these matters could be settled only if it was known who was seised, common law required that every transfer of a freehold estate be effected by an open and public delivery of seisin, either upon or within view of the land conveyed. The merit of this was that in the event of a dispute the actual freehold tenant would be well known to the neighbourhood. The method itself was called *feoffment with livery of seisin*, but the operative part of the transaction was the delivery, and a charter of feoffment, which only served to authenticate the transaction, was not strictly necessary.[3]

There were other kinds of common law assurances, but it may be said of them all that they were open and notorious, although, when the feudal vigour began to abate, they gradually ceased to bear this characteristic.[4] It often happens that a man, instead of publishing his dealings with land to the world at large, prefers to resort to some transaction which is secret and free from ceremony, but at common law this was a desire that was unattainable, at any rate in the early days.

B Types of Interests were Strictly Limited

As it was essential that the seisin should not be in abeyance for an instant, but should always be vested in a freehold tenant, it followed that every conveyance of freehold had to be made

---

[1] See Co Litt 342b, Butler's note (1).   [2] Challis, *Law of Real Property*, p. 100.
[3] Co Litt 271b, note 1.
[4] Hayes, *Introduction to Conveyancing*, vol. i. pp. 29–30. For the history of the subject, see Holdsworth, *History of English Law*, vol. iii. pp. 220–46; vol. vii. pp. 353 et seq.

to take immediate effect, so that the seisin passed at once to the grantee. This meant that many dispositions which a tenant might legitimately desire to make were rendered impossible. For instance, a gift of a freehold interest which was to vest in the donee if and when he attained twenty-one years of age was void, since such a gift had to be completed by delivery of seisin, and if seisin were delivered at once, it would, having been parted with by the donor, be vested in nobody until the donee attained twenty-one. If a grant were made to A for life and after his death to B when he attained twenty-one, the grant to the latter failed unless he had reached that age at the death of A, because otherwise an abeyance of seisin would have occurred. Again, under a grant to A for life and after his death to the future children of B, only children who were in existence at A's death could take, for to allow later children to come in would have broken still another general principle, namely, that a transfer of a freehold interest had to be carried out by a public transaction.

Thus it is clear that the concentration of the common law upon the simple fact of possession led to extreme simplicity in the interests that might be created, and restricted within narrow bounds the limitation of future interests.[5]

C A Tenant at Common Law could not Devise his Freehold Estate

Whatever may have been the rule in Anglo-Saxon days, one of the effects of the introduction of feudal tenure into this country was to abolish the right of leaving freeholds by will, except in a few particular localities and boroughs. To have allowed such wills would not only have diminished the lord's right of taking the land by escheat and have been a hardship to the heir, but it would have run counter to a feudal policy which demanded that every transfer should be notorious and public.[6]

D A Tenant at Common Law was Liable to Certain Onerous Feudal Incidents[7]

This is not the place to elaborate the burdensome nature of the tenurial dues that have already been briefly described. It must suffice to cite an expressive passage in which Blackstone sums up the position of one who held his lands in knight service:[8]

In the meantime the families of all our nobility and gentry groaned under the intolerable burthens, which (in consequence of the fiction adopted after the Conquest) were introduced and laid upon them by the subtlety and finesse of the Norman lawyers. For, besides the scutages to which they were liable in defect of personal attendance, which however were assessed by themselves in parliament, they might be called upon by the king or lord paramount for aids, whenever his eldest son was to be knighted or his eldest daughter married; not to forget the ransom of his own person. The heir, on the death of his ancestor, if of full age, was plundered of the first emoluments arising from his inheritance, by the way of relief and primer seisin; and, if under age, of the whole of his estate during infancy. And then, as Sir Thomas Smith very feelingly complains, "when he came to his own, after he

---

5 Pp. 509 et seq, post.   6 Holdsworth, *History of English Law*, vol. iii. pp. 75–6.
7 See pp. 19–20, ante.   8 Blackstone, vol. ii. p. 76.

was out of wardship, his woods decayed, houses fallen down, stock wasted and gone, lands let forth and ploughed to be barren," to reduce him still farther, he was yet to pay half a year's profit as a fine for suing out his livery; and also the price or value of his marriage, if he refused such wife as his lord and guardian had bartered for, and imposed upon him; or twice that value, if he married another woman. Add to this, the untimely and expensive honour of knighthood; to make his poverty more completely splendid. And when by these deductions his fortune was so shattered and ruined that perhaps he was obliged to sell his patrimony, he had not even that poor privilege allowed him, without paying an exorbitant fine for a licence of alienation.

There were additional disadvantages that resulted directly from the important part played by the feudal services. Thus, for instance, several of the feudal dues consisted of payments which were made by the newcomer upon the death of a tenant, and, as these would never be enforceable if the lands were granted to a body which never died, the rule soon became established that lands, granted to an association such as a monastery without the licence of the King and the lord paramount, were forfeited. Such a grant was called a *grant in mortmain*, and statutes were passed from time to time maintaining the rule as to forfeiture.[9]

Enough has now been said to show that the position of a freehold tenant at common law, as regards freedom of disposition, was not enviable. To quote Hayes:[10]

Large deductions must, therefore, be made from the praise lavished on the ancient common law, when its provisions are said to have promoted security of enjoyment, simplicity of title and notoriety of transfer. As civilization advanced, it proved less and less sufficient to attain those favourite objects of its founders, while it was manifestly ill-adapted to meet the growing demands of freedom and commerce. The rules of ownership and modes of assurance which we have endeavoured to explain, composed an unbending and oppressive code, utterly inadequate to the extended view and complicated interests of an intelligent and wealthy community. The progress of society called for a more pliant and liberal policy.

II Disadvantages of Common Law Tenures Avoided by the Device of Putting Lands in Use

History shows us that whenever a grievance presses hardly on the greater part of the population, it is not long before a remedy is discovered, and it was certainly not long before a "more pliant and liberal policy" was introduced with regard to the rights and powers of landowners in general. But the new policy did not come from the common law. It was the sole work of the Chancellor, who made it possible by means of the protection which he gave in his court of equity to the new conception called the *use* of lands. It was due to this alone that a tenant was enabled to retain the ordinary advantages of landholding which were assured to him by the common law while escaping some of the worst disabilities of that system.

---

[9] Blackstone, vol. ii. p. 268; p. 926, post.
[10] Hayes, *Introduction to Conveyancing*, vol. i. pp. 30–1.

A Origin and Effect of Putting Lands in Use

(1) Origin of the Use

The word "use" is derived not from the Latin *usus* but from *opus*.[11] Maitland has shown us that before Domesday it was a common practice for one man to deal with land *ad opus*—on behalf of—another, as, for instance, where the sheriff seized lands *ad opus domini Regis*, where a knight about to go to the Crusades conveyed his property to a friend on behalf of his wife and children, or where the vendor of an unfree tenement surrendered it to the lord to hold on behalf of the purchaser.[12] The word *opus*, which was in such connections commonly adopted, became gradually transformed into *oes*, *ues*, and thence into *use*. Now, if one person could deal with land on behalf of or to the use of another for a particular purpose, the question that inevitably occurred to men was why one person should not in a *general* way be allowed to hold land to the use of another. This, as a matter of fact, is exactly what was done in course of time. The tenant A would transfer his land by a common law conveyance to B, who undertook to hold it on behalf of, or, adopting the correct expression, to the use of, A. In such a case B was called the *feoffee to uses*, that is, the person to whom the feoffment had on certain conditions been made; while A went by the name of the *cestui que use*, which meant the person on whose behalf the land was held.

The practice did not spring into life all at once, and Maitland believed that 1230 was the earliest time at which one man was holding land permanently and generally to the use of another.[13]

In the second quarter of the thirteenth century came hither the Franciscan friars. The rule of their order prescribes the most perfect poverty: they are not to have any wealth at all. . . . Still, despite this high ideal, it becomes plain that they must have at least some dormitory to sleep in. They have come as missionaries to the towns. The device is adopted of having land conveyed to the borough community to the use of the friars.

By the fourteenth century this device had become more extensive and there is evidence that it was a common practice for a landholder to convey his land to two or more friends *ad opus suum*—to his own use[14]—or to the use of a third person.

(2) Legal Effect of Putting Lands in Use

(a) Cestui que use *lost his rights at common law*

The important point to observe is the legal effect of this practice. It was to cut off the *cestui que use* in the eyes of the *common law* from all connection with the land. By an assurance operating at common law he had conveyed his estate to the feoffees to uses, and was therefore deprived of all common law rights over the land. He was nothing, the feoffees were everything; he had exchanged an actual estate for an intangible right, for instead of keeping seisin he had decided to rely upon the confidence that he had reposed in the feoffees.

---

[11] Maitland, *Collected Papers*, vol. ii. p. 403; Pollock and Maitland, *History of English Law*, vol. ii. p. 228. For the origin and history of uses, see Holdsworth, *History of English Law*, vol. iv. pp. 407 et seq; (1965) 81 LQR 562 (J. L. Barton); Simpson, *A History of the Land Law*, pp. 173 et seq; Bean, *The Decline of English Feudalism*, esp. chap. 3; Baker, *Introduction to English Legal History*, chap. 14.   [12] Maitland, supra.

[13] Maitland, *Equity*, p. 25; and see *Collected Papers*, vol. ii. p. 408. A Papal Bull ordained in 1279 that a use was not property.   [14] Ibid., pp. 25–6.

If, therefore, B (the feoffee) refused to account to his *cestui que use* A for the profits, or wrongfully conveyed the estate to another, this was merely a breach of confidence on the part of B, for which the common law gave no redress; much less did that law acknowledge any right in A to the possession or enjoyment of the land. The ordinary judicature knew no other proprietor than B; to him, and to him alone, attached the privileges and liabilities of a landholder; for he it was, to whom the possession was legally delivered. To have regarded A in any other light than that of a mere stranger to the soil would have been to subvert a system raised upon investiture and tenure. It was accordingly decided at a very early period[15] that the common law judges had no jurisdiction whatever in regard to the use.[16]

If the feoffees failed or refused to carry out the directions imposed upon them,[17] or if they deliberately alienated the land for their own purposes,[18] there was no common law action by which they could be rendered liable, and as a *cestui que use* who was let into possession of the land was regarded as a mere tenant at will of the feoffees to uses, he could be turned out by the latter at any moment, and in the event of contumacy could be sued in trespass.[19]

(b) Uses protected by Chancellor

This absence of all remedy seems at first sight to stultify the practice of putting lands in use, and it would have been fatal had no alternative means been discovered for protecting the *cestui que use*. But an adequate form of protection was ready to hand. From about the year 1400 the Chancellor, in the first blush of his growing jurisdiction, stepped in and interceded on behalf of the *cestui que use*. He could not interfere with the jurisdiction of the common law courts by proceeding in a direct fashion against the land itself, because the absolute title to the land was vested in the feoffees by operation of the immutable principles enforced in those courts, but his role was to see that men acted honestly according to the precepts of good morality, and, in accordance with the principle that equity acts *in personam*, he did not hesitate to proceed against feoffees who disregarded the moral rights of the *cestui que use*. He was in a stronger position than the common law courts, for not only could he order a person to perform some definite act under pain of attachment, but his power of viva voce examination enabled him to discover breaches of good faith.

The spectacle of feoffees retaining for themselves land which they had received upon the faith of their dealing with it for the benefit of others was too repugnant to the sense of justice of the community to be endured. The common law could give no remedy, for by its principles the feoffee was the absolute owner of the land. A statute might have vested, as the Statute of Uses a century later did vest, the legal title in the *cestui que use*. But in the absence of a statute the only remedy for the injustice of disloyal feoffees to uses was to compel them to convey the title to the *cestui que use* or hold it for his benefit. Accordingly the right of the *cestui que use* was worked out by enforcing the doctrine of personal obedience.[20]

In other words, the wrong which an unfaithful feoffee committed was breach of contract, but it was a breach for which at that time no remedy lay in the ordinary courts, since the general principle of the enforceability of contracts was still undeveloped. Further, it was

---

[15] 4 Edw. 4.   [16] Hayes, *Introduction to Conveyancing*, vol. i. p. 33.
[17] 3 Rot Parl 511, No. 112, cited Ames (1907–8) 21 Harv L Rev, p. 265; *Select Essays in Anglo-American Legal History*, vol. ii. p. 741.   [18] Sanders, *Uses and Trusts*, vol. i. p. 67.
[19] *Preston on Estates*, vol. i. p. 145.
[20] Ames, *Select Essays in Anglo-American Legal History*, vol. ii. p. 741.

common for a use to be declared in favour of a third party, and even if the modern doctrine of contract had been perfected, the rules as to privity of contract[21] would have precluded the grant of a remedy to the *cestui que use*.

B Creation of the Distinction Between the Legal and the Equitable Estate

We have seen that from the year 1400 the Chancellor began to build up a comprehensive
jurisdiction over uses, but it is especially important to observe that his intervention in this
field led to the introduction into English law of what is generally described as a duality of
land ownership. He did not deny that the *feoffee* was entitled at common law to the exclusion of the *cestui que use*, since the land had been conveyed to him by a conveyance effective at common law. That fact was inescapable, but what the Chancellor insisted upon was
that the *feoffee* should scrupulously observe the directions imposed upon him by the *feoffor*. The feoffment had not been made to him for his own benefit.

In other words, while the *feoffee* was regarded as owner by the common law, the *cestui
que use* was considered to be the true owner by equity: the former had the legal ownership,
the latter the equitable ownership of the same piece of land. Thus we get the essentially
English distinction between the legal and the equitable estate—the legal estate recognised
and protected by the common law courts, and the equitable estate recognised and
protected only by the Chancellor. This is what is meant by *duality of ownership*. Starting
with the assumption that A had conveyed land to B to be held to the use of A, or to the use
of C, Hayes, writing in 1840, described the position that arose:[22]

But, under the auspices of an ecclesiastical chancellor, the use, though alien to the soil, took root in
our civil jurisprudence, and attained to a degree of influence and importance which at length almost
superseded the ancient polity. Means were soon devised for compelling B, the owner in point of law,
to keep good faith towards A or C, the owner in point of conscience. The king, in his Court of
Chancery, assumed jurisdiction to extort a disclosure upon oath of the nature and extent of the confidence reposed in B, and to enforce a strict discharge of the duties of his trust. Hence Equity arose.
From this period, when the right of A (or C) became cognizable in the Court of Chancery, we may
speak of him as the equitable or beneficial owner, and of B as the legal owner. But in order to preserve a clear perception of the twofold character of the system, we must keep steadily in view the fact
that B had still the *real* right, to be enforced, on one side of Westminster Hall, by judgment of law *in
rem*, which went at once to the possession of the land itself; while A (or C) had nothing more than a
mere right *in personam*, to be enforced on the other side of the Hall, by subpoena, directed against
the individual trustee. The Chancery, in assuming jurisdiction over the use, left untouched and invi-
olate the ownership at the common law. It exercised no direct control over the land, but only coerced
and imprisoned the person of the legal owner who obstinately resisted its authority. It usurped none
of the powers or functions of a court of law, but, leaving to the latter the redress of wrongs done to
the realty, confined its jurisdiction to matters of trust and confidence, which could not be reached by
the arm of ordinary justice.

---

[21] It was only in 1999 that a general rule was created allowing a contract to create rights enforceable directly
by third parties: Contracts (Rights of Third Parties) Act 1999; p. 676, post.

[22] Hayes, *Introduction to Conveyancing*, vol. i. pp. 33–4.

C Advantages of Putting Lands in Use

Before we proceed any further it is desirable to notice how some of the worst burdens incidental to tenure at common law might be avoided by the device of a use.

There were at least six substantial advantages that might accrue to the *cestui que use*.

(1) Lands became Devisable

That very natural desire that the power of testamentary disposition, which already applied to goods and chattels, should be extended to land, contributed more largely than any other factor to the rapid establishment of the use. The obligation of the feoffees to administer the legal estate according to the wishes of the *cestui que use* was not confined to the lifetime of the latter, and from an early date it was the usual practice for the beneficial owner to specify what the destination of the use should be after his death. In this indirect way, by making a testamentary disposition of the equitable as distinct from the legal estate, men were accustomed to provide for their younger sons, daughters and other relatives, to ensure the payment of their debts and to make charitable gifts.[23]

(2) Conveyances of Land Facilitated[24]

The common law principle that a conveyance should be open and notorious could easily be evaded by means of the use, for just as the *cestui que use* could direct what dispositions of the land should be made after his death, so he could give similar directions that would be operative during his life. A transfer of the use required no formality; the one essential was that the intention of its owner should be clearly manifested. Moreover, the system of conveyancing was radically affected as the result of an equitable doctrine which applied even where land had not deliberately been put in use. This was that a mere contract to sell a legal estate raised a use in favour of the purchaser immediately on payment of the purchase money. Such a contract was called a *bargain and sale*, and though at first it passed merely an equitable estate to the purchaser, it gained a far wider operation after the Statute of Uses in 1535 and developed into the normal method of conveying *legal* estates.[25]

---

[23] Holdsworth, *History of English Law*, vol. iv. pp. 438–9.   [24] Ibid., pp. 424–7.

[25] For the history of the matter, see Holdsworth, *History of English Law*, vol. vii. pp. 356–60. The process of development may be briefly described as follows: (1) A, having bargained and sold land to B for a fee simple estate and having received the purchase money, was implicitly seised to the use of B. (2) The Statute of Uses provided that when A stood seised to the use of B, the latter should acquire the *legal* estate (p. 50, post). Had this been the only enactment, therefore, a bargain and sale after the statute would have provided a secret method of conveying *legal* estates. (3) The Statute of Enrolments, however, passed at the same time, enacted that no estate of *inheritance or freehold* should pass, nor should any use be raised, by a bargain and sale, unless the bargain and sale was made by deed and enrolled in one of the King's Courts of Record. (4) The last statute applied only to sales of freehold or inheritable estates. Therefore a bargain and sale of a leasehold might be made privately without enrolment. This fact was quickly appreciated (certainly before 1620), and it became usual to transfer a fee simple as follows: A bargained and sold Blackacre to B *for one year*. On payment of the purchase money A became seised to the use of B. The Statute of Uses operated upon this state of affairs and passed the legal possession to B, leaving the reversion in A. Next day A executed a deed of *release* which extinguished his reversion and consequently enlarged B's leasehold into the fee simple. This form of conveyance, which was called a *lease and release*, remained the normal method of conveyance until 1841, when it was enacted that a release alone should be as effectual as a lease and release. A simple deed of grant was substituted for a release in 1845. See (1988) 104 LQR 617 (J. M. Kaye), arguing that the object of the Statute of Enrolments was not to prevent secret conveyancing,

(3) Settlements of Land Facilitated

We have already mentioned,[26] and indeed shall have occasion to explain more fully later,[27] that the power of a landowner at common law to create future interests was so severely restricted that only the simplest forms of settlements of a legal estate were possible. This stringency was relaxed upon the introduction of uses. The use, to which the restrictive rules of common law were wholly inapplicable, conferred upon its owner an almost unrestrained liberty to specify who the future beneficiaries should be, upon what events their interests should arise, and in what order the interests should take effect. The equitable estate was, in fact, a pliable instrument, a subject-matter that could be moulded by its owner into such forms as might appear desirable to him. Thus arose what were called shifting and springing uses.[28]

(4) Avoidance of Feudal Burdens

The most oppressive of the feudal burdens to which a tenant was liable at common law[29] were those that became exigible at his death, namely, wardship, marriage, reliefs and primer seisin. No relief from these would be gained by the appointment of a sole feoffee to uses, for the latter, in his capacity as tenant at law, would be caught in the feudal net and *his* death would entitle the lord to exact such dues as might be demandable. The usual practice, therefore, was to enfeoff, not one, but several, persons as joint tenants. The rule of joint tenancy is that the share of a tenant who dies does not pass to his heir but accrues to the surviving tenants.[30] He leaves nothing for which his heir can be made to pay a relief, he leaves nobody over whom the lord can claim the right of wardship or of marriage. The one essential, therefore, was to ensure that the number of feoffees never fell below two. The death of the *cestui que use* himself, despite his position as the true beneficial owner, created no right to feudal dues, since they were the consequence of tenure, and the use "being the creature of conscience, the offspring of moral obligation, could not be the subject of tenure".[31] "The lord could not look behind the feoffees; they were his tenants: it was nothing to him that they were allowing another person to enjoy land which by law was theirs."[32]

(5) Avoidance of Forfeiture and Escheat

Land held by tenure at common law was forfeited to the Crown if the tenant committed high treason, and upon his conviction or outlawry for felony it passed to the Crown for a year and a day and then escheated to the lord.[33] These unpleasant consequences, however, were avoided, if a tenant, before embarking upon some doubtful enterprise, had the prescience to vest his lands in a few confidential friends. The delinquent might possibly suffer the extreme penalty, but at least his family would not be destitute.

---

but that "it was foreseen that, without it, the Statute of Uses would have had some unfortunate effects upon security of titles".   [26] P. 40–1, ante.

[27] Pp. 510–14, post.   [28] Pp. 514–5, post.   [29] Pp. 19–20, ante.   [30] P. 455, post.
[31] Hayes, *Introduction to Conveyancing*, vol. i. p. 34.   [32] Maitland, *Equity*, p. 27.
[33] See Challis, *Law of Real Property*, pp. 33 et seq.

(6) Evasion of the Mortmain Statutes

We have noticed that, since those feudal dues that became exigible at the death of a tenant would be lost to the lord if land came into the hands of a body that might never die, such as a corporation, a series of Acts, generally called the Mortmain Statutes, were passed from an early date providing that land granted to a corporation without the licence of the King and lord paramount should be forfeited.[34] Uses, however, provided an obvious means of evading this prohibition, and, until the practice was finally stopped in 1392,[35] it was a common plan for a donor to enfeoff a number of persons to hold to the use of a monastery or other corporation.

D Influence of Common Law Doctrines on the Use

We should next notice how the Chancellor dealt with this new form of ownership called the use or equitable estate. It was his own creation. He had invented something hitherto unknown to the law. He was free to do what he liked with his own. In the quaint language of an old judge, the use was as clay in the hands of the potter,[36] and, as the owner of a use was in theory allowed to give any imaginable directions as to its enjoyment, the Chancellor might have allowed it to be moulded into forms entirely subversive of common law principles. There were, in fact, several forms of landed interests, unattainable at common law, which he did permit to be carved out of the use, but they were mostly confined to the realm of future interests. Thus, for instance, the dispositions mentioned on page 41, which would have been void at common law, were open to a landowner if he was content to create them by way of use.

It may be said in general, indeed, that in framing rules for the governance of the use the Chancellor refused to be bound, or to let the development of the use be hampered, by any of the common law rules connected with tenure. And yet it was certainly not his policy to encourage wide deviations from the established tenets of the law. The exact contrary was the case. Having begun by affording an adequate protection to the use, he then to some extent allowed the fact that its basis rested on personal confidence to fade into the background, and proceeded to regard it as a kind of interest in land, "a sort of immaterialized piece of land", in which actual estates might be created just as they might be created at common law.[37]

In other words, the general policy of the Chancellor in his development of the use was to adopt the accepted rules of common law. When necessary he was prepared to depart from those rules on the ground of convenience, but he usually took them as his guide. It can, indeed, be said "that there scarcely is a rule of law or equity of more ancient origin, or which admits of fewer exceptions, than the rule that Equity followeth the law."[38]

Thus upon the death of the *cestui que use*, Equity applied the common law rules of descent; the common law rights of a husband to the wife's property after her death were extended to the equitable interest, though a wife was not dowable out of her husband's equitable estates until 1833; and estates, similar in extent to those possible at law, might be created in the use. As Butler noted: "There is the same division in Equity as there is at law, of estates of freehold and inheritance, of estates of freehold only, and of estates less than

---

[34] P. 926, post.   [35] 15 Ric. 2, c. 5.   [36] *Brent's Case* (1583) 2 Leon 14 at 16, per MANWOOD J.
[37] Maitland, *Equity*, p. 31.   [38] Butler's note to Co Litt 250b, xvi.

freehold; of estates in possession, remainder or reversion; and of estates several and of estates undivided."[39]

To sum up this part of the discussion we may say that a use of lands existed where the legal estate was vested in A in such circumstances that he was subject to a trust enforceable in equity to convey the legal estate to such persons, and in the meantime to apply the rents and profits in such manner, as the *cestui que use* should direct; and, failing directions, should hold the land and pay the profits to the use of the *cestui que use* himself.[40]

E The Later History of Uses and the Rise of the Modern Trust Estate

What, then, is the essential difference between the legal and the equitable estate? It is clear at first sight that the legal estate carries the bare technical ownership, while its equitable counterpart gives the *cestui que use* beneficial ownership. One is the nut, the other the kernel. If land is conveyed to

A and his heirs to the use of B and his heirs,

there is no doubt that A is the true *legal* owner. But it is an unprofitable ownership, for unless he succeeds in some fraudulent enterprise he will be compelled to deal with the land as B desires. In truth, the difference goes much deeper than this, but before stating wherein it lies we should say something of the subsequent history of uses.

(1) Statute of Uses 1535

(a) Object of statute

The equitable estate, which was the greatest achievement of the Chancellor, was not allowed to pursue its course of development undisturbed. It was assailed by the legislature under Henry VIII, who, with a view to the "extirping and extinguishment of all such subtle practised feoffments, fines, recoveries, abuses", procured the passing of the Statute of Uses in 1535.[41] Many reasons were alleged in justification of this statute, but the real object of the King's action was to restore to something like their ancient buoyancy and dimensions those feudal dues of which the collection had been rendered so much less fruitful by the practice of conveying land to uses. The simplest remedy was to abolish uses altogether, and this the King tried to do. In 1532 a Bill was presented to Parliament in an attempt to limit the consequences of uses. This met with strong opposition, however, and Henry warned the Commons in March 1532 that he would "search out the extremity of the law". This he did by obtaining, in the case of *Lord Dacre* in 1535, a decision that any devise of lands by a tenant in chief who died leaving an heir under age was *ipso facto* fraudulent. Parliament, thus faced with a fait accompli which undermined the title of many tenants in chief, was prevailed upon to pass the Statute of Uses.[42]

---

[39] Ibid.   [40] *Gilbert on Uses*, p. 1; Fearne, *Contingent Remainders*, p. 291, note *h*.

[41] 27 Hen. 8, c. 10.

[42] (1967) 82 EHR 673 (E. W. Ives); Bean, *The Decline of English Feudalism*, chap. 6. For an earlier view of the origins of the Statute, see Holdsworth, *History of English Law*, vol. iv. pp. 450–61; (1912–13) 26 Harv L Rev, pp. 108–27.

The Act contained a very long preamble, the general object of which was to denigrate as grievances the advantages which uses conferred upon the landowning class as a whole, while keeping in the background the real purpose of the statute, which was to replenish the royal coffers. The preamble made the statute look as if it were a highly popular measure, but Maitland put the matter in its true historical setting when he said:[43]

A long preamble states the evil effects of the system [of uses], and legal writers of a later day have regarded the words of this preamble as though they stated a generally admitted evil. As a matter of historical fact this is not true. The Statute of Uses was forced upon an extremely unwilling parliament by an extremely strong-willed King. It was very unpopular and was one of the excuses, if not one of the causes, of the great Catholic Rebellion known as the Pilgrimage of Grace. It was at once seen that it would deprive men of that testamentary power, that power of purchasing the repose of their souls, which they had long enjoyed. The King was the one person who had all to gain and nothing to lose by the abolition of uses.

(b) Effect of statute

The statute was passed, however, and its effect was to abolish the distinction between the legal and the equitable estate in the case of the passive use, that is to say where the feoffees stood seised to the use of B and were the mere passive instruments for carrying out the directions of B. A conveyance to

A and his heirs to the use of B and his heirs,

which before the statute would have carried only the equitable estate to B, operated after 1535 to pass the legal estate to him. This was so because the statute provided in effect that, when any person was seised of lands to the use of any other person, the *cestui que use* should be deemed to have lawful seisin of the land to the extent of his interest in the use, and the seisin that prior to the statute would have been in the feoffee to uses, A, should be deemed to be in the *cestui que use*, B. In other words, the statute brought about two results:

First, to adopt a technical expression it *executed the use*, that is to say, it turned B's former equitable estate into a legal estate carrying common law seisin; and

Secondly, the common law seisin, which would normally have been vested in A as a consequence of the conveyance, was taken away from him entirely.[44]

A was a mere nonentity, and as a general rule nothing was to be gained by conveying to A to the use of B instead of making a direct conveyance at common law to B, since in both cases B was seised of the legal estate, and by reason of that fact was in both cases subject to the dues, burdens and incapacities that had always affected an estate at common law.

(c) Advantages and disadvantages of statute

The advantages of the statute lay with the common lawyers and with the King, its disadvantages with the general class of landowners. The common lawyers profited because they

---

[43] Maitland, *Equity*, p. 34; and see Froude, *History of England*, vol. iii. pp. 91, 105, 158.
[44] Fearne, *Contingent Remainders*, p. 273, Butler's note.

acquired a profitable jurisdiction over the uses that had been turned into legal estates. The King profited because the conversion of uses into legal estates involved the abolition of the power to devise lands, and this, in itself, increased very considerably the value of the tenurial incidents.[45]

The statute was a real grievance in many ways. For one thing the common belief was that it prevented wills of land, and, though this was a misapprehension,[46] it caused such irritation[47] that it was found necessary in 1540 to pass the Statute of Wills which permitted a tenant to devise all his socage lands and two-thirds of his lands held in knight service.

It would seem, then, if we proceeded no further with the history of uses, as if COKE was right when he said that:[48]

the makers of the statute at last resolved, that uses were so subtle and perverse, that they could by no policy or provision be governed or reformed; and therefore, as a skilful gardener will not cut away the leaves of the weeds, but extirpate them by the roots, and as a wise householder will not cover or stir up the fire which is secretly kindled in his house, but utterly put it out; so the makers of the said statute did not intend to provide a remedy and reformation by the continuance or preservation, but by the extinction and extirpation of uses; and because uses were so subtle and ungovernable, they have with an indissoluble knot coupled and married them to the land, which of all the elements is the most ponderous and immovable.

(d) Uses not executed by statute

This, however, was to go too far, for the Act did not entirely abolish uses. There were at least two cases in which the grantees to uses retained the legal estate and were still compelled by the Chancellor to fulfil the intention of the grantor.

(1) USES OF LEASEHOLDS

First, since the statute applied only where a feoffee was seised to the use of another, it was necessarily inoperative where a term of years, as distinct from a freehold estate, was given to A to the use of B, for A was possessed, not seised, of the subject-matter.

(2) ACTIVE USES

Secondly, the exclusion of the statute was admitted where an active duty was imposed upon the feoffees to uses, as for instance where they were directed to collect the rents and profits and to pay them to B. In these circumstances it was recognised that the legal estate must remain with the feoffees, for otherwise they could not justify their right to the rents.

In both these instances, the conscience of the feoffees to uses was affected and they came under a moral duty to deal with the legal estate on behalf of the beneficiary—in the one case to transfer the term to him, in the other to secure the rents for him—and it was a duty that was enforceable only by the Chancellor. As regards terminology, however, it became usual to describe the person whose conscience was affected in these cases as being under a *trust* to carry out the directions of the grantor.[49] The uses were not those which the statute could execute, yet they were trusts which in conscience ought to be performed.[50]

---

[45] Holdsworth, *History of English Law*, vol. iv. pp. 463–4.   [46] See (1944) 7 CLJ 354 (R. E. Megarry).
[47] Froude, *History of England*, vol. iii. p. 89.   [48] *Chudleigh's Case* (1595) 1 Co Rep 113b.
[49] Plucknett, *Concise History of the Common Law*, pp. 598–9.   [50] Blackstone, vol. ii. p. 336.

The statutory abolition of the passive use, of course, was in no way affected by this exercise of the Chancellor's jurisdiction. It long remained true that if the fee simple were granted to A to the use of B, A was divested of the legal estate and deprived of his former functions. Nevertheless, the principle that a moral duty must be performed was developed with such insistence that the passive use was ultimately restored in the shape of the passive trust, for the courts of equity gradually extended the circumstances in which the person upon whom the statute conferred the legal estate was bound in conscience to hold it in trust for some other person in accordance with the intention of the grantor.[51]

(e) The use upon a use

A striking example of this enduring concern of Chancery with the problem of conscience is furnished by the ancient rule that there could be no use upon a use. The rule established before the statute was that if land were conveyed to

A and his heirs to the use of B and his heirs to the use of C and his heirs.

it was only the use in favour of B that took effect. He acquired the equitable estate, and the second use in favour of C was ruled out as being repugnant to the first.[52] This was confirmed at common law soon after the statute in *Jane Tyrrel's Case*,[53] the result of which was that B, not A, acquired the legal estate and the limitation in favour of C was still nugatory. The repugnancy of his use with that of B was, of course, apparent, for as was said in another case, "The use is only a liberty to take the profits, but two cannot severally take the profits of the same land, therefore there cannot be an use upon an use."[54]

(2) Development of Modern Trust

(a) Passive use finally restored

Although it was equally apparent, as Blackstone remarks,[55] that B was never intended by the parties to have any beneficial interest in the land, the Chancery court at first came to the same conclusion and repudiated the second use.[56] Ultimately, however, and certainly by 1700, it reversed this view and restored the passive use by holding that B must be regarded as holding the legal estate in trust for C. It was against conscience for one man to retain what was clearly intended for another. The exact stages by which this result was reached are not discernible. It was long thought that *Sambach v Dalston* (or *Darston*)[57] in 1634 was the decisive authority, but research has shown that this is to go too far.[58] The

---

[51] Plucknett, *Concise History of the Common Law*, p. 599.

[52] (1532) Bro Ab, Feoff. al Uses, 40; cited Ames, *Select Essays in Anglo-American Legal History*, vol. ii. p. 748.

[53] (1557) 2 Dyer 155a; Digby, *History of the Law of Real Property*, p. 375. Jane bargained and sold land (p. 46, ante) to her son, G, and his heirs, upon the understanding that G was to hold to the use of Jane for life and thereafter to the use of himself in tail. The purchase money was paid, and therefore by implication of law Jane was seised to the use of G. The statute operated upon this use, and gave G the legal fee simple. But further uses had been declared, namely, to Jane for life and then to G in tail, and the question was whether these were valid or not. It was held that they were void.

[54] *Daw v Newborough* (1716) 1 Com 242; cited Ames, vol. ii. p. 748.   [55] Vol. ii. p. 336.

[56] *Girland v Sharp* (1595) Cro Eliz 382; Digby, *History of the Law of Real Property*, p. 375.

[57] (1635) Toth 188; Nelson 30, sub nom. *Morris, Lambeth et Margery v Darston*.

[58] (1958) 74 LQR 550 (J. E. Strathdene); Simpson, *A History of the Land Law*, p. 202; see further (1957) CLJ 72 (D. E. C. Yale); (1966) 82 LQR 215 (J. L. Barton), arguing that "the trust of freehold was an accepted

importance of that decision was the refusal of the court to ignore the grantor's intention. In the actual circumstances of the case he intended to benefit not only C, but also an infant after the death of C and therefore the court directed B to make such dispositions of the land as would fulfil the whole of the grantor's design. This direction, however, did not involve the restoration of the passive use or any recognition of the modern passive trust, for B's obligation was to divest himself of the legal estate, not to retain it and hold it on behalf of C.[59]

(b) Rise of modern passive trust

Eventually, however, a change in the political situation facilitated the restoration of the passive use. The passive use had been abolished in 1535 for the sole reason that the King laid the loss of his feudal revenue at its door. But towards the end of the seventeenth century a complete revolution had occurred in the political sphere. Owing to the abolition of the military tenures in 1660 and to the gradual fall in the value of money, the feudal dues had become of little consequence and, indeed, the royal finances had been put on a more satisfactory footing. This fact, coupled with an almost universal desire for the old liberty of action, enabled the Chancellor once more to recognise the former distinction between the legal and the equitable estate whenever the intention was that B should hold land on behalf of C. The device eventually adopted by conveyancers to make this intention effective was merely to limit a use upon a use.[60] Thus, if it was desired to create an equitable estate in favour of C, instead of adopting the pre-statute method of a conveyance to A to the use of C, all that was necessary was to add a second use and make the conveyance run to A to the use of B to the use of C. The effect of this was that the statute divested A of his interest and passed the legal estate to B, with the result that, since the second use was not executed by the statute, C was left with a mere equitable estate corresponding with the equitable estate that existed in the pre-statute days under the name of the use.

(c) Creation and terminology

Thus the old distinction was retained in spite of the statute, but both the method of creating the distinction and the terminology adopted to describe it were changed. The first use in favour of B, which was executed by the statute, was still called a use, but the second one in favour of C, on which the statute did not operate, was for greater clearness always designated a "trust".[61]

The practice ultimately adopted was to leave A out altogether and to create the equitable estate by conveying the land

unto and to the use of B and his heirs in trust for C and his heirs.

The effect of this was that B, called the *trustee*, acquired the legal estate by virtue of the common law; but he also obtained the use, and though he was deemed to take the legal estate at common law and not under the statute, for there was no other person seised to

institution at any rate in the latter part of the sixteenth century"; and this is supported by two manuscripts: (1977) 93 LQR 33 (J. H. Baker).

[59] Plucknett, *Concise History of the Common Law*, pp. 601–2.　　[60] Ibid., p. 602.

[61] Hayes, *Introduction to Conveyancing*, vol. i. p. 54. See Holdsworth, *History of English Law*, vol. v. pp. 307–9; vol. vi. pp. 641–4.

this use,[62] yet, since a use had been declared in his favour, the rule that there could be no use upon a use prevented the statute from operating upon the second use and passing the legal estate to C.[63]

Thus, despite the complacent optimism of COKE, the old distinction between the legal and the equitable estate was fully restored by at any rate the early eighteenth century. In 1738, Lord HARDWICKE stated the position in these words:[64]

Yet [after 1535] the judges still adhered to the doctrine, that there could be no such thing as *an use upon an use*, but where the first use was declared, there it was executed, and must rest for that estate: therefore, on a limitation to A and his heirs, to the use of B and his heirs, in trust for D, B's estate was held there to be executed by the statute, and D took nothing.

Of this construction equity took hold, and said that the intention was to be supported. It is plain B was not intended to take, his conscience was affected. To this the reason of mankind assented, and it has stood on this foot ever since, and by this means a statute made upon great consideration, introduced in a solemn and pompous manner, by this strict construction, has had no other effect than to add at most three words to a conveyance.

The last remark of the Lord Chancellor, however, though picturesque and arresting, was scarcely accurate, for, as we shall see, the statute had a vital and a lasting effect in so far as it enabled a class of future interests (springing and shifting uses), hitherto unknown to the common law, to be carved out of the legal estate.[65]

F The Essential Difference Between the Legal and the Equitable Estate

The position with regard to equitable estates remained as indicated above until 1 January 1926. If, that is to say, it was desired to create a trust estate, all that was necessary was to convey land *unto and to the use of* trustees in fee simple, in trust for the *cestui que trust*— or beneficiary, as we will designate him in the future.

The questions that now require answering are:

(1) What is the nature of trust estates, and

(2) What is the exact point of difference between them and legal estates?

(1) Nature of the Trust Estate

In the first place it may be said in a general way that the uses which continued, after and in spite of the statute, to have their old effect were simply the same original uses appearing under the different name of trusts.[66] But this is not the whole story. As Lord

---

[62] "The statute ought to be expounded that, where the party seised to the use and the *cestui que use* is one person, he never taketh by the statute, except there be a direct impossibility or impertinency for the use to take effect by the common law": Bacon, *Reading on the Statute of Uses*, p. 440.

[63] *Samme's Case* (1609) 13 Co Rep 54; *Doe d Lloyd v Passingham* (1827) 6 B & C 305; *Orme's Case* (1872) LR 8 CP 281; *Hadfield's Case* (1873) LR 8 CP 306; *Cooper v Kynock* (1872) 7 Ch App 398; *Sanders on Uses and Trusts*, vol. i. p. 89; Hargreaves, *Introduction to Land Law*, pp. 96–8.

[64] *Hopkins v Hopkins* (1738) 1 Atk 581 at 591.   [65] Pp. 514–5, post.

[66] *Lloyd and Jobson v Spillet* (1741) 2 Atk 148, per Lord HARDWICKE.

MANSFIELD said in *Burgess v Wheate*,[67] "An use and a trust may essentially be looked upon as two names for the same thing; but the opposition consists in the difference of the practice of the Court of Chancery." As is inevitable in the development of any legal conception equitable interests became much more elaborate and were adapted to many more purposes than in the days before the Statute of Uses. Lord Keeper HENLEY said in the same case:[68]

Geometry was the same in the time of Euclid as in that of Sir Isaac Newton, though he applied the principles and rules to effect greater discoveries and more important demonstrations . . . An use, say the older books, was neither *jus in re*, nor *ad rem*, but a confidence resting in privity of person and estate, without remedy but in a court of equity. What else is a trust? What other definition can be given of it? No other is attempted. But it is said since the existence of trusts (since the statute), equity has modelled them into the shape and quality of real estates, much more than it did in earlier times when they were called uses. It has made tenants by the curtesy, permitted tenants in tail to suffer common recoveries etc. And why? Because equity follows the law. And between *cestui que trust* and those claiming by, from and under him, it is equity that he should be considered as formally possessed of that estate of which he is and appears substantial owner. But this is only the effect of the equitable jurisdiction's growing to maturity, and was an accident that to a degree accompanied uses as well as trusts. Lord Bacon observes that they grew to strength and credit by degrees and as the Chancery grew more eminent.

Thus uses required that the feoffee to uses should have the fee simple estate, but trusts could be declared upon the estates of tenants in tail, for life or for years; uses were generally passive, that is, the feoffee was a dormant instrument compelled by equity to obey the directions of the *cestui que use*, but later development allowed the creation of special trusts under which the trustee might be directed to perform such duties as the sale of land, the accumulation of profits, the management of estates and so on. Again, the use applied only to land, but the subject-matter of trusts has expanded to such a degree that at the present day it includes, not only every conceivable kind of property, but even objects unconnected with property. The trust, for instance, has enabled unincorporated associations, such as clubs, trade unions and nonconformist bodies, which, owing to the indefinite and fluctuating character of their personnel, are not persons in the legal sense, both to own property and to fulfil the objects of their formation. The ownership of premises cannot reside in an unincorporated club, but it may be vested in a few persons, who, in the capacity of trustees, will not only have a legally protected ownership but will be amenable to the jurisdiction of the court if they fail to administer the property on behalf of the members and in accordance with the rules.[69] Then again the trust is not the only form of equitable interest known to the law. The interest that arises in favour of a person who has made a valid contract for the purchase of land or a valid contract for a lease; the right which an owner possesses to enforce certain restrictive covenants; the interest in land retained by a person before 1926 who mortgaged the land in return for a loan of money—these are all equitable interests[70] and exhibit the one great characteristic that distinguishes them from legal estates.

---

[67] (1759) 1 Eden 177 at 217.   [68] Ibid., at 248.

[69] See Maitland, *Collected Papers*, vol. iii. pp. 271–84 (*The Unincorporate Body*); pp. 321–404 (*Trust and Corporation*); Warburton, *Unincorporated Associations: Law and Practice*; Maudsley and Burn, *Trusts and Trustees*, pp. 354–72.   [70] Pp. 65–6, post.

(2) Difference between Legal and Equitable Estate

That brings us to the second point. What is that characteristic, or, in other words, what is the difference between the legal and the equitable estate?

As we have said, the difference is not adequately defined by the statement that the legal estate confers an empty title, while the equitable estate amounts to beneficial ownership of the land. The fundamental distinction is this: a legal estate is a right *in rem*, an equitable estate a right *in personam*, that is to say, the former confers a right enforceable against the whole world, the latter one which can be enforced only against a limited number of persons.

(a) *Legal estate*

If A is entitled to the legal estate in Blackacre, then as a general rule it is true to say that, apart from some voluntary act of his own, he cannot be deprived of his rights in the land by the fraud of some third person. If, for instance, the owner of a fee simple grants a legal term of years in the land to A and then sells and conveys the fee simple to X, fraudulently concealing the existence of the lease, the rights of A as the owner of a legal estate are entirely unaffected by the transaction.

Exactly the same principle applies to all legal as distinct from equitable interests.[71] For instance, a landowner may allow his neighbour to enjoy some right over his land such as a right of way. If the right which is so enjoyed exhibits certain characteristics (to be described in chapter 18), it is known as an easement, and an easement is capable of being a legal interest and, if so, is permanently enforceable against all subsequent owners of the land over which it is exercisable. That land may very well be bought by a person who does not know of the right and has no reason to know of it, but nevertheless it will be binding upon him. The person entitled to enjoy the right has a legal interest which can be enforced against all persons whether they know of it or not.

(b) *Equitable estate*

So then the legal estate, or in fact any legal interest however small, is binding against all people, no matter how they have obtained what seem to be absolute and unrestricted rights over the land. But the rights conferred upon the owner of an equitable estate are not and never have been so extensive as this, though they are enforceable against so many people that they come to look very like rights *in rem*. The general principle is that they are enforceable only against those persons who, owing to the circumstances in which they have acquired the land, ought in conscience to be held responsible. This principle derives from the consistent refusal of the Chancellor to enforce the use against a person who acquired the land from the feoffee to uses unless he was affected by the confidence that had been reposed in the original feoffee. "As the use had its beginning in personal confidence, so its continuance, as a binding obligation on the legal owner of the land, was measured by the continuance of that confidence."[72] The number of persons who were deemed to be affected by this confidence gradually grew in number.

---

[71] The operation of the principles described here were modified by the introduction of the registration of estates and interests in 1925 (in both registered and unregistered land); but, as we shall see, the underlying principles, and the distinction between legal and equitable estates and interests, are unchanged: chap. 5, post.

[72] Hayes, *Introduction to Conveyancing*, vol. i. p. 42. See also Sanders, *Uses and Trusts*, vol. i. pp. 55–6.

(c) Extension of enforceability of equitable estate

The starting point was of course that the trustee himself, or the *feoffee to uses* as he was originally called, was permanently bound to observe the trust. The first extension of this was made in 1465, when it was held that a person who bought the land from the trustee with notice of the conditions upon which the land was held was bound by the trust.[73] The next stage, reached in 1522, was that all those who came to the trustee's estate by way of succession, such as his heir or doweress, were held responsible for carrying out the trust.[74] The law, which had reached this point at the time when the Statute of Uses was passed, was adopted and carried further by the courts when equitable estates reappeared under the name of trusts. Thus it was decided by *Chudleigh's Case* in 1595[75] that a voluntary alienee from the trustee, that is to say, a person who had acquired the estate without giving valuable consideration for it, was bound by the trust even though he had no notice of its existence. Therefore a trust was enforceable both against a man who bought the land *with notice* of the trust, and against one who received it by way of gift but without notice. Again, at some date after 1660,[76] trusts were made enforceable against creditors of the trustee who had seized the trust estate with a view to obtaining satisfaction for the debts due to them.

The one person, therefore, whose conscience was unaffected and against whom the equitable estate became unenforceable was the purchaser for value of the legal estate *without notice* of the rights of the *cestui que use*. If the feoffee to uses fraudulently sold and conveyed the land to an unsuspecting purchaser, the equity of the *cestui que use* was gone so far as the land was concerned and he could not claim relief against the purchaser. Nevertheless his equity remained in full force against the fraudulent trustee. "The *very* land was irrecoverably gone, but the use remained; and while the conscience of the person *to* whom the possession had passed was unaffected, the person *from* whom it had passed was still liable, as before, to fulfil the equities tacitly included in the use."[77]

(d) Summary

We are now in a position to summarise the essential difference between the legal and equitable estate as it stood before the reforms of 1925. We have said that a legal interest is enforceable against all the world, while an equitable interest can be enforced only against a limited number of persons. To be more precise, if an equitable interest in Blackacre was created in favour of X, the following were the persons who, if they subsequently acquired an interest in land, would take that interest subject to X's right:

(1) a person who acquired Blackacre as the heir, devisee or personal representative of the trustee;

(2) a person who had acquired the legal estate in Blackacre *without the payment of valuable consideration*, even though he had no notice of the equitable interest;

(3) a creditor of the trustee, whether with or without notice of the trust; or

---

[73] YB 5 Ed IV, Mich pl 16, fo. 7. For the whole of this subject, see the account given by Jenks in his *Modern Land Law*, pp. 141 et seq.   [74] YB 14 Hen VIII, Mich pl 5 fo. 8, cited Jenks; Maitland, *Equity*, p. 117.
[75] 1 Co Rep 113b at 122b; *Mansell v Mansell* (1732) 2 P Wms 678.
[76] See Maitland, *Equity*, p. 112.   [77] Hayes, *Introduction to Conveyancing*, vol. i. p. 43.

(4) a person who had given valuable consideration for the legal estate in Blackacre, but who was affected by notice of the equitable interest.

An equitable interest such as a trust is, then, if we put the matter with strict regard to historical accuracy, one that can be enforced only against those particular persons, but a definition which is almost equally accurate[78] is that an equitable interest is one that is enforceable against the whole world *except a bona fide purchaser for valuable consideration of the legal estate which is subject to the equitable interest, provided that, when the purchaser acquired the legal estate, he had no notice of the equitable interest.* In the case of such a person there is no reason why equity should not allow the common law to run its normal course. Equity follows the law, and will not interfere with the law unless there is some very strong equitable ground for doing so. Where a person has paid for the interest which is secure at law, and moreover has acted honestly and diligently there is no equitable reason for postponing him to somebody who from the point of view of equity is in no stronger position, and from the point of view of law is in a far inferior position.

The position was put very forcibly by JAMES LJ in *Pilcher v Rawlins:*[79]

I propose simply to apply myself to the case of a purchaser for valuable consideration, without notice, obtaining, upon the occasion of his purchase, and by means of his purchase deed, some legal estate, some legal right, some legal advantage; and, according to my view of the established law of this court, such a purchaser's plea of a purchase for valuable consideration without notice is an absolute, unqualified, unanswerable defence, and an unanswerable plea to the jurisdiction of this court. Such a purchaser, when he has once put in that plea, may be interrogated and tested to any extent as to the valuable consideration which he has given in order to shew the *bona fides* or *mala fides* of his purchase, and also the presence or the absence of notice; but when once he has gone through that ordeal, and has satisfied the terms of the plea of purchase for valuable consideration without notice, then this court has no jurisdiction whatever to do anything more than to let him depart in possession of that legal estate, that legal right, that legal advantage which he has obtained whatever it may be. In such a case the purchaser is entitled to hold that which, without breach of duty, he has had conveyed to him.

Apparently, the only exception to this immunity enjoyed by the purchaser for value without notice arose where in fact the vendor's only title to convey the fee simple was that he was tenant for life under a settlement, but he fraudulently concealed the existence of the settlement.[80]

(3) The Doctrine of the Bona Fide Purchaser for Value of the Legal Estate Without Notice

There thus emerged the doctrine of the bona fide purchaser for value of the legal estate without notice. Maitland has called such a purchaser "Equity's darling".[81] This doctrine is a cardinal principle of the land law, and, although it has been shorn of much of its importance by subsequent legislation, it still remains a basis of the law and is even used as a residuary principle in unregistered land to solve problems of the enforceability of third-party rights for which statute makes no provision. We must now look at the details of the doctrine as it was devised by the courts of equity.

[78] But see Maitland, *Equity*, pp. 120–1.
[79] (1872) 7 Ch App 259 at 268, M & B p. 26; p. 65, post.
[80] *Weston v Henshaw* [1950] Ch 510, M & B p. 335; see, however, *Re Morgan's Lease* [1972] Ch 1, M & B p. 335; pp. 995–6, post.   [81] See Maitland, *Collected Papers*, vol. iii. p. 350.

(a) Purchaser for value

The purchaser must have given consideration in money or money's worth[82] or marriage. Otherwise he is a donee and is bound by the equitable interest whether he has notice of it or not. The consideration need not be adequate, and may even be nominal.[83] Money's worth extends to all forms of non-monetary consideration, such as other land or chattels or stocks and shares. Marriage is limited to a future marriage; a promise in consideration of a future marriage, called an ante-nuptial agreement, is deemed to have been made for value,[84] but a promise made in consideration of a past marriage, called a post-nuptial agreement, is not.

A purchaser is not limited to a person who acquires the fee simple, but includes a mortgagee[85] or lessee.

(b) Legal estate

The purchaser must normally show that he has acquired a legal estate in the land. The doctrine is based on the maxim that where the equities are equal the law prevails; and as between the beneficiary's equitable interest and the innocent purchaser's legal estate, the equities are equal, and the purchaser's legal estate prevails.

On the other hand, the purchaser of an equitable interest in land takes the land subject to existing equitable interests in the same land whether he has notice of them or not.[86] The competition here is between two equitable interests and the rule is that the first in time prevails: *qui prior est tempore potior est jure*.[87]

The purchaser for value of an equitable interest without notice, however, takes free of an *equity* or a *mere equity*. An equitable interest is distinguishable from what is generally called an *equity* or a *mere equity*. This is a concept that defies precise definition, but it includes a right to enforce an equitable remedy, such as specific performance, or to set aside or rectify a conveyance for fraud, undue influence, misrepresentation and similar reasons.[88]

The defence of the purchaser for value without notice thus avails the purchaser of an equitable interest against the owner of an earlier equity, but not against the owner of an earlier equitable interest.

(c) Without notice

(1) ACTUAL NOTICE

A purchaser of the land for valuable consideration from the trustee was not liable to carry out the trusts provided that he had no notice of them when he acquired the legal estate,

---

[82] *Thorndike v Hunt* (1859) 3 De GF & J 563.

[83] *Bassett v Nosworthy* (1673) Cas temp Finch 102; *Midland Bank Trust Co Ltd v Green* [1981] AC 513, M & B p. 38.   [84] *A-G v Jacobs-Smith* [1895] 2 QB 341.

[85] *Caunce v Caunce* [1969] 1 WLR 286, M & B p. 311; *Kingsnorth Finance Co Ltd v Tizard* [1986] 1 WLR 783, M & B p. 156.

[86] It has, however, been held that, if B, an equitable incumbrancer for value without notice of A's prior equitable incumbrance, gets in the legal estate, he takes precedence over A, even if he then has notice; *Bailey v Barnes* [1894] 1 Ch 25; cf *McCarthy and Stone Ltd v Julian S Hodge & Co Ltd* [1971] 1 WLR 1547, M & B p. 49.

[87] *Phillips v Phillips* (1861) 4 De GF & J 208 at 215; *Cave v Cave* (1880) 15 Ch D 639. But see pp. 804–5, post for the modification of this principle by LPA 1925, s. 137(1).

[88] *Phillips v Phillips*, supra, at 218, per Lord WESTBURY; *National Provincial Bank Ltd v Ainsworth* [1965] AC 1175 at 1238, per Lord UPJOHN; at 1252–3, per Lord WILBERFORCE; (1955) 71 LQR 480 (R. E. Megarry); *Shiloh Spinners Ltd v Harding* [1973] AC 691 at 721, per Lord WILBERFORCE. See generally chap. 22, post.

but it is obvious that, unless a careful watch had been kept on the conduct of such a purchaser, he would have taken care not to have notice. The definition of notice was therefore
made elastic. If a purchaser was diligent enough and acted in a reasonable and sensible
manner, making all those investigations which the purchaser of land normally did make,
then he was affected only by actual notice of trusts. If, however, he omitted to make the
usual investigations then he might be affected by constructive notice.

(2) CONSTRUCTIVE NOTICE

Constructive notice[89] is generally taken to include two different things:[90]

(1) The notice which is implied when a purchaser omits to investigate the vendor's title
properly or to make reasonable inquiries as to deeds or facts which come to his
knowledge.

(2) The notice which is imputed to a purchaser by reason of the fact that his solicitor or
other legal agent has actual or implied notice of some fact. This is generally called
"imputed notice".[91]

Now the question is: what ought a prudent, careful man to do when he is purchasing an
estate? The answer will afford us an insight into the equitable doctrine of notice, and at the
same time will show us in what circumstances a purchaser takes an estate free from any
trust or other equitable interests to which it may be subject.

It is not necessary to go back further than the Conveyancing Act 1882 (now re-
enacted by the Law of Property Act 1925[92]), which contained a section designed to protect purchasers against a doctrine that had been refined to the point of unfairness. The
Act provides that no purchaser is to be affected by notice of any instrument, fact or
thing unless he actually knows of it, or unless he would have known of it had such
inquiries and inspections been made, as ought reasonably to have been made by him,
or unless his solicitor, while carrying out that particular transaction, actually obtains
knowledge of that instrument, etc., or would have obtained it had he made reasonable
inquiries and inspections. What it comes to, then, is that a purchaser is deemed to have
notice of anything which he has failed to discover either because he did not investigate
the title properly, or because he did not inquire for deeds relating to the land, or
because he did not inspect it.

We will take these three cases separately:

(i) Notice from not investigating title

For centuries it has been regarded as essential that a man who is purchasing land should
investigate the title of his vendor, that is to say, should require the vendor to "prove his
title" by producing evidence to show that the interest which he has contracted to sell is
vested in him, and that it is unincumbered by rights and interests enforceable against the
land by third parties. Under the system of unregistered conveyancing,[93] proof of the

---

[89] Sugden, *Law of Vendors and Purchasers*, p. 755.
[90] White and Tudor, *Leading Cases in Equity*, vol. ii. p. 172.
[91] *Kingsnorth Finance Co Ltd v Tizard* [1986] 1 WLR 783, M & B p. 156. See also *Sharpe v Foy* (1868) 4 Ch
App 35; *Re Cousins* (1886) 31 Ch D 671; *Woolwich plc v Gomm* (2000) 79 P & CR 61 (imputed notice under
LPA 1925, s. 199(1)(ii)(b)).   [92] S. 199(1)(ii).
[93] For registered conveyancing, see pp. 100 et seq, post.

title[94] takes the form of requiring the vendor to set out the history of the land in what is called an *abstract of title* with a view to showing how the interest he has contracted to sell became vested in him, so as to prove that for a given number of years he and his predecessors have rightfully exercised dominion over the land consistent with that interest. The old rule both at law and in equity was that, if a vendor could adduce evidence of acts of ownership for a period of not less than sixty years, he had satisfied the obligation which lay upon him, and, unless anything appeared to the contrary, had proved a title which the purchaser was bound to accept. But there was no rigid rule about the length of this period, for it was useless to trace the title for sixty years unless the result was to show that the vendor was entitled to convey that interest which he had agreed to sell.[95] For instance, a vendor might very well show sixty years' possession in himself, but if this possession was held under a long lease, something more was obviously required to substantiate a right to sell the fee simple. The vendor's proof must always begin with a "good root of title", in other words, with some instrument transferring the interest that the purchaser now seeks to obtain.

The Vendor and Purchaser Act 1874 provided that in an open contract of sale, that is, where no express stipulation had been entered into fixing a precise date from which title should be traced, forty years should be substituted for the old period of sixty years. Thus under the law as it existed in 1925 a vendor who failed to persuade the purchaser to accept a shorter title was obliged to adduce evidence of acts of ownership stretching over a period of at least forty years. This obligation was satisfied by the vendor showing what conveyances of the estate—whether *inter vivos* or as a result of death—had been effected, for, to take a simple illustration, if documents could be produced showing that forty-five years earlier X had bought the estate for valuable consideration and then left it by will to the vendor, it was clear that the latter could make a good title.

If, then, on the sale of a freehold in fee, the vendor produces the title-deeds for the last forty years, and these show that the fee simple in the land sold has been conveyed to him, free from incumbrances, and if there be satisfactory evidence that the deeds produced relate to the land sold, and the vendor be in possession of the land and of the deeds, he has shown a good title to the land.[96]

The general obligations of a vendor in unregistered land are the same under the modern law, except that the period for which title must be traced under an open contract, reduced from forty to thirty years in 1925,[97] has been further reduced to fifteen years.[98]

The first duty of the vendor is to prepare an abstract of title, that is, a statement of the material parts of all deeds and other instruments by which the property has been disposed of during the period in question, and also of all facts, such as births, deaths and marriages, which affect the ownership of the land. But in addition to producing this abstract the vendor is required to verify its contents by producing either the actual documents abstracted or the best possible evidence of the contents of those which he is not in a position to produce, and by proving facts, such as births and deaths, which are material to the title.

---

[94] For a fuller account of investigation of title, see pp. 931 et seq, post.
[95] Williams, *Vendor and Purchaser* (1st edn), p. 76.   [96] Ibid., p. 84.   [97] LPA 1925, s. 44(1).
[98] LPA 1969, s. 23, in respect of contracts made on or after 1 January 1970. See Law Commission Interim Report on Root of Title to Freehold Land (1967) (Law Com. No. 9).

We can now understand what is meant by constructive notice. One object of investigating title is to discover whether the land is subject to rights vested in persons other than the vendor, and the equitable doctrine of notice ordains that a purchaser is bound by any right which he would have discovered had he made the ordinary investigations as sketched above. Moreover, if the vendor has imposed conditions requiring a purchaser to accept a title shorter than the statutory period, the doctrine of notice is extended to rights which would have been disclosed had title been shown for the full period.[99]

In general, then, it may be said that a purchaser will be bound by equitable interests of which he may in fact be ignorant but whose existence he would have discovered had he acted as a prudent man of business, placed in similar circumstances, would have acted.[100]

(ii) Notice from not inquiring for deeds

As we have just seen, the system of unregistered conveyancing requires that a person who is buying land should examine the vendor's deeds, in order both to ascertain whether a good title can be made and to ensure that no third person possesses rights enforceable against the land. It follows from this that, if a purchaser makes no inquiries for the title deeds, and allows them to remain in the possession of a third person, he will be deemed to have notice of any equitable claims which the possessor of the deeds may have against the land.[101] If, however, he makes inquiry but fails to secure their production, his liability for any equity that they would have disclosed depends upon whether or not his failure was due to his own gross negligence. If he is satisfied with an unreasonable excuse for their non-production, he is liable;[102] but if the excuse is reasonable, he may successfully shelter behind the plea of purchaser of the legal estate for valuable consideration without notice.[103]

(iii) Notice from not inspecting land

A purchaser should inspect the land and make such inquiries as a reasonable purchaser would make; what those inquiries are depends on the circumstances of each individual case.[104] He will have constructive notice of any rights which are reasonably discoverable.[105] In particular he should make inquiries of any tenant or other person in occupation of the land, since the occupation of a person is constructive notice to a purchaser of the interest of that person; not only indeed of his interest, but of his other rights.[106] "A tenant's

---

[99] Re Cox and Neve's Contract [1891] 2 Ch 109 at 117–18.   [100] Bailey v Barnes [1894] 1 Ch 25 at 35.

[101] Walker v Linom [1907] 2 Ch 104, M & B p. 910.

[102] Oliver v Hinton [1899] 2 Ch 264 at 274, M & B p. 906

[103] Hewitt v Loosemore (1851) 9 Hare 449, M & B p. 905. On the subject generally, see pp. 784 et seq, post especially p. 786, n. 464.

[104] Midland Bank Ltd v Farmpride Hatcheries Ltd (1980) 260 EG 493 at 498, per OLIVER LJ; M & B p. 28.

[105] Hervey v Smith (1856) 22 Beav 299 (purchaser of house held to have constructive notice of equitable easement to use two chimneys for the passage of smoke from the mere fact of there being fourteen chimney pots on top of the chimney stack and only twelve flues in the house); Kingsnorth Finance Co Ltd v Tizard [1986] 1 WLR 783, M & B, p. 156; p. 409 post (mortgagee held to have constructive notice of mortgagor's wife's equitable interest in matrimonial home due to (a) his agent's inspection at a time prearranged with the mortgagor (b) his failure to make further inquiries after his agent (i) found evidence of occupation by twin fifteen-year-old children of the mortgagor and (ii) was informed by the mortgagor, who had described himself as single on the mortgage application form, that he was separated from his wife who was residing nearby). The decision is criticised in [1986] Conv 283 (M. P. Thompson); (1986) 136 NLJ 771 (P. Luxton); [1986] All ER Rev 181 (P. J. Clarke). See also Northern Bank Ltd v Henry [1981] Ir 1; Barclays Bank plc v O'Brien [1994] 1 AC 180, p. 751 post (bank's constructive notice of wife's suretyship agreement induced by misrepresentation of husband).

[106] Barnhart v Greenshields (1853) 9 Moo PCC 18. But not of an equity to rectification of a tenancy agreement which the tenant may have against the vendor: Smith v Jones [1954] 1 WLR 1089, M & B p. 47. Cf Nurdin & Peacock plc v D B Ramsden & Co Ltd [1999] 1 EGLR 119, p. 980, n. 390 post.

occupation is notice of all that tenant's rights,[107] but not of his lessor's title or rights."[108] This is known as the rule in *Hunt v Luck* and it was further elaborated in that case by VAUGHAN WILLIAMS LJ as follows:[109]

If a purchaser or a mortgagee has notice that the vendor or mortgagor is not in possession of the property, he must make inquiries of the person in possession—of the tenant who is in possession—and find out from him what his rights are, and, if he does not choose to do that, then whatever title he acquires as purchaser or mortgagee will be subject to the title or right of the tenant in possession.

If, however, the person in occupation of the land deliberately puts the inquirer off the scent by withholding information about his interest, he will be estopped from relying on the defence that the inquirer had constructive notice arising from the occupation.[110]

Finally, it is now clear that the rule operates to give a purchaser or mortgagee constructive notice of the interest of a person in occupation, even if the vendor or mortgagor is also in occupation.[111]

(3) SUMMARY

In *Royal Bank of Scotland plc v Etridge (No. 2)*,[112] STUART-SMITH LJ summarised constructive notice as follows:

Where there is a standard procedure for investigating title, a purchaser is fixed with constructive notice of everything which he would have discovered if he had followed the standard procedure. The doctrine of constructive notice is, however, wider than this. It also applies whenever a party is put on inquiry as to the existence of another's rights. If he makes no inquiry he is fixed with constructive notice of whatever he would have discovered if he had made reasonable inquiry: see Law of Property Act 1925, section 199(1)(ii)(*a*).

If he does make inquiry, the question depends in the first instance on whether he has made reasonable inquiry. If he has, and the results of his inquiries are such as would reasonably allay

---

[107] E.g., an option to purchase: *Daniels v Davison* (1809) 16 Ves 249.

[108] *Hunt v Luck* [1901] 1 Ch 45 at 51 per FARWELL J; approved by CA [1902] 1 Ch 428 at 432. The principle is preserved by LPA 1925, s. 14: *City of London Building Society v Flegg* [1988] AC 54 at 80, per Lord OLIVER OF AYLMERTON; p. 998 post. [109] *Hunt v Luck*, supra, at 433.

[110] *Midland Bank Ltd v Farmpride Hatcheries Ltd*, supra (where a company mortgaged its property to a bank, a contractual licensee who was in occupation of a house under a licence from the company, of which he and his wife were in complete control, was held to be estopped from relying on the doctrine; he had "set up a smoke-screen designed to hide even the possible existence of some interest in himself which could derogate from the interest of the company ostensibly conferred by the mortgage", per SHAW LJ at 497); OLIVER and BUCKLEY LJJ held that the bank did not have constructive notice, because the licensee was not only in control of the company but also had been negotiating as agent on his principal's behalf. "He does not thereby make any representation that his principal has an indefeasible title to the property offered as security . . . but he does at least represent that he has his principal's authority to offer the property free from any undisclosed adverse interest of his own" (per OLIVER LJ at 498). His failure to disclose that interest entitled the bank to assume that there was no such interest. See (1982) 132 NLJ 68 (H. W. Wilkinson); *Abbey National plc v Tufts* [1999] EGCS 24 (bank had no constructive notice of wife's credit status where bankrupt husband had fraudulently applied for loan on her behalf).

The issues of the binding effect of a licence on a third party (p. 836, post) and of the lifting of the veil of corporate personality were not raised. See (1982) 132 NLJ 68 (H. W. Wilkinson); [1982] Conv 67 (R. E. Annand); (1982) 79 LSG 464 (H. Lawless and J. Alder). Cf, in registered land, LRA 2002, Sch. 3, para. 2(b).

[111] *Kingsnorth Finance Co Ltd v Tizard*, supra, not following *Caunce v Caunce* [1969] 1 WLR 286; cf the position in registered land: *Hodgson v Marks* [1971] Ch 892 at 934–5 and *Williams & Glyn's Bank Ltd v Boland* [1981] AC 487 M & B p. 136; p. 981, post.

[112] [1998] 4 All ER 705 at 718; for HL, see pp. 749 et seq, post. See also *Macmillan Inc v Bishopsgate Investment Trust plc (No. 3)* [1995] 1 WLR 978, where MILLETT J said at 1000: "In English law notice . . . includes not only

suspicion, then he takes free from the other's rights. If he has taken reasonable steps to allay suspicion, the question is not whether he could reasonably have done more, but whether, in the light of all the information, including the results of his inquiries, at his disposal at the time when he gave value, any suspicions have reasonably been allayed.

(d) Bona fide

This requirement is not synonymous with absence of notice. As Lord WILBERFORCE said in *Midland Bank Trust Co Ltd v Green*:[113]

The character in the law known as the bona fide (good faith) purchaser for value without notice was the creation of equity. In order to affect a purchaser for value of a legal estate with some equity or equitable interest, equity fastened upon his conscience and the composite expression was used to epitomise the circumstances in which equity would or rather would not do so. I think that it would generally be true to say that the words "in good faith" related to the existence of notice. Equity, in other words, required not only absence of notice, but genuine and honest absence of notice. As the law developed, this requirement became crystallized in the doctrine of constructive notice which assumed a statutory form in the Conveyancing Act 1882, section 3. But it would be a mistake to suppose that the requirement of good faith extended only to the matter of notice, or that when notice came to be regulated by statute, the requirement of good faith became obsolete. Equity still retained its interest in and power over the purchaser's conscience. The classic judgment of James LJ in *Pilcher v Rawlins*[114] is clear authority that it did: good faith there is stated as a separate test which may have to be passed even though absence of notice is proved. And there are references in cases subsequent to 1882 which confirm the proposition that honesty or bona fides remained something which might be inquired into.[115]

The burden of proving all the elements of the defence is on the purchaser.[116]

(e) Purchaser with notice from purchaser without notice

A bona fide purchaser for value of a legal estate without notice, who takes free from equitable interests, may nevertheless pass a good title to a purchaser who *has* notice of them.[117] Otherwise the owner of the equitable interest, by proclaiming his right, could make it difficult for the purchaser without notice to sell the land which he had purchased. There is an exception to this rule; where a trustee who is bound by equitable interests sells the trust property in breach of trust to a purchaser without notice, and then re-acquires the property, he will again hold it subject to the equitable interests. He cannot take advantage of the purchaser's immunity under the doctrine.[118]

---

actual notice (including 'wilful blindness' or 'contrived ignorance', where the purchaser deliberately abstains from an inquiry in order to avoid learning the truth) but also constructive notice, that is to say notice of such facts as he would have discovered if he had taken proper measures to investigate them."

[113] [1981] AC 513 at 528; p. 946, post. *Grindal v Hooper* [1999] EGCS 150 (actual notice an essential but not exclusive element of good faith).   [114] (1872) 7 Ch App 259 at 269; p. 58, ante.

[115] *Berwick & Co v Price* [1905] 1 Ch 632 at 639; *Taylor v London and County Banking Co* [1901] 2 Ch 231 at 256; *Oliver v Hinton* [1899] 2 Ch 264 at 273.

[116] *Re Nisbet and Potts' Contract* [1906] 1 Ch 386 at 398; *Barclays Bank plc v Boulter* [1999] 1 WLR 1919 at 1924, per Lord HOFFMANN.   [117] *Wilkes v Spooner* [1911] 2 KB 473, M & B p. 27.

[118] *Bovey v Smith* (1682) 1 Vern 84; *Lowther v Carlton* (1741) 2 Atk 242; *Sweet v Southcote* (1786) 2 Bro CC 66; *Re Stapleford Colliery Co* (1880) 14 Ch D 432.

(f) Effect on equitable estate

In brief, then, an equitable estate is not so safe as a legal estate. An equitable owner may find himself, without any fault or negligence on his part, postponed to a third person who has obtained the legal estate in the same land, and his remedy will be reduced to that of recovering the value of the estate from the fraudulent or negligent trustee. The facts of *Pilcher v Rawlins*[119] will serve to illustrate this proposition.

Pilcher, who was the sole surviving trustee of £8,373, which he held in trust for X for life and after his death for X's children, lent the money to Rawlins on a legal mortgage of Blackacre. This was a perfectly legitimate transaction, the effect of which was to vest the legal estate of Blackacre in Pilcher as trustee on the same trusts for X, so that until the mortgage was redeemed by Rawlins, Pilcher acquired the legal and X the equitable estate of the lands.

Rawlins then arranged to grant a legal mortgage of Blackacre to Z in return for a loan of £10,000. As things stood this was impossible because a legal mortgage before 1926 necessitated the transfer to the lender of the legal fee simple, and this was vested in Pilcher. Pilcher, however, decided to abet Rawlins in the fraudulent scheme. First of all Rawlins (who was a solicitor) prepared an abstract of title to Blackacre which stopped short of and excluded the mortgage to Pilcher and thus made it appear that the legal fee simple was still vested in himself. Of course it was not, but at this point Pilcher came into the plot by re-conveying his legal estate in Blackacre to Rawlins in consideration of a repayment of X's trust moneys. This repayment was never in fact made, but Rawlins, having thus attained the legal estate, was enabled to transfer it to Z, who paid over the £10,000. The deed of re-conveyance was suppressed. When the fraud was discovered, the question was, which of the two innocent parties, X or Z, had the better right to Blackacre. It was held that, as Z had acted reasonably and honestly, the legal interest which had passed to him must prevail over the mere equitable interest vested in X. Pilcher was the sole trustee and as such had the legal estate and the title-deeds. That being so, the effect of his reconveyance was to give the legal estate to Rawlins, and, as the whole mortgage transaction was concealed, there was no document to put Z on inquiry.

G Other Forms of Equitable Interests

Throughout the preceding account we have principally considered one form of equitable interest, the trust, but though this is the most important species, we must observe that it is not the only one. The trust, already described, is an interest which corresponds with a legal interest in the sense that just as, before 1926, there could be a legal fee simple, entailed interest or life interest, so also may there be equitable counterparts possessing the same incidents, for equity follows the law.[120] But other equitable interests may exist which have no analogy at common law. The more important of these, which will require a more detailed discussion later, are the following:

(1) Estate Contract

This arises where the owner of a legal estate either agrees to convey it to the other contracting party or to create a legal estate out of it in favour of that other. Thus, if A, the

---

[119] (1872) 7 Ch App 259, M & B p. 26.

[120] We shall see later (pp. 93–4, post) that by the legislation of 1925 it became impossible for entailed and life interests to subsist as *legal* as distinct from equitable estates.

owner of the fee simple absolute in Blackacre, agrees to sell it to B or to create a term of years absolute out of it in favour of B, the equitable interest in the land as measured by the terms of the contract passes at once to B, although the legal estate remains with A until an actual conveyance or lease has been executed. This is an application of a general doctrine, commonly known as the doctrine of *Walsh v Lonsdale*,[121] under which a specifically enforceable contract to create or convey a legal estate or interest is treated in equity as creating the equivalent estate or interest.

(2) Restrictive Covenant

This is a covenant by which the use of the covenantor's land is restricted for the benefit of the covenantee's adjoining land, for example, where it is agreed that it shall not be used for the purpose of trade. The effect of such a covenant, if the necessary conditions are satisfied,[122] is that the covenantee acquires an equitable interest in the burdened land.

(3) Equity of Redemption

This is the right of a mortgagor to redeem the mortgaged property upon payment of all that is due by way of capital or interest.[123]

(4) Equitable Charge

This arises where, without the transfer of any definite estate, land is designated as security for the payment of a sum of money.[124] In such a case, the chargee acquires an equitable interest that entitles him to take proceedings for the sale of the land.[125]

(5) Equitable Lien

This is similar in effect to the equitable charge, and most generally arises when the vendor conveys the land to the purchaser before he has been paid. If so, he becomes entitled by operation of law to an equitable lien on the land for the amount of the unpaid purchase money which is enforceable by a sale under the direction of the court.[126]

(6) Equity by Estoppel

This right, which emerged during the twentieth century, arises, for example, where A encourages B to believe that he has or will acquire an interest in A's land, and B relies on this encouragement to his detriment. A is estopped (i.e. prevented) from insisting on his strict legal rights where it would be unconscionable for him to do so. B has an interest which in equity is enforceable against A and his successors in title.[127]

---

[121] (1882) 21 Ch D 9, M & B p. 85; pp. 223–5, 877, post.   [122] Pp. 666 et seq, post.
[123] P. 735, post.   [124] Land can be similarly charged at law. See pp. 724, 726, post.
[125] P. 773, post.   [126] P. 878, post.   [127] Pp. 825–7, post.

4

SETTLEMENTS BEFORE 1926[1]

SUMMARY

An owner of property may need to do more than to own it during his lifetime and then to pass it on to someone else when he dies. He may desire to create successive interests, as, for example, by giving it in his will to his widow for her life, with a remainder to the children; or by providing on a son's marriage a life interest for the son, and after the son's death for the daughter-in-law, and after her death for their children. He may even wish to found a family dynasty.

Any historical survey must begin with this latter type of settlement which has been a feature of English social life for many centuries. It was the desire of the aristocracy to order the future destiny of their land and to prevent its sale out of the family which decisively affected the form and substance of real property law. A fee simple owner makes what is called a *settlement* by which he retains the benefit of ownership during his own life, but withholds the entire ownership in the shape of the fee simple from his descendants for as long as possible by reducing them, one after the other, to the position of mere limited owners. The English doctrine of estates is ideally adapted to the achievement of this object. The fee simple of infinite duration is divisible into shorter periods of time each of which may be allotted successively to a number of persons, with the result that while these periods are running there is no person able to dispose of the entire ownership.

---

[1] Simpson, *A History of the Land Law*, pp. 233–41; Harvey, *Settlements of Land*; Bonfield, *Marriage Settlements 1601–1740*; English and Saville, *Strict Settlement*, which contains details of several dynastic settlements of land; and essays in Rubin and Sugarman, *Law, Economy and Society*, pp. 1–123 (D. Sugarman and G. R. Rubin), 124–67 (M. R. Chesterman), 168–91 (E. Spring) and 209–10 (B. English); Spring, *Strict Settlement: its Role in Family History* (1988) EHR 454; Spring, *Law, Land and Family*; (1998) 61 MLR 162 (A. Pottage).

I The Strict Settlement

A *Form of Settlement*

(1) Settlement

Settlements in one form or another have been common since at any rate the early thirteenth century,[2] and indeed for some two hundred years after the statute *De Donis Conditionalibus* in 1285,[3] it was possible to grant an estate tail that would perforce descend from heir to heir and would permanently remain inconvertible into a fee simple. Although by the end of the fifteenth century means had been contrived to cut short such an impolitic tying-up of the land, by allowing any tenant in tail in possession and of full age to bar the entail and so to acquire the fee simple,[4] the urge to keep the land in the family for as long as the law would permit still persisted, and by the time of the Restoration the general form of the *strict settlement* had been established. It is desirable to appreciate its general design even at this early stage in the book if the significance of much of the existing legislation is to be grasped. Suppose, for instance, that a fee simple owner, A, a widower, has decided to use the land as a source of endowment for his only son B, who is about to be married, and for B's issue. In such a case the practice for several centuries was for A to execute a deed of settlement by which he limits the land to himself for life; then to B for life and then, after making provision for B's widow and younger children, to the first and every other son of B successively in tail.

Under such a settlement the desire of A to keep the land in the family is at least partly achieved, for no one will be able to acquire complete control over the land before the eldest son of B, who may bar the entail and so convert it into a fee simple as soon as he attains his majority. To create a fee simple absolute, however, the disentailment must either be effected by him after he has become entitled in possession on the deaths of A and B or, if he desires to act earlier, it must be effected with the collaboration of the present possessor. There is no difficulty, therefore, if he waits until the successive life tenants, A and B, are dead, for in that case he is tenant in tail in possession and free to act independently. But even while, say, B is tenant for life in possession, he may join as party to the disentailment and thus enable his son to acquire the fee simple absolute.

(2) Resettlement

This collaboration of life tenant in possession and tenant in tail in remainder—usually of father and son—was consistently utilised by conveyancers as part of the scheme to prolong the retention of the land in the family. That scheme will, of course, succeed automatically if the eldest son or other heir in each generation refrains throughout his life from barring the entail, for in that event the entailed interest will descend in due course to his own heir. But the danger is that he will bar the entail when he becomes entitled in possession and will then acquire and sell the fee simple. Hence the long-established practice of making what is called

---

[2] By gifts to a person and a special class of heirs; p. 481, post.
[3] P. 482, post. For the effect of this statute, see Plucknett, *Legislation of Edward I*, pp. 125–35.
[4] P. 484, post, common recovery.

a *resettlement* by which the eldest son, on the attainment of his majority, is in most cases persuaded to bar the entail with the concurrence of his father and then voluntarily to settle the fee simple thus acquired upon himself for a mere life interest with a further limitation in favour of his own sons successively in tail. This ensures that the land will remain in the family for yet another generation. If, therefore, a resettlement is effected in each generation, the land is held by a succession of limited owners and there is nobody who can claim to be owner of the fee simple.[5]

(3) Effect of Statute of Uses 1535

Settlements, as we have said, are of respectable antiquity, but at common law the opportunities of carving up the *legal* fee simple so as to anticipate events that might affect the family in the future were severely restricted, for limitations only of the simplest nature were allowed. The Chancellor, on the other hand, had never imposed restrictions upon limitations of the *equitable* estate. The use might be moulded into any form congenial to its creator and adapted to solve the riddles of the future. The Statute of Uses 1535, therefore, played an important part in the evolution of the strict settlement, an evolution that was complete towards the end of the seventeenth century. The flexibility of the use was imparted to the legal estate by the statute. What was impossible at common law might now be achieved by a single assurance, either a grant to uses or a will. The simple expedient of vesting the legal estate in feoffees with a declaration of the uses to which they were to hold, entitled the beneficiaries to legal interests in the land, as and when their rights matured.

(a) Grant of fee simple defeasible by later events

The opportunities of a settlor were now greater. For instance, common law did not permit a man to convey a freehold estate to himself, nor did it recognise any estate limited to take effect after the grant of a fee simple.[6]

Neither of these rules, however, affected the use and they ceased to affect the legal estate into which the use was converted by the Statute of Uses, if the limitation was made by a grant to uses or by will. The normal method of creating a marriage settlement was for the settlor to grant his fee simple to feoffees to the use of himself in fee simple until the intended marriage, and thereafter to the use of himself for life with remainder to such uses in favour of his wife and issue as his fancy might dictate. Thus, after the statute he acquired a determinable fee simple during the interval between the settlement and the marriage, but on his marriage it was displaced in favour of the subsequent limitations, which were themselves legal.[7]

(b) Springing and shifting uses

Again, at common law a freehold estate could not be given to a man to begin at some future date,[8] nor was it permissible to annex to a grant a condition that the freehold should shift from the donee to another person upon the happening of a prescribed event.[9]

Yet, the Chancellor had always protected such limitations of the equitable estate and therefore when uses were statutorily converted into legal estates, a limitation to feoffees to the use of X when he married (springing use) or to the use of Y for life, but if he became

---

[5] For a clear account, see Elphinstone, *Introduction to Conveyancing*, pp. 638 et seq.   [6] P. 514, post.
[7] Digby, *History of the Law of Real Property*, pp. 357–8.   [8] P. 514, post.   [9] P. 514, post.

insolvent then to the use of Z for life (shifting use), operated to vest a legal estate in X and Z upon the occurrence of the prescribed events.

(c) Powers of appointment

Another innovation of the Chancellor that greatly increased the pliability of settlements was the *power of appointment*. The normal procedure upon the creation of a use was for the feoffor to declare then and there the exact uses to which the land should be held. But such a definitive declaration was not essential. The feoffor might reserve to himself or to a third person a power to declare in the future what uses should arise or to revoke existing uses and substitute new ones in their place. The donee of such a power, who might be a stranger having no proprietary interest, present or future, in the land, was thus enabled before the Statute of Uses to give fresh directions as to the enjoyment of the equitable estate. If, for example, in place of an existing use in favour of A for life, he *appointed* to the use of B in tail, the original feoffees immediately stood seised to the use of B who consequently acquired an equitable estate tail. If the appointment were made after the statute, B would take a legal estate tail.

Thus, through the machinery of powers, an appointor was able to dispose of an estate that he did not own, and the legal ownership might at his instance be freely shifted and modified to suit exigencies occurring after the date of the settlement.

B Disadvantages of Settlement

A settlement of land, though it afforded a convenient means of providing for descendants and, when followed by periodic resettlements, of keeping the land in the family, suffered from three particular disadvantages. It tended to render land inalienable, it might have an adverse effect upon the prosperity of the family and it complicated conveyancing.

(1) Inalienability of the Land

The first of these dangers was inherent in the pliability that the legal estate had inherited from the use. It soon became obvious that, unless some limit of time was imposed upon the power to create future interests, an astute employment of a series of springing and shifting clauses might well render the fee simple inalienable for an unreasonable period. Thus, the general employment in settlements of such devices to create a series of merely limited interests, enduring far into the future, would have starved the market of land to the detriment of the community. The courts have always fought against the creation of inalienable interests and have held them void.[10] Further, they developed what is now called the *rule against perpetuities*, which looks to the date at which a contingent interest will vest, if it vests at all, and hold it to be void as a perpetuity if the date is too remote. The common law rule, which will require detailed treatment later,[11] allows a settlor to provide that an estate will shift to a person or spring up in his favour upon the occurrence of a prescribed contingency, but it ordains that the estate shall be void unless the contingency, if it ever happens at all, will necessarily happen not later than twenty-one years from the death of some person or persons alive when the settlement takes effect.

---

[10] P. 574, post.

[11] Chap. 16, post. The common law perpetuity rule was amended by PAA 1964, to allow "wait and see": pp. 545 et seq, post.

(2) Impoverishment of the Land

(a) Effect of settlement on power of alienation

The chief defect inherent in a system of strict settlements and of periodic re-settlements is that at no point of time is there any beneficiary competent to exercise many of the powers of a fee simple owner, unless indeed a right to do so is reserved by the settlement or granted by some statute. The person who under this system has every appearance of being owner is the life tenant in possession, but since his beneficial interest must necessarily determine with his death it follows that any interest granted by him must also determine at that moment. A conveyance by him purporting to pass the fee simple will at common law pass to the grantee nothing more than an estate *pur autre vie*, and a lease for any number of years will automatically determine on his death unless saved by statute or permitted by the settlement. The grave effects resulting from this limited power of alienation in the days when the strict settlement was the foundation of landed society can easily be realised. Given a system whereby it is usual for a fee simple owner, in view of his approaching marriage, to limit the land to himself for life and then to his eldest son in tail, and given further the inclination to resettle the land in each generation on the eldest son for life, with remainder in tail to *his* eldest son, a moment's reflection will show what a prejudicial effect such a perpetual series of life tenants, each devoid of the power to convey the fee simple estate, must have not only on the supply of land available for purposes of trade, but also on the prosperity of the settled land itself.

The common practice, by which the eldest son under a strict settlement was persuaded on reaching his majority to convert his estate tail into a fee simple and then to resettle the fee simple upon himself for a mere life estate with remainder to his own issue in tail, was stigmatised as follows by a critic:[12]

It is commonly supposed that a son acts with his eyes open and with a special eye to the contingencies of the future and of family life. But what are the real facts of the case? Before the future owner of the land has come into possession, before he has any experience of his property, or of what is best to be done, or what he can do with regard to it, before the exigencies of the future or his own real position are known to him, before the character, number and wants of his children are learned, or the claims of parental affection and duty can make themselves felt, while still very much at the mercy of a predecessor desirous of posthumous greatness and power, he enters into an irrevocable disposition by which he parts with the rights of a proprietor over his future property for ever, and settles its devolution, burdened with charges, upon an unborn heir.

Under such a system there never exists, apart from statute, a beneficial owner capable of selling or dealing with the fee simple. In the words of Sir Frederick Pollock:[13]

The lord of this mansion is named by all men its owner; it is said to belong to him; the park, the demesne, the farms are called his. But we shall be almost safe in assuming that he is not the full and free owner of any part of it. He is a "limited owner", having an interest only for his own life. He might have become the full owner . . . if he had possessed the means of waiting, the independence of thought and will to break with the tradition of his order and the bias of his education, and the energy to persevere in his dissent against the counsels and feelings of his family. But he had every inducement to let things

---

[12] Cliffe Leslie, *Fraser's Magazine*, February 1867, cited Scrutton, *Land in Fetters*, p. 135.
[13] Pollock, *Land Laws*, p. 9.

go their accustomed way. Those whom he had always trusted told him, and probably with sincere belief, that the accustomed way was the best for the family, for the land, for the tenants and for the country. And there could be no doubt that it was at the time the most agreeable to himself.

(b) Economic disadvantages

It is clear, in fact, that an uncontrolled system of settlements and re-settlements is an evil—both social and economic—to any country which tolerates it, though it was not one that was apparent to the lawyers of the early nineteenth century. Thus we find the Real Property Commissioners in their report of 1829 stating:

The owner of the soil is, we think, vested with exactly the dominion and power of disposition over it required for the public good, and landed property in England is admirably made to answer all the purposes to which it is applicable. Settlements bestow on the present possessor of an estate the benefits of ownership, and secure the property to his posterity . . . In England families are preserved and purchasers always find a supply of land in the market.

This language is specious. It is true in the sense that settled land could usually be sold in fee simple, because a settlement might contain, and a well-drawn settlement would contain, powers enabling the tenant for life to deal with the land by way of sale, lease, mortgage and so on.[14] If he took advantage of such a power and for instance sold the land to X, the fact that he was a mere life tenant was no obstacle to the transfer of the fee simple, for the feoffees had been directed by the settlement to hold to such uses as might be appointed by the donee of the power and therefore they now held to the use of the appointee X. Thus under the Statute of Uses, X acquired a legal fee simple. But, although the land could be rendered manageable and saleable by this device, it happened only too often that powers were either omitted altogether or were too restricted in character. Speaking broadly, land was kept in families only at the expense of removing it from commerce and too often starving it of money necessary for its development and improvement. No doubt the evil was not so great under the rural conditions prevalent until the early nineteenth century, but it became urgent when the vast spread of industrialism produced a demand for coal and other minerals, and converted England from an agricultural to a trading community. To appreciate the nature of the problem it is only necessary to examine the position of a life tenant of settled land in, say, 1835. This was admirably summed up by Underhill:[15]

Unless the will or settlement . . . contained express powers (which was frequently not the case) a tenant for life could neither sell, exchange, nor partition the settled property, however desirable it might be. If the estate consisted of a large tract of poor country, fruitful in dignity but scanty in rent, and specially if the portions of younger children charged on it were heavy, he too often found it a damnosa hereditas; the rents, after payment of interest on the portions, leaving a mere pittance for the unfortunate life tenant to live on, and quite disabling him from making improvements, or even keeping the property in a decent state of repair. Nay more, if he did spend money in improvements, the money was sunk in the estate to the detriment of his younger children. He could not pull down the mansion-house, however old or inconvenient it might be, nor even, strictly, make any substantial alteration in it. Unless expressly made unimpeachable for waste, he could not open new mines. But in addition to these disabilities, what pressed still more hardly upon him, and on the development of the estate

---

[14] For a seventeenth-century precedent, see Holdsworth, *History of English Law*, vol. vii. p. 547.
[15] Underhill, *Century of Law Reform*, pp. 284–5.

generally, was his inability to make long leases.[16] Consequently when valuable minerals lay beneath a settled property, or the growth of the neighbouring town made it ripe for building sites (the rents for which would greatly exceed the agricultural rent) nothing could lawfully be done. The tenant for life could not open mines himself, even if he had the necessary capital for working them; nor, even if unimpeachable for waste, could he grant leases of them to others for a term which would repay the lessees for the necessary expenditure in pits and plant; nor could he grant building leases or sell for building purposes at fee farm rents. In some settlements powers were expressly inserted, enabling the trustees to grant such leases and to sell, exchange and partition. But frequently, especially in wills, such powers were omitted, and in such cases the only means of doing justice to the land was to apply for a private Act of Parliament authorizing the trustees or life tenant to sell, exchange, partition or lease. But such Acts were expensive luxuries, only open to the rich, and beyond the means of most country gentlemen of moderate means.

C Statutory Reform

(1) Before 1882

When, however, the modern industrial era set in, the legislature took the matter in hand, and in a tentative manner began to pass a series of public Acts of Parliament which enabled settled land to be dealt with in a manner likely to enhance its prosperity. A start was made in the 1840s with statutes which empowered tenants for life to borrow money for the purpose of carrying out permanent drainage improvements and to charge the loan on the inheritance. Then the Improvement of Land Act 1864 enabled a tenant for life to raise money with the consent of the Ministry of Agriculture in order to execute certain specified improvements, and to charge the loan on the corpus of the property.[17] Further examples were the Limited Owners Residences Acts 1870 and 1871, which allowed money to be raised for completing or adding to a mansion-house; and the Limited Owners Reservoirs Act 1877, which sanctioned the same method for the construction of permanent waterworks.

But in 1856 the much more important Settled Estates Act had been passed which contained the germ of all the future legislation on the subject. Its object was to facilitate leases and sales of settled estates, and after being amended by several statutes in the succeeding generation, it was replaced in 1877 by the Settled Estates Act of that year. This allowed the Chancery Division of the High Court to sanction the sale, exchange or partition of the settled land, and the grant of leases of twenty-one years for an agricultural or occupation lease, forty years for a mining lease, and ninety-nine years for a building lease. It also allowed the tenant for life without resorting to the court to make a valid lease up to a period of twenty-one years. So this Act made great strides towards permitting all opportunities for the proper development of the land to be seized, but its weakness was that, except in the case of short leases, its enabling powers could not be exercised without an order of the court. It had in truth facilitated dealings, since it substituted an order of the court for a private Act of Parliament, but it stopped short of placing the powers unreservedly in the hands of the tenant for life.

---

[16] A tenant *in tail*, however, was empowered by the Fines and Recoveries Act 1833, s. 41, to grant a lease for a term not exceeding twenty-one years.   [17] P. 710, post.

About this time an agitation sprang up for the total abolition of life estates and the restriction of grants to the creation of a fee simple, the argument being that settlements, besides making conveyances difficult and costly, deprived a father of a much-needed power of control over his eldest son, and prevented an estate from being thrown on the market when its poverty made such a course desirable. For better or for worse the argument did not prevail. It was realised that settlements enabled a fair and reasonable provision to be made for all the members of a family, and therefore, while the general features of the time-honoured system were retained, a plan was evolved to prevent settled land from becoming an inert mass through lack of capital or of adequate powers of management.[18]

(2) Settled Land Act 1882

The principle adopted by Lord CAIRNS and incorporated in the famous Settled Land Act of 1882 was to put the entire management of the land into the hands of the tenant for life for the time being, and to give him, at his own sole discretion and without asking the permission of the court or the trustees of the settlement, wide powers of selling, leasing, mortgaging and otherwise dealing with the property. These powers were independent of, and could not be restrained by, the settlement itself, but they were subject to certain statutory provisions designed to protect the interests of all persons entitled under the settlement, and to prevent the tenant for life from acquiring more than a life interest in the income or profits.

The objects of the Act were lucidly explained by CHITTY LJ in the following words:[19]

The object is to render land a marketable article, notwithstanding the settlement. Its main purpose is the welfare of the land itself, and of all interested therein, including the tenants and not merely the persons taking under the settlement. The Act of 1882 had a much wider scope than the Settled Estates Acts. The scheme adopted is to facilitate the striking off from the land of the fetters imposed by settlement; and this is accomplished by conferring on *tenants for life in possession*, and others considered to stand in a like relation to the land, large powers of dealing with the land by way of sale, exchange, lease and otherwise, and by jealously guarding those powers from attempts to defeat them or to hamper their exercise. At the same time the rights of persons claiming under the settlement are carefully preserved in the case of a sale by shifting the settlement from the land to the purchase money which has to be paid into court or into the hands of trustees.

The Act of 1882 was amended in small particulars by further statutes passed in 1884, 1887, 1889, and 1890, but its policy has stood the test of time, and though it was repealed and replaced by the Settled Land Act 1925, its general principles still continue to govern the rights and the liabilities of a tenant for life under a strict settlement.

(a) *The legal title*

The third disadvantage of a settlement—its aggravation of the complexity of conveyancing—became evident when a tenant for life, by virtue of a power conferred upon him, had agreed to sell the fee simple to a purchaser. In this event, he would prove the title down to the date of the settlement in the normal fashion by tracing the history of the land back to a good root of title, in order to show that the fee simple was owned by the original settlor. So far there was nothing abnormal, but at this point arose the difficulty that the vendor himself did not

---

[18] Underhill, *Century of Law Reform*, pp. 287–90.
[19] *Re Mundy and Roper's Contract* [1899] 1 Ch 275 at 288.

own the estate that he had contracted to sell. His case would be, of course, that as tenant for life under a settlement he possessed a power, conferred upon him either by the settlement itself or after 1882 by the Settled Land Act, to convey the fee simple. The general rule on this matter is that the exercise of a power, whether it is given by act of parties or by statute, is void unless all the conditions imposed by the instrument or statute from which it derives are literally observed. If attention is concentrated on a sale after 1882, the governing factors in this respect were that the Act of that year empowered a tenant for life under a settlement to convey a good title to the fee simple, provided that the purchase money was paid to the trustees. In other words, before the statutory power of sale or any other statutory power was validly exercisable, it was essential that, *within the meaning of the Act*,

the instrument under which the vendor held was a "settlement";

the vendor himself was a "tenant for life" or one of the persons to whom the statutory powers were given;

the trustees were properly appointed.

In order, therefore, to verify that these conditions were satisfied, it was necessary for the original deed of settlement and, in fact, several further deeds if there had been one or more resettlements, to be abstracted by the vendor and investigated by the purchaser. Thus, in order to satisfy himself that a good title would be made, the purchaser was confronted with the formidable task of scrutinising a series of transactions and documents stretching back perhaps for very many years.

(b) Overreaching of beneficial interests

In contrast to this complication which beset a purchaser of settled land, his position vis-à-vis the beneficial interests under the settlement was simple. This was due to the doctrine of overreaching: it originated in conveyancing practice and was adopted by the Settled Land Act 1882. The Act provides that if the purchaser pays the purchase money to at least two trustees or into Court (and not to the tenant for life) the interests of the beneficiaries under the settlement shall be transferred from the land to the purchase money.[20] Thus the purchaser by virtue of the Act takes the land free from the beneficial interests; and he does this even though he has notice of them and even though the interests may be legal. The conveyancing advantage to the purchaser is obvious. So far as the beneficiaries are concerned, they lose their opportunity of enjoying the land qua land, but, instead, they have equivalent interests in the purchase money. A beneficial interest in a fund of £50,000 is just as valuable as the same interest in land worth £50,000; more valuable, if the money is invested more profitably; less valuable, if the land was a better investment. The question is one of choice of investment of the family capital.

II The Trust for Sale

So far we have concentrated attention upon the strict settlement. An entirely different way of applying the principle of the settlement to land was by means of a trust for sale, a method

---

[20] SLA 1882, ss. 20, 22(5), 39(1).

that was common in wills for some five hundred years and in deeds since the early nineteenth century.[21] By 1997, when it was replaced by the trust of land,[22] it had almost superseded the strict settlement.

If it were used to create a family settlement *inter vivos* as described in Section I, the transaction would fall into two parts and, though not strictly necessary, would usually be effected by two separate deeds. If, for instance, it preceded the marriage of the settlor:

The first deed in its opening clause conveyed the fee simple to the trustees upon trust (with the consent of the husband until the intended marriage, and after the marriage with the consent of the husband and wife, or of the survivor, and after the death of the survivor at the discretion of the trustees) to sell the said fee simple.

The second clause of the deed directed the trustees to hold the money arising from the sale and the rents and profits accruing prior to the sale upon such trusts as were declared by a deed already engrossed and made between the same parties and on the same date as the present deed.[23]

According to the equitable doctrine of conversion the effect of the execution of this deed was that in the eyes of equity the land was notionally converted into money, for that doctrine, based on the principle that equity looks on that as done which ought to be done, insisted that an imperative direction to turn land into money should impress the land with the quality of money no matter how long the sale might be postponed.[24] The important point to notice, therefore, is that a trust for sale relating to the fee simple and containing a succession of beneficial limitations was a settlement of personalty, not of realty.

The second deed set out the beneficial trusts of the personalty into which the realty had already been notionally converted. It would usually provide in the first place that the income, whether arising from the invested purchase money or from the rents and profits prior to the sale, should be held in trust for the husband during his life and after his death in trust for his wife if she survived him. Secondly, it would provide that after the death of the husband and wife the capital should be divided among the children or remoter issue of the marriage in such shares as the husband and wife or the survivor should appoint, and, failing appointment, among the children equally.[25]

The investigation of title upon a sale by the trustees raised none of the difficulties that, as we have already seen, formerly attended a sale by a tenant for life under a strict settlement. The legal fee simple was vested in the trustees for sale and it was from them that the purchaser took his title. His main concern was to ascertain that the settlor was entitled to the fee simple that was conveyed to the trustees for sale. As far as the interests of the beneficiaries were concerned, the purchaser took free from them if he paid the purchase money to at least two trustees.[26] In contrast to the position under the strict settlement, overreaching under the trust for sale was automatic: no statutory intervention was necessary. The legal estate was held by the trustees for sale on trust to sell, and the beneficial interests were imposed upon the proceeds of sale or upon the rents and profits until sale. They were not upon the land. The only trust upon the land was the trust to sell. Where therefore the trustees for sale sold the land in performance of their duty to sell, the land which the

---

[21] (1929) 3 CLJ, p. 63 (J. M. Lightwood). [22] TLATA 1996, chap. 12, post.

[23] See Burnett, *Elements of Conveyancing*, pp. 455–6.

[24] *Fletcher v Ashburner* (1779) 1 Bro CC 497. The reverse was also true.

[25] Burnett, *Elements of Conveyancing* (8th edn), pp. 456–8.

[26] Or to a trust corporation: LPA 1925, ss. 2(1)(ii), 27(2); LP(A)A 1926, Schedule.

purchaser took was unaffected by any trusts; the trusts were and always had been imposed upon the purchase money.

Furthermore, the purchaser was not responsible for the proper application of the money, provided that he paid it to at least two trustees.[27] The beneficiaries must then look to the trustees and to them alone. This was not always so. In earlier days it was considered that the purchaser, since he had notice of the existence of beneficial limitations, was bound to see that the money was applied in accordance with the trust,[28] and it therefore became the usual practice to insert a clause in the first deed authorising the trustees to give the purchaser a receipt exonerating him from liability in this respect. This was made unnecessary, however, by a series of statutes dating from 1859,[29] culminating in:

The receipt in writing of a trustee for any money . . . payable to him under any trust or power shall be a sufficient discharge to the person paying . . . the same and shall effectually exonerate him from seeing to the application or being answerable for any loss or misapplication thereof.[30]

III Summary of the Two Methods of Settling Land before 1926

Before 1926 there had been evolved two methods of settling land: the strict settlement, in which the purchaser took his title from the tenant for life under the Settled Land Act 1882; and the trust for sale in which he took it from the trustees for sale. In both he might overreach the interests of the beneficiaries, even though he had notice of them. As to which was used depended on the object of the settlor. The strict settlement was appropriate where "land was settled with the object of founding a family or continuing the possession of family estates in the line of primogeniture";[31] here the tenant for life would reside on the land and himself exercise control over it. On the other hand the trust for sale was convenient where the property settled was not to be kept in the family, but was to be treated as an investment and as a source of income for the beneficiaries. It was especially useful where the fund settled was a mixture of personalty and realty and where the ultimate object was the division of land among children equally.

In 1925, the legislature, impressed by the advantages that the trust for sale imparted to the practice of conveyancing, made it the basis of several of the reforms introduced in that year. In particular, it was by extending the machinery and principle of the trust for sale that the law relating to concurrent interests[32] was strikingly simplified.

As we shall see,[33] the simplification of settlements was continued by the Trusts of Land and Appointment of Trustees Act 1996, which replaced the dual system of strict settlement and trust for sale by a unitary trust of land which applies to both successive and concurrent interests.

---

[27] Or to a trust corporation: LPA 1925, ss. 2(1)(ii), 27(2); LP(A)A 1926, Schedule.

[28] Vaizey, *The Law of Settlements of Property*, pp. 1409–12.

[29] LP(A)A 1859, s. 23; Conveyancing Act 1881, s. 36; Trustee Act 1893, s. 20.

[30] Trustee Act 1925, s. 14(1).   [31] (1929) 3 CLJ, p. 63 (J. M. Lightwood).

[32] Pp. 463, et seq, post.   [33] Chap. 12, post.

B. The Modern Law

SUMMARY

5

THE SIMPLIFICATION OF THE
LAW: 1925, 1996 AND 2002

SUMMARY

I	Simplification of the Law of Real Property	82
	A The Reduction of Tenures to One Common Form	82
	B The Assimilation of Real and Personal Property Law	86
	C The Abolition of Certain Anachronisms	90
II	Simplification of Conveyancing in 1925, 1996	
	and 2002. The Cult of the Estate Owner	91
	A Contract before Conveyance	91
	B Unregistered Conveyancing	92
	C Registered Conveyancing	100
	D Comparison of Unregistered and Registered Systems	111

Even as late as the conclusion of the war of 1914–1918 there were many features of the land law which seemed unnecessarily cumbrous and antiquated to a generation that, for the moment at any rate, considered itself destined to effect a general simplification of life. There was certainly much in the fundamentals of the subject that would seem strange to an impartial critic. Thus land was the subject of tenure, not of ownership, but instead of there being one common form of tenure with incidents of universal application, there were the two distinct forms, socage and copyhold, with various divergent offshoots such as gavelkind and borough-English. This division of tenures, which led to differences in the ordinary incidents of ownership and in the modes of conveyance, was complicated by a cross-division under which estates were classified as being either freehold or leasehold. The main object of the legislation of 1925 was the simplification of conveyancing, and the committee that was appointed to suggest alterations was instructed by its terms of reference "to consider the present position of land transfer, and to advise what action should be taken to *facilitate and cheapen the transfer of land*". It was found, however, that a necessary preliminary to the attainment of this object was the simplification of the law of real property. It is scarcely possible to modernise a system of transfer if the subject-matter of the transfer is itself governed by antiquated rules. An analysis of the legislation of 1925, therefore, requires us to consider how it simplified, first the law of real property, and then the system of conveyancing.

I Simplification of the Law of Real Property

In 1925 land was subject, not to one system, but to three systems of law. This surprising result was caused by the distinction between freeholds and chattels real,[1] and by the existence of two forms of tenure—socage and copyhold.

The law of real property strictly so-called, which governed freehold interests in land, was still different in several respects from that which governed chattels real. Furthermore, whether the interest enjoyed by a proprietor was a freehold or a chattel real, the land affected would be held either by socage or by copyhold tenure. This was an added complication, since in several important respects the rules governing socage and copyhold lands were divergent. There was thus a law of freeholds, a law of leaseholds and a law of copyholds. The obvious solution, therefore, and the one adopted by the legislature, was first to institute one common form of tenure by the abolition of copyhold; then to assimilate as far as practicable the law of real property and of chattels real; finally, to abolish certain anachronisms of the common law—irritating survivals that were inimical to a simplified legal system. We shall consider these three improvements separately.

A *The Reduction of Tenures to One Common Form*

(1) History of Simplification of Tenures

The account that we have already given of tenure shows that for a long period there has been a gradual but continuous reduction in the number of possible tenures. This process was far advanced before 1926, but in that year uniformity was at last attained.

Seven hundred years ago the law on this subject was complicated. In the time of Edward I there were four distinct and important varieties of tenure, distinguished from each other by the different kinds of services due and each exhibiting fundamental differences in the substantive rules of law to which they were subject.[2] This led to the growth of a mass of confused and intricate law, and it was only by slow degrees that simplification began to emerge.

(a) *Statute Quia Emptores 1290*

The Statute *Quia Emptores*, though it was not concerned with the actual reduction of the several varieties, at least stemmed the increasing confusion, since it forbade the creation of any further tenures within each variety. The introduction of the doctrine of *uses* led indirectly to a decline in the importance of tenures, for the relationship of lord and tenant would lose much of its value and significance if it was freed from those tenurial incidents, the avoidance of which was one of the chief inducements to put land in use.

(b) *Statute of Uses 1535*

The Statute of Uses, on the other hand, was a retrograde step in the process of simplification, though it was only for a time that it restored the importance of tenures. Before another century had passed the King no longer looked to the feudal incidents for a revenue, while the country as a whole evinced a desire to regain the advantages which had disappeared with the

---

[1] Pp. 37–8, ante.   [2] Pp. 17 et seq, ante.

abolition of uses, and to be rid of the burdensome incidents that were a feature of the law of tenures.

(c) Tenures Abolition Act 1660

In fact, even before the ultimate re-establishment of uses in the seventeenth century the first direct simplification of tenures was effected by the Tenures Abolition Act in 1660. The effect of this Act was the reduction of tenures to socage, copyhold and frankalmoin, though the honorary incidents of grand sergeanty were retained, and various customary modes of holding land, such as gavelkind, borough-English and ancient demesne, continued to exist in certain parts of the country. In effect only two important tenures remained—namely, socage and copyhold.

(d) Conveyancing complicated by copyhold

The position, then, long before 1926, showed a vast improvement upon that of the time of Edward I, but, as we have already seen, the continued existence of copyhold as a distinct tenure not only disturbed the simplicity of conveyancing, but also tended to embarrass the full exploitation of the land.[3] Not only did the form of conveyance vary according as the land was socage or copyhold, but, what was a far more serious blemish, such legal incidents as the mode of descent and the types of interest created often differed from those recognised by the general law. In this respect, indeed, there was not even a system of law common to all copyholds, for the actual customs upon which the legal incidents were dependent frequently varied from manor to manor. There was thus room for reform in this particular field of law, and the opportunity was seized by the legislature.

(2) Abolition of all Tenures except Socage

All previous modes of descent, whether operating by the general law or by the custom of gavelkind or borough-English or by any other custom of any county, locality or manor, were abrogated.[4] Escheat[5] *propter defectum sanguinis* was discarded and replaced by the right of the Crown to take as *bona vacantia* the interest of a tenant who died intestate and heirless.[6] The honorary services incident to tenure by sergeanty, where they still existed, were expressly reserved, but the tenure itself had already disappeared.[7] An attempt was also made to abolish frankalmoin, though whether it succeeded is doubtful. The Statute of 1660, which by its first section abolished knight service, provided in section 7 that nothing in the first section was to affect frankalmoin. The Administration of Estates Act 1925, instead of abolishing frankalmoin by express language, merely repealed section 7 of the Statute of 1660.[8] This repeal, however, would appear to be fruitless, for even if the seventh section had been omitted from the Statute, frankalmoin would have been unaffected by an enactment that merely abolished knight service. The matter is indeed of little importance, for no land can be held by frankalmoin at the present day unless it has been continuously so held by the same ecclesiastical tenant since before *Quia Emptores* 1290.[9] Finally, and at long last, the decisive step was taken of abolishing copyhold tenure. As from 1 January 1926, every parcel of copyhold land was enfranchised and converted into freehold land held by socage tenure.[10]

---

[3] P. 25, ante.   [4] AEA 1925, s. 45(1)(*a*).   [5] Pp. 19–20, ante.   [6] AEA 1925, s. 45(1)(*d*).
[7] LPA 1922, s. 136.   [8] Sch. 2.   [9] P. 21, n. 31, ante.
[10] LPA 1922, Part V, ss. 128–37, and Sch. 2 as amended by LP(A)A 1924, s. 2 and Sch. 2; LPA 1922, s. 189.

(3) Extinguishment of Manorial Incidents

It was realised, of course, that copyhold tenure could not be dismissed in this peremptory manner, for certain manorial incidents had long been associated with it, and to extinguish without compensation such of those as possessed a money value would obviously be unjust to the beneficiary, whether lord or copyholder. The solution adopted was based upon a tripartite classification of these incidents.

(a) Extinguished at once

The first class, consisting of those that had become anachronisms were extinguished immediately subject to a single payment of compensation.[11]

(b) Continued until 1950

The second class consisted of those incidents that still possessed a money value. These were temporarily saved,[12] but it was provided that they should be extinguished upon the payment of compensation, the amount of which was to be determined either by agreement or by the Minister of Agriculture and Fisheries at the instance of either party. The final date of extinction was to be 31 December 1935, though if by then no agreement upon the amount of compensation had been reached either party might apply to the Minister requiring the amount to be determined, provided that the application was made before 31 December 1940. Owing to the war, this was later extended to 1 November 1950.[13]

(c) Continued indefinitely

The following incidents, falling within the third class, were permanently saved and they continue to attach to the land, unless the parties agree to their extinction upon payment of compensation:[14]

   (a) any commonable rights to which the tenant is entitled;[15]

   (b) any right of the lord or the tenant to mines, minerals, gravel pits or quarries, whether in or under the land;[16]

   (c) any rights of the lord in respect of fairs, markets or sporting;

   (d) any liability for the construction, maintenance, cleansing or repair of any dykes, ditches, canals, sea or river walls, bridges, levels, ways, etc.[17]

Lordships of manors continue to exist;[18] they represent mesne tenure between the Crown and the freeholders. In addition to potential manorial rights, the owner is entitled to be

---

[11] LPA 1922, Sch. 12, para. 1; forfeiture for an alienation without the lord's licence; liability of the copyholder to customary suits and to do fealty; customary modes of descent or any custom relating to dower, curtesy (p. 486, post) or freebench (Blackstone, vol. ii. p. 337).

[12] Ibid., s. 128(2): *rents*; fines payable to the lord in certain circumstances; *reliefs* payable to the lord upon descent of the land; *heriots*, the right of the lord to seize the best beast or best chattel upon the tenant's decease; *forfeitures* for a variety of acts by the tenant; the right of the lord to fell *timber* trees.

[13] SI 1949 No. 836.   [14] LPA 1922, s. 138(12).   [15] Ibid., Sch. 12, para. 4, p. 643, post.

[16] Ibid., Sch. 12, para. 5. As to the right to work out coal in former copyhold land, see Coal Industry Act 1994, s. 49.   [17] Ibid., Sch. 12, para. 6.

[18] Manors could be registered: LRR 1925, rr. 50, 51; but this is no longer possible under LRA 2002. A manor which was registered under LRA 1925 may now be removed from the register on the application of the proprietor: LRA 2002, s. 119. See generally Land Registry Practice Guide 22.

called "Lord of the Manor" and has the right to the manorial records, which may date from before the Norman Conquest.[19]

(4) Unimportance of Doctrine of Tenure

Thus, after some nine hundred years of development the doctrine of tenure still characterises the English law of real property. Land is still incapable of ownership by a subject. Every acre is held by a tenant, not owned, though by a gradual process of elimination the various forms of tenure that complicated the law in former days have at last been reduced to the one type—socage. And, given that there is now no distinction between different types of tenure, even the term "socage" is rarely invoked. But what are the practical effects of the doctrine? Are the rights that the English tenant in fee simple enjoys any less valuable, for instance, than those of an absolute owner of land in the State of New York where all feudal tenures have been expressly abolished? Is tenure a mere name, a reminder only of the pomp and splendour of former days? The truth is, of course, that it is a mere historical survival that now has little practical effect. To have styled the tenant a landowner some centuries ago would have been inaccurate, since his very right to retain the land was conditional on his performance of the tenurial liabilities. But in course of time these liabilities have almost entirely disappeared, and it is only on the rarest occasion that anything of value can now be claimed by virtue of tenure. Until 1926, indeed, a lord, if he were still able to establish his lordship, might be fortunate enough to derive an unearned increment under the doctrine of escheat, but he lost even this when the Administration of Estates Act 1925 provided that the land of a tenant who dies intestate without leaving near relatives shall pass to the Crown.[20] The feudal doctrine of tenure has no doubt impressed an indelible mark upon the framework of the law, but it no longer affects the tenant's rights of enjoyment, though the modern tendency to stress the rights of the community at large has resulted in the imposition of restrictions upon him that were unknown to earlier ages. The living results of feudalism must be sought, not in the realm of tenures, but in that classification of estates which is a peculiarity of English law. Apart from this "wonderful calculus of estates", as Maitland expressed it, perhaps the sole feudal incident that is a living force at the present day consists of those rights of common which the successors of the copyhold lord and tenant may still hold in the manorial waste. To quote Maitland again:[21]

Everyone knows that this doctrine [of tenure], however indispensable as an explanation for some of the subtleties of real property law, is, in fact, untrue. "The first thing the student has to do is to get rid

---

[19] For a discussion of the contemporary significance of manors by Lord DENNING who, as Master of the Rolls, had charge and superintendence of manorial documents, see *Corpus Christi College, Oxford v Gloucestershire County Council* [1983] QB 360 at 364–6. In 1985, twenty-nine Lordships were sold at public auction; the highest price paid was £21,200 for the Lordship of Codicote in Hertfordshire. This included a right to hold a fair in the manor on the Vigil and Feast of St James and the two following days: (1985) 274 EG 15.

[20] Ss. 45, 46(1)(vi). Escheat may, however, still exist if a trustee in bankruptcy of a landowner disclaims the land: *British General Insurance Co Ltd v A-G* [1945] LJNCCR 113; (1946) 62 LQR 223 (R. E. Megarry), or if a corporation (other than a company incorporated under the Companies Acts) holding real property is dissolved: *Re Sir Thomas Spencer Wells* [1933] Ch 29 at 54; *Re Strathblaine Estates Ltd* [1948] Ch 228. See too (1954) 70 LQR 25 (D. W. Elliott); *Re Lowe's Will Trusts* [1973] 1 WLR 882 at 884, where RUSSELL LJ said: "By a happy chance [escheat to the Crown of realty *propter defectum sanguinis*] has arisen from the past in connection with the Phoenix Inn in Stratford-on-Avon". See also *Scmilla Properties Ltd v Gesso Properties (BVI) Ltd* [1995] NPC 48.

[21] *Collected Papers*, vol. i. p. 196. See also Challis, *Law of Real Property*, p. 3.

of the idea of absolute ownership." So says Mr. Williams;[22] but we may add, with equal truth, that the second thing he has to do is to learn how, by slow degrees, the statement that there is no absolute ownership of land has been deprived of most of its important consequences.

If this was true in 1880 when Maitland wrote, how unsubstantial must the doctrine of tenure be after the abolition of copyholds in 1925.

It should be observed that, although the substance has gone, the form remains. To quote MEGARRY J: "Hundreds of . . . phrases and concepts which permeate our law will have to be remembered if reforming zeal ever proposes to sweep away the theoretical structure of tenures and estates upon which English land law rests."[23]

There is indeed a reforming zeal at the start of the twenty-first century. The Law Commission is proposing to review feudal land law:[24]

Reform is necessary for a number of technical and practical reasons. First, it makes little sense to have a partial retention of feudal land law for 21st century land holdings. Land law has, in most major respects, moved on from ancient concepts and practices and it is inconsistent that remnants remain in operation. Secondly, the remnants that do remain cause uncertainty to members of the public, to practitioners and to the courts due to their complex and archaic nature and their incompatibility with modern case and statute law. Finally, there is an unnecessary and confusing overlap in the main area in which feudal land law finds modern expression: the treatment of ownerless land.[25]

The Commission initially sought to reform this area of the law as part of its project on Land Registration.[26] During the course of the project, however, far-ranging reform of feudal land law was postponed and "stop-gap" measures substituted. It was felt that more time and further research was needed to understand fully both the law and the best means of reforming it and to gain the agreement of interested parties.[27] Nevertheless, the report called in very strong terms for wholesale reform to follow as "the present law is indefensible".[28] Feudal land law is included in the Ninth Programme of Law Reform . . .

B The Assimilation of Real and Personal Property Law

Originally, as we have seen, there were wide distinctions between the law of real and of personal property, but there has been a tendency ever since an early age to make both these departments of the law subject to the same legal rules, and in the main the rules that have been adopted are those that govern personal property. Thus the legislation of 1925 attempted to complete a process of assimilation that was already far advanced. We shall perhaps gain a greater clearness of view if we first consider in what particulars a common body of legal rules had been created before 1926, and then review the contents of the statutes designed to procure as complete a unification as possible.

---

[22] Williams, *The Law of Real Property*, p. 17.

[23] *Lowe (Inspector of Taxes) v J W Ashmore Ltd* [1971] Ch 545 at 554.

[24] Thirty-ninth Annual Report 2004–05 (Law Com No. 294), paras. 6.24. The feudal system of land tenure was formally abolished in Scotland by Abolition of Feudal Tenures etc (Scotland) Act 2000 (asp 5), implementing the Scottish Law Commission's Report on Abolition of the Feudal System 1999 (Scots Law Com No. 168). The modern law of immovable property in Scotland is substantially civilian in nature: Zimmermann, Visser and Reid, *Mixed Legal Systems in Comparative Perspective*, pp. 643–4 (K. Reid and G. G. van de Merwe); Reid, *The Abolition of Feudal Tenure in Scotland*.   [25] That is, the doctrines of escheat and bona vacantia.

[26] Land Registration for the Twenty-First Century—A Conveyancing Revolution 2001 (Law Com No. 271). This joint project with HM Land Registry was implemented in the Land Registration Act 2002.

[27] Law Com No. 271, para 11.27.   [28] Ibid., para 11.26.

(1) Matters in which Assimilation had been Effected Prior to 1926

(a) Remedies for dispossession

The original rule that leaseholds, unlike freeholds, were not specifically recoverable[29] ceased to be true towards the middle of the fifteenth century, by which time the action *de ejectione firmae* was available to the termor or lessee. The actions that lay for recovery of land were still, indeed, different according as the demandant's interest was freehold or leasehold, but complete assimilation in this particular was attained in the seventeenth century, by which time the *de ejectione firmae* had been borrowed from the law of chattels real and, under the name of the action of ejectment, had been adapted to the recovery of freeholds.[30]

(b) Power of testamentary disposition

It was always possible to bequeath leaseholds and other forms of personal property, but the feudal law would not admit a will of freeholds. A partial power of testamentary disposition over real property was obtained, however, in 1540, when the Statute of Wills permitted tenants to devise all their socage lands and two-thirds of their land held in knight service. This testamentary power was completed by the Tenures Abolition Act of 1660, which converted knight service tenure into free and common socage.

(c) Availability of property for creditors

While at an early date leaseholds and other forms of personal property belonging to a deceased debtor constituted assets available for all creditors, the general rule was that a fee simple estate passed directly to the heir or devisee of a deceased tenant and could not be seized by his creditors. Gradual inroads upon this immunity of real property were, however, made by statute and by equity, and assimilation was almost attained in 1833, when the Administration of Estates Act made all land belonging to a deceased debtor available as assets for the one class of creditors—namely, simple contract creditors—who had not already obtained a remedy against freeholds. There was, however, still a difference in respect of remedies, for to render personal property available a creditor had to proceed against the personal representatives, while to satisfy his claim against real property, which did not vest in the personal representatives, he had to bring a suit in equity for administration. Assimilation on this point came with the Land Transfer Act 1897, which provided that realty should vest in the personal representatives, as had always been the practice with personalty.

The law that regulated the right of a creditor to seize the land of his *living* debtor was also assimilated before 1926. At common law all the chattels, real and personal, of a judgment debtor might be seized, but there was no right to satisfaction out of his freeholds. The Statute of Westminster 1285 made half the debtor's land available for creditors, and this was extended to the whole of the land by the Judgments Act of 1838.

(2) Matters in which Assimilation was Effected by the Legislation of 1925

The process of assimilation was carried further by the legislation of 1925 in the following respects.

---

[29] P. 36, ante. [30] Holdsworth, *History of English Law*, vol. vii. pp. 4 et seq.

(a) Size and nature of estates and interests

Before 1926 there was a fundamental distinction between realty and personalty with regard to the interests that might be created.

In the case of real property it has been possible for many centuries to create not only legal and equitable estates of different sizes—namely, the fee simple, the estate tail and the life estate—but also to split the full fee simple up into a series of partial and successive legal or equitable interests, as for example by a grant to A for life, then to B in tail, and then to C in fee simple.

The position with regard to personal property was different. Pure personalty (goods and money) and chattels real (such as an unexpired lease for twenty years) were *at common law* the subjects of absolute ownership only. They were outside the doctrine of estates altogether and they could not be divided into successive interests. A grant of an existing term of years to A for life or in tail made A at common law the owner of the entire term. A gift for an hour was a gift for ever. The position *in equity* was different, for to a limited extent equity did permit successive interests to be created in personalty if the device of a grant to trustees was adopted. If the owner of a leasehold for thirty years granted it to trustees

upon trust for A for life and then upon trust for B for life,

A did not become absolute owner of the whole term as he would have done at common law, but held merely for life, while on his death B similarly became entitled to a life estate. The interests of both A and B were of course equitable. There was one method, however, though it was seldom used, by which even at common law an effective life estate might be given in personalty—namely, by will. Without adopting the instrument of a trust a testator might make a direct bequest of a leasehold

to A for life with a further gift to B for life,

and the bequests would be upheld. But it is important to observe that before 1926 it was impossible to create an estate tail in leaseholds either by a direct bequest or through the instrumentality of trustees. A term of years, not being an estate of inheritance, could not be entailed.[31]

(1) SUMMARY OF PRE-1926 LAW

A summary of the law is, then, that in real property there might be legal or equitable fees simple, estates tail or life interests, either alone or in succession, but that in personal property there was normally only absolute ownership, though there might be equitable and, exceptionally, legal life interests.

(2) ASSIMILATION BY LAW OF PROPERTY ACT 1925

Assimilation, as regards both the size of the interests creatable and their nature when created, was, however, effected as from 1 January 1926 by the Law of Property Act 1925. In the first place this provided that personalty could be entailed.[32] The result was that the nature of the subject-matter no longer affected the quantitative interest that could be carved out of it.

---

[31] *Leventhorpe v Ashbie* (1635) 1 Roll Abr 831.
[32] LPA 1925, s. 130 (1); p. 495, post. Entails can no longer be created after 1996: TLATA 1996; p. 500, post.

In realty there may be a fee simple estate, in personalty absolute ownership; while in both cases either entailed interests or life interests could validly be created. Secondly, as we shall see later,[33] entailed and life interests, whether in real or in personal property, can no longer exist as legal estates, but must always be equitable. Moreover, it is no longer possible to have a future *legal* estate in freeholds.

(b) Descent on intestacy

Perhaps the most striking difference between realty and personalty in 1925 lay in the rules that regulated their descent or distribution upon the death of the owner intestate. The old canons of descent, based upon feudal doctrines as amended by statute, governed the descent of fee simple and entailed estates, while the Statutes of Distribution contained a different set of rules prescribing what relatives were entitled to share the leaseholds and personal chattels of the deceased. Both these systems, together with various customary modes of descent, were abolished and new distributive rules were introduced which apply to both real and personal property.[34] The old canons of descent have, however, been retained for entailed interests.

(c) Order in which assets were applied for payment of debts

It is essential that definite rules shall prescribe the order in which the beneficiaries under a will must be deprived of their interests for the benefit of the unpaid creditors of the testator. The rules before 1926 on this matter represented another difference between real and personal property, for they required the exhaustion of the general personal estate before recourse was had to the realty. They were replaced by new provisions in the Administration of Estates Act 1925 which, from this point of view, put realty and personalty on the same footing.[35]

(d) Necessity for words of limitation

A conveyance which was intended to pass the whole fee simple had under the old law to contain technical words of limitation, namely, to A and *his heirs* or to A *in fee simple*, otherwise it operated to pass only a life estate. Such words were not necessary in the case of a transfer of leaseholds; a simple grant to A, without more, was sufficient to transfer the whole interest of the grantor. Assimilation on this point, however, was effected by the Law of Property Act 1925,[36] which provides that a conveyance of freehold land without words of limitation shall pass the whole interest held by the grantor unless a contrary intention appears in the conveyance.

(e) Method of creating legal mortgages

The method of creating a legal mortgage of the fee simple before 1926 was by a conveyance of the legal fee simple to the mortgagee with a proviso that he should re-convey the estate upon repayment of the loan; but where the subject-matter of the mortgage was a leasehold

---

[33] Ibid., s. 1(1)–(3); p. 94, post.
[34] AEA 1925, ss. 45, 46, as amended by IEA 1952, Family Provision Act 1966, Law Reform (Succession) Act 1995, s. 1 and Civil Partnership Act 2004. For the detail of the law of intestate succession see the 16th edn of this book, chap. 26.   [35] Ibid., s. 34(3), Sch. 1, Part II.
[36] S. 60(1); p. 172, post.

interest, the almost universal practice was for the mortgagor to grant a sub-lease of the property to the mortgagee. This particular difference between freeholds and leaseholds disappeared, for the practice of conveying the fee simple was forbidden, and it was enacted that a legal mortgage of freeholds must be made by the grant of a lease or its equivalent.[37]

(f) Application of rule in Dearle v Hall

If successive assignments or mortgages of an *equitable* interest in property were made before 1926, the order in which the several assignees or mortgagees were entitled to repayment out of the property depended upon the nature of the property. If it was land, whether freehold or leasehold, they ranked for payment according to the order of time in which they had taken their assignment or mortgage; but if it was pure personalty, the rule in *Dearle v Hall*[38] applied, and the priorities were governed by the order of time in which the assignments or mortgages had been notified to the trustees of the personalty. This rule now applies to equitable interests in unregistered land, so that a later assignee who is the first to notify the estate owner of the land affected ranks prior to an earlier assignment of which he had no notice when he took his own assignment.[39]

(3) Remaining Differences Between Realty and Personalty

The above review of those differences between realty and personalty that were eradicated by the legislation of 1925 shows that the law relating to the two forms of property has been assimilated as far as is possible. Certain differences must, of course, inevitably persist. For instance, easements and profits may subsist in land, but not in pure personalty; time under the Limitation Act 1980 varies according as the subject-matter is realty or personalty; the forms of alienation are different; so is the procedure on alienation, for investigation of title, though not usual in the case of personalty, is essential upon the transfer of an interest in land—and, indeed, the very system of registration of title to estates in land emphasises the different significance of realty as compared with personalty. It would seem that most of the divergences must always in the nature of things continue to exist, since they result inevitably from the physical difference between the two forms of property.

C The Abolition of Certain Anachronisms

A subsidiary part of the simplification of land transfer was the abolition of certain real property rules and doctrines which, though they had originally been introduced to preserve principles of importance in feudal days, were nothing more than obstructive anachronisms in 1925. The abolitions and alterations of this character effected by the various Acts will be described later, and we shall therefore content ourselves for the moment with a mere enumeration of those that are the most important:

(1) the abolition of the rule in *Shelley's Case*;[40]

(2) the indirect abolition of the old contingent remainder rules;[41]

---

[37] LPA 1925, s. 85(1). Under LRA 2002 it is now no longer possible to create a mortgage of registered land by the grant of a lease; p. 724, post.   [38] (1823) 3 Russ 1; M & B p. 912.

[39] LPA 1925, s. 137; pp. 804 et seq, post. Priority in registered land has a different rule: p. 807, post.

[40] P. 492, post.   [41] P. 511, post.

(3) the abolition of the rule in *Whitby v Mitchell*;[42]

(4) the almost complete abolition of the old canons of descent;[43]

(5) the final abolition of the doctrine of *Dumpor's Case* so far as it related to leases;[44]

(6) the reversal of the rule that husband and wife were always one person for the purposes of the acquisition of land;[45]

(7) the abolition of special occupancy.[46]

II Simplification of Conveyancing in 1925, 1996 and 2002. The Cult of the Estate Owner

There are two systems of conveyancing in England and Wales today; the unregistered system, under which title to land is deduced from past transactions relating to the property, and the registered system, where the title is recorded on a national register and is guaranteed by the State. The registered system under the Land Registration Acts 1925 and 2002 has gradually superseded the unregistered system and since 1990 has been made compulsory over the whole of England and Wales; compulsory in the sense that dealings in land must now be carried out under the new and not the old system of conveyancing.[47] A detailed discussion of both systems will be found in Part III.[48] In this section we are concerned with a general outline of the two systems, and with a comparison of their main features from the point of view of a purchaser.

A Contract before Conveyance

It should first be noticed that, both in unregistered conveyancing and in registered conveyancing, a contract for the sale of land usually precedes the conveyance of the legal estate to the purchaser.[49] As a matter of common practice, the purchaser will make some of his inquiries in relation to the property before the contract is entered into; others in the period between the contract and the conveyance. We shall consider the law and practice governing the contract, and its effect, in detail in chapter 24. From the outset, however, it should be realised that since 1989 a contract for the sale or other disposition of land must be in writing, signed by both parties.[50] And that the effect of a contract for the sale of land is very significant: under the doctrine of *Walsh v Lonsdale*,[51] a specifically enforceable contract to

---

[42] P. 519, post.   [43] P. 89, ante.   [44] P. 264, post.   [45] P. 917, post.

[46] See the 16th edn of this book, p. 294, n. 19.   [47] Pp. 100 et seq, post.   [48] Pp. 929 et seq, post.

[49] Similarly, a contract for a lease may be made first, and then followed at a later date by a formal grant of the legal term of years absolute; p. 219, post. And (although this is less common) the owner of an estate in land may contract to create an interest in it, such as an easement or a charge, the actual creation of the interest to follow later.

[50] LP(MP)A 1989, s. 2 (contracts entered into after 26 September 1989). A contract entered into before 27 September 1989 was valid even if not made in writing, but would only be enforceable by action if evidenced by a signed memorandum (LPA 1925, s. 40), or if there was a sufficient act of part performance by the party seeking to enforce it; pp. 864 et seq, post.   [51] (1882) 21 Ch D 9, M & B p. 85; pp. 223–5, 877, post.

create or convey a legal estate or interest is treated in equity as creating the equivalent estate or interest. A contract for the sale of land—commonly termed an *estate contract*[52]—therefore has the effect of creating an immediate equitable interest in favour of the purchaser.

B Unregistered Conveyancing

Under the system of unregistered conveyancing, a purchaser must make inquiries and bear the responsibility of satisfying himself on two matters—first, that the vendor is entitled to convey the estate which he has contracted to sell, and, secondly, that there are no incumbrances in favour of third parties that will continue to affect the land after the conveyance.

The legislation of 1925 made no fundamental alteration in the practice relating to the former matter,[53] but devoted its main attention to the question of incumbrances. In the normal case there will be no undisclosed incumbrances, but nevertheless the doctrine of constructive notice exists and a purchaser dare not do otherwise than institute an expensive inquiry. The danger is obvious. Land is different from such subjects of ownership as goods, since more often than not it is affected by rights vested in parties other than the ostensible owner.

A may appear to be absolute unincumbered tenant in fee simple of Blackacre, but investigation may disclose that B has an easement of way over the land, that C has a right to prevent the erection of buildings upon it, or that D, having lent £10,000 to A, has taken a mortgage upon Blackacre as security for repayment of the loan.

The power to create rights of this description in favour of third parties, and enforceable primarily against the land itself rather than against its owner, is a valuable, in fact an inevitable, feature of our social life. For the sake of brevity, we will describe them in future as third-party rights.

(1) Classification of Third-party Rights

In some cases (as for instance in the case of easements and restrictive covenants), third-party rights are a necessary local complement of land ownership; in others they originate in the financial requirements of owners (as for instance mortgages); while in others (as for instance in the rights of a wife who has contributed to the purchase price where the legal estate is vested in the husband alone), they are due to the social traditions of family life. They may be conveniently divided into two cases:

(1) Those arising either under a settlement or a trust of land, as for instance the wife's beneficial share in the family home, or financial provisions made for a widow and after her death for the children of the marriage;

(2) Those arising under some other transaction connected with the landowner's activities as a landowner or business man. Examples of this second class are easements, profits, restrictive covenants, estate contracts, mortgages and annuities.

But whatever their origin or character, it is obvious that the possibility of their existence and the risk that they may continue to bind the land after its sale, must cause a purchaser to walk warily and with no undue haste.

---

[52] Pp. 65–6, ante.   [53] Pp. 60 et seq, ante.

(2) Extent to which a Purchaser was Bound by Third-party Rights before 1926

The extent to which a purchaser was affected by third-party rights before 1926 depended upon the fundamental distinction between the legal and the equitable estate.[54] A bona fide purchaser for value of the legal fee simple which was subject to third-party rights was absolutely bound by them if they amounted to legal estates or interests, the question of his actual knowledge or ignorance of their existence being irrelevant. On the other hand, he was not bound by rights that were merely equitable in nature, unless he had actual or constructive notice of their existence. Thus:

An easement in perpetuity or a lease for a definite number of years would be enforceable against even an innocent purchaser because each is a legal interest, i.e. a right *in rem* enforceable against the whole world. On the other hand, if a fee simple owner had made an estate contract with X (e.g. had agreed to sell him the legal fee simple or to grant him a lease), or if he had subjected the land to a restrictive covenant in favour of Y (as for instance by covenanting that he would erect no business premises), the rights thus vested in X and Y, since they are merely equitable in nature, would not bind a subsequent purchaser for value who took a conveyance of the legal estate from the fee simple owner, unless he was affected with notice.

The significant points, then, are that a purchaser had more to fear from legal than from equitable third-party rights, and conversely that the third-party himself was less secure with an equitable than a legal right.

(3) Outline of Statutory Changes by Legislation of 1925 and 1996

The following is a bare sketch of how the legislation attempted to simplify the problem of third-party rights.

(a) It drastically curtailed the category of legal estates and legal third-party rights. The result is that after 1925 most third-party rights are equitable.

(b) It made the legal estate the basis of conveyancing. The principal effect of this is that the legal estate can be conveyed only by its owner, not, as frequently occurred under the former law, by a person who had no estate in the land at all.[55]

(c) The existing system by which in certain circumstances the conveyance of a legal estate by way of sale overreached equitable third-party rights, that is, it encumbered the purchase money instead of the land with their payment and relieved the purchaser of the duty to investigate them, was extended. In the result,

(i) these rights are cleared off the land altogether if they can equally well be satisfied out of the purchase money; but

(ii) if this is not possible, then they can be registered as *land charges* in a public register, so that their owners are protected and a purchaser is warned.

This sketch now requires a little elaboration.

(a) Reduction in number of legal estates

Before 1926 any recognised interest in land, regarded quantitatively, might be either legal or equitable. The Law of Property Act 1925, however, reduced the possible legal estates to the

---

[54] Pp. 54 et seq, ante.   [55] Pp. 74–5, ante.

fee simple absolute in possession in the case of freeholds, and the term of years absolute in the case of leaseholds.

The person in whom such an estate is vested is called the *estate owner*. All other estates, interests and charges in or over the land can exist only as equitable interests,[56] with the exception of those interests permitted to exist at law by section 1(2) of the Act.[57]

In the case of freeholds, for instance, the:

> determinable fee simple,[58]
>
> entailed interest,[59]
>
> life interest,[60]
>
> future interest of whatever size,[61]

can subsist only in equity, not at law. Each one must be created behind a trust, that is, the legal estate in the land affected must be held by an *estate owner* whose function it is to give effect to the equitable interest. The very terminology, indeed, is changed. The correct expression now, for instance, is "entailed interest" not "estate tail", and "life interest" instead of "life estate".

Section 1 of the Law of Property Act 1925 runs as follows:

(1) The only estates in land which are capable of subsisting or of being conveyed or created at law are
(a) An estate in fee simple absolute in possession;[62]
(b) A term of years absolute.[63]

(2) The only interests or charges in or over land which are capable of subsisting or of being conveyed or created at law are
(a) An easement, right, or privilege in or over land for an interest equivalent to an estate in fee simple absolute in possession or a term of years absolute;[64]
(b) A rentcharge in possession issuing out of or charged on land being either perpetual or for a term of years absolute;[65]
(c) A charge by way of legal mortgage;[66]
(d) Land tax,[67] tithe rentcharge,[68] and any other similar charge on land which is not created by an instrument;
(e) Rights of entry exercisable over or in respect of a legal term of years absolute, or annexed, for any purpose, to a legal rentcharge.

(3) All other estates, interests, and charges in or over land take effect as equitable interests.

It will be observed that in referring in the first sub-section to *estates* and in the second to *interests* the Act invented a new terminology[69] that depends upon the difference between a right to the land itself and a right to some claim against the land of another person.

---

[56] LPA 1925, s. 1(1)–(3).   [57] Infra.   [58] Chap. 17, post.   [59] Chap. 14, post.
[60] Chap. 15, post.   [61] Chap. 16, post.   [62] Chap. 8, post.   [63] Chap. 10, post.
[64] Chap. 18, post.
[65] Chap. 20, post. The Rentcharges Act 1977 is phasing out the creation of certain kinds of rentcharge.
[66] Chap. 21, post.   [67] Abolished by the Finance Act 1963, s. 73, Sch. 14, Part VI.
[68] Extinguished by the Tithe Act 1936, s. 48, Sch. 9 and replaced by a sixty years' redemption annuity payable to the Crown. This is a legal interest within the meaning of "any other similar charge . . ." of para. (d). This was itself extinguished as from 2 October 1977 by FA 1977, s. 56.
[69] However, the term "legal estate" is still used as shorthand to refer to both the two legal estates (property so-called) and legal interests and charges: LPA 1925, s. 1(4).

To be entitled to a legal as distinct from an equitable interest in the land itself it is necessary to hold an estate, and the only estate that qualifies for this purpose is either the fee simple absolute in possession or the term of years absolute according as the subject-matter is freehold or leasehold.

On the other hand, a claim against the land of another, if falling within the five items in the Law of Property Act 1925, s. 1(2) is termed an *interest* in that land, but to constitute a *legal* interest it must correspond in duration to one of the two legal estates. A person entitled in perpetuity or for twenty-one years to an easement, such as a right of way over Blackacre, owns a legal interest in Blackacre provided that the easement is created in the appropriate form. If he is only entitled to it for life, he is an equitable owner.

Thus, the ancient doctrine of estates under which the fee simple, the entail and the life interest were recognised as estates at common law, has been drastically abridged. There is only the one freehold estate at law—the fee simple absolute in possession. The doctrine, however, has only been "as it were, pushed back into equity"[70] in the sense that the interests that were formerly estates at law still subsist with equal vigour as equitable interests.

(b) *Legal estate as basis of conveyancing*

This may be illustrated by two observations.

(1) POWERS OF APPOINTMENT NOW EQUITABLE

First, we have seen that it was a common practice before 1926 to limit land to A and B in fee simple to such uses as X might appoint, with the result that if X, who had no proprietary interest in the land, "appointed" to the use of Y and his heirs, A and B thereupon stood seised to the use of Y and he took a *legal* fee simple under the Statute of Uses.[71] This is no longer possible. The Statute of Uses has been repealed[72] and, though land may still be limited to A and B upon such trusts as X shall appoint, this merely empowers X to dispose of the equitable interest. With very few exceptions powers are now equitable.[73]

(2) TITLE TO LEGAL ESTATE ALONE INVESTIGATED

Secondly, if a legal estate that is held in trust for beneficiaries is offered for sale, the purchaser's sole concern in the normal case is to trace the title of the vendors to the legal estate. As we have seen,[74] he is entirely unaffected by the beneficial interests, for these are overreached, that is, once the legal estate has been conveyed to a purchaser, they are no longer binding on the land but are transferred to the purchase money which has been paid to the trustees.[75]

---

[70] Lawson, *Rational Strength of English Law*, p. 94.   [71] P. 69, ante.   [72] LPA 1922, s. 207, Sch. 7.

[73] LPA 1925, ss. 1(7), 3 as amended by TLATA 1996, s. 25(2), Sch. 4. Section 205(1)(xi) contains the following definitions: "Legal powers" include the powers vested in a chargee by way of legal mortgage or in an estate owner under which a legal estate can be transferred or created, and "equitable powers" mean all the powers in or over land under which equitable interests or powers only can be transferred or created.

[74] P. 75, ante.   [75] For details, see pp. 994, 997–1002, post.

(c) Strict settlements: Settled Land Act 1925

(1) CONVEYANCING DIFFICULTIES

The policy of freeing the title to the legal estate from beneficial interests to which it may be subject, had begun in 1882 in the case of settled land. This was continued by the 1925 legislation. Furthermore the conveyancing machinery was greatly simplified. Before 1926 a strict settlement was created by a single deed which conferred legal estates and interests upon the successive beneficiaries, so that for instance the husband acquired a legal estate for life and the eldest son a legal estate tail.[76] When the tenant for life exercised, say, his statutory power of sale under the Settled Land Act 1882, his conveyance did, indeed, overreach these legal interests, but, as we have seen, the conveyancing difficulties were not inconsiderable.[77] These derived mainly from the fact that, since the fee simple was not vested in the tenant for life, his right to convey it rested solely upon the statutory powers of sale. The whole settlement required investigation, and before the purchaser was relieved from liability in respect of the beneficial limitations, it was incumbent upon him to make sure that the statutory conditions for the exercise of the power had been satisfied.

(2) SETTLED LAND ACT 1925

These conveyancing difficulties, however, were removed by the Settled Land Act 1925. Owing to the reduction in the number of legal estates, the limited and beneficial interests arising under a strict settlement are now necessarily equitable, and the legal fee simple out of which they have been carved must, in accordance with the statutory provisions, be vested in the first tenant for life and be transferred to each subsequent tenant for life as and when he becomes entitled to possession.[78]

(3) DUAL POSITION OF TENANT FOR LIFE

Thus the tenant for life occupies a dual position. Although he is a mere tenant for life as regards beneficial enjoyment, he is the owner of the legal fee simple for conveyancing purposes. This means that within the scope of his statutory powers he can dispose of the legal estate, whether it be the fee simple absolute in possession or the term of years absolute, so as to pass to the purchaser a title free from the rights under the settlement; but it does not mean that he becomes entitled to the capital money arising from the transaction. It is, in fact, a condition of the purchaser's immunity that the money should be paid to the trustees.

(4) METHOD OF CREATING A STRICT SETTLEMENT AFTER 1925

In order to emphasise this separation of the legal estate from the beneficial and equitable interests and to facilitate conveyancing, a new method of creating a strict settlement, framed on the pattern of the trust for sale, was introduced by the Settled Land Act 1925. Every settlement *inter vivos* had to be made by two deeds. One (*the vesting deed*) vested the legal fee simple in the tenant for life, described the property and named the trustees; the other (the

---

[76] These interests could also be equitable. After the re-introduction of the use in the form of the trust (pp. 52–4, ante) it was, of course, possible to create a strict settlement by the alternative method of a grant unto and to the use of trustees to hold the legal estate upon the requisite trusts, in which case the beneficiaries would be entitled to equitable interests.   [77] Pp. 74–5, ante.

[78] Pp. 403, 405 post.

trust instrument) declared the beneficial interests of the tenant for life and the other persons entitled under the settlement.[79]

(5) OVERREACHING OF EQUITABLE INTERESTS

The effect of a conveyance made by the tenant for life in his capacity as estate owner is to overreach the equitable interests of the beneficiaries, that is, it clears them off the title to the legal fee simple and converts them into equivalent interests in the purchase money. Their fate is of no concern to the purchaser, provided that he pays the purchase money to the trustees, and not to the tenant for life. His sole object is to investigate the title to the *legal* estate. He must, therefore, trace that title down to the first vesting deed, that is, he must require the vendor to show that the person who purported to vest the legal estate in the first tenant for life was in fact entitled to do so. He does not see, nor in general may he demand to see, the trust instrument. That instrument is solely the charter of the beneficiaries. The rights that it grants to the beneficiaries are still intact, still secure, but they are now transferred to the purchase money. The whole operation set in motion upon a conveyance by the tenant for life is an illustration of what is called the *curtain* principle. The vesting deed is, as it were, a curtain that veils the equitable interests.[80]

(d) Trusts of land

A major change was made by the Trusts of Land and Appointment of Trustees Act 1996.[81] The Act applies to trusts of land created before or after the date of its commencement on 1 January 1997. Under it the dual system of strict settlement and trust for sale is replaced by a trust of land which applies to both successive and concurrent interests. Existing strict settlements continue, but no new strict settlements can be created. Existing express trusts for sale, whether of successive or of concurrent interests, also continue, and may still be expressly created so as to come within the wide definition of the trust of land.[82] Trusts of concurrent interests which were implied by statute, are converted into trusts of land.[83] Under the trust of land the legal estate to the land is vested in trustees who are given all the powers of an absolute owner for the purpose of exercising their functions as trustees. The trustees have a power, but not a duty, to sell, and the interests of the beneficiaries are still overreachable on sale, as they were under the previous dual system. The doctrine of conversion is abolished in respect of all trusts for sale, whenever created,[84] and consequently the interests of the beneficiaries cease to be interests in personalty and become interests in land. The Act is another and welcome measure in the long line of measures which over the centuries have sought to develop and simplify the land law; it is an important gloss on the 1925 legislation, and gives to the trustees broad and flexible powers to enable them to manage the land more effectively, and to the beneficiaries more scope in the control of those powers.

(e) Registrable third-party rights

In the case, then, of a settlement, whether it be a strict settlement, a trust for sale, or, after 1996, a trust of land, the beneficial interests are cleared altogether off the title to the legal

---

[79] SLA 1925, s. 4; pp. 403–5, post. In the case of a settlement made by a testator, the legal estate devolved upon his executors who held it upon trust to convey it to the tenant for life. The will itself constituted the trust instrument and the executors made a *vesting assent*, corresponding to the vesting deed, in favour of the tenant for life; p. 405, post.   [80] For a detailed account, see pp. 991 et seq, post.

[81] Chap. 12, post.   [82] P. 438, post.   [83] P. 465, post.

[84] Except for a trust for sale created in the will of a testator dying before 1997.

estate and, since they are transferred to the purchase money, no harm is done to their owners. Family rights and incumbrances in the nature of pecuniary claims do not impede a conveyance of the legal estate. There are, however, other equitable third-party rights to which the doctrine of overreaching is necessarily inapplicable, since they are incapable of being attached to money. For instance, an estate contract or a restrictive covenant of which a purchaser has had notice must continue to affect the land after conveyance to him of the legal estate. In such cases the obvious method of simplifying the task of the purchaser and at the same time of protecting the equitable owner is to require rights of this nature to be publicly recorded if they are to remain binding against purchasers. This was the policy adopted by the legislature in 1925.

Legislation enabling rights against land to be registered has long been in force, but it has appeared in successive and somewhat slow stages. Thus life annuities charged upon land were made registrable as far back as 1777, and the system was extended to judgments in 1838, to pending land actions in 1839, to deeds of arrangement in 1887, and to what are called land charges in 1888. These several topics are the subject of full discussion later,[85] but what should be observed at once is that a great extension of the system of registration was made by the Land Charges Act 1925. Without going into details, it may be said that almost all equitable rights against land, except those which arise under a settlement and are therefore overreachable, may be entered in one of the registers kept at the Land Charges Department of the Land Registry in Plymouth.[86] Registration of a registrable right constitutes notice of it to the whole world; failure to register it carries the penalty that it is void against a purchaser;[87] and this is so even if the purchaser has actual notice of the unregistered right. Therefore in the case of a third-party right that falls within the provisions of the Act, all now turns on registration; its owner can secure complete protection for himself by registration, while a purchaser need do no more than search at the Land Registry to discover whether the land is incumbered or not. An examination of section 2(2) of the Land Charges Act 1972[88] will show that most of the charges which are registrable are equitable. The important exception is the puisne mortgage, that is to say, any legal mortgage not being a mortgage protected by a deposit of documents relating to the legal estate affected.[89] A puisne mortgage, although a legal interest, does not therefore bind a purchaser for value unless registered. It is made registrable, as will be seen later, in order to comply with the post-1925 scheme for the priority of mortgages.[90]

(4) Summary of Changes Made by Legislation of 1925

(a) Conveyance by estate owner

By way of summary, it may be said, then, that one of the principal objects of the 1925 legislation was to simplify and clear the title to the legal fee simple, which is the estate that

---

[85] Pp. 937 et seq, post.   [86] Land Registry Practice Guide 63.

[87] Some unregistered charges are void against a purchaser for value of any estate, legal or equitable; others are void only against a purchaser of a legal estate for money or money's worth: LCA 1972, s. 4(5), (6); pp. 944–5, post.

[88] LCA 1925 has been replaced by LCA 1972 and LLCA 1975.

[89] Class C(i); p. 940, post.

[90] P. 794, post. The Matrimonial Homes Act 1967, now replaced by Family Law Act 1996 and amended by Civil Partnership Act 2004, added a new Class F land charge which does not owe its origin to equity or to common law; p. 478, post.

the majority of purchasers wish to obtain. As a result of the legislation the general position is now as follows:

The only legal freehold estate in Blackacre is the fee simple absolute in possession. In all cases this will be vested in a definite person or body of persons called the *estate owner*. According to the circumstances the estate owner will be one of the following:

A beneficial owner entitled in his own right.

Trustees for sale.

The tenant for life or "statutory owners"[91] in the case of settled land.

Trustees of land.

Personal representatives.

A mortgagor.[92]

A bare trustee.[93]

A conveyance of the legal fee simple must be made by or in the name of the estate owner, not by anybody else. Thus the exercise of a power of appointment can no longer affect the legal estate,[94] and in the case of a strict settlement the tenant for life conveys the legal fee simple because the Settled Land Act 1925 requires that it shall be vested in him, not as formerly because he had a statutory power to convey what he had not got.

(b) Third-party rights

The conveyance of a legal fee simple that is subject to equitable third-party rights is considerably simplified:

(i) Rights which arise under a settlement (whether it be a strict settlement, a trust for sale, or, after 1996, a trust of land) continue to be overreached by the conveyance[95] and cleared off the title, for no injury is done to their owners by converting them into rights against the purchase money.

(ii) If the rights do not arise in that way (i.e. they came into existence before the creation of the settlement) but are nevertheless convertible into rights against the money, the estate owner may clear them off the title by creating a settlement for that particular purpose, called an *ad hoc* settlement.[96]

(iii) If the rights do not arise under a settlement and are not convertible into money rights, such as an estate contract or a restrictive covenant, their continued enforcement depends in general on their registration as land charges.

---

[91] These are the persons who take the legal fee simple in settled land when there is no person entitled to take it as tenant for life; p. 409, post.

[92] In a mortgage of a legal fee simple, the mortgagor remains the estate owner of the legal fee simple, but nevertheless the mortgagee is entitled by virtue of his power of sale to convey it to a purchaser.

[93] A bare or naked trustee is one who holds property for the absolute benefit of a beneficiary of full age, and who himself has no beneficial interest in the property and no duty except to transfer it to its owner: *Christie v Ovington* (1875) 1 Ch D 279; and, for an example in registered land, *Hodgson v Marks* [1971] Ch 892. See p. 439, post.   [94] Save in a few exceptional cases; p. 95, n. 73, ante.

[95] P. 97, ante; pp. 994 et seq, post.   [96] Pp. 1000–1, post.

(c) Effect on doctrine of bona fide purchaser for value of legal estate without notice

We have already seen the curtailment of the doctrine of the bona fide purchaser,[97] where overreaching operates in the case of beneficial interests under a settlement.[98] It has been further dramatically curtailed by the extension of the system of registration of land charges. In the case of registrable third-party rights, their enforceability no longer depends on the state of the purchaser's mind; it is the state of the register which is crucial.

The doctrine, however, continues to apply to a residual category of equitable third-party rights which are neither overreachable nor registrable. Here a purchaser is bound unless he is a bona fide purchaser of the legal estate for value without actual or constructive notice. This category is necessarily limited, because most equitable third-party rights are in practice susceptible to overreaching or registration. Certain situations where the old rules concerning notice continue to apply were contemplated by the draftsmen of the 1925 legislation, for instance, a restrictive covenant entered into before 1926.[99] But in recent years the old rules have been applied in a number of situations which were presumably not foreseen.[100]

(d) Reconciliation of family and commercial needs

One aspect of the clear-cut distinction between the legal estate and the equitable interest deserves attention. Land is employed to satisfy at least two requirements, one affecting the family of its owner, the other affecting its commercial exploitation. It must be subject to rules that facilitate its employment as a continuing source of income for the present and future members of a family, but at the same time it must be under effective administration and above all be readily transferable by way of sale, lease, mortgage and similar transactions if good estate management so demands. These two requirements, at first sight contradictory, have been reconciled by English law. The estate owner, despite the existence of family trusts, is given full powers of management and disposal in respect of the land, but he holds them as trustee for such equitable beneficiaries as may exist. In this way the well-being of the land, the needs of the market and the prosperity of the family are harmonised.[101]

C Registered Conveyancing

So far we have discussed the changes made by the 1925 legislation which were intended to simplify the law of real property within the framework of the system of unregistered conveyancing. The intention was that the unregistered system should be replaced by a simplified system of registered conveyancing.

---

[97] For the doctrine, see pp. 58 et seq, ante.   [98] P. 97, ante.   [99] P. 673, post.

[100] *E R Ives Investment Ltd v High* [1967] 2 QB 379, M & B p. 665 (equity by estoppel), p. 825, post; *Poster v Slough Estates Ltd* [1968] 1 WLR 1515 (right of entry to remove a fixture on termination of lease); *Caunce v Caunce* [1969] 1 WLR 286, M & B p. 311 (beneficial interest of wife who had contributed towards purchase price); *Kingsnorth Finance Co Ltd v Tizard* [1986] 1 WLR 783, p. 62, n. 105, ante; *Shiloh Spinners Ltd v Harding* [1973] AC 691, especially at 720–1, per Lord WILBERFORCE; M & B p. 34 (equitable right of re-entry on breach of covenant); *Midland Bank Ltd v Farmpride Hatcheries Ltd* (1980) 260 EG 493 (contractual licence); M & B p. 28; p. 63, n. 110, ante.   [101] Lawson, *Rational Strength of English Law*, pp. 91–2.

(1) Introduction and Extension of Registration of Title

Registration of title was introduced into England as long ago as 1862.[102] At first it was voluntary, and little used.[103] In 1897 provision was made to extend it compulsorily to areas to be defined from time to time by Orders in Council on the request of a county council,[104] but progress in this respect was slow and by the time that the Land Registration Act 1925 replaced the old statutes with a new system for registration of title as part of the great reforms of land law, only the county of London had become an area of compulsory registration. Although the 1925 Act had a renewed purpose of producing a complete register of title to land in England and Wales, the compulsion necessary to achieve this was not yet put in place: the central Government's power to initiate compulsory registration in any area was delayed for ten years;[105] and it took a further fifty-five years before compulsory registration was finally extended to the whole of England and Wales with effect from 1 November 1990.[106] It should be realised, however, that "compulsory registration" does not mean that every acre of land has to be registered: only that dealings in land must now be carried out under the new and not the old system of conveyancing. The 1925 Act[107] defined transactions with unregistered land that, in any area of compulsory registration, would require the title to be placed on the register. The triggers for compulsory registration were increased by the Land Registration Act 1997;[108] and have been further increased by the Land Registration Act 2002.[109] The present intention is to create a Land Register with comprehensive content and national coverage by 2012.[110] This will require in due course the further extension of triggers for first registration, including the requirement that all land be registered, whether or not

[102] Land Registry Act 1862, replaced by Land Transfer Act 1875. For a history of land registration before 1926, see (1972) 36 Conv (NS) 390 (H. W. Wilkinson); Rowton Simpson, *Land Law and Registration*, pp. 39–47. See also *City of London Building Society v Flegg* [1988] AC 54 at 84, per Lord OLIVER OF AYLMERTON. The Torrens system of registration of title was first introduced in South Australia by Sir Robert Torrens in 1858. It operates in many Commonwealth countries. For land registration systems in European countries, see Cooke, *The New Law of Land Registration*, chap. 9. Registered conveyancing must be distinguished from the system of registration of assurances practised in parts of Yorkshire which merely recorded conveyances and devises in a public register. These deeds registries are closed: LPA 1969, ss. 16–22.

[103] By December 1885 only 113 titles had been registered: Rowton Simpson, *Land Law and Registration*, p. 44.

[104] Land Transfer Act 1897.

[105] LRA 1925, s. 120(2)(b). From 1926 until the end of 1935 the power of initiation was left in the hands of county councils, and only two took advantage of it: Middlesex, and Eastbourne and Hastings: see the 4th edn of this book (1937), pp. 95–6.

[106] Registration of Title Order 1989, SI 1989 No. 1347. Earlier attempts were made to advance this plan, but all failed because of the administrative burdens involved in such an enormous task: Rowton Simpson, *Land Law and Registration*, p. 49.

[107] S. 123: sale of freehold; grant of lease for not less than forty years; and assignment of lease with not less than forty years still to run.

[108] S. 1: conveyance of freehold, grant of lease for more than twenty-one years; assignment of lease having more than twenty-one years still to run; assent or vesting deed of freehold or leasehold having more than twenty-one years still to run; first legal mortgage of freehold or leasehold having more than twenty-one years still to run; first legal mortgage of freehold or leasehold having more than twenty-one years still to run, protected by deposit of documents.

[109] S. 4: the most significant change is to reduce the length of leaseholds triggering registration on grant or assignment to those granted for more than seven years, or having more than seven years still to run. For first registration under LRA 2002, see pp. 954 et seq., post.

[110] By 2005 the freehold title to 48% of the area of England and Wales had been registered, comprising 19.9 million titles: Land Registry Annual Report 2004–05, p. 8.

there is any disposition of it. The register must be complete in order to facilitate the full introduction of electronic conveyancing.[111]

(2) General Principles of Registered Conveyancing

Under the system of registered conveyancing contained in the Land Registration Acts 1925 and 2002 a registered title is guaranteed by the State. We have seen that the conveyancing of unregistered land depends upon the production by a vendor of a series of documents which recount previous transactions affecting the land and demonstrate to a purchaser the ability of a vendor to convey what he has agreed to convey. Title to the interest to be conveyed is thus something deduced from evidence. It has to be proved afresh each time a disposition of land is made. The conveyancing of registered land is different in principle and in practice. Once the title to land is registered, its past history is irrelevant. The title thenceforth is guaranteed by the State, and a purchaser can do no other than rely on it. Title has now become something more than evidence; in a sense, it is itself the subject-matter of the conveyance. Transfer of land becomes the substitution of one person's name for another person's name on a register. That transfer necessarily shifts the whole title registered in the former proprietor's name. Under the 1925 Act the landowner received from the registry a land certificate reproducing the relevant entries on the register,[112] but the source of title was the register, not the land certificate.

Registered conveyancing is not, however, a new system of land law. It is based on such familiar concepts as estates and interests, settlements, leases, mortgages, easements and covenants,[113] and the system introduced by the Land Registration Act 1925 was an integral part of the 1925 legislation. The Land Registration Act 2002 has made significant changes to the detail of the system contained in the 1925 Act, but the general approach remains the same. These Acts provide mechanisms for the authoritative recording of certain interests in land in a public register, the guarantee by the State of their validity and the accuracy of the record, and a system by which dealings in land can be conducted: a system of conveyancing. But what constitutes an estate or interest in land that is capable of being so recorded, is logically a prior question. The Land Registration Acts presuppose the identification and categorisation of interests in land under the general law. For this reason we shall defer a detailed consideration of the principles of registered conveyancing until we have considered the estates and interests in land recognised at law and in equity.[114] However, we shall here give an outline of the scheme as it was set out in the Land Registration Act 1925, together with a note of the significant points of comparison between that Act and the Land Registration Act 2002.

(3) Land Registration Act 1925

As we have seen, the scheme of the 1925 legislation was to reduce the number of legal estates to two: the fee simple absolute in possession and the term of years absolute;[115] and to provide simplified mechanisms to protect the holder of other rights in unregistered land. Beneficial interests under a settlement or trust for sale,[116] which are capable of being

---

[111] Pp. 110–1, post.   [112] Land certificates are no longer issued under the 2002 Act: p. 109, post.
[113] See *First National Bank plc v Thompson* [1996] Ch 231 (estoppel).
[114] Pp. 929 et seq, post.   [115] P. 94, ante.   [116] Or, since 1997, a trust of land; p. 77, ante.

converted into money, were overreached on a sale[117] of the legal estate and the beneficiary was protected by having a continuing property right in the purchase money instead of in the land. And most other property rights could be protected by their holder registering them as land charges, so as ensure that they would remain enforceable as rights in or over the land itself even as against a transferee.[118] Those property rights that were neither overreached[119] nor capable of being registered as land charges could still bind a transferee as long as he was not a bona fide purchaser of the legal estate for value without notice (actual, imputed or constructive) of the right in question.[120]

Under the Land Registration Act 1925 the fee simple absolute in possession and the term of years absolute[121] were the only two legal estates which could be registered under separate titles.[122] Other interests were dealt with in one of three ways:

(a) by the doctrine of overreaching, which operates in registered land in the same way as in unregistered land;[123]

(b) as "overriding interests", which bind a registered proprietor and his transferees whether or not they are entered on the register;[124]

(c) as "minor interests", which must be entered on the register of the land affected, if they are not to be overridden by a subsequent registered disposition of the land for value.[125]

(a) Registration and entry on the register

It is important to grasp the distinction between interests which could be *registered* under the Land Registration Act 1925, and interests which could be *entered on the register*. The former were confined to the two legal estates,[126] the titles to which were substantively registered under their own separate title numbers. Minor interests, as the name implies, were interests, lesser than registered interests, which could be protected by the entry of a notice, caution, inhibition, or restriction[127] on the register of the title affected. The entry was made on the proprietorship or charges register[128] of that title, and operated by way of an incumbrance against it. The proper person to be registered proprietor was the person holding the legal estate under the general law: in the case of a strict settlement, this would therefore be the tenant for life, and in the case of a trust for sale (or, after 1996, a trust of land), the trustees. In these cases, warning was given to a purchaser by the entry of a restriction on the

---

[117] By at least two trustees or a trust corporation: pp. 76–7, ante.   [118] P. 98, ante.

[119] Either because they were not overreachable (e.g. *E R Ives Investment Ltd v High* [1967] 2 QB 379: equity by estoppel) or because they were overreachable but not in fact overreached because the sale was by a sole trustee (e.g. *Kingsnorth Finance Co Ltd v Tizard* [1986] 1 WLR 783: beneficial interest under a trust for sale).

[120] P. 100, ante.

[121] Not all leases were registrable: the general effect of the legislation was that only leases with more than twenty-one years to run could be registered: LRA 1925, s. 8.

[122] LRA 1925, s. 2(1); for the suggestion that the Act creates a statutory estate, distinct from the fee simple or term of years at common law, see p. 173, post. Legal interests which could be registered in addition to those in corporeal land, were those in manors, mines and minerals, advowsons and rents (in practice, rentcharges): LRR 1925, r. 50. But legal easements could only be registered as appurtenant to the registered title of the dominant tenement: LRR 1925, r. 257.

[123] *City of London Building Society v Flegg* [1988] AC 54 (interest of beneficiary under trust for sale over-reached even though beneficiary was in actual occupation).   [124] Pp. 107–8, post.

[125] P. 107, post.   [126] Supra.   [127] Pp. 106, post.   [128] P. 104, post.

registered title that the settlement or trust existed, without however telling him what the individual beneficial interests were. Thus the doctrine of overreaching applied to the interests of the beneficiaries, and the curtain principle was retained. "References to trusts shall, so far as is possible, be excluded from the register."[129]

The Land Registration Act 1925 laid down precise rules for dealings in the land, and attempted an enumeration of the powers of an owner under the Act.[130] In order to be effectual at law a disposition of registered land had to be completed by registration. Thus a transfer for value of registered freehold or leasehold land had to be completed by the Registrar entering on the register the transferee as the registered proprietor[131] and until he had done this the transferor was deemed to remain the proprietor.[132] As soon as he had done this, however, the legal estate passed at once to the transferee.[133]

(b) The register

(1) TRIPARTITE

The separate register for each individual title under the Land Registration Act 1925 was divided into three parts, a property register, a proprietorship register, and a charges register.[134] It was intended that the register should "mirror" the title, though, as we shall see, it did so in only a qualified manner. The register was originally kept on a card index system, but was gradually computerised.[135] It was a register of title, so that where there was more than one legal title subsisting in one piece of land (the obvious case is that of a registered reversion subject to a registered lease) there would be one register for each title. A copy of the various entries on the register and of the filed plan of the title, called a land certificate,[136] was given to the registered proprietor of the title, and could be retained by him or deposited in the registry. It was not, however, the certificate but the register retained in the registry which was the title.

The property register described and identified the land, and the interest in the land which was the subject-matter of the title, whether it be freehold or leasehold. As we have said

---

[129] LRA 1925, s. 74; cf s. 88(1); *Abigail v Lapin* [1934] AC 491 at 500.

[130] ibid., ss. 18, 21, 25, 40, 101, 104, 106, 107, 109; LRR 1925, r. 74, as substituted by LRR 1997, r. 2(1), Sch. 1, para. 18.

[131] LRA 1925, ss. 19(1), 22(1). A prescribed form had to be used: LRR 1925, r. 98, as substituted by LRR 1999, r. 2(1), Sch. 1, para. 4. Registration was completed as of the day on which the application was delivered to the Registrar: LRR 1925, r. 83(1), as substituted by LRR 1978, r. 8; LR (Delivery of Applications) R 1986.

[132] Before registration, there might be a complete transfer in equity: *Mascall v Mascall* (1984) 50 P & CR 119 (intending donor executed transfer which he handed to donee together with land certificate: even though donee had not applied for registration, held to be complete gift in equity, since donor had done everything that he had to do to perfect gift: *Re Rose* [1952] Ch 499, Maudsley and Burn, *Trusts and Trustees*, p. 108). See also *E S Schwab & Co Ltd v McCarthy* (1975) 31 P & CR 196 at 212; *Brown & Root Technology Ltd v Sun Alliance and London Assurance Co Ltd* [1996] Ch 51 (reversed on other grounds (1996) 75 P & CR 223).

[133] LRA 1925, ss. 20(1), 23(1) as amended by FA 1975, s. 52, Sch. 12, para. 5, which set out in detail what appurtenances passed to the transferee, and also the matters subject to which his title subsisted. See also LRR 1925, r. 251.   [134] LRR 1925, r. 2.

[135] LRA 1925, s. 1, was amended by AJA 1982, s. 66(1) to provide that the register need not be kept in documentary form.

[136] For a specimen land certificate, see M & B (7th edn, 1998) pp. 105–7. A new design for the cover was introduced in 1986: ibid, p. 108. Where the property was mortgaged by way of legal charge, the charge was completed by registration and a charge certificate was issued to the chargee, the land certificate being deposited at the Registry until the charge was cancelled. LRA 1925, ss. 63, 65; LRR 1925, r. 262 as amended by LRR 1993 (SI 1993 No. 3275), r. 7.

already, the interest had to be legal. There might also appear on this register mention of specific benefits capable of subsisting as legal interests, such as legal easements, and the effect would be to create a registered title of the same nature in them. There could also be a reference to other benefits, for instance, to the freedom of the land from specific overriding interests.[137]

The proprietorship register stated the nature of the title, that is, absolute, good leasehold, possessory or qualified, the name, address and description of the proprietor, and also any entries that affected his right of disposing of the land. As from 1 April 2000 there could also be entered, on first registration or following the transfer of land (be it freehold or leasehold) the price paid or its value.[138] The entry only remained on the register until a further change of proprietorship. The charges register contained entries of incumbrances which burdened the land, such as restrictive covenants and mortgages.

(2) INSPECTION OF REGISTER

Originally, the register was accessible only to the proprietor of the land or of a registered charge, or persons authorised by them or by the court,[139] but the Land Registration Act 1988 opened it to inspection by the public.[140] It was also possible to discover whether or not a particular plot of land was registered by searching the Index Map and Parcels Index.[141]

(c) *Classes of title*

The purpose of the land register under the Land Registration Act 1925 was to provide an authoritative record of estates and interests in land, guaranteed by the State. In furtherance of this, the Act[142] recognised four different classes of title, which provided more or less full assurance as to the owner's title to the legal estate: absolute title, good leasehold title (for a lessee only), possessory title, and, finally, qualified title, where an application for one of the other titles could not be substantiated. The classes of title are unchanged under the Land Registration Act 2002, and are discussed in detail the context of the new Act.[143] It suffices here to notice that an absolute title was the most frequent,[144] and that a title registered in this

---

[137] LRR 1925, r. 197; *Re Dances Way, West Town, Hayling Island* [1962] Ch 490.

[138] LRR (No. 3) R 1999 (SI 1999 No. 3462); [2000] EG 11 March p. 169 (A. Judge). See the Consultation Paper published by the Land Registry in 1997.

[139] LRA 1925, s. 112. This corresponded broadly to the position in unregistered land, where documents of title are private, although the register of land charges is open to the public: Barnsley, *Conveyancing Law and Practice*, pp. 40–2.

[140] Substituting LRA 1925, ss. 112–13; *Mortgage Corpn v Halifax (SW) Ltd* The Times, 15 July 1998 (inherent jurisdiction to disclose transfer including purchase price of land). LRA 1988 was based on the Second Report on Land Registration: Inspection of the Register 1985 (Law Com No. 148). See (1990) 49 EG 44 (C. Coombe and H. Lewis); (1990) 41 LSG 19 (E. J. Pryer).

[141] LRR 1925, r. 8, as amended by LRR (No. 2) 1999, r. 2(1), Sch. 1, para. 2; LR (Open Register) R 1991 (SI 1991 No. 122) as amended by LRR 1999, r. 2(3), Sch. 3 and LRR 2000 (SI 2000 No. 429), r. 2(2), Sch. 2; LRR 1993 (SI 1993 No. 3275); LRR 1995 (SI 1995 No. 1354), rr. 5–7. On searching the Index Map, see [1991] 6 LSG 24 (M. J. Russell).   [142] Ss. 4–12.

[143] P. 956, post.

[144] On first registration of freehold land under LRA 1925, over 99 per cent of applications were registered with absolute title. The majority of the remainder relate to titles founded purely on adverse possession. See [1980] Conv, pp. 7–9, 96–8, 165–7. "Possessory titles are granted in less than one in a hundred applications for first registration. Qualified titles are virtually unknown. Good leasehold titles are common": Ruoff and Pryer, *Land Registration Handbook*, p. 36.

way could actually be improved by registration. Any technical defect was cured, for no one could subsequently raise it, save in the exceptional case of a rectification action.[145]

(d) Rectification and indemnity

Once the title to the land had been registered under the Land Registration Act 1925, it vested in the registered proprietor, and was thenceforth guaranteed by the State. But, as in unregistered conveyancing, the title was still less than absolute. Section 82 of the Land Registration Act 1925 gave to the court and to the registrar wide powers to rectify the register where there was any error or omission. Section 83,[146] however, provided for an indemnity for those who suffered loss in certain cases by reason of such rectification or by refusal of rectification. So the system of registered conveyancing is to some extent an insurance system.[147]

(e) Protection of third party rights

We must now briefly consider the scheme of the Land Registration Act 1925 for the protection of third-party rights, and how they affected a purchaser from the proprietor of registered land.

The scheme was simple. A party who had an interest, other than a legal estate which was itself capable of substantive registration,[148] should normally protect it by an entry on the register of the title affected by it. The Land Registration Act 1925 designated such an interest a *minor interest*. There were four different forms of entry on the register,[149] each suitable to different categories of interest and different circumstances of their entry, and each having their own effect: a notice,[150] restriction,[151] caution[152] or inhibition.[153] The common theme,

---

[145] Infra.   [146] As substituted by LRA 1997, s. 2.

[147] This is discussed further in the context of the new system under LRA 2002: pp. 961–2 et seq, post. The sums paid are not significant when viewed against the Land Registry's fee income. In 2004–05 £3,516,061 was paid for 914 claims, the largest of which was in excess of £240,000: Land Registry Annual Report 2004–05, p. 23. The fee income in the same year was over £397 million: ibid., p. 80.

[148] I.e., the fee simple or a lease for more than twenty-one years: p. 103, ante.

[149] For a more detailed discussion, see the 16th edn of this book, pp. 872–6.

[150] LRA 1925, ss. 48–52; LRR 1925, rr. 7, 190. In most cases the entry of a notice required the land certificate to be produced to the Registry, if not already on deposit there—and so could usually be entered only with the co-operation of the owner of the land affected. The notice was entered on the charges register, and disposition of the land took effect subject to all estates, rights and claims which were protected by entry on the register, if the claim was valid and not (independently of the Act) overriden by the disposition: LRA 1925, s. 52.

[151] Ibid., s. 58; LRR 1925, r. 6: an entry which prevents dealings in registered land until certain specified conditions or requirements have been complied with. It therefore recorded, on (normally) the proprietorship register, any impediment to the proprietor's freedom of disposal, such as the requirement to pay capital money to two trustees or a trust corporation (or into court) in the case of the restriction entered to protect the beneficial interests under a settlement or trust for sale (or, after 1996, trust of land). As with a notice, the land certificate generally had to be produced.

[152] Ibid., ss. 53–6, LRR 1925, rr. 6, 7. A caution against dealings was a hostile act, used to protect a claim to an interest or right over land without the need to produce the land certificate. The registered proprietor could "warn off" the cautioner and force him either to withdraw his caution or to have the dispute about it adjudicated by the registrar or the court. If a caution was on the register (in the proprietorship register or the charges register) no dealing with the title could be registered without the registrar serving notice on the cautioner, which then served as a "warning off" notice. For the court's exercise of its jurisdiction to order the vacation of cautions, see the 16th edn of this book, p. 874, n. 3. A caution against first registration was a similar procedure to protect an interest or claim where the land was not yet registered: LRA 1925, s. 53.

[153] Ibid., s. 57: a hostile act which prevented any dealings with the registered land; rarely used except in the case of bankruptcy inhibitions entered by the registrar: ibid., s. 61.

however, is that a third party who claimed an interest in the land had a means of placing his claim on the register of title itself—and therefore any purchaser[154] of the land had the opportunity, on searching the register before committing himself to the transaction,[155] to discover it.

Some minor interests were incapable of binding a purchaser even if protected by entry, but nevertheless affected the method of disposing of land. Thus, in the case of beneficial interests under a settlement or trust of land that would be overreached on a sale of the land, a restriction would be entered on the proprietorship register indicating that the proprietor of the legal title was limited in his powers, but, if the terms of the restriction were complied with, a purchaser for value was not concerned with such beneficial interests. But other minor interests such as restrictive covenants, equitable easements, legal and equitable rentcharges, and estate contracts did bind purchasers for valuable consideration, if protected by entry on the register. Conversely, a purchaser would take free from them if they were not so protected by entry; and, as in unregistered conveyancing, this was so even if he had actual notice of their existence. But no place was to be left in the system of registered conveyancing for the doctrine of notice.[156]

Such an approach, if strictly applied, would however work to protect only those persons having a right over land who had in fact made an entry on the register of the land affected. We here find one of the perennial problems of land law: finding the proper balance to strike between the need to protect a purchaser, who ought to be able to discover the rights affecting the title which he is purchasing, and the desire to protect third parties, who may often have very good reasons for not having protected their rights explicitly—for example, where the right is itself created informally in a third party who is acting without legal advice.[157] The Land Registration Act 1925 sought to strike a balance, by designating as *overriding interests* certain interests that would bind a registered proprietor and his transferee, where they had not been protected by entry on the register.[158] They were "overriding" because they overrode, or assumed superiority over, the transferee's estate. Section 70(1) of the Act listed overriding interests, most of which were particular categories of interest in land, such as profits à prendre, legal easements, leases for not more than twenty-one years, local land charges, and rights acquired or being acquired under the Limitation Act. Of more significance, however was the inclusion in paragraph (g) of:[159]

the rights of every person in actual occupation of the land or in receipt of the rents and profits thereof, save where enquiry is made of such person and the rights are not disclosed.

[154] A. donee would be bound by minor interests even if they were not protected by entry: LRA 1925, ss. 20(4), 23(5).

[155] Before the register became open to public inspection, the purchaser would see it because the vendor would give the purchaser authority to search the register: Barnsley, *Conveyancing Law and Practice*, p. 335.

[156] *Hodges v Jones* [1935] Ch 657 at 671, per LUXMOORE J; *De Lusignan v Johnson* (1973) 230 EG 499; LRA 1925, s. 59(6). See, however, the much criticised decisions in *Peffer v Rigg* [1977] 1 WLR 285, M & B p. 176; *Lyus v Prowsa Developments Ltd* [1982] 1 WLR 1044, M & B p. 176; p. 972, n. 334, post. For further discussion about the extent to which the doctrine of notice is contained (or hidden) within the various categories of overriding interests under LRA 2002, see pp. 634 and 984–5, post.

[157] For the informal creation of interests in land, see pp. 905 et seq, post.

[158] LRA 1925, ss. 3(xvi), 70.

[159] For some discussion, and a comparison with the equivalent provision under LRA 2002 (Sch. 1, para. 2 and Sch. 3, para. 2), see pp. 979 et seq, post.

All overriding interests, which do not appear on the register, detract from the principle that the register should be a mirror of the vendor's title. Their existence will only be discovered by a purchaser if he resorts to the older methods of investigation. But this is particularly so in the case of paragraph (g). As Lord DENNING MR said in *Strand Securities Ltd v Caswell*:[160]

Section 70(1)(g) is an important provision. Fundamentally, its object is to protect a person in actual occupation of land from having his rights lost in the welter of registration. He can stay there and do nothing. Yet he will be protected. No one can buy the land over his head and thereby take away or diminish his rights. It is up to every purchaser before he buys to make inquiry on the premises. If he fails to do so, it is at his own risk. He must take subject to whatever rights the occupier may have. Such is the doctrine of *Hunt v Luck*,[161] for unregistered land. Section 70(1)(g) carries the same doctrine forward into registered land . . .

(4) The New Law: Land Registration Act 2002

The Land Registration Act 2002 repealed the 1925 Act, and replaced it with a revised scheme of registration of title to land. The new Act, together with the Land Registration Rules 2003,[162] came into force on 13 October 2003.[163] The new scheme is presented in a more coherent and logical form.[164] There are some significant changes from the 1925 Act, but the essential elements of the former scheme are still recognisable, and cases decided under the former Act may still be relevant in interpreting the new Act on points where the substance remains the same. The detail of the system of registered conveyancing, as it now exists under the 2002 Act, will be considered later.[165] For the moment we shall limit ourselves to a brief summary of the key points of similarity and difference between the two Acts.

(a) Similarities between the 1925 and 2002 Acts

The fundamental principles of the scheme of registration of title, set out in the Land Registration Act 1925, are continued by the 2002 Act. The register of title is conclusive, and so the State guarantee of title remains—subject only to the powers of the court and the registrar to alter the register. Dispositions of registered land do not take effect at law until the registration requirements are met; and the new Act maintains the distinction between interests which can be registered under their own separate title numbers, and interests

---

[160]   [1965] Ch 958 at 979–80; see also RUSSELL LJ at 984.

[161]   [1902] 1 Ch 428. See p. 63, ante. But, as we shall see, LRA 1925, s. 70(1)(g) (and its successor in LRA 2002) and the doctrine of *Hunt v Luck* are by no means identical.

[162]   SI 2003 No. 1417, amended by SI 2005 No. 1766; SI 2005 No. 1982. LRR 1925 lapsed on repeal of LRA 1925.

[163]   SI 2003 No. 1725. For transitional provisions, see LRA 2002, s. 134, Sch. 12, paras. 1–3 (existing entries in the register); 4 (existing cautions against first registration); 5–6 (pending applications); 7–13 (former overriding interests); 14–16 (cautions against first registration); 17 (applications under ss. 34 or 43 by cautioners); 18 (adverse possession); 19 (indemnities); 20 (implied indemnity covenants on transfer of pre-1996 leases); LRR 2003, rr. 218–23 (caution against dealings); 224 (registered rentcharges); LRA 2002 (Transitional Provisions) Order 2003 (SI 2003 No. 1953), arts. 2–5 (general and administrative), 6–9 (disputes, objections, appeals and proceedings); 10–13 (souvenir land); 14–18 (cautions); 19 (outline applications); 20 (matrimonial home rights cautions); 21 (index of relating franchises and manors); 22–3 (compulsory first registration); 24 (land and charge certificates); 25 (obligation to make further advances); 26–7 (Forms); 28–9 (official searches and official copies); LRA 2002 (Transitional Provisions) (No. 2) Order 2003 (SI 2003 No. 2431) (right to repair of church chancel).

[164]   LRA 1925 was the only part of the 1925 Legislation that was not drafted by Sir Benjamin Cherry.

[165]   Pp. 952 et seq, post.

which should be protected by entry on the register against a registered estate. Moreover, the new scheme, like the old, admits overriding interests which bind even though they do not appear on the register[166]—and this includes a revised version of the broad principle which used to be found in section 70(1)(g) of the 1925 Act.[167] A third party should therefore, in principle, protect his interest over a registered estate by making an entry on the register if it is to bind a purchaser; but the new Act continues to recognise the need to balance the protection of the purchaser (through a complete register which will disclose all incumbrances affecting the title) against the protection of the third party (who may not have been able to enter his interest on the register). No change is made to the operation of the doctrine of overreaching; and (as under the 1925 Act) the registrar is not to be affected by notice of a trust: the policy is still to keep beneficial interests off the register.

The tripartite structure of the register is unchanged. And the 2002 Act, like its predecessor, contains provisions for both voluntary and compulsory registration of title, the latter being triggered by specified events.

(b) Changes made by the Land Registration Act 2002

Although the main principles of the 1925 scheme are maintained, there are significant changes of detail in the 2002 Act.

A number of the changes are designed to make the register more complete, in two respects. In the first place, the aim is to hasten the day when all the land in England and Wales is on the register, in furtherance of which there is an increase in the number of triggers for first registration, with the promise of more to come until the register is complete; the length of leases subject to compulsory registration is reduced from twenty-one to seven years; land held by Her Majesty as demesne land now becomes registrable;[168] and there is a new law of adverse possession, which makes it much more difficult for a squatter to obtain title in registered land (so much so that owners of hitherto unregistered land may have an incentive to register their title voluntarily). Voluntary registration now has a reduced fee.[169] In the second place, the register is to be a more complete mirror of the title to land once it has been registered: although overriding interests are still admitted, there is a decrease in their number and extent, as well as an increased effort to place incumbrances on the register so as to avoid the need to rely on overriding interests.

There are many changes designed to simplify registered conveyancing. The classes of title are redrafted; the methods of protection of minor interests are simplified (and the terminology of "minor interests" is abandoned); the principles of rectification and indemnity are restructured (and rectification is absorbed into a wider principle of "alteration" of the register); the principles of priority of interests are simplified; and the creation of mortgages by demise and sub-demise, already obsolescent, is made obsolete.

Other changes include a new system of independent adjudication arising out of disputed applications to the registrar; and the abolition of land and charge certificates,[170] which more

---

[166] LRA 2002, Schs. 1 (first registration), 3 (registered dispositions).

[167] Ibid., Sch. 3, para. 2 (broadly, the interest belonging to a person in discoverable actual occupation; for the detail, see pp. 979 et seq, post).

[168] LRA 2002, s. 79 (voluntary registration). This includes extensive parts of the foreshore.

[169] LR Fee Order 2004 (SI 2004 No. 595), art. 2.

[170] No further certificates will be issued, and if a certificate is lodged with the Land Registry it will be destroyed: LRA 2002 (Transitional Provisions) Order 2003, supra, art. 24. In its place a Title Information

properly reflects the position that it is the register, rather than any document issued by the registrar, that constitutes the title to the land.

(5) The Future: Electronic Conveyancing

Many of the changes made by the Land Registration Act 2002 are designed to pave the way for the introduction of a system of paperless transfer of land by electronic conveyancing. As the Law Commission said in proposing the Bill which became the Land Registration Act 2002:[171]

The fundamental objective of the Bill is that, under the system of electronic dealing with land that it seeks to create, the register should be a complete and accurate reflection of the state of the title of the land at any given time, so that it is possible to investigate title to land on line, with the absolute minimum of additional enquiries and inspections.

This will be the next step in the evolution of the land law of England and Wales. The Act[172] puts in place the mechanisms for fully electronic conveyancing, under which parties no longer submit documents to the Land Registry for the registrar's staff to process, but the register will be changed automatically to give effect to electronic dealings in registered land:[173]

It is envisaged that, within a comparatively short time, it will be the only method of conducting registered conveyancing . . . An essential feature of the electronic system when it is fully operational is that it will be impossible to create or transfer many rights in or over registered land expressly except by registering them. Investigation of title will be almost entirely online. It is intended that the secure electronic communications network on which the system will be based, will be used to provide information about properties for intending buyers. It will also provide a means of managing a chain of transactions by monitoring them electronically. This will enable the cause of delays in any chain to be identified and remedial action encouraged. It is anticipated that far fewer chains will break in consequence and that transactions will be considerably expedited. Faster conveyancing is also likely to provide the most effective way of curbing gazumping. The process of registration under the electronic system will be initiated by solicitors and licensed conveyancers, though the Land Registry will exercise control over the changes that can be made to the register. Electronic conveyancing will not come into being as soon as the Bill is brought into force. It will be introduced over a number of years, and there will be a time when both the paper and electronic systems co-exist.

The movement towards electronic conveyancing is gaining momentum. Although 2012 is the target for the Land Registry to create a register with comprehensive content and national coverage,[174] the electronic lodgement of forms for certain transactions is already in place, and the Registry aims to pilot the e-conveyancing service during the spring of 2006 and to start a gradual roll-out across England and Wales in 2007.[175] It must, however, be noted that this will be a new system of conveyancing, not a new system of land law.[176] The

Document will be issued which comprises a copy of the register and a copy of the title plan. In consequence, equitable mortgages by deposit of the land certificate are no longer possible: p. 732, post.

[171] Report on Land Registration for the Twenty-First Century 2001 (Law Com No. 271), para. 1.5.

[172] LRA 2002, Part 8, which will be supplemented by rules in due course. For electronic contracts, see p. 873, post.   [173] Law Com No. 271, para. 1.12.

[174] Land Registry Annual Report 2004–05, p. 50.   [175] Ibid., pp. 48–9, 51–2.

[176] In introducing the Law of Property Bill 1922, Sir Leslie Scott said (p. 8, n. 4, ante): "The Bill is not a brand-new invention. It is not a new-fangled, ready-made scheme of law. It is not revolution, it is evolution."

estates and interests which are capable of being substantively registered or entered on the register remain those which are identified under the existing law—and in particular under the great reforms of land law which were achieved in the 1925 legislation. However, the Land Registration Act 2002 will have significant effects on the substantive law. It will change the way in which title to land is perceived, since it is the fact of registration and registration alone that confers title.[177] Relativity of seisin, or possession, is no longer the test for title to land, as we shall see in chapter 6.

D Comparison of Unregistered and Registered Systems

We may now compare the position of a purchaser of the legal fee simple of Blackacre under the two systems of conveyancing. Under both systems he must satisfy himself on two separate matters: first, that the vendor is entitled to convey the fee simple, and, secondly, that there are no incumbrances in favour of third parties which will continue to bind the land after the conveyance.

As far as the first matter is concerned, the task of a purchaser is clearly simplified under the registered system. An investigation of the vendor's title deeds is replaced by a search of the register at the Land Registry. There is, however, no such clear cut difference in the matter of third-party rights. Under the unregistered system since 1925, a purchaser must first search the Land Charges Register. He is bound by any registrable interests which have been registered at the time when he takes his conveyance from the vendor; if a registrable interest is not so registered, he takes free from it, even though he actually knows of its existence. Further, if the vendor is a tenant for life under a strict settlement or if the vendors are trustees under a trust of land, the purchaser takes free from the equitable interests of the beneficiaries under the doctrine of overreaching. Thirdly, under the unregistered system, a vendor is bound by certain rights which are neither registrable nor overreachable but which in the last resort can only be discovered by his own inquiries and inspection of Blackacre. These include: (a) legal third-party rights, whether he knows about them or not, for example, a legal estate, such as a lease, or a legal interest, such as a legal easement;[178] and (b) a residual category of equitable interests, unless he is a bona fide purchaser for value of the legal estate in Blackacre without actual or constructive notice, for example, a pre-1926 restrictive covenant or an equity by estoppel.[179]

Under the registered system the position of a purchaser of Blackacre is different. On the one hand he is bound by interests which are entered on the register: if an interest is not so entered, he takes free from it even though he actually knows of its existence. In this context an entry on the register has the same function that registration in the Land Charges Register has in unregistered conveyancing. If, however, the vendor is a tenant for life or if the vendors are trustees of land, the interests of the beneficiaries may be overreached. On the other hand

Similarly, in spite of the Law Commission's Report being sub-titled *A Conveyancing Revolution*, the 2002 Act is is effect a further evolutionary stage in the development of English land law, which enables conveyancing to take advantage of information technology and develop alongside similar transactions in banking and business.

[177] Ibid., paras. 1.1, 1.10; Geztler, *Rationalizing Property, Equity and Trusts*, chap. 9 (C. Harpum).

[178] He is not bound by a puisne mortgage (any legal mortgage not being a mortgage protected by a deposit of documents relating to the legal estate affected) unless it is registered as a land charge; p. 98, ante, p.940, post.

[179] P. 100, n. 100, ante.

a purchaser is bound by overriding interests, even though he has no knowledge of them and even though they are not entered on the register. The statutory list of overriding interests is a collection of interests which it is held desirable to be binding on a purchaser but which, for some reason or another, do not fit into the pattern of the register. They are discoverable by, but only by, the purchaser's inspection of Blackacre and by inquiries which he must make without assistance from the register. They not only include legal rights which are familiar in unregistered conveyancing, for example, legal easements and certain leases, but they also include interests belonging to a person in discoverable actual occupation of the land.[180]

Thus in registered conveyancing there is no residual category of equitable interests to which the doctrine of the bona fide purchaser is applicable; that doctrine has been replaced by the provisions of the Land Registration Acts for the protection of interests by notice on the register, and overriding interests. Several judges have discussed this in the context of the 1925 Act, but in terms which apply equally to the Land Registration Act 2002. Lord WILBERFORCE stated emphatically in *Williams & Glyn's Bank Ltd v Boland* that:[181]

the registered land system is designed to free the purchaser from the hazards of notice—real or constructive . . . The only kind of notice recognised is by entry on the register

and PLOWMAN J, in *Parkash v Irani Finance Ltd*, found a plaintiff's reliance on the doctrine:[182]

a little surprising, since one of the essential features of registration of title is to substitute a system of registration of rights for the doctrine of notice.

The residual category of equitable interests can exist under registered conveyancing, but any such interests which are not overriding interests must appear on the register if they are to bind a purchaser.

Third-party rights are treated differently under the two systems of conveyancing. The difference was strikingly illustrated in *Lloyds Bank plc v Carrick*,[183] where:

Mrs Carrick, a purchaser of unregistered land from her brother-in-law, paid the purchase price in full and entered into possession of the land under an oral contract of sale. The contract, though oral, was at that time enforceable.[184] The contract was registrable as an estate contract (class C (iv)) under the Land Charges Act 1972, but had not been so registered. The vendor then charged the land to Lloyds Bank plc.

The Court of Appeal held that the bank was not bound by the rights of Mrs Carrick. The estate contract was void for non-registration against a purchaser of the legal estate for money or money's worth, even though Mrs Carrick was in possession of the land. However, if the land had been registered land under the Land Registration Act 1925, Mrs Carrick would have been in actual occupation of the land, and her rights would have been binding on the bank as an overriding interest under section 70(1)(g), even though she had not protected them by an entry on the register of the vendor's title.

In commenting on the important difference between the Draconian solution in unregistered land, and the safety net of overriding interests in registered land, MORRITT LJ said:[185]

---

[180] LRA 2002, Sch. 3, para. 2; p. 979, post.   [181] [1981] AC 487 at 503.
[182] [1970] Ch 101 at 109; *Hodgson v Marks* [1971] Ch 892.   [183] [1996] 4 All ER 630.
[184] Under the doctrine of part performance, now abolished by LP(MP)A 1989, s. 2(8); p. 866, post.
[185] At 642.

This result seems to me to be inevitable in the light of the provisions of the Land Charges Act 1972 and of the Law of Property Act 1925 . . . However, it should be noted that the result would have been different if the title to the maisonette had been registered. In such a case the interest of Mrs Carrick, who was in possession of the maisonette and of whom no enquiry had been made, would have been an overriding interest under section 70(1)(g) of the Land Registration Act 1925. As such it would have been binding on the Bank. . . . It must be for others to consider and for Parliament to decide whether this distinction between registered and unregistered land should continue.

It is this different treatment that gives rise to differences in the substance of the land law; these differences we shall consider under the various topics in which they occur.

6

ADVERSE POSSESSION.
LIMITATION OF ACTIONS

SUMMARY

I Introductory Note

A *The Significance of Possession in the Modern Law*

We saw in chapter 2 that the common law developed the doctrine of the *estate*: the "owner" of land was not absolute owner of the land itself in the manner recognised by the civil law. Rather, he held an estate in the land: the right to seisin, or possession,[1] of the land for

---

[1] For the technical usage of "seisin" (for freeholds) and "possession" (for leaseholds), see p. 32, ante.

a period. The fee simple owner, for example, had the right to possession—and was therefore entitled to exercise proprietary rights over the land—for as long as he or his successors had heirs. The holder of a life estate had the similar right, but only for his own life. The tenant under a lease had the right to possession for the term of the lease. Since the enactment of the Law of Property Act 1925, the estates that can exist at common law are limited to the fee simple absolute in possession, and the term of years absolute.[2] But that Act did not change the nature of land ownership or of the doctrine of the estate. Thus from 1926 in English law the "ownership" of land was still based on the doctrine of the estate, which is itself inextricably linked to the notion of the right to possession of the land.

We also saw[3] that this reliance on possession as the basis of land ownership resulted in the common law taking the view that the acquisition of possession of the land was itself the acquisition of a title to the land. Possession was a *root of title*. From the first day of his possession, the disseisor had full beneficial rights over the land, holding a fee simple estate—although this was only a *relative* title, since if anyone could show a better right to possession, he could recover the land.[4]

Two separate issues arise from this view, taken by the common law, of the significance of possession.[5] First, if possession is a root of title, how, in practice, will a vendor of land establish his title to sell? We shall reserve the discussion of this for Part III, when we consider the mechanisms for the transfer of estates and interests in land. Secondly, what is the significance of the loss of possession: in what circumstances does a squatter not only oust the owner from possession of his land, but also deprive him of the right any longer to claim that he is owner? This is the question for the present chapter. We consider it here because it tells us much about the contemporary development of land law, and completes the picture we have been viewing in Part I of the nature of land ownership as it stands at the start of the twenty-first century—because the changes made in this area by the Land Registration Act 2002 have fundamentally changed the significance of possession in the modern law.

B Lapse of Time, Prescription and Limitation of Actions

Most systems of law have realised the necessity of fixing some definite period of time within which persons who have been unlawfully dispossessed of their land must pursue their claims. It is, no doubt, an injustice that after this period has elapsed the wrongdoer should be allowed to retain the land against the person whom he has ousted, but it would be an even greater injustice to the world at large if the latter were allowed after any interval of time, however long, to commence proceedings for recovery of possession. If A, having ejected B, is allowed to remain in long and undisturbed possession of the land, the impression will grow that his title is superior to B's, and the public should be allowed to deal safely with him on that footing. As Lord ST LEONARDS remarked:[6] "All statutes of limitation have for their object the prevention of the rearing up of claims at great distances of time when evidences

---

[2] LPA 1925, s. 1(1); pp. 93–4, ante.   [3] P. 30, ante.   [4] Pp. 28–9, ante.

[5] Possession, or the right to possession, of land also has other significance; e.g. in the law of tort it gives standing to sue in trespass, or in nuisance: *Powell v McFarlane* (1977) 38 P & CR 452 at 469, per SLADE J; *Malory Enterprises Ltd v Cheshire Homes (UK) Ltd* [2002] Ch 216; *Hunter v Canary Wharf Ltd* [1997] AC 655.

[6] *Dundee Harbour Trustees v Dougall* (1852) 1 Macq 317. See too *R B Policies at Lloyd's v Butler* [1950] 1 KB 76 at 81; [1985] Conv 272 (M. Dockray).

are lost; and in all well-regulated countries the quieting of possession is held an important point of policy."

(1) Limitation and Prescription

The effect of a person remaining in possession of the land of another for the period of time fixed by law varies in different countries and in different ages. Thus the effect of *usucapio* in Roman law was to confer a positive title to the land upon a person who had remained in possession for a certain time.[7] Under the Statutes of Limitation which were in force in England prior to 1833 the effect of remaining in possession for the prescribed period was to bar only the remedy of the person dispossessed, not his right. His *title* remained intact, and if he came lawfully into possession of the land again, his title might prevail against the possessor.[8] Under the statutes that have been in force from time to time since 1833[9] the effect of remaining in possession for the statutory period of twelve years in unregistered land is still merely negative, but in the sense that the right as well as the remedy of the person dispossessed is extinguished. The *usucapio* of Roman law exemplified what is sometimes called acquisitive prescription in the sense that possession of another's land for a given period conferred a positive title upon the occupier, but English law has never adopted this theory in its treatment of corporeal hereditaments and chattels, though it has done so in the case of easements and profits.[10]

(2) The Modern Acts

The English law relating to the period within which an action for the recovery of land must be brought was recast and simplified by the Real Property Limitation Act of 1833; was consolidated and amended by the Limitation Act 1939; and, after further amendment by the Limitation Amendment Act 1980, was again consolidated by the Limitation Act 1980. In relation to registered land, this has now been further changed by the Land Registration Act 2002. Originally the period was fixed at the discretion of individual judges. Later, certain dates (such as the first coronation of Henry II) were chosen from time to time by the legislature. Then in 1623 the Limitation Act introduced the modern principle that actions must be brought within a fixed number of years. But even so the state of the law was unsatisfactory owing to the variety of remedies that lay for the recovery of land, and to the fact that the period of limitation varied according to the nature of the remedy adopted. An account of the old law must be sought in works on legal history.[11] We confine ourselves to

---

[7] Similarly, modern French law adopts the Roman principle, and allows a possessor to acquire a positive title by *usucapion*—after a period (between ten and thirty years) which depends on whether the acquisition of possession was in good faith, and whether the previous owner is still living in the same district: Bell, Boyron and Whittaker, *Principles of French Law*, pp. 285–7. See also *International Encyclopedia of Comparative Law*, vol. VI, *Property and Trust*, chap. 2, para. 2–23 (J. H. Beekhuis), discussing the role of possession and ownership in modern civil law jurisdictions.

[8] Lightwood, *Possession of Land*, p. 153. See *Buckinghamshire County Council v Moran* [1990] Ch 623 at 644, per NOURSE LJ; *R v Oxfordshire County Council, ex p Sunningwell Parish Council* [2000] 1 AC 335 at 349, per Lord HOFFMANN.

[9] Real Property Limitation Act 1833; Real Property Limitation Act 1874; LA 1939; Limitation Amendment Act 1980; LA 1980, as amended by Latent Damage Act 1986.　　　　　　　　[10] Pp. 613 et seq, post.

[11] See especially Hayes, *Introduction to Conveyancing*, vol. i. pp. 222 et seq; Holdsworth, *History of English Law*, vol. iv. p. 484; vol. vii. pp. 29 et seq; Simpson, *A History of the Land Law*, pp. 151–5.

describing the current law as it has been established by the Limitation Act 1980[12] and now varied, in relation to registered land, by the Land Registration Act 2002.[13]

II Limitation Act 1980

A Period of Limitation for Actions to Recover Land

Under the Limitation Act 1980, which applies in relation to unregistered land,[14] no action can be brought to recover any land after the expiration of twelve years from the date on which the *right of action accrued* to the claimant,[15] or to the person through whom he claims.[16] This limitation applies to a foreclosure action.[17]

Land is defined in wide terms. It includes:[18] "corporeal hereditaments, tithes[19] and rentcharges and any legal or equitable estate or interest therein, . . . but except as provided above in this definition does not include any incorporeal hereditament."

There are certain exceptional cases[20] in which the ordinary period of twelve years is increased.

(1) Actions by the Crown

The Crown Suits Act 1769, generally called the *Nullum Tempus* Act, altered the ancient rule that Statutes of Limitations do not bind the Crown and prescribed a period of sixty years in the case of an action to recover land. This period is now thirty years,[21] and there is a general provision that the "Act shall apply to proceedings by or against the Crown in like

---

[12] This is based on the Law Reform Committee 21st Report (Final Report on Limitations of Actions) 1977 (Cmnd 6923), which contains a valuable discussion of all aspects of limitation. The Act came into force on 1 May 1981. See the annotation in Current Law Statutes 1980 (D. Morgan); and generally Franks, *Limitation of Actions*; McGee, *Limitation Periods*; Preston and Newsom, *Limitation of Actions* (3rd edn 1953; 4th edn 1989); Prime and Scanlan, *Modern Law of Limitation*; Redmond-Cooper, *Limitation of Actions*; Josling, *Periods of Limitation*; Oughton, Lowry and Merkin, *Limitation of Actions*; Jourdan, *Adverse Possession*.

In 2001 the Law Commission published a report on Limitation of Actions (Law Com No. 270), M & B pp. 242–4, which proposed the repeal of the 1980 Act, and its replacement by a new, simplified regime for limitation periods. It included proposals relating to land, although substantial reforms were later made in relation to registered land by the Land Registration Act 2002; pp. 145 et seq, post. The Government accepted the Report in principle in July 2002.   [13] Pp. 145 et seq, post.

[14] P. 145, post.

[15] After a judgment for possession has been obtained in an action begun in due time, the successful plaintiff has twelve years from the date of judgment: *BP Properties Ltd v Buckler* (1987) 55 P & CR 337.

[16] LA 1980, s. 15(1). Action means proceedings in court for possession, but not an application to the Land Registry to rectify the register: *J A Pye (Oxford) Ltd v Graham* [2000] Ch 676 (this point was not further argued on appeal to CA or HL). For possession claims generally, see CPR Pt 55, Part I; and (for summary proceedings for possession) CPR Sch. 1 RSC Ord 113; Sch. 2 CCR Ord 24. An appointee under a special power is not deemed to claim through the appointor: s. 38(6).

[17] ibid., s. 20(4). There can be adverse possession of a party wall: *Prudential Assurance Co Ltd v Waterloo Real Estate Inc* [1999] 2 EGLR 85.   [18] ibid., s. 38(1), as amended by TLATA 1996, s. 25(2), Sch. 4.

[19] P. 94, n. 68, ante.

[20] The special period of limitation in respect of an advowson (the right to present to or bestow any ecclesiastical benefice) was repealed by Patronage (Benefices) Measure 1986, s. 4(3); p. 933, n. 26, post.

[21] LA 1980, s. 15(7), Sch. 1, para. 10. It remains sixty years where foreshore is owned by the Crown: para. 11; *Secretary of State for Foreign and Commonwealth Affairs v Tomlin* The Times, 4 December 1990 (former embassy of Government of Cambodia in St John's Wood, London).

manner as it applies to proceedings between subjects".[22] An action to recover land brought *against* the Crown, however, is subject to the twelve years' period.

(2) Action by Corporation Sole

An action to recover land by a spiritual or an eleemosynary corporation sole, such as a bishop, dean or master of a hospital, must be brought within thirty years after the date on which the right of action accrued to the corporation or to the person through whom the corporation claims.[23] The ordinary period of twelve years applies in the case of a corporation aggregate, such as one of the colleges of Oxford or Cambridge.

In the case of the Crown or a spiritual or eleemosynary corporation the position with regard to *claiming through a person* may be illustrated by examples:

The Crown purchased from A in 2000 land which was then in the wrongful possession of a third party, X.

If a right of action to recover the land from the wrongful possessor accrued to A more than twelve years before 2000, A's title is extinguished and the Crown acquires nothing. If, however, A's right of action accrued less than twelve years before 2000, say in 1995, then the Crown can sue the wrongdoer at any time within thirty years after 1995.[24]

The reverse case arises where a person claims through the Crown or a corporation sole after a cause of action has already accrued, as for example where:

In 2000 the Crown conveyed to A land which had been in the wrongful possession of X since 1980.

The statutory rule here is that A's remedy against X is barred either thirty years after 1980, when the cause of action accrued to the Crown, or twelve years after the cause of action accrued to himself, *whichever period expires first.*[25] The cause of action accrued to A by virtue of the conveyance of 1980, but nevertheless his remedy is barred in 2010.

B The Date from which Time Begins to Run

(1) The General Rule

(a) Accrual of right of action

Time begins to run against a claimant only from the date on which the right of action accrued to him or to the person through whom he claims. In the case of land, as distinct from other cases such as contract or tort, the Act lays down specific rules fixing the date at which in varying circumstances this accrual occurs.[26] It deals separately with present interests, future interests, settled land, land held on trust, tenancies and forfeiture or breach of condition.

---

[22] LA 1980, s. 37(1). This applies to proceedings by or against the Duke of Cornwall or the Duchy of Lancaster.   [23] Ibid., s. 15(7), Sch. 1, para. 10.

[24] Ibid., s. 15(7), Sch. 1, paras. 10, 13.

[25] Ibid., para. 12. This provision applies whether or not the Crown was the owner when the adverse possessor first took possession; the Crown's thirty-year period is available from the moment when it acquires the title as long as the title has not already been extinguished by adverse possession (supra), and this longer period can then benefit a successor to the Crown: *Hill v Transport for London* [2005] Ch 379.

[26] For accrual in negligence cases in respect of latent damage to property, see the Latent Damage Act 1986, which is based on the recommendations of the Law Reform Committee 24th Report on Latent Damage (1984

(b) "Adverse possession"

Before dealing with these different cases, however, it is necessary to notice an overriding provision of the greatest importance. This is that time does not begin to run from the specified dates unless there is some person in "adverse possession" of the land. It does not run merely because the land is vacant.[27] There must be both absence of possession by the claimant and adverse possession by the defendant.

This rule, founded on the obvious reason that a right of action cannot accrue unless there is somebody against whom it can be asserted, was well established after the Real Property Limitation Act 1833, in the case where an *actual possessor* left possession vacant, though there was some doubt whether it applied where the land of a deceased owner remained vacant owing to the failure of the person entitled thereto to take possession. All doubts are now removed, for each statutory rule fixing the date at which the right of action accrues is subject to the overriding condition that there must be some person in possession of the land in whose favour time can run. This condition is enacted in the following words:[28]

No right of action to recover land shall be treated as accruing unless the land is in the possession of some person in whose favour the period of limitation can run (referred to below in this paragraph as "adverse possession"); and where . . . any such right of action is treated as accruing on a certain date and no person is in adverse possession on that date, the right of action shall not be treated as accruing unless and until adverse possession is taken of the land.[29]

The term "adverse possession" must not, however, be misunderstood. It does not mean that the possessor must act adversely to the paper title owner, or "oust" him, or intend to exclude the whole world including the true owner, or that his use of the land has to be inconsistent with any present or future use by the true owner.

In *J A Pye (Oxford) Ltd v Graham*[30]

P was the registered proprietor of land which it intended to develop. In February 1983 P entered into a contract with G to allow G to use a portion of the land, which was adjacent to G's farm, and was accessible only through G's own land, for the purposes of grazing. This grazing contract ended on 31 December 1983, and P required G to vacate the land but G continued to use it for grazing and P took no steps to evict him. G knew of P's intention to develop the land, and continued to use it knowing that he might be requested to vacate it or to pay for its continued use for grazing, but no such request was made by P. In August 1984 P allowed G to cut and remove hay, in return for payment. In December 1984 G asked P whether he might have a further formal grazing contract, but P did not reply. G made no further attempts to contact P, but would have been prepared to pay for occupation if asked. In 1997 G registered a caution at the Land Registry claiming that he had obtained title by adverse possession. On 30 April 1998 P brought an action challenging this.

Cmnd 9390); McGee, *Limitation Periods* (2nd edn), chap. 6; (1991) 54 MLR 345 (N. J. Mullany); Emmet, para. 1.036A.

[27] *M'Donnell v M'Kinty* (1847) 10 ILR 514; *Smith v Lloyd* (1854) 9 Exch 562.

[28] LA 1980, s. 15(6), Sch. 1, para. 8(1).

[29] *Moses v Lovegrove* [1952] 2 QB 533. The mere fact that the premises become subject to the Rent Acts, so that possession cannot be recovered without a court order, does not prevent the tenant's possession from being adverse. See too *Hughes v Griffin* [1969] 1 WLR 23.   [30] [2003] 1 AC 419; [2003] CLJ 36 (L. Tee).

The question was whether, by that date, G had been in adverse possession for a period of 12 years. It was held that he had; and that P's title to the land had therefore been extinguished.[31] Lord BROWNE-WILKINSON said:

much confusion and complication would be avoided if reference to adverse possession were to be avoided so far as possible and effect given to the clear words of the Acts. The question is simply whether the defendant squatter has dispossessed the paper owner by going into ordinary possession of the land for the requisite period without the consent of the owner.[32]

(c) Successive adverse possessors

This general principle may be illustrated by the case where the adverse possessor (let us call him X) fails for one reason or another to occupy for the full period of twelve years. In this connection there are four possible situations which must be considered separately.

(1) X DIES OR TRANSFERS HIS INTEREST TO ANOTHER PERSON BEFORE THE LAPSE OF TWELVE YEARS

The principle obtaining here is that since possession is prima facie evidence of seisin in fee,[33] X holds a transmissible interest in the land. The time during which he has possessed is available to his successor in title, and therefore a purchaser or devisee who immediately follows him into possession and holds for the remainder of the twelve years acquires as good a right to the land as if he himself had been in possession for the whole period.[34]

(2) POSSESSION IS ABANDONED BY X AND IS NOT RETAKEN BY ANOTHER PERSON

After this abandonment the dispossessed person is in the same position as if he had never been deprived of possession by X. There is no one whom he can now sue. There is no need

---

[31] LA 1980, s. 17, p. 135, post; LRA 1925, s. 75, p. 145, post. For subsequent proceedings arising from this case in which the European Court of Human Rights held by a majority that the operation of these statutory provisions was incompatible with Article 1 of the First Protocol to ECHR, see p. 150, post.

[32] [2003] 1 AC 419 at [36], per Lord BROWNE-WILKINSON. "Adverse possession" bore a technical meaning before the Real Property Limitation Act 1833. Before that date wrongful possession did not ripen into a claim to bar the owner's remedy unless there had been ouster of the seisin in one of five ways (for which see Carson, *Real Property Statutes*, notes to RPLA 1833, s. 2). Moreover, possession where possible was referred to a lawful title, and there were several cases where possession obviously held without title was held not to be "adverse". For instance, possession of a younger brother was possession of the heir; possession of one co-parcener, joint tenant or tenant in common was the possession of all, unless an intention to claim the whole was expressed; a tenant for years continued to hold for the landlord after the lease ended; if a squatter was entitled to an interest in the land less in extent than that which he claimed under the statute, his possession was referred to his lawful title; see *Lightwood on Possession*, pp. 159 et seq. Lord ST LEONARDS described the effect of the 1833 Act in these words: "It is perfectly settled that adverse possession is no longer necessary in the sense in which it was formerly used, but that mere possession may be and is sufficient under many circumstances to give a title adversely": *Dean of Ely v Bliss* (1842) 2 De GM & G 459 at 476–7. The effect of the Act was "to substitute for a period of adverse possession in the old sense a simple period of time calculated from the accrual of the right of action": Preston and Newsom (3rd edn), p. 87. So "adverse possession" is now used by the statute simply to describe the possession of those against whom a right of action has accrued to the owner. However, it has been held that, in relation to the acquisition of title by a trespasser between October 2000 and October 2003, it is necessary to use the former sense in order to construe the provisions of LA 1980 and LRA 1925 as compatible with HRA 1998: *Beaulane Properties Ltd v Palmer* [2006] Ch 79; p. 149, post.   [33] P. 29, ante.

[34] *Asher v Whitlock* (1865) LR 1 QB 1, M & B p. 233; *Mount Carmel Investments Ltd v Peter Thurlow Ltd* [1988] 1 WLR 1078.

for him to perform some act or ceremony in order to rehabilitate himself. The former possession of X, as Lord Macnaghten said, is not available to "some casual interloper or lucky vagrant".[35] This rule is now statutory:

Where a right of action to recover land has accrued and after its accrual, before the right is barred, the land ceases to be in adverse possession, the right of action shall no longer be treated as having accrued and no fresh right of action shall be treated as accruing unless and until the land is again taken into adverse possession.[36]

(3) POSSESSION IS ABANDONED BY X AND AFTER AN INTERVAL OF TIME IS TAKEN BY Y

It follows from what was said by Lord Macnaghten and from what is now enacted, that in this case the time during which X has occupied is not available to Y, for during a distinct and definite period there was no person against whom the person ousted by X could bring an action for the recovery of the land. Y is not a successor in title of X, and his intrusion causes a fresh right of action to accrue in favour of the person dispossessed by X.

(4) X LOSES POSSESSION AND IS FOLLOWED BY A SUCCESSION OF TRESPASSERS EACH CLAIMING ADVERSELY TO THE OTHERS

Here there is no distinct interval of time during which the possession is vacant. X, for instance, ejects V, Y ejects X, Z ejects Y, and is in actual possession when the statutory period of twelve years has run from the time of V's ejectment. Who is entitled to succeed in an action to recover the land?[37] Objection may be taken to the title of each of these persons, for V has been out of possession for more than twelve years, and yet none of the trespassers has been in possession for that period. Nevertheless, V is barred: "A continuous adverse possession for the statutory period, though by a succession of persons not claiming under one another, does, in my opinion, bar the true owner."[38] As for the trespassers, something might be said by the moralist for the earliest possessor, also for the one who has possessed for the longest period, and again for the latest possessor,[39] but it is clear that these conflicting claims must be decided in accordance with the general principle that possession is evidence of title.[40] X, while in possession, is ejected by Y. His possession, therefore, entitles him to recover the land from the wrongdoer, Y. If he takes no proceedings, then Y, upon being ejected by Z, may recover upon the strength of his existing possession: "Possession being once admitted to be a root of title, every possession must create a title which, as against all subsequent intruders, has all the incidents and advantages of a true title."[41]

We are now in a position to deal with the accrual of the cause of action in the different cases described by the statute.

---

[35] *Trustees, Executors and Agency Co Ltd v Short* (1888) 13 App Cas 793 at 798; explained by Parker J in *Samuel Johnson & Sons Ltd v Brock* [1907] 2 Ch 533 at 538; (1956) 19 MLR p. 22, n. 11 (A. D. Hargreaves).

[36] LA 1980, s. 15(6), Sch. 1, para. 8(2).

[37] See Pollock and Wright, *Possession in the Common Law*, pp. 95 et seq; Lightwood, *Possession of Land*, pp. 275 et seq. [38] *Willis v Earl Howe* [1893] 2 Ch 545 at 553, per Kay LJ.

[39] *Dixon v Gayfere* (1853) 17 Beav 421 at 430, per Lord Romilly.

[40] *Asher v Whitlock* (1865) LR 1 QB 1 at 6, M & B p. 233; approved *Perry v Clissold* [1907] AC 73; Pollock and Wright, p. 98. [41] Pollock and Wright, p. 95.

(2) Accrual of Rights of Action

(a) Present interests

Time does not begin to run against a person in present possession of land until possession has been taken by another person. The Act states the rule in this way:[42]

Where the person bringing an action to recover land, or some person through whom he claims, has been in possession of the land, and has while entitled to the land been dispossessed or discontinued his possession, the right of action shall be treated as having accrued on the date of the dispossession or discontinuance.

(1) DISCONTINUANCE OR DISPOSSESSION

The language of the above paragraph is not altogether happy, for it might be thought that a mere abandonment of possession is sufficient to set time running. This is not so, however, for the factor common to dispossession and discontinuance is entry upon the land by a stranger.[43] And there will be a "dispossession" of the paper owner whenever the squatter takes possession:[44]

Except in the case of joint possessors, possession is single and exclusive. Therefore if the squatter is in possession the paper owner cannot be. If the paper owner was at one stage in possession of the land but the squatter's subsequent occupation of it in law constitutes possession the squatter must have "dispossessed" the true owner for the purposes of Schedule 1, paragraph 1.[45]

(i) "Possession"

"Possession" requires both the *fact* of possession, and the *intention* to possess. As Lord BROWNE-WILKINSON has said:[46]

there are two elements necessary for legal possession: (1) a sufficient degree of physical custody and control ("factual possession"); (2) an intention to exercise such custody and control on one's own behalf and for one's own benefit ("intention to possess") ...

... there has always, both in Roman law and in common law, been a requirement to show an intention to possess in addition to objective acts of physical possession. Such intention may be, and frequently is, deduced from the physical acts themselves. But there is no doubt in my judgment that there are two separate elements in legal possession. So far as English law is concerned intention as a separate element is obviously necessary. Suppose a case where A is found to be in occupation of a locked house. He may be there as a squatter, as an overnight trespasser, or as a friend looking after the house of the paper owner during his absence on holiday. The acts done by A in any given period do not tell you whether there is legal possession. If A is there as a squatter he intends to stay as long as he can for his own benefit: his intention is an intention to possess. But if he only intends to trespass for the

---

[42] LA 1980, s. 15(6), Sch. 1, para. 1.

[43] Preston and Newsom (3rd edn), p. 99. See *Rains v Buxton* (1880) 14 Ch D 537, per FRY J; *Tecbild Ltd v Chamberlain* (1969) 20 P & CR 633.

[44] *J A Pye (Oxford) Ltd v Graham* [2003] 1 AC 419 at [38], per Lord BROWNE-WILKINSON. See also *Powell v McFarlane* (1977) 38 P & CR 452 at 470, per SLADE J.

[45] *Treloar v Nute* [1976] 1 WLR 1295 at 1300, per Sir John PENNYCUICK; [1982] Conv 256 (M. Dockray).

[46] *J A Pye (Oxford) Ltd v Graham* [2003] 1 AC 419 at [40]. In this context the word "possession" has its ordinary meaning, which is the same as in the law of trespass or conversion: ibid., at [42]. For a useful summary of the general propositions, see *Topplan Estates Ltd v Townley* [2005] 1 EGLR 89 at [70]–[76], per JONATHAN PARKER LJ.

night or has expressly agreed to look after the house for his friend he does not have possession. It is not the nature of the acts which A does but the intention with which he does them which determines whether or not he is in possession.

(ii) Factual possession

Leaving aside for the moment the "special type of case", the question whether there is factual possession does not always admit of a ready answer. The test was well put by Lord O'HAGAN:[47]

As to possession, it must be considered in every case with reference to the peculiar circumstances. The acts, implying possession in one case, may be wholly inadequate to prove it in another. The character and value of the property, the suitable and natural mode of using it, the course of conduct which the proprietor might reasonably be expected to follow with a due regard to his own interests—all these things, greatly varying as they must, under various conditions, are to be taken into account in determining the sufficiency of a possession.

Some cases, of course, may be obvious, as for instance, where a stranger occupies the house of another or encloses and cultivates a strip of his neighbour's land.[48] It must be a very exceptional case in which enclosure will not demonstrate the relevant adverse possession required for a possessory title;[49] but enclosure is not necessarily conclusive.[50] And cultivation without fencing may amount to adverse possession.[51]

---

[47] Lord Advocate v Lord Lovat (1880) 5 App Cas 273 at 288; cited in Treloar v Nute [1976] 1 WLR 1295 at 1299.

[48] Marshall v Taylor [1895] 1 Ch 641.

[49] George Wimpey & Co Ltd v Sohn [1967] Ch 487 at 512, per RUSSELL LJ.

[50] ibid. (where the stranger had an easement over the land in question). See also Littledale v Liverpool College [1900] 1 Ch 19; Hughes v Cork [1994] EGCS 25.

[51] Seddon v Smith (1877) 36 LT 168. See also Tecbild Ltd v Chamberlain, n. 43 supra (playing by children and tethering of ponies held to be acts too trivial for adverse possession); Basildon DC v Manning (1975) 237 EG 879 (erecting fence and dumping poultry manure held not to be adverse possession); Red House Farms (Thorndon) Ltd v Catchpole (1976) 244 EG 295 (shooting over marshy ground held to be adverse possession); Treloar v Nute [1976] 1 WLR 1295 (grazing of two cows and a yearling, storing timber and stone and filling in a gully held to be adverse possession); Hyde v Pearce [1982] 1 WLR 560 (continued occupation by purchaser, after termination of licence to occupy pending completion, held not to be adverse possession since "he had at no time made it clear that he was no longer bound by the contract of sale"); cf Bridges v Mees [1957] Ch 475 (contracting purchaser having equitable ownership held adverse possession); [1982] Conv 383 (J.E.M.); 46 MLR 89 (M. Dockray); Bills v Fernandez-Gonzalez (1981) 132 NLJ 60 (compost pens, bonfires, free-ranging chickens and planting trees and shrubs, together with adjoining owner's walking along line of fence for purposes of his garden, held not to be adverse possession); Williams v Usherwood (1983) 45 P & CR 235 (enclosure of land by fence, parking of three cars in enclosed curtilage of private dwelling house and paving of driveway with decorative crazy-paving stones held to be adverse possession); [1983] Conv 398 (M. Dockray); 134 NLJ 144 (H. Wilkinson); Dear v Woods [1984] CA Transcript 318 (playing of children, single perambulation by male plaintiff and laying of tar macadam on strip half the width of a brick held not to be adverse possession; this note was cited by Sir David CAIRNS as containing examples of trivial acts that will not suffice); Boosey v Davis (1987) 55 P & CR 83 (grazing of goats, cutting down of scrub and erection of secondary wire mesh fence held not to be adverse possession); Buckinghamshire County Council v Moran [1990] Ch 623 (placing of new lock and chain on access gate held to be adverse possession); Bladder v Phillips [1991] EGCS 109 (cleaning of ditch at defendant's request ("thinking it was my ditch") held not to be adverse possession); Ellett-Brown v Tallishire Ltd (CA 29 March 1990) (clipping of hedge, filling in ditch, planting of daffodils and building of brick pillar to serve as gatepost held not to be adverse possession); Marsden v Miller (1992) 64 P & CR 239 (erection of fence for twenty-four hours held not to be adverse possession by person having no documentary title against another such person); Wilson v Martin's Executors [1993] 1 EGLR 178 (walking boundary, cutting chestnuts for repair of fence, clearing fallen timber for

Once he has taken possession, the adverse possessor can still exclude himself from possession, and thereby lose his claim; but there must be an exclusion from possession, as opposed merely to a temporary absence.[52]

(iii) Intention to possess

Not only must the stranger establish factual possession; he must also show that he has the requisite intention to possess (*animus possidendi*). It used to be said that the stranger must take occupation with the intention of excluding the owner as well as others,[53] but this has now been disapproved. Instead, what is required is an

intention, in one's own name and on one's own behalf, to exclude the world at large, including the owner with the paper title if he be not himself the possessor, so far as is reasonably practicable and so far as the processes of the law will allow.[54]

It is not therefore inconsistent with the squatter's possession that he knows that, until the full time has run, the paper owner can recover the land from him; nor that he would be willing to pay the paper owner if asked. An admission of title by the squatter is not inconsistent with his being in possession in the meantime.[55]

In *Powell v McFarlane*[56] SLADE J's elaboration of the requirement of intention shows how heavy the burden of proof is on a stranger whose alleged possession originates in a trespass:

An owner or other person with the right to possession of land will be readily assumed to have the requisite intention to possess, unless the contrary is clearly proved. This, in my judgment, is why the

firewood, repairing wire fence and cutting trees for sale held not to be adverse possession); *Stacey v Gardner* [1994] CLY 568 (incinerator on concrete base on small part of land held not to be adverse possession, even though it was a substantial piece of machinery and a prominent feature); *Hughes v Cork* [1994] EGCS 25 (enclosure of triangular shaped plot "most cogent evidence" of adverse possession); *Basildon DC v Charge* [1996] CLY 4929 (keeping of geese within chestnut paling fence, digging of vegetable patch and storage of sawed wood held not to be adverse possession); *London Borough of Hounslow v Minchinton* (1997) 74 P & CR 221 (keeping of compost heap, trimming of hawthorn and elderberry hedges and erection of fencing to prevent dogs from escaping held to be adverse possession); (1997) 147 NLJ 1662 (H. W. Wilkinson); *Prudential Assurance Co Ltd v Waterloo Real Estate Inc* [1998] EGCS 51, affd. [1999] 2 EGLR 85 (adverse possession of one face of a divided wall); *Central Midlands Estates Ltd v Leicester Dyers Ltd* [2003] 2 P & CR DG1 (no possession where car parking was on an unenclosed strip of land with no erection of car parking signs; cf p. 596, post for the relationship between taking possession and the enjoyment of an easement); *Inglewood Investment Co Ltd v Baker* [2003] 2 P & CR 23 (erection of portakabins for use as lavatories for those attending car boot sales; shooting of rabbits and foxes; children playing and deposit of rubbish held not to be adverse possession; nor was the erection of a fence, the object of which was to keep sheep in and not to keep the paper owner out); *Purbrick v Hackney LBC* [2004] 1 P & CR 34 (placing makeshift door with two locks on entrance to dilapidated "burnt-out shell" held to be adverse possession, even though squatter was aware that he was liable to be dispossessed); *Topplan Estates Ltd v Townley* [2005] 1 EGLR 89 (no obligation in law on squatter to alert owner that time is running against him).

   52   *Generay Ltd v Containerised Storage Co Ltd* [2005] 2 EGLR 7 (three months' exclusion from part of land by erection of line of rods and orange tape).

   53   *Littledale v Liverpool College* [1900] 1 Ch 19 at 23, per LINDLEY MR.

   54   *Powell v McFarlane* (1977) P & CR 452 at 471–2, per SLADE J, approved in *J A Pye (Oxford) Ltd v Graham* [2003] 1 AC 419 at [43], per Lord BROWNE-WILKINSON.

   55   *J A Pye (Oxford) Ltd v Graham*, supra, at [46].

   56   (1977) 38 P & CR 452 (infant who at age of fourteen began to graze the cow Kashla, otherwise known as Ted's cow, held not to have requisite intent); (1980) 96 LQR 333 (P. Jackson); [1982] Conv 256, 345 (M. Dockray); *Lodge v Wakefield Metropolitan City Council* [1995] 2 EGLR 124 (occupier who wrongly believed that he was a rent paying tenant held to have necessary animus possidendi); *Ellis v Lambeth LBC* (2000) 32 Harv L Rev 596 (squatter not estopped by failure to return community charge form); *Battersea Freehold and Leasehold Property Co Ltd v Wandsworth LBC* (2001) 82 P & CR 137 (distribution of access keys to other persons entitled to use land indicates lack of animus); *Clowes Developments (UK) Ltd v Walters* [2006] 1 P & CR 1 (daughter and son-in-law of former licensee had no intention to possess; intention to remain in factual possession only for so long as the true owner continues so to permit not sufficient animus); *Tennant v Adamczyk*

slightest acts done by or on behalf of an owner in possession will be found to negative discontinuance of possession. The position, however, is quite different from a case where the question is whether a trespasser has acquired possession. In such a situation the courts will, in my judgment, require clear and affirmative evidence that the trespasser, claiming that he has acquired possession, not only had the requisite intention to possess, but made such intention clear to the world.[57] If his acts are open to more than one interpretation and he has not made it perfectly plain to the world at large by his actions or words that he has intended to exclude the owner as best he can, the courts will treat him as not having had the requisite *animus possidendi* and consequently as not having dispossessed the owner.[58]

In the absence of concealed fraud,[59] it is irrelevant that the true owner is ignorant that he has been dispossessed. As SLADE J said:[60]

In view of the drastic results of a change of possession, a person seeking to dispossess an owner must at least make his intentions sufficiently clear so that the owner, if present at the land, would clearly appreciate that the claimant is not merely a persistent trespasser, but is actually seeking to dispossess him.[61]

(iv) Intention of true owner

Difficulties have arisen where the owner of a strip of land who has no immediate use for it, retains it for some specific purpose in the future, and meanwhile some other person has physical possession of it. Until recently the owner was not treated as dispossessed. In *Leigh v Jack*,[62] for instance, where a stranger deposited heavy factory materials on a strip of land which the owner intended to dedicate as a highway at a future date, it was held that there was neither discontinuance nor dispossession. BRAMWELL LJ said:[63]

In order to defeat a title by dispossessing the former owner, acts must be done which are inconsistent with his enjoyment of the soil for the purposes for which he intended to use it: that is not the case here, where the intention of the plaintiff and her predecessor in title was not either to build upon or to cultivate the land, but to devote it at some future time to public purposes.

However, this has been doubted at first instance,[64] and rejected by the Court of Appeal,[65] and again most recently in very firm terms by the House of Lords:[66]

The suggestion that the sufficiency of the possession can depend on the intention not of the squatter but of the true owner is heretical and wrong. It reflects an attempt to revive the pre-1833 concept of adverse possession requiring inconsistent user.... The highest it can be put is that, if the squatter is aware of a special purpose for which the paper owner uses or intends to use the land and the use made

[2005] 41 EG 205 (CS) (mere intention to use own land and to make additional use of other land only so far as necessary for parking and unloading not sufficient).

[57] This requirement applies to an unconscious as well as to a conscious trespasser: *Prudential Assurance Co Ltd v Waterloo Real Estate Inc* [1999] 2 EGLR 85.

[58] *Morrice v Evans* [1989] EGCS 26 (claimant accepted an assertion by the true owner of a right to restrict the claimant's activities on the land); *Pavledes v Ryesbridge Properties Ltd* (1989) 58 P & CR 459 (claimant of land for car-parking asked the true owner "to do its duty as the person entitled to possession to keep out trespassers").

[59] P. 140, post.   [60] *Powell v McFarlane* (1977) 38 P & CR 452 at 480.

[61] *Wilson v Martin's Executors* [1993] 1 EGLR 178.   [62] (1879) 5 Ex D 264.   [63] At 273.

[64] *Powell v McFarlane* (1977) 38 P & CR 452 at 469, per SLADE LJ

[65] *Buckinghamshire County Council v Moran* [1990] Ch 623 at 645, per NOURSE LJ. See also *London Borough of Hounslow v Minchinton* (1997) 74 P & CR 221.

[66] *J A Pye (Oxford) Ltd v Graham* [2003] 1 AC 419 at [45], per Lord BROWNE-WILKINSON. For the re-introduction of this "heresy", however, in relation to the acquisition of title by a trespasser between October 2000 and October 2003, in order to construe the provisions of LA 1980 and LRA 1925 as compatible with HRA 1998, see *Beaulane Properties Ltd v Palmer* [2006] Ch 79; pp. 149–50, post.

by the squatter does not conflict with that use, that may provide some support for a finding as a question of fact that the squatter had no intention to possess the land in the ordinary sense but only an intention to occupy it until needed by the paper owner. For myself I think there will be few occasions in which such inference could be properly drawn in cases where the true owner has been physically excluded from the land. But it remains a possible, if improbable, inference in some cases.

(v) Implied licence

If the owner gives permission to a stranger to commit the acts of possession upon which he seeks to rely, then the latter cannot succeed, because time does not run in favour of a licensee.[67] The reliance in some earlier cases on a doctrine of an implied or hypothetical licence[68] was rejected by the Limitation Act 1980. The doctrine was explained by SLADE J as follows:[69]

Very broadly . . . it would appear that in any case where the acts of an intruder, however continuous and far-reaching, do not substantially interfere with any present or future plans which the owners may have for the use of unbuilt land, the court will not treat the intruder as having dispossessed the owner for the purpose of the Limitation Act 1939 because it will treat him as having been there under some implied or hypothetical licence.

The Limitation Act 1980 rejected this doctrine while preserving the possibility of a licence being implied where the actual facts of the case warrant it:[70]

For the purpose of determining whether a person occupying any land is in adverse possession of the land it shall not be assumed by implication of law that his occupation is by permission of the person entitled to the land merely by virtue of the fact that his occupation is not inconsistent with the latter's present or future enjoyment of the land.

This provision shall not be taken as prejudicing a finding to the effect that a person's occupation of any land is by implied permission of the person entitled to the land in any case where such a finding is justified on the actual facts of the case.

(2) DECEASED PERSON IN POSSESSION AT DEATH

When A, the person entitled to land, dies while still in possession, and a stranger seizes possession after his death, time begins to run from the date of his death, not from the wrongful seizure, against those who claim under his will or upon his intestacy.[71] The same rule applies to a rentcharge created by will or taking effect upon death.[72]

---

[67] *BP Properties Ltd v Buckler* [1987] 2 EGLR 168 (possession ceased to be adverse when claimant occupied by unilateral licence from true owner), [1994] Conv 196 (H. Wallace); *Sze To Chun Keung v Kung Kwok Wai David* [1997] 1 WLR 1232 (licence from by someone other than the dispossessed) (the last appeal to PC from Hong Kong); *Smith v Lawson* (1997) 75 P & CR 466 (time held not to run against freeholder in favour of occupier of land protected by promissory estoppel).

[68] *Wallis's Cayton Bay Holiday Camp Ltd v Shell-Mex and BP Ltd* [1975] QB 94 at 103, per Lord DENNING MR; *Gray v Wykeham-Martin and Goode* [1977] Bar Library Transcript No. 10A (where there had first been an express licence); *Powell v McFarlane* (1977) 38 P & CR 452. The contrary approach along traditional lines was demonstrated in *Treloar v Nute* [1976] 1 WLR 1295. See (1980) 77 LSG 270 (P. A. Kay).

[69] *Powell v McFarlane*, supra, at 484. See also *J A Pye (Oxford) Ltd v Graham* [2003] 1 AC 419 at [32].

[70] S. 15(6), Sch. 1, para. 8(4), replacing Limitation Amendment Act 1980, s. 4. Implied licences were found on the facts in *Colin Dawson Windows Ltd v King's Lynn and West Norfolk BC* [2005] 2 P & CR 19; *Batsford Estates (1983) Co Ltd v Taylor* [2005] 2 EGLR 12.

[71] LA 1980, s. 15(6), Sch. 1, para. 2; *James v Williams* [2000] Ch 1 (executor de son tort).

[72] LA 1980, s. 15(6), Sch. 1, para. 2.

(3) GRANT OF PRESENT INTEREST

Where an interest in possession has been granted to A, or where the land has been charged in his favour with the payment of a rentcharge, and he has not taken possession or has not received the rent, time begins to run against him from the date of the grant.[73]

So far as a rentcharge is concerned this rule meets the case where the rent payer has never made a payment of the money due.

Where, however, he wrongfully makes payment to a stranger,[74] the statutory rule is that time shall begin to run against the owner of the rentcharge from "the date of the last receipt of rent" by him.[75] The result of this is to reduce the limitation period of twelve years, for normally a right of action would accrue and time would begin to run, not from the last receipt of rent, but from the date when the rent again became due. If, for example, the rent is payable annually on 29 September and payment is duly made on that date in 2005, no *right of action or of distraint* accrues until 29 September 2006. Nevertheless time begins to run under the statute on 29 September 1999, so that in effect the period of limitation is reduced to eleven years.[76]

(b) Future interests

(1) ALTERNATIVE PERIODS

The date upon which time begins to run against the owner of a future interest depends upon whether the person entitled to the preceding estate was in possession when it came to an end. Suppose that there is a:

grant to A for life, remainder to B in fee simple,

and that B fails to take possession on the death of A. In such a case the statute enacts alternative rules.

(i) If A dies while still possessed of the land, B's right of action accrues upon the determination of the life interest, i.e. he must sue within twelve years from the death of A.[77]

(ii) If A is not in possession at death, e.g. where he has been dispossessed by a stranger, B has the longer of two alternative periods within which he may bring his action, namely, twelve years from the time when the cause of action accrued to A, or six years from the death of A.[78]

This second rule does not apply where the preceding estate is a term of years absolute.[79] Thus time does not begin to run against a landlord until the lease determines, even though the tenant may have been ejected before that date.[80]

---

[73] LA 1980, s. 15(6), Sch. 1, para. 3.   [74] See generally Preston and Newsom, *Limitation of Actions*, para. 6.6.4.
[75] LA 1980, s. 38(8).   [76] *Owen v De Beauvoir* (1847) 16 M & W 547.
[77] LA 1980, s. 15(6), Sch. 1, para. 4.
[78] ibid., s. 15(2). The corresponding periods are thirty years and twelve years where the Crown or a spiritual or eleemosynary corporation is entitled to the future interest: s. 15(6), Sch. 1, para. 13.   [79] ibid.
[80] P. 131, post.

(2) ENTAILED INTEREST

Neither rule applies to an interest limited after an entailed interest which is capable of being barred by the tenant in tail.[81] In this case the remainderman "claims through" the tenant in tail, so that if time has commenced running against the latter it continues to run against the remainderman, and does not start afresh upon the determination of the entail.

(3) SETTLEMENT MADE BY PERSON OUT OF POSSESSION

Future interests created by a settlor after time has commenced to run against him are subject to a different rule. The second case given above contemplates that *after* the settlement in favour of B has been made, a right of action accrues to A, the owner of the preceding estate, against an adverse possessor. In those circumstances, as we have seen, B may recover the land within six years from the death of A, though it may be more than twelve years since A was wrongfully dispossessed. But if time once begins to run against a settlor, no *subsequent* alteration in his title, for example, by the later creation of future interests, will prevent the bar from operating after the lapse of twelve years. The persons deriving title from the settlor cannot be in a better position than he is:[82] "Thus, if A, seised in fee in possession, were dispossessed by X, and were afterwards to settle the estate upon B for life, remainder to C in fee, the time would run from the dispossession, in the same manner as if no such settlement had been made."[83]

(4) SAME PERSON ENTITLED TO SUCCESSIVE INTERESTS

Where a person is entitled to successive interests in land, one present, the other future, the general principle is that, if his present interest is barred, the bar shall extend also to his future right.[84] Thus if land stands limited:

to A for life, remainder to B for life, remainder to A in fee simple,

and A is dispossessed for twelve years, he and those claiming under him lose the right to recover both the life interest and the fee simple in remainder. The right to recover the fee simple, however, is not barred if, to quote the words of the Act, "possession has been recovered by a person entitled to an intermediate estate or interest".[85] If, for instance, in the example just given, B were to recover possession after A had been dispossessed for twelve years, a right of recovery in respect of the fee simple would accrue to A and those claiming under him, upon the death of B.

(c) *Forfeiture or breach of condition*

A right of action to recover land by virtue of a forfeiture or breach of condition accrues on the date on which the forfeiture was incurred or the condition broken. If, however, a reversioner or remainderman fails to take advantage of the forfeiture or breach of condition he still retains the right of recovery that accrues to him when his estate falls into possession.[86] So if A, tenant for years, subject to a condition of re-entry, breaks the condition, the time runs against the reversioner in respect of his right of entry for the breach from its occurrence; but a bar to such right of entry will not affect his right to enter on the expiration of the lease by effluxion of time.[87]

---

[81] LA 1980, s. 15(3).   [82] ibid., s. 15(4).   [83] Hayes, *Introduction to Conveyancing*, vol. i. p. 257.
[84] LA 1980, s. 15(5).   [85] ibid., s. 15(5).   [86] ibid., s. 15(6), Sch. 1, para. 7.
[87] Hayes, *Introduction to Conveyancing*, vol. i. p. 252.

(d) Settled land and land held on trust

Equitable interests in land, such as a life interest under a strict settlement and equitable interests under a trust of land, are land within the meaning of the Limitation Act 1980.[88] In general, the provisions of the Act apply to these interests in like manner as they apply to legal estates, and the right to sue for the recovery of the land is deemed to accrue to the person entitled in possession on the date on which it would accrue if his interest were a legal estate.[89] Where such equitable interests exist the legal estate will, according to the circumstances, be vested in a tenant for life or statutory owner, or in personal representatives or in trustees of land, all of whom are trustees for the purposes of the Act.[90]

There are two circumstances in which the beneficiaries entitled to the equitable interests may be affected by wrongful possession:

(1) The trustee in possession may disregard the rights of the beneficiaries.

(2) A stranger may seize possession and hold it adversely to the beneficiaries.

(1) ADVERSE POSSESSION BY TRUSTEE

The first case raises no difficulty, for a trustee cannot obtain a title to the land by adverse possession against the beneficiaries. It is expressly enacted that no period of limitation shall apply to an action brought by a beneficiary:[91]

(a) in respect of any fraud or fraudulent breach of trust to which the trustee was a party or privy;

In the context of this paragraph, fraud and fraudulent breach of trust are limited to cases involving dishonesty. The result is that in the absence of deliberate concealment,[92] liability for an honest breach of trust endures without limitation of time.[93]

(b) to recover from the trustee trust property or the proceeds of trust property in the possession of the trustee or previously received by the trustee and converted to his use.

Thus, if a person, who is in possession of land as trustee for A and B, pays the whole of the profits to A, time does not run against B.[94] Even a notional receipt of property may come within this enactment. Thus, a trustee who remains in occupation of trust land for his own benefit is deemed to have received profits belonging to the beneficiaries, since in the circumstances he is chargeable with an occupation rent. Therefore, he can never escape liability for payment of this by pleading lapse of time, unless, indeed, under the equitable doctrine of laches, a beneficiary has been so tardy in bringing his action that it would be practically unjust to grant him relief.[95]

(i) Tenancies in common

The statutory provision (b) has an important effect upon tenancies in common. Where land is limited to A and B as tenants in common in fee simple, the beneficiaries become joint tenants and trustees of the legal estate upon trust to give effect to their own beneficial

---

[88] LA 1980, s. 38(1), as amended by TLATA 1996, s. 25(2), Sch. 4.
[89] ibid., s. 18(1), as amended by TLATA 1996, s. 25(2), Sch. 4.   [90] ibid., s. 38(1).
[91] ibid., s. 21(1).   [92] P. 140, post.   [93] *Armitage v Nurse* [1998] Ch 241 at 260.
[94] *Knight v Bowyer* (1858) 2 De G & J 421; see Preston and Newsom (3rd edn), pp. 148, 169.
[95] *Re Howlett* [1949] Ch 767; p. 133, post.

interests.[96] If, therefore, A appropriates the whole of the rents and profits to himself for many years, he does not acquire a title against B, for, since the land is in his possession as trustee, time does not run in his favour.[97]

If a beneficiary is entitled to a future interest in the trust property, his right of action does not accrue until the interest falls into possession; otherwise he would be compelled to litigate in respect of any injury to an interest which he may never live to enjoy.[98]

Where the claim is not comprised in provisions (a) and (b), as for instance where it concerns an unauthorised investment, the beneficiary must sue the trustee within six years from the accrual of his cause of action.[99]

(ii) *Relief for trustee–beneficiary*

In one case a trustee who is *also a beneficiary* under the trust is entitled to some relief from the effect of these provisions. If he distributes the trust property amongst himself and, for example, A and B, two other beneficiaries under the trust, and then another beneficiary C appears more than six years after the distribution, under these provisions C would be able to claim from the trustee the full amount of the share of the trust property to which he would have been entitled if all the beneficiaries had claimed in time. The law was amended in 1980 to limit the liability of a trustee who has acted honestly and reasonably in making the distribution: he has to pay to C only the excess over his, the trustee's, proper share.[100]

(2) ADVERSE POSSESSION BY STRANGER

Where a stranger seizes possession, the rule stated above, that the statutory provisions apply to equitable interests as well as to legal estates, if it stood alone, would mean that twelve years' possession held by the stranger adversely to the trustee would extinguish the legal estate and bar the remedy of the beneficiaries. This, however, is not so. It is provided by another section[101] that where possession of land has been held for twelve years adversely to the trustee (i.e. adversely to a tenant for life or statutory owner of settled land, or to trustees of land), the legal estate shall not be extinguished so long as the right of a beneficiary to recover the land has not accrued or has not been barred.

Thus the legal estate is not extinguished until the right of action of the *beneficiary* is barred. There is a further provision that a statutory owner or a trustee may sue for the recovery of the land on behalf of a beneficiary whose title to the equitable interest has not been barred.[102] By way of illustration:

Suppose that land is settled under a strict settlement upon A for life with remainder to B in fee simple, and that a stranger seizes the land in A's lifetime and remains in adverse possession for twelve years.

In these circumstances the *beneficial* life interest of A is extinguished, with the result that the adverse possessor acquires an equitable interest *pur autre vie*. Nevertheless the *legal fee*

---

[96] P. 465, post.
[97] *Re Landi* [1939] Ch 828; *Re Milking Pail Farm Trusts* [1940] Ch 996; Preston and Newsom (3rd edn), pp. 149–51. See (1941) 57 LQR 26 (R.E.M.); (1971) 35 Conv (NS) 6 (G. Battersby).
[98] *Armitage v Nurse* [1998] Ch 241 at 261, per MILLETT LJ.
[99] LA 1980, s. 21(3). The section does not apply to an action by the Attorney-General to enforce a charitable trust, because there is no relevant beneficiary: *A-G v Cocke* [1988] Ch 414.
[100] ibid., s. 21(2), replacing Limitation Amendment Act 1980, s. 5.   [101] ibid., s. 18(2), (3).
[102] ibid., s. 18(4).

simple, held by A under the provisions of the Settled Land Act 1925, remains intact, and therefore B, as the owner of a future interest, will be able to enforce his right of action when it accrues to him upon the death of A. When that event occurs, the representatives of A, upon whom his legal fee simple devolves, may recover the land on behalf of B.[103]

(3) ADVERSE POSSESSION BY BENEFICIARY

The only case remaining for consideration is where a *beneficiary* claims title by virtue of adverse possession for twelve years. Under the law as it stood before the Limitation Act 1939, such a person, although he was ordinarily regarded as tenant at will of the trustee, acquired a title by twelve years' possession if he occupied the land to the exclusion of the trustees and the other beneficiaries.[104] Now, however, his possession cannot be adverse to these persons, for it is enacted that during his occupation of the land time shall not run against a tenant for life, statutory owner, trustee or beneficiary.[105]

(e) Tenancies

(1) RECOVERY OF POSSESSION FROM THE TENANT

The right of action of a landlord to recover the land from the tenant accrues when the lease determines.[106] He must, therefore, sue within twelve years from this date. The mere fact that he has received no rent for many years does not affect his right to recover the land within this period.[107]

(i) Encroachment

If a tenant avails himself of the opportunity afforded him by his tenancy to encroach on other land (whether belonging to the landlord or to a third party), he is presumed to have done so for the benefit of his landlord.[108] But this presumption may be rebutted by showing that there are circumstances pointing to an intention to take the land for his own benefit exclusively. Although a tenant may thus acquire a title by adverse possession over other land, he must give it up to the landlord at the end of his lease.[109]

(ii) Forfeiture

If the lease contains a clause providing for the forfeiture of the premises upon non-payment of the rent, and if the rent is not paid within the stipulated period, the landlord acquires by virtue of this clause a right to recover the land during the continuance of the tenancy.[110] This right accrues to him, as we have seen, when the forfeiture is incurred,[111] but the fact that he

---

[103] See generally Preston and Newsom (3rd edn), pp. 143–6.

[104] *Burroughs v M'Creight* (1844) 1 Jo & Lat 290 (Ireland).

[105] LA 1980, s. 15(6), Sch. 1, para. 9, as amended by TLATA 1996, s. 25(1), (2), Sch. 3, para. 18, Sch. 4. But see Preston and Newsom (3rd edn), p. 148. [106] ibid., para. 4.

[107] *Doe d Davy v Oxenham* (1840) 7 M & W 131.

[108] A "rather esoteric doctrine", but too well established to be overruled by CA: *Tower Hamlets LBC v Barrett* [2006] 1 P & CR 9 at [21], [30], per NEUBERGER LJ, who at [31] was "sceptical about the application of the doctrine (especially in relation to land owned by a third party), unless the land to which possessory title is acquired is very close to the demised land and occupied by the tenant together with that demised land".

[109] *Kingsmill v Millard* (1855) 11 Exch 313; *Whitmore v Humphries* (1871) LR 7 CP 1; *Smirk v Lyndale Developments Ltd* [1975] Ch 317, M & B p. 225; *Kensington Pension Developments Ltd v Royal Garden Hotel (Oddenino's) Ltd* [1990] 2 EGLR 117. [110] P. 273, post.

[111] P. 128, ante.

fails to enforce it does not affect his right to recover the land within twelve years after the determination of the term. Moreover, his failure to enforce one forfeiture does not prejudice him with regard to the future. A fresh right of re-entry accrues to him on each occasion that the tenant defaults in payment.[112]

(2) RECOVERY OF POSSESSION FROM A STRANGER

If a stranger enters upon land which is held by lease, time begins to run in his favour against the *tenant* from the moment when the latter is dispossessed; but it does not begin to run against the *landlord* until the end of the lease, for it is only then that the landlord's right of action arises. The landlord must sue within the next twelve years, even though the existing lease is renewed in favour of the tenant while the stranger is still in possession.[113]

But since the receipt of rent is the only fact that symbolises the landlord's title to the land, and since an adverse receipt by a stranger is really tantamount to dispossession, it is enacted that:[114]

Where—

(a) any person is in possession of land by virtue of a lease in writing by which a rent of not less than ten pounds a year is reserved; and

(b) the rent is received by some person wrongfully claiming to be entitled to the land in reversion immediately expectant on the determination of the lease; and

(c) no rent is subsequently received by the person rightfully so entitled;

the right of action to recover the land of the person rightfully so entitled shall be treated as having accrued on the date when the rent was first received by the person wrongfully claiming to be so entitled and not on the date of the determination of the lease.

Thus, if the rent is wrongfully received by a stranger for twelve years, both the right of action and the title of the landlord are irretrievably barred, but if before the twelve years have elapsed rent is once more received by him, his right of action revives. If the lease is not in writing or if the annual rent is less than ten pounds, adverse receipt of the rent does not set time running against the landlord.

(3) TENANCIES AT WILL, FROM YEAR TO YEAR AND AT SUFFERANCE

Tenancies at will and from year to year have received special treatment.

(i) *Tenancy at will*[115]

Time begins to run against the landlord from the determination of the tenancy. The landlord may determine the tenancy either by demanding possession or by exercising some act of ownership on the land which is inconsistent with the right of the tenant.

Until the rule was abolished in 1980,[116] in the absence of determination, time began to run against the landlord at the end of one year from the beginning of the tenancy.[117]

---

[112] *Barratt v Richardson and Cresswell* [1930] 1 KB 686.

[113] *Ecclesiastical Commrs of England and Wales v Rowe* (1880) 5 App Cas 736; *Gray v Wykeham-Martin and Goode* [1977] Bar Library Transcript No. 10A, M & B p. 226.

[114] LA 1980, s. 15(6), Sch. 1, para. 6. Limitation Amendment Act 1980, s. 3(2) had substituted ten pounds for twenty shillings.   [115] Pp. 212–3, post.

[116] Limitation Amendment Act 1980, ss. 3(1), 13(2), Sch. 2.   [117] LA 1939, s. 9(1).

If, therefore, the landlord did nothing that constituted a positive determination, his title was extinguished in thirteen years from the commencement of the tenancy.

This rule was confined to a tenancy at will properly so called. If, for instance, A were given exclusive occupation of the land of B for an indefinite period and the circumstances showed that all that was intended was that he should have a personal privilege with no interest in the land, he was not a tenant at will, but a licensee, and time did not run against B while the licence subsisted.[118]

A tenancy at will and a licence are in this respect now on the same footing.

(ii) Tenancy from year to year[119]

In the case of a tenancy from year to year or other period *without a lease in writing*,[120] the right of the landlord to recover the land accrues either at the end of the first of such years or other period, or at the last receipt of rent, whichever shall last occur.[121] If the tenant remains in possession without paying rent for twelve years after the right of action has arisen, and without giving a written acknowledgment of the landlord's title, the cause of action is effectually barred,[122] and subsequent acknowledgment or payment of rent does not start time running afresh.[123]

If the lease is in writing the present rule does not apply, and the landlord's right of action accrues when he determines the tenancy by notice to quit.

(iii) Tenancy at sufferance[124]

In the case of a tenancy at sufferance, time runs from the beginning of the tenancy.

(3) The Doctrine of Laches

Despite the general rule that the provisions of the Limitation Act apply to equitable interests in land,[125] there are certain cases in which an equitable claim is unaffected by the statutory bars just discussed. Thus, as we have seen, a claim by a beneficiary to recover trust property retained by a trustee or to recover damages from a fraudulent trustee is subject to no period of limitation.[126] Again, the statutory bars do not apply to any claim for specific performance, an injunction or other equitable relief, except in so far as they may be applied by analogy to the Act.[127]

---

[118] *Cobb v Lane* [1952] 1 All ER 1199; *Hughes v Griffin* [1969] 1 WLR 23; *Heslop v Burns* [1974] 1 WLR 1241.

[119] P. 214, post.

[120] The possession by the tenant of a rent book does not covert an oral into a written lease: *Moses v Lovegrove* [1952] 2 QB 533. A document is not a lease in writing unless it is dispositive, that is a document which at law creates, of and by itself, a leasehold estate in land. A document which is merely a contract for a lease, or merely evidential of the terms of a lease is not a lease in writing: *Long v Tower Hamlets LBC* [1998] Ch 197 at 208; *Perry v New Islington and Hackney Housing Association* (2004) 14 January, discussed in [2004] EG 138 (G. Featherstonhaugh and S. Woodhead).

[121] LA 1980, s. 15(6), Sch. 1, para. 5(1).

[122] *Hayward v Chaloner* [1968] 1 QB 107, M & B p. 224; *Jessamine Investment Co v Schwartz* [1978] QB 264; *Lodge v Wakefield Metropolitan City Council* [1995] 2 EGLR 124, p. 124, n. 56, ante; *Price v Hartley* [1995] EGCS 74 (weekly tenant, who remained in occupation without paying rent, held to be a trespasser for purposes of Limitation Act only and therefore extinguished his landlord's title).

[123] *Nicholson v England* [1926] 2 KB 93.   [124] P. 213, post.

[125] LA 1980, s. 18(1), as amended by TLATA 1996, s. 25(2), Sch. 4.   [126] ibid., s. 21(1); p. 129, ante.

[127] ibid., s. 36(1).

Nevertheless, whenever a plaintiff seeks to enforce an equitable right to which no statute of limitation applies or to obtain a form of relief unknown to the common law, courts of equity have always required him to prosecute his claim with due diligence. In pursuance of the maxim *vigilantibus non dormientibus iura subveniunt*— "equity aids the vigilant, not those who sleep over their rights"—they discourage what is called *laches*, a word that signifies the negligent failure of a plaintiff to take proceedings for the enforcement of his claim within a reasonable time after he has become aware of his rights.[128] But the application of the doctrine of laches has always depended upon whether or not the suit in equity corresponds to an action at law that is within a statute of limitation.

If the equitable claim is substantially similar to a legal right that is subject to a statutory bar, the courts act by analogy to the statute and enforce the same bar upon the equitable right of action.[129] Thus an action by a widow for the assignment to her of specific land in satisfaction of her right to dower, which lay in Chancery before the abolition of dower, would fail unless she started proceedings within the statutory period prescribed for an action of ejectment.[130] The court, however, will not adopt the analogous statutory bar if the equitable claim has been deliberately omitted from the Act as a matter of policy. Relevant examples are the right of a mortgagor to redeem a mortgage of personalty,[131] or of a beneficiary to recover trust property retained by a trustee.

This principle of analogous application is now of much diminished importance, for the legislation of the nineteenth century, fortified by the Limitation Act 1980, has imposed a statutory bar upon most equitable claims.

If there is no corresponding claim or remedy at common law, or if, despite such correspondence, the equitable claim has been omitted from the statutory limitation as a matter of policy, equity applies its own test of unreasonable delay. Mere delay is seldom sufficient to constitute laches. It must be considered in the light of the circumstances.

The modern approach to laches or acquiescence has recently been set out by the Court of Appeal:[132]

It should not require an exhaustive enquiry into whether the circumstances could fit within the principles established in previous cases. Instead a broader approach should be adopted, namely whether it was unconscionable for the party concerned to be permitted to assert his beneficial rights.

And in *Nelson v Rye*[133] LADDIE J indicated some of the factors to be considered in deciding whether this defence runs:

Those factors include the period of the delay, the extent to which the defendant's positon has been prejudiced by the delay, and the extent to which that prejudice was caused by the actions of the plaintiff. I accept that mere delay alone will almost never suffice, but the court has to look at all the circumstances, including in particular those factors set out above, and then decide whether the balance of justice or injustice is in favour of granting the remedy or withholding it. If substantial prejudice will

---

[128] For a detailed discussion, see Brunyate, *Limitation of Actions in Equity*, pp. 185 et seq; Preston and Newsom (3rd edn), pp. 256–64; *Snell's Equity*, paras. 5–16 to 5–19.

[129] *Knox v Gye* (1872) LR 5 HL 656 at 674, per Lord WESTBURY.

[130] *Williams v Thomas* [1909] 1 Ch 713.

[131] Waldock, *Law of Mortgages*, p. 199. An action to foreclose a mortgage of personalty is barred by the LA after twelve years, but not an action to redeem such a mortgage.

[132] *Frawley v Neill* The Times, 5 April 1999, per ALDOUS LJ; *Patel v Shah* [2005] 8 EG 190 (cs).

[133] [1996] 1 WLR 1378 at 1382, citing *Lindsay Petroleum Co v Hurd* (1874) LR 5 PC 221 at 239, 240, and *Erlanger v New Sombrero Phosphate Co* (1878) 3 App Cas 1218 at 1279–80, per Lord BLACKBURN.

be suffered by the defendant, it is not necessary for the defendant to prove that it was caused by the delay. On the other hand, the plaintiff's knowledge that the delay will cause such prejudice is a factor to be taken into account.

Such will be the nature of the inquiry if laches is pleaded as a defence to an action by a beneficiary to recover property retained by a trustee;[134] by a mortgagor, to redeem a mortgage of pure personalty.[135] The doctrine of laches, which is of ancient origin, is preserved by the Limitation Act 1980 which provides that "Nothing in this Act shall affect any equitable jurisdiction to refuse relief on the ground of acquiescence or otherwise."[136]

C Nature of Title Acquired under the Limitation Act 1980

(1) Title to Land

It is necessary to consider what effect the expiration of the statutory period produces upon the title to the land.

What is the effect upon the legal position, first, of the person dispossessed, secondly of the person who has held adverse possession for twelve years?

(a) Title of person dispossessed

When time has run against a claimant, the effect in every case, no matter whether his claim is founded on tort, breach of contract, dispossession of land or some other wrong, is to bar his *remedy*. As a general rule, however, his *right* is not barred. He is precluded by the extinction of his remedy from a resort to legal proceedings, but he is free to enforce his still-existent right by any other method that may be available. Before 1833 this was the effect of adverse possession of land for the required period, but the Real Property Limitation Act[137] of that year provided that at the end of the statutory period the right, as well as the remedy, of the dispossessed owner should be extinguished. This rule is retained by the Limitation Act 1980 which provides that:[138]

At the expiration of the period prescribed by this Act for any person to bring an action to recover land (including a redemption action) the title of that person to the land shall be extinguished.

There is, however, an exception in the case of settled land and land held on trust where, as we have already seen, the title of the trustee to the legal estate is not extinguished until all the beneficiaries have been barred.[139]

In considering the extent to which the *status quo ante* of the parties is affected by the statutory extinguishment of the right of action, we will deal first with the former possessor and then with the squatter.

---

[134] See e.g. *Baker v Read* (1854) 18 Beav 398; *Re Jarvis* [1958] 1 WLR 815.

[135] *Weld v Petre* [1929] 1 Ch 33.

[136] S. 36(2); *Filross Securities Ltd v Midgeley* [1998] 3 EGLR 43 (equitable set-off held to be within s. 36(2) and not statute-barred). [137] S. 34.

[138] S. 17 (disapplied in relation to registered land by LRA 2002: p. 145, post). Similarly for an action to enforce an advowson: s. 25(3). The extinguishment of title also extinguishes the rights to claim rent and mesne profits during the period of adverse possession: *Mount Carmel Investments Ltd v Peter Thurlow Ltd* [1988] 1 WLR 1078. [139] P. 130, ante.

The dispossessed person and those who claim through him lose the title to possession that he could previously have enforced against the squatter. To that extent, his title is finally destroyed and there is no method by which it can be revived, not even by a written acknowledgment given by the squatter.[140]

But the restricted effect of the extinguishment must be realised. It extinguishes nothing more than the title of the dispossessed *against the squatter*.[141] Thus, the dispossession of a tenant does not destroy his lease. His title against the landlord remains good, so that, for instance, he is entitled to resume possession if the land is vacated by the squatter. Likewise, the landlord remains entitled to sue the tenant on the covenants or indeed to re-enter the land for a forfeiture committed by the squatter if the lease contains a proviso for forfeiture.[142]

A fortiori, the titles of third parties who have enforceable interests in the land, such as those entitled to the benefit of a restrictive covenant, are unaffected by the adverse possession of the land, for no remedy accrues to them until *their* rights have been infringed.[143]

(b) Title of squatter

It follows from what has been said, that the sole, though substantial, privilege acquired by a squatter is immunity from interference by the person dispossessed. In other words, the statutory effect of twelve years' adverse possession is merely negative; not, as Baron Parke once said,[144] "to make a parliamentary conveyance to the person in possession". This judicial heresy has long been exploded and it is now recognised that we must not confound the negative effect of the statute with the positive effect of a conveyance.[145]

There is no transfer, statutory or otherwise, to the squatter of the very title held by the dispossessed person. As Lord RADCLIFFE said:[146]

He is not at any stage of his possession a successor to the title of the man he has dispossessed. He comes in and remains in always by right of possession, which in due course becomes incapable of disturbance as time exhausts the one or more periods allowed by statute for successful intervention. His title, therefore, is never derived through but arises always in spite of the dispossessed owner.

Thus if a man ejects a tenant for years and remains in possession for the statutory period, he cannot be sued for breach of a repairing covenant contained in the lease, for there has been no transfer to him of the tenant's estate.[147] Again, any right enjoyed by the dispossessed person that is based upon an implied grant, such as a way of necessity, will not avail an adverse possessor, for the doctrine of implication cannot be imported into a statutory provision that is purely negative.[148]

---

[140] *Nicholson v England* [1926] 2 KB 93.

[141] *Fairweather v St Marylebone Property Co Ltd* [1963] AC 510 at 539, per Lord RADCLIFFE.

[142] ibid., at 545, per Lord DENNING. See also *Jessamine Investment Co v Schwartz* [1978] QB 264 (sub-tenant, protected as statutory tenant under Rent Act 1968, acquired title by adverse possession against his immediate landlord. Held (1) title of immediate landlord not extinguished as against the freeholder until head-lease expired; (2) when it did expire, sub-tenant still protected against freeholder under the Rent Act).

[143] *Re Nisbet and Potts' Contract* [1905] 1 Ch 391, M & B p. 241; p. 672, post.

[144] *Doe d Jukes v Sumner* (1845) 14 M & W 39 at 42.

[145] Hayes, *Introduction to Conveyancing*, vol. i. p. 269.

[146] *Fairweather v St Marylebone Property Co Ltd* [1963] AC 510 at 535.

[147] *Tichborne v Weir* (1892) 67 LT 735, M & B p. 241; p. 307, post.

[148] *Wilkes v Greenway* (1890) 6 TLR 449; similarly, in registered land, *Palace Court Garages (Hampstead) Ltd v Steiner* (1958) 108 LJ 274.

(1) DISPOSSESSION OF TENANT

The decision of the House of Lords in *Fairweather v St Marylebone Property Co Ltd*,[149] is a further illustration of the rule that there is no transfer to a squatter of an interest commensurate with that held by the person dispossessed. The facts relevant to the present inquiry may be stated in a much simplified form as follows:

A house and garden containing a shed were leased by X to Y for ninety-nine years. The shed was occupied by a neighbour, Z, for more than twelve years adversely to Y. While the lease was still running, Y surrendered it to the freeholder, X.

The question was whether, X, *qua* freeholder, could resume possession immediately or whether he had no such right until the lease determined by effluxion of time.

The majority of the House of Lords, overruling *Walter v Yalden*,[150] gave judgment for X. Despite the title acquired by the squatter against Y the tenant, the relationship between X and Y still continued with all its implications, including the right of Y to retain possession as against X. By surrendering the lease, Y had abandoned the right to possession, with the result that his tenancy had merged in the freehold and had disappeared. Therefore, the landlord could recover the shed on the strength of his own right to immediate possession of the freehold.[151]

The earlier decision of *Taylor v Twinberrow*[152] was approved. In that case, the facts were in effect as follows:

X, a yearly tenant, allowed Y to occupy a cottage for more than thirteen years as a tenant at will. X then bought the fee simple, with the result that the yearly tenancy was determined by its merger in the freehold. It was argued that the title acquired by Y was commensurate with that lost by X and that therefore he was entitled to the half a year's notice to quit appropriate to a yearly tenancy.

This argument was fallacious. All that the squatter had acquired was a title to possession indefeasible by the yearly tenant. With the disappearance of the yearly tenancy, the former yearly tenant had become the freeholder, and as such he had an immediate right to recover possession.

In *Chung Ping Kwan v Lam Island Development Co Ltd*,[153] the Privy Council held that, where a tenant has been dispossessed, he cannot recover possession against the squatter, if the tenant exercises an option to renew the lease. The tenant's right of action is not revived by his exercise of the option because he acquires a new legal estate by virtue only of a right included in the lease whose title has been extinguished as against the trespasser.[154]

If, however, the landlord grants a new lease even to the original tenant the new tenant is entitled to recover possession from the squatter by virtue of the landlord's title.

---

[149] [1963] AC 510, M & B p. 237.　　[150] [1902] 2 KB 304.

[151] Lord MORRIS dissented. He took the view that the tenant could not surrender what he had not himself got, namely, a right to immediate possession. *Nemo dat quod non habet*. For a criticism of the decision, see (1962) 78 LQR 541 (H. W. R. Wade). For a discussion of the difficulty of terminology in this context, see (1964) 80 LQR 63 (B. Rudden). See also (1973) 37 Conv (NS) 85 (J. A. Omotola).　　[152] [1930] 2 KB 16.

[153] [1997] AC 38, M & B p. 234. *Taylor v Twinberrow*, supra, was expressly approved: at 47.

[154] At 48, per Lord NICHOLLS OF BIRKENHEAD.

One effect of these decisions is that the landlord and tenant can combine to defeat the squatter. If the landlord accepts a surrender of the term, he is then able to grant a new lease to the tenant.[155]

(2) SUBSEQUENT IMPROVEMENT OF TITLE

Nevertheless, despite the negative operation of the Limitation Act, the title to possession acquired by a squatter against the person dispossessed may ultimately ripen into an indefeasible title to the fee simple. As Cozens-Hardy MR said:

Whenever you find a person in possession of property, that possession is prima facie evidence of ownership in fee, and that prima facie evidence becomes absolute once you have extinguished the right of every other person to challenge it.[156]

In other words, a squatter, though a wrongdoer, acquires by virtue of his possession a new independent title to the fee simple which prevails against all persons except those who can rely on an earlier and therefore a better title. Moreover, it is a title that will prevail against those with better titles if they fail to assert their rights within the period prescribed by the Limitation Act. Thus, a title originally defeasible may in course of time become indefeasible.[157]

For instance:

X dispossesses W, the fee simple owner of Blackacre, and remains in possession for eight years when he himself is dispossessed by Y.

As between X and Y, X's is the earlier and therefore the stronger title of the two, but he must assert it against the weaker within the statutory period. If Y is allowed to remain in possession for twelve years without being challenged either by W or by X, his title to possession of the fee simple becomes indefeasible. It rests on the infirmity of the right of others to eject him.[158]

Again, if some lesser title than that to the fee simple is destroyed, as when a tenant is ejected, the squatter may still be challenged by the landlord, the freeholder. So, if the lease terminates by effluxion of time or becomes forfeitable for breach of condition,[159] the freeholder's right to recover possession accrues and prevails over that of the squatter. Relatively to the tenant, the squatter's right is the stronger; relatively to the freeholder, it is the weaker. But if the freeholder does not pursue his remedy within twelve years from the end of the lease, the squatter's title to the fee simple becomes indefeasible.

(2) Proof of Title

A consequence of the negative effect of the Limitation Act 1980 is that as between vendor and purchaser a title based on adverse possession alone for the limitation period or longer is not necessarily a good title. The claims of a reversioner or a remainderman may have yet to be extinguished;[160] the reversion may be on a ninety-nine year lease; the remainderman's

---

[155] *Fairweather v St Marylebone Property Co Ltd* [1963] AC 510 at 547, per Lord Denning.

[156] *Re Atkinson and Horsell's Contract* [1912] 2 Ch 1 at 9.

[157] *St Marylebone Property Co Ltd v Fairweather* [1962] 1 QB 498 at 513, per Holroyd Pearce LJ.

[158] Darby and Bosanquet, *Statutes of Limitation* (2nd edn), p. 493, adopted by Bowen LJ in *Tichborne v Weir* (1892) 67 LT 735.   [159] *Tickner v Buzzacott* [1965] Ch 426.

[160] LA 1980, ss. 15, 18.

interest may not vest in possession for over a hundred years.[161] But if a vendor can establish that the flaw in an otherwise good title is one that can be cured by the running of time in his favour under the Act, he can force a purchaser of unregistered land to take the title.[162] Proof that rival claims have been extinguished by the lapse of time may be very difficult, and in practice a purchaser often agrees to accept an imperfect title.[163]

D Circumstances in which the Statutory Period is Extended

In three cases, namely:

(1) where the person entitled to recover land is under a disability;

(2) where there has been fraud or deliberate concealment of a cause of action; and

(3) where a person seeks relief from the consequences of a mistake;

the period of twelve years within which an action must normally be brought is lengthened.

(1) Disability

A person is deemed to be under a disability for the purposes of the Act while he is a minor or of unsound mind.[164]

If, on the date when a right of action for the recovery of land accrues, the person to whom it has accrued is under a disability, the action may be brought at any time within six years from the removal of the disability or from his death, whichever event first occurs, notwithstanding that the period of limitation has expired.[165] No action, however, to recover land or money charged on land may be brought after the expiration of thirty years from the date on which the right accrued.[166] A disability which begins *after* the accrual of a right of action does not prevent time from continuing to run against the disabled person.[167]

If before the cessation of one disability another one supervenes, time does not begin to run until both have ceased.[168] For instance:

A dispossesses B, who is six years of age. When fifteen years old B becomes of unsound mind, and is still in this state upon the attainment of his majority. Time does not begin to run until he recovers his sanity.

If the person entitled to the right of action dies while still under a disability, his successor in title must sue within six years even though he himself is under a disability.[169]

---

[161] *Cadell v Palmer* (1833) 1 Cl & Fin 372; vesting postponed for over a hundred years (note to *Re Villar* [1928] Ch 471 at 478); p. 526, post.

[162] *Re Atkinson and Horsell's Contract* [1912] 2 Ch 1; *Re Spencer and Hauser's Contract* [1928] Ch 598; distinguished in *George Wimpey & Co Ltd v Sohn* [1967] Ch 487.

[163] Farrand, *Contract and Conveyance* (4th edn), pp. 108–9.

[164] LA 1980, s. 38(2)–(4); *Kirby v Leather* [1965] 2 QB 367. The terminology of "infant" remains in LA 1980, s. 38(2), although the usual term is now "minor"; p. 911, post.   [165] ibid., s. 28(1).

[166] ibid., s. 28(4).   [167] ibid., s. 28(1), (2).   [168] *Borrows v Ellison* (1871) LR 6 Exch 128.

[169] LA 1980, s. 28(3).

(2) Fraud or Deliberate Concealment of Right of Action

Section 32(1) of the Limitation Act 1980 provides that where:

(a) the action is based upon the fraud of the defendant; or

(b) any fact relevant to the plaintiff's right of action has been deliberately concealed from him by the defendant

time shall not begin to run until the plaintiff has discovered the fraud or concealment, or could with reasonable diligence have discovered it.[170] The defendant includes the defendant's agent and any person through whom the defendant claims and his agent.[171]

The section, however, provides that the enactment shall not enable a person to recover the land or its value from a purchaser for valuable consideration who was not a party to the fraud or to the concealment, and who at the time of the purchase did not know and had no reason to believe that the fraud or concealment had taken place.[172]

"Fraud" in paragraph (a) bears its usual meaning,[173] but deliberate concealment in paragraph (b) is more difficult. It is presumably intended to take account of the restrictive interpretation placed by the courts on the words "concealed fraud" in the corresponding section of the Limitation Act 1939.[174] The word "deliberate" is not defined, but section 32(2) provides that: "deliberate commission of a breach of duty in circumstances in which it is unlikely to be discovered for some time amounts to deliberate concealment of the facts involved in that breach of duty". Deliberate concealment is clearly less than fraud, and in essence:[175] "denotes conduct by the defendant or his agent such that it would be 'against conscience' for him to avail himself of the lapse of time." Thus, wrongfully to enter land without the knowledge of the owner would not constitute deliberate concealment.[176] It would, however, be deliberate concealment in the context of adverse possession where a person, knowing that the land belongs to X, conceals from X the circumstances which confer the right upon him, and thus enables himself to enter and hold.[177] Examples are the destruction of title deeds,[178] the intentional concealment of a voluntary conveyance to the plaintiff,[179] the passing off of an illegitimate son as the eldest legitimate son,[180] the procuring of a conveyance from a person of unsound mind,[181] and where a builder covers up what he knows to be rubbishy foundations and does not tell the owner anything about it.[182]

---

[170] *Peco Arts Inc v Hazlitt Gallery Ltd* [1983] 1 WLR 1315 at 1323 (drawing Études Pour le Bain by Ingres).

[171] *Eddis v Chichester Constable* [1969] 2 Ch 345 (painting attributed to Caravaggio).

[172] LA 1980, s. 32(3), (4).   [173] See *Beaman v ARTS Ltd* [1949] 1 KB 550 at 558, per Lord GREENE.

[174] S. 26. See *Applegate v Moss* [1971] 1 QB 406 at 413, per Lord DENNING; *Clark v Woor* [1965] 1 WLR 650 at 654; *King v Victor Parsons & Co* [1973] 1 WLR 29 at 33; *Tito v Waddell (No 2)* [1977] Ch 106 at 224–5; *Lewisham London Borough v Leslie & Co Ltd* (1978) 250 EG 1289; *Bartlett v Barclays Bank Trust Co Ltd* [1980] Ch 515 at 537.

[175] *Applegate v Moss*, supra, at 413, per Lord DENNING; *Westlake v Bracknell DC* [1987] 1 EGLR 161; *Johnson v Chief Constable of Surrey* The Times, 23 November 1992; *Sheldon v RHM Outhwaite (Underwriting Agencies) Ltd* [1996] AC 102. Cf *Cave v Robinson Jarvis & Rolf* [2003] 1 AC 384 (deliberate concealment does not include failure to disclose a negligent breach of duty which the actor was unaware of committing). See Emmet, para. 1.010B.   [176] *Rains v Buxton* (1880) 14 Ch D 537.

[177] *Petre v Petre* (1853) 1 Drew 371 at 397, per KINDERSLEY V-C.

[178] *Lawrance v Lord Norreys* (1890) 15 App Cas 210.   [179] *Re McCallum* [1901] 1 Ch 143.

[180] *Vane v Vane* (1873) 8 Ch App 383.   [181] *Lewis v Thomas* (1843) 3 Hare 26.

[182] *Applegate v Moss* supra; *King v Victor Parsons & Co* supra.

Finally, even though time has started to run after a cause of action has arisen, subsequent concealment starts time running again.[183]

(3) Mistake

Similar provisions apply where the action is for relief from the consequences of a mistake.[184] The period of limitation does not begin to run until the plaintiff has discovered the mistake or could with reasonable diligence have discovered it. The relief, however, is only available "where the mistake is an essential ingredient of the cause of action",[185] as for instance where the action is to recover money paid under a mistake. There is no general rule that a mistake prevents time from running under the Act.

In *Kleinwort Benson Ltd v Lincoln City Council*,[186] the House of Lords held that this provision applies where the claim is for recovery of money paid under a mistake of law, including the case where the plaintiff's mistake was based on a settled understanding of the law which is shown by a later judicial decision to have been mistaken. The effect is that rent paid under a mistake (even a mistake of law[187]) made many years ago may be recoverable well beyond the normal limitation period.

E Methods by which Time may be Prevented from Running

Time which has begun to run under the Act is stopped, either when the owner asserts his right or when his right is admitted by the adverse possessor.

(1) Assertion of Owner's Right

Assertion of right occurs when the owner takes legal proceedings or makes an effective entry onto the land.

(2) Admission of Owner's Right

An admission of the right of the person entitled occurs when the adverse possessor acknowledges the right, or, if the right is to the payment of money, where he makes a part payment.

(a) Acknowledgment

Where a right of action to recover land or an advowson or to foreclose a mortgage has already accrued to X and his title is later acknowledged by the person in possession, his right is treated as having accrued on and not before the date of the acknowledgment.[188] The effect is that the owner's right of action recommences, not only against the person who makes the admission, but also against all later possessors, and remains effective until there has been

---

[183] *Sheldon v RHM Outhwaite (Underwriting Agencies) Ltd* [1996] AC 102. "In the case of subsequent concealment, the clock is turned back to zero", per Lord NICHOLLS at 152; criticised by Law Commission Consultation Paper No. 151 on Limitation of Actions 1998, paras. 8.17–8.20.   [184] LA 1980, s. 32(1)(c).

[185] *Phillips-Higgins v Harper* [1954] 1 QB 411 at 419, per PEARSON J.

[186] [1999] 2 AC 349; [1999] CLJ 478 (G. Virgo).

[187] *Nurdin & Peacock plc v D B Ramsden & Co Ltd* [1999] 1 WLR 1249.   [188] LA 1980, s. 29(1), (2)(a).

adverse possession for a further period of twelve years.[189] An acknowledgment, however, has no effect if it is given after the period of limitation has run its full course.[190]

Every acknowledgment must be in writing and signed by the person by whom it is made.[191] It must be made to the person whose title or claim is being acknowledged or to his agent.[192] Any written statement is sufficient that implicitly recognises the title of the person to whom it is made, as for instance an offer by a squatter to purchase the land from the freeholder;[193] or a request for further time within which to pay made by the possessor of land in response to a demand for rent.[194]

(b) Part payment

If, after a right of foreclosure or other cause of action has accrued to a mortgagee, the possessor of the land or the person liable for the mortgage debt makes any payment of principal or interest, there is a fresh accrual of the right of action from the date of payment.[195]

Where a right of action has accrued to recover any debt or other liquidated pecuniary claim, as for instance rent due under a lease, and the person liable acknowledges the claim or makes any payment in respect of it, the right is treated as accruing on and not before the date of the acknowledgment or payment.[196] A payment of part only of rent does not, however, enable the remainder then due to be recovered more than six years after it became due.[197] An acknowledgment to be effective for this purpose must admit the existence of the debt, but it need not state its precise amount, provided that this is ascertainable by extrinsic evidence.[198]

(c) Persons bound by acknowledgment and part payment

There is a distinction between acknowledgment and part payment with regard to the persons upon whom they are binding. An acknowledgment binds only the acknowledgor and his successors,[199] in other words, persons who claim through him, such as a trustee in bankruptcy or an executor.[200] A part payment of a debt or other liquidated money claim, on the other hand, binds all persons liable in respect of it,[201] for since they derive advantage from the payment it is only just that they should share the disadvantage of a fresh accrual of a right of action to the creditor. Thus a part payment of rent by a tenant revives the landlord's right of action against a surety.[202]

---

[189] LA 1980, s. 31(1).   [190] ibid., s. 29(7), infra; *Sanders v Sanders* (1881) 19 Ch D 373.

[191] ibid., s. 29(1). See *Browne v Perry* [1991] 1 WLR 1297 at 1301, per Lord TEMPLEMAN.

[192] ibid., s. 29(2).

[193] *Edginton v Clark* [1964] 1 QB 367 (letter to owner's agent offering to purchase land held to be effective acknowledgment); *Re Compania de Electricidad de la Provincia de Buenos Aires Ltd* [1980] Ch 146 (balance sheet effective acknowledgment if received by creditor). But an offer to purchase is not a sufficient acknowledgment where it is made by the landlord of the person in possession, even though the tenant was by his possession acquiring title for the landlord: the acknowledgment must be made by the person in possession: *Tower Hamlets LBC v Barrett* [2006] 1 P & CR 9 at [95].   [194] *Fursdon v Clogg* (1842) 10 M & W 572.

[195] LA 1980, s. 29(3).   [196] ibid., s. 29(5).   [197] ibid., s. 29(6).

[198] *Dungate v Dungate* [1965] 1 WLR 1477, explaining *Good v Parry* [1963] 2 QB 418; *Surrendra Overseas Ltd v Government of Sri Lanka* [1977] 1 WLR 565; *Kamouh v Associated Electrical Industries International Ltd* [1980] QB 199; *Re Overmark Smith Warden Ltd* [1982] 1 WLR 1195.   [199] LA 1980, s. 31(6).

[200] ibid., s. 31(9).   [201] ibid., s. 31(7).

[202] *Re Powers* (1885) 30 Ch D 291; *Re Frisby* (1889) 43 Ch D 106.

(d) Acknowledgment or part payment after time has run

No acknowledgment or part payment can revive any right to recover land if it is made after the full period of limitation has run. The reason is that the effect of the Limitation Act is to bar not only the remedy of an owner for recovering the land but also his right to it;[203] and, since the right as well as the remedy is barred, there is nothing left to acknowledge. Where, however, the remedy alone is barred, for example, in the case of an action for the payment of a debt, the rule used to be that an acknowledgment or part payment was effective even if given after the period had elapsed.[204] This rule was changed in the Limitation Act 1980, where it was enacted[205] that: "a current period of limitation may be repeatedly extended by further acknowledgments or payments, but a right of action, once barred by this Act, shall not be revived by any subsequent acknowledgment or payment".

III Registered Land. Land Registration Acts 1925 and 2002

A Land Registration Act 1925

(1) Title of Person Dispossessed

Before the Land Registration Act 2002,[206] the Limitation Act 1980 applied to registered land, and a title to a registered estate could be acquired by adverse possession,[207] as long as the required period had already been completed by the date the 2002 Act came into force.[208] There was, however, one important difference which sprang from the mechanics of registration. When a squatter acquires a legal title to unregistered land by adverse possession, the former owner's estate is automatically extinguished. With registered land, however, there was no automatic extinction of the proprietor's title but it was deemed to be held by the proprietor on trust for the squatter.

This was without prejudice to the rights of any other person interested in the land whose estate or interest was not extinguished by the limitation. Anyone claiming to have acquired a title to registered land under the Act could apply to be registered as proprietor and he could be registered with an absolute, good leasehold, qualified or possessory title, as the case may be, but his registration would have the same effect as that of a first proprietor.[209]

Rights acquired or in course of being acquired under the Limitation Act were overriding interests under the Land Registration Act 1925,[210] and therefore a registered purchaser for value could never be in a better position than his predecessor in title and must take subject to the rights of the squatter.[211] The purchaser's registered title, even if absolute, could be rectified in favour of the squatter,[212] but the purchaser would not be entitled to an indemnity, as he

---

[203] P. 116, ante.   [204] See LA 1939, s. 25(5), (6).

[205] S. 29(7), replacing Limitation Amendment Act 1980, s. 6. A squatter may be estopped from asserting his title: *Colchester BC v Smith* [1991] Ch 448.   [206] Infra.

[207] See generally R & R (1991 edn), chap. 32.   [208] 13 October 2003; n. 223, infra.

[209] LRA 1925, s. 75; *Fairweather v St Marylebone Property Co Ltd* [1963] AC 510 at 541, 548; *Spectrum Investment Co v Holmes* [1981] 1 WLR 221 at 229; (1981) 131 NLJ 718 (P. F. Smith); 774 (E. G. Nugee); [1981] Conv 155 (R. E. Annand); [1982] Conv 201 (P. H. Kenny).

[210] S. 70(1)(f); *Bridges v Mees* [1957] Ch 475; ibid., s. 70(1)(g).   [211] *Bridges v Mees*, supra.

[212] *Chowood Ltd v Lyall (No 2)* [1930] 2 Ch 156.

had only lost thereby a valueless asset, that is, a title barred by adverse possession on the part of the squatter.[213]

(2) Dispossession of Tenant

The rule in *Fairweather* did not, however, apply to registered land. This has been decided twice at first instance.

First, where the squatter had acquired a title as against the tenant and had then been registered under section 75 as proprietor in place of the tenant. It was then no longer possible for the tenant "to do a Marylebone",[214] and thereby enable the freeholder to dispossess the squatter.

In *Spectrum Investment Co v Holmes*[215] the question arose whether the rule in *Fairweather v St Marylebone Property Co Ltd*[216] applied to registered land:

In 1902 a registered freeholder granted a registered lease of a house to T. In 1968 H acquired a title by adverse possession against D, a registered assignee of T, under the Limitation Act 1939. H applied for and obtained registration as proprietor of the leasehold interest with possessory title, and the title under which D was registered was closed. In 1975 D "woke up" and purported to surrender the lease to S the freeholder's successor in title, who was then the registered proprietor with absolute title to the freehold. S then claimed possession against H, the registered squatter.

BROWNE-WILKINSON J held that the rule in *Fairweather* did not apply to registered land. Since D's title had been closed, D was no longer the registered proprietor of the lease, and was therefore unable to surrender it. In any event the surrender itself was invalid as not having been effected by a registered disposition.[217]

Secondly, where the squatter had acquired a title as against the tenant but had not yet exercised his right to register it in his place. In *Central London Commercial Estates Ltd v Kato Kagaku Ltd*,[218]

a freeholder granted a long lease in 1935 of land forming part of Bush House in the Strand. Both titles were registered. The squatter had been in continuous adverse possession of a courtyard for more than twelve years before 1996, using it as a paying car park. The lease was surrendered by a successor in title of the tenant to the freeholder.

SEDLEY J held that here too the tenant cannot do a Marylebone. He held his estate on trust for the squatter under section 75, and the squatter's rights under the trust were overriding interests under section 70(1)(f) or (g), or both, of the Land Registration Act 1925. Therefore, any disposition by the tenant (and surrender is a disposition) was ineffective to override the rights of the squatter.

---

[213] See *Re Chowood's Registered Land* [1933] Ch 574, M & B p. 193.

[214] Per Christopher Nugee QC, counsel in *Central London Commercial Estates Ltd v Kato Kagaku Ltd* [1998] 4 All ER 948.

[215] [1981] 1 WLR 221, M & B p. 245; (1981) 131 NLJ 718 (P. F. Smith); 774 (E. G. Nugee); [1981] Conv 155 (R. E. Annand); [1982] Conv 201 (P. H. Kenny); [1984] LS 1 (C. E. Cooke).

[216] [1963] AC 510; p. 137, ante.

[217] LRA 1925, ss. 21, 22, 69(4). D's claim to rectification of the register to enable her to executed a valid surrender was rejected. H was properly registered under the mandatory requirements of s. 75(5). See also *Mount Carmel Investments Ltd v Peter Thurlow Ltd* [1988] 1 WLR 1078 at 1089 (original squatter forged a long lease from the registered freeholder and assigned it to another squatter).

[218] [1998] 4 All ER 948; (1999) 115 LQR 187 (C. Harpum); [1999] 149 NLJ 118 (H. W. Wilkinson); [1999] Conv 136 (E. J. Cooke), 329 (S. Pascoe); [1998] All ER Rev 272 (P. J. Clarke).

We have seen that in unregistered land there is no Parliamentary conveyance of the title of the dispossessed person to the squatter. In registered land, however, the wording and operation of section 75 of the 1925 Act could not be reconciled with that view. Under section 75(1) the estate of the registered proprietor was not extinguished, but was deemed to be held in trust for the squatter. And section 75(2) assumed that the squatter acquired title under the Act to a "registered estate"—in other words, the estate of the registered proprietor against whom he had been adversely dispossessing. Both subsections suggested that the squatter succeeded to the title of the dispossessed proprietor.[219] As SEDLEY J said in *Kato*:[220]

In relation to a registered leasehold, section 75 lifts the extinguishing effect of the Limitation Acts and substitutes a trust of the leasehold title. The squatter becomes entitled, without regard to merits, to be placed in the same relationship with the freeholder as had previously been enjoyed by the leaseholder. The trust preserves not the squatter's common law title but a new statutory right to be substituted by registration for the leaseholder—carrying with it an obligation to indemnify the leaseholder against outgoings. This is to all appearances a statutory conveyance of the entire leasehold interest.

B Land Registration Act 2002[221]

The Land Registration Act 2002 changed fundamentally the position of the squatter in relation to registered land. In short, it disapplies the law of adverse possession described earlier in this chapter, and substitutes a new scheme which reflects the fact that the basis of title to registered land is registration, not possession.[222] In so doing, the Act also makes a fundamental change to the role of possession in the modern land law.

(1) Disapplication of the Limitation Periods

In relation to registered estates and rentcharges in land, section 96 of the Land Registration Act 2002 disapplies the limitation periods which apply to unregistered land:[223]

(1) No period of limitation under section 15[224] of the Limitation Act 1980 (time limits in relation to recovery of land) shall run against any person, other than a chargee,[225] in relation to an estate in land or rentcharge the title to which is registered.

(2) No period of limitation under section 16[226] of that Act (time limits in relation to redemption of land) shall run against any person in relation to such an estate in land or rentcharge.

---

[219] (1999) 115 LQR 187 at 189 (C. Harpum).   [220] [1998] 4 ALLER 948 at 959.

[221] LRA 2002, Sch. 6; LRR 2003, rr. 187–94; R & R, chap. 33; H & B, Part 6; Law Commission Report on Land Registration for the Twenty-First Century 2001 (Law Com No. 271), Part XIV, M & B pp. 252–9; Land Registry Practice Guide 4.   [222] Law Com No. 271, para. 1.13.

[223] Where the limitation period running under the old law had already expired before the 2002 Act came into force (13 October 2003) the position of the parties under LRA 1925 is preserved: i.e., the registered estate is held in trust (indefinitely) for the adverse possessor: LRA 2002, Sch. 12, para. 18. The adverse possessor's right remains an overriding interest until 13 October 2006: ibid., para. 7, but thereafter his right will be protected as an overriding interest only if he is in discoverable actual occupation: LRA 2002, Sch. 3, para. 2; p. 979, post.

[224] P. 117, ante.

[225] The exclusion of a chargee in sub-s. (1) avoids any change to the position of mortgagors in possession: the mortgagee's rights to possession or foreclosure as against the mortgagor in possession remain subject to the limitation provisions of LA 1980: H & B, para. 29.6.   [226] P. 772, post.

Since no limitation period runs against the paper owner in these circumstances, there can be no automatic extinction of his title.[227] In other words, adverse possession of registered land, for however long, does not of itself extinguish the paper owner's title, nor confer any title on the adverse possessor.

(2) Registration of Adverse Possessor as Proprietor

This does not, however, mean that an adverse possessor cannot acquire title to registered land. A new regime is laid down by the 2002 Act.

A person who has been in adverse possession of the estate for a period of ten years may apply to the Registrar to be registered as proprietor.[228] This still requires the possessor to prove his adverse possession; and "adverse possession" has the same meaning as under the Limitation Act 1980.[229] But the applicant must normally still be in possession on the date of his application in order to qualify.[230]

The Registrar must give formal notice of the adverse possessor's application to the registered proprietor.[231] Once the registered proprietor has been served with the notice, he may consent to the application, and the applicant will then be registered as the new proprietor.[232] However, he may oppose the application by serving a counter-notice.[233] In such a case, the applicant will be registered as proprietor only if one of three conditions is met:[234] (i) that the applicant has the benefit of an equity by estoppel by virtue of which he should be registered as proprietor;[235] (ii) that he is for some other reason entitled to be registered; or (iii) that the land in question is involved in a boundary dispute in relation to adjacent land belonging to the applicant, and the applicant is in adverse possession on the basis of a reasonable mistake as to title. These grounds are very limited, and only the third is based on the applicant's adverse possession. It will therefore be evident that the mere fact of adverse possession will rarely result in the squatter acquiring the registered estate after ten years' adverse possession if the paper owner does not consent to it.

However, the squatter may have a further opportunity to acquire the registered title. If he has made a first application to be registered, which has been opposed by the proprietor and

---

[227] LRA 2002, s. 96(3).

[228] LRA 2002, Sch. 6, para. 1(1). The estate need not have been registered throughout the ten-year period, as long as it is registered by the time the application is made: para. 1(4).

[229] ibid., para. 11(1). A possessor can include in the calculation periods of adverse possession by his predecessor in title, and any period within the ten-year period when he was himself dispossessed by an adverse possessor: para. 11(2). For the meaning of "adverse possession", see pp. 119 et seq, ante.

[230] He still qualifies, however, if he has been evicted by the paper owner, without a judgment for possession, within the last six months: ibid., para. 1(2). But he may not make application if he is defendant in proceedings for possession of the land: para. 1(3). These rules encourage the paper owner to use the legal process to recover his land, to bar the squatter's right to apply for registration.

[231] And to certain others, such as registered chargees, and the proprietor of the superior estate if the estate in question is leasehold: ibid., para. 2(2). In practice, however, the registered proprietor is given an earlier, informal notice because the Land Registry, before accepting that the applicant has an arguable case for registration, will normally require one of its own surveyors to inspect the land; both the registered proprietor and the applicant are notified of the inspection: Land Registry Practice Guide 4, para. 5.1.

[232] If he does not serve a counter-notice, infra, the applicant is entitled to be registered: LRA 2002, Sch. 6, para. 4. Any person on whom the notice of application is served may, however, dispute the applicant's right to make the application, and such a dispute may be referred to the Adjudicator: LRA 2002, s. 73(1); Land Registry Practice Guide 4, para. 6.   [233] LRA 2002, Sch. 6, para. 3.

[234] ibid., para. 5.   [235] [2004] Conv 123 (S. Nield).

rejected, he may make a further application if he is in adverse possession of the estate from the date of the first application for a period ending two years after the date of the rejection, and as long as he is not then a defendant in proceedings for possession of the land, and no judgment for possession has been given against him.[236] In such a case he is entitled to be entered in the register as the new proprietor of the estate, and the paper owner has no further right to object.[237]

The purpose of this provision is to allow the registered proprietor to take steps to recover possession of the land once the first application has been rejected. But if he takes no steps for a further period of two years, he loses his right to recover possession, and also loses his registered title.

(3) Effect of Registration of Adverse Possessor

Where the adverse possessor is registered under these provisions, he becomes the new registered proprietor of the estate, as the successor in title to the previous proprietor.[238] As with the position in relation to registered land under the Land Registration Act 1925,[239] therefore, and unlike the position in unregistered land,[240] he takes in effect a Parliamentary transfer of the title, rather than simply having a new, original title.

Registration of the adverse possessor as proprietor does not affect the priority of any interest affecting the estate,[241] and so he takes it subject to the estates and interests that bound the original paper owner. He is not, however, normally bound by any registered charge affecting the estate immediately before his registration.[242]

(4) Impact of Changes made by Land Registration Act 2002

The changes to the law of limitation of actions made by the Land Registration Act 2002, therefore, are of immense significance.

Most obviously, they significantly reduce the ability of a squatter to obtain title to the land. The mere passage of time does not give a person in adverse possession of the land the right to an estate. At most, it gives him the right to *apply* to be registered—an application which then necessarily alerts the registered proprietor to the claim which is being asserted. With limited exceptions[243] the registered proprietor can resist the application, and take steps to recover possession against the squatter. Only if he does not do so within a further period does the squatter acquire an indefeasible right to the transfer of the registered estate.

The corollary of this is that the registered proprietor's estate is more secure.[244] Under the Land Registration Act 1925,[245] to which the same essential rules of limitation of actions applied as in unregistered land, the register could fail to reflect the underlying rights to the

---

[236] LRA 2002, Sch. 6, para. 6.   [237] ibid., para. 7.

[238] His own former title based on possession is extinguished: ibid., para. 9(1).   [239] P. 145, ante.

[240] P. 136, ante. Where the estate is a lease, the effect of registration is an assignment of the lease, but as an assignment by operation of law, it will be an "excluded assignment" under LT(C)A 1995, p. 315, post, and so the former tenant will remain liable on the covenants: H & B, para. 31.3.   [241] LRA 2002, Sch. 6, para. 9(2).

[242] ibid., para. 6(3). This is because the chargee will have received notice of the squatter's application and could himself have taken steps to obtain possession: H & B, para. 31.6. There is an exception where he is registered on one of the three grounds in the paper owner's counter-notice, supra: para. 6(4).

[243] ibid., para. 5; supra.

[244] This as a further consequence in relation to the protection of the registered proprietor's human rights: infra.

[245] P. 143, ante.

estate, in the sense that the registered proprietor could (even without his own knowledge) be holding the registered estate on trust for the adverse possessor who had the right to be substituted as proprietor. Now, however, the registered proprietor is and remains the estate owner vis-à-vis an adverse possessor of the estate, both at law and in equity, unless and until the adverse possessor is registered. The register is a more complete mirror of the title to the estate.[246]

A further consequence of this change is that it encourages the owners of unregistered land to register their title. Since the new rules apply to all registered estates, whether or not they have been registered throughout the period of the squatter's adverse possession,[247] the effect of registration of an unregistered estate is now to defeat the potential title of a squatter, even if he is already in adverse possession. As we have already seen,[248] a principal aim of the Land Registration Act 2002 was to facilitate the completion of the register of title, in order to allow the introduction in due course of electronic conveyancing. The provisions on adverse possession are designed to further this aim.

At a more fundamental theoretical level, however, the effect of the new regime for adverse possession and limitation of actions is to change the very basis of title to land. We have already seen in chapter 5 that the introduction of registration of title, coupled with the State guarantee of the title, has shifted the basis of land ownership to the fact of registration. The Land Registration Act 1925 took this a long way forward, but still left unchanged the basic principle: that the underlying estate in the land, which is subject to registration, is based on possession, and therefore a registered estate could still be defeated by adverse possession. The Land Registration Act 2002, however, has taken this still further. Relativity of seisin, or possession, is no longer the test for title to land. The registered proprietor cannot lose his title without having the opportunity to take steps to recover possession; in that sense, registration is everything.

IV Adverse Possession and Human Rights

In recent years questions have been asked about the compatibility of the rules on adverse possession of land with the European Convention on Human Rights. This issue has come into sharp focus with the enactment of the Human Rights Act 1998.

A Limitation Act 1980 and Land Registration Act 1925

We have seen that, both in relation to unregistered land, and in relation to registered land where the period of adverse possession was completed under the Land Registration Act 1925,[249] the paper owner could lose his title in favour of an adverse possessor. There is no requirement for the adverse possessor to give him any formal notice of his possession, or that he is approaching the completion of the limitation period;[250] nor is there any provision for the paper owner to be compensated for his loss of title. These features of the law have

---

[246] Pp. 104 et seq, ante.   [247] LRA 2002, Sch. 6, para. 1(4).   [248] P. 110, ante.
[249] I.e., before 13 October 2003, when the Land Registration Act 2002 came into force: p. 145, ante.
[250] *Topplan Estates Ltd v Townley* [2005] 1 EGLR 89 at [85], per Jonathan PARKER LJ. It would be otherwise if the squatter had acted dishonestly: ibid.

prompted the question whether the statutory provisions constitute an interference with the paper owner's rights under Article 1 of the First Protocol to the European Convention, which provides:[251]

Every natural or legal person is entitled to the peaceful enjoyment of his possessions. No one shall be deprived of his possessions except in the public interest and subject to the conditions provided for by law and by the general principles of international law.

The preceding provisions shall not, however, in any way impair the right of a State to enforce such laws as it deems necessary to control the use of property in accordance with the general interest or to secure the payment of taxes or other contributions or penalties.

The most likely challenge is based on the second rule within this Article: the *deprivation of possessions*.

The first indications were that the courts would not hold that the statutory provisions relating to adverse possession were contrary to this rule.[252] However, this has given way to later decisions, both at first instance in the domestic courts, and by the European Court of Human Rights, that Article 1 of the First Protocol is engaged in a case in which the adverse possessor of registered land claims to have acquired title under the combined effect of the Limitation Act 1980 and the Land Registration Act 1925.

In *Beaulane Properties Ltd v Palmer*[253] Nicholas Strauss QC held that the effect of section 17 of the Limitation Act 1980[254] is to deprive the owner of the land of all his right to it, and therefore is a deprivation of his possessions.[255] And even if there might be an argument in relation to unregistered land that the effect of section 17 is merely to enlarge the adverse possessor's (relative) title rather than to deprive the paper owner of his property, this cannot apply in registered land, where the basis of title is registration, rather than simply relative possession.[256] The loss of registered title in favour of an adverse possessor under section 75 of the Land Registration Act 1925[257] was therefore contrary to Article 1:[258]

the expropriation of registered land without compensation in circumstances such as exist in this case does not advance any of the legitimate aims of the statutory provisions and is disproportionate. Nor is it justified . . . by the need to have a uniform rule applicable across the board. In essence, the registered owner loses his land because he has failed to take steps to get rid of a trespasser within a 12-year period. But . . . the acts of trespass may not be obvious, or may be trivial and entirely harmless. Further, the owner may not know the law, and may not realise that the failure to take steps to put an end to a situation which is doing him no harm may be prejudicing his position. There is little or no fault involved. On the other side, the trespasser will usually know that he is trespassing, will already have benefited from the acts of trespass, and will have done nothing whatsoever to deserve the windfall of being given the property in return for having illegitimately used it for a long time.

[251] For further discussion, see Rook, *Property Law and Human Rights*, esp. chap. 4 and section 8.5 (written before the development of the case law set out infra); Allen, *Property and the Human Rights Act 1998*.
[252] *Family Housing Association v Donnellan* [2002] 1 P & CR 34, following the approach taken (obiter) by CA in *J A Pye (Oxford) Ltd v Graham* [2001] Ch 804.
[253] [2006] Ch 79; [2005] Conv 345 (M. Dixon). An "impressive judgment": *Tower Hamlets LBC v Barrett* [2006] 1 P & CR 9 at [120], per NEUBERGER LJ. [254] P. 135, ante.
[255] At [136].
[256] At [139]–[140], relying on the difference between registered and unregistered land set out in Law Commission Consultative Document on Land Registration for the Twenty-First Century 1998 (Law Com No. 254), para. 10.3. [257] P. 145, ante.
[258] At [196].

Rather than simply declaring the domestic statutory provision incompatible with the Convention, however, the judge re-interpreted[259] it so as to make it compatible—and held that "adverse possession" should be construed as covering only the case where the possession is inconsistent with the use or intended use of the land by the registered proprietor. The effect of this, as the judge noted, is to re-introduce the test of "adverse possession" which was rejected by the House of Lords in *J A Pye (Oxford) Ltd v Graham*.[260]

The European Court of Human Rights has also now held, in a claim brought in relation to the *Pye* case itself, that the combined operation of the Limitation Act 1980 and the Land Registration Act 1925 was incompatible with Article 1 of the First Protocol.[261]

B Land Registration Act 2002

In *Beaulane Properties Ltd v Palmer*[262] the Judge expressed the view that the new regime for adverse possession under the Land Registration Act 2002 is not open to the same objections:

What the 2002 Act does is to place the burden where it lies, on the party seeking to override a registered title. This reflects the Law Commission's view that there is no need for an owner who has established his claim by registering it to make a further claim. It is for the trespasser to establish his claim, if he has good grounds to do so.

What happens under the new provisions is that notice is given to the registered owner of the application, so that, as the Law Commission says, at paras 10.45 and 10.47 of the consultative document,[263] the registered owner would have "ample opportunity ... to evict the squatter". The squatter would not normally be awarded a title to the land, unless the registered owner did not oppose the application. If he did, the application would succeed only in the limited classes of cases envisaged by the Law Commission and provided for in Schedule 6.

---

[259] HRA 1998, s. 3.

[260] P. 119, ante. The judge (at [214]) thought that this interpretation would be necessary only in relation to the acquisition of title by a trespasser between October 2000 (when HRA came into force) and October 2003 (when LRA 2002 superseded LRA 1925). For a contrary view, see [2005] Conv 345 at 350–1 (M. Dixon). The *Beaulane* interpretation of "adverse possession" is now applied by the Land Registry in relation to unregistered land and the transitional provisions for registered land: Additional Practice Note affecting Practice Guide 5.

[261] *J A Pye (Oxford) Ltd v United Kingdom* [2005] 3 EGLR 1; (2005) 155 NLJ 1912 (S. Murch), 1921 (E. Peters) [2006] 10 EG 150 (N. Thomas); [2006] Conv 179 (M. Dixon). The Court was divided four to three; in the view of the dissenting judges "the applicant companies have not had to bear an excessive or individual burden. They lost their land as a result of the foreseeable operation of legislation on limitation of actions which had recently been consolidated by the legislator, and the applicant companies could have stopped time running against them by taking minimal steps to look after their interests. We therefore take the view that the deprivation of possessions was compatible with Article 1 of Protocol No. 1, even in the absence of compensation."

HL in *J A Pye (Oxford) Ltd v Graham* did not consider the matter because the facts arose before HRA 1998 came into force, and they found no ambiguity in LA 1980: [2003] 1 AC 419 at [65]. There is no immediate substantive effect on domestic law of the decision of the European Court of Human Rights: Land Registry Addendum to Practice Guide 5 (January 2006). The claim in the European Court was by the party who lost title (Pye) against the UK Government, on the basis that it should be compensated by the Government, given that it was the Government's failure to ensure that UK legislation is in conformity with the ECHR. The European Court reserved the question of the quantification of compensation in this case.

[262] [2006] Ch 79, at [198]–[200].

[263] Law Commission Consultative Document on Land Registration for the Twenty-First Century 1998 (Law Com No. 254).

Thus, the objectionable feature of the pre-2003 law, which as Lord Hope said in the *Pye* case[264] is the inadvertent loss of land, sometimes without any fault, and sometimes in favour of the deliberate land-grabber, is avoided. Save in the exceptional cases, the title to the land can only be lost by ten years' adverse possession, followed by a failure to respond to notification of the application, in which case it is legitimate for the law to infer abandonment.

[264] [2003] 1 AC 419 at [73].

REAL PROPERTY. PROPERTY RIGHTS AND THE MEANING OF LAND

SUMMARY

In this book we are concerned with the law of *real property*. There are two separate aspects to this which should be clarified, in order that the detailed discussion in the following chapters can be properly understood. First, the concept of *property rights*, as opposed to purely personal rights. Second, within the law of property, how the law defines *real* property—in other words, the meaning attributed by the law to the word "land".

I Property Rights

The notion of "property", or property rights, is deceptively simple, and cannot be fully treated here.[1] We shall confine ourselves to drawing attention, by way of introduction, to matters which are relevant to an understanding of to the topics which follow in Part II.

---

[1] See, e.g., Lawson and Rudden, *The Law of Property;* Bright and Dewar, *Land Law Themes and Perspectives,* chaps. 1 (K. Gray and S. F. Gray), 18 (P. Birks); Tee, *Land Law Issues, Debates, Policy,* chap. 1 (M. Dixon); Harris, *Property and Justice;* Honoré, *Oxford Essays in Jurisprudence* (ed. Guest), pp. 107 et seq; Rudden, *Oxford Essays in Jurisprudence* (3rd series, eds. Eekelaar and Bell), pp. 239 et seq. For the protection of property rights under the ECHR, see generally Rook, *Property Law and Human Rights;* Allen, *Property and the Human Rights Act 1998;* Tee, chap. 7 (K. Gray).

A Property Rights and Personal Rights

Property rights are to be contrasted with personal rights. This contrast, in English law, can be expressed in the same essential terms as were developed in Roman law:[2] property rights are rights *in rem*; personal rights are rights *in personam*. To say that one has a property right in relation to land is to say that one has a right over, or in respect of, the land itself. A personal right, however, is a right against a person, generated by the act of the person or imposed on him by the law, but in every case the right is against—and so the correlative duty is owed by—the particular individual concerned. Obligations arising from contract, for example, are personal: the reason that the defendant is bound to the claimant is because he has (expressly or impliedly) undertaken the obligation.

B Third Parties and Property Rights

The significance of the distinction between personal rights and property rights, for our purposes, lies in the case where third parties become involved. As Lord WILBERFORCE said:[3]

Before a right or an interest can be admitted into the category of property, or of a right affecting property, it must be definable, identifiable by third parties, capable in its nature of assumption by third parties, and have some degree of permanence or stability.

This emphasises the link between property rights and third parties. And the focus here is on the burden of rights affecting property. A contract creates a personal relationship in law between the contracting parties; and although English law allows the *benefit* of a contractual right to be transferred by assignment,[4] a third party cannot generally be *bound* by an obligation in a contract without himself accepting it—and in that case he is bound by his own act rather than simply as successor to the original obligor under the contract.[5] By contrast, proprietary rights are inherently capable of both benefiting and binding parties who were not involved in their original creation. The fundamental point, therefore, is that—to take the example of land law—a property right is either the right to the land itself (in some sense, the "ownership" of the land); or a right owned by a third party in or over that land, which means that it is a right which is capable of binding the owner for the time being of the land: his acquisition of the land brings with it the burdens which are in law recognised as attaching to the land.

As we have already said, this is only an introduction—a starting-point for a further analysis of the notion of property rights as recognised by English law. In some respects the history of the land law, and in particular the fact that the common law does recognise absolute property rights in land[6] but that equity developed the protection of property rights through the concept of the trust,[7] immediately complicates the simplicity of the notion of rights in land as rights *in rem*. Not every successor in title to the land will necessarily be bound by every right attached to the land.[8] And it should not be assumed that a person cannot create

---

[2] Nicholas, *Introduction to Roman Law*, pp. 99–103; Bright and Dewar, supra, p. 472 (P. Birks).

[3] *National Provincial Bank Ltd v Ainsworth* [1965] AC 1175 at 1247–8; p. 789, post.

[4] Anson, chap. 11. Even so, this involves a recognition of the benefit of a contractual right as having proprietary characteristics: it is a chose in action: ibid., p. 470; LPA 1925, s. 136(1). [5] Ibid., pp. 484–6.

[6] Unlike Roman law and modern civil law systems; p. 34, ante. [7] Chap. 3, ante.

[8] Pp. 56–8, ante, noting that an equitable estate can be characterised as a right *in personam*, since the category of persons who are bound by it are limited by the doctrine of the bona fide purchaser for value without notice. For the use of registration to supersede the doctrine of the bona fide purchaser in the modern law, see chap. 5, ante.

an interest in the land which has inherent limits on its alienability.[9] But the underlying principle still holds. The principal concern of the law of property—and in particular land law—is with what is meant by saying that a person is the "owner" of the property; what other rights of third parties are recognised by the law as being capable of existing in or over that property; and in what circumstances a successor to the owner is bound to give effect to those third-party rights.

We shall consider in more detail in Part III the mechanisms for the creation and transfer of property rights, and the extent to which, in the modern law, a third-party right is enforceable against a successor to the owner. Before that, in Part II, we must identify, first, those interests in the land itself that can be characterised, either at common law or in equity, as rights of "ownership"; and then those rights which the law recognises as property rights in or over the land, inherently capable of binding the owner of the land for the time being.

First, however, we must complete this introductory section by explaining what in law constitutes "land".

II The Meaning of Land

A Distinction between Corporeal and Incorporeal Hereditaments

Law is at one with the layman in agreeing that "land" includes the surface of the earth, together with all the sub-jacent and super-jacent things of a physical nature such as buildings, trees and minerals,[10] but it also gives the word a far wider meaning, and one which would not occur to those unversed in legal terminology. Using the word "hereditament" to signify a right that is heritable, that is, capable of passing by way of descent to heirs, our legal ancestors reached the remarkable[11] conclusion that hereditaments are either corporeal or incorporeal. As Blackstone said:

Hereditaments, then, to use the largest expression, are of two kinds, corporeal and incorporeal. Corporeal consist of such as affect the senses; such as may be seen and handled by the body; incorporeal are not the object of sensation, can neither be seen nor handled, are creatures of the mind and exist only in contemplation. Corporeal hereditaments consist of substantial and permanent objects.[12]

What this comes to is that the subject-matter of estate ownership may consist either of corporeities or of incorporeities. There is nothing remarkable in this, for it is obvious that an incorporeity such as a right of way may, equally with a house or a piece of land, be held in fee simple or for life. What is remarkable, however, is a terminology which declares that an interest in a corporeity, that is a physical thing capable of carrying seisin, is itself a corporeal *interest*, but that an interest in an incorporeity is an incorporeal *interest*. This nomenclature will not bear a moment's examination, for no proprietary interest can be other than a mere *right* of ownership, and no matter what the nature of its subject matter

---

[9] But a total restraint on alienation is inconsistent with the conception of ownership: p. 547, post; *Re Brown* [1954] Ch 39, M & B p. 9.

[10] See p. 174, post. As to waste products dumped on land, see *Rogers (Inspector of Taxes) v Longsdon* [1967] Ch 93.   [11] Co Litt 6a; *Lloyd v Jones* (1848) 6 CB 81 at 90.

[12] Blackstone, *Commentaries*, vol. ii. p. 17.

may be, it must always be incorporeal: "All property, of whatever kind, is an *incorporeal* right to the *corporeal* use and profit of some *corporeal* thing."[13] It is difficult to answer the following criticism of Austin:

With us *all* rights and obligations are not *incorporeal things*; but certain rights are styled *incorporeal hereditaments*, and are opposed by that name to *hereditaments corporeal*. That is to say, *rights* of a certain species . . . are absurdly opposed to the *things* (strictly so called) which are the *subjects* or *matter* of rights of another species. The word *hereditaments* is evidently taken in two senses in the two phrases which stand to denote the species of hereditaments. A corporeal hereditament is the thing itself which is the subject of the right; an incorporeal hereditament is not the subject of the right, but the right itself.[14]

The continued use to the present day of this unscientific terminology need not, however, disturb us. The two facts to bear in mind are: first, that whether an interest, such as a fee simple estate, exists in a corporeity or an incorporeity, it is an interest in *land*; secondly, that the number of incorporeities recognised by English law is considerable. Blackstone described no fewer than ten *incorporeal hereditaments* some of which are no longer of practical importance.[15] The most important now are easements,[16] profits[17] and rentcharges.[18]

The following is the definition of *land* for the purposes of the Law of Property Act 1925:

"Land" includes land of any tenure, and mines and minerals, whether or not held apart from the surface, buildings or parts of buildings (whether the division is horizontal, vertical or made in any other way) and other corporeal hereditaments; also a manor, an advowson, and a rent and other incorporeal hereditaments, and an easement, right, privilege, or benefit in, over, or derived from land . . .[19]

There is one class of corporeal things, namely *fixtures*, which are regarded as "land" and which are sufficiently important to merit a somewhat extensive treatment.

---

[13] (1857) 1 Jurid Soc, p. 542 (S. M. Leake).

[14] Austin, *Jurisprudence* (5th edn) vol. i. p. 362; but see Sweet's answer in Challis, *Law of Real Property*, pp. 48–58. LPA 1925, s. 1(2), p. 94, ante, perpetuates the confusion in describing a right to, for instance, an easement as an interest in land, notwithstanding that in s. 205(1)(ix) it includes an easement in the definition of "land". The truth is that an incorporeity, such as an easement, is neither an estate nor an interest, but something in which an estate or an interest can exist.

[15] Blackstone, *Commentaries*, vol. ii. c. iii. The list is: advowsons, tithes, commons, ways, offices, dignities, franchises, corodies (a right to receive victuals for one's maintenance), annuities and rents. "Whether the benefit of a restrictive covenant can be described as an incorporeal hereditament is a very doubtful question": *Earl of Leicester v Wells-next-the-Sea UDC* [1973] Ch 110 at 119, per PLOWMAN J. On franchises, see *Sevenoaks DC v Pattullo & Vinson Ltd* [1984] Ch 211 (right of market); *R (Corporation of London) v Secretary of State for the Environment, Food and Rural Affairs* [2005] 1 WLR 1286 (Smithfield and Billingsgate common law markets).

[16] P. 586, post. "An easement is that familiar creature of English land law: an estate or interest carved out of a larger estate or interest, but nevertheless constituting a hereditament in its own right. It is a burden on the servient tenement, but also 'land' vested in the proprietor of the dominant tenement": *Willies-Williams v National Trust for Places of Historic Interest or Natural Beauty* (1993) 65 P & CR 359 at 361, per HOFFMANN LJ.   [17] P. 640, post.

[18] Chap. 20, post.

[19] Section 205(1)(ix), as amended by TLATA 1996, s. 25(2), Sch. 4; cf the definitions in SLA 1925, s. 117(1)(ix), as amended by TLATA 1996, s. 25(2), Sch. 4; TA 1925, s. 68(6), as amended by TLATA 1996, s. 25(2), Sch. 4; LRA 1925, s. 3(viii), as amended by TLATA 1996, s. 25(2), Sch. 4; LCA 1972, s. 17(1). See also Interpretation Act 1978, s. 5, Sch. 1; *Starke v IRC* [1995] 1 WLR 1439. As to whether land includes an interest under a trust for sale, see pp. 429–30, 439, post.

B Fixtures

(1) Distinction Between Land and Chattels

The primary meaning from a historical point of view of "fixtures" is chattels which are so affixed to land or to a building on land as to become in fact part of it.[20] Such chattels lose the character of chattels and pass with the ownership of the land, for the maxim of the law is, *quicquid plantatur solo, solo cedit*: whatever is affixed to the soil accedes to the soil.

This question whether a chattel has been so affixed to land as to become part of it is sometimes difficult to answer. It is a question of law for the judge,[21] but the decision in one case is no sure guide in another, for everything turns upon the circumstances and mainly, though not decisively, upon two particular circumstances, namely, the *degree of annexation* and the *object of annexation*.[22] We will take these considerations separately.

(a) Degree of annexation

The general rule is that a chattel is not deemed to be a fixture unless it is actually fastened to or connected with the land or building. Mere juxtaposition or the laying of an article, however heavy, upon the land does not prima facie make it a fixture, even though it subsequently sinks into the ground. If a superstructure can be removed without losing its identity, it will not in general be regarded as a fixture. Examples are a Dutch barn, consisting of a roof resting upon wooden uprights, the uprights being made to lie upon brick columns let into the ground;[23] or a printing machine weighing several tons, standing on the floor and secured by its own weight;[24] or a white marble statue of a Greek athlete weighing half a ton and standing on a plinth.[25] The case is the same if the posts that support the roof of a corrugated iron building are not embedded in the concrete floor, but are held in position by iron strips fixed into the floor. The concrete foundation, which is of course a fixture, is regarded as a separate unit from the superstructure.[26] Again, a printing machine that stands by its own weight upon the floor is not a fixture, even though the driving apparatus is attached to the building at certain points.[27] On the other hand, a chattel that is attached to

---

[20] Leake, *Uses and Profits of Land*, p. 103. In *Elitestone Ltd v Morris* [1997] 1 WLR 687, M & B p. 98, HL preferred a tripartite classification into chattels, fixtures and objects which are part and parcel of the land; [1998] Conv 418 (H. Conway).   [21] *Reynolds v Ashby & Son* [1904] AC 466.

[22] *Holland v Hodgson* (1872) LR 7 CP 328 at 334, per BLACKBURN J. See *Melluish v BMI (No 3) Ltd* [1996] AC 545 (contractual term that object shall remain a chattel not decisive: "The concept of a fixture which remains personal or removable property is a contradiction in terms and an impossibility in law"; [1995] Ch 90 at 115 per DILLON LJ in CA). For a useful summary of the principles, see *Wessex Reserve Forces and Cadets Association v White* [2005] 3 EGLR 127 at [21]–[23], per Michael Harvey QC.

[23] *Elwes v Maw* (1802) 3 East 38 at 55; *Wiltshear v Cottrell* (1853) 1 E & B 674; *Deen v Andrews* (1986) 52 P & CR 17; *Hynes v Vaughan* (1985) 50 P & CR 444 (chrysanthemum growing frame and sprinkler system held not to be fixtures); *Kennedy v Secretary of State for Wales* [1996] EGCS 17 (three massive ormulu bronze chandeliers and carillon turret clock at Neo-Gothic Grade II listed Leighton Hall, Welshpool, held to be fixtures).

[24] *Hulme v Brigham* [1943] KB 152.

[25] *Berkley v Poulett* [1977] 1 EGLR 86; cf *Hamp v Bygrave* [1983] 1 EGLR 174 (stone and lead garden ornaments held to be fixtures); *Berkley v Poulett*, supra, was not cited; [1983] NZLJ 256 (H. W. Wilkinson).

[26] *Webb v Bevis Ltd* [1940] 1 All ER 247; cf *Jordan v May* [1947] KB 427 (electric lighting engine and dynamo bolted to a concrete bed. These were held to be fixtures, but not the batteries). The degree of affixation is not necessarily the same in every type of case; see, e.g., *London County Council v Wilkins* [1955] 2 QB 653; affd. [1957] AC 362 (whether a wooden sectional hut is exempt from rateability).

[27] *Hulme v Brigham* [1943] KB 152.

land, however slightly, is prima facie to be deemed a fixture. Thus, a verandah connected with a house is a fixture,[28] as also are doors, windows, chimney-pieces, ovens and other similar things.

Nevertheless the extent of annexation is not a decisive test. As BLACKBURN J said:[29]

Perhaps the true rule is, that articles not otherwise attached to the land than by their own weight are not to be considered as part of the land, unless the circumstances are such as to shew that they were intended to be part of the land, the onus of showing that they were so intended lying on those who assert that they have ceased to be chattels; and that, on the contrary, an article which is affixed to the land even slightly is to be considered as part of the land, unless the circumstances are such as to shew that it was intended all along to continue a chattel, the onus lying on those who contend that it is a chattel.

(b) Object of annexation

The test here is to ascertain whether the chattel has been fixed for its more convenient use as a chattel, or for the more convenient use of the land or building.[30] BLACKBURN J gave the following example:

Blocks of stone placed one on the top of another without any mortar or cement for the purpose of forming a dry stone wall would become part of the land, though the same stones, if deposited in a builder's yard and for convenience sake stacked on the top of each other in the form of a wall, would remain chattels.[31]

Again, a comparatively durable method of affixation will not render a chattel a fixture, if the method of annexation is necessary to its proper enjoyment as a chattel. Thus in the case of *Leigh v Taylor*[32] a tenant for life, the owner of some valuable tapestry, laid strips of wood over the drawing-room paper and fixed them to the walls with two-inch nails. Canvas was stretched over these strips, and the tapestry was fastened by tacks to the strips. It was held that the tapestry had not become a fixture. VAUGHAN WILLIAMS LJ said:[33]

In my judgment it is obvious that everything which was done here can be accounted for as being absolutely necessary for the enjoyment of the tapestry, and when one arrives at that conclusion there is an end of the case.

The principle of this decision was adopted where a lessee had erected some oak and pine panelling and a chimney-piece;[34] and where a vendor had screwed pictures while still in their frames into the recesses in the panelling of a dining-room.[35]

On the other hand, chattels may be annexed to or placed on land in circumstances which show an obvious intention to benefit the use of the land, and if this is so they become fixtures. Examples are seats secured to the floor of a cinema hall,[36] and such objects as

---

[28] *Buckland v Butterfield* (1820) 2 Brod & Bing 54.
[29] *Holland v Hodgson* (1872) LR 7 CP 328 at 335; *Bradshaw v Davey* [1952] 1 All ER 350 (yacht mooring in the Hamble River held intended to be a chattel); *Chelsea Yacht and Boat Co Ltd v Pope* [2000] 1 WLR 1941 (houseboat moored by ropes and connected to services which could be untied and disconnected without undue effort not annexed to the land; leave to appeal to HL refused: [2000] 1 WLR 2469).
[30] *Wake v Hall* (1883) 8 App Cas 195 at 204.   [31] *Holland v Hodgson*, supra, at 335.
[32] [1902] AC 157.   [33] In CA sub nom. *Re De Falbe* [1901] 1 Ch 523 at 537.
[34] *Spyer v Phillipson* [1931] 2 Ch 183.   [35] *Berkley v Poulett* [1977] 1 EGLR 86.
[36] *Vaudeville Electric Cinema Ltd v Muriset* [1923] 2 Ch 74. Cf *Lyon & Co v London City and Midland Bank* [1903] 2 KB 135.

statues, stone seats and ornamental vases, held in position merely by their own weight, which are part of the architectural design of a house and its grounds.[37]

Similarly, a wooden bungalow resting on its own weight on concrete pillars has been held to be part of the land, whereas a greenhouse resting on its own weight on concrete dollies has been held not to be a fixture.[38] As Lord LLOYD OF BERWICK said:[39] "It is obvious that a greenhouse which can be moved from site to site is a long way removed from a two bedroom bungalow which cannot be removed at all without being demolished."

In *Botham v TSB Bank plc*,[40] the Court of Appeal examined household appliances and held that baths, lavatories and bathroom fittings, as well as fitted kitchen units and sinks will usually be fixtures; but not so carpets, curtains, most light fittings and gas fires whose only connection with the building is by a pipe to the gas supply; and white goods, such as refrigerators, dishwashers and washing machines, where the degree of annexation is slight and no more that needed, to allow normal use. In emphasising that the purpose of annexation is the key issue, ROCH LJ said:

If the item viewed objectively, is intended to be permanent and to afford a lasting improvement to the building, the thing will have become a fixture. If the attachment is temporary and is no more than is necessary for the item to be used and enjoyed, then it will remain a chattel.

(2) Right to Remove Fixtures

Even if a chattel is affixed to the land so as to become part of the land, the person who affixed it or his successors in title may have a right to remove it. The question arises as between the following parties:[41]

(a) Landlord and tenant

In the course of time, the rule that an article becomes part of the land to which it has been affixed has been relaxed in favour of the tenant for years, and he is now allowed to remove three particular classes of articles notwithstanding that they are fixtures in the strict sense of the term:

(1) TRADE FIXTURES

First, it has long been the rule that during the term the tenant may remove fixtures that have been attached to the land for the purpose of carrying on his particular trade, since it is in the public interest that industry should be encouraged. Thus in *Poole's Case*[42] in 1703 it was held by Lord HOLT

that during the term the soap-boiler might well remove the vats he set up in relation to trade, and that he might do it by the common law (and not by virtue of any special custom), in favour of trade and to

---

[37] *D'Eyncourt v Gregory* (1866) LR 3 Eq 382; *Monti v Barnes* [1901] 1 KB 205; cf *Berkley v Poulett*, n. 35, ante, where the statue was not an integral part of the design.

[38] *H E Dibble Ltd v Moore* [1970] 2 QB 181; *Hynes v Vaughan* (1985) 50 P & CR 444, n. 23, ante.

[39] *Elitestone Ltd v Morris* [1997] 1 WLR 687 at 693; (1997) 147 NLJ 1031 (H. W. Wilkinson); [1997] CLJ 498 (S. Bridge).

[40] (1996) 73 P & CR D1; *Chelsea Yacht and Boat Co Ltd v Pope* [2000] 1 WLR 1941 (mooring of houseboat was not with the object of providing a permanent home, but to prevent it from being carried by the tide or the weather and to provide services to it).

[41] See too *Simmons v Midford* [1969] 2 Ch 415 (plaintiff's drainpipe under roadway held to be chattel with which neighbour claiming an easement of drainage could not interfere); cf *Montague v Long* (1972) 24 P & CR 240.

[42] (1703) 1 Salk 368.

encourage industry: but after the term they become a gift in law to him in reversion, and are not removable.

Engines for working collieries,[43] salt pans,[44] coppers and pipes erected by a brewing tenant,[45] the fittings of a public house,[46] petrol pumps installed at a wayside garage[47] and floor coverings and light fittings[48] have been held to come within the description of trade fixtures.

(2) ORNAMENTAL AND DOMESTIC FIXTURES

Secondly, it is now well established that during the term a tenant may remove such chattels as he has affixed to a house for the sake either of ornament or of convenience, but this relaxation of the strict rule is not supported by such strong reasons as apply in the case of trade fixtures and it will not be extended. Examples of objects which have been held removable on this ground are ornamental chimney-pieces, wainscot fixed to the wall by screws, fixed water-tubs, stoves and grates, ranges and ovens.[49]

But any fixture which is in the nature of a permanent improvement and which cannot be removed without substantial damage to the house, such as a conservatory connected by a door with one of the living rooms, does not come within the exception of an ornamental fixture.[50]

Trade, ornamental and domestic fixtures must be removed before the end of the tenancy, otherwise they become a gift in law to the reversioner,[51] but a further period of grace is allowed when the tenant continues in possession after the term under a reasonable supposition of consent on the part of the landlord.[52] Where the tenant surrenders his tenancy to his landlord, he loses the right to remove these fixtures if the surrender is express, in the absence of agreement to the contrary; but he does not lose the right if the surrender is implied by operation of law, as where the lease has expired by effluxion of time and is replaced by a new lease between the same parties.[53] If tenant's fixtures are removed, the premises must be made good to the extent of being left in a reasonable condition.[54]

(3) AGRICULTURAL FIXTURES

The third exception relates to agricultural fixtures. Formerly, a farmer was in an unfavourable position with regard to chattels that he had fixed to his holding, for it was held in *Elwes v Maw*[55] in 1802 that, although the sole purpose of their affixation was to further and improve his agricultural operations, they could not be regarded as trade fixtures. In that case, the tenant farmer had built at his own cost a beast-house, a carpenter's shed, a fuel-house, a wagon-house and a fold-yard, each of which he removed before the end of the lease,

---

[43] *Lawton v Lawton* (1743) 3 Atk 13. Cf *Herbert v British Railways Board* (2000) 4 L & T Rev D13 (rails and sleepers removed by tenant railway board from disused railway line held to be landlord's fixtures, not tenant's).

[44] *Mansfield v Blackburne* (1840) 6 Bing NC 426.   [45] *Lawton v Lawton,* supra.

[46] *Elliott v Bishop* (1854) 10 Exch 496.   [47] *Smith v City Petroleum Co Ltd* [1940] 1 All ER 260.

[48] *Young v Dalgety plc* [1987] 1 EGLR 116.

[49] See Hill and Redman, *Landlord and Tenant*, paras. A1681–A1687.

[50] *Buckland v Butterfield* (1820) 2 Brod & Bing 54.   [51] *Poole's Case* (1703) 1 Salk 368.

[52] *Ex parte Brook* (1878) 10 Ch D 100 at 109; *Leschallas v Woolf* [1908] 1 Ch 641.

[53] *New Zealand Government Property Corpn v HM & S Ltd* [1982] QB 1145; [1987] Conv 253 (G. Kodilinye).

[54] *Mancetter Developments Ltd v Garmanson Ltd* [1986] QB 1212 (holes left behind in landlord's brickwork).

[55] (1802) 3 East 38; *Smith's Leading Cases*, vol. ii. p. 193.

leaving the premises in the same state as when he first became tenant. He was held liable to pay damages to the landlord. The only mitigation at common law of this rigour came in 1901, when it was decided that, although buildings put up by a farmer were not trade fixtures, glasshouses built by a market-gardener did come within this description and could be removed before the end of the tenancy.[56]

This particular matter has, however, been put upon a more equitable footing by a succession of statutes and the position now is as follows:

In the case of a tenancy within the Agricultural Holdings Act 1986,[57] which cannot normally begin on or after 1 September 1995, any fixture affixed to the agricultural holding by a tenant and any building erected by him on the holding, for which he is not otherwise entitled to compensation, becomes his property and is removable by him during the tenancy or within two months after its termination. After the expiration of this period the property in fixtures is no longer vested in him.[58] Within at least a month before the termination of the tenancy written notice of removal must be given to the landlord, who thereupon acquires an option to purchase the fixture.[59] There is no right of removal until the tenant has paid all rent and satisfied his other obligations under the tenancy.

The provisions which apply to a farm business tenancy beginning on or after 1 September 1995 under the Agricultural Tenancies Act 1995[60] are broadly similar, although somewhat more favourable to the tenant. Any fixture affixed by the tenant to the holding and any building erected by him on the holding may be removed by the tenant during the tenancy or so long as he remains in possession as tenant after its termination.[61] This is subject to exceptions, for example where the tenant was under an obligation to affix the fixture or erect the building, or where he has obtained compensation.[62] Unlike the position under the Agricultural Holdings Act 1986, the right to remove fixtures does not depend on compliance with the terms of the tenancy, nor is the tenant required to give notice of intention to remove, nor does the landlord acquire any option to purchase the fixture. The right to remove fixtures under section 8 of the 1995 Act may not be excluded, nor may the farm business tenant exercise any right to remove fixtures save that conferred by the section.[63]

The result of these developments is that if a landlord disputes the right of his tenant to remove a certain chattel from the premises, there are two separate questions to be answered. First, has the chattel become a fixture by reason of its affixation to the land? If not, no issue arises. If, however, the answer is in the affirmative, the further question arises whether it is a landlord's or a tenant's fixture, and this of course depends upon whether the chattel falls within one of the three categories already described.[64]

(b) Mortgagor and mortgagee

Fixtures pass with the land to the mortgagee even though not mentioned in the deed,[65] as also do those which are added later by the mortgagor himself while in possession. Moreover, a mortgagor in possession is not entitled to remove "tenant's" fixtures, whether they have

---

[56] *Mears v Callender* [1901] 2 Ch 388.   [57] P. 386, post.

[58] Agricultural Holdings Act 1986, s. 10(1), (2).

[59] Ibid., s. 10(3)(b). Under s. 10(5) the tenant must make good any damage done when removing the fixture. Likewise under s. 8(3), (4) of the Agricultural Tenancies Act 1995, infra.   [60] P. 388, post.

[61] Agricultural Tenancies Act 1995, s. 8(1).   [62] Ibid., s. 8(2).   [63] Ibid., s. 8(6), (7).

[64] *Bain v Brand* (1876) 1 App Cas 762 at 767, per Lord CAIRNS.

[65] *Vaudeville Electric Cinema Ltd v Muriset* [1923] 2 Ch 74; LPA 1925, ss. 62(1), 205(1)(ii).

been annexed to the land before or after the mortgage transaction.[66] These rules apply whether the mortgage is legal or equitable, and whether it affects freehold or leasehold premises. Where, however, fixtures have been annexed to land by a *third party* under an agreement between him and the mortgagor which permits him to remove them in certain circumstances, his right of removal cannot in general be defeated by the mortgagee. The mortgagee, by allowing the mortgagor to remain in possession, implicitly authorises him to make agreements usual and proper in his particular trade.[67]

(c) Vendor and purchaser

A conveyance of land, in the absence of express reservation, passes fixtures, but not chattels[68] to the purchaser without special mention,[69] and they cannot be removed by a vendor who remains in possession between the contract of sale and the completion of the transaction, even though they consist of articles which, as between landlord and tenant, would be "tenant's fixtures".[70] The fixtures are deemed to have been paid for by the price fixed for the land, and if the vendor desires to remove them or to receive an additional sum in respect of them a clause to that effect must be inserted in the contract.[71]

(d) Tenant for life and reversioner or remainderman

The general rule obtains that chattels annexed by a tenant for life so as to become part of the land belong to the owner of the fee simple. Nevertheless the personal representatives of a deceased tenant for life are entitled to remove "such fixtures as are removable by a tenant for years", that is, objects affixed for purposes of trade, ornamentation or domestic use.[72]

(e) Executor of fee simple owner and devisee

If A, the tenant in fee simple of Blackacre, devises Blackacre to B, it might be argued that A's executors are entitled to remove, at any rate, "tenant's fixtures". The rule, however, is well established that all fixtures, no matter of what description, pass with the land to the devisee.[73]

---

[66] *Longbottom v Berry* (1869) LR 5 QB 123.   [67] *Gough v Wood & Co* [1894] 1 QB 713.

[68] *Moffatt v Kazana* [1969] 2 QB 152; *H E Dibble Ltd v Moore* [1970] 2 QB 181; *Deen v Andrews* (1986) 52 P & CR 17. See also *Berkley v Poulett* [1977] 1 EGLR 86 (sub-purchaser).

[69] LPA 1925, s. 62(1). The section is set out, p. 603, post.

[70] *Gibson v Hammersmith & City Rly Co* (1863) 32 LJ Ch 337; *Phillips v Lamdin* [1949] 2 KB 33.

[71] On hire-purchase agreements and fixtures, see (1963) 27 Conv (NS) 30 (A. G. Guest and J. Lever); [1990] Conv 275 (G. McCormack).

[72] *Lawton v Lawton* (1743) 3 Atk 13. There is some question whether the power of removal by the personal representative is not more restricted than in the case of a tenant for years.

[73] *Re Whaley* [1908] 1 Ch 615; *Re Lord Chesterfield's Settled Estates* [1911] 1 Ch 237 (ornamental wood carvings by Grinling Gibbons).

PART II

ESTATES AND INTERESTS IN LAND

After this brief introductory survey, the next task is to describe the estates and interests that may subsist in land in the modern law. The general arrangement of this Part is to consider, first, the estates that may subsist at common law—whether freehold (the fee simple, or commonhold) or leasehold; second, those estates and interests in the land that may subsist in equity under a settlement or a trust of land; and third, those interests that third parties may hold, whether at law or in equity, in or over an estate in land—easements, profits à prendre, covenants, rentcharges, mortgages and equities (including proprietary estoppel). A final chapter in this Part, devoted to licences, will assist in drawing the line between property rights—rights in or over the land itself—and personal rights, which we have already seen briefly in chapter 7.

A. Freehold Estates

SUMMARY

8

THE ESTATE IN FEE SIMPLE
ABSOLUTE IN POSSESSION

SUMMARY

I Definition

A *Fee Simple*

The first essential is to investigate the precise meaning of the statutory expression *fee simple absolute in possession* which, as we have seen, is the only *freehold* interest capable of existing as a legal estate.[1] The word *fee* had by Littleton's day come to denote that the estate was inheritable, that is to say, that it would endure until the person entitled to it *for the time being*—whether the original donee or some subsequent alienee—died intestate and left no heir.[2] The word *simple* showed that the fee was one which was capable of passing to the heirs *general* and was not restricted to passing to a particular class of heirs.[3] This last fact therefore distinguishes a fee simple from another kind of fee which used to be called a fee tail and is now called an entailed interest, for this is a freehold that passes, on the intestacy of its owner, only to the particular class of lineal descendants specified in the instrument of creation.[4] Thus if a tenant in fee simple died intestate before 1926, his estate passed to his nearest heir, who according to the circumstances might be a descendant or an ascendant, a lineal or a collateral relative.

---

[1] LPA 1925, s.1(1)(a); p. 94, ante. For the registration of the freehold estate in land as *commonhold*, see chap. 9, post.   [2] Pollock and Maitland, *History of English Law*, vol. ii, p. 14.
[3] Co Litt 1a, b, 18a, Blackstone, vol. ii. p. 105.   [4] Pp. 485–8, post.

An entailed interest, on the other hand, was capable of passing only to lineal descendants, and these might, according to the terms of the instrument of gift, be either lineal descendants in general or a restricted class of descendants, such as male heirs or the issue of the tenant by a specified wife. The characteristic of general inheritability is still the attribute of a fee simple, but the significance of this is now modified by the abolition of the doctrine of heirship on intestacy except in the case of the entailed interest. The land itself no longer passes to the nearest heir but upon the death of the owner intestate is held by the administrators on trust, for distribution among the nearest relatives according to a scheme introduced by the Administration of Estates Act 1925, as amended by subsequent legislation. The relatives specified by the Act, however, comprise descendants and ascendants, both lineal and collateral, and it is therefore still true to say that a fee simple is an estate which is the subject of general inheritability.[5]

B Absolute

It is not every fee simple that is a legal estate, for the Law of Property Act 1925 confines that attribute to a fee simple absolute in possession. Postponing for the moment the consideration of the last two words, we must inquire what is meant by the word "absolute". This is not defined in the Act, but it clearly excludes an estate that is defeasible either by the breach of a condition or by the possibility that it may pass to some new owner upon the happening of a specified event. Preston explained the purport of *absolute* in the following words:[6]

The epithet *absolute* is used to distinguish an estate extended to any given time, without any condition to defeat, or collateral limitation to determine the estate in the mean time, from an estate subject to a condition or collateral limitation. The term absolute is of the same signification with the word pure, or *simple*, a word which expresses that the estate is not determinable by any event besides the event marked by the clause of limitation.

Thus a fee simple absolute is distinguished from a *determinable* fee simple, that is, one which according to the express terms of its limitation may determine by some event before the completion of the full period for which it may possibly continue.[7]

If, for instance, premises are limited in fee simple to an incorporated golf club "so long as the premises are used for the purposes of the Club", the interest is a fee simple because it may possibly continue for ever, but it is not a fee simple absolute since it will cease and will return to the grantor or his successors if at some time in the future the premises are used for other purposes.

Again, the limitation of a fee simple may be accompanied by an executory limitation over which provides that if a certain event happens the estate shall pass from the grantee to another person. As, for instance, where there is a grant of Whiteacre,

to A in fee simple, but if he becomes entitled to Blackacre, then to B in fee simple.

Here the fee simple given to A is not absolute, since it is liable to be divested from him on the occurrence of the specified event. There is one exception to this rule, for the Law of Property Act 1925 provides that a fee simple which is liable to be divested under the provisions of the

---

[5] For detail of the rules of intestate succession before 1926, see the 16th edn of this book, pp. 947–50; and for the modern rules of distribution, see ibid., pp. 950 et seq.   [6] *Preston on Estates*, vol. i. pp. 125–6.
[7] See p. 567, post.

Lands Clauses Acts or any similar statute is "for the purposes of the Act" a fee simple *absolute*.[8] The effect of this provision is that the interest is a legal estate within section 1(1) of the Law of Property Act 1925, and not an equitable interest giving rise to a strict settlement under the Settled Land Act before 1997.[9] The conditions attached to the fee simple are not affected. Statutes of this type, which enable land to be acquired for certain public purposes, generally provide expressly that if the purpose fails or is not carried out the land shall revert to the original owner or shall vest in some other person. An express provision to this effect is not, however, essential to bring a statute within the exception. It is sufficient if the implication is that the grantee shall be divested of his interest upon the fulfilment or failure of the purpose for which the land was acquired.[10]

The Law of Property Act 1925 also provides that a fee simple vested in a corporation shall be regarded as absolute notwithstanding its liability to determine upon the dissolution of the corporate body.[11]

If a condition is annexed to the limitation of a fee simple providing that the grantor shall be entitled to re-enter and recover his interest if a certain event happens or does not happen, it is equally clear on general principles that the estate is not a fee simple absolute within the meaning of the description given by Preston. Nevertheless the provision of the Law of Property Act 1925, which denied the character of a legal estate to an interest of this nature, caused considerable difficulty. In the North West of England and in the county of Avon (and especially in Manchester and Bristol), it has been a common practice for a purchaser of a fee simple, instead of paying the purchase money in a lump sum, to enter into a covenant to pay a perpetual annual rentcharge.[12] The payment of the rent is secured to the vendor and his successors by the reservation of either a right of entry or a right of re-entry. The former permits the vendor and his successors to enter the land at any time in the future if the annual payment falls into arrear and to hold the land *as a leasehold interest* until the arrears are paid.[13] The right of re-entry (which is more common in the case of a lease[14]) arises where the conveyance contains a condition that the purchaser and his successors will pay the rent and provides that the vendor shall be entitled to re-enter if this condition is broken. In this

---

[8] LPA 1925, s. 7(1), as amended by Reverter of Sites Act 1987, which excludes from s. 7(1) the School Sites Acts, the Literary and Scientific Institutions Act 1854 and the Places of Worship Sites Act 1873. The right of reverter in those cases is replaced by a trust of land. Where, for example, a school site ceases to be used for purposes for which it was originally granted, the charitable trustees continue to hold the legal estate on trust for the revertee: s. 1, as amended by TLATA 1996, s. 5, Sch. 2, para. 6; *Marchant v Onslow* [1995] Ch 1; [1994] Conv 489 (J. Hill); *Habermehl v A-G* [1996] EGCS 148; *Fraser v Canterbury Diocesan Board of Finance (No 1)* [2001] Ch 669; *Fraser v Canterbury Diocesan Board of Finance (No 2)* [2006] 1 AC 377. They may apply to the Charity Commissioners to have the interests of the revertee extinguished: s. 2; Charities Act 1993, s. 23. A revertee in some circumstances may be entitled to compensation: s. 2(4). For the difficulties caused by the original s. 7(1), see Law Commission Report on Rights of Reverter 1981 (Law Com No. 111, Cmnd 8410). The Act departs in a significant number of respects from the Report's recommendations. See Current Law Statutes Annotated (J. Hill); [1987] Conv 408 (D. Evans).

[9] Strict settlements can no longer be created after 1996: TLATA 1996, s. 2(1), p. 437, post.

[10] *Tithe Redemption Commission v Runcorn UDC* [1954] Ch 383 (highway vested in the local highway authority; Local Government Act 1929 held to be "a similar statute" within LPA 1925, s. 7(1)).

[11] S. 7(2). As to whether the lands of a corporation upon its dissolution reverted to the donor or escheated to the lord, see Co Litt 13b; Gray, *Rule against Perpetuities*, ss. 44–52; Challis, *Law of Real Property*, pp. 35–6, 467–8; *Hastings Corpn v Letton* [1908] 1 KB 378; *Re Woking UDC* [1914] 1 Ch 300; *Re Sir Thomas Spencer Wells* [1933] Ch 29; (1933) 49 LQR 240; (1934) 50 LQR 33 (F. E. Farrer); (1935) 51 LQR 347 (M. W. Hughes), 361 (F. E. Farrer).

[12] Pp. 707 et seq, post.　　[13] Litt s. 327; Co Litt 202b; ibid., note 93 by Hargrave and Butler.

[14] Pp. 273, 280 post.

case the person entitled to the rent may either re-enter upon the land or bring proceedings for its recovery, whereupon the interest of the purchaser is forfeited and the vendor *reacquires his old estate*.[15]

The fact that a fee simple liable to interruption in either of these ways was not a legal estate within the meaning of the Law of Property Act 1925 operated to the prejudice of a landowner, for not only did it seem to make the land subject to the Settled Land Act and thus to require the execution of a vesting deed, but it made it difficult to discover where the legal estate resided.[16]

In view of this inconvenience it was later enacted that: "a fee simple subject to a legal or equitable right of entry or re-entry is for the purposes of this Act a fee simple absolute".[17]

The word "absolute" does not imply freedom from incumbrances. Thus a fee simple, though subject to a lien or a mortgage, whether legal or equitable, or to a mere charge, is none the less absolute.

C In Possession

Finally, to have the character of a legal estate, a fee simple absolute must be *in possession*. "Possession" is not here confined to its popular meaning, for it includes receipt of rents and profits or the right to receive the same.[18] Therefore a tenant in fee simple who has leased the land to a tenant for years is the owner of a legal estate even though he is not in physical possession of the land. If, however, he is entitled to the fee simple only at some time in the future, as for instance in the case of a limitation:

to A for life and then to B in fee simple,

A has an equitable life interest and B has an equitable fee simple. Before 1997 the land was settled land under the Settled Land Act 1925; since then the limitation takes effect under a trust of land.[19]

II Mode of Creation

A *Words of Limitation*

We must first distinguish between "words of limitation" and "words of purchase". "Words of limitation" indicate the size of the interest given by some instrument; they limit or define it. On the other hand, "words of purchase" (*perquisitio*) point out, by name or description, the person who is to acquire (*perquirit*) an interest in land. A "purchaser" in this technical sense does not denote a person who buys land, but one to whom land is expressly transferred by *act of parties*, as for instance by conveyance on sale, by gift or by will. If land is given "to A and his heirs", A is a purchaser since he is personally designated as the transferee, but the words "and his heirs" are words of limitation. They merely indicate the quantum of interest

---

[15] Litt s. 325.   [16] (1926) 61 LJ News 49 (F. E. Farrer). See also M & B p. 7, n. 5.

[17] LP(A)A 1926, Schedule. The rentcharge, being perpetual, is a *legal* interest under LPA 1925, s. 1(2)(b), p. 94, ante; and under s. 1(2)(e), the right of entry, being "annexed to a legal rentcharge", is also a *legal* interest.

[18] LPA 1925, ss. 205(1)(xix), 95(4); *District Bank Ltd v Webb* [1958] 1 WLR 148, M & B p. 8.

[19] P. 502, post.

that A is to take, and give the heirs nothing by direct gift. The lands may, of course, descend to them as heirs if A dies intestate, but they will not be purchasers since the land comes to them by operation of law and not by act of parties.[20]

(1) Natural Persons

Whether a fee simple passes to a grantee or a devisee of land depends upon the words of limitation contained in the deed or will. In the case of deeds the law was in former times exceedingly strict upon this point. If certain expressions were adopted the effect was to create a fee simple; if others, a fee tail or life estate. Thus before 1882 the only way of creating a fee simple by a direct grant *inter vivos* was by a limitation to the grantee *and his heirs*. This expression has been common form since the birth of English law, and perhaps its original implication was that the tenant could not alienate his interest without first consulting the apparent heirs. In the thirteenth century, however, all restraints of that kind on alienation disappeared and it became settled that the expression did not confer rights of any sort upon the heir, but was used merely to show that the tenant had an estate that would endure at least as long as his heirs endured.[21]

If in a *deed* there was for instance a grant to:

A and his assignees;
A for ever;
A and his descendants;
A and his successors,[22]

then, however untechnical the expression might be, and however obvious the intention of the parties might be to convey the fee simple, the only effect was to pass a life estate to A. This strictness was mitigated and an alternative form of words was permitted by the Conveyancing Act 1881, which provided that in deeds executed after 31 December 1881, the fee simple should pass if the expression "in fee simple" was adopted.

In the case of land *devised by will* the law was more liberal in its definition of words of limitation than it was in the case of deeds. Thus in addition to the technical expression "and his heirs", any informal words which clearly showed that the testator intended to give the fee simple were allowed to have that effect,[23] but notwithstanding this more lenient attitude the fact remained that laxity in the use of words of limitation frequently defeated intention. The Wills Act 1837 therefore provided that: "where any real estate shall be devised to any person without any words of limitation, such devise shall be construed to pass the fee simple, or other the whole estate or interest which the testator had power to dispose of by will in such real estate, unless a contrary intention shall appear by the will."[24] The effect of this enactment was to reverse the former law.

[20] See Fearne, *Contingent Remainders*, pp. 79–80; and *IRC v Gribble* [1913] 3 KB 212, where at 218 Buckley LJ said: " 'Purchaser', as it seems to me, may mean any one of four things. First, it may bear what has been called the vulgar or commercial meaning; purchaser may mean a buyer for money. Secondly, it may also include a person who becomes a purchaser, for money's worth, which would include the case of an exchange. Thirdly, it may mean a purchaser for valuable consideration, which need not be money or money's worth, but may be, say, a covenant on the consideration of marriage. Fourthly it may bear that which in the language of real property lawyers is its technical meaning, namely a person who does not take by descent."

[21] Pollock and Maitland, *History of English Law*, vol. ii. p. 13.

[22] *Bankes v Salisbury Diocesan Council of Education Inc* [1960] Ch 631.   [23] *Jarman on Wills*, p. 1802.

[24] S. 28.

Before 1837 the effect of using a non-technical expression was to pass only a life estate, unless an intention to pass the whole fee simple could be clearly deduced; but since 1837 the effect is to pass the entire interest which the testator happens to have in the lands, unless his intention clearly is to give some smaller interest. The burden of proving that a smaller interest passes lies on those who maintain that hypothesis.

The rule thus introduced for wills by the Act of 1837 was extended to deeds by the Law of Property Act 1925. It provides that:[25]

a conveyance of freehold land to any person without words of limitation, or any equivalent expression, shall pass to the grantee the fee simple or other the whole interest which the grantor had power to convey in such land, unless a contrary intention appears in the conveyance.

It will be noticed that the language of this section corresponds closely with that of the Wills Act 1837.

The position, then, at the present day, both for deeds and for wills, is that, if it is desired to confer a fee simple upon X, land may be limited "to X in fee simple" or "to X and his heirs"; but that, if any other expression is used, as for instance, "to X", or "to X for ever", the fee simple, if owned by the alienor, will pass unless the instrument clearly shows that there was no such intention.[26] In practice the words "to X in fee simple" are used, in order to avoid the possibility of a contrary intention appearing in the instrument.

A limitation before 1926, not "*to A and his heirs*", but to "A for life, remainder to his heirs" would have conferred a fee simple estate upon A under the rule known as the *Rule in Shelley's Case*. This rule, which is described below,[27] has, however, been abolished, and the effect of such a limitation now is to give a life interest to A and a fee simple estate to his heir.

(2) Corporations

Where it was desired to grant a fee simple to a corporation sole,[28] that is, a body politic having perpetual succession and consisting of a single person, such as a bishop, a parson, the Crown or the Public Trustee, the old law was that the grant must be made to the person in question *and his successors*, otherwise it merely operated to confer an estate for life on the actual holder of the office.[29] This rule has, however, been altered,[30] and a conveyance of freehold land in which the word "successors" has been omitted passes to the corporation the fee simple or other the whole interest which the grantor has, unless a contrary intention appears in the conveyance.

In the case of a corporation aggregate,[31] that is, a collection of several persons united into one body under a special name and having perpetual existence, such as a limited liability company incorporated under the Companies Act 1985, it is sufficient to grant to the corporation under its corporate name.[32]

B *Voluntary Conveyance*

If a feoffment were made before the Statute of Uses to a stranger in blood without the receipt of a money consideration (i.e. a voluntary conveyance), and *without declaring a use* in favour

---

[25] LPA 1925, s. 60(1).   [26] See, for example, *Quarm v Quarm* [1892] 1 QB 184.   [27] P. 492, post.
[28] P. 923, post.   [29] Co Litt 8b, 94b.   [30] LPA 1925, s. 60(2).   [31] P. 923, post.
[32] Co Litt 94b.

of the feoffee, the rule was that the land must be held by the feoffee to the use of the feoffor.[33] The equitable interest that thus returned by implication to the feoffor was called a resulting use. The effect of the enactment by the Statute of Uses that a *cestui que use* should have the legal estate was, of course, that the legal estate resulted to the feoffor.[34] In order to prevent this it became the practice in the case of such a conveyance to declare in the deed that the land was granted "unto and to the use of" the grantee. The repeal of the Statute of Uses by the legislation of 1925 would, in the absence of a further enactment, have restored the original rule, and it might have led practitioners to believe that the expression "to the use of" was still necessary in order to render a voluntary conveyance effective. It is, however, enacted that:

in a voluntary conveyance a resulting trust for the grantor shall not be implied merely by reason that the property is not expressed to be conveyed for the use or benefit of the grantee.[35]

C Registered Land

In registered land there are two points to notice about the fee simple absolute in possession. First, where the registered proprietor transfers it *inter vivos*, no words of limitation are required in the transfer.[36] Secondly, as we have seen, the legal estate will not pass to the transferee until the transfer is completed by registration.[37] For this reason it has been suggested[38] that the Land Registration Acts really provide a new statutory title to land, one that is not the fee simple, but a new fee based on it. But the argument is really a verbal one as to how the consequences of registration affect the character of what is registered. Section 11 of the Land Registration Act 2002 provides that the effect of registration is to vest the freehold estate—that is, the fee simple absolute in possession[39]—in the proprietor, and so it is still, in law, the fee simple estate that he holds.

III The Legal Position of a Tenant in Fee Simple

A Extent of Ownership

A tenant in fee simple has extensive property rights in the subject-matter of his interest. In accordance with the maxim, *cujus est solum, ejus est usque ad coelum et ad inferos*[40] the common law principle is that a tenant in fee simple is owner of everything in, on and above his

---

[33] Sanders, *Uses and Trusts*, vol. i. p. 60.   [34] Ibid., p. 97; *Beckwith's Case* (1589) 2 Co Rep 56b.

[35] LPA 1925, s. 60(3).

[36] P. 963, post; *A J Dunning & Sons (Shopfitters) Ltd v Sykes & Son (Poole) Ltd* [1987] Ch 287 at 302.

[37] LRA 2002, s. 27; pp. 104,108, ante; p. 970, post; replacing LRA 1925, ss. 19(1), 20(1).

[38] See (1949) 12 MLR 139, 477 (A. D. Hargreaves); 205 (H. Potter); (1947) 11 Conv (NS) 184, 232 (R. C. Connell); (1972) 88 LQR 93 (D. Jackson); Farrand, *Contract and Conveyance* (2nd edn), pp. 178–80; Barnsley, *Conveyancing Law and Practice*, pp. 36–8.

[39] "Legal estate" has the same meaning as in LPA 1925, s. 1: LRA 2002, s. 132(1). See also s. 3(1)(a). LRA 1925 referred more particularly to the proprietor having the fee simple absolute in possession vested in him: ss. 5, 20(1), 69(1).

[40] "The owner of the soil owns it up to the sky and down to the depths below": "A colourful phrase often upon the lips of lawyers since it was first coined by Accursius in Bologna in the 13th century": *Baron Bernstein of Leigh v Skyviews and General Ltd* [1978] QB 479 at 485, per GRIFFITHS J.

land. As Lord WILBERFORCE said:[41] "At most the maxim is used as a statement, imprecise enough, of the extent of the rights, prima facie, of owners of land: Bowen LJ was concerned with these rights when . . . he said 'Prima facie the owner of the land has everything under the sky down to the centre of the earth' ."[42] The rights are as extensive as common law and statute permit.[43]

(1) In and On the Land

(a) Mines and minerals

At common law all mines and minerals that lie beneath the soil belong absolutely to the tenant in fee simple but by statute all interests in coal are vested in the Coal Authority[44] and petroleum existing in its natural condition in strata in Great Britain or beneath the territorial sea adjacent to the United Kingdom is vested in the Crown.[45] Further, the Crown is entitled to all gold and silver in gold and silver mines.[46]

(b) Chattels

In the absence of trustworthy evidence of ownership, there is a legal presumption that the fee simple owner, if in possession, is owner of chattels found on or under his land.[47]

(c) Treasure trove

The proprietary rights of the tenant do not extend to treasure trove.

(1) AT COMMON LAW

The common law definition of treasure was stated by Chitty as follows:[48]

Treasure trove is, where any gold or silver in coin, plate, or bullion is found concealed in a house, or in the earth, or other private place, the owner thereof being unknown, in which case the treasure belongs

---

[41] *Railways Comr v Valuer-General* [1974] AC 328 at 351–2. The maxim was applied in *Grigsby v Melville* [1974] 1 WLR 80 (cellar underneath drawing-room floor); *Graystone Property Investments Ltd v Margulies* (1983) 47 P & CR 472 (void space between false ceiling and underneath of floor of flat above).

[42] *Pountney v Clayton* (1883) 11 QBD 820 at 838.

[43] "It is quite plain that airspace is not something which even the most ingenious conveyancer of Lincoln's Inn has ever dealt with as an item of property unrelated to the ground over which it lies": *Rolfe v Wimpey Waste Management Ltd* [1988] STC 329 at 357, per HARMAN J.

[44] Coal Act 1938; Coal Industry Nationalisation Act 1946; Coal Industry Act 1987, s. 1(2), Sch. 1, para. 1; Coal Industry Act 1994.

[45] Petroleum Act 1998, s. 2. See *Earl of Lonsdale v A-G* [1982] 1 WLR 887 ("mines and minerals" in 1880 conveyance held not to include oil and natural gas).

[46] *Mines Case* (1567) 1 Plowd 310. Royal Mines Acts 1688, 1693.

[47] *South Staffordshire Water Co v Sharman* [1896] 2 QB 44; *Hannah v Peel* [1945] KB 509; *Hibbert v McKiernan* [1948] 2 KB 142; *Re Cohen* [1953] Ch 88; *City of London Corpn v Appleyard* [1963] 1 WLR 982; *Moffatt v Kazana* [1969] 2 QB 152; *Parker v British Airways Board* [1982] QB 1004 especially at 1017–18 (gold bracelet found on floor in international executive lounge at Heathrow held to belong to finder); [1990] Conv 348 (D. C. Hoath); *Tamworth Industries v A-G* [1991] 3 NZLR 616; [1993] CLP Part I, p. 81 (P. Kohler). See Goodhart, *Essays in Jurisprudence and the Common Law*, pp. 75–90; Harris, *Oxford Essays in Jurisprudence* (ed. Guest), pp. 69–106.

[48] *Chitty on the Prerogative*, p. 152, cited *A-G v Moore* [1893] 1 Ch 676 at 683; *A-G v British Museum Trustees* [1903] 2 Ch 598; *Waverley BC v Fletcher* [1996] QB 334 (mediaeval gold brooch found in park held not treasure but to belong to local authority); [1996] Conv 216 (J. Stevens). On treasure generally, see Hill, *Treasure Trove in Law and Practice*.

to the King or his grantee having the franchise of treasure trove; but if he that laid it be known or after-wards discovered, the owner and not the King is entitled to it; this prerogative right only applying in the absence of an owner to claim the property. If the owner, instead of hiding the treasure, casually lost it, or purposely parted with it,[49] in such a manner that it is evident he intended to abandon the prop-erty altogether, and did not purpose to resume it on another occasion, as if he threw it on the ground, or other public place, or in the sea, the first finder is entitled to the property as against every one but the owner, and the King's prerogative does not in this respect obtain. So that it is the hiding, and not the abandonment, of the property that entitles the King to it.

Whether a coin or object is made of silver or gold is a question of fact. It must contain a substantial proportion of gold or silver. Thus, Roman coins of the third century AD with a silver content ranging from 0.2 to 18 per cent have been held not to be treasure trove.[50]

(2) TREASURE ACT 1996

The Treasure Act 1996 widens the definition of treasure.[51] It is any object which is at least three hundred years old when found and, if not a coin, has a metallic content of which at least 10 per cent by weight is gold or silver.

There are special rules for coins. To be treasure they must be at least three hundred years old and be one of at least two coins with the same percentage of gold or silver. Alternatively, if a coin is at least three hundred years old and is one of at least ten coins in the same find, it is treasure regardless of its metallic percentage. If a coin is found alone, it is not treasure. Objects found as part of the same find are also treasure; for example the pot in which the coins are found. Objects of historical or archaeological or cultural importance are not included within the statutory definition, but the Secretary of State may designate as treasure by statutory instrument any such objects which are over two hundred years old.[52]

(d) Sea-shore

An owner of land adjoining the sea is entitled to the sea-shore[53] down to a point which is reached by an ordinary high tide, but all the shore below that is vested in the Crown or its grantee.[54]

He is also entitled to land which is added by gradual and imperceptible accretion from the sea.[55]

---

[49] On whether a possessor can divest himself of possession of a thing by its deliberate abandonment, see Pollock and Wright, *Possession in the Common Law*, p. 124; *Haynes' Case* (1613) 12 Co Rep 113; *Arrow Shipping Co v Tyne Improvement Comrs* [1894] AC 508 at 532.

[50] *A-G of the Duchy of Lancaster v G E Overton (Farms) Ltd* [1982] Ch 277; [1980] CLJ 281 (D. E. C. Yale); (1981) 44 MLR 178 (N. E. Palmer).

[51] Ss. 1, 3(3); (1996) 146 NLJ 1346 (C. MacMillan); [1997] Conv 273; [1998] Conv 252 (J. Marston and L. Ross). It is a criminal offence not to notify the coroner within fourteen days of the find: s. 8. See also the reports of the Treasure Valuation Committee (available on the web site of the Department for Culture, Media and Sport).   [52] S. 2; Treasure Designation Order 2002 (SI 2002 No. 2666).

[53] See *Government of Penang v Beng Hong Oon* [1972] AC 425 at 435, 439.

[54] *Lowe v Govett* (1832) 3 B & Ad 863; *Blundell v Catterall* (1821) 5 B & Ald 268; *Alfred F Beckett Ltd v Lyons* [1967] Ch 449. For the rights of the public over the sea-shore, see [1974] JPL 705 (A. Wharam).

[55] *Gifford v Lord Yarborough* (1828) 5 Bing 163. See *Baxendale v Instow Parish Council* [1982] Ch 14 at 23; Wisdom, *Law of Watercourses* (5th edn), chap. 2. The rule of accretion also applies to inland lakes: *Southern Centre of Theosophy Inc v State of South Australia* [1982] AC 706 (accretion by fluvial action and river-blown sand); (1983) 99 LQR 412 (P. Jackson); [1986] Conv 255 (W. Howarth).

(e) Wild creatures

The owner's rights in respect of wild animals, such as game,[56] depend upon the circumstances. Such animals are not within the absolute ownership of any particular person. There are two exceptions, for wild animals which have been tamed belong to the person who has tamed them, and animals too young to escape belong to the occupier of the land on which they are until they gain their natural liberty.[57] In other cases the tenant in fee simple or, indeed, the occupier of the land, has not an absolute, but a qualified, right of ownership over the animals within the confines of his property in the sense that the exclusive right to catch and appropriate them belongs to him *ratione soli*.[58] Thus, game which is killed by a trespasser belongs to the occupier of the land on which it is killed. The only exception to this principle and one not altogether free from doubt is that if A starts game on the land of B, and hunts it on to the ground of C and kills it there, the ownership of the game belongs to A the hunter, though of course he is liable in trespass both to B and to C.[59]

(2) Above the Land

Although the tenant does not acquire the ownership of anything that overhangs his land, such as a cornice, an illuminated advertisement, telephone wires or the bough of a tree, he can maintain an action of nuisance or of trespass against the person who allows it to be there,[60] unless it has been acquired by that person as an easement.[61] A tenant's rights in the airspace above the property do not, however, extend to an unlimited height, but are restricted to such height as is necessary for the ordinary use and enjoyment of his land. Thus, where an aircraft flew over land for the purpose of taking an aerial photograph of a house on it, an action for trespass failed.[62] And there is also a defence under the Civil Aviation Act 1982,[63] which provides that no action shall lie in respect of trespass or nuisance by reason only of the flight of an aircraft over any property at a height which is reasonable under the circumstances, provided that certain regulations are complied with.

[56] See *Inglewood Investment Co Ltd v Forestry Commission* [1988] 1 WLR 1278 (game construed to mean feathered game and not deer).   [57] *Case of Swans* (1592) 7 Co Rep 15b.

[58] *Blades v Higgs* (1865) 11 HL Cas 621, per WESTBURY LC. The Crown has a prerogative right to swans, and royal fish, e.g. whales and sturgeon. Any such right to other wild creatures was abolished by the Wild Creatures and Forest Laws Act 1971, s. 1(1)(a).

[59] *Sutton v Moody* (1697) 1 Ld Raym 250, criticised by Lord CHELMSFORD in *Blades v Higgs* (1865) 11 HL Cas 621 at 639. It is a criminal offence under the Protection of Badgers Act 1992 to kill badgers, and under the Wildlife and Countryside Act 1981 to kill wild animals listed in Sch. 5 (for example, swallowtail butterfly, common otter and red squirrel), and wild birds in Sch. 1 (for example, bee-eater, chough, fieldfare, hoopoe, kingfisher and barn owl). The Act was amended by the Wildlife and Countryside Act 1981 (Variation of Schedules) Order 1988 (SI 1988 No. 288); SI 1989 No. 906; and by the Wildlife and Countryside (Amendment) Act 1991. See also the Deer Act 1991; Wild Animals Protection Act 1996; Wildlife and Countryside Act 1981 (Variation of Schedules 5 and 8) Order 1998 (SI 1998 No. 878). The Hunting Act 2004 makes it a criminal offence to hunt a wild mammal with a dog save in limited circumstances; *Jackson v A-G* [2006] 1 AC 262.

[60] *Wandsworth Board of Works v United Telephone Co* (1884) 13 QBD 904; *Lemmon v Webb* [1895] AC 1; *Gifford v Dent* [1926] WN 336; *Kelsen v Imperial Tobacco Co (of Great Britain and Ireland) Ltd* [1957] 2 QB 334; *Woollerton and Wilson Ltd v Richard Costain Ltd* [1970] 1 WLR 411; *Anchor Brewhouse Developments Ltd v Berkley House (Docklands Developments) Ltd* [1987] 2 EGLR 173 (tower cranes oversailing adjoining land held to be infringement of airspace and therefore trespass: injunction granted).

[61] *Simpson v Weber* (1925) 41 TLR 302.

[62] *Baron Bernstein of Leigh v Skyviews and General Ltd* [1978] QB 479. See McNair, *Law of the Air*, pp. 31 et seq.

[63] S. 76(1).

(3) Water[64]

A landowner has certain valuable rights over water that may run through or be situated on his land.

The right of abstraction at common law, however, has been substantially modified by statute. Under the Environment Act 1995 the Environment Agency is responsible for running a compulsory system of licensing for the abstraction of water.[65]

(a) Ponds and lakes

Water standing upon his land in a lake or pond is part of the land and belongs to him. If it stands partly upon his land and partly upon that of another, each is probably entitled to such part as lies opposite his own bank, but only up to a point half way between his and the opposite bank.[66]

(b) Percolating water

Water percolating underneath the land and not contained in a defined and contracted channel is a common supply in which nobody has any property, but at common law it becomes the absolute property of any occupier by whom it is appropriated.[67]

If an occupier abstracts percolating water, he becomes the owner of it and may take it regardless of the consequences, whether physical or pecuniary, to his neighbours.[68] Thus he will not be liable to his neighbours, though the effect may have been to dry up a spring or a well on their land.[69]

(c) Streams and rivers

The next type of case is where a river or stream runs in a *definite channel*, whether above or below the surface, though it must be noted that an underground stream does not come within this category until it is established that it follows a definite course.[70] Underground water, the course of which cannot be ascertained without excavation, ranks as percolating water. Two questions arise where a stream follows a definite course; first, the rights of the riparian owner or owners in the *bed*, secondly, their rights in the *water*.

(1) RIGHTS IN THE BED

The bed of a *non-tidal* river belongs, when there is no evidence of acts of ownership to the contrary, to the owner of the land through which it flows, but when the lands of two

[64] See generally Waite and Jewell, *Environmental Law in Property Transactions*, chap. 17; Getzler, *A History of Water Rights at Common Law*; Bates, *Water and Drainage Law*.

[65] S. 2, which transfers to the Environment Agency from the National Rivers Authority the functions set out in Water Resources Act 1991, ss. 24–72.   [66] See *Mackenzie v Bankes* (1878) 3 App Cas 1324.

[67] *Ballard v Tomlinson* (1885) 29 Ch D 115 at 121, per BRETT MR.

[68] *Stephens v Anglian Water Authority* [1987] 1 WLR 1381 at 1387, per SLADE LJ; [1988] Conv 175 (M. Harwood).

[69] *Acton v Blundell* (1843) 12 M & W 324; *Chasemore v Richards* (1859) 7 HL Cas 349; *Rugby Joint Water Board v Walters* [1967] Ch 397; *Langbrook Properties Ltd v Surrey County Council* [1970] 1 WLR 161; *Thomas v Gulf Oil Refining Ltd* (1979) 123 SJ 787; *Brace v South Eastern Regional Housing Association Ltd* (1984) 270 EG 1286; *Home Brewery Co Ltd v William Davis & Co (Leicester) Ltd* [1987] QB 339; *Palmer v Bowman* [2000] 1 WLR 842 (natural right to drain surface and percolating water onto lower neighbouring land not capable of being an easement), p. 591, n. 47, post. See too *Bradford Corpn v Pickles* [1895] AC 587.

[70] *Bleachers' Association Ltd and Bennett and Jackson Ltd v Chapel-en-le-Frith RDC* [1933] Ch 356; *R v Falmouth and Truro Port Health Authority, ex p South West Water Ltd* [2001] QB 445 (a watercourse does not include a river or an estuary for the purposes of Public Health Act 1936, s. 259).

owners are separated by a running stream, each owner is prima facie owner of the soil of the bed of the river up to the mid-point of the stream. The soil of the bed is not the common property of the two owners, but the share of each belongs to him separately, so that, if from any cause the stream becomes diverted, each owner may use his share of the bed in any way he chooses.[71] On the other hand, the bed of a *tidal* river, up to a point where the water flows and reflows regularly, belongs to the Crown unless it has been granted to a subject.[72]

(2) RIGHTS IN THE WATER

But the water as distinct from the bed of a river is not the subject of absolute ownership, and, though subject to certain rights exercisable by the owners of the lands through which it flows, it does not belong to them in the ordinary sense of the term. Such a riparian owner has at common law, as a natural incident of his ownership, certain riparian rights, which have been authoritatively described as follows:[73]

A riparian proprietor is entitled to have the water of the stream on the banks of which his property lies, flow down as it has been accustomed to flow down to his property, subject to the ordinary use of the flowing water by upper proprietors, and to such further use, if any, on their part in connection with their property as may be reasonable under the circumstances.

The common law, as thus stated, may be elaborated into three propositions:[74]

(1) A riparian owner may take and use the water for ordinary purposes connected with his riparian tenement (such as domestic purposes or the watering of his cattle),[75] even though the result may be to exhaust the water altogether.

(2) A riparian owner may take the water for extraordinary purposes, provided, first that such user is connected with the riparian land, and secondly that he restores the water substantially undiminished in volume and unaltered in character. Common examples are where water is employed in the irrigation of the adjoining land or the working of a mill, for in such cases practically the same amount of water ultimately returns to the stream.[76] Manufacture, in the present connection, is prima facie an extraordinary purpose, though the ultimate solution of this question depends upon local trading conditions, and on the use to which the water of rivers is put in the adjoining district.[77]

---

[71] *Bickett v Morris* (1866) LR 1 Sc & Div 47 (especially at 58).

[72] *A-G v Earl of Lonsdale* (1868) LR 7 Eq 377 at 388.

[73] *John Young & Co v Bankier Distillery Co* [1893] AC 691 at 698, per Lord MACNAGHTEN; *Provender Millers (Winchester) Ltd v Southampton County Council* [1940] Ch 131; *Tate & Lyle Industries Ltd v Greater London Council* [1983] 2 AC 509; *Scott-Whitehead v National Coal Board* (1985) 53 P & CR 263; [1987] Conv 368 (S. Tromans); *Home Brewery Co Ltd v William Davis & Co (Leicester) Ltd* [1987] QB 339; (1987) 137 NLJ 867 (H. W. Wilkinson). On water pollution, see *Cambridge Water Co v Eastern Counties Leather plc* [1994] 2 AC 264 (civil liability); [1994] Conv 309 (M. P. Gravells); (1994) 57 MLR 799 (D. Wilkinson); *Alphacell Ltd v Woodward* [1972] AC 824; *National Rivers Authority v Sir Alfred McAlpine Homes (East) Ltd* [1994] 4 All ER 286; *Empress Car Co (Abertillery) Ltd v National Rivers Authority* The Times, 9 February 1998 (criminal liability).

[74] *Attwood v Llay Main Collieries Ltd* [1926] Ch 444 at 458.

[75] But not spray irrigation: *Rugby Joint Water Board v Walters* [1967] Ch 397.

[76] *Embrey v Owen* (1851) 6 Exch 353; cf *Rugby Joint Water Board v Walters*, supra.

[77] *Ormerod v Todmorden Joint Stock Mill Co Ltd* (1883) 11 QBD 155 at 168, per Lord ESHER; see (1959) 22 MLR 35 (A. H. Hudson).

(3) A riparian owner has no right whatever to take the water for purposes unconnected with the riparian tenement.[78] Thus it has been held that the mere possession of a mill on the bank of a stream does not entitle a waterworks company to collect the water in a reservoir for the benefit of a neighbouring town.[79]

(d) Abstraction under Water Resources Act 1991

The rights of taking water at common law have been curtailed by section 24(1) of the Water Resources Act 1991,[80] as amended and supplemented by the Water Act 2003.[81] Under the 1991 Act:[82]

no person shall

(a) abstract water from any source of supply; or

(b) cause or permit any other person so to abstract any water,

except in pursuance of a licence under this Chapter granted by the [Environment] Agency and in accordance with the provisions of that licence.

The 2003 Act makes provision for different categories of licence for the abstraction of water. There is, however, an exemption for[83]

any abstraction of a quantity of water not exceeding twenty cubic metres in any period of twenty-four hours, if the abstraction does not form part of a continuous operation, or of a series of operations,[84] by which a quantity of water which, in aggregate, is more than twenty cubic metres is abstracted during the period.

(e) Public rights in a river

The public have a common law right to navigation in a tidal river up to the point where the tide ebbs and flows,[85] but the non-tidal part of a river is analogous to a road running between two properties, and though the public may by dedication acquire the right of navigation on it, it must be proved in case of dispute that this has been established by long enjoyment or by Act of Parliament.[86] Such a right of navigation, if established, prevails over the ordinary rights of a riparian owner, and he cannot make any use of the bed of the river or of its water which will prejudice enjoyment by the public; he is not, for instance, entitled to erect a wharf or other building on the bed so as to obstruct to the smallest extent the passage of boats.[87]

---

[78] *McCartney v Londonderry and Lough Swilly Rly Co* [1904] AC 301; *Attwood v Llay Main Collieries,* supra.

[79] *Swindon Waterworks Co v Wilts and Berks Canal Navigation Co* (1875) LR 7 HL 697.

[80] Replacing the provisions of the Water Resources Act 1963 as amended. The functions were transferred to the Environment Agency by Environment Act 1995, s. 2; see also Sch. 23, para. 20.

[81] See also report by the Department for Environment, Food and Rural Affairs, *Taking Water Responsibly* (March 1999).   [82] S. 24.

[83] Water Resources Act 1991, s. 27(1), substituted by Water Act 2003, s. 6(1).

[84] *Cargill v Gotts* [1981] 1 WLR 441 (series depends on taking, not quantity or frequency); (1981) 97 LQR 382 (P. Jackson).

[85] *A-G v Tomline* (1880) 14 Ch D 58. See *Iveagh v Martin* [1961] 1 QB 232; *Evans v Godber* [1974] 1 WLR 1317. See Caffyn, *The Right of Navigation on Non-Tidal Rivers and the Common Law.*

[86] *Orr Ewing v Colquhoun* (1877) 2 App Cas 839.

[87] *A-G v Terry* (1874) 9 Ch App 423. *Tate & Lyle Industries Ltd v Greater London Council* [1983] 2 AC 509 (construction of ferry terminals in River Thames caused silting at jetty of plaintiffs who succeeded in claim for special damage for public nuisance). Salvage is not recoverable on a non-tidal navigable river: *The Goring*

(f) Fishing

As regards the person who possesses the right of fishing in a river, a distinction must again be drawn between tidal and non-tidal rivers, for while all members of the public are entitled to fish[88] in the former up to the point where the tide ebbs and flows,[89] the right in the case of a non-tidal river belongs to the owner of the bed of the stream, or to any person who has acquired a right from or against him. It is often thought that if a river is navigable the public have a right to fish in it, but this is not true in respect of that part of a river which lies above the flow of the tide, for the privilege of navigation no more confers a right to fish than the right to pass along a public highway entitles a member of the public to shoot upon it.[90] BOWEN LJ said:[91]

There is another most important matter to be recollected as regards such streams as the Thames, viz. that although the public have been in the habit, as long as we can recollect, and as long as our fathers can recollect, of fishing in the Thames, the public have no right to fish there—I mean they have no right as members of the public to fish there. That is certain law. Of course they may fish by the licence of the lord or the owner of a particular part of the bed of the river, or they may fish by the indulgence, or owing to the carelessness or good nature, of the person who is entitled to the soil, but right to fish themselves as the public they have none, and whenever the case is tried the jury ought to be told this by the judge in the most emphatic way, so as to prevent them from doing injustice under the idea that they are establishing a public right. There is no such right in law . . .

The position is, then, that the owner of the bed of a river is presumptively entitled to the fishing, and if, for instance, the opposite banks are in different hands, each proprietor is owner of the fishing *usque ad medium filium aquae*: up to the mid-point of the river.[92] But this fishing may become separated from the ownership of the bed and be vested as an incorporeal right in the hands of another person, and when this has been done it exists either as a several fishery or as a common of fishery. Both these rights are instances of what is called a *profit à prendre*. A several fishery is, as was said by Lord COLERIDGE: "a right to take fish *in alieno solo*, and to exclude the owner of the soil from the right of taking fish himself".[93] A right to fish in the river of another in common with the owner, or in common with others to whom the same right has been granted, is called a "common of fishery", or "common of piscary".[94]

[1988] AC 831 (River Thames above Reading Bridge); [1987] CLJ 153 (D. E. C. Yale); *Rowland v Environment Agency* [2005] Ch 1 (public right of navigation on non-tidal stretch of River Thames below Cookham existing since time immemorial not extinguished by Thames Preservation Act 1885).

[88] And to take worms on the foreshore as bait in exercise of their right to fish: *Anderson v Alnwick DC* [1993] 1 WLR 1156; *Adair v National Trust for Places of Historic Interest or Natural Beauty* The Times, 19 December 1997.

[89] It is an offence under the Salmon and Freshwater Fisheries Act 1975, s. 6(1) to place a net in tidal and inland waters which obstructs the passage of salmon and migratory trout: *Champion v Maughan* [1984] 1 WLR 469; *Gray v Blamey* [1991] 1 WLR 47. See generally Salmon Act 1986, s. 33 and Robinson, *Law of Game, Salmon and Freshwater Fishing in Scotland*.

[90] *Smith v Andrews* [1891] 2 Ch 678 at 696. It is an offence to fish in such a river even though the fish are returned alive to the water: *Wells v Hardy* [1964] 2 QB 447.

[91] *Blount v Layard* [1891] 2 Ch 681n at 689.

[92] *Hanbury v Jenkins* [1901] 2 Ch 401. If he is fishing for salmon by rod and line, he is entitled to stand on his own bank or to wade out to the mid-point, and to fish as far across the river as he can reach by normal casting or spinning: *Fothringham v Kerr* (1984) 48 P & CR 173 (River Tay). See also *Welsh National Water Development Authority v Burgess* (1974) 28 P & CR 378 at 383 (salmon and trout-fishing in River Dovey).

[93] *Foster v Wright* (1878) 4 CPD 438 at 449. See *Loose v Castleton* (1978) 41 P & CR 19; *Lewis v Cavaciuti* [1993] NLJR 813 (extent of profit of piscary in River Usk).

[94] Leake, *Uses and Profits of Land*, p. 176; p. 644, post.

(4) Flying Freeholds

A fee simple can exist in an upper storey of a building, separate and distinct from the rest. As COKE said: "A man may have an inheritance in an upper chamber though the lower buildings and soil be in another."[95] This is known as a flying freehold. Land can thus be divided horizontally as well as vertically.

A fee simple may also be[96] "a movable fee where 'the fee itself is a continuing estate, but it is an estate in land which from time to time changes its location'; as, for example, where it varies with changes of a boundary such as the foreshore." A more sophisticated form of flying freeholds has now been created in the form of *commonhold*. This is discussed in chapter 9.

B Restrictions on Ownership

In his account of the fee simple estate, written in 1885, Challis was able to give a comforting description of the extensive powers of enjoyment available to its owner:[97] "It confers, and since the beginning of legal history it always has conferred, the lawful right to exercise over, upon, and in respect, to the land, every act of ownership which can enter into the imagination, including the right to commit unlimited waste." Challis would, no doubt, have agreed with Samuel Johnson that a man cannot be allowed by society to be complete master of what he calls his own, and that he must submit to the restrictions placed by the law upon the exercise of his proprietary rights.[98] There is little doubt, however, that the restrictions now imposed by statute upon a landowner's right to enjoy what at common law is his own would have passed the understanding of both those writers. Even in Challis' time, of course, statutory interference with the freedom of a landowner was not unknown. He was obliged, for instance, to erect new buildings in conformity with local by-laws, and he might be compelled to demolish houses that were unfit for habitation. Later he became subject to legislation passed in the interests of the poorer sections of the community, such as the Housing Acts and the Rent Acts,[99] which further increased his burdens and circumscribed his proprietary rights. Also, from earlier times Parliament has frequently authorised the compulsory purchase or redistribution of land by private and public Acts, for purposes of inclosure or the provision of docks, canals, railways, utility undertakings and public works of all kinds.[100]

But the most vigorous attack upon the right of an owner to do what he likes with his land has been made by the various Town and Country Planning Acts, which seek to prevent the evils that inevitably arise if no public control is placed upon the development of land. That building operations need to be controlled in the interests of the community is, of course, obvious. Land is scarce, the demand for houses increases with a rapidly rising population, the profit instinct is no weaker than formerly, and unless something is done to curb the activities of the speculative developer certain unfortunate results must inevitably ensue. Too often, uncontrolled development sacrifices agricultural land and places of natural beauty,

---

[95] Co Litt 48b; Lincoln's Inn Act 1860 which regulates flying freeholds in New Square, Lincoln's Inn. See the claim to a "subterranean flying freehold" of a cellar in *Grigsby v Melville* [1974] 1 WLR 80 at 83.

[96] *Baxendale v Instow Parish Council* [1982] Ch 14 at 20, per MEGARRY V-C; *Welden v Bridgewater* (1592) Cro Eliz 421 (lot meadows, where two or more have a fee simple in a measured part of a meadow, but the precise part owned is determined by lots at specified times). See [1982] Conv 208 (R. E. Annand).

[97] *Law of Real Property*, p. 218.   [98] In a letter to Boswell, 3 February 1776.

[99] Pp. 336 et seq, post.

[100] See Blackstone, *Commentaries*, vol. i. p. 139; Dicey, *Law of the Constitution* (10th edn) p. 48.

defaces the countryside with unco-ordinated buildings sprawling along the main roads and causing embarrassment to the sanitary and educational authorities, and in general it is effected with little thought for the amenities of the neighbourhood or for the problems that it will raise in the future. Nevertheless, there is a need to preserve a just balance between the rights of landowners and the interests of the community.

Planning law and compensation rules together have produced a situation in which the market value of land, which includes development potential in addition to the value of the land in its existing use, is affected in a striking manner. The withholding of planning permission will deprive land of development value which market demand would otherwise confer upon it. Compensation is payable only rarely for this loss of development value (except where land is compulsorily purchased).[101]

To give an adequate account of these matters in the present chapter would upset the balance of the book and divert the attention of the reader from fundamental principles, but they are of such importance in the modern law that they are dealt with at a later stage in Part IV.[102]

---

[101] Pp. 1038, et seq, post.   [102] P. 1009, post.

9

COMMONHOLD[1]

SUMMARY

I Nature of Commonhold

Commonhold was introduced by Part I of the Commonhold and Leasehold Reform Act 2002, which came into force on 27 September 2004. It is not a new form of tenure, but is a new form in which the *freehold* estate in *registered* land can be held. In outline, it is a means of providing for the registered freehold ownership of two or more units of land,[2] for example in a block of flats or offices. A commonhold association is the registered proprietor of the common parts, but the holder of each unit is registered as the proprietor of the freehold estate in that unit.

II Aims of the Legislation Introducing Commonhold

The introduction of commonhold was recommended in 1987 by the Aldridge Working Group on Freehold Flats and Freehold Ownership of Other Interdependent Buildings:[3]

The purpose of the scheme is to regulate relations between owners of separate properties which lie in close proximity to each other and are interdependent. The scheme is suitable for, but not limited to,

---

[1] Fetherstonhaugh, Sefton and Peters, *Commonhold*; Cowen, Driscoll and Target, *Commonhold Law and Practice*; Hill and Redman, *The Commonhold and Leasehold Reform Act 2002*, chap. 2; Clarke, *Commonhold: The New Law*; *Clark on Commonhold: Law, Practice and Precedents*; Aldridge, *Commonhold Law*; R & R, chap. 22. Developers have been slow to adopt commonhold: (2006) 156 NLJ 226 (F. Larcombe); [2005] 35 EG 104 (G. Fetherstonhaugh); but are now beginning to do so: [2006] 09 EG 173; (2005) 154 PLJ 5 (J. Hopkins).

[2] There must be at least two units, although a unit need not contain all or any part of a building: CLRA 2002, s. 11(2)(a), (4). Any commonhold property that is not comprised within a defined unit will be "common parts": s. 25(1).

[3] Cmnd 79. The Working Group was established in 1986 by the Chairman of the Law Commission as a result of the initiative of the Lord Chancellor: p. v.

residential property. It gives people the chance to own flats freehold, without the present drawbacks, but the scheme can also apply to offices, commercial and industrial premises and other properties.[4]

The Commonhold scheme is similar to Condominium legislation in Canada, the United States of America and, under the name of strata titles, in Australia and New Zealand.[5]

The "present drawbacks" which the new scheme was designed to overcome are, first, the difficulty which an owner of freehold property has in enforcing a positive covenant, for example, to repair or to pay service charges, against a purchaser from his original covenantor.[6] Hitherto this difficulty has been avoided by the owner of a block of flats granting *leases* of each separate unit within it. In this case any positive covenant that relates to the property is enforceable against successive owners of the unit, in accordance with the rules for the running of leasehold covenants.[7] The system of leasehold flats, however, has brought a second drawback. Many leasehold schemes were evolved in the 1930s when leases were granted for ninety-nine years. Today a lease with less than forty years to run is an unattractive security for a mortgagee, and so the unit in many cases becomes unsaleable.

The general scope of commonhold was outlined by Mr Aldridge himself as follows:[8]

Like other condominium systems, [commonhold] would allow the freehold ownership of separate parts of a building. The problem of passing the benefit of positive obligations is overcome by legislation laying down the content of mutual obligations and easements, and making them bind the owners for the time being of each unit for the benefit of the rest of the development. Many see the standardisation of the mutual rights and obligations as a recommendation of the system.

There would be an incorporated management association, the members of which are the owners of the freehold units. It is responsible for repairs and services and any common parts are vested in it. That structure is, of course, familiar here for leasehold flat schemes. When the commonhold is brought to an end, the owners would cease to have an exclusive interest in their respective units. They would then become equitable tenants in common of the whole property in pre-determined proportions. The legal estate would be vested in the association on trust for them. This avoids possible difficulties with the freehold ownership of blocks of air on a complete or partial destruction.

The aim of the Working Group is to recommend a property ownership system which could be freely adopted by owners or developers for all types of property: existing or new, purpose-built in separate units or converted, of any type of construction, and put to any use, whether or not residential. With the progress of compulsory registration of title, it seems to us appropriate to base a new commonhold system wholly on registration. Commonholds would only be possible with a registered title. This should ensure that they are properly constituted, and will give easy access to the basic documentation.

---

[4] The commonhold scheme "will be as useful for a business park or a large out-of-town shopping centre as it will for mansion flats in Kensington or leafy suburban housing estates. It could be employed for something as mundane as a shared car park": per Lord IRVINE OF LAIRG LC, *Hansard*, HL (series 4) vol. 626, col. 886 (5 July 2001). For a comparison of commonholds and leaseholds, see Cowan, Driscoll and Target, *Commonhold Law and Practice*, chap. 15; Fetherstonhaugh, Sefton and Peters, *Commonhold*, para. 1.3.7 (in tabular form).

[5] Cmnd 79, para. 1.7. Similar legislation has been in force in Europe since the 1930s, and it has been introduced in many other parts of the world. On strata titles in Australia, see (1991) 9107 EG 92 (N. Carter); and for other comparisons, see [2005] Conv 53 (C. G. van der Merwe and P. F. Smith). The suggestion that "strata title" be introduced in England was first made in the Report of the Committee on Positive Covenants Affecting Land 1965, Cmnd 2719.   [6] Pp. 663 et seq, post.

[7] Pp. 230 et seq, post.

[8] [1986] Conv 361. On the relationship between commonhold and leasehold, see (2004) 8 L & T Rev 100 (T. Aldridge).

In 1991 the Government announced its proposals for the introduction of commonhold,[9] although the legislation was not finally enacted until 2002.[10]

III The Commonhold Scheme

A Commonhold Land

Land is commonhold land if three conditions are satisfied:[11]

(a) the freehold estate in the land is *registered* as a freehold estate in commonhold land;

(b) the land is specified in the memorandum of association of a *commonhold association* as the land in relation to which the association is to exercise functions, and

(c) a *commonhold community statement* makes provision for rights and duties of the commonhold association and unit-holders.

B Registration of the Title to Commonhold Land

Only freehold land, registered with absolute title,[12] can be held as commonhold land.[13] The application must be made by the person who is already registered as proprietor of the land, or a person who is entitled to be registered.[14] The application for registration as commonhold must be accompanied by certain specified documents, including the certificate of incorporation and other documents relating to the commonhold association, the community commonhold statement, and evidence of the consent of certain persons with an interest in the land.[15] The estate may not be registered as commonhold without the consent of anyone who is the registered proprietor of the freehold in the whole or any part of the land, or of a lease granted for more than twenty-one years, or the registered proprietor of a charge over it,[16] or the holder of the equivalent unregistered interests in or over the land, or the

---

[9] A Consultation Paper in 1990 (Cm 1345) contained a draft Bill; [1991] Conv 170 (H. W. Wilkinson). In 1996 the Lord Chancellor's Department issued a further Consultation Paper and draft Bill; [1997] Conv 6; (1996) IL & T Rev 3 (J. C. Williams); a third draft Bill published in 2000 (Cm 4843) fell when the general election of 2001 was called. See also Blundell Memorial Lecture 1991: *Commonhold–Can we make it work* (J. Wylie and E. Nugee QC); [1997] Conv 169 (L. Charlebois); [1998] Conv 283 (L. Crabb); [2006] Conv 14 (S. M. J. Wong).

[10] CLRA 2002, Part I; [2002] Conv 349 (D. N. Clarke); Commonhold Regulations 2004 (SI 2004 No. 1829); Commonhold (Land Registration) Rules 2004 (SI 2004 No. 1830). See also LCD Consultation Paper on Proposals for Commonhold Regulations 2002 and Analysis of the Responses to the Consulation Paper 2003; DCA Non-Statutory Guidance on the Commonhold Regulations 2004; Guidance on the Drafting of a Commonhold Community Community Statement including Specimen Local Rules 2005; all are available on the DCA web site. [11] CLRA 2002, s. 1(1).

[12] Ibid., s. 2(3)(a); for absolute title, see pp. 105–6, ante, pp. 956–7, post.

[13] Flying freeholds (p. 181, ante), certain agricultural land, and contingent estates (liable to revert or vest in another on particular events) cannot be commonhold: ibid., s. 4, Sch. 2.

[14] CLRA 2002, s. 2(1), (3). This therefore includes a transferee of a registered estate who has not yet been registered, and a transferee of unregistered land where the estate is now to be registered for the first time. The application for first registration is completed first, before the title is then re-registered as commonhold: Land Registry Practice Guide 60, para. 4.1.

[15] Ibid., s. 2(2), Sch. 1; Commonhold Regulations, reg. 4; C(LR)R 2004, rr. 5–7; Land Registry Practice Guide 60. [16] Ibid., s. 3.

holder of a lease granted for twenty-one years or less which will be extinguished by virtue of the registration as commonhold.[17]

The commonhold association is registered as proprietor of the freehold estate in the common parts, and each of the unit-holders is registered as proprietor of the freehold estate in the unit.[18]

C The Commonhold Association

The commonhold association is a private company limited by guarantee.[19] Its purpose is to hold the registered commonhold title to the common parts of the property, and to manage the commonhold scheme: the directors must exercise their powers so as to permit or facilitate each unit-holder to exercise his rights, and enjoy the freehold estate in his unit.[20] The unit-holders for the time being are the members of the association.[21]

In substance, therefore, the commonhold association will be responsible for the repair and maintenance of the common parts, and to give effect to the individual parties' rights and duties in respect of the whole commonhold scheme under the commonhold community statement.

D The Commonhold Community Statement

The commonhold community statement makes provision for the rights and duties of the commonhold association, and of the unit-holders. It must take a prescribed form.[22] This is the legal heart of the commonhold scheme which, amongst other things, must define the several commonhold units,[23] make provision regulating the use of units, impose duties (on either the commonhold association or the unit-holder) in respect of the insurance, repair and maintenance of each unit,[24] and make provisions regulating the use of the common parts and imposing on the commonhold association the duty to insure, repair and maintain the common parts.[25] It may also impose duties on either the association or individual unit-holders:[26]

(a) to pay money;

(b) to undertake works;

---

[17] Commonhold Regulations 2004, reg. 3. Registration of the freehold as commonhold extinguishes prior leases, whatever the length of the term: CLRA 2002, ss. 7(3)(d), 9(3)(f). If a tenant or sub-tenant was not required to give consent, he has an action for against his superior landlord or the freeholder who did give consent: s. 10.

[18] CLRA 2002, s. 9. The land may be registered initially as commonhold land without unit-holders being identified and registered; the applicant then continues to be registered as the proprietor of the freehold estate in the commonhold land, and the commonhold community statement does not come into effect, until at least one unit-holder becomes entitled to be registered: ibid., s. 7.   [19] Ibid., s. 34; Sch. 3.

[20] Ibid., s. 35.

[21] Ibid., Sch. 3, paras. 7, 12. The initial subscribers to the company's memorandum will also be members, as may any developer in respect of the scheme during the period before the commonhold was established with the registration of the unit-holders. The subscribers and any developer may resign, but the unit-holders may not: para. 13; and no other person may become a member: para. 10.

[22] Ibid., ss. 31–33; Commonhold Regulations 2004, reg. 15, Sch. 3. For an example, see Cowan, Driscoll and Target, *Commonhold Law and Practice*, Appendix B.

[23] Ibid., s. 11(2)(b). A plan must be included: s. 11(3)(a).   [24] Ibid., s. 14.

[25] Ibid., s. 26. The commonhold association will in practice maintain a reserve fund, to which the unit holders are required to contribute, to provide for such expenditure: s. 39. For mandatory provisions for allocation of costs between unit-holders, see s. 38.   [26] Ibid., s. 31(5).

(c) to grant access;

(d) to give notice;

(e) to refrain from entering into transactions of a specified kind in relation to a commonhold unit;

(f) to refrain from using the whole or part of a commonhold unit for a specified purpose or for anything other than a specified purpose;

(g) to refrain from undertaking works (including alterations) of a specified kind;

(h) to refrain from causing nuisance or annoyance;

(i) to refrain from specified behaviour;

(j) to indemnify the commonhold association or a unit-holder in respect of costs arising from the breach of a statutory requirement.

In other words, it provides a complete set of rules for the enjoyment and management of the property, and covenants (both positive and negative) which bind and benefit both the unit-holders and the commonhold association which is charged with its enforcement. This set of rules, which are enforceable in the courts,[27] is designed to fulfil one of the principal aims of the introduction of commonhold: to facilitate the enforcement of covenants between freehold owners of shared property.[28]

E Transfer of Commonhold Units

Commonhold units must be freely alienable: the commonhold community statement may not prevent or restrict the transfer of a unit.[29] On a sale or gift of the registered proprietor's estate in a unit, the new unit-holder must notify the commonhold association of the transfer,[30] and he will be entitled to be registered as the proprietor.

Since the unit-holder has the benefit and burden of rights and obligations under the commonhold community statement, it is crucial—as with the rights and liabilities of a former tenant in the case of the assignment of a lease[31]—to know what rights and liabilities, if any, attach to former unit-holders, and at what moment the benefit and burden of such rights and liabilities passes to the transferee. Under the Act[32] the new unit-holder acquires the rights and duties from the moment of the transfer, and not only from the moment when he is registered as proprietor of his unit. Similarly, the former unit-holder ceases to incur any new liability or acquire any right once he has transferred his unit, even if his name still appears on the register as proprietor.

F Leases and Charges of Commonhold Units

The Act draws a distinction between residential and non-residential commonhold units as regards the unit-holder's power to grant leases. In the case of residential commonhold,[33] the principal restriction is that the lease must not be granted for a premium, nor for longer than

---

[27] CLRA 2002, s. 37; Commonhold Regulations 2004, reg. 17.   [28] P. 184, ante.

[29] CLRA 2002, s. 15(2).   [30] Ibid., s. 15(3).   [31] Pp. 312 et seq, post.

[32] CLRA 2002, s. 16.

[33] A unit is residential if provision is made in the commonhold community statement for it to be used only for residential purposes, or for residential and other incidental purposes: ibid., s. 17(5).

seven years.[34] There is no general restriction on leasing of non-residential commonhold units, which is instead governed by the provisions of the commonhold community statement.[35]

The unit-holder is not generally restricted by the Act or by the commonhold community statement from creating, granting or transferring any other interests in the whole or part of his unit, or a charge over his unit.[36] This is particularly significant in allowing the unit-holder to mortgage his interest. Since his interest in the unit is a freehold, not a wasting asset such as a leasehold, this therefore fulfils another principal aim of the introduction of commonhold: to facilitate the raising of funds on mortgage by owners of shared property by ensuring that it continues to constitute good security, and thereby to maintain its value as a transferable asset.[37]

G Termination of Commonhold

The Act makes provision for both voluntary winding up of the commonhold association[38] and for winding-up by the court,[39] and for the registrar to make arrangements, in consequence, for the freehold estate in land to cease to be registered as a freehold estate in commonhold land.

---

[34] CLRA 2002, s. 17; Commonhold Regulations 2004, reg. 11.   [35] Ibid., s. 18.

[36] Regulations may, however, impose limits and require the consent of the commonhold association: ibid., s. 20(3). For restrictions on the creation of interests in, and charges over, part only of a commonhold unit, see ss. 21, 22.

[37] P. 184, ante. The ability of the commonhold association to charge the common parts, of which it is the registered proprietor, is limited by CLRA 2002, ss. 28, 29.   [38] CLRA 2002, ss. 43 et seq.

[39] Ibid., ss. 50 et seq.

B. Leasehold Estates

SUMMARY

10

LEASEHOLD INTERESTS[1]

SUMMARY

[1] See generally Aldridge, *Leasehold Law*; Bright and Gilbert, *Landlord and Tenant Law*; Hill and Redman's *Landlord and Tenant*; Woodfall, *Landlord and Tenant*; Evans and Smith, *Law of Landlord and Tenant*; Hill and Redman, *Guide to Landlord and Tenant Law*; Sparkes, *A New Landlord and Tenant*; M & B, chap. 8; Foa, *Law of Landlord and Tenant*.

The Law Commission has published numerous reports on the law of landlord and tenant: (*a*) The Obligations of Landlords and Tenants 1975 (Law Com No. 67); (*b*) Covenants Restricting Dispositions, Alterations and Change of User 1985 (Law Com No. 141); (1985) 135 NLJ 991, 1015 (P. F. Smith); (*c*) Forfeiture of Tenancies 1985 (Law Com No. 142); (*d*) Leasehold Conveyancing 1987 (Law Com No. 161); (*e*) Landlord and Tenant: Reform of the Law 1987 (Law Com No. 162, Cm 145) which reviews the law and identifies areas which require reform; (*f*) Privity of Contract and Estate 1988 (Law Com No. 174); (*g*) Compensation for Tenants' Improvements 1989 (Law Com No. 178); (*h*) Distress for Rent 1991 (Law Com No. 194); (*i*) Business Tenancies: A Periodic Review of the Landlord and Tenant Act 1954 Part II 1992 (Law Com No. 208); [1993] Conv 334 (M. Haley); (*j*) Implied Covenants for Title 1991 (Law Com No. 199); (*k*) Termination of Tenancies Bill 1994 (Law Com No. 221); (*l*) Responsibility for State and Condition of Property 1996 (Law Com No. 238); (*m*) Land, Valuation and Housing Tribunals 2003 (Law Com No. 281); (*n*) Renting Homes 2003 (Law Com No. 284; a "narrative report"). Consultation papers have been published by

(a) the Law Commission on Termination of Tenancies for Tenant Default 2004 (Law Com No. 174);

(b) the Lord Chancellor's Department on Distress for Rent 2001 (Cm 5096);

(c) the DTLR on Landlord and Tenant: Responsibility for State and Condition of Property (2001); and on Business Tenancies Legislation in England and Wales: The Government's Proposals for Reform (2001); [2002] Conv 261 (R. Hewitson). On the voluntary Code of Practice for Commercial Leases, see (2002) 152 NLJ 1033 (J. Keating);

(d) the Office of the Deputy Prime Minister on Commercial Property Leases (2004);

(e) the Department of the Environment on the Reform of the Caravan Sites Act 1968 (1992); [1993] Conv 39, 111 (G. Holgate); LTA 1954 Part II (1996); Residential Leasehold Reform (1999).

Many cases on leases are reported only in the Property, Planning and Compensation Reports (until 1967, Planning and Compensation Reports; from 1968 until 1985, Property and Compensation Reports); the Estates Gazette (issued weekly); the Estates Gazette Digest (published annually until 1984) and (since 1985) the Estates Gazette Law Reports; Landlord and Tenant Reports (since 1998). Specialist periodicals are Landlord and Tenant Law Review (which began in 1997) and Rent Review and Lease Journal (1981).

The history of leasehold interests is—and continues to be—one of tension: where should the lease be placed within the structure of private law? We have seen[2] how the leasehold developed during the Middle Ages: it became accepted as a property right, but not a freehold

[2] Pp. 36–8 et seq, ante.

estate; it was not even recognised as real property even though its significance, and in particular its commercial significance, was already well established. It was personalty but, since it is an estate in land, was classified as a "chattel real". Even today it remains technically personalty, but we have seen how realty and personalty were assimilated before and by the 1925 legislation to such an extent that there is now no significant practical distinction between realty and leasehold interests.[3]

More recently a different question has arisen in relation to the proper place for the lease: the extent to which it should be characterised in contractual, rather than proprietary terms. In a sense this is returning the lease to its fundamental origins: before it was recognised as an estate in land, it was seen as a purely personal covenant between the landlord and the tenant. We shall see that the courts have begun to re-emphasise the contractual nature of the lease, and sometimes to apply contractual rules, rather than property rules; and even to recognise that a lease can exist that is not an estate in land—a purely personal relationship without proprietary characteristics.[4]

We begin this chapter with an examination of the general principles of leasehold law. However, it is important to understand that that the lease may be used in significantly different commercial and social contexts.[5] A lease may be a weekly tenancy or a term of 999 years. It may be a private residential letting, a (secure) public sector tenancy, an agricultural tenancy or a commercial letting. The application of the general principles of leasehold law will therefore in some measure reflect the context of the particular letting. But, more than that, superimposed on the general law is a large body of statutory material dealing with specialised topics which reflect these different commercial and social contexts. There are many distinct statutory codes, in various respects radically different from each other, but with the general policy of limiting the rent which a landlord can obtain, and of restricting his right to recover possession of the premises at the end of the lease; and sometimes of granting to the tenant the right to acquire an extended lease or even the freehold. An outline of these codes is given in Section IX below.

I General Characteristics of a Lease

A Terminology

We sometimes refer to a "lease", or a "leasehold" estate or interest; sometimes to a "term of years"; sometimes to a "tenancy". These expressions[6] are, for most practical purposes, synonymous in the sense that they all refer to the relationship between a landlord (or "lessor")

---

[3] Pp. 38, 83 et seq, ante. The lease, as a chattel real, is however to be distinguished in many significant respects from *pure* personalty: ibid.

[4] *Bruton v London and Quadrant Housing Trust* [2000] 1 AC 406, M & B p. 441; p. 195, post.

[5] Office for National Statistics, Social Trends 35 (2005), chap. 10. For an extract from the 2004 edn, see M & B pp. 434–5.

[6] And others, such as a "letting"; or a "demise" (the latter expression now most commonly used in relation to mortgages *by demise*, which are no longer possible under LRA 2002, although the principles of leasehold interests still underpin the mortgage: p. 725, post). In earlier days, the language was more significant, in that the landlord's covenant for quiet enjoyment was implied only if the word "demise" was used in the grant: n. 275, post. A "sub-lease", "under-lease" or "sub-tenancy" similarly refers to the relationship of landlord and tenant, but where the landlord is himself a tenant under a superior lease. See also LPA 1925, s. 205(1)(xxiii).

and a tenant (or "lessee") which we shall discuss in detail in this chapter. As we shall see, each expression may more commonly be used in certain contexts: for example, a leasehold estate which continues only from week to week may generally be referred to as a weekly *tenancy*; whereas a lease for a fixed number of years may naturally be referred to as a *term of years*. However, for the general purposes of this chapter, they may be taken to be different names for the same legal entity.[7] The interest retained by the landlord is the *reversion*.

B The Lease as an Estate or Interest in Land. Legal and Equitable Leases

A leasehold is capable of subsisting as a legal estate,[8] but to do so it must be created in the manner required by the law[9] and satisfy the definition of a "term of years absolute" contained in the Law of Property Act 1925.[10] A "term of years absolute" means a term that is to last for a certain fixed period, even though it may be liable to come to an end before the expiration of that period by the service of a notice to quit, the re-entry of the landlord,[11] operation of law,[12] or a provision for cesser on redemption (as in the case of a mortgage term[13]). It includes a term for less than a year,[14] or for one year, or for a year or years and a fraction of a year, and also a tenancy from year to year or for any other period such as a weekly or monthly tenancy. A term of years absolute is a legal estate notwithstanding that it does not entitle the tenant to enter into immediate possession, but is limited to begin at a future date. Such a lease is called a reversionary lease.[15]

The Act provides that:[16] "A legal estate may subsist concurrently with or subject to any other legal estate in the same land in like manner as it could have done before the commencement of this Act" and it therefore follows, for example, that A, who owns the legal fee simple in Blackacre, may grant a legal lease to B, who then grants a legal sub-lease to C. In such a case three legal estates exist together in the same land.

A lease which does not satisfy the definition of a term of years absolute, or which has not been created in the required manner,[17] can take effect only as an equitable interest.[18]

C The Lease as a Contract

A lease is not only an interest in property—a legal estate or an equitable interest; it is also a contract between landlord and tenant. "A lease is a hybrid, part contract, part property."[19] This hybrid nature gives rise to a tension between contractual rules and property rules

---

[7] For the purpose of LPA 1925 the "term of years" includes a term for less than a year, or from year to year (a periodic tenancy): s. 205(1)(xxvii). However, other statutes might not necessarily by the use of one expression include the others; it depends on the construction of the enactment: *Re Land and Premises at Liss, Hants* [1971] Ch 986 at 990, per GOULDING J.   [8] LPA 1925, s. 1(1)(b).

[9] Pp. 219 et seq, post.   [10] LPA 1925, s. 205(1)(xxvii).   [11] Pp. 273, 280, post.

[12] For example, where the purposes for which a term has been created are satisfied, the term merges in the reversion and ceases accordingly: LPA 1925, s. 5.

[13] Mortgages by demise are no longer possible under LRA 2002: p. 724, post.

[14] *Re Land and Premises at Liss, Hants* [1971] Ch 986 at 991, per GOULDING J; *EWP Ltd v Moore* [1992] QB 460.

[15] P. 208, post. It must however take effect in possession within twenty-one years of its creation: ibid.

[16] LPA 1925, s. 1(5)   [17] *R v Tower Hamlets LBC, ex p Von Goetz* [1999] QB 1019.

[18] LPA 1925, s. 1(3). For this important aspect of leases under the doctrine of *Walsh v Lonsdale*, see pp. 223 et seq, post.

[19] *Linden Gardens Trust Ltd v Lenesta Sludge Disposals Ltd* [1994] 1 AC 85 at 108, per Lord BROWNE-WILKINSON.

applicable to a lease. The courts have held that certain essential characteristics of a lease cannot be overridden by the contract between the parties.[20] However, in recent years they have emphasised the contractual nature of a lease and have sometimes applied contractual rules. A lease is now subject to the doctrine of frustration,[21] and can be terminated by the tenant in response to the repudiatory conduct of the landlord.[22] A tenancy agreement which one party is induced to enter into by the fraud of the other can be rescinded at the election of the innocent party.[23] A notice to terminate a periodic joint tenancy has been explained in contractual terms;[24] and rent is no longer conceived of as a proprietary interest but rather as a payment which a tenant is contractually bound to make to his landlord for the use of the land.[25] A person cannot grant a lease to himself because of his inability to contract with himself.[26] Terms may be implied into a lease on the same principles as other contracts.[27] And some of the statutory controls on unfair contract terms apply also to leases.[28]

However, in *Bruton v London & Quadrant Housing Trust*[29] the House of Lords went further, and held that an agreement to grant exclusive possession[30] of a flat created a tenancy, even though the landlord housing trust had no freehold or leasehold estate out of which it could grant a leasehold estate to the tenant, but was only a licensee from the freehold owner; and this was the basis on which the tenant agreed to the arrangement. This is not simply a

[20] *Prudential Assurance Co Ltd v London Residuary Body* [1992] 2 AC 386, M & B p. 447, p. 211, post (maximum duration of the term must be ascertainable at the outset: see, however, Lord BROWNE-WILKINSON at 397 who hoped that "the Law Commission might look at the subject to see whether there is in fact any good reason now for maintaining a rule which operates to defeat contractually agreed arrangements between the parties"); *Street v Mountford* [1985] AC 809, M & B p. 473, p. 198, post (lease distinguished from (contractual) licence); *PW & Co v Milton Gate Investments Ltd* [2004] Ch 142 (it is not possible to contract out of the general rule (p. 329, post) that a sub-tenancy comes to an end on determination of the head tenancy: "a tenancy is not merely a contract: it is and it creates an estate in land", per NEUBERGER J at 164; see, however, *Bruton v London & Quadrant Housing Trust* [2000] 1 AC 406, M & B p. 441, infra). See also *Linden Gardens Trust Ltd v Lenesta Sludge Disposals Ltd*, supra, at 108–9 (covenant against assignment in lease, unlike similar covenant in any other contract, does not prevent the assignment taking effect because of the proprietary nature of a lease; p. 256, post).

[21] *National Carriers Ltd v Panalpina (Northern) Ltd* [1981] AC 675, p. 328, post.

[22] *Hussein v Mehlman* [1992] 2 EGLR 87, M & B p. 437, p. 324, post, per Smedley QC, holding that the decisions of the House of Lords in *United Scientific Holdings Ltd v Burnley BC* [1978] AC 904 (rent review clause in lease to be interpreted on normal contractual principles) and *National Carriers Ltd v Panalpina (Northern) Ltd*, supra (lease may be frustrated) have superseded the decision of the Court of Appeal in *Total Oil Great Britain Ltd v Thompson Garages (Biggin Hill) Ltd* [1972] 1 QB 318 to the effect that a lease cannot be repudiated.

[23] *Killick v Roberts* [1991] 1 WLR 1146 at 1150; [1992] Conv 269 (J. Martin); [1992] CLJ 21 (L. Tee).

[24] *Hammersmith and Fulham LBC v Monk* [1992] 1 AC 478, p. 323, post.

[25] *C H Bailey Ltd v Memorial Enterprises Ltd* [1974] 1 WLR 728, p. 266, post, approved in *United Scientific Holdings Ltd v Burnley BC*, supra.

[26] *Rye v Rye* [1962] AC 496, M & B p. 521: "A man cannot make himself his own tenant", per Lord RADCLIFFE at 512. [27] *Liverpool City Council v Irwin* [1977] AC 239.

[28] The Unfair Contract Terms Act 1977 does not apply to a covenant in a lease "in so far as it relates to the creation or transfer of an interest in land": Sch. 1, para. 1(b); *Electricity Supply Nominees Ltd v IAF Group Ltd* [1993] 1 WLR 1059 (anti-set off clause excluded); *Star Rider Ltd v Inntrepreneur Pub Co* [1998] 1 EGLR 53 (agreement for lease). But the Unfair Terms in Consumer Contract Regulations 1999 do apply to contracts relating to land, and therefore to a lease: *R (Khatun) v Newham LBC* [2005] QB 37; Office of Fair Trading, Guidance on Unfair Terms in Tenancy Agreements 2005 (OFT 356). The Law Commission proposes to replace the Unfair Contract Terms Act 1977 and the Unfair Terms in Consumer Contracts Regulations 1999 with a single statute which, in relation to land contracts, would apply only to *consumer* contracts (thereby broadly maintaining the position under the 1977 Act and the 1999 Regulations): Unfair Terms in Contracts 2005 (Law Com No. 293) paras. 3.80, 4.84, 5.77. [29] [2000] 1 AC 406, M & B, p. 441; p. 205, post.

[30] Applying the indicia of a tenancy set out in *Street v Mountford* [1985] AC 809, M & B p. 473; pp. 196 et seq, post.

decision that a lease has the characteristics of a contract, creating personal obligations between the parties; but a decision that a lease can exist that is *only* personal to the parties and need not create an estate in the land at all:[31]

The term "lease" or "tenancy" describes a relationship between two parties who are designated landlord and tenant. It is not concerned with the question of whether the agreement creates an estate or other proprietary interest which may be binding upon third parties. A lease may, and usually does, create a proprietary interest called a leasehold estate or, technically, a "term of years absolute." This will depend upon whether the landlord had an interest out of which he could grant it. Nemo dat quod non habet. But it is the fact that the agreement is a lease which creates the proprietary interest. It is putting the cart before the horse to say that whether the agreement is a lease depends upon whether it creates a proprietary interest.

This decision is surprising, and not uncontroversial.[32] It might be understood as a purposive interpretation of the meaning of a particular statutory provision: the question at issue in the case was whether the tenant could require the landlord to fulfil the obligation to repair the premises implied by section 11 of the Landlord and Tenant Act 1985, which applies to a "lease of a dwelling-house granted . . . for a term of less than seven years".[33] By holding that the contract constituted such a "lease", the House of Lords has ensured that landlords bear the obligation to repair, and cannot escape it by showing that they do not have a sufficient estate themselves out of which the tenant's leasehold could be granted. However, the approach taken in the case was not to restrict the decision to an interpretation of the particular statutory provision, but instead to make a general statement about the nature of a lease, applicable not only to the Landlord and Tenant Act 1985, but also to other legislation which refers to a lease or tenancy.[34]

D The Essentials of a Lease

For a lease to be created, the landlord must confer on the tenant the right to exclusive possession of certain land for a term—a period that is definite or capable of definition. Discussing the case of a residential tenancy, Lord TEMPLEMAN said:[35]

where . . . the only circumstances are that residential accommodation is offered and accepted with exclusive possession for a term at a rent, the result is a tenancy . . .

---

[31] [2001] 1 AC 406 at 415, per Lord HOFFMANN.

[32] For trenchant criticism, see S. Bridge in *Land Law Issues, Debates, Policy*, ed. L. Tee, chap. 4, M & B p. 445. See [1999] All ER Rev 229 (P. J. Clarke); (1999) 3 L & TR 124 (M. Pawlowski); (2000) 4 L & TR 119 (M. Pawlowski and J. Brown); (2000) 116 LQR 7 (S. Bright); [2000] CLJ 25 (M. Dixon); [2002] Conv 550 (M. Pawlowski); [2005] Conv 114 (J.-P. Hinojosa). See also, for an analysis of the nature of a lease which was rejected by the House of Lords, the judgment of MILLETT LJ in the Court of Appeal: [1998] QB 834.

[33] LTA 1985, s. 13; pp. 234–6, post.

[34] [2000] 1 AC 406 at 413, per Lord HOFFMANN. For discussion of the problems to which this gives rise (e.g. in relation to covenants under LT(C)A 1995) see (2000) 4 L & TR 119 (M. Pawlowski and J. Brown). However, the consequences of the decision will be limited, since a "*Bruton* tenancy"(as it is now commonly called see, e.g., *Kay v Lambeth LBC* [2006] 2 WLR 570 at [143]) does not create an estate, but only a personal relationship between the parties, and so its incidents take effect only as between the parties themselves; third parties will not be bound: *Kay v Lambeth LBC*, supra; *Islington LBC v Green* [2005] L & TR 24 (both cases holding, on facts similar to those in *Bruton*, that the lease was not binding on the freeholder).

[35] *Street v Mountford* [1985] AC 809 at 827, p. 198, post.

If these three hallmarks—exclusive possession, for a term, at a rent—are present, then there will be a tenancy unless there are exceptional circumstances to negative it.[36] The payment of rent, though normally required under the terms of a lease, is not, however, essential.[37] We shall consider the obligation to pay rent in the context of the tenant's covenants, later in this chapter;[38] but here we consider the essential elements of a lease: the grant of exclusive possession, for a term.

E The Right to Exclusive Possession

A necessary feature of a lease is that the tenant shall be given the right to exclude all other persons from the land, including the landlord.[39] This does not mean, however, that whenever a person is let into exclusive possession he necessarily becomes a tenant. It may well be that he obtains only a personal privilege in the shape of a licence which may be revoked according to the express or implied terms of the contract.[40] There are a number of reasons why it is important to determine whether a transaction creates a lease or a licence. The plethora of cases on this in recent years has arisen from the applicability of the Rent Acts which conferred substantial security of tenure and other rights on a residential tenant but not on a licensee.[41] Changes to the statutory regimes governing tenancies[42] have reduced the rights of tenants to the point where there is now less incentive for the owner of residential property to seek to create a licence rather than a lease.[43] However, questions may still arise in relation to the construction of occupation agreements which were entered into during the time of the Rent Acts. And the distinction between a lease and a licence is still relevant to business tenancies,[44] as well as to determine the nature, content and legal consequences more generally of agreements to occupy land.[45] Most important, however, is that a lease is

---

[36] For such exceptional circumstances, see pp. 205 et seq, post.

[37] LPA 1925, s. 205(1)(xxvii); *Ashburn Anstalt v Arnold* [1989] Ch 1, n. 64, post (occupier let into possession for business purposes under rent-free arrangement pending redevelopment; only outgoings payable during occupation; held to be a tenant); *Skipton Building Society v Clayton* (1993) 66 P & CR 223; [1993] Conv 478 (L. Crabb).

For a residential tenancy to be protected under the Rent Act 1977, the rent had to be not less than two-thirds of the rateable value or, if not in money, quantifiable: *Barnes v Barratt* [1970] 2 QB 657; *Bostock v Bryant* (1990) 61 P & CR 23 (Uncle Joe who owned a house and lived in one room paid general and water rates in respect of the whole house, and the respondents, who lived in the rest of the house, the gas and electricity likewise for the whole; CA held that, assuming the respondents were tenants, the rent was not quantifiable).

Where, however, no rent is payable, a licence may be the more likely construction: *Barnes v Barratt*, supra; *Onyx (UK) Ltd v Beard* [1996] ECGS 55. [38] Pp. 241 et seq, post.

[39] *London and North Western Rly Co v Buckmaster* (1874) LR 10 QB 70 at 76. [40] Pp. 833 et seq, post.

[41] In particular, Rent Act 1977; section IX, pp. 336 et seq, post. The context in which this question has arisen (statutory provisions designed to protect residential tenants) has no doubt influenced the courts' interpretation of the test to distinguish between a lease and a licence: see *Street v Mountford* [1985] AC 809, infra.

[42] In particular, HA 1988 which phased out the Rent Act 1977 by introducing the assured and assured shorthold tenancy (pp. 338 et seq, post); and HA 1996 which further extended the application of assured shorthold tenancies (pp. 344 et seq, post). [43] Pp. 198 et seq, post.

[44] LTA 1954 Part II; pp. 377 et seq, post.

[45] E.g. the duty of care owed to an occupier in respect of his chattels by a licensor but not by a landlord: *Appah v Parncliffe Investments Ltd* [1964] 1 WLR 1064; the warranty of suitability of premises for their intended purpose implied into a licence: *Wettern Electric Ltd v Welsh Development Agency* [1983] QB 796; (1983) 80 LSG 2195 (H. W. Wilkinson): there is generally no such warranty in respect of a lease, in the absence of an express covenant by the landlord: p. 232, post; the length of notice required for the termination of a licence: *Smith v Northside Developments Ltd* [1987] 2 EGLR 151; and under FA 2003, s. 48(1) and (2) a lease is a stamp duty chargeable interest, but a licence to use or occupy land (or a tenancy at will) is not. Certain other differences have been removed

generally[46] capable of being enforced against third parties as a legal estate or an equitable interest, whereas generally[47] a licence is not.

In deciding whether a transaction creates a lease or a licence,[48] the test has now come full circle. In the nineteenth century the crucial issue was whether the occupier had exclusive possession of the land or not;[49] if he was in exclusive possession, other than as a freeholder or copyholder, he was a tenant; if not, he was a licensee.[50] From the middle of the twentieth century the emphasis shifted from the rigid test of exclusive possession to the flexible test of the intention of the parties to be inferred from all the circumstances. For example, in *Marchant v Charters*[51] Lord DENNING MR said:

What is the test to see whether the occupier of one room in a house is a tenant or a licensee? It does not depend on whether he or she has exclusive possession or not. It does not depend on whether the room is furnished or not. It does not depend on whether the occupation is permanent or temporary. It does not depend on the label which the parties put upon it. All these are factors which may influence the decision but none of them is conclusive. All the circumstances have to be worked out. Eventually the answer depends on the nature and quality of the occupancy. Was it intended that the occupier should have a stake in the room or did he have only permission for himself personally to occupy the room, whether under a contract or not? In which case he is a licensee.

In 1985, however, the House of Lords in *Street v Mountford*[52] considered the distinction for the first time and decisively rejected the flexible test. In that case

there was a licence agreement under which it was conceded that Mrs Mountford was given exclusive possession of furnished rooms for £37 a week. She had signed a statement at the end of the agreement that she understood and accepted that it "does not and is not intended to give me a tenancy protected

in recent years, e.g. the doctrines of frustration and termination for repudiatory breach now apply to leases as well as to licences: p. 195, ante. It can sometimes also be necessary for the purposes of value added tax to know whether a transaction is a lease or a licence to occupy land: VAT Act 1994, s. 31 and Sch. 9 Part II Group 1. This provision, which implements Council Directive 77/388, must however be construed in accordance with Community law: *Sinclair Collis Ltd v Customs and Excise Commissioners* [2001] STC 989 (HL); [2003] STC 898 (ECJ); *Belgium v Temco Europe SA* [2005] STC 1451; *Abbey National plc v Customs and Excise Commissioners* [2005] 3 EGLR 73 190.

46 Not, however, a "*Bruton* lease": p. 195, ante. This is a further confusion thrown up by the House of Lords' acceptance of the concept of a "lease" that is not an estate or interest in land. See also (2000) 4 L & TR 119 (M. Pawlowski and J. Brown).

47 Unless the circumstances give rise to a constructive trust: *Ashburn Anstalt v Arnold* [1989] Ch 1, M & B pp. 612, 618; or proprietary estoppel: pp. 841 et seq, post.

48 Megarry, *Rent Acts*, vol 1, chap. 3; Evans and Smith, *Law of Landlord and Tenant*, chap. 3; Martin, *Residential Security*, 2nd edn, pp. 7–31. On the distinction between a lease and a sale, see *Paper Properties Ltd v Power Corpn plc* (1994) 69 P & CR D 16 ("It is a clear that at one end of the range of possibilities a letting at a rack rent for no premium cannot be a sale. At the other end the grant of a leasehold interest at a peppercorn rent for a premium of £6.5 million would be a sale", per PETER GIBSON LJ).

49 The giving of a right of exclusive possession should be distinguished from the giving of an exclusive or sole right to use the premises for a particular purpose which has never been held to create a tenancy: *Hill v Tupper* (1863) 2 H & C 121; *Wilson v Tavener* [1901] 1 Ch 578; *Clore v Theatrical Properties Ltd and Westby & Co Ltd* [1936] 3 All ER 483.

50 In *Lynes v Snaith* [1899] 1 QB 486, LAWRENCE J said: "As to the first question, I think it is clear [the defendant] was a tenant at will and not a licensee; for the admissions state that she was in exclusive possession, a fact which is wholly inconsistent with her having been a mere licensee"; *Allan v Liverpool Overseers* (1874) LR 9 QB 180; *Glenwood Lumber Co Ltd v Phillips* [1904] AC 405. Cf *Taylor v Caldwell* (1863) 3 B & S 826.

51 [1977] 1 WLR 1181 at 1185. See also *Abbeyfield (Harpenden) Society Ltd v Woods* [1968] 1 WLR 374 at 376, per Lord DENNING MR; *Barnes v Barratt* [1970] 2 QB 657 at 669, per SACHS LJ; *Shell-Mex and BP Ltd v Manchester Garages Ltd* [1971] 1 WLR 612; *Somma v Hazlehurst* [1978] 1 WLR 1014, p. 202, post.

52 [1985] AC 809, M & B p. 473; [1985] All ER Rev 190 (P. J. Clarke); [1985] Conv 328 (R. Street); [1985] CLJ 351 (S. Tromans); 48 MLR 712 (S. Anderson); (1986) 130 SJ 3, 27 (P. M. Rank); [1986] Conv 39 (D. N. Clarke); [1986] Conv 344 (S. Bridge); Lewison, *Lease or Licence: The Law after Street v Mountford*.

under the Rent Acts". As SLADE LJ said in the Court of Appeal: "It was a plain expression of the intentions of both parties that what she was being given was a licence rather than a tenancy. There is no plea by her of misrepresentation, undue influence or *non est factum* and no claim to rectification."[53]

The House of Lords reversed the Court of Appeal and held that the agreement was a tenancy. Lord TEMPLEMAN said:[54]

where . . . the only circumstances are that residential accommodation is offered and accepted with exclusive possession for a term at rent, the result is a tenancy . . .

Henceforth the courts which deal with these problems will, save in exceptional circumstances, only be concerned to inquire whether as a result of an agreement relating to residential accommodation the occupier is a lodger or a tenant.

The intentions of the parties as to the nature of the agreement are irrelevant; the only intention which is relevant is the intention to grant exclusive possession:

The manufacture of a five-pronged implement for manual digging results in a fork even if the manufacturer, unfamiliar with the English language, insists that he intended to make and has made a spade.[55]

(1) Exclusive Possession

(a) *Tenant or lodger*

Sometimes it may be difficult to discover whether, on the true construction of an agreement, exclusive possession is conferred. As JESSEL MR said:[56]

I think it wiser and safer to say that the question whether a man is a lodger, or whether he is an occupying tenant, must depend on the circumstances of each case.

It is clear that the reservation by the landlord of the right to enter and view the state of the premises and to repair and maintain them does not derogate from the exclusive possession of the tenant. It merely serves to emphasise the fact that the occupant is entitled to exclusive possession and is a tenant.[57] It is also clear that the occupier of residential accommodation at a term for a rent is a lodger, if the landlord provides attendance or services which require the landlord or his servants to exercise unrestricted access to and use of the premises.[58] But

---

[53] (1984) 271 EG 1261 at 1262.

[54] [1985] AC 809 at 827. A simple example of the rule is *Caplan v Mardon* [1986] CLY 1873 (held in the county court that three students were joint tenants in spite of a signed agreement that nothing in it should create a tenancy).

[55] Ibid., at 819. See *Antoniades v Villiers* [1990] 1 AC 417 at 444, where BINGHAM LJ said: "The House of Lords [in *Street v Mountford*] has not, I think, held that assertions in a document that it is a licence should be ignored. It has held that the true legal nature of a transaction is not to be altered by the description the parties choose to give it. A cat does not become a dog because the parties have agreed to call it a dog. But in deciding whether an animal is a cat or a dog the parties' agreement that it is a dog may not be entirely irrelevant." See also Lewison, *Interpretation of Contracts*, para. 9.07. In *Brooker Settled Estates v Ayers* [1987] 1 EGLR 50 O'CONNOR LJ said at 51: "Lord Templeman reviewed the authorities dealing with this tortured question, and sought to introduce some order into the law for the better administration of the law and guidance of the learned judges, particularly in the county courts, who have to deal with this problem."

[56] *Bradley v Baylis* (1881) 8 QBD 195 at 218.   [57] *Street v Mountford* [1985] AC 809 at 818.

[58] At 818. See also *Royal Philanthropic Society v County* [1985] 2 EGLR 109; *Brillouet v Landless* (1996) 28 HLR 836. But the fact that the occupier chooses not to avail himself of the attendance or services cannot convert a licence into a tenancy: *Uratemp Ventures Ltd v Collins* [2000] 1 EGLR 156 at 157, per PETER GIBSON LJ. The presence or absence of cooking facilities is not relevant: *Uratemp Ventures Ltd v Collins* [2002] 1 AC 301. On the equivocal significance of the retention of keys by the landlord, see *Aslan v Murphy* [1990] 1 WLR 766, M & B p. 498.

such provision, or the lack of it, is not by itself decisive. Lord TEMPLEMAN did not say in *Street v Mountford* that the occupier was a lodger if, and only if, such attendance or services were provided.[59] And in *Brooker Settled Estates Ltd v Ayers*[60] the Court of Appeal reversed the county court judge who had held that there was a tenancy where:

a written agreement purported to license an individual occupier of one room in a three room flat to occupy the whole flat, repeatedly asserting that nobody had exclusive possession of anything and reserving to the licensor the right to put another person into that room. "There is no evidence that Brooker & Co provided any attendance or services to Miss Ayers. By that definition, she must have had the exclusive use of the room. She was not a lodger, *ergo* she was a tenant."

In reversing the judgment, the Court of Appeal pointed out that in *Street v Mountford* the right to exclusive possession had been conceded, and ordered a new trial as to the nature of the possession given when the agreement was made and as to the credibility and honesty of the licensor as a witness.

Useful guidance was given in *Crancour Ltd v Da Silvaesa*,[61] where PURCHAS LJ considered the signals for which the court should look in order to decide whether the occupier is a tenant or a lodger. He identified the criteria which the court should ignore or, alternatively, should not be treated as decisive; namely:

(a) the description of the agreement chosen by the parties, for example, "lease" or "licence";

(b) the actual subjective intention of the parties, even if they are *ad idem*;[62]

(c) the effects of the Rent Acts are irrelevant to the construction of the document;

(d) the exercise or failure to exercise rights provided by the agreement by one, other or both parties to the agreement is not of decisive importance;

(e) the court should not draw up a "shopping list" of clauses;

(f) the court should not award marks for drafting.

(b) Business tenant or licensee

The decision in *Street v Mountford*, which related to residential accommodation, has been applied to business tenancies not only where the three indicia of exclusive possession and payment of rent for a term are present,[63] but even where the indicium of rent is

---

59 *Crancour Ltd v Da Silvaesa* [1986] 1 EGLR 80 at 85, per RALPH GIBSON LJ; *Huwyler v Ruddy* (1996) 72 P & CR D3 (provision of cleaning and linen once a week which entailed only twenty minutes' labour held to be unrestricted access).

60 [1987] 1 EGLR 50.

61 [1986] 1 EGLR 80 at 88. These criteria mainly summarise points raised by Lord TEMPLEMAN in *Street v Mountford*. See (1987) 50 MLR 226 (A. J. Waite). See also Lord DONALDSON OF LYMINGTON in *Aslan v Murphy* [1990] 1 WLR 766 at 770–1, M & B p. 498.

62 Unless they do not intend to enter into the agreement at all: *Isaac v Hotel de Paris Ltd* [1960] 1 WLR 239, cited in *Street v Mountford* [1985] AC 809 at 823.

63 *London and Associated Investment Trust plc v Calow* [1986] 2 EGLR 80, M & B p. 486; [1987] Conv 137 (S. Bridge); *Dellneed Ltd v Chin* (1986) 53 P & CR 172 (Mai Toi agreement); [1987] Conv 298 (S. Bridge); cf *Smith v Northside Developments Ltd* [1987] 2 EGLR 151 (*oral* agreement where occupier said that he "would take unit 17 on my own" held not to be grant of exclusive possession). See also *Bracey v Read* [1962] 3 All ER 472 at 475, per CROSS J; *University of Reading v Johnson-Houghton* (1985) 276 EG 1353 (grant of right to "gallops for race-horses at Blewbury in Berkshire" held to be a lease on the balance of probabilities . . . despite its title ("licence"))

lacking.[64] The Court of Appeal, however, held in *Dresden Estates Ltd v Collinson*[65] that "an unusual provision" in a licence agreement which reserved to the licensor of an industrial unit the right to relocate the licensee to an adjoining unit effectively deprived the licensee of the right to exclusive possession. GLIDEWELL LJ said[66] that the test in relation to residential premises as to whether the occupier is a tenant or a lodger:

is of course of itself not applicable to business tenancies because there is no such person as a lodger in relation to business premises. For myself, I think that the indicia, which may make it more apparent in the case of a residential tenant or a residential occupier that he is indeed a tenant, may be less applicable or be less likely to have that effect in the case of some business tenancies.

The decision of the Court of Appeal in *IDC Group Ltd v Clark*,[67] holding that an agreement for the occupation of business premises, which was made by a deed which was *professionally* drawn and described as a licence, was a licence and not an easement, may be significant in the construction of an agreement for business, but not for residential, accommodation. As JONATHAN PARKER LJ said in *Clear Channel UK Ltd v Manchester City Council*:[68]

I find it surprising and (if I may say so) unedifying that a substantial and reputable commercial organisation ... having (no doubt with full legal assistance) negotiated a contract with the intention *expressed in the contract* that the contract should *not* create a tenancy, should then invite the court to conclude that it did ...

I do not intend to cast any doubt whatever upon the principles established in *Street v Mountford*. On the other hand, the fact remains that this was a contract negotiated between two substantial parties of equal bargaining power and with the benefit of full legal advice. Where the contract so negotiated contains not merely a label but a clause that sets out in unequivocal terms the parties' intention as to

and much of its language), per LEONARD J at 1356; [1986] Conv 275 (C. P. Rodgers); *Graysim Holdings Ltd v P & O Property Holdings Ltd* [1996] AC 329 (stallholder in covered market at Wallasey held to be tenant); *Hunts Refuse Disposals v Norfolk Environmental Waste Services Ltd* [1997] 1 EGLR 16 (agreement giving waste disposal firm access to part of active quarry for twenty-one years for disposal of waste on payment held to be licence); *Venus Investments Ltd v Stocktop Ltd* [1996] EGCS 173 (vendor of garage permitted to remain after completion under written agreement intended to create licence and not lease held to be licensee); *Clear Channel UK Ltd v Manchester City Council* [2006] 04 EG 168 (20-metre high advertising hoarding on supports which were set in one-metre deep concrete base, which covered significant area of a roundabout, but where exact site for placing bases and hoardings was undefined: licence).

[64] *Ashburn Anstalt v Arnold* [1989] Ch 1, n. 37, ante: "We are unable to read Lord Templeman's speech in *Street v Mountford* as laying down a principle of 'no rent, no lease'", per FOX LJ at 9.

[65] [1987] 1 EGLR 45, M & B p. 485; [1987] Conv 220 (P. E. Smith); (1987) 50 MLR 655 (S. Bridge); *Esso Petroleum Co Ltd v Fumegrange Ltd* [1994] 2 EGLR 90 (three-year "partnership licence" agreement, which reserved control to licensor over physical layout of premises and way in which the business was run, held to be licence); *National Car Parks Ltd v Trinity Development Co (Banbury) Ltd* [2002] 2 P & CR 18 (agreement to operate shoppers' car park held to be licence because grantee had no right to exclude grantor).

[66] At 47. See also *London and Associated Investment Trust plc v Calow*, [1986] 2 EGLR 80 at 84, where Judge Baker QC said: "There might be special cases of some sort of trading properties, areas in shops and so forth, or stalls in markets, and there might be difficulties with agricultural properties, where licences are frequent"; *McCarthy v Bence* [1990] 1 EGLR 1 (joint venture in form of sharing milk arrangement held to be licence for purposes of s. 2(2)(b) of the Agricultural Holdings Act 1986; agreement would not involve "exclusive occupation", and area of land and fields available for licensee's cows might be altered from time to time by the licensor, who also enjoyed access for several purposes such as the exercise of sporting rights, felling dead elm trees, hedging and ditching and "walking with his dog, taking his thistle spud in the thistle season to pull out thistles or doing any other minor tidying up that caught his eye"; [1991] Conv 58 (C. Rodgers), 207 (M. Slater)); *Wigan BC v Green & Son (Wigan) Ltd* [1985] 2 EGLR 242 ("permission to use exclusively" stalls in covered market for "a very substantial butcher's shop" held to be tenancy). [67] (1992) 65 P & CR 179, p. 598, post.

[68] [2006] 04 EG 168 at [28]–[29].

its legal effect, I would in any event have taken some persuading that its true effect was directly contary to that expressed intention.

The policies underlying the statutory regulation of business tenancies may also differ from those underlying the regulation of residential tenancies. In so far as the courts have been reluctant to allow parties to draft licences to avoid the policy of the Rent Acts[69] in relation to residential tenancies, their approach to business tenancies or licences may therefore not be so strict.[70]

(2) Sham or Genuine. Multiple Occupation

Before 1985 some landlords had drafted occupation agreements in terms designed to ensure that the premises were occupied under a licence and not under a lease. Their object was to avoid the application of the Rent Acts. Thus in *Somma v Hazelhurst*:[71]

Mr H and Miss S each entered into separate but identical agreements with the owner of a dwelling-house to occupy a double bed-sitting room. Each agreement repeatedly proclaimed itself to be a licence and stated that the licensor was not willing to grant exclusive possession of any part of the rooms, and that the use of the rooms was to be "in common with the licensor and such other licensees as the licensor may permit to use the said rooms". Each occupant was severally liable for his or her rent.

The Court of Appeal held that each agreement was a licence, CUMMING-BRUCE LJ saying:[72]

We can see no reason why an ordinary landlord . . . should not be able to grant a licence to occupy an ordinary house. If that is what both he and the licensee intend and if they can frame any written agreement in such a way as to demonstrate that it is not really an agreement for a lease masquerading as a licence, we can see no reason in law or justice why they should be prevented from achieving that object. Nor can we see why their common intentions should be categorised as bogus or unreal or as sham merely on the ground that the court disapproves of the bargain.

In *Street v Mountford* the House of Lords strongly disapproved of this case saying that both agreements were a sham:[73]

Although the Rent Acts must not be allowed to alter or influence the construction of an agreement, the court should be astute to detect and frustrate sham devices and artificial transactions whose only object is to disguise the grant of a tenancy and to evade the Rent Acts.[74]

---

[69] P. 337, post.

[70] In particular, it should be noted that the parties to a business tenancy are permitted by LTA 1954, Part II, to contract out of the provisions that are designed to protect the tenant: p. 385, post.

[71] [1978] 1 WLR 1014. Followed in *Aldrington Garages Ltd v Fielder* (1978) 247 EG 557; *Sturolson & Co v Weniz* (1984) 272 EG 326. Cf *O'Malley v Seymour* (1978) 250 EG 1083; *Walsh v Griffiths-Jones* [1978] 2 All ER 1002, where the agreements were held to be sham. For a detailed review, see (1980) 130 NLJ 939, 959 (A. Waite).

[72] At 1024. HL Appellate Committee (Lords WILBERFORCE, SALMON and FRASER OF TULLYBELTON) refused leave to appeal: [1978] 2 All ER 1011 at 1025.

[73] "It would have been more accurate and less liable to give rise to misunderstandings if I had substituted the word 'pretence' for the references to 'sham devices' and 'artificial transactions'": *AG Securities v Vaughan* [1990] 1 AC 417 at 462, per Lord TEMPLEMAN. See also *Stribling v Wickham* [1989] 2 EGLR 35 at 38, per Sir Denys BUCKLEY. See *Snook v London and West Riding Investments Ltd* [1967] 2 QB 786 at 802, where DIPLOCK LJ defines "this popular and pejorative word": "If it has any meaning in law, it means acts done or documents executed by the parties to the 'sham' which are intended by them to give to third parties or to the court the appearance of creating between the parties legal rights and obligations different from the actual legal rights and obligations (if any) which the parties intend to create."

[74] [1985] AC 809 at 825. Cf the similar approach in the House of Lords to tax avoidance schemes which involve "a pre-ordained series of transactions (whether or not they include the achievement of a legitimate

In *AG Securities v Vaughan* and *Antoniades v Villiers*[75] (which were heard simultaneously) the House of Lords went further and overruled *Somma v Hazelhurst*. Both cases concerned separate flat-sharing agreements, both were described as "licences", and both denied exclusive possession (in terms drafted before *Street v Mountford*). In both cases the House of Lords reversed the Court of Appeal, holding that in the first there was a licence, and in the second a joint tenancy.

In *AG Securities v Vaughan*:

Four young men signed separate agreements on different dates with different amounts of payment. The documents were described as licences, denied exclusive possession of any part and required the occupier to share with not more than three other persons. When there was a change, there was a pecking order for the best rooms.

The House of Lords held that the four occupiers were individual licensees, and not joint tenants. The differences of date and payment made it impossible for the four unities (of possession, interest, time and title) of a joint tenancy to exist.[76] As Lord BRIDGE OF HARWICH said:[77]

The arrangement seems to have been a sensible and realistic one to provide accommodation for a shifting population of individuals who were genuinely prepared to share the flat with others introduced

commercial end) into which there are inserted steps which have no commercial purpose apart from the avoidance of a liability to tax which in the absence of those particular steps would have been payable": *IRC v Burmah Oil Co Ltd* [1982] STC 30 at 32, per Lord DIPLOCK. See also *W T Ramsay v IRC* [1982] AC 300; *Furniss v Dawson* [1984] AC 474; *Craven v White* [1989] AC 398; *Hatton v IRC* [1992] STC 140; *IRC v Fitzwilliam* [1993] 1 WLR 1189; *IRC v McGuckian* [1997] 1 WLR 991; *MacNiven v Westmoreland Investments Ltd* [2003] 1 AC 311. See Maudsley and Burn, *Trusts and Trustees*, pp. 613–21. See also *Gisborne v Burton* [1989] QB 390, where CA invoked the tax doctrine to strike down a scheme to deny a sub-tenant the protection of the Agricultural Holdings Act 1948, s. 24(1); cf *Hilton v Plustitle Ltd* [1989] 1 WLR 149 (company let scheme held not to be a sham because the company tenant, rather than the occupier, performed all the obligations under the tenancy), distinguished in *Bankway Properties Ltd v Pensfold-Dunsford* [2001] 1 WLR 1369 (*non-negotiated* provision for five-fold rent increase in assured tenancy, designed to give landlord right to possession contrary to purpose of HA 1988, held unenforceable); [2001] CLJ 146 (S. Bright); *Kaye v Massbetter Ltd* (1990) 62 P & CR 558 (letting to limited company tenant with a view to excluding the Rent Acts held to be genuine); [1992] Conv 58 (P. Luther); *Estavest Investments Ltd v Commercial Express Travel Ltd* [1988] 2 EGLR 91; [1991] 11 OJLS 136 (S. Bright); *Belvedere Court Management Ltd v Frogmore Developments Ltd* [1997] QB 858. See also the 1986 Blundell Memorial Lecture, summarised at (1986) 83 LSG 3736 (K. Lewison); (1987) 84 LSG 403 (P. Freedman); (2001) 117 LQR 575 (Lord TEMPLEMAN); Getzler, ed., *Rationalizing Property, Equity and Trusts*, chap. 7 (Lord TEMPLEMAN); chap. 8 (B. McFarlane and E. Simpson).

[75] [1990] 1 AC 417, M & B p. 488; [1989] 1 CLJ 19 (C. Harpum); (1989) 105 LQR 165 (P. V. Baker); (1989) Conv 128 (P. F. Smith); (1989) 52 MLR 408 (J. Hill); [1988] All ER Rev 171 (P. J. Clarke); (1992) 142 NLJ 575 (S. Bright) (arguing that the co-occupants may be tenants in common; note, however, that as against the landlord, the (legal) lease must be held as a joint tenancy).

[76] On the four unities, see pp. 454–5, post; cf *Mikeover Ltd v Brady* [1989] 3 All ER 618, M & B p. 496 (where each of two occupants was liable for his or her own share of the payments, CA held that there was no unity of interest and therefore each had a licence). See, however, Lord TEMPLEMAN in *Antoniades v Villiers* at 461 ("a tenancy remains a tenancy even though the landlord may choose to require each of two joint tenants to agree expressly to pay one-half of the rent").

AG Securities v Vaughan was followed *in Stribling v Wickham* [1989] 2 EGLR 35, M & B p. 493; [1989] Conv 192 (J. E. Martin) (three friends signed identical agreements; on change of occupation the new occupant signed an agreement ending on expiry of agreements of the remaining occupiers; on that date all then in occupation signed new arrangements with common expiry date; CA held each occupier to have a separate licence).

[77] At 454.

from time to time who would, at least initially, be strangers to them. There was no artificiality in the contracts concluded to give effect to this arrangement.

In *Antoniades v Villiers*:

There were two separate agreements based on the *Somma v Hazelhurst* precedent. They were entered into by a man and a woman who wished to live together in a small flat in undisturbed quasi-connubial bliss.[78] They chose a double rather than single beds. They were to use the flat in common with the owner or other licensees permitted by him.

Unlike *AG Securities v Vaughan*, "the two agreements were interdependent, not independent of one another. Both would have signed or neither. The two agreements must therefore be read together".[79] The sharing term was "contrary to the provisions of the Rent Acts and, in addition was, in the circumstances, a pretence intended only to get round the Rent Acts".[80]

    Lord TEMPLEMAN set out the matters to be taken into consideration when construing one or more documents in order to decide whether a tenancy has been created.[81]

The court must consider the surrounding circumstances including any relationship between the prospective occupiers, the course of negotiations[82] and the nature and extent of the accommodation and the intended and actual mode of occupation of the accommodation.

This approach appears to resurrect some aspects of the earlier, more flexible test for distinguishing between a lease and a licence.[83]

(3) Licensee or Sub-tenant

The status of sharers of residential accommodation was further considered by the Court of Appeal in *Monmouth Borough Council v Marlog*.[84]

Mr Roberts, the secure tenant of a house, shared it with Mrs Marlog and her two children. There were three bedrooms; he occupied one, and they occupied the other two. The kitchen, bathroom and living accommodation were shared. Mrs Marlog paid a weekly rent to Mr Roberts.

The Court held that, although Mrs Marlog and her children had exclusive occupation of their two bedrooms, she was not the sub-tenant of Mr Roberts, but only his licensee, and therefore not entitled to remain as a secure tenant when Mr Roberts' tenancy from the local authority came to an end. NOURSE LJ said:[85]

Where two persons move into residential premises together under a tenancy granted to one but not the other of them, each occupying a bedroom or bedrooms and the remainder of the premises being

---

[78] *Street v Mountford* [1985] AC 809 at 825, per Lord TEMPLEMAN.

[79] At 460, per Lord TEMPLEMAN. Followed in *Aslan v Murphy* [1990] 1 WLR 766, M & B p. 498; [1989] All ER Rev 172 (P. J. Clarke); *Nicolaou v Pitt* [1989] 1 EGLR 84 ("after a certain amount of humming and hawing the owner said he did contemplate introducing a stranger into the flat. I do not believe him." CA held that there was a tenancy, even though the flat had a spare bedroom and had been previously occupied by three persons).

[80] At 464.   [81] At 458.

[82] The negotiations, however, are of limited relevance in construing a written contract: Lewison, *Interpretation of Contracts*, para. 3.05. On the relevance of subsequent conduct Lord OLIVER OF AYLMERTON said in *AG Securities v Vaughan* [1990], AC 417 at 469: "though subsequent conduct is irrelevant as an aid to construction, it is certainly admissible as evidence on the question of whether the documents were or were not genuine documents giving effect to the parties' true intentions".

[83] See, e.g., *Marchant v Charters* [1977] 1 WLR 1181 at 1185, per Lord DENNING MR; p. 198, ante.

[84] [1994] 2 EGLR 68, M & B p. 495.   [85] At 70.

shared between them, the court will be slow to infer a common intention that the one who is not the tenant shall be the subtenant of the one who is. The natural inference is that what is intended is a contractual house-sharing arrangement under the tenancy of one of them. The inference is greatly strengthened where, as here, there is a written agreement between the landlord and the tenant and none between the tenant and the other occupant.

(4) Exceptional Circumstances

Where the occupier has the right to exclusive possession, there are certain exceptional circumstances where he may nevertheless only be a licensee. In *Street v Mountford* Lord TEMPLEMAN identified as exceptional[86] those cases where:

(a) *the occupancy is within one of a number of special categories*, that is, under a contract for the sale of land, or pursuant to a contract of employment or referable to the holding of an office.[87] The Court of Appeal has interpreted the first exception narrowly, in holding that a *potential* purchaser of a dwelling-house who entered into exclusive possession for a term at a rent under an arrangement with the ultimate intention of negotiating for its sale was a tenant;[88]

(b) *the owner has no power to grant a tenancy*.[89] This exception has been controversially whittled down by the House of Lords in *Bruton v London and Quadrant Housing Trust*.[90] In this case:

> a local authority owned a block of flats of which it had no statutory authority to grant a tenancy. It therefore entered into a licence agreement with the Housing Trust, which prohibited it from granting a tenancy. The Trust then entered into a "weekly licence agreement" with

[86] [1985] AC 809 at 826. The categories are "illustrative and not exhaustive": *Dellneed Ltd v Chin* (1986) 53 P & CR 172 at 187, per MILLETT J. See *Royal Philanthropic Society v County* [1985] 2 EGLR 109, where CA rejected a number of submitted exceptional circumstances; [1986] Conv 215 (P. F. Smith); *Whitbread West Pennines Ltd v Reedy* [1988] ICR 807.

[87] *Mayhew v Suttle* (1854) 4 E & B 347; *Smith v Seghill Overseers* (1875) LR 10 QB 422. Distinguish a service occupant who is a licensee from a service tenant who is not. The latter is a person to whom a dwelling-house is let in consequence of his employment, but who is not required to live there for the better performance of his duties: *Torbett v Faulkner* [1952] 2 TLR 659. See *Royal Philanthropic Society v County*, supra; *Norris v Checksfield* [1991] 1 WLR 1241 (semi-skilled mechanic held to be service licensee, even though he was never in a position to perform the duties required of him); *Burgoyne v Griffiths* [1991] 1 EGLR 14 (farm cottage); *South Glamorgan County Council v Griffiths* [1992] 2 EGLR 232; *Hughes v Greenwich LBC* [1994] 1 AC 170; *Surrey County Council v Lamond* [1999] 1 EGLR 32 (employer providing facility, but not imposing obligation). The occupant may also be an object of charity; *Gray v Taylor* [1998] 1 WLR 1093 (occupant of Peterborough Almshouse held to be a licensee); [1998] 2 L & TR 40.

[88] *Bretherton v Paton* [1986] 1 EGLR 172. See also *Essex Plan Ltd v Broadminster* (1988) 56 P & CR 353 (licence where occupier continued in possession after expiry of option; no exclusive possession); [1989] Conv 55 (J. E. Martin); cf *Heslop v Burns* [1974] 1 WLR 1241, M & B p. 508, p. 212, post, where SCARMAN LJ held that occupation prior to a contract of sale was a paradigm case of a tenancy at will; *Vandersteen v Agius* (1992) 65 P & CR 266 (occupation pursuant to sale of goodwill of osteopathy practice not an exception). On purchasers in possession generally, see [1987] Conv 278 (P. Sparkes).

[89] *Street v Mountford* [1985] AC 809 at 821; *Camden LBC v Shortlife Community Housing Ltd* (1992) 90 LGR 358 (which contains a critique on the exceptions by MILLETT J); [1993] Conv 157 (D. S. Cowan).

[90] [2000] 1 AC 406; (1999) 3 L & TR 124 (M. Pawlowski); [1998] Conv 524 (D. Rook); [2000] CLJ 25 (M. Dixon). The doctrine of tenancy by estoppel was held to be irrelevant; the sole issue was whether the agreement created a tenancy; pp. 195–6, ante. See *Mehta v Royal Bank of Scotland* [1999] 3 EGLR 153 (licence even though the three hallmarks of *Street v Mountford* were present; ten other equally significant factors based on the parties' intentions and surrounding circumstances to be taken into account; no deliberate intention to exclude the Rent Acts); (1999) 3 L & TR 64.

Mr Bruton, who had exclusive possession of his flat. He brought an action against the Trust for breach of repairing obligations implied by section 11 of the Landlord and Tenant Act 1985.[91]

In holding the Trust liable, the House of Lords held that, although the Trust had no estate out of which it could grant a tenancy, nevertheless the agreement satisfied the criteria of *Street v Mountford*. It was not a special circumstance that the Trust was "a responsible landlord performing socially valuable functions".[92] It seems, however, that Mr Bruton had no estate binding on third parties.

(c) *the circumstances show that there is no intention to create legal relationships* as, for example, "where there has been something in the circumstances, such as a family arrangement, an act of friendship or generosity, or such like, to negative any intention to create a tenancy".[93]

It would appear that the test of intention is relevant in deciding whether there is an intention to create a legal relationship, but irrelevant in deciding which legal relationship is created.

(5) Examples of Licences

Licences rather than leases have been created where an employer allowed his retiring servant to remain in his cottage rent free for the rest of his life;[94] where a father, wishing to provide a home for his son and daughter-in-law, allowed them to occupy a house that he had bought in return for their promise to pay the instalments still due to a building society;[95] where a

---

[91] P. 234, post.

[92] See Lord HOFFMANN at 414. Cf *Westminster City Council v Clarke* [1992] 2 AC 288; [1992] Conv 112 (J. E. Martin), 285 (D. S. Cowan); [1992] All ER Rev 225 (P. J. Clarke) (grant of "licence to occupy" to occupant of single room in men's hostel run by appellant council, in pursuance of its duty to house the homeless under HA 1985, s. 65(2), held to be a licence and not a secure tenancy; "a very special case which depends on the peculiar nature of the hostel maintained by the council, the use of the hostel by the council, the totality, immediacy, and objectives of the powers exercisable by the council and the immediate restrictions imposed on Mr. Clarke. The decision in this case will not allow a landlord, private or public, to free himself from the Rent Acts or from the restrictions of a secure tenancy merely by adopting or adapting the language of the licence to occupy": per Lord TEMPLEMAN at 302); *Parkins v Westminster City Council* [1998] 1 EGLR 22. See also HA 1985, s. 79(2)(a), Sch. 1, para. 4, which excludes most tenancies granted in such circumstances from statutory protection. See also HA 1996, Part VII, Pp. 358–9, post.

[93] *Facchini v Bryson* [1952] 1 TLR 1386 at 1389–90, per DENNING LJ, cited *Street v Mountford* at 821. See *Booker v Palmer* [1942] 2 All ER 674; *Marcroft Wagons Ltd v Smith* [1951] 2 KB 496; *Heslop v Burns* [1974] 1 WLR 1241; *Sharp v MacArthur* (1987) 19 HLR 364, where owner of flat, with empty "For Sale" notice board prominently displayed, let defendant into possession as a favour pending sale. Held by CA to be a licence, even though defendant had exclusive possession and was given a rent book for the purpose of enabling him to obtain payment from the DHSS for outgoings for accommodation; *Carr Gomm Society v Hawkins* [1990] CLY 2811 (self-employed gardener held to be licensee of registered charity which had sixty homes in London and a continuing need to move people if necessary); *Westminster City Council v Basson* [1991] 1 EGLR 277 (girl friend who remained in exclusive possession of flat after her boy friend's tenancy had been terminated held to be licensee, even though she had received rent rebates from the council, which had made it clear that no tenancy was intended); [1992] Conv 113 (J. E. Martin); *Colchester BC v Smith* [1991] Ch 448 at 485–6 (no intention to create legal relations where occupant's implied offer to pay reasonable rent was rejected, and where there was insistence on his occupation at his own risk and on his giving up possession at short notice if land required for other purposes). Cf *Nunn v Dalrymple* (1989) 59 P & CR 231; *Ward v Warnke* (1990) 22 HLR 496 (in both cases a *family* arrangement in which exclusive possession of a cottage in return for regular payments was held to be a tenancy). See also *Abbeyfield (Harpenden) Society Ltd v Woods* [1968] 1 WLR 374; *Barnes v Barratt* [1970] 2 QB 657 (house-sharing arrangement without rent or fixed term held to be licence).

[94] *Foster v Robinson* [1951] 1 KB 149; *Binions v Evans* [1972] Ch 359, M & B p. 617 (widow of deceased employee). [95] *Errington v Errington and Woods* [1952] 1 KB 290.

landlord allowed the daughter of his deceased employee to remain in her father's cottage rather than evict her immediately;[96] where a woman bought a house and allowed her brother to occupy it, rent free;[97] where a man aged eighty-five occupied a room in an old people's home;[98] where a lodger occupied a room in a self-contained residential hotel for men;[99] where "under an informal family arrangement" a mother bought a house and allowed her son and his second wife to live there on payment of £7 a week;[100] where a gardener-handyman occupied a cottage rent and rates free;[101] where a petrol company granted what purported to be a one-year licence of a petrol filling station;[102] and where a company was permitted to sink concrete bases into the ground and to fix to them substantial advertising hoardings.[103]

F The Term

There is no limit of time for which a lease may be made to endure; periods of 99 or 999 years are common, and longer periods are possible,[104] but a lease cannot exist for an indeterminate period, such as in perpetuity.[105]

It may be limited to certain hours of the day.[106] It may even be for a discontinuous period, for example, a single letting for three successive bank holidays. In the context of time-sharing of holiday homes, it was held that the lease of a cottage for one week in each year for eighty consecutive years was a lease for a discontinuous period of eighty years.[107]

(1) The Term must be Certain. Commencement of Period

The term must be for a definite period in the sense that it must have a certain beginning[108] and a certain ending. This does not necessarily mean that the parties must immediately fix

---

96 *Marcroft Wagons Ltd v Smith* [1951] 2 KB 496.

97 *Cobb v Lane* [1952] 1 All ER 1199. See also *Heslop v Burns* [1974] 1 WLR 1241.

98 *Abbeyfield (Harpenden) Society Ltd v Woods*, supra.

99 *Marchant v Charters* [1977] 1 WLR 1181. The decision was approved, but not its reasoning, in *Street v Mountford* at 824.

100 *Hardwick v Johnson* [1978] 1 WLR 683, M & B, p. 608; cf *Tanner v Tanner* [1975] 1 WLR 1346, M & B p. 600.

101 *Scrimgeour v Waller* (1980) 257 EG 61; *De Rothschild v Wing RDC* [1967] 1 WLR 470.

102 *Shell-Mex and BP Ltd v Manchester Garages Ltd* [1971] 1 WLR 612; *Esso Petroleum Co Ltd v Fumegrange Ltd* [1994] 2 EGLR 90, p. 201, n. 65, ante.

103 *Clear Channel UK Ltd v Manchester City Council* [2006] 04 EG 168, p. 201, ante.

104 The length of a lease can be significant for tax purposes, since stamp duty land tax is payable under FA 2003, Part 4 and Sch. 5, on the net present value of the lease, which is the discounted aggregate of the rents payable over the whole of the term. A shorter lease with an option to renew may therefore be more tax efficient than a longer lease with a break clause: [2004] Conv 167 (M. Blackwell); [2005] Conv 7 (E. Slessenger).

105 *Sevenoaks, Maidstone and Tunbridge Rly Co v London, Chatham and Dover Rly Co* (1879) 11 Ch D 625 at 635–6. The effect of an instrument purporting to create a perpetual lease at a rent may perhaps be either to create a yearly tenancy or to pass the fee simple to the lessee subject to the payment of an annual rentcharge in perpetuity: *Doe d Roberton v Gardiner* (1852) 12 CB 319 at 333. Contrast a *perpetually renewable* lease, which is converted by statute into a term of 2000 years: p. 209, post.

106 *Graysim Holdings Ltd v P & O Property Holdings Ltd* [1996] AC 329.

107 And not for "a term certain exceeding 21 years" within VATA 1983, s. 1, Sch. 2, para. 4. VAT was therefore chargeable: *Cottage Holiday Associates Ltd v Customs and Excise Comrs* [1983] QB 735. See Timeshare Act 1992; Timeshare Directive (94/47/EC); Timeshare Regulations 1997 (SI 1997 No. 1081); Timeshare Act 1992 (Amendment) Regulations 2003 (SI 2003 No. 1922); Timeshare (Cancellation Information) Order 2003 (SI 2003 No. 2579); [1992] Conv 30; [1993] Conv 248 (H. W. Wilkinson).

108 *Harvey v Pratt* [1965] 1 WLR 1025 (contract for lease void for failing to specify date of commencement); *Liverpool City Council v Walton Group plc* [2001] 1 EGLR 149 (uncertainty in respect of two dates six weeks apart in 999-year term could be resolved).

the exact date of commencement, for it is open to them to agree that the lease shall *begin* upon the occurrence of an uncertain event as, for example, upon the declaration of war by Great Britain;[109] or: "upon possession of the premises becoming vacant".[110]

Such an agreement, though at first conditional, becomes absolute and enforceable as soon as the event occurs.[111]

(2) *Interesse Termini* Abolished

There was a troublesome doctrine of the common law which provided, in the case of a lease not operating under the Statute of Uses, that the lessee acquired no estate in the land until he actually entered into possession. Until that time he was said to have a mere right to take possession, and this right was called an *interesse termini*. This requirement of entry to perfect a lease was, however, abolished by the Law of Property Act 1925, and all terms of years absolute, created before or after the commencement of the Act, take effect from the date fixed for the commencement of the term without actual entry.[112]

(3) Reversionary Leases

A term expressed to begin from a past date[113] or, as is more usual, from the date of the lease is called a lease *in possession*. It is also possible to create a *reversionary* lease, by which the term is limited to commence at some future date.[114] Formerly such a term might be granted so as to commence at any time in the future, as, for instance, where a lease was made in 1917 to commence in 1946,[115] but a restriction was imposed upon this right by the Law of Property Act 1925, which provides that:

A term, at a rent or granted in consideration of a fine, limited after the commencement of this Act to take effect more than 21 years from the date of the instrument purporting to create it, shall be void, and any contract made after such commencement to create such a term shall likewise be void.[116]

The first limb of this enactment nullifies the creation of a reversionary lease limited to take effect more than twenty-one years from the date of the lease, for example, a lease executed in 2006 for a term of ten years to run from 2030. The second limb nullifies a contract to create *such a term*, that is, a term that will commence more than twenty-one years from the date of the lease by which it will eventually be created. For example, a contract,

---

[109] *Swift v Macbean* [1942] 1 KB 375.
[110] *Brilliant v Michaels* [1945] 1 All ER 121. In this case, however, it was held that no final agreement had been made.   [111] Ibid., at 126, citing Fry, *Specific Performance* (6th edn), p. 458.
[112] LPA 1925, s. 149(1), (2).
[113] *James v Lock* (1977) 246 EG 395. Such a lease cannot retrospectively vest an estate in the lessee. A grant of a term of seven years from this day a year ago merely creates a term of six years from today. See *Bradshaw v Pawley* [1980] 1 WLR 10 at 14.
[114] The lease must be created by deed: *Long v Tower Hamlets LBC* [1998] Ch 197; the law was different before 1926. See the detailed historical analysis by James Munby QC; [1998] Conv 229 (S. Bright). See also *Wolff v Wolff* [2004] STC 1633 (reversionary lease executed by parents in favour of daughters as part of inheritance tax saving scheme set aside for parents' mistake as to its legal effect).
[115] *Mann, Crossman and Paulin Ltd v Registrar of the Land Registry* [1918] 1 Ch 202.
[116] S. 149(3). This restriction does not affect terms, such as portions terms, taking effect in equity under a settlement.

which is made in 2006 to grant a lease for ten years in 2008, the term to run from 2030 is void.[117]

Thus, the Act relates the period of twenty-one years to the date of the lease, not to the date of the contract. Therefore a contract in a lease for thirty-five years giving the tenant an option to renew it for a further period of thirty-five years by making a written request to this effect twelve months before the expiration of the current term, is not void, since the contractual option, if exercised, will result in a term to begin upon the execution of the second lease. It is immaterial that it will be more than twenty-one years before the contractual right is exercised.[118]

(4) Perpetually Renewable Leases and Other Renewal Clauses

The nearest approach to a perpetual lease before 1926 was one which was perpetually renewable; that is, one in which the landlord covenanted that he would from time to time grant a new lease on the determination of the one then existing, if the tenant should so desire and should pay a fine[119] for the privilege.

Perpetually renewable leases were inconvenient[120] and were modified by the Law of Property Act 1922. A lease made after 1925 which contains a covenant which, when properly construed, provides for perpetual renewal, operates as the grant of a lease for 2,000 years.[121] A term for 2,000 years that arises as a result of this legislation is in general subject to the covenants, conditions and provisions of the original lease, but the following special incidents have been attached to it by statute:

(a) The lessee or his successor in title may terminate the lease by giving at least ten days' written notice before any date at which, but for its conversion, it would have expired if no renewal had taken place.[122]

(b) The lessee is bound to register with the lessor every assignment or devolution of term within six months of its taking place.[123]

(c) A lessee who assigns the term to another ceases after the assignment to be liable on the covenants contained in the lease.[124]

Great care must be taken in drafting renewal clauses, since a landlord may find that a lease, though not expressly made perpetually renewable, is converted, by reason of the language used in a renewal clause, into a term that will endure for 2,000 years unless the tenant chooses to determine it sooner. This will be the case, for instance, if a lease for three years

---

[117] *Re Strand and Savoy Properties Ltd* [1960] Ch 582, M & B p. 454; *Weg Motors Ltd v Hales* [1961] Ch 176; affd. [1962] Ch 49, M & B p. 455; see (1960) 76 LQR, pp. 352–4 (R.E.M.).

[118] *Re Strand and Savoy Properties Ltd*, supra.

[119] A fine is usually the single payment of a lump sum made by the tenant, and is additional to the rent. See also n. 131 post.

[120] See remarks by JESSEL MR in *Re Smith's Charity* (1882) 20 Ch D 516.

[121] Perpetually renewable leases which already existed on 1 January 1926 were converted into leases for 2,000 years calculated from the date at which the existing term began; and any perpetually renewable sub-lease granted by the tenant out of his interest was converted into a term of 2,000 years less one day: LPA 1922, s. 145, Sch. 15, para. 1. Any fine that was due on renewal became payable as additional rent: ibid., para. 12. Where a lease made after 1925 containing a covenant for perpetual renewal is converted into a term of 2,000 years, the lessor is not entitled to convert into any additional rent any fine that may have been reserved: ibid., para. 5.

[122] LPA 1922, Sch. 15, para. 10(1)(i).   [123] Ibid., para. 10(1)(ii).

[124] Ibid., para. 11(1). Until LT(C)A 1995, p. 312 et seq, post, this was an exception to the general rule that an original lessee remained liable on the covenants in a lease despite the assignment of his interest.

contains a covenant that: "the lessor will on the request of the tenant grant him a tenancy at the same rent containing the like provisions as are herein contained including the present covenant for renewal".[125] Such a clause contains the seeds of its own reproduction[126] in the sense that a lease granted for a second period of three years would also contain a covenant for renewal, and so on *ad infinitum*.

It should, however, be noted that, in construing renewal clauses, the courts lean against perpetual renewals.[127] In *Marjorie Burnett Ltd v Barclay*[128] a perpetual lease was not created where a seven-year lease contained a covenant by the landlord to grant to the tenant at his request:

a new lease of the premises hereby demised for a further term of seven years, to commence from and after the expiration of the term hereby granted at a rent to be agreed between the parties . . .

And such lease shall also contain a like covenant for renewal for a further term of seven years on the expiration of the term thereby granted.

Nourse J held that the second paragraph of the covenant was not part of the covenant for renewal, and the notion of a 2,000-year term was completely inimical to a lease containing provision for rent review every seven years.[129]

The result, then, of the legislation is that there may be a valid contract for renewal, but not for perpetual renewal. In order to keep permissible renewals within reasonable bounds, however, it was also enacted by the Law of Property Act 1922[130] that an agreement to renew for a longer period than sixty years from the end of the lease in question shall be void.

(5) Leases for Lives or until Marriage

Certain other leases were also modified by the Law of Property Act 1925.

A lease at a rent, or in consideration of a fine,[131] made:

  (i) for life or lives, e.g. to T for life or during the lives of A and B; or

 (ii) for any term of years determinable with a life or lives, e.g. to T for nine years or to T for ninety-nine years, if X shall so long live; or

(iii) for any term of years determinable on the marriage of the tenant, e.g. to T for twenty years until T marries,

now takes effect as a lease for ninety years.[132] This lease may be terminated upon the death or the marriage, as the case may be, of the original tenant: after these events have occurred a

---

[125] *Parkus v Greenwood* [1950] Ch 644; *Northchurch Estates Ltd v Daniels* [1947] Ch 117; *Caerphilly Concrete Products Ltd v Owen* [1972] 1 WLR 372 at 376, M & B p. 457, where Sachs LJ referred to "an area of the law in which the courts have manoeuvred themselves into an unhappy position. . . . The use of a certain set of words . . . causes the lease to be perpetually renewable, even when no layman—at least if he has some elementary knowledge of business—would dream of granting such a lease and, if aware of the technical meaning of the particular phraseology would almost certainly be aghast at its devastating effect and refuse to sign. One reason for the courts so binding themselves is said to be that the formula is one the effect of which is well-known to trained conveyancers, and that this is advantageous, however much of a trap it may constitute for others."

[126] An expression used by counsel in the court below: [1950] Ch 33 at 34.

[127] *Marjorie Burnett Ltd v Barclay* (1980) 258 EG 642 at 644, per Nourse J.

[128] Ibid.; (1981) 131 NLJ 683 (H. W. Wilkinson), M & B p. 459.   [129] Ibid., at 644.

[130] Sch. 15, para. 7(2).

[131] See n. 119, ante. By statute the word includes "a premium or foregift and any payment, consideration or benefit in the nature of a fine, premium or foregift": LPA 1925, s. 205(1)(xxiii). *Skipton Building Society v Clayton* (1993) 66 P & CR 223 (transfer of freehold at two-thirds discount was "benefit in the nature of a premium" for grant of lease-back to vendor). The rent or fine excludes beneficial tenancies for life under a settlement; these are equitable interests and subject to SLA 1925 or, after 1996, to a trust of land: *Binions v Evans* [1972] Ch 359 at 366; *Ivory v Palmer* [1975] ICR 340; p. 848, n. 125, post.   [132] LPA 1925, s. 149(6).

month's notice in writing to terminate the tenancy on one of the usual quarter days may be given by either side.[133]

The policy of the Act is not altogether clear. In the case of a lease for life, ninety years is chosen as a term long enough to exceed the specified life, but it is difficult to see why *all* terms determinable with life or lives should be converted into ninety years irrespective of the term actually granted:

Why should a term of 3 years if X shall so long live automatically become a term of 90 years determinable by notice after X's death? It is possible (although one hardly dares whisper such a suggestion about the great conveyancers who drafted the statute) that it was simply a mistake.[134]

(6) Ending of Period

The date upon which a lease is to terminate is generally expressed specifically, but it is sufficient if made to depend upon some uncertain event, provided that the event occurs before the lease takes effect; as for example where lands are let to A for so many years as B shall fix. On the other hand a lease is void if the date of its termination remains uncertain after it has taken effect.[135] It was accordingly held in *Lace v Chantler*[136] that an agreement to let a house for the duration of the war did not create a valid tenancy.[137]

This principle, which has been judicially accepted for 500 years, was reaffirmed by the House of Lords in *Prudential Assurance Co Ltd v London Residuary Body*[138] in which: the London County Council granted a lease of a strip of land fronting a road on terms that "the tenancy shall continue until the land is required by the council for the purposes of widening the road". The lease was held to be void for uncertainty, since it was not possible to say at the outset what the maximum duration of the lease would be.

II Tenancies at Will and at Sufferance, Periodic Tenancies, and Tenancies by Estoppel

This section deals with various types of tenancy, apart from a lease for a fixed period of time.

---

[133] Ibid.

[134] *Bass Holdings Ltd v Lewis* (1986) unreported, per HOFFMANN J; affd. [1986] 2 EGLR 40, M & B p. 400.

[135] A tenancy at will, p. 212, post, is of infinite duration, but in other respects it shares the characteristics of a tenancy: *Ramnarace v Lutchman* [2001] 1 WLR 1651 at 1656, per Lord MILLETT.   [136] [1944] KB 368.

[137] A conveyancing device by which the difficulty may be surmounted is to grant a lease for a fixed period determinable upon the happening of the uncertain event, e.g. to A for 99 years terminable on the cessation of hostilities: *Prudential Assurance Co Ltd v London Residuary Body* [1992] 2 AC 386 at 389, per Lord TEMPLEMAN. In *Great Northern Rly Co v Arnold* (1916) 33 TLR 114, ROWLATT J managed even to construe a lease similar to that in *Lace v Chantler* as a lease for 999 years terminable on the cessation of the 1914 War. The effect of *Lace v Chantler* was to defeat so many leases made before and during the war of 1939 that it was found necessary to save them by a temporary measure, the Validation of War-time Leases Act 1944.

[138] Supra, M & B p. 447; (1993) 109 LQR 93 (P. Sparkes); [1993] Conv 461 (P. F. Smith); (1994) 57 MLR 117 (D. Wilde); [1993] CLJ 26 (S. Bridge); (1992) 13 LS 38 (S. Bright); [1992] All ER Rev 223 (P. J. Clarke); [1993] CLP Part I 69 (P. Kohler). For the subsequent holding that the purported lease was valid as a periodic tenancy on the terms of the agreement in so far as they were consistent with a yearly tenancy, see p. 214, post.

A   *Tenancy at Will*

A tenancy at will exists when A occupies the land of B as tenant with B's consent, on the understanding that either A or B may terminate the tenancy when he likes. Littleton says:

Tenant at will is where lands or tenements are let by one man to another, to have and to hold to him at the will of the lessor, by force of which lease the lessee is in possession. In this case the lessee is called tenant at will, because he hath no certain or sure estate, for the lessor may put him out at what time it pleaseth him.[139]

But such a tenancy equally arises when possession is held at the will of the lessee, and indeed it is important to notice that, even though a lease is made determinable at the will of the lessor only, it is also by implication determinable at the will of the lessee. In other words, every tenancy at will must be at the will of both parties.[140] In the words of Lord SIMONDS:

A tenancy at will, though called a tenancy, is unlike any other tenancy except a tenancy at sufferance, to which it is next-of-kin. It has been properly described as a personal relation between the landlord and his tenant: it is determined by the death of either of them or by one of a variety of acts, even by an involuntary alienation, which would not affect the subsistence of any other tenancy.[141]

A tenancy at will may be created either expressly[142] or by implication, as, for example, where a tenant, with the consent of his landlord, holds over after the expiry of the lease;[143] or where he goes into possession under a contract for a lease or under a void lease;[144] or where a purchaser goes into possession prior to completion, or a prospective tenant goes into possession during negotiations for a lease.[145] These situations apart, the courts have restricted the scope of implied tenancies at will. They are now disinclined to infer such a tenancy from an exclusive possession of premises for an indefinite period.[146] As SCARMAN LJ said in 1974:[147]

It may be that the tenancy at will can now serve only one legal purpose, and that is to protect the interests of an occupier during a period of transition. If one looks to the classic cases in which tenancies at will continue to be inferred, . . . one sees that in each there is a transitional period during which negotiations are being conducted touching the estate or interest in the land that has to be protected, and the tenancy at will is an apt legal mechanism to protect the occupier during such a period of transition: he is there and can keep out trespassers: he is there with the consent of the landlord and can keep out the landlord as long as that consent is maintained.

---

[139] Litt, s. 68.   [140] Co Litt 55a; *Fernie v Scott* (1871) LR 7 CP 202.

[141] *Wheeler v Mercer* [1957] AC 416 at 427.

[142] E.g. *Manfield & Sons Ltd v Botchin* [1970] 2 QB 612; *Hagee (London) Ltd v AB Erikson and Larson* [1976] QB 209.

[143] On the level of rent payable during the holding over period, see *Cathedral and Metropolitan Church of Christ Canterbury (Dean and Chapter) v Whitbread plc* (1996) 72 P & CR 9. Cf the tolerated trespasser, who is a public sector tenant who remains in possession after the tenancy has been ended by a possession order, and pays for occupation, without the local authority taking any active steps to evict: *Burrows v Brent LBC* [1996] 1 WLR 1448; *Newham LBC v Hawkins* [2005] 2 EGLR 51; (2003) 119 LQR 495 (S. Bright); p. 359, post.

[144] P. 222, post.

[145] *British Railways Board v Bodywright Ltd* (1971) 220 EG 651; *Ramnarace v Lutchman* [2001] 1 WLR 1651, M & B p. 508, which contains a useful summary of the law. See also *City of Westminster Assurance Co Ltd v Ainis* (1975) 29 P & CR 469; p. 288, post. Where the potential purchaser has exclusive possession and pays rent the result may be a (periodic) tenancy: *Bretherton v Paton* [1986] 1 EGLR 172, p. 205, ante, n. 88, ante (where, however, the Court did not consider the possibility of a tenancy at will). For an order for payment for use and occupation enjoyed during the period of negotiations for a lease, where the tenant at will left without the lease being concluded, see *Mayor and Burgesses of the London Borough of Lewisham v Masterson* (1999) 80 P & CR 117.

[146] As in *Lynes v Snaith* [1899] 1 QB 486.   [147] *Heslop v Burns* [1974] 1 WLR 1241 at 1253.

Where, therefore, there is a grant of exclusive possession at a rent, a court is more likely to find that a lease has been created; and, in particular, the payment of rent by reference to a yearly (or other) period is presumptive evidence of a periodic tenancy.[148]

The tenant at will therefore holds a position somewhere between a lease and a licence. Like the licensee, he has no estate: no interest in the land to which his possession can be referred,[149] and therefore has no property right to assign to another, nor anything that can bind a successor of the landlord. And his "tenancy" may be less secure than a lease, since some of statutes giving protection to tenants under residential or business leases do not apply to tenancies at will.[150] On the other hand, he has possession; and therefore as long as his tenancy at will endures, he can maintain against third parties actions to which that possession entitles him.[151] Moreover, despite the termination of his tenancy, a tenant at will has a right to emblements, that is, a right to re-enter the land at harvest to recover the crops that he has sown.[152]

B Tenancy at Sufferance

COKE said that: "Tenant at sufferance is he that at first comes in by lawful demise and after his estate ended continueth in possession and wrongfully holdeth over".[153] For example, a tenant for a fixed term becomes a tenant at sufferance if he "holds over", that is, remains in possession without the consent of the landlord, after the term has come to an end. Such a person differs from a tenant at will because his holding over after the determination of the term is a wrongful act, and he differs from a disseisor in that his original entry upon the land was lawful.[154]

A tenant at sufferance, unless he is a tenant of premises within the Rent Acts,[155] is in a precarious position. He may be ejected at any moment and has no right to emblements, while he becomes liable to statutory penalties if he remains in occupation after he should have departed. In the view of the common law tenants at sufferance came under no liability to pay rent, since it was the folly of the owners that suffered them to continue in possession after their estate had ended,[156] but under the Landlord and Tenant Act 1730[157] any tenant (or any other person getting possession under or by collusion with him) who wilfully holds over after the determination of the term, and after demand made and written notice given for delivery up of possession, is liable to pay double the yearly value of the lands for the time the

[148] P. 215, post.   [149] *Ramnarace v Lutchman* [2001] 1 WLR 1651 at 1657.

[150] LTA 1954 Part II, p. 377, post, does not apply to a tenancy at will: *London Baggage Co (Charing Cross) Ltd v Railtrack (No 2)* [2003] 1 EGLR 141. For doubts whether HA 1985 Part IV, p. 358, post, applies, see *Banjo v Brent LBC* [2005] 1 WLR 2520 at [25]–[26], [31]–[35], per CHADWICK LJ, and [40]–[43], per BUXTON LJ. However, the Rent Acts did apply to a tenancy at will, and some of the modern statutory codes which replaced them similarly apply: e.g. assured tenancies under HA 1988, p. 338, post; Megarry, *Rent Acts*, vol. 1, p. 66; vol. 3, p. 72.

[151] Such as trespass: *Heslop v Burns*, supra, per SCARMAN LJ; and, presumably, nuisance: *Hunter v Canary Wharf* [1997] AC 655; *Pemberton v Southwark LBC* [2000] 1 WLR 1672 ("tolerated trespasser"; n. 143, ante). On the significance of possession in the modern law generally, see chap. 6.

[152] This situation, in which the land reverted to the lessor but the right to enjoyment remained in effect with the tenant, seemed unsatisfactory to the common law courts and was a further reason for the preference, if the circumstances warranted it, for holding that the tenancy at will had been converted into one from year to year: Smith's *Leading Cases* (13th edn), notes to *Clayton v Blakey* (1798) 8 Term Rep 3, vol. ii, 120; p. 215, post.

[153] Co Litt 57b.   [154] Co Litt 57b, and Butler's note to 270b.

[155] Megarry, *Rent Acts*, vol. 1, p. 66; vol. 3, p. 72.   [156] Cruise, *Digest*, Tit. ix., c. ii. s. 5.   [157] S. 1.

premises are detained. A tenant is not deemed to hold over "wilfully" unless he is well aware that he has no right to retain possession.[158]

Similarly, by the Distress for Rent Act 1737,[159] a tenant holding under a periodic tenancy who gives notice to quit and who does not give up possession in accordance with his notice is liable to pay double the rent for the time he remains in possession after the notice expires. The tenant must not only become a trespasser as a result of his own notice to quit; the landlord must also treat him as such.[160] Such a person is not a tenant at sufferance, but his tenancy is statutorily prolonged at double rent.

On the other hand, a tenant at sufferance, since he is in possession, may maintain trespass against a third party or recover in an action for possession of land against a mere wrongdoer,[161] and, in unregistered land, if he remains in possession for twelve years without paying rent, he defeats the right of the landlord and of those claiming under the landlord to recover the land.[162]

C Tenancy from Year to Year and Other Periodic Tenancies

(1) Nature

A tenancy from year to year, or another periodic tenancy such as a tenancy from week to week, or from month to month, differs from a tenancy for a fixed number of years, in that, unless terminated by a proper notice to quit, it may last indefinitely; and from a tenancy at will, in that the death of either party or the alienation of his interest by either party does not effect its determination. It is practically the universal form of letting in the case of agricultural land.[163]

The rule in *Lace v Chantler*[164] that requires certainty of duration in the case of a lease for a fixed term applies also to a tenancy from year to year (or to any other periodic tenancy). The term, although originally indeterminate, is determinable by either party.[165] As Lord TEMPLEMAN explained:[166]

A tenancy from year to year is saved from being uncertain because each party has power by notice to determine at the end of the year. The term continues until determined as if both parties made a new agreement at the end of each year for a new term for the ensuing year. A power for nobody to determine or for one party only to be able to determine is inconsistent with the concept of a term from year to year.

(2) Creation

A tenancy from year to year, or any other periodic tenancy, may arise from express agreement, or by operation of law.

---

158   *French v Elliott* [1960] 1 WLR 40; *Dun & Bradstreet Software Services (England) Ltd v Provident Mutual Life Assurance Association* [1998] 2 EGLR 175.   159   S. 18.

160   *Ballard (Kent) Ltd v Oliver Ashworth (Holdings) Ltd* [2000] Ch 12.

161   *Asher v Whitlock* (1865) LR 1 QB 1, M & B p. 233 (ejectment).

162   *Re Jolly* [1900] 2 Ch 616. For registered land, see pp. 143 et seq, ante.

163   It is greater than a tenancy for one year: *Bernays v Prosser* [1963] 2 QB 592. See p. 386, post.

164   [1944] KB 368; p. 211, ante.   165   Partington, *Landlord and Tenant*, p. 45.

166   *Prudential Assurance Co Ltd v London Residuary Body* [1992] 2 AC 386 at 394; p. 211, ante.

(a) Express

Where a tenancy from year to year is created by express agreement, the phrase best adopted for carrying out the intention of the parties is "from year to year", since this enables the tenancy to be determined at the end of the first or any subsequent year.[167] But it sometimes happens that the parties by inadvertence use expressions which have the effect of creating a tenancy for at least two years, as for example, "for one year and so on from year to year" in which case the tenancy can be determined only by notice in the second or any later year.[168]

(b) Implied

A tenancy from year to year will arise by operation or presumption of law when a person is in possession of land with the permission of the owner, not as a licensee nor for an agreed period, and rent measured by reference to a year is paid and accepted.[169] Two important cases[170] where this occurs are where either a tenant at will or a tenant at sufferance pays a yearly rent.

(1) WHERE A TENANT AT WILL PAYS A YEARLY RENT

It has been the law from an early date that the payment and acceptance of rent is presumptive evidence of an intention by the parties to establish a yearly tenancy, provided that the rent is contractually assessed on a yearly basis.[171] CHAMBRE J said:

> If he accepts yearly rent, or rent measured by any aliquot part of a year, the courts have said that is evidence of a taking for a year.[172]

The assessment of rent on a yearly basis is evidence of an intention to create a yearly tenancy, even though payment may fall due at more frequent intervals such as every quarter or month. If the rent is fixed by reference to some period less than a year it creates a shorter tenancy.[173] Where, for example, a lease for one year reserves a rent of £3 weekly, the tenant holds under a weekly tenancy if he remains in possession after the end of the year.[174]

But the presumption in favour of a periodic tenancy raised by the payment and acceptance of rent may be rebutted by contrary evidence, as for instance by proof that, unknown to the lessor, the payments have been made by a squatter who disseised the original occupier,[175] or where the tenant has a right to remain in possession as a statutory tenant of a residential letting within the Rent Act.[176] As DENNING LJ said:[177]

> If the acceptance of rent can be explained on some other footing than a contractual tenancy, as, for instance, by reason of an existing or possible statutory right to remain, then a new tenancy should not be inferred.

---

[167] *Doe d Clarke v Smaridge* (1845) 7 QB 957. For termination of yearly or other periodic tenancies, see p. 321, post.   [168] *Re Searle* [1912] 1 Ch 610; *Cannon Brewery v Nash* (1898) 77 LT 648.

[169] Similarly, a weekly or monthly rent will create a weekly or monthly tenancy: infra.

[170] For the situation where the tenant under a void lease takes possession and pays rent, see *Walsh v Londsale*, p. 223, post.   [171] *Clayton v Blakey* (1798) 8 Term Rep 3.

[172] *Richardson v Langridge* (1811) 4 Taunt 128 at 132.

[173] *Ladies' Hosiery and Underwear Ltd v Parker* [1930] 1 Ch 304.

[174] Ibid., at 327–9; *Adler v Blackman* [1953] 1 QB 146, M & B p. 509.

[175] *Tickner v Buzzacott* [1965] Ch 426. In this case, the original occupier was not a tenant at will but was holding under a lease for an unexpired period of 75 years. See too *Manfield & Sons Ltd v Botchin* [1970] 2 QB 612.

[176] *Marcroft Wagons Ltd v Smith* [1951] 2 KB 496. The same applies to renewable business tenancies: *Lewis v MTC (Cars) Ltd* [1975] 1 WLR 457, and to long leases under the Leasehold Reform Act 1967: *Baron v Phillips* (1978) 38 P & CR 91.   [177] Ibid., at 506.

In *Javad v Aqil*,[178] where a prospective tenant was let into possession of premises during negotiations, NICHOLLS LJ thought that it would be artificial to impose a periodic tenancy on the parties, and said:[179]

They cannot sensibly be taken to have agreed that he shall have a periodic tenancy, with all the consequences flowing from that, at a time when they are still not agreed about the terms on which the prospective tenant shall have possession under the proposed lease, and when he has been permitted to go into possession or remain in possession merely as an interim measure in the expectation that all will be regulated and regularised in due course when terms are agreed and a formal lease granted.

In essence, the court must look at all the circumstances of the case and determine what is a fair inference to be drawn.[180]

(2) WHERE A TENANT AT SUFFERANCE PAYS A YEARLY RENT

This is the second case in which a periodic tenancy may arise by presumption of law. A. L. SMITH LJ explained this in *Dougal v McCarthy*:[181]

If the landlord consents to such holding over by the tenant, and the tenant consents to remain in possession as tenant, then the implication of law is, unless there is evidence to rebut it, that the tenant holds over as tenant from year to year on the terms of the old tenancy so far as they are not inconsistent with a tenancy from year to year.

The best evidence of this consent is the payment and acceptance of rent on a yearly basis. But other indications suffice. Thus in *Dougal v McCarthy*:

Premises were let at an annual rent of £140 for one year ending 1 February. The tenants remained in possession after 1 February and on 25 February they received a demand from the landlord for £35, being one quarter's rent due in advance. The tenants did not answer this demand, but wrote on 26 March intimating their intention to discontinue the tenancy.

It was held that under the circumstances the parties must be taken to have consented to a tenancy from year to year on the terms of the original lease. A. L. SMITH LJ said:

In the present case there is a direct statement by the landlord to the tenants that he consents to their holding over, because on 25 February, three weeks after the expiration of the tenancy, he writes asking for a quarter's rent as on a fresh tenancy. For a whole month the tenants do nothing, but hold over with notice that the landlord is demanding rent from them as tenants on the terms of the agreement which expired on 1 February. Speaking for myself, I should say that the proper inference from that was that the tenants consented to hold over on the terms of the old agreement.

---

[178] [1991] 1 WLR 1007, M & B p. 510; [1991] CLJ 232 (S. Bridge); (1990) 140 NLJ 1538 (H. W. Wilkinson). The possibility of a licence was not raised: pp. 205–6, ante. See also *Cricket Ltd v Shaftesbury plc* [1999] 3 All ER 283; (1999) 143 SJ 1174 (M. Draper).

[179] At 1012; *Brent LBC v O'Bryan* [1993] 1 EGLR 59.

[180] *Longrigg, Burrough and Trounson v Smith* (1979) 251 EG 847, per Lord SCARMAN; *Cardiothoracic Institute v Shrewdcrest Ltd* [1986] 1 WLR 368; *Dreamgate Properties Ltd v Arnot* (1998) 76 P & CR 25 (new tenancy not implied after expiry of lease: demand for rent computer generated and not result of conscious decision); *London Baggage Co (Charing Cross) Ltd v Railtrack plc (No 1)* [2000] L & TR 439 (test of intention objective); *Walji v Mount Cook Land Ltd* [2002] 1 P & CR 13.

[181] [1893] 1 QB 736; *Lowther v Clifford* [1926] 1 KB 185; affd. [1927] 1 KB 130.

If, however, the contractual tenant who holds over occupies premises that are within the Rent Acts, the landlord has no alternative but to accept the rent, for the tenant becomes a "statutory tenant" and not a tenant holding under a new contractual agreement.[182]

(3) Terms of Tenancy from Year to Year

Where a yearly tenancy arises by implication of law there is often some instrument of agreement under which the premises were formerly held, or under which it was intended that they should be held. For instance, there is the old lease when a tenant holds over with the consent of the landlord and, as in *Walsh v Lonsdale*,[183] there is the void lease or the contract for a lease where the parties have failed to comply with the formalities for the creation of the lease. In such a case the tenant holds the land subject to all the terms of the old or the void lease or the contract, as the case may be, where they are not inconsistent with the general nature of a yearly tenancy.

Examples of terms which in this way will be read into an implied yearly tenancy are agreements to pay rent,[184] to keep a house in repair,[185] to keep the premises open as a shop and to promote its trade as far as possible.[186]

On the other hand, covenants by the tenant to build,[187] or to paint every three years,[188] and a covenant by the landlord giving the tenant an option to purchase the freehold at a certain price[189] are incompatible with a yearly tenancy and will not be enforced.

D Tenancy by Estoppel[190]

(1) The Doctrine

If a person purports to grant, in favour of another, a lease of land in which he has no estate, both the grantor and the grantee may be estopped from denying that a tenancy has been created.

The estoppel arises when one or other of the parties wants to deny one of the ordinary incidents or obligations of the tenancy on the ground that the landlord had no legal estate. The basis of the estoppel is that having entered into an agreement which constitutes a lease or tenancy, he cannot repudiate that incident or obligation.[191]

There thus arises what is called a *tenancy by estoppel* which, as between the parties estopped, possesses the attributes of a true tenancy:[192] "It is true that a title by estoppel is

---

[182] *Morrison v Jacobs* [1945] KB 577; p. 337, post.   [183] P. 223, post.

[184] *Lee v Smith* (1854) 9 Exch 662.

[185] *Cole v Kelly* [1920] 2 KB 106; *Felnex Central Properties Ltd v Montague Burton Properties Ltd* (1981) 260 EG 705.   [186] *Sanders v Karnell* (1858) 1 F & F 356.

[187] *Bowes v Croll* (1856) 6 E & B 255 at 264.   [188] *Pinero v Judson* (1829) 6 Bing 206.

[189] *Re Leeds and Batley Breweries Ltd* [1920] 2 Ch 548.

[190] For a full discussion, see Spencer Bower and Turner, *Estoppel by Representation*, paras. IX.3.1–IX.3.32; (1964) 80 LQR 370 (A. M. Prichard). For the origin of the word, see p. 815, post.

[191] *Bruton v London & Quadrant Housing Trust* [2000] 1 AC 406 at 416, per Lord HOFFMANN. "It is the fact that the agreement between the parties constitutes a tenancy that gives rise to an estoppel, and not the other way round": ibid.

[192] *Bank of England v Cutler* [1908] 2 KB 208 at 234, per FARWELL LJ; *Bell v General Accident Fire & Life Assurance Corpn Ltd* [1998] 1 EGLR 69 (tenant by estoppel of business premises entitled to protection of LTA 1954).

only good against the person estopped and imports from its very existence the idea of no real title at all, yet as against the person estopped it has all the elements of a real title." Thus, the covenants contained in the lease are enforceable by the landlord against the tenant, and the successors in title to either party are themselves equally estopped.[193] The estoppel does not, however, bind strangers to it; for example, the landlord cannot exercise his right to distrain goods, which are not owned by the tenant, for rent in arrear.[194]

The estoppel operates from the time when the landlord puts the tenant into possession, and continues to operate after the tenant has given up possession, unless he has been evicted by someone claiming by title paramount.[195] Thus the covenants contained in the lease are enforceable by the landlord in respect of breaches which occurred before the tenant surrendered his lease.[196] The tenant, however, can show that the landlord no longer has a title; if, for example, the landlord assigns his reversion to A and then sues the tenant for rent, the tenant can deny the landlord's title and claim that the rent is now due to A. Similarly, if the landlord's title is a lease which has expired, the tenant can withhold the rent even though no third party is claiming it.[197]

The doctrine applies to all types of tenancy.

(2) Feeding the Estoppel

A tenancy by estoppel, however, may be transformed into an effective tenancy. The rule is that if the landlord later acquires the legal estate in the land, the effect is to "feed the estoppel" and to clothe the tenant also with a legal estate. The tenant then acquires a legal tenancy and ceases to rely on the estoppel. The tenancy commenced by estoppel, but for all purposes it has now become an estate or interest.[198] Formerly this gave rise to difficulties where the landlord purchased land on mortgage. For instance:

P agrees to purchase a house from V and is let into possession before completion. Though at present entitled only to an equitable interest, he purports to lease the premises to T, whereupon a tenancy by estoppel arises between these two parties. The conveyance of the legal estate to P is completed some weeks later and this is followed immediately by a mortgage of the premises to M who has agreed to advance the purchase money and who pays it direct to V.

It had been held[199] that there was a *scintilla temporis* between the conveyance to P (which fed the estoppel and gave T a legal tenancy) and the mortgage to M, with the result that the legal tenancy acquired by T preceded and took priority over M's mortgage.

---

[193] *Cuthbertson v Irving* (1859) 4 H & N 742. If the lessor has any legal estate in the land, though one less in extent than that which he purports to lease, there is no estoppel. The tenant acquires the interest, whatever it may be, that the lessor holds: *Hill v Saunders* (1825) 4 B & C 529. There may be an estoppel if the lessor has an equitable interest: *Universal Permanent Building Society v Cooke* [1952] Ch 95 at 102.

[194] *Tadman v Henman* [1893] 2 QB 168. For distress, see p. 267, post.

[195] Or the equivalent, e.g. where the tenant, without going out of possession, recognises the title of a third person by attorning tenant to him (i.e., acknowledging that he is the third party's tenant).

[196] *Industrial Properties (Barton Hill) Ltd v Associated Electrical Industries Ltd* [1977] QB 580, M & B p. 515, where CA did not follow its own previous decision in *Harrison v Wells* [1967] 1 QB 263 on the ground that it was decided per incuriam; (1977) 40 MLR 718 (P. Jackson); [1978] Conv 137 (J. Martin).

[197] *National Westminster Bank Ltd v Hart* [1983] QB 773, M & B p. 517; [1984] Conv 64 (J. W. Price). But if the plaintiff is an assignee of the reversion from the landlord the tenant must prove a valid title paramount.

[198] *Webb v Austin* (1844) 7 Man & G 701 at 724, per TINDAL CJ, citing Preston, *Treatise on Abstracts*; M & B p. 515.   [199] *Church of England Building Society v Piskor* [1954] Ch 553.

In *Abbey National Building Society v Cann*[200] the House of Lords reversed this approach and held that the transactions are "not only precisely simultaneous but indissolubly bound together", with the result that M takes free from T's tenancy.

III Creation of a Lease

A Contract for a Lease

We shall discuss later the requirements for a valid and enforceable contract for the sale or other disposition of an interest in land.[201] For a contract for a lease to be valid, there must be a final agreement on the terms of the lease,[202] that is to say, on the parties, the property, the consideration or rent, the commencement and period of the lease and any other special terms. The contract must also comply with the formalities required for a contract for the sale or other disposition of land.[203]

It is usual for a contract for the sale of land to precede the conveyance of the legal estate to the purchaser. However, this is the exception rather than the rule in the case of a lease.[204] Where there is a building lease, a contract is often made first, and then a lease is subsequently granted when the building is complete. But in most cases, the transaction is effected either by a contract for a lease, or by a lease, but rarely by a combination of both.[205]

B Lease

A lease may be brought into existence either *at law* or *in equity*.

If made in the form required by law, and if the term created satisfies the definition of a "term of years absolute" contained in the Law of Property Act 1925,[206] it passes a legal term of years to the tenant and creates the legal relationship of landlord and tenant—either at once in the case of an immediate letting or at the agreed future date in the case of a reversionary lease. The formalities required to create a legal lease depend on the length of the term; and whether the title to the estate out of which it is granted is unregistered or registered.

If the formalities required to create a legal lease are not complied with, the transaction may still create a lease in equity. In particular, although a *contract* for a lease does not operate to create the relationship of landlord and tenant at law,[207] an *equitable* term of years may pass to the person who holds under a contract for a lease.[208] As we shall see, if the contract is capable of being enforced by specific performance, then he will hold under the same terms in equity as if a lease had actually been granted to him. The relationship of landlord and tenant will be created *in equity*, and as between the parties the rights and duties of that

---

[200] [1991] 1 AC 56, M & B p. 519; preferring *Coventry Permanent Economic Building Society v Jones* [1951] 1 All ER 901; *Security Trust Co v Royal Bank of Canada* [1976] AC 503; (1992) 108 LQR 380 (G. Goldberg). See also *Walthamstow Building Society v Davies* (1989) 60 P & CR 99 (where mortgagee took a second charge to replace a first charge, held no *scintilla temporis* between discharge of first and creation of second charge during which unauthorised tenancy granted by mortgagor became binding on mortgagee).   [201] Chap. 24.

[202] See e.g. *Fletcher v Davies* (1980) 257 EG 1149 (flat in Inner Temple).   [203] Pp. 863 et seq, post.

[204] See *Hollington Bros Ltd v Rhodes* [1951] 2 TLR 691 at 694.   [205] Emmet, para. 26.001.

[206] S. 205(1)(xxvii); p. 194, ante.

[207] *Borman v Griffith* [1930] 1 Ch 493, M & B p. 524 (contract for lease not a "conveyance" for the purposes of LPA 1925, ss. 62, 205(1)(ii)).

[208] *National Carriers Ltd v Panalpina (Northern) Ltd* [1981] AC 675 at 704 (Lord SIMON OF GLAISDALE, citing the 12th edn of this book).

relationship will be the same as if the lease had been granted.[209] In such a case, however, the tenant has only an equitable interest in the land.[210]

The grant of a legal lease may take the form of more or less technical language;[211] and the mere fact that an instrument is drafted as a contract does not preclude it from taking effect as an actual demise. Whether a contract operates as a lease or as only a contract depends on the intention of the parties, which must be gathered from all the circumstances. Moreover, as we shall see,[212] the courts have sometimes construed a document which purported to be the grant of a lease, but which failed to satisfy the formality requirements for the grant, as having the force of a contract between the parties and therefore effective to create a lease in equity.

(1) Formalities Necessary to Create a Legal Lease under Law of Property Act 1925

We here consider the requirements set by the Law of Property Act 1925 for the creation of a lease at common law. The further registration requirements set by the Land Registration Act 2002 in the case of certain legal leases which satisfy the Law of Property Act 1925 are considered below.[213]

(a) Lease not exceeding three years

At common law a parol (oral) lease was sufficient to create the relation of landlord and tenant in the case of corporeal hereditaments, and there was no necessity to employ either a deed or a writing. This is still the law with regard to leases *not exceeding three years*, for the Law of Property Act 1925,[214] re-enacting in effect the Statute of Frauds 1677, provides that:

the creation by parol of leases taking effect in possession for a term not exceeding three years (whether or not the lessee is given power to extend the term) at the best rent which can be reasonably obtained without taking a fine,

shall be valid.

Thus a mere oral lease suffices to create a *legal* term of years, provided that it is to take effect in possession, that it reserves the best rent reasonably obtainable, and that it is not to last for longer than three years. A lease exceeds three years within the meaning of the Act only if it is for a definite term longer than that period. It is immaterial in such a case that it contains a provision allowing its earlier determination by notice.[215] On the other hand, a periodic tenancy for an indefinite period, such as one from year to year or week to week, may be validly created by a parol lease, for, though it may endure for much longer than three years, each party has power to determine it at the end of each period.[216]

Although a lease not exceeding three years may be created orally, it cannot be assigned at law without a deed.[217]

---

[209]   *Walsh v Lonsdale* (1882) 21 Ch D 9, M & B p. 85; p. 223, post.

[210]   For the differences between a legal lease and an equitable lease, see pp. 225 et seq, post.

[211]   The usual words by which a lease is made are "demise" and "let", but any words which amount to a grant are sufficient: Woodfall, para. 5.016. In early days, the language was significant in that the landlord's covenant for quiet enjoyment would only be implied if the word "demise" was used: p. 230, n. 275, n. 0, post. For precedents, see *Encyclopedia of Forms and Precedents*, vols. 22 (business tenancies) and 23 (residential tenancies).

[212]   P. 222, post.   [213]   Pp. 228 et seq, post.   [214]   S. 54(2).

[215]   *Kushner v Law Society* [1952] 1 KB 264.   [216]   P. 214, ante.

[217]   *Crago v Julian* [1992] 1 WLR 372, M & B p. 504; [1992] Conv 375 (P. Sparkes); *Camden LBC v Alexandrou* (1997) 74 P & CR D33. For assignment of a lease, see pp. 294 et seq, post. On informal short-term leases, see [1992] Conv 252, 337 (P. Sparkes).

(b) Lease exceeding three years

A lease which exceeds three years, however, will not pass a legal estate to the tenant unless it is made by deed. The history of this requirement is as follows. Section 1 of the Statute of Frauds 1677 enacted that:

All leases . . . or terms of years . . . made or created . . . by parol, and not put in writing, and signed by the parties so making or creating the same, or their agents thereunto lawfully authorized by writing, shall have the force and effect of leases or estates *at will* only.

The second section excepted leases not exceeding three years at a rent of two-thirds at least of the full improved value of the land.

The next enactment was the Real Property Act 1845, section 3, which required a further formality by providing that:

A lease, required by law to be in writing, of any tenements or hereditaments . . . made after the first day of October, 1845, shall be void at law unless also made by deed.

Thus it was only in the case of leases exceeding three years that a deed became necessary, since it was these alone that had previously been "required by law to be in writing". A lease exceeding three years and not executed as a deed had and still has a greater effect than is indicated by the language of the two statutes cited but since 1845 it has never sufficed to pass to the tenant an immediate legal interest equivalent to that which the parties intended to create. The Statutes of 1677 and 1845 have been in effect re-enacted by the Law of Property Act 1925 in the two following sections:

54.—(1) All interests in land created by parol and not put in writing and signed by the persons so creating the same, or by their agents thereunto lawfully authorized in writing, have, notwithstanding any consideration having been given for the same, the force and effect of interests at will only.

(2) Nothing in the foregoing provisions . . . shall affect the creation by parol of leases taking effect in possession for a term not exceeding three years . . . at the best rent which can be reasonably obtained without taking a fine.

52.—(1) All conveyances of land or of any interest therein are void for the purpose of conveying or creating a legal estate unless made by deed.

(2) This section does not apply to—

(d) leases or tenancies or other assurances not required by law to be made in writing.

We must now attempt to define the exact effect of a lease exceeding three years which fails to satisfy the statutory requirements.

(2) Effect of a Lease Exceeding Three Years which is not made in Accordance with the Formalities Required by Law of Property Act 1925

The scope of the following inquiry is to ascertain, first what was the legal effect between 1677 and 1845 of a lease not put into writing as required by the Statute of Frauds; secondly, what has been the effect since 1845 of a lease not made by deed as required by the Real Property Act of that year. Since these statutes were re-enacted by the Law of Property Act 1925, the result of this inquiry will be a statement of the present law on the subject.

(a) Effect at common law

The Statute of Frauds said that a lease which was not put in writing should create a mere tenancy at will, and this was the view taken by the common law when a tenant did nothing more than enter into possession of the premises under a parol lease. But this was not the final word. The common law went further and presumed that a tenant who had not merely gone into possession, but had also paid rent on a yearly basis, became tenant from year to year, and that he held this yearly tenancy subject to such of the terms and conditions of the unwritten lease as were consistent with a yearly tenancy.[218]

The provision of the Real Property Act 1845 that a lease that was not made by deed should be *void at law* was construed in the same manner. The document was void as a lease in the sense that it did not create the agreed term of years, but if the intended tenant entered into possession and paid rent at a yearly rate, he was presumed to be a yearly tenant.[219]

Moreover the above represents the legal position at the present day *if we confine our attention to the common law*. A conveyance of land, and this includes a lease,[220] is void under the Law of Property Act 1925 for the purpose of creating a legal estate unless made by deed (except of course in the case of a lease not exceeding three years), but nevertheless, if the tenant enters into possession and pays a yearly rent, he will become a yearly tenant. Again, by the same Act a term exceeding three years which is not put in writing is to have the force and effect of an interest at will only, but, given the same two facts of possession and payment of rent, it also will be converted into a legal yearly tenancy. It is expressly provided that the requirements of the Act with regard to formalities shall not "affect the right to acquire an interest in land by virtue of taking possession".[221]

(b) Effect in equity

Equity, however, took a very different view of the effect of a lease for more than three years which was not put in writing as required by the Statute of Frauds, or which, after 1845, was not made by deed. While admitting that the statutes rendered such a lease incapable of passing the term agreed upon by the parties, courts of equity held that the abortive lease must be regarded as *a contract for a lease*, provided, of course, that the constituents of an enforceable contract were present. When this principle was devised by the courts of equity,[222] this meant that an *oral* lease followed by an act of part performance, and a *written* lease signed by the party to be charged and constituting a sufficient memorandum of the terms of the bargain, were both allowed to have the same effect as a contract for a lease. It becomes necessary, therefore, to ascertain what the effect has always been in equity of such a contract.

A contract for a lease is a contract to which the equitable remedy of specific performance is peculiarly appropriate. If a party can prove to the satisfaction of the court that such a contract has been entered into, he can bring an action for specific performance requiring the other party to execute a deed in the manner required by statute so as to create that legal term which the parties intended to create. One effect, therefore, of such a specifically enforceable

---

[218] *Doe d Rigge v Bell* (1793) 5 Term Rep 471; *Mann v Lovejoy* (1826) Ry & M 355; *Clayton v Blakey* (1798) 8 Term Rep 3; *Richardson v Gifford* (1834) 1 Ad & El 52; *Hamerton v Stead* (1824) 3 B & C 478 at 483, per LITTLEDALE J. See p. 217, ante.

[219] *Martin v Smith* (1874) LR 9 Exch 50; *Rhyl UDC v Rhyl Amusements Ltd* [1959] 1 WLR 465, where the lease was void for lack of compliance with the Public Health Act 1875, s. 177.   [220] S. 205(1)(ii).

[221] S. 55(c).

[222] Under Statute of Frauds 1677, s. 4; p. 864, post. Since 26 September 1989 a contract for lease must be *in writing*: LP(MP)A 1989, s. 2; p. 868, post.

contract is that the prospective tenant immediately acquires an equitable interest in the land in the sense that he has an equitable right to a legal estate.[223] As was said in a case prior to 1845:[224]

The defendant was let into possession under an agreement, which gave the parties a right to go to equity to compel the execution of it by making out a formal lease.

The same view was upheld even when the Real Property Act 1845 had enacted that a lease exceeding three years made otherwise than by deed should be void at law. As Lord CHELMSFORD said in *Parker v Taswell*:[225]

The legislature appears to have been very cautious and guarded in language, for it uses the expression "shall be void at law". If the legislature had intended to deprive such a document of all efficacy, it would have said that the instrument should "be avoided to all intents and purposes". There are no such words in the Act. I think it would be too strong to say that because it is void at law as a lease, it cannot be used as an agreement enforceable in Equity, the intention of the parties having been that there should be a lease, and the aid of Equity being only invoked to carry that intention into effect.

(3) Doctrine of *Walsh v Lonsdale*

(a) *The doctrine*

The effect of this divergence between the views of common law and equity was that, prior to the passing of the Judicature Act 1873, a lease that was not made by deed and a contract for a lease resulted in the creation of two entirely different interests, according as the common law or the equitable doctrine was invoked. At common law the tenant acquired the interest of a tenant from year to year if he paid rent and entered into possession: in equity he was entitled to call for the execution of a legal lease and to have inserted therein all the provisions of the void lease or of the contract.

The Judicature Act, however, materially affected the position. It provided in effect that, whenever an action is brought in any court, the plaintiff may set up equitable claims and the defendant may raise equitable defences, and that:

[Where] there is any conflict or variance between the rules of equity and the rules of the common law with reference to the same matter, the rules of equity shall prevail.[226]

The particular point of variance which existed in the case of a lease that was not made by deed fell to be considered in the leading case of *Walsh v Lonsdale*,[227] decided in 1882. In that case:

the plaintiff agreed in writing to take a lease of a mill for seven years, and part of the agreement was that a deed should be executed containing inter alia a provision that *on any given day* the lessor might require the tenant to pay one year's rent in advance. No deed was executed, and the plaintiff, who was let into possession, paid rent quarterly, but not in advance, for a year and a half. The landlord then demanded a year's rent in advance and upon refusal distrained for the amount. The plaintiff brought an action to recover damages for illegal distress, for specific performance of the contract for a lease and for an interim injunction to restrain the distress.

---

[223] *Palmer v Carey* [1926] AC 703 at 706.
[224] *Doe d Thomson v Amey* (1840) 12 Ad & El 476 at 479, per Lord DENMAN CJ.
[225] (1858) 2 De G & J 559 at 570.
[226] Supreme Court of Judicature Act 1873, s. 25(11); now SCA 1981, s. 49(1).
[227] (1882) 21 Ch D 9, M & B p. 85; (1988) 8 OJLS 350 (P. Sparkes).

The main ground upon which he rested his claim was that, as he had been let into possession and had paid rent under a contract which did not operate as a lease, he was in the position of a tenant from year to year and held the mill upon such of the agreed terms as were consistent with a yearly tenancy. The condition making a year's rent always payable in advance was obviously inconsistent with a yearly tenancy which could be determined by half a year's notice, and for this reason it was argued that the distress was illegal.

This argument did not prevail. It was decided that a tenant who holds under a contract for a lease of which specific performance will be decreed occupies the same position *vis-à-vis the landlord*, as regards both rights and liabilities, as he would occupy if a formal lease had been executed as a deed.

If a lease by deed had been executed in this case on the lines of the contract, the defendant would have been entitled to distrain for rent not paid in advance, and the mere fact that the formal lease had not been actually made was not to prejudice his rights. Sir George JESSEL MR put the matter thus:

There is an agreement for a lease under which possession has been given. Now since the Judicature Act the possession is held under the agreement. There are not two estates as there were formerly—one estate at common law by reason of the payment of the rent from year to year, and an estate in equity under the agreement. There is only one court, and the equity rules prevail in it. The tenant holds under an agreement for a lease. He holds, therefore, under the same terms in equity as if a lease had been granted, it being a case in which both parties admit that relief is capable of being given by specific performance. That being so, he cannot complain of the exercise by the landlord of the same rights as the landlord would have had if a lease had been granted. On the other hand, he is protected in the same way as if a lease had been granted; he cannot be turned out by six months' notice as a tenant from year to year. He has a right to say: "I have a lease in equity and you can only re-enter if I have committed such a breach of covenant as would, if a lease had been granted, have entitled you to re-enter according to the terms of a proper proviso for re-entry". That being so, it appears to me that being a lessee in equity he cannot complain of the exercise of the right of distress merely because the actual parchment has not been signed and sealed.

Such, then, is the doctrine of *Walsh v Lonsdale*. It is one example of the principle that equity regards as already done what the parties to a transaction have agreed to do—a principle that is by no means confined to a contract for a lease, for it applies to any contract to convey or create a legal estate or an interest in land of which equity will order specific performance.[228]

(b) Application of doctrine

In the context of landlord and tenant, *Walsh v Lonsdale* has been followed,[229] qualified[230] and explained[231] in later cases. It has also been applied "once removed",[232] as where V entered into a contract to sell the fee simple of land to P, who then agreed to grant a lease of the land

---

[228] P. 877, post.

[229] *Lowther v Heaver* (1889) 41 Ch D 248; *Coatsworth v Johnson* (1885) 55 LJQB 220, M & B p. 87; *Tottenham Hotspur Football and Athletic Co Ltd v Princegrove Publishers Ltd* [1974] 1 WLR 113; (1974) 90 LQR 149 (M. Albery); *Re A Company (No 00792 of 1992), ex p Tredegar Enterprises Ltd* [1992] 29 EG 122.

[230] *Cornish v Brook Green Laundry Ltd* [1959] 1 QB 394, where it was held that it cannot be invoked if the contract to grant a term of years is subject to a condition precedent performable by the proposed tenant and not yet performed; *Shelley v United Artists Corpn Ltd* [1990] 1 EGLR 103.

[231] *Manchester Brewery Co v Coombs* [1901] 2 Ch 608, M & B p. 576; *Gray v Spyer* [1922] 2 Ch 22.

[232] *Industrial Properties (Barton Hill) Ltd v Associated Electrical Industries Ltd* [1977] QB 580, M & B p. 86.

to T. T was treated as a lessee in equity by virtue of a double application of the doctrine. T could not become a lessee at common law until a legal lease had been properly granted. As Lord DENNING said:[233]

It is quite plain that, if the lease to T was defective in point of law, nevertheless it was good in equity, and for this simple reason. There were two agreements of which specific performance would be granted. One was the agreement by V to convey to P. The other was the agreement by P to grant a lease to T. In respect of each of these agreements, equity looks upon that as done which ought to be done. It follows that, by combining the two agreements, the tenant, T, holds upon the same terms as if a lease had actually been granted by V to T. This is, of course, an extension of the doctrine of *Walsh v Lonsdale* where there was only one agreement. But I see no reason why the doctrine should not be extended to a case like the present, where there were two agreements, each of which was such that specific performance would be granted.

The doctrine is now the governing rule whenever it is necessary to ascertain the effect of a lease or contract for a lease which is not made by deed as required by the Law of Property Act 1925. Section 52(1)[234] of the Act provides that all conveyances of land "are void for the purpose of conveying or creating a legal estate unless made by deed", but, if a tenant has an enforceable right to call for a deed, he is, as far as his rights and liabilities in relation to the landlord are concerned, in practically the same position as if he actually had a deed.

(4) A Contract for a Lease is not Equal to a Lease

It must not, however, be concluded that a contract for a lease is as effective in all respects and against all persons as a lease. This is not so.[235] What Sir George JESSEL MR meant in *Walsh v Lonsdale* was that if, in litigation between the parties, the circumstances would justify a decree for the execution of a lease by deed, then both in the Queen's Bench Division and in the Chancery Division, the case must be treated as if such a lease had been granted. There are at least three points which illustrate the limitations of the doctrine, and the advantages of a lease as compared with a contract for a lease.

(a) *Specific performance*

First, the doctrine is excluded if the contract is one of which equity will not grant specific performance.[236] This is still a discretionary remedy and will not be granted in all cases, as for instance where a tenant who seeks the aid of the court will be unable to perform the covenants in the lease owing to his insolvent state, or where he has already committed a breach of covenant that would have formed part of the lease. Thus, in *Coatsworth v Johnson*:[237]

The plaintiff entered into possession under an agreement that the defendant would grant him a lease for twenty-one years. Before any rent was due or had been paid, the defendant gave him notice to quit and evicted him on the ground that he had done that which amounted to a breach of a covenant contained in the agreement and intended to be inserted in the lease.

---

[233] ibid., at 598. Letters have been substituted for the names of the parties.   [234] P. 221, ante.
[235] *Manchester Brewery Co v Coombs* [1901] 2 Ch 608 at 617.
[236] For criticism of this requirement, see (1987) 7 OJLS 60 (S. Gardner).
[237] (1886) 55 LJQB 220, M & B p. 87.

The plaintiff sued in trespass, but failed. At common law, having paid no rent, he was a mere tenant at will and as such could be evicted at the pleasure of the defendant; in equity he was precluded from obtaining a decree of specific performance, since he had broken a covenant into which he had entered.

STAMP J, in explaining that the doctrine only applies where the tenant is entitled to specific performance, said in *Warmington v Miller*:[238]

The equitable interests which the intended lessee has under an agreement for a lease do not exist in vacuo, but arise because the intended lessee has an equitable right to specific performance of the agreement. In such a situation that which is agreed to be and ought to be done is treated as having been done and carrying with it in equity the attendant rights.

Further, specific performance will not be granted if the court has no jurisdiction to grant it. Thus a county court has such jurisdiction only where the value of the property claimed by the plaintiff does not exceed £30,000.[239]

(b) Conveyance

Secondly, the statutory definition of "conveyance"[240] includes a lease but not a contract for a lease. Thus, a tenant under a contract cannot claim those privileges which are granted by section 62 of the Law of Property Act 1925[241] to one who takes a "conveyance" of land.[242]

(c) Third parties

Thirdly, an equitable lease, including one created under the doctrine in *Walsh v Lonsdale*, does not in all cases affect the rights of third parties.

For instance, privity of estate[243] exists at common law between the landlord and the assignee from the tenant holding under a lease, but not the assignee from a person "whose only title to call himself a lessee depends on his right to specific performance of an agreement".[244] In consequence, covenants in a lease were enforceable by and against the assignee under a lease but, until this rule was changed by statute in relation to agreements for lease created after 1995,[245] it was not entirely certain that the same was true for covenants in an agreement for lease.[246]

But more important is that, since a specifically enforceable contract confers only an equitable interest on the lessee, its potency against third parties is less than that of a legal lease, as is the case with all equitable interests by comparison with legal estates and interests.[247] Writing at a time when the old general principle of notice was still applied, Maitland said:[248]

An agreement for a lease is not equal to a lease. An equitable right is not equal to a legal right; between the contracting parties an agreement for a lease may be as good as a lease; just so between the

---

[238] [1973] QB 877 at 887.

[239] County Courts Act 1984, s. 23(d); County Courts Jurisdiction Order 1981, SI 1981 No. 1123; *Foster v Reeves* [1892] 2 QB 255; cf *Cornish v Brook Green Laundry Ltd* [1959] 1 QB 394; *Kingswood Estate Co Ltd v Anderson* [1963] 2 QB 169; *Rushton v Smith* [1976] QB 480.   [240] LPA 1925, s. 205(1)(ii).

[241] P. 603, post.   [242] *Borman v Griffith* [1930] 1 Ch 493, M & B p. 524.

[243] Pp. 302 et seq, post.

[244] *Purchase v Lichfield Brewery Co* [1915] 1 KB 184 at 188, per LUSH J, M & B p. 579. See also *Manchester Brewery Co v Coombs* [1901] 2 Ch 608, M & B p. 576; (1978) 37 CLJ 98 (R. J. Smith)

[245] LT(C)A 1995, pp. 309 et seq, post, which defines "tenancy" as including "an agreement for a tenancy": s. 28(1).   [246] Pp. 302–3, post.

[247] Pp. 302 et seq, ante.   [248] Maitland, *Equity*, p. 158.

contracting parties an agreement for the sale of land may serve as well as a completed sale and conveyance. But introduce the third party and then you will see the difference. I take a lease; my lessor then sells the land to X; notice or no notice my lease is good against X. I take a mere agreement for a lease, and the person who has agreed to grant the lease then sells and conveys to Y, who has no notice of my merely equitable right. Y is not bound to grant me a lease.

The current position depends on whether the land is still unregistered, or already registered, at the time when it is purchased by the third party.

(1) UNREGISTERED LAND

In unregistered land a contract for a lease is now an estate contract within the meaning of the Law of Property Act 1925[249] and will therefore be enforceable against a purchaser for money or money's worth of the legal estate from the landlord only if it has been registered as a land charge under the Land Charges Act 1972[250] at the Land Registry. Thus

if A takes a contract for lease from B and then B sells and conveys the land to C, A's estate contract if registered will prevail against C, but if not registered will be defeated by the conveyance, even if C actually knew that it had been made.[251]

If, however, A goes into possession of the land before the sale to C and pays rent on a yearly (or other periodic) basis, he acquires a legal periodic tenancy which will be binding on C.[252] This is not affected by A's failure to register his equitable lease, although of course the basis on which A holds of C is under the terms of the periodic tenancy (which is therefore terminable accordingly[253]) rather than under the terms of the contract for lease.

(2) REGISTERED LAND

Under the Land Registration Act 2002 the purchaser from the landlord will be bound by a legal lease.[254] But the purchaser for value[255] will take free of an equitable lease unless it is protected by a notice or, failing that, if it takes effect as an overriding interest by virtue of the tenant being in discoverable actual occupation.[256]

---

[249] S. 2(3)(iv).   [250] Formerly LCA 1925; class C(iv).

[251] LPA 1925, s. 199(1)(i); *Sharp v Coates* [1948] 1 All ER 136; on appeal, [1949] 1 KB 285. See *Midland Bank Trust Co Ltd v Green* [1981] AC 513, M & B p. 38; *Hollington Bros Ltd v Rhodes* [1951] 2 TLR 691, M & B p. 46; *Markfaith Investment Ltd v Chiap Hua Flashlights Ltd* [1991] 2 AC 43 ("indistinguishable from the decision of Harman J in *Hollington Bros Ltd v Rhodes*", per Lord TEMPLEMAN, at 60). See also *Lyus v Prowsa Developments Ltd* [1982] 1 WLR 1044, p. 972, post, where a sale expressly subject to an estate contract gave rise to a constructive trust; *Ashburn Anstalt v Arnold* [1989] Ch 1, p. 838, post, per Fox LJ, at 25.

[252] See, e.g., *Bell Street Investments Ltd v Wood* (1970) 216 EG 585. As a tenancy not exceeding three years it can take effect at law without a deed: p. 220, ante.

[253] For example, a yearly tenancy will be terminable at the end of each year by half a year's notice: p. 321, post.

[254] Either because it is registered with an individual title: p. 955, post; or because it is an overriding interest under LRA 2002, Sch. 3, para. 1. An equitable lease is not included as an overriding interest within this provision because it has not been "granted": *City Permanent Building Society v Miller* [1952] Ch 840 at 852, M & B p. 505, per JENKINS LJ, on equivalent wording in LRA 1925, s. 70(1)(k). LRA 2002 is also more explicit in referring to a "leasehold *estate*" rather than just a "lease".   [255] LRA 2002, s. 29.

[256] Ibid., Sch. 3, para. 2; pp. 979 et seq, post. This provision superseded LRA 1925, s. 70(1)(g). Where the tenant under an equitable lease goes into possession and pays rent, the legal periodic tenancy which thereby arises (supra) will therefore be binding as an overriding interest under Sch. 3, para. 1. But possession will generally constitute discoverable actual occupation and therefore give rise to an overriding interest under para. 2—which will render the terms of the contract for lease itself binding on the purchaser.

(5) Registered Land. Formalities Necessary to Create a Legal Lease under Land Registration Act 2002

(a) The requirement of registration

A lease which complies with the formalities required by the Law of Property Act 1925 in order to create a legal estate will none the less not take effect at law if it is in addition required to comply with registration requirements set by the Land Registration Act 2002 but fails to do so. Under the 2002 Act the grant of a term of years absolute out of a registered estate in land is required to be completed by registration if it is:[257]

    (i) for a term of more than seven years[258] from the date of the grant,

    (ii) to take effect in possession after the end of the period of three months beginning with the date of the grant,

    (iii) under which the right to possession is discontinuous,[259]

    (iv) in pursuance of Part 5 of the Housing Act 1985 (the right to buy), or

    (v) in circumstances where section 171A of that Act applies (disposal by landlord which leads to a person no longer being a secure tenant).

Until the relevant registration requirements are met, it does not operate at law,[260] and therefore if it is to bind a purchaser from the landlord it requires protection by notice on the register unless it is an overriding interest by virtue of the tenant being in discoverable actual occupation.[261]

(b) Requirements as to form and content

Most leases which are required to be completed by registration must also, if granted on or after 19 June 2006, comply with requirements as to their form and content.[262] Certain

---

[257] LRA 2002, s. 27(2)(b). See also s. 27(2)(c) (grant of a lease out of a registered franchise or manor).

[258] The Lord Chancellor has power to shorten the seven-year period: LRA 2002, s. 5. It is intended that, when electronic conveyancing is introduced, the period will be reduced to three years so as to bring the registration requirement into line with the rules requiring leases to be granted by deed, p. 221, ante; H & B, para. 2.14.

Under LRA 1925, s. 123, as substituted by LRA 1997, s. 1, only leases granted for more than twenty-one years out of registered land were substantively registrable and were required to be registered. Leases for twenty-one years or less were overriding interests: s. 70(1)(k). For further details, see the 16th edn of this book, pp. 561–3. At first sight, the effect of the reduction by LRA 2002 of the length of leases required to be registered will be to render many business leases, which have generally been granted for ten or fifteen years, registrable. However, the average length of a commercial lease has been reduced in recent years: Reading University Report *Monitoring the 2002 Code of Practice for Commercial Leases* (March 2005), discussed (2005) EG 179 (N. Crosby, S. Murdoch, C. Hughes), 186 (M. Hull); (2004) 8 L & TR 1 (J. Bignell). See also n. 104, supra (impact on introduction in 2003 of stamp duty land tax on length of leases). [259] E.g. a timeshare lease: n. 107, ante.

[260] LRA 2002, s. 27(1). Under LRA 1925, s. 123A, as substituted by LRA 1997, s. 1, the legal estate passed by virtue of the disposition, but became void as regards the legal estate if not registered within two months, and thereafter took effect as a contract for lease. [261] Ibid., s. 29; Sch. 3, para. 2.

[262] LRR 2003, r. 58A, Sch. 1A, inserted by Land Registration (Amendment) (No 2) Rules 2005 (SI 2005 No. 1982), r. 5; Land Registry Practice Guide 64. The new rule came into force on 9 January 2006; from that date until 18 June 2006 compliance was voluntary. The new rule does not apply to leases granted in a form expressly required by an agreement entered into before 19 June 2006, by an order of the court, by or under an enactment, or by a necessary consent or licence for the grant of the lease given before 19 June 2006: ibid., r. 58A(4). For the consultation leading up to the introduction of these requirements, see Land Registry Consultation Document on Presentation of Prescribed Information in Registrable Leases (September 2004); Report on Consultation

prescribed clauses must be set out at the beginning of the lease, dealing with the date of the lease; the title number(s) of the property out of which the lease is granted (if already registered); the parties to the lease; the property; certain prescribed statements (if applicable[263]); the term for which the property is leased; any premium paid; a statement indicating whether or not the lease contains any prohibition or restriction on dispositions; any rights of renewal or surrender; restrictive covenants given in the lease by the landlord in respect of other property; easements granted or reserved by the lease; any estate rentcharge burdening the property; an application, if appropriate, for any standard form restriction which should be entered on the register; and a declaration of trust where the tenant comprises more than one person. The failure to comply with these requirements will result in the Land Registry rejecting the application for registration as defective.[264]

The purpose of these requirements is to to facilitate quicker and more accurate registration of leases, and to prepare for e-conveyancing.[265] They will also have the consequence of standardising the form of leases and thereby simplifying conveyancing.

(6) Summary

We have now reviewed the methods whereby the relation of landlord and tenant may be constituted, and it may be helpful in conclusion to summarise the present state of the law:

(a) A lease not exceeding three years, whether by parol, in writing or by deed, confers a legal term of years upon the tenant.[266]

(b) A lease by deed exceeding three years has the same effect,[267] unless it is granted out of registered land; in that case, if the grant is for more than seven years it does not operate at law until the registration requirements are met.[268]

(c) A lease exceeding three years which is not executed as a deed, but which complies with the formalities for a contract for the sale or other disposition of an interest in land, confers an equitable term upon the tenant by virtue of the doctrine of *Walsh v Lonsdale*.[269] There may be a concurrent legal periodic tenancy by virtue of possession plus payment of rent by the tenant; but as long as the equitable term is enforceable against a purchaser from the landlord,[270] the tenant need not rely on the periodic tenancy.

(d) A contract for a lease of any period (which, if for three years or longer, complies with the relevant formalities for land contracts[271]), confers an equitable term on the tenant by virtue of the doctrine of *Walsh v Lonsdale*.[272]

(July 2005); [2006] Conv 282 (E. J. Slessenger); (2004) 45 LSG 34 (J. Jenkins); [2005] EG 270 (P. J. G. Williams, K. Fenn and A. Colby).

[263] LRR 2003, rr. 179 (dispositions in favour of a charity), 180 (dispositions by a charity), 196 (leases under the Leasehold Reform, Housing and Urban Developments Act 1993).

[264] Land Registry Practice Guide 64, para. 6; Practice Guide 49.

[265] Land Registry Consultation Document, supra. See also Explanatory Note to SI 2005 No. 1982.

[266] P. 220, ante.   [267] P. 221, ante.

[268] P. 228, ante; and the lease must contain the prescribed clauses: supra.   [269] P. 223, ante.

[270] By (in unregistered land) registration of the estate contract as a land charge; or (in registered land) by registration of a notice or as an overriding interest by virtue of the tenant's discoverable actual occupation: p. 227, ante.

[271] LP(MP)A 1989, s. 2; chap. 24, post. A lease for less than three years need not be in writing: ibid., s. 2(5)(a).

[272] Whether it binds a purchaser from the landlord depends on whether it is protected by registration or as an overriding interest: n. 270, supra.

IV Rights and Liabilities of Landlord and Tenant

In the majority of cases the rights and the liabilities of a landlord and a tenant are fixed by
the express covenants that, having been settled by the parties, are incorporated in the lease
or the contract under which the premises are held. But a contract may be silent on several
matters of importance, or there may be no agreement at all, and therefore it is necessary to
consider, first, what the position of the parties is where there are no express covenants, and
then to notice shortly the usual covenants common to all ordinary leases.[273]

A Position where there are no Express Covenants or Conditions

(1) Implied Obligations of the Landlord

(a) Quiet enjoyment

A covenant that the tenant shall have quiet enjoyment[274] of the premises is implied in every
lease that does not expressly deal with the matter.[275] The meaning of this is that the tenant shall
be put into possession[276] and that he shall be entitled to recover damages[277] if his enjoyment
is substantially disturbed by acts either of the landlord or of somebody claiming under
the landlord.[278] "It is a covenant for freedom from disturbance by adverse claimants to the
property."[279] Instances are, where the landlord, having reserved the right to work minerals
under the land, so works them as to cause the land to subside;[280] or where, in a lease of shooting
rights, he erects buildings so as substantially to reduce the area over which the rights are exercisable,[281] or where, with a view to getting rid of the tenant, he removes the doors and windows of the demised premises,[282] or subjects him to persistent and prolonged intimidation,[283]

---

[273] For the application of the Unfair Contract Terms Act 1977 and the Unfair Terms in Consumer Contracts
Regulations 1999 to covenants in leases, see p. 195, n. 28, ante.

[274] See (1976) 40 Conv (NS) 427; (1977) 40 MLR 651; [1978] Conv 419 (M. J. Russell).

[275] *Markham v Paget* [1908] 1 Ch 697. In early days there was no such implication unless the word "demise"
had been used in the lease; ibid. See *Gordon v Selico Co Ltd* [1986] 1 EGLR 71 at 77, where Slade LJ held that no
covenants were to be implied "where it was intended by all parties to provide a comprehensive code in regard to
repair and maintenance".   [276] *Miller v Emcer Products Ltd* [1956] Ch 304.

[277] For criminal offences, see p. 332, post.

[278] *Jones v Lavington* [1903] 1 KB 253; *Sanderson v Berwick-upon-Tweed Corpn* (1884) 13 QBD 547 at 551;
Matania v National Provincial Bank Ltd and Elevenist Syndicate Ltd [1936] 2 All ER 633; *Sampson v Hodson-
Pressinger* [1981] 3 All ER 710 at 714; *Guppys (Bridport) Ltd v Brookling* (1983) 269 EG 846 (exemplary dam-
ages); *Mira v Aylmer Square Investments Ltd* [1990] 1 EGLR 45 (damages for loss of revenue from sublettings).
An express right of entry in the lease must be construed consistently with the covenant for quiet enjoyment:
Yeoman's Row Management Ltd v Bodentien-Meyrick [2002] 2 EGLR 39 (express covenant); and where there is
a covenant to repair the landlord must take all reasonable precautions (but not all possible precautions) before
causing a disturbance by carrying out the repairs: *Goldmile Properties Ltd v Lechouritis* [2003] 1 EGLR 60
(express covenants).   [279] *Hudson v Cripps* [1896] 1 Ch 265 at 268 per North J.

[280] *Markham v Paget*, supra.   [281] *Peech v Best* [1931] 1 KB 1 (a case, however, of an express covenant).

[282] *Lavender v Betts* [1942] 2 All ER 72.

[283] *Kenny v Preen* [1963] 1 QB 499; *Branchett v Beaney* [1992] 3 All ER 910, where CA reviewed the authorities
and held that damages are not recoverable for mental distress; doubting *Sampson v Floyd* [1989] 2 EGLR 49 (constructive eviction where tenant was frightened for himself and for his wife; damages awarded for loss of lease, conveyancing costs and distress). On the recoverability of damages for mental distress for breach of contract generally,
see *Farley v Skinner* [2002] 2 AC 732; Treitel, pp. 987–94. Such conduct might however constitute a tort, such as

or inflicts physical discomfort on him by cutting off his gas and electricity,[284] or where he erects scaffolding which obstructs access to the premises.[285] However, there is no liability under the covenant which would impose on the landlord an obligation to alter or improve the premises so as to provide adequate sound-proofing against noise penetration from his adjoining premises.[286] There is also no liability under the covenant if the act of disturbance is committed by a person claiming not under the landlord, but under a title paramount to his;[287] nor is there liability if a landlord enters into possession as a result of a court order on the ground of forfeiture of the lease, which is subsequently reversed on appeal.[288] And the tenant must expect some disruption with his enjoyment of the premises when the landlord fulfils his duty to repair.[289]

(b) Non-derogation from grant[290]

Closely related to the covenant for quiet enjoyment[291] is the landlord's implied covenant that he shall not derogate from his grant. He must not frustrate the use of the land for the purposes for which it was let;[292] or, as Bowen LJ put it, "a grantor having given a thing with one hand is not to take away the means of enjoying it with the other".[293] Wood V-C in one case said:

If a landowner conveys one of two closes to another, he cannot afterwards do anything to derogate from his grant; and if the conveyance is made for the express purpose of having buildings erected upon the land so granted, a contract is implied on the part of the grantor to do nothing to prevent the land from being used for the purpose for which to the knowledge of the grantor the conveyance is made.[294]

In the case of leases this general principle of law becomes particularly applicable when the landlord makes an inconsiderate use of land adjacent to the tenant's holding. Thus where lands were leased to a tenant for the purpose of carrying on the business of a timber merchant, and the landlord proceeded to erect buildings on adjoining land in such a way as to

---

[284] trespass or assault; and damages may be recoverable in tort for distress: *Branchett v Beaney*, at 918. See also Protection from Harassment Act 1997, s. 3 (civil remedy may include damages for anxiety).

[284] *Perera v Vandiyar* [1953] 1 WLR 672.

[285] *Owen v Gadd* [1956] 2 QB 99, a case of an express covenant, but equally applicable to an implied covenant: *Queensway Marketing Ltd v Associated Restaurants Ltd* (1984) 271 EG 1106; *Lawson v Hartley-Brown* (1995) 71 P & CR 242 (erection of scaffolding outside shop and construction of flat roof above it).

[286] *Southwark LBC v Tanner* [2001] 1 AC 1 (eighteen flats built at the end of First World War which had fallen short of modern standards); [2000] Conv 161 (D. Rook).

[287] *Jones v Lavington* [1903] 1 KB 253. See also *Celsteel Ltd v Alton House Holdings Ltd (No 2)* [1987] 1 WLR 291 (lessor not liable on covenant for what predecessor in title had done).

[288] *Hillgate House Ltd v Expert Clothing Service & Sales Ltd* [1987] 1 EGLR 65.

[289] *Goldmile Properties Ltd v Lechouritis* [2003] 1 EGLR 60 (covenants to repair and to give quiet enjoyment must be construed and applied so as to coexist on a basis of parity, not priority). For covenants to repair, see pp. 245 et seq, post.

[290] For a comprehensive discussion, see (1964) 80 LQR 244 (D. W. Elliott); criticised in part, (1965) 81 LQR 28 (M. A. Peel); Gale, paras. 3–31 to 3–51.   [291] Ibid., at 273–6.

[292] *Browne v Flower* [1911] 1 Ch 219 at 225–7, where illustrations are given by Parker J.

[293] *Birmingham, Dudley and District Banking Co v Ross* (1888) 38 Ch D 295 at 313; *Johnston & Sons Ltd v Holland* [1988] 1 EGLR 264 at 267–8, per Nicholls LJ: "The expression 'derogation from grant' conjures up images of parchment and sealing wax, of copperplate handwriting and fusty title deeds. But the principle is not based on some ancient technicality of real property . . . it is a principle which merely embodies in a legal maxim a rule of common honesty."   [294] *North Eastern Rly Co v Elliott* (1860) 1 John & H 145 at 153.

interrupt the free flow of air to the tenant's drying sheds, it was held that damages were recoverable against the landlord's assigns for breach of the implied covenant.[295] Again, where a flat is leased in a building, the whole of which is clearly intended to be used solely by residential tenants, the landlord commits a breach of the covenant if he subsequently lets the greater part of the premises for business purposes.[296]

The covenant is enforceable against the landlord and his successors not only by the original tenant but also by those claiming under him.[297]

(c) Fitness for habitation

In general, there is no implied undertaking by the landlord that the premises are or will be fit for habitation; and no covenant is implied that he will do any repairs.[298] Caveat lessee.[299] There are, however, exceptions to this rule.

(1) FURNISHED HOUSES

Upon the letting of a furnished house, there is at common law an implied warranty, in the nature of a condition,[300] that the premises shall be reasonably fit for habitation at the date

---

[295] *Aldin v Latimer Clark, Muirhead & Co* [1894] 2 Ch 437; *Harmer v Jumbil (Nigeria) Tin Areas Ltd* [1921] 1 Ch 200 (landlord unable to build on land acquired after lease granted); *Port v Griffith* [1938] 1 All ER 295; *Romulus Trading Co Ltd v Comet Properties Ltd* [1996] 2 EGLR 70 (grant of adjoining premises to competing business held not to be derogation); cf *Chartered Trust plc v Davies* [1997] 2 EGLR 83 (held to be derogation where landlord failed to use his powers to prevent another tenant of his from substantially interfering with the way in which the tenant ran his business of selling puzzles and executive toys in a "niche" shop in Bognor Regis); (1998) 148 NLJ 57 (H. W. Wilkinson); *Yankwood Ltd v Havering LBC* [1998] EGCS 75. See also *Lyme Valley Squash Club Ltd v Newcastle under Lyme BC* [1985] 2 All ER 405 (easement of light); *Oceanic Village Ltd v Shirayma Shokusan Co Ltd* [2001] L & TR 35 (implied term in lease of gift shop at London Aquarium restricting landlord from permitting sale of aquarium-related goods from other nearby premises).

The principle is also applicable if the tenant is prevented from entering the lessor's land in order to execute essential repairs to the demised premises: *Ward v Kirkland* [1967] Ch 194 at 226–7.

The Access to Neighbouring Land Act 1992 enables a person to obtain an order of the County Court for access to neighbouring land, in order to carry out works which are reasonably necessary for the preservation of his own land (land includes a party-wall: *Dean v Walker* (1996) 73 P & CR 366). The Act is based on the Law Commission Report on Rights of Access to Neighbouring Land 1985 (Law Com No. 151, Cmnd 9692). The Act had a chequered history: [1992] 26 EG 136 (J. Adams). It came into force on 31 January 1993. An access order is registrable as a writ or order under LCA 1925, s. 6(1)(d), and is regarded as a pending land action under s. 5(1). If the land is registered, the order is registrable by way of agreed notice under LRA 2002, s. 34; LRR 2003, r. 80, and cannot be an overriding interest: Access to Neighbouring Land Act 1992, s. 5. See Gale, *Easements*, paras. 11–41 to 11–69.

[296] *Newman v Real Estate Debenture Corpn Ltd and Flower Decorations Ltd* [1940] 1 All ER 131; distinguished in *Kelly v Battershell* [1949] 2 All ER 830.

[297] *Molton Buildings Ltd v City of Westminster LBC* (1975) 30 P & CR 182 at 186, per Lord DENNING MR.

[298] The Law Commission has proposed that an (excludable) covenant to repair should be implied into all leases, and not only those exceptional cases discussed infra; and that a (non-excludable) covenant should be implied into a lease of a dwelling-house for a term of less than seven years that the lessor will keep it fit for human habitation during the term of the lease: Responsibility for State and Condition of Property 1996 (Law Com No. 238), Parts VII and VIII; p. 254, post. In *Wettern Electric Ltd v Welsh Development Agency* [1983] QB 796 was implied into a contractual *licence* of business premises that they were of sound construction and would be reasonably fit for the purposes required by the licensee; (1983) 80 LSG 2195 (H. W. Wilkinson); cf *Morris-Thomas v Petticoat Lane Rentals* (1986) 53 P & CR 238.

[299] *Southwark LBC v Tanner* [2001] 1 AC 1 at 12, per Lord HOFFMANN.

[300] For the technical difference between a "condition", a "warranty" and an "intermediate" contractual term as now applied in the law of contract, see Anson, pp. 134–5. The language of the older cases must be understood in the light of this.

fixed for the commencement of the tenancy. As McCARDIE J said:[301]

What is the meaning of "fit for habitation"? The meaning of the phrase must vary with the circumstances to which it is applied. In the case of unclean furniture or defective drains or a nuisance by vermin the matter is not, as a rule, one of difficulty. The eye or the nostrils can detect the fault and measure its extent. But in the case of a house lately occupied by a person suffering from an infectious disease, the eye and other senses are of no avail. The bacilli of infection are not apparent to the eye. Yet a peril is none the less grave because it is hidden.

Thus, if the house is infested with bugs,[302] if its drainage is defective,[303] or if it has been lately occupied by a person suffering from tuberculosis,[304] the tenant is entitled to repudiate the tenancy and to recover damages. But provided that the house is fit for habitation at the beginning of the tenancy, the fact that it later becomes uninhabitable imposes no liability upon the landlord.[305]

This implied condition does not extend to unfurnished premises.[306]

(2) PREMISES IN MULTIPLE OCCUPATION

A landlord who retains control of the means of access to demised premises in a high-rise block of flats, such as lifts and staircases and other common facilities such as rubbish chutes or lighting, is under an implied duty to keep them in repair. The duty, implied into the lease at common law, is not absolute, but only a duty to take reasonable care to maintain them in a state of reasonable repair and usability.[307]

(3) CORRELATIVE OBLIGATION ON LANDLORD

A repairing covenant may be implied against a landlord where a tenant's express covenant as to internal repairs would eventually become impossible to perform in the absence of a cor-relative obligation on the landlord as to outside repairs. The imposition of such an obliga-tion on the landlord is necessary in order to give business efficacy to the lease.[308]

(4) HOUSES LET AT LOW RENT

The Landlord and Tenant Act 1985[309] provides for the protection of persons taking houses at a low rent. Where a contract is made on or after 6 July 1957 for letting for human habitation a house or part of a house at a rent not exceeding £80 a year in Greater London and £52 elsewhere, there shall be implied a condition by the landlord, notwithstanding any stipulation to the contrary, that the house is fit for human habitation at the

---

[301] *Collins v Hopkins* [1923] 2 KB 617 at 620–1.   [302] *Smith v Marrable* (1843) 11 M & W 5.

[303] *Wilson v Finch Hatton* (1877) 2 Ex D 336.   [304] *Collins v Hopkins,* supra.

[305] *Sarson v Roberts* [1895] 2 QB 395.

[306] *Hart v Windsor* (1843) 12 M & W 68; *Robbins v Jones* (1863) 15 CBNS 221; *Cruse v Mount* [1933] Ch 278; *Cavalier v Pope* [1906] AC 428; *Bottomley v Bannister* [1932] 1 KB 458; *Otto v Bolton and Norris* [1936] 2 KB 46.

[307] *Liverpool City Council v Irwin* [1977] AC 239, p. 235, post; Treitel, p. 208. It was held on the facts that there was no breach of the duty. Cf *Duke of Westminster v Guild* [1985] QB 688 (no repairing covenant implied on part of landlord in respect of drains running under retained land).

[308] *Barrett v Lounova (1982) Ltd* [1990] 1 QB 348; cf *Demetriou v Poolaction Ltd* [1991] 1 EGLR 100 (busi-ness premises and no correlative obligation on the landlord); *Adami v Lincoln Grange Management Ltd* [1998] 1 EGLR 58.

[309] Ss. 8–10, replacing HA 1957, ss. 4, 6 and 7. See commentary on LTA 1985 in *Current Law Statutes Annotated* by A. Arden and S. McGrath.

commencement of the tenancy, and an undertaking that he will keep it so throughout the tenancy.[310] There is no such stipulation, however, if the letting is for at least three years upon the terms that the tenant will put the house into a condition reasonably fit for human habitation, and if the lease is not determinable by either party before the expiration of three years.[311]

Whether the statutory condition has been broken is a question of fact and one not always easy to determine, but the Act provides that a house shall be deemed to be unfit for human habitation if and only if it is unreasonably defective in respect of one or more of the following matters: repair; stability; freedom from damp; internal arrangement; natural lighting; ventilation; water supply; drainage and sanitary conveniences; facilities for preparation and cooking of food and for the disposal of waste water.[312]

In the event of a breach of the implied condition, the tenant may repudiate the tenancy and recover damages for breach of the undertaking,[313] providing that the landlord had notice of the existence of the defect and failed to remedy it.[314] The landlord's obligation is restricted to cases where the house is capable of being made fit at reasonable expense for human habitation.[315]

(5) HOUSES LET FOR SHORT TERM

The Landlord and Tenant Act 1985[316] imposes further obligations on the landlord, where he has granted a lease of a dwelling-house after 24 October 1961 for a term of less than seven years.[317]

---

[310] LTA 1985, s. 8. In the case of a contract made before 6 July 1957 and after 31 July 1923, the equivalent figures are £40 for London and £26 elsewhere. In view of inflation, the section must now have remarkably little application: *Quick v Taff Ely BC* [1986] QB 809 at 817, per DILLON LJ; *Issa v Hackney LBC* [1997] 1 WLR 956 at 964, per BROOKE LJ (Parliament's failure to increase rental values makes the implied covenant a "dead letter"). In 1996 the Law Commission recommended that LTA 1985 ss. 8–10 be repealed, and that a covenant should be implied into a lease of a dwelling-house for a term of less than seven years that the lessor will keep it fit for human habitation during the term of the lease: Responsibility for State and Condition of Property (Law Com No. 238); p. 254, post. This would have the effect of removing the present archaic rent limits. See also *Lee v Leeds City Council* [2002] 1 WLR 1488 at 1499 per CHADWICK LJ, criticising the delay in giving effect to the Law Commission's Report.

[311] Ibid., s. 8(5). The Law Commission's proposed reforms, n. 310, supra, would remove this exception: Law Com No. 238, para. 8.40.

[312] Ibid., s. 10. As to the test of unfitness in the case of disrepair, see *Summers v Salford Corpn* [1943] AC 283 at 293, per Lord ATKIN; and generally M.H.L.G. circular 69/67.

[313] *Walker v Hobbs & Co* (1889) 23 QBD 458.

[314] *Morgan v Liverpool Corpn* [1927] 2 KB 131; *McCarrick v Liverpool Corpn* [1947] AC 219.

[315] *Buswell v Goodwin* [1971] 1 WLR 92 at 96–7; *Hillbank Properties Ltd v Hackney LBC* [1978] QB 998; [1979] Conv 414 (D. Morgan); *FFF Estates Ltd v Hackney LBC* [1981] 1 All ER 32; *Phillips v Newham LBC* (1981) 43 P & CR 54; *Kenny v Kingston upon Thames Royal London Borough Council* [1985] 1 EGLR 26; *R v Ealing London Borough* (1982) 265 EG 691.

[316] Ss. 11–16, as amended by HA 1988, s. 116, replacing HA 1961, ss. 32, 33. See the commentary in *Current Law Statutes Annotated* (1985). S. 11 does not bind the Crown: s. 15(5). See *Department of Transport v Egoroff* [1986] 1 EGLR 89. For the Law Commission's proposal that an (excludable) covenant should be implied into other leases (retaining, however, the provisions of LTA 1985 ss. 11–15), see Responsibility for State and Condition of Property 1996 (Law Com No. 238), Part VII; p. 254, post.

[317] A lease is treated as one for less than seven years if, though made for that period or longer, it is determinable at the lessor's option within seven years: LTA 1985, s. 13(2)(c). See *Parker v O'Connor* [1974] 1 WLR 1160; *Brikom Investments Ltd v Seaford* [1981] 1 WLR 863. For the meaning of a "lease" within LTA 1985, s. 11, see *Bruton v London & Quadrant Housing Trust* [2000] 1 AC 406, M & B p. 441, pp. 195–6, ante.

In the case of such a lease or an agreement for a lease,[318] he is subjected to an implied covenant:

(a) to keep in repair the structure and exterior[319] of the dwelling-house[320] (including drains, gutters and external pipes); and

(b) to keep in repair and proper working order[321] the installations in the dwelling-house—
   (i) for the supply of water,[322] gas and electricity, and for sanitation (including basins, sinks, baths and sanitary conveniences); and
   (ii) for space heating or heating water.[323]

This implied covenant was extended by the Housing Act 1988 to include any part of the building in which the landlord has an estate or interest, if the disrepair is such as to affect the tenant's enjoyment of the dwelling-house or of any common parts which the tenant is entitled to use.[324]

The duty to repair means that the tenant must show physical damage to that part of the premises which has to be made good; it is not enough to show that it is defective or inherently inefficient for living in or ineffective in providing the condition of ordinary habitation.[325]

The statutory obligations do not require the landlord to reinstate the premises if they are damaged by fire or by tempest, flood or other inevitable accident; or to effect repairs necessitated by the tenant's failure to use the premises in a tenant-like manner.[326] In determining the standard of repair, regard must be had to the age, character and prospective life of the

---

[318] Brikom Investments Ltd v Seaford, supra; [1981] Conv 396.

[319] Brown v Liverpool Corpn [1969] 3 All ER 1345 (outside steps and path held to be essential part of access and therefore included): cf Hopwood v Cannock Chase DC [1975] 1 WLR 373 (backyard path not giving access excluded); King v South Northamptonshire DC [1992] 1 EGLR 53. See also Campden Hill Towers Ltd v Gardner [1977] QB 823 (exterior of flat not exterior of whole building). The decision was reversed by HA 1988, s. 116. See also Douglas-Scott v Scorgie [1984] 1 WLR 716 (roof over a top-floor flat); Irvine v Moran [1991] 1 EGLR 261, where structure was defined as consisting of those elements of the overall dwelling-house which gave it its essential appearance, stability and shape; Staves & Staves v Leeds City Council (1990) 23 HLR 107 (plaster part of structure).   [320] As to the meaning of a dwelling-house, see Okereke v Brent LBC [1967] 1 QB 42.

[321] But not to put in a new efficient system: Liverpool City Council v Irwin [1977] AC 239 at 269–70 (water closet cistern which flooded due to bad design held not to be in proper working order); nor to lag water pipes: Wycombe Health Authority v Barnett (1982) 47 P & CR 394; nor to install a damp-course: Wainwright v Leeds City Council (1984) 270 EG 1289. In relation to supply of water, gas and electricity, the duty is to ensure that the installation is so designed and constructed as to be capable of performing its function at the start of the tenancy, under conditions of supply which it is reasonable to anticipate will prevail; and might also require a landlord to make necessary modifications during the tenancy to accommodate unanticipated alterations in quantity or character of supply from external utility provider: O'Connor v Old Etonian Housing Association Ltd [2002] Ch 295; [2003] Conv 80 (M. P. Thompson).   [322] Sheldon v West Bromwich Corpn (1973) 25 P & CR 360.

[323] For a miscellany of "severe defects" leading to repudiation of lease, see Hussein v Mehlman [1992] 2 EGLR 87, p. 324, post.

[324] LTA 1985, s. 11(1A), (1B), as added by HA 1988, s. 116; Niazi Services Ltd v van de Loo [2004] 1 WLR 1254 (covenant does not extend to installation not owned or controlled by lessor and located in part of building in which lessor does not have estate or interest); [2004] Conv 330 (D. W. Potts); [2005] Conv 123 (I. Loveland).

[325] Quick v Taff Ely BC [1986] QB 809 (living conditions appalling due to condensation, but no damage to walls or windows of house); McNerny v Lambeth LBC [1989] 1 EGLR 81; Lee v Leeds City Council [2002] 1 WLR 1488 (rejecting arguments (i) that Quick v Taff Ely BC was wrongly decided; and (ii) that the interpretation of "repair" in LTA 1985, s. 11 contained in Quick is incompatible with Convention rights and so should be reinterpreted under HRA 1998, s. 3); [2003] Conv 112 (P. F. Smith)   [326] LTA 1985, s. 11(2).

dwelling-house and to the locality.[327] The landlord is liable for any consequential expenditure to which the tenant is put, such as redecoration or alternative accommodation during the repairs.[328] But he is only liable for defects of which notice[329] is given, and only then if after a reasonable time, he fails to remedy the defect.[330]

The parties cannot contract out of the Act,[331] but with their consent the county court may exclude or modify the repairing obligations of the landlord if it is considered reasonable to do so.[332] It is further enacted that any covenant to repair by the tenant shall be of no effect in so far as it relates to the matters covered in the landlord's statutory obligations.[333]

Local housing authorities have wide powers under the Housing Act 2004[334] to enforce housing standards in relation to residential premises. A tenant may prefer to invoke action by the local authority rather than to enforce his rights directly under the covenant.

(6) LOCAL AUTHORITY LANDLORD'S DUTIES UNDER HUMAN RIGHTS ACT 1998

Section 6(1) of the Human Rights Act 1998 provides that it is unlawful for a public authority to act in a way which is incompatible with a Convention right.[335] This imposes on a local authority landlord an obligation to take steps to ensure that the condition of a dwelling-house

---

[327] LTA 1985, s. 11(3); *Newham London Borough v Patel* [1979] JPL 303; *McClean v Liverpool City Council* [1987] 2 EGLR 56; *Hungerford (Dame Margaret) Charity (Trustees) v Beazeley* [1993] 29 EG 100; [1994] Conv 145 (J. Morgan). On whether the obligation to repair can extend to merely preventative works, see *Mason v Totalfinaelf UK Ltd* [2003] 3 EGLR 91 at [17]–[23].

[328] *McGreal v Wake* (1984) 269 EG 1254; *Bradley v Chorley BC* [1985] 2 EGLR 49.

[329] *O'Brien v Robinson* [1973] AC 912; *McGreal v Wake*, supra; *Al Hassani v Merrigan* [1988] 1 EGLR 93; *Passley v Wandsworth LBC* (1998) 30 HLR 165. The notice may be from a person other than the tenant: *Dinefwr BC v Jones* [1987] 2 EGLR 58; and may be by way of a valuation report sent to the landlord: *Hall v Howard* [1988] 2 EGLR 75.

[330] *Porter v Jones* [1942] 2 All ER 570 (landlord who failed for eight months from notice to remedy disrepair held liable in damages); *Morris v Liverpool City Council* [1988] 1 EGLR 47 (delay of one week for emergency repairs held unreasonable).   [331] LTA 1985, s. 12(1).

[332] Ibid., s. 12(2). For the extension of the obligations by express provision in the lease or by any subsequent variation of its terms, see *Palmer v Sandwell Metropolitan Borough* [1987] 2 EGLR 79.   [333] Ibid., s. 11(4).

[334] Part I (which came into force in April 2006: SI 2006 No. 1060). This Act replaced HA 1985, Part VI, under which local authorities could require the person who has control of residential premises to make it fit for human habitation, or to carry out repairs where, even though the house was not unfit, substantial repairs were necessary to bring it up to a reasonable standard, having regard to its age, character and locality. HA 2004 provides a new system for assessing the condition of residential premises, and provides new kinds of enforcement action, to enforce housing standards: ss. 1(1), (3). The condition of the premises is now to assessed by reference to defined "hazards" (to be prescribed by Regulations), to replace the former system based on the test of fitness for human habitation contained in HA 1985, s. 604: s. 1(2). The test of "fitness for human habitation" under HA 1985 was the same as that under LTA 1985 s. 10, but HA 2004 does not make any change to LTA 1985 in this respect. However, the Law Commission's proposals to replace LTA 1985 ss. 8–10 by a more general provision for implied covenants of fitness for purpose for human habitation, n. 310, supra, has not yet been accepted by the Government, which will reconsider the proposals following the enactment of HA 2004: Law Commission 38th Annual Report 2003/04 (Law Com No. 288), para. 3.37.

See also Environmental Protection Act 1990, Part III (statutory nuisances). On noise, see Noise and Statutory Nuisance Act 1993; Noise Act 1996; Environment Act 1995. See Waite and Jewell, *Environmental Law in Property Transactions* (3rd edn, 2005); McCracken, Jones, Pereira and Payne, *Statutory Nuisance Law and Practice; Encyclopedia of Environmental Law*.

[335] For the rights and freedoms under the European Convention for the Protection of Human Rights and Fundamental Freedoms included within "Convention rights" for the purposes of the Act, see HRA 1998, s. 1, Sch. 1.

which it has let for social housing is such that the tenant's right to respect for private and family life[336] is not infringed.[337] Whether the condition of the dwelling-house is such that the tenant's Convention right is infringed depends on the circumstances of the particular case, having due regard to the needs and resources of the community and of individuals. However, it appears that a local authority landlord, which lets a house unfit for habitation or in a state prejudicial to health, will not generally be in breach of this obligation.[338] It is clear that the Act does not impose some general and unqualified obligation on local authorities in relation to the condition of their housing stock.[339]

(7) DUTY OF CARE IN TORT OR UNDER DEFECTIVE PREMISES ACT 1972 FOR SAFETY

At common law a landlord of unfurnished premises does not owe a duty of care in tort to his tenant or the tenant's guests in respect of the state of the premises at the time when they are let, even in relation to personal injury suffered in consequence of the state of the premises. ERLE CJ said in 1863:[340]

A landlord who lets a house in a dangerous state is not liable to the tenant's customers or guests for accidents happening during the term: for, fraud apart, there is no law against letting a tumble-down house; and the tenant's remedy is upon his contract, if any.

This rule was confirmed by the House of Lords in *Cavalier v Pope*[341] and remains the position at common law.[342] However, persons, such as designers or builders, involved in the construction of premises owe a duty of reasonable care at common law to those who may reasonably be expected to be affected by their work, although the duty extends only to the physical injury or property damage suffered in consequence of the failure to take reasonable care.[343] Although, therefore, the landlord owes no duty of care at common law *qua landlord* to his

---

[336] Art. 8 of the Convention; HRA 1998, Sch. 1.

[337] *Lee v Leeds City Council* [2002] 1 WLR 1488 at 1506.

[338] "The allocation of resources to meet the needs of social housing is very much a matter for democratically determined priorities": ibid., per CHADWICK LJ, relying on *Southwark LBC v Mills* [2001] 1 AC 1 at 9–10, per Lord HOFFMANN.

[339] *Lee v Leeds City Council*, supra, at 1506.

[340] *Robbins v Jones* (1863) 15 CB (NS) 221 at 240.

[341] [1906] AC 428.

[342] *McNerny v Lambeth LBC* [1989] 1 EGLR 81; [1989] Conv 216 (P. F. Smith). The common law might have developed otherwise on this point, since the rule was based on certain assumptions of the law of tort which are no longer correct: in particular, the "privity fallacy" which provided that a party, such as a landlord, who undertook contractual obligations should be liable only under the contract for the consequences of breach, and could not be liable directly to third parties in tort. This was corrected in *Donoghue v Stevenson* [1932] AC 562, but the absence of the landlord's duty in tort then was already well established. See Smith, *Liability in Negligence* (1984), p. 18. Development of the common law rule is now unlikely, given its effective reversal by Defective Premises Act 1972, s. 4; infra. See generally *Salmond and Heuston on the Law of Torts* (21st edn, 1996), pp. 284–91.

[343] *D & F Estates Ltd v Church Comrs for England* [1989] AC 177; *Murphy v Brentwood DC* [1991] 1 AC 398; *Department of the Environment v Thomas Bates & Son Ltd* [1991] 1 AC 499. For an exceptional case in which HL held that the duty could extend to economic loss, see *Junior Books Ltd v Veitchi Co Ltd* [1983] 1 AC 520, which was distinguished but not overruled in the later HL cases. The exclusion of economic loss (including therefore the cost of repair incurred by the building owner or tenant) has not been followed in Australia: *Bryan v Maloney* (1995) 182 CLR 609; nor in Canada: *Winnipeg Condominium Corpn No 36 v Bird Construction Co Ltd* [1995] 1 SCR 85; (1995) 111 LQR 362 (J. G. Fleming); nor in New Zealand: *Invercargill City Council v Hamlin* [1996] AC 624; (1996) 112 LQR 369 (I. N. Duncan Wallace); (1996) 3 LS 387 (C. F. Stychin).

tenant or his guests, if the landlord is also involved in the design or construction of the premises he will owe the duty *qua designer* or *qua builder*.[344]

These common law rules were however changed by statute. Under the Defective Premises Act 1972, section 4,[345] the landlord's immunity under *Cavalier v Pope* is effectively removed. A landlord owes to all persons[346] who might reasonably be expected to be affected by defects[347] in the state of the premises, a duty to take reasonable care to see that they are reasonably safe from personal injury or from damage to their property. Such a duty arises when the land-lord is under an obligation to the tenant for the maintenance or repair of the premises, or when he has an express or implied right[348] to enter the premises[349] in order to maintain and repair them. The duty is only owed, however, if the landlord knows or ought to have known of the defect,[350] and if the defect arises from his failure to carry out his obligation or right to maintain or repair.

Furthermore, a landlord of residential property may sometimes be liable to a tenant or to third parties under section 1 of the Defective Premises Act 1972,[351] which provides that any person who takes on work[352] for or in connection with the provision of a dwelling,[353] whether by the erection, conversion or enlargement of a building, is under a duty to see that the work is done in a workmanlike or professional manner, with proper materials, and so that as regards that work the dwelling will be fit for habitation when completed. The duty is owed to the person to whose order the building is provided and to every person who acquires an interest (whether legal or equitable) in it,[354] including therefore a tenant under a legal or equitable lease, and is not limited to damages in respect of physical damage. The duty is not imposed on the landlord *qua landlord*, but will apply to him if he takes on work within the meaning of the section.[355]

---

[344] *Rimmer v Liverpool City Council* [1985] QB 1 (tenant injured by defective glass panel; the Defective Premises Act 1972, infra, did not apply: at 7); *Targett v Torfaen BC* [1992] 3 All ER 27 (CA held that *Rimmer* was not overruled by *Murphy v Brentwood DC*, supra).

[345] Replacing Occupiers' Liability Act 1957, s. 4. The Act was based on the Law Commission Report on Civil Liability of Vendors and Lessors for Defective Premises 1970 (Law Com No. 40). See generally Holyoak and Allen, *Civil Liability for Defective Premises*, as supplemented by (1984) 134 NLJ 347, 369, 411, 425; Speaight and Stone, *Law of Defective Premises* (1982); *Salmond and Heuston on the Law of Torts*, pp. 287–91; [1974] CLJ 307, [1975] CLJ 48, esp. at 62–8 (J. R. Spencer).

[346] Including a tenant: *Smith v Bradford Metropolitan Council* (1982) 44 P & CR 171; *McNerny v Lambeth LBC* [1989] 1 EGLR 81; *Sykes v Harry* [2001] QB 1014 at 1025; and a contractual licensee: s. 4(6). The Act applies to all types of tenancy: s. 6(1). The damages may be reduced for the claimant's contributory negligence: *Sykes v Harry* (80% reduction).

[347] There must be a defect which constitutes *disrepair*, and not just a defect inherent in the design of the property: *Lee v Leeds City Council* [2002] 1 WLR 1488 at 1497, 1515.

[348] *McAuley v Bristol City Council* [1992] QB 134; [1992] Conv 346 (J. Martin).

[349] Including a back concrete patio: ibid.

[350] But this does not require him to have notice, actual or constructive, of the *actual* defect which gave rise to the injury: *Sykes v Harry*, supra, at 1025–6.

[351] The statutory duty under this section does not apply to dwellings build in accordance with an "approved scheme" of purchaser protection: s. 2. Schemes run by the National House-Building Council, under which the Council in effect guaranteed the building for a period of ten years from completion against defects arising from non-compliance with the Council's standard specifications, were approved until 1979, but the last approved scheme came to an end on 31 March 1979: *Keating on Building Contracts*, para. 15–01.

[352] *Alexander v Mercouris* [1979] 1 WLR 1270; (1980) 255 EG 241 (H. W. Wilkinson); *Smith v Drumm* [1996] EGCS 192. "Work" includes non-feasance: *Andrews v Schooling* [1991] 1 WLR 783.

[353] *Jacobs v Moreton* (1996) 72 BLR 92.   [354] S. 1(1).

[355] It will, however, apply to such persons as the builder and the architect.

(2) Implied Obligations and Rights of the Tenant

(a) Obligations

(1) GENERAL

A tenant, including one from year to year,[356] is subject to an implied obligation to keep and to deliver up the premises in a tenant-like manner and to keep the fences in a state of repair.[357]

(2) LIABILITY FOR WASTE

Further, tenants are subject to the doctrine of waste,[358] though in varying degrees.

A tenant for a fixed number of years is liable for voluntary and also for permissive waste.[359]

A tenant from *year to year* is liable for voluntary waste, but otherwise his only obligation, it would seem, is to use the premises in a "tenantlike" manner.[360] This expression is obscure if not unintelligible,[361] and all that it means apparently is that the tenant must do such work as is necessary for his own reasonable enjoyment of the premises. DENNING LJ gave some illustrations in *Warren v Keen*:[362]

The tenant must take proper care of the place. He must, if he is going away for the winter, turn off the water and empty the boiler.[363] He must clean the chimneys, when necessary, and also the windows. He must mend the electric light when it fuses. He must unstop the sink when it is blocked by his waste. In short, he must do the little jobs about the place which a reasonable tenant would do. In addition, he must, of course, not damage the house, wilfully or negligently; and he must see that his family and guests do not damage it: and if they do, he must repair it. But apart from such things, if the house falls into disrepair through fair wear and tear or lapse of time, or for any reason not caused by him, then the tenant is not liable to repair it.

There is however some authority for the view that he must keep the premises wind and water tight in the sense that, although he is not bound to do anything of a substantial nature, he must carry out such repairs as are necessary to prevent the property from lapsing into a state of decay.[364] But the existence of this obligation was doubted by the Court of Appeal in *Warren v Keen*.

---

[356] *Marsden v Edward Heyes Ltd* [1927] 2 KB 1.

[357] *Cheetham v Hampson* (1791) 4 Term Rep 318; *Goodman v Rollinson* (1951) 95 SJ 188. For the tenant of an agricultural holding, see *Wedd v Porter* [1916] 2 KB 91.

[358] Pp. 504–8, post. The Law Commission has proposed that the law of waste be abolished as between landlord and tenant and that it, and the duty of tenant-like user, be replaced by a modern implied covenant to similar effect: Responsibility for State and Condition of Property 1996 (Law Com No. 238), Part X; p. 254, post.

[359] *Yellowly v Gower* (1855) 11 Exch 274; *Mancetter Developments Ltd v Garmanson Ltd* [1986] QB 1212; *Dayani v Bromley LBC* [1999] 3 EGLR 144 (a detailed analysis referring to authorities from the tenth century), p. 507, post.

[360] *Warren v Keen* [1954] 1 QB 15; (1954) 70 LQR 9 (R.E.M.); [1954] CLJ 71 (H. W. R. Wade).

[361] Law Com No. 238, paras. 10.26–10.29, 10.31(vi).

[362] Supra, at 20. The expression is an extension to tenants generally of the rule that the agricultural tenant must farm the land in a "husbandlike" manner. In this context, "husbandlike" has a definite meaning. The tenant must observe the custom of the country, i.e. the local usages of husbandry.

[363] Not, however, for two nights, even when the temperature fell to below 6 or 7 degrees below freezing. The test is reasonable foresight of frozen pipes in a cold climate: *Wycombe Health Authority v Barnett* (1982) 47 P & CR 394.   [364] *Ferguson v —* (1797) 2 Esp 590; *Wedd v Porter* [1916] 2 KB 91 at 100.

A tenant *at will* is not liable for either kind of waste, though the effect of the commission by him of any act of voluntary waste is to terminate his tenancy and to render him liable to an action of trespass.[365] A tenant *at sufferance* is liable for voluntary waste, but probably not for permissive waste.[366]

(b) Rights

(1) ESTOVERS

A tenant for years, notwithstanding the doctrine of waste, is entitled to take estovers from the land, that is to say, wood, even though it be timber,[367] for the purpose of carrying out certain repairs. Estovers fall into three classes, namely: house-bote (wood to be used either as fuel or for building purposes); plough-bote (wood for making and repairing agricultural implements); and hay-bote (wood for repairing hedges).[368]

This right is limited by immediate necessity: a tenant cannot cut and store wood with a view to future requirements.

(2) EMBLEMENTS

A tenant for years is entitled at common law to emblements, that is, a right to re-enter the land at harvest to recover the crops that he has sown.[369] It is obvious that a tenant for a fixed term of years cannot be entitled to this right, because he knows when his tenancy will end, and it his own fault if he sows crops which will not come to maturity until after that date. But there may be cases where a tenancy comes to an end unexpectedly, as for instance upon the sudden determination of a tenancy at will or upon the determination of the estate out of which the term has been created, in which the common law right to emblements exists. The right is obviously inconvenient to both parties, and in one type of case, that is, where the landlord's estate ended prematurely, it was modified by the Landlord and Tenant Act 1851. This provided that a tenant for years at a rack rent (i.e. a rent which represents the full annual value of the land[370]) whose lease expired owing to the failure of his landlord's estate, should in lieu of emblements be entitled to remain in occupation until the end of the current year of tenancy.

In the case of agricultural tenancies, however, the Agricultural Holdings Act 1986[371] provides that a tenant at a rack rent, whose term ceases by the death, or the cesser of the estate, of a landlord entitled only for life or for any other uncertain interest, shall continue to hold and occupy the holding until the occupation is determined by a twelve-month notice to quit, expiring at the end of a year of the tenancy. This provision has no counterpart in the Agricultural Tenancies Act 1995 in relation to a farm business tenancy.

(3) RIGHT TO REMOVE CERTAIN FIXTURES

The extent of this right of removal has already been discussed.[372]

---

[365] *Countess of Shrewsbury's Case* (1600) 5 Co Rep 13b.   [366] *Burchell v Hornsby* (1808) 1 Camp 360.
[367] For the definition of "timber", see p. 506, post.   [368] Co Litt 41b; cf p. 506, post.
[369] P. 504, post. The tenant at will is similarly entitled: p. 213, ante.
[370] *Re Sawyer and Withall* [1919] 2 Ch 333.
[371] S. 21(1). The Act does not apply, subject to exceptions, to tenancies beginning on or after 1 September 1995, although it may still apply to tenancies entered into *in succession* to tenancies already governed by the 1986 Act: Agricultural Tenancies Act 1995, s. 4. For further discussion of the policies underlying the Agricultural Holdings Act 1986 and the Agricultural Tenancies Act 1995, see pp. 386 et seq, post.   [372] Pp. 158–60, ante.

B Position where there are Express Covenants and Conditions

In the majority of cases the rights and the liabilities of a landlord and a tenant are regulated by express covenants inserted in the lease,[373] but, as the number of matters that may be the subject of agreement is infinite, and as the agreed terms will naturally vary widely in different cases, in a treatise of this limited scope we cannot do more than notice shortly the more important covenants that find a place in a normal lease.

Generally speaking, and where no exceptional circumstances exist, a tenant will enter into covenants with regard to the payment of rent, rates and taxes, and the maintenance, repair and insurance of the premises; while the landlord will undertake to keep the tenant in quiet enjoyment, and may perhaps take upon himself part of the burden of repairs. The following covenants require special mention.

(1) Covenant by Tenant to Pay Rent

(a) Rent service

The rent payable by a tenant for years is properly called a rent service,[374] and though it generally consists of the payment of money, it may equally well take the form of the delivery of personal chattels,[375] such as corn, or the performance of personal services;[376] and there may even be no rent at all.[377]

(b) Certainty of rent

The rent must be certain,[378] but this does not mean that it must be certain at the date of the lease. Rent is sufficiently certain if it can be calculated with certainty at the time when payment comes to be made. Thus a condition in a council tenant's rent book, providing that the rent was "liable to be increased or decreased on notice being given" was held to be valid.[379] So also was an option to renew a lease "at a rent to be fixed at a price to be determined having regard to the market valuation of the premises at the time of exercising the option".[380] The parties

---

[373] For the modern approach to the interpretation of contracts in general, and covenants in leases in particular, see *Investors' Compensation Scheme Ltd v West Bromwich Building Society* [1998] 1 WLR 896; *Holding & Barnes plc v Hill House Hammond Ltd* [2002] 2 P & CR 11. And for the jurisdiction of the Lands Tribunal to modify a restrictive covenant in a lease of more than forty years after the expiration of twenty-five years of the term, see LPA 1925, s. 84(12); p. 694, post.   [374] P. 265, post.

[375] Co Litt 142a.   [376] *Duke of Marlborough v Osborn* (1864) 5 B & S 67.

[377] LPA 1925, s. 205(1)(xxvii); *Ashburn Anstalt v Arnold* [1989] Ch 1, M & B p. 612.

[378] This is an application of the general principle of contract law that the terms must be certain: Treitel, pp. 49–62. The cases discussed in this section therefore include, but are not limited to, those relating to rent. As will be seen from the cases discussed, questions have most commonly arisen over the certainty of rent in relation to the validity of an option to renew an lease; the validity of a rent review clause within an existing lease, p. 243, post; and the rent payable on renewal of a lease.   [379] *Greater London Council v Connolly* [1970] 2 QB 100.

[380] *Brown v Gould* [1972] Ch 53, M & B p. 461; *Smith v Morgan* [1971] 1 WLR 803 (right of pre-emption "at a figure to be agreed upon" held to be valid); cf *King's Motors (Oxford) Ltd v Lax* [1970] 1 WLR 426 (option for lease "at such rental as may be agreed upon between the parties" held to be void for uncertainty); *Courtney and Fairbairn Ltd v Tolaini Bros (Hotels) Ltd* [1975] 1 WLR 297 (building agreement to "negotiate fair and reasonable contract sums" held to be void for uncertainty); *Bushwall Properties Ltd v Vortex Properties Ltd* [1976] 1 WLR 591 (contract for sale of 51½ acres of land for £50,000 payable in three unequal instalments held unenforceable because of provision that on each payment "a proportionate part of the land shall be released"); cf *Hackney LBC v Thompson* [2001] L & TR 7 (covenant requiring transferee to "pay a due proportion of

may also provide machinery for the application of the formula, such as by directing that the rent shall be fixed by a third party;[381] but, if that machinery proves to be ineffective, the court may substitute its own. In *Sudbrook Trading Estate Ltd v Eggleton*:[382]

a lease gave to the lessees an option to purchase the reversion "at such a price not being less than £12,000 as may be agreed upon by two valuers one to be nominated by the lessor and the other by the lessees or in default of such agreement by an umpire appointed by the said valuers". The lessor refused to appoint a valuer.

In granting specific performance of the option at "a fair and reasonable price", the House of Lords held that, if the ineffective machinery is merely subsidiary and inessential, the court will provide its own, but it will not do so if the machinery constitutes an essential term of the contract. As Lord FRASER OF TULLYBELTON said:[383]

Where an agreement is made to sell at a price to be fixed by a valuer who is named, or who, by reason of holding some office such as auditor of a company whose shares are to be valued, will have special knowledge relevant to the question of value, the prescribed mode may well be regarded as essential. Where, as here, the machinery consists of valuers and an umpire, none of whom is named or identified,

management costs" held valid: construable as meaning an appropriate or reasonable proportion); *ARC Ltd v Schofield* [1990] 2 EGLR 52 (option to renew lease at a rent "to be agreed between the landlord and tenant, being a fair and reasonable market rent at that time" held valid); *Corson v Rhuddlan BC* [1990] 1 EGLR 255, M & B p. 464 (option to renew lease of golf course for further twenty-one years "at a rental to be agreed" [but not to exceed £1,150 per annum] held valid with implication of term that rent was to be a fair rent with an upper limit of £1,150); [1990] Conv 290 (J. E. Martin); *Miller v Lakefield Estates Ltd* [1989] 1 EGLR 212 (option to purchase "at a price to be agreed", but if no sale took place within six months of notice given to exercise option, then property should be sold at public auction, held valid); *Lambert v HTV Cymru (Wales) Ltd* [1998] EMLR 629 (clause obliging purchaser "to use all reasonable endeavours to obtain rights of first negotiation from any assignee" for benefit of seller held not enforceable for lack of certainty); *King's Motors (Oxford) Ltd v Lax* was doubted in *Corson v Rhuddlan BC*; and *Smith v Morgan* was doubted in *Miller v Lakefield Estates Ltd*; *Walford v Miles* [1992] 2 AC 128, p. 861, post (agreement to continue to negotiate "in good faith" held void for uncertainty). For the validity of an index-linked rent, see *Blumenthal v Gallery Five Ltd* (1971) 220 EG 31 (index of retail prices); *Cumshaw Ltd v Bowen* [1987] 1 EGLR 30; (1987) 132 NLJ 288 (H. W. Wilkinson); (1994) 138 SJ 552 (R. Castle and A. MacFarquhar).

[381] *Lloyds Bank Ltd v Marcan* [1973] 1 WLR 1387 (rent to be fixed by person chosen by President of the Royal Institution of Chartered Surveyors).

[382] [1983] 1 AC 444, M & B p. 465; [1983] Conv 76 (K. Hodkinson). Followed in *Re Malpass* [1985] Ch 42 (testamentary option to purchase farm "at the agricultural value thereof determined for agricultural purposes . . . as agreed with the District Valuer"; the valuer declined to act). See also *Campbell v Edwards* [1976] 1 WLR 403 (valuation fixed by an agreed valuer held binding); *Trustees of National Deposit Friendly Society v Beatties of London Ltd* [1985] 2 EGLR 59, where GOULDING J held valid an option agreement for a new lease in favour of tenants who had carried on a business of selling model railways for seventy-five years "the rent payable . . . to be the greater of £33,000 per annum exclusive or such rent as may be agreed as from the architect's certificate of completion". In rejecting claims that it was void for uncertainty in regard to the date of the commencement of the term, the amount of rent and the covenants and conditions, he said at 61: "There has been such performance on the tenant's side as to justify the court in a much more liberal approach to the validity of the document than in the case of a purely executory option where nothing but perhaps a nominal consideration has been given on either side"; *R & A Millett (Shops) Ltd v Leon Allen International Fashions Ltd* [1989] 1 EGLR 138 (sub-lease rent to be 78/85ths of fair market rent as fixed in manner provided by head lease); *Harben Style Ltd v Rhodes Trust* [1995] 1 EGLR 118 (only landlord had power to apply to President of RICS for appointment of third party to determine rent; on his refusal to apply, tenant not entitled to have rent determined by court); cf *Royal Bank of Scotland v Jennings* [1997] 1 EGLR 101 (where both landlord and tenant had such power); *Addin v Secretary of State for the Environment* [1997] 1 EGLR 99; *Black Country Housing Association v Shand and Shand* [1998] NPC 92 (land to be transferred at a price which reflected its use being restricted as a garden held valid). [383] At 483.

it is in my opinion unrealistic to regard it as an essential term. If it breaks down there is no reason why the court should not substitute other machinery to carry out the main purpose of ascertaining the price in order that the agreement may be carried out.

(c) Date of payment

The covenant should state precisely the dates at which rent is payable, but if no mention is made of the matter, payment is due at the end of each period by reference to which the rent has been assessed. Thus in the case of a yearly rent nothing need be paid until the end of each year of the term.[384] If a day for payment is fixed, it becomes due on the first moment of that day and is held to be in arrear if it is not paid by midnight.[385]

(d) Rent review clauses

Many leases today contain a rent review clause,[386] the object of which is to enable the rent to be raised[387] at regular intervals to what is then the fair market value of the property let. The clause may provide for a revision to be made every seven years, and, not infrequently, every four or even three years. Institutional leases now commonly have a five-yearly review. In some leases of commercial premises granted for longer terms, there may be a provision to allow the landlord to reduce the interval between rent reviews after, for example, the first thirty-five years; this "review of reviews" operates in the same way as a rent review.[388] The clause usually lays down the administrative procedure or machinery by which the fair market rent is to be ascertained. Wide varieties of formulae are used.[389] In practice many clauses have not been well drawn,[390] and, in particular, there has been considerable litigation on the question of whether time is of the essence in construing clauses

---

384 Coomber v Howard (1845) 1 CB 440; Collett v Curling (1847) 10 QB 785.

385 Dibble v Bowater (1853) 2 E & B 564.

386 See generally Aldridge, Leasehold Law, paras. 4.045–4.060; Reynolds and Fetherstonhaugh, Handbook of Rent Review; Hill and Redman's Guide to Rent Review (2001); Emmet, paras. 26.031–26.051; Barnsley, Land Options, chap. 9; Bernstein and Reynolds, Essentials of Rent Review (1995); Rent Review Journal (which began in 1981), superseded in 1992 by Rent Review and Lease Renewal Journal. There is no presumption that a rent review clause (even one incorporating an open review) ought to be exercisable by both parties: it depends on the proper construction of the clause: Hemingway Realty Ltd v Clothworkers' Company [2005] 2 EGLR 36.

387 In May 2004 the Office of the Deputy Prime Minister issued a consultation paper, Commercial Property Leases, which asked whether upwards only rent reviews should be prohibited or deterred. The Reading University Report Monitoring the 2002 Code of Practice for Commercial Leases (March 2005), para. 8.4.3, found that neither tenants nor their agents were seeking alternatives to upwards only rent reviews, and the Government is no longer pursuing this.   388 Aldridge, Leasehold Law, para. 4.046.

389 For precedents, see Aldridge, Leasehold Law, paras. P.016–P.029; Conv Prec, Part 5H, including revised model forms by the Joint Working Party of the Law Society and the Royal Institution of Chartered Surveyors (2nd edn, 1986) as Precedent 5–H5.

390 United Scientific Holdings Ltd v Burnley BC [1976] Ch 128 at 146, per ROSKILL LJ. See London Regional Transport v Wimpey Group Services Ltd [1986] 2 EGLR 41 at 42 where HOFFMANN J said: "Rent formulae can often be expressed more simply and unambiguously in algebraic form and this case shows that a very modest degree of numeracy can save a great deal of money", and Freehold & Leasehold Shop Properties Ltd v Friends Provident Life Office (1984) 271 EG 451, where OLIVER LJ referred to the "somewhat Delphic pronouncement" of the definition of rent for the D. H. Lawrence House, Nottingham: "It may be doubted whether the distinguished author after whom the premises were named would have approved of the obscurity of language with which the parties have chosen to veil their intentions". See (1992) 12 LS 349 (G. D. Goldberg and P. F. Smith).

On professional negligence in connection with a rent review clause in a commercial lease, see County Personnel (Employment Agency) Ltd v Alan R Pulver & Co [1987] 1 WLR 916.

which specify time limits for the operation of the rent review procedure. In *United Scientific Holdings Ltd v Burnley Borough Council*[391] the House of Lords held that there was a presumption that time was not of the essence of the contract. Accordingly a landlord who fails to serve a notice on the tenant by a specified date may still serve a notice late and implement the rent review. Unreasonable delay, and even delay which causes hardship to the tenant, will not disentitle him from exercising his contractual right to claim a rent review which will be retrospective to the relevant date. The right continues to exist unless and until it is abrogated by mutual agreement, breach of contract or frustration, or by an estoppel by words or conduct.[392] The tenant, however, can serve a counter-notice making time of the essence.[393]

The presumption may be rebutted either expressly,[394] or impliedly by other provisions in the lease or by inference from surrounding circumstances; as where the tenant has an option

---

[391] [1978] AC 904; [1979] Conv 10 (P. F. Smith); *Chichester Cathedral (Dean and Chapter) v Lennards Ltd* (1977) 35 P & CR 309; cf *Commission for the New Towns v R Levy & Co Ltd* [1990] 2 EGLR 121; *Lancecrest Ltd v Asiwuju* [2005] 1 EGLR 40.

[392] *Amherst v James Walker Goldsmith & Silversmith Ltd* [1983] Ch 305, per OLIVER LJ at 316; per LAWTON LJ at 320; cf *Barclays Bank plc v Savile Estates Ltd* [2003] 2 EGLR 16.

[393] *Factory Holdings Group Ltd v Leboff International Ltd* [1987] 1 EGLR 135.

[394] On the construction and effect of an express provision,

(a) where time has been held to be of the essence, see *Drebbond Ltd v Horsham DC* (1978) 37 P & CR 237 (reference to arbitration within three months of original notice "but not otherwise"); *Weller v Akehurst* [1981] 3 All ER 411; *Pips (Leisure Productions) Ltd v Walton* (1980) 43 P & CR 415 ("would use their best endeavours"); *Lewis v Barnett* (1981) 264 EG 1079 (notice to review "shall be void and of no effect"); *Henry Smith's Charity Trustees v Awada Trading and Promotion Services Ltd* (1983) 47 P & CR 607 ("shall be deemed to be a market rent"); *Greenhaven Securities Ltd v Compton* (1985) 275 EG 628 (rent to be "a sum equal to the rent payable immediately before the review date"); *Mammoth Greeting Cards Ltd v Agra Ltd* [1990] 2 EGLR 124 (rent "shall be conclusively fixed"; "This evinces the concept of finality", per MUMMERY J at 125); *Norwich Union Life Insurance Society v Sketchley plc* [1986] 2 EGLR 126 ("but not otherwise"); *Chelsea Building Society v R & A Millett (Shops) Ltd* (1994) 67 P & CR 319 ("it shall be a condition precedent": "clearest possible intention"); *Central Estates Ltd v Secretary of State for the Environment* [1997] 1 EGLR 239 (mutuality arising from interrelationship between break clause and relevant review period); *Banks v Kokkinos* [1999] 3 EGLR 133;

(b) where time has been held not to be of the essence, see *Amherst v James Walker* (1980) 254 EG 123 (two time-limit steps out of three stated to be "of the essence"; held third step to be not of the essence); *Laing Investment Co Ltd v GA Dunn & Co* (1981) 262 EG 879; *Touche Ross & Co v Secretary of State for the Environment* (1982) 46 P & CR 187 (reference to surveyor "as soon as practicable but in any event not later than three months"); *Thorn EMI Pension Ltd Trust v Quinton Hazell plc* (1983) 269 EG 414; *Starmark Enterprises Ltd v CPL Distribution Ltd* [2002] Ch 306 (if lessees fail to serve counter-notice within period, "they shall be deemed to have agreed to pay increased rent specified in the rent notice"); Emmet, para. 26.050a; *Taylor Woodrow Property Co Ltd v Lonrho Textiles Ltd* (1985) 52 P & CR 28; *Phipps-Faire Ltd v Malbern Construction Ltd* [1987] 1 EGLR 129; cf *Banks v Kokkinos*, supra; *Power Securities (Manchester) Ltd v Prudential Assurance Co Ltd* [1987] 1 EGLR 121 (rent to be agreed between landlord and tenant within six months after end of second term; *Panavia Air Cargo Ltd v Southend-on-Sea BC* (1988) 56 P & CR 365 (if review not completed until twelve months of relevant period, rent payable during the period would be current rent increased by 25%); *Kings (Estate Agents) Ltd v Anderson* [1992] 1 EGLR 121 (determination of rent (time to be of the essence) "three months prior to commencement of second or third rent period", failure to mention fourth period); *North Hertfordshire DC v Hitchin Industrial Estate Ltd* [1992] 2 EGLR 121 (service of landlord's notice "shall be a condition precedent"); *Richurst Ltd v Pimenta* [1993] 1 WLR 159 (acknowledgment of receipt of late service of notice held not to be agreement to extend time); [1993] Conv 382 (M. Haley); *Woolwich Property Services Ltd v Capital Land Holdings Ltd* (1992) 66 P & CR 378 (effective counter-notice); *Bickenhall Engineering Co Ltd v Grandmet Restaurants Ltd* [1995] 1 EGLR 110 (rent specified by landlord should be market rent payable "if no such counter-notice served" held not certain enough to rebut presumption); *Fordgate (Bingley) Ltd v National Westminster Bank plc* [1995] EGCS 97; *Fox & Widley v Guram* [1998] 1 EGLR 91 (extension of time limit under Arbitration Act 1996, s. 12: purpose of Act to restrict power of court to extend time).

to determine the lease which is linked to the rent review.[395] Where time is of the essence, the court will not intervene to impose a rent review, if notice is served out of time.[396]

The doctrine of time not being of the essence is one of substance and not of form. The fact that the time limit is to be found partly in a definition and partly in a substantive clause of the lease makes no difference.[397]

A rent review clause usually contains a formula for the assessment of the revised rent. In this context,[398] where rent has been paid and accepted up to the review date, the courts have been astute not to hold a formula void for uncertainty; they are more concerned with the amount of rent payable for the remainder of the term, and with the construction of the formula in such a way as to render the clause effective. Thus in *Beer v Bowden*[399] the court held that "such rent as shall thereupon be agreed" should be construed to mean "such fair rent as shall thereupon be agreed", and this formed the basis for the valuation of the revised rent.[400]

(e) Recovery of rent

The landlord's remedies for the recovery of rent will be considered later.[401]

(2) Covenant by Landlord or Tenant to Repair[402]

Various expressions are used to describe the extent of the obligation imposed by a covenant to repair the premises. The following are typical examples:

good tenantable repair;

good and tenantable order and repair;

---

[395] *United Scientific Holdings Ltd v Burnley BC* [1978] AC 904 at 929, per Lord DIPLOCK; *Al Saloom v Shirley James Travel Service Ltd* (1981) 42 P & CR 181; *Rahman v Kenshire* (1980) 259 EG 1074; *Coventry City Council v J Hepworth & Son Ltd* (1982) 265 EG 608; *Legal and General Assurance (Pension Management) Ltd v Cheshire County Council* (1983) 269 EG 40; *William Hill (Southern) Ltd v Govier & Govier* (1983) 269 EG 1168; *Edwin Woodhouse Trustee Co Ltd v Sheffield Brick Co plc* (1983) 270 EG 548; *McLeod Russel (Property Holding) Ltd v Emerson* (1985) 51 P & CR 176; *Metrolands Investments Ltd v J H Dewhurst Ltd* [1986] 3 All ER 659; *Stephenson & Son v Orca Properties Ltd* [1989] 2 EGLR 129.   [396] *Weller v Akehurst* [1981] 3 All ER 411.

[397] *Pembroke St Georges Ltd v Cromwell Developments Ltd* [1991] 2 EGLR 129.

[398] For the general rules relating to certainty of rent, see pp. 241 seq, ante.

[399] [1981] 1 WLR 522, M & B p. 467; *Corson v Rhuddlan BC* [1990] 1 EGLR 255 at 257.

[400] *Thomas Bates & Son Ltd v Wyndham's (Lingerie) Ltd* [1981] 1 WLR 505, M & B p. 468; *Beer v Bowden*, supra; *Lear v Blizzard* [1983] 3 All ER 662, M & B p. 468, n. 6; *British Railways Board v Mobil Oil Co Ltd* (1994) 68 P & CR 446 (rise in rents of comparable properties).

For rent reviews where improvements have been made to the premises, see *Ponsford v HMS Aerosols Ltd* [1979] AC 63, approving *Cuff v J & F Stone Property Co Ltd* [1979] AC 87; *Hambros Bank Executors and Trustee Co Ltd v Superdrug Stores Ltd* [1985] 1 EGLR 99; *Lear v Blizzard*, supra; *Pleasurama Properties Ltd v Leisure Investments (West End) Ltd* [1986] 1 EGLR 145 (conversion of shop premises into a dolphinarium); *Brett v Brett Essex Golf Club Ltd* (1986) 52 P & CR 330; *Panther Shop Investments Ltd v Keith Pople Ltd* [1987] 1 EGLR 131; *Ravenseft Properties Ltd v Park* [1988] 2 EGLR 164; *Ipswich Town Football Club Co Ltd v Ipswich BC* [1988] 2 EGLR 146; *Laura Investment Co Ltd v Havering LBC* [1992] 1 EGLR 155 (where HOFFMANN J reviews the authorities); ibid. *(No. 2)* [1993] 08 EG 120; *Historic House Hotels Ltd v Cadogan* [1995] 1 EGLR 117 (improvements to be disregarded in spite of provision that premises so altered were to be comprised in lease at outset); *Ocean Accident & Guarantee Corpn v Next plc* [1996] 2 EGLR 84 (tenant's fixtures not be taken into account, even if affixed by tenant under obligation in lease, unless expressly provided); cf *Daejan Properties Ltd v Mahoney* [1995] 2 EGLR 75; *Braid v Walsall MBC* (1999) 78 P & CR 94.   [401] Pp. 265 et seq, post.

[402] See generally West and Smith's *Law of Dilapidations*; Williams, *Handbook of Dilapidations*; Dowding and Reynolds, *Dilapidations: the Modern Law and Practice*. Whether the matter has been dealt with by covenant or not, the lessor is under a statutory obligation to repair a dwelling-house that has been let for less than seven years; p. 234, ante.

well and substantially repair;

perfect repair.

By the use of appropriate language, the parties can, of course, settle the standard of repair as high or as low as they choose, but it is generally admitted that such epithets as "good", "perfect" or "substantial" do not increase the burden connoted by the simple word "repair".[403] By way of caution, it should be noticed that, if the premises are in a state of disrepair at the beginning of the lease, a covenant by the tenant to "keep" them in repair requires him to put them into the required state at his own expense.[404] A state of disrepair means a deterioration in the condition of the premises from a former better condition.[405]

In *Brew Brothers Ltd v Snax (Ross) Ltd*,[406] SACHS LJ set out the approach to be adopted in construing a covenant to repair:

It seems to me that the correct approach is to look at the particular building, to look at the state which it is in at the date of the lease, to look at the precise terms of the lease, and then come to a conclusion as to whether, on a fair interpretation of those terms in relation to that state, the requisite work can fairly be termed repair. However large the covenant it must not be looked at in vacuo.[407]

(a) Extent of obligation

The extent of the obligation assumed by a covenantor who has agreed to repair the premises is that, after making due allowance for the locality, character and age of the premises at the time of the lease, he must keep them in the condition in which they would be kept by a reasonably minded owner.[408]

(1) LOCALITY AND CHARACTER OF PREMISES

The locality and character of the premises are material. The essential fact to notice, however, is that it is the character of the premises and of the locality at the beginning, not at the end, of the lease that is material in this context. Thus in one case:[409]

a new house, situated in what was then a fashionable part of London was let in 1825 to a good class of tenant on a 95-year lease. In course of time the character of the neighbourhood deteriorated to such

---

403 *Anstruther-Gough-Calthorpe v McOscar* [1924] 1 KB 716 at 722–3; but see at 731–2. A covenant to "maintain . . . in good condition" adds a great deal to "repair", and may extend to the general state of the premises and not just the structure: *Welsh v Greenwich LBC* [2000] 3 EGLR 41 (severe condensation and mould growth).

404 *Payne v Haine* (1847) 16 M & W 541; *Proudfoot v Hart* (1890) 25 QBD 42; *Crédit Suisse v Beegas Nominees Ltd* [1994] 4 All ER 803; [1995] 145 NLJ 718 (H. W. Wilkinson).

405 *Post Office v Aquarius Properties Ltd* [1987] 1 All ER 1055, per RALPH GIBSON LJ; *Plough Investments Ltd v Eclipse Radio and Television Services Ltd* [1989] 1 EGLR 244.

406 [1970] 1 QB 612 at 640; *Smedley v Chumley and Hawke Ltd* (1981) 44 P & CR 50 at 54; *McDougall v Easington DC* [1989] 1 EGLR 93.

407 "I have found most assistance in the judgment of SACHS LJ . . . It contains a timely warning against attempting to impose the crudities of judicial exegesis upon the subtle and often intuitive discriminations of ordinary speech": *Post Office v Aquarius Properties Ltd* [1985] 2 EGLR 105 at 107, per HOFFMANN J.

408 *Proudfoot v Hart* (1890) 25 QBD 42; *Lurcott v Wakely and Wheeler* [1911] 1 KB 905; *Anstruther-Gough-Calthorpe v McOscar* [1924] 1 KB 716; *Lloyds Bank Ltd v Lake* [1961] 1 WLR 884; *Firstcross Ltd v Teasdale* (1982) 47 P & CR 228; *Crédit Suisse v Beegas Nominees Ltd*, supra. See also *British Glass Manufacturers' Corporation v University of Sheffield* [2004] 1 EGLR 40 (demolition of laboratory and other buildings not a breach of repairing obligation in lease granted in 1957 for a term of 1000 years); *Riverside Property Investments Ltd v Blackhawk Automotive* [2005] 1 EGLR 114; *Fitzroy House Epworth Street (No 1) Ltd v Financial Times Ltd* [2006] 02 EG 112 (summarising the general principles) affd. on other grounds [2006] 14 EGCS 175(CS).

409 *Anstruther-Gough-Calthorpe v McOscar*, supra; *Ladbroke Hotels Ltd v Sandhu* (1995) 72 P & CR 498 (repairs not limited to those necessary to maintain building for its commercial life); (1997) 147 NLJ 420 (H. W. Wilkinson).

an extent that the only persons willing to occupy the house expected nothing more than that the rain should be kept out.

The covenantor, therefore, argued that the standard of repair required of him was to be measured by the needs and expectations of prospective tenants in 1920. The argument failed. The obligation of a covenantor is neither increased nor diminished in extent by a change in the character of the neighbourhood.

(2) AGE OF PREMISES

The age of a house is also material, though only in the sense that the covenantor's obligation is not to bring it up to date, but to keep it in a reasonably good condition for a building of that age. He cannot escape liability by the allegation that to keep so old a building in the covenanted condition requires renewal, not mere repairs. Repair always involves renewal. The covenant must be fulfilled, even though this necessitates the replacement of part after part until the whole is renewed.[410] The correct antithesis is between renewal and reconstruction. The former is required, the latter not. Whether the work necessary for the maintenance of a building is renewal or reconstruction is a question of degree, the test being whether the replacement affects a subordinate part or substantially the whole of the building.[411] Thus the tenant of an old house is not bound to replace defective foundations by foundations of an entirely different character;[412] but he must demolish and replace a dangerous wall if it is but a subsidiary part of the whole building.[413]

An inherent defect of design in the premises may be within the ambit of a covenant to repair, but the covenantor is not liable to remedy a design fault, unless that fault has caused or contributed to a proved state of disrepair.[414] As FOSTER J said:[415] "the true test is that it is always a question of degree whether that which the tenant is being asked to do can properly

---

[410] *Lurcott v Wakely and Wheeler* [1911] 1 KB 905 at 916–17, per FLETCHER-MOULTON LJ.

[411] Ibid.; *Sotheby v Grundy* [1947] 2 All ER 761; *Minja Properties Ltd v Cussins Property Group plc* [1998] 2 EGLR 52 (replacement of window frames held to be repair); *Creska Ltd v Hammersmith and Fulham LBC* [1998] 3 EGLR 35.

[412] *Lister v Lane and Nesham* [1893] 2 QB 212; *Sotheby v Grundy*, supra; *Pembery v Lamdin* [1940] 2 All ER 434 (landlord's covenant); *Brew Bros Ltd v Snax (Ross) Ltd* [1970] 1 QB 612 (tenant's covenant).

[413] *Lurcott v Wakely and Wheeler*, supra; cf *Smedley v Chumley and Hawke Ltd* (1981) 44 P & CR 50 (under-pinning of foundations of *recently* constructed restaurant in motel complex held to be work of repair). Cf *Halliard Property Co Ltd v Nicholas Clarke Investments Ltd* (1983) 269 EG 1257 (no duty to rebuild jerry-built structure); *Post Office v Aquarius Properties Ltd* [1985] 2 EGLR 105 (remedial scheme for failure of "kicker joint" more than repair); affd. on other grounds [1987] 1 All ER 1055; *Elmcroft Developments Ltd v Tankersley-Sawyer* (1984) 270 EG 140 (defective damp course below ground level to be repaired by silicone injection); cf *Yanover v Romford Finance & Development Co Ltd* (1983) unreported but noted at (1984) 272 EG 250 (D. W. Williams); *Elite Investments Ltd v T I Bainbridge Silencers Ltd* [1986] 2 EGLR 43 (replacement of roof held to be repair) where the authorities are reviewed; [1987] Conv 140 (P. F. Smith); *New England Properties v Portsmouth News Shops* [1993] 1 EGLR 84.

[414] *Ravenseft Properties Ltd v Davstone (Holdings) Ltd* [1980] QB 12; [1979] Conv 429 (P. F. Smith); *Quick v Taff Ely BC* [1986] QB 809; *Post Office v Aquarius Properties Ltd* [1985] 2 EGLR 105; [1987] Conv 224 (P. F. Smith); *Stent v Monmouth DC* [1987] 1 EGLR 59; *Murray v Birmingham City Council* [1987] 2 EGLR 53; *Staves & Staves v Leeds City Council* [1992] 2 EGLR 36 (condensation affecting plasterwork); *Crédit Suisse v Beegas Nominees Ltd* [1994] 4 All ER 803.

[415] *Ravenseft Properties Ltd v Davstone (Holdings) Ltd*, supra, at 21. For more detailed formulations of the test, see *McDougall v Easington DC* [1989] 1 EGLR 93 at 95–6, per MUSTILL LJ; [1990] Conv 735 (P. F. Smith); *Holding and Management Ltd v Property Holding and Investment Trust plc* [1990] 1 EGLR 65 at 68, per NICHOLLS LJ.

be described as repair, or whether on the contrary it would involve giving back to the land-lord a wholly different thing from that which he demised".

(b) Exception of fair wear and tear

It is usual to qualify the covenant to repair by a clause to the effect that the covenantor shall not be liable for "fair wear and tear", or, what signifies the same thing, for "reasonable wear and tear". The effect of these words is to exempt the covenantor from liability for damage that is due to the ordinary operation of natural causes, always presuming that he has used the premises in a reasonable manner.[416] As Tindal CJ put it in a case where a tenant had invoked such a clause:

What the natural operation of time flowing on effects, and all that the elements bring about in dimin-ishing value, constitute a loss which, so far as it results from time and nature, falls upon the landlord.[417]

But where the defect, though initially due to natural causes, will obviously cause further and lasting damage unless rectified, the clause will not continue to avail a covenantor who stands idly by and allows the ravages of time and nature to take their course. Talbot J made this clear in a passage later adopted by the House of Lords:

The tenant is bound to do such repairs as may be required to prevent the consequences flowing originally from wear and tear from producing others which wear and tear would not directly produce. For example, if a tile falls off the roof, the tenant is not liable for the immediate consequences; but, if he does nothing and in the result more and more water gets in, the roof and walls decay and ultimately the top floor, or the whole house, becomes uninhabitable, he cannot say that it is due to reasonable wear and tear. . . . On the other hand, take the gradual wearing away of a stone floor or staircase by ordinary use. This may in time produce a considerable wear and tear, and the tenant is not liable in respect of it.[418]

(c) Covenant not to make improvements without consent

A covenant against the making of improvements without consent is by statute[419] subject to a proviso that consent shall not unreasonably be withheld, though the landlord is entitled to demand the payment of a reasonable sum for any damage or loss of value that may be caused to the premises or to neighbouring premises belonging to him. The word "improvements" refers to improvements from the point of view of the tenant, and the statute applies even though what he proposes to do, for example, the demolition of part of the main structure of a building, will temporarily diminish the value of the premises.[420] In such a case no injury is,

---

[416] *Haskell v Marlow* [1928] 2 KB 45 at 59.

[417] *Gutteridge v Munyard* (1834) 1 Mood & R 334 at 336. The words quoted do not appear in the report at 7 C & P 129.

[418] *Haskell v Marlow*, supra, at 59. This decision was overruled by the Court of Appeal in *Taylor v Webb* [1937] 2 KB 283, but the principles laid down in this second case, after being stigmatised as inconsistent with earlier authorities by a later Court of Appeal in *Brown v Davies* [1958] 1 QB 117 were finally overruled by the House of Lords in *Regis Property Co Ltd v Dudley* [1959] AC 370, and the authority of *Haskell v Marlow* restored.

[419] LTA 1927, s. 19(2). The tenant may apply to the High Court or the county court for a declaration that the landlord has unreasonably withheld his consent: LTA 1954, s. 53(1)(b) as amended by County Courts Act 1984, s. 148(1), Sch. 2, para. 23. For the application of s. 19(2) see *Iqbal v Thakrar* [2004] 3 EGLR 21 at [26], per Peter Gibson LJ (adopting with variations the principles set out by Balcombe LJ in relation to s. 19(1) in *International Drilling Fluids Ltd v Louisville Investments (Uxbridge) Ltd* [1986] Ch 513 at 519–20, p. 261, post); *Sergeant v Macepark (Whittlebury) Ltd* [2004] 4 All ER 662.

[420] *Lambert v Woolworth & Co Ltd* [1938] Ch 883.

in theory, suffered by the landlord, since he is permitted by the statute to demand an undertaking from the tenant that the premises will be reinstated.[421]

(d) Landlord's right of entry

If the landlord is to perform his covenant to repair, he must have a right of entry to the premises. This may be expressly authorised by the terms of the lease or by statute; and if the landlord is liable to repair the premises he has an implied right to enter for a reasonable time to carry out the work.[422] Otherwise he has no right to enter during the currency of the lease,[423] because, as we have seen, the tenant has the right to exclusive possession.[424]

(e) Remedies for breach of covenant to repair

(1) REMEDIES OF LANDLORD

(i) Specific performance

Apart from forfeiture,[425] the usual remedy for breach of a covenant to repair is damages. The landlord may himself do the work, if the lease authorises him to enter to do repairs.[426] Until recently, it had been generally accepted that a landlord could not obtain specific performance to enforce his tenant's covenant. In *Rainbow Estates Ltd v Tokenhold Ltd*, however, it was held that the court has power to grant such a decree in appropriate circumstances. Lawrence Collins QC said:[427]

Subject to the overriding need to avoid injustice or oppression, the remedy should be available when damages are not an adequate remedy or, in the more modern formulation, when specific performance is the appropriate remedy. This will be particularly important if there is substantial difficulty in the way of the landlord effecting repairs: the landlord may not have a right of access to the property to effect necessary repairs, since (in the absence of contrary agreement) a landlord has no right to enter the premises, and the condition of the premises may be deteriorating . . .

It follows that not only is there a need for great caution in granting the remedy against a tenant, but also that it will be a rare case in which the remedy of specific performance will be the appropriate one: in the case of commercial leases, the landlord will normally have the right to forfeit or to enter and do the repairs at the expense of the tenant; in residential leases, the landlord will normally have the right to forfeit in appropriate cases.

(ii) Damages

The measure of damages *at common law* for breach of a contract to repair varies according as the breach occurs during the tenancy or at the end of the tenancy. In the first case the measure is the amount by which the value of the reversion has diminished; but in the second

---

[421] LTA 1927, s. 19(2). In 1989 the Law Commission published a Report: Compensation for Tenants' Improvements (No. 178), which recommended that (a) the statutory scheme in Part I of the Landlord and Tenant Act 1927 for compensating tenants of business properties for improvements which they have made should be abolished; and (b) there should not be a statutory compensation scheme for residential tenants who improve their premises. The Government rejected the Report.

[422] *Saner v Bilton* (1878) 7 Ch D 815; *Mint v Good* [1951] 1 KB 517.

[423] *Stocker v Planet Building Society* (1879) 27 WR 877.   [424] P. 197, ante.   [425] P. 280, post.

[426] *Regional Properties Ltd v City of London Real Property Co Ltd* (1979) 257 EG 64; *Stocker v Planet Building Society* (1879) 27 WR 877, per JAMES LJ.

[427] [1999] Ch 64 at 73–4; (1998) 148 NLJ 1475 (H. W. Wilkinson); [1995] Conv 495 (M. Pawlowski and J. Brown). In particular it should not be used to avoid the safeguards for tenants in the Leasehold Property (Repairs) Act 1938, p. 286, post.

case, where the premises are delivered up in disrepair, it is the amount that it will cost to carry out the repairs required by the covenant.[428] If, for instance, a tenant converts into flats a house which he has covenanted to keep suitable for single occupation, the first rule applies and the measure of damages is not necessarily the full cost of reinstatement, but the sum that represents the loss which the landlord has sustained.[429] It was found that the second rule might inflict unnecessary hardship upon an outgoing tenant, since it enabled a landlord to recover substantial damages even though the performance of the covenant would have been entirely useless, as, for instance, where the premises were to be demolished, or where the want of repair would not diminish by one penny the rent obtainable on a re-letting. It is, therefore, provided by the Landlord and Tenant Act 1927[430] that whether the breach is of a covenant to repair during the currency of a lease or to leave premises in repair at the termination of a lease: "the damages shall in no case exceed the amount (if any) by which the value of the reversion (whether immediate or not) in the premises is diminished, owing to the breach of the covenant or agreement". The diminution in the value of the reversion is the amount that it will cost within the terms of the covenant to make the house reasonably fit for the class of tenant likely to take it. The fact that the landlord has been able to re-let it, though spending less than that amount on repairs, is an irrelevant consideration.[431] In other words the primary test of the measure of damages still seems to be the cost of doing the covenanted repairs. There are many cases where the sale of the property unrepaired will fetch as high a price as its sale in a state of good repair, so that in one sense the value of the reversion as a whole is undiminished, as, for example, where the tenancy relates only to a few rooms in a large building and they cannot be made fit for occupation unless the covenanted repairs are done. In such a case it is now recognised that the cost of the necessary repairs prima facie represents the diminution in value of the reversion.[432] However, if the landlord has sold the premises for a price which shows that the tenant's failure to repair has not damaged the value of his reversion he can recover nothing.[433]

In one particular case the landlord is denied any right to damages. The Act provides that no damages shall be recoverable for breach of the covenant: "if it is shown that the premises, in whatever state of repair they might be, would at or shortly after the termination of the tenancy have been or be pulled down, or such structural alterations made therein as would render valueless the repairs covered by the covenant or agreement".[434]

---

[428]　*Joyner v Weeks* [1891] 2 QB 31; *Crewe Services & Investment Corporation v Silk* [1998] 2 EGLR 1.

[429]　*Duke of Westminster v Swinton* [1948] 1 KB 524. See also *James v Hutton and J Cook & Sons Ltd* [1950] 1 KB 9.

[430]　S. 18(1); *Haviland v Long* [1952] 2 QB 80; *Mather v Barclays Bank plc* [1987] 2 EGLR 254; (1988) 104 LQR 372 (D. N. Clarke).

[431]　*Jaquin v Holland* [1960] 1 WLR 258; *Hanson v Newman* [1934] Ch 298. Cf *Family Management v Gray* (1979) 253 EG 369; [1980] Conv 244; *Crown Estate Comrs v Town Investments Ltd* [1992] 1 EGLR 61; *Mason v Totalfinaelf UK Ltd* [2003] 3 EGLR 91 (terminal dilapidations award cannot exceed the amount by which the disrepair diminishes the value of the premises).

[432]　*Jones v Herxheimer* [1950] 2 KB 106; *Smiley v Townshend* [1950] 2 KB 311 at 322–3; *Drummond v S & U Stores Ltd* (1980) 258 EG 1293 (where the landlord was awarded the bulk of the cost of repairs, including Value Added Tax, and a sum representing three months' loss of rent); *Culworth Estates Ltd v Society of Licensed Victuallers* [1991] 2 EGLR 54 (damage to reversion greater than cost of carrying out necessary repairs); *Shortlands Investments Ltd v Cargill plc* [1995] 1 EGLR 51 (negative value of landlord's reversion; quantum of damages was that by which the want of repair further diminished that value).

[433]　*Simmons v Dresden* (2004) 97 Con LR 81. The burden of proof that the value of the reversion has been diminished, and by how much, is on the landlord: ibid., at [88]; *Craven (Builders) Ltd v Secretary of State for Health* [2000] 1 EGLR 128 at 131; *Crown Estate Commissioners v Town Investments Ltd* [1992] 1 EGLR 61 at 64–5.

[434]　LTA 1927, s. 18(1).

Thus the Act requires the tenant to prove that the landlord had decided to demolish the premises and that this decision still held at the end of the lease. If this be shown, it is immaterial that the decision is later changed and the premises not demolished.[435] Damages are irrecoverable.[436] The onus, therefore, that lies upon the tenant is to show that the demolition or structural alteration of the premises was firmly intended, not merely contemplated, by the landlord and also that the achievement of the plan was reasonably possible.[437] Damages will, however, be recoverable if the premises are demolished as a result of the tenant's breach of his covenant to repair.

(2) REMEDIES OF TENANT

The landlord is not liable on his covenant to repair until he has notice of the need to repair and has also a reasonable period in which to remedy the defect.[438] The notice is usually given to him by the tenant, but notice from any source is probably sufficient.[439]

The remedies of the tenant are:

(i) Specific performance

Where it is the landlord who breaks the covenant, damages may be an inadequate remedy for the tenant; and, in the case of dwellings, the Landlord and Tenant Act 1985 gives the court discretion to order specific performance of the covenant whether or not the breach relates to part of the premises let to the tenant.[440] Further, where a landlord has failed to carry out repairs within his express or implied covenant, the tenant, after giving due notice, may carry out the repairs himself and deduct the proper costs of repair from future payments of rent.[441] The right of set-off may be excluded by clear words in the lease.[442]

---

[435] *Keats v Graham* [1960] 1 WLR 30.   [436] *Salisbury v Gilmore* [1942] 2 KB 38.

[437] *Cunliffe v Goodman* [1950] 2 KB 237.

[438] *Torrens v Walker* [1906] 2 Ch 166; *McCarrick v Liverpool Corpn* [1947] AC 219; *O'Brien v Robinson* [1973] AC 912 (extending the rule to implied covenant under LTA 1985, s. 11, p. 234 ante). See also *Sheldon v West Bromwich Corpn* (1973) 25 P & CR 360 (landlord liable for damage of which he ought to have recognised warning signs on inspection); *Dinefwr BC v Jones* [1987] 2 EGLR 58 ("actual notice from some responsible source"). For the landlord's liability to all persons likely to be affected by his failure to repair under Defective Premises Act 1972, s. 4, see p. 238, ante. For the enforceability by the tenant of the landlord's covenant to repair where the covenant is expressly subject to payment of maintenance charges by the tenant, see *Bluestorm Ltd v Portvale Holdings Ltd* [2004] 2 EGLR 38; cf *Yorkbrook Investments Ltd v Batten* [1985] 2 EGLR 100.

[439] *British Telecommunications plc v Sun Life Assurance Society plc* [1996] Ch 69; (1995) 145 NLJ 1793 (H. W. Wilkinson).

[440] Ss. 17, 32(1). *Jeune v Queens Cross Properties Ltd* [1974] Ch 97 (specific performance granted before the Act); *Francis v Cowcliffe Ltd* (1976) 33 P & CR 368; *Parker v Camden LBC* [1986] Ch 162; *Posner v Scott-Lewis* [1987] Ch 25 (covenant to employ resident porter). See (1975) 119 SJ 362, (1976) 120 SJ 428 (H. E. Markson).

[441] *Lee-Parker v Izzet* [1971] 1 WLR 1688; (1976) 40 Conv (NS) 190 (P. M. Rank). See *Asco Developments Ltd v Gordon* (1978) 248 EG 683 at 683, where MEGARRY V-C said that this right of deduction was equally applicable to arrears of rent. See also *British Anzani (Felixstowe) Ltd v International Marine Management (UK) Ltd* [1980] QB 137; *Melville v Grapelodge Developments Ltd* (1978) 39 P & CR 179; (1980) 131 NLJ 330 (P. F. Smith); [1981] Conv 199 (A. Waite); *Muscat v Smith* [2003] 1 WLR 2853 (tenant entitled to set off cross-claim for unliquidated damages relating to former landlord's breaches of repairing covenant: see general discussion by SEDLEY LJ of right of set-off against landlords' claims for rent at [9] et seq); cf *Edlington Properties Ltd v J H Fenner & Co Ltd* [2006] 1 All ER 98, affd. [2006] 13 EG 141 (CS) (claim for damages for defective construction against original landlord cannot be set off against rent due for periods following assignment by that landlord). On set-off generally, see Derham, *Law of Set-off*.

[442] *Connaught Restaurants Ltd v Indoor Leisure Ltd* [1994] 1 WLR 501 (payment of rent "without any deduction" ambiguous and insufficient to exclude right of set-off). For the application of the Unfair Contract Terms Act 1977 and the Unfair Terms in Consumer Contracts Regulations 1999 to covenants in leases, see p. 195, n. 28, ante.

(ii) Damages

Damages are awarded on the same principle as for other breaches of contract: to place the tenant in the position he would have been in if the landlord's obligation to repair had been performed.[443] He may recover the cost of repairs and redecoration, the cost of reasonable alternative accommodation and of storage of furniture, and general damages for inconvenience and discomfort. In *Marshall v Rubypoint Ltd*[444] the Court of Appeal held that the tenant was entitled to recover damages for personal injury, consequential expenses and items stolen in three burglaries at his flat, due to the landlord's failure to repair the front door to the block of flats, in one of which the tenant was living. The burglars had forced the internal front door of the flat, which was the tenant's responsibility. In holding that the loss was not too remote, and that the burglars did not break the chain of causation, Buckley J said: "The main purpose of a front door, apart from affording access and egress, is to keep out uninvited visitors and that includes burglars."

If the premises, to the knowledge of the landlord, had been purchased for re-sale or subletting or if the tenant was forced to sell because of the breach of covenant, then he can recover the loss in market value or of rental value as the case may be.[445]

(iii) Appointment of a receiver [446]

Where the landlord is in breach of his covenant to repair and neglects the property, the court may appoint a receiver to collect the rent and to carry out repairs "if it is just and convenient to do so".

(iv) Appointment of a manager: leasehold flats

The Landlord and Tenant Act 1987[447] makes special provision for tenants of residential[448] premises consisting of the whole or part of a building[449] which contains two or more flats.[450] Part II of the Act applies where the leasehold valuation tribunal is satisfied that the

---

[443] *Wallace v Manchester City Council* [1998] 3 EGLR 38; *English Churches Housing Group v Shine* [2005] L & TR 7 (*Wallace* is "plainly the leading case on the subject": per WALL LJ at [94]).   [444] [1997] 1 EGLR 69.

[445] *Calabar Properties Ltd v Stitcher* [1984] 1 WLR 287; *McGreal v Wake* (1984) 269 EG 1254; *Bradley v Chorley BC* [1985] 2 EGLR 49; (1984) 134 NLJ 379 (H. W. Wilkinson); *Chiodi's Personal Representatives v De Marney* [1988] 2 EGLR 64; *Wallace v Manchester City Council* [1998] 3 EGLR 38 (calculation of damages when tenant remained in occupation after breach by landlord).

See Secure Tenancies (Right to Repair Scheme) Regulations 1985 (SI 1985 No. 1493), which entitles a secure tenant (p. 358, post) to carry out his landlord's repairs ("other than a repair to the structure or exterior of a flat"), the cost of which may then be recouped from the landlord; cf *Lee-Parker v Izzet* [1971] 1 WLR 1688; (1986) 83 LSG 1376 (P. M. Rank).

[446] SCA 1981, s. 37(1); *Hart v Emelkirk Ltd* [1983] 1 WLR 1289; *Daiches v Bluelake Investments Ltd* [1985] 2 EGLR 67; cf *Parker v Camden LBC* [1986] Ch 162; *Evans v Clayhope Properties Ltd* [1988] 1 WLR 358; [1988] Conv 363 (C. P. Rodgers); *Blawdziewicz v Diadon Establishment* [1988] 2 EGLR 52 (balance of convenience).

[447] As amended by HA 1988, Sch. 13 and HA 1996, s. 86. The Act implements the main recommendations of the Nugee Committee of Inquiry on the Management of Privately Owned Blocks of Flats (1985). This valuable report contains statistics about private sector flats in England and Wales in chap. 3, and discusses the problems of owning a flat in chap. 6. See (1988) 51 MLR 97 (M. E. Percival).

[448] Tenancies under LTA 1954, Part II are excluded: ss. 21(7), 26(1).

[449] A building means either a single building or one or more buildings where the occupants of qualifying flats in each of those buildings shares the use of the same appurtenant premises: *Long Acre Securities Ltd v Karet* [2005] Ch 61.   [450] Ss. 21(2), 25(1).

landlord[451] is in breach of any obligations under the tenancy that relate to the management of the premises, including their repair, maintenance and insurance.[452] The tribunal must also be satisfied that it is just and convenient to make the order in all the circumstances of the case. The tribunal then has power under Part II to appoint a manager to carry out:[453]

(a) such functions in connection with the management of the premises, or

(b) such functions of a receiver,

or both, as the tribunal thinks fit.

Part III of the Act makes provision for a person to be nominated by the tenants to acquire their landlord's interest in the premises without his consent.[454] In order to qualify under this Part, the tenants must be tenants of residential premises under a *long* lease[455] (i.e. a lease granted for a term exceeding twenty-one years[456]). On the application by not less than two-thirds[457] of the qualified tenants, the court may make an acquisition order[458] if the landlord is in breach, and is likely to continue to be in breach, of his obligations, or if the appointment of a manager under Part II has been in force for at least two years, and, in either case, the court considers it appropriate to make the order in the circumstances. Under the order the nominated person is entitled to acquire the landlord's interest on such terms as may be determined by agreement between the parties, or, in default of agreement, by a rent assessment committee.[459]

(3) APPORTIONMENT OF LIABILITY

There are circumstances in which liability may be apportioned between landlord and tenant on the basis of causation; for example, where a tenant was in breach of his covenant to

---

[451] Or any other person (other than the landlord) by whom obligations relating to the management of the premises or any part of them are owed to the tenant under his tenancy: LTA 1987, ss. 22(1)(ii), 24(2za), as amended by CLRA 2002, s. 160. This allows tenants to apply for a new manager where an existing manager is failing properly to manage the premises. "Landlord" also includes an RTM ("right to manage") company appointed under CLRA 2002: s. 102, Sch. 7, para. 8.

[452] On service charges, see LTA 1987, s. 24(2A); HA 1996, ss. 85–8; on the determination of reasonableness of a service charge, see LTA 1985, s. 19, as amended by HA 1996, s. 83, and CLRA 2002, s. 180, Sch. 14; and on consultation with the tenant see LTA 1985, s. 20 as substituted by CLRA 2002, s. 151; Service Charges (Consultation Requirements) (England) Regulations 2003, SI 2003 No. 1987, amended by SI 2004 Nos. 2665 and 2939; Freedman, Shapiro and Slater, *Service Charges Law and* Practice (3rd edn, 2002); Sherriff, *Service Charges in Leases: A Practical Guide*. For a new no-fault right for tenants of certain long leases to manage the property, see CLRA 2002, Part 2; p. 376, post.

[453] LTA 1987, s. 24(1). If a tenant could apply for an order under s. 24, he may not apply for the appointment of a receiver under Supreme Court Act 1981, s. 37(1), supra: s. 21(6). See *Howard v Midrome Ltd* [1991] 1 EGLR 58 (manager of a company owned by the tenants).

[454] Part III is disapplied where the tenants have exercised their right to manage under CLRA 2002: s. 102, Sch. 7, para. 8; n. 451, supra; p. 376, post.

[455] LTA 1987, s. 26. A lease includes a sub-lease, and an agreement for a lease or for a sub-lease: s. 59(1).

[456] Or a perpetually renewable lease, or a lease granted in pursuance of Part V of HA 1985 (the right to buy): ss. 59(3), 60.

[457] LTA 1987, ss. 25, 27(4), as amended by Leasehold Reform, Housing and Urban Development Act 1993, s. 85. In addition, at least two-thirds of the flats in the premises must be held by qualifying tenants: LTA 1987, s. 25(2)(c), as amended by Leasehold Reform, Housing and Urban Development Act 1993, s. 85.

[458] LTA 1987, s. 29.

[459] Ibid., s. 30. See also Part IV, as amended by Leasehold Reform, Housing and Urban Development Act 1993, s. 86, and CLRA 2002, s. 162, under which the court may vary the terms of any long lease of a flat if they fail to make satisfactory provision for repair or maintenance, insurance, provision or maintenance of services,

repair, but had a claim against the landlord in tort for nuisance and negligence in respect of neglect which contributed to the damage, liability was apportioned 90 per cent to the landlord and 10 per cent to the tenant.[460]

(f) Law reform

In 1996 the Law Commission published a Report on Landlord and Tenant: Responsibility for State and Condition of Property,[461] which is intended to create a more coherent and principled code for regulating the responsibilities of the parties to a lease. Four discrete areas are addressed:[462]

First, the allocation of responsibility for repairs where the lease is silent; secondly, repairing obligations and fitness for human habitation in short residential leases; thirdly, the landlord's remedies for breach of repairing obligations; and finally, the law of waste. If enacted, the reforms will:

(a) ensure that someone will always be responsible for the repair of the premises, unless the parties expressly agree otherwise;[463]

(b) revive the statutory implied covenant that residential accommodation should be fit for human habitation,[464] by removing the present archaic rent limits,[465] and applying the covenant instead to all leases of residential accommodation for a term of less than seven years;

(c) confirm that specific performance is available as a remedy in actions for breach of covenant by tenants, and make the remedy available for landlords as well; and

(d) abolish the law of waste as between landlord and tenant, and replace both the duty not to commit waste and the duty of tenantlike user by a modern implied covenant to similar effect.[466]

With the exception of (b) above, these reforms are in essence a straightforward modernisation and clarification of the present law. They will not impose any obligation which the parties cannot avoid by express provision, nor will they affect existing leases or tenancies.

However, the Government has not yet indicated whether it proposes to accept the Report.[467]

recovery of expenditure or computation of a service charge payable under the lease or such other matters as may be prescribed by regulations.

[460] *Tennant Radiant Heat Ltd v Warrington Development Corpn* [1988] 1 EGLR 41.

[461] Law Com No. 238; [1996] Conv 342 (S. Bridge); [1998] Conv 189 (P. F. Smith). Forerunners of the Report are Law Commission Report on Obligations of Landlords and Tenants 1975 (Law Com No. 67); Law Commission Consultation Paper on Landlord and Tenant: Responsibility of State and Condition of Property 1992 (Law Com No. 123).

[462] Law Commission Thirtieth Annual Report 1995 (Law Com No. 238), paras. 5.10–5.11.

[463] We intend to achieve this by implying an excludable obligation to repair into every lease. This will remove the need to rely on the notoriously uncertain operation of general contractual principles to imply a term as to repair (see e.g. *Liverpool City Council v Irwin* [1977] AC 239; *Duke of Westminster v Guild* [1985] QB 688; and *Hafton Properties Ltd v Camp* [1994] 1 EGLR 67), p. 233, ante.

[464] LTA 1985, s. 8, which consolidated earlier legislation, p. 233, ante.

[465] £80 p.a. for houses in London and £52 p.a. elsewhere. These limits have not been changed since 1957, p. 234, n. 310 ante.   [466] This recommendation also applies to licences and tenancies at sufferance.

[467] Following the enactment of HA 2004, which modernised the enforcement regime in respect of residential property found to be in an unsatisfactory condition for occupation, the Office of the Deputy Prime Minister will reconsider the proposals: Law Commission Thirty-eighth Annual Report 2003/2004, Law Com No. 288, para. 3.37.

(3) Covenant to Insure Against Fire

By the Fires Prevention (Metropolis) Act 1774[468] no action may be brought against any person in whose house a fire shall *accidentally* begin, though it is expressly enacted that this provision shall not defeat an agreement made between landlord and tenant. The result is that, when the property has been burnt, a landlord can maintain an action against his tenant in two cases: first, where the tenant has covenanted to repair, for his contractual liability is not excluded by the happening of an inevitable accident against which he might have expressly protected himself;[469] and secondly, where the fire has begun or been allowed to spread by reason of the negligence of the tenant or of those for whom he is responsible.[470]

But, in addition, it is usual for a tenant to covenant that he will insure the demised buildings to their full value and will keep them insured during the term, or for the landlord to covenant to insure but to have the right to charge the premiums to the tenant. There is no implied term which requires the landlord to show that the amount of the premium is fair and reasonable. He does not "have to shop around", but must prove either that the rate of premium is representative of the market rate, or that the contract was negotiated at arm's length and in the market place, whether literal or metaphorical.[471] The omission to keep the premises insured for any period, no matter how short, and even though no fire breaks out during the period, constitutes a breach of the covenant.[472]

A covenant to insure is usually coupled with a covenant to apply any insurance moneys received in the reinstatement of the premises,[473] and this is effective unless it is impossible to rebuild. There is an implied duty to lay out the insurance moneys within a reasonable time.[474]

If the landlord himself takes out a policy without having agreed to do so, he is not liable to expend the insurance money on the reinstatement of the premises in the event of their destruction, unless the cost of the premiums is reflected in the rent.[475] Reinstatement of the premises may be impossible, for example, because of restrictions on building or compulsory acquisition of the site. In that case the insurance proceeds belong to the party who paid the premium.[476]

(4) Covenant by Tenant not to Assign or Under-let or Part with Possession[477]

Unless there is a special agreement to the contrary, a tenant is free to grant his interest to a third party either by assignment or by underlease,[478] but as it is undesirable from the

---

[468] S. 86. The Act applies to the whole of England. As to its interpretation, see *Goldman v Hargrave* [1967] 1 AC 645; *Mason v Levy Auto Parts of England Ltd* [1967] 2 QB 530; *Reynolds v Phoenix Assurance Co Ltd* (1978) 247 EG 995.   [469] *Redmond v Dainton* [1920] 2 KB 256.

[470] *Musgrove v Pandelis* [1919] 2 KB 43.   [471] *Havenridge Ltd v Boston Dyers Ltd* [1994] 49 EG 111.

[472] *Penniall v Harborne* (1848) 11 QB 368 (tenant's covenant).

[473] *Lonsdale & Thompson Ltd v Black Arrow Group plc* [1993] Ch 361; [1983] All ER Rev 270 (P. H. Pettit).

[474] *Farimani v Gates* (1984) 271 EG 887.

[475] *Mumford Hotels Ltd v Wheler* [1964] Ch 117. Cf *Re King* [1963] Ch 459, M & B p. 565; *Mark Rowlands Ltd v Berni Inns Ltd* [1986] QB 211; (1986) 83 LSG 1046 (H. W. Wilkinson).

[476] *Re King*, supra; cf *Beacon Carpets Ltd v Kirby* [1985] QB 755.

[477] Crabb, *Leases: Covenants and Consents* (1991).

[478] *Keeves v Dean* [1924] 1 KB 685 at 691; *Leith Properties Ltd v Byrne* [1983] QB 433.

landlord's point of view that the premises should fall into the hands of an irresponsible person, it is usual to provide for the matter by express covenant. In this case, even though the assignment or underlease is made in breach of the covenant, it is nevertheless valid, but the breach may give rise to forfeiture or to a claim for damages.[479]

(a) Construction of covenant

The courts, however, have always construed this covenant with great strictness and have insisted that the restraint imposed upon the tenant shall not go beyond the letter of the express agreement.[480] Thus, a covenant *not to assign or underlet* is not broken by an equitable mortgage accompanied by deposit of title deeds,[481] nor by a deed of arrangement whereby the tenant constitutes himself trustee for his creditors,[482] nor by permitting another person to have the use of the premises without giving him legal possession,[483] nor in general by any transfer which is involuntary, as, for instance, one which results from the bankruptcy of the tenant.[484] A provision that "this lease shall be non-assignable" does not embrace a sub-lease of the premises.[485] An agreement *not to sub-let* is not broken by a sub-lease of part of the premises;[486] but a covenant *not to assign or underlet any part of the premises* is broken if the tenant assigns or underlets the whole of the premises.[487] A covenant *not to part with the possession of the premises or any part thereof* is not broken by the grant of a licence to place an advertisement hoarding on the wall of the demised premises, since the tenant is not thereby deprived of legal possession;[488] but a covenant "*not to underlet or part with possession of the premises*" is broken if the tenant assigns his lease, since this involves a parting with possession.[489]

---

[479] *Old Grovebury Manor Farm Ltd v W Seymour Plant Sales and Hire Ltd (No 2)* [1979] 1 WLR 1397; *Governors of the Peabody Donation Fund v Higgins* [1983] 1 WLR 1091. The purported assignment of the benefit of a contractual right in breach of a non-assignment provision is ineffective; but although a lease is "a hybrid, part contract, part property", p. 194, ante, "so far as rights of alienation are concerned a lease has been treated as a species of property" and the law has allowed the assignment to transfer the property rights although liable to forfeiture for breach of the covenant: *Linden Gardens Trust Ltd v Lenesta Sludge Disposals Ltd* [1994] 1 AC 85 at 108–9, per Lord Browne-Wilkinson.

It may also constitute a breach of a restrictive covenant: chap. 20, post; or an inducement of a breach of contract by the tenant: *Hemingway Securities Ltd v Dunraven Ltd* [1995] 1 EGLR 61, [1995] Conv 416 (P. Luxton and M. Wilkie).

[480] *Church v Brown* (1808) 15 Ves 258 at 265, per Lord Eldon; *Grove v Portal* [1902] 1 Ch 727 at 731.

[481] *Doe d Pitt v Hogg* (1824) 4 Dow & Ry KB 226; p. 729, post. A mortgage of registered land can no longer be made by demise or sub-demise: LRA 2002, s. 23(1); there can therefore be no argument that such a mortgage constitutes a breach of a covenant against assignment or underletting.

[482] *Gentle v Faulkner* [1900] 2 QB 267.   [483] *Chaplin v Smith* [1926] 1 KB 198.

[484] *Re Riggs* [1901] 2 KB 16; *Marsh v Gilbert* (1980) 256 EG 715 (vesting in new trustee by order of court). As to whether a bequest of a leasehold interest breaks a covenant not to assign, see (1963) 27 Conv (NS) 159 (D. G. Barnsley).   [485] *Sweet and Maxwell Ltd v Universal News Services Ltd* [1964] 2 QB 699.

[486] *Cook v Shoesmith* [1951] 1 KB 752; *Esdaile v Lewis* [1956] 1 WLR 709.

[487] *Field v Barkworth* [1986] 1 WLR 137, approved in *Troop v Gibson* [1986] 1 EGLR 1 (landlord estopped from enforcing covenant); (1985) 129 SJ 781, 867.

[488] *Stening v Abrahams* [1931] 1 Ch 470; *Lam Kee Ying Sdn Bhd v Lam Shes Tong* [1975] AC 247. Whether the grant of the right to occupy premises constitutes an "underletting" or parting with "possession" ought to depend on whether a lease, rather than a licence, has been granted: pp. 197 et seq, ante; *Victoria Dwellings Association Ltd v Roberts* [1947] LJNCCR 177. Cf *Doe d Pitt v Laming* (1814) 4 Camp 73 at 77, doubted (on the question of whether there was not in the case a grant of exclusive possession) in *Greenslade v Tapscott* (1834) 1 Cr M & R 55 at 59, per Parke B; *Akici v L R Butlin Ltd* [2006] 1 WLR 201 (distinction between "parting with possession" and "sharing possession").   [489] *Marks v Warren* [1979] 1 All ER 29.

(b) Effect of breach of covenant

The result of a tenant's breach depends upon the nature of the covenant by which he has bound himself. A covenant is either absolute or qualified.[490]

(1) ABSOLUTE COVENANT

An absolute covenant is one which imposes an unconditional prohibition upon the tenant, there being no provision for its relaxation at the will of the landlord. In this case any assignment contrary to the terms of the covenant renders the tenant liable,[491] notwithstanding that it is in no way prejudicial to the landlord's interest.

(2) QUALIFIED COVENANT

(i) Unreasonable withholding of consent by landlord

A qualified covenant, which is far more common in practice, is one which merely prohibits an assignment without the consent of the landlord. It has long been usual to qualify this type of covenant even further by a provision that the landlord's consent shall not be unreasonably withheld, and the Landlord and Tenant Act 1927 makes this qualification inevitable by providing that:

> In all leases whether made before or after the commencement of this Act containing a covenant condition or agreement against assigning, underletting, charging or parting with the possession of demised premises or any part thereof without licence or consent, such covenant condition or agreement shall, notwithstanding any express provision to the contrary, be deemed to be subject to a proviso to the effect that such licence or consent is not to be unreasonably withheld.[492]

Thus, the Act requires that the grounds for the refusal of consent shall in fact be reasonable, and therefore its operation cannot be curtailed by a provision in the lease that certain specified grounds shall not be deemed unreasonable.[493] But if the lease contains a covenant that, before the tenant assigns or underlets, he must first offer to surrender his lease to the landlord, the landlord may demand surrender and so obtain the value of a premium obtainable on an assignment.[494] In relation to non-residential leases granted after 1995, however, a

---

[490] It may also be conditional: *Prudential Assurance Co Ltd v Mount Eden Land Ltd* [1997] 1 EGLR 37 (subject to formal execution of licence); cf *Next plc v National Farmers Union Mutual Insurance Co Ltd* [1997] EGCS 181.

[491] The sub-tenant who knowingly accepts an underlease in breach of the tenant's covenant in the lease and thereby intends to procure a breach of the covenant, can be liable in the tort of wrongful interference with contract; the remedy may be not only damages, but also an order against tenant and sub-tenant for surrender of the underlease: *Crestfort Ltd v Tesco Stores Ltd* [2005] 3 EGLR 25.

[492] S. 19(1)(a); this section does not apply to an absolute covenant: per ROMER LJ in *F W Woolworth & Co Ltd v Lambert* [1937] Ch 37 at 58, 59; and MEGAW LJ in *Bocardo SA v S & M Hotels Ltd* [1980] 1 WLR 17 at 22, but see DANCKWERTS LJ in *Property and Bloodstock Ltd v Emerton* [1968] Ch 94 at 119–20; *Vaux Group plc v Lilley* [1991] 1 EGLR 60 at 63, per KNOX J. Nor does it apply to the lease of an agricultural holding or a farm business tenancy: s. 19(4). [493] *Re Smith's Lease* [1951] 1 All ER 346.

[494] *Bocardo SA v S & M Hotels Ltd*, supra; *Adler v Upper Grosvenor Street Investment Ltd* [1957] 1 WLR 227; (1957) 73 LQR 157 (R.E.M.); *Creer v P and O Lines of Australia Pty Ltd* (1971) 45 ALJR 697; (1972) 88 LQR 317; *Allied Dunbar Assurance plc v Homebase Ltd* [2002] 2 EGLR 23. This surrender proviso was doubted by CA in *Greene v Church Comrs for England* [1974] Ch 467. It is registrable in unregistered land as an estate contract: LCA 1972, s. 2(4): *Greene v Church Comrs for England*, supra; in registered land it must be protected by a notice on the register: LRA 2002, s. 29. For the position of business tenancies under LTA 1954, Part II, see *Allnatt London Properties Ltd v Newton* [1981] 2 All ER 290; [1980] Conv 418 (C. G. Blake); (1983) 127 SJ 855 (C. Coombe).

significant change was made by the Landlord and Tenant (Covenants) Act 1995 in relation to covenants against assignment.[495] If the landlord and tenant have agreed (whether in the lease or not, and at the time of the lease or later) any circumstances in which the landlord may withhold his consent to an assignment of the demised premises or any part of them, or any conditions subject to which any such consent may be granted, then the landlord is not to be regarded as unreasonably withholding his consent, or subjecting it to unreasonable conditions, if he withholds it or makes it conditional on that ground. This gives landlords much greater control over the assignment of leases to which it applies.

Under the Law of Property Act 1925[496] the landlord may not require the payment of a fine in return for his consent unless express provision for such a payment is contained in the lease.

The tenant must apply for consent to assign, even if it could not reasonably be refused; the landlord must be given a reasonable opportunity to consider whether to give his consent or not.[497] If the tenant assigns the premises without asking for consent, he is in breach of covenant, and liable to pay damages, and also at common law to the forfeiture of his interest.[498] He may, however, apply to the court for relief against such forfeiture.[499] If, on the other hand, the tenant asks for consent and the landlord refuses consent unreasonably, the tenant may proceed with the assignment without consent.[500]

(ii) Landlord and Tenant Act 1988

This "curious little Act"[501] imposes statutory duties on a landlord in relation to applications for consent to an assignment, underletting, charging or parting with possession. It applies to applications served after 28 September 1988, and only affects qualified covenants.[502] Its object is to prevent undue delay by the landlord in dealing with a consent application by the tenant, especially where the landlord decides to refuse consent.[503]

Where the landlord receives written application for consent from the tenant,[504] he owes a duty to the tenant within a reasonable time:[505]

(a) to give consent, except in a case where it is reasonable not to give consent,

---

[495] S. 22, inserting new subsections (1A)–(1E) into LTA 1927, s. 19; p. 314, post.

[496] S. 144; *Gardner & Co Ltd v Cone* [1928] Ch 955; *Comber v Fleet Electrics Ltd* [1955] 1 WLR 566. An increase in rent as a condition to giving consent is in the nature of a fine: *Jenkins v Price* [1907] 2 Ch 229. See also LTA 1927, s. 19(3); *Barclays Bank plc v Daejan Investments (Grove Hall) Ltd* [1995] 1 EGLR 68.

[497] *Wilson v Fynn* [1948] 2 All ER 40.   [498] *Barrow v Isaacs & Son* [1891] 1 QB 417.

[499] *Lambert v F W Woolworth & Co Ltd (No 2)* [1938] Ch 883 at 893.

[500] The tenant may apply to the High Court or to the county court for a declaration that the landlord has unreasonably withheld his consent: LTA 1954, s. 53(1)(a), as amended by County Courts Act 1984, s. 148(1), Sch. 2, para. 23.

[501] *Venetian Glass Gallery Ltd v Next Properties Ltd* [1989] 2 EGLR 42 at 46, per HARMAN J. The Act is based on Law Commission Report: Leasehold Conveyancing 1987 (Law Com No. 161, HC 360); [1989] Conv 1. See also the earlier Report on Covenants Restricting Dispositions, Alterations and Change of User 1985 (Law Com No. 141, HC 278), paras. 8.50–8.131: (1985) 135 NLJ 491, 1015 (P. F. Smith); [1986] Conv 240 (A. J. Waite). For a general review of the Act, see [2004] Conv 453 (J. A. Sandham).

[502] S. 1(1). It does not apply to a secure tenancy under HA 1985: s. 5(3).

[503] See *29 Equities Ltd v Bank Leumi (UK) Ltd* [1986] 1 WLR 1490 at 1494, per DILLON LJ.

[504] On what constitutes a sufficient application, see *Norwich Union Mercantile Linked Life Assurance Co Ltd v Mercantile Credit Co Ltd* [2003] EWHC 3064 (Ch), [2004] 4 ECGS 109.

[505] S. 1(3); *Go West Ltd v Spigarolo* [2003] QB 1149 (service of request for consent is the commencement of reasonable time. The length of reasonable time depends on the circumstances and is the time reasonably required by the landlord to do the things required of him by the Act); *NCR Ltd v Riverland Portfolio No 1 Ltd* [2005] 2 EGLR 42.

(b) to serve on the tenant written notice of his decision whether or not to give consent specifying in addition—

    (i) if the consent is given subject to conditions, the conditions,

    (ii) if the consent is withheld, the reasons for withholding it.

The landlord is also under a duty to forward the application to any other person whose consent to the transaction is needed, for example, to a superior landlord or to a mortgagee. In this case the superior landlord owes a similar duty.[506]

Where any duty imposed by the Act is broken, an action lies for the tort of breach of statutory duty.[507]

The burden of proof, which at common law was placed on the tenant to prove that consent cannot be unreasonably refused, is reversed by the Act in regard to all the duties, that is, as to reasonable time, reasonable conditions and reasonable refusal.[508] The Act contains no definition of reasonableness in any of its connotations.[509] These matters will still depend on the application of common law principles.[510]

(iii) Giving of consent by landlord

The 1988 Act changed the law on the giving of consent by the landlord. As Sir Richard Scott V-C said in *Norwich Union Life Insurance Society v Shopmoor Ltd*:[511]

The Act of 1998 has altered the law in this respect. It has done so by necessary implication, although not explicitly. The landlord has a statutory duty to the tenant within a reasonable time to give consent, except in a case where it is reasonable not to give consent. In judging whether it is reasonable not to give consent, the position must, in my view, be tested by reference to the state of affairs at the expiry of the reasonable time. If, at that time, the landlord has raised no point and there is no point outstanding which could constitute a reasonable ground for refusal of consent, then it seems to me that the landlord's duty is positively, as expressed by s. 1(3), to give consent.

It follows that a landlord who has not given his reasons for refusing consent within a reasonable time cannot thereafter justify his refusal of consent by putting forward any reasons, even though he had them in his mind.[512]

The landlord must give his reasons in writing; reasons given orally are not sufficient and must be confirmed in writing within the reasonable period required by the Act.

---

[506] Ss. 2, 3.   [507] S. 4; *Berkeley Leisure Group Ltd v Lee* [1995] EGCS 162.

[508] S. 1(6). Exemplary damages may be awarded: *Design Progression Ltd v Thurloe Properties Ltd* [2005] 1 WLR 1 (deliberate obstruction by the landlord frustrating the tenants' attempt to assign: £25,000); [2006] Conv 37 (T. Fancourt). The Act has not changed the rule that it is not necessary for the landlord to prove that his conclusions were justified if he can show that they were reasonably reached in the circumstances: *Air India v Balabel* [1993] 2 EGLR 66; *Beale v Worth* [1993] EGCS 135.

[509] In the 1985 Report the Law Commission had recommended a twenty-eight-day period: para. 8.125. On the obscure s. 1(5), see (1989) 133 SJ 1277 (T. Aldridge).

[510] *Midland Bank plc v Chart Enterprises Inc* [1990] 2 EGLR 59 (gap of two and a half months between application and notice of decision held unreasonable).

[511] [1999] 1 WLR 531 at 545, [1998] All ER Rev 282 (P. H. Pettit).

[512] *Footwear Corpn Ltd v Amplight Properties Ltd* [1999] 1 WLR 551 at 559, per Neuberger J. See also *Dong Bang Minerva (UK) Ltd v Davina Ltd* [1995] 1 EGLR 41; *Kened Ltd and Den Norske Bank plc v Connie Investments Ltd* [1997] 1 EGLR 21; *CIN Properties Ltd v Gill* [1993] 2 EGLR 97; *Go West Ltd v Spigarolo* n.505 above at [40], per Munby J (where landlord has given reasons he does not require any further time, and so cannot assert that the reasonable time he requires has not yet elapsed; premature unreasonable refusal of consent therefore constituted actionable breach of duty and could not be cured by anything that happened later to render refusal reasonable).

(iv) Test of reasonableness

The crucial question is—What does the law regard as a reasonable refusal? This was answered in *Houlder Bros & Co Ltd v Gibbs*,[513] where TOMLIN J at first instance said:

It is by reference to the personality of the lessee or the nature of the user or occupation of the premises that the court has to judge the reasonableness of the lessor's refusal.

And where SARGANT LJ in the Court of Appeal said:[514]

I was very much impressed by counsel's argument that in a case of this kind the landlord's reason must be something affecting the subject matter of the contract which forms the relationship between the landlord and the tenant, and that it must not be something wholly extraneous and completely dissociated from the subject matter of the contract.

In that case it was held that: it was unreasonable for a landlord, who had let Blackacre to X and Whiteacre to Y, to forbid an assignment of Blackacre by X to Y, on the ground that Y might terminate his tenancy of Whiteacre.

Although this approach has been criticised by the House of Lords on the ground that it involved adding glosses to the plain words of the covenant,[515] it has been generally followed by the Court of Appeal.[516] The question of reasonableness is essentially a question of fact depending on all the circumstances of the case;[517] and there is now more emphasis on this approach.[518] As Lord DENNING MR said:[519]

Seeing that the circumstances are infinitely various, it is impossible to formulate strict rules as to how a landlord should exercise his power of refusal. The utmost that the Courts can do is to give guidance to those who have to consider the problem. As one decision follows another, people will get to know the likely result in any given set of circumstances. But no one decision will be a binding precedent as a strict rule of law. The reasons given by the judges are to be treated as propositions of good sense—in relation to the particular case—rather than propositions of law applicable to all cases.

---

[513] [1925] Ch 198 at 209. See generally [1988] Conv 45 (G. Kodilinye).

[514] [1925] Ch 575 at 587; *Bromley Park Garden Estates Ltd v Moss* [1982] 1 WLR 1019 (where the object of the refusal was to promote good estate management); *Anglia Building Society v Sheffield City Council* (1982) 266 EG 311.   [515] *Viscount Tredegar v Harwood* [1929] AC 72 at 78, 81.

[516] *Lee v K Carter Ltd* [1949] 1 KB 85 at 96; *Swanson v Forton* [1949] Ch 143 at 149; *Pimms Ltd v Tallow Chandlers in the City of London* [1964] 2 QB 547; *Bickel v Duke of Westminster* [1977] QB 517, per ORR and WALLER LJJ; contra, Lord DENNING MR, who considered that no such rule bound the Court of Appeal; *Bromley Park Garden Estates Ltd v Moss*, supra; *International Drilling Fluids Ltd v Louisville Investments (Uxbridge) Ltd* [1986] Ch 513.

[517] *Brann v Westminster Anglo-Continental Investment Co Ltd* (1975) 240 EG 927 at 931; *Bickel v Duke of Westminster*, supra, at 524, per Lord DENNING MR; *West Layton Ltd v Ford* [1979] QB 593 at 605, 606, per ROSKILL and LAWTON LJJ; *Ashworth Frazer Ltd v Gloucester City Council* [2001] 1 WLR 2180.

[518] See e.g. *Leeward Securities Ltd v Lilyheath Properties Ltd* (1983) 271 EG 279 at 282, per OLIVER LJ; *International Drilling Fluids Ltd v Louisville Investments (Uxbridge) Ltd*, infra, at 521.

[519] *Bickel v Duke of Westminster* [1977] QB 517 at 524, approved by HL in *Ashworth Frazer v Gloucester City Council*, supra.

In *International Drilling Fluids Ltd v Louisville Investments (Uxbridge) Ltd*,[520] BALCOMBE LJ deduced the following propositions of law from the authorities:

(1) The purpose of a covenant against assignment without the consent of the landlord, such consent not to be unreasonably withheld is to protect the lessor from having his premises used or occupied in an undesirable way, or by an undesirable tenant or assignee.

(2) As a corollary to the first proposition, a landlord is not entitled to refuse his consent to an assignment on grounds which have nothing whatever to do with the relationship of landlord and tenant in regard to the subject matter of the lease.

(3) The onus of proving that consent has been unreasonably withheld is on the [landlord].[521]

(4) It is not necessary for the landlord to prove that the conclusions which led him to refuse consent were justified, if they were conclusions which might be reached by a reasonable man in the circumstances.

(5) It may be reasonable for the landlord to refuse his consent to an assignment on the ground of the purpose for which the proposed assignee intends to use the premises, even though that purpose is not forbidden by the lease.

(6) There is a divergence of authority on the question, in considering whether the landlord's refusal of consent is reasonable, whether it is permissible to have regard to the consequences to the tenant if consent to the proposed assignment is withheld.

(7) Subject to the propositions set out above, it is in each case a question of fact, depending upon all the circumstances, whether the landlord's consent to an assignment is being unreasonably withheld.

Two further propositions on a covenant against sub-letting were added by PHILLIPS LJ in *Mount Eden Land Ltd v Straudley Investments Ltd*:[522]

(1) It will normally be reasonable for a landlord to refuse consent or impose a condition if this is necessary to prevent his contractual rights under the headlease from being prejudiced by the proposed assignment or sublease.

(2) It will not normally be reasonable for a landlord to seek to impose a condition which is designed to increase or enhance the rights that he enjoys under the headlease.[523]

The essential question is: "Has it been shown that no reasonable landlord would have withheld consent?"[524]

---

[520] [1986] Ch 513 at 519–20; *Jaison Property Development Co Ltd v Roux Restaurants Ltd* (1996) 74 P & CR 357. See generally [1998] 2 L & TR 117 (J. Brock).

[521] See LTA 1988, s. 1(3)(a), p. 258, ante, reversing the burden of proof.

[522] (1996) 74 P & CR 306 at 310. These propositions also apply where there is a management scheme for enfranchisement for property enfranchised under Leasehold Reform Act 1967; *Estates Governors of Alleyn's College of God's Gift at Dulwich v Williams* [1994] 1 EGLR 112.

[523] *London & Argyll Developments Ltd v Mount Cook Land (No 1)* [2002] 50 EGCS 111 (unreasonable to impose new surety condition); cf *Mount Eden Land Ltd v Towerstone Ltd* [2003] L & TR 4 (guarantors required for assignee under terms of the lease: implied term that request for guarantors must be genuinely for the purpose of improving the landlords' financial security. They could not, in circumstances in which they were amply secured, request a large number of guarantors with the object of making it impossible for the tenant to comply and thus prevent an assignment).

[524] *Kened Ltd and Den Norske Bank plc v Connie Investments Ltd* [1997] 1 EGLR 21 at 25, per MILLETT LJ.

In considering whether the landlord's refusal of consent is reasonable, there is a divergence of authority as to whether it is permissible to have regard to the consequences to the tenant if consent is withheld. In *International Drilling Fluids Ltd v Louisville Investments (Uxbridge) Ltd*, BALCOMBE LJ reconciled this divergence by saying that:[525]

while a landlord need usually only consider his own relevant interests, there may be cases where there is such a disproportion between the benefit to the landlord and the detriment to the tenant if the landlord withholds his consent to an assignment that it is unreasonable for the landlord to refuse consent.

In that case it was held that, where a user clause permitted only one specified type of use ("for any purpose other than as offices"), it was unreasonable to refuse consent to an assignment on the grounds of use (being within the only specified type of use) where the result would be that the property was left vacant and where the landlord was fully secured for payment of the rent.

Finally, even if a landlord was misled by a tenant as to the circumstances surrounding the tenant's application for a licence to assign his lease, the landlord's refusal of consent to it could be treated as unreasonably withheld, if disclosure of the full facts would not have justified refusal.[526]

(v) Examples of reasonable refusal

It has been held that a landlord has a valid reason for withholding his consent:

if the assignee's references[527] or financial standing[528] are unsatisfactory; or if he considers that other property belonging to him will be injured by the use that the assignee intends to make of the demised premises;[529] or if, where the lease is of a tied public-house, he fears that the value of the trade will depreciate because the assignee is a foreigner who does not intend to reside on the premises;[530] or,

if the effect of the assignment will be to nullify a collateral agreement made at the time of the lease;[531] or

---

[525] [1986] Ch 513 at 521; *Leeward Securities Ltd v Lilyheath Properties Ltd* (1983) 271 EG 279 at 283, per OLIVER LJ. Cf *Ponderosa International Development Inc v Pengap Securities (Bristol) Ltd* [1986] 1 EGLR 66 ("nothing like as grave a detriment as was in question in *International Drilling*"); *F W Woolworth plc v Charlwood Alliance Properties Ltd* [1987] 1 EGLR 53; [1987] Conv 381 (L. Crabb).

[526] *Storehouse Properties Ltd v Ocobase Ltd* The Times, 3 April 1988.

[527] *Shanly v Ward* (1913) 29 TLR 714; *Rossi v Hestdrive Ltd* [1985] 1 EGLR 50. See also *Shires v Brock* (1977) 247 EG 127 (fictitious transaction by tenant in favour of nominee with first class references, the object being to give difficult landlord "a bit of a fright"); *City Hotels Group Ltd v Total Property Investments Ltd* [1985] 1 EGLR 253 (extent of inquiries for information of tenant's capabilities); *Warren v Marketing Exchange for Africa Ltd* [1988] 2 EGLR 247 ("references of a particularly qualified and non-enthusiastic character").

[528] *Ponderosa International Development Inc v Pengap Securities (Bristol) Ltd*, supra; *British Bakeries (Midlands) Ltd v Michael Testler & Co Ltd* [1986] 1 EGLR 64. Cf *NCR Ltd v Riverland Portfolio No 1 Ltd* [2005] 2 EGLR 42 (prospective sub-tenant's financial standing can sometimes be relevant also to consent to underletting).

[529] *Governors of Bridewell Hospital v Fawkner and Rogers* (1892) 8 TLR 637; *Sportoffer Ltd v Erewash BC* [1999] 3 EGLR 136.

[530] *Mills v Cannon Brewery Co Ltd* [1920] 2 Ch 38; cf *Parker v Boggon* [1947] KB 346; *Rayburn v Wolf* (1985) 50 P & CR 463 (absentee American attorney resident in Washington).

[531] *Wilson v Fynn* [1948] 2 All ER 40.

if the assignment will enable the assignee to acquire a statutory tenancy protected by the Rent Acts,[532] or in due course to acquire the freehold under the Leasehold Reform Act 1967;[533] or

if the rent reserved in a proposed sub-lease is well below that obtainable in the open market, but the sub-lessee agrees to pay a large sum by way of premium;[534] or

if the assignment will embarrass the future development of the property of which the demised premises form part;[535] or

if, where there are breaches of a covenant to repair, he is not really sure that the assignee will remedy them;[536] or

if the assignment will undermine the estate management considerations for its strategic development;[537] or

if the motive of the assignee is to acquire a ransom position with regard to a proposed development by the landlord;[538] or

if the purpose of the assignment is to enable the original tenant to exercise his option to determine the lease.[539]

(vi) Discrimination

It is unlawful to discriminate on grounds of race,[540] sex[541] or disability[542] by withholding consent for assignment or sub-letting. These provisions do not generally apply[543] if the person withholding consent, or a near relative of his, resides and intends to continue to reside on the premises, there is shared accommodation, and the premises are small premises.

[532] *Lee v K Carter Ltd* [1949] 1 KB 85; *Swanson v Forton* [1949] Ch 143; *Dollar v Winston* [1950] Ch 236; cf *Thomas Bookman Ltd v Nathan* [1955] 1 WLR 815; *Re Cooper's Lease* (1968) 19 P & CR 541; *Brann v Westminster Anglo Continental Investment Co Ltd* (1975) 240 EG 927; *West Layton Ltd v Ford* [1979] QB 593; cf *Deverall v Wyndham* [1989] 1 EGLR 57 (unreasonable).

[533] *Norfolk Capital Group Ltd v Kitway Ltd* [1977] QB 506; *Bickel v Duke of Westminster* [1977] QB 517. See also *Welch v Birrane* (1974) 29 P & CR 102; *Leeward Securities Ltd v Lilyheath Properties Ltd* (1983) 271 EG 279. For the Leasehold Reform Act 1967, see pp. 364 et seq, post.

[534] *Re Town Investments Ltd Underlease* [1954] Ch 301. Cf *Blockbuster Entertainment Ltd v Leakcliff Properties Ltd* [1997] 1 EGLR 28 (rent within open market band of validity).

[535] *Pimms Ltd v Tallow Chandlers in the City of London*, [1964] 2 QB 547.

[536] *Orlando Investments Ltd v Grosvenor Estate Belgravia* [1989] 2 EGLR 74; [1989] Conv 371 (P. F. Smith); cf *Farr v Ginnings* (1928) 44 TLR 249.

[537] *Crown Estates Comrs v Signet Group plc* [1996] 2 EGLR 200 (freehold of Regent Street, London); (1999) 115 LQR 191 (L. Crabb).

[538] *BRS Northern Ltd v Templeheight and Sainsbury's Supermarkets Ltd* [1998] 2 EGLR 182.

[539] *Olympia & York Canary Wharf Ltd v Oil Property Investment Ltd* (1994) 69 P & CR 43.

[540] Race Relations Act 1976, s. 24, as amended by SI 2003 No. 1626, introducing also a prohibition on harassment on racial grounds of the person who applies for consent or from whom the consent is withheld. For the meaning of racial discrimination, see ss. 1–3, as amended by SI 2003 No. 1626.

[541] Sex Discrimination Act 1975, s. 31. For the meaning of discrimination, see s. 1. S. 31 refers to discrimination against a woman, but this is to be read as applying equally to men: s. 2.

[542] Disability Discrimination Act 1995, s. 22(4). For the meaning of disability, see s. 1; and for the meaning of discrimination, see s. 24; [2000] Conv 128 (A. Lawson).

[543] Sex Discrimination Act 1975, s. 31(2); Disability Discrimination Act 1995, s. 23. A similar general exclusion in Race Relations Act 1976, s. 24(2), was amended by SI 2003 No. 1626, reg. 26(2)(b), to apply only to discrimination on grounds other than those of race or ethnic or national origins. The Secretary of State has power to amend or remove the small premises exemption in relation to disability discrimination: Disability Discrimination Act 2005, s. 14.

(3) BUILDING LEASES

It is also provided by the Landlord and Tenant Act 1927 that in the case of a lease for more than forty years made in consideration of the erection or the substantial improvement, alteration or addition of buildings, the tenant may, notwithstanding a prohibition of assignment without the landlord's consent, assign the premises without such consent, provided that the assignment is made more than seven years before the end of the term, and provided that within six months after its completion it is notified in writing to the landlord.[544]

(4) RULE IN *DUMPOR'S CASE*

The rule at common law as laid down in *Dumpor's Case*[545] is that a condition is an entire and indivisible thing and therefore incapable of enforcement if the person entitled to enforce it has once allowed it to be disregarded. The effect of this doctrine was that, if a lease from A to B contained a covenant or condition against assigning without licence, and A permitted B to assign to C, A's right to stop further assignments was utterly gone. Once consent had been given to an assignment, the term became freely assignable. Again, and as a result of the same doctrine, if a lease was made to several tenants, upon condition that neither they nor any one of them should assign without a licence, a licence given to one of the tenants destroyed the condition with regard to the others. Again, if a tenant was allowed to assign part of the land leased, the condition ceased to apply to the whole of the land. This absurd doctrine was, however, abrogated by statute[546] in 1859 so far as conditions contained in leases were concerned, and the present position is regulated by the Law of Property Act 1925.[547] This provides that:

where a licence is granted to a lessee to do any act, the licence, unless otherwise expressed, extends only

  (a) to the permission actually given; or

  (b) to the specific breach of any provision or covenant referred to; or

  (c) to any other matter thereby specifically authorised to be done; and the licence does not prevent any proceeding for any subsequent breach unless otherwise specified in the licence.

Moreover, it is enacted that where a lease contains a covenant or condition against assigning or doing any other act without licence, and a licence is granted to one or more of several lessees, or is granted in respect of part only of the property, it shall not operate to extinguish the landlord's remedy in case the covenant is broken either by the other lessees or with regard to the rest of the property.[548]

The result is that the rule in *Dumpor's Case* no longer applies to leases.

(5) The usual covenants

Although there are many other covenants which may figure in a lease, those that are normally found have been mentioned. It should be noticed that, where the lease is preceded by a contract for a lease,[549] there is an implied term of the contract that it shall include the *usual*

---

[544] S. 19(1)(b). This section does not apply if the lessor is a Government department, a local or public authority, or a statutory or public utility company. See *Vaux Group plc v Lilley* [1991] 1 EGLR 60.

[545] (1603) 4 Co Rep 119b; *Smith's Leading Cases* (13th edn), vol. i. p. 35; Holdsworth, *History of English Law*, vol. vii. p. 282. In *GMS Syndicate Ltd v Gary Elliott Ltd* [1982] Ch 1, NOURSE J relied on *Dumpor's Case* as establishing that a landlord can in certain circumstances forfeit a lease in part only; p. 288, post.

[546] LP(A)A 1859, s. 1.　　　　[547] S. 143(1).　　　　[548] LPA 1925, s. 143(3).　　　　[549] P.219, ante.

covenants. At one time it was generally considered, on the authority of *Hampshire v Wickens*,[550] that the only covenants by a tenant which could be described as "usual" were:

to pay rent;

to pay tenant's rates[551] and taxes;

to keep and deliver up the premises in repair;

to allow the lessor to enter and view the state of repair;

and that the covenant for quiet enjoyment was the only usual covenant binding the landlord.

However, the list is neither fixed nor closed. The question whether particular covenants are usual is a question of fact dependent upon the circumstances of each case, which can be resolved only after considering the evidence of conveyancers, the books of precedents, the practice in the particular district and the character of the property.[552]

V Remedies of the Landlord for the Enforcement of the Covenants

We have already noticed some of the remedies available to the landlord[553] or tenant[554] for breach of particular covenants (express or implied) in a lease. We shall here discuss in general terms the landlord's remedies for breach of covenant by the tenant. However, in so doing, the covenant to pay rent must be treated separately from all other covenants entered into by the tenant.

A Covenant to Pay Rent

(1) Meaning of Rent

The rent payable to a landlord by the tenant holding from him under a lease is technically called *rent service*. This must be distinguished from a *rentcharge*, which will be discussed in detail later.[555]

(a) Rent service

A brief account of the history of rent service is necessary in order to understand some of the modern features of the law of rent as between landlord and tenant—and in particular distress for rent, which is a very significant remedy available to a landlord for enforcement of the covenant to pay rent.

---

[550] (1878) 7 Ch D 555 at 561, per JESSEL MR; *Charalambous v Ktori* [1972] 1 WLR 951.

[551] On rates and taxes, see Aldridge, *Leasehold Law*, paras. 4.116–4.120.

[552] *Flexman v Corbett* [1930] 1 Ch 672. For usual covenants where there was a contract for a lease of garage workshops in Chelsea in 1971, see *Chester v Buckingham Travel Ltd* [1981] 1 WLR 96; (1981) 97 LQR 385 (G. Woodman).

[553] Pp. 249–51, ante (specific performance and damages for breach of tenant's covenant to repair).

[554] Pp. 232 et seq (repudiation and/or damages for breach of landlord's implied obligations in respect of the state of the premises); pp. 251–253, ante (specific performance, damages, or appointment of a receiver or of a manager for breach of landlord's covenant to repair).

[555] Chap. 21, post. A third form of rent, *rent-seck*, no longer exists: p. 267, post.

Historically, rent service consisted of an annual return, made by the tenant in labour, money or provisions, for the land.[556] This is the rent which is due whenever a tenant holds his lands of a reversioner.[557] A reversion is the residue of the estate out of which the estate owner has carved a smaller estate, called a *particular estate*, in favour of another.[558]

Thus, where lands are leased at a rent for a term of years, the landlord is the *reversioner* and the rent payable by the tenant is called a *rent service*. Since, however, rent service is that rent which is due from a tenant who holds of a reversioner, it follows that rent which is reserved on the grant of an estate in fee simple cannot be a rent service, for since *Quia Emptores* 1290 such a grantee no longer holds of the grantor, but is substituted for him.[559] There is no reversion, no residue left in the grantor.

The origin of the term rent service lies far back in legal history. Originally the services due from a tenant took many forms, but in course of time they were commuted into fixed money payments called rents service, since they represented the services that formerly issued out of the land. If the tenant failed to perform the services or to pay the rent into which they had been commuted, the lord enjoyed of common right, that is, independently of statute or agreement, the remedy of distress, a feudal institution of very ancient origin, which entitled him to seize cattle and other chattels found upon the land. This remedy existed of common right only where the distrainor had an interest in the shape of a reversion in the land upon which the chattels lay, for otherwise it could scarcely be said with justice that there was anything he was entitled to seize.[560]

Today rent is regarded as a contractual sum to which a landlord becomes entitled for the use of his land, and, therefore, "the time and manner of the payment is to be ascertained according to the true construction of the contract, and not by reference to out-dated relics of medieval law".[561] As Lord DIPLOCK said:[562] "The mediaeval concept of rent as a service rendered by the tenant to the landlord has been displaced by the modern concept of a payment . . . for the use of his land. The mediaeval concept has, however, left as its only surviving relic the ancient remedy of distress."

(b) Rentcharge

From a rent service must be distinguished a rentcharge. This differs from rent service in that its owner has no tenurial interest in the land out of which it is payable, and having no such interest, is not entitled as of common right to the remedy of distress. It is, then, any rent *expressly* made payable out of land, other than rent payable by a tenant to a reversioner. For instance, if A sells land to B in fee simple, he may agree to accept an annual sum of money from B in perpetuity instead of an immediate lump sum, and it is expressly agreed that the fee simple estate shall be charged in favour of A with a power of distress should the rent fall into arrears, the rent (whatever name may be given to it by local usage, such as quit rent,

---

[556] *Gilbert on Rents*, p. 9. For the history of the subject, see Holdsworth, *History of English Law*, vol. vii. pp. 262 et seq.   [557] Litt, s. 213.

[558] Co Litt 22b.   [559] P. 16, ante.

[560] Litt, s. 213; *Gilbert on Rents*, p. 9; Co Litt 78b, 142b; Bacon's *New Abridgement of the Law* under the title Rent (A) 1.

[561] *C H Bailey Ltd v Memorial Enterprises Ltd* [1974] 1 WLR 728 at 732, per Lord DENNING MR, approved in *United Scientific Holdings Ltd v Burnley BC* [1978] AC 904 at 956, per Lord SALMON; *Homes (T & E) Ltd v Robinson* [1979] 1 WLR 452; *Bradshaw v Pawley* [1980] 1 WLR 10 (rent payable under contract from a date prior to execution of lease). See also *Property Holding Co Ltd v Clark* [1948] 1 KB 630 at 648, per EVERSHED LJ; [1991] Conv 270 (R. G. Lee).   [562] *United Scientific Holdings Ltd v Burnley BC*, supra, at 935.

ground rent, chief rent, etc.) is a rentcharge. "It is called a rentcharge because the land for payment thereof is charged with a distresse."[563] The circumstances in which rentcharges can now be created have been curtailed by the Rentcharges Act 1977, and most existing rentcharges are being phased out. The detail of the law of rentcharges will be considered in chapter 20.

(c) Rent-seck

Formerly, if a rent was made payable out of a fee simple and for some reason an express power of distress was not reserved, the rent was called a *rent-seck* or dry rent—*dry* because it did not confer the power to distrain.[564]

Thus, at common law the three kinds of rent are rentservice, rentcharge and rent-seck. But rents-seck have long ceased to exist, for the inability of their owners to distrain was removed by the Landlord and Tenant Act 1730,[565] which enacted that the owners of rents-seck, rents of assize and chief rents should have the same remedy by distress as was available to the owner of a rentservice.

LINDLEY LJ said:

Bearing in mind what was done by the Act of Geo. II, which by section 5 gave a power of distress for all rents, there is now no magic in the word rentcharge. Whether you speak of a rentcharge or only of a rent, if it is a rent and not merely a sum covenanted to be paid, seems to me to be utterly immaterial, because under the Act of Geo. II you have a power of distress in respect of it.[566]

The same remedy is given by the Law of Property Act 1925.[567] For the purpose of this Act, rent "includes a rentservice or a rentcharge, or other rent, toll, duty, royalty, or annual or periodical payment, in money or money's worth, reserved or issuing out of or charged upon land, but does not include mortgage interest."[568]

We may now proceed to set out the remedies that are available to a landlord for the recovery of the rentservice due to him.

(2) Distress[569]

The right of distress which has existed in England since the Conquest was originally allowed for the enforcement of a great number of services that in feudal days might be incidental to tenure, such as rentservice, suit-service, heriot-service, aids, reliefs and so on,[570] but most of these are now obsolete, and practically the only purpose for which common law distress is exercisable is the recovery of rent in arrear.[571] It is not dependent on an express right of re-entry, and the landlord is entitled to exercise it unless he contracts not to do so.[572]

The value of the remedy to a landlord is that he can seize and sell the chattels found on the land and thus procure the rent without the necessity of taking legal proceedings. It is a

---

[563] Co Litt 144a. See also *Jenkin R Lewis & Sons Ltd v Kerman* [1971] Ch 477 at 484.   [564] Litt, s. 218.

[565] S. 5.   [566] *Re Lord Gerard and Beecham's Contract* [1894] 3 Ch 295 at 313.   [567] S. 121.

[568] S. 205(1)(xxiii).

[569] See generally Tanney and Travers, *Distress for Rent* (2000); Rook, *Distress for Rent* (1999).

[570] Pp. 41–2, 84–5, ante.

[571] The common law right to recover compensation by way of distress for damage caused by trespassing livestock was replaced by a statutory provision for detention and sale: Animals Act 1971, s. 7.

[572] *Homes (T & E) Ltd v Robinson* [1979] 1 WLR 452 at 453, per TEMPLEMAN LJ.

self-help remedy[573] which operates outside the machinery of the courts except in the case of tenancies subject to the Rent Acts.

(a) The right to distrain

It is essential that the reversion should be vested in the distrainor at the time when the rent falls due and also when the distress is levied. Thus if L has assigned the reversion to X at a time when rent is due, L cannot distrain, since he no longer holds the reversion; and X is under the same disability, since he was not the reversioner at the critical moment.

(b) Time and place

Distress cannot be made until the rent is in arrear, which does not occur until the day after it is due,[574] nor can it be levied between sunset and sunrise.[575]

As a general rule the right of seizure is confined to chattels upon the actual land out of which the rent issues, but it may be extended by agreement to other premises, and by the Distress for Rent Act 1737 goods which have been fraudulently and secretly removed by a tenant after the rent became due, in order to avoid distress, may be seized by the landlord within thirty days wherever found.

A distrainor must enter the demised premises[576] and in so doing may commit what in anyone else would be a trespass,[577] as for example by entry through an unlocked door;[578] but he may neither break open a door, whether of a dwelling-house or of an outhouse,[579] nor effect an entrance through a closed but unfastened window.[580]

(c) Distrainable goods

The general rule of the common law is that all personal chattels found upon the premises out of which the rent issues, whether they belong to the tenant or to a stranger, can be distrained, but this extensive power is cut down in two ways.

(1) PRIVILEGED GOODS

It is outside the scope of this work to deal with this question in detail. It will suffice here to say that the following articles are absolutely privileged in the sense that they can never be seized:[581]

machinery belonging to a third person which is on an agricultural holding under a contract of hire;[582]

---

[573] At common law he could only retain the goods: a power of sale was given by the Distress for Rent Act 1689, s. 1. For proposals for reform, see p. 271, post.

[574] *Duppa v Mayo* (1669) 1 Wms Saund 275; *Re Aspinall* [1961] Ch 526.

[575] *Tutton v Darke* (1860) 29 LJ Ex 271.

[576] *Evans v South Ribble BC* [1992] QB 757; [1993] Conv 77 (J. E. M. Sulek) (posting draft walking possession agreement and distress notice through letter-box in sealed envelope insufficient).

[577] *Long v Clarke* [1894] 1 QB 119 at 122.   [578] *Southam v Smout* [1964] 1 QB 308.

[579] *American Concentrated Must Corpn v Hendry* (1893) 62 LJQB 388.

[580] *Nash v Lucas* (1867) LR 2 QB 590.

[581] For further detail, see *Smith's Leading Cases* (13th edn), vol. 1, p. 137 (notes on *Simpson v Hartopp* (1744) Willes 512).

[582] Agricultural Holdings Act 1986, s. 18. The Act does not apply to tenancies beginning on or after 1 September 1995. In the case of a farm business tenancy the Agricultural Tenancies Act 1995 contains no restrictions on distress.

livestock belonging to a third person which is on an agricultural holding solely for breeding purposes;[583]

animals *ferae naturae* (wild animals) in which there is no right of property;[584]

things delivered to a person in the way of his trade, such as cloth given to a tailor to be made into a suit;

things in actual use, such as a horse drawing a cart;

things in the custody of the law, such as property already taken in execution;

such tools, books, vehicles and other items of equipment as are necessary for the tenant's personal use in his employment, business or vocation;[585]

such clothing, bedding, furniture, household equipment and provisions as are necessary for satisfying the basic domestic needs of the tenant and his family.[586]

The following things are conditionally privileged, that is to say, they can be seized only if there is not a sufficiency of other distrainable goods to be found upon the premises:

beasts of the plough;

sheep and instruments of husbandry;

the instruments of a man's trade or profession, such as the text-books of a solicitor;

the livestock of a third person found on an agricultural holding as a result of a contract of agistment.[587]

(2) GOODS BELONGING TO THIRD PARTIES

BLACKBURN J said:

The general rule at common law was that whatever was found upon the demised premises, whether belonging to a stranger or not, might be seized by the landlord and held as a distress till the rent was paid or the service performed. This state of things produced no harm, because at common law the landlord not being able to sell the distress he generally gave up the goods as soon as he found they were not the tenant's, as his continuing to hold them would not induce the tenant to pay. But in the reign of William and Mary a very harsh and unjust law was passed by which the right was given to the landlord to sell any goods seized, and to apply the proceeds to the payment of the rent unless the tenant or the owner of the goods first paid it; and this held out a great temptation to a landlord to seize the goods of a stranger although he knew they were not the tenant's.[588]

This has gradually been put on a more equitable footing, and at the present day the Law of Distress Amendment Act 1908,[589] except in the case of certain specified goods,[590] provides

---

[583] Ibid., s. 18.

[584] Co Litt 47a. For discussions of the acquisition and retention of property in animals *ferae naturae*, see *Hamps v Darby* [1948] 2 KB 311 (racing pigeons); *Kearry v Pattinson* [1939] 1 KB 471 (bees).

[585] Law of Distress Amendment Act 1888, s. 4; County Courts Act 1984, s. 89(1), as substituted by Courts and Legal Services Act 1990, s. 15(2).   [586] Ibid.

[587] Agricultural Holdings Act 1986, s. 18. "Agisted livestock" means livestock belonging to another person which has been taken in by the tenant of an agricultural holding to be fed at a fair price: s. 18(5). If distrained because of an insufficiency of other goods the landlord cannot thereby recover more than the amount due and unpaid under the contract of agistment. For farm business tenancies, see n. 582, supra.

[588] *Lyons v Elliott* (1876) 1 QBD 210 at 213.   [589] S. 1.

[590] I.e. goods belonging to the husband, wife or civil partner of the tenant; goods comprised in a settlement made by the tenant; goods of which the tenant is the reputed owner: *Perdana Properties Bhd v United Orient*

a means by which a lodger or under-tenant or indeed any person not being a tenant of the premises and not having any beneficial interest in the tenancy, may avoid the seizure of his belongings. Suppose for instance that:

L has leased premises to T, and that X is the lodger or the under-tenant of T. If in such a case L levies a distress on any goods belonging to X for arrears of rent due from T, X may serve L with a notice declaring that:

T has no right of property in the goods;

the goods are not goods excepted from the Act;

so much rent is due from X to T;

future instalments will become due on stated days;

he will pay such rent to L.

With this notice, which is of no effect unless it contains the requisite written declarations,[591] X must also send an inventory of his goods. If L distrains on the goods of X after receipt of this notice and inventory, he is guilty of an illegal distress, and X may apply to a justice of the peace or to a magistrate for the restoration of his goods. The protection afforded by the Act applies only to a tenant whose rent equals the full annual value of the premises.

(d) Levying of distress

A landlord may distrain in person, or by employing a certificated bailiff, who has been authorised to levy distress (either in the one particular case or in general cases) by a certificate in writing under the hand of a county court judge.[592]

Such a bailiff should be provided by the landlord with a distress warrant authorising him to make the levy. The first step is to seize and impound the goods. At common law the impounding had to take place off the premises but now it is lawful to secure the goods in some part of the premises themselves.[593]

The usual practice is to leave someone in possession, but this is not essential, for goods are deemed to be impounded if "walking possession" is taken of them, that is, if they are left on the premises but periodically inspected by the bailiff.[594] If the bailiff is in walking possession of the goods and is later disbarred from entering the premises, he is not entitled forcibly to re-enter them, unless he has been expelled by force or deliberately excluded by the tenant.[595] Anyone who interferes with goods after they have been impounded is liable in treble damages for pound breach.[596] As soon as the seizure is complete, the landlord is bound to give the tenant[597] notice of the distress and of the place, if any, to which the goods have been

---

Leasing Co Sdn Bhd [1981] 1 WLR 1496; and agisted livestock on an agricultural holding: Law of Distress Amendment Act 1908, s. 4(1), as amended by Civil Partnership Act 2004, s. 261, Sch. 27; Agricultural Holdings Act 1986, s. 100, Sch. 14.

591 *Druce & Co Ltd v Beaumont Property Trust Ltd* [1935] 2 KB 257. It may be signed by an agent: *Lawrence Chemical Co Ltd v Rubenstein* [1982] 1 WLR 284. See *Rhodes v Allied Dunbar Pension Services Ltd* [1987] 1 WLR 1703.

592 Law of Distress Amendment Act 1888, s. 7; Distress for Rent Rules 1988 (SI 1988 No. 2050), rr. 3–5, as amended by SI 1999 Nos. 2360 and 2564. See also *Rhodes v Allied Dunbar Pension Services Ltd* [1989] 1 WLR 800.

593 Distress for Rent Act 1737, s. 10.   594 *Lavell & Co Ltd v O'Leary* [1933] 2 KB 200.

595 *Mcleod v Butterwick* [1998] 1 WLR 1603.   596 Distress for Rent Act 1689, s. 3.

597 Ibid., s. 1; Distress for Rent Rules 1988 (SI 1988 No. 2050), r. 12, Appendix 2, Form 7.

removed,[598] and he is not at liberty to sell them until five days have elapsed since the service of the notice. Thus a tenant is allowed five days within which to pay what is due, but he is entitled to an extension of this period to fifteen days if he makes a request in writing to this effect to the landlord and gives security for any additional expense that the delay may involve.[599] The sale is generally, though not necessarily, by auction, and it usually takes place on the premises unless the tenant has requested in writing that the goods shall be removed to a public auction-room. If it does not produce sufficient proceeds, no second sale is as a general rule permissible.[600]

Only six years' arrears of rent may be recovered by the remedy of distress, whether or not the lease is by deed.[601] When the demised premises consist of an agricultural holding with the Agricultural Holdings Act 1986 only one year's arrears are recoverable by this method.[602] No such restriction applies in the case of a farm business tenancy under the Agricultural Tenancies Act 1995.

(e) Amount recoverable

The tenant may set off any sums due to him from the landlord against a claim to levy distress. Otherwise a landlord would be able to recover more by distress than he could in an action for the debt.[603]

(f) Law reform

In 1969 the Payne Committee recommended the abolition of the "highly complex technical and archaic law" of distress for rent.[604] This was also the view of the Law Commission in 1991, which, however, recommended[605] that distress should not be abolished until improvements to the court system make the other remedies available to landlords effective alternatives to distress. In 2003 the Lord Chancellor's Department published a White Paper[606]

---

[598] Distress for Rent Act 1737, s. 9.   [599] Law of Distress Amendment Act 1888, s. 6.

[600] *Rawlence and Squarey v Spicer* [1935] 1 KB 412.   [601] Limitation Act 1980, s. 19.

[602] Agricultural Holdings Act 1986, s. 16. The Act does not apply to tenancies beginning on or after 1 September 1995.

[603] *Eller v Grovecrest Investments Ltd* [1995] QB 272; *Fuller v Happy Shopper Markets Ltd* [2001] 1 WLR 1681 at 1692, per Lightman J ("a landlord is bound to take the greatest care before levying distress that there are no claims on the part of the tenant which may be available by way of equitable set-off . . . he would be well advised to give notice of his intention and invite the tenant to agree what is owing . . . the human rights implications of levying distress must be in the forefront of the mind of the landlord").

[604] Report of the Committee on the Enforcement of Judgment Debts (1969), Cmnd 3909, paras. 912–32. See also Law Commission Interim Report on Distress for Rent 1966; Law Commission Report on Rentcharges 1975 (Law Com No. 68), para. 94.

[605] Report on Distress for Rent (Law Com No. 194). See [1985] Conv 451 (A. Hill-Smith) and (1985) Law Notes 21 (M. Maddock), arguing that distress is speedier and more comprehensive than an action for the arrears of rent. In *Wharfland v South London Co-operative Building Society Co Ltd* [1995] 2 EGLR 21 at 22 (landlord may not levy distress against goods of assignee in respect of arrears of rent due before assignment and owed by the assignor) Crowley QC said: "At one stage the remedy of distress seemed to be passing out of use, but it appears that it has come back into fashion." Cf, however, *Salford Van Hire (Contracts) Ltd v Bocholt Developments Ltd* [1995[2 EGLR 50 where Hirst LJ said at 52: "The remedy of distress, on the terms set out in the current legislation, appears to have outlived its usefulness as a just remedy."

[606] *Effective Enforcement* (March 2003, Cm 5744), following (in this respect) a consultation paper, *Distress for Rent* (Enforcement Review Consultation Paper 5, May 2001). It is understood that the Government proposes to implement these changes as soon as Parliamentary time allows: Law Commission Thirty-Eighth Annual Report 2003/04 (Law Com No. 288), para 3.36; Thirty-Ninth Annual Report 2004/05 (Law Com No. 294), para. 3.20.

setting out the Government's view that the current procedures for distress for rent are not an appropriate or proportionate[607] remedy and should be abolished for residential properties, but that a modified form of enforcement, with additional safeguards, should continue to be available in relation to commercial properties through a new system of "Commercial Rent Arrears Recovery". The terminology is to be modernised: the words "distress", "distraint", "execute", "levy" and "walking possession" will no longer be used, and will be replaced by the phrase "taking legal control of goods".[608] The Commercial Rent Arrears Recovery system will be available only for the collection of rent (and not service charges or any other variable charge collected under commercial leases); its use must be proportionate to the amount of rent owed;[609] and it will no longer be permitted for landlords to carry out enforcement action for themselves, but they may use licensed enforcement agents (without the need first to apply to court for prior authority); and fourteen days' notice must be given to the tenant before sale of the goods.[610]

(3) Action for Arrears of Rent

(a) Arrears recoverable

Whether a lease is made by deed or not, only six years' arrears of rent are recoverable by action.[611] Thus a landlord must bring his action within six years after the rent has become due or has been acknowledged in writing to be due, or after some payment has been made by the tenant.[612] A payment of part of the rent does not entitle the landlord to sue for the remainder more than six years after it became due.[613]

But while the relation of landlord and tenant continues under a lease for a fixed term of years, the right of the landlord to recover rent is not *totally* barred by non-payment no matter how long the rent is in arrear.[614] Suppose, for instance, that: A holds lands of B for ninety-nine years at £100 a year, and that A has not paid rent for twenty-five years. B's right to recover rent is not extinguished, but is limited to the recovery of the last six years' arrears.

The only case in which the right of a landlord is extinguished altogether occurs in unregistered land where for a period of twelve years the rent has been paid to a third person who wrongfully claims to be entitled to the reversion.[615]

---

[607] For a discussion of the vulnerability of the law of distress to challenge under the European Convention on Human Rights, see *Independent Review of Bailiff Law* (the Beatson Report), June 2000, paras. 2.21–2.26, summarised in *Effective Enforcement*, supra, p. 36, n. 30; *Fuller v Happy Shopper Markets Ltd* [2001] 1 WLR 1681 at 1692.   [608] *Effective Enforcement*, supra, p. 8.

[609] The details of this have not yet been worked out: ibid., p. 45.   [610] Ibid., pp. 44–6.

[611] Limitation Act 1980, s. 19. *Romain v Scuba TV Ltd* [1997] QB 887 (time limit applies to guarantor in respect of his undertaking to pay rent reserved by lease); *Tabarrok v EDC Lord & Co* The Times, 14 February 1997 (where negligent advice causes plaintiff to guarantee another's debts, time runs as soon as plaintiff suffers loss).

For the recovery of rent overpaid by the tenant whether due to mistake of fact or law, see *Kleinwort Benson Ltd v Lincoln City Council* [1999] 1 AC 153; (1999) 115 LQR 170 (J. M. Finnis); [1999] Conv 40 (M. P. Thompson); [1999] 3 L & TR 12 (C. Lamont); *Nurdin & Peacock plc v D B Ramsden & Co Ltd* [1999] 1 WLR 1249, p. 141, ante.   [612] Limitation Act 1980, s. 29(5).

[613] Ibid., s. 29(6).   [614] *Grant v Ellis* (1841) 9 M & W 113; *Archbold v Scully* (1861) 9 HL Cas 360.

[615] *Lehain v Philpott* (1875) LR 10 Exch 242; pp. 132, ante. Where the lease is registered, see p. 145, ante.

(b) Inter-relation of remedies

A landlord cannot pursue the two remedies of action and distress at one and the same time. If he has levied a distress, he cannot bring an action for recovery until he has sold the distrained articles and found the purchase money insufficient to satisfy his demand.[616] If he has sued to judgment first, then, even though the judgment remains unsatisfied, he loses his remedy of distress altogether for that particular rent.[617]

(4) Forfeiture[618]

(a) Right to forfeit

(1) DISTINCTION BETWEEN COVENANT AND CONDITIONS

The breach of a covenant by a tenant does not entitle the landlord to resume possession by a re-entry upon the premises, unless the right to do so is expressly reserved in the lease. On the other hand, an undertaking by the tenant which is framed not as a mere covenant, but as a condition, carries with it at common law a right of re-entry if the condition is broken. Whether a stipulation amounts to a covenant or a condition is sometimes a question of considerable nicety, but it depends entirely upon the intention of the parties. A condition is a clause which shows a clear intention on the part of the landlord, not merely that the tenant shall be personally liable if he fails in his contractual duties, but that the landlord shall have the right to determine the lease in the event of such a failure. The tenancy is to remain conditional upon the fulfilment by the tenant of his obligations. In an early case, BAYLEY J said:[619] "In a lease for years no precise form of words is necessary to make a condition. It is sufficient if it appears that the words used were intended to have the effect of creating a condition. They must be the words of the landlord, because he is to impose the condition."

In this case it was "stipulated and conditioned" in the lease that the tenant should not assign or underlet the premises, otherwise than to his wife or children, and it was held that these words were sufficient to create a condition. Mere words of agreement, however, as for example when the tenant "agrees that he will not assign the premises without the consent of the landlord", create nothing more than a covenant.[620]

(2) EXPRESS PROVISO FOR RE-ENTRY AND FORFEITURE OF LEASE

It is, however, the usual practice for a lease to contain, in clear and unmistakable language, an express clause which reserves to the landlord the right of re-entry[621] if one or more of the covenants are broken, and which provides that upon re-entry the lease shall be forfeited.[622]

---

[616] *Archbold v Scully* (1861) 9 HL Cas 360.   [617] *Chancellor v Webster* (1893) 9 TLR 568.

[618] Pawlowski, *The Forfeiture of Leases* (1993), which contains a useful overview of the whole subject in chap. 1; Kenny, *Forfeiture of Tenancies* (1999).   [619] *Doe d Henniker v Watt* (1828) 8 B & C 308 at 315.

[620] *Crawley v Price* (1875) LR 10 QB 302.

[621] A right of re-entry is capable of subsisting as a legal interest: LPA 1925, s. 1(2)(e), and the express grant of such a right is a registrable disposition: LRA 2002, s. 27(2)(e). However, no entry need be noted in the title of the reversionary estate: LRR 2003, r. 77; H & B, paras. 8.17, 8.20.

[622] See *Richard Clarke & Co Ltd v Widnall* (1976) 33 P & CR 339, where a clause in a lease under which the landlord was entitled to serve a notice to terminate in the event of a breach of covenant to pay rent was

The virtue of this is that the landlord,[623] if he finds himself saddled with an impecunious tenant who is a persistent defaulter in the payment of rent, may regain possession instead of being driven to constant litigation.

The following is a precedent of a proviso for forfeiture:

Provided always that if any part of the said rent shall be in arrears for 21 days, whether lawfully demanded or not, the landlord or his assigns may re-enter upon the said premises, and immediately thereupon the said term shall absolutely determine.

(b) Effect of breach

Where the lease contains such a proviso, the effect of allowing the rent to fall into arrears for more than twenty-one days is to render the tenant's interest liable to forfeiture, and not *ipso facto* to cause a forfeiture. However clearly the proviso may state that the lease shall "be void" or "determine" on breach of condition, it has been held in a long series of decisions that its only effect is to render the lease liable to be determined at the option of the landlord.[624] It is only if he does some unequivocal act which shows his intention to end it that the lease will be terminated.[625] Thus an actual entry by the landlord[626] or the grant of a lease to a new tenant works a forfeiture,[627] but the usual practice at the present day is to sue for the recovery of possession instead of making a re-entry;[628] for, as WILLES J said: "The bringing of an action of ejectment is equivalent to the ancient entry. It is an act unequivocal in the sense that it asserts the right of possession upon every ground that may turn out to be available to the party claiming to re-enter."[629] Under the Civil Procedure Rules

construed as a proviso for re-entry. Cf *Clays Lane Housing Cooperative Ltd v Patrick* (1984) 49 P & CR 72 (for a clause to be a forfeiture clause it must bring the lease to an end earlier than the actual termination date).

[623] Cf *Rother District Investments Ltd v Corke* [2004] 1 EGLR 47 (purchaser of head lease not entitled to re-enter and forfeit sub-lease until it became legal proprietor by registration of transfer; but as against the sub-lessee could not deny the effectiveness of purported forfeiture. LIGHTMAN J found four interrelated grounds, including (at [16]): "as between what had been a 'forfeiture by estoppel' between [purchaser] and [sub-lessee] was 'fed' and became a full legal forfeiture valid against the world" when purchaser registered as proprietor of head lease).

[624] *Davenport v R* (1877) 3 App Cas 115 at 128–9. This case, and many others, refer to the lease being "voidable" on forfeiture, but this language is misleading: the lease is not annulled *ab initio*. From the moment the forfeiture takes effect, the tenant's estate no longer exists and the landlord again holds his own estate as if there had been no lease. But the tenant's estate was (and remains) good up to the moment of forfeiture, so rendering his possession lawful and maintaining his liability for payment of rent; he is liable for damages or mesne profits for trespass for wrongful possession only thereafter: *Hartshorne v Watson* (1838) 4 Bing NC 178 at 182–3, per TINDAL CJ; *Elliott v Boynton* [1924] 1 Ch 236.

[625] *Toleman v Portbury* (1871) LR 6 QB 245 at 250; *Eaton Square Properties Ltd v Beveridge* [1993] EGCS 91 ("it is difficult to imagine a more unequivocal act than changing the locks", per LLOYD LJ).

[626] See *Hone v Daejan Properties Ltd* (1976) 239 EG 427, where re-entry by a landlord who had taken an assignment of his tenant's mortgage did not effect a forfeiture. He was "wearing two hats" (of landlord and mortgagee in possession) and that was equivocal.

[627] But not an agreement with a sub-lessee that he remain in occupation as lessee of a term of an *existing* sub-lease: *Ashton v Sobelman* [1987] 1 WLR 177.

[628] In the case of tenancies of residential premises a re-entry other than pursuant to a court order for possession is prohibited. See p. 331, post.   [629] *Grimwood v Moss* (1872) LR 7 CP 360 at 364.

1998 it is the issue by the court[630] of a claim form at the request of the claimant which is equivalent to re-entry.[631] But the forfeiture does not become final until the landlord has obtained judgment for possession. Until then, for example, the covenants in a lease remain potentially good, since the forfeiture may not be established; or relief against forfeiture may be granted to the tenant, in which case the lease is re-established as from the beginning.[632] But where an application for relief is pending the position appears to be one-sided. As STEPHENSON LJ said:[633]

A landlord who has unequivocally elected to determine a lease by serving a writ and forfeiting it cannot himself rely on any covenants of the lease in any shape or form, or any covenants in it, but the tenant who has not elected to determine the lease can do so.

The landlord may forfeit a lease in respect of part only of the premises where that part is physically separate and capable of being distinctly let.[634]

(c) Waiver of right to forfeit

The question whether the landlord has by some unequivocal act elected to treat the lease as forfeited is an important one from the point of view of waiver. Common law dislikes conditions of forfeiture, and it will always treat such a condition as waived and therefore unenforceable if, after the act of forfeiture has been committed, the landlord clearly shows that he regards the tenancy as still existing. The two essentials for waiver are that:

(1) the landlord must be aware of the commission of an act of forfeiture by the tenant, and

(2) he must do "some unequivocal act recognizing the continued existence of the lease".[635]

Thus a merely passive attitude on his part has no effect,[636] nor does his failure to take action because he thinks that he will not be able to prove a suspected breach of covenant;[637]

---

[630] CPR, r. 7.2. For possession claims generally, see pp. 117, ante; 330, post. The landlord cannot then withdraw and reinstate the lease: G. S. Fashions Ltd v B & Q plc [1995] 1 WLR 1088; and it is open to the tenant to accept the forfeiture and so terminate future rights and liabilities under the lease: Kingston upon Thames Royal London Borough Council v Marlow [1996] 17 EG 187.

[631] Under the old law it was the service of the writ of possession: Canas Property Co Ltd v KL Television Services Ltd [1970] 2 QB 433; Richards v De Freitas (1975) 29 P & CR 1; Ashton v Sobelman [1987] 1 WLR 177; Hammersmith and Fulham LBC v Top Shop Centres Ltd [1990] Ch 237; Capital and City Holdings Ltd v Dean Warburg Ltd (1988) 58 P & CR 346.

[632] Driscoll v Church Comrs for England [1957] 1 QB 330 at 339, per DENNING LJ. For the effect of relief against forfeiture, see p. 277, post.

[633] Peninsular Maritime Ltd v Padseal Ltd (1981) 259 EG 860 at 866. See also Meadows v Clerical, Medical and General Life Assurance Society [1981] Ch 70 ("The tenancy has a trance-like existence pendente lite; none can assert with assurance whether it is alive or dead", per Sir Robert MEGARRY at 75); Associated Deliveries Ltd v Harrison (1984) 50 P & CR 91; Official Custodian for Charities v Mackey (No 2) [1985] 1 WLR 1308; Hillgate House Ltd v Expert Clothing Service & Sales Ltd [1987] 1 EGLR 65; Ivory Gate Ltd v Spetale (1998) 77 P & CR 141; Mount Cook Land Ltd v Media Business Centre Ltd [2004] 2 P & CR 25 (discontinuance of claim terminated lease's "shadowy state").

[634] GMS Syndicate Ltd v Gary Elliott Ltd [1982] Ch 1, p. 288, post. See LT(C)A 1995, s. 21.
For restrictions on forfeiture of a residential lease for non-payment of a service charge, see HA 1996, s. 81, as amended by CLRA 2002, s. 170; and for other restrictions on forfeiture of residential leases, see CLRA 2002, ss. 167, 168; [2005] EG 185 (J. Driscoll).

[635] Matthews v Smallwood [1910] 1 Ch 777 at 786, per PARKER J, M & B p. 548; Dendy v Nicholl (1858) 4 CBNS 376.   [636] Perry v Davis (1858) 3 CBNS 769.

[637] Chrisdell Ltd v Johnson [1987] 2 EGLR 123.

but on the other hand (and this applies to all conditions of forfeiture, whether in respect of the non-payment of rent or of the non-performance of other covenants), a waiver will be implied if a landlord, with knowledge of the breach:[638]

(1) demands or sues for rent,[639] or accepts payment of it notwithstanding that his acceptance is stated to be "without prejudice",[640] or a clerk of his agents accepts it by mistake;[641] or

(2) distrains for rent whether due before or after the breach;[642] or

(3) grants a new lease to the defaulting tenant.[643]

It is a question of fact whether money has been tendered and accepted as rent,[644] and its acceptance as such is in law conclusive against the landlord. Intention is irrelevant. As Lord DENNING MR said: "It does not matter that the landlords did not intend to waive. The very fact that they accepted the rent with the knowledge constitutes the waiver." [645]

The waiver of a covenant or of a condition does not operate as a general waiver, but extends only to the particular breach in question.[646] An important distinction should be noticed between continuing and non-continuing breaches of covenant, for acceptance of rent or the levy of distress after the breach of a continuing covenant, for example, to keep in repair the premises,[647] waives the forfeiture only up to the date of distress or payment of rent. The proviso for re-entry may be enforced if the breach subsequently continues.[648]

But when once a landlord unequivocally and finally elects to treat a lease as determined, as, for instance, where he serves a writ for recovery of the land, no subsequent receipt of rent or other act will amount to waiver so as to deprive him of his right to enforce the clause of re-entry.[649]

---

[638] *Metropolitan Properties Co Ltd v Cordery* (1979) 39 P & CR 10 (landlords' acceptance of rent for flat with knowledge, through their porters, of facts which pointed to breach of covenant held to be waiver). Cf *Trustees of Henry Smith's Charity v Willson* [1983] QB 316 (uncommunicated rent demand); *Re A Debtor (No 13A-IO-1995)* [1995] 1 WLR 1127 (demand for rent due before right to forfeit not waiver); *Official Custodian for Charities v Parway Estates Developments Ltd* [1985] Ch 151 (publication in London Gazette of compulsory liquidation held not to be imputed knowledge so as to constitute waiver); *Cornillie v Saha* (1996) 72 P & CR 147.

[639] *Dendy v Nicholl*, supra; dist. *Clarke v Grant* [1950] 1 KB 104.

[640] *Segal Securities Ltd v Thoseby* [1963] 1 QB 887.

[641] *Central Estates (Belgravia) Ltd v Woolgar (No 2)* [1972] 1 WLR 1048. See also *Expert Clothing Service & Sales Ltd v Hillgate House Ltd* [1986] Ch 340, M & B p. 542 (proffering of negotiating document held not to be waiver where no acceptance of rent or demand for rent involved): *Church Comrs for England v Nodjoumi* (1985) 51 P & CR 155 (service of s. 146 notice held not to be waiver of right to forfeit lease on grounds other than those set out in notice); *Re National Jazz Centre Ltd* [1988] 2 EGLR 57 (mere entry into negotiations held not to be waiver).   [642] *Doe d David v Williams* (1835) 7 C & P 322.

[643] *Ward v Day* (1864) 5 B & S 359.

[644] *John Lewis Properties plc v Viscount Chelsea* [1993] 2 EGLR 77 ("arguments very finely balanced").

[645] *Windmill Investments (London) Ltd v Milano Restaurant Ltd* [1962] 2 QB 373; see also *Bader Properties Ltd v Linley Property Investments Ltd* (1967) 19 P & CR 620 at 638–41; *Central Estates (Belgravia) Ltd v Woolgar (No 2)*, supra; *David Blackstone Ltd v Burnetts (West End) Ltd* [1973] 1 WLR 1487; *Welch v Birrane* (1974) 29 P & CR 102; (1988) 138 NLJ 95 (H. W. Wilkinson); *Van Haarlam v Kasner* [1992] 2 EGLR 59; [1993] Conv 288 (J. Martin); *Iperion Investments Corpn v Broadwalk House Residents Ltd* [1992] 2 EGLR 235.

[646] LPA 1925, s. 148.

[647] *Penton v Barnett* [1898] 1 QB 276; *Cooper v Henderson* (1982) 263 EG 592 (covenant as to user); *City and Westminster Properties (1934) Ltd v Mudd* [1959] Ch 129, M & B p. 550; cf *Farimani v Gates* (1984) 271 EG 887.

[648] *Doe d Hemmings v Durnford* (1832) 2 Cr & J 667; *Doe d Baker v Jones* (1850) 5 Exch 498.

[649] *Civil Service Co-operative Society Ltd v McGrigor's Trustee* [1923] 2 Ch 347; *Evans v Enever* [1920] 2 KB 315.

(d) Formal demand for rent

In the precedent which is set out above it will be noticed that the landlord reserves a power of re-entry for non-payment of rent *whether lawfully demanded or not*. The object of inserting these words is to avoid the strictness of the common law which requires the landlord, failing a contrary agreement, to make a formal demand upon the premises themselves for the exact amount of rent due, and to make it between the hours of sunrise and sunset so as to afford the tenant an opportunity of counting out the money while light remains.[650] This common law rule has, however, been partly abrogated by a statute which enacts that, even though the formal demand has not been dispensed with in the lease, yet, if one-half year's rent is in arrear and there are not sufficient distrainable goods upon the premises and a power of re-entry has been reserved, the landlord can recover the premises by action at the end of the period fixed in the proviso for re-entry without making any formal demand of rent.[651] The restricted nature of this statutory modification makes it desirable, in the interests of a sure and speedy remedy, to obviate by express words the necessity for a formal demand.

(e) Relief against forfeiture

One of the aims of the old Court of Chancery was to prevent the enforcement of a legal right from producing hardship, and therefore, since the sole object of a right of re-entry was to give a landlord security for the rent, it was always prepared to relieve the tenant against the forfeiture, provided that he paid all that was due by way of arrears of rent, together with costs and interest. In this way, the landlord obtained all that the right of re-entry was intended to secure to him, and it would be inequitable for him to take advantage of the forfeiture.[652] However, as ARDEN J has said:[653]

It can . . . be seen that the discretion to grant relief is based on solid principle and not simply to be exercised in a manner that the court considers fair on the particular facts before it. Apart from history, there are, no doubt, sound reasons of policy why the discretion should be circumscribed and consistently exercised. If the courts do not uphold the terms of the lease except in limited situations, there will be a strong disincentive to landlords to invest in property and let it out on lease. By enforcing rights of property, the law promotes the use and availability of this resource within society, and property can be used, as in this case, for commercial purposes, which can serve to increase society's prosperity. Not all landlords are large corporations. The principles have been established by the higher courts and over centuries. They cannot be swept aside by this court.

Originally a tenant might petition for and obtain this relief at any time after he had been ejected under the power of re-entry, but his right has been restricted by statute. The present position depends upon sections 210–12 of the Common Law Procedure Act 1852 and section 38 of the Supreme Court Act 1981.[654] The result of these Acts is as follows.

[650] Notes to *Duppa v Mayo* (1669) 1 Wms Saund 275 at 287.

[651] Common Law Procedure Act 1852, s. 210.

[652] *Howard v Fanshawe* [1895] 2 Ch 581, and authorities there cited; *Inntrepreneur Pub Co (CPC) Ltd v Langton* [2000] 1 EGLR 34 (possibility of successful claim by tenant to set off potential damages for breach of EC Treaty, art. 85 (now art. 81 EC), in respect of challenge to beer tie not sufficient evidence of ability to pay: relief against forfeiture refused). For a solicitor's liability in negligence for failing to make application for relief from forfeiture, see *Vision Golf Ltd v Weightmans* [2005] All ER (D) 379 (Jul).

[653] *Inntrepreneur Pub Co (CPC) Ltd v Langton*, supra, at 38.

[654] Replacing Landlord and Tenant Act 1730, ss. 2, 4, and Supreme Court of Judicature (Consolidation) Act 1925, s. 46 respectively. Once the Constitutional Reform Act 2005 is in force, SCA 1981 will be known as the

If the landlord sues for possession and the tenant at any time before the trial pays or tenders to the landlord or pays into court the rent and arrears and costs, all further proceedings are stayed and he regains possession under the old lease.[655] It has been held, however, that there is no case for such a stay of proceedings unless six months' rent is in arrear.[656]

If the tenant does not, or cannot, take this opportunity and judgment is given against him, he may, nevertheless, apply for relief within six months after execution of the judgment.[657] If he applies within this period, the court is empowered to relieve him from the forfeiture subject to such terms and conditions as to payment of rent, costs and otherwise, as could formerly have been imposed by the old Court of Chancery. The effect of a grant of relief is that he holds the land according to the terms of the original lease without the necessity of a new lease.[658]

The grant of relief within this extended time of six months, however, is a matter of discretion, the general principle being that, so far as rent is concerned, the landlord can claim nothing more than to be restored to the position that he would have occupied had the forfeiture not been incurred. The position has been stated in the following authoritative passage:

The function of the court in exercising this equitable jurisdiction is to grant relief when all that is due for rent and costs has been paid up, and (in general) to disregard any other causes of complaint that the landlord may have against the tenant. The question is whether, provided all is paid up, the landlord will not have been fully compensated; and the view taken by the court is that if he gets the whole of his rent and costs, then he has got all that he is entitled to so far as rent is concerned, and extraneous matters of breach of covenant, and so forth, are, generally speaking, irrelevant.[659]

Even so, however, exceptional circumstances may justify the refusal of relief, such as the inordinate conduct of the tenant himself or the fact that the landlord has altered his position in the belief that the forfeiture is effective. Thus, for instance, relief was refused to a tenant who did not apply until just before the six months had elapsed, by which time the landlord, after incurring expenditure upon the maintenance of the property, had "made an arrangement" to let another party into possession.[660]

If relief is granted upon conditions to be performed within a limited time, the court has jurisdiction to extend the time if it is just and equitable to do so.[661]

Relief may be granted to the tenant where the landlord, instead of bringing an action for recovery of the land, enters into peaceable possession. In such a case the tenant cannot claim relief under the Act which only applies where the landlord sues for possession. He may, however, rely on the ancient inherent equitable jurisdiction of the court, and, provided that he acts with reasonable promptness, may obtain relief even if he brings his action more than six months after the landlord resumes possession.[662]

Senior Courts Act. A useful summary of the law is given by Sir Nicolas BROWNE-WILKINSON V-C in *Billson v Residential Apartments Ltd* [1992] 1 AC 494 at 510.

[655] Common Law Procedure Act 1852, s. 212. For a "trial" to come within the meaning of this section, it must be an effective trial binding on all the necessary parties: *Gill v Lewis* [1956] 2 QB 1, where judgment was signed against only one of two joint tenants.

[656] *Standard Pattern Co Ltd v Ivey* [1962] Ch 432, criticised (1962) 78 LQR pp. 168–71 (R.E.M.).

[657] Common Law Procedure Act 1852, ss. 210–12.   [658] SCA 1981, s. 38(2).

[659] *Gill v Lewis* [1956] 2 QB 1 at 13, per JENKINS LJ. See also *Belgravia Insurance Co Ltd v Meah* [1964] 1 QB 436.

[660] *Stanhope v Haworth* (1886) 3 TLR 34.   [661] *Chandless-Chandless v Nicholson* [1942] 2 KB 321.

[662] *Howard v Fanshawe* [1895] 2 Ch 581; *Lovelock v Margo* [1963] 2 QB 786; *Thatcher v C H Pearce & Sons (Contractors) Ltd* [1968] 1 WLR 748 (four days over six months); *Ladup Ltd v Williams & Glyn's Bank plc* [1985]

(f) Relief to under-lessees

Where a lease is forfeited, any under-leases created out of it automatically come to an end. But an under-lessee[663] has the same right of applying to the court for relief against forfeiture of the head lease as the tenant has under the head lease.[664] The Law of Property Act 1925,[665] provides that where a head lessor proceeds by action or otherwise to enforce a forfeiture, the court may, on the application of an under-lessee, make an order vesting the whole or any part of the property in the under-lessee "for the whole term of the lease or any less term" upon such conditions as it thinks fit,[666] "but in no case shall any such under-lessee be entitled to require a lease to be granted to him for any longer term than he had under his original sub-lease".[667]

There is an important difference between relief granted to an under-lessee and relief granted to a tenant. In the case of the under-lessee a new term is created in him; the lease which has been forfeited is not revived and continued. Accordingly the rent from any under-lease is payable to the landlord between the forfeiture of the old lease and the creation of the new one.[668]

Relief is available to the mortgagee of a leasehold interest holding under a sub-demise or under a charge by way of legal mortgage.[669] An equitable chargee has no claim to relief because he is not an "under-lessee"; nor directly under the court's inherent jurisdiction which extends only to granting relief to one entitled to possession of the land or who has a legal or equitable interest in it. However, he may obtain relief indirectly under the inherent jurisdiction by making the application for relief which the lessee could himself have made.[670] Relief is not available to a squatter who has dispossessed a lessee.[671]

1 WLR 851. See [1969] JPL pp. 251–2. See also *Billson v Residential Apartments Ltd* [1992] 1 AC 494 at 516, where CA held that there was no similar inherent jurisdiction in the case of relief for breach of covenant other than the covenant to pay rent; p. 289, post.

For the statutory jurisdiction of the county court to grant relief, see the County Courts Act 1984, s. 138, as amended by AJA 1985, s. 55; High Court and County Courts Jurisdiction Order 1991, art. 2 (SI 1991 No. 724); *United Dominions Trust Ltd v Shellpoint Trustees Ltd* [1993] 4 All ER 310 (containing a detailed examination of the sections); (1994) 110 LQR 15 (N. P. Gravells); *Maryland Estates Ltd v Bar-Joseph* [1999] 1 WLR 83; *Croydon (Unique) Ltd v Wright* [2001] Ch 318 (charging order); *Bland v Ingrams Estates Ltd* [2001] Ch 767 (equitable chargee. CA discussed the relationship between County Courts Act 1984, s. 138, and the inherent jurisdiction).

[663] And so has a person deriving title under a lessee: LPA 1925, s. 146(5)(b); *High Street Investments Ltd v Bellshore Property Investments Ltd* [1996] 2 EGLR 40 (equitable assignee); *Escalus Properties Ltd v Robinson* [1996] QB 231 (mortgagee by sub-demise).

[664] Common Law Procedure Act 1852, s. 210; *Doe d Wyatt v Byron* (1845) 1 CB 623. See generally [1986] Conv 187 (S. Tromans).

[665] S. 146(4). This is the only part of s. 146 which applies to forfeiture for non-payment of rent.

[666] See *Chatham Empire Theatre (1955) Ltd v Ultrans Ltd* [1961] 1 WLR 817 (relief granted on payment of proportionate share of rent by applicant sub-lessees).

[667] *Factors (Sundries) Ltd v Miller* [1952] 2 All ER 630; *Cadogan v Dimovic* [1984] 1 WLR 609.

[668] *Official Custodian for Charities v Mackey* [1985] Ch 168; [1985] Conv 50 (J. Martin).

[669] *Belgravia Insurance Co Ltd v Meah* [1964] 1 QB 436; *Hammersmith and Fulham LBC v Top Shop Centres Ltd* [1990] Ch 237; [1989] All ER Rev 194; *Escalus Properties Ltd v Robinson*, supra (relief granted retrospectively under s. 146(2) to mortgagee by sub-demise); [1995] All ER Rev 334 (P. J. Clarke); cf *Pellicano v MEPC plc* [1994] 1 EGLR 104 (vesting order under s. 146(4) not retrospective; sub-lessee had no right to possession between date of forfeiture and grant of relief); *Barclays Bank plc v Prudential Assurance Co Ltd* [1998] 1 EGLR 44 (disclaimer of lease held not to prevent granting of relief to mortgagee as under-lessee). As to these forms of mortgage, see p. 725, post.

[670] *Bland v Ingrams Estates Ltd* [2001] Ch 767; [2002] All ER Rev 737 (P. H. Pettit); leave to appeal to HL refused: [2003] 1 WLR 1810. [671] *Tickner v Buzzacott* [1965] Ch 426.

B Covenants Other than the Covenant to Pay Rent

(1) Damages or Injunction

If the tenant fails to observe any of the covenants contained in the lease, it is open to the landlord either to sue for damages for breach or to seek an injunction to restrain the breach.[672]

(2) Forfeiture

As a further safeguard to the landlord it is the common practice, just as in the case of the covenant to pay rent, to ensure the observance of all other covenants by inserting an express proviso for re-entry and forfeiture in the event of their breach. The following is a typical clause in a lease:

If there shall be any breach or non-observance of any of the covenants by the tenant hereinbefore contained, then and in any such case the lessor may, at any time thereafter, into and upon the demised premises, or any part thereof, in the name the whole, re-enter, and the same have again, repossess and enjoy as in his former estate.[673]

In two respects, what has already been said above about forfeiture for non-payment of rent applies equally to these other covenants, namely, the effect of a breach is to render the lease liable to be determined by the landlord, and not to terminate it automatically; and the right of termination is lost by any act on the part of the landlord which amounts to a waiver of the condition.[674] But until the legislature intervened, the jurisdiction of the court to relieve the tenant varied according as the forfeiture was due to non-payment of rent or to the breach of a covenant relating some other matter. The question soon arose whether equity would protect a tenant against the loss of his interest under such a clause if, having incurred a forfeiture by breaking one of the covenants, he was prepared to put the matter right by paying all costs and compensation. To cite the words of KAY LJ:[675]

At first there seems to have been some hesitation whether this relief [grantable in the case of non-payment of rent] might not be extended to other cases of forfeiture for breach of covenants such as to repair, to insure, and the like, where compensation could be made; but it was soon recognized that

---

[672] *Coward v Gregory* (1866) LR 2 CP 153. For the landlord's remedies for breach of the covenant to repair, see pp. 249 et seq, ante.

[673] In this case forfeiture is provided for the acts of the tenant contrary to the terms of the lease, but the landlord may also forfeit if the tenant asserts a title in himself adverse to the landlord (e.g. by a written declaration that he, not the landlord, is entitled to the freehold), or if he lets a stranger into possession with the intention of enabling him to set up such an adverse title. But in all cases, it is a question of fact whether the tenant's act shows an intention to deny the landlord's title: *Wisbech St Mary Parish Council v Lilley* [1956] 1 WLR 121; *Warner v Sampson* [1959] 1 QB 297; *W G Clark (Properties) Ltd v Dupre Properties Ltd* [1992] Ch 297; [1993] Conv 299 (J. Martin); *British Telecommunications plc v Department of the Environment* [1996] NPC 148 (denial must be unequivocal); *Abidogun v Frolan Health Care Ltd* [2002] L & TR 16 (no denial of title by submitting question of title to the court for determination. The right to forfeiture for denial of title has been said to arise by operation of law, but is better described as an implication into the lease: at [41]–[42], per ARDEN LJ); [2001] Conv 399 (M. Pawlowski). The Law Commission propose removing the *implied* term that a tenant should not deny or disclaim his landlord's title: Termination of Tenancies for Tenant Default 2004 (Consultation Paper No. 174), para. 4.16. See *Hill and Redman's Landlord and Tenant*, para. A 8626.   [674] Pp. 275–6, ante.

[675] *Barrow v Isaacs & Son* [1891] 1 QB 417 at 425; *Shiloh Spinners Ltd v Harding* [1973] AC 691 at 722 et seq, per Lord WILBERFORCE.

there would be great difficulty in estimating the proper amount of compensation; and since the decision of Lord ELDON in *Hill v Barclay*[676] it has always been held that equity would not relieve, merely on the ground that it could give compensation, upon breach of any covenant in a lease except the covenant for payment of rent. But of course this left unaffected the undoubted jurisdiction to relieve in case of breach occasioned by fraud, accident, surprise, or mistake.

This denial of relief was maintained even though the breach, instead of causing loss to the landlord, operated to his advantage by restoring to him, at a much earlier date than he had a right to expect, premises upon which the tenant, in the expectation of continued tenure, might have already expended large sums of money. The strongest example of this was where a tenant failed to re-insure for a short time after the previous year's policy had run out. If in such a case no fire had occurred in the uninsured period the landlord had obviously lost nothing, and yet it was held in several cases that such a breach was sufficient to produce a forfeiture against which no relief could be given.[677] This particular case of forfeiture (by failure to insure) received legislative attention in 1859,[678] when relief was made possible on certain conditions, but it still remained true that the merely technical and innocuous breach of any other covenant inevitably led to the loss of his interest by the tenant if the landlord chose to take advantage of a proviso for re-entry.

The law, however, was fundamentally changed in two respects by the Conveyancing Act of 1881,[679] which first required certain conditions to be satisfied before forfeiture could be enforced, and then gave to the tenant the right to petition for relief.

These provisions were re-enacted by section 146 of the Law of Property Act 1925 and amended by three further Acts in 1927, 1938 and 1954.[680] The law now stands as follows.

(a) The statutory restriction on the landlord's right to enforce a forfeiture

(1) THE NOTICE

Section 146 of the Law of Property Act 1925 provides as follows:

A right of re-entry or forfeiture under any proviso or stipulation in a lease for a breach of any covenant or condition in the lease shall not be enforceable, by action or otherwise, unless and until the lessor serves on the lessee a notice

(a) specifying the particular breach complained of;[681] and

(b) if the breach is capable of remedy, requiring the lessee to remedy the breach; and

(c) in any case, requiring the lessee to make compensation in money for the breach;

and the lessee fails, within a reasonable time thereafter, to remedy the breach, if it is capable of remedy, and to make reasonable compensation in money, to the satisfaction of the lessor, for the breach.

A period of three months is normally regarded as a "reasonable time", but in special circumstances it may be much less.[682] This statutory rule is designed to afford the tenant an

---

[676] (1810) 16 Ves 402.　　[677] See e.g. *Doe d Muston v Gladwin* (1845) 6 QB 953.

[678] LP(A)A 1859, ss. 4–9; later repealed by the Conveyancing Act 1881.　　[679] S. 14.

[680] LTA 1927; Leasehold Property (Repairs) Act 1938; LTA 1954.

[681] The landlord is not required to give particulars of each defect: *Fox v Jolly* [1916] 1 AC 1; *Adagio Properties Ltd v Ansari* [1998] 2 EGLR 69.

[682] *Civil Service Co-operative Society Ltd v McGrigor's Trustee* [1923] 2 Ch 347; *Scala House and District Property Co Ltd v Forbes* [1974] QB 575, M & B p. 537 (fourteen days held to be sufficient where breach of

opportunity of considering the matter before an action is brought against him and of making up his mind whether he can admit the breach and whether he ought to offer compensation.[683]

The section has effect notwithstanding any stipulation to the contrary.[684] The parties cannot even contract out of its requirements indirectly. Thus, where a tenant agreed to lodge a deed of surrender executed in escrow with the president of the local law society, who had authority to deliver it to the landlord if the tenant committed a breach of covenant, it was held that the deed was void as being a device to circumvent the section.[685] As PLOWMAN J said:[686]

A forfeiture in the guise of a surrender . . . remains a forfeiture for the purposes of section 146.

(2) METHOD OF SERVICE

The notice may be served in accordance with the general provisions of section 196 of the Law of Property Act 1925 governing all notices under the Act. It can be sent to "the lessee"[687] or to "the persons interested", and may be left at the tenant's address[688] or sent there by registered letter or recorded delivery.[689] The notice may also be served by affixing it to or leaving it for the tenant at the demised premises,[690] but will only be valid if it is "required" to be served by the tenancy agreement.[691]

In the case of a covenant to repair, it is enacted by the Landlord and Tenant Act 1927[692] that a right of re-entry shall not be enforceable unless the lessor proves that

covenant against assigning or sub-letting held to be incapable of remedy); *Cardigan Properties Ltd v Consolidated Property Investments Ltd* [1991] 1 EGLR 64 (ten days to comply with insurance covenant held to be insufficient); [1991] Conv 223 (J. E. Martin); *Bhojwani v Kingsley Investment Trust Ltd* [1992] 2 EGLR 70; [1993] Conv 296 (J. E. Martin); *Courtney Lodge Management Ltd v Blake* [2005] 1 P & CR 17 (four working days insufficient to remedy nuisances caused by sub-underlessee).

[683] *Horsey Estate Ltd v Steiger* [1899] 2 QB 79 at 91.   [684] LPA 1925, s. 146(12).

[685] *Plymouth Corpn v Harvey* [1971] 1 WLR 549, M & B p. 546.   [686] At 554.

[687] Lessee includes an under-lessee and the persons deriving title under the lessee: LPA 1925, s. 146(5)(b). Where a lessee assigns his lease in breach of covenant, the assignment is effective and the notice must be served on the assignee and not on the original lessee: *Old Grovebury Manor Farm Ltd v W Seymour Plant Sales and Hire Ltd (No 2)* [1979] 1 WLR 1397; *Governors of the Peabody Donation Fund v Higgins* [1983] 1 WLR 1091; *Fuller v Judy Properties Ltd* [1992] 1 EGLR 75; [1992] Conv 343 (J. E. Martin); *Greenwich LBC v Discreet Selling Estates Ltd* [1990] 2 EGLR 65; [1991] Conv 222 (J. E. Martin) (a landlord, who had served notice for breach of covenant to repair and then waived breach by acceptance of rent, need not serve a fresh notice). The notice should be served on the tenant, and not on any mortgagee of the term: *Church Commissioners for England v Ve-Ri-Best Manufacturing Co Ltd* [1957] 1 QB 238, even if the mortgagee has taken possession: *Smith v Spaul* [2003] QB 983. On problems with LPA 1925, s. 196, see [2005] Conv 191 (E. Slessenger).

[688] Even though the lessee is in prison and unlikely to receive it: *Van Haarlam v Kasner* [1992] 2 EGLR 59; and even though the recipient is suffering from mental disorder; *Tadema Holdings Ltd v Ferguson* [1999] 14 NPC 144 (notice served under HA 1988, s. 13(2)); *WX Investments Ltd v Begg* [2002] 1 WLR 2849 (service deemed to have occurred on first occasion Post Office attempted to deliver, notwithstanding that it was not actually received by landlord until much later); [2003] Conv 90 (M. Haley); *Beanby Estates Ltd v Egg Stores (Stamford Hill) Ltd* [2003] 1 WLR 2064 (where notice sent by recorded delivery to addressee at place of abode, it was irrebuttably deemed to have been served). See also *C A Webber (Transport) Ltd v Railtrack plc* [2004] 1 WLR 320 (*Beanby Estates* not inconsistent with HRA 1998); [2003] Conv 268 (J. E. Adams).

[689] Recorded Delivery Service Act 1962, s. 1; [1990] Conv 147 (J. E. Adams).

[690] *Blunden v Frogmore Investments Ltd* [2002] 2 EGLR 29, [2002] Conv 312 (J. E. Adams).

[691] *Trustees of Henry Smith's Charity v Kyriakou* [1989] 2 EGLR 110; *Wandsworth LBC v Attwell* [1996] 1 EGLR 57.   [692] S. 18(2).

service of the notice was known either:

(a) to the lessee; or

(b) to an under-lessee holding under an under-lease which reserved a nominal reversion only to the lessee; or

(c) to the person who last paid the rent,

and that a reasonable interval had elapsed since the time when the fact of service was *known to* such person. In this case, the sending of the notice by registered letter or recorded delivery to a person is only to be regarded prima facie as good service.[693]

(3) CONTENTS OF NOTICE

It is now established that the statutory notice need not contain a demand for compensation if the lessor does not desire to be compensated.[694] We must now see whether the statutory notice will be ineffective if it omits to require a breach to be remedied.

If a *positive* covenant has been broken, for example, a covenant to repair, that is clearly capable of remedy and accordingly the notice must require it to be remedied. In *Expert Clothing Service and Sales Ltd v Hillgate House Ltd*[695] the Court of Appeal held that, where a tenant had committed a once-and-for-all breach of a covenant to reconstruct premises by a certain date, the breach was capable of remedy even after that date. SLADE LJ said:[696]

The breach of a positive covenant (whether it be a continuing breach or a once-and-for-all breach) will ordinarily be capable of remedy. The concept of capability of remedy for the purpose of section 146 must surely be directed to the question whether the harm that has been done to the landlord by the relevant breach is for practical purposes capable of being retrieved. In the ordinary case, the breach of a promise to do something by a certain date can for practical purposes be remedied by the thing being done, even out of time.

In my judgment on the remediability issue, the ultimate question for the court was this: if the section 146 notice had required the lessee to remedy the breach and the lessors had then allowed a reasonable time to elapse to enable the lessee fully to comply with the relevant covenant, would such compliance, coupled with the payment of any appropriate monetary compensation, have effectively remedied the harm which the lessors had suffered or were likely to suffer from the breach? If, but only if, the answer to this question was "No," would the failure of the section 146 notice to require remedy of the breach have been justifiable.

There may, however, be rare cases where the breach of a positive covenant is incapable of remedy, for example, where there is a breach of a covenant to insure at a time when the premises have already been burnt down.

Where, however, the covenant which has been broken is *negative*, there is some difficulty. At first it was held that the breach of *all* negative covenants was incapable of remedy. This

---

[693] If a tenant is making a claim under the Leasehold Reform Act 1967 (p. 364, post), no proceedings to enforce any right of re-entry or forfeiture may be brought during the currency of the claim without the leave of the court, which shall not be granted unless it is satisfied that the claim was not made in good faith, i.e. to avoid forfeiture: ss. 22, 34, Sch. 3, para. 4(1); *Central Estates (Belgravia) Ltd v Woolgar* [1972] 1 QB 48.

[694] *Lock v Pearce* [1893] 2 Ch 271; *Governors of Rugby School v Tannahill* [1935] 1 KB 87, M & B p. 536.

[695] [1986] Ch 340, M & B p. 542.   [696] At 355.

"attractive and easy ratio"[697] was, however, rejected. The matter has arisen in the Court of Appeal in different situations:

(i) Not to use premises for illegal or immoral purposes. Stigma

If, for instance, the tenant has agreed not to permit the premises to be used for illegal or immoral purposes and he is convicted of using them for habitual prostitution, it may be that the landlord is already branded locally as the owner of a brothel. If so, the tenant may discontinue his immoral use of the premises, his only mode of redemption, but mere cesser will not wipe out the past and remove the stigma on the landlord's reputation. In this sense the breach is not capable of remedy. If, therefore, the landlord can show that he has suffered lasting damage of this nature, his statutory notice need not require the breach to be remedied.[698] But the position is different where the action for forfeiture is brought against the original tenant in respect of immoral user permitted not by him, but by his sub-tenant or assignee. In these circumstances, it is the duty of the original tenant to take immediate steps to stop the wrongful user and also to enforce the forfeiture against the wrongdoer. It is only if he fails to do so within a reasonable time after learning the facts that the breach will be regarded as incapable of remedy.[699]

(ii) Not to assign or sub-let without consent of landlord. Other breaches of negative covenants

In *Scala House and District Property Co Ltd v Forbes*[700] the Court of Appeal held that a covenant not to assign or sub-let without the consent of the landlord is a once for all breach which cannot be remedied, even by obtaining a surrender from the tenant of the sub-lease. "Whatever events follow the breach they cannot wipe the slate clean."[701] In reaching that decision RUSSELL LJ reviewed the cases of *user* of premises in breach of covenant and said:[702]

We have a number of cases . . . in which the decision that the breach is not capable of remedy has gone upon the "stigma" point, without considering whether a short answer might be—if the user had ceased before the section 146 notice—that it was *ex hypothesi* incapable of remedy, leaving the lessee only with the ability to seek relief from forfeiture and the writ unchallengeable as such.

---

[697] *Hoffman v Fineberg* [1949] Ch 245 at 254, per HARMAN J, referring to the ratio of MACKINNON J in *Governors of Rugby School v Tannahill* at first instance [1934] 1 KB 695 at 700–1. While affirming his decision, CA rejected his view that all breaches of negative covenants were irremediable: [1935] 1 KB 87 at 90, 92. If it were held that breaches of negative covenants were incapable of remedy, recovery of possession by the landlord would depend solely upon whether the court would grant relief from forfeiture to the tenant.

[698] *Governors of Rugby School v Tannahill*, supra; *Egerton v Esplanade Hotels, London Ltd* [1947] 2 All ER 88 (immoral use of hotel); *Hoffman v Fineberg*, supra (breach of health regulations in restaurant); *Ali v Booth* (1966) 110 SJ 708; *D R Evans & Co Ltd v Chandler* (1969) 211 EG 1381 (pornographic literature); *Dunraven Securities Ltd v Holloway* (1982) 264 EG 709 (illegal pornography); *British Petroleum Pension Trust Ltd v Behrendt* (1985) 52 P & CR 117 (prostitution); *Van Haarlam v Kasner* [1992] 2 EGLR 59 (paraphernalia for spying found in flat).

[699] *Glass v Kencakes Ltd* [1966] 1 QB 611. These difficulties will be avoided if the statutory notice requires the tenant to remedy the breach *if it is capable of remedy*. The landlord can then claim in his action (1) that the breach is incapable of remedy, or (2) if it is capable of remedy that it has not been remedied: at 629–30.

[700] [1974] QB 575, M & B p. 537, (1973) 89 LQR 460 (P.V.B.); (1973) 37 Conv (NS) 455 (D. Macintyre); *Billson v Residential Apartments Ltd* [1992] 1 AC 494 (where Sir Nicolas BROWNE-WILKINSON V-C doubted whether breach of covenant not to make alterations without prior consent of landlord was irremediable).

[701] At 591, per JAMES LJ.

[702] At 588. For criticism of some of the reasoning in this decision, see *Expert Clothing Service and Sales Ltd v Hillgate House Ltd* [1986] Ch 340 at 364, M & B p. 540 n. 8, per O'CONNOR LJ.

However, more recent decisions of the Court of Appeal cast doubt on this decision, and its authority has been severely qualified.

In *Savva v Houssein*[703] the tenant covenanted not to display on the outside of the premises any sign or advertisement and not to make any alterations to them without the prior consent of the landlords. The tenant broke both covenants. The Court of Appeal, while leaving in place the solutions in the former two categories,[704] held that the breaches were capable of remedy. In so doing, it adopted the approach of SLADE LJ in *Expert Clothing Service and Sales Ltd v Hillgate House Ltd* and considered whether the harm caused by the breaches was remediable rather than whether the breach itself could be remedied. There was nothing in the statute, nor in logic, which required different considerations between a positive and a negative covenant, although it might be right to differentiate between particular covenants. The test was one of effect. If a breach had been remedied then it must have been capable of being remedied.[705] As STAUGHTON LJ said:[706]

In my judgment, except in a case of breach of a covenant not to assign without consent, the question is: whether the remedy referred to is the process of restoring the situation to what it would have been if the covenant had never been broken, or whether it is sufficient that the mischief resulting from a breach of the covenant can be removed. When something has been done without consent, it is not possible to restore the matter wholly to the situation which it was in before the breach. The moving finger writes and cannot be recalled. This is not to my mind what is meant by a remedy, it is a remedy if the mischief caused by the breach can be removed. In the case of a covenant not to make alterations without consent or not to display signs without consent, if there is a breach of that, the mischief can be removed by removing the signs or restoring the property to the state it was in before the alterations.

In *Akici v L R Butlin Ltd*[707] the Court of Appeal went further. Holding that the breach of a covenant against parting with possession of the premises is capable of remedy, NEUBERGER LJ accepted that *Scala House* might be binding authority on whether the breach of a covenant against assignment can be remedied, but said that it should not be given any wider authority:

Unless there is some binding authority, which either calls into question the conclusion or renders it impermissible, both the plain purpose of section 146(1) and the general principles laid down in two relatively recent decisions in this court, namely the *Expert Clothing* and *Savva* cases[708] point strongly to the conclusion that, at least in the absence of special circumstances, a breach of covenant against parting with possession or sharing possession, falling short of creating or transferring of legal interest, are breaches of covenant which are capable of remedy within the meaning of section 146.

The only authority which could be cited to call that conclusion into question is the *Scala House* case itself, but that does not deter me from my conclusion. First, it was only concerned with underletting; secondly, the reasoning of the leading judgment in the case is, at least in part, demonstrably fallacious and inconsistent with common sense and many other authorities; thirdly, it has been overtaken and marginalised by the *Expert Clothing* and *Savva* cases; fourthly, there is no reason of logic or principle why the reasoning or conclusion in the *Scala House* case should be extended to apply to a breach which falls short of creating a legal interest.

---

[703] [1996] 2 EGLR 65, M & B p. 541; (1997) 1 L & TR 70 (J. Brown and R. Doddridge).
[704] See *Expert Clothing Service and Sales Ltd v Hillgate House Ltd*, supra, at 358; *Savva v Houssein* [1996] 2 EGLR 65 at 66. [705] At 67.
[706] At 66. [707] [2006] 1 WLR 201 at [73]–[74]. [708] Supra.

There must be some doubt whether *Scala House* will survive, even in the context of covenants against assignment.

As regards the details which must be brought to the knowledge of the tenant, the rule has been laid down that the notice must be sufficiently precise to direct his attention to the particular things of which the landlord complains, so that he may understand with reasonable certainty what he is required to do and may be in a position to put matters right before the action is brought.[709] If, for instance the tenant holds six houses from the landlord and he is merely notified that he has broken his covenant to repair, the notice will be bad as not indicating which of the houses are involved.

(4) EXCEPTIONAL CASE OF COVENANT TO REPAIR

Where a landlord sues for damages or to enforce a forfeiture in respect of a covenant to keep or put the premises in repair,[710] he is subject to a further statutory restriction under the Leasehold Property (Repairs) Act 1938.[711] This Act applies to premises, other than an agricultural holding, which have been let for a period of not less than seven years, of which at least three years remain unexpired. The landlord must serve on the tenant a notice under section 146 of the Law of Property Act 1925 not less than one month before the commencement of the action, and inform him in that notice of his right to serve a counter-notice.[712] The tenant may within twenty-eight days of receiving the notice serve a counter-notice on the landlord claiming the benefit of the Act.

The effect of a counter-notice is that no proceedings whatsoever may be taken by the landlord for the enforcement of any right of re-entry or forfeiture, or for the recovery of damages, in respect of a breach of the repairing covenant, unless he first obtains the leave of the court. But as soon as the lease has less than three years to run, there is no longer any need to apply for this leave.[713] The circumstances in which leave is to be given are specifically enumerated by the statute.[714] At this stage of the proceedings the landlord need only show a prima facie case of a breach by the tenant.[715]

---

[709] *Fletcher v Nokes* [1897] 1 Ch 271 at 274; approved *Fox v Jolly* [1916] 1 AC 1; *John Lewis Properties plc v Viscount Chelsea* [1993] 2 EGLR 77.

[710] An obligation to cleanse is not an obligation to repair: *Starrokate Ltd v Burry* (1982) 265 EG 871.

[711] S. 1(1); as extended by LTA 1954, s. 51(1).

[712] S. 1(4); *Middlegate Properties Ltd v Messimeris* [1973] 1 WLR 168; *BL Holdings Ltd v Marcolt Investments Ltd* (1978) 249 EG 849. See *Swallow Securities Ltd v Brand* (1983) 45 P & CR 328 (where a landlord failed in his attempt to circumvent the requirement of serving a notice).

[713] *Baker v Sims* [1959] 1 QB 114.

[714] Leasehold Property (Repairs) Act 1938, s. 1(5); (a) where substantial damage has been caused, or will be caused if breach not remedied; (b) where an immediate remedy is required for giving effect to any enactment, by-law or order of a local authority respecting the safety, repair, maintenance or sanitary condition of the house; (c) where the tenant does not occupy the whole of the house and the breach is injurious to the other occupant; (d) where the cost of repair is relatively small as compared with the much greater expense that a postponement will involve; or (e) where it is "just and equitable" that leave should be given. It is sufficient to give the court jurisdiction if the landlord proves any one of these five grounds: *Phillips v Price* [1959] Ch 181. And he must prove it on the balance of probabilities: *Associated British Ports v C H Bailey plc* [1990] 2 AC 703; [1990] CLJ 401 (S. Bridge); [1990] Conv 305 (P. F. Smith). The relevant date for proving one or more of the s. 1(5) grounds is the date of the application for leave to bring forfeiture proceedings: *Landmaster Properties Ltd v Thackeray Property Services Ltd* [2003] 2 EGLR 30 (leave granted under s. 1(5)(e) where premises destroyed by fire before the hearing, but tenant's breach of covenant to repair was a direct cause of vandalism and arson).

[715] *Sidnell v Wilson* [1966] 2 QB 67; *Land Securities plc v Receiver for Metropolitan Police District* [1983] 1 WLR 439 (Scotland Yard).

The Act applies where the landlord is claiming forfeiture or damages, but not where he is claiming for a contract debt. A claim for expenses incurred in the preparation and the service of a section 146 notice is a claim for a contract debt and therefore no leave to enforce it under the Act is required.[716] There are conflicting decisions at first instance as to whether this extends to a case where the lease contains a covenant that the landlord can enter and carry out repairs at the tenant's expense, if the tenant fails to do them, and that the tenant will reimburse his proper expenditure. The better view is that an action for the recovery of the cost of repair is an action for debt and therefore no leave of the court is required under the Act.[717]

(b) Suspension of covenant

There may exist lawful excuses for the non-performance of a covenant in a lease. If so, the lease is not forfeitable; the covenant is merely suspended, but the lease remains valid. Lord RUSSELL OF KILLOWEN recognised obiter that there may be excuses for the non-performance of a building covenant short of full frustration:[718]

It may well be that circumstances may arise during the currency of the term which render it difficult, or even impossible, for one party or the other to carry out some of its obligations as landlord or tenant, circumstances which might afford a defence to a claim for damages for their breach, but the lease would remain.

This dictum was applied in *John Lewis Properties plc v Viscount Chelsea*[719] where a tenant was unable to perform a covenant to demolish and rebuild property owing to his inability to obtain planning permission, which had become necessary on its subsequent listing as a Grade II building.

(c) The statutory right of the tenant to claim relief

(1) POWER OF COURT TO GRANT OR REFUSE RELIEF

After requiring the above preliminaries from a lessor before he can enforce a forfeiture the Act of 1925 then provides that, when the lessor is proceeding by action[720] or entry to recover the premises, the lessee may apply to the court for relief,[721] and the court may, after reviewing the circumstances of the case and the conduct of the parties, refuse such relief, or grant it upon such terms as to costs, expenses, damages, compensation, penalty, etc, as seem fit.[722] This application must be made by all the tenants if the premises are held by joint lessees.[723]

---

[716] *Bader Properties Ltd v Linley Property Investments Ltd* (1967) 19 P & CR 620; *Middlegate Properties Ltd v Gidlow-Jackson* (1977) 34 P & CR 4.

[717] *Hamilton v Martell Securities Ltd* [1984] Ch 266; *Jervis v Harris* [1996] 1 All ER 303; [1997] Conv 299 (R. Hewitson). See also *SEDAC Investments Ltd v Tanner* [1982] 1 WLR 1342; (1984) 134 NLJ 791 (H. W. Wilkinson); [1986] Conv 85 (P. F. Smith).

[718] *Cricklewood Property and Investment Trust Ltd v Leighton's Investment Trust Ltd* [1945] AC 221 at 233–4; so too Lord GODDARD at 244.

[719] [1993] 34 EG 116(25 Cadogan Gardens "once described as the most wonderful house in the world"); [1995] Conv 74 (J. Morgan). Frustration was not pleaded; p. 328, post.

[720] Such an action is a pending land action under LCA 1972, s. 17(1) and is registrable under s. 5; and, in the case of registered land, is required to be protected by a notice under LRA 2002, s. 87; H & B, paras 10.102–10.105; *Selim Ltd v Bickenhall Engineering Ltd* [1981] 1 WLR 1318.

[721] He may apply as soon as the s. 146 notice has been served: *Pakwood Transport Ltd v 15 Beauchamp Place Ltd* (1977) 36 P & CR 112.   [722] LPA 1925, s. 146(2).

[723] *T M Fairclough and Sons Ltd v Berliner* [1931] 1 Ch 60.

Where the court grants relief, the effect is as if the lease had never been forfeited.[724] If the relief is granted upon terms to be performed by the tenant in the future, the order for relief falls to the ground if they are not performed; but, until the time comes for performance, the tenant who remains on the premises is there not as a tenant under the lease, but as a tenant at will or on sufferance.[725] The court has jurisdiction to extend the time.[726]

Further, where the tenant has under-let the premises, if the court grants relief to the tenant, the effect is to revive the under-lease in its entirety. In a case, however, where part of the demised premises had been under-let by the tenant, and where those premises were physically separated and the breach of covenant was committed by the under-lessee on his part of the property only, it was held that relief could be granted to the tenant without reviving the under-lease.[727]

Attempts have been made to specify the principles upon which this relief should be granted or withheld,[728] but the House of Lords has held that though such statements are useful and may reflect the judicial view for normal cases, yet the discretion given by the statute is so wide that it is better not to lay down rigid rules for its exercise.[729] Although the court will rarely exercise its discretion in favour of a lessee who knowingly suffers premises to be used for immoral purposes, it may nevertheless do so where there are special mitigating circumstances.[730]

(2) TIME OF APPLICATION

After the statutory notice under section 146 has been served, the tenant may apply for relief under subsection (2). He may do so not only where the landlord proceeds by action, but also where he peaceably re-enters without a court order. The latter was decided by the House of Lords in *Billson v Residential Apartments Ltd*,[731] as a result of a purposive interpretation of

---

[724] *Dendy v Evans* [1910] 1 KB 263; *Meadows v Clerical, Medical and General Life Assurance Society* [1981] Ch 70; *Hynes v Twinsectra Ltd* [1995] 2 EGLR 69.

[725] *City of Westminster Assurance Co Ltd v Ainis* (1975) 29 P & CR 469.

[726] *Chandless-Chandless v Nicholson* [1942] 2 KB 321; *Starside Properties Ltd v Mustapha* [1974] 1 WLR 816.

[727] *GMS Syndicate Ltd v Gary Elliott Ltd* [1982] Ch 1, relying on *Dumpor's Case* (1603) 4 Co Rep 119b, p. 264, ante. For an under-lessee's independent right to claim relief, see infra.

[728] E.g. *Rose v Hyman* [1911] 2 KB 234.

[729] *Hyman v Rose* [1912] AC 623 at 631, per Lord ELDON LC; *Southern Depot Co Ltd v British Railways Board* [1990] 2 EGLR 39; *Darlington BC v Denmark Chemists Ltd* [1993] 1 EGLR 62.

[730] *Borthwick-Norton v Romney Warwick Estates Ltd* [1950] 1 All ER 798; *Borthwick-Norton v Dougherty* [1950] WN 481; *Central Estates (Belgravia) Ltd v Woolgar (No 2)* [1972] 1 WLR 1048; *Burfort Financial Investments Ltd v Chotard* (1976) 239 EG 891; *British Petroleum Pension Trust Ltd v Behrendt* (1985) 52 P & CR 117; *Ropemaker Properties Ltd v Noonhaven Ltd* [1989] 2 EGLR 50; (1989) 139 NLJ 1747 (H. W. Wilkinson). See also *Earl Bathurst v Fine* [1974] 1 WLR 905 (relief refused to unsatisfactory tenant, where personal qualifications were important); *Southern Depot Co Ltd v British Railways Board* [1990] 2 EGLR 39 (relief granted despite wilful breaches involving "a thoroughly deceptive course of conduct" towards the landlord); *Mount Eden Land Ltd v Towerstone Ltd* [2003] L & TR 4 (relief refused where assignee had failed to provide guarantors as required by the lease and had failed to tell landlord that (a) it had taken possession under assignment for which consent had not been given, (b) part of premises were occupied by others ("deliberate and reprehensible" silence), and (c) one of its directors was a discharged bankrupt (a "lack of frankness"); and it had not been shown that the tenant could not find alternative premises); *Mount Cook Land Ltd v Hartley* [2000] EGCS 26 (relief granted where landlord was using the breach of covenant against underletting as an opportunity to seize a valuable asset, and the landlord would have had to give consent to the underletting if it had been applied for).

[731] [1992] 1 AC 494, M & B p. 551; [1992] CLJ 216 (S. Bridge); [1992] Conv 273 (P. F. Smith); (1992) 02 EG 154 (P. Dollar and C. Peet).

the opening words of the section: "Where a lessor is proceeding, by action or otherwise, to enforce such a right of re-entry or forfeiture."

Before *Billson*, these words had been construed to mean that the tenant could only apply for relief during the time when *the lessor is proceeding*, and that, once the lessor had recovered possession, it would be too late. The House of Lords has now held that the effect of the subsection is that the tenant may apply for relief if the landlord *proceeds or has proceeded* to forfeit by action or otherwise. Accordingly, the tenant may apply where the landlord has peaceably re-entered without first obtaining a court order.[732]

Where the landlord proceeds by action, the tenant must apply before the landlord has entered into possession pursuant to a final judgment; but where the landlord forfeits by peaceable re-entry, there is no time limit. In deciding whether to grant relief, the court will take into account all the circumstances, including delay on the part of the tenant.[733]

(3) UNDER-LESSEES

The jurisdiction of the court to relieve an under-lessee, or a person deriving title under him,[734] against a forfeiture due to the under-lessor's failure to pay rent[735] is equally exercisable where the failure relates to some other covenant.[736] This is so, even though the nature of the breach, for example, the bankruptcy of a publican, precludes the under-lessor from applying for relief.[737] It is a jurisdiction that should be sparingly exercised.[738]

(4) INHERENT EQUITABLE JURISDICTION

The Court of Appeal in *Billson*[739] first decided that there was no statutory jurisdiction to grant relief against forfeiture and then held by a majority that it had no inherent equitable jurisdiction either. The section was an exhaustive provision. As Sir Nicolas BROWNE-WILKINSON V-C said:[740] "If Parliament intended the court to be able to grant relief even when the landlord is *not* proceeding to enforce his rights but has enforced them, what was the reason for including in section 146 (2) and (4) the limitation that the powers of relief could be exercised only when the landlord is proceeding?"

The House of Lords did not refer to this equitable jurisdiction, since it had reversed the Court of Appeal and held that it had statutory jurisdiction to grant relief.

(5) DECORATIVE REPAIRS

A special rule was introduced by the Law of Property Act 1925 for covenants relating to the internal decorative repair of a house.[741] It is provided that where a statutory notice has been

---

[732] An application for relief was subsequently refused: *Billson v Residential Apartments Ltd (No 2)* [1993] EGCS 155.

[733] [1992] 1 AC 494 at 539–40, per Lord TEMPLEMAN; at 543–4, per Lord OLIVER OF AYLMERTON.

[734] *Re Good's Lease* [1954] 1 WLR 309; as for example, a mortgagee by way of sub-demise: *Grand Junction Co Ltd v Bates* [1954] 2 QB 160.   [735] Pp. 279, ante.

[736] LPA 1925, s. 146(4).   [737] LP(A)A 1929, s. 1.

[738] *Creery v Summersell and Flowerdew & Co Ltd* [1949] Ch 751; *Hill v Griffin* [1987] 1 EGLR 81; *Duarte v Mount Cook Land Ltd* [2002] L & TR 21 (relief granted where landlord was extremely anxious to have sub-tenant as its direct tenant, and had used forfeiture as a negotiating tactic for grant of a new lease).

[739] [1992] 1 AC 494, supra.

[740] Ibid., at 517. The equitable jurisdiction is available in cases of non-payment of rent, see p. 278, ante. CPR Part 55, PD, para. 2.4 requires a landlord of a residential tenancy to notify any person entitled to relief against forfeiture of whom he is aware.   [741] S. 147.

served by the landlord indicating a breach of such a covenant, the court, after reviewing all the circumstances and in particular the length of the term, may wholly or partially relieve the tenant from liabilities for such repairs. But this power to set a covenant aside is not exercisable when a tenant, having expressly agreed to put the property in a decorative state of repair, has never performed the covenant, nor is it to apply to anything which is necessary for keeping the property in a sanitary condition or in a state which makes it fit for human habitation.

(d) Exceptions to the statutory requirements

The particular subsections of the Act already considered are general in nature and would, without more, apply to every covenant contained in a lease, but there are three covenants for the breach of which a lessor need not serve the statutory notice as a preliminary to enforcing the forfeiture, and in respect of which relief is not grantable. The covenants so excepted are the following.

(1) COVENANT TO PAY RENT[742]

(2) COVENANT FOR INSPECTION IN MINING LEASE

If a mining tenant, under obligation to pay royalties according to the quantity of minerals mined, breaks the covenant by which he has agreed to give access to his books, accounts, records, weighing machines or other things, or to the mine itself, forfeiture may be enforced without service of the statutory notice and no relief is grantable.[743]

(3) CONDITION OF FORFEITURE ON THE BANKRUPTCY OF TENANT OR WHERE LEASE IS TAKEN IN EXECUTION

It is common to provide in a lease that the premises shall be forfeited to the lessor if the tenant becomes bankrupt[744] or if his interest is taken in execution. There are certain classes of property in which it is vital to the landlord that he should recover his property in either of these events, and where the lease relates to such property the Act provides that the statutory provisions shall be excluded. The following are the leases concerned:[745]

(a) agricultural or pastoral land,

(b) mines or minerals,

(c) a house used or intended to be used as a public house or beer shop,

(d) a house let as a dwelling-house, with the use of any furniture, books, works of art, or other chattels not being in the nature of fixtures,

(e) any property with respect to which the personal qualifications of the tenant are of importance[746] for the preservation of the value or character of the property, or on the ground of neighbourhood to the lessor,[747] or to any person holding under him.

In such a lease, then, the lessor can proceed to enforce a forfeiture as soon as the bankruptcy occurs, and the tenant has no claim to relief.

---

[742] LPA 1925, s. 146(11); pp. 273, et seq, ante.   [743] Ibid., s. 146(8)(ii).
[744] But not if his surety does: *Halliard Property Co Ltd v Jack Segal Ltd* [1978] 1 WLR 377.
[745] LPA 1925, s. 146(9).   [746] *Earl Bathurst v Fine* [1974] 1 WLR 905.
[747] *Hockley Engineering Co Ltd v V & P Midlands Ltd* [1993] 1 EGLR 76.

If the demised land is not within one of the classes enumerated above, the extent to which the statutory provisions concerning notice and relief apply depends upon whether the lessee's interest is sold, or is not sold, for the benefit of his creditors within one year from the bankruptcy or taking in execution. The two rules on the matter, which are designed to enable the trustee in bankruptcy to decide whether he will disclaim the lease or use it for the benefit of the creditors, are as follows:[748]

(a) If the interest is sold within the year, the statutory provisions apply without any limit of time. This means, in the case of bankruptcy, that if the trustee in bankruptcy is able to sell the tenant's interest under the lease within the year for the benefit of the creditors, then, despite proceedings for forfeiture, he can apply for relief even after the year has elapsed, and the court may grant the application and confirm the title of the purchaser.

(b) If the interest is not sold within the year, the statutory provisions apply only during that year, i.e., although the landlord cannot take steps to regain possession during that period without serving the statutory notice and without the risk of defeat by a successful application for relief, yet, after the year has elapsed, his right to recover the premises is absolute. No notice need be served; no relief can be granted.[749]

In practice, however, leases do not usually contain a proviso for forfeiture on the bankruptcy of the tenant, except in the five cases enumerated above, since it is troublesome for the landlord to be deprived of his rent until a decision has been reached by the trustee, and if he accepts rent falling due after the date of bankruptcy the forfeiture is thereby waived.[750]

(e) Law reform

In recent years there have been several proposals to reform the law of forfeiture, none of which has yet been implemented.[751]

In 1985 the Law Commission[752] said that the law of forfeiture was "complex and confused; its many features fit together awkwardly; and it contains a number of uncertainties, anomalies and injustices". It identified two major defects.

First,[753] the doctrine of re-entry under which a landlord forfeits a tenancy by re-entry upon the property let, and the tenancy terminates on the date on which re-entry takes place. As a result, the obligations which the tenancy imposes upon the tenant terminate also at that time. So, although the tenant may remain in possession for several months afterwards, he is not obliged to pay rent or to perform any of his other covenants unless he is granted relief, in which case the tenancy is taken never to have ended at all, and his liability revives retrospectively.

---

[748] LPA 1925, s. 146(10). Any wider equitable jurisdiction is ousted by s. 10: *Official Custodian for Charities v Parway Estates Developments Ltd* [1985] Ch 151; *Billson v Residential Apartments Ltd* [1992] 1 AC 494, p. 289, ante.

[749] *Civil Service Co-operative Society v McGrigor's Trustee* [1923] 2 Ch 347 at 355; *Horsey Estate Ltd v Steiger* [1899] 2 QB 79; *Gee v Harwood* [1933] Ch 712; affd. sub nom. *Pearson v Gee and Braceborough Spa Ltd* [1934] AC 272.   [750] *Doe d Gatehouse v Rees* (1838) 4 Bing NC 384.

[751] For a general overview, see Law Commission Consultation Paper No. 174, Termination of Tenancies for Tenant Default 2004, paras. 1.16 et seq.

[752] Forfeiture of Tenancies (Law Com No. 142) at para. 3.2; [1986] Conv 165 (P. F. Smith); [1987] LSG 1042 (J. Cherryman). The new scheme proposed by the Law Commission would apply to existing tenancies as well as to those created in the future: para. 3.29.   [753] Ibid., paras. 3.3–3.10.

Secondly,[754] in relation to relief against forfeiture, there are two almost entirely separate regimes, one for cases involving non-payment of rent and the other for all other cases. There are also uncertainties, including the fact that the courts' ancient equitable jurisdiction to grant relief exists, though to an extent not altogether certain, side by side with their statutory powers.

The Law Commission's Report in 1985 recommended that the present law of forfeiture, both statutory and non-statutory, be swept away, and with it the doctrine of re-entry, to be replaced by a scheme under which there would be no distinction between termination for non-payment of rent and termination for other reasons, and under which the tenancy would continue in force until the date on which the court orders that it should terminate. The court would have power to make a *termination order* which could be applied for only on the occasion of a *termination order event*: (a) breach of covenant by the tenant; or (b) disguised breach of covenant (that is, broadly, a breach by the tenant of an obligation imposed on him otherwise than by covenant); or (c) insolvency of the tenant. The order may be either *absolute* (to terminate the tenancy unconditionally on a date specified) or *remedial* (to terminate the tenancy on a date specified unless the tenant takes remedial action by that time). In both cases the court may grant or refuse to grant the order according to a discretion exercisable within guidelines.[755] Finally, the tenant would be given a new right to terminate the tenancy in cases of fault on the part of the landlord.[755a] The right is analogous to the landlord's right to terminate, and the tenant exercising this right is given a right to claim damages from the landlord for the loss of his tenancy.[756]

Subsequent proposals for reform have built upon the 1985 Report. In 1994 the Law Commission published a further Report, which was in effect a republication of the 1985 Report,[757] together with minor amendments and a draft Termination of Tenancies Bill. This was however limited to the *landlord's* termination order scheme; the Law Commission found that there was no consensus on its proposals for a tenant's termination order scheme and therefore shelved that part of the 1985 proposals in order to facilitate the implementation of the other elements of the proposals.[758] However they were still not implemented. After further consideration and discussion with Government departments and property professionals, in 1998 the Law Commission published a consultative document[759] in which it provisionally concluded that, although the common law doctrine of re-entry should be abolished, there should be a new statutory right of re-entry so that, in appropriate cases, the landlord would be able to terminate a tenancy by physical re-entry without the need for court proceedings. This proposal stemmed from the view that the landlord's ability to determine a tenancy in appropriate circumstances without recourse to the courts is an effective management tool, and fears that its abolition might have an adverse effect on the commercial property sector and on the availability of rented property.[760] Although the Law Commission's

---

[754] Forfeiture of Tenancies (Law Com No. 142) at paras. 3.11–3.13, 3.16.   [755] Ibid., paras. 3.25–3.71.

[755a] This has now been given effect by *Hussein v Mehlman* [1992] 2 EGLR 87, p. 324, post.

[756] Ibid., paras. 3.72–3.93.

[757] Termination of Tenancies Bill (Law Com No. 221). Appendix C contains an updated summary of the law of forfeiture and its defects.

[758] Ibid., para. 1.13: "reforms to cure the evident defects in the law of forfeiture should take precedence over implementing proposals for innovation, for which there has been no great support . . . It would not be helpful for the landlords' termination order scheme to be unnecessarily embroiled in controversy".

[759] Termination of Tenancies by Physical Re-entry; (1998) 2 L & TR 24 (M. Pawlowski); Law Commission Thirty-Second Annual Report 1997 (1998, Law Com No. 250), paras. 5.3–5.5; Thirty-Third Annual Report 1998 (1999, Law Com No. 258), paras. 5.5–5.6.

[760] Law Commission Thirty-Second Annual Report, supra, para. 5.3.

consultation exercise led it to conclude that this proposal should be finalised and implemented, there was further delay. Finally, a new Consultation Paper on Termination of Tenancies for Tenant Default[761] was published in 2004, which again makes proposals for the abolition of the remedy of forfeiture, building on the original 1985 Report but with modifications to take into account significant developments since the earlier proposals.[762] The key elements of the present proposals, which will apply to all leases except residential tenancies for a term of less than twenty-one years,[763] are as follows:[764]

(1) The principal means of termination of a tenancy for tenant default[765] will be by means of an order of the court: a "termination order".

(2) The effect of a termination order will be to terminate the tenancy at a specified date and to extinguish all interests (such as sub-tenancies and mortgages) which derive from it. Unless and until such an order takes effect, the tenancy will remain in existence.

(3) In all cases, prior to commencing any proceedings, the landlord must serve a notice, in pre-scribed form, on the tenant and any sub-tenants or mortgagees (the "pre-action notice").

(4) The pre-action notice will inform the tenant of the details of the default. The tenant may refer the pre-action notice to the court. The court may then exercise its case management powers to safeguard the parties' interests and to ensure that the court's overriding objective (of dealing with cases justly) is complied with.

(5) The court will be able to make an absolute termination order terminating the tenancy from a stated future date (without giving the tenant any further chances) or a remedial order adjourning the application on terms that the tenant be allowed to continue as tenant (provided that certain conditions are satisfied).

(6) There will be four specific grounds on which an absolute termination order can be sought. The pre-action notice must state which of these is relied upon by the landlord.

(7) Greater protection will be given to sub-tenants and mortgagees and possibly others holding interests deriving out of the tenancy. They will be entitled to be served with the pre-action notice and may protect their interests by applying for relief from the court.

(8) Exceptionally, in tightly defined circumstances, a landlord may instigate the termination process by recovering possession unilaterally without the prior sanction of a court order. The landlord will only be able to do this where due warning has been given in the pre-action notice, and where the premises are not currently occupied as a residence. In every case, the tenant may refer the matter to court. If the landlord does recover possession unilaterally, the tenancy will terminate (in the absence of any application by the tenant) on the expiry of one month.

(9) Special provision is made concerning termination of tenancy for nonpayment of service or administration charges.

(10) The inter-related doctrines of re-entry and waiver should both be abolished.

The Law Commission expects to produce its final report and a draft Bill during 2006.

---

[761] Consultation Paper No. 174; (2004) 154 NLJ 113 (S. Bridge); (2004) 8 L & T Rev 32, 119 (M. Pawlowski).

[762] In particular, the new Civil Procedure Rules and the Human Rights Act 1998: ibid., paras. 1.31–1.32. The Law Commission began again with a Consultation Paper, because of the lack of consultation responses by participants and advisers currently involved in the property industry, given the length of time since the original consultation: ibid., para. 1.30.

[763] Shorter residential tenancies are considered in the Narrative Report on Renting Homes 2003 (Law Com No. 284). A court order is to be necessary before a landlord can regain possession: Part IX; pp. 331 et seq, post.

[764] Law Commission Thirty-Eighth Annual Report 2003/04 (2004, Law Com No. 288), para. 7.2.

[765] "Tenant default" will comprise breaches of covenant or obligation, including certain "disguised" breaches, i.e. where the tenancy provides that it will determine on the occurrence of a specified event.

VI The Effect of Assignment on Covenants[766]

A covenant in a lease is prima facie a contract binding only on the landlord and the tenant—the actual contracting parties. But it was early seen that to enforce this doctrine of privity of contract was highly undesirable in the case of leases, since both parties had transmissible interests the value of which depended largely upon the obligations that each had assumed. Thus the mediaeval land law, although it never lost sight of the general principle that a stranger to a contract cannot sue or be sued upon it, did recognise that covenants contained in a lease might have a wider operation than ordinary contracts. As Holdsworth remarked, "they were regarded in a sense as being annexed to an estate in the land, so that they could be enforced by anyone who took that estate in the land." [767]

The scope, then, of our present inquiry is to ascertain in what circumstances persons other than the original landlord and tenant can sue or be sued upon the covenants.[768] Two events may occur—an assignment of the term by the tenant or an assignment of the reversion by the landlord.[769] In each case the two questions that arise are whether the benefit and burden of the covenants pass to the assignee. In short, do the covenants run with the land and with the reversion? Four cases, therefore, fall to be considered:

(1) The tenant assigns his interest to A. Can A enforce the covenants inserted in the lease in favour of the tenant? *Does the benefit of these covenants run with the land?*

(2) The tenant assigns his interest to A. Can A be sued on the covenants inserted in the lease in favour of the landlord? *Does the burden of the covenants entered into by the tenant run with the land?*

(3) The landlord assigns his interest, i.e. the reversion, to Z. Can Z enforce the covenants inserted in the lease in favour of the landlord? *Does the benefit of the covenants run with the reversion?*

(4) The landlord assigns his reversion to Z. Can Z be sued upon the covenants inserted in the lease in favour of the tenant? *Does the burden of the landlord's covenants run with the reversion?*

We must first notice that the Landlord and Tenant (Covenants) Act 1995 radically changed the law.[770] It is not retrospective,[771] but provides a new statutory code for covenants in leases granted after 1995. The existing law, which is an amalgam of rules laid down by common law and statute, continues in force where the lease was granted before 1996. The effect therefore is that we now have two separate sets of rules for the enforcement of covenants in leases; and that the existing rules will continue in force for many years to come; for example, covenants in a lease granted in 1990 for 99 or 999 years will attract those rules for decades or even centuries.

---

[766] Holdsworth, *History of English Law*, vol. vii. pp. 287–92; Fancourt, *Enforceability of Landlord and Tenant Covenants.*   [767] Holdsworth, *History of English Law*, vol. iii. p. 158.

[768] We are generally concerned here only with the enforceability between landlord (and his successors) and tenant (and his successors). For circumstances in which a covenant can benefit and burden a *sub*-tenant, see pp. 306–7, 312 and 671, post.   [769] For the meaning of assignment, see pp. 306, post.

[770] (1996) 59 MLR 78 (M. Davey); [1996] CLJ 313 (S. Bridge); [1996] Conv 432 (P. Walter); (1996) 49 CLP Part I 95 (A. Clarke). In *First Penthouse Ltd v Channel Hotels & Properties (UK) Ltd* [2004] 1 EGLR 16 at [43] LIGHTMAN J said: "The 1995 Act is the product of rushed drafting, and its provisions create exceptional difficulties."

[771] Except for ss. 17–20 which apply to all leases whenever granted; p. 308, post.

A Covenants in Leases Granted Before 1996

(1) Covenants Touching and Concerning the Land

It will simplify our task if, before dealing separately with the four divisions of the subject given above, we describe what is meant by covenants that *touch and concern the land demised*, for it is only these, as distinct from those merely affecting the person, that are capable of running either with the reversion or with the land.

From the present point of view all covenants fall into one or other of two classes, being either personal to the contracting parties, or such as touch and concern the land.

The time-honoured[772] expression "touching and concerning the land" was replaced in the Law of Property Act 1925[773] by the phrase *having reference to the subject-matter of the lease*. This affords a clue to the meaning of what is at first sight a little vague. If the covenant has direct reference to the land, if it lays down something which is to be done or is not to be done upon the land, or, and perhaps this is the clearest way of describing the test, *if it affects the landlord in his normal capacity as landlord or the tenant in his normal capacity as tenant*, it may be said to touch and concern the land. Lord RUSSELL CJ said:[774] "The true principle is that no covenant or condition which affects merely the person, and which does not affect the nature, quality, or value of the thing demised or the mode of using or enjoying the thing demised, runs with the land", and BAYLEY J at an earlier date asserted the same principle:[775] "In order to bind the assignee, the covenant must either affect the land itself during the term, such as those which regard the mode of occupation, or it must be such as per se, and not merely from collateral circumstances, affects the value of the land at the end of the term."

If a simple test is desired for ascertaining into which category a covenant falls, it is suggested that the proper inquiry should be whether the covenant affects either the landlord qua landlord or the tenant qua tenant. A covenant may very well have reference to the land, but, unless it is reasonably incidental to the relation of landlord and tenant, it cannot be said to touch and concern the land so as to be capable of running therewith or with the reversion.[776] Tested by this principle the following covenants have been held to touch and concern the land.

(a) Examples of covenants touching and concerning the land

Covenants by the tenant:

to pay rent or taxes;[777]

to repair or leave in repair;[778]

---

[772] A "somewhat archaic expression": *Cardwell v Walker* [2004] 2 P & CR 9 at [41], per NEUBERGER J.

[773] Ss. 141, 142.   [774] *Horsey Estate Ltd v Steiger* [1899] 2 QB 79 at 89.

[775] *Mayor of Congleton v Pattison* (1808) 10 East 130 at 138.

[776] Cited with approval in *Hua Chiao Commercial Bank Ltd v Chiaphua Industries Ltd* [1987] AC 99 at 107, M & B p. 562, per Lord OLIVER OF AYLMERTON; and in *Breams Property Investment Co Ltd v Stroulger* [1948] 2 KB 1 at 7, per SCOTT LJ. See also formulations of the test by Sir Nicolas BROWNE-WILKINSON V-C in *Kumar v Dunning* [1989] QB 193 at 204; and by Lord OLIVER OF AYLMERTON in *P & A Swift Investments v Combined English Stores Group plc* [1989] AC 632 at 642, M & B pp. 561–2. And generally [1989] 47 LSG 24, 48 LSG 22 (J. Adams and H. Williamson).

[777] *Parker v Webb* (1693) 3 Salk 5. Cf a premium payable by instalments: *Hill v Booth* [1930] 1 KB 381. A covenant by a surety guaranteeing the tenant's rent also touches and concerns the land: *Kumar v Dunning, supra*.

[778] *Martyn v Clue* (1852) 18 QB 661.

to spend a stated yearly sum on repairs, or in default to pay to the landlord the difference between this sum and the amount actually expended;[779]

to lay dung on the land annually;[780]

to renew tenant's fixtures;[781]

to reside on a farm during the term;[782]

to insure the premises against fire;[783]

by a publican tenant to buy all beer from the landlord;[784]

not to assign or under-let without the landlord's consent;[785]

not to allow a third party, X, to be concerned in the conduct of the business carried on at the demised premises.[786]

Covenants by the landlord:

to renew the lease;[787]

to supply the demised house with good water;[788]

not to build on adjoining land so as to depreciate the amenity of the demised land;[789]

to erect a new building in place of an old one;[790]

to keep a housekeeper to act as servant of the lessee;[791]

not to serve a notice to quit for three years, unless he requires the premises for his own occupation;[792]

to accept a surrender of the lease.[793]

Covenant by a third party:

to guarantee the tenant's performance of his obligations.[794]

(b) Examples of personal covenants

On the other hand personal, or collateral, covenants do not touch and concern the land, since they have no direct reference to the subject-matter of the lease. The word *collateral*, admittedly ambiguous in this context, indicates a covenant relating to a matter not normally

---

[779] *Moss' Empires Ltd v Olympia (Liverpool) Ltd* [1939] AC 544.

[780] *Sale v Kitchingham* (1713) 10 Mod Rep 158.   [781] *Williams v Earle* (1868) LR 3 QB 739.

[782] *Tatem v Chaplin* (1793) 2 Hy Bl 133.   [783] *Vernon v Smith* (1821) 5 B & Ald 1.

[784] *Clegg v Hands* (1890) 44 Ch D 503; *Caerns Motor Services Ltd v Texaco Ltd* [1994] 1 WLR 1249 (solus agreement to purchase products held to touch and concern).   [785] *Goldstein v Sanders* [1915] 1 Ch 549.

[786] *Lewin v American and Colonial Distributors Ltd* [1945] Ch 225 at 236.

[787] *Muller v Trafford* [1901] 1 Ch 54; *Weg Motors Ltd v Hales* [1961] Ch 176; affd. [1962] Ch 49.

[788] *Jourdain v Wilson* (1821) 4 B & Ald 266.   [789] *Ricketts v Enfield (Churchwardens)* [1909] 1 Ch 544.

[790] *Easterby v Sampson* (1830) 6 Bing 644.

[791] *Barnes v City of London Real Property Co* [1918] 2 Ch 18.

[792] *Breams Property Investment Co Ltd v Stroulger* [1948] 2 KB 1.

[793] *System Floors Ltd v Ruralpride Ltd* [1995] 1 EGLR 48; *Harbour Estates Ltd v HSBC Bank plc* [2005] Ch 194 (an unusually framed clause which allowed the first tenant and only a limited group of assigns, if permitted, to break the lease: benefit passed to assignee with the term under LPA 1925, s. 63).

[794] *Kumar v Dunning* [1989] QB 193; [1988] CLJ 180 (C. Harpum); approved *P & A Swift Investments v Combined English Stores Group plc* [1989] AC 632, where Lord TEMPLEMAN said at 637: "A surety for a tenant is a quasi tenant who volunteers to be a substitute or twelfth man for the tenant's team and is subject to the same rules and regulations as the player he replaces. A covenant which runs with the reversion against the tenant runs with the reversion against the surety"; *Milverton Group Ltd v Warner World Ltd* [1995] 2 EGLR 28 at 31. See also

relevant to the relationship of landlord and tenant. For instance, a covenant by either party to pay a sum of money to the other is merely collateral,[795] unless it is inextricably bound up with other covenants that touch and concern the land.[796] Thus a covenant by a tenant, in furtherance of his express undertaking to repair, to expend £500 yearly upon repairs, or to pay the landlord the difference between this amount and what is actually expended, is not a bare obligation personal to the contracting parties. It touches and concerns the land, since it is part and parcel of the repairing covenant.[797]

In *Thomas v Hayward*,[798] where the landlord of a public house had covenanted that he would not open another beer or spirit house within half a mile of the demised premises, the question arose whether this covenant could be enforced by an assignee of the tenant. It was held that it could not, because it was collateral in the sense that it did not oblige the landlord to do or to refrain from doing anything on the demised premises. On the other hand a covenant by the tenant of a public house to conduct the business in such a manner as to afford no ground for the suspension of the licence, was held to touch and concern the land, since it concerned the manner in which the covenantor was to use the premises as tenant.[799]

A covenant that entitles the tenant to purchase the fee simple at a given price at any time during the term, affects the parties qua vendor and purchaser, not qua landlord and tenant. It is collateral to the lease and as such it cannot run as a matter of course with the land or with the reversion as being one that touches and concerns the land.[800] Nevertheless, if it does not infringe the rule against perpetuities,[801] its effect is to confer upon the tenant an equitable interest in the land[802] which, like any other piece of property, is freely assignable unless the terms of its grant show that it is personal to him. Therefore, the option will pass on an assignment of the demised land and will be enforceable by an assignee of the tenant against the landlord; and if protected by registration or as an overriding interest[803] it will be enforceable against an assignee of the reversion.[804]

It has also been held that a covenant by the tenant to pay to the landlord a substantial security deposit on the terms that it would be repayable at the end of the lease if there was no breach of the tenant's covenants did not touch and concern the land.[805] The obligation was entered into with the landlord qua payee rather than qua landlord.[806]

Finally, a covenant may be personal to one party but not to the other, for example, the benefit of a term expressed to be personal to an original tenant may nevertheless bind an assignee of the reversion.[807]

Coronation Street Industrial Properties Ltd v Ingall Industries plc [1989] 1 WLR 304 (covenant by surety of tenant to accept new lease replacing lease granted to tenant, where that lease was disclaimed by liquidator on tenant's insolvency, held to touch and concern).

[795] *Re Hunter's Lease* [1942] Ch 124. The tenant's covenant to pay rent of course touches and concerns the land: supra.

[796] *Moss' Empires Ltd v Olympia (Liverpool) Ltd*, supra; *Boyer v Warbey* [1953] 1 QB 234.   [797] Ibid.

[798] (1869) LR 4 Exch 311.   [799] *Fleetwood v Hull* (1889) 23 QBD 35.

[800] A right of pre-emption over adjoining land is also collateral: *Collison v Lettsom* (1815) 6 Taunt 224; *Charles Frodsham & Co Ltd v Morris* (1972) 229 EG 961.   [801] P. 559, ante.

[802] *London and South Western Rly Co v Gomm* (1882) 20 Ch D 562; p. 880, post.

[803] In registered land, by notice on the register or by discoverable actual occupation: pp.972 et seq, post; in unregistered land, by registration as an estate contract: p. 940, post.

[804] *Griffith v Pelton* [1958] Ch 205, explaining *Woodall v Clifton* [1905] 2 Ch 257; *Re Button's Lease* [1964] Ch 263. See generally (1958) 74 LQR 242 (W. J. Mowbray).

[805] *Hua Chiao Commercial Bank Ltd v Chiaphua Industries Ltd* [1987] AC 99, M & B p. 562.

[806] At 107, per Lord OLIVER OF AYLMERTON.

[807] *System Floors Ltd v Ruralpride Ltd* [1995] 1 EGLR 48.

(2) Running of Covenants at Common Law and by Statute

We can now take up the four cases that have been indicated above and determine in what circumstances the covenant will run in each case. The rules depend partly upon the common law as finally enunciated in 1583 in *Spencer's Case*[808] and partly upon statutes. The statutes that formerly regulated the matter were the Grantees of Reversions Act, passed in 1540[809] after the dissolution of the monasteries, and the Conveyancing Act 1881,[810] but these were both repealed and replaced by the Law of Property Act 1925.[811]

(a) Benefit of covenant runs with land

The tenant assigns his interest to A. Can A enforce the covenants which were inserted in the lease in favour of the tenant? The rule even at common law is that the benefit of the covenants runs with the land, enabling an assignee (A) from the tenant to sue the landlord on any covenants which touch and concern the land demised and which enure for the benefit of the tenant, such as a covenant by the landlord to supply the demised premises with pure water. The authority for this rule is *Spencer's Case*, in the fourth resolution of which the court, dealing with a covenant for quiet enjoyment, said:

for the lessee and his assignee hath the yearly profits of the land, which shall grow by his labour and industry for an annual rent; and therefore it is reasonable when he hath applied his labour and employed his cost upon the land, and be evicted (whereby he loses all), that he shall take such benefit of the demise and grant, as the first lessee might . . .

(b) Burden of covenant runs with land

The tenant assigns his interest to A. Can A be sued upon the covenants which were inserted in the lease in favour of the landlord? The common law answers this also in the affirmative, provided that the covenant touches and concerns the land, for it was said in *Spencer's Case* that:

When the covenant extends to a thing *in esse*, parcel of the demise, the thing to be done by force of the covenant is *quodammodo* annexed and appurtenant to the thing demised, and shall go with the land and shall bind the assignee, although he be not bound by express words.

It is true that the judgment drew a distinction between a covenant which referred to something "*in esse*", already in existence (such as to repair an existing wall), and one which related to a thing not in existence at the time of the lease (such as a covenant to build a new wall), and laid down that though the former would bind assignees in all cases, the latter would not do so unless the original tenant had covenanted for himself *and his assigns*.

This distinction rested upon no solid basis, but, though adversely criticised,[812] it remained law until 1926. It was abolished by the Law of Property Act 1925, which provides that:[813]

(1) A covenant relating to any land of a covenantor or capable of being bound by him, shall, unless a contrary intention is expressed,[814] be deemed to be made by the covenantor on behalf of

---

[808] (1583) 5 Co Rep 16a, M & B p. 563.   [809] 32 Hen. 8, c. 34, s. 1.   [810] Ss. 10, 11.
[811] Ss. 141, 142.
[812] *Minshull v Oakes* (1858) 2 H & N 793. See Behan, *Covenants Affecting Land*, pp. 75 et seq.
[813] S. 79.
[814] I.e. unless an indication to the contrary is found in the instrument, and this may be expressed or implied: *Re Royal Victoria Pavilion, Ramsgate* [1961] Ch 581, per PENNYCUICK J at 589, M & B p. 949.

himself his successors in title and the persons deriving title under him or them, and, subject as aforesaid, shall have effect as if such successors and other persons were expressed.

This subsection extends to a covenant to do some act relating to the land, notwithstanding that the subject-matter may not be in existence when the covenant is made.

(2) For the purposes of this section in connexion with covenants restrictive of the user of land "successors in title" shall be deemed to include the owners and occupiers for the time being of such land.

This section, however, applies only to covenants made on or after 1 January 1926.[815] In the case of a lease executed before 1926, the burden of a covenant relating to something not in existence will not run with the land unless it was expressly imposed upon the tenant *and his assigns.*

(c) Benefit of covenant runs with reversion

The landlord assigns his interest, that is, the reversion, to Z. Can Z enforce the covenants which were inserted in the lease in favour of the landlord? The rule at common law is that the grantee of a reversion can sue upon an implied covenant, that is, one which automatically results from the relationship of landlord and tenant (such as a covenant to pay rent), but he cannot sue upon express covenants contained in the lease.[816] The difficulty is said to be that in the case of a reversion there is no corporeal thing to which the covenant can be regarded as annexed, such as there is where the land is assigned.[817]

A mitigation of this strict rule of the common law became urgent when the monasteries were dissolved by Henry VIII in 1539, because, if the law had not been altered, it would have precluded the grantees of the monastic lands from enforcing against existing tenants the express covenants in leases granted by the monasteries before their dissolution. Hence the Grantees of Reversions Act 1540, which, though designed merely to accommodate grantees of monastic lands, soon came to be regarded as having universal application and as laying down the law for assignees of reversions in general. This statute, which remained the only law on the subject until the Conveyancing Act 1881, enacted that assignees of reversions should have the same right of enforcing forfeitures, and the same right of suing for a breach of any covenant, as the original lessors.[818]

Both these statutes have been repealed, and the right of an assignee of a reversion to enforce the covenants now rests upon the Law of Property Act 1925,[819] which, in a section that applies to all leases whether made before or after the Act[820] provides that:

(1) Rent reserved by a lease, and the benefit of every covenant or provision therein contained, having reference to the subject-matter thereof,[821] and on the lessee's part to be observed or performed, and every condition of re-entry and other condition therein contained, shall be annexed and incident to and shall go with the reversionary estate in the land, or in any part thereof, immediately expectant on the term granted by the lease, notwithstanding severance of that reversionary estate, and without prejudice to any liability affecting a covenantor or his estate.[822]

---

[815] S. 79 does not, however, apply to covenants in leases granted after 1995: LT(C)A 1995, s. 30(4)(a); pp. 310, et seq, post.   [816] *Platt on Covenants,* p. 531; *Wedd v Porter* [1916] 2 KB 91 at 100–1.
[817] E.g. *Smith's Leading Cases* (13th edn), vol. i. pp. 61–2.   [818] S. 10.   [819] S. 141.
[820] S. 141 does not, however, apply to covenants in leases granted after 1995: LT(C)A 1995, s. 30(4)(b); pp. 310, et seq, post.   [821] I.e., touching and concerning the land demised: p. 295, ante.
[822] *London and County (A & D) Ltd v Wilfred Sportsman Ltd* [1971] Ch 764, M & B p. 567.

(2) Any such rent, covenant or provision shall be capable of being recovered, received, enforced and taken advantage of, by the person from time to time entitled, subject to the term, to the income of the whole or any part, as the case may require, of the land leased.

(3) Where that person becomes entitled by conveyance or otherwise, such rent, covenant or provision may be recovered, received, enforced or taken advantage of by him notwithstanding that he becomes so entitled after the condition of re-entry or forfeiture has become enforceable, but this subsection does not render enforceable any condition of re-entry or other condition waived or released before such person becomes entitled as aforesaid.

(1) FORM OF LEASE

One result of this enactment, which provides, in repetition of the Conveyancing Act 1881, that "rent reserved by a lease,[823] and the benefit of every covenant or provision therein contained" shall pass with the reversion, is to abolish the old construction that was put upon the Grantees of Reversions Act 1540, to the effect that the assignee of a reversion could not sue upon the covenants unless the original lease was under seal. The rule now is that the assignee can sue if the lease is in writing or if the tenancy is the result of a written agreement for a lease.[824] The same is the case if a parol lease is made for a period not exceeding three years[825] or where the assignment is effective only to transfer the title to the landlord in equity.[826]

(2) BREACH OF COVENANT COMMITTED BEFORE ASSIGNMENT

The Court of Appeal has held that, under this section of the Act, the assignee of the reversion is the only person entitled to sue the tenant for any breach of covenant, whether of a continuous nature or not and even though committed before the date of the assignment:[827]

The expression "go with" must be intended to add something to the concept involved in the expression "annexed and incident to" and in my view connotes the transfer of the right to enforce the covenant from the assignor to the assignee with the consequent cessation of the right of the assignor to enforce the covenant against the tenant.[828]

So, where arrears of rent have accrued before the landlord has assigned his reversion, it is the assignee who is entitled to sue for them; he may, however, assign his right to collect those arrears to his predecessor and still retain his right to forfeit the lease for non-payment of rent.[829]

(d) Burden of covenant runs with reversion

The landlord assigns his reversion to Z. Can Z be sued upon the covenants which were inserted in the lease in favour of the tenant? There was no right of action against Z at

---

[823] "Lease" includes "an under-lease or other tenancy": s. 154.

[824] *Rickett v Green* [1910] 1 KB 253, M & B p. 578; *Rye v Purcell* [1926] 1 KB 446; *Boyer v Warbey* [1953] 1 QB 234, M & B p. 580; [1978] 37 CLJ 98 (R. J. Smith).

[825] See M & B pp. 575–8; Smith, *Property Law*, pp. 447–9.

[826] *Scribes West Ltd v Relsa Anstalt (No 3)* [2005] 1 WLR 1847 (transfer of legal title, not yet registered).

[827] *Re King* [1963] Ch 459, M & B p. 565 (covenant to repair and reinstate); *London and County (A & D) Ltd v Wilfred Sportsman Ltd* [1971] Ch 764, M & B p. 567 (covenant to pay rent); *Arlesford Trading Co Ltd v Servansingh* [1971] 1 WLR 1080; *Electricity Supply Nominees Ltd v Thorn EMI Retail Ltd* [1991] 2 EGLR 46.

[828] Ibid., at 497, per DIPLOCK LJ.

[829] *Kataria v Safeland plc* [1998] 1 EGLR 39. For post-1995 tenancies under LT(C)A 1995, see s. 3(3), where the position is the same.

common law, but a right was given by the Grantees of Reversions Act 1540 which enacted that a lessee and his assigns should have the same remedy against the assignees of the lessor as the original lessee would have had against the lessor. This enactment was attended by certain difficulties, which are no longer of interest, since they were removed by the Conveyancing Act 1881,[830] in a section now replaced by section 142(1) of the Law of Property Act 1925, and applicable to all leases whenever made:[831]

The obligation under a condition or of a covenant entered into by a lessor[832] with reference to the sub-ject-matter of the lease shall, if and as far as the lessor has power to bind the reversionary estate imme-diately expectant on the term granted by the lease, be annexed and incident to and shall go with that reversionary estate, or the several parts thereof, notwithstanding severance of that reversionary estate, and may be taken advantage of and enforced by the person in whom the term is from time to time vested by conveyance, devolution in law, or otherwise; and, if and as far as the lessor has power to bind the person from time to time entitled to that reversionary estate, the obligation aforesaid may be taken advantage of and enforced against any person so entitled.

The word "covenant" as used in this section is not confined to its strict meaning of a contract under seal, but includes any promise touching and concerning the land[833] that is contained in a tenancy agreement made otherwise than by deed.[834]

(1) BREACH OF COVENANT COMMITTED BEFORE ASSIGNMENT

Section 142 differs in one respect from its counterpart, section 141. It does not contain subsections corresponding to subsections (2) and (3) of section 141. As a result of the omission, it has been held that, although a tenant can sue the assignee of the reversion for breach of a repairing covenant which occurred before the assignment, because the prop-erty is still in disrepair, he cannot sue him for consequential damages flowing from the breach.[835]

(2) SEVERANCE OF REVERSION

One particular difficulty which arose under the Grantees of Reversions Act was that, owing to its indivisible nature, a condition could not be enforced by an assignee of *part* of the reversion. If the reversion was severed, the condition could not be apportioned. The statu-tory rule now, however, is that, where such a severance has taken place, every condition contained in the lease is apportioned and remains annexed to the severed parts of the rever-sion.[836] The tenancy itself, however, is not severed, with the result that there is still a single

---

[830] S. 11.

[831] S. 142 does not, however, apply to covenants in leases granted after 1995: LT(C)A 1995, s. 30(4)(b); pp. 310, et seq, post.

[832] The obligation may be expressed in a side letter: *System Floors Ltd v Ruralpride Ltd* [1995] 1 EGLR 48; *Lotteryking Ltd v AMEC Properties Ltd* [1995] 2 EGLR 13; cf s. 141, where the covenant must be contained in the lease: *Weg Motors Ltd v Hales* [1962] Ch 49 at 73.

[833] *Davis v Town Properties Investment Corpn Ltd* [1903] 1 Ch 797.

[834] *Weg Motors Ltd v Hales* [1962] Ch 49.

[835] *Duncliffe v Caerfelin Properties Investment Corpn Ltd* [1989] 2 EGLR 38; [1990] Conv 127 (J. E. Martin). For another difference between the sections, see *City and Metropolitan Properties Ltd v Greycroft Ltd* [1987] 1 WLR 1085, p. 305, post.

[836] LPA 1925, s. 140(1); replacing LP(A)A 1859, s. 3, and Conveyancing Act 1881, s. 12.

tenancy, even though the reversion has been severed.[837] If the owner of a severed part of the reversion determines the tenancy by a notice to quit,[838] the tenant is permitted within one month to determine the whole tenancy by serving notice on the owner in whom the rest of the reversion is vested.[839]

(3) Essentials of Enforceability

Before we conclude the subject of covenants that run with the land or the reversion in leases granted before 1996, there are two general observations of considerable importance to be made.

(a) Privity of contract or estate

First, the enforcement of covenants between two parties depends upon the existence between them of either privity of contract or privity of estate.

We have seen[840] that a lease is a contract, as well as an interest in property. *Privity of contract* denotes the relationship which exists between the landlord and the tenant by virtue of the contract, and under it each party[841] is entitled by the law of contract to enforce those covenants contained in the contract of which he has the benefit, and bound by those covenants of which he has the contractual burden. This relationship continues to subsist between the landlord and tenant despite an assignment of their respective property interests in the lease.[842] The covenants in a contract for a lease, which is not completed by the grant of a lease, will similarly be enforceable between the parties under the general law of contract.

Privity of estate describes the relationship between two parties who respectively hold the same legal estates as those created by the lease. This is the position where one holds the original reversion and the other the original term, or rather, the whole of what is left of the original term. Thus there is privity of estate between the landlord and an assignee from the tenant of the residue of the term; also between the tenant and an assignee of the reversion; also between an assignee of the reversion and an assignee of the residue of the term. In the absence of assignment, therefore, there is privity both of contract and of estate between the landlord and tenant.[843]

There is privity of estate only between the parties holding the *legal* estates created by the original lease. There is therefore no privity between persons who have entered into

---

[837] LPA 1925, s. 140(2). The severance must be genuine, and not, e.g., where the landlord conveys part of the reversion to bare trustees for himself: *Persey v Bazley* (1983) 47 P & CR 37.

[838] See, e.g., *Smith v Kinsey* [1936] 3 All ER 73.

[839] *Jelley v Buckman* [1974] QB 488; *Nevill Long & Co (Boards) Ltd v Firmenich & Co* (1983) 47 P & CR 59.

[840] Pp. 194 et seq, ante.

[841] In relation to the leases we are here considering (leases granted before 1996), only the parties themselves acquired original contractual rights; cf Contracts (Rights of Third Parties) Act 1999, under which the benefit of a term in a contract (including a lease) may now in certain circumstances be enforced by a person who is not a party to it: p. 676, post.

[842] The benefit of contractual rights may be assigned at law under LPA 1925, s. 136, but then the assignor will lose the right to enforce them. The burden of contractual rights cannot be assigned, but can be novated. See generally Treitel, chap. 16.

[843] *Bickford v Parson* (1848) 5 CB 920 at 929. See also *Platt on Leases*, vol. ii. p. 351: "Privity of estate is the result of tenure; it subsists by virtue of the relation of landlord and tenant, and follows alike the devolution of the reversion, and of the term"; *City of London Corpn v Fell* [1994] 1 AC 458 at 464, per Lord TEMPLEMAN, M & B p. 569.

a contract for a lease[844] or between their assigns;[845] nor between the landlord and one who has only contracted to take an assignment from a tenant.[846] Such situations therefore raise certain difficulties in relation to the enforcement of covenants. Since the benefit of a covenant can be assigned at law, the courts had little difficulty in holding that the benefit of a covenant in a contract for a lease could pass to the assignee of the reversion;[847] and it appears that the benefit will also run by virtue of Law of Property Act 1925, section 141, which has been interpreted as applying to contracts for a lease as well as to leases.[848] Similarly, the benefit of the landlord's covenant is capable of assignment with the assignment of the benefit of the contract for a lease; and it appears that the burden of the landlord's covenant in a contract for a lease should pass to the assignee of the reversion under Law of Property Act 1925, section 142.[849] However, it has been held that the burden of covenants in an equitable lease does not run with the land,[850] although there are more recent dicta to the effect that the rules relating to the running of covenants in leases should be the same, whether the lease which has been assigned is legal or equitable.[851] Whatever the proper legal analysis of this proposition,[852] it is submitted that the better view is that the court should hold that the assignee of an equitable lease, and that the equitable assignee of a legal lease, should be both bound by and able to enforce the covenants.[853]

We shall see that there are no such problems in relation to covenants in equitable leases granted after 1995, since the Landlord and Tenant (Covenants) Act 1995 treats equitable leases and equitable assignments in the same way as their legal counterparts.[854]

(1) ORIGINAL TENANT ALWAYS LIABLE TO ORIGINAL LANDLORD

There are certain important rules that flow from this general principle. Thus:

It is perfectly settled by a multitude of decisions that, notwithstanding an assignment of his lease, the lessee continues liable on the personal privity of the contract to the payment of the rent and the performance of the covenants during the whole term; although the lessor concur in the assignment, or, by acceptance of rent or otherwise, recognize the assignee as his tenant.[855]

---

[844] Which can take effect as an equitable lease under the doctrine of *Walsh v Lonsdale* (1882) 21 Ch D 9, p. 223, ante.   [845] *Purchase v Lichfield Brewery Co* [1915] 1 KB 184, M & B p. 579.

[846] An equitable assignment; *Cox v Bishop* (1857) 8 De GM & G 815, M & B p. 578; *Friary, Holroyd, and Healey's Breweries Ltd v Singleton* [1899] 1 Ch 86.

[847] *Manchester Brewery Co v Coombs* [1901] 2 Ch 608, M & B p. 576, applying the doctrine of *Walsh v Lonsdale* (1882) 21 Ch D 9, M & B p. 86, p. 223, ante.   [848] P. 299, ante.

[849] P. 301, ante: both ss. 141 and 142 refer to a "lease", which is defined in LPA 1925, s. 154, as including "an under-lease or other tenancy".

[850] *Purchase v Lichfield Brewery Co*, supra, which was a case, however, of assignment by mortgage.

[851] *Boyer v Warbey* [1953] 1 QB 234 at 246, per DENNING LJ, M & B p. 580.

[852] The "fusion of law and equity": per DENNING LJ in *Boyer v Warbey*, supra; or, more particularly, an application of the doctrine of *Walsh v Lonsdale*: *Manchester Brewery Co v Coombs*, supra; *Industrial Properties (Barton Hill) Ltd v Associated Electrical Industries Ltd* [1977] QB 580; Smith, *Property Law*, pp. 451–2; [1978] CLJ 98 (R. J. Smith).

[853] The technical case for extending this to the equitable assignee of the legal lease is more problematic than the case of the equitable lease: Smith, *Property Law*, p. 453.   [854] S. 28(1); p. 310, post.

[855] *Platt on Leases*, vol. ii. pp. 352–3; *Warnford Investments Ltd v Duckworth* [1979] Ch 127 at 137. Distinguish, however, the liability of a lessee who acquires a statutory term of 2,000 years under the provisions for converting perpetually renewable leases; p. 209, ante.

This continuing liability of the original tenant for all breaches of covenant throughout the duration of the lease, even after he has assigned it, is a hazard for the tenant.[856] Several cases have highlighted this, and in one of them:[857]

a warehouse was let for 21 years at a rent of £17,000 a year, subject to a rent review at the end of 14 years. The original tenant assigned the lease and in the following year the landlord and the assignee agreed a revised rent of £40,000 a year. When the assignee failed to pay the rent for two quarters, the tenant was held liable to pay the £20,000 then outstanding.

As HARMAN J said:[858]

Each assignee is the owner of the whole estate and can deal with it so as to alter it or its terms. The estate as so altered then binds the original tenant, because the assignee has been put into the shoes of the original tenant and can do all such acts as the original tenant could have done.

In *Friends' Provident Life Office v British Railways Board*,[859] however, the Court of Appeal rejected this approach and held that:

If the contract in the original lease itself provides for some variation in the future of the obligations to be performed by the tenant (for example by a rent review clause), the original tenant may be bound to

---

[856] The original tenant is released if the landlord unconditionally releases the assignee by accord and satisfaction: *Deanplan Ltd v Mahmoud* [1993] Ch 151; (1993) 143 NLJ 28 (H. W. Wilkinson); cf *Sun Life Assurance Society plc v Tantofex (Engineers) Ltd* [1999] 2 EGLR 135; *City of London Corpn v Fell* [1994] 1 AC 458 (where lease, assigned by original lessee, had run its term and had been extended under Landlord and Tenant Act 1954, original lessee's obligations held to cease on completion of term); [1994] CLJ 28 (S. Bridge); [1994] Conv 247 (M. Haley); cf *Herbert Duncan Ltd v Cluttons* [1993] QB 589; [1993] Conv 164 (P. F. Smith). See also *Norwich Union Life Insurance Society v Low Profile Fashions Ltd* [1992] 1 EGLR 86; [1992] CLJ 425 (S. Bridge) (no duty of care on landlord to ensure solvency of assignee when consenting to assignment, and no equitable principle which obliges landlord to sue assigns and his surety before original tenant); *Becton Dickinson UK Ltd v Zwebner* [1989] QB 208, 217 (original tenant entitled to be indemnified by solvent guarantor of later assignee). *Re A Debtor (No 21 of 1995)* [1995] NPC 170. Other defences available are fraught with difficulty:

  (a) surrender and regrant: *Jenkin R Lewis Ltd v Kerman* [1971] Ch 477; [1995] Conv 124 (A. Dowling); *Friends' Provident Life Office v British Railways Board* [1996] 1 All ER 336;
  (b) release by accord and satisfaction: *Deanplan Ltd v Mahmoud* [1993] Ch 151; [1993] 143 NLJ 23 (H. W. Wilkinson); *Allied London Investments Ltd v Hambro Life Assurance Ltd* [1984] 1 EGLR 16; *Mytre Investments Ltd v Reynolds* [1995] 3 All ER 588; *March Estates plc v Gunmark Ltd* [1996] 2 EGLR 38;
  (c) disclaimer by liquidator or trustee in bankruptcy: *Hindcastle Ltd v Barbara Attenborough Associates Ltd* [1997] AC 70; [1997] Conv 24 (T. Taylor); *Scottish Widows plc v Tripipatkul* [2004] 1 P & CR 29. See generally [1996] CLJ 313 at 319 (S. Bridge); *Groveholt Ltd v Hughes* [2005] 2 BCLC 421.

[857] *Centrovincial Estates plc v Bulk Storage Ltd* (1983) 46 P & CR 393; [1984] Conv 443 (P. McLoughlin). The other cases are *Allied London Investments Ltd v Hambro Life Assurance Ltd* [1985] 1 EGLR 45; *Selous Street Properties Ltd v Oranel Fabrics Ltd* (1984) 270 EG 643 (tenant liable for rent increase under review clause where landlord permitted improvements otherwise forbidden by terms of original lease); *Thames Manufacturing Co Ltd v Perrotts (Nichol & Peyton) Ltd* (1984) 50 P & CR 1; *GUS Property Management Ltd v Texas Homecare Ltd* [1993] 27 EG 130.
  For the continuing liability of a surety for the original lessee, see *P & A Swift Investments v Combined English Stores Group plc* [1989] AC 632; *Becton Dickinson UK Ltd v Zwebner* [1989] QB 208; *Johnsey Estates Ltd v Webb* [1990] 1 EGLR 80. For his liability to an assignee of the lessee, see *Cerium Investments Ltd v Evans* [1991] 1 EGLR 80. And for release of a surety by variation, see *Metropolitan Properties Co (Regis) Ltd v Bartholomew* [1996] 1 EGLR 82; *Howard de Walden Estates Ltd v Pasta Place Ltd* [1995] 1 EGLR 79.
[858] At 396; Jackson and Wilde, *The Reform of Property Law*, p. 73 (S. Bright); *Beegas Nominees Ltd v BHP Petroleum Ltd* [1998] 2 EGLR 57; *Metropolitan Properties Co (Regis) Ltd v Bartholomew*, supra.
[859] [1995] 2 EGLR 55 at 60, per Sir Christopher SLADE. See also his other three propositions. BELDAM LJ thought at p. 59 that *Centrovincial* might be justified on the ground that the original covenant contained a promise to pay not only the original but also the reviewed rent.

perform the obligations as so varied, even though the variations occur after the assignment of the lease—this will depend on the construction of the relevant covenant(s) in the original lease.

Although the point does not often arise, the landlord is in the same position as the tenant. He remains personally liable on his covenants in the lease even after he has assigned his reversion.[860] Likewise he remains liable to the tenant, even after the tenant has assigned his lease.[861]

(2) ASSIGNEE LIABLE AND ENTITLED ONLY IN RESPECT OF MATTERS OCCURRING WHILE HE HOLDS THE LAND

Again, as the liability of an assignee of the tenant is based upon the privity[862] of estate between him and the landlord or the latter's assignee, it follows that the tenant's assignee cannot be liable for a breach of covenant committed before he took the estate under the assignment,[863] and cannot sue the landlord for breaches committed prior to that time. Lastly, and consistently with the same principle, an assignee ceases to be liable for breaches occurring after he has assigned his interest to a third party, for such a re-assignment obviously destroys the privity of estate which previously existed.[864] He is liable, however, even for these subsequent breaches, if he expressly covenants with the landlord at the time of taking the assignment that he will perform the terms of the lease.[865] Moreover, in any event, he remains liable after reassignment for any breaches which occurred while the tenancy was vested in him.[866]

(3) IMPLIED INDEMNITY BY ASSIGNEE

It will thus be seen that, where one of the tenant's covenants has been broken after an assignment of the term, the landlord has the option of suing either the original tenant on the privity of contract or the particular assignee who had the estate when the breach occurred, but although this joint liability undoubtedly exists, the rule is that the assignee in possession is the principal debtor, while the original tenant occupies the position of a surety.[867] Nevertheless the continuing liability of the original tenant is an obvious menace to him, and it became the invariable practice for every assignee expressly to covenant to indemnify his assignor against future breaches of the provisions contained in the lease. This is no longer necessary, for it is now enacted that every assignment for valuable consideration[868] shall be deemed to include a covenant by the assignee that he will pay all rent falling due in the future and will perform all the covenants, agreements and conditions binding upon the original tenant. This implied covenant of indemnity binds all persons, such as later assignees, deriving title under the assignee.[869] To take an example:

L leases land to T. Later successive assignments of the land are made first to U, then to V, and finally to W. If L sues T for the breach committed by W of some condition contained in the lease, the implied

---

860 *Stuart v Joy* [1904] 1 KB 362, M & B p. 572; (1996) 59 MLR 79 at p. 83 (M. Davey).

861 *City and Metropolitan Properties Ltd v Greycroft* [1987] 1 WLR 1085, M & B p. 568 (tenant who assigned lease at reduced value because of landlord's breach of covenant to repair held able to recover damages from landlord after assignment); [1987] Conv 374 (P. F. Smith); *Celsteel Ltd v Alton House Holdings Ltd (No 2)* [1987] 1 WLR 291 at 296.   862 *Purchase v Lichfield Brewery Co* [1915] 1 KB 184, M & B p. 579.

863 *Grescot v Green* (1700) 1 Salk 199.   864 *Paul v Nurse* (1828) 8 B & C 486.

865 *J Lyons & Co Ltd v Knowles* [1943] 1 KB 366; *Estates Gazette Ltd v Benjamin Restaurants Ltd* [1994] 1 WLR 1528.   866 *Harley v King* (1835) 2 Cr M & R 18; cf *Richmond v Savill* [1926] 2 KB 530.

867 *Humble v Langston* (1841) 7 M & W 517 at 530, per PARKE B.

868 On valuable consideration, see *Johnsey Estates Ltd v Lewis & Manley (Engineering) Ltd* [1987] 2 EGLR 69.

869 LPA 1925, s. 77(1)(c); Sch. 2, Part IX; and in registered land, LRA 2002, s. 134(2), Sch. 12, para. 20, replacing LRA 1925, s. 24 (whether or not there is valuable consideration). The implied statutory covenant is one of

covenant of indemnity entitles T to make U a party to the action. Similarly U can join V, and V can join W as a party. In this way judgment can be given against the person who has actually committed the breach.[870]

(b) Assignment

(1) WHOLE INTEREST MUST BE TRANSFERRED.

ASSIGNEE AND SUB-TENANT

The second observation is that the rules laid down above with regard to the running of covenants apply only where there has been an assignment in the proper sense of that term, for it is only then that privity of estate exists between the reversioner and the person who is in occupation of the land. The term "assignee" is very comprehensive: it applies to all persons who take the estate either by act of party[871] or by act of law, such as the executors of a tenant or assignee, and persons taking the premises by way of execution for debt, but in the eyes of the law no person occupies the position of assignee of the land unless he takes the *identical term* which the tenant had, and also takes the *whole of that term*.[872]

Thus if the tenant, on making what purports to be an assignment of his term, reserves to himself a reversion, no matter how trifling it may be—as where he assigns the remainder of his lease less one day—the transaction amounts to a sub-lease and not to an assignment. In such a case it is obvious that there is neither privity of contract nor privity of estate between the superior landlord and the sub-tenant, and therefore neither of them can sue or be sued *at law* upon the covenants of the lease,[873] though as we shall see later the sub-tenant may be liable under the equitable doctrine of *Tulk v Moxhay* on purely negative covenants.[874] But there is no magic in words. If one has acquired an interest in the tenancy and a question arises with regard to his position, the first point that falls to be considered is whether he has taken the whole of the tenant's interest. Thus where the tenant executes a deed couched in the form of a sub-lease, which purports to sub-let the property for the whole of the remainder of his term or for a longer period, the transaction amounts to an assignment.[875]

---

indemnity, not guarantee: *Scottish & Newcastle plc v Raguz* [2004] L & TR 11; and may be excluded by an express term of the contract: *Re Healing Research Trustee Co Ltd* [1992] 2 All ER 481. For a later assignee's obligation at common law to indemnify the original lessee for breaches of covenant in the lease committed during his own tenancy, see *Moule v Garrett* (1872) LR 7 Exch 101; Goff and Jones, para. 15–006.

870 As to the nature of this covenant, see *Butler Estates Co Ltd v Bean* [1942] 1 KB 1. See also *Re Mirror Group (Holdings) Ltd* (1992) 65 P & CR 252 (original lessee cannot compel his assignee to enforce the benefit of its own indemnity covenant against an ultimate assignee if the latter has re-assigned the lease).

871 *Old Grovebury Manor Farm Ltd v W Seymour Plant Sales and Hire Ltd (No 2)* [1979] 1 WLR 1397; p. 282, n. 687, ante.   872 *Platt on Leases*, vol. ii. pp. 419–20.

873 *South of England Dairies Ltd v Baker* [1906] 2 Ch 631, M & B p. 574.

874 P. 666, post; *Hemingway Securities Ltd v Dunraven Ltd* [1995] 1 EGLR 61 (enforceability of restrictive covenant against sub-letting). The burden of a restrictive covenant in the head lease is binding on the sub-tenant in unregistered land if he has actual, imputed or constructive notice of it (which he will have, having being entitled to call for sight of the head lease before signing the under-lease: *Gosling v Woolf* [1893] 1 QB 39, p. 935, post): LPA 1925, s. 199(1)(ii); a restrictive covenant between lessor and lessee is not registrable as a Class D(ii) land charge: LCA 1972, s. 2(5)(ii). In registered land it is binding automatically: LRA 2002, ss. 29(2)(b), 30(2)(b); H & B, para. 9.8. For restrictive covenants in post-1995 leases, see p. 312, post.

875 *Beardman v Wilson* (1868) LR 4 CP 57; *Hallen v Spaeth* [1923] AC 684; *Milmo v Carreras* [1946] KB 306, M & B p. 574 (sub-lease for a term longer than that of lease is an assignment of the lease); *Parc Battersea Ltd v Hutchinson* [1999] 2 EGLR 33 (oral sub-lease effective as assignment by operation of law).

Although there is no privity of estate between landlord and sub-tenant, nevertheless the sub-tenant may be able to enforce a covenant which touches and concerns the land against the landlord. In Caerns Motor Services Ltd v Texaco Ltd[876] L granted a lease to T and T then sub-let to S. S could enforce the benefit of any landlord covenants which touched and concerned the land against L, despite the absence of privity of contract. This is because the benefit of such covenants was annexed under section 78 of the Law of Property Act 1925 and could be enforced by a person with a derivative interest.[877]

(2) IDENTICAL INTEREST MUST BE TRANSFERRED

The other point, as we have observed, is that if there is to be an assignment, the assignee must take the identical interest which the assignor possessed. If, for instance, a tenant deposits his lease with X by way of mortgage, X obtains a mere equitable right to the land and not the legal term to which the tenant was entitled. Therefore, whether he goes into possession or not, he can neither sue nor be sued on the covenants.[878] A similar result again ensues where a person obtains a title under the Limitation Act against the tenant, as was decided in *Tichborne v Weir*.[879] The facts of this case were as follows:

In 1802 D leased land to B for 89 years.

In 1836 G seized the land and remained in possession of it until 1876, paying D the rent which had been fixed by the lease of 1802.

In 1876 G by deed assigned all his interest to the defendant, who remained in possession until 1891, paying the same rent to the plaintiff, who had succeeded to D.

The original lease between D and B contained a covenant by B to keep the premises in repair, and the plaintiff now sued the defendant for breach of that covenant. The right of the original covenantor B to his tenancy of the land had been extinguished by lapse of time when the defendant came to the land in 1876, but the question that arose was whether the defendant was an assignee of B through G. It was clear, if the identical lease which was vested in B had passed to G and from him to the defendant, that the latter would be liable as assignee on the repairing covenant, and it was strenuously argued that the effect of the Real Property Limitation Act 1833, which was the statute then in force, was to transfer the term from B to G.

It was held that the only effect of the statute was to extinguish B's right of recovering the land and not to convey what he had to G. It therefore followed that the defendant was not liable on the repairing covenant, because, not possessing the very estate to which it was attached,

---

[876] [1994] 1 WLR 1249; Law Commission Report on Contracts for the Benefit of Third Parties 1996 (Law Com No. 242, Cm 3329), para. 2.11(iii)). See also Contracts (Rights of Third Parties) Act 1999, under which, in relation to covenants entered into by L on or after the Act came into force, S may have a direct right against L under s. 1; p. 676, post. See the remarks of the Parliamentary Secretary of the Lord Chancellor's Department in the Standing Committee Proceedings in HL on 15 July 1999. See also (2000) 4 L & TR D10 (D. R. Perks).

[877] *Smith and Snipes Hall Farm Ltd v River Douglas Catchment Board* [1949] 2 KB 500 (lessee able to enforce annexed freehold covenant on the wording of s. 78). As it is clear that s. 78 applies to leases as well as to freeholds, S must be able to enforce the covenant against L.

[878] *Cox v Bishop* (1857) 8 De GM & G 815, M & B p. 578. He may, however, be liable under the doctrine of *Tulk v Moxhay*, pp. 666 et seq, post.

[879] (1892) 67 LT 735, M & B pp. 241, 946, followed in *Taylor v Twinberrow* [1930] 2 KB 16.

he was not an assignee. But the limits of the decision must be noted. It was said by a learned Irish judge:[880]

It appears to me to decide only this, that the Statute of Limitations operates by way of extinguishment, and not by way of assignment of the estate, which is barred; and that a person who becomes entitled to a leasehold interest by adverse possession for the prescribed period is not liable to be sued *in covenant as assignee* of the lease, unless he has estopped himself from denying that he is assignee.

So, in the first place, the decision will not apply where the occupier of the land has estopped himself from denying that he holds on all the terms of the original lease,[881] but although this point was pressed in *Tichborne v Weir*, it was held that the terms under which the defendant paid rent did not warrant the conclusion that he stood for all purposes in the shoes of the original tenant B.[882] But where a lease contains a proviso that the rent shall be reduced by half if all the covenants are duly observed, and an adverse possessor avails himself of the privilege, he is estopped from denying that he is subject to the burden of the lease.[883]

Secondly, the case only goes to show that an adverse possessor cannot be sued in covenant as assignee. When we come to deal with equitable doctrines, we shall see that he is liable on such negative covenants as create an equitable burden on the estate he takes.[884]

(4) Statutory Protection for Former Tenants

Sections 17–20 of the Landlord and Tenant (Covenants) Act 1995 impose restrictions on the liability of a former tenant and his guarantor after assignment of the tenancy. The restrictions apply to *all* tenancies, whether created before or after the Act.

(a) *Restriction on liability for fixed charge*[885]

Under section 17, a former tenant (and his guarantor) is not liable for a "fixed charge", unless the landlord serves a prescribed notice[886] informing him that the charge is now due and that the landlord intends to recover a specified sum and, where payable, interest. The notice must be served within six months of the charge becoming due.

A fixed charge is defined as rent, service charge or any liquidated sum payable in the event of failure on breach of a covenant in the lease.

The object of the section is to give protection to former tenants against a landlord who allows arrears of payment to accumulate without their knowledge.

---

[880] FITZGIBBON LJ in *O'Connor v Foley* [1906] 1 IR 20 at 26.
[881] As for instance in *Rodenhurst Estates Ltd v Barnes Ltd* [1936] 2 All ER 3.
[882] For another instance, see *Official Trustee of Charity Lands v Ferriman Trust Ltd* [1937] 3 All ER 85.
[883] *Ashe v Hogan* [1920] 1 IR 159.
[884] *Re Nisbet and Potts' Contract* [1905] 1 Ch 391, M & B pp. 241, 948; p. 672, post.
[885] See Fancourt, chap. 20.
[886] LT(C)A 1995 (Notices) Regulations 1995 (SI 1995 No. 2964), Schedule Form 1; *Cheverell Estates Ltd v Harris* [1998] 1 EGLR 27 (where guarantor is to be sued, notice need not also be served on former tenant as well); *Commercial Union Life Assurance Co Ltd v Moustafa* [1999] 2 EGLR 44 (notice is properly served if sent to intended recipient at his last residential address, whether it was received by that recipient or not). The amount recoverable may be less than the amount specified in the notice under s. 17(4); *Kellogg v Tobin* [1999] L & TR 513; [1999] EG 25 May p. 152 (D. Stevens) (former tenants must receive notices from landlord in order to obtain indemnity).

(b) Right to overriding lease [887]

Sections 19 and 20 entitle the tenant (or his guarantor), who has made full payment of a fixed charge under section 17, to "have the landlord under that tenancy grant him an overriding lease of the premises demised by the tenancy".[888] The effect is to insert a lease between the interest of the landlord and that of a defaulting assignee.

It will be for a term equal to the remainder of the term of the relevant tenancy[889] plus three days,[890] and on essentially the same terms.

Thus, if L has granted a lease to T, who then assigns it to A, T, who has paid the fixed charge to L, is entitled to call upon L to grant him an overriding lease. This makes T the landlord of A and gives him control over A for the duration of the lease; he can pursue remedies directly against A for breach of covenant or forfeit his lease, and thus either take possession himself or assign it to a more attractive and solvent assignee.

A claim to an overriding lease must be made in writing within twelve months of the date of payment of the fixed charge.[891] In order to be enforceable against a successor in title of the landlord, it must be registered under the Land Charges Act 1972, if it is unregistered land, or protected by a notice, if it is registered land, as if it were an estate contract. It cannot be an overriding interest under paragraph 2 of Schedule 1 or 3 of the Land Registration Act 2002.[892] It is expressly provided that an overriding lease will be binding on a mortgagee of the landlord.[893]

(c) Restriction on liability for post-assignment variation[894]

As we have seen, the Court of Appeal considered the effect of post-assignment variation in *Friends' Provident Life Assurance v British Railways Board*[895] a week after the passing of the Landlord and Tenant (Covenants) Act 1995 and declined to follow the reasoning in *Centrovincial Estates plc v Bulk Storage Ltd*.[896] Section 18 is anticipated by the protection given to the tenant in that case.[897] Under the section a former tenant or his guarantor are not liable to pay any amount which is solely attributable to a relevant variation of a tenant covenant by the landlord and the assignee effected after the assignment.

A relevant variation is one where the landlord either has the absolute right to refuse to allow it, or would have had such a right if the former tenant had sought a variation immediately before he assigned the tenancy but, between then and the time of the variation, the tenant covenants had been varied so as to deprive the landlord of his rights.[898]

B Covenants in Leases Granted After 1995

(1) Introduction

We have seen the hazards which beset a tenant who has assigned his lease granted before 1996. These were exacerbated by the recession of the late 1980s and early 1990s.

---

[887] Fancourt, chap. 21. See Land Registration (Overriding Leases) Rules 1995 (SI 1995 No. 3154), r. 2.

[888] S. 19(1). Failure of the landlord to grant the lease within a reasonable time renders him liable in tort for breach of statutory duty: ss. 19(6)(a), 20(3).

[889] I.e. the lease to which the overriding lease is immediately in reversion and under which the tenant defaulted.   [890] S. 19(2)(a).

[891] S. 19(5)   [892] S. 20(6), as amended by LRA 2002, s. 133, Sch. 11, para. 33.   [893] S. 20(4).

[894] Fancourt, chap. 21.   [895] [1995] 2 EGLR 55, in which reference is made to s. 18, p. 304, ante.

[896] (1983) 46 P & CR 393, p. 304, ante.

[897] Nothing in the section applies to any variation effected before 1996: s. 18(6).

[898] S. 18(4). See [1996] CLJ 313 (S. Bridge) at pp. 317, 335.

The Landlord and Tenant (Covenants) Act 1995, which came into effect on 1 January 1996, radically changed the law and provides a new code for covenants in leases granted after 1995. It follows the Law Commission Report of 1988[899] (with substantial amendments introduced during the debate in the House of Lords), which sets out the object of the legislation:

First, a landlord or tenant of property should not continue to enjoy rights nor be under any obligation arising from a lease once he has parted with all interest in the property. Second, all the terms of the lease should be regarded as a single bargain for letting the property. When the interest of one of the parties changes hands, the successor should fully take his predecessor's place as landlord and tenant, without distinguishing between the different categories of covenant.

The Bill, as amended during the debates in the House of Lords, was the result of a concordat reached between the United Kingdom's major property organisations; the British Property Federation (for the landlord) and the British Retail Consortium (for the tenant). Without it the Bill would not have been passed. At the same time, the opportunity was taken to extend the original object and to enact a code which would contain complete provisions for the running of covenants in a lease.

The essence of the change is that the contractual liability of original tenants and landlords after they have assigned their interests is terminated, and that all landlord and tenant covenants, other than those which are expressed to be personal,[900] are enforceable and binding upon successors in title of the original parties. Accordingly the principles of privity of contract and privity of estate no longer apply, and sections 78, 79, 141 and 142 of the Law of Property Act 1925[901] cease to have effect in the new statutory code.[902]

(2) Terminology

The code is new, and so is the terminology. The leases to which the Act applies are called "new tenancies", to be distinguished from other tenancies.[903] However some leases granted after 1995 are not new tenancies; for example, where a lease is granted as a result of an option or a right of first refusal which was granted before 1996, even though it was exercised after 1995.[904]

A tenancy includes a sub-tenancy and an agreement for a tenancy but not a mortgage term, thereby avoiding any technical difficulties that have arisen in connection with pre-1996 agreements for leases.[905]

Covenants are either "landlord covenants" or "tenant covenants" which fall to be complied with by the landlord or tenant of premises demised by the tenancy. It is immaterial

---

[899] Privity of Contract and Estate (Law Com No. 174). See Aldridge, *Privity of Contract: Landlord and Tenant (Covenants) Act 1995*.

[900] A covenant is not personal if it would endure throughout the term and be binding on the landlord's successors in title, even though the liability of one particular landlord's liability under the covenant is limited to the period during which it holds the reversion: *London Diocesan Fund v Phithwa* [2005] 1 WLR 3956 at [27], per Lord NICHOLLS OF BIRKENHEAD. For a personal covenant, see *BHP Petroleum Great Britain Ltd v Chesterfield Properties Ltd* [2002] Ch 194 (landlord's obligations, contained in agreement for lease and expressed to be personal to the landlord, to remedy defects in building within specified period).

[901] Pp. 298, 299, 301, 307, ante. Sections 78 and 79 continue to apply in the running of freehold covenants.

[902] LT(C)A 1995, s. 30(4).   [903] S. 1(1). The word "old" is not used for pre-1995 tenancies.

[904] Ss. 1(6), (7), 28(1).

[905] S. 28(1); pp. 302–3, ante. Agreements for tenancies must comply with the formalities of LP(MP)A 1989, s. 2, p. 868, post.

whether or not the covenant has reference to the subject matter of the tenancy and whether the covenant is implied or imposed by law.[906]

(3) Anti-avoidance Provisions[907]

The anti-avoidance provisions are widely drawn. Section 25 makes void any agreement to the extent that

    (a) it would . . . have effect to exclude, modify or otherwise frustrate the operation of any provision of this Act, or

    (b) it provides for—
        (i) the termination or surrender of the tenancy, or
        (ii) the imposition on the tenant of any penalty, disability or liability, in the event of the operation of any provision of this Act.

However, paragraph (a) does not limit the parties' freedom to define the scope of their obligations at the outset of the tenancy, and therefore does not prevent a landlord from defining his liability as being limited to the period when he holds the reversion. In *London Diocesan Fund v Phithwa*[908] a lease contained a covenant in the following terms: "The landlord covenants with the tenant as follows (but not, in the case of Avonridge Property Co Ltd only, so as to be liable after the landlord has disposed of its interest in the Property) . . ." The House of Lords held[909] that this provision did not frustrate the operation of the Act, and was therefore effective. Lord NICHOLLS OF BIRKENHEAD said:[910]

Section 25 is of course to be interpreted generously, so as to ensure the operation of the Act is not frustrated, either directly or indirectly. But there is nothing in the language or scheme of the Act to suggest the statute was intended to exclude the parties' ability to limit liability under their covenants from the outset in whatever way they may agree. An agreed limitation of this nature does not impinge upon the operation of the statutory provisions.

It is, however, always possible for one party to a tenancy to release the other from a covenant.[911]

(4) Transmission of Benefit and Burden of Covenants[912]

The requirement of touching and concerning[913] does not feature in the running of new covenants. The Act provides for the automatic running of *all* landlord and tenant covenants, unless they are (in whatever terms) expressed to be personal to any person. Section 3(1) provides:

The benefit and burden of all landlord and tenant covenants of a tenancy—

    (a) shall be annexed to the whole, and to each and every part, of the premises[914] demised by the tenancy and of the reversion in them, and

[906] S. 2(1). S. 2(2), as amended by SI 1996 No. 2325, art. 5, Sch. 2, excludes covenants under HA 1985, ss. 35, 155; Sch. 6A, para. 1; Housing Associations Act 1985, Sch. 2, paras. 1, 3; HA 1996, ss. 11, 13; *First Penthouse Ltd v Channel Hotels (UK) Ltd* [2004] 1 EGLR 16 (obligations to grant sub-lease and pay commission held not to be tenant covenants). [907] Fancourt, chap. 23.
[908] [2005] 1 WLR 3956; [2006] 05 EG 97 (S. Murdoch).
[909] Lord WALKER OF GESTINGTHORPE dissenting. [910] At [18]. [911] LT(C)A 1995, s. 26(1)(a).
[912] Fancourt, chaps. 11–13. [913] P. 295, ante.
[914] The wording of annexation is taken from the formula in *Rogers v Hosegood* [1900] 2 Ch 388, after some discussion of a looser formula in the House of Lords debate.

(b) shall in accordance with this section pass on an assignment of the whole or any part of those premises or of the reversion of them.

(a) Assignees and sub-tenants

The running of the covenants is still limited to cases of assignment.[915] As far as sub-tenancies are concerned, section 3(5) expressly preserves the equitable doctrine that any landlord and tenant covenant which is restrictive of the user of land: "shall, as well as being capable of enforcement against an assignee, be capable of being enforced against any other person who is the owner or occupier of any demised premises[916] to which the covenant relates, even though there is no express provision in the tenancy to that effect". The effect is that such a restrictive covenant in the head tenancy binds any sub-tenant automatically.[917]

However, *Caerns Motor Services Ltd v Texaco Ltd*[918] would be decided differently. In a new tenancy the sub-tenant could not enforce any covenant in the head lease against the landlord. Section 78 of the Law of Property Act 1925 does not apply to new tenancies and the effect of that section is not replicated in the Act.[919]

Where, however, the Contracts (Rights of Third Parties) Act 1999 applies, a sub-tenant may be able to enforce covenants in a lease against the landlord.[920]

(b) Enforcement of covenants by persons other than landlord and tenant

Section 15 of the Act makes special provision for mortgagees of the reversion and of the tenancy. The benefit and burden of the landlord and tenant covenants run, if the mortgagee is in possession of the reversion or of the premises.[921]

(5) Release of Tenant Covenants on Assignment

Section 5 is the centre piece of the Act. Under it a tenant, who has assigned the premises, is automatically released from his tenant covenants as from the date of the assignment. He also ceases to be entitled to the benefit of the landlord covenants.[922] This automatic release and cessation also applies where only part of the premises is assigned; the release and cessation

---

[915] P. 306, ante.

[916] *Oceanic Village Ltd v United Attractions Ltd* [2000] Ch 234 ("any demised premises" refers only to premises demised by the lease in question, and not to all premises demised by the landlord, if only to have conformity with s. 3(2) and (3) where "any demised premises" can only refer to the premises comprised in the relevant lease).

[917] Law Commission Report on Privity of Contract: Contracts for the Benefit of Third Parties 1996 (Law Com No. 242 Cm 3329), para. 2.11(iii). See also Emmet, para. 26.121. For the mechanisms by which a restrictive covenant in a lease binds a sub-tenant, see p. 307, n. 878, ante.

[918] [1994] 1 WLR 1249, p. 307, ante.

[919] LT(C)A 1995, s. 30(4); s. 15. For the transmission of rights of re-entry, see s. 4. A landlord's right of re-entry is not a landlord covenant. In pre-1996 leases, the right passed with the reversion under LPA 1925, s. 141. Since this section does not apply to new tenancies, a specific provision is necessary. S. 3(7) abolishes as far as necessary the rule in *Spencer's Case* (1583) 5 Co Rep 16a, p. 298, ante.

[920] The Act allows a third party (such as a sub-tenant in relation to the head lease) to enforce a term in the contract if it was the contracting parties' express or implied intention that he should, and as long as he was expressly identified in the contract by name or as a member of a class or by description, even if he was not yet in existence when the contract was entered into: s. 1; p. 676, post. On the Act generally, see Treitel, pp. 651 et seq.

[921] So too where a landlord grants a further lease of his reversionary interest in the premises, for example, in the case of an overriding lease under s. 19; p. 309, ante.

[922] For a similar release of a guarantor and to the same extent, see s. 24(2).

are effective only to the extent that the covenants fail to be complied with in relation to the part assigned.[923]

This statutory rule is not retrospective; the release is from future liability for breach of covenant. Thus, the tenant remains liable for any breach of covenant committed before assignment;[924] but he also retains his right to sue the landlord for breaches of landlord covenants committed before assignment.[925] However, as has been well said:[926]

The relative purity of the Law Commission proposals has been tainted by the Parliamentary process, and the euphoria of the tenant on being rid of privity of contract liability will soon be dampened by acquaintance with the other secrets of the Act. Although the assigning tenant is released from the covenants on assignment, it is almost certain that the *quid pro quo* for release will be a requirement to guarantee the liability of the immediate assignee.

And it is to that guarantee that we must now turn.

(6) Authorised Guarantee Agreement (AGA)

An authorised guarantee agreement is an agreement whereby a tenant who has assigned his new tenancy to A, guarantees to his landlord the performance of tenant covenants by A.[927] It guarantees the performance by A only, and does not extend to the breach of covenants by B to whom A subsequently assigns the tenancy.[928] The landlord may, however, be able to enter into an AGA with B when A assigns the tenancy to B.

(a) Conditions of entering into agreement

Under section 16(2) of the Act an AGA is only effective if:

(a) under it the tenant guarantees the performance of the relevant covenant to any extent by the assignee; and

(b) it is entered into in the circumstances set out in subsection (3); and

(c) its provisions conform with subsections (4) and (5).[929]

Subsection (3) defines the circumstances as follows:

(a) by virtue of a covenant against assignment (whether absolute or qualified) the assignment cannot be effected without the consent of the landlord under the tenancy or some other person;[930]

(b) any such consent is given subject to a condition (lawfully imposed[931]) that the tenant is to enter into an agreement guaranteeing the performance of the covenant by the assignee; and

(c) the agreement is entered into by the tenant in pursuance of that condition.

---

[923] LT(C)A 1995, s. 5(3).   [924] Ibid., s. 24(1).   [925] Ibid., s. 24(4).

[926] [1996] CLJ 313 at p. 337 (S. Bridge).   [927] LT(C)A 1995, s. 16.   [928] Ibid., s. 16(4).

[929] Ibid., supra. Under s. 16(5) the liability of the tenant may be as a principal debtor or as a guarantor, in which case the rules of law relating to guarantees apply: s. 16(8). On disclaimer of the tenancy, see s. 16(5), (7).

[930] For example, a head landlord.

[931] *Wallis Fashion Group Ltd v CGU Life Assurance Ltd* [2000] 2 EGLR 49 (where an assignment of a lease requires the landlord's consent, and the alienation covenant is silent as to whether he can demand an AGA, the landlord can only refuse consent if it is reasonable to do so: LTA 1927, s. 19(1). Therefore a landlord can only "lawfully impose" an AGA condition in the alienation provisions of a new lease granted under LTA 1954, Part II if it is qualified as being enforceable "where reasonable").

(b) Consent and reasonableness

As to whether a landlord, when giving consent to an assignment, may lawfully make it conditional on the tenant entering into an AGA, depends, first, on the type of tenancy. Residential
new tenancies, which are defined as being "a lease by which a building or part of a building is
let wholly or mainly as a single private residence"[932] continue to be governed by section 19 of
the Landlord and Tenant Act 1927, which, as we have seen, implies into a covenant by a tenant not to assign without the landlord's consent a proviso that the consent of the landlord
shall not be unreasonably withheld.[933] There is nothing in the Landlord and Tenant
(Covenants) Act 1995 to suggest that it is always reasonable for the landlord of a residential
new tenancy to make consent to an assignment conditional on the tenant entering into an
AGA. Accordingly, the onus is on the landlord to prove that refusal to consent is reasonable
within section 1(6) of the Landlord and Tenant Act 1988,[934] and, as was said in *International
Drilling Fluids Ltd v Louisville Investments (Uxbridge) Ltd*,[935] each case turns on its own facts.
In the case of a tenancy containing an *absolute* covenant not to assign, however, the landlord
has an absolute discretion as to whether or not to give his consent, and so it will always be
lawful to make the consent conditional on the tenant entering into an AGA.[936]

The position is different, however, if the new tenancy does not come within the definition
of a residential tenancy.[937] Here section 22 of the 1995 Act adds a new section 19(1A) to the
Landlord and Tenant Act 1927,[938] by providing that a landlord may specify in advance the
conditions subject to which consent may be granted. A condition to the effect that a tenant
must enter into an AGA comes within the amended section 19 and will be "lawfully imposed".

The new section 19 (1A) of the 1927 Act[939] provides that where the parties specify in
their AGA

(a) any circumstances in which the landlord may withhold his licence or consent to an assignment
of the demised premises of any part of them, or

(b) any conditions subject to which any such licence or consent may be granted,

then the landlord—

(i) shall not be regarded as unreasonably withholding his licence or consent to any such assignment
if he withholds it on the ground (and this is the case) that any such circumstances exist, and

(ii) if he gives such licence or consent subject to any such conditions, shall not be regarded as giving
it subject to unreasonable conditions.

However, if these predetermined circumstances or conditions are not purely factual, but are
at the discretion of the landlord or any other person, then the agreement must either state
that the discretion is to be exercised reasonably, or give to the tenant an unrestricted right to
have its exercise reviewed by an independent third party, whose determination is to be conclusive.

The agreement specifying these terms need not be set out in the new tenancy itself and
may be made at any time before the tenant makes application for consent to the assignment.

---

932 LTA 1927, s. 19(1E)(a).   933 P. 257, ante.   934 P. 258, ante.
935 [1986] Ch 513 at 521, p. 261, ante.   936 Emmet, para. 26.133E.
937 An agricultural tenancy is also outside s. 19: Agricultural Holdings Act 1986; and so too is a farm business tenancy: Agricultural Tenancies Act 1995.   938 P. 257, ante.
939 *Legends Surf Shops plc v Sun Life Assurance Society plc* [2005] 3 EGLR 43 (whether landlord could insist
on personal guarantees in AGA where former tenant in administrative receivership).

(c) Statutory protection for former tenants

Sections 17–20 of the Act,[940] which impose restrictions on the liability of a former tenant or his guarantor for a fixed charge, for post-assignment variations and for his right to the grant of an overriding lease, have already been set out in connection with covenants in pre-1996 leases to which the restrictions also apply.

(7) Excluded Assignments

Section 11 of the Act excludes two cases of assignment in which the tenant is not released from liability. First, where the tenant assigns his tenancy in breach of his covenant not to assign; and secondly, where the assignment is by operation of law. Examples of the latter are an assignment on the death of a tenant when the tenancy will vest in his personal representatives; on the death of a joint tenant of a legal estate, when it vests in the other joint tenant; on the bankruptcy of an individual tenant, when it vests in his trustee in bankruptcy; and on registration of a squatter as the new proprietor of a registered estate.[941]

The effect of an excluded assignment is to defer the release to the next assignment which is not an excluded assignment.[942]

(8) Release of Landlord Covenants on Assignment

There are two separate situations to consider: where the landlord is released and where a former landlord is released.

(a) Release of landlord

Unlike the tenant, the landlord is not automatically released from the landlord covenants when he assigns his reversion. If he were, a tenant would have no way of vetting the landlord's assignee and preventing assignment to a man of straw. Instead, he must apply to the tenant to be released under section 6 of the Act. He can do this by serving a notice on him under section 8 of the Act,[943] informing him of the assignment and requesting the release of the covenants. The notice must be served either before or within four weeks from the date of the assignment. If the tenant either consents or fails to object within this strict time limit, the landlord is released. If the tenant objects, he must serve a counter-notice objecting to the release within four months of the service of the notice on him. If he does so, the landlord may then apply to the county court for a declaration that it is reasonable for the covenant to be released. If the covenant is released, then the landlord ceases to be bound by the landlord covenants and loses their benefit.

---

[940] P. 308, ante.

[941] Law Commission Report on Land Registration for the Twenty-First Century 2001 (Law Com No. 271), para. 14.71, n. 242; H & B, paras. 31.2, 31.3.

[942] LT(C)A 1995, s. 11(5). The implied indemnity covenants given by an assignee to a tenant on assignment with regard to future performance of the covenants in a lease under LPA 1925, s. 77(1)(c) and (d) and LRA 1925, s. 24(1)(b) and (2) (now LRA 2002, s. 134(2), Sch. 12, para. 20), p. 305, ante, are repealed by the Act in respect of new tenancies: s. 30(2), Sch. 2.

[943] S. 27; SI 1995 No. 2964, Sch., Forms 3–6. S. 8 allows the landlord to obtain release only of "landlord covenants": i.e., a covenant which is capable of binding the person from time to time entitled to the reversion. It does not apply to a covenant entered into by a landlord but expressed to be personal to him: *BHP Petroleum Great Britain Ltd v Chesterfield Properties Ltd* [2002] Ch 194.

Similarly, when the landlord assigns part of the reversion, the release relates to the covenants only to the extent that they fall to be complied with in relation to that part of the demised premises.

(b) Release of former landlord

If the landlord fails to apply for release within the four-month period, or fails in his application, he is nevertheless entitled under section 7 to make a further application when the reversion is next assigned.

(9) Joint Liability under Covenants

As a result of the provisions of the Act, a situation may arise where two or more persons are bound by the same covenant. Under section 13(1) they are jointly and severally liable under the covenant; the Civil Liability (Contribution) Act 1978 applies for the purposes of contribution between the joint covenantors. An example may make this clearer. In the context of the release of landlord covenants:

One landlord (A) may assign his interest to B and decide to serve no notice on the tenant, with the result that his liability continues. B may in turn decide to assign to C, serving notice on him. If the tenant takes no action and the property is assigned to C, B escapes liability. At that point, C is fully liable to comply with the landlord's covenants, and he is jointly and severally liable with A.[944]

VII Termination of a Lease

A lease may be terminated on various grounds. The lease may provide for its own termination without fault of either party—for example, by allowing either party to serve on the other a notice[945] to terminate; and by being of its very nature limited in time by reference to the term granted.[946] The conduct of one party in breach of his obligations under the lease may be accepted by the other as grounds to terminate, either under an express provision contained in the lease,[947] or under general principles of law.[948] The parties may agree to terminate the lease during its currency,[949] or circumstances may occur which are not provided for in the lease but which have the effect in law of terminating the lease.[950] And sometimes statute provides a particular mechanism for termination.[951]

---

[944] Law Commission Report: Privity of Contract and Estate 1988 (Law Com No. 174). A similar joint liability may arise in the context of tenant covenants: for example, where a tenant assigns the whole of the demised premises in breach of assignment (an excluded assignment), p. 315, ante; or where a tenant assigns part of the demised premises, where no apportionment has occurred. For apportionment of liability, see LT(C)A 1995, ss. 9 and 10; [1986] CLJ 313 at 343 (S. Bridge).

[945] A notice is commonly referred to as a "notice to quit", particularly where given by a landlord; a notice given by the tenant is often the exercise of its right under the terms of the lease to "break" the term. We shall however see that a "notice to quit" can operate in different ways: p. 317, post.

[946] For the different operation of termination by effluxion of time in fixed term and periodic tenancies, however, see pp. 317, 321, post.

[947] E.g. re-entry and forfeiture by the landlord under an express provision in the lease: p. 324, post.

[948] E.g. acceptance by the landlord or the tenant of the other's repudiation, under general contractual principles: p. 324, post.   [949] Surrender: p. 325, post.

[950] Frustration: p. 328, post; merger: p. 327, post.

[951] E.g. enlargement under LPA 1925, s. 153: p. 327, post. For termination by disclaimer of the lease as onerous property by the tenant's liquidator or trustee in bankruptcy, see Insolvency Act 1986, ss. 178, 179, 182, 315, 317, 321; *Christopher Moran Holdings Ltd v Bairstow* [2000] 2 AC 172.

We have seen[952] that a lease is both a contract and an estate or interest in land. The rules for termination generally follow from one or other of these characteristics.[953] It should be noted from the outset, however, that the common law rules, in so far as they give the landlord the right to terminate, are in many cases limited by statutory rules designed to protect the tenant. In this section we shall notice some of these statutory rules, applicable to the termination of leases in general, but in Section IX[954] we shall discuss the statutory protections afforded to particular types of tenancy.

A Effluxion of Time

In principle there is no need for a notice to quit in the case of a lease for a definite term, since the tenancy terminates automatically upon the expiration of the agreed period. The scope of this rule, however, has been drastically restricted by legislation, for there are several cases in which there is no automatic cessation of a tenancy upon the expiration of the period for which it was granted. These cases are the following:

private residential lettings;[955]

public sector housing (secure tenancies);[956]

long tenancies;[957]

business tenancies;[958] and

agricultural tenancies.[959]

In the result there are comparatively few cases in which effluxion of time has its normal effect.

B Termination by Notice

If the lease so provides, it may be terminated by notice by either the landlord or the tenant.[960] A notice operates differently in terminating a tenancy for a fixed period, and a periodic tenancy.

(1) Special Rule in Case of Lease of a Dwelling

There is special protection in the case of premises let as a dwelling. The Protection from Eviction Act 1977[961] provides that no notice by a landlord or a tenant shall be valid unless it

---

[952] Pp. 194, ante.

[953] E.g. the contractual doctrines of frustration and repudiation have been applied in recent years to leases; whereas the doctrine of merger follows from the nature of a lease as an estate in land as well as being a consequence of the principle that one cannot contract with oneself.   [954] Pp. 336 et seq, post.

[955] P. 337, post.   [956] P. 358, post.   [957] P. 363, post.   [958] P. 377, post.

[959] P. 386, post.

[960] A termination clause will benefit and bind the assignees of the original parties, unless it is expressed to be personal: *Harbour Estates Ltd v HSBC Bank plc* [2005] Ch 194, p. 296, n. 793, ante (pre-1996 lease); *Brown & Root Technology Ltd v Sun Alliance and London Assurance Co Ltd* [2001] Ch 733 (tenant's option to break expressed to be personal); LT(C)A 1995, ss. 2(1), 3(1), (6), p. 311, ante.

[961] S. 5 (1)(b). This section only applies where the true relation between the parties is that of landlord and tenant: *Alliance Building Society v Pinwill* [1958] Ch 788 (mortgagor/mortgagee); *Crane v Morris* [1965] 1 WLR 1104 (tenancy at will); *Peckham Mutual Building Society v Registe* (1980) 42 P & CR 186 (mortgagor/

is given not less than four weeks before the date on which it is to expire; the notice must be in writing and contain such information as may be prescribed by the Secretary of State.[962] The common law rule[963] applies in this context and the provision is satisfied by a notice given on one day to expire that day four weeks hence.[964]

(2) Notice to Terminate a Tenancy for a Fixed Period

Since the notice is a unilateral act performed in the exercise of a contractual right, it must conform strictly to the terms of the contract.[965] The onus of proving its validity lies upon the person by whom it is given.[966] Three matters in particular upon which its validity depends may be observed.

(a) Must indicate correct day

First, it is void unless it either names the correct date for the termination of the tenancy[967] or uses a formula from which the correct date is ascertainable with certainty. A familiar example of the latter is when the notice requires the yearly tenant to quit the premises: "at the expiration of the year of your tenancy, which shall expire next after the end of one half-year from the service of this notice".[968]

This rigid rule has, however, been relaxed where the date in the notice is one which no reasonable tenant could possibly have supposed was the date correctly intended by the landlord. Thus, where by a clerical error a notice served in 1974 referred to a 1973 date instead of a 1975 date, GOULDING J held the notice valid and said:[969] "I would put the test generally applicable as being this: 'is the notice quite clear to a reasonable tenant reading it? Is it plain that he cannot be misled by it?' "

mortgagee). However, s. 5(1A), inserted by HA 1988, s. 32(2), applies the same rule to a periodic *licence* to occupy premises as a dwelling: s. 5(1A). Four weeks is also the minimum notice for a residential contract in respect of a caravan: Caravan Sites Act 1968, s. 2.

962   Protection from Eviction Act 1977., s. 5(1)(a). See Notices to Quit (Prescribed Information) Regulations 1988 (SI 1988 No. 2201), Sched. This includes notifying the tenant that the landlord cannot evict him without first obtaining a court order for possession: p. 331, post. Even if the notice is ineffective as a notice to quit under the 1977 Act, if given by the tenant it can still be evidence of the tenant's intention to surrender the lease: *Ealing Family Housing Association Ltd v McKenzie* [2004] L & TR 15; *Lewisham LBC v Lasisi-Agiri* [2003] 45 EGCS 175; *Laine v Cadwallader* (2001) 33 HLR 36 (depositing keys through letterbox amounted to offer by tenant to surrender tenancy).   963   P. 320, post.

964   *Schnabel v Allard* [1966] 3 All ER 816.

965   *Dagger v Shepherd* [1946] KB 215 at 220; *Hankey v Clavering* [1942] 2 KB 326 at 330. Cf *Brown & Root Technology Ltd v Sun Alliance and London Assurance Co Ltd* [2001] Ch 733 (break clause personal to original tenant who had assigned lease but not yet registered the transfer: still exercisable because, on proper construction, right to exercise break clause ceased only after there had been a *legal* assignment). For service of a notice affecting land where intended recipient is dead, see LP(MP)A 1994, s. 17; [1995] Conv 476 (L. Clements).

966   *Lemon v Lardeur* [1946] KB 613; *Lemmerbell Ltd v Britannia LAS Direct Ltd* [1998] 3 EGLR 67 (wrong person identified in notice); [2004] Conv 361 (J. L. Diamond and J. A. Sandham).

967   *Hankey v Clavering*, supra; *Keepers and Governors of John Lyon Grammar School v Secchi* [1999] 3 EGLR 49.

968   *Addis v Burrows* [1948] 1 KB 444. See (1974) 38 Conv (NS) 312.

969   *Carradine Properties Ltd v Aslam* [1976] 1 WLR 442, approved and followed by CA in *Germax Securities Ltd v Spiegal* (1978) 37 P & CR 204 (where the clerical error was not in the operative part of the notice, and was clear from association of the notice with a covering letter from the landlord); (1977) 40 MLR 490 (P. F. Smith). See also *Safeway Food Stores Ltd v Morris* (1980) 254 EG 1091 (notice, which failed to identify subsidiary part of property necessarily enjoyed with main part of it, held to apply to whole); *Crawford v Elliott* [1991] 1 EGLR 13; *Divall v Harrison* [1992] 2 EGLR 64 (notice which failed to identify correct landlord held invalid); *Trafford MBC v Total Fitness (UK) Ltd* [2003] 2 P & CR 2.

A gloss was put on this test in *Land v Sykes*,[970] where Scott LJ held that it was: "subject perhaps to the qualifications that the reasonable tenant reading the notice is to be taken to have had the knowledge of the surrounding facts and circumstances which the actual landlord and tenant enjoyed".

In *Mannai Investment Co Ltd v Eagle Star Life Assurance Co Ltd*,[971] the House of Lords, by a majority of three to two, approved this "ordinary commonsense interpretation of what people say". In that case a tenant served a notice purporting to operate a break clause in a lease by specifying 12 January 1995, instead of 13 January 1995, as the date for expiry. In holding that the notice was valid, Lord Steyn said:

In determining the meaning of the language of a commercial contract, and unilateral contractual notices, the law therefore generally favours a commercially sensible construction. The reason for this approach is that a commercial construction is more likely to give effect to the intention of the parties. Words are therefore interpreted in the way in which a reasonable commercial person would construe them. And the standard of the reasonable commercial person is hostile to technical interpretations and undue emphasis on niceties of language.

Lord Hoffmann added the graphic comment:

I propose to begin by examining the way we interpret utterances in everyday life. It is a matter of constant experience that people can convey their meaning unambiguously although they have used the wrong words. We start with an assumption that people will use words and grammar in a conventional way but quite often it becomes obvious that, for one reason or another, they are not doing so and we adjust our interpretation of what they are saying accordingly. We do so in order to make sense of their utterance: so that the different parts of the sentence fit together in a coherent way and also enable the sentence to fit the background of facts which plays an indispensable part in the way we interpret what anyone is saying. No one, for example, has any difficulty in understanding Mrs. Malaprop. When she says "She is as obstinate as an allegory on the banks of the Nile," we reject the conventional or literal meaning of allegory as making nonsense of the sentence and substitute "alligator" by using our background knowledge of the things likely to be found on the banks of the Nile and choosing one which sounds rather like "allegory".

In commenting on these two speeches, Neuberger J said in *Proctor & Gamble Technical Centres Ltd v Brixton plc*:[972] "like Lord Hoffmann, Lord Steyn did not give a green light to inaccurate and sloppily drafted notices. The test, even in relation to the construction of notices, is relatively strict".

(b) Must be unconditional

Secondly, a notice to quit must be unconditional. It must be expressed in such decisive and unequivocal terms, that the person to whom it is directed can entertain no reasonable doubt

---

[970] [1992] 1 EGLR 1 at 3 (9 ft by 200 ft strip not material in context of 290 acre farm).

[971] [1997] AC 749; [1987] Conv 326 (P. F. Smith); (1999) 115 LQR 389 (M. Robinson); [1998] CLJ 29 (L. Tee). Followed in *Garston v Scottish Widows' Fund and Life Assurance Society* [1998] 1 WLR 1583, where Nourse LJ said at 1585: "In the company of 'the man on the Clapham Omnibus', 'the officious bystander', and 'the man skilled in the art', there has now been added 'the reasonable recipient', a formidable addition to the imagery of our law." See also *York v Casey* [1998] 2 EGLR 25; *Investors' Compensation Scheme Ltd v West Bromwich Building Society* [1998] 1 WLR 896; *National Bank of Sharjah v Dellborg* (CA, 9 July 1997); *Scottish Power plc v Britoil (Exploration) plc* The Times, 2 December 1998; (1998) 142 SJ 176 (S. Price); [1999] 3 L & T Rev 88 (P. Morgan); *Havant International Holdings Ltd v Lionsgate (H) Investment Ltd* [2000] L & TR 297 (lessee's break notice mistakenly given by director of associated company having very similar name held valid); *Peer Freeholds Ltd v Clean Wash International Ltd* [2005] 1 EGLR 47.   [972] [2003] 2 EGLR 24 at [35].

as to its intended effect. In particular, although no precise form is required, "there must be plain unambiguous words claiming to determine the existing tenancy at a certain time".[973] Thus a notice given by a tenant would be ineffective if it expressed his intention to quit the premises on 25 March unless he was unable to obtain alternative accommodation.

Where, however, the naming of a certain day for the termination of the tenancy is followed by an intimation that the lease shall continue if the other party assents to certain terms, as for example to an increase[974] or diminution[975] of rent, the courts are inclined to treat the document as a valid notice accompanied by an offer of a new tenancy capable of acceptance or refusal by the other party.

Similarly, the courts will treat as valid a notice which gives only a long-stop date for termination. In *Dagger v Shepherd*,[976] for instance, the question arose whether a notice, given on 21 December, directing the tenant to quit the premises "on or before the 25th March next", was valid and effective. It was objected by the tenant that the notice was void for uncertainty, since he was left in doubt as to its intended effect. In his submission the document contained nothing more than a statement that the tenancy was to end on some unspecified date between 21 December and 25 March. The court, however, rejected this submission. It construed the document as an irrevocable notice to quit on 25 March in any event, but followed by an offer to accept the termination of the tenancy at an earlier date at which the tenant might elect to give up possession. Similarly, a notice to quit "by" a certain day is valid.[977] And, where the landlord has a right to determine a lease by giving to the tenant "not less than three months' notice", a notice to vacate the premises "within a period of three months from the date of the service of the notice" is valid. As NOURSE LJ said:[978] "I see no difference between the meanings of 'within' and 'during' . . . If someone is required to vacate premises within or during a specified period, he will comply with the requirement by walking out of the door either before, or on, the stroke of midnight on the last day of that period."

(c) *Must relate to whole of premises*

A notice to quit given by a landlord must relate to the whole of the premises. It is void if it directs the tenant to surrender possession of part only of what he holds, unless this is permitted by the lease itself or by statute.[979] Such a statutory power is vested in the landlord of an agricultural holding if he requires part of the land for certain purposes, such as the erection of cottages or the provision of allotments, specified by the Agricultural Holdings Act 1986.[980] If, however, he takes advantage of this power, the tenant may treat the notice as a notice to quit the entire holding.[981]

In the case of a farm business tenancy any notice to quit part which is permitted by the lease must be in writing and be given at least twelve months but less than twenty-four months before the date on which it is to take effect.[982]

---

[973] *Gardner v Ingram* (1889) 61 LT 729 at 730, per Lord COLERIDGE.

[974] *Ahearn v Bellman* (1879) 4 Ex D 201; but Lord ESHER vigorously dissented.

[975] *Bury v Thompson* [1895] 1 QB 696.   [976] [1946] KB 215.

[977] *Eastaugh v Macpherson* [1954] 1 WLR 1307.

[978] *Manorlike Ltd v Le Vitas Travel Agency and Consultancy Services Ltd* [1986] 1 All ER 573.

[979] *Re Bebington's Tenancy* [1921] 1 Ch 559. The actual decision is now out of date owing to LPA 1925, s. 140(1), (2).

[980] S. 31. The Act does not apply to tenancies beginning on or after 1 September 1995.   [981] S. 32.

[982] Agricultural Tenancies Act 1995, ss. 6, 7, apply only to tenancies for more than two years or for year to year. In the latter case the notice must take effect at the end of the year of the tenancy.

(3) Notice to Terminate a Yearly or Other Periodic Tenancy

As we have seen,[983] a periodic tenancy is one which is renewed at the end of each period unless determined by notice to quit. As Lord TEMPLEMAN said:[984]

The term continues until determined as if both parties made a new agreement at the end of each year for a new term for the ensuing year.

In the case of a periodic tenancy, therefore, a notice to quit does not involve the premature termination of the term, but causes the tenancy to terminate at the end of a period—therefore, by effluxion of time—without being renewed.[985]

(a) Tenancies from year to year

(1) HALF A YEAR'S NOTICE NECESSARY

A tenancy from year to year does not expire at the end of the first or any subsequent year, but continues until it is determined at the end of a year by a notice served by either the landlord or the tenant.[986] It has been the rule since the reign of Henry VIII that not less than half a year's notice is necessary, unless a different agreement has been made by the parties.

It is well established what is meant by "half a year". If the tenancy began on one of the usual quarter days,[987] it means the interval between a quarter day and the next quarter day but one, notwithstanding that, measured by days, such a period may not amount to half a year.[988] Thus in a Lady Day tenancy notice to quit will be good if given on or before Michaelmas Day, though the actual period is five days short of 182. If the tenancy began at some day falling between two quarter days, then the length of notice must be 182 days at least.[989]

(2) EXCEPTIONS

There are two exceptions to the rule requiring half a year's notice.

(i) Contrary agreement

First, where the parties have made a different arrangement:

I know of nothing which prevents parties, in entering into an agreement for a tenancy from year to year, from stipulating that it should be determinable by a notice to quit shorter than the usual six months' notice; or that the notices to quit to be given by the landlord and the tenant respectively should be of unequal length; or that the tenancy should be determinable by the one party only by notice to quit and by the other party either by notice to quit or in some other way.[990]

Any such agreement must not be repugnant to the nature of a yearly tenancy. Thus a term under which neither of the parties may determine, or under which only one of them may

---

[983] P. 214, ante.

[984] *Prudential Assurance Co Ltd v London Residuary Body* [1992] 2 AC 386 at 394. See also *Hammersmith and Fulham LBC v Monk* [1992] 1 AC 478 at 490, per Lord BRIDGE OF HARWICH; p. 323, post.

[985] *Newlon Housing Trust v Alsulaimen* [1999] AC 313 (notice to quit therefore not a disposition of property for the purposes of Matrimonial Causes Act 1973).

[986] See *Youngmin v Heath* [1974] 1 WLR 135 (personal representative of deceased weekly tenant liable for rent until notice to quit given).

[987] Lady Day (25 March); Midsummer Day (24 June); Michaelmas (29 September); Christmas (25 December).

[988] *Right d Flower v Darby and Bristow* (1786) 1 Term Rep 159.

[989] 1 Wms Saunders 276 C; *Sidebotham v Holland* [1895] 1 QB 378 at 384.

[990] *Allison v Scargall* [1920] 3 KB 443 at 449, per SALTER J.

determine, is inconsistent with the concept of a yearly tenancy,[991] and will be struck out, thereby enabling a landlord to terminate on giving the appropriate notice.

(ii) Agricultural holding

Secondly, it is provided by statute in the case of an agricultural holding, that, notwithstanding any express stipulation to the contrary, a notice to quit shall be invalid if it purports to terminate the tenancy before the expiration of twelve months from the end of the current year of the tenancy.[992]

(3) NOTICE TO EXPIRE AT END OF CURRENT YEAR

A yearly tenancy is terminable only at the end of the current year, and therefore a notice, given for example by the landlord, must require the tenant to quit the holding on that date—no earlier, no later. Literally interpreted, the end of the current year is midnight of the day prior to the anniversary of the day on which the tenancy began.

For instance, if a yearly tenancy began on 29 September,[993] its current period ends each year on 28 September. In strictness, therefore, a notice given, say, by the landlord, must direct the tenant to quit on 28 September and it must reach the tenant at least half a year before that day. A notice, for instance, that is not served upon him till after 25 March, and which directs him to quit on the next ensuing 28 September is bad, and he will be entitled to remain until 28 September in the following year.

The courts, however, after some hesitation, extended the strict meaning of the expression "end of the current year" to include the anniversary of the day on which the tenancy began. "A notice to quit at the first moment of the anniversary," said LINDLEY LJ, "ought to be just as good as a notice to quit on the last moment of the day before."[994] A notice, therefore, given not later than Lady Day, will be good if it purports to terminate a Michaelmas tenancy on 29 September.[995]

(b) Other periodic tenancies

Similar rules apply in the case of other periodic tenancies. Subject to the statutory rule in the case of premises let as a dwelling,[996] the length of the notice must be not less than the length of the tenancy, for example, at least seven days' notice is necessary to terminate a weekly

---

[991] *Prudential Assurance Co Ltd v London Residuary Body* [1992] 2 AC 386 at 394, p. 214, ante (reversing *Re Midland Rly Co's Agreement* [1971] Ch 725); *Doe d Warner v Browne* (1807) 8 East 165; *Cheshire Lines Committee v Lewis & Co* (1880) 50 LJQB 121.

[992] Agricultural Holdings Act 1986, s. 25(1); p. 387, post.

[993] There is a presumption that a tenancy from a named date commences on the first moment of the day following: *Ladyman v Wirral Estates Ltd* [1968] 2 All ER 197. The presumption was rebutted in *Whelton Sinclair v Hyland* [1992] 2 EGLR 158 (application of presumption would have left premises undemised for one day, where parties were mistaken as to correct date of renewed lease under Landlord and Tenant Act 1954); *Meadfield Properties Ltd v Secretary of State for the Environment* [1995] 1 EGLR 39 (term expressed as "from 24 June 1984 until 24 December 2003" held to include both specified days).

[994] *Sidebotham v Holland* [1895] 1 QB 378 at 383.

[995] *Sidebotham v Holland*, supra; *Crate v Miller* [1947] KB 946 (dealing with the analogous case of a weekly tenancy); *Yeandle v Reigate and Banstead BC* [1996] 1 EGLR 20. Where notice is given in months, the period of notice ends on the day of the month which bears the same number as that on which the notice was given. February, having only twenty-eight or twenty-nine days, is an exception: *Dodds v Walker* [1981] 1 WLR 1027; *E J Riley Investments Ltd v Eurostile Holdings Ltd* [1985] 1 WLR 1139.

[996] Protection from Eviction Act 1977, s. 5(1); p. 317, ante.

tenancy, and the notice must purport to terminate the tenancy at the end of the current period,[997] that is, either on the anniversary of the date of its commencement[998] or on the preceding day. In computing the period of seven days or the other appropriate period, the day of expiry but not the day of service is included. Thus, a tenancy that began on a Saturday may be terminated by a notice to quit given on a Saturday, notwithstanding that this does not give the tenant seven clear days' notice. In *Lemon v Lardeur*,[999] a tenant who held on a four-weekly tenancy was given "a month's notice as from 1 August, 1945, to vacate" the premises. No evidence was given of the date on which the tenancy began. The notice was invalid, for, since it had not been shown that 1 August was the first day of one of the four-weekly periods, it was impossible to ascertain whether the month's notice would expire at the end of the current period.

These rules may be varied by the parties. Subject to the statutory rule that four weeks' notice is necessary to terminate a lease of premises let as a dwelling,[1000] the length of the notice and the date at which it may be given are matters upon which the parties may make what arrangement they like.[1001]

(c) Termination of joint periodic tenancy

A notice to quit given by one of two joint landlords[1002] or by one of two joint tenants is effective to determine a periodic tenancy, even though the other joint owner does not concur.[1003]

In *Hammersmith and Fulham London Borough Council v Monk*[1004] the House of Lords held that this was so, in spite of the law that a single joint tenant cannot exercise a break clause in a lease,[1005] surrender the term, make a disclaimer, exercise an option to renew the lease or apply for relief against forfeiture. As Lord BRIDGE OF HARWICH said:[1006]

All these positive acts which joint tenants must concur in performing are said to afford analogies with the service of notice to determine a periodic tenancy, which is likewise a positive act. But this is to

---

[997] *Lemon v Lardeur* [1946] KB 613; *Queen's Club Gardens Estates Ltd v Bignell* [1924] 1 KB 117; *Bathavon RDC v Carlile* [1958] 1 QB 461. The payment period of a week is not necessarily the appropriate test in the case of a licence: in that case, the test is: what is the reasonable period in all the circumstances of the case? *Smith v Northside Developments Ltd* (1987) 283 EG 1211; [1992] Conv 263 (E. Cooke).

[998] *Crate v Miller* [1947] KB 946.   [999] [1946] KB 613.

[1000] Protection from Eviction Act 1977, s. 5(1); p. 317, ante.

[1001] *Land Settlement Association Ltd v Carr* [1944] KB 657. As regards the actual decision in this case, see Agricultural Holdings Act 1986, s. 2(1). See also *Harler v Calder* [1989] 1 EGLR 88.

[1002] *Doe d Aslin v Summersett* (1830) 1 B & Ad 135; *Parsons v Parsons* [1983] 1 WLR 1390 (two of four joint tenants); criticised in [1983] Conv 194 (F. Webb). For a similar rule in licences, see *Annen v Rattee* (1985) 273 EG 503; [1985] Conv 218 (J. Martin).

[1003] The giving of a notice is not an exercise of any *function* relating to land subject to the trust under which the joint owners hold their respective interests, and therefore there is no requirement for one to consult the other under TLATA 1996, s. 11: *Notting Hill Housing Trust v Brackley* [2001] 3 EGLR 11; [2004] Conv 370 (S. Pascoe). Nor is the failure to consult a breach of trust: *Crawley BC v Ure* [1996] QB 13. For problems which can arise for the remaining tenant when one joint tenant under a secure tenancy, in ignorance of the law, gives notice to quit intending simply to bring her own liability to an end but to safeguard the position of the other joint tenant, see *Bradney v Birmingham City Council* [2004] HLR 27; see also *Harrow LBC v Qazi* [2004] 1 AC 983; (2004) 120 LQR 398 (S. Bright).

[1004] [1992] 1 AC 478; [1992] Conv 279 (S. Goulding); CLJ 218 (L. Tee); 108 LQR 375 (J. Dewar); *Crawley BC v Ure* [1996] QB 13 (no obligation on one joint tenant to consult other joint tenant before serving notice); *Burton v Camden LBC* [2000] 2 AC 399; p. 455, post (deed of release by one joint tenant); *Osei-Bonsu v Wandsworth LBC* [1999] 1 WLR 1011. For discussion of possible challenges to the rule in *Hammersmith v Monk* based on the ECHR, see [2005] Conv 123 (I. Loveland).   [1005] *Hounslow LBC v Pilling* [1993] 1 WLR 1242.

[1006] At 490.

confuse the form with the substance. The action of giving notice to determine a periodic tenancy is in form positive; but both on authority and on the principle so aptly summed up in the pithy Scottish phrase "tacit relocation" the substance of the matter is that it is by his omission to give notice of termination that each party signifies the necessary positive assent to the extension of the term for a further period.

C Forfeiture

The landlord's remedy of forfeiture, which has the effect of terminating the lease, has been discussed already.[1007]

D Repudiation

A contract may be terminated by one party's acceptance of the other's repudiatory breach.[1008] Although it used to be said that a repudiatory breach of a lease is not possible,[1009] it has been held more recently that it is. In *Hussein v Mehlman*,[1010] there was a miscellany of serious breaches of the implied covenant to repair (one of which "vitiated the central purpose of the contract of letting"[1011]) by the landlord who persistently attempted to evade compliance with his covenant. It was held that the tenant had accepted the landlord's repudiation by vacating the premises and returning the keys.

The judge[1012] held that in a line of nineteenth-century cases it had been "treated as axiomatic that a contract of letting could be terminated by the innocent party without notice if the other party failed to fulfil a fundamental term of the contract", but this case also forms part of the modern approach under which the lease is seen as a contract as much as an estate or interest in land.[1013] Whether a breach of covenant by landlord or tenant justifies the other terminating the lease must therefore depend upon the application of the normal principles of contract law.[1014] However, it is important to note that the landlord cannot, by appealing to a contractual analysis in order to obtain termination of the lease for the tenant's

---

[1007] Pp. 273 et seq, ante (forfeiture for breach of covenant to pay rent); 280 et seq, ante (forfeiture for breach of other covenants). [1008] Anson, chap. 15.

[1009] *Total Oil Great Britain Ltd v Thompson Garages (Biggin Hill) Ltd* [1972] 1 QB 318 at 324; rejected in Australia in *Progressive Mailing House Pty Ltd v Tabili Pty Ltd* (1985) 157 CLR 17; [1986] Conv 262 (J. Carter and J. Hill); (1988) Monash LR 83 (J. Effron). It was, however, clear that a *contract* for a lease could be terminated by acceptance of a repudiatory breach, on normal contractual principles: *Sweet & Maxwell Ltd v Universal News Services Ltd* [1964] 2 QB 699.

[1010] [1992] 2 EGLR 87, M & B p. 437; [1993] CLJ 212 (C. Harpum); [1993] Conv 71 (S. Bright); [1995] Conv 379 (M. Pawlowski). See also *W G Clark (Properties) Ltd v Dupre Properties Ltd* [1992] Ch 297 (tenant's disclaimer of a lease a repudiation); *Kingston upon Thames Royal London Borough Council v Marlow* [1996] 1 EGLR 101 at 102, per SIMON BROWN LJ (tenant's acceptance of landlord's wrongful claim to forfeit would be acceptance of repudiation by landlord); *Chartered Trust plc v Davies* [1997] 2 EGLR 83 (landlord's failure to prevent nuisance constituted repudiatory breach of covenant against derogation from grant or of quiet enjoyment); *Nynehead Developments Ltd v Fibreboard Containers Ltd* [1999] 1 EGLR 7 (landlord's breaches not repudiatory); *Petra Investments Ltd v Jeffrey Rogers plc* (2000) 81 P & CR 21 (no breach, so no repudiation).

[1011] Ibid., at 90, per Stephen SEDLEY QC.

[1012] Ibid., at 89, drawing also on the development by which a lease can now in principle be frustrated: p. 328, post. [1013] P. 194, ante.

[1014] *Nynehead Developments Ltd v Fibreboard Containers Ltd*, supra; [1999] Conv 150 (M. Pawlowski and J. Brown).

repudiatory breach, avoid the limitations on the forfeiture of leases put in place by Parliament for the protection of tenants.[1015]

E Surrender

Surrender occurs where the tenant yields up his estate to the landlord and the landlord accepts it. Termination by surrender is distinct from termination by notice, because a notice to quit served in accordance with the provisions of a lease does not require the consent of the other party to be effective, whereas a surrender by the tenant constitutes the premature determination of the tenancy and is ineffective without the landord's consent given at the time of surrender.[1016]

In the case of a joint tenancy, a surrender is not effective unless made by all tenants.[1017]

(1) Express Surrender

The express surrender of a lease not exceeding three years must be made by deed.[1018] If an express surrender is not made by deed, but complies with the formalities required for a contract for the sale or other disposition of land[1019] and is made for value (for example, where the landlord releases the tenant's arrears of rent), it is effective in equity only as a contract to surrender the lease.[1020]

(2) Surrender by Operation of Law

If, however, the intention of the parties as inferred from their conduct is that the lease should be yielded up,[1021] surrender results by operation of law without the necessity either of a writing or a deed.[1022] This doctrine rests upon the principle of estoppel.

As PETER GIBSON J said:[1023]

In my judgment, it is indeed estoppel that forms the foundation of the doctrine. The doctrine operates when the tenant is a party to a transaction that is inconsistent with the continuation of his tenancy, but

---

[1015] LPA 1925, s. 146; *Abidogun v Frolan Health Care Ltd* [2002] L & TR 16 at [48]–[49], per ARDEN LJ ("the right to bring the lease to an end by accepting repudiation is, in my judgment, a forfeiture" within s. 146), [52], per BUXTON LJ.

[1016] *Barrett v Morgan* [2000] 2 AC 264 at 272, per Lord MILLETT, listing four major differences between surrender and termination by notice to quit.

[1017] *Leek and Moorlands Building Society v Clark* [1952] 2 QB 788; *Greenwich LBC v McGrady* (1982) 46 P & CR 223 at 224. For the effect of surrender by a tenant on his sub-tenant's estate, see pp. 327, 1005, post; *Bromley Park Garden Estates Ltd v George* [1991] 2 EGLR 95; *Barrett v Morgan*, supra, at 272.

[1018] LPA 1925, s. 52. This will be so even if the lease was for a period not exceeding three years, and could therefore be created orally; the exception in s. 54(2) applies only to the *creation* of a lease: *Crago v Julian* [1992] 1 WLR 372, M & B p. 504, p. 220, ante. [1019] Chap. 24, post.

[1020] *Tarjomani v Panther Securities Ltd* (1982) 46 P & CR 32 at 37–8, per PETER GIBSON J (doubting whether the doctrine of *Walsh v Lonsdale*, p. 223, ante, applies to a contract to surrender). It is not an actual surrender as required by Landlord and Tenant Act 1954, s. 24(2): ibid.

[1021] *John Laing Construction Ltd v Amber Pass Ltd* [2004] 2 EGLR 128 (if there is no prescribed process, the tenant yields up when, objectively, his acts manifest a clear intention to terminate the tenancy, and the landlord can, if he wants to, occupy the premises without difficulty or objection: at [45]).

[1022] LPA 1925, s. 52(2)(c).

[1023] *Tarjomani v Panther Securities Ltd*, supra at 41. Followed in *Mattey Securities Ltd v Ervin* [1988] 34 EG 91 (payment of rent); *McDougalls Catering Foods Ltd v BSE Trading Ltd* [1997] 2 EGLR 65. See also *Chamberlaine v Scally* [1992] EGCS 90. For operation of estoppel in the creation of a tenancy, see p. 217, ante.

in my judgment the conduct of the tenant must unequivocally amount to an acceptance that the tenancy has been terminated. There must be either relinquishment of possession and its acceptance by the landlord or other conduct consistent only with the cesser of the tenancy, and the circumstances must be such as to render it inequitable for the tenant to dispute that the tenancy has ceased.[1024]

It operates where the owner of a particular estate, such as a tenant for years, is a party to some transaction that would not be valid if his estate continued to exist.[1025] If, for example, the landlord grants to him a new lease which is to begin during the currency of the existing lease, the latter is implicitly surrendered and the tenant is estopped from disputing the validity of the new lease.[1026] Before there can be such an implied surrender,[1027] there must be something in the nature of an agreement, and that agreement must amount to more than a mere variation of the terms of an existing tenancy.[1028] In particular, an agreed increase in rent does not necessarily amount to an implied surrender.[1029]

Other examples of implied surrender occur, if:

possession is delivered by the tenant to the landlord and accepted by the latter.[1030] The delivery of the keys to the landlord is commonly regarded as a symbolic delivery of possession; and where the circumstances show that they were handed over by the tenant and accepted by the landlord with the intention of bringing the tenancy to an end then it is sufficient to do so;[1031]

the tenant is permitted to remain in occupation of the premises as a licensee paying no rent;[1032]

[1024] It may be the landlord who does the disputing. See *Proudreed Ltd v Microgen Holdings plc* [1996] 1 EGLR 89 at 90, where Schiemann LJ said: "The circumstances must be such as to render it inequitable for the tenant to dispute that the tenancy has ceased, or such as to render it inequitable for the landlord to dispute that the tenancy has ended"; *Bellcourt Estates Ltd v Adesina* [2005] 2 EGLR 33 (no unequivocal act by landlord to show it had accepted surrender: "the parties must have acted towards each other in a way that is inconsistent with the continuation of the tenancy. That imposes a high threshold": per Peter Gibson LJ at [30]).

[1025] *Allen v Rochdale BC* [2000] Ch 221 (Council, holding freehold as trustee, in which it also held leasehold interest as local education authority, sold part of freehold: implied surrender only in relation to the part sold).

[1026] *Lyon v Reed* (1844) 13 M & W 285; *Fenner v Blake* [1900] 1 QB 426; *Knight v Williams* [1901] 1 Ch 256. To produce a surrender, the new lease must be effective, not, for example, one which is beyond the powers of the lessor: *Barclays Bank Ltd v Stasek* [1957] Ch 28.

[1027] This may be expressly given or inferred from the landlord's conduct: *Phene v Popplewell* (1862) 12 CBNS 334 (act amounting to taking of possession or which would otherwise be a trespass).

[1028] *Smirk v Lyndale Developments Ltd* [1975] Ch 317 at 339, per Lawton LJ; *Bush Transport Ltd v Nelson* [1987] 1 EGLR 71 (oral agreement).

[1029] *Jenkin R Lewis & Son Ltd v Kerman* [1971] Ch 477; *Take Harvest Ltd v Liu* [1993] AC 552. See also *J W Childers Trustees v Anker* [1996] 1 EGLR 1 (addition to premises); *Friends' Provident Life Office v British Railways Board* [1996] 1 All ER 336; cf *Francis Perceval Saunders' Trustees v Ralph* (1993) 66 P & CR 335 (addition of tenant); [1995] Conv 124 (A. Dowling).

[1030] *Dodd v Acklom* (1843) 6 Man & G 672. See *Chamberlaine v Scally* [1992] EGCS 90 (no unequivocal conduct which was inconsistent with continuance of existing tenancy; tenant's belongings and two cats still on premises, which she visited to attend to them); cf *Brent London Borough v Sharma* (1993) 25 HLR 2570.

[1031] *Bolnore Properties Ltd v Cobb* (1996) 75 P & CR 127 at 13, per Millett LJ. See *Filering Ltd v Taylor Commercial Ltd* [1996] EGCS 95 (surrender only reason for handing over keys); cf *Oastler v Henderson* (1877) 2 QBD 575 (keys taken in order to try to re-let); *Relvok Properties Ltd v Dixon* (1972) 25 P & CR 1 (in order to change locks to improve security); *Proudreed Ltd v Microgen Holdings plc* [1996]1 EGLR 89 (keys accepted for six days, but surrender intended only when new lease granted); *John Laing Construction Ltd v Amber Pass Ltd* [2004] 2 EGLR 128 (retention of keys by tenant did not signify any rights in respect of the tenancies).

[1032] *Foster v Robinson* [1951] 1 KB 149; *Scrimgeour v Waller* (1980) 257 EG 61; *Tarjomani v Panther Securities Ltd* (1982) 46 P & CR 32.

the landlord grants a new lease to a third party, or accepts a third party as the new tenant, with the assent of the existing tenant;[1033]

the tenant has been absent from the premises for a substantial period and owes a substantial amount of rent;[1034]

the tenant has served on the landlord a notice to terminate the tenancy with effect from a date on which she then moves to a new flat, owned by the same landlord, and the landlord terminates her rent account for the first flat and opens a new account for the second flat, even though the tenant's husband remains in the old flat.[1035]

F Merger

The term of years and the reversion are concurrent interests that cannot be held by one and the same person at the same time. If, therefore, they become united in one person in the same right,[1036] as for example where the landlord conveys the fee simple to the tenant, the term is at common law immediately destroyed. It is said to be "merged", that is, sunk or drowned in the greater estate.[1037] It will be explained later, however, that in equity the union of a smaller and a greater estate in one person does not always result in merger.[1038]

G Enlargement

A tenant may by deed enlarge his lease into a fee simple under the Law of Property Act 1925.[1039]

Before the enlargement can be effected, however, the following conditions must exist:

(i)   The term must originally have been created for not less than 300 years, and at the time of the proposed enlargement there must be at least 200 more years to run.

(ii) There must be no trust or right of redemption[1040] still existing in favour of the reversioner.

(iii) The term must not be one which is liable to be determined by re-entry for condition broken.

(iv) There must be no rent of any money value.[1041]

[1033] *Wallis v Hands* [1893] 2 Ch 75; *Metcalfe v Boyce* [1927] 1 KB 758.

[1034] *Preston BC v Fairclough* (1982) 8 HLR 70 (test not satisfied).

[1035] *Ealing Family Housing Association Ltd v McKenzie* [2004] L & TR 15 (landlord treated tenant's husband as an illegal occupier from that date, showing that it regarded the tenancy as terminated).

[1036] *Allen v Rochdale BC* [2000] Ch 221 at [4] (freehold held by Council in capacity as trustee; leasehold as local education authority: no merger).   [1037] Blackstone, vol. ii. p. 177.

[1038] P. 1005, post.

[1039] S. 153, as amended by TLATA 1996, s. 25(1), Sch. 3, para. 4(16). See (1958) 22 Conv (NS) 101 (T. P. D. Taylor).

[1040] I.e., under a mortgage. See p. 735, post.

[1041] *Re Chapman and Hobbs* (1885) 29 Ch D 1007; *Re Smith and Stott* (1883) 29 Ch D 1009n.

A fee simple, so acquired by enlargement, is subject to all the same covenants, provisions and obligations as the lease would have been subject to if it had not been so enlarged.[1042]

As we shall see, this statutory power provides a possible, but as yet untried, method of making the burden of positive covenants run with freehold land.[1043]

H Frustration

In *National Carriers Ltd v Panalpina (Northern) Ltd*,[1044] the House of Lords, by a majority of four to one, held that the doctrine of frustration is applicable to leases. In so doing, it reconsidered its former opinions in *Cricklewood Property and Investment Trust Ltd v Leighton's Investment Trust Ltd*,[1045] in which Viscount SIMON LC and Lord WRIGHT were of opinion that the doctrine could apply; the second Lord RUSSELL OF KILLOWEN and Lord GODDARD that it never could, and Lord PORTER reserved his opinion. The effect of the decision is unlikely to produce any dramatic change, and as Lord HAILSHAM OF ST MARYLEBONE LC said:[1046]

It is the difference immortalised in *H.M.S. Pinafore* between "never" and "hardly ever", since both Viscount SIMON and Lord WRIGHT conceded that, though they thought the doctrine applicable in principle to leases, the cases in which it could properly be applied must be extremely rare.

As a result of this decision,[1047] it is no longer necessary to draw the anomalous distinctions between:[1048]

(i) a lease and a licence. Hitherto the doctrine has been applicable to a licence, as in *Krell v Henry*[1049] and the other Coronation cases, where an agreement to let a room for the purpose of viewing the coronation procession of Edward VII was frustrated when the procession was cancelled owing to the illness of the King;

(ii) a lease and a contract for a lease. In *Rom Securities Ltd v Rogers (Holdings) Ltd*[1050] GOFF J had assumed, without deciding, that the doctrine was applicable to a contract for a lease;

(iii) the charter of a ship by demise[1051] and a demise of land, for example, a short lease of an oil storage tank and a demise charter for the same term of an oil tanker to serve

---

[1042] LPA 1925, s. 153(8); p. 665, post.   [1043] P. 665, post.

[1044] [1981] AC 675; (1981) 131 NLJ 189 (H. W. Wilkinson). For the doctrine generally, see Treitel, chap. 20, esp. pp. 894–5.   [1045] [1945] AC 221.

[1046] At 688.

[1047] The third Lord RUSSELL OF KILLOWEN, with filial piety, dissented; and followed the views of the second Lord RUSSELL and Lord GODDARD in the *Cricklewood case*. For him also "the second answer of the *Pinafore's* captain on the subject of mal de mer is to be preferred to his first". He was prepared to accept the doctrine where the lease is merely incidental to an overall commercial adventure, or where the subject-matter has totally disappeared. Lord SIMON OF GLAISDALE noted at 701 that the majority decision had a theoretical anomaly of its own: that a conveyance of freehold cannot be frustrated, but a lease of 999 years can; but it would be only in exceptional circumstances that a lease for as long as 999 years would be susceptible of frustration.

For the effect of the unforeseen event of "mountainous inflation and the pound dropping to cavernous depths" on the construction of the terms of a covenant in a lease, see *Staffordshire Area Health Authority v South Staffordshire Waterworks Co* [1978] 1 WLR 1387; *Pole Properties Ltd v Feinberg* (1981) 43 P & CR 121.

[1048] See Lord SIMON OF GLAISDALE at 701.   [1049] [1903] 2 KB 740.   [1050] (1967) 205 EG 427.

[1051] See *Blane Steamships Ltd v Minister of Transport* [1951] 2 KB 965; LR (Frustrated Contracts) Act 1943, s. 2(5)(a).

such a storage tank, and a supervening event then frustrating the demise charter and equally affecting the use of the storage tank.

In the *National Carriers* case the House of Lords held unanimously that a ten-year lease of a warehouse was not in fact frustrated when it was made unusable for twenty months by the closing of an access street to it. Previous cases are also examples of a lease not being frustrated.

In the *Cricklewood* case itself, a building lease for 99 years from May 1936 was not frustrated by war-time legislation prohibiting building. It has also been held that a tenant must continue to pay his rent notwithstanding that the premises are utterly destroyed by fire,[1052] or by a hostile bomb,[1053] or are requisitioned by the Crown acting under statutory powers or under the prerogative,[1054] even though the Crown itself is the landlord.[1055]

Similarly, a covenant to repair imposes an absolute obligation for the non-performance of which the covenantor remains liable, notwithstanding that owing to some extraneous cause beyond his control, such as the refusal of the authorities to grant him a building licence[1056] or the requisitioning of the premises,[1057] he is unable to execute the necessary work.[1058]

I *Effect of Termination of Head Tenancy on Sub-tenants*

At common law the general rule is that, when the head tenancy comes to an end, any sub-tenancy derived out of it also automatically and simultaneously comes to an end. This general rule applies without question when the head tenancy comes to an end by effluxion of time, by a landlord's notice to quit or by forfeiture.[1059] It is equally beyond question that the general rule does not apply in cases of surrender[1060] or merger.

The general rule also applies when the notice to quit is served by the head tenant.[1061]

If the sub-tenancy is determined, the sub-tenant may still be protected by statute, for example under the Rent Act 1977.[1062] If it is determined by forfeiture, he may apply to the court for relief.[1063]

[1052] *Matthey v Curling* [1922] 2 AC 180.

[1053] See *Redmond v Dainton* [1920] 2 KB 256; *Denman v Brise* [1949] 1 KB 22.

[1054] *Whitehall Court Ltd v Ettlinger* [1920] 1 KB 680. But see the Landlord and Tenant (Requisitioned Land) Act 1942, which allows a tenant to disclaim a lease if the land is requisitioned by the Crown.

[1055] *Crown Lands Comrs v Page* [1960] 2 QB 274.   [1056] *Eyre v Johnson* [1946] KB 481.

[1057] *Smiley v Townshend* [1950] 2 KB 311. But the Landlord and Tenant (Requisitioned Land) Act 1944 relieves the tenant of liability for damages to the land during the period of requisition.

[1058] See *John Lewis Properties plc v Viscount Chelsea* [1993] 34 EG 116 (excuse for non-performance short of full frustration).

[1059] *Pennell v Payne* [1995] QB 192 at 197, per SIMON BROWN LJ. See *Barrett v Morgan* [2000] 2 AC 264 (notice to quit served by landlord by pre-arrangement with head tenant effective to terminate both head tenancy and sub-tenancy; it was not to be construed as a surrender which would have preserved the sub-tenancy); *PW & Co v Milton Gate Investments Ltd* [2004] Ch 142 (where NEUBERGER J held that as a matter of law, it was not possible to contract out of the general rule in *Pennell v Payne*).

[1060] *Mellor v Watkins* (1874) LR 9 QB 400. But the *Mellor v Watkins* principle and the *Pennell v Payne* principle have no relevance to a "*Bruton* tenancy", pp. 195–6, ante, because it is not a derivative estate and therefore cannot bind the freeholder if the licence of the party who granted the *Bruton* tenancy is terminated: *Kay v Lambeth LBC* [2006] UKHL 10 at [140]–[147], per Lord SCOTT OF FOSCOTE.

[1061] *Pennell v Payne*, supra; [1995] Conv 263 (P. Luxton and M. Wilkie).

[1062] S. 137(2); *Keepers and Governors of the Free Grammar School of John Lyon v James* [1996] QB 163; *Basingstoke and Deane BC v Paice* [1995] 2 EGLR 9 (HA 1985, s. 79(1)).   [1063] P. 287, ante.

J Termination of Tenancy at Will

A tenancy at will may be expressly terminated at any time by either party. The strict rules that govern a notice to quit do not, however, apply in this case, for, as has been said by TINDAL CJ:

Anything which amounts to a demand of possession, although not expressed in precise and formal language, is sufficient to indicate the determination of the landlord's will.[1064]

Thus a declaration that the landlord will take steps to recover possession unless the tenant complies with certain conditions, determines the tenancy if the conditions are not accepted.[1065]

The tenancy is also implicitly determined if the landlord does acts inconsistent with its continuance, as for instance if he alienates the reversion or removes material, such as stones, from the land.[1066] Implicit determination also occurs if the tenant does acts incompatible with his limited rights, as for instance if he commits waste or assigns the land to a stranger.[1067]

The death of either party also determines the tenancy.

A premature determination is not allowed to prejudice the rights of either party. If the tenant quits before the day on which his rent is due, he does not escape liability;[1068] while if he has sown crops he has a right at common law to re-enter and reap them if the landlord determines the tenancy before they are ripe.[1069]

VIII Recovery of Possession by the Landlord

Even if the lease has been terminated on one of the grounds described in the previous section, the landlord may still need to take positive steps to recover possession of the premises. For example, the landlord may have lawfully terminated the lease but the tenant is refusing to leave; or the tenant may have given notice to quit, but a member of the tenant's family is still on the premises. We shall see in the next section that certain special rules have been laid down by statute to protect tenants holding under certain special types of lease, and that this sometimes extends to requiring the landlord to obtain a court order in order to terminate the tenancy, as well as to recover possession of the premises. In this section, however, we notice the general rules applicable to a landlord's attempt to recover possession of premises, whether against the former tenant or against another person present on the premises.

A Re-entry by the Landlord

We have already seen that the landlord's right to re-enter the premises in the event of breach of covenant by the tenant will commonly be reserved by the lease, and that at common law re-entry is a means by which forfeiture of the lease may be effected; but that

---

[1064] *Doe d Price v Price* (1832) 9 Bing 356 at 358.

[1065] ibid.; *Fox v Hunter-Paterson* [1948] 2 All ER 813.

[1066] *Doe d Bennett v Turner* (1840) 7 M & W 226.   [1067] *Pinhorn v Souster* (1853) 8 Exch 763 at 772.

[1068] Cruise, *Digest*, Tit. ix., c. 1, s. 13.   [1069] Co Litt 55b; see p. 213, ante.

the usual practice is for the landlord to sue for possession, rather than to exercise his right of re-entry, in order to forfeit the lease.[1070] Once the lease has been terminated, however—for example, by the expiry of a fixed term, or by notice to quit—at common law the landlord has the right to enter and re-take possession.[1071] This can be a useful right, allowing the landlord quickly and efficiently to recover possession in order to use the premises himself or to re-let them, although the landlord may still prefer to seek a court order which will delay matters but in a clear case may be relatively speedy.[1072] Where the landlord has a right to possession, the court has a duty to make an order to enforce it, subject to any inherent or statutory power to defer the landlord's taking possession.[1073] The right of the landlord to re-take possession without a court order is however restricted by statute in the case of a lease of a dwelling; and the unlawful eviction or harassment of a residential occupier constitutes a criminal offence.

B Leases of Dwellings. Requirement of Court Order to Recover Possession

Where premises have been let as a dwelling, and the tenancy has come to an end but the occupier continues to reside in the premises or part of them, it is not lawful for the owner to enforce his right to recover possession of the premises without a court order.[1074] This rule is subject to certain exceptions, for example where the tenant or licensee shares accommodation with the owner or occupies it for a holiday, or where it has been granted in order to provide accommodation for asylum-seekers.[1075] Similarly, the right of re-entry or forfeiture of a lease of premises let as a dwelling cannot be enforced without court proceedings while any person is residing in the premises or part of them.[1076]

[1070] P. 273, ante. In the case of a tenancy of residential premises, re-entry without a court order is prohibited: infra. The Law Commission has proposed that the doctrine of re-entry be abolished, and replaced by the requirement to obtain a court order to terminate a lease: Termination of Tenancies for Tenant Default 2004, Consultation Paper No. 174; p. 293, ante.

[1071] *Sheffield Corporation v Luxford* [1929] 2 KB 180 at 184; *Jones v Savery* [1951] 1 All ER 820 at 822.

[1072] The procedure for a claim for the recovery of possession of land (including a claim brought by a landlord against a tenant or sub-tenant, or former tenant or sub-tenant, or against a trespasser) is set out in CPR Part 55. Default judgment cannot be given even if the defendant does not acknowledge service or file a defence: CPR, r. 55.7(4), although where the tenant has no real prospect of defending the landlord's claim to possession, summary judgment can be given as long as it is not a claim for possession of residential premises against a tenant or a person holding over after the end of his tenancy whose occupancy is protected within the meaning of the Rent Act 1977 or HA 1988: CPR, r. 24.3(1)(a)(ii). There is an accelerated procedure for claims for possession of property let on an assured shorthold tenancy: CPR, Part 55, Section II. For such tenancies, see pp. 344 et seq, post.

[1073] *Sheffield Corporation v Luxford*, supra; *Jones v Savery*, supra. Under HA 1980, s. 89, the court has power in most cases to postpone the giving up of possession for only fourteen days after its order or (if it appears to the court that exceptional hardship would be caused by requiring possession to be given up by that date) up to six weeks.

[1074] Protection from Eviction Act 1977, s. 3, as amended by HA 1988, s. 30. "Occupier" means any person lawfully residing in the premises or part of them at the termination of the former tenancy: s. 3(2). The provision applies to licences, as well as to leases: s. 3(2A), (2B).

[1075] Ibid., s. 3A, inserted by HA 1988, s. 31, and amended by Immigration and Asylum Act 1999, s. 169(1), Sch. 14; Nationality, Immigration and Asylum Act 2002, s. 32(5). Certain statutorily protected tenancies, including assured tenancies, protected tenancies under the Rent Act 1977, tenancies under L & TA 1954, Part II, agricultural holdings and farm business tenancies, are excluded and governed by their own particular rules. s. 8(1).   [1076] Protection from Eviction Act 1977, s. 2.

C Criminal Offences of Unlawful Eviction and Harassment

There are a several criminal offences relating to the entry onto premises or harassment of occupiers of them, even where the entry is effected by the owner of premises in order to enforce his right to possession against a person who has no right to possession.

It is an offence of *unlawful eviction* for any person unlawfully to deprive the residential occupier of his occupation of the premises, or any part thereof, or to attempt to do so, unless he proves that he believed, and had reasonable cause to believe, that the occupier had ceased to reside.[1077] Furthermore, it is an offence of *harassment*[1078] for any person, with the intention[1079] of causing a residential occupier to give up the occupation of all or part of the premises or to refrain from exercising any of his rights, to do acts[1080] likely to interfere with the peace or comfort of the occupier or members of his household, or persistently to withdraw services reasonably required for the occupation of the premises as a residence. These offences are not aimed solely at, but will include, acts done by landlords. However, the Housing Act 1988 introduced a further offence of harassment, directed at the conduct of landlords and their agents. This offence[1081] is committed where the landlord or his agent commits acts of harassment similar to those set out above, but it suffices that the landlord (or agent, as the case may be) knows or has reasonable cause to believe that his conduct is likely to cause the occupier to give up occupation or refrain from exercising his rights. In this offence specific intent is not required, and it is therefore easier to prove. Prosecutions for these offences can be brought by the victim, the police or the local authority, although in practice the police refer complaints to the local authority.

D Damages for Unlawful Eviction or Harassment

Section 27 of the Housing Act 1988 confers a civil action for damages against the landlord[1082] for unlawful eviction or harassment causing the occupier to give up occupation. The measure of damages is the difference in value (if any[1083]) between the landlord's interest in the building subject to the occupier's rights and not so subject.[1084] Although the liability is said to be in the nature of a tort,[1085] in substance it is calculated to expropriate the landlord's

---

[1077] Protection from Eviction Act 1977, s. 1(2). See also Criminal Law Act 1977, s. 6 (offence of using or threatening violence for the purpose of securing entry into premises).

[1078] Protection from Eviction Act 1977, s. 1(3), amended by HA 1988, s. 29(1). See also Protection from Harassment Act 1977, s. 1 (general criminal offence of harassment; actionable in damages by the victim: s. 3); *Daiichi Pharmaceuticals UK Ltd v Stop Huntingdon Animal Cruelty* [2004] 1 WLR 1503 (interlocutory injunction refused to corporate claimants but granted to individual claimants on behalf of themselves and employees of claimant companies).

[1079] " 'Intention' in this context meaning with the purpose or motive of causing the occupier to give up occupation of the premises": *R v Burke* [1991] 1 AC 135 at 147, per Lord GRIFFITHS.

[1080] It is not necessary for an act by the defendant to be an actionable civil wrong in order to be an offence under s. 1(3): *R v Burke*, supra (preventing tenant from using shared bathroom and lavatories, and disconnecting front door bell).   [1081] Protection from Eviction Act 1977, s. 1(3A), inserted by HA 1988, s. 29(2).

[1082] Only the landlord is liable: *Sampson v Wilson* [1996] Ch 39.

[1083] *Melville v Bruton* (1996) 29 HLR 319 (no damages where no difference in value because other tenants not evicted).

[1084] HA 1988, s. 28; *Tagro v Cafane* [1991] 1 WLR 378 (£31,000); *Jones v Miah* [1992] 2 EGLR 50 (£8,000); *Haniff v Robinson* [1993] QB 419 (£26,000). See also *Osei-Bonsu v Wandsworth LBC* [1999] 1 WLR 1011 (defences). For county court decisions on the measure of damages, see the monthly issues of *Legal Action*.

[1085] HA 1988, s. 27(4)(a).

notional gain from his wrongful conduct.[1086] Where section 27 is not satisfied, remedies in the general law of contract or tort are likely to be available to the occupier for the acts of harassment. These remedies are available in addition to the statutory remedy, but damages may not be awarded twice for the same loss.[1087]

E Impact of Human Rights Act 1998 on Landlord's Claim for Possession

In recent years the question has been asked whether the Human Rights Act 1998 has an impact on the landlord's right to possession on termination of the lease. In 2003, in *Harrow London Borough Council v Qazi*,[1088] the House of Lords by a bare majority gave an emphatic negative answer to this question. In 2006, in *Kay v Lambeth London Borough Council*,[1089] the House, again by a bare majority, substantially reaffirmed its decision in *Qazi*.

Under the Act, it is unlawful for a public authority to act in a way which is incompatible with "Convention rights"—certain rights under the European Convention for the Protection of Human Rights and Fundamental Freedoms.[1090] This includes, under article 8.1 of the Convention, everyone's "right to respect for . . . his home"; and, under article 8.2:

There shall be no interference by a public authority with the exercise of this right except such as is in accordance with the law and is necessary in a democratic society in the interests of national security, public safety or the economic well-being of the country, for the prevention of disorder or crime, for the protection of health or morals, or for the protection of the rights and freedoms of others.

The question therefore arises whether the exercise by a public authority landlord[1091] of its right to possession of premises against a residential occupier—a former tenant or another member of his family still living on the premises—is subject to these Convention rights, and therefore whether the court in hearing a claim for possession should make an assessment of the compatibility of the claim to possession on the facts of the case with the occupant's rights under article 8.2. In Harrow London Borough Council v Qazi:[1092]

[1086] *Sampson v Wilson* [1996] Ch 39 at 49, per Sir Thomas BINGHAM MR: the formula is "very apt to prevent the landlord profiting from his 'Rachmannite' activities".   [1087] HA 1988, s. 27(4), (5).

[1088] [2004] 1 AC 983; [2004] Conv 406 (J. Howell); (2004) 120 LQR 398 (S. Bright); [2004] PL 594 (I. Loveland).   [1089] [2006] 2 WLR 570.

[1090] S. 6. The court may grant such relief or remedy, or make such order, within its powers as it considers just and appropriate: s. 8(1).

[1091] "Public authority" under HRA 1998, s. 6, includes the court: s. 6(3)(a). However, in *R v Hounslow LBC* [2003] HLR 68 at [48]–[49] MOSES J firmly rejected the argument that s. 6 and art. 8 imposed on the *court* the duty to adjudicate on the compatibility of a order for possession in every case, even those in which the landlord was a private person: such an argument "would fundamentally transform our law as to enforcement of property rights into one where such rights could only be enforced when the court thinks it justifiable to seek possession and proportionate to make an order". See also *Harrow LBC v Qazi*, supra, at [108]–[109], per Lord MILLETT, and at [143], per Lord SCOTT OF FOSCOTE. In *Kay v Lambeth LBC*, supra, the application to private landlords of the principles enunciated in *Qazi* and *Kay* was left open by Lord BINGHAM OF CORNHILL at [28], Lord NICHOLLS OF BIRKENHEAD at [61] and Lord HOPE OF CRAIGHEAD at [64], although given the narrow scope of application of HRA 1998 even to public landlords, in the view of the majority of the House in both cases, there is no significant scope for challange on this basis to claims to possession by private landlords.

[1092] Supra.

the defendant, together with his wife, had occupied a house under a secure joint tenancy[1093] granted by the local authority. His wife left, and gave notice to quit which terminated the tenancy.[1094] The local authority sought possession.

The House of Lords held that, although the defendant was a trespasser, he was occupying a house as his "home" within the meaning of article 8.1 of the Convention. However, by a majority of three to two, the House went on to hold that, since English domestic law in these circumstances gave the authority an unqualified right to possession, article 8.2 did not apply. As Lord SCOTT OF FOSCOTE said:[1095]

If Mr Qazi has no contractual or proprietary right under the ordinary law to resist the council's claim for possession, and it is accepted he has not, the acceptance by the court of a defence based on article 8 would give him a possessory right over 31 Hutton Lane that he would not otherwise have. It would deprive the council of its right under the ordinary law to immediate possession. It would constitute an amendment of the domestic social housing legislation. It would give article 8 an effect it was never intended to have and which it has never been given by the Strasbourg tribunals responsible for implementing the Convention.

This was not, however, the last word on this matter. After the decision of the House of Lords in *Qazi*, the European Court of Human Rights held in *Connors v United Kingdom*[1096] that article 8 of the Convention was violated where a local authority obtained, and executed, an order for summary possession of land occupied by gypsies under a licence which had been terminated, and who therefore had in domestic law no answer to the claim for immediate possession. It was held that the eviction was not attended by the requisite procedural safeguards—the requirement to establish proper justification for the serious interference with the occupier's rights—and so could not be regarded as justified by (within the meaning of article 8.2) a "pressing social need" or proportionate to the legitimate aim being pursued.

In the light of the decision in *Connors*, in *Kay v Lambeth London Borough Council*[1097] the House of Lords reviewed its own decision in *Harrow London Borough Council v Qazi*.

[1093] P. 358, post.   [1094] *Hammersmith and Fulham LBC v Monk* [1992] 1 AC 478; p. 323, ante.

[1095] [2004] 1 AC 983 at [151]. See also Lord HOPE OF CRAIGHEAD at [74], [84], and Lord MILLETT at [103], [109]. Lord BINGHAM OF CORNHILL and Lord STEYN dissented vigorously; see at [27], per Lord STEYN: "It would be surprising if the views of the majority on the interpretation and application of art. 8 . . . withstood European scrutiny. . . . it empties art. 8(1) of any or virtually any meaningful content. The basic fallacy in the approach is that it allows domestic notions of title, legal and equitable rights, and interests, to colour the interpretation of art. 8(1). The decision of today does not fit into the new landscape created by the 1998 Act." However, the European Court of Human Rights has held that Mr Qazi's application to it did not disclose any appearance of a violation of the Convention or its protocols and declared it inadmissible. The House of Lords has disagreed over the significance of this: *Kay v Lambeth LBC* [2006] 2 WLR 570 at [23], per Lord BINGHAM OF CORNHILL ("the refusal of leave does not necessarily import approval of the reasoning of the judgment which it is sought to challenge"); cf. at [107], per Lord HOPE OF CRAIGHEAD, at [154], per Lord SCOTT OF FOSCOTE, and at [179], per Baroness HALE OF RICHMOND. The general rule stated in *Qazi* was applied in *Newham LBC v Kibata* [2004] 1 FLR 690; *Bradney v Birmingham City Council* [2004] HLR 27; *Hounslow LBC v Adjei* [2004] 2 All ER 636; *McCann v Birmingham City Council* [2005] 1 P & CR DG5 (proceedings for judicial review).

[1096] (2005) 40 EHRR 9. The decision of the House of Lords in *Qazi* was not cited. See also *Blecic v Croatia* (2005) 41 EHRR 13 (tenant lost flat in Croatia in consequence of absence abroad during Balkan war: art. 8 ECHR engaged, but interference with rights was justified).

[1097] [2006] 2 WLR 570. Two appeals were consolidated: *Kay v Lambeth LBC* and *Leeds City Council v Price*. In the *Leeds* case, CA had held at [2005] 1 WLR 1825 that the decision of HL in *Qazi* was incompatible with the later decision in *Connors*, but that *Qazi* remained the binding authority in English law. On appeal, HL held by a majority that there was no such inconsistency, but that, if there were, the English courts below HL should follow the binding precedent of HL: at [43], per Lord BINGHAM OF CORNHILL.

By a decision of four to three, it reaffirmed its earlier decision with only minor qualifications. There was agreement amongst their Lordships that a possession order made by a court in respect of a defendant's home will be an interference with the right to respect for his home, and therefore article 8 of the Convention will normally be engaged where a public authority landlord seeks possession. There was also agreement that, if the ratio of *Qazi* was that the enforcement of a right to possession in accordance with the domestic law of property can *never* be incompatible with article 8, it must now be modified in the light of the decision in *Connors*. However, there was disagreement over the circumstances in which a defendant can challenge the claim to possession on the basis of the Convention. The minority would have held that the defendant must be given a fair opportunity to contend that the excepting conditions of article 8.2 have not been met on the facts of the case, and that if he so pleads, it is for the public authority to establish that the conditions have been met—even though in the overwhelming majority of cases the authority will be be able to do so without difficulty.[1098] The majority, however, held that the defendant's right, under the Convention and therefore under the Human Rights Act 1998, to challenge the claim to possession is not based on his individual personal circumstances, or the particular facts of the case. The challenge can be only to the compatibility with the Convention of the domestic rules under which the possession order is sought. As Lord HOPE OF CRAIGHEAD said:[1099]

The contrary conclusion, for which the appellants contend, is that procedures must exist in the domestic system for a consideration of the interests safeguarded by article 8 in every case where a person is evicted from his home by the making of a possession order. A requirement that the article 8 issue must be considered by the court in every case by taking into account the defendant's personal circumstances would ... drive a deep wedge into the domestic system for the handling of possession cases and would be a colossal waste of time and money ... Judges in the county courts, when faced with such a defence, should proceed on the assumption that domestic law strikes a fair balance and is compatible with the occupier's Convention rights.

But, in agreement with Lord Scott, Baroness Hale and Lord Brown, I would go further. Subject to what I say below, I would hold that a defence which does not challenge the law under which the possession order is sought as being incompatible with the article 8 but is based only on the occupier's personal circumstances should be struck out. ... Where domestic law provides for personal circumstances to be taken into account, as in a case where the statutory test is whether it would be reasonable to make a possession order, then a fair opportunity must be given for the arguments in favour of the occupier to be presented. But if the requirements of the law have been established and the right to recover possession is unqualified, the only situations in which it would be open to the court to refrain from proceeding to summary judgment and making the possession order are these: (a) if a seriously arguable point is raised that the law which enables the court to make the possession order is incompatible with article 8, the county court in the exercise of its jurisdiction under the Human Rights Act 1998 should deal with the argument in one or other of two ways: (i) by giving effect to the law, so far as it is possible for it do so under section 3, in a way that is compatible with article 8, or (ii) by adjourning the proceedings to enable the compatibility issue to be dealt with in the High Court; (b) if the defendant wishes to challenge the decision of a public authority to recover possession as an improper exercise of its powers at common law on the ground that it was a decision that no reasonable person would consider justifiable, he should be permitted to do this provided again that the point is seriously arguable: *Wandsworth London Borough Council v Winder*.[1100] The common law as explained in that case is, of course, compatible with article 8. It provides an additional safeguard.

[1098] See at [29], per Lord BINGHAM OF CORNHILL, at [56], per Lord NICHOLLS OF BIRKENHEAD and at [176], per Lord WALKER OF GESTINGTHORPE.   [1099] At [109]–[110].
[1100] [1985] AC 461 (judicial review).

IX Statutory Codes for Special Leases.
Security of Tenure and Control of Rent

Land in overcrowded England is a scarce commodity which all need but many cannot afford to own. The forces of supply and demand, if left unchecked, would give landlords a bargaining superiority over their tenants which modern ideas of social justice have been unwilling to accept. As Lord DENNING said:[1101]

No bargain will be upset which is the result of the ordinary interplay of forces. There are many hard cases which are caught by this rule. Take the case of a poor man who is homeless. He agrees to pay a high rent to a landlord just to get a roof over his head. The common law will not interfere. It is left to Parliament.

In consequence, ever since the First World War, legislation has been used to redress the balance in favour of the tenant.[1102] Restrictions have been imposed upon the amount of rent chargeable and the landlord's common law right to recover possession. With changes in Government the tide of protection has ebbed and flowed—most particularly in relation to residential tenancies, where the policy in favour of social protection has most commonly been seen to outweigh the policy of freedom of contract.[1103] The high water-mark of residential tenants' rights in the private sector was the Labour Government's Rent Act of 1974. However, the Conservative Governments between 1979 and 1997 reduced the tenant's protection very significantly, through the Housing Acts of 1980, 1988 and 1996; and the Labour Governments since 1997 have shown no sign of a return to the extreme protective measures of the mid-1970s. But the need for protection of some kind is today generally accepted and it is highly unlikely that landlord and tenant will ever be restored to their nineteenth-century freedom of contract.

Statutory protection was at first afforded only to tenants who held periodic tenancies or short leases of unfurnished residential premises;[1104] but protection has been extended to most residential lettings by private landlords who do not themselves reside in the same house,[1105] while different systems of control have been devised for public sector housing,[1106] long leaseholders,[1107] business tenants,[1108] and agricultural holdings.[1109] The result of somewhat haphazard historical development is that there are today many distinct statutory codes of protection, in various respects radically different from each other. The detailed provisions of this legislation are extremely complex and the subject matter of a number of specialised works. What follows is no more than a brief outline of how the various codes operate.

[1101] *Lloyds Bank Ltd v Bundy* [1975] QB 326 at 336.

[1102] See *Johnson v Moreton* [1980] AC 37 at 65, per Lord SIMON OF GLAISDALE; *R v Secretary of State for the Environment, Transport and the Regions, ex p Spath Holme Ltd* [2001] 2 AC 349 at 378–379, per Lord BINGHAM OF CORNHILL.

[1103] For an overview, see Megarry, *Rent Acts*, Introductory Survey, esp. pp. 1–3.

[1104] Increase of Rent and Mortgage Interest (War Restrictions) Act 1915.

[1105] Rent Act 1977; HA 1988.   [1106] Part IV of HA 1985, p. 358, post.

[1107] Part I of LTA 1954; Local Government and Housing Act 1989; Leasehold Reform Act 1967; Leasehold Reform, Housing and Urban Development Act 1993; Commonhold and Leasehold Reform Act 2002, Part 2, pp. 363 et seq, post.   [1108] Part II of the Landlord and Tenant Act 1954; p. 377, post.

[1109] Agricultural Holdings Act 1986; Agricultural Tenancies Act 1995; p. 386, post.

A *Private Residential Lettings*[1110]

Statutory control of residential lettings dates back to 1915, but almost all the provisions now in force will be found in the Rent Act 1977 and the Housing Act 1988, as amended by the Housing Act 1996.

A tenancy falling within the Rent Act 1977 is known as a "protected tenancy". Tenants under protected tenancies are given security of tenure by the mechanism of the "statutory tenancy"—a status of irremovability which attaches to a tenant remaining in occupation after his protected tenancy has come to an end and which cannot be terminated by the landlord except by an order of the court made upon limited and specified grounds. For the purposes of rent regulation, both protected and statutory tenancies are termed "regulated tenancies" and are subject to machinery for determining a "fair rent" which is the maximum that the tenant can be required to pay. "Fair rent" does not simply mean a "reasonable rent", but takes as its starting point the open market rent for the premises in their current state,[1111] although it is usually lower than the open market rent because it must be assumed that the demand for similar dwellings in the locality is not substantially greater than the supply.[1112]

One consequence of the expansion of the rental market following the Housing Act 1988 has been to reduce the gap between supply and demand, and therefore to increase the open market rental value of premises. This has led to a corresponding increase in "fair rents", but to avoid hardship to tenants the growth in "fair rents" is controlled by a cap on the maximum permitted rent rise.[1113]

The philosophy behind the Housing Act 1988 was that the reduction of security and rent control would increase the supply of rented accommodation by encouraging owners to let. The effect of the 1988 Act was to phase out the regulated tenancy (and also the "restricted contract", an inferior form of protection under the Rent Act 1977 applying primarily to tenants of resident landlords). The operation of the Rent Act 1977 has been much reduced in that, subject to narrow exceptions,[1114] no new protected tenancies may be granted after 15 January 1989, the date upon which the 1988 Act came into operation. Tenancies created before that date continue to enjoy the protection of the Rent Act 1977, but the 1988 Act hastens their termination by diminishing the succession rights which previously existed on the death of a protected or statutory tenant.

[1110] For detailed discussion, see Megarry *Rent Acts*, vol. 3; Martin, *Residential Security*; Rodgers, *Housing Law Residential Security and Enfranchisement*; Evans and Smith, *Law of Landlord and Tenant*, Part D.

[1111] *Spath Holme Ltd v Greater Manchester and Lancashire Rent Assessment Committee* (1995) 28 HLR 107; *Curtis v London Rent Assessment Committee* [1999] QB 92.

[1112] Rent Act 1977, s. 70(2). Certain other matters are also to be disregarded: ibid., s. 70(3).

[1113] Rent Acts (Maximum Fair Rent) Order 1999 (SI 1999 No. 6) caps the increase by reference to the increase in the UK Retail Prices Index plus 7.5% (first applications after the Order comes into force) or 5% (any subsequent applications). A challenge to the Order was rejected in *R v Secretary of State for the Environment, Transport and the Regions, ex p Spath Holme Ltd* [2001] 2 AC 349. For an account of the background to the Order, see at 378–80, per Lord BINGHAM OF CORNHILL, pointing out that the earlier reluctance of rent officers and rent assessment committees properly to operate the provisions of Rent Act 1977, s. 70, when combined with the expansion of the rental market (and therefore higher open market rents) after HA 1988, led to "very sharp and unexpected increases in the rent payable" under regulated tenancies. See also Department of the Environment, Transport and the Regions Consultation Paper on Limiting Fair Rent Increases (1998), paras. 2.3–2.5.

[1114] HA 1988, s. 34; *Laimond Properties Ltd v Al-Shakarchi* (1998) 30 HLR 1099.

The key concepts of the Housing Act 1988 are the "assured tenancy" and its variant the "assured shorthold tenancy". The basic principle of security of tenure remains, but the grounds for possession are strengthened and there are only very limited rights of succession and rent control. In order to dissuade landlords from evicting Rent Act tenants unlawfully in order to get the benefit of the new Housing Act regime, the 1988 Act strengthened the Protection from Eviction Act 1977 by extending criminal and civil liability for unlawful eviction and harassment.[1115]

The Housing Act 1996 gave landlords further incentive to let by removing some of the restrictive conditions formerly necessary for the creation of the less secure shorthold tenancy. The broad effect of the 1996 Act is that most assured tenancies granted after its commencement are shorthold tenancies.

The account which follows deals only with assured and assured shorthold tenancies under the Housing Act 1988 as amended. Much of the Rent Act case law, however, remains relevant, as many provisions of the 1988 Act are modelled on those of the 1977 Act, in particular in relation to the conditions for protected status, the exceptions to protection and the grounds for possession.

It appears, however, that the Housing Acts 1988 and 1996 have not had the effect of increasing the pool of private rented accommodation.[1116]

(1) The Assured Tenancy[1117]

(a) Definition

By section 1 of the Housing Act 1988, a tenancy under which a dwelling-house is let as a separate dwelling is an assured tenancy if and so long as:

(a) the tenant or each of joint tenants is an individual; and

(b) the tenant or at least one of joint tenants occupies the dwelling-house as his only or principal home; and

(c) the tenancy is not one which cannot be an assured tenancy by virtue of the exclusions in Schedule 1[1118] or by virtue of section 1(6).[1119]

Further, the tenancy cannot be assured unless it was entered into on or after the commencement of the 1988 Act on 15 January 1989.[1120]

Each part of the definition will now be examined.

(1) DWELLING-HOUSE . . . LET AS A SEPARATE DWELLING

Every word of this phrase has been the subject of judicial interpretation and the last five words are among the most litigated on the statute book.

[1115] P. 332, ante.

[1116] The percentage of private renter households decreased from 19% in 1971 to 10% in 1995; since 1995 there have been no significant changes and it has remained relatively constant (between 10% and 11%): Office for National Statistics, Living In Britain: Results from the General Household Survey 2002 (published 2004).

[1117] Bridge, *Assured Tenancies*.   [1118] P. 341, post.

[1119] This excludes tenancies granted to homeless persons by private landlords by arrangement with the local authority.   [1120] HA 1988, Sch. 1, para. 1.

(i) Dwelling-house

A "dwelling-house", which may be a house or part of a house, includes a flat and even an hotel,[1121] but the premises must be structurally suitable for occupation as a residence and must have some degree of permanence.[1122] Caravans are therefore not normally within the definition and their occupants are protected, if at all, by different legislation.[1123]

(ii) Let

The use of the word "let" connotes the relationship of landlord and tenant. Contractual licensees are therefore not within the Act.[1124]

The most common examples of residential licensees are lodgers, who lack exclusive possession because the owner provides attendance or services which require him to exercise unrestricted access to the premises,[1125] and the "service occupant", that is, the employee who is required by his contract of employment to occupy a particular dwelling for the better performance of his duties.[1126] Caretakers occupying flats in blocks or office buildings usually come within this category. Agricultural workers in tied cottages also do so, but they are now subject to a separate code under the Rent (Agriculture) Act 1976. But a service occupant must be distinguished from a "service tenant", that is, a person to whom a dwelling-house is let in consequence of his employment, but who is not required to live there for the better performance of his duties.[1127] Service tenants are within the Housing Act 1988, although the Act contains a special provision to enable the employer to recover possession from a tenant who has left his service.[1128]

(iii) As

The requirement that the house must be let *as* a separate dwelling means that one has regard to the purpose for which it was let, which will not necessarily be the same as the purpose for which it is actually being used. If a lease contains a covenant confining the use of the premises to business purposes, the tenancy will not be protected merely because the tenant in fact uses them as a dwelling.[1129] If there is no specific user covenant in the lease, the question will turn upon the use contemplated by the parties at the time of the letting,[1130] and if they had no particular use in mind, it will depend upon the nature of the premises and their *de facto* use at the time when the question arises for decision.

[1121] *Luganda v Service Hotels Ltd* [1969] 2 Ch 209.

[1122] See *Elitestone Ltd v Morris* [1997] 1 WLR 687(chalet part of realty), M & B p. 98; *Chelsea Yacht and Boat Co Ltd v Pope* [2000] 1 WLR 1941 (houseboat moored by ropes and connected to services which could be untied and disconnected without undue effort not part of the land, and therefore not occupied as a dwelling for HA 1988 which only applies to the letting of land). On 29 November 2005, ODPM issued a Consultation Paper on security of tenure and additional contract rights of occupants of residential boats and long-term moorings. For fixtures generally, see pp. 156 et seq, ante.

[1123] The Caravan Sites Act 1968 and the Mobile Homes Act 1983; *R v Rent Officer of Nottinghamshire Registration Area, ex p Allen* (1985) 52 P & CR 41.

[1124] For the distinction between a lease and a licence, see pp. 197 et seq, ante.

[1125] See *Street v Mountford* [1985] AC 809; p. 198, ante.

[1126] *Norris v Checksfield* [1991] 1 WLR 1241.

[1127] *Royal Philanthropic Society v County* [1985] 2 EGLR 109   [1128] HA 1988, Sch 2, Ground 16.

[1129] *Wolfe v Hogan* [1949] 2 KB 194.   [1130] Ibid.

(iv) A

The house (or part of a house) must be let as a single dwelling. A house let to one person as a number of separate dwellings in multiple occupation is not protected.[1131] Similarly, in *St Catherine's College v Dorling*,[1132] the owner of a house in Oxford let it to the college for the purpose of enabling it to grant sub-tenancies or licences of rooms to undergraduates. The Court of Appeal held that a letting for the purpose of permitting a number of people the exclusive use of particular rooms was not a letting of the house as a single dwelling.

(v) Separate

The requirement that the premises must be let as a separate dwelling would, if unqualified, exclude all cases where the tenant shares some living accommodation, either with another tenant or with his landlord.[1133] This was in fact the position before 1949, by which time the courts had evolved a great deal of learning on what constituted sharing and what amounted to "living accommodation". Now, however, the tenant who shares with another tenant nevertheless has an assured tenancy,[1134] while a tenant who shares with his landlord is normally excluded by the resident landlord exception.[1135]

(vi) Dwelling

The word "dwelling" has its ordinary meaning of premises used for normal domestic purposes such as cooking, feeding and sleeping, of which sleeping seems to be the most important.[1136] If premises are let partly as a dwelling and partly for business purposes (as in the common case of a shop with living accommodation above) the tenancy will be subject only to the code governing business tenancies[1137] and not come within the Housing Act 1988 at all.[1138]

(2) THE TENANT IS AN INDIVIDUAL

This part of the definition makes it clear that a corporate tenant cannot have an assured tenancy. It has long been established that a "company let" cannot attract security of tenure under the Rent Act 1977 because that Act, although not expressly requiring the tenant to be an "individual", imposes a residence requirement[1139] which corporate tenants cannot satisfy.[1140] The courts have been reluctant to regard company lettings as shams even where the mechanism has clearly been adopted solely as a device to avoid statutory protection,[1141] although it remains possible that a letting to a company could be construed as a letting to the individual who occupies.[1142]

[1131] *Horford Investments Ltd v Lambert* [1976] Ch 39.   [1132] [1980] 1 WLR 66.

[1133] *Neale v Del Soto* [1945] KB 144; *Goodrich v Paisner* [1957] AC 65.   [1134] HA 1988, s. 3.

[1135] Ibid., Sch. 1, para. 10. See p. 342, post.

[1136] *Wright v Howell* (1947) 92 SJ 26; *Palmer v McNamara* [1991] 1 EGLR 121; *Westminster City Council v Clarke* [1992] 2 AC 288. Cooking facilities need not be available: *Uratemp Ventures Ltd v Collins* [2002] 1 AC 301.   [1137] See p. 377, post.

[1138] HA 1988, Sch. 1, para. 4. Unless the business element is "de minimis": *Lewis v Weldcrest Ltd* [1978] 1 WLR 1107.   [1139] Rent Act 1977, s. 2.

[1140] *Hiller v United Dairies (London) Ltd* [1934] 1 KB 57; *Firstcross Ltd v East-West (Export/Import) Ltd* (1980) 41 P & CR 145.

[1141] *Hilton v Plustitle Ltd* [1989] 1 WLR 149; *Kaye v Massbetter Ltd and Kanter* (1990) 62 P & CR 558.

[1142] See *Gisborne v Burton* [1989] QB 390 (tax doctrine of "artificial transaction" applicable in landlord and tenant context); cf *Belvedere Court Management Ltd v Frogmore Developments Ltd* [1997] QB 858.

(3) OCCUPATION AS ONLY OR PRINCIPAL HOME

The purpose of the Housing Act 1988 and its predecessors is to protect a tenant in the occupation of his home, not to confer rights on those who do not occupy, because they have sub-let[1143] or for some other reason. The occupation requirement of the 1988 Act may be best understood by first considering the authorities under the Rent Act 1977, which remain to a great extent relevant. The rule under section 2 of the 1977 Act is that the tenant must occupy the dwelling-house as his residence. Clearly he need not be there all the time, so long as he preserves a sufficient intention to return and leaves some visible indication of continued occupation. In other words, he must establish the necessary *animus possidendi* and *corpus possessionis*.[1144] The presence of the tenant's furniture and effects, his wife[1145] or other member of his family are the usual ways in which the latter requirement is satisfied while the tenant is away on business, at sea or in prison.[1146] A tenant who has sub-let part of the premises continues to satisfy the requirement so long as he resides in the other part.

The "only or principal home" requirement of the assured tenancy is stricter. Although a tenant who has two homes is not excluded, he can only have an assured tenancy in relation to his principal home. This is a question of fact. The requirement is the same as that which applies to public sector secure tenants under the Housing Act 1985.[1147] Decisions concerning secure tenancies may thus afford guidance.[1148] In the case of joint tenancies, only one need occupy as his only or principal home.[1149] Hence assured status is not lost if the tenants are a married couple who separate. As in the case of the Rent Act 1977, occupation by the tenant's spouse or civil partner (where there is no joint tenancy) will satisfy the requirement.[1150]

(b) The exceptions

The Act contains a fairly long list of exceptions.[1151] Only the more important ones will be considered here.

(1) HOUSES LET BY AN EXEMPTED BODY

Tenancies granted by certain specified bodies, which include local authorities, the Commission for the New Towns, and housing action trusts are not assured.[1152] They are instead subject to the code of protection for public sector housing now found in the Housing Act 1985.[1153] Similar exemption from the Housing Act 1988 (and from the public sector code)

[1143] *Ujima Housing Association v Ansah* (1997) 30 HLR 831.

[1144] *Brown v Brash and Ambrose* [1948] 2 KB 247; *Skinner v Geary* [1931] 2 KB 546. This is a question of fact and degree. For the meaning of possession (both *animus* and *corpus*), see p. 122, ante.

[1145] Occupation by the tenant's spouse or civil partner satisfies the requirement even if the tenant does not intend to return: Family Law Act 1996, s. 30(4), as amended by Civil Partnership Act 2004, s. 82, Sch. 9.

[1146] *Brown v Brash and Ambrose*, supra.   [1147] S. 81.

[1148] See *Peabody Donation Fund Governors v Grant* (1982) 264 EG 925; *Crawley BC v Sawyer* (1987) 20 HLR 98. See also, on the Leasehold Reform Act 1967, *Dymond v Arundel-Timms* [1991] 1 EGLR 109.

[1149] HA 1988, s. 1.

[1150] Family Law Act 1996, s. 30(4), as amended by Civil Partnership Act 2004, s. 82, Sch. 9. The exception extends to former spouses or civil partners, cohabitants or former cohabitants who have obtained occupation orders: ibid., ss. 35(13), 36(13). The court may order the transfer of the tenancy on divorce, or on the separation of cohabitants; see p. 343, post.   [1151] See HA 1988, Sch. 1.

[1152] Ibid., para. 12.   [1153] See p. 358, post.

has been conferred upon educational institutions and similar bodies who let premises to students,[1154] and upon Crown lettings.[1155] Housing associations are not, however, exempted.

(2) LETTINGS BY RESIDENT LANDLORDS

A tenancy is not assured if the dwelling forms part of a building[1156] (other than a purpose-built block of flats) in which the landlord was also residing when the tenancy began and in which he has since continued to reside.[1157]

This exception was introduced by the Rent Act 1974 and is hedged about with qualifications of great complexity which can only be explained (though not excused) by its legislative history. Until 1974 the law took no account of whether or not the landlord resided on the premises. Instead, there was a general exception for furnished lettings. The furnished tenancy exception was socially controversial because it was comparatively easy and inexpensive for a landlord to provide enough furniture to prevent the tenant from acquiring security of tenure.[1158] This was hard on the many persons (including a substantial proportion of recent immigrants and single-parent families) who had to take furnished accommodation because they could not find or afford any other. On the other hand, there is a need for a pool of short-term accommodation which would dry up if all tenants were given full protection. The Rent Act 1974 compromised by abolishing the furnished lettings exception and trying to preserve the pool of short-term accommodation by introducing an exception for resident landlords.

The 1988 Act deals in two ways with the amount of residence which a landlord must put in to keep his tenant within the exception. In the first place, it provides that the landlord, or at least one of joint landlords, must occupy as his only or principal home.[1159] Secondly, the Act specifies periods of non-residence which may be overlooked, such as up to six months for a purchaser landlord to move in and up to two years after a landlord has died and while the premises are vested in his estate.[1160]

Finally, where the landlord is not only resident but also shares accommodation with the tenant, the tenancy is excluded from the requirements of the Protection from Eviction Act 1977 relating to notices to quit and recovery of possession by court order.[1161]

(3) HOLIDAY LETTINGS

These are outside the Housing Act 1988[1162] or any other system of control.[1163] The lack of statutory definition of "holiday" has facilitated attempts to avoid the Act. In the leading case of *Buchmann v May*[1164] there was a three-month letting in Norbury to an Australian with a temporary visitor's permit, who had already occupied under a series of short lettings. The document, signed by her, stated that the letting was "solely for the purpose of the tenant's holiday in the London area".

The Court of Appeal held that where the tenancy is stated to be for a holiday, the onus is on the tenant to establish that the document is a sham or the result of mistake or

---

[1154] HA 1988, Sch. 1, para. 8; HA 1985, Sch. 1, para. 10.
[1155] Ibid., para. 11 (no exemption for Crown Estate Commissioners or Duchies of Lancaster or Cornwall).
[1156] See *Bardrick v Haycock* (1976) 31 P & CR 420; *Griffiths v English* (1982) 261 EG 257.
[1157] HA 1988, Sch. 1, para. 10.   [1158] See *Woodward v Docherty* [1974] 1 WLR 966.
[1159] HA 1988, Sch. 1, para. 10(1)(b). See p. 341, ante.   [1160] Ibid., paras. 17, 20.
[1161] Protection from Eviction Act 1977, s. 3A, p. 331, ante.
[1162] HA 1988, Sch. 1, para. 9.   [1163] Protection from Eviction Act 1977, s. 3A, p. 331, ante.
[1164] [1978] 2 All ER 993.

misrepresentation, but added that the court would be astute to detect a sham if evasion was suspected. On the facts, the tenant failed.

(4) TENANCIES AT A LOW RENT

Tenancies under which no rent is payable[1165] or, if entered into on or after 1 April, 1990 (when domestic rating was abolished), at a rent not exceeding £1,000 a year in Greater London or £250 elsewhere[1166] are excluded. Tenancies entered into before that date are excluded if the current rent is less than two thirds of the rateable value on 31 March 1990.[1167] The effect of these provisions is to exclude tenants under leases, usually for long terms such as ninety-nine years, which have been granted at a low or "ground" rent in return for payment of a substantial premium. Such tenants are, from an economic point of view, owner-occupiers, and the machinery of the 1988 Act is not appropriate for them. As we shall see, they have substantial protection under other statutory codes.[1168]

(5) TENANCIES AT A HIGH RENT

Tenancies granted on or after 1 April 1990 cannot be assured if the current rent exceeds £25,000 a year.[1169] At this level there is no hardship in allowing a free market. Tenancies granted prior to that date, before the abolition of domestic rating, are excluded if the property (or such part as is subject to the tenancy) had a rateable value on 31 March 1990 exceeding £1,500 in Greater London or £750 elsewhere.[1170]

(c) Implied terms of the assured tenancy

The most important implied term relates to assignment and sub-letting. In the case of an assured periodic tenancy, there is an implied term that the tenant shall not assign, sub-let or part with possession (in whole or in part) without the landlord's consent.[1171] Section 19 of the Landlord and Tenant Act 1927,[1172] implying that the landlord's consent shall not be unreasonably withheld, is excluded.

No such term is implied in the case of a periodic tenancy (which is not a statutory periodic tenancy[1173]) if there is an express term either prohibiting or permitting assignment and so forth (absolutely or conditionally).[1174] In the case of an express conditional prohibition, section 19 of the 1927 Act will apply.

Nor is such a term implied in the case of a fixed-term assured tenancy, where the general law on assignment and sub-letting (including section 19 of the 1927 Act) applies. It should be noted that the court has power to order the transfer of an assured tenancy to the other spouse, civil partner of cohabitant on divorce, on making a property adjustment order with respect to a civil partnership, or on separation of cohabitants.[1175]

[1165] HA 1988, Sch. 1, para. 3.

[1166] Ibid., para. 3A, inserted by References to Rating (Housing) Regulations 1990 (SI 1990 No. 434).

[1167] Ibid., para. 3B.   [1168] See p. 363, post.

[1169] HA 1988, Sch. 1, para. 2, as substituted by References to Rating (Housing) Regulations 1990 (SI 1990 No. 434); R v London Rent Assessment Panel, ex p Cadogan Estates Ltd [1998] QB 398.

[1170] Ibid., Sch. 1, para. 2A.   [1171] Ibid., s. 15.   [1172] See p. 257, ante.

[1173] See p. 346, post.

[1174] HA 1988, s. 15(3)(a). Nor is such a term implied where a premium is payable on the grant or renewal of the tenancy: s. 15(3)(b).

[1175] Family Law Act 1996, Sch. 7, as amended by Civil Partnership Act 2004, s. 82, Sch. 9.

In the case of all assured tenancies there is an implied term that the tenant shall afford the landlord access for doing repairs which the landlord is entitled to execute.[1176]

The jurisdiction of the rent assessment committee to vary the terms of a statutory periodic tenancy is dealt with below.[1177]

(2) The Assured Shorthold Tenancy

An assured shorthold tenancy is one which is within the definition of an assured tenancy, as discussed above, and which satisfies further conditions. In the case of tenancies granted before 28 February 1997 (when the amending provisions of the Housing Act 1996 came into operation) the conditions were as follows:[1178]

(a) it is a fixed-term tenancy granted for a term certain of not less than six months; and

(b) the landlord has no power to determine[1179] the tenancy at any time earlier than six months from the beginning of the tenancy; and

(c) a notice in prescribed form[1180] was served by the prospective landlord on the prospective tenant[1181] before the assured tenancy was entered into, stating that the tenancy was to be a shorthold tenancy.[1182]

Subject to certain exceptions,[1183] failure to satisfy the three conditions resulted in the creation of an assured tenancy, so long as section 1 of the 1988 Act was satisfied.

The attraction of the assured shorthold tenancy to landlords is that they may recover possession more easily than in the case of an assured tenancy because of the availability of a special mandatory ground of possession applicable only to assured shorthold tenancies. This ground, which is available in addition to the grounds which apply to assured tenancies generally, is explained below.[1184] The other distinction between assured tenancies and assured shorthold tenancies is that a greater degree of rent control applies to assured shortholds.[1185]

The Housing Act 1996 gave landlords further inducement to let by providing that assured tenancies granted on or after 28 February 1997 are shortholds unless they fall within certain narrow exceptions. In other words, the shorthold is the norm and positive steps must be taken to create a full assured tenancy, which is the converse of the previous position. The simple definition is that an assured tenancy entered into after the 1996 Act is an assured shorthold unless it falls within the exceptions mentioned below.[1186] Thus there is no minimum term, no prohibition on landlord's break clauses, periodic tenancies are included, and there is no need to serve prior notice on the prospective tenant. The tenant no longer has a

---

[1176] HA 1988, s. 16.   [1177] See p. 346, post.

[1178] HA 1988, s. 20(1). See also s. 20(3) (anti-avoidance).

[1179] The existence of a right of re-entry is not treated as a power to determine the tenancy; ibid., s. 45(4). Forfeiture is not a means of determining assured tenancies; see p. 348, post.

[1180] The question is whether the notice is substantially to the same effect as the prescribed form in accomplishing the statutory purpose of telling the proposed tenant the special nature of an assured shorthold tenancy, even if it is wrong in some detail: Assured Tenancies and Agricultural Occupancies (Forms) Regulations 1988, SI 1988 No. 2203, reg. 2; *Ravenseft Properties Ltd v Hall* [2002] 1 EGLR 9.

[1181] Or the tenant's authorised agent: *Yenula Properties Ltd v Naidu* [2002] 3 EGLR 28.

[1182] See *Panayi v Roberts* [1993] 2 EGLR 51. The court has no power to dispense with this requirement.

[1183] HA 1988, s. 20(4) (where prior assured shorthold); s. 34(2) (where prior shorthold tenancy under Rent Act 1977); s. 39(7) (succession on death of shorthold tenant under Rent Act 1977).

[1184] Ibid., s. 21, p. 352, post.   [1185] See p. 346, post.

[1186] HA 1996, s. 96, inserting s. 19A into the 1988 Act. A statutory periodic tenancy arising under s. 5 of the 1988 Act at the end of a fixed term falling within s. 19A is also shorthold, as explained below.

warning as to the nature of the tenancy. As explained below, the tenant is protected by the rule that possession cannot be recovered during the first six months.

The main exceptional cases where a full assured tenancy may still be created are as follows.[1187]

(a) *Excluded by notice* Where the prospective landlord serves notice on the prospective tenant before the tenancy is entered into, stating that the tenancy is not to be shorthold; or, where the landlord serves a notice on the tenant after an assured tenancy has been entered into, stating that it is no longer shorthold.

(b) *Excluded by tenancy provision* Where the tenancy itself contains a provision to the effect that it is not shorthold.

(c) *Successor to Rent Act tenant* An assured tenancy arising under section 39 of the 1988 Act in favour of a successor to a deceased Rent Act tenant (whose tenancy was not a protected shorthold) takes effect as a full assured tenancy.

(d) *Tenancies replacing non-shortholds* Where immediately before[1188] the grant of a tenancy the tenant (alone or jointly with others) had a full assured tenancy, then the new tenancy is also a full assured tenancy, if granted by the same landlord (or one of the joint landlords). There is no requirement that the premises be the same. The replacement tenancy will, however, be a shorthold if the tenant serves a prescribed form notice before the grant of the replacement tenancy stating that the new tenancy is to be shorthold.

As it is now possible to grant a shorthold informally, for example a weekly or monthly periodic tenancy, the Act[1189] provides a means for the tenant to acquire a written statement of the terms of the tenancy. A tenant who has an assured shorthold granted on or after 28 February 1997 may by notice in writing require the landlord to provide a written statement of any of the following terms which is not already evidenced in writing:

(a) the date the tenancy began or, if it is a statutory periodic tenancy, the date it arose;

(b) the rent and the dates on which it is payable;

(c) any term providing for rent review;

(d) the length of the term if it is a fixed term.

Such a statement is not conclusive evidence of what was agreed. A landlord who fails to comply without reasonable excuse is liable to a fine.

The result of the 1996 Act is that most private landlords will create only assured shortholds, while full assured tenancies continue to be granted by "social landlords" such as housing associations.[1190] Thus the private rental sector has been substantially deregulated.

[1187] HA 1996, Sch. 7, inserting Sch. 2A into the 1988 Act. Other exceptions relate to assured agricultural occupancies, tenancies which transfer from the secure to the assured regime when the landlord ceases to be a local authority, and assured tenancies arising on termination of long leaseholds.

[1188] See *Dibbs v Campbell* [1988] 2 EGLR 122 (no assured tenancy immediately before the grant where effectively surrendered). [1189] HA 1996, s. 97, inserting s. 20A into the 1988 Act.

[1190] If the landlord is a registered social landlord, the landlord may apply to a county court for a demotion order under HA 1998, s. 6A, inserted by Anti-social Behaviour Act 2003, s. 14(4), under which the assured tenancy is terminated and replaced by a demoted assured shorthold tenancy. This demoted tenancy lasts for at least one year: HA 1988, s. 20B, inserted by Anti-social Behaviour Act 2003, s. 15(1); and during the demotion period

(3) Control of Rent

Rent control under the "fair rent" system of the Rent Act 1977[1191] took the form of keeping the rent below market levels. In order to encourage letting, the philosophy of the Housing Act 1988 is to impose a form of rent control which seeks merely to prevent excessive rents and does not prohibit the recovery of a market rent. Unlike the Rent Act 1977, the payment of a premium on the grant or assignment of an assured tenancy is not prohibited.

(a) Fixed-term assured tenancy

The rent control scheme of the 1988 Act does not apply to such a tenancy during the period of the fixed term. The rent under such a tenancy is that which the parties have agreed. It may be increased if there is a rent review clause (or by agreement).

(b) Periodic assured tenancy and statutory periodic assured tenancy

As will be explained below,[1192] the scheme of the Housing Act 1988 is that a periodic assured tenancy continues until a ground for possession becomes available, and cannot be terminated by a landlord's notice to quit. The security mechanism for a fixed-term assured tenancy is that, on expiry of the fixed term, a statutory periodic assured tenancy arises, which continues until a ground for possession becomes available and cannot be ended by a landlord's notice to quit. In both of these cases section 13 of the 1988 Act provides a means of increasing the rent.

The landlord may serve on the tenant a notice in prescribed form proposing a new rent to take effect at the beginning of a new period of the tenancy specified in the notice.[1193] Except in the case of a statutory periodic tenancy, the increase cannot take effect within a year of the commencement of the tenancy. If the rent has already been increased under this procedure, no further increase can take effect within a year of the date on which the previous increase took effect. Subject to these two rules, the Act provides that the increased rent cannot take effect within certain minimum periods from the date of service of the notice, such as six months in the case of a yearly tenancy.[1194]

The rent specified in the landlord's notice will take effect unless the tenant refers the notice to a rent assessment committee before the beginning of the new period specified in the notice.[1195] Alternatively, the rent may be varied by agreement without following these procedures.[1196]

If the tenant refers the landlord's notice to a rent assessment committee, the committee will determine the rent which the dwelling "might reasonably be expected to be let in the open market by a willing landlord under an assured tenancy".[1197] In assessing the market rent, certain matters must be disregarded, such as any increase in value attributable to relevant improvements by the tenant or any decrease in value attributable to a breach of

---

the landlord can obtain an order for possession without having to establish grounds: HA 1988, s. 21, as amended by Anti-social Behaviour Act 2003, s. 15(2). For demotion orders in relation to secure tenancies under HA 1985, see p. 360, post.

[1191] P. 337, ante.   [1192] P. 348, post.   [1193] HA 1988, s. 13(2), as amended by SI 2003 No. 259.
[1194] HA 1988, s. 13(2), (3), as amended by SI 2003 No. 259.   [1195] Ibid., s. 13(4).
[1196] Ibid., s. 13(5).
[1197] Ibid., s. 14(1). An assessment above £25,000 a year will take the tenancy out of assured status; *R v London Rent Assessment Panel, ex p Cadogan Estates Ltd* [1998] QB 398.

covenant by the tenant, such as a failure to repair.[1198] The rent determined by the committee takes effect from the beginning of the new period specified in the landlord's notice (unless the parties agree otherwise), although a later date may be substituted if it appears that the earlier date would cause undue hardship to the tenant.[1199]

(c) Assured shorthold tenancy

The procedures described above can apply to assured shorthold tenancies provided they are periodic.[1200] Shorthold tenancies granted before the operation of the Housing Act 1996 were normally fixed-term,[1201] and, accordingly, outside these provisions unless they had become statutory periodic tenancies on expiry of the fixed term. There is no requirement of a minimum six-month fixed term in the case of assured shortholds granted after the commencement of the 1996 Act. Thus the provisions discussed in (b) above are now of wider application.

The 1988 Act provides a further procedure which is applicable only to assured shorthold tenancies, and which enables the tenant to refer the rent initially agreed to a rent assessment committee.[1202] This differs from the procedure already discussed, which merely facilitates a review of the rent after it has operated for a certain period. A shorthold tenant may apply by notice in prescribed form for a determination by the committee, which will then determine the rent which "the landlord might reasonably be expected to obtain under the assured shorthold tenancy".[1203] This procedure may be invoked only once, and is not available in the case of a statutory periodic tenancy which has arisen on the expiry of a fixed-term shorthold tenancy.[1204] In the case of an assured shorthold granted on or after 28 February 1997 the tenant may refer the rent under this procedure only within the period of six months from the beginning of the tenancy.[1205]

The committee is not to make a determination unless it considers that there is a sufficient number of similar dwellings in the locality let on assured tenancies (whether or not short-hold), and that the agreed rent is significantly higher than the rent which the landlord might reasonably be expected to be able to obtain.[1206] The committee has no power to increase the rent. The effect of these limitations is that the tenant will not succeed if there are insufficient comparables nor if the rent is insufficiently excessive. His lack of security of tenure may in any event make him reluctant to apply.

If the committee does determine the rent, it takes effect from such date as it directs, not being earlier than the date of the application.[1207]

Finally, information as to rents which have been the subject of applications to rent assessment committees is publicly available, to assist in the establishment of comparables.[1208]

(4) Security of Tenure

An assured tenancy may be terminated only in the manner laid down by the Housing Act 1988, as amended by the Housing Act 1996. As in the case of the Rent Act 1977, it is clear

---

[1198] Ibid., s. 14(2). The default must be that of the present tenant: *N & D (London) Ltd v Gadsdon* [1992] 1 EGLR 112.   [1199] Ibid., s. 14(7).

[1200] Ibid., s. 14(9), inserted by HA 1996, s. 104, Sch. 8.   [1201] See p. 344, ante.

[1202] HA 1988, s. 22.   [1203] Ibid., s. 22(1).   [1204] Ibid., s. 22(2).

[1205] Ibid., s. 22(2)(aa), inserted by HA 1996, s. 100.   [1206] Ibid., s. 22(3).

[1207] Ibid., s. 22(4). Any excess is irrecoverable from the tenant. The landlord cannot serve a notice of increase under s. 13 within a year of this date.   [1208] Ibid., s. 42.

from the mandatory wording of the Act that the parties cannot contract out of security of tenure.[1209] If, however, the tenancy has ceased to be assured, as where the tenant no longer occupies as his only or principal home, the landlord may terminate it by any methods which are available under the general law.

(a) Periodic assured tenancy

In the case of a periodic tenancy, section 5 of the 1988 Act provides that service of a notice to quit by the landlord shall be of no effect.[1210] Such a tenancy may be terminated by a tenant's notice to quit[1211] or by a court order based on a ground for possession, as explained below.

(b) Fixed-term assured tenancy

Such a tenancy may be terminated by "surrender or other action on the part of the tenant".[1212] The "other action" would include the operation of a break clause (a provision permitting premature termination of a fixed term) by the tenant. The landlord cannot terminate the tenancy except by a court order based on a ground for possession or, "in the case of a fixed-term tenancy which contains a power for the landlord to determine the tenancy in certain circumstances, by the exercise of that power".[1213] It is further provided that, unless the tenancy is terminated by the tenant or by a court order, the tenant is entitled to remain after termination of the fixed term as a statutory periodic tenant.[1214] This will occur, for example, where the fixed term ends by expiry or is determined by the exercise of a break clause by the landlord. The provisions relating to forfeiture are obscurely drafted, but the position has been held to be as follows. The reference in section 5 to ending the tenancy by the exercise of a landlord's power to determine it does not include forfeiture,[1215] which is not, therefore, an available method of terminating an assured tenancy.[1216] A notice under section 146 of the Law of Property Act 1925[1217] would be ineffective, and the concept of relief from forfeiture does not apply. A landlord who would have had grounds for forfeiture may, however, be able to invoke a statutory ground for possession. Only certain grounds are available during the currency of a fixed term,[1218] and the terms of the tenancy must provide for termination on the ground in question (whether by forfeiture, notice or otherwise).[1219] It appears that the forfeiture clause or other terminating provision in the tenancy need not

---

[1209]   *Bankway Properties Ltd v Pensfold-Dunsford* [2001] 1 WLR 1369 (provision for five-fold rent increase, designed to give landlord right to possession, held unenforceable as being an improper attempt to evade the mandatory scheme for security of tenure: per ARDEN LJ at [56]; or as being inconsistent with the statutory purpose of security of tenure which the parties, by choosing to contract in the form of an assured tenancy under HA 1988, had incorporated into their agreement: per PILL LJ at [70]).

[1210]   See *Love v Herrity* [1991] 2 EGLR 44.

[1211]   Notice by one of joint tenants will suffice; *Hammersmith and Fulham LBC v Monk* [1992] 1 AC 478, p. 323, ante.   [1212]   HA 1988, s. 5(2).

[1213]   Ibid., s. 5(1). See *Aylward v Fawaz* (1996) 29 HLR 408. For the termination of an assured tenancy and its replacement by a demoted assured shorthold tenancy, see p. 345, n. 1190, ante.

[1214]   HA 1988, s. 5(2). For the avoidance of doubt, a statutory periodic tenancy arising after the commencement of HA 1996 on the termination of an assured tenancy which was not a shorthold will not itself be a shorthold: HA 1996, Sch. 7, para. 8.   [1215]   Ibid., s. 45(4).

[1216]   *Artesian Residential Investments Ltd v Beck* [2000] QB 541.   [1217]   See p. 281, ante.

[1218]   The available grounds are the mandatory Grounds 2 and 8 and the discretionary grounds other than Grounds 9 and 16. These are explained at pp. 349–56, post.

[1219]   HA 1988, s. 7(6). See (1989) 139 NLJ 326 (C. Rodgers).

refer specifically to the grounds for possession, although the safest course would be to make specific reference.

Where a statutory periodic tenancy arises on termination of the fixed term, it can be ended only by the tenant[1220] or by a court order based on a ground for possession, as described in (a) above. The periods of this tenancy are the same as those for which rent was last payable under the fixed term. The other terms (including rent) are the same as those of the fixed term immediately before it ended.[1221] The implied terms relating to assignment and sub-letting and the procedure for increasing the rent have already been discussed.[1222] Either party may seek a variation in the terms of the tenancy (other than rent) by serving a notice proposing different terms on the other party. If the other party does not accept the new terms he may refer the notice to a rent assessment committee, which will determine whether those terms or some other terms might reasonably be expected in an assured periodic tenancy of the dwelling-house in question.[1223]

(c) The grounds for possession

The court may make an order for possession, which determines the assured tenancy, only if the judge is satisfied of the existence of one of the grounds for possession specified in the Act.[1224] In some cases the establishment of a statutory ground for possession concludes the matter. An order for possession is then mandatory.[1225] In other cases, the judge may not make such an order unless he considers it reasonable to do so.[1226] The requirement gives the judge a wide discretion, enabling him to consider all relevant circumstances at the date of the hearing. There are eighteen grounds for possession, eight mandatory and ten discretionary. In addition, there is the special mandatory ground which applies only to assured shorthold tenancies.[1227] The position as to termination during the currency of a fixed-term assured tenancy has already been discussed.[1228] Where a fixed-term tenancy has come to an end, the possession order operates to terminate also any statutory periodic tenancy which has arisen.[1229]

In order to invoke a ground for possession, the landlord must serve a notice[1230] in prescribed form under section 8 of the 1988 Act, specifying the ground or grounds relied on.[1231] He must then begin proceedings within the time limits laid down by section 8, which vary according to the ground in question.[1232]

(1) MANDATORY GROUNDS

The following grounds are those upon which the court must order possession.

[1220] As in the case of any tenancy of premises let as a dwelling, the tenant must give four weeks' notice: Protection from Eviction Act 1977, s. 5, p. 317, ante; *Laine v Cadwallader* (2001) 33 HLR 36.

[1221] HA 1988, s. 5(3).   [1222] See s. 15 (assignment etc.), p. 343, ante, and s. 13 (rent), p. 346, ante.

[1223] HA 1988, s. 6.   [1224] As to consent orders, see *Baygreen Properties Ltd v Gil* [2002] 3 EGLR 42.

[1225] HA 1988, Sch. 2, Part I.   [1226] Ibid., Sch. 2, Part II.   [1227] Ibid., s. 21, post.   [1228] Supra.

[1229] HA 1988, s. 7(7).

[1230] The court may dispense with this requirement (except in the case of Ground 8) if it considers it just and equitable to do so: ibid., s. 8(1)(b). *Kelsey Housing Association v King* (1995) 28 HLR 270.

[1231] The statutory grounds need not be set out verbatim in the notice but the substance must be fully set out; *Mountain v Hastings* (1993) 25 HLR 427 (Ground 8).

[1232] The time limits have been amended by s. 151 of HA 1996. The main effect is to enable proceedings based on Ground 14 to be commenced more speedily.

(i) Ground 1: Landlord occupied or intends to occupy

This ground applies either where the landlord (or at least one of joint landlords) occupied the dwelling as his only or principal home at some time before the beginning of the tenancy or, without any such condition, the landlord (or at least one of joint landlords) requires the dwelling as his, his spouse's, or his civil partner's[1233] only or principal home. In the latter case the landlord must not have acquired the reversion for money or money's worth. In the former case there is no requirement that the landlord intends to occupy. In both cases the ground is available only if the landlord gave written notice no later than the beginning of the tenancy that possession might be recovered on this ground, although the court may dispense with this requirement if of the opinion that it is just and equitable to do so.[1234]

Compensation is payable where the landlord recovers possession but it later appears that he obtained the order by misrepresentation or concealment of material facts.[1235]

(ii) Ground 2: Mortgagee's power of sale

Where the landlord mortgaged the property before granting the tenancy, this ground is available where the mortgagee requires possession in order to exercise the power of sale. Written notice[1236] must have been given before the beginning of the tenancy, unless the court dispenses with the requirement, as in the case of Ground 1.

Where the mortgage was granted after the tenancy, the mortgagee's power of sale can be exercised only subject to the tenancy,[1237] and so this ground is not available. A tenancy granted after the mortgage will be binding on the mortgagee only if the mortgagor's leasing power under section 99 of the Law of Property Act 1925[1238] has not been excluded, or if he has consented to the grant or accepted the tenant. It is in these cases that Ground 2 is relevant. Where the tenancy is not binding on the mortgagee, the latter may recover possession under the general law without regard to the Housing Act 1988,[1239] although the landlord could not do so. If the subject of the mortgage is the assured tenancy itself, the mortgagee's right to possession is not affected by the Housing Act 1988.[1240]

(iii) Ground 3: Out-of-season lettings

This ground applies to a fixed-term tenancy not exceeding eight months where the dwelling has been occupied for a holiday within the twelve-month period before the beginning of the tenancy. The landlord must have given written notice to the tenant no later than the beginning of the tenancy that possession might be recovered on this ground. The effect of this ground is that landlords may let holiday accommodation out of season and be able to recover possession when the property is again required for holiday lettings, which, as has been seen, cannot be assured tenancies.[1241]

(iv) Ground 4: Vacation lettings of student accommodation

This is based on the same principle as Ground 3. Student lettings themselves cannot be assured.[1242] If the landlord wishes to utilise the accommodation in the vacation,

---

[1233] As amended by Civil Partnership Act 2004, s. 81, Sch. 8.
[1234] See *Boyle v Verrall* [1997] 1 EGLR 25; *Mustafa v Ruddock* (1998) 30 HLR 495.   [1235] HA 1988, s. 12.
[1236] It appears that the notice in question must have been a notice under Ground 1.
[1237] See p. 769, post; *Barclays Bank plc v Zaroovabli* [1997] Ch 321.   [1238] See p. 760, post.
[1239] See, on the Rent Act 1977, *Britannia Building Society v Earl* [1990] 1 WLR 422.   [1240] S. 7(1).
[1241] See p. 342, ante.   [1242] See p. 342, ante.

possession may be recovered on this ground when the property is again required for student lettings. The vacation letting must be for a fixed term not exceeding twelve months, the dwelling must have been subject to an excluded student letting during the twelve-month period before the beginning of the tenancy, and written notice must have been given to the tenant no later than the beginning of the tenancy that possession might be recovered on this ground.

(v) Ground 5: Occupation by minister of religion

This ground applies to a dwelling which is held for the purposes of being available as a residence for a minister of religion, where the court is satisfied that the dwelling is now required for that purpose. Notice must have been given to the tenant not later than the beginning of the tenancy that possession might be recovered on this ground.

(vi) Ground 6: Intention to demolish or reconstruct

A landlord who intends to demolish or reconstruct the whole or a substantial part of the dwelling or to do substantial works may invoke this ground, which is based on one of the business tenancy grounds in the Landlord and Tenant Act 1954.[1243] The landlord will not succeed if the work could reasonably be done without the tenant giving up possession. The tenant may, for example, be willing to take an assured tenancy of a reduced part of the dwelling or to give the landlord access and facilities, where the nature of the work is such that either course would be practicable.

This ground is available only to the original landlord or a successor who acquired the reversion other than for money or money's worth. In other words, he must not have purchased the property subject to the tenancy.

Where Ground 6 is established, the landlord must pay reasonable removal expenses to the tenant.[1244] Compensation is also payable in cases of misrepresentation or concealment, as mentioned in relation to Ground 1, above.

(vii) Ground 7: Death of periodic tenant

Where a periodic assured tenant dies without leaving a spouse or civil partner who is qualified to succeed to the assured tenancy,[1245] it devolves under his will or intestacy and becomes subject to termination by Ground 7. The landlord must begin proceedings not later than twelve months after the death or after the date on which the court considers that the landlord became aware of it. If the landlord does not act in time, the tenancy will continue until some other ground for possession becomes available, provided the beneficiary satisfies the conditions required for an assured tenancy. If he does not, the tenancy may be terminated by a notice to quit, without recourse to Ground 7.

Ground 7 does not apply to a fixed-term assured tenancy. On the death of the tenant such a tenancy will pass under his will or intestacy and will continue assured if the beneficiary satisfies the conditions required for an assured tenancy. A statutory periodic tenancy will then arise at the end of the fixed term, which will be subject to Ground 7 on the tenant's death. If the beneficiary does not satisfy the conditions required for an assured tenancy, the tenancy will terminate on expiry of the fixed term.

[1243] S. 30(1)(f), p. 382, post.   [1244] HA 1988, s. 11.   [1245] See p. 356, post.

(viii) Ground 8: Two months' rent unpaid[1246]

There are three grounds for possession relating to rent, one mandatory and two discretionary.[1247] Ground 8 applies where the arrears exist both at the date of service of the notice of proceedings under section 8[1248] and at the date of the hearing. The amount of arrears necessary to establish the ground varies according to how frequently the rent is payable under the tenancy, but broadly at least two months' rent must be unpaid. The rent must be "lawfully due", which will not be the case, for example, so far as it exceeds any figure determined by a rent assessment committee.[1249]

As the ground is mandatory, the court has no power to suspend or postpone the order subject to conditions as to payment.[1250] If, however, the tenant pays the arrears before the hearing, Ground 8 will no longer apply.[1251] The discretionary grounds applicable to rent may still apply, and so the landlord should include these in his section 8 notice.

(ix) Assured shorthold tenancy

Section 21 provides a further mandatory ground which is confined to assured shorthold tenancies. Where the tenancy has ended and no further tenancy is in existence other than a statutory periodic tenancy, the court must make a possession order if the landlord has given the tenant not less than two months' notice in writing[1252] stating that he requires possession.[1253] The court cannot stay or suspend the order.[1254] The notice may be given on or before the day on which a fixed-term tenancy ends, although the order cannot be made before the fixed term has ended.[1255]

Where a fixed-term tenancy has already become a statutory periodic tenancy before the notice is served, the date specified in the landlord's notice cannot be earlier than the earliest date upon which the tenancy could have been ended[1256] by notice to quit.

In the case of a shorthold granted on or after 28 February 1997, a possession order may not be made so as to take effect earlier than six months after the beginning of the tenancy.[1257]

[1246] Reduced from three months by HA 1996, s. 101.   [1247] Grounds 10 and 11, post.

[1248] P. 349, ante. See *Mountain v Hastings* (1993) 25 HLR 427; *Marath v MacGillivray* (1996) 28 HLR 484.

[1249] HA 1988, ss. 14, 22; see p. 346, ante. Other examples would include non-compliance with Landlord and Tenant Act 1987, ss. 47, 48 (duty to provide information to tenant). The rent "lawfully due" is the rent after deduction of the amount of any equitable set-off: *Baygreen Properties Ltd v Gil* [2002] 3 EGLR 42.

[1250] Ibid., s. 9(6). See *North British Housing Association Ltd v Matthews* [2005] 1 WLR 3133 (court has power to adjourn *before* being "satisfied" (by judgment, given in a perfected order of the court) that the landlord is entitled to possession, but such adjournment can be granted in order to enable tenant to reduce arrears of rent below Ground 8 threshold only in exceptional circumstances and cannot be used to defeat the policy of the Act); [2005] EG 165 (S. Murdoch).

[1251] An uncleared cheque delivered to the landlord or his agent at or before the hearing and which is accepted by him, or which he is bound by earlier agreement to accept, is to be treated as payment at the date of delivery provided the cheque is subsequently paid at first presentation; and an adjournment is appropriate to see if the cheque will clear: *Day v Coltrane* [2003] 1 WLR 1379; [2004] Conv 152 (J. Morgan).

[1252] HA 1988, s. 21(1), as amended by HA 1996, s. 98.

[1253] A notice of proceedings under s. 8 is not required; *Panayi v Roberts* [1993] 2 EGLR 51.

[1254] HA 1988, s. 9(6). An accelerated possession procedure is available: CPR, Part 55, Section II.

[1255] See *Lower Street Properties Ltd v Jones* (1996) 28 HLR 877 (landlord may not start proceedings before expiry of notice).

[1256] But for s. 5(1), which prohibits termination by a landlord's notice to quit.

[1257] HA 1988, s. 21(5), inserted by HA 1996, s. 99. The proceedings may be commenced within this period. This restriction does not apply to a demoted assured shorthold tenancy: HA 1988, s. 21(5A), as inserted by Antisocial Behaviour Act 2003, s. 15(2); p. 345, n. 1190, ante.

Where the tenancy is a "replacement tenancy", coming into being at the end of an assured shorthold with the same parties and premises, the six-month period runs from the beginning of the original tenancy. Thus a landlord who renews the shorthold or does not act to prevent a statutory periodic tenancy arising on termination of a fixed-term shorthold is not prejudiced. These provisions thus provide minimum security to shorthold tenants in the light of the fact that the former requirement of a fixed term of at least six months does not apply to shortholds granted after the commencement of the 1996 Act. However short the term, the landlord cannot regain possession for at least six months.

(2) DISCRETIONARY GROUNDS

The grounds discussed below are those upon which the court may make an order for possession if it considers it reasonable to do so.[1258] In the case of these discretionary grounds the court may adjourn the proceedings or stay or suspend execution of the order or postpone the date of possession for such period as it thinks just.[1259] In such a case the court will impose conditions as to the payment of any rent arrears or such other conditions as it thinks fit. Where the tenant complies with the conditions, the possession order may be discharged.

(i) Ground 9: Alternative accommodation

The court can make an order for possession if it is satisfied that "suitable alternative accommodation" is available for the tenant or will be available for him when the order takes effect. Alternative accommodation is suitable if (as will normally be the case) the tenant will have an assured tenancy or equivalent security of tenure,[1260] and if the premises are reasonably suitable to the means of the tenant and the needs of his family as regards proximity to place of work, extent and character.[1261] Although the alternative accommodation must be suitable for the tenant and his family, it need not be as pleasant and commodious as the existing premises.[1262] The test is suitability to the means and needs of the tenant and not comparison with what the tenant has got.[1263] Indeed, landlords would seldom in practice offer alternative accommodation if it had to be in all respects equivalent to the existing premises. Furthermore, the rent may be higher than that of the existing premises. If the tenant has the means to pay, the accommodation will nevertheless be suitable.[1264] It should however be observed that although comparisons with the existing premises and rent are not admissible on the question of suitability, they are nevertheless matters which the judge may take into account in deciding whether or not it is reasonable to make an order for possession.[1265]

[1258] Ibid., s. 7(4).

[1259] Ibid., s. 9. As to the mandatory grounds, see HA 1980, s. 89 (fourteen days or up to six weeks if exceptional hardship).

[1260] Ibid., Sch. 2, Part III, para. 2. A tenancy subject to Grounds 1–5 or an assured shorthold will not suffice. Whether a residential property owned by the tenant but let out to another person will be "suitable alternative accommodation" depends on whether it is reasonable to expect the tenant to take steps to recover possession of it: *Amrit Holdings Co Ltd v Shahbakhti* [2005] L & TR 18.

[1261] HA 1988, Sch. 2, Part III, para. 3. See *Siddiqui v Rashid* [1980] 1 WLR 1018, in which a room in a house in Luton (where the tenant worked) was held to be a suitable alternative to a room in Islington, where the tenant had cultural, social and religious connections. The Rent Act cases discussed in this section remain authoritative, as Ground 9 is closely modelled on the equivalent Rent Act provisions.

[1262] *Hill v Rochard* [1983] 1 WLR 478 (proximity to sport, entertainment and recreation not relevant).

[1263] *Warren v Austen* [1947] 2 All ER 185.   [1264] *Cresswell v Hodgson* [1951] 2 KB 92.

[1265] *Warren v Austen*, supra; *Redspring Ltd v Francis* [1973] 1 WLR 134 (relevance of environmental factors).

An ingenious piece of judicial interpretation has made the "alternative accommodation" provision a means of regaining possession of parts of the premises which the tenant has sub-let. We have seen that as long as the tenant himself resides somewhere on the premises as his only or principal home, he may sub-let the rest and retain his assured tenancy of the whole.[1266] An assured tenant may thus be able to make more out of sub-lettings of parts than he pays his landlord for the whole premises. But the landlord may be able to put an end to this situation by offering the tenant as "alternative accommodation" a tenancy of the part of the premises which he is actually occupying, and on this ground seeking an order for possession of the whole.[1267] As the tenant is voluntarily confining himself to the part in question, it is difficult for him to say that it is not suitable to his needs. The end result is that the tenant obtains a new tenancy of his part, while the landlord takes over his sub-tenants.

Finally, a landlord who recovers possession under Ground 9 must pay reasonable removal expenses to the tenant.[1268]

(ii) Ground 10: Some rent unpaid

This ground applies where some rent lawfully due was unpaid at the date on which the possession proceedings were begun and was in arrears at the date of service of the notice under section 8.[1269] Unlike mandatory Ground 8, the rent need not be unpaid at the date of the hearing, and may be less than two months in arrears. The possibility of suspension or postponement of the order has been dealt with.[1270] It is most unlikely that an immediate possession order will result from an isolated breach.

(iii) Ground 11: Persistent delay in paying rent

Persistent delay in paying rent which is lawfully due is a ground for possession even if there are no arrears on the date on which possession proceedings are begun. Again, the court may suspend or postpone the execution of the order, subject to conditions.[1271]

(iv) Ground 12: Other breaches

Breach of any obligation of the tenancy other than non-payment of rent affords a ground for possession. Where the breach is not serious or can be remedied, the order is likely to be refused or suspended, as is also the case with the following grounds.

(v) Ground 13: Condition of the dwelling-house

This ground applies where the dwelling (or common parts) has deteriorated owing to the act, neglect or default of the tenant or other person residing in the tenant's dwelling. If the guilty party is the tenant's lodger or sub-tenant, the ground applies only if the tenant has not taken reasonable steps to remove him.

(vi) Ground 14: Nuisance or annoyance or certain criminal offences

It is a ground for possession if the tenant or any person residing in or visiting the dwelling has been guilty of conduct causing or likely to cause a nuisance or annoyance to a person

---

[1266] For terms as to sub-letting, see p. 343, ante.
[1267] *Mykolyshyn v Noah* [1970] 1 WLR 1271; cf *Yoland Ltd v Reddington* (1982) 263 EG 157.
[1268] HA 1988, s. 11.   [1269] See p. 349, ante.   [1270] See p. 352, ante.
[1271] HA 1988, s. 9. Ground 11 is modelled on the business tenancy ground in s. 30(1)(b) of LTA 1954.

residing, visiting or otherwise engaging in a lawful activity in the locality, or has been convicted of using the dwelling-house or allowing it to be used for immoral or illegal purposes,[1272] or of an arrestable offence committed in, or in the locality of, the dwelling-house.[1273] The degree of control which the tenant could have exercised over the person in question will be taken into account in deciding whether it is reasonable to make an order.[1274] In deciding whether to grant a possession order on Ground 14 the court must give particular consideration to the actual or likely effect which the nuisance or annoyance has had or could have on others.[1275]

(vii) Ground 14A: Domestic violence

This ground was introduced by section 149 of the Housing Act 1996. It may be used only where the landlord is a registered social landlord (primarily a housing association) or a charitable housing trust. The ground applies where the dwelling was occupied by a married couple, a couple who are civil partners, or a couple living together as husband and wife or as civil partners,[1276] one or both of whom is the tenant, and one partner has left the dwelling because of the violence or threats of violence by the other towards that partner or a member of the family[1277] of that partner who was residing with that partner immediately before he or she left. The court must be satisfied that the partner who has left is unlikely to return.

(viii) Ground 15: Condition of furniture

Deterioration in the condition of furniture provided under the tenancy owing to ill-treatment by the tenant or any other person residing in the dwelling is a ground for possession. Where the person responsible is the tenant's lodger or sub-tenant, the ground applies only if the tenant has not taken reasonable steps to remove him.

(ix) Ground 16: Tenant ceasing to be in landlord's employment

This ground for possession lies only against a "service tenant", that is, a person to whom the premises were let in consequence of his employment.[1278] The court may make an order for possession if the tenant has ceased to be in the landlord's employment, whether or not the premises are needed for another employee.

[1272] See *Abrahams v Wilson* [1971] 2 QB 88 (possession of drugs).

[1273] This ground, substituted by HA 1996, s. 148, replaces a similar but narrower ground. Proceedings based on Ground 14 may be commenced more speedily than those based on other grounds; HA 1988, s. 8(4), as amended by HA 1996, s. 151.

[1274] *West Kent Housing Association Ltd v Davies* (1999) 31 HLR 415.

[1275] HA 1988, s. 9A, inserted by Anti-social Behaviour Act 2003, s. 16(2); *London Quadrant Housing Trust v Root* [2005] L & TR 23 (tenant's partner ran business of repairing and scrapping cars at the premises; garden and surrounding areas were littered with general debris, especially car parts; partner had terrorised the neighbours and also the landlord's representatives by his intimidation and threats; "there is a limit to which the courts can be willing to tolerate behaviour of this kind out of the kindness of their hearts to a woman and three children when their neighbours have suffered as much as they have on this occasion": per BROOKE LJ at [30]).   [1276] As amended by Civil Partnership Act 2004, s. 81, Sch. 8.

[1277] As defined by HA 1996, s. 62. See also HA 1988, s. 8A, introduced by s. 150 of the 1996 Act, relating to the service of the s. 8 notice (p. 349, ante) on the partner who has left.   [1278] See p. 339, ante.

(x) Ground 17: Grant of tenancy induced by false statement

This ground, introduced by section 102 of the Housing Act 1996 and modelled on Ground 5 of the Housing Act 1985 (secure tenancies),[1279] applies when the landlord was induced to grant the tenancy by a false statement made knowingly or recklessly by the tenant (or one of joint tenants) or a person acting at the tenant's instigation.[1280]

(d) Succession to an assured tenancy

Section 17 of the 1988 Act creates succession rights to an assured periodic tenancy (including a statutory periodic tenancy). In its original drafting it provided that on the death of a sole[1281] tenant under such a tenancy, the tenancy vests in the tenant's spouse provided that the spouse was occupying as his or her only or principal home immediately before the death. "Spouse" includes a person living with the tenant as his or her wife or husband.[1282] No minimum period of cohabitation is specified. Cases arose in which the issue was whether a same-sex partner could succeed to a tenancy under this provision. In construing a similar provision in the Rent Act 1977,[1283] the House of Lords first held that the words "living with the . . . tenant as his or her wife or husband" were gender-specific, connoting a relationship between a man and a woman and therefore could not include a same-sex relationship.[1284] However, in *Ghaidan v Godin-Mendoza*[1285] the House reviewed this in the light of the requirement of the Human Rights Act 1998[1286] that, so far as it is possible to do so, legislation must be read and given effect in a way which is compatible with Convention rights, and held that the Rent Act provision could be construed as extending to same-sex partners so as to eliminate its discriminatory effect[1287] on such persons without contradicting the underlying social policy of the Rent Act.[1288] The decision in *Ghaidan v Godin-Mendoza* has since been applied to similar language in section 17 of the Housing Act 1988,[1289] but the section has now itself been amended by the Civil Partnership Act 2004[1290] to provide explicitly that

---

[1279] P. 359, post. In practice this ground is rarely used by a private landlord but is more likely to be provable where false statements have been made in order to influence the way in which a public sector or social landlord allocates its housing: [2005] 25 EG 191 (S. Murdoch).

[1280] *Merton LBC v Richards* [2005] HLR 44 (secure tenancy under HA 1985).

[1281] On the death of a joint tenant, the other joint tenant will take by survivorship, and no further succession will be possible: HA 1988, s. 17(2), post.   [1282] HA 1988, s. 17(4).

[1283] Sch. 1, para. 2, as substituted by HA 1980, s. 76, and amended by HA 1988, s 39, Sch. 4, Pt I, para. 2.

[1284] *Fitzpatrick v Sterling Housing Association Ltd* [2001] 1 AC 27. The Rent Act 1977 also allowed succession by a member of the tenant's "family", and it was held that this was capable of a construction which included the same-sex partner.

[1285] [2004] 2 AC 557; [2005] PL 23 (A. Young). The original tenant in the *Fitzpatrick* case, supra, died in 1994, before the coming into force of the Human Rights Act 1998.   [1286] S. 3.

[1287] ECHR, art. 14, as read with art. 8.

[1288] Lord MILLETT dissented on the question of whether it was proper to construe the Rent Act provision by "adopting an interpretation of the existing legislation which it not only does not bear but which is manifestly inconsistent with it": at [101]. He drew attention (at [96]) to the fact that Parliament was already considering corrective legislation in the Civil Partnership Bill; infra.

[1289] *Nutting v Southern Housing Group Ltd* [2005] 2 P & CR 14; however, the claim failed: the relationship must be openly and unequivocally displayed to the outside world; and "without a lifetime commitment at least at some point in the relationship there is no sufficient similarity to marriage": per EVANS-LOMBE J at [17]. Cf *Westminster City Council v Peart* (1992) 24 HLR 389 (for a couple to be "living together as man and wife" it is necessary to show that the parties have a settled intention to be so regarded).

[1290] S. 81, Sch. 8 (with effect from 5 December 2005: SI 2005 No. 3175).

the succession right extends also to a surviving civil partner and a person living with the tenant as if they were civil partners.[1291]

In the unlikely event of more than one claimant, only one can be the successor. Failing agreement, the county court will decide the matter.[1292] Where succession rights are established, the tenancy will not devolve under the tenant's will or intestacy.[1293] It appears that these provisions apply also to a shorthold periodic tenancy although in such a case the succession right would be of minimal value.[1294]

Succession can occur only once, because section 17 applies only where the deceased tenant was not himself a successor.[1295] On the death of the successor a mandatory ground for possession becomes available.[1296]

These succession rights do not apply on the death of a tenant holding under a fixed-term assured tenancy.[1297] If the beneficiary who acquires the tenancy on the death satisfies the assured tenancy requirements, the tenancy will continue to be assured.[1298] If the beneficiary does not qualify as an assured tenant (for example because he does not occupy as his only or principal home), the tenancy will terminate under the general law at the end of the term.

Where there is no person who qualifies to be a successor on the death of an assured periodic tenant, the tenancy will devolve as part of the deceased tenant's estate, but a mandatory ground for possession is available.[1299]

(e) Sub-tenants

The Housing Act 1988 applies between tenant and sub-tenant in the same way as between landlord and tenant. The question to be considered here is whether the sub-tenant has any security of tenure against the head landlord when the tenancy terminates. In addition to any rights he may have at common law,[1300] he will retain security if he falls within section 18 of the 1988 Act. This section protects only lawful sub-tenants (whose presence does not constitute a breach of a covenant against sub-letting) and who qualify as assured tenants against their immediate landlord. Its effect is that, on termination of the superior tenancy (in any way), the sub-tenant becomes assured tenant of the superior landlord.[1301] There is no requirement that the mesne landlord should have had an assured tenancy, and it seems unlikely that this could have been the case. If the mesne landlord was not also occupying as his only or principal home, he would not have satisfied the residence requirement of an

---

[1291] A civil partnership is a relationship between two people of the same sex ("civil partners") which has been formalised by registration: Civil Partnership Act 2004, s. 1. It remains to be seen what the courts will require to be satisfied that same-sex cohabitants are living together "as if they were civil partners" without having entered into a civil partnership; cf *Nutting v Southern Housing Group Ltd*, supra. See also [2005] Conv 318 (M. Davis and D. Hughes).   [1292] HA 1988, s. 17(5).

[1293] Ibid., s. 17(1).   [1294] See *Lower Street Properties Ltd v Jones* (1996) 28 HLR 877.

[1295] HA 1988, s. 17(1)(c). "Successor" has an extended meaning, including, for example, the survivor of joint tenants or a person who inherited a fixed-term assured tenancy by will or intestacy: s. 17(2), (3).

[1296] Ground 7, p. 351, ante.   [1297] Nor does Ground 7 apply.

[1298] If a statutory periodic tenancy subsequently arises, there can be no succession rights under s. 17 on the tenant's death (see s. 17(2)), and Ground 7 will be available.

[1299] Ground 7, p. 351, ante. The tenancy ceases to be assured if the person entitled to it does not occupy, in which case it may be terminated by notice to quit.   [1300] P. 279, ante.

[1301] Unless the landlord's interest is such that the tenancy cannot be assured, for example where the superior landlord is the Crown: HA 1988, s. 18(2).

assured tenancy,[1302] whereas if he was occupying part as his only or principal home, the sub-tenancy would not have been assured because of the resident landlord exception.[1303]

B Public Sector Housing. Secure Tenancy

Until the Housing Act 1980 the residential tenants of landlords in the public sector (by far the most numerous category of tenants) were altogether excluded from statutory protection. They may now enjoy a "secure tenancy", which is modelled upon the Rent Act protected tenancy with certain variations and modern improvements. The provisions are now found in the Housing Act 1985.[1304]

(1) Definition of a Secure Tenancy

A secure tenancy is a tenancy:

(i) under which a dwelling-house is let as a separate dwelling;[1305]

(ii) in respect of which the interest of the landlord belongs to one or other of a list of "public sector" bodies such as local authorities, new town corporations, and housing action trusts;[1306]

(iii) in respect of which the tenant is an individual who occupies the house as his only or principal home or, where the tenancy is a joint tenancy, each of the joint tenants is an individual and at least one of them occupies the house as his only or principal home;[1307]

(iv) which does not fall within any of the exceptions listed in the Housing Act 1985.

The first of these conditions reproduces part of the definition of a protected or assured tenancy in the private sector. The second mirrors (with certain exceptions) the list of tenancies excluded from the definition of a protected or assured tenancy on account of the identity of the landlord.[1308] The third is the same as the conditions as to occupation which apply to assured tenancies.[1309] The list of exceptions has some common ground with the exceptions for protected tenancies (long tenancies,[1310] student lettings,[1311] business tenancies,[1312] farm business tenancies and agricultural holdings[1313]) but also includes important arrangements which exist only in the public sector, such as the provision of accommodation for homeless

---

[1302] See p. 341, ante.   [1303] See p. 342, ante.

[1304] Part IV. See also Part V and Leasehold Reform, Housing and Urban Development Act 1993, Part II (the right to buy). See generally Hughes and Lowe, *Public Sector Housing Law*; Evans and Smith, *Law of Landlord and Tenant*, chap. 16.   [1305] HA 1985, s. 79. Certain licences are included: s. 79(3), (4).

[1306] Ibid., s. 80, as amended by HA 1988, s. 83.

[1307] Ibid., s. 81. Ss. 80 and 81 have an "ambulatory" effect in that occupiers may pass in or out of "secure" status, depending on either a change of landlord or a change in the tenant's own circumstances: *Kay v Lambeth LBC* [2005] QB 352 at [53], per AULD LJ. But a secure tenancy for the purpose of HA 1985, s. 79 is one in which there is a direct landlord and tenant relationship between a landlord, satisfying the landlord condition in s. 80, and a tenant, satisfying the tenant condition in s. 81: ibid., at [67]. It most probably does not include a tenancy at will: *Banjo v Brent LBC* [2005] 1 WLR 2520 at [25]–[26], [31]–[35], per CHADWICK LJ, and [40]–[43], per BUXTON LJ.   [1308] Rent Act 1977, ss. 14–16; HA 1988, Sch. 1, para. 12.

[1309] See p. 338, ante.   [1310] HA 1985, Sch. 1, para. 1.   [1311] Ibid., para. 10.

[1312] Ibid., para. 11.   [1313] Ibid., para. 8, as substituted by the Agricultural Tenancies Act 1995.

persons under Part VII of the Housing Act 1996[1314] or for asylum-seekers under Part VI of the Immigration and Asylum Act 1999,[1315] lettings of "short-life" premises acquired for development,[1316] the provision of temporary accommodation for persons who have come to the area to seek employment[1317] and lettings to local authority or other public sector employees.[1318]

(2) No Control of Rents

There is no control of the rents which may be charged in the public sector in any way analogous to the machinery provided by rent officers and rent assessment committees in the private sector.

(3) Security of Tenure

The mechanism for giving security of tenure in the public sector resembles that which applies to assured tenancies in the private sector.[1319] The scheme of the Act is that the landlord cannot recover possession without obtaining a court order based on one of the grounds for possession.[1320] Thus a periodic tenancy cannot be terminated by notice to quit[1321] unless a ground for possession is available. Where the tenancy is for a fixed term, a periodic tenancy automatically arises on its expiry,[1322] which cannot be terminated without a ground for possession. A similar principle applies to the forfeiture of a fixed-term tenancy: on termination by forfeiture a periodic tenancy arises, which again cannot be terminated without a ground for possession.[1323] There is a list of cases in which orders for possession may be made, and the order has the effect of terminating the tenancy on the date when the tenant is ordered to give up possession.[1324] The secure tenancy can be revived, however, if the court order is varied or rescinded before it has been executed, but if, without a further order, the tenant remains in possession and pays for occupation with the local authority's agreement, no new secure tenancy is created, but the former tenant is a "tolerated trespasser".[1325] A new tenancy may, however, subsequently be created by agreement between the landlord and tenant,[1326] although this will be rare.[1327]

Several of the grounds upon which orders for possession may be made are the same or similar to the grounds upon which the court may make such an order in the private sector.

[1314] HA 1985, Sch. 1, para. 4, substituted by HA 1996, s. 216, Sch. 17. Homeless persons are not excluded in all cases. See *Westminster City Council v Clarke* [1992] 2 AC 288; p. 206, n. 92, ante.

[1315] Ibid., para. 4A, inserted by Immigration and Asylum Act 1999, s. 169(1), Sch. 14.

[1316] Ibid., para. 3.   [1317] Ibid., para. 5.   [1318] Ibid., para. 2.

[1319] See p. 347, ante. For the position of sub-tenants, see *Basingstoke and Deane BC v Paice* [1995] 2 EGLR 9.

[1320] HA 1985, s. 82(1), amended by Anti-social Behaviour Act 2003, s. 14. It is otherwise if the tenancy is not secure: *Sevenoaks DC v Emmott* (1979) 39 P & CR 404.

[1321] Except by the tenant: *Hammersmith and Fulham LBC v Monk* [1992] 1 AC 478.

[1322] HA 1985, s. 86.

[1323] Ibid., ss. 82(3), 86(1)(b). The ground for forfeiture will not necessarily constitute a ground for possession.   [1324] Ibid., s. 82(2).

[1325] *Burrows v Brent LBC* [1996] 1 WLR 1448; *Lambeth LBC v Henry* [2000] 1 EGLR 33; *Pemberton v Southwark LBC* [2000] 1 WLR 1672 ("a recent, somewhat bizarre, addition to the dramatis personae of the law": per Clarke LJ at 1683); *Newham LBC v Hawkins* [2005] 2 EGLR 51 (no succession rights); *Lambeth LBC v O'Kane* [2006] HLR 2; (2003) 119 LQR 495 (S. Bright); [2006] Conv 48 (S. Bright).

[1326] *Swindon BC v Aston* [2003] 2 P & CR 22.

[1327] *Newham London BC v Hawkins, supra;* [2005] 29 EG 97 (S. Murdoch).

Non-payment of rent or breach of covenant,[1328] nuisance or annoyance to neighbours or visitors,[1329] neglect of the premises,[1330] furniture[1331] or common parts, and inducement of the tenancy by a false statement made knowingly or recklessly[1332] are examples. A new "domestic violence" ground was added by the Housing Act 1996.[1333] There are also other grounds special to public sector dwellings, for example where that the dwelling has features designed to make it suitable for occupation by a physically disabled person and such a person no longer resides in the dwelling-house.[1334] In such a case suitable alternative accommodation must be available for the tenant.[1335]

It should be noted that all the grounds for possession are to some degree discretionary; for secure tenancies there are no mandatory grounds for possession comparable to those in relation to assured tenancies.[1336] In most cases the court must be satisfied not only that a ground for possession has been made out, but also that it is reasonable to make the order, although there are four grounds (overcrowding, proposed demolition of the premises, proposed disposal under a redevelopment scheme and conflict with purposes of a charity landlord) where there is no requirement of reasonableness, but the court must still be satisfied that there is suitable alternative accommodation for the tenant.[1337]

(4) Demoted Tenancies

The Anti-social Behaviour Act 2003 introduced the "demoted tenancy". If the landlord is a local housing authority, a housing action trust or a registered social landlord, it may apply to a county court for a "demotion order". The court may make an order if the tenant, or a person residing in or visiting the dwelling-house, has engaged in or threatened to engage in certain forms of anti-social behaviour, or the use of the premises for unlawful purposes,[1338] and if the court is satisfied that it is reasonable to make the order.[1339] The effect of the order

---

[1328]   HA 1985, Sch. 2, Part 1, Ground 1.

[1329]   Ibid., Ground 2, as amended by HA 1996, s. 144. In deciding whether to grant a possession order on Ground 2 the court must give particular consideration to the actual or likely effect which the nuisance or annoyance has had or could have on others: HA 1985, s. 85A, inserted by Anti-social Behaviour Act 2003, s. 16(1); *Manchester City Council v Higgins* [2006] 1 All ER 841 (judge wrong to suspend possession order, which was necessary and proportionate under ECHR in order to protect the rights and freedoms of neighbours where tenant showed no remorse for son's bullying towards neighbour and her mentally disabled sons). For other provisions concerning anti-social behaviour in relation to public sector and social housing, see Anti-social Behaviour Act 2003, ss. 12 and 13, inserting into HA 1996 new ss. 218A (anti-social behaviour: landlords' policies and procedures) and 153A–E (injunctions against anti-social behaviour); and ss. 14 and 15 (demoted tenancies), infra.   [1330]   HA 1985, Sch. 2, Ground 3.

[1331]   Ibid., Ground 4.

[1332]   Ibid., Ground 5, amended by HA 1996, s. 146; *Merton LBC v Richards* [2005] HLR 44.

[1333]   S. 145, introducing Ground 2A; amended by Civil Partnership Act 2004, s. 81, Sch. 8.

[1334]   HA 1985, Sch. 2, Part III, Ground 13. Cf. *Freeman v Wansbeck DC* [1984] 2 All ER 746.

[1335]   See *Enfield LBC v French* (1984) 49 P & CR 223; *Wandsworth LBC v Fadayomi* [1987] 1 WLR 1473 (wife's position).   [1336]   P. 349, ante.

[1337]   HA 1985, s. 84(2); Sch. 2, Part II as amended by Housing and Planning Act 1986, s 9(1). See also *Manchester City Council v Romano* [2005] 1 WLR 2775 (relevance of tenant's disability, under Disability Discrimination Act 1995, in deciding whether reasonable to order possession on ground of nuisance or annoyance to neighbours).

[1338]   HA 1996, s. 153A or 153B, inserted by Anti-social Behaviour Act 2003, s. 13; *Manchester City Council v Higgins*, supra; [2006] Conv 85 (S. Bright); cf *Moat Housing Group-South Ltd v Harris* [2005] 3 WLR 69.

[1339]   HA 1996, s. 82A, inserted by Anti-social Behaviour Act 2003, s. 14.

is that the secure tenancy is terminated and replaced by a demoted tenancy,[1340] which lasts for at least one year and during the demotion period the landlord can obtain an order for possession without having to establish grounds.[1341]

The purpose of these provisions is to encourage landlords not to seek possession immediately in all cases of anti-social behaviour:[1342]

Demoted tenancies have been designed to be both a warning and a last chance. We want to encourage landlords to use them instead of seeking suspended or outright possession orders. Demotion is not a soft option. As well as being a warning and an incentive to behave, it is a real sanction. The tenant, through his or her actions, has lost security; we want him to understand that this may have serious consequences. Tenants need to understand that when they are considering how to conduct themselves in the first instance.

(5) Introductory Tenancies

The Housing Act 1996[1343] introduced the introductory tenancy regime, which a local authority may elect to operate. While such an election is in force, any new periodic tenancy (or licence) which would otherwise have qualified as secure takes effect as introductory for a trial period of one year. The Housing Act 2004[1344] permits landlords to extend the trial period by six months. During the trial period the landlord may terminate the tenancy by obtaining a court order. No ground for possession needs to be established, nor has the court any discretion to refuse the order,[1345] but the landlord must state its reasons, as to which the tenant may request that the landlord review its decision.[1346] If not ended during the trial period, the introductory tenancy becomes secure at the end of that period.

(6) Succession

As in the case of the private sector, the Housing Act confers certain rights of succession to the secure tenancy. As with an assured tenancy, succession can occur once only.[1347] The

---

[1340] If the landlord is a registered social landlord, the demoted tenancy takes effect as a demoted assured shorthold tenancy under HA 1988, s. 20B, inserted by Anti-social Behaviour Act 2003, s. 15; p. 345, n. 1190, ante. Otherwise, it takes effect as a demoted tenancy under HA 1996, chap. 1A, inserted by Anti-social Behaviour Act 2003, s. 14(5), Sch. 1.

[1341] In the case of a demoted tenancy under HA 1996, chap. 1A, however, the tenant may request a review by the landlord of its decision: ibid., s. 143F. For the procedure to be followed in such a review, see Demoted Tenancies (Review of Decisions) (England) Regulations 2004, SI 2004 No. 1679.

[1342] Lord Bassam of Brighton, *Hansard* HL (Series 5), vol. 653, col. 1805 (23 October 2003) (Report stage).

[1343] Part V, ss. 124–43. The tenancy will not be introductory if granted to a tenant who, immediately beforehand, was a secure tenant of the same or another dwelling-house.

[1344] S. 179, inserting ss. 125A and 125B into HA 1996, with effect for introductory tenancies entered into on or after the section came into force (6 June 2005: SI 2005 No. 1451). The landlord must give reasons: s. 125A(5), and the tenant can request a review by the landlord of its decision: s. 125B. Regulations will make provision for the procedures to be followed in such a review.

[1345] *Manchester City Council v Cochrane* [1999] 1 WLR 809.

[1346] For the procedure to be followed in a review, including a requirement that the review be undertaken by a person who was not involved in the decision to apply for an order for possession, see Introductory Tenants (Review) Regulations 1997, SI 1997 No. 72.

[1347] HA 1985, s. 87. The succession provisions do not infringe ECHR arts 8 and 14: *R (Gangera) v Hounslow LBC* [2003] HLR 68. Succession rights exist also in the case of demoted tenancies, infra: HA 1996, s. 143H, inserted by Anti-social Behaviour Act 2003, s. 14(5), Sch. 1; and introductory tenancies, infra: HA 1996, s. 131.

successor must have occupied the dwelling-house as his only or principal home[1348] at the time of the tenant's death, and must either be the tenant's spouse or civil partner, or another member of his family. In the latter case he must have resided with the tenant for the period of twelve months ending with the tenant's death,[1349] although not necessarily in the same dwelling.[1350] If there is more than one claimant, the landlord selects the successor in default of agreement.[1351] The Housing Act contains a definition of "family",[1352] which includes persons who live together as husband and wife[1353] and, after it was amended by the Civil Partnership Act 2004,[1354] same-sex partners who live together "as if they were civil partners".[1355]

(7) The Right to Buy

The Housing Act 1980 first gave the secure tenant the "right to buy" the property. These provisions were amended in 1984[1356] and are now contained in Part V of the Housing Act 1985, as further amended by the Leasehold Reform, Housing and Urban Development Act 1993[1357] and the Housing Act 2004. The right is now to acquire the freehold if the dwelling-house is a house and the landlord owns the freehold, or the right to a lease if it is a flat, or if the landlord does not own the freehold.[1358] The tenant must have been a public-sector tenant (although not necessarily of the same premises, or of the same landlord) for at least five years before the right to buy arises,[1359] and he is then entitled to purchase at a discount to the market value reflecting the length of the period he has been a public-sector tenant.[1360] There

---

[1348] See *Peabody Donation Fund Governors v Grant* (1982) 264 EG 925.

[1349] HA 1985, s. 87; amended by Civil Partnership Act 2004, s. 81, Sch. 8.

[1350] *Waltham Forest LBC v Thomas* [1992] 2 AC 198.   [1351] HA 1985, s. 89(2).

[1352] Ibid., s. 113; amended by Civil Partnership Act 2004, s. 81, Sch. 8. A minor may be the successor: *Kingston upon Thames BC v Prince* [1999] 1 FLR 593; but the legal estate must be held on trust for the minor: *Newham LBC v R* [2004] EWCA Civ 41; (2004) 148 SJLB 113; (2004) 8 L & T Rev 61 (M. Pawlowski). The definition of "family" is exhaustive, and should not be interpreted more widely under HRA 1998, s. 3: *Wandsworth LBC v Michalak* [2003] 1 WLR 617.   [1353] See *Westminster City Council v Peart* (1991) 24 HLR 389.

[1354] S. 81, Sch. 8. The definition in HA 1980, s. 50(3) (the predecessor of HA 1985, s. 113) was originally interpreted as not including same-sex partners: *Harrogate BC v Simpson* [1986] 2 FLR 91. Although the term "family" in the Rent Act 1977 was held to be capable of a construction which included a same-sex partner (*Fitzpatrick v Sterling Housing Association Ltd* [2001] 1 AC 27), that Act contained no definition of "family", thus permitting a more flexible approach. However, the decision in *Ghaidan v Godin-Mendoza* [2004] 2 AC 557, p. 356, ante, would equally apply to the original language of HA 1985, and therefore allow it to be interpreted as extending to same-sex partners even without the amendment of the Civil Partnership Act 2004.

[1355] For a couple to be "living together as man and wife" it is necessary to show that the parties have a settled intention to be so regarded: *Westminster City Council v Peart* (1992) 24 HLR 389. For the meaning of living together "as" civil partners, see p. 356, n. 1289, ante.   [1356] Housing and Building Control Act 1984, Part I.

[1357] Part II.

[1358] A dwelling-house which is a commonhold unit is treated as a house, rather than a flat: HA 1985, s. 118(3), inserted by CLRA 2002, s. 68, Sch. 5.

[1359] HA 1985, s. 119 and Sch. 4 as amended by HA 2004, s. 180 (originally three years under HA 1980, and then two years under Housing and Building Control Act 1984).

[1360] Ibid., s. 129. If within five years the tenant disposes of the whole or part of the property or grants a lease of it for more than twenty-one years, he is required to repay (on a sliding scale) a proportion of the discount: ibid., ss. 155 (as amended by HA 2004, s. 185), 159; and if the tenant wishes to resell within ten years of exercising the right to buy the landlord has a right of first refusal: ibid., s. 156A, inserted by HA 2004, s. 188; Housing (Right of First Refusal) Regulations 2005 (SI 2005 No. 1917).

is also a list of exceptions to the right to buy, such as where the landlord is a charitable housing trust or housing association, or where the dwelling is one of a group let to the physically disabled, persons suffering from a mental disorder, or the elderly.[1361]

C Long Tenancies

A long tenancy for the purposes of the landlord and tenant codes means primarily a tenancy granted for a term exceeding twenty-one years.[1362] In 1967 it was estimated that about a million and a quarter houses in England and Wales were let on long tenancies. Most of them originate in the Victorian and Edwardian practice of developing land for residential purposes by means of "building leases". This usually involved an agreement between a landowner and a speculative builder. The builder would enter upon the land and put up houses. When the houses were completed, the landowner would let them to the builder on long leases. Ninety-nine years was a common period.[1363] The leases would reserve a rent representing the value of the site as building land but ignoring the value of the houses, which the builder had erected at his own expense. It was therefore called a "ground rent". The landowner would thus obtain an immediate enhanced return on his land and the somewhat distant prospect of the reversion in the houses when the leases came to an end. The builder would make his profit by selling the leases to individual purchasers for capital sums. Or sometimes the landowner would grant the leases directly to individual purchasers nominated by the builder, in return for payment of a capital sum to the builder and the reservation of a ground rent for himself. In all these cases the main object of the builder was to take his profit and disappear from the scene, but more recently some developers of residential estates have chosen to grant long leases rather than sell freeholds in order to retain control over the management of the estate. Positive covenants are easier to enforce against tenants than against freeholders[1364] and the expiry of all leases simultaneously would allow the landlords to undertake a comprehensive redevelopment.

Long tenancies seldom fall within the Rent Act 1977 or the Housing Act 1988. This is not because the Acts exclude long tenancies as such but because they are usually within the exception for tenancies granted at a low rent.[1365] Such tenancies are, however, by no means lacking in statutory protection. The Leasehold Reform Act 1967 allows a duly qualified long leaseholder of a house to acquire the freehold or an extended long tenancy upon terms which the Act describes as "fair"[1366] but which can be highly advantageous to the tenant. The existence of these rights has reduced the importance of the second code, contained in Part I of the Landlord and Tenant Act 1954, which merely allows the tenant to remain in possession at a regulated rent after the expiration of his lease. Now long leaseholders of flats may collectively purchase the freehold of their block[1367] or may individually extend their leases

---

[1361] HA 1985, Sch. 5. The landlord may apply to the court for suspension of the right to buy because of anti-social behaviour of the tenant: ibid., s. 121A, inserted by HA 2004, s. 192.

[1362] LTA 1954, s. 2(4); Leasehold Reform Act 1967, s. 3(1). See generally Hague, *Leasehold Enfranchisement* (4th edn); Barnes, *Leasehold Reform Act 1967*.

[1363] Because leases for 100 years and over attracted a higher rate of stamp duty.   [1364] P. 663, post.

[1365] Rent Act 1977, s. 5; HA 1988, Sch. 1, paras. 3, 3A, 3B, substituted by SI 1990 No. 434.

[1366] Leasehold Reform Act 1967, s. 1(1).

[1367] Long leaseholders of flats cannot convert their title to commonhold, chap. 11, post, without first acquiring the freehold themselves, or persuading the freeholder to apply for conversion, since the application must be

under the Leasehold Reform, Housing and Urban Development Act 1993. The following is a brief account of these statutes.

(1) Leasehold Reform Act 1967

The Act confers upon a duly qualified tenant the right to acquire the freehold (commonly called "enfranchisement" of the tenancy) or an extended long lease of his house and premises. Contracting out is not permitted.[1368] The discussion of the Act can conveniently be divided into four parts. First, the conditions which must be satisfied by the tenant; secondly, the procedure by which he must exercise his rights; thirdly, the nature of the interests he may acquire and finally the terms upon which he may do so.

(a) The qualifying conditions

The qualifying conditions concern the terms of the tenancy, the character and value of the premises and the way in which they have been occupied.

(1) LONG TENANCY

A tenant must hold under a tenancy[1369] granted originally for a term of years certain exceeding twenty-one years.[1370] He need not of course be the original tenant. It is possible to buy a long lease which has only a short time left to run and then (subject only to the residence requirements discussed below) claim the benefits of the Act. A tenant who had bought the short residue of a long lease in the years immediately before the passing of the Act found that Parliament had given him a substantial windfall gain.

(2) AT A LOW RENT

The 1967 Act originally provided that the tenancy must be at a rent which is less than two-thirds of the rateable value of the premises.[1371] This was modified for tenancies created after the abolition of domestic rating on 1 April 1990, under which the rent must not exceed £1,000 in Greater London or £250 elsewhere.[1372] Further reforms to the "low rent" rule were

---

made by the freeholder: CLRA 2002, s. 2(1)(a). If the freeholder does make application, all long leaseholders must consent: ibid., s. 3(1)(b).

[1368] Leasehold Reform Act 1967, s. 23. See *Rennie v Proma Ltd* [1990] 1 EGLR 119.

[1369] The enfranchisement provisions of the 1967 Act do not apply to tenants holding directly of the Crown, but the Crown has given an undertaking to Parliament to comply with the legislation voluntarily in most cases. Enfranchisement will not be permitted by the Crown (but new leases instead may be negotiated) where the property, or the area in which it is situated, has long, historic or particular association with the Crown; where it is within (or intimately connected with) the historic Royal Palaces and Parks (including properties adjacent to Regent's Park); or where there are special security considerations: *Hansard* HC vol. 213, col. 19 (2 November 1992) (replacing, in relation to both the Leasehold Reform Act 1967 and the Leasehold Reform, Housing and Urban Development Act 1993, p. 372, post, the original undertaking reported at *Hansard* HC (series 5) vol. 747, col. 42 (31 May 1967)); *Hansard* HC (series 5) vol. 628, col. 927 (19 November 2001) (extending the undertaking to amendments made by CLRA 2002).

[1370] Leasehold Reform Act 1967, s. 3(1); *Roberts v Church Comrs for England* [1972] 1 QB 278.

[1371] Ibid., s. 4; *Duke of Westminster v Johnston* [1986] AC 839.

[1372] Local Government and Housing Act 1989, s. 149; SI 1990 No. 434.

introduced in 1993[1373] and 1996,[1374] and the rule was finally abolished by the Commonhold and Leasehold Reform Act 2002[1375] for tenancies granted on or after 26 July 2002. Whether the "low rent" test is a qualifying condition and, if so, in what form, therefore now depends on the date at which the lease was granted.

(3) HOUSE, NOT FLAT

The Act applies to houses in the ordinary sense of that word ("any building designed or adapted for living in and reasonably so called"[1376]) but not to flats or maisonettes. Where a building is horizontally divided into flats or maisonettes, the building itself can be a "house", but the units cannot. For the avoidance of conveyancing difficulties, it is further provided that the Act does not apply to a house "of which a material part lies above or below a part of the structure not comprised in the house".[1377] "House" has been widely interpreted, and, according to a majority of the House of Lords, even includes a purpose-built shop with a flat above in a parade, where the shop constituted 75 per cent of the total area of the property.[1378] Flats and maisonettes were excluded because their conversion into freeholds would present problems over the enforceability of positive covenants.[1379] The White Paper which preceded the Act also said rather mysteriously that "different considerations of equity" applied to flats,[1380] although it is not easy to guess what these could be. However, the sale of flats on long leases has continued to be a widespread practice, being considered a more profitable proposition than letting them on regulated or assured tenancies.[1381] Steps have, however, been taken in recent years to increase the rights of long leaseholders of flats. Qualifying leaseholders may acquire a new extended lease or may collectively acquire the freehold of the block under the Leasehold Reform, Housing and Urban Development Act 1993, discussed below.[1382] And the introduction of the system of commonhold, discussed in chapter 9, has extended the freehold ownership of flats.

[1373] Leasehold Reform, Housing and Urban Development Act 1993 introduced an alternative rule which may be satisfied if the rent during the first year of the tenancy did not exceed specified limits: Leasehold Reform Act 1967, ss. 1A(2), 4A. HA 1996, s. 105, amended ss. 4 and 4A in cases where the rateable value was nil.

[1374] HA 1996, s. 106 and Sch. 9, inserting Leasehold Reform Act 1967, s. 1AA (primarily tenancies granted for a term not exceeding thirty-five years).

[1375] S. 141, amending Leasehold Reform Act 1967, s. 1AA. Certain properties in designated rural areas are excluded, in order to prevent the break-up of country estates.   [1376] Leasehold Reform Act 1967, s. 2(1).

[1377] Ibid., s. 2(2); see *Parsons v Viscount Gage (trustees of Henry Smith's Charity)* [1974] 1 WLR 435; *Duke of Westminster v Birrane* [1995] QB 262.

[1378] *Tandon v Trustees of Spurgeons Homes* [1982] AC 755; *Hareford Ltd v Barnet LBC* [2005] 2 EGLR 72; [2005] 28 EG 119 (S. Murdoch).

[1379] "Flying freeholds . . . give rise to peculiarly difficult conveyancing problems": *Gaidowski v Gonville and Caius College, Cambridge* [1975] 1 WLR 1066 at 1069, per ORMROD LJ. For the problems of enforcing positive covenants, see pp. 663 et seq, post.

[1380] *Leasehold Reform in England and Wales* (1966) Cmnd 2916, para. 8. For the White Paper's statement on the consideration of equity applicable to houses, see p. 369, post.

[1381] Pp. 337, et seq, ante. The market in short lettings has, by contrast, been substantially deregulated and therefore made more accessible to landlords who wish to retain short-term control of their properties, through the extended use of shorthold tenancies, especially after HA 1996: ibid.   [1382] P. 372, post.

(4) RATEABLE VALUE

Formerly the Act did not apply if the rateable value of the house exceeded certain limits or, after the abolition of domestic rating, if the premium paid for the lease exceeded a specified figure.[1383] Tenants of houses previously so excluded have now been given the right to acquire the freehold by the Leasehold Reform, Housing and Urban Development Act 1993.[1384] As will be explained below, the price to be paid by such tenants is assessed in a manner more favourable to the landlord.

(5) QUALIFYING PERIOD

Until it was amended by the Commonhold and Leasehold Reform Act 2002, the 1967 Act contained a qualifying condition that the tenant must have been occupying the house or some part of it in right of his tenancy as his only or main residence for a particular period.[1385] Now, however, the residence test has been largely abolished,[1386] and in most cases the only question is whether the tenant has held his tenancy for a qualifying period—which is now two years.[1387] This therefore enables non-resident tenants, such as companies, to exercise the right to acquire the freehold.[1388] The removal of the residence requirement has made it necessary to deal explicitly with the case were there are two or more long tenancies in respect of the same house (for example, if there is both a long tenancy and a long sub-tenancy). In such a case, the superior tenant has no right under the 1967 Act as long as the inferior tenancy subsists.[1389]

(b) Enfranchisement procedure

A tenant exercises his rights under the Act by serving upon his landlord a notice in the prescribed statutory form, stating that he desires to acquire the freehold or an extended lease.[1390] In particular the notice must make it clear whether he wants the one or the other. A notice claiming the freehold or an extended lease in the alternative is invalid.[1391] The effect

---

[1383] Leasehold Reform Act 1967, s. 1(1)(a), as amended.

[1384] S. 63, introducing s. 1A(1) of the 1967 Act.

[1385] Leasehold Reform Act 1967, s. 1(1); originally the last five years or for five out of the last ten years; in both cases "five" was reduced to "three" by HA 1980, s. 141, Sch. 21. The residence test involved difficult questions of fact and degree: *Poland v Earl Cadogan* [1980] 3 All ER 544; *Dymond v Arundel-Timms* [1991] 1 EGLR 109. For further discussion, see the 16th edn of this book, pp. 536–7.

[1386] CLRA 2002, s. 138. The residence requirement (now reduced to the last two years, or two years in the last ten years) is retained for tenancies of a house to which LTA 1954, Part II applies (business tenancies; p. 337, post; *Smith v Titanate Ltd* [2005] 2 EGLR 63). The right for business tenants to enfranchise is further restricted by CLRA 2002, s. 140, inserting s. 1(1ZC) into Leasehold Reform Act 1967 (in particular, only leases granted for a term exceeding thirty-five years can now be enfranchised). The residence requirement is also retained to prevent a non-resident landlord of the house, who has sub-let the premises in parts under long leases of flats to which Leasehold Reform, Housing and Urban Development Act 1993 applies, pp. 372 et seq, post, from making a windfall profit at the freeholder's expense through acquiring the freehold: CLRA 2002, s. 138(2), inserting s. 1(1ZB) into Leasehold Reform Act 1967; *Earl Cadogan v Search Guarantees plc* [2004] 1 WLR 2768.

[1387] CLRA 2002, s. 139.   [1388] *Hareford Ltd v Barnet LBC* [2005] 2 EGLR 72.

[1389] CLRA 2002, s. 138(2), inserting s. 1(1ZA) into Leasehold Reform Act 1967.

[1390] For the position where there is a claim to forfeiture, see Sch. 3, para. 4(1); *Central Estates (Belgravia) Ltd v Woolgar* [1972] 1 QB 48.

[1391] *Byrnlea Property Investments Ltd v Ramsay* [1969] 2 QB 253. The prescribed form has since been amended. See *Speedwell Estates Ltd v Dalziel* [2002] 1 EGLR 55 (certain omissions did not invalidate notice, on construction under *Mannai Investment Co Ltd v Eagle Star Life Assurance Co Ltd* [1997] AC 749, p. 319, ante; other omissions however rendered notice invalid). On irregularities in a tenant's notice, see *Malekshad v Howard de Walden Estates Ltd (No 2)* [2004] 1 WLR 3106; *Earl Cadogan v Strauss* [2004] 2 P & CR 16.

of service of the notice is to create rights and obligations which have the same effect as a contract between landlord and tenant, registrable as if it were an estate contract[1392] under which the one is bound to grant and the other to take the freehold or an extended lease, as the case may be, on the terms laid down by the Act.[1393] The landlord can oppose enfranchisement or extension if the house is reasonably required for occupation as the only or main residence of the landlord or an adult member of his family.[1394]

(c) Freehold or extended lease

(1) FREEHOLD

A tenant who claims the freehold is entitled to have it conveyed to him free of incumbrances.[1395] Any intermediate leasehold interests will be merged in the freehold and there are provisions for dividing up the purchase money between the freeholder and intermediate leaseholders according to the value of their respective interests.[1396]

The effect of enfranchisement is of course ordinarily to extinguish the covenants between landlord and tenant in the lease and thereby to deprive the landlord of all rights which he may have had under the lease to control the use, appearance or state of repair of the house. The Act did, however, provide for exceptional cases in which the former landlord was allowed to retain limited "powers of management".[1397] This exception was intended to apply to substantial residential estates which were held from one landlord where the Secretary of State for the Environment certified that it was in the general interest "in order to maintain adequate standards of appearance and amenity and regulate development in the area" that the landlord should retain some control. Applications for the Minister's certificate had to be made before 1 January 1970.[1398] If the certificate was granted, the landlord could apply to the High Court for approval of a scheme giving him the appropriate powers.

(2) EXTENDED LEASE

A tenant who claims an extended lease is entitled to the grant of a new tenancy, in substitution for the existing tenancy, for a term expiring fifty years after the term date of the existing tenancy[1399] and on terms as to rent which will be considered in the next paragraph.

Compared with the freehold, the extended tenancy is weak, although it has recently been made more attractive. Until reforms introduced by the Commonhold and Leasehold Reform Act 2002,[1400] the extended lease carried no further rights, either to claim the freehold or to another extension, and the tenant under the extended tenancy had no security of tenure after the expiry of his term. However, although there can be no further extension of

---

[1392] Leasehold Reform Act 1967, s. 5(1), (5). Protection is (in unregistered land) by registration as a land charge; or (in registered land) by registration of a notice. It cannot take effect as an overriding interest: ibid., s. 5(5). [1393] Ibid., ss. 8(1), 14 (1).

[1394] Ibid., s. 18. Compensation is payable. [1395] Ibid., s. 8(1). [1396] Ibid., Sch. 1.

[1397] Ibid., s. 19.

[1398] For houses which became enfranchisable only by virtue of the increases in rateable value limits effected by HA 1974, s. 118, the date was 31 July 1976. For houses brought within the 1967 Act by Leasehold Reform, Housing and Urban Development Act 1993, the landlord's application must be made within two years of the coming into force of the 1993 Act.

[1399] Leasehold Reform Act 1967, s. 14(1). This option is not available to tenants given enfranchisement rights by Leasehold Reform, Housing and Urban Development Act 1993 or HA 1996.

[1400] S. 143, amending s. 16 of the 1967 Act in relation to all tenancies, whether extended before or after the amendment comes into force: s. 143(3).

the lease,[1401] the restriction on the tenant claiming the freehold has been removed;[1402] and some security of tenure is now afforded to the leaseholder under an extended lease.[1403]

Furthermore, the landlord may at any time from twelve months before the commencement of the last fifty years of the term apply to the court for an order terminating the tenancy (on payment of compensation) if he can show that he intends to demolish or reconstruct the whole or a substantial part of the house and premises.[1404]

(d) Terms of acquisition

(1) EXTENDED TENANCY

The rent for the new substituted tenancy is the old rent for the remainder of the old term and then, for the fifty-year extension, a "modern ground rent" representing the letting value of the site without including anything for the value of the buildings on the site, calculated at the date when the extension commences, with a review after twenty-five years.[1405]

(2) FREEHOLD

The Act now contains three different methods of calculating the price which the tenant must pay for the freehold. The first, contained in the original Act, now applies to houses of a rateable value on 31 March 1990 of less than £500 (£1,000 in Greater London). The second, introduced by the Housing Act 1974, applies to houses of which the rateable value exceeds those figures but does not exceed £750 (£1,500 in Greater London).[1406] The third applies to high-value houses brought within the 1967 Act by the Leasehold Reform, Housing and Urban Development Act 1993 and to houses brought within the 1967 Act by the Housing Act 1996 where the tenancy fails the "low rent" test.

Under the original scheme, the price of the freehold is the price which it would fetch if sold in the open market by a willing seller subject to the lease, on the assumption that the lease had already been extended by fifty-years in accordance with the Act,[1407] but without regard to any enhanced bid which might be expected from the tenant himself or a member of his family.[1408] In practice, therefore, the price will be the capitalised value of the rent payable under the lease as extended together with the value (if any) of the reversion. In the case of a lease which still has a very long time to run, the calculation is comparatively easy because the reversion has no value. No one will give anything simply for the right to possession of a property in ninety years' time. The value is therefore simply a capitalisation of the rent. Thus the freehold reversion upon a lease of a house at a ground rent of £20 a year with seventy years unexpired is likely to be worth today about eight years' purchase or £160. On the other hand, as the term date approaches, the reversion begins to acquire some value. However, because of the deemed extension, there will always be at least fifty years to run. If

---

[1401] Leasehold Reform Act 1967, s. 16(1)(b).

[1402] CLRA 2002, s. 143(1)(a), deleting s. 16(1)(a) and amending s. 16(4) of the 1967 Act.

[1403] Ibid., s. 143(2), inserting s. 16(1B) into the 1967 Act, applying Local Government and Housing Act 1989, Sch. 10, p. 370, post, whether or not the extended lease would otherwise fulfil the low rent qualifying condition of that Schedule. LTA 1954, Part II continues, however, to be excluded: Leasehold Reform Act 1967, s. 16(1)(c).

[1404] Leasehold Reform Act 1967, s. 17.   [1405] Ibid., s. 15(2).

[1406] See p. 369, post. For houses built after the abolition of domestic rating, see post.

[1407] Leasehold Reform Act 1967, s. 9(1). See also Leasehold Reform Act 1979, protecting a tenant against artificial inflation of the price he has to pay; the Act negatives the effect of the device considered by HL in *Jones v Wrotham Park Settled Estates* [1980] AC 74.   [1408] HA 1969, s. 82.

the reversion does have any value, this must be added to the value of the right to receive the rent for the rest of the term. If the parties cannot agree on the value, it must be determined by the Leasehold Valuation Tribunal.[1409]

The terms upon which the freehold can be acquired are perhaps the most controversial feature of the Leasehold Reform Act 1967. The effective disregard of the value of the reversion to the building means that the terms can be highly advantageous to the tenant whose lease has a short period left unexpired. This method of calculation was intended to give effect to the Government's declaration in the White Paper that "the price of enfranchisement must be calculated in accordance with the principle that in equity the bricks and mortar belong to the qualified leaseholder and the land to the landlord".[1410] The word "equity" is clearly used in the sense of social justice and not in any sense which would have been recognised by Lord ELDON. Even so, it is not easy to understand. It is presumably intended to reflect the situation on the grant of a building lease, when the landlord reserves a rent which reflects the value of the land alone and the builder is able to dispose at a profit of the building which he has erected.[1411] At this stage, however, the reversion is so remote that the question of whether it should in equity be a reversion in the land alone or the land and building is entirely academic; in either case it will have no value. But the position is very different when the lease is approaching its end, as was the case with many Victorian building leases at the time when the Act was passed. At this point the reversion has a value which is enhanced by the fact that it includes the house as well as the land and a person who bought the reversion would have paid a price which reflected this enhanced value. A purchaser of the residue of the term will have paid a price which was correspondingly lower in order to allow for the fact that he was buying a wasting asset. The "equity" of the Act deprives the landlord of part of the value of his reversion and gives the tenant a windfall gain. It can be justified only on the general ground that it is desirable to enrich tenants at the expense of their landlords.[1412]

It was no doubt for these reasons that a different method of calculating the price was applied to the more expensive houses which were brought within the scope of the Act by the Housing Act 1974. In the case of houses that had a rateable value on 31 March 1990 of between £500 and £750 (the figures are £1,000 and £1,500 in Greater London) the price is calculated upon a set of assumptions which result in the tenant paying more or less the market value of the reversion, including the reversion to the building as well as the site.[1413] Instead of assuming a fifty-year extension, as in the case of low rateable value properties, it is assumed that the tenant has the right to remain at the end of his contractual term as an assured tenant under the Housing Act 1988.[1414] Unlike the low rateable value properties, the fact that the tenant himself might make an enhanced bid is not to be disregarded. The price, therefore, includes the value of the rent for the residue of the contractual term, the value of

---

[1409] Leasehold Reform Act 1967, s. 21(1), as amended by HA 1980.

[1410] *Leasehold Reform in England and Wales* 1966 (Cmnd 2916), para. 4.   [1411] See p. 363, ante.

[1412] A claim that the Act contravened ECHR was rejected in *James v United Kingdom* (1986) 8 EHRR 123 (trustees of the Grosvenor Estate in Mayfair compelled under 1967 Act to sell eighty houses to long-lease tenants at a loss of £2,529,903). See also *Di Palma v United Kingdom* (1988) 10 EHRR 149.

[1413] Leasehold Reform Act 1967, s. 9(1A); *Shalson v Keepers and Governors of John Lyon School* [2004] 1 AC 802; *Fattal v Keepers and Governors of John Lyon School* [2005] 1 WLR 803 (leave to appeal refused by HL: [2005] 1 WLR 1285). This method applies also to leases of houses built after the abolition of domestic rating if the premium paid for the lease exceeds a limit based on a mathematical formula. Otherwise the original method applies: Local Government and Housing Act 1989, s. 149 and SI 1990 No. 434. See generally [1998] 14 EG 122 (C. Boston).   [1414] Formerly the assumption was that the tenant had security under Part I of LTA 1954.

the market rent for the dwelling-house (not just the site) during continuation under the 1988 Act, the value of the reversion to the site and building subject to these rights, and an addition to reflect the higher bid a sitting tenant would make.

It became apparent that a tenant of a high rateable value property could achieve a substantial reduction in the price by first extending the lease for fifty years under the 1967 Act prior to enfranchising.[1415] This effectively gave the tenant the benefit of the formula applicable to low rateable value properties, and thereby diminished the value of the reversion. This is now prohibited by the Housing and Planning Act 1986, whereby it is assumed, for the purpose of calculating the price, that the tenant has no right to an extension, and that, where the lease has been extended, that it will end on the original term date.[1416]

In the case of high-value houses brought within the 1967 Act by the Leasehold Reform, Housing and Urban Development Act 1993, the price of the freehold is calculated on a basis similar to the second method described above, but with certain modifications which operate in the landlord's favour.[1417] For example, there is no assumption that the tenant has any statutory right to remain in possession at the end of the tenancy. This, accordingly, increases the value of the freehold. Further, compensation is payable to the landlord if the enfranchisement causes the value of his other property to diminish.[1418] This third method applies also to houses brought within the 1967 Act by the Housing Act 1996, where the tenancy fails the "low rent" test.[1419]

(2) Landlord and Tenant Act 1954, Part I. Local Government and Housing Act 1989

Part I of the Landlord and Tenant Act 1954 gave security of tenure to long leaseholders who, at common law, would have been obliged to give up possession on the ground that their leases had terminated by effluxion of time. In effect, it allowed them to remain in possession as Rent Act statutory tenants. In the case of long leases entered into on or after 1 April 1990 or those created before that date but still existing on 15 January 1989, Part I of the 1954 Act is replaced by a new regime under the Local Government and Housing Act 1989.[1420] Under this system the leaseholder becomes entitled to an assured tenancy on termination of the long lease. Even after the Housing Act 1996, the entitlement is to a full assured tenancy as opposed to an assured shorthold.[1421] Only the new rules will be examined in this section. Nowadays, however, long leaseholders of houses will usually also be entitled to the more attractive privileges of the Leasehold Reform Act 1967,[1422] while long leaseholders of flats have been given enhanced rights by the Leasehold Reform, Housing and Urban Development Act 1993.[1423]

[1415] *Mosley v Hickman* (1986) 52 P & CR 248.

[1416] S. 23, amending s. 9 of the 1967 Act, but not retrospectively; further amended by CLRA 2002, ss. 143(4), 180; Sch. 14.

[1417] S. 9(1C) of the 1967 Act, introduced by s. 66 of the 1993 Act, and as further amended by CLRA 2002, ss. 145–7, inserting also ss. 9(1D) and 9(1E) into the 1967 Act.

[1418] S. 9A, introduced by s. 66 of the 1993 Act. See [1996] 50 EG 93 (J. Briant).

[1419] S. 9(1C), as amended by HA 1996, Sch. 9, para. 2(4).   [1420] S. 186 and Sch. 10.

[1421] HA 1988, Sch. 2A, para. 6, introduced by HA 1996, Sch. 7; p. 338, ante.   [1422] P. 364, ante.

[1423] P. 372, post.

(a) The qualifying tenancy

The 1989 Act protects the tenant if he holds under a long tenancy at a low rent[1424] and if he satisfies the "qualifying condition".[1425] This requires him to show that, if the tenancy had not been at a low rent, it would for the time being qualify as an assured tenancy under the Housing Act 1988. Thus the premises must have been let as a separate dwelling,[1426] they must fall within the appropriate limits of rent or rateable value,[1427] the tenant must have been occupying them wholly or in part as his only or principal home,[1428] and so forth. The crucial moment when the qualifying condition must be satisfied is on "the term date",[1429] that is, the date on which the tenancy would expire at common law.

(b) Security of tenure

At common law the landlord would be entitled to possession on the term date. But the 1989 Act provides that he shall be entitled to possession only if he can show the existence of certain specified grounds.[1430] These grounds are broadly similar to those upon which a court may make an order for possession under the Housing Act 1988.[1431] If the landlord is unable to prove the existence of any of the statutory grounds, the tenant is entitled to an assured tenancy.[1432] Possession may thereafter be recovered under the Housing Act 1988 grounds for possession.

The machinery by which the Act provides security of tenure is rather different from that applicable to ordinary short protected tenancies. The Act artificially prolongs the existence of the long tenancy until it has been determined in accordance with a complicated procedure of notices, counter-notices and (if necessary) applications to the county court. While thus prolonged, the tenancy remains "property", capable of vesting in the tenant's trustee in bankruptcy.[1433] If the landlord wishes to retake possession, he must serve the appropriate notice on the tenant at least six months but less than twelve months in advance, stating the ground upon which he claims that he is entitled to possession.[1434] If the tenant replies with a counter-notice electing to remain in possession, or simply stays there and continues to fulfil the "qualifying condition",[1435] the landlord must apply to the court for an order for possession.[1436] If he is successful, the tenancy will of course come to an end. If he is unsuccessful, or if he did not want to retake possession in the first place, he may terminate the long tenancy by a notice proposing an assured monthly periodic tenancy.[1437] Such a notice must specify the date upon which the long tenancy is to come to an end. Except in the case of a notice served after an unsuccessful application for possession, the notice must also be given at least six months but

---

[1424] As defined in Sch. 10, para. 2. For tenancies granted on or after 1 April 1990, the rent must not exceed £1,000 a year in Greater London or £250 elsewhere. A rateable value formula applies to those granted before that date.   [1425] HA 1988, Sch. 10, para. 1.

[1426] See p. 338, ante.

[1427] Defined in HA 1988, Sch. 1, para. 2A. For tenancies granted on or after 1 April 1990, the requirement is that the premium paid for the tenancy did not exceed a limit based on a mathematical formula: Local Government and Housing Act 1989, Sch. 10, para. 1(2A).   [1428] See p. 341, ante.

[1429] Local Government and Housing Act 1989, Sch. 10, para. 3.   [1430] Ibid., para. 5.

[1431] For example, breach of covenant, nuisance or annoyance, redevelopment, or requirement for occupation by landlord or family.

[1432] Local Government and Housing Act 1989, Sch. 10, paras. 4, 9.

[1433] De Rothschild v Bell [2000] QB 33 (LTA 1954, Part I).

[1434] Local Government and Housing Act 1989, Sch. 10, para. 4.   [1435] Ibid., para. 1, ante.

[1436] Ibid., para. 13.   [1437] Ibid., para 4.

less than one year in advance. The notice must also propose the terms of the new assured tenancy. If these are not agreed, they must be settled by an application to the rent assessment committee.[1438] The committee will assess the open market rent and, if other terms are disputed, the terms which might reasonably be expected to be found in an assured monthly periodic tenancy of the dwelling-house (not being an assured shorthold).[1439]

(3) Leasehold Reform, Housing and Urban Development Act 1993

Long leases of flats have been a source of dissatisfaction to tenants for two reasons. First, they are wasting assets which in time become unsaleable. Secondly, the tenants have insufficient control over the level of service charges and the standard of maintenance. We have seen that flat-dwellers have no rights of enfranchisement under the Leasehold Reform Act 1967.[1440]

The Leasehold Reform, Housing and Urban Development Act 1993 sought to improve the position of long leaseholders of flats by giving them a collective right to acquire the landlord's interest in the building. It should be appreciated that this Act does not enable a leaseholder to acquire the freehold of his *flat*, as the system of commonhold tenure does.[1441] Also, such a leaseholder is given an individual right to an extended lease of his flat. Contracting out of either of these rights is prohibited.[1442] Significant amendments were made to the 1993 Act by the Commonhold and Leasehold Reform Act 2002, which further improved the leaseholder's position.

(a) *Conditions for enfranchisement*

The 2002 Act relaxed the conditions for enfranchisement. Formerly, only tenants of flats under a long lease (granted for a term exceeding twenty-one years) at a low rent,[1443] or a "particularly long" term if not at a low rent,[1444] qualified for enfranchisement; and a proportion of the qualifying tenants had to satisfy a residence condition.[1445] Now, however, a "qualifying tenant"[1446] is any person who is the tenant of the flat[1447] under a long lease—still defined[1448] primarily as a term exceeding twenty-one years—but without restriction as to the level of rent and without any residence condition.[1449] The premises must still be a self-contained building or a self-contained part of a building containing at least two flats held by

---

[1438] Local Government and Housing Act, para. 10.

[1439] Ibid., para 11. An interim monthly rent may be fixed during the statutory continuation of the long tenancy; ibid., para. 6.

[1440] The tenants of flats (including, but not limited to, long leaseholders) were first given limited rights to acquire the landlord's interest, by way of a right of first refusal on disposal by the landlord, under LTA 1987, amended by HA 1996, ss. 89–91 and Sch. 6; p. 391, post.   [1441] Chap. 9, ante.

[1442] Leasehold Reform, Housing and Urban Development Act 1993, s. 93.

[1443] Ibid., s. 8, as amended by HA 1996, s. 105. The requirement of low rent related to the first year of the lease. For leases granted on or after 1 April 1990 the limits were £1,000 per annum in Greater London or £250 elsewhere. In other cases the limit was based on the letting value or the rateable value.

[1444] Ibid., s. 8A, inserted by HA 1996, s. 106, Sch. 9. "Particularly long" meant, primarily, a term exceeding thirty-five years.

[1445] Ibid., s. 6: occupation of the flat as the tenant's only or principal home for the last twelve months or for periods amounting to three years in the last ten years. Occupation by a company or other artificial person did not suffice.

[1446] Ibid., s. 5. Business leases are excluded: s. 5(2)(a). The 1993 Act does not apply to tenants holding directly of the Crown, but for the application of the provisions of the 1993 Act to Crown leaseholders, see p. 364, n. 1369, ante.

[1447] Defined ibid., s. 101; *Slamon v Planchon* [2005] Ch 142 (meaning of resident landlord exemption).

[1448] Ibid., s. 7.   [1449] CLRA 2002, ss. 117, 120.

qualifying tenants, and such tenants must hold at least two-thirds of the total number of flats in the premises.[1450] The right to enfranchisement is excluded if there is a resident landlord and the premises contain no more than four units,[1451] or if more than 25 per cent of the internal floor area (disregarding common parts) is non-residential.[1452] Until 2002 the mixed-use exclusion was defined as applying where more than 10 per cent was non-residential, thus excluding from the operation of the Act a building consisting of a row of flats above shops, but the new definition is likely to bring some such properties within the scope of collective enfranchisement.

(b) Procedure

The right to collective enfranchisement can[1453] be exercised only by a "RTE company",[1454] a private company limited by guarantee which has as its object (or one of its objects[1455]) the exercise of the right to collective enfranchisement of the premises, which has among its participating members qualifying tenants of at least one-half of the flats contained in the premises.[1456]

The statutory procedure requires the RTE company to serve a notice on the landlord, who must respond by counter-notice.[1457] The purpose of the counter-notice by the landlord is meant[1458] "to define the basic issues before proceedings start, and the landlord should not be entitled then to depart from that position and keep other matters up its sleeve".

In outline, the RTE company's notice must provide the landlord with information such as the names of the qualifying tenants and must propose a purchase price. The landlord's counter-notice must state whether he accepts the right to enfranchise and whether the price is acceptable. If the right is denied, the matter will be resolved by the court.[1459] If the

---

[1450] Leasehold Reform, Housing and Urban Development Act 1993, s. 3, as amended by HA 1996, s. 107, to include premises owned by multiple freeholders.

[1451] Ibid., s. 4(4). "Resident landlord" is defined in s. 10, amended (and narrowed) by CLRA 2002, s. 118; and "unit" in s. 38.

[1452] Ibid., s.4(1), as amended by CLRA 2002, s. 115; *Indiana Investments Ltd v Taylor* [2004] 3 EGLR 63 (non-residential portion was 24.11126%).

[1453] The provisions for RTE companies, and the amendments to the 1993 Act and to other legislation which follow from these provisions, are complex: CLRA 2002, ss. 121–3 and Sch. 8, and no date has yet been set for them to be brought into force.

[1454] Leasehold Reform, Housing and Urban Development Act 1993, s. 13(2)(b), amended by CLRA 2002, s. 121. Formerly the qualifying tenants themselves gave the notice to exercise the right to enfranchise, and could choose whom to nominate as "nominee purchaser", to conduct the proceedings arising out of the initial notice and to take the conveyance of the freehold under s. 15 of the 1993 Act. The "RTE" company is so-called because it exercises the Right To collective Enfranchisement: 1993 Act, s. 4A(1)(b); cf "RTM company" which exercises the "right to manage" under CLRA 2002, s. 71.

[1455] It may have other objects, including the right to manage the premises: p. 376, post. The same company could therefore be both the RTM company and the RTE company in relation to the same premises.

[1456] If there are only two qualifying tenants, both must be participating members: 1993 Act, s. 13(2ZA), inserted by CLRA 2002, s. 121. All qualifying tenants must be given the opportunity to participate: s. 12A (inserted by CLRA 2002, s. 123: a change from the previous law, under which a group of at least two-thirds of the qualifying tenants, of at least one-half of the total number of flats, could give the notice without involving the others).

[1457] Leasehold Reform, Housing and Urban Development Act 1993, ss. 13, 21. By s. 28, the RTE company's notice may be withdrawn before a binding contract is made. Leasehold Reform (Collective Enfranchisement) (Counter-notices) (England) Regulations 2002 (SI 2002 No. 3208); *7 Strathay Gardens Ltd v Poinstar Shipping & Finance Ltd* The Times 10 January 2005.

[1458] *Bishopsgate Foundation v Curtis* [2004] 3 EGLR 57 at [13], per Judge Cooke.

[1459] Leasehold Reform, Housing and Urban Development Act 1993, s. 22.

landlord accepts the right but rejects the proposed price, his counter-notice must include a counter-offer.

The landlord may defeat the claim by applying to court and establishing an intention to redevelop the whole or a substantial part of the premises. This course is open to him only if at least two-thirds of all the long leases of flats in the premises are due to end within five years from the date of the tenants' notice.[1460]

The RTE company must grant a lease back to the former landlord of any flats subject to secure tenancies. This lease will be for 999 years at a peppercorn rent. The former landlord may also require such a lease of non-residential units or flats having no qualifying tenant.[1461]

It will be appreciated that, after enfranchisement, the tenants (via the RTE company) will be responsible for the management of the premises.

Where it is necessary for the maintenance of standards of appearance and amenity of an estate, the former landlord may be permitted to retain limited control over an enfranchised building by means of a management scheme along the lines of section 19 of the Leasehold Reform Act 1967.[1462]

(c) The price[1463]

The tenants must pay the market value[1464] of the landlord's interest, which includes the capitalised value of the rents for the residue of the leases and the value of the reversion on expiry of the leases, allowing for the tenants' rights to remain in possession (i.e. as assured tenants), but disregarding the right to enfranchise or to extend the lease. If the landlord does not take a lease of any non-qualifying parts, the value of the reversion to these parts must be included. In addition, except in relation to any lease which has more than eighty years still to run, the tenants must pay half of the "marriage value"[1465] of the landlord's and tenants' interests. This means that the landlord can share in the increased value accruing to the tenants as a result of their ability to acquire new long leases from the RTE company without paying a premium. The price must also include any compensation payable to the landlord on account of loss or damage to his other property as a result of the enfranchisement.

(d) Extended lease

The 1993 Act also confers on long leaseholders individual rights to a new lease of their flats, on payment of a premium. Again, the Commonhold and Leasehold Reform Act 2002 made significant amendments which have enhanced the rights of leaseholders. As with the right to collective enfranchisement,[1466] the 2002 Act has removed both the "low rent"

[1460] Leasehold Reform, Housing and Urban Development Act 1993, s. 23.

[1461] Ibid., s. 36, Sch. 9. Likewise a flat occupied by a resident landlord (i.e. where the right to enfranchise is not excluded because the premises contain more than four units: s. 4).

[1462] Ibid., s. 69. The landlord must apply to a leasehold valuation tribunal for approval within two years of the coming into force of s. 70. The time limits were modified by HA 1996, s. 118, where properties become newly enfranchisable.

[1463] Ibid., Sch. 6, as amended by HA 1996, s. 109 and CLRA 2002, ss. 126–8 and Sch. 8. Only an outline can be given here. Failing agreement, the price will be determined by a leasehold valuation tribunal; s. 24.

[1464] Before the amendments made by CLRA 2002, the valuation was made on the date when the interest to be acquired by the tenants was agreed or otherwise determined by a leasehold valuation tribunal. It is now the date on which the notice to exercise the right to enfranchise is given by the RTE company.

[1465] Leasehold Reform, Housing and Urban Development Act 1993, Sch. 6, para. 4, amended by CLRA 2002, ss. 127, 128.   [1466] P. 372, ante.

requirement and the residence condition which used to apply to the right to a new lease. Now the only condition is that the leaseholder must have been a qualifying tenant under a long lease of the flat for the last two years before exercising the right to the new lease.[1467] This greatly extends the scope of operation of the 1993 Act.[1468] The statutory procedure requires a tenant's notice and a landlord's counter-notice.[1469] The tenant's rights may be assigned along with the lease of the flat, but cannot be exercised during the currency of any claim to acquire the freehold of the block.[1470] Where the original lease is due to end within five years from the date of the tenant's notice, the landlord may defeat the right to a new lease by applying to court and establishing his intention to redevelop the premises in which the flat is contained.[1471]

A qualifying tenant is entitled, on payment of premium, to a new lease at a peppercorn rent for a term expiring ninety years after the term date of his existing lease.[1472] This lease, which replaces the existing lease, is otherwise on the same terms as the original lease, but excluding any express renewal right or option to purchase.[1473] The tenant is not entitled to any security of tenure (i.e. as an assured tenant) at the end of the new lease, but the new lease may itself be renewed under the statutory procedure.[1474]

The premium which the tenant must pay for the new lease is the aggregate of (a) the diminution in the value of the landlord's interest in the flat (on the assumption that the tenant had no enfranchisement or extension rights, but not disregarding his right to the existing and extended tenancy), (b) the landlord's share (50 per cent) of the "marriage value", and (c) any compensation payable to the landlord on account of loss or damage to his other property as a result of the grant of the new lease.[1475]

The landlord may subsequently terminate the new lease if he satisfies the court of his intention to redevelop the premises in which the flat is contained.[1476] In such a case he must pay compensation to the tenant based on the open market value of the new lease.[1477]

It is likely in practice that this right to a new lease will be more attractive to tenants than the collective right to acquire the freehold of the block, not least because the conditions are easier to satisfy.

[1467] Leasehold Reform, Housing and Urban Development Act 1993, s. 39, amended by CLRA 2002, ss. 130, 131. "Qualifying tenant" and "long lease" are given the same definition as for the right to collective enfranchisement: primarily, a term exceeding twenty-one years, but excluding a business lease: ibid., ss. 5, 7, incorporated by s. 39(3).

[1468] *Maurice v Hollow-Ware Products Ltd* [2005] 26 EG 132 (tenant of block of twenty-eight flats, which were sub-let, entitled to new lease in respect of each of the flats); [2005] 26 EG 129 (S. Murdoch).

[1469] Leasehold Reform, Housing and Urban Development Act 1993, ss. 42, 45. See *Cadogan v Morris* (1998) 77 P & CR 336 (unrealistic proposal by tenant on price can invalidate notice); *9 Cornwall Crescent London Ltd v Kensington and Chelsea Royal London Borough Council* [2005] 4 All ER 1207 (no such rule as regards landlord's counter-notice); (2005) 155 NLJ 942 (J. Driscoll); *Lay v Ackerman* [2004] HLR 40 (misdescription of landlord did not invalidate notice, on construction under *Mannai Investment Co Ltd v Eagle Star Life Assurance Co Ltd* [1997] AC 749, p. 319, ante); cf *Burman v Mount Cook Land Ltd* [2002] Ch 256 (counter-notice did not contain matters required by the Act and so could not be construed under *Mannai* to be valid).

[1470] Ibid., s. 54.   [1471] Ibid., s. 47.   [1472] Ibid., s. 56.   [1473] Ibid., s. 57.   [1474] Ibid., s. 59.

[1475] Ibid., Sch. 13, as amended by HA 1996, s. 110 and CLRA 2002, ss. 134—6. Only an outline is given here. For "marriage value", see p. 374, ante.

[1476] Ibid., s. 61. The application may be during the twelve months ending with the original term date or during the period of five years ending with the term date of the new lease.   [1477] Ibid., Sch. 14.

(4) The "Right to Manage"

We have seen that many amendments were made by the Commonhold and Leasehold Reform Act 2002 to the existing provisions for enfranchisement of long leases and the rights of long leaseholders to new or extended leases, and that the general purpose of the Act was to enhance tenants' rights. The Act also introduced an entirely new provision: the right[1478] for long leaseholders, who have a greater present interest in the state of the premises than the landlord, to acquire and exercise the right to manage their premises. It may well be that the very existence of such a right will act as an inducement for landlords to exercise their own management functions in such a way as to avoid a claim by the tenants to take over the management, but the exercise of the right does not depend on the tenants' showing any failing on the part of the landlord.

Many of the provisions regarding the right to manage are similar to those elsewhere in the 2002 Act which modified existing legislation on long leases, and in particular the Leasehold Reform, Housing and Urban Development Act 1993. The right to manage applies only to a self-contained building or part of a building which contains two or more flats held by qualifying tenants, where the total number of flats held by such tenants is not less than two-thirds of the total number of flats contained in the premises.[1479] A "qualifying tenant" is any person who is the tenant of the flat under a long lease—defined primarily as a term exceeding twenty-one years—but without restriction as to the level of rent and without any residence condition.[1480] The right to manage must be acquired and exercised through a "RTM company", which has among its participating members qualifying tenants of at least one-half of the flats contained in the premises.[1481]

The RTM company must serve a notice on the landlord claiming to acquire the right to manage, and the landlord must serve a counter-notice either accepting or denying the company's right.[1482] Once the company has acquired the right to manage,[1483] it takes over all the management functions that the landlord formerly had under the lease: functions with respect to services, repairs, maintenance, improvements, insurance and management.[1484] The terms of the lease on these matters are overridden.[1485] The company has the right to any uncommitted service charges which have already been collected by the landlord,[1486] and has the right to collect service charges from the tenants thereafter.[1487]

[1478] The parties cannot contract out of the "right to manage" provisions: CLRA 2002, s. 106.

[1479] CLRA 2002, s. 72(1). The right to manage is excluded if there is a resident landlord and the premises contain no more than four units, or if more than 25 per cent of the internal floor area (disregarding common parts) is non-residential: ibid., s. 72(6) and Sch. 6, paras. 1, 3. These are the new rules also for enfranchisement under the 1993 Act; p. 372, ante.

[1480] CLRA 2002, ss. 75–7; business tenancies are excluded. Again, this follows the definition of "qualifying tenant" for the purposes of the 1993 Act.

[1481] Ibid., ss. 71(1), 73, 74, 79. All qualifying tenants must be given the opportunity to participate: s. 78. Cf the RTE company for the purpose of exercising the right to collective enfranchisement under the 1993 Act.

[1482] Ibid., ss. 79–81, 84. The company bears the landlord's reasonable costs: s. 88. In the case of a dispute the matter is resolved by a leasehold valuation tribunal: s. 84(3).

[1483] The right to manage is registrable as a notice in registered land: CLRA 2002, s. 104 (amending LRA 1925, s. 49); LRA 2002, s. 32. Cf, however, R & R, para. 26.027 (the right to manage is not considered an interest adversely affecting the estate, so no notice is appropriate).

[1484] CLRA 2002, s. 96. Functions concerning only part of the premises not held under a lease by a qualifying tenant, and functions relating to re-entry or forfeiture, are excluded.   [1485] Ibid., s. 96(4).

[1486] Ibid., s. 94.

[1487] The landlord must also contribute to the service charges in certain cases where the premises contain excluded units and the landlord has the right to service charges from his tenant: ibid., s. 103.

D Business Tenancies[1488]

Protection is necessary for business tenants principally because a tenant with an established business is in a vulnerable position. If he has built up a goodwill attaching to the premises, such as that of a successful shopkeeper, he may suffer a severe loss of custom if he is required to remove elsewhere at the end of his tenancy. Furthermore, he will often have adapted the premises at his own cost to the needs of his particular business, so that removal would involve him in considerable further outlay. A landlord may therefore be able to extract a higher rent from his sitting tenant than he would obtain by letting the premises to a new tenant in the open market. Parliament thought it unfair that the landlord should be able to force the tenant to pay this additional rent merely to preserve goodwill and improvements[1489] created by his own effort and expense. The need to protect the tenant became more acute after the Second World War, when bomb damage had caused a shortage of business accommodation and a consequent increase in the landlord's bargaining power. The provisions for security of tenure and rent control are now contained in Part II of the Landlord and Tenant Act 1954, as amended by Part I of the Law of Property Act 1969 and the Regulatory Reform (Business Tenancies) (England and Wales) Order 2003.[1490]

(1) The Qualifying Tenancy

A tenancy qualifies for the protection of Part II of the Landlord and Tenant Act 1954 if the property comprised in the tenancy "is or includes" premises which are occupied by the tenant "and are so occupied for the purposes of a business carried on by him or for those and other purposes".[1491] There are some features of this definition which require closer examination.

(a) "Is or includes premises . . . occupied by the tenant . . ."

A tenant will enjoy the protection of the Act if he occupies any part of the property comprised in his lease for the purposes of his business, although his protection extends only to what the Act defines as his "holding". This means the part of the property occupied by the tenant himself (whether for business or other purposes) or by a person employed in his business.[1492] Thus the tenant of a shop with a flat above who carries on business in the shop

---

[1488] Woodfall, *Landlord and Tenant*, chap. 22; Aldridge, *Letting Business Premises*; Lewison, *Drafting Business Leases*; Bell, *Drafting and Negotiating Commercial Leases*; Tromans, *Commercial Leases*; Reynolds and Clark, *Renewal of Business Tenancies*; Williams, Brand and Hubbard, *Handbook of Business Tenancies*; Haley, *Statutory Regulation of Business Tenancies*; Hewitson, *Business Tenancies*; Evans and Smith, *Law of Landlord and Tenant*, Part E; Government's Code of Practice for Commercial Leases (April 2002).

[1489] As to compensation for improvements, see LTA 1927, Part I.

[1490] SI 2003 No. 3096, which came into force on 1 June 2004. The reforms introduced by the 2003 Regulations amended many details of the Act while leaving the fundamentals undisturbed, largely following the recommendations of the Law Commission: Landlord and Tenant: Business Tenancies 1992, Law Com No. 208; [1993] Conv 334 (M. Haley). See also Department of the Environment, Transport and the Regions' Consultation Paper on Business Tenancies Legislation in England and Wales 2001. Regulatory Reform Orders are made under the Regulatory Reform Act 2001 and are designed to remove burdens on businesses. See [2006] Conv 137 (S. Bright), advocating improved protection for the Small Business Tenant.

[1491] LTA 1954, s. 23(1). The definition includes a tenancy by estoppel: *Bell v General Accident Fire & Life Assurance Corpn Ltd* [1998] 1 EGLR 69.

[1492] Ibid., s. 23(3). Occupation or the carrying on of a business by a company in which the tenant has a controlling interest are treated as occupation or the carrying on of a business by the tenant: LTA 1954, s. 23(1A), (1B), inserted by SI 2003 No. 3096.

and lives in the flat, or sub-lets it to an assistant or manager working in the shop will enjoy protection in respect of the whole premises. If he has sub-let the flat to someone who does not work in the shop, the tenancy will be within the Act but his "holding" will be the shop alone.[1493] If he has sub-let the whole premises, his tenancy will not be protected at all, although that of the sub-tenant probably will be. Difficult questions can arise as to the meaning of "occupation". Where the tenant maintains a presence on the premises but his business in reality involves no more than the receipt of income from sub-tenants, he will not be protected. Thus the operator of a market hall who had sub-let the market stalls was not entitled to a renewal even though he was occupying the common parts, which alone could be the "holding".[1494] It was left open whether the tenant was outside the 1954 Act or was a business tenant with no right of renewal (in which case the statutory termination procedure would nevertheless apply). The former approach seems preferable.

(b) "Occupied for the purposes of a business"

"Business" is very widely defined, to include a "trade, profession or employment" and, rather curiously, "*any* activity carried on by a body of persons, whether corporate or unincorporate". Thus the tenancy of a members' tennis club has been held within the Act, because playing tennis is undoubtedly an activity and it was carried on by a body of persons.[1495] For an individual, on the other hand, activity is not enough. It must be a "trade, profession or employment". Accordingly a tenant who ran a free Sunday school in a disused shop was held to be outside the definition.[1496]

Under the Housing Act 1988, where the key phrase is "let as a separate dwelling", attention is concentrated on the purpose for which the premises were let rather than the purpose for which they are actually being used.[1497] The business code, on the other hand, is more concerned with actual user at the time when the question has to be decided.[1498] Prima facie, the fact that the tenant is carrying on business upon the premises is enough. But in some cases the fact that the business user is in breach of covenant will exclude the application of the Act.[1499] And there is nothing in the Act to restrict the landlord's common law right to forfeit the tenancy for breach of covenant.[1500]

(c) "Or for those and other purposes"

The tenant need use only a part of the premises for the purposes of his business, or he may use the same part for business purposes some of the time and other purposes at other times.

[1493] *Narcissi v Wolfe* [1960] Ch 10.

[1494] *Graysim Holdings Ltd v P & O Property Holdings Ltd* [1996] AC 329; [1997] Conv 119 (S. Higgins). Where the sub-letting is of a residential premises covered by the Rent Acts, or is a residential licence, rather than a tenancy, it might be possible for the tenant still to be in occupation but only if it retains such use and control of the sub-occupied parts as can be regarded as business occupation: [2005] 20 EG 259 (S. Murdoch); *Lee-Verhulst (Investments) Ltd v Harwood Trust* [1973] QB 204; *Smith v Titanate Ltd* [2005] 2 EGLR 63.

[1495] *Addiscombe Garden Estates Ltd v Crabbe* [1958] 1 QB 513; *Hawkesbrook Leisure Ltd v Reece-Jones Partnership* [2004] 1 L & TR 28 (non-profit-making company managing sports grounds).

[1496] *Abernethie v A M and J Kleiman Ltd* [1970] 1 QB 10; see also *Lewis v Weldcrest Ltd* [1978] 1 WLR 1107 (taking lodgers).   [1497] See p. 338, ante.

[1498] The critical dates are the contractual term date (because unless the premises are then being used for business purposes the term will not be artificially prolonged: *Esselte AB v Pearl Assurance plc* [1997] 1 WLR 891, p. 381, post) and the date when a notice to determine the tenancy is served: *Cheryl Investments Ltd v Saldanha* [1978] 1 WLR 1329 at 1337, per GEOFFREY LANE LJ.

[1499] LTA 1954, s. 23(4); see *Bell v Alfred Franks and Bartlett Co Ltd* [1980] 1 WLR 340.

[1500] Ibid., s. 24(2).

If the premises are used partly for business and partly for residential purposes, residential security is excluded and only the Landlord and Tenant Act 1954 applies.[1501] But the business user must be significant "and not merely ancillary to the residential user" such as maintaining a study where one can work in the evenings or at weekends.[1502]

(2) Exclusions

Expressly excluded from the protection of the Act are short fixed-term lettings not exceeding six months,[1503] tenancies excluded by agreement,[1504] and certain other tenancies such as agricultural holdings, farm business tenancies, and mining leases.[1505] Although not expressly excluded, the Act does not apply to tenancies at will, even if expressly created,[1506] nor to licences. With respect to the latter, the effect of the decision in *Street v Mountford*[1507] must be considered.[1508]

(3) Security of Tenure and Rent

The Act gives a business tenant security of tenure by providing, first, that his tenancy (whether periodic or for a term certain) cannot be terminated except by the notice procedure laid down by the Act, and secondly, that upon the termination of his tenancy the tenant shall be entitled as of right to the grant of a new tenancy unless the landlord can establish one of a list of specified grounds of opposition.

(a) *Termination procedure*

A business tenancy can be terminated only in accordance with the provisions of the Act.[1509] Until then, the tenancy continues, whatever its term might be. At common law, if a tenant for a term certain at an annual rent holds over after the end of the term and rent continues to be paid at the old rate, the normal inference is that he is holding over as a tenant from year to year.[1510] But a business tenant who stays after the term date is not holding over. There can be no inference of a tenancy from year to year because the old tenancy has not yet come to an end. In the case of a tenancy granted before the Landlord and Tenant (Covenants) Act 1995,[1511] the original tenant who has assigned the tenancy during the contractual term is not liable for the defaults of the assignee during the statutory continuation period.[1512] The landlord may, however, ensure that guarantors remain liable during the continuation period by appropriate wording in the guarantee, whether the tenancy was granted before or after the 1995 Act.

[1501] HA 1988, Sch. 1, para. 4.   [1502] *Cheryl Investments Ltd v Saldanha*, supra.

[1503] LTA 1954, s. 43(3).   [1504] Ibid., s. 38A, p. 385, post.

[1505] Ibid., s. 43(1), as amended by the Agricultural Tenancies Act 1995. Tenancies of public houses are no longer excluded: Landlord and Tenant (Licensed Premises) Act 1990.

[1506] *Manfield & Sons Ltd v Botchin* [1970] 2 QB 612.

[1507] [1985] AC 809, M & B p. 473; p. 198, ante.

[1508] See *University of Reading v Johnson-Houghton* [1985] 2 EGLR 113; *London & Associated Investment Trust plc v Calow* (1986) 53 P & CR 340; *Dellneed Ltd v Chin* (1986) 53 P & CR 172; *Dresden Estates Ltd v Collinson* [1987] 1 EGLR 45; *Vandersteen v Agius* (1992) 65 P & CR 266; p. 200, ante.

[1509] LTA 1954, s. 24(1). For the procedure to be followed, see CPR Part 56, PD; (2004) 154 NLJ 1620 (D. Mo).

[1510] See p. 214, ante.   [1511] See p. 304, n. 856, ante.

[1512] *City of London Corpn v Fell* [1994] 1 AC 458.

(1) TERMINATION BY LANDLORD

The landlord may terminate the tenancy by a notice in a prescribed form, specifying the date of termination.[1513] This must be at least six months but not more than twelve months after service of the notice and not earlier than the date on which the tenancy would have terminated, or could have been terminated, at common law.[1514] A landlord's notice to terminate is commonly known as a "section 25 notice".

The notice must state whether the landlord is opposed to the grant of a new tenancy to the tenant; and, if he is so opposed, the statutory grounds for his opposition or, if he is not so opposed, his proposals for the property, rent and other terms of the new tenancy.[1515] Until the reform of the 1954 Act effected by the 2003 Regulations, the tenant was required to serve a counter-notice within two months if he wished to resist the landlord's claim to terminate the tenancy, and then to make application to the court for a new tenancy not less than two months nor more than four months after the service of the section 25 notice. These requirements constituted something of a trap for tenants, who could find that the failure to take the required steps within the strict time limits had resulted in their losing all their rights.[1516] No counter-notice is now required.[1517] Instead, the landlord may apply to the court for an order for termination of the tenancy, as long as neither he nor the tenant has yet made application to the court for a new tenancy,[1518] and as long as he applies before the date specified for termination in his section 25 notice.[1519] The court will order the termination of the current tenancy, but in order to resist the grant of a new tenancy, the landlord must satisfy the court of one or more grounds of opposition; failing that, the court will order the grant of a new tenancy.[1520] Alternatively, before the date specified for termination, the tenant may himself make an application to the court for a new tenancy.[1521]

(2) TERMINATION BY TENANT

A tenant who simply wants to go out of possession can terminate his contractual tenancy in any way open to him at common law.[1522] If the tenancy cannot be terminated, the tenant may nevertheless serve a notice on the landlord to indicate that he does not wish it to continue under the Act.[1523] The Act has no further scope for application if the tenant simply

---

[1513] LTA 1954, s. 25(1).   [1514] Ibid., s. 25(2).

[1515] Ibid., s. 25(6), (7), (8), substituted by SI 2003 No. 3096. For the construction of notices in the light of the principles set out in *Mannai Investment Co Ltd v Eagle Star Life Assurance Co Ltd* [1997] AC 749, see *Barclays Bank plc v Bee* [2002] 1 WLR 332.

[1516] See, e.g., *Beanby Estates Ltd v Egg Stores (Stamford Hill) Ltd* [2003] 1 WLR 2064 (s. 25 notice, sent by recorded delivery, deemed by LTA 1927, s. 23 to have been served on posting, not receipt, so application to court out of time).

[1517] The abolition was proposed by Law Commission Report on Business Tenancies 1992 (Law Com No. 208), para. 2.39. The original LTA 1954, s. 29(2) was replaced by SI 2003 No. 3096, reg. 5.

[1518] LTA 1954, s. 29(2), (3), substituted by SI 2003 No. 3096. On the application for a new tenancy, see infra.

[1519] Ibid., s. 29A, inserted by SI 2003 No. 3096. The parties may agree to extend the period before it expires: s. 29B.

[1520] Ibid., s. 29(2), substituted by SI 2003 No. 3096. If the court orders that the current tenancy be terminated without the grant of a new tenancy, the termination takes effect three months after the proceedings have been finally disposed of: ibid., s. 64.

[1521] Ibid., s. 24(1). The time limit is set out in s. 29A, inserted by SI 2003 No. 3096. The parties may agree to extend the period before it expires: s. 29B.

[1522] Ibid., s. 24(2); *Bentley & Skinner (Bond St Jewellers) Ltd v Searchmap Ltd* [2003] 2 P & CR DG18 (grant of new lease operated by reason of estoppel as a surrender of the old lease); [2004] Conv 61 (M. Haley).

[1523] Ibid., s. 27(1), (2).

ceases to occupy before the contractual termination date.[1524] If the tenant ceases to occupy during the continuation period, the tenancy will continue until terminated by notice by either party.[1525] Where the tenant desires a renewal, he may take the initiative by serving a notice requesting the grant of a new tenancy, provided he holds under a tenancy for a term of years certain exceeding one year, or a term of years certain and thereafter from year to year.[1526] This notice is the counterpart of the landlord's section 25 notice. Like the section 25 notice, it must specify the date on which the current tenancy is to terminate, and it is subject to the same time limits.[1527] A landlord who wishes to oppose the grant of a new tenancy may serve a counter-notice stating his grounds of opposition within two months of the tenant's notice,[1528] but whether he does so or not, the tenant will lose his right to a new tenancy unless he follows up his notice by an application to the court before the date specified in his request for the beginning of a new tenancy.[1529]

(3) WHO IS THE LANDLORD?

The scheme of the Act contemplates an exchange of notices followed by negotiations for a new tenancy and, if necessary, the adjudication of the court, between landlord and tenant. "Tenant", however, includes a sub-tenant;[1530] the immediate landlord of the tenant carrying on the business may himself hold only a leasehold interest. But there is little point in the grant of a new tenancy by a "landlord" whose own interest in the premises is shortly about to expire. The Act deals with this problem by disregarding altogether a landlord who has himself only a short remaining leasehold interest. For the purposes of the Act, the "landlord" must be the owner of the fee simple or a leasehold interest which will not come to an end within fourteen months by effluxion of time and in respect of which no notice to terminate has been served under the Act.[1531] If the immediate landlord does not fulfil these conditions, the competent landlord for the purposes of the Act will be the next superior landlord who does.

(b) The grounds of opposition

The Act specifies seven grounds upon which a landlord may oppose the grant of a new tenancy.[1532] These may be briefly summarised as follows: (a) the tenant's failure to repair, (b) persistent delay in paying rent, (c) other misbehaviour by the tenant, (d) alternative accommodation available, (e) that the tenant is, in relation to the landlord, a sub-tenant of part of the property originally let and that the landlord could realise a better rent by reletting the property as a whole, (f) the landlord's intention to demolish or reconstruct the premises, and (g) the landlord's intention to occupy the premises himself, either for the purposes of

---

[1524] LTA 1954, s. 27(1A), inserted by SI 2003 No. 3096 to confirm the decision in *Esselte AB v Pearl Assurance plc* [1997] 1 WLR 891; [1998] Conv 218 (M. Haley).   [1525] See LTA 1954, ss. 24(3), 27(2).
    [1526] Ibid., s. 26(1).
    [1527] Ibid., s. 26(2). The tenant cannot operate the s. 26 procedure when exercising a break clause; *Garston v Scottish Widows' Fund and Life Assurance Society* [1998] 1 WLR 1583.   [1528] Ibid., s. 26(6).
    [1529] Ibid., s. 29A, inserted by SI 2003 No. 3096. The parties may agree to extend the period before it expires: s. 29B. The tenant's notice has the effect of terminating the current tenancy immediately before the date specified in his request: ibid., s. 26(5), and is subject to the rule that once an application has been made to the court for a new tenancy, the old tenancy continues until three months after the proceedings have been finally disposed of: s. 64.   [1530] Ibid., s. 69(1).
    [1531] Ibid., s. 44(1), substituted by LPA 1969, s. 14(1).   [1532] Ibid., s. 30(1)(a) to (g).

his business or of a business of a company in which he has a controlling interest,[1533] or as a residence. The last two grounds are in practice the most frequently relied upon and the only ones upon which any further comment will be made.

(1) INTENTION TO DEMOLISH OR RECONSTRUCT

The burden is upon the landlord to establish the necessary intention at the time of the hearing.[1534] "Intention" involves more than thinking that demolition or reconstruction would be desirable. The landlord must be able to show that he means business. As Lord ASQUITH said in a famous passage:[1535]

An "intention" . . . connotes a state of affairs which the party "intending" . . . does more than merely contemplate: it connotes a state of affairs which, on the contrary, he decides, so far as in him lies, to bring about, and which, in point of possibility, he has a reasonable prospect of being able to bring about, by his own act of volition . . . The term "intention" [is] unsatisfied if the person professing it has too many hurdles to overcome, or too little control of events . . . [The scheme must have] moved out of the zone of contemplation—out of the sphere of the tentative, the provisional and the exploratory—into the valley of decision.

The landlord may therefore have to satisfy the court that his scheme of redevelopment is commercially viable, that he has the means to carry it through and the necessary planning permissions and other consents, or a reasonable prospect[1536] of obtaining them. His motive, however, is not relevant.[1537]

The landlord must also show that he could not reasonably carry out his work of demolition or reconstruction without obtaining possession of the holding.[1538] "Possession" in this context means legal possession, not merely physical occupation of the premises. Thus a landlord who has reserved a right to enter and do works upon the premises may be entitled to go into occupation for a lengthy period without ousting his tenant from legal possession.[1539] Such a right will prevent him from opposing the grant of a new tenancy in similar terms. Even if the lease does not include such rights of entry, the tenant may be able to preserve his right to a new lease by offering to include them. The Act provides that the landlord cannot oppose the grant of a new tenancy on this ground, if the tenant agrees to the inclusion of terms giving the landlord reasonable access and other facilities and the work could then be carried out without obtaining possession and without interfering "to a substantial extent or for a substantial time" with the use of the holding for the purposes of the tenant's business.[1540] Similarly, the tenant may be entitled to claim a new tenancy of "an economically separable part"[1541] of the holding, if possession of the rest and (if necessary) access and

---

[1533] LTA 1954, s. 30(1A), (1B), inserted by SI 2003 No. 3096.

[1534] *Betty's Cafés Ltd v Phillips Furnishing Stores Ltd* [1959] AC 20.

[1535] *Cunliffe v Goodman* [1950] 2 KB 237 at 253–4.

[1536] " 'Reasonable prospect' is a low threshold, not to be equated with probability": *Dogan v Samali Investments Ltd* [2005] 3 EGLR 51 at [35], per MANCE LJ.

[1537] See *Turner v London Borough of Wandsworth* (1994) 69 P & CR 399.   [1538] LTA 1954, s. 30(1)(f).

[1539] *Health v Drown* [1973] AC 498.

[1540] LTA 1954, s. 31A(1)(a), inserted by LPA 1969, s. 7(1). See *Cerex Jewels Ltd v Peachey Property Corpn plc* (1986) 52 P & CR 127; *Romulus Trading Co Ltd v Trustees of Henry Smith's Charity* (1989) 60 P & CR 62.

[1541] Defined in LTA 1954, s. 31A(2).

facilities over the part retained would be reasonably sufficient to enable the landlord to carry out his work.[1542]

(2) INTENTION TO USE FOR OWN BUSINESS OR RESIDENCE

Again the burden is upon the landlord to establish the necessary intention at the time of the hearing.[1543] He must show that he has a reasonable prospect of achieving his genuine intention to occupy for business within a reasonable time, but he is not required to establish that the business is likely to be successful.[1544] The Act provides, however, that the landlord cannot rely upon this ground if his own interest has been purchased or created less than five years before "the termination of the current tenancy".[1545] The purpose of this provision, as in the case of the parallel provision in the Housing Act 1988,[1546] is to prevent persons wanting premises with vacant possession from buying them over the heads of sitting tenants and then opposing their normal security of tenure on the ground that they are required for the landlord's own use.

(c) Compensation

A tenant who is unable to obtain a new tenancy because the landlord can establish one of the grounds of opposition listed above as (e), (f) or (g) is entitled to be paid compensation for disturbance.[1547] If his business has been carried on at the premises (whether by himself or a predecessor) for more than fourteen years, the compensation will be twice the rateable value of the premises. Otherwise it will be the rateable value.[1548] A tenant need not go to court and lose merely in order to claim his compensation. If the landlord states in his section 25 notice, or his counter-notice opposing the tenant's request for a new tenancy, that he intends to rely on grounds (e), (f) or (g), the tenant will be entitled to his compensation if he makes no application to court, or makes one and later withdraws it.[1549]

(d) Terms of the new tenancy

If the parties cannot agree on the terms of the new tenancy, they must be fixed by the court. The court has a discretion in fixing the length of the term but it must not exceed fifteen years.[1550] Other terms (apart from rent) must be fixed by having regard to the terms of the current tenancy and to "all relevant circumstances".[1551] This means in practice that the court will follow the terms of the current tenancy unless there is a good reason for not doing so. In

---

[1542] LTA 1954, s. 31A(1)(b). On the other hand, if the landlord wants to use the whole holding for the purposes of the work, the tenant cannot argue that the landlord could do as well or better by using only a part. See *Decca Navigator Co Ltd v Greater London Council* [1974] 1 WLR 748.

[1543] See *Westminster City Council v British Waterways Board* [1985] AC 676.

[1544] *Dolgellau Golf Club v Hett* (1998) 76 P & CR 526.   [1545] LTA 1954, s. 30(2).

[1546] HA 1988, Sch. 2, Ground 1. See also Ground 6.

[1547] LTA 1954, s. 37. For contracting out under s. 38(3), see *Bacchiocchi v Academic Agency Ltd* [1998] 1 WLR 1313.

[1548] LTA 1954, s. 37(2) and (3); Local Government and Housing Act 1989, Sch. 7; LTA 1954 (Appropriate Multiplier) Order 1990 (SI 1990 No. 363).

[1549] Until the Act was amended by LPA 1969 the tenant had to go to court.

[1550] LTA 1954, s. 33, amended by SI 2003 No. 3096.

[1551] Ibid., s. 35. Amendments to ss. 34 and 35 by LT(C)A 1995, Sch. 1, paras. 3 and 4, reflect the changes made by that Act to the liability of original tenants; p. 310, ante.

O'May v City of London Real Property Co Ltd[1552] the current tenancy made the landlord responsible for repair and services, the tenant paying a fixed service charge. The House of Lords refused to alter the tenancy to make the tenant liable for repairs and the full cost of services, paying a correspondingly lower rent, because the effect would be to transfer the risk of indeterminate financial burdens to the tenant.

(e) Rent

The rent under the new tenancy is that which the premises could command if let in the open market, but disregarding any effect on the rent of the fact that the tenant or his predecessors in title have been in occupation, or any goodwill attaching to the holding on account of the tenant's business, or any improvements made during the current tenancy or in certain cases in previous tenancies within the past twenty-one years.[1553] When the court has to determine the rent, it will usually do so after hearing the evidence of expert surveyors, giving their opinions of the letting value of the premises supported by evidence of lettings of comparable properties in the same area. It may be questioned whether the court's function could not be better performed by a body which was itself expert in these matters, such as the Lands Tribunal.

Until 1970, the tenant continued to be liable only for the rent under the old tenancy until it was duly terminated in accordance with the Act and the new tenancy had begun. In the absence of contrary agreement, the old tenancy could not terminate until three months after the proceedings for the grant of the new tenancy had been finally disposed of.[1554] In times of inflation, when the difference between the old rent and the new might be very considerable, it was therefore greatly in the tenant's interest to prolong the proceedings (and his tenancy) as much as possible. Time might be gained by taking fine points on the validity of the section 25 notice and similar procedural matters, while even an unsuccessful appeal to the House of Lords might be financed out of the difference in rents. This situation led to an amendment in 1969.[1555] In a rising market, the interim rent will commonly be more than the current rent; but in a falling market it could be lower. Accordingly, the 2003 Regulations introduced a further amendment to allow the application to be made by either the landlord or the tenant,[1556] and also made other changes to the rules governing the interim rent. Now the application cannot be made more than six months after the termination of the tenancy,[1557] and the interim rent becomes payable from the earliest date that could have been specified in the landlord's section 25 notice, or the earliest date that could have been specified in the tenant's request for a new tenancy, depending on whether the assessment is initiated by the landlord's or the tenant's notice.[1558] Where the landlord is not opposed to the grant of the new tenancy

---

[1552] [1983] 2 AC 726. See also *Cairnplace Ltd v CBL (Property Investment) Co Ltd* [1984] 1 WLR 696 (guarantor term imposed).   [1553] LTA 1954, s. 34, amended by LPA 1969, s. 1.

[1554] Ibid., s. 64. See p. 379, ante.

[1555] LPA 1969, s. 3(1), inserting LTA 1954, s. 24A. See *Stream Properties Ltd v Davis* [1972] 1 WLR 645.

[1556] SI 2003 No. 3096, substituting LTA 1954, s. 24A; Law Commission Report on Business Tenancies 1992, n. 1490, supra, para. 2.63.   [1557] LTA 1954, s. 24A(3), substituted by SI 2003 No. 3096.

[1558] Ibid., s. 24B. Under the original s. 24A, introduced by LPA 1969, the interim rent was payable from the date of termination actually specified in the section 25 notice or in the tenant's request for a new tenancy, or the date of the application to fix the interim rent, whichever was the later.

the interim rent is normally the rent payable at the commencement of the new tenancy.[1559] Where, however, the landlord is opposed, the interim rent is that which it is reasonable for the tenant to pay while the old tenancy continues.[1560] This will generally be lower than the rent which would be payable under statutory renewal of the tenancy, for two reasons. First, it is fixed upon the assumption that a new tenancy from year to year is being granted, the rent for such a tenancy normally being less than that of a tenancy for a fixed term. Secondly, the court must "have regard" to the rent payable under the existing tenancy in determining the interim rent.[1561] In a rising market this usually has the effect of reducing the interim rent below a market rent in order to provide a "cushion" for the tenant against the shock of a steep increase if a market rent were to be imposed.[1562]

(f) Contracting out

Until 1970 the parties could not by agreement exclude the provisions of the Act.[1563] Although landlords could avoid the Act by granting terms not exceeding six months or licences,[1564] it was found that this prohibition discouraged landlords from letting premises which they intended eventually to use themselves or redevelop. Whatever the terms of the letting, the protected tenant will be entitled to at least six months' notice to terminate[1565] and can usually prolong his tenancy for several months more by an unsuccessful application for a new tenancy.[1566] When it finally expires, he may delay the landlord still further by compelling him to commence proceedings for possession. Many landlords therefore preferred to leave their building temporarily empty. The Law of Property Act 1969 introduced an amendment allowing the parties to agree to exclude the Act if their agreement was approved by the court, which would have to be satisfied that the tenant understood his position and had not been oppressed or overborne.[1567] This was further relaxed under the 2003 Regulations: the parties may now agree that the provisions of the 1954 Act giving security of tenure shall be excluded, or that the tenancy shall be surrendered on a specified date, or in specified circumstances, and there is no longer a requirement that the parties apply to court for approval of their agreement. However, the agreement is void unless the landlord has served a prescribed notice on the tenant, normally at least fourteen days before they enter into the agreement, and the tenant must sign a declaration that he has received the notice and accepts its consequences.[1568]

[1559] LTA 1954, s. 24C. This is adjusted if the rent under the new tenancy would have been substantially different if it had been assessed at the date when the interim rent first becomes payable (i.e., the market conditions change substantially during the interim period), or if the terms of the new tenancy differ to such an extent that the rent under it is substantially different from the rent which would otherwise have been assessed had the terms remained as under the old tenancy: s. 24C(3).   [1560] Ibid., s. 24D(1).

[1561] Ibid., s. 24A(3).

[1562] See *English Exporters (London) Ltd v Eldonwall Ltd* [1973] Ch 415; *Charles Follett Ltd v Cabtell Investments Co Ltd* [1987] 2 EGLR 88. In a falling market, it would similarly cushion the landlord.

[1563] LTA 1954, s. 38(1); *Allnatt London Properties Ltd v Newton* [1984] 1 All ER 423 (effect of s. 38(1) on "offer to surrender" clause), p. 257, ante.   [1564] P. 379, ante.

[1565] See p. 380, ante.   [1566] See p. 384, ante.   [1567] LTA 1954, s. 38(4), inserted by LPA 1969, s. 5.

[1568] Ibid., s. 38A. The parties can agree to waive the fourteen-day period, but then the tenant's declaration has to be in the form of a *statutory* declaration. The form of notice is set out at SI 2003 No. 3096, Sch. 1, and the requirements of a valid agreement (including the prescribed forms of declaration) in Sch. 2. But it is not sufficient that the landlord's wife will occupy the premises to carry on her own business: *Zafiris v Liu* The Times, 3 March 2005.

E Agricultural Tenancies

Some statutory protection for tenant farmers was introduced soon after the First World War,[1569] but this was greatly strengthened and improved during and after the Second World War as part of the general effort made to increase home food production at the time. The principle upon which the legislation was based was that tenant farmers needed security of tenure to encourage them to spend money on improving the land and buying stock and other capital equipment. This principle is reflected in the Agricultural Holdings Act 1986, but has been departed from in the "farm business tenancy" code introduced by the Agricultural Tenancies Act 1995. The purpose of the 1995 Act was to encourage new lettings of farmland by removing security of tenure and to encourage diversity in the use of the land. The Agricultural Holdings Act 1986 applies to tenancies granted before 1 September 1995; the Agricultural Tenancies Act 1995 applies to tenancies granted on or after that date.

(1) Agricultural Holdings[1570]

(a) The agricultural holding

The key concept in the Agricultural Holdings Act 1986 is the "agricultural holding". This is defined as[1571] "the aggregate of the land (whether agricultural land or not) comprised in a contract of tenancy which is a contract for an agricultural tenancy". A contract for an agricultural tenancy is one where, having regard to the terms of the tenancy, the actual or contemplated use of the land at the date of the contract or subsequently and any other relevant circumstances, substantially the whole of the land is let for use as agricultural land.[1572] "Agriculture" is very widely defined[1573] and there is no minimum size for an agricultural holding. "Agricultural land" means land which is not merely used for agriculture but is "so used for the purposes of a trade or business".[1574] Provided the use is agricultural, the business need not be,[1575] but non-commercial agricultural use does not qualify.

(b) Security of tenure

(1) THE DEEMED YEARLY TENANCY

The Act confers security of tenure by limiting the circumstances in which a landlord can validly serve a notice to quit. Prima facie this machinery can operate only on periodic tenancies, because only in such cases is a notice to quit necessary to terminate the tenancy. But the Act deals with this problem in sweeping fashion by providing that tenancies for an interest less than a tenancy from year to year take effect as if they were yearly tenancies,[1576] while a tenancy for a term certain of two years or upwards (unless a notice to quit has been served) thereafter continues as a yearly tenancy.[1577] Licences to occupy the land for any period also take effect as

---

[1569] Agricultural Holdings Act 1923.

[1570] See Muir Watt and Moss, *Agricultural Holdings*; Scammell and Densham's *Law of Agricultural Holdings*; Evans and Smith, *Law of Landlord and Tenant*, chap. 26.

[1571] Agricultural Holdings Act 1986, s. 1(1).   [1572] Ibid., s. 1(2). S. 1(3) deals with change of user.

[1573] Ibid., s. 96(1).   [1574] Ibid., s. 1(4). See *Brown v Teirnan* [1993] 1 EGLR 11.

[1575] *Rutherford v Maurer* [1962] 1 QB 16 (grazing horses of a riding school).

[1576] Agricultural Holdings Act 1986, s. 2(1). See *Calcott v J S Bloor (Measham) Ltd* [1998] 1 WLR 1490.

[1577] Ibid., s. 3(1). Subject to an exception in s. 5, it is not possible to contract out of this provision.

tenancies from year to year.[1578] Thus most agricultural tenancies granted before 1 September 1995, whatever their express terms, are deemed to be or become yearly tenancies.

It will be noticed, however, that there is a curious gap in these provisions. A tenancy for a term certain which is more than a year but less than two is not converted into a yearly tenancy. It therefore expires by effluxion of time and the security of tenure machinery cannot apply to it.[1579] Furthermore, the Act contains an express exception in the case of a letting or licence "in contemplation of the use of the land only for grazing or mowing (or both) during some specified period of the year".[1580] The owner of a country house who had some surplus fields could therefore let them to a neighbouring farmer for grazing for up to 364 days at a time[1581] without committing himself to the security of tenure provisions of the Act. Finally, the security provisions do not protect sub-tenants against the head landlord.[1582]

(2) THE NOTICE TO QUIT

At common law a yearly tenancy may be terminated by at least six months' notice expiring on the anniversary of the tenancy.[1583] For an agricultural holding the notice period is extended to one year.[1584] The common law requirement that the notice must terminate on the anniversary is retained. It may therefore be up to two years before a notice to quit can expire.

(3) VALIDITY OF NOTICE TO QUIT

A notice to quit an agricultural holding can operate effectively in only two kinds of circumstances. The first is when the landlord at the time of service can rely upon one of eight specified grounds.[1585] The second is when the local Agricultural Land Tribunal consents to the operation of the notice after it has been served.[1586] This consent also may be given only upon certain specified grounds, for example, that greater hardship would be caused by withholding than by giving consent. Compensation is payable except in default cases.

The grounds upon which a notice may be served and operate without further consent include bad husbandry; failure to pay rent or to remedy remediable breach; irremediable breach of covenant; bankruptcy; and death of the tenant or sole surviving tenant.

The last of these is important because it is the only ground which (unless the tenant is a company) must become available sooner or later. Its significance was reduced when the Agriculture (Miscellaneous Provisions) Act 1976 gave certain members of the deceased

---

[1578] Agricultural Holdings Act 1986, s. 2(2); *Bahamas International Trust Co Ltd v Threadgold* [1974] 1 WLR 1514 (exclusive occupation necessary). See also *McCarthy v Bence* [1990] 1 EGLR 1, discussing the effect on this subsection of *Street v Mountford* [1985] AC 809, p. 198, ante.

[1579] *Gladstone v Bower* [1960] 2 QB 384; *Keen v Holland* [1984] 1 WLR 251. Nor is it protected as a business tenancy: *EWP Ltd v Moore* [1992] QB 460.   [1580] Agricultural Holdings Act 1986, s. 2(3).

[1581] *Reid v Dawson* [1955] 1 QB 214; *Scene Estate Ltd v Amos* [1957] 2 QB 205; *Stone v Whitcombe* (1980) 40 P & CR 296; *Watts v Yeend* [1987] 1 WLR 323.

[1582] See, however, *Gisborne v Burton* [1989] QB 390 (sub-tenant treated as tenant under "artificial transaction" doctrine); cf *Barrett v Morgan* [2000] AC 264 (notice to quit served on tenant by head landlord effective to terminate sub-tenancy also), p. 329, ante.   [1583] See p. 321, ante.

[1584] Agricultural Holdings Act 1986, s. 25(1). Contracting out is not permitted; cf *Elsden v Pick* [1980] 1 WLR 898 (waiver). This applies to notices given by the tenant, as well as by the landlord.

[1585] Ibid., Sch. 3. The 1986 Act is not contrary to the ECHR in distinguishing between different grounds of termination, and in providing different routes for challenging a notice to quit for different grounds of termination: *Lancashire County Council v Taylor* [2005] 1 WLR 2668.   [1586] Ibid., ss. 26, 27.

tenant's family a right to succeed to the tenancy. These succession rights, however, have now been largely confined to tenancies granted before 12 July 1984.[1587]

(4) NOTICE PROCEDURE

A tenant who has been served with a notice to quit and wishes to invoke the security of tenure provisions of the Act must serve a counter-notice.[1588] If the notice does not purport to have been given on one of the permitted grounds, he must simply claim the protection of the relevant section whereby the Tribunal's consent is required.[1589] If the notice relies on certain of the permitted grounds, the tenant's notice must claim an arbitration on whether the appropriate ground existed.[1590] There are stringent time limits for these notices and the tenant may lose all protection if they are not correctly served.[1591]

(c) Rent

The rent for an agricultural holding is, in the absence of agreement, fixed by an arbitrator as the rent at which the holding might reasonably be expected to be let by a prudent and willing landlord to a prudent and willing tenant, taking into account the current level of rents for comparable lettings (as to which any scarcity element must be disregarded).[1592] Certain matters must be disregarded, including the fact that the tenant is in occupation, any improvements he has made and any deterioration for which he is responsible.[1593] The rent may be reviewed (by agreement or arbitration) at intervals of not less than three years.[1594]

(2) Farm Business Tenancies[1595]

The steady decline in tenant farming led Parliament to deregulate agricultural lettings and return in substance to freedom of contract. The Agricultural Tenancies Act 1995, which applies to lettings on or after 1 September 1995, introduces the concept of the farm business tenancy. The policy of the Act is to encourage new lettings and to facilitate diversification into non-agricultural business use such as, for example, the provision of golfing or equestrian facilities.[1596] Although the 1995 Act regulates the form and duration of notices to quit, it does not confer security of tenure. This is a radical departure from the previous legislation, although it must be said that many agricultural tenants before the 1995 Act did not enjoy security of tenure because of the loopholes in the previous legislation.[1597] The farm

---

[1587] Agricultural Holdings Act 1986, s. 34. Where succession rights are available, they apply also on the tenant's retirement.

[1588] It is not possible to deprive the tenant by contract of his right to serve a counter-notice: *Johnson v Moreton* [1980] AC 37. See also *Featherstone v Staples* [1986] 1 WLR 861.

[1589] Agricultural Holdings Act 1986, s. 26(1). See *Crawford v Elliott* [1991] 1 EGLR 13. The inclusion of a dwelling on the holding does not make s. 5 of the Protection from Eviction Act 1977 applicable; *National Trust for Places of Historic Interest or Natural Beauty v Knipe* [1998] 1 WLR 230.

[1590] Ibid., ss. 83, 84; Agricultural Holdings (Arbitration on Notices) Order 1987 (SI 1987 No. 710), Part III. But a notice containing statements which the landlord knows to be false is of no effect: *Rous v Mitchell* [1991] 1 WLR 469.   [1591] As in *Magdalen College, Oxford v Heritage* [1974] 1 WLR 441.

[1592] Agricultural Holdings Act 1986, s. 12.   [1593] Ibid., Sch. 2, paras. 1–3.

[1594] Ibid., para. 4. See *Mann v Gardner* (1990) 61 P & CR 1.

[1595] See Rodgers, *Agricultural Law*; Sydenham and Mainwaring, *Farm Business Tenancies—The Agricultural Tenancies Act 1995*; Scammell and Densham's *Law of Agricultural Holdings*; Muir Watt and Moss, *Agricultural Holdings*; Evans and Smith, *Law of Landlord and Tenant*, chap. 27.

[1596] See [1995] Conv 445 (S. Bright); [1996] Conv 164 (C. Rodgers) and 243 (J. Bishop).

[1597] P. 387, ante (for example, fixed terms of between one and two years).

business tenant will, however, be entitled to compensation for improvements on quitting. It is still too early to say whether the 1995 Act will reverse the decline in tenant farming.

(a) *The farm business tenancy*

The farm business tenancy is defined in section 1 of the 1995 Act as a tenancy which meets the business conditions together with either the agriculture condition or the notice conditions of the section, and is not excluded by section 2.[1598] Genuine licences fall outside the Act, as do tenancies at will, but sub-lettings are included.[1599]

The "business conditions" are that all or part of the land is farmed for the purpose of a trade or business, and has been so farmed since the beginning of the tenancy.[1600] The "agriculture condition" is that the character of the tenancy is primarily or wholly agricultural, having regard to the terms of the tenancy, the use of the land, the nature of any commercial activities carried on on the land,[1601] and any other relevant circumstances. The "notice conditions" are that, on or before the "relevant day",[1602] the landlord and tenant gave each other a written notice identifying the land to be comprised in the tenancy and stating that the person giving the notice intends the tenancy to be and remain a farm business tenancy, and that, at the beginning of the tenancy, its character was primarily or wholly agricultural, having regard to the terms and any other relevant circumstances.

It will be seen that there are thus two kinds of farm business tenancy. Where the notice conditions are not satisfied, the tenancy ceases to be a farm business tenancy if its character ceases to be primarily or wholly agricultural. Where the notice conditions are satisfied, the tenancy will remain within the 1995 Act even if diversification into a non-agricultural business causes it to cease to be primarily or wholly agricultural, provided that at least part continues to be farmed for the purpose of a trade or business. In such a case the non-agricultural business will not result in the acquisition of security of tenure under the Landlord and Tenant Act 1954, Part II.[1603] Thus the notice conditions should be complied with if the landlord wishes to protect himself against the possibility of the tenancy moving into the 1954 Act. Presumably, such a transfer may occur even if the notice conditions have been complied with, if, without any breach of the terms of the tenancy, all farming activity is discontinued.

(b) *Termination of the tenancy*

Although the farm business tenant enjoys no security of tenure, the common law rules as to termination are modified to some extent. A fixed term of two years or less will terminate by expiry or, whatever its duration, may be terminated by forfeiture in the ordinary way. Nor does the 1995 Act regulate the termination by notice to quit of periodic tenancies which are for periods other than from year to year.

[1598] A tenancy beginning before 1 September 1995 is excluded, and also one which, although beginning on or after that date, falls within the Agricultural Holdings Act 1986 pursuant to the transitional provisions in s. 4 of the 1995 Act.   [1599] See s. 38(1).

[1600] By s. 1(6), there is a rebuttable presumption that the second condition is established if the first is proved.

[1601] By s. 1(8), activities in breach of the terms of the tenancy must be disregarded unless the landlord has consented or acquiesced or his predecessor in title has consented.

[1602] By s. 1(5), this is the beginning of the tenancy or the day the parties entered into any instrument creating the tenancy, whichever is the earlier. By s. 1(6), the notice must not be included in the instrument creating the tenancy.

[1603] Farm business tenancies are excluded from the business tenancy code by s. 43(1)(aa) of the 1954 Act, inserted by Agricultural Tenancies Act 1995, s. 40, Sch., para.10(b).

The 1995 Act does, however, provide a special code for the termination of a farm business tenancy which is for a fixed term of more than two years or which is a yearly tenancy. A fixed term of more than two years does not terminate by expiry but continues as from its term date as a tenancy from year to year unless either party has given a written notice at least twelve months but less that twenty-four months before the term date of his intention to terminate.[1604] In such a case the tenancy will end on the term date. Where the tenancy continues, it does so on the terms of the original fixed term, so far as applicable to a yearly tenancy.

In the case of a yearly tenancy (either originally granted or arising after a fixed term, as described above) a notice to quit is invalid unless it is in writing, is to take effect at the end of a year of the tenancy, and is given at least twelve months but less than twenty-four months before the date on which it is to take effect.[1605] Where a farm business tenancy for a fixed term of more than two years contains a provision permitting the service of a notice to quit the whole or part during the fixed term (a "break clause"), the notice is valid only if in writing and if given at least twelve months but less than twenty-four months before the date on which it is to take effect.[1606] Presumably, where such a notice is validly served, no yearly tenancy will arise under section 5(1) of the Act.

These modifications of the common law termination rules apply notwithstanding any contrary provision in the tenancy.[1607] Where the statutory rules as to the form and duration of a notice are complied with, the tenancy will end as if terminated in the ordinary way at common law, without any right of renewal. This absence of any necessity for the landlord to establish a specified ground for possession is a significant distinction from the scheme of the Agricultural Holdings Act 1986.

(c) Rent

The initial rent is that which is agreed by the parties. The 1995 Act provides a statutory framework for subsequent rent review which operates, notwithstanding any agreement to the contrary, unless the document creating the tenancy expressly states that the rent is not to be reviewed or provides for review (so long as not upwards only) in a manner which does not involve the exercise of any judgment or discretion.[1608] Thus the statutory review procedure does not apply if the tenancy provides for an index-linked review.

Subject to the above exception, either party to a farm business tenancy may give the other a written "statutory review notice", requiring that the rent to be payable from the "review date" shall be referred to arbitration. This review date must be at least twelve months but less than twenty-four months after the day on which the notice is given. Unless the parties have otherwise agreed in writing, the review date must be an anniversary of the beginning of the tenancy and must not be within a period of three years from the beginning of the tenancy or from any previous review (by arbitration or agreement).[1609]

After the notice has been served, the parties are free to agree on the machinery for rent review (for example, review by an expert), but in default of agreement an arbitrator will be

---

[1604] Agricultural Tenancies Act 1995, s. 5(1).

[1605] Ibid., s. 6(1). The notice may be given before the end of a fixed term, to end the yearly tenancy on the first anniversary of the term date: s. 6(2).   [1606] Ibid., s. 7.

[1607] Ibid., ss. 5(4), 6(1), 7(1).   [1608] Ibid., s. 9.

[1609] Ibid., s. 10. The parties may agree in writing that the intervals between review shall be greater or less than three years.

appointed.[1610] Where the rent is referred to arbitration, the arbitrator may increase or reduce the rent, or direct it to continue unchanged. The rent properly payable is the rent at which the holding might reasonably be expected to be let on the open market by a willing landlord to a willing tenant, taking into account the terms of the tenancy and other relevant factors. Certain matters are to be disregarded, such as any increase in the rental value due to any tenant's improvement which he was not obliged by the tenancy to provide and for which he has received no consideration or compensation, any decrease in the rental value due to any deterioration or damage caused or permitted by the tenant, and any effect on the rent of the fact that the tenant is a sitting tenant.[1611]

(d) Compensation for improvements

The absence of security of tenure is to some extent mitigated by the provisions of the 1995 Act allowing compensation for improvements when the farm business tenancy ends. Thus the tenant may acquire funds for relocation. When the tenant quits, he is entitled to compensation from the landlord in respect of any physical improvement made by him on the holding (such as a building) and of any "intangible advantage" obtained by him for the holding (such as an unimplemented planning permission).[1612] Although a compensation regime existed under the earlier legislation, the latter aspect was new in 1995. The landlord must have given written consent to the making of the improvement or the application for planning permission.[1613] The compensation is generally the amount equal to the increase in the value of the holding at the end of the tenancy attributable to the improvement or to the securing of planning permission.[1614] The compensation provisions apply notwithstanding any agreement to the contrary.[1615] The right of a farm business tenant to remove fixtures has already been discussed.[1616]

F Residential Flats. Tenants' Rights of First Refusal

The Landlord and Tenant Act 1987, Part I,[1617] introduced a right for certain tenants of flats to have the first refusal on their immediate landlord's disposal of his interest in the property. The general principle was not to deprive the unwilling landlord of his interest, as in the case of a tenant's right of enfranchisement of a long lease;[1618] nor to require the landlord to accept a lower price from a tenant than he would be willing to accept on a sale to a third party. It was simply to give the sitting tenants preferential treatment over a third party

---

[1610] Ibid., s. 12. Either party may, at any time during the period of six months ending with the review date, apply to the President of the Royal Institution of Chartered Surveyors for the appointment of an arbitrator.

[1611] Ibid., s. 13.

[1612] Ibid., ss. 15, 16. No compensation is payable if the improvement is removed or the intangible advantage does not remain attached to the holding. Where planning permission has been implemented, the tenant will be able to claim for any improvements made as a result.

[1613] Ibid., ss. 17, 18. Disputes are to be referred to arbitration: s. 19.

[1614] Ibid., ss. 20, 21. The procedure for claims (which must be made within two months of termination) and for arbitration in the absence of agreement is laid down by s. 22. [1615] Ibid., s. 26.

[1616] See p. 160, ante.

[1617] Implementing recommendations of the Committee of Inquiry on the Management of Privately Owned Blocks of Flats (1985). For other recommendations, implemented by other Parts of the 1987 Act, see pp. 252–3, ante. [1618] Pp. 364, et seq, post.

purchaser, as part of a broader recognition of the stake that residential tenants have in their flats. Certain problems were discovered in the workings of the 1987 Act, including the fact that some landlords appeared to seek to avoid the proper exercise of their rights by their tenants, and the provisions were amended and strengthened by the Housing Act 1996.[1619]

The right is given to "qualifying tenants" of flats:[1620] tenants holding under tenancies other than protected shorthold or assured tenancies,[1621] business tenancies to which Part II of the Landlord and Tenant Act 1954 applies,[1622] and tenancies terminable on cessation of the tenant's employment. It therefore includes, although it is not limited to, residential tenants holding under a long lease. As long as the premises consist of the whole or part of a building, and contain two or more flats held by qualifying tenants (who together hold more than half of the total number of flats in the premises),[1623] the landlord[1624] must not make a "relevant disposal"[1625] affecting the premises without first serving on the qualifying tenants a notice offering to enter into the transaction in question with them.[1626] The offer need not be accepted by all the qualifying tenants, but acceptance will be effective and will irrevocably bind the landlord if it is made by at least a requisite majority. The tenants who accept the landlord's offer nominate a person to enter into the transaction with him.[1627]

If the landlord makes a relevant disposal to a third party without complying with the requirements of the Act, the qualifying tenants are entitled to compel the third party to dispose of the premises to them, on the same terms as the landlord's disposal to him.[1628] In effect, therefore, the third party is bound by the tenants' right of first refusal.[1629]

G Law Reform

We have seen that in recent years there have been many significant reforms of the special rules relating to security of tenure and control of rent: for example, the extension of the scope of assured shorthold tenancies by the Housing Act 1996;[1630] the introduction of

---

[1619] Ss. 89–92 and Sch. 6. The Act was described as "ill-drafted, complicated and confused" by Sir Nicolas BROWNE-WILKINSON in *Denetower Ltd v Toop* [1991] 1 WLR 945 at 952. See also *Mainwaring v Trustees of Henry Smith's Charity* [1998] QB 1 at 17–18, 20. HA 1996 introduced into the 1987 Act a new s. 10A which makes it a criminal offence for the landlord to fail to comply with the requirements of Part I.

[1620] LTA 1987, s. 3, as amended by HA 1988, s. 119, Sch. 13.   [1621] P. 337, ante.   [1622] P. 377, ante.

[1623] LTA 1987, s. 1(2). The Act does not apply to premises of which more than half of the floor area (disregarding common parts) is occupied or intended to be occupied otherwise than for residential purposes: ibid., s. 1(3).

[1624] The landlord may be the freeholder or a leaseholder. If he is a leaseholder holding under a lease for less than seven years, or terminable by the landlord within seven years, the superior landlord is also to be regarded as the qualifying tenant's landlord for the purposes of the Act.

[1625] Defined as (with certain exclusions) the disposal of any estate or interest (legal or equitable) in the premises: LTA 1987, s. 4. It includes a *contract* to make such a disposal: LTA 1987, s. 4A, inserted by HA 1996, s. 89(1).

[1626] LTA 1987, s. 1(1). The requirements of the offer notice are set out in ss. 5–5E, as substituted by HA 1996, s. 92(1), Sch. 6.

[1627] Ibid., s. 6. "Requisite majority" is defined in s. 18A, inserted by HA 1996, s. 92(1), Sch. 6: qualifying tenants of constituent flats with more than 50% of the available votes. Procedures for the subsequent stages of the process are set out at ss. 6–10, as substituted by HA 1996, s. 92 (1), Sch. 6.

[1628] Ibid., ss. 11–12D, as substituted by HA 1996, s. 92(1), Sch. 6.

[1629] It takes effect, however, as a direct right under the terms of the statute, rather than by the third party being bound by a pre-existing right of pre-emption. The prospective purchaser of premises to which the Act applies may serve notices on the tenants to ensure that rights of first refusal do not arise which could be enforced against him: ibid., s. 18.   [1630] P. 344, ante.

introductory tenancies by the Housing Act 1996,[1631] and demoted tenancies by the Anti-social Behaviour Act 2003;[1632] significant changes to long leaseholders' rights made by the Commonhold and Leasehold Reform Act 2002;[1633] and amendment of the rules relating to business tenancies made by the Regulatory Reform (Business Tenancies) (England and Wales) Order 2003.[1634] Further, far-reaching reforms can be expected in housing law, which the Law Commission is currently considering.

In 2003 the Law Commission published a "Narrative Report" on Renting Homes.[1635] This was in interim report, following two Consultation Papers which had been published in 2002,[1636] and was designed to give the outline of the scheme which the Commission was likely to recommend, in order to allow for the preparation for its implementation in advance of the (delayed) publication of the final Report and draft Bill.[1637]

The Law Commission's recommendations for the reform of housing law represent radical legislative change to the regulation of the rented sector of the housing market:[1638]

The proposed Bill will not only include detailed changes to the existing rules, but also fundamental change to the legislative approach to the regulation of this sector of the housing market. In particular the historic linkage between principles of property law and housing legislation will, so far as is practicable, be abandoned; instead, a new approach based on contract which incorporates consumer law principles of fairness and transparency is proposed.

It is recommended that there should be two basic agreement types.[1639] "Type I" agreements will have a high degree of security of tenure protected by the Act; these will be periodic agreements only, and are similar to the existing secure tenancy under the Housing Act 1985. "Type II" agreements will have a low degree of security of tenure provided by statute, and can be either fixed-term or periodic. They are based on the assured shorthold tenancy agreement. Normally social landlords will be required to use type I agreements; by default, private landlords' agreements will be type II.[1640]

The broad objective is that, unless there are compelling reasons for excluding them, all occupation agreements should come within the scheme.[1641] A number of types of agreement currently outside the statutory schemes of protection for residential tenancies will be brought within the scheme, such as service occupancies and student accommodation provided by universities and local authorities. The distinction between the lease and the licence will therefore no longer be of importance for the purpose of rent control or security of tenure:[1642]

While the practical importance of the distinction has receded in recent years, it nonetheless retains its potential for complexity. We think this distinction is out of place in a modern system of housing law. We recommend that our scheme should apply to all contractual occupation arrangements, not just those classifiable as tenancies.

[1631] P. 361, ante.   [1632] P. 360, ante.   [1633] Pp. 366, 372, 373, 374 and 376, ante.

[1634] P. 380, ante.

[1635] Law Com No. 284; (2004) 8 L & T Rev 26 (M. Partington); (2004) 7 JHL 9 (M. Partington); [2005] L & T Rev 26 (M. Partington); [2005] Conv 207 (W. Barr and N. Glover-Thomas).

[1636] Renting Homes 1: Status and Security 2002 (Consultation Paper 162), and Renting Homes 2: Co-occupation, Transfer and Succession 2002 (Consultation Paper 168).   [1637] Law Com No. 284, paras. 1.2–1.4.

[1638] Ibid., para. 2.5.   [1639] Ibid., para. 3.7. The details are set out in Part V of the Report.

[1640] Ibid., paras. 3.9, 3.10.   [1641] Ibid., para. 3.12.

[1642] Ibid., para. 6.19. For the lease/licence distinction, see pp. 197 et seq, ante.

However, there will be two classes of exclusion from the new scheme:[1643]

(1) Agreements covered by other statutory schemes. These include business tenancies, agricultural holdings, and mobile homes.

(2) Certain types of agreement excluded on social policy grounds. These include holiday lets; agreements granted as a temporary expedient to persons who entered the premises as trespassers; agreements where the occupier is sharing accommodation with the landlord; agreements relating to certain categories of sheltered accommodation; and agreements relating to accommodation provided on a temporary basis to meet duties to house the homeless under Part VII of the Housing Act 1996.

Under the scheme there must be a contractual agreement between the landlord and the occupier; if it is made orally, a written statement of it must be provided by the landlord to the occupier.[1644] Model forms of agreement will be provided by Statutory Instrument, which will assist those drafting written agreements, and will operate as a default where a landlord fails to meet the requirement to put an agreement into writing.[1645] The agreement must contain four categories of terms:[1646]

(1) *Key* terms, providing information about the parties and setting out the fundamentals of the agreement such as the description/address of the property and the rent payable.

(2) *Compulsory-minimum* terms. These will (a) prescribe the circumstances in which a landlord may seek possession against an occupier; and (b) set down the duties imposed by law on landlords (such as statutory repairing obligations). It will be possible for parties to agree to amend these terms but only so that they are rendered more favourable to the occupier.

(3) *Special* terms, which impose obligations on occupiers for social policy reasons (in particular, those relating to anti-social behaviour).

(4) *Other* terms. This part will include *default* terms, which will deal with a list of issues needed to make the contract work. The model agreements will contain default terms covering these matters, though the parties may substitute their own terms for the default terms. Any *substitute* term will have to be fair and transparent. In addition, this part of the agreement will contain *additional* terms dealing with other matters not otherwise considered.

It is also recommended that the existing schemes should, as far as possible, be brought within the scope of the new scheme.[1647] If enacted, therefore, the law applicable to residential tenancies will be greatly simplified.

[1643] Law Com. No. 284, para. 3.15. The Law Commission believes that the actual number of agreements affected by these exclusions will be very modest: ibid. Further details of the scope of the scheme, and exclusions from it, are set out in Part VI of the Report.   [1644] Ibid., Part VII.

[1645] Ibid., para. 7.2(7). The model forms will, by definition, be "fair" for the purposes of the Unfair Terms in Consumer Contracts Regulations 1999, which will apply to all occupation agreements covered by the scheme: ibid., paras. 3.4, 3.5.   [1646] Ibid., para. 3.29.

[1647] With two exceptions: tenancies still covered by the Rent Act 1977, and by the Rent (Agriculture) Act 1976: Law Com No. 284, para. 3.20.

The Law Commission now expects to produce its final proposals, and a draft Bill, during 2006. It has also now begun work on two further related topics:[1648]

(1) *Resolving Housing Disputes*, which will consider the law and procedure relating to the resolution of housing disputes, and how in practice they serve landlords, tenants and other users; and

(2) *Ensuring Responsible Renting*, which will consider the legal framework necessary to promote and secure compliance by both landlords and occupiers with their legal obligations (both under the present law and, if implemented, the law as reformed in the light of the Law Commission's proposals on *Renting Homes*), and the procedures (including through the criminal law) available to landlords, occupiers and third parties, with particular regard to preventing or remedying anti-social behaviour by both rental-occupiers and owner-occupiers.

Consultation Papers are promised on both topics during 2006.

[1648] Law Commission, Thirty-ninth Annual Report 2004–05 (Law Com No. 294), paras. 7.2–7.17.

C. Equitable Beneficial Interests in Land

SUMMARY

In this section we consider those estates and interests in the land that may subsist in equity under a settlement or a trust of land: equitable *beneficial* interests in the land. As we shall see, before 1926 a range of interests could be held at law in the land. In addition to the fee simple absolute and the leasehold estate, this included such things as concurrent interests (tenancies in common, as well as joint tenancies), entailed interests and life interests. Under section 1 of the Law of Property Act 1925, however, the only legal estates that can subsist at law are now the fee simple absolute in possession and the term of years absolute, which we have discussed in the earlier sections of this Part. All other beneficial estates and interests in land can subsist only in equity. These are the beneficial interests we shall consider in this section.

In chapters 11 and 12 we first consider the *legal framework* within which equitable beneficial interests have been held in land since 1925: until 1996, within a strict settlement or a trust for sale; and since 1997 within a trust of land. We shall then consider the different *substantive forms* of equitable beneficial interest which can be so held: concurrent beneficial interests, entailed interests, life interests, future interests and certain determinable interests.

11

THE STRICT SETTLEMENT AND THE TRUST FOR SALE BEFORE 1997

SUMMARY

The evolution of the strict settlement and the trust for sale has already been described in the historical introduction.[1]

The system of settlements was radically changed as from 1 January 1997, when the Trusts of Land and Appointment of Trustees Act 1996 came into operation. Thereafter no new strict settlements can be created, existing trusts for sale are retrospectively modified, and a new trust of land is invented.

Since strict settlements created before 1997 continue to exist, it is still important to understand their continuing operation. And an understanding of the trust for sale as it existed before 1997 is also important in order to understand fully the changes made by the 1996 Act in introducing the trust of land. In this chapter we shall discuss the strict settlement and the trust for sale before 1997, and in chapter 12 the trust of land which arises under the Trust of Land and Appointment of Trustees Act 1996 and applies to all settlements thereafter.

---

[1] Pp. 68 et seq, ante.

The general idea of a settlement is to create, by either deed or will, out of real or personal property, a series of beneficial interests in favour of a succession of persons. Before 1997 there were two methods of settling land: either by strict settlement under the Settled Land Act 1925, or by trust for sale under the Law of Property Act 1925.[2] They were mutually exclusive. Indeed it was expressly enacted that the statutory definition of a settlement contained in the Settled Land Act 1925 should not apply to land held upon trust for sale.[3]

It is vital to distinguish the two methods of settlement. The chief practical importance of the distinction is that, upon the occasion of a conveyance, title to settled land must be made by the tenant for life, since the legal estate is vested in him, while title to land held upon trust must be made by the trustees. The result of a mistake in this regard is troublesome and expensive, for a purchaser who takes a conveyance from the trustees when the instrument is a settlement or from the tenant for life in the reverse case, does not thereby acquire the legal estate. We must also reiterate at the outset of the discussion that a purchaser, who takes a conveyance from the correct vendor, takes the land free from the interests of the beneficiaries under the settlement, provided that he pays the purchase money to at least two trustees or to a trust corporation. The interests of the beneficiaries are transferred from the land to the purchase money and are overreached.[4]

Of these two methods of settling land we shall discuss first the strict settlement under the Settled Land Act 1925. Even before 1997, however, mainly due to considerations of taxation, the strict settlement had become less widely used. In particular, the classic strict settlement, which was created on the occasion of a marriage so as to provide for all members of the family and thereby to keep the land as far as possible within the family,[5] was unlikely to be created. The trust for sale was mainly used for family settlements, whether created *inter vivos* or by will; and furthermore its conveyancing machinery was extended by the 1925 legislation to concurrent interests[6] and intestacy.[7]

I The Strict Settlement

A The Definition of a Settlement under the Settled Land Act 1925

The word *settlement* properly so called connotes succession. Its normal meaning is any instrument or series of instruments by which successive interests are carved out of realty or personalty and under which, in the case of land, there will usually be at any given time some person entitled in possession to a beneficial interest for life. But the Settled Land Act 1925 was not content to stop short at cases where there was a succession properly so called. Its further aim was to facilitate dealings wherever the disposition of the land is retarded or obstructed by some impediment affecting its title.

Minority affords a simple illustration. If a favourable offer has been made for the purchase of land to which a minor is entitled in fee simple under a will, the rule that no person

---

[2] See Harvey, *Settlements of Land*.   [3] SLA 1925, s. 1(7).

[4] P. 75, ante. For a full discussion of overreaching, see pp. 994, 997–1002, post.

[5] Pp. 68–9 ante. For a detailed account see Cheshire, *Modern Real Property* (10th edn), pp. 126–31.

[6] Pp. 452, et seq, post.   [7] For a detailed account, see the 16th edn of this book, chap. 26.

under eighteen years of age[8] can execute a valid conveyance will cause the loss of a profitable bargain, unless some way out of the impasse can be found. But all difficulty disappears if the will is regarded as a "settlement" and if some person of full age is designated to exercise the statutory power of sale.

In a case of this nature there is, of course, no settlement and no tenant for life as usually understood, but any device which renders the statutory powers exercisable in respect of the minor's land is an undoubted advantage to all concerned. What the Act did, therefore, with the object of rendering an absolute title easily transferable despite the existence of what would normally be inhibitory factors, was to define "settlement" in broad terms so as to include a number of cases where there was no succession in the ordinary sense, and also, where necessary, to grant the statutory powers to a person who according to ordinary language is not a tenant for life. In fact, not only was the statutory definition of a "settlement" very wide, but wherever there is a settlement within the meaning of the Act and no tenant for life properly so called, and therefore no person normally competent to exercise the statutory powers, one of two things will occur, namely, either some person will be designated by the Act as entitled to exercise the powers; or the powers will be exercisable by trustees, who in this context are called "statutory owners".[9]

A settlement for the purposes of the Act exists in each of the following cases, as long as it was created before 1 January 1997:[10]

(1) Succession

Where land stands limited in trust for any persons by way of succession.

This refers to the normal case where land is limited to a series of persons by way of succession, as for instance to A for life, remainder to B for life, remainder to C in fee simple.[11]

(2) Extended meaning of settlement

We now come to six cases where an extended meaning is given to the word "settlement".

(i) *Entailed interest* Where land stands limited in trust for any person in possession for an entailed interest whether or not capable of being barred or defeated.

(ii) *Base or determinable fee*[12] Where land stands limited in trust for any person in possession for a base or determinable fee or any corresponding interest in leasehold land.

---

[8] P. 911, post. For the terminology of "minor" or "infant" in relation to settled land, see p. 402, n. 14, post.

[9] P. 409, post.   [10] SLA 1925, s. 1; TLATA 1996, s. 2.

[11] It need not be expressly limited. The trust could arise by operation of law, as, for instance, where there is a constructive trust under which the court gives protection to a licensee for the period of his life: *Bannister v Bannister* [1948] 2 All ER 133, M & B p. 615; *Binions v Evans* [1972] Ch 359, M & B p. 617 (Lord DENNING MR dissented on this point at 366); p. 838, post; *Ungurian v Lesnoff* [1990] Ch 206, especially at 224; [1990] CLJ 25 (M. Oldham); [1990] Conv 223 (P. Sparkes); [1991] Conv 596 (J. Hill); *Costello v Costello* (1994) 70 P & CR 297; [1994] Conv 391 (M. P. Thompson). See also *Ivory v Palmer* [1975] ICR 340 at 347, where CAIRNS LJ said "*Binions v Evans* stretched to the very limit the application of the Settled Land Act"; (1977) 93 LQR 561 (J. A. Hornby); *Dent v Dent* [1996] 1 WLR 683 (where the agreement was construed as an irrevocable licence and not a SLA settlement); [1996] All ER Rev 258 (P. J. Clarke). See Harvey, pp. 54, 82 et seq; *Emmet on Title*, paras. 23.004–23.004.3; (1977) 93 LQR 561 (J. A. Hornby); Law Commission Report on Trusts of Land 1989 (Law Com No. 118), para. 4.2. On avoidance of an unintentional creation of a strict settlement in this situation, see *Griffiths v Williams* (1977) 248 EG 947, M & B p. 673, p. 844, post; [1978] Conv 250. For similar problems arising in connection with settlements on divorce, see *Morss v Morss* [1972] Fam 264; *Martin v Martin* [1978] Fam 12; [1978] Conv 229 (P. Smith). See also *Allen v Allen* [1974] 1 WLR 1171 (trust for sale).

[12] Including a fee determinable by condition: SLA 1925, s. 117(1)(iv).

Thus, under (i) and (ii), where the possessor is a tenant in tail or tenant of a base fee, the instrument of creation is a settlement, and the tenant holds the land under a settlement.

(iii) Limitation subject to gift over   Where land stands limited in trust for any person in possession for an estate in fee simple or for a term of years absolute subject to an executory gift over on failure of issue or in any other event.

Thus, where a house is devised to A in fee simple subject to a condition that he resides and provides a home for X there, and if he breaks this condition, then devise over to B in fee simple, the will is a settlement and A is tenant for life within the meaning of the Act.[13]

(iv) Minor   Where land stands limited in trust for any person in possession being a minor, for an estate in fee simple or for a term of years absolute.

A conveyance which purports to grant a fee simple absolute to a minor cannot take effect according to its terms, for a minor is incapable of holding a legal estate. Instead, the conveyance operates as an agreement by the grantor to execute a settlement by means of a vesting deed in favour of trustees (statutory owners),[14] and a trust instrument in favour of the minor.

(v) Springing interests   Where land stands limited in trust for any person to take effect as a fee simple or term of years absolute on the happening of some event.

If, for instance, a fee simple estate is limited in trust for the two sons of X, who attain the age of eighteen years, the first son to reach that age becomes absolutely entitled to a half share, but also entitled to the fee simple in the entirety of the land contingent on the death of his brother before reaching his majority.[15] This is one of the cases where, pending the occurrence of the contingency, the powers are exercisable by the statutory owners.[16]

(vi) Family charges   Where land stands charged voluntarily,[17] or in consideration of marriage or by way of family arrangement[18] with the payment of any rentcharge for the life of any person, or any lesser period,[19] or of any sums for the portions, advancement, maintenance or otherwise for the benefit of any persons.[20]

If, for example, A charges his fee simple absolute with an annuity for his wife and capital sums for his children, the instrument which creates the charge is a "settlement", and, although the rentchargor, A, is not a tenant for life, yet by section 20(1)(ix) of the Settled Land Act 1925 he is given the powers of a tenant for life. Strictly speaking, therefore, he should execute a vesting deed and appoint trustees. If he does so, he may sell the fee simple under the Act, and overreach the rentcharges so as to make them recoverable from the trustees to whom payment will have been made. If, however, the purchaser is willing to buy subject to the charges, A is permitted by the Law of Property (Amendment) Act 1926 to sell

---

[13]   *Re Richardson* [1904] 2 Ch 777.

[14]   SLA 1925, s. 27(1); p. 409, post. SLA 1925 refers to an "infant" rather than a minor. Under Family Law Reform Act 1969, s. 12, "A person who is not of full age may be described as a minor instead of as an infant", and most, but not all, statutes now refer accordingly to "minors". However, the terminology of "infant" in SLA 1925 was not amended. In this book the term "minor" is generally used, in accordance with modern usage: p. 911, post.

[15]   *Re Bird* [1927] 1 Ch 210.   [16]   SLA 1925, s. 23.   [17]   I.e. not for valuable consideration.

[18]   Presumably "family arrangement" in this context includes an arrangement made not voluntarily, but for valuable consideration; cf *Williams v Williams* (1867) 2 Ch App 294 at 301.   [19]   Chap. 20, p. 705, post.

[20]   SLA 1925, s. 1(1)(v); *Re Austen* [1929] 2 Ch 155.

as absolute owner without the necessity of executing a vesting deed. Section 1(1) of this Act provides that: "[n]othing in the Settled Land Act 1925 shall prevent a person on whom the powers of a tenant for life are conferred by section 20(1)(ix) from conveying or creating a legal estate subject to a prior interest as if the land had not been settled land."

(3) Compound settlement

What emerges from the account given above is that a settlement may consist of a number of instruments. This will occur, for instance, where lands, which in the first place have been settled on A for life with remainder in tail to his eldest son, are resettled on A for life, remainder (subject to the charges created by the original settlement) to the eldest son for life, with remainder over. In this case the two settlements may be read as one, being together called a *compound settlement*, [21] and the Act provides that the word *settlement* shall be construed as referring to such compound settlement where it exists.[22]

B The Machinery of a Settlement after 1925

We have already seen that in order to emphasise the separation of the legal estate from the equitable interests of the beneficiaries and also to facilitate a conveyance of the former, the Settled Land Act 1925 introduced a new method for the creation of a settlement by enacting as follows:[23]

Every settlement of a legal estate in land *inter vivos* shall, save as in this Act otherwise provided, be effected by two deeds, namely, a vesting deed and a trust instrument and if effected in any other way shall not operate to transfer or create a legal estate.[24]

This method must now be examined in more detail. We shall first consider the machinery of settlements in unregistered land, which will have been the original method of creation of most settlements that remain in existence today. Then we shall consider briefly the impact of registration of title on settled land.

(1) Settlement *inter vivos*

(a) The vesting deed

The function of the vesting deed is to vest the legal fee simple in the person who for the time being is to have the actual enjoyment of the land, or, if he is a minor or otherwise legally incapable, then to vest it in some other person who is denominated a *statutory owner*.[25] The virtue of thus passing the legal fee simple to a person who is beneficially entitled to some lesser interest is that, should he later desire, in the interests of the beneficiaries generally, to dispose of the fee simple by way of sale, lease or otherwise under one of the powers conferred upon him by the Settled Land Act 1925, he can produce a document which not only shows that the legal estate is vested in him, but also certifies the facts essential to a valid exercise of the statutory power.

This vesting deed, then—called the *principal vesting deed*—conveys to the tenant for life or the statutory owner the whole legal estate which is held upon trust for persons by

---

[21] *Re Ogle's Settled Estates* [1927] 1 Ch 229 at 232–3.　　　[22] SLA 1925, s. 1(1)(i), proviso.

[23] Pp. 96–7, ante.

[24] SLA 1925, s. 4(1). In the case of registered land, a disposition does not operate at law until the registration requirements are met: LRA 2002, s. 27(1); p. 970, post.　　　[25] ibid., ss. 23, 26, 117(1)(xxvi).

way of succession. It is a short document and must contain the following statements and particulars:[26]

(i)   a description, either specific or general, of the settled land;

(ii) a statement that the settled land is vested in the person or persons to whom it is conveyed or in whom it is declared to be vested upon the trusts from time to time affecting the settled land;

(iii) the names of the trustees of the settlement;

(iv) a statement of any powers, over and above those conferred upon every tenant for life by the Act, which it is desired to give to the tenant for life under the settlement;

(v)   the name of any person entitled to appoint new trustees of the settlement.

If after the execution of a principal vesting deed more land is acquired which is to become subject to the settlement, it is conveyed to the tenant for life by what is called a *subsidiary vesting deed*.[27]

(b) The trust instrument

At the same time a second deed, called the trust instrument, is executed which:[28]

(i)   declares the trusts affecting the settled land;

(ii) appoints trustees of the settlement;

(iii) contains the power, if any, to appoint new trustees of the settlement;

(iv) sets out, either expressly or by reference, any powers intended to be conferred by the settlement in extension of those conferred by the Act;

(v)   bears any ad valorem stamp duty which may be payable in respect of the settlement.

Thus it is the trust instrument which declares the trusts upon which the legal estate is to be held. If we look at the vesting deed alone, the tenant for life seems to be fully entitled to sell the fee simple. So he is. An intending purchaser need not look beyond the deed, but at the same time such a person is told in the vesting deed that the land is held upon trust and that there are trustees, and this knowledge places upon him the obligation to pay the purchase money, not to the tenant for life, but to the trustees. If he does this, his obligations are at an end, and it is no concern of his what is done with the money. But what we need to look at is the trust instrument, since it records the equitable interests which it is the object of the settlement to confer upon the beneficiaries. The property comprised in the settlement, whether it remains in the form of land or is sold and converted into money, is actually enjoyed by the persons who are described in, and upon the conditions which are prescribed by, the trust instrument. We must not be misled by the vesting deed into thinking that the

---

[26] SLA 1925, s. 5(1). SLA, Sch. 1, Form No. 2 contained a precedent of a vesting deed. The Schedule was repealed by Statute Law Repeals Act 2004, s. 1, Sch. 12, following a recommendation of the Law Commission on the ground that the guidance contained in such forms, necessary in 1925 when the SLA was new, is no longer necessary as there are now modern precedents in relation to the dwindling number of strict settlements in existence: Statute Law Revision: Seventeenth Report 2003 (Law Com No. 285). For precedents generally, see *Encyclopaedia of Forms and Precedents*, vol. 40(2), part 9.   [27] Ibid., s. 10.

[28] Ibid., s. 4(3). SLA, Sch. 1, Form No. 3 contained a precedent of a trust instrument. The Schedule was repealed by Statute Law Repeals Act 2004, s. 1, Sch. 12; see n. 26, supra.

tenant for life, who is thereby declared to be the fee simple owner, can sell the whole estate and pocket the proceeds.

(2) Settlement by Will

The rule that an *inter vivos* settlement must be created by two contemporaneous deeds called the principal vesting deed and the trust instrument, applies differently to a settlement by will. In this case the legal estate devolves upon the personal representatives of the settlor, who hold it upon trust to convey it to the person entitled to the tenancy for life under the will.[29] This conveyance may be made by a *vesting assent*, that is, by an assent in writing but not under seal.[30] The position then is, that the vesting assent corresponds to the vesting deed that forms part of a settlement *inter vivos*, and the will itself is deemed to be the trust instrument.

(3) Effect of Machinery

(a) Legal estate separated from equitable interests

As a result of this machinery, the legal estate conveyed to the tenant for life by the vesting deed is kept rigorously separate from the equitable interests of the beneficiaries which are created by and contained in the trust instrument. Throughout the duration of the settlement, and however long that duration may be, the legal estate must and will be vested in a person or persons competent to deal with it as permitted by the Act. If no vesting deed has been executed, the tenant for life or statutory owner[31] can require the trustees of the settlement to repair the omission.[32] Normally, the legal estate will remain with the first tenant for life until his death, though in certain exceptional circumstances, as for example where his equitable life interest is forfeited under the terms of the settlement, it will pass to the trustees. On his death it will devolve on the trustees who will as soon as practicable convey it by a vesting assent to the person next entitled.[33]

(b) Evasion of Act prevented

The evasion of the statutory requirement of a vesting deed is prevented by section 13 of the Settled Land Act 1925.[34] This provides that where a tenant for life or statutory owner has become entitled to have a vesting deed or assent executed in his favour, then, until such an instrument has in fact been executed, no disposition of the land made *inter vivos* by any person shall operate to pass a legal estate, unless it is made in favour of a purchaser having no notice that the tenant for life or statutory owner has become so entitled. Such a purported disposition operates as a contract to convey the legal estate as soon as the vesting deed has been executed.[35]

There is an exception, however, in favour of personal representatives, for they are allowed to sell settled land in the ordinary course of administration even though no vesting deed has been executed when their title accrues.[36]

---

[29] SLA 1925, s. 6.   [30] Ibid., s. 8(1).   [31] P. 409, post.   [32] SLA 1925, s. 9(2).
[33] P. 991, post.   [34] SLA 1925, s. 13, as amended by LP(A)A 1926, Schedule.
[35] It should be protected by (in registered land) entry of a notice in the register, or by (in unregistered land) registration as a land charge: p. 880, post.   [36] SLA 1925, s. 13.

(c) Where vesting deed not necessary

Moreover, there are three cases in which there is no necessity for a vesting deed:

(1) WHERE LAND CEASES TO BE SETTLED

If, for instance, a tenant in tail in possession of settled land, free from any trusts or incumbrances, bars the entail before a vesting deed is executed in his favour, he thereby terminates the settlement, and can make title as a fee simple owner.[37]

(2) WHERE BENEFICIARIES TERMINATE SETTLEMENT

Beneficiaries, if of full age, may terminate the settlement and so avoid the necessity for a vesting deed. If, for instance, an owner devised his residence to his wife for life with remainder to his children in fee simple, the widow becomes tenant for life on his death and, as such, entitled to a vesting deed. Instead, however, she may surrender her life interest to the remaindermen in fee, and then all the parties can create a trust for sale—or, since 1997, a trust of land—with themselves as trustees, the income until sale and the ultimate proceeds to be held on trusts corresponding to those of the settlement.

(3) WHERE LAND SUBJECT TO FAMILY CHARGES

If the land has become settled merely because it has been voluntarily subjected to family charges,[38] the tenant for life, as we have seen, is allowed by the Law of Property (Amendment) Act 1926 to convey a legal estate subject to the charges without being required to procure the execution of a vesting deed.[39]

(4) Settlements in Registered Land

Although most settlements that exist today may have been created when the land was unregistered and not yet subject to compulsory registration,[40] the transfer of the legal estate will now require the title to be registered;[41] and dispositions thereafter will be subject to the principles of registered land.[42]

The application of the principles of registered land to settlements under the Settled Land Act 1925 is governed by Schedule 7 of the Land Registration Rules.[43] The legal estate in the settled land must be registered in the name of the tenant for life or statutory owner,[44] and the beneficial interests under the settlement must be protected by the entry of a restriction on the register:[45] they cannot be protected by entry of a notice in the register,[46] nor can they

---

[37] *Re Alefounder's Will Trusts* [1927] 1 Ch 360.   [38] SLA 1925, s. 20(1)(ix).   [39] Pp. 402–3, ante.

[40] P. 101, ante.

[41] LRA 2002, s. 4(1)(a), expressly including a transfer by means of a vesting assent.

[42] Ibid., s. 27.   [43] Ibid., s. 89; LRR 2003, r. 186, Sch 7; H & B, paras. 13.42, 13.43.

[44] LRR 2003, Sch. 7, para. 1. The transfer of registered land into a settlement, and the transfer of the settled land on the succession of a new tenant for life, must contain provisions which mirror those of the vesting deed in unregistered land: (a) that the property is vested on trust (identifying the trust deed or will); (b) the names of the trustees; (c) the name of the person entitled to appoint new trustees; and (d) powers, additional to those conferred by SLA 1925, conferred by the trust deed or will on the tenant for life: ibid., paras. 4(1), 6(1), 12(1).

[45] Ibid., paras. 2, 3. The restriction must be in one of three forms (G, H or I) specified in Sch. 4, depending on whether the tenant for life or statutory owners are registered proprietor, and whether there are trustees of the settlement.   [46] LRA 2002, s. 33(a)(ii).

take effect as overriding interests, even where the beneficiaries are in actual occupation.[47] The restrictions, which are designed to ensure that any sale by the tenant for life complies with the requirements of overreaching,[48] are binding on the registered proprietor during his life but do not affect a disposition by his personal representatives.[49]

Thus, if X is the tenant for life and Y and Z are the trustees of a settlement, X will be the registered proprietor of the fee simple of the settled land and the register will contain a dual restriction, first preventing the registration of any disposition not authorised by the Settled Land Act 1925, and then preventing the registration of any disposition under which capital money arises unless the money is paid to Y and Z or into court.[50] By this means, the beneficial interests of a strict settlement are protected without their details being brought onto the register. There is still a curtain, and a purchaser who complies with the restrictions will overreach the beneficial interests in the same way that he would overreach them in the case of unregistered land.

C The Tenant for Life

(1) Definition of Tenant for Life

A tenant for life is defined as follows in section 19(1) of the Settled Land Act 1925:[51]

The person of full age who is for the time being beneficially entitled under a settlement to possession of settled land for his life is for the purposes of this Act the tenant for life of that land and the tenant for life under that settlement.

He is deemed to be such, notwithstanding that the land or his estate therein is charged with the payment of incumbrances.[52] If two or more persons are jointly entitled to possession they together constitute the tenant for life.[53]

(a) Persons with powers of tenant for life

Obviously however there are several cases where land is settled in the sense that it is subject to a "settlement" within the statutory meaning of that word,[54] and yet where there is no tenant for life as defined in section 19. A tenant in tail in possession is a simple example of the situation.[55] The Act, therefore, takes care to ensure that wherever there is a "settlement" there

---

[47] LRA 2002, Sch. 1, para. 2; Sch. 3, para. 2(a). This was also the position under LRA 1925, s. 86(2); (1958) 22 Conv (NS) 14 at 23–4 (F. R. Crane). Law Commission Third Report on Land Registration 1987 (Law Com No. 158) para. 2.69 recommended that interests under settlements should be capable of being overriding interests; and so did the Law Commission Consultative Document 1998 (Law Com No. 254), para. 5.63.

[48] P. 994, ante.

[49] LRR 2003, Sch. 7, para. 3(3). When the settlement ends on the death of the proprietor, the personal representatives must apply for cancellation of the restriction, but the Registrar does not investigate whether the personal representatives are acting correctly and within their powers: ibid., para. 12(2), (3).

[50] Ibid., Sch. 4, Form G.

[51] Re Jefferys [1939] Ch 205 (an annuitant is not a tenant for life); Re Carne's Settled Estates [1899] 1 Ch 324 ("to occupy the land rent free so long as she might wish to do so" held to be a tenant for life); Ayer v Benton (1967) 204 EG 359; Re Catling [1931] 2 Ch 359 (wife as tenant at a nominal annual sum, the tenancy not to be determined so long as she made the property her principal place of residence; held not to be a tenant for life; and indeed there was no settlement); Re Waleran Settled Estates [1927] 1 Ch 522 (a term to a woman "for 99 years if she should so long live" held to be a tenant for life); Re Ogle's Settled Estates [1927] 1 Ch 229, p. 403, ante; Re Cayley and Evans' Contract [1930] 2 Ch 143; Re Gallenga Will Trusts [1938] 1 All ER 106.

[52] SLA 1925, s. 19(4).   [53] Ibid., s. 19(2).   [54] Pp. 400-3, ante.   [55] P. 401, ante.

shall always be some person with the powers of a tenant for life. In the first place section 20 provides that the following persons shall have the powers of a tenant for life and shall be included in the expression "tenant for life".[56]

(i)   A tenant in tail, including both a tenant after possibility[57] and one who is by Act of Parliament restrained from barring his estate tail, but excluding a tenant in tail whose land has been bought with money provided by Parliament in consideration of public services.

(ii) A person entitled to land for an estate in fee simple or for a term of years absolute, subject to a gift over on failure of his issue or in any other event.[58]

(iii) A person entitled to a base[59] or a determinable fee[60] or a corresponding interest in leaseholds.

(iv) A tenant for years determinable on life, not holding merely under a lease at a rent.

We have seen that leases *at a rent* for a term of years determinable at the death of the tenant are now converted into terms for ninety years,[61] and that such a person cannot have the powers of a tenant for life,[62] but this conversion does not operate where such a term takes effect under a settlement. For instance, a devisee to whom lands are given for thirty years if he should so long live has the powers of a tenant for life.

(v)   A tenant pur autre vie not holding merely under a lease at a rent.[63]

(vi) A tenant for his own or any other life, or for years determinable on life, whose interest is liable to cease in any event during that life, or is subject to a trust for accumulation of income.

For instance, a devise to A so long as he shall live on the estate for at least three months in each year, with a gift over to B upon failure to observe this condition, makes A tenant for life within section 20.[64]

(vii) A tenant by the curtesy.[65]

(viii) A person entitled to the *income* of land under a trust for payment thereof to him during his own or any other life,[66] or until sale of the land, or until some event (e.g. bankruptcy) terminates his interest. But if the land is subject to an immediate binding trust for sale, the person so entitled does not have the powers of a tenant for life.

(ix) A person beneficially entitled to land for an estate in fee simple or for a term of years absolute subject to any estates, interests, charges or powers of charging, subsisting or capable of being exercised under a settlement.

If, for instance, lands are settled on A for life with remainder in fee simple to his eldest son B, with powers for A to charge the land with portions for his younger children, B, on the

---

[56] SLA 1925, s. 117(1)(xxviii).   [57] P. 488, post.

[58] But a gift over on failure of issue becomes incapable of taking effect as soon as there is any issue who attains eighteen: LPA 1925, s. 134(1), as amended by Family Law Reform Act 1969, s. 1(3), Sch. 1.

[59] Pp. 498–9, post.   [60] Pp. 567 et seq, post.   [61] LPA 1925, s. 149(6), p. 210, ante.

[62] *Re Catling* [1931] 2 Ch 359.   [63] *Re Johnson* [1914] 2 Ch 134.

[64] *Re Paget* (1885) 30 Ch D 161.   [65] P. 486, post.

[66] *Re Llanover Settled Estates* [1926] Ch 626.

death of A, will hold the fee simple subject to any such charges that may have been created. He is tenant for life under the above clause and as such can deal with the estate, notwithstanding the charge to which it is subject.[67]

(b) Statutory owners

Comprehensive though this list is, it still fails to provide for the case of every settlement. For instance, a settlement within the meaning of the Settled Land Act 1925 exists if land is limited in trust for any person in fee simple contingently upon the happening of some event,[68] or when the person entitled in possession is entitled only to a *part* of the income from the trust[69] or where no person is entitled to any of its income at all as in the case of a discretionary strict settlement where the trustees are directed to pay the income to such members of a class of persons as they may think fit.[70] In none of these cases is the beneficiary a tenant for life or a person who has the powers of a tenant for life. The Act, therefore, provides that where such a situation arises the legal estate shall be vested in statutory owners—that is to say:

(a) any person of full age on whom they are conferred by the settlement; and

(b) in any other case the trustees of the settlement.[71]

Further, where the person who would otherwise be a tenant for life is a minor, the legal estate and statutory powers are vested during the minority of the minor in:

(a) a personal representative, if the settled land is vested in him and no vesting instrument has yet been executed; and

(b) in every other case, the trustees of the settlement.[72]

(2) Powers of Tenant for Life

In accordance with the policy that has prevailed since the Settled Land Act 1882, the person vested with the legal estate, normally the tenant for life in actual possession, is empowered by the Settled Land Act 1925 to manage and even to dispose of the fee simple, an aspect of his position that must now be developed in some detail. The general policy is that he shall have many of the powers of dealing with the land that are available to an estate owner entitled beneficially in his own right, but subject to this overriding proviso, that any gain accruing from the exercise of a power shall be held on trust for the equitable beneficiaries according to the limitations of the settlement. To this end the Act confers upon the tenant for life the right to exercise any of the following powers:

(a) Powers exercisable by tenant for life

(1) POWERS TO SELL OR EXCHANGE

The tenant for life may sell the settled land, or any part thereof, or any easement, right or privilege of any kind over or in relation to the land.[73] Every sale must be made for the best

---

[67] He also has the option under LP(A)A 1926, s. 1(1), pp. 402–3, ante, of conveying the legal estate to a purchaser subject to the charge, provided that the purchaser is agreeable.   [68] *Re Bird* [1927] 1 Ch 210; p. 402, ante.
[69] *Re Frewen* [1926] Ch 580.   [70] *Re Gallenga Will Trusts* [1938] 1 All ER 106.
[71] SLA 1925, ss. 23, 117(1)(xxvi).
[72] Ibid., s. 26; pp. 420–2, post. For the terminology of "minor" or "infant" in relation to settled land, see p. 402, n. 14, ante.   [73] Ibid., s. 38(i).

consideration in money that can reasonably be obtained,[74] but instead of being made in return for a lump sum it may be made in consideration, wholly or partly, of a rent payable yearly or half-yearly and secured upon the land sold. Such a rent may be perpetual or terminable, and in the latter case—that is to say, when it will cease to be payable after a certain number of years—it must be treated partly as principal and partly as interest, and the part constituting principal must be dealt with as capital money. The interest accruing on the principal sum must be accumulated by way of compound interest and added each year to capital.[75] The rent must be the best that can reasonably be obtained, though for a period not exceeding five years from the sale it may be nominal.[76] The statutory remedies for the recovery of a rentcharge given by the Law of Property Act 1925[77] lie for recovery of the rent.[78]

It is also provided that where the land is sold to any company incorporated by special Act of Parliament or by any order having the force of an Act of Parliament, the purchase money may consist, either wholly or partially, of fully-paid securities of any description of the purchasing company.[79]

The tenant for life may make an exchange of the whole or part of the land, or of any easement, right, or privilege over it, for other land or for an easement, right, or privilege over other land, and he may pay or accept money in order to render the exchanges equal in value.[80]

When a sale or exchange is made, the tenant for life is permitted to except the mines and minerals, and in such a case to reserve for the settled land all proper rights and powers incidental to mining purposes.[81]

The powers of sale and exchange are exercisable with regard to any principal mansion-house which stands on the settled land, but in two cases mere notice to the trustees of the proposed transaction[82] does not suffice, and the tenant for life must first obtain either the consent of the trustees or an order of the court, namely:

(i)   where the settlement existed before 1926, and does not expressly dispense with the necessity for such consent or order; and

(ii)   where the settlement came into operation after 1925, but contains a provision that such consent or order is necessary.

The court must determine as a fact whether any particular house is a principal mansion-house,[83] but it is enacted that a house which is usually occupied as a farmhouse, or which, together with its pleasure-grounds and park and lands, does not exceed 25 acres in extent, is not a principal mansion-house within the meaning of the Act and can in all cases be disposed of without the consent of the trustees.[84]

(2)   POWER TO GRANT LEASES

The tenant for life may lease the whole or part of the land or any easement, right, or privilege incidental thereto for any purpose whatever, whether involving waste or not, for any of the following maximum periods:[85]

(a)   999 years for a building lease;

(b)   100 years for a mining lease;

---

[74] SLA 1925, s. 39(1); *Wheelwright v Walker* (1883) 31 WR 912.   [75] Ibid., s. 39(2).
[76] Ibid., s. 39(3).   [77] S. 121; p. 712, post.   [78] LP(A)A 1926, Schedule.
[79] SLA 1925, s. 39(5).   [80] Ibid., ss. 38(iii), 40.   [81] Ibid., s. 50.   [82] P. 415, post.
[83] *Re Feversham Settled Estate* [1938] 2 All ER 210.   [84] SLA 1925, s. 65.   [85] Ibid., s. 41.

(c) 999 years for a forestry lease;

(d) 50 years for any other kind of lease.[86]

When any of the above leases is made:

(i)   the tenant for life must give one month's notice in writing to the trustees;[87]

(ii) he must procure the best rent reasonably obtainable;[88] and

(iii) the lease must be by deed and must contain a covenant by the lessee for payment of the rent, and a condition allowing the tenant for life to re-enter if the rent is not paid within a specific time not exceeding thirty days.

The deed must be so framed that the lessee will take possession within twelve months, but if the land is already leased to a third person, then, provided that such existing lease has no more than seven years to run, it is lawful to grant a reversionary lease to take effect in possession when the existing one determines.[89]

Without any notice to the trustees, a lease may be granted for a term not exceeding twenty-one years at the best rent that can reasonably be obtained without a fine, provided that the lessee is made impeachable for waste.[90] If the lease does not exceed three years, it may be made by writing without a deed, but the lessee must enter into a written agreement to pay the rent.[91]

As in the case of the power of sale, the tenant for life may lease the land and reserve the minerals,[92] and if he desires to lease the principal mansion-house, he must obtain the consent of the trustees in the cases which have been specified above.[93]

Special provisions are inserted in the Act with regard to building, mining and forestry leases:

(i) Building leases

A building lease[94] must be made partly in consideration of the lessee or some other person erecting new or additional buildings or improving or repairing buildings, and partly in consideration of the payment of rent. A peppercorn or nominal rent may be reserved for the first five years of the term.[95] A lease is valid although it does not specify a definite time within which the building or rebuilding shall begin.[96]

(ii) Mining leases

As regards minerals the rule at common law was that a tenant for life unimpeachable for waste[97] could *open* and work mines and retain the whole profits, though this right can no longer be exercised without the permission of the local planning authority, since it involves a material change in the user of land within the meaning of the Town and Country Planning Act 1990.[98] A tenant for life impeachable for waste cannot *open* mines, but he can continue

---

[86] Law Reform Committee 23rd Report (The Powers and Duties of Trustees) 1982 (Cmnd 8733), para. 8.6 recommended that this period be increased to 99 years.   [87] SLA 1925, s. 101.

[88] Ibid., s. 42(1)(ii); *Re Morgan's Lease* [1972] Ch 1; (1971) 87 LQR 338 (D. W. Elliott). As to whether a tenant for life has power to insert a rent review clause in the lease, see [1979] Conv 258 (M. Dockray); Law Reform Committee 23rd Report, supra, para. 8.4, recommended that this doubt be removed.

[89] Ibid., s. 42(1)(i).   [90] For the meaning of waste, see p. 505, post.   [91] SLA 1925, s. 42(5)(ii).

[92] Ibid., s. 50.   [93] Ibid., s. 65, p. 410, ante.   [94] P. 363, ante.   [95] SLA 1925, s 44

[96] *Re Grosvenor Settled Estates* [1933] Ch 97.   [97] For the meaning of waste, see p. 505, post.

[98] P. 1019, post.

to work to his own profit those that have already been lawfully opened by a predecessor.[99] These rules were varied by the Settled Land Act 1925. If the tenant for life is impeachable for waste in respect of minerals, three-quarters of the rent arising from a mining lease becomes capital; if unimpeachable, one-quarter becomes capital and the residue goes to him as income.[100] A tenant for life who is impeachable for waste under the settlement is not impeachable in respect of mines that have been lawfully opened by a predecessor, and therefore he is entitled to three-fourths of the rents.[101] These rules with regard to minerals have lost much of their importance since the passing of the Coal Industry Nationalisation Act 1946, but they are still material, for "minerals" include "all substances in, on or under the land, obtainable by underground or by surface working".[102]

(iii) Forestry lease

A forestry lease is defined by the Act as a "lease to the Forestry Commissioners for any purpose for which they are authorized to acquire land by the Forestry Act [1967]",[103] but this is now to be construed as a reference to the Minister of Environment, Food and Rural Affairs, in whom the former powers of the Commissioners to acquire land are now vested.[104] In a forestry lease the rent may be nominal for any period not exceeding the first ten years or may be made to vary according to the value of the timber cut in any one year, and any other provisions may be made for the sharing of the profits of the user of the land between the tenant for life and the Minister.[105]

(3) POWER TO RAISE MONEY BY THE GRANT OF A LEGAL MORTGAGE OF THE SETTLED LAND

A capital sum of money may be raised by mortgage in order to meet some expense that is connected with the settled land or desirable in the interests of its prosperity. There are nine different purposes specified by the Act for which a tenant for life may raise money in this manner, but as five of these are connected with the conversion of copyhold into socage[106] and perpetually renewable leases into long terms, it is only necessary to notice that a mortgage of the legal estate is permissible when the object is:[107]

(a) The discharge of an incumbrance on the settled land.

If, for instance, different parts of the land are subject to three separate mortgages, the tenant for life may grant a new mortgage of the entire land to another mortgagee and use the money to pay off the three original debts.[108]

The incumbrance must be permanent, thus excluding any annual sum payable only during a life or for a term of years.[109]

---

[99] *Re Hall* [1916] 2 Ch 488.
[100] SLA 1925, s. 47. These provisions may be displaced by the settlement: s. 48.
[101] *Re Chaytor* [1900] 2 Ch 804; *Re Fitzwalter* [1943] Ch 285.   [102] SLA 1925, s. 117(1)(xv).
[103] Ibid., s. 117(1)(x); Forestry Act 1967, Sch. 6, para. 5.
[104] Forestry Act 1967, s. 50, Sch. 6, para. 5. In this capacity the Minister is the successor in England to the Minister of Agriculture, Fisheries and Food, referred to in the Forestry Act. The National Assembly for Wales has responsibility for forestry in Wales: SI 1999 No. 672, art. 2, Sch. 1.   [105] SLA 1925, s. 48.
[106] P. 83, ante.
[107] SLA 1925, s. 71. See also Leasehold Reform Act 1967, s. 6(5); CLRA 2002, s. 109(4)(b).
[108] *Re Clifford* [1902] 1 Ch 87.   [109] SLA 1925, s. 71(2).

(b) Payment for any improvement authorised by the Settled Land Act 1925 or by the settlement.

This is a valuable power that was introduced in 1925. A tenant for life may spend existing capital money on carrying out any of the improvements authorised by the Act.[110]

(c) Equality of exchange.

(d) Payment of the costs of any transaction effected under (a) to (c) above.

A legal mortgage by the tenant for life may take the form either of a charge by deed by way of legal mortgage or of a long lease,[111] and a tenant for life who grants a mortgage term for any of the above four purposes is not subject to those provisions of the Settled Land Act[112] which in a normal case restrict the length of lease that may be made.[113]

This must be distinguished from the case where the tenant for life borrows money for his own purposes by mortgaging his beneficial interest, as for instance his equitable life interest.[114]

(4) POWER TO EFFECT IMPROVEMENTS

The tenant for life is empowered to effect certain authorised improvements on the land and to have the cost defrayed out of capital.[115] Moreover, his right to this payment, unlike the practice prevailing before 1926, is no longer conditional on his submitting a scheme of operations to the trustees or to the court before the work is done.[116] The Act authorises thirty-four specific improvements which are classified into three categories according to the permanence or impermanence of their results:[117]

Part I improvements comprise twenty-five different works that clearly increase the permanent capital value of the land, such as drainage, irrigation, bridges, defences against water, the provision of farmhouses and cottages for labourers and the rebuilding of the mansion house.

Part II improvements are those, the lasting value of which is more doubtful, such as the erection of houses for land agents, the repair of damage due to dry rot or boring for water.

Part III improvements are those whose value is transitory, as, for example, the installation of a heating or electric power apparatus for buildings, the wiring of a house for electricity or the purchase of moveable machinery for farming or other purposes.

(5) POWER TO ACCEPT LEASES OF OTHER LAND

A new power was introduced by the Settled Land Act 1925 allowing the tenant for life to accept a lease of any other land[118] or of mines and minerals, or of any easement, right or privilege, "convenient to be held or worked with or annexed in enjoyment to the settled land", and there is no limit to the length of the term which he may so accept.[119]

---

[110] SLA 1925, s. 83, infra.

[111] Pp. 725, et seq, post. A mortgage of registered land can no longer be made by demise: p. 724, post.

[112] P. 410, ante.   [113] SLA 1925, s. 71(3).   [114] P. 732, post.   [115] SLA 1925, s. 83.

[116] Ibid., s. 84(1).   [117] Ibid., Sch. 3. For the significance of this classification, see p. 425, post.

[118] This includes a power to accept an extended lease under Leasehold Reform Act 1967, s. 6(2)(a); p. 367, ante.   [119] SLA 1925, s. 53.

(6) MISCELLANEOUS POWERS

There are several miscellaneous powers which the tenant for life is entitled to exercise, and of these the following may be mentioned:

(i) *Power to contract*

Power to contract to make any sale, exchange, mortgage, charge or other disposition authorised by the Act.[120] The transaction must be in conformity with the Act at the time of the performance of the contract. Thus in the case of a contract for a lease the lease must satisfy the requirement that the rent must be the best reasonably obtainable when the lease is granted.[121] Such contracts are enforceable by and against every successor in title of the tenant for life.[122]

(ii) *Power to grant options*

Power to grant, by writing, with or without consideration, an option to purchase or take a lease of settled land, or any easement, right, or privilege over it.[123] The price or rent must be the best reasonably obtainable and must be fixed when the option is granted.[124] The option must be made exercisable within an agreed number of years not exceeding ten.

(iii) *Power to accept surrender of leases*

Power to accept, with or without consideration, a surrender of any lease of settled land.[125]

(iv) *Power to grant land for public purposes*

Power, if the result will be for the general benefit of the settled land, to make grants or leases at a nominal price or rent for certain public and charitable purposes, for example, the grant of land not exceeding one acre for a village institute or a public library.[126]

(v) *Power to provide land for working classes*

Power to grant or lease a restricted amount of land at a nominal price or rent for the purpose of providing allotments or dwellings for the working classes.[127]

(vi) *Power to sell timber*

Power with the consent of the trustees or under an order of the court for a tenant for life who is impeachable for waste to sell timber that is ripe and fit for cutting, provided, however, that three-quarters of the net proceeds become capital money and one-quarter becomes income.[128]

(vii) *Power to sell heirlooms*

Power under an order of the court to sell heirlooms, but in such a case the money arising from the sale becomes capital money, which in this case may be spent on the purchase of other heirlooms.[129]

---

[120] SLA 1925, s. 90.   [121] *Re Rycroft's Settlement* [1962] Ch 263.   [122] SLA 1925, s. 90(2).
[123] Ibid., s. 51.
[124] *Re Morgan's Lease* [1972] Ch 1; Law Reform Committee 23rd Report (The Powers and Duties of Trustees) 1982 (Cmnd 8733), para. 8.10 recommended that the tenant for life should be given the power to grant an option at a price to be fixed at the time of the exercise of the option.   [125] SLA 1925, s. 52.
[126] Ibid., s. 55.   [127] Ibid., s. 57(2).   [128] Ibid., s. 66.   [129] Ibid., s. 67.

(viii) Power to appoint agents

Power to appoint agents, subject to certain restrictions; and to remunerate them and to reimburse their expenses.[130]

(ix) Power to insure

Power to insure under the terms of the Trustee Act 1925, section 19.[131]

(7) POWER TO EFFECT ANY TRANSACTION UNDER ORDER OF COURT

"Any transaction" within the powers of an absolute owner may be sanctioned by the court if this will be for the benefit of the settled land or the beneficiaries, even though it is a transaction not otherwise authorised by the Act or the settlement.[132] Thus approval was given to a scheme to raise money out of capital to enable the tenant for life to continue to reside in the mansion house;[133] and it has been held that the court has jurisdiction to authorise the tenant for life to vary the beneficial interest of an ascertained beneficiary of full age and capacity, even if that beneficiary did not consent.[134] Moreover the width of the definition of "transaction" enables the court to alter the beneficial interests under the settlement. This was commonly done for the purpose of saving estate duty on the death of beneficiaries, and the jurisdiction was largely superseded by that given to the court under the Variation of Trusts Act 1958.[135] Both jurisdictions still remain.

(b) Notice, consent or court order

As a general rule a tenant for life need not obtain the consent of the trustees to his exercise of a power, but if he intends to sell, exchange, mortgage or charge the land, to make a lease exceeding twenty-one years or to grant an option to purchase or to take a lease of the land, he must notify the trustees of his intention at least one month before he completes the transaction.[136] Except in the case of a proposed mortgage or charge, it is permissible, indeed usual, to give a general notice, that is one which states his intention to grant, for example, leases from time to time, without mentioning any specific lease already arranged.[137] There

---

[130] SLA 1925, s. 107(1A)(a) and (b), inserted by TA 2000, s. 40(1), Sch. 2, Pt II, para. 17. The exercise of this power is subject to the duty of care under TA 2000, s. 1 and Sch. 1: ibid., s. 107(1A)(d).

[131] Ibid., s. 107(1A)(c), inserted by TA 2000, s. 40(1), Sch. 2, Pt II, para. 17. The exercise of this power is subject to the duty of care under TA 2000, s. 1 and Sch. 1: ibid., s. 107(1A)(d). TA 1925 s. 19 was substituted by TA 2000, s. 34(1).

[132] Ibid., s. 64(1). "Transaction" is defined in s. 64(2) as amended by Settled Land and Trustee Acts (Court's General Powers) Act 1943, s. 2. *Re White-Popham Settled Estates* [1936] Ch 725; *Re Scarisbrick Re-Settlement Estates* [1944] Ch 229; *Re Earl of Mount Edgcumbe* [1950] Ch 615; *Re Simmons* [1956] Ch 125; *Re Rycroft's Settlement* [1962] Ch 263; *Raikes v Lygon* [1988] 1 WLR 281. For a brief summary of these cases, see M & B p. 344.

[133] *Re Scarisbrick Re-Settlement Estates*, supra.

[134] *Hambro v Duke of Marlborough* [1994] Ch 158, M & B p. 345; [1994] Conv 492 (E. Cooke) (Blenheim Parliamentary Estates).   [135] See generally H & M, chap. 22; Harris, *Variation of Trusts*, pp. 19–22.

[136] SLA 1925, s. 101(1). Law Reform Committee 23rd Report, para. 8.9, recommended that on receipt of the notice the trustees should require the tenant for life to submit to them a valuation, so that they may control the transaction more effectively.   [137] Ibid., s. 101(2).

are, however, as we have seen, several cases in which something more than notice is required, and it may be helpful to restate these in summary form:

First, an order of the court must be obtained before the tenant for life may:

   (i)   grant more than the amount of land specified in the Act for providing allotments or dwellings for the working classes;[138]

  (ii) buy or sell heirlooms;[139]

 (iii) grant building or mining leases for terms longer than those specified in the Act.[140]

Secondly, *either* an order of the court *or* the consent of the trustees must be obtained before the tenant for life may:

   (i)   sell or lease the principal mansion-house in the cases specified above;[141]

  (ii) sell the timber in the event of his being impeachable for waste.[142]

Thirdly, there are two cases in which the tenant for life must obtain the consent in writing of the trustees, namely, before he:

   (i)   compromises or otherwise settles any claim or dispute relating to the settled land;[143]

  (ii) releases, waives or modifies a right imposed on other land for the benefit of the settled land, as, for instance, an easement or a covenant.[144]

(3) Position of Tenant for Life

(a) Additions to and reductions from powers

Such, then, are the powers conferred upon the tenant for life by the Act, but it must be remembered that there is nothing to prevent additional powers being given to him by the settlement, for it is expressly provided[145] that when a settlor authorises the exercise of any powers additional to or larger than those enumerated above, they shall operate in exactly the same manner and with the same results as if they had been permitted by the Act. Thus a settlement may allow the tenant for life:

   (i)   to grant a lease to take effect in possession not later than three years after its date;

  (ii) to use as income the whole of the rent reserved on a mining lease; or

 (iii) to raise money on mortgage for the purchase of a dwelling house.[146]

In fact all the powers given by a settlement are expressly preserved, for it is provided that nothing in the Act shall take away, abridge or prejudicially affect any power under the settlement which is exercisable by the tenant for life or by the trustees with the consent of the tenant for life.[147] If, however, there is any conflict between the Act and the settlement, the Act prevails, and any power (not being a mere power of revocation or appointment[148]) conferred on the trustees becomes exercisable by the tenant for life as an additional power.[149]

---

[138] SLA 1925, s. 57(2).   [139] Ibid., s. 67.   [140] Ibid., s. 46.

[141] Ibid., s. 65; p. 410, ante.   [142] Ibid., s. 66.   [143] Ibid., s. 58(1).   [144] Ibid., s. 58(2).

[145] Ibid., s. 109.

[146] For an example of such an express power, see *City of London Building Society v Flegg* [1988] AC 54.

[147] SLA 1925, s. 108(1).

[148] As, for example, where land is limited upon such trusts as T shall appoint, and subject thereto to A for life. Here, T's power to revoke the life interest and to appoint new interests remains exercisable by him: Wolstenholme and Cherry, *Conveyancing Statutes*, 13th edn, vol. 3, p. 222.   [149] SLA 1925, s. 108(2).

Such a conflict occurs, for instance, if the settlement empowers the tenant for life to sell with the consent of a third person, for such a conditional power is inconsistent with the unfettered power of sale given by the Act.[150] Though a settlor is allowed to confer upon the tenant for life the right to exercise powers additional to those permissible under the statute, it is enacted that any provisions inserted in the settlement with a view to cutting down the statutory powers shall be void. Section 106 of the Settled Land Act 1925 provides:

If in a settlement, will, assurance, or other instrument ... a provision is inserted:

(a) purporting or attempting, by way of direction, declaration, or otherwise, to forbid a tenant for life or statutory owner to exercise any power under this Act, or his right to require the settled land to be vested in him; or

(b) attempting, or tending, or intended, by a limitation, gift, or disposition over of settled land, or by a limitation, gift, or disposition of other real or any personal property, or by the imposition of any condition, or by forfeiture, or in any other manner whatever, to prohibit or prevent him from exercising, or to induce him to abstain from exercising, or to put him into a position inconsistent with his exercising, any power under this Act, or his right to require the settled land to be vested in him;

that provision, as far as it purports, or attempts, or tends, or is intended to have or would or might have, the operation aforesaid, shall be deemed to be void.[151]

A condition that is sometimes inserted in settlements requiring the tenant for life to reside on the settled land will serve to illustrate the application of this section. Suppose that land is settled on X for life with a proviso that if he does not reside on the settled land for at least three months in each year he shall forfeit his interest. Such a clause is void so far as it "tends" to hinder or obstruct the exercise by X of his statutory powers. This, of course, is its natural tendency, for if he sells or leases the estate he must necessarily infringe the condition as to residence. It is a deterrent of this nature that is within the mischief of the section, and the rule therefore is that, notwithstanding a disposition of the land under his statutory powers, his life interest in the income remains intact.[152] If, on the other hand, there is no question of the exercise of the powers, his failure to satisfy the condition operates as a forfeiture of his interest.[153] If it has never been his intention to exercise the powers, it cannot be said that the condition has in any way hampered his freedom of action.

Another example of the operation of the section is this:

If the settlor vests a fund of money in the trustees, with authority to apply the income thereof upon the maintenance of the estate and to pay any surplus not required for that purpose to the tenant for life, X, the prospect of losing this income might tend to dissuade X from exercising his power of sale. As a general rule, therefore, if X sells the land he still remains entitled to the income for life.[154]

---

[150] *Re Jefferys* [1939] Ch 205, M & B p. 346; (1939) 55 LQR 22 (H.P.).

[151] *Re Aberconway's Settlement Trusts* [1953] Ch 647.

[152] *Re Paget's Settled Estates* (1885) 30 Ch D 161; *Re Patten* [1929] 2 Ch 276 (an excellent example of the principle); *Re Orlebar* [1936] Ch 147.

[153] *Re Acklom* [1929] 1 Ch 195, M & B p. 347; *Re Haynes* (1887) 37 Ch D 306; *Re Trenchard* [1902] 1 Ch 378.

[154] *Re Ames* [1893] 2 Ch 479, M & B p. 346; *Re Herbert* [1946] 1 All ER 421; cf *Re Burden* [1948] Ch 160; *Re Aberconway's Settlement Trusts*, supra; [1954] CLJ 60 (R. N. Gooderson).

(b) Non-assignability of powers

Again, as long as the land remains settled, the powers of a tenant for life are indestructible in the sense that they are not capable of assignment or release, but remain exercisable by him notwithstanding any assignment by operation of law or otherwise of his beneficial interest under the settlement.[155] Thus:

If land stands settled on A for life, remainder to B for life with remainder over, and B sells his reversionary life interest for value to X, the statutory power to grant leases after the death of A is exercisable by B, for the design of the Act is to enable a tenant for life to exercise his powers whether he has disposed of his beneficial interest or not.[156]

In such a case as this the former rule was that B could not exercise his powers without the consent of his assignee for value, X, but the necessity for such consent has now been removed by the Act.[157] The rights of the assignee are, however, protected, for whatever interest he had in the property originally assigned to him he has a corresponding interest in any money, securities or land into which that property may have been converted as a result of the exercise of some power.[158] Moreover, notice of an intended transaction must be given to him.[159]

If, however, it is shown to the satisfaction of the court that a tenant for life has by reason of bankruptcy, assignment, incumbrance, or otherwise ceased to have a substantial interest in the settled land, and has unreasonably refused to exercise the statutory powers, an order may be made authorising the trustees of the settlement to exercise the powers in his name.[160] The mere fact that he has grossly neglected the land and has allowed it to become derelict does not justify the making of an order. The court must be satisfied that there has been an unreasonable refusal to exercise the powers.[161]

Although any attempted assignment of the powers by the tenant for life is void, it is provided that if the life interest, with the intention of causing its extinction, is surrendered to the remainderman or reversioner next entitled under the settlement, the statutory powers shall cease to be available to the tenant for life and shall be exercisable as if he were dead.[162] For instance, if a tenant for life becomes bankrupt and the trustee sells his life interest to the tenant in tail in remainder,[163] or if a father surrenders his life interest to the tenant in tail in remainder, the statutory powers become exercisable by the tenant in tail.

(c) Fiduciary nature of powers

(1) TENANT FOR LIFE A TRUSTEE

Finally, it must be observed that the tenant for life, though he is given an almost unfettered liberty to exercise the statutory powers, is at the same time constituted trustee for all interested

---

155 SLA 1925, s. 104(1).
156 *Re Barlow's Contract* [1903] 1 Ch 382; *Earl of Lonsdale v Lowther* [1900] 2 Ch 687.
157 SLA 1925, s. 104(4).   158 Ibid., s. 104(4)(a).   159 Ibid., s. 104(4)(c).
160 Ibid., s. 24(1). This section does not apply to a statutory owner: *Re Craven Settled Estates* [1926] Ch 985.
161 *Re Thornhill's Settlement* [1940] 4 All ER 83; affd. [1941] Ch 24, M & B p. 349.
162 SLA 1925, s. 105(1). LP(A)A 1926, Sch. A remainderman or reversioner does not qualify if there is an intervening limitation which may take effect: *Re Maryon-Wilson's Instruments* [1971] Ch 789.
163 *Re Shawdon Estates Settlement* [1930] 1 Ch 217; affd. [1930] 2 Ch 1, M & B p. 349.

parties. Section 107(1) of the Settled Land Act 1925 provides that:

A tenant for life or statutory owner shall, in exercising any power under this Act, have regard to the interests of all parties entitled under the settlement, and shall, in relation to the exercise thereof by him, be deemed to be in the position and to have the duties and liabilities of a trustee for those parties.[164]

Several judicial pronouncements have placed those duties on a high level. It has been said that the duty to "have regard to the interests of all parties" requires the tenant for life to consider all the interests in the widest sense, not merely pecuniary interests, but even the aspirations and sentiments of the family.[165] As Lord ESHER said:

He must take all the circumstances of the family, and of each member of the family who may be affected by what he is about to do; he must consider them all carefully, and must consider them in the way that an honest outside trustee would consider them; then he must come to what, in his judgment, is the right thing to do under the circumstances—not the best thing, but the right thing to do.[166]

Nevertheless, having regard to the deliberate policy of the Act in conferring upon the tenant for life virtually the status of absolute owner, this super-imposed trusteeship is somewhat abnormal, for in the nature of things it must inevitably be "a highly interested trusteeship".[167] The mere imposition of a trust is insufficient to ensure that powers, so freely confided to the judgment of the tenant for life, will not be exercised from motives of selfishness and personal aggrandisement. A tenant for life, who, with the object of securing a larger income in order to meet his debts or to indulge expensive tastes, or to relieve himself from the cares of management, or because he is hostile to the remainderman, sells land that will obviously be of far greater value in a few years' time, owing perhaps to rapidly changing conditions in the neighbourhood, can scarcely be described as acting "as an upright independent and righteous man would act in dealing with the affairs of others",[168] and yet none of these facts alone is sufficient to render him liable, provided that he obtains the best price reasonably obtainable and otherwise observes the requirements of the Act.[169]

The Court may, however, intervene upon clear proof that the tenant for life has exercised a power with the sole object of conferring some benefit upon himself or upon some relative other than the remainderman, as, for example, where he accepts a bribe from a lessee,[170] where he makes an unsuitable investment,[171] or where a widow entitled for life *durante viduitate* makes a lease to her second intended husband in order to ensure her continued occupation of the premises.[172]

---

[164] SLA 1925, s. 107(1) re-enacting s. 53 of the 1882 Act; *Re Pelly's Will Trusts* [1957] Ch 1 at 18.

[165] *Re Marquis of Ailesbury's Settled Estates* [1892] 1 Ch 506, at 536, per LINDLEY LJ; and see BOWEN LJ passim. "He must act as an upright, independent and righteous man would act in dealing with the affairs of others," at 546, per FRY LJ.   [166] *Re Earl of Radnor's Will Trusts* (1890) 45 Ch D 402 at 417.

[167] *Re Stamford and Warrington* [1916] 1 Ch 404 at 420, per YOUNGER J. TA 2000 extended the powers of the tenant for life in relation to the employment and remuneration of agents, and insurance, subject however to the duty of care under TA 2000, s. 1 and Sch. 1: SLA 1925, s. 107(1A), inserted by TA 2000, s. 40(1), Sch. 2, Pt II, para. 17; p. 415, ante.   [168] See note 165, supra.

[169] Cf the remarks of PEARSON J in *Wheelwright v Walker* (1883) 23 Ch D 752 at 761–2, M & B p. 351. See too *England v Public Trustee* (1967) 205 EG 651 where SELLERS LJ suggested that SLA 1925 should be amended to provide that notice of an intended sale by the tenant for life should be given to the other beneficiaries under the settlement.   [170] *Chandler v Bradley* [1897] 1 Ch 315.

[171] *Re Hunt's Settled Estates* [1906] 2 Ch 11.   [172] *Middlemas v Stevens* [1901] 1 Ch 574, M & B p. 352.

(2) ACQUISITIONS BY TENANT FOR LIFE

Subject to certain restrictions, a tenant for life may deal with the settled land for his own purposes. When a tenant for life exercises his statutory powers, he is normally dealing with persons who have no connection with the estate, but it may happen that in his private capacity and not as tenant for life he wishes to exercise one of the powers in favour of himself. The possibility of such a dealing between him and the settled estate was first allowed to a restricted extent by the Settled Land Act 1890, but his freedom in this respect has been extended by the Act of 1925, and it is now provided that any disposition of the settled land may be made to him, that capital money may be advanced on mortgage to him, and that land may be bought from or exchanged with him.[173]

Since a person can scarcely negotiate a transaction with himself, it is provided that in all such cases the trustees shall have all the powers of a tenant for life in reference to negotiating and completing the transaction, and the right to enforce any covenants entered into by the tenant for life.[174] Where the tenant for life is himself one of the trustees, he should be a conveying party as well as the person in whose favour the conveyance is made.[175]

D   The Trustees of the Settlement

(1) Definition of Trustees

Section 30(1) of the Settled Land Act 1925 gives a list of five different classes of persons competent to act as trustees of the settlement and arranges them in a binding order of priority as follows:[176]

(a) The persons who, under the settlement, are trustees with power to sell the settled land.

A power given to trustees to sell settled land is in fact abortive, since the Act provides that it shall be exercisable not by them, but by the tenant for life.[177] The only effect is to make the persons to whom it is given trustees of the settlement.

(b) The persons who are declared by the settlement to be trustees thereof for the purposes of the Settled Land Act.

These persons will normally constitute the trustees, for an express reservation of the power of sale contemplated by the first paragraph will rarely occur in practice.

(c) The persons who, under the settlement, are trustees with a power or duty to sell[178] any *other* land comprised in the settlement which is subject to the same limitations as the land that is being dealt with.

(d) The persons who, under the settlement, are trustees with a *future* power or duty to sell the settled land.[179]

If, for example, a testator devises his land to his wife for life and after her death to X and Y upon trust to sell the fee simple, then, failing persons qualified under the first three paragraphs, X and Y will be the trustees of the settlement during the wife's life.

---

[173] SLA 1925, s. 68(1).   [174] Ibid., s. 68(2).   [175] *Re Pennant's Will Trusts* [1970] Ch 75.
[176] SLA 1925, s. 30(1)(i)–(v).   [177] Ibid., s. 108(2).
[178] As amended by TLATA 1996, s. 25(1), Sch. 3, para. 2(9)(b).   [179] Ibid.

(e) The persons appointed by deed by the beneficiaries, provided that the beneficiaries are of full capacity and entitled to dispose of the whole equitable interest in the settled land.

Where a settlement is created by will, or has arisen by reason of an intestacy, and there are no trustees, the personal representatives of the deceased are trustees of the settlement until others are appointed; but if there is only one personal representative, not being a trust corporation, he must appoint an additional trustee to act with him.[180]

If at any time there are no trustees as defined above, or if for any reason it is expedient that new trustees should be appointed, the court may appoint fit persons to hold the office.[181]

(2) Compound Settlement

(a) Definition

Where land is settled by a series of separate instruments, the instruments together form one settlement which is called a *compound settlement*.[182] The commonest example of this occurs in the case of a resettlement, which, as we have seen, involves three instruments, that is, the original settlement, the disentailment and the resettlement.[183] The principle that the several instruments may be regarded as constituting one settlement becomes important when the tenant for life, in exercise of his statutory power of sale, desires to convey the fee simple to the purchaser free from the limitations of the various instruments.

(b) Conveyance by tenant for life

If, after a resettlement, a sale is effected by the father as first tenant for life he can execute the conveyance in any one of three capacities:

(i) He may convey as tenant for life under the original settlement.

The merit of this is that his conveyance overreaches the limitations of both settlements, and if the purchase money is paid to the trustees of the original settlement the purchaser acquires a title free from the rights of the beneficiaries. The disadvantage is that the tenant for life, since he is acting under the original settlement, cannot avail himself of any additional powers which may have been reserved by the deed of resettlement.

(ii) He may convey as tenant for life under the resettlement.

The position here is reversed, for although he can exercise any additional powers, he cannot convey a title free from the rights of beneficiaries that have been created by the original settlement. Conveyancers sought before 1926 to overcome this difficulty by reciting in the resettlement that the life interest resettled upon the father was "in restoration and by way of confirmation of" his life interest under the original settlement, but it was only on the eve of a statutory amendment of the law[184] that this device was held to be effective.[185] It had previously been held that "when once conveyancers have in fact transmuted the old body into a new body, they cannot claim to have retained the old body, whatever incantations they may use in the process".[186]

---

[180] SLA 1925, s. 30(3).   [181] Ibid., s. 34.
[182] *Re Ogle's Settled Estates* [1927] 1 Ch 229 at 233–4, per ROMER J; M & B p. 328.   [183] Pp. 68–9, ante.
[184] Infra.   [185] *Parr v A–G* [1926] AC 239 (18 December 1925).
[186] *A-G v Parr* [1924] 1 KB 916 at 931, per ATKIN LJ; *Re Constable's Settled Estates* [1919] 1 Ch 178.

(iii)   He may convey as tenant for life under the compound settlement.

This plan combines the advantages of the two preceding methods, since the tenant for life can exercise additional powers given by the resettlement and can overreach, within the statutory limits,[187] the limitations of both settlements. Under the old law, however, this method was often open to a fatal objection, for its efficacy depends upon the existence of compound trustees, and before the legislation of 1925, it frequently happened that there were no such trustees. If compound trustees had not been appointed in the original settlement it was impossible to rectify the omission in the resettlement, and unless all the beneficiaries were of full age (an improbable event), it was necessary to incur the expense of making an application to the court.

(c) *Compound trustees*

The difficulty that there may be no compound trustees was avoided by the legislation of 1925 which is retrospective and to the following effect:

(i)   trustees under an instrument which is a settlement are trustees also of a settlement constituted by that instrument and any subsequent instruments, i.e. the original trustees are trustees of any compound settlement which later comes into being;[188]

(ii)   trustees under a resettlement, where there are no trustees under the original settlement, are trustees of the compound settlement;[189]

(iii) where a resettlement states that a life interest limited to a tenant for life is *in restoration or confirmation* of his interest under the original settlement, he is entitled as of his former interest, and can exercise the statutory powers both under the original settlement and under the resettlement.[190]

(3) Protection of Trustees

It is not the policy of the legislature to subject the trustees of the settlement to a strict liability for the acts of the estate owner. Provisions are therefore inserted in the Settled Land Act 1925 designed to protect them in certain circumstances, and they now enjoy a greater measure of immunity than under the Act of 1882. Thus they are not liable for giving any consent or for not bringing any action which they might have brought, and, in the case of a purchase of land with capital money or in the case of a lease of the settled land by the tenant for life, they are not bound to investigate the propriety of the disposition.[191] Again, they are not liable for having delivered documents of title to the tenant for life, though they are responsible for securities representing capital money.[192] In short, the role of the trustees is to manage and protect the money that is paid to them.[193]

---

[187] P. 994, post.   [188] SLA 1925, s. 31.   [189] Ibid., as added by LP(A)A 1926, Schedule.

[190] Ibid., s. 22(2); *Re Cradock's Settled Estates* [1926] Ch 944.   [191] Ibid., s. 97.

[192] Ibid., s. 98(3).

[193] It must, however, be remembered that, in exercising their functions the trustees of the settlement have (except as limited by SLA 1925 or by the trust instrument) the general powers and duties of trustees, including the duty of care under TA 2000, s. 1 and Sch. 1. TA 2000, s. 40(1), Sch. 2, para. 12 repealed SLA 1925, s. 96, which had provided that each trustee was answerable only for what he actually receives, notwithstanding his signing any receipt for conformity, and he was not answerable for the acts and defaults of his co-trustees or for any loss not due to his own wilful default.

E Capital Money

(1) Definition of Capital Money

It is obvious that in several cases the exercise of a statutory power will result in the payment of money to the trustees; this is called *capital money*. Thus, for instance:

(i) money which becomes due on the sale of the land or of heirlooms;[194]

(ii) fines paid by lessees in consideration of obtaining a tenancy;[195]

(iii) three-quarters or one-quarter (as the case may be) of a mining rent;[196]

(iv) three-quarters of the money arising from the sale of timber by a tenant for life who is impeachable for waste;[197]

(v) consideration paid for an option to purchase or take a lease of the settled land;[198]

(vi) damages or compensation received by the tenant for life in respect of a breach of covenant by his lessee or grantee;[199] and

(vii) raised by a mortgage of the land for the purposes authorised by the Act,[200]

are all examples of capital money.[201] The expression also covers money arising otherwise than under the Act which ought to be treated as capital,[202] as for example money paid under a fire insurance policy which the tenant for life was under an obligation to maintain.

(2) Application of Capital Money

As regards the manner in which capital money must be disposed of, the first point is that if raised for some particular purpose, it must be applied accordingly. Thus, money that has been borrowed on mortgage in order to carry out some specific improvement on the land must be so spent. If, however, the money has not been raised for some particular object, but is due, for instance, to the sale of the land, it must be applied in one or more of the modes set out in the Settled Land Act 1925.[203] In addition to any special mode permitted by the settlement itself twenty-one different modes were originally indicated by the Act.[204] It would be inappropriate in a book of this nature to set out the whole list, but a few of the more important methods will be noted:

(a) Investment

Wide investment powers are usually included in most modern trusts so that the trustees may make any investment which they could make if they were the absolute owners of the trust. However, the trustees of older trusts may not have been given these powers, in which case their powers are governed by the Trustee Act 2000,[205] which also gives trustees a

---

[194] SLA 1925, s. 67(2).   [195] Ibid., s. 42(4).   [196] Ibid., s. 47; p. 412, ante.
[197] Ibid., s. 66(2).   [198] Ibid., s. 51(5).   [199] Ibid., s. 80(1).   [200] Ibid., s. 71; p. 412, ante.
[201] Similarly, ibid., ss. 52, 54(4), 55(2), 56(4), 57(3), 58–61.   [202] Ibid., s. 81.   [203] Ibid., s. 73(1).
[204] Three have since been repealed: Statute Law Repeals Act 1969, s. 1, Sch., Part III; Statute Law Repeals Act 1998, s. 1, Sch. 1, Part II. Others have been added, not by amendment of SLA itself, but in particular enactments; e.g. Leasehold Reform Act 1967, s. 6(5); Leasehold Reform, Housing and Urban Development Act 1993, ss. 9(4), 40(5), Sch. 2 para. 6; CLRA 2002, s. 109(4)(a). The provisions relating to investment were replaced by TA 2000: infra.
[205] Part II, replacing narrower provisions of Trustee Investments Act 1961; SLA 1925, s. 73(1)(i), substituted by TA 2000, s. 40(1), Sch. 2, Pt II, para. 9. See generally H & M paras. 18–005 to 18–023; Snell, paras. 26–12 et seq;

"general power of investment": the power to make any kind of investment that they could make if they were absolutely entitled to the assets of the trust, with certain exceptions and always subject to the provisions of the trust instrument. Capital money arising under the settlement is paid to the trustees or into court at the option of the tenant for life, and the investment is made in the name or under the control of the trustees and (subject to the directions contained in the settlement) according to the discretion of the trustees. In exercising the power to invest or apply capital money, the trustees must, so far as practicable, consult the tenant for life and, so far as consistent with the general interest of the settlement, give effect to his wishes. The money, either before or after investment, represents the land from which it originated, and it is held in trust for the same persons for whom the land was held under the settlement and for the same interests, so that, for instance, the income arising from the investments is paid to the tenant for life in the same way as the annual profits of the land would have been paid prior to its sale.[206]

(b) Charge on sale of settled land

When the settled land is sold in fee simple or for a term having at least 500 years to run, a sum not exceeding two-thirds of the purchase money may be allowed to remain on mortgage of the land sold.[207]

(c) Purchase of land

Capital money may also be expended in the purchase of land or of mines or minerals convenient to be worked with the settled land, provided that the interest so bought is either the fee simple or a leasehold having at least sixty more years to run.[208] Again, it may be used to finance a person who has agreed to take a lease or grant for building purposes of the settled land, advances being made to him on the security of an equitable mortgage of his building agreement.[209]

(d) Improvements

Lastly, capital money may be used in payment for any improvement authorised by the Settled Land Act 1925.

(1) PAYMENT FOR IMPROVEMENT

The procedure that governs payment varies according as the capital money is in the hands of the trustees or in court. In the former case the trustees, unless ordered by the court, must not pay for the improvement until they have obtained from a competent engineer or able practical surveyor, employed independently of the tenant for life, a certificate certifying that the

Law Commission Report on Trustees' Powers and Duties (1999 Law Com No. 172), Part II, which recommended the reform of the 1961 Act.

[206] SLA 1925, s. 75, as amended by TA 2000, s. 40(1), Sch. 2, Pt II, para. 10. See *Re Cartwright* [1939] Ch 90. Delegation by the trustees of their power of investment cannot circumvent their duty consult the tenant for life: ibid., s. 75(4B).

[207] Ibid., s. 75A, inserted by by TA 2000, s. 40(1), Sch. 2, Pt II, para. 11, replacing TA 1925, s. 10(2). The power is exercisable by the tenant for life or statutory owner with the consent of the trustees, subject to the consent of any person required by the trust instrument. The mortgagor must covenant to insure any buildings comprised in the mortgage security.   [208] Ibid., s. 73(1)(xi) and (xii).

[209] Ibid., s. 73(1)(xviii).

improvement has been properly executed and declaring the amount that ought to be paid.[210] Where the capital money is in court, the court may, on a report or certificate of the Secretary of State for Environment, Food and Rural Affairs, or of a competent engineer or able practical surveyor, approved by it, or on such other evidence as it may think sufficient, make what order it thinks fit for the application of the money in payment of the improvement.[211]

(2) REPAYMENT OF COST

In cases where the work done is not of lasting value it is economically sound that the tenant for life should ultimately restore the amount expended to capital by the creation of a sinking fund out of income, and it is with this object in view that the Act classifies the authorised improvements into the three categories that have already been mentioned.[212] The position is this:

Part I improvements The tenant for life cannot be required to set up a sinking fund.

Part II improvements Before meeting the cost out of capital, the trustees *may* if they think fit, and must if so directed by the court, require that the money shall be repaid to them out of the income of the settled land by not more than fifty half-yearly instalments.[213]

Part III improvements The trustees *must* require the whole cost to be paid out of income in the manner mentioned above.[214]

The court, when in possession of the capital money, is in the same position as the trustees with regard to requiring repayment of the money, except that it is not bound to require repayment in twenty-five years.

The effect of an order requiring repayment by instalments is that the settled land becomes subject to a yearly rentcharge which takes effect as if it were limited by the settlement prior to the estate of the tenant for life.[215] If, however, the subject matter of the settlement is agricultural land used as such for the purposes of a trade or business,[216] capital money may be applied in the execution of any improvements specified in the Agricultural Holdings Act 1986,[217] without any provision being made for the replacement of the cost out of income.[218] How prejudicial this may be to remaindermen is evident from the inclusion in the specified improvements of the execution of running repairs other than those which the tenant is under an obligation to carry out.[219] In the case of a farm business tenancy of settled land, capital money may be applied in the payment of the landlord's expenses in the making of any physical improvement on the holding or the payment of statutory compensation for any tenant's improvement.[220] The Agricultural Tenancies Act 1995 is silent on whether such expenditure is repayable out of income. It appears, therefore, that this aspect is governed by section 84 of the Settled Land Act 1925. The power under the Agricultural Holdings Act 1986 to pay for improvements out of capital was not exercisable by trustees for sale without regard to their duty to preserve the capital.[221] Trustees of a trust of land have the powers of an

---

[210] SLA 1925, s. 84(2).   [211] Ibid., s. 84(3), amended by SI 2002 No. 794.

[212] Ibid., Sch. 3. Law Reform Committee 23rd Report, supra, para. 8.4 said that the provisions of this Schedule "undoubtedly require modernisation".   [213] Ibid., s. 84(2)(a).

[214] Ibid., s. 84(2)(b).   [215] Ibid., s. 85.   [216] Agricultural Holdings Act 1986, s. 1(4).

[217] Ibid., Sch. 7.   [218] Ibid., s. 89(1), as amended by TLATA 1996, s. 25(2), Sch. 4.

[219] *Re Duke of Northumberland* [1951] Ch 202; *Re Sutherland Settlement Trusts* [1953] Ch 792; *Re Lord Brougham and Vaux's Settled Estates* [1954] Ch 24.   [220] Agricultural Tenancies Act 1995, s. 22.

[221] *Re Wynn* [1955] 1 WLR 940; *Re Boston's Will Trusts* [1956] Ch 395.

absolute owner in relation to the land, but must have regard to the rights of the beneficiaries and to general rules such as the duty to hold the balance between income and capital beneficiaries.[222]

II The Trust for Sale Before 1997

An alternative method of settling land before 1997 was to adopt the device of a trust for sale.

In general this arose where land was transferred by deed or will to trustees with an imperative direction that they were to effect a sale and to hold the proceeds thereof upon certain specified trusts. The manner of its formation has already been sufficiently described,[223] though it should be recalled that owing to the doctrine of conversion in equity, the land notionally became money, with the result that the interests of the beneficiaries were in the proceeds of sale and not in the land,[224] and were automatically overreached on a sale of the land by the trustees for sale.[225]

It is essential to define a trust for sale. As we have seen, the strict settlement and the trust for sale were mutually exclusive, and successive or limited interests in land created a settlement under the Settled Land Act 1925, unless the land was held upon trust for sale.[226]

A The Definition of a Trust for Sale

Until it was amended by the Trusts of Land and Appointment of Trustees Act 1996,[227] the definition in section 205(1)(xxix) of the Law of Property Act 1925 reads as follows:

"Trust for sale", in relation to land, means an immediate binding trust for sale, whether or not exercisable at the request or with the consent of any person, and with or without a power or discretion to postpone the sale.

We must now consider the meaning of the words "trust", "immediate", and "binding".

(1) Trust

An instrument did not create a trust for sale unless it contained a direction imposing a duty upon the trustees to sell. A *duty* to sell must always be distinguished from a *power* to sell. A trust is obligatory upon the trustee, a power leaves it to his discretion whether he will sell or not. It was, indeed, enacted that a disposition coming into operation after 1925 which directed that the trustees should *either retain or sell* land should constitute a trust for sale with power to postpone the sale,[228] but, apart from this statutory provision, whether an instrument created a trust or confers a power was a question that could be answered only by construing its terms. What was in form a trust for sale might be nothing more than a discretionary power; what was in form a power might, when properly construed, be an imperative trust.[229]

---

222 TLATA 1996, s. 6(1), (5), (6), p. 441, post.   223 Pp. 75–7, ante.

224 See *Irani Finance Ltd v Singh* [1971] Ch 59 at 80, per CROSS LJ; pp. 428, et seq, post.

225 Pp. 76–7, ante; pp. 997–1000, post.   226 SLA 1925, s. 1(7); p. 400, ante.

227 TLATA 1996, s. 25(1), Sch. 4 repeals the words "binding" and the phrase "with or without a power of discretion to postpone the sale".   228 LPA 1925, s. 25(4).

229 *Re Newbould* (1913) 110 LT 6, per SWINFEN EADY LJ: cf *Re White's Settlement* [1930] 1 Ch 179. For the distinction between a power and a trust, see H & M, paras. 2-021 to 2-027, chap. 6; Maudsley and Burn, *Trusts and Trustees*, pp. 37 et seq; *Farwell on Powers*; Maclean, *Trusts and Powers*; *Thomas on Powers*.

The distinction is of great importance in conveyancing, for if what was given to the trustees was a mere power of sale, it was exercisable not by them but by the tenant for life.[230] The trustees became trustees within the Settled Land Act 1925, the land was settled land within the meaning of that Act and was not subject to a trust for sale, and the proper person to make title was the tenant for life.[231]

(2) Immediate

The word "immediate" did not mean that the land must be sold at once, for power to postpone the sale was implied in every case, unless a contrary intention appeared.[232] Its significance was to distinguish a trust for sale from a *future* trust for sale. A future trust was not immediately effective, and it was enacted that where it was imposed upon land, the trustees were to be trustees for the purposes of the Settled Land Act, not trustees for sale.[233] Thus, if land was devised to a wife for life and after her death upon trust for sale, the land *during her life* was settled land and was governed by the Settled Land Act.[234]

(3) Binding

In its natural meaning "binding trust" is tautologous. A trust is different from a power because it is obligatory, not discretionary: the trustees are bound to sell the land ultimately, though the actual time of the sale is left to their discretion. A trust which imposes a duty upon the trustees as distinct from one which gives them a mere power may rightly be described as binding. Yet the word was inserted in a statutory definition and the courts searched for a secondary meaning. ROMER J suggested that, if it was not surplusage, the object of its insertion might be to emphasise the exclusion of a revocable trust for sale.[235] The cases in which the word was discussed were concerned with the situation where settled land had been resettled by way of trust for sale before the Settled Land Act settlement had been exhausted, and the judges sought to find a solution in the word "binding" to the problem of whether the unexhausted settlement had precedence over the trust for sale or vice versa.

Thus in *Re Leigh's Settled Estates:*[236]

X was tenant in tail of settled land which was subject to an equitable jointure rentcharge in favour of her mother. In 1923 X disentailed and conveyed the fee simple, still subject to the charge, to trustees upon trust for sale. The question arose whether in 1926 the land was settled land or whether it was held upon trust for sale.

---

[230] SLA 1925, s. 108(2).

[231] Ibid., ss. 30(1)(i), 108, 109; p. 420, ante. The position before 1926 involved a conflict of powers, since the tenant for life had a statutory, the trustees an express, power of sale. SLA 1882, s. 56 provided that in such a case the tenant for life should be unfettered in the exercise of the power, and that the trustees should not sell without his consent.   [232] LPA 1925, s. 25(1).

[233] SLA 1925, s. 30(1)(iv).

[234] *Re Jackson's Settled Estate*[1902] 1 Ch 258; *Re Hanson*[1928] Ch 96; *Re Herklots' Will Trusts*[1964] 1 WLR 583; *Re Nierop's Will Trusts* (Ch D, 23 April 1986), discussed in *Williams on Wills* (7th edn), pp. 1008, 1174–8 (trust to sell with consent of beneficiary combined with trust to permit beneficiary to reside while property remains unsold qualifies as trust for sale).   [235] *Re Parker's Settled Estates* [1928] Ch 247 at 261.

[236] [1926] Ch 852.

It was clearly settled land[237] unless the conveyance made by X in 1923 was an "immediate binding trust for sale" within the meaning of the Law of Property Act 1925. TOMLIN J held that the land remained settled land and was not subject to a binding trust for sale, since in his opinion the word "binding" was not used to indicate that the trustees for sale were bound to sell sooner or later but referred to the interests that would be bound, that is, overreached, when the trustees conveyed. To be "binding", the trust must enable the trustees to execute a conveyance which would bind the whole subject matter of the settlement, that is, interests prior to the trust as well as those arising under its provisions. This test was not satisfied in the present case, for a conveyance in 1923 could not overreach the widow's prior equitable charge. To do this it would be necessary to obtain the additional powers of overreaching by creating an ad hoc trust for sale,[238] and this could only be done by replacing the trustees by a trust corporation or by having them approved by the court.[239]

This restricted view of the scope of the ordinary trust for sale was implicitly[240] and expressly rejected.[241] In *Re Parker's Settled Estates*[242] ROMER J came to the conclusion that there could be a binding trust for sale notwithstanding that the trustees for sale were unable to overreach all charges having, under the settlement, priority to the trust for sale. He, however, then held that land could not be described as held upon trust for sale so as to take it out of the Settled Land Act unless the *whole legal estate* was vested in the trustees. He was of the opinion that if there were prior *equitable* interests the trust for sale excluded the Settled Land Act, since the whole legal estate was in the trustees; but if there were prior *legal* estates or interests then the trust for sale was not sufficient to exclude that Act, since the *whole* legal estate was not in the trustees. In *Re Parker's Settled Estates* there was a prior legal term of years to secure portions and accordingly the land remained settled land.[243]

B The Doctrine of Conversion

As we have seen, the doctrine of conversion applied as soon as a trust for sale came into operation.[244] As a result of this doctrine, the interests of the beneficiaries under the trust became automatically interests in the proceeds of the sale of land and not in the land itself. As CROSS LJ said:[245]

The whole purpose of the trust for sale is to make sure, by shifting the equitable interests away from the land and into the proceeds of sale, that a purchaser of the land takes free from the equitable interests.

[237] SLA 1925, s. 1(1)(v).   [238] LPA 1925, s. 2(2); pp. 1000 et seq, post.

[239] After the trustees had been approved by the court TOMLIN J upheld the trust for sale: *Re Leigh's Settled Estates (No 2)* [1927] 2 Ch 13.

[240] *Re Ryder and Steadman's Contract* [1927] 2 Ch 62 (land vested in X, Y and Z as tenants in common subject to an equitable jointure rentcharge in favour of A. CA held that after 1925 X, Y and Z held on a *statutory* trust for sale although they could not overreach A's prior equitable interest).

[241] *Re Parker's Settled Estates* [1928] Ch 247; see (1928) 65 LJ News 248, 272, 293 (J.M.L.).   [242] Supra.

[243] See too *Re Norton* [1929] 1 Ch 84, (1929) 67 LJ News 24 at 44 (J.M.L.). ROMER J held that there was no binding trust for sale since the trustees could not call for the legal estate from personal representatives due to a prior *equitable* charge: SLA 1925, s. 7(5); *Re Beaumont Settled Estates* [1937] 2 All ER 353; *Re Sharpe's Deed of Release* [1939] Ch 51.

[244] P. 76, ante; (1971) 34 MLR 441 (S. M. Cretney); [1971] CLJ 44 (M. J. Prichard); [1978] Conv 194 (H. Forrest); [1981] Conv 108 (A. E. Boyle); [1986] Conv 415 (J. Warburton); M & B (6th edn), pp. 292–301. See generally (1984) 100 LQR 86 (S. Anderson); Law Commission Report on Trusts of Land 1989 (No. 181), paras. 3.4–3.7.

[245] *Irani Finance Ltd v Singh* [1971] Ch 59 at 80. For a critical analysis of the statutory provisions on overreaching and its relationship to the doctrine of conversion, see [1990] CLJ 277 (C. Harpum).

To hold these to be equitable interests in the land itself would be to frustrate this purpose. Even to hold that they have equitable interests in the land for a limited period, namely, until the land is sold, would, we think, be inconsistent with the trust for sale being an "immediate" trust for sale working an immediate conversion, which is what the Law of Property Act 1925 envisages (see section 205 (1) (xxix)).[246]

A simple example of the effect of the doctrine is that, where a testator had left all his personal estate to P and all his real estate to R, an interest under a trust for sale passed to P and not to R.[247] The full logic of the doctrine of conversion was not, however, applied by the courts. There were various situations where an interest under a trust for sale was treated as if it were an interest in land. Thus, a beneficiary under a trust for sale could, with the consent of the other beneficiaries, if he and they were all adult and of sound mind, terminate the trust and call for a transfer of the land itself;[248] he was a "person interested" who might apply to the court for an order relating to the land under section 30 of the Law of Property Act 1925;[249] in the case of a statutory trust for sale, he had a right to be consulted by the trustees as to the exercise of their powers over the land;[250] and, within the discretion of the court, he might be protected from eviction from the land by the holder of the legal estate.[251]

The nature of a beneficiary's interest also arose in the context of the interpretation of a statute. The question was whether a reference in a statute to "land" included an interest under a trust for sale. Sometimes the statute dealt expressly with the point; as in the Limitation Act 1980, where land includes "an interest in the proceeds of the sale of land held upon trust for sale".[252] Even though the Law of Property Act 1925 contains no such provision, it was held that a contract for the sale of a beneficial interest under a trust for sale was a contract for the sale of "land or any interest in land" within section 40 and so required a memorandum for its enforceability.[253] Similarly, under the Land Registration Act 1925, a beneficiary was held to be a person interested in land within section 54(1) and thereby entitled to lodge a caution to protect his interest as a minor interest;[254] and also to have "an interest subsisting in reference to" registered land for the purpose of an overriding interest under section 70(1)(g).[255] The latter point was decided by the House of Lords in *Williams & Glyn's Bank Ltd v Boland*,[256] where it was held unanimously that the wife's interest was valid; her interest under the trust for sale was capable of existing as an overriding interest.[257] It was "an interest subsisting in reference to" registered land. Lord WILBERFORCE said that: "to describe

---

[246] P. 426, ante. See *City of London Building Society v Flegg* [1988] AC 54 at 82, where Lord OLIVER OF AYLMERTON quotes CROSS LJ verbatim as "a useful general analysis". The case is discussed p. 998, post.

[247] *Re Kempthorne* [1930] 1 Ch 268; *Re Newman* [1930] 2 Ch 409; *Re Cook* [1948] Ch 212.

[248] *Saunders v Vautier* (1841) 4 Beav 115, p. 563, post.   [249] P. 432, post.

[250] LPA 1925, s. 26(3); p. 432, post.

[251] *Bull v Bull* [1955] 1 QB 234 (order for possession refused); *Cook v Cook* [1962] P 235; *Gurasz v Gurasz* [1970] P 11; cf *Barclay v Barclay* [1970] 2 QB 677 (order for possession granted).   [252] S. 38(1).

[253] *Cooper v Critchley* [1955] Ch 431; (1955) 71 LQR 177 (R.E.M.); *Steadman v Steadman* [1974] QB 161 at 167. S. 40 has been repealed in respect of contracts entered into after 26 September 1989: LP(MP)A 1989, s. 2(8), p. 868, post. The replacement s. 2(6) expressly includes "any interest in or over the proceeds of sale of land". Cf *Re Rayleigh Weir Stadium* [1954] 1 WLR 786 (such a contract held not registrable under LCA 1925, where the definition of land expressly excludes an undivided share in land s. 17(1)). See also *Cedar Holdings Ltd v Green* [1981] Ch 129.

[254] S. 3(xv); *Elias v Mitchell* [1972] Ch 652; cf *Lynton International Ltd v Noble* (1991) 63 P & CR 452 (contractual right to share in proceeds of sale).   [255] P. 107, ante, pp. 979–81, post.

[256] [1981] AC 487 at 507; p. 981, post.

[257] Her interest could not be valid as a minor interest, since it had not been so protected on the register. Her only hope was in the safety-net provision of s. 70(1)(g).

the interests of spouses in a house jointly bought to be lived in as a matrimonial home as merely an interest in proceeds of sale, or rents and profits until sale is just a little unreal".[258]

C   The Powers of the Trustees for Sale

The powers of the trustees for sale were set out in the Law of Property Act 1925.

(1) Postponement of Sale

Under section 25 a power to postpone a sale was implied in every trust for sale unless a contrary intention appeared, and the trustees were not liable for an indefinite postponement in the absence of an express direction to the contrary.[259] A disregard of such an express direction, however, did not prejudice a purchaser of a legal estate, for it was enacted that he should not be concerned with directions that relate to postponement.[260] The power to postpone must, like any other power given to trustees, be exercised unanimously by them;[261] if there was disagreement between the trustees for sale, the court might at its discretion direct them to carry out the sale.[262]

(2) Management and Sale

The power of postponement might lead to the land remaining unsold for a considerable period, and it was essential that during the interval between the creation of the trust and the actual sale, the trustees should possess powers of disposition and management. These were given to them in abundance by the Law of Property Act 1925.

(a) Settled Land Act powers

Despite the fundamental distinction between a settlement and a trust for sale, it was provided by section 28 of the Law of Property Act 1925 that the trustees for sale, in relation to the land and the proceeds of sale, should have all the powers both of a tenant for life and of trustees of a settlement under the Settled Land Act 1925.[263] Thus, for example, they might grant leases, raise money on mortgage for improvements and, so long as they retained some land, might invest the proceeds of sale in the purchase of other land.[264] It was further provided by the same section that they should have the powers of management that were exercisable by trustees under section 102 of the Settled Land Act 1925 during the minority of a tenant for life of *settled* land.[265] Although, in the case of settled land, these powers given by

---

258   [1981] AC 487 at 507. See also Ormrod LJ in CA [1979] Ch 312 at 316, describing the doctrine as "in effect a legal fiction, at least in so far as the implied trusts are concerned".

259   LPA 1925, s. 25(1), (2); *Re Rooke* [1953] Ch 716 (direction by testator to sell farm "as soon as possible after my death" held to be contrary intention); *Re Atkins' Will Trusts* [1974] 1 WLR 761, M & B p. 388.

260   Ibid., s. 25(2).

261   *Re Roth* (1896) 74 LT 50; *Re Hilton* [1909] 2 Ch 548; *Re Mayo* [1943] Ch 302; cf *Re 90 Thornhill Rd, Tolworth, Surrey* [1970] Ch 261 (sale not ordered under SLA 1925, s. 93 when joint tenants for life disagreed as to the exercise of the power of sale). A power to act by a majority may be given in the trust deed, but it will be strictly construed: *Re Butlin's Settlement Trusts* (1974) 118 SJ 757; see also [1976] Ch 251 at 253, 259.

262   LPA 1925, s. 30; pp. 432, 449, post.

263   Ibid., s. 28(1), as amended by LP(A)A 1926, s. 7. For the SLA powers, see pp. 409–15, ante.

264   *Re Wakeman* [1947] Ch 607; *Re Wellsted's Will Trusts* [1949] Ch 296.   265   P. 916, post.

section 102 were exercisable only during the minority of the tenant for life, they might be exercised by trustees for sale whether there was a minority or not.[266]

(b) Delegation

In many cases the trustees for sale would not wish themselves to exercise the powers that were given to them by section 28. Section 29(1), therefore, provided that while the land remained unsold they might revocably and in writing delegate from time to time the *powers of leasing, of accepting surrenders of leases, and of management* to any person of full age (not merely being an annuitant), who was beneficially entitled in possession to the net rents and profits for his life or for any less period.[267] He must exercise the powers so delegated only in the names and on behalf of the trustees.[268] They were not liable for his acts or defaults. He alone was personally liable and in relation to the exercise of a power was deemed to be in the position of a trustee.[269] Thus, pending sale, the welfare of the land might be entrusted to the person most anxious to promote it. It must be noticed, however, that only those powers that were set out in section 29 might be delegated. The legal estate remained in the trustees for sale, and only they could convey the fee simple. That was the basis of their trust.

(c) Consents

The exercise of their powers by the trustees for sale, including that of sale itself, might be made subject to the consent of any persons.[270]

If the consent of not more than two persons was required, a purchaser[271] must ascertain that the requirement had been satisfied. If, however, the consent of more than two persons was required his obligation was satisfied if any two of the persons specified gave their consent.[272] If the person whose consent was required was not sui juris or became subject to a disability, his consent, in favour of a purchaser, should not be deemed to be required. But in the case of a minor the trustees should obtain the consent of his parent or guardian, and in the case of a mental patient that of the receiver.[273]

(d) Curtailment of powers

As we have seen, the powers of a tenant for life under the Settled Land Act 1925 could not be cut down by any provisions inserted in the settlement.[274] There is no similar provision in the Law of Property Act 1925 for the curtailment of the powers of trustees for sale. Indeed their power of sale could be restricted by the imposition of a requirement of consent and the power to postpone sale might be excluded by a contrary intention. Apart from these cases, however, it would appear that the powers of trustees for sale, like those of a tenant for life, were irreducible.[275]

---

[266] *Re Gray* [1927] 1 Ch 242.

[267] LPA 1925, s. 29(1); *Stratford v Syrett* [1958] 1 QB 107; *Napier v Light* (1974) 236 EG 273.

[268] Ibid., s. 29(2).   [269] Ibid., s. 29(3).

[270] If they refuse to give it, any person interested may apply to the court for an order of sale: LPA 1925, s. 30; *Re Beale's Settlement Trusts* [1932] 2 Ch 15.   [271] As defined by LPA 1925, s. 205(1)(xxi).

[272] Ibid., s. 26(1).   [273] Ibid., s. 26(2) as amended by the Mental Health Act 1959, s. 149, Sch. 7.

[274] SLA 1925, s. 106; p. 417, ante.

[275] See *Re Davies' Will Trusts* [1932] 1 Ch 530 (life interest to nephew "so long as he shall reside upon and assist in the management of the farm" held not forfeitable by exercise of powers inconsistent with such condition. The decision related to statutory trusts for sale under LPA 1925, s. 35, but the principle would appear to apply to express trusts for sale as well; [1978] Conv 229 (P. Smith)).

(e) Consultation

We must now consider how far the trustees for sale were required to observe the wishes of the beneficiaries. Under a statutory trust for sale[276] it was their duty, so far as practicable, to consult the persons of full age for the time being beneficially interested in possession in the rents and profits of the land until sale, and, so far as was consistent with the general interest of the trust, to give effect to the wishes of such persons, or, in the case of dispute, of the majority according to the value of their combined interests. A purchaser was not, however, concerned to see that this provision had been complied with.[277] It did not apply to express trusts for sale, unless a contrary intention appeared in the instrument creating the trust. Thus a settlor or testator might either give the trustees for sale complete freedom of discretion or compel them to consult the beneficiaries; but in the case of a statutory trust for sale there must be consultation.[278]

(f) Application to court

Finally, if the trustees for sale refused to sell or to exercise any of the powers conferred on them by sections 28 and 29 of the Law of Property Act 1925 or if any requisite consent could not be obtained, any person interested might apply to the court under section 30 for an order directing the trustees to act accordingly, and the court might make such order as it thought fit.[279] The court had the widest possible discretion under this section, and would take into account all the circumstances of the case. In order to qualify as a person interested, the applicant must have some proprietary interest in the land.[280]

The powers of the court under section 30 were entirely discretionary. In exercising this discretion the court had regard to the underlying purpose of the trust for sale and would not order a sale if some purpose of the trust remained to be discharged. Thus the court would refuse a sale on an application by A, if he had covenanted to sell only with the consents of B and C.[281] And likewise the court would refuse a sale where land had been acquired with some particular purpose in mind, as for instance, the joint occupation of a house and that purpose still subsisted.[282]

Thus, if the purpose was that the house should be the matrimonial home, then so long as that purpose is still alive, the court will not allow the husband or the wife arbitrarily to insist on a sale. But if the

---

[276] P. 433, post.

[277] LPA 1925, s. 26(3), as substituted by LP(A)A 1926, Sched. (1973) 117 SJ 518 (A. M. Prichard).

[278] If the trustees failed to consult the beneficiaries it might be a breach of trust; *Re Jones* [1931] 1 Ch 375 at 377 per BENNETT J; *Crawley Borough Council v Ure* [1996] QB 13 (notice to quit given to landlord by one joint tenant without consultation with other joint tenant not a "positive" act for which consultation was necessary, and therefore, not a breach of trust).

[279] See *Dennis v McDonald* [1981] 1 WLR 810 at 819 per PURCHAS J; affd [1982] Fam 63 (where an order for sale was refused, but one co-owner was ordered to pay an occupation rent to the other co-owner); *Bernard v Josephs* [1982] Ch 391 at 411, per KERR LJ; Law Commission Report on Trusts of Land 1989 (Law Com No. 181), paras. 12.6–12.13.

[280] *Stevens v Hutchinson* [1953] Ch 299 at 305 (chargee); *Re Solomon* [1967] Ch 573 (trustee in bankruptcy); see also *First National Securities Ltd v Hegerty* [1985] QB 850; *Harman v Glencross* [1986] Fam 81 (judgment creditor under Charging Orders Act 1979, s. 3 (5)). For an application by a trustee in bankruptcy, see Insolvency Act 1986, s. 336 and the 14th edn of this book, p. 231.

[281] *Re Buchanan-Wollaston's Conveyance* [1939] Ch 738; *Re Citro* [1991] Ch 142, M & B p. 284; cf *Abbey National plc v Moss* [1994] 1 FLR 307.

[282] *Bull v Bull* [1955] 1 QB 234; cf *Barclay v Barclay* [1970] 2 QB 677.

parties are divorced and in consequence the contemplated purpose is dead, then the trust for sale will take effect, subject always to the discretion of the court to postpone it.[283]

Litigation was mainly concerned with the matrimonial or quasi-matrimonial home, where, on the breakdown of the relationship, A wanted the house to be sold in order to realise his or her share of the proceeds of sale, and B wanted it to be retained as accommodation for himself or herself and the children, if any.

In the matrimonial homes[284] cases the main question was whether the marriage still subsisted in law[285] or in fact.[286] The court had regard to all the circumstances of the case, and, in particular, to the provision of a home for young and dependent children. Other factors to be taken into account included the conduct of the parties, their financial circumstances and the contribution which each has made to the acquisition of the property. Where children were concerned, however, there were conflicting approaches in the Court of Appeal. In *Re Evers's Trust*[287] the underlying purpose of the trust was to provide a *family* home, so that a sale would not be ordered while that purpose still existed; in *Re Holliday*[288] the purpose of the trust was to provide a *matrimonial* home and the interests of the children were only to be taken into account "so far as they affect the equities in the matter as between the two persons entitled to the beneficial interests in the property". It has been suggested that the conflict was really a matter of language rather than substance.[289]

D Statutory Trusts for Sale

A trust for sale might either be created expressly by act of parties or be imposed by statute. The following is a summary of the circumstances in which a statutory trust for sale was imposed by the 1925 legislation in pursuance of its policy to simplify conveyancing by separating the legal estate from the equitable interests:

(i) Where an estate owner died intestate.[290]

(ii) Where property vested in trustees by way of security became discharged from the debtor's right of redemption.[291]

If, for example, trust money had been invested in a mortgage of a legal estate and the right of the mortgagor to redeem the land had been extinguished under the Limitation Act 1980[292] or by a foreclosure order,[293] the land, being thus subjected to a trust for sale, was regarded as converted into money and it would pass as such under a beneficiary's will.

In the following cases an express trust for sale was usually created, but, if not, a statutory trust for sale arose automatically.

---

[283] *Bedson v Bedson* [1965] 2 QB 666 at 678, per Lord DENNING MR.

[284] See generally Cretney and Masson, *Principles of Family Law* (6th edn), pp. 162–8; M & B (6th edn), pp. 238–58.   [285] *Jones v Challenger* [1961] 1 QB 176.

[286] *Rawlings v Rawlings* [1964] P 398; *Re Solomon* [1967] Ch 573; *Bernard v Josephs* [1982] Ch 391 (cohabitees).

[287] [1980] 1 WLR 1327.

[288] [1981] Ch 405. The final judgment was delivered on the day after *Re Evers' Trust* was heard, and neither case refers to the other. See (1980) 77 LSG 288 (A. J. Oakley and D. Marks); [1981] Conv 79 (A. Sydenham); (1981) 97 LQR 200 (C. Hand); (1982) 98 LQR 519 (F. Webb); [1984] Conv 103 (M. P. Thompson).

[289] *Cousins v Dzosens* The Times, 12 December 1981. See also *Chhokar v Chhokar* [1984] FLR 313.

[290] AEA 1925, s. 33(1); See also pp. 988–9, post.   [291] LPA 1925, s. 31(1).   [292] P. 756, post.

[293] P. 775, post.

(iii) Where land was devised or conveyed to two or more persons as tenants in common.[294]

(iv) Where land was devised or conveyed beneficially to two or more persons as joint tenants.[295]

(v) Where a legal estate was conveyed to a minor jointly with one or more persons of full age other than trustees or mortgagees.[296]

(vi) Where the trustees of a *personalty* settlement or trustees for sale of land purchased land in virtue of a power contained in the settlement.[297] The effect of this, having regard to the doctrine of conversion, was that the land remained money in the eyes of equity and thus the original character of the settlement was preserved.

III Defects in the Dual System of Settlements

The criticism of the existing system of settlements made by the Law Commission in its Reports on Trusts of Land[298] and Overreaching: Beneficiaries in Occupation[299] was summarised in the Notes on Clauses to the Trust of Land and Appointments of Trustees Bill (HL) as follows:

21. The Law Commission criticised the existing law on three grounds:
    (a) it is unnecessarily complex, and the provisions governing strict settlements particularly so;
    (b) it is ill-suited to the conditions of modern property ownership, and the imposition of a trust for sale in all cases of conveyance to more than one person particularly so;
    (c) it is liable to give rise to unforeseen conveyancing complications.

22. The complexity of the existing law was the main criticism. The Commission argued that the existence of a dual system with two different ways of creating successive interests is unnecessarily complicated, given the very limited difference in substance between the two systems. It argued further that the machinery of the Settled Land Act is in any event unnecessarily complex and cumbersome for its purpose, requiring both a vesting deed and a trust instrument for its creation (and thus requiring a string of subsidiary vesting deeds where additional land is brought into the settlement or a new principal vesting deed where land is brought into a settlement presently containing only capital money); requiring special personal representatives to deal with settled land where the settlement still subsists after the death of a tenant for life (and thus requiring those responsible for administering the estate to distinguish between land which ceased to be settled on the deceased's death and that which remains settled); requiring complicated and detailed provisions for strict settlements to come about in such cases as a conveyance to a minor; and giving priority to the lesser-used and more complicated Settled Land Act regime (so that an unwary grantor or testator, or one acting without legal advice, is likely to create a strict settlement inadvertently if he wishes to include any element of successive ownership in his disposition).

23. The Commission also criticised the co-ownership trust for sale as being an inappro-prate legal vehicle for modern home ownership. At the time of the 1925 property legislation,

---

[294] LPA 1925, s. 34(2), (3); p. 466, post.   [295] ibid., s. 36(1); p. 468, post.
[296] Ibid., s. 19(2); p. 912, post.
[297] Ibid., s. 32(1). The statutory trust could be excluded by a contrary intention.
[298] Law Com No. 181 (1989).   [299] Law Com No. 188 (1989).

owner-occupation of dwellings in England and Wales was far less usual than it is today (the proportion of owner-occupied dwellings growing from 7% in 1914 to 43% in 1938 and 66% by 1992), and where it did exist, it was much less likely that a house would be purchased in joint names. The sort of co-ownership envisaged by the 1925 legislation would have tended to arise in other contexts, for example property left by a testator to his children in equal shares, where a sale would be the most likely outcome. In contrast, under modern conditions most co-ownership of property involves a shared home, and the imposition in such circumstances of a duty to sell (albeit with an implied power to postpone sale) seemed to the Law Commission to be inconsistent with the interests and intentions of the majority of owners who buy a house to use, not purely to hold it pending sale as an investment asset.

24. The Commission considered the unsuitability of the trust for sale to be compounded by the doctrine of conversion, it being even more artificial to treat a person with a half-share in his house as having an interest only in the proceeds of sale and not in the house itself. The courts have made efforts to reduce this artificiality by developing the principle of "collateral purpose" (that is, the purpose of providing a family home, collateral to the principal purpose of sale) under which the court may refuse to order a sale in the case of dispute, and have done the same with the doctrine of conversion: this has, however, had the unfortunate result that in some cases an interest under a trust for sale will count as an interest in land while in others it will not, and it may not be clear which is to apply, since there are conflicting Court of Appeal authorities.

25. The Commission's third main head of criticism was the tendency of the existing dual system to cause conveyancing difficulties, particularly arising from "imperfect" or "inadvertent" strict settlements, where in some cases involving more informal personal rights of occupation it may not be apparent even with the benefit of legal advice that a settlement has been created until after the conveyance. Particular problems may arise where there is no vesting deed, resulting in "paralysis" of the conveyance, or where the conveyance is taken from the wrong person (that is, from the tenant for life rather than the trustees).

In the next chapter we shall consider the reforms made by the Trusts of Land and Appointment of Trustees Act 1996, which were designed to address the defects of the old system of settlements and trusts for sale.

12

THE TRUST OF LAND

SUMMARY

I The Trust of Land

The Trusts of Land and Appointment of Trustees Act 1996, which came into force on 1 January 1997, changed the structure of settlements.[1] The object of the Act is to replace the two methods of settling land,[2] the strict settlement and the trust for sale, by a single system—the *trust of land*—modelled on the trust for sale, which can be used as the framework

---

[1] For commentaries on the Act, see TLATA Bill (House of Lords) *Notes on Clauses*; Whitehouse and Hassall, *Trusts of Land, Trustee Delegation and the Trustee Act 2000* (a very useful commentary which is referred to throughout this chapter); Barraclough and Matthews, *Trusts of Land and Appointment of Trustees Act 1996*; Kenny and Kenny, *The Trusts of Land and Appointment of Trustees Act 1996* (with the principal sections of the 1925 legislation as amended, and the Law Commission Report on Trusts of Land 1988 (Law Com No. 181)); Sydenham and Sydenham, *Trusts of Land—The New Law*. See also Emmet, chap. 22; R & R, chap. 37; [1996] Conv 401 (A. J. Oakley); 411 (N. Hopkins); (1998) 61 MLR 56 (L. M. Clements); [1999] Liverpool LR 21(1), pp. 97–121 (M. Draper).

[2] See chap. 11, Section I (strict settlement); Section II (pre-1997 trust for sale), pp. 399 et seq, ante. For criticism of the dual system, see pp. 434–5, ante.

for the creation not only of successive beneficial interests but also of concurrent interests in land.

As we have seen, no new strict settlement can be created or be deemed to be made after 1996, but existing strict settlements remain, and, where a settlement exists before 1997, any later resettlement creates a new strict settlement. However, a trust for sale created before 1997 takes effect as a trust of land. However, unlike a strict settlement, a trust for sale can still be created after 1996 but with important modifications.

A No New Strict Settlements after 1996

Schedule 1 to the Act provides for situations where the Settled Land Act 1925 imposes a strict settlement. As from 1 January 1997 a trust of land is imposed instead where:

(i)   an attempt is made to convey a legal estate to a minor alone, or to two or more minors; or to a minor or two or more minors and to another person, or other persons who are not of full age;[3]

(ii) land is charged voluntarily (or in consideration of marriage) or by way of family arrangement with the payment of a rentcharge for the life of a person or a shorter period;[4]

(iii) land is held on charitable, ecclesiastical or public trusts;[5]

(iv) an attempt is made to grant an entailed interest (in which case the property is held in trust absolutely for the grantee);[6] and

(v)   a settlement ceases to be a settlement because no property is subject to it (any property which is, or later becomes, subject to it is held in trust for those entitled under the settlement).

B Meaning of Trust of Land

The definition of a trust of land is widely drawn so as to include all types of trust, however and whenever created. Section 1 of the Act provides:

(1) (a) "trust of land" means (subject to subsection (3)) any trust of property which consists of or includes land, and

(b) "trustees of land" means trustees of a trust of land.

(2) The reference in subsection (1)(a) to a trust—

(a) is to any description of trust (whether express, implied, resulting or constructive[7]), including a trust for sale[8] and a bare trust,[9] and

(b) includes a trust created, or arising, before the commencement of this Act.

(3) The reference to land in subsection (1)(a) does not include land which (despite section 2) is settled land or which is land to which the Universities and College Estates Act 1925 applies.

We must first consider the trust for sale and the bare trust as examples of a trust of land.

---

[3] Pp. 914–5, post.   [4] P. 402, ante.   [5] P. 927, post.   [6] P. 401, ante.

[7] For such trusts in the cases of co-ownership, see pp. 472 et seq, post. On resulting trusts and registered land, see [1999] Conv 382 (D. Wilde).   [8] Infra.

[9] P. 439, post.

(1) Trust for Sale

(a) Definition

The definition of a trust for sale has been amended retrospectively and now reads as follows:[10]

"Trust for sale", in relation to land, means an immediate trust for sale, whether or not exercisable at the request or with the consent of any person: "trustees for sale" mean the persons (including a personal representative) holding land on trust for sale.

Before 1997 it was necessary to distinguish between a trust for sale and a strict settlement. An interest in succession created a strict settlement unless it satisfied the then definition of a trust for sale which included the word "binding" between "immediate" and "trust". There must be a trust which imposes on the trustees a duty to sell and not merely a power of sale; the trust for sale must be immediate in that a trust to sell at some future date does not prevent land from being settled land for the time being.[11] It must also be binding. The apparent tautology of this word caused difficulty; trusts are by their very nature binding.[12]

After 1996 it is necessary to discover whether an interest in succession is a trust for sale within the overall definition of a trust of land. To do this it must satisfy the amended definition which excises the word binding.

(b) Express trust for sale as a trust of land

After 1996 a trust for sale can still be expressly created, but it takes effect as a trust of land. It has been suggested that it may be desirable to create an express trust for sale where there is a trust in the residue clause of a will, or where there is a conveyance to co-owners.[13] In any event section 1 of the Act ensures that if a trust for sale is created in ignorance of the new legislation it will be valid under it.

Before 1997, section 25 of the Law of Property Act 1925 gave to trustees for sale the power to postpone sale indefinitely, unless a contrary intention was expressed in the trust instrument.[14] After 1996 this power still exists but under section 4(1) cannot be excluded by the settlor. The sale can only be postponed if the trustees for sale unanimously decide to exercise the power;[15] if they are not unanimous, then the land must be sold.[16]

An express trust for sale created before 1997 becomes a trust of land. There are, however, differences between a trust for sale created before 1997, and a trust for sale created after 1996. The trustees retain the *duty* to sell imposed on them by the settlor, but this duty is subject to the mandatory power to postpone sale indefinitely.[17] Presumably, if the trustees retain this duty, there will have to be a sale if they do not unanimously exercise their discretion to postpone it. Further, their duty to sell does not prevent them from delegating the

---

[10] LPA 1925, s. 205(1), as amended by TLATA 1996, s. 25(2), Sch. 4.   [11] Pp. 426–7, ante.

[12] Pp. 427–8, ante. It may be necessary to interpret "binding" when deciding whether there is a pre-existing strict settlement before 1997, but this will be very rare.

[13] W & H, paras. 2.26, 2.159, 6.41; Sydenham and Sydenham, *Trusts of Land*, para. 3.8.3; [1998] Conv 84 (R. Mitchell), doubting whether a trust for sale should continue to be used in a will.

[14] P. 426, ante. S. 25 was repealed by TLATA 1996, s. 25(2), Sch. 4.

[15] *Re Mayo* [1943] Ch 302 (where the power to retain required unanimity). Charitable trustees may act by a majority: *Re Whiteley* [1910] 1 Ch 600 at 607.

[16] Subject to an order of the court under TLATA 1996, ss. 14 and 15, p. 449, post.   [17] Supra.

duty, since they have a statutory power to delegate their functions under the trust.[18] And finally the settlor or surviving settlors may, if they wish, opt in to the consultation provisions of section 11 by an irrevocable deed executed after 1996.[19]

(c) Implied trust for sale as a trust of land

All trusts for sale, which are implied by statute, including those arising before 1997, are converted into trusts of land by section 5(1) of the Act.

Schedule 2 identifies these former statutory trusts for sale. Statutory provisions throughout the 1925 legislation have been amended so as to replace the duty to sell by a power to sell and a power to retain. Schedule 2 refers to:

(a) Mortgaged property held by trustees after redemption barred.[20]

(b) Land purchased by trustees of personal property.[21]

(c) Dispositions to tenants in common.[22]

(d) Joint tenancies.[23]

(e) Intestacy.[24]

(f) Reverter of sites.[25]

(d) Doctrine of conversion

Before 1997 the doctrine of conversion applied as soon as a trust for sale came into operation; the interests of the beneficiaries were thus automatically interests in the proceeds of sale of land and not in the land itself. As we have seen,[26] this doctrine gave rise to difficulties and in certain situations it was found undesirable to apply its full logic. As Lord WILBERFORCE said in *Williams & Glyn's Bank Ltd v Boland*:[27] "To describe the interests of spouses in a house jointly bought to be lived in as a matrimonial home as merely an interest in proceeds of sale, or rents and profits until sale, is just a little unreal."

Section 3 of the Act abolished the doctrine retrospectively, and the interests of beneficiaries under a trust for sale of land are now interests in the land itself. This has felicitous consequences for their rights of occupation[28] and for the powers of the court to resolve disputes.[29]

The doctrine is not abolished where a trust is created by a will, if the testator died before 1997.[30]

(2) Bare Trusts

A bare trust arises when a trustee holds property on trust for an adult beneficiary absolutely.[31] He must permit the beneficiary to occupy the property and he must obey instructions about its disposition. The beneficiary can call for an outright conveyance of the

---

[18] S. 9, pp. 442–3, post.   [19] S. 11(3), (4), p. 445, post.   [20] LPA 1925, s. 31; p. 433, ante.
[21] Ibid., s. 32, p. 434, ante.   [22] Ibid., s. 34, p. 466, post.   [23] Ibid., s. 36, p. 468, post.
[24] AEA 1925, s. 33.   [25] Reverter of Sites Act 1987, s. 1; p. 169, n. 8, ante.
[26] Pp. 428–30, ante.   [27] [1981] AC 487 at 507.   [28] P. 445, post.   [29] P. 449, post.
[30] TLATA 1996, s. 3(2). See also s. 25(5). The side heading of s. 3 is misleading. The doctrine still subsists for example, in specifically enforceable contracts for the sale of land. (1997) 113 LQR 207 at p. 209 (P. H. Pettit); W & H, para. 2.23.   [31] H & M, para. 2–034.

legal estate at any time. A bare trustee into whose name an absolute owner transfers property is sometimes called a nominee.[32]

Before 1997 bare trusts fell outside the dual system of strict settlement and trust for sale. This caused difficulty, especially in that interests under a bare trust could not be overreached. After 1996 bare trusts come within the definition of a trust of land,[33] and are therefore overreachable.

(3) The Trust of Land in Registered Land

In registered land the legal estate must be registered in the name of the trustees (not exceeding four in number),[34] and the beneficial interests under the trust must be protected by the entry of a restriction on the register.[35] The application for the entry of a restriction may be made by the trustees as registered proprietors, or by any person with the proprietor's consent or who has a sufficient interest in the making of the entry— including a beneficiary under the trust.[36] The beneficial interests cannot be protected by a notice in the register;[37] but, unlike beneficial interests under a strict settlement,[38] they can be overriding interests under Schedules 1 and 3 of the Land Registration Act 2002 where the beneficiary is in discoverable actual occupation of the land.[39] The interests may, however, be overreached by the payment of the purchase money to two trustees or to a trust corporation.[40]

II Functions of Trustees of Land

A General Powers[41]

Before 1997 section 28 of the Law of Property Act 1925 gave to trustees for sale "all the powers of a tenant for life and the trustees of a settlement under the Settled Land Act

---

[32] To be distinguished from the situation where trustees vest securities in a nominee to facilitate dealings with shares; here the nominee is in effect an agent of the trustees.

[33] TLATA 1996, s. 1(2)(a), p. 437, ante.

[34] The transfer or grant of unregistered land for the purpose of constituting the trust (other than a bare trust) triggers compulsory first registration: LRA 2002, s. 4(7); Law Commission Report on Land Registration for the Twenty-First Century 2001 (Law Com No. 271), p. 466.

[35] LRA 2002, ss. 40–7; LRR 2003, rr. 91–9, as amended by SI 2005 No. 1766. The standard forms of restriction are Sch. 4, Forms A (sole proprietor), B (trustees as proprietor) and C (personal representatives); R & R, chap. 37; H & B, paras. 10.72 et seq; Land Registry Practice Guide 19, section 4.

[36] LRA 2002, s. 43(1); LRR 2003, r. 93.   [37] Ibid., s. 33(a)(i).   [38] Pp. 406–7, ante.

[39] P. 979, post; *Williams & Glyn's Bank Ltd v Boland* [1981] AC 487, M & B p. 136 (a decision under LRA 1925, s. 70(1)(g)).

[40] Pp. 447, ante; 997, post; *City of London Building Society v Flegg* [1988] AC 54, M & B p. 316 (LRA 1925, s. 70(1)(g)).

[41] Trustees are usually appointed by the settlor when creating the trust; in default the court may appoint them. See Trustee Act 1925, ss. 34–43, as amended by TLATA 1996, s. 25(1) Sch. 3, paras. 3(9)–(14); LPA 1925, s. 24, as substituted by TLATA 1996, s. 25(1), Sch. 3, para. 4(1), (7); TLATA 1996 Part II: ss. 19 (appointment and retirement of trustee at instance of beneficiaries); 20 (appointment of substitute for trustee who lacks capacity, as amended by Mental Capacity Act 2005, s. 67, Sch. 6, para. 42); 21 (supplementary). See generally Maudsley and Burn, *Trusts and Trustees*, chap. 16; H & M, chap. 17; W & H, chap. 3; Law Commission Report 1999 (Law Com No. 260).

In respect of deaths after 1996, the provisions of Part I of the Act relating to trustees apply to personal representatives, other than ss. 10, p. 444, post; 11, p. 445, post; and 14, p. 449, post; s. 18.

1925".[42] This section is repealed and replaced by section 6 of the Trusts of Land and Appointment of Trustees Act 1996, which applies to all trusts of land whether arising before or after the commencement of the Act. The scope of the new section is much wider than its predecessor and is designed 'to make the scheme of powers as broadly based and as flexible as possible.'[43]

Section 6(1) provides that:

For the purpose of exercising their functions as trustees, the trustees of land have in relation to the land subject to the trust, all the powers of an absolute owner.

Functions include both powers and duties of trustees. The trustees of land have no duty to sell, unless they are trustees for sale, when the duty is combined with a mandatory power to postpone sale.[44]

There are, however, limitations on the exercise by the trustees of their general powers. Even though they enjoy all the powers of an absolute owner, section 6(6) provides that they shall not exercise them in contravention of, or of any order made in pursuance of, any other enactment or any rule of law or equity.

In other words, they are subject when exercising their functions to the normal fiduciary duties of trustees. These were spelt out by MEGARRY V-C in *Cowan v Scargill*:[45]

The starting point is the duty of trustees to exercise their powers in the best interest of the present and future beneficiaries of the trust, holding the scales impartially between different classes of beneficiaries. This duty of the trustees towards their beneficiaries is paramount. They must, of course, obey the law; but subject to that, they must put the interests of their beneficiaries first.

Moreover, in exercising their powers the trustees must have regard to the rights of the beneficiaries;[46] and since 1 February 2001 trustees of land have been subject to the general duty of care owed by trustees under section 1 of the Trustee Act 2000.[47]

The exercise of the powers only applies in relation to the land subject to the trust. The trustees therefore have no power to enlarge the investment powers which they have under the trust.[48]

Finally, section 6 specifically mentions

(a) the power to acquire land under the power conferred by section 8 of the Trustee Act 2000;[49] that is, to acquire freehold or leasehold land in the United Kingdom as an investment, for occupation by a beneficiary or for any other reason. In relation to land in England and Wales, this confers a power to acquire only a legal estate: there is no power to acquire an equitable interest in the land, although such a power could be included expressly in the instrument creating the trust.

---

[42] P. 430, ante, TLATA 1996, s. 25(2), Sch. 4.

[43] See Law Commission Report No. 181, paras. 10.4–10.5; [1998] Conv 178 (G. Ferris and G. Battersby).

[44] TLATA 1996, s. 4, p. 438, ante.   [45] [1985] Ch 270 at 287.   [46] TLATA 1996, s. 6(5).

[47] Ibid., s. 6(9), inserted by TA 2000, s. 40(1), Sch. 2, para. 45(3); H & W, paras. 2.53–2.55, chap. 10; H & M, para. 17–003. For the application of the duty of care, see W & H, chap 10; Maudsley and Burn, *Trusts and Trustees*, pp. 679–84.

[48] Pp. 423–4, ante. An application to court under the Variation of Trusts Act 1958 is necessary; p. 415, ante.

[49] TLATA 1996, s. 6(3), amended by TA 2000, s. 40(1), Sch. 2, para. 45(1). See TLATA 1996, s. 17(2), for the treatment of the proceeds of sale of land subject to the trust.

(b) the power to transfer the land to the beneficiaries when all are of full age and capacity, even though they have not required the trustees to do so.[50]

B Exclusion and Restriction of Powers

The powers given under section 6 may be excluded or restricted by the disposition creating the trust. Section 8 provides:[51]

Sections 6 and 7[52] do not apply in the case of a trust of land created by a disposition in so far as provision to the effect that they do not apply is made by the disposition.

This is an important new provision which may have an unintended consequence. On the face of it a settlor could by express words take away the power of the trustees to sell or otherwise dispose of the land and tie it up for a long period in conformity with the rule against perpetuities.[53] If this were possible, it would be contrary to the statutory policy of unrestricted alienation by the tenant for life under a strict settlement,[54] and of only partial and indirect restriction on trustees for sale.[55] It is also inconsistent with the rule that a restraint on alienation is contrary to public policy.[56]

C Delegation by Trustees

Under section 29 of the Law of Property Act 1925[57] trustees for sale were empowered to delegate revocably their powers of leasing, accepting surrenders of leases and management to any person of full age for the time being beneficially entitled in possession to the net rents and profits of the land during his life or for any less period. The duty to sell could not be delegated. The trustees were not liable for the acts or defaults of the delegate, but the delegate was, in relation to the exercise of the power by him, deemed to be in the position, and to have the duties and liabilities, of a trustee.

This section has been repealed by the Trusts of Land and Appointment of Trustees Act 1996,[58] and replaced by a wider provision for delegation by the trustees acting together.[59]

---

[50] TLATA 1996, s. 6(2). On the power of the trustees to partition the land, see s. 7, replacing LPA 1925, s. 28(3), without change of substance.

[51] W & H, paras. 2.68–2.76. S. 8(1) does not apply to charitable, ecclesiastical or public trusts.

[52] S. 7 deals with partition by trustees, p. 470, post.

[53] The Law Commission in its Report on The Rules against Perpetuities and Excessive Accumulations 1998 (Law Com No. 251) paras. 8.13–8.24, pp. 564–5, post, recommends that there should be one fixed perpetuity period of 125 years.   [54] SLA 1925, s. 106, p. 417, ante.

[55] LPA 1925, s. 26(3), replaced by TLATA 1996, s. 11(1)(a) (duty to consult); LPA 1925, s. 26(1), replaced by TLATA 1996, s. 11(1)(b) (to give effect to wishes of beneficiaries), p. 445, post.

[56] *Re Brown* [1954] Ch 39, M & B p. 9 (in the context of a conditional fee simple). See Emmet, para. 22.029; [1997] Conv 263 (G. Watt) (suggesting that the court might make an order under TA 1925, s. 57, which enables trustees to carry out any disposition or transaction where expedient).

[57] P. 431, ante. Any delegation made before 1997 under s. 29 is not affected; TLATA 1996, s. 9(9).

[58] TLATA 1996, s. 25(2), Sch. 4. See W & H, paras. 2.77–2.99.

[59] It seems that the power to delegate under s. 9 cannot be excluded: Kenny and Kenny, para. 47-11.

Section 9 (1) provides that:

The trustees of land may, by power of attorney[60] delegate to any beneficiary or beneficiaries[61] of full age and beneficially entitled to an interest in possession in land subject to the trust any of their functions as trustees which relate to the land.[62]

The powers of delegation under this section are wider than those under section 29 of the Law of Property Act 1925 in that sale and mortgage can now be delegated. Further changes to the powers of delegation have also been made by the Trustee Delegation Act 1999[63] and the Trustee Act 2000.

We must notice several points of detail. Where there is more than one trustee of land, the delegation must be made by all the trustees jointly. If a trustee wishes to delegate his own functions, he must do so under section 25 of the Trustee Act 1925.[64]

Since the delegation must be unanimous, it follows that a delegation may be revoked by any one of the trustees. It is also automatically revoked where there is a change of trustees, or where a beneficiary delegate ceases to be beneficially entitled.[65]

The delegation may be for any period or it may be indefinite.[66] It must be made by power of attorney, and therefore executed as a deed by the donor of the power.[67] Detailed protection is given to a purchaser from an attorney by section 9 (2) as follows:

Where trustees purport to delegate to a person by a power of attorney under subsection (1) functions relating to any land and another person in good faith deals with him in relation to the land, he shall be presumed in favour of that other person to have been a person to whom the functions could be delegated unless that other person has knowledge at the time of the transaction that he was not such a person.

Protection is also given to a later purchaser from the original purchaser:

And it shall be conclusively presumed in favour of any purchaser whose interest depends on the validity of that transaction that that other person dealt in good faith and did not have such knowledge if that other person makes a statutory declaration to that effect before or within three months after the completion of the purchase.

If the trustees refuse to delegate their functions, an application may be made to court under section 14 of the Trust of Land and Appointment of Trustees Act[68] by any person with

---

[60] It cannot be an enduring power or lasting power of attorney under Mental Capacity Act 2005: s. 9(6), amended by Mental Capacity Act 2005, s. 67(1), Sch. 6, para. 42; p. 922, post.

[61] For the definition of a beneficiary, see s. 22(1): "In this Act 'beneficiary', in relation to a trust, means any person who under the trust has an interest in property subject to the trust (including a person who has such an interest as a trustee or a personal representative)." This does not include a beneficiary who has an interest only by reason of being a trustee or personal representative; nor an annuitant: ibid., s. 22(2), (3). For a detailed analysis, see W & H, paras. 4.1–4.8.   [62] See ss. 6 and 7, pp. 441–2, ante.

[63] Law Commission Report on Delegation by Individual Trustees 1994 (Law Com No. 220); W & H, Part II.

[64] As substituted by Trustee Delegation Act 1999, s. 5(1). For delegation of general powers by trustees, see TA 2000, Part IV, which creates a new statutory regime. For delegation by trustees of land who are also beneficiaries, see Trustee Delegation Act 1999, ss. 1 and 2. See generally Maudsley and Burn, *Trusts and Trustees*, pp. 799–804; H & M, paras. 20-012 to 20-021; W & H, chaps. 7, 8 and 12.   [65] TLATA 1996, s. 9(3), (4).

[66] Ibid., s. 9(5).

[67] On powers of attorney generally, see Cretney and Lush, *Enduring Powers of Attorney*.

[68] P. 449, post.

an interest, for example, a beneficiary under the trust who wishes a delegation to be made to him.

Finally, we must consider the position of the delegate beneficiary. He has the same duties and liabilities as a trustee, but he cannot sub-delegate, nor can he receive capital money.[69] As originally drafted[70] the Act provided that the liability of the trustees for any act or default of a beneficiary was limited: it arose if, and only if, the trustees did not exercise reasonable care in deciding to delegate the relevant function to the beneficiary. Since 1 February 2001, however,[71] the duty of care under the Trustee Act 2000[72] applies to trustees of land in deciding whether to delegate any of their functions under section 9 of the 1996 Act, and, if the delegation is not irrevocable, as long as the delegation continues. In the latter case, the trustees must keep the delegation under review, and consider in appropriate circumstances whether to exercise any power of intervention they may have (including intervention by giving directions to the beneficiary or by revoking the delegation). It is still provided that the liability of the trustees for any act or default of the beneficiary is limited to the case where the they fail to comply with the duty of care; and it appears that this imposes on the trustee liability for his own breach of the duty of care, not vicarious liability for the act or default of the beneficiary.[73]

III Beneficiaries Under a Trust of Land

Sections 10 to 13 of the Trusts of Land and Appointment of Trustees Act 1996 are mainly concerned with the rights of beneficiaries under a trust of land and with the duties owed to them by their trustees.

A Consents

Section 10[74] of the Act is based on section 26 of the Law of Property Act 1925, which has been repealed.[75] Settlors may wish to make the sale of trust land dependent on the consent of the interest in possession beneficiary who will then be able to enjoy the use of the land and prevent the trustees from selling it over his head and thereby overreaching his interest. Section 10(1) provides that:

If a disposition creating a trust of land requires the consent of more than two persons to the exercise by the trustees of any function relating to the land, the consent of any two of them to the exercise of the function is sufficient in favour of a purchaser.

This sub-section[76] protects a purchaser from any requirement in the trust instrument to obtain more than two consents to a disposition, but the trustees remain under a duty to obtain

---

[69] TLATA 1996, s. 9(7).

[70] Ibid., s. 9(8); repealed by TA 2000, s. 40(1), (3), Sch. 2, para. 46, Sch. 4, Pt II.

[71] Ibid., s. 9A, inserted by TA 2000, s. 40(1), Sch. 2, para. 47. Delegations effected before 1 February 2001 are not affected: ibid., s. 9A(7).   [72] S. 1; p. 441, ante.

[73] TLATA 1996, s. 9A(6); W & H, para. 2.99. Before TLATA 1996 was enacted, the Law Commission had proposed that the liability should be extended to cover all the acts or defaults of the beneficiary: Trusts of Land 1988, Law Com No. 181, para. 11.3. See generally W & H, paras. 2.93–2.98.

[74] W & H, paras. 2.100–2.106.   [75] P. 431, ante. TLATA 1996, s. 25(2), Sch. 4.

[76] S. 10(1) does not apply to charitable, ecclesiastical or public trusts: s. 10(2).

all the specified consents; if they do not, they are liable for breach of trust. Sub-section (3) provides that, where the consent of a minor is required, then in favour of a purchaser the minor's consent is not required, but the trustees are under a duty to obtain the consent of a parent who has parental responsibility for him or a guardian on his behalf.[77]

B Consultation with Beneficiaries

Section 11 of the Trusts of Land and Appointment of Trustees Act 1996[78] is based on section 26(3) of the Law of Property Act 1925, which has been repealed and extends to express trusts a rule which applied before 1997 to implied trusts for sale only.[79] It applies to trusts expressly created after 1996 unless excluded by the disposition; it also applies to implied trusts, whenever arising. As far as pre-1997 express trusts for sale are concerned, the section does not apply unless it is included by a deed made by the settlor or surviving settlors after 1996. It does not apply to trusts created by will before 1997.[80]

Such a deed opting into the section is irrevocable, and binds not only the beneficiary but also his successors in title.[81]

The revised wording of section 11(1) is as follows:

The trustees of land shall in the exercise of any function[82] relating to land subject to the trust—

(a) so far as practicable, consult the beneficiaries of full age and beneficially entitled to an interest in possession in the land, and

(b) so far as consistent with the general interest of the trust, give effect to the wishes of those beneficiaries, or (in case of dispute) of the majority (according to the value of their combined interests).

There are no cases on the interpretation of the words "so far as practicable" in this context,[83] nor on "so far as consistent with the general interest of the trust". If the trustees fail to consult the beneficiaries, they may be liable for breach of trust.[84]

C Rights of Occupation

Section 12 of the Trusts of Land and Appointment of Trustees Act 1996[85] gives to a beneficiary, who is beneficially entitled to an interest in possession in land, the right to occupy

---

[77] It was not thought necessary to reproduce the provision of LPA 1925, s. 26(2) relating to consent on behalf of a mentally incapacitated beneficiary.   [78] W & H, paras. 2.107–2.119.

[79] P. 432, ante. TLATA 1996, s. 25(2), Sch. 4.   [80] TLATA 1996, s. 11(2)–(4).   [81] Ibid., s. 11(4).

[82] The giving of a notice to quit by one of joint tenants under a lease is not an exercise of any function relating to land subject to the trust: *Notting Hill Housing Trust v Brackley* [2001] 3 EGLR 11.

[83] Cf, discussing such language in regulations under the Industrial Relations Act 1971, *Dedman v British Building & Engineering Appliances Ltd* [1974] 1 WLR 171 at 179, per SCARMAN LJ: "The word 'practicable' is an ordinary English word of great flexibility: it takes its meaning from its context. But, whenever used, it is a call for the exercise of common sense, a warning that sound judgment will be impossible without compromise. Sometimes the context contemplates a situation rarely to be achieved, though much to be desired: the word then indicates one must be satisfied with less than perfection: see, for example, its use in section 5 of the Matrimonial Property Act 1970. Sometimes, as is submitted in the present case, what the context requires may have been possible, but may not for some reason have been 'practicable'. Whatever its context, the quality of the word is that there are circumstances in which we must be content with less than 100%: and it calls for judgment to determine how much less."

[84] *Re Jones* [1931] 1 Ch 375 at 377; *Crawley BC v Ure* [1996] QB 13, p. 432, n. 278, ante.

[85] [1998] CLJ 123 (D. G. Barnsley).

trust land. Section 13 provides that the trustees may exclude, restrict or impose conditions on such occupation.[86]

Before 1997 there were difficulties concerning the occupation of beneficiaries under a trust for sale, especially where the beneficiaries were co-owners under an implied trust. This was due to the doctrine of conversion under which the interests of beneficiaries under a trust for sale were in the proceeds of sale and not in the land itself. As we have seen, the courts regarded the doctrine as artificial.[87]

In *Bull v Bull*,[88] for example, a mother and son were equitable tenants in common of residential accommodation and the son was trustee of the legal estate which he held upon an implied trust for sale in favour of his mother and himself. The question was whether the son could obtain vacant possession against his mother. In holding that the son failed, Lord DENNING MR treated the mother as having an interest in land, and a right to occupy it. The doctrine of conversion has been abolished[89] retrospectively, and the matter is now regulated by sections 12 and 13.

Under section 12(1):

A beneficiary who is beneficially entitled to an interest in possession in land subject to a trust of land is entitled by reason of his interest to occupy the land at any time if at that time—

(a) the purposes of the trust include making the land available for his occupation (or for the occupation of beneficiaries of a class of which he is a member or of beneficiaries in general), or

(b) the land is held by the trustees so as to be so available.

No right to occupy arises if the land is "either unavailable or unsuitable for occupation" by the beneficiary in question. The term "unsuitable" was added in order to ensure that a right to occupy does not arise where premises are empty (and therefore not "unavailable" for occupation) but it would be inappropriate for the particular beneficiary to occupy them; for example, where the land is a working farm but the beneficiary is not, and has no intention, of becoming a farmer.[90]

Section 13 gives to the trustees of land the power to exclude or restrict the right to occupy conferred by section 12. This power arises where two or more beneficiaries are entitled to occupy land; the trustees may exclude or restrict the right of one or more beneficiaries in favour of another beneficiary, but may not exclude the rights of occupation of all the beneficiaries.[91] They may not unreasonably exclude any beneficiary's entitlement to occupy, or restrict any such entitlement to an unreasonable extent.

---

[86] W & H, paras. 2.120–2.138; [1997] Conv 254 (J. G. Ross Martyn); [2006] Conv 54 (S. Pascoe).

[87] P. 429, ante.

[88] [1955] 1 QB 234; cf *Barclay v Barclay* [1970] 2 QB 677 (express testamentary trust for sale of bungalow intended to be sold and the proceeds divided). Before 1926 the answer depended very much on the discretion of the trustees: (1955) 19 Conv (NS) 146 at p. 147 (F. R. Crane).   [89] TLATA 1996, s. 3, p. 439, ante.

[90] TLATA Bill (House of Lords) Notes on Clauses, para. 129; *Chan Pui Chun v Leung Kam Ho* [2003] 1 FLR 23 at [100]–[103].

[91] *Rodway v Landy* [2001] Ch 703 (partition of property jointly owned by two medical practitioners prohibited by National Health Service Act 1977, but order made under TLATA 1996, s. 13, to effect de facto partition by excluding one of the practitioners from one part of the property, and the other practitioner from the remainder of the property. The section prohibits only exclusion of the beneficiaries collectively: at [32]–[33], per PETER GIBSON LJ).

Section 13(3) enables the trustees to impose conditions on occupation by a beneficiary. Guidelines are set out in sub-section (4) and particular examples of conditions in
sub-section (5). Sub-section (4) specifies matters to which the trustees must have
regard in exercising their powers to exclude or restrict the right to occupy; these include
the intentions of the creator of the trust, the purposes for which the land is held, and
the circumstances and wishes of the beneficiaries who are, or would be but for restriction or exclusion, entitled to occupy the land. Sub-section (5) lists particular conditions
which the trustees may impose on a beneficiary. The list is not exhaustive; it includes
conditions requiring him to pay outgoings or other expenses in respect of the land; or
to assume some other obligation, such as to ensure that planning requirements are
complied with.

Sub-section (6) provides for the payment of compensation to an excluded beneficiary.
A beneficiary already in occupation cannot be excluded unless he consents or the court has
given approval.

IV Protection of Purchasers

Purchasers[92] are protected by the doctrine of overreaching and also by limitations on
powers and consent requirements.

A Overreaching

The main object of the doctrine is a compromise between, on the one hand, the interest of
the public in securing that land held in trust is freely marketable and, on the other hand, the
interests of beneficiaries in preserving their rights under the trust. The overreaching provisions under section 2(1) of the Law of Property Act 1925 are routinely amended by the
Trusts of Land and Appointment of Trustees Act 1996, and continue to operate.[93] They are
improved in that bare trusts are included in the definition of a trust of land by section
1(2)(a) and interests under them are now overreachable.[94]

B Limitation on Powers and Consent Requirements

Further detailed protection is given to a purchaser by section 16 of the Trusts of Land and
Appointment of Trustees Act 1996. This section applies only to unregistered land.[95]
A purchaser of registered land is left to rely on restrictions which must be placed on the
register.[96]

---

[92] A purchaser has the same meaning as in Part I of the Law of Property Act 1925: TLATA 1996, s. 23(1): i.e.,
a person who acquires an interest in or charge on property for money or money's worth, and in reference to a
legal estate includes a chargee by way of legal mortgage: LPA 1925, s. 205(1)(xxi).   [93] P. 997, post.

[94] Pp. 439–40, ante.

[95] TLATA 1996, s. 16(7). See [1998] Conv 168 at pp. 179–88 (G. Ferris and G. Battersby); [2005] Conv 140
(S. Pascoe, suggesting amendments to s. 16).

[96] LRA 2002, ss. 42–3; LRR 2003, rr. 93, 94 (3)–(5), Sch. 4, Forms B (trustees as proprietor) and C (personal
representatives); H & B, paras. 10.77–10.78; Land Registry Practice Guide 19, para. 4.4.4; p. 440, ante.

Section 16 provides that a purchaser of unregistered land from trustees "need not be concerned to see" that they have:

(i) had regard to the rights of beneficiaries in exercising their general powers under section 6(5);[97]

(ii) obtained the consent of beneficiaries before partition of land under section 7(3);[98]

(iii) consulted the beneficiaries and given effect to their wishes in exercising powers under section 11.[99]

A purchaser, however, needs only to be concerned in cases where he has actual notice that:

(i) the trustees are exercising their general powers in contravention of sections 6(6) (the exercise of powers which are in contravention of any other enactment or any rule of law or equity)[100] or 6(8) (in contravention of a limitation on powers conferred by any other enactment).[101] An example would be where absolutely entitled beneficiaries call for the trust land to be conveyed to them, but the trustees in breach of trust convey the land to a third party. The conveyance is valid in the absence of actual notice on the part of the purchaser.

(ii) the trustees are exercising powers which are limited by section 8.[102] Here the trustees are under a duty to take all reasonable steps to bring the limitation to the notice of a purchaser; if they do not, a purchaser without actual notice takes free from the limitation.

(iii) the trustees convey land to beneficiaries where the beneficiaries are not absolutely entitled. Here the purchaser is protected if he has no actual notice of the trustees' mistake and has obtained a deed executed by the trustees that they are discharged from the trust.

C Deed of Discharge

As we have seen, where a strict settlement comes to an end, the trustees should execute a deed of discharge; but there was no similar provision in relation to land held on trust for sale before 1997.[103] Section 16(4) of the Trusts of Land and Appointment of Trustees Act 1996 introduced a deed of discharge in relation to trusts of unregistered land.[104] Where trustees of land convey land to persons whom they believe to be beneficiaries absolutely entitled to the land and of full and capacity, the trustees must execute a deed of discharge, which declares that they are discharged from the trust; and, if they fail to do so, the court may make an order requiring them to do so.

Section 16(5) provides that a subsequent purchaser of land, to which the deed of discharge relates, is entitled to assume that, as from the date of the deed, the land is not subject to the trust, unless he has actual notice that the trustees were mistaken in their belief.

---

[97] P. 441, ante.   [98] P. 470, post.   [99] P. 445, ante.   [100] P. 441, ante.   [101] P. 441, ante.

[102] P. 442, ante.   [103] P. 992, post.

[104] In registered land the purchaser is protected by the restriction required to be placed on the register: n. 96, supra. When registering the disposition of a registered estate, the registrar must cancel the restriction if he is satisfied that the estate is no longer subject to the trust of land: LRR 2003, r. 99. For applications to cancel or withdraw a restriction, see ibid., rr. 97, 98.

V Powers of the Court

A General

Section 14 of the Trusts of Land and Appointment of Trustees Act 1996[105] gives to the court wide powers to interfere with the trustees' exercise of any of the trust powers, to dispense with their obligation to obtain any consents[106] or to consult, or to regulate occupation of land by the beneficiaries. Section 15 sets out the matters to which the court must have regard in determining an application under section 14.

The sections apply to all applications whether made before or after the commencement of the Act. In particular, an application may be made by a trustee;[107] an interest in possession beneficiary; a remainderman (whether vested or contingent); a discretionary beneficiary; the secured creditor of a beneficiary;[108] and trustees (and beneficiaries) of a sub-trust (because the "interest" does not have to be owned beneficially).

There is a considerable body of case law on section 30 of the Law of Property Act 1925, which has been repealed.[109] Those decisions were influenced by the primacy of the trustees' *duty* to sell. The courts invented the doctrine of a secondary or collateral purpose to help them to decide whether that primary purpose could be displaced. They could then exercise their discretion as to whether to make an order for sale or not. As the Law Commission Report said: "there is something odd about a doctrine whose essential purpose is so obviously the circumvention of an inconvenient position".[110]

Section 15(1) puts on a statutory footing the criteria which the courts have developed for settling disputes over trusts for sale under section 30 of the Law of Property Act 1925. They include:

(a) the intentions of the person or persons (if any) who created the trust,[111]

(b) the purposes for which the property subject to the trust is held,

---

[105] W & H, paras. 2.139–2.164. S. 14 also applies in relation to a trust of proceeds of sale: s. 17(1). Where the issue is the sale of a matrimonial home, as between husband and wife the claim should be heard by the court with jurisdiction in relation to ancillary relief under the Matrimonial Causes Act 1973, which overrides TLATA 1996: *Tee v Tee* [1999] 2 FLR 613; even where the spouses are co-owners with a third party: *Laird v Laird* [1999] 1 FLR 791. However, the jurisdictions under TLATA and the Children Act 1989 are concurrent: *White v White* [2004] 2 FLR 321 at [27], per ARDEN LJ.   [106] *Abbey National plc v Powell* (1999) 78 P & CR D 16.

[107] But not a trustee in bankruptcy: s. 15(4); p. 450, post. See *Oke v Ridout* [1998] CLY 4876 (resulting trust).

[108] Before 1997 the courts had treated a secured creditor in the same way as a trustee in bankruptcy, and therefore entitled to an order for sale save in exceptional circumstances: *Lloyds Bank plc v Byrne & Byrne* [1993] 1 FLR 369. Now, however, although "to put it at its lowest, it does not seem to me unlikely that the legislature intended to relax the fetters on the way in which the court exercised its discretion . . . and so as to tip the balance somewhat more in favour of families and against banks and other chargees": *Mortgage Corpn v Shaire* [2001] Ch 743, at 760, M & B p. 289, per NEUBERGER J, yet a "powerful consideration is and ought to be whether the creditor is receiving proper recompense for being kept out of his money, repayment of which is overdue": *Bank of Ireland Home Mortgages Ltd v Bell* [2001] 2 FLR 809 at [31], per PETER GIBSON LJ. See also *First National Bank plc v Achampong* [2004] 1 FCR 18 at [62]; [2003] Conv 314 (M. P. Thompson); *Edwards v Lloyds TSB Bank plc* [2005] 1 FCR 139 at [30].   [109] Pp. 432–3, ante. TLATA 1996, s. 25(2), Sch. 4.

[110] Law Com No. 181, para. 12.3.

[111] This refers only to the *common* intention of *all* those who created the trust, and only those held at the time the trust was created: *White v White* [2004] 2 FLR 321 at [22]–[23], per ARDEN LJ

(c) the welfare of any minor who occupies or might reasonably be expected to occupy any land subject to the trust as his home, and

(d) the interests of any secured creditor of any beneficiary.

The court is also required to have regard to the circumstances and wishes of any beneficiaries who are of full age and entitled in possession to property subject to the trust, or, in the case of dispute, of the majority (according to the value of their interests), except in the case of occupation disputes where regard is to be had to the circumstances and wishes of each of the beneficiaries entitled to occupy.[112] The court will also be able to take into account any other matters which it considers to be relevant.

These criteria are not exhaustive, and there is no guide as to the priorities to be accorded to each of them.[113] The relevance of the welfare of any minor as an independent criterion is welcome and comes after uncertainty in the case law on it under section 30.

However, it is clear that section 15 has changed the law.[114] In consequence, the old authorities on section 30 of the Law of Property Act 1925 must be treated with caution, and in many cases they are unlikely to be of great, let alone decisive, assistance.[115]

B Bankruptcy

There are different considerations where the application is made by the trustee in bankruptcy of a bankrupt who is beneficially interested in land held in trust. The application must be made to the court which has jurisdiction in the bankruptcy proceedings. Section 335A(2) of the Insolvency Act 1986[116] sets out an exhaustive list of criteria:[117]

On such an application the court shall make such order as it think just and reasonable having regard to—

(a) the interests of the bankrupt's creditors;

(b) where the application is made in respect of land which includes a dwelling house which is or has been the home of the bankrupt or the bankrupt's spouse or civil partner or former spouse or former civil partner—

(i)   the conduct of the spouse, civil partner, former spouse or former civil partner, so far as contributing to the bankruptcy,

---

[112] And also save where the trustees wish to transfer the land to such beneficiaries pursuant to s. 6(2).

[113] *White v White*, supra, at [26], per ARDEN LJ. See *Bank of Ireland Home Mortgages Ltd v Bell* [2001] 2 FLR 809 at [24]–[32], considering, inter alia, value of beneficiary's equity (nil) compared with interest of chargee; purpose of occupation as family home (already ended once husband left); welfare of minor (only a slight consideration where son not far short of eighteen); beneficiary's poor health (a reason for postponing, not refusing, sale): sale ordered; [2001] All ER Rev 262 (P. J. Clarke); *First National Bank plc v Achampong* [2004] 1 FCR 18 at [65] (sale ordered); *Edwards v Lloyds TSB Bank plc* [2005] 1 FCR 139 (sale postponed for five years until youngest child reached full age).

[114] *Mortgage Corpn v Shaire* [2001] Ch 743 at 758–60, M & B p. 289, per NEUBERGER J, giving eight reasons to support this; [2002] Conv 329 (M. P. Thompson); [2000] Conv 315 (S. Pascoe); [2001] CLJ 43 (M. Oldham); [2001] All ER Rev 258 (P. J. Clarke).   [115] [2001] Ch 743 at 761.

[116] As added by TLATA 1996, s. 25(1), Sch. 3, para. 23 and amended by Civil Partnership Act 2004, s. 261(1), Sch. 27, para. 118. The section is retrospective.

[117] For pre-1996 cases on which the criteria are based, see *Re Solomon* [1967] Ch 573; *Re Turner* [1974] 1 WLR 1556; *Re McCarthy* [1975] 1 WLR 807; *Re Densham* [1975] 1 WLR 1519; *Re Bailey* [1977] 1 WLR 278; *Re Lowrie* [1981] 3 All ER 353, M & B p. 288; *Re Citro* [1991] Ch 142 at 159, M & B p. 284. See also *Abbey National plc v Moss* [1994] 1 FLR 307; [1994] Conv 331 (D. N. Clarke); (1995) 111 LQR 72 (N. Hopkins).

    (ii)   the needs and financial resources of the spouse, civil partner, former spouse or former civil partner, and

    (iii)   the needs of any children; and

  (c)   all the circumstances of the case other than the needs of the bankrupt.

Where, however, an application is made after one year from the vesting of the bankrupt's estate in a trustee, the court must assume that the interests of the creditors outweigh all other considerations, unless the circumstances of the case are exceptional.[118] By delaying the sale, protection is given to the family to enable it to make arrangements either for alternative accommodation or for the buying out of the bankrupt's interest in the property.

---

[118] *Re Citro* [1991] Ch 142, M & B p. 284; (1991) 107 LQR 177 (S. M. Cretney); [1991] CLJ 45 (J. C. Hall); [1991] Conv 302 (A. M. M. Lawson); (1992) 15 MLR 284 (D. Brown) (inability to buy alternative home and disruption of children's schooling held not to be exceptional circumstances: "they are those melancholy consequences of debt and improvidence", per NOURSE LJ at 157); *TSB Bank plc v Marshall* [1996] 1 FLR 258. Cf *Re Mott* [1987] CLY 212, M & B p. 288 ("it would be difficult to imagine a more extreme case of hardship than this one", per HOFFMANN J); *Judd v Brown* [1998] 2 FLR 360 (cancer); *Re Raval* [1998] 2 FLR 718 (mental illness of wife); *Claughton v Charalambous* [1999] 1 FLR 740 (60-year-old with chronic disease, who had great difficulty in walking in house adapted to her needs); *Re Bremner* [1999] 1 FLR 912 (wife needed to care for 79-year-old bankrupt with only six months to live); *Barca v Mears* [2005] 2 FLR 1 (requirements of child with special educational needs not, on the facts, exceptional circumstances); [2005] Conv 161 (M. Dixon). See *Re Bennett* [2000] EGCS 41, applying the same test for exceptional circumstances as was applied in pre-1996 Act decisions. It may, however, be arguable that the approach to "exceptional circumstances" adopted in *Re Citro* is not consistent with the ECHR, and there needs to be a shift in emphasis to recognise that although, in the general run of cases, the creditors' interests will outweigh all other interests, a court may find, on proper consideration of the facts of a particular case, it is one of the exceptional cases in which that proposition is not true: *Barca v Mears*, supra, at [33]–[42], per Nicholas Strauss QC; [2005] Conv 161 at 165–7 (M. Dixon). See [2006] Conv 157 (P. Omar) on the paramount status of creditors in proceedings involving recovery of the family home.

13

CONCURRENT INTERESTS[1]

SUMMARY

As we have already observed,[2] the 1925 legislation used the statutory trust for sale to solve the conveyancing problems which arose before 1926 from the holding of concurrent interests. And since 1997 the trust for sale has been replaced by the trust of land.[3] The trust for sale, and the trust of land, are the legal framework within which successive and concurrent interests in land can be held. We have already considered successive interests.[4] In this chapter, we consider the forms of concurrent interest in land recognised by the law.

I Concurrent Ownership at Law and in Equity

A Several and Concurrent Ownership

Several and concurrent ownership must first be distinguished. The owner of an interest in land may be entitled to possession either alone or in conjunction with other persons, and in both cases he may be entitled to take possession either now or at some time in the future. If

---

[1] See generally Thompson, *Co-ownership*; Smith, *Plural Ownership*.   [2] Pp. 426 et seq, ante.
[3] Chap. 12, ante.   [4] Chap. 11, ante.

he is entitled in his own right without having any other person joined with him in point of interest, he is said to hold in severalty; but where he and other persons have simultaneous interests in the land, they are said to hold concurrently, or in co-ownership, and to have concurrent interests. In other words, land may be the subject of several, that is, separate ownership, or of co-ownership.

B Co-ownership at Law and in Equity

The forms of co-ownership which are discussed in the following section were originally recognised by both the common law and equity. However, as we shall see, the 1925 legislation made fundamental changes in the principles applicable to concurrent interests, so that in the modern law the basis on which concurrent interests may be held in the legal estate—only under a joint tenancy—is different from the basis on which equitable beneficial concurrent interests may be held—under either a joint tenancy or a tenancy in common. We must first explain the characteristics of, and the differences between, the various forms of concurrent ownership, drawing on both older authorities and examples from the modern law in order to do so. Thereafter we shall consider how they are treated in the law today.

II Forms of Concurrent Ownership

At common law there were four possible forms of co-ownership, one of which, tenancy by entireties, is now defunct;[5] while another, coparcenary, seldom arises.[6] The two found in practice are joint tenancy and tenancy in common.

A Joint Tenancy

(1) Nature of Joint Tenancy

A joint tenancy arises whenever land is conveyed or devised to two or more persons without any words to show that they are to take distinct and separate shares, or, to use technical language, without words of severance.[7] If an estate is given, for instance, to:

A and B in fee simple,

without the addition of any restrictive, exclusive or explanatory words, the law feels bound to give effect to the whole of the grant, and this it can do only by creating an equal estate in them both.[8] From the point of view of their interest in the land they are united in every respect. But if the grant contains words of severance showing an intention that A and B are to take separate and distinct interests, as for instance where there is a grant to:

A and B equally,

the result is the creation not of a joint tenancy, but of a tenancy in common.

---

[5] For a discussion, see 11th edn of this book, p. 338.   [6] P. 462, post.
[7] Litt s. 277; Blackstone, vol. ii. p. 179.   [8] Blackstone, vol. ii. p. 180.

The two essential attributes of joint tenancy which must be kept in mind if the true meaning of the legislation of 1925 is to be grasped are the absolute unity which exists between joint tenants, and the right of survivorship.

(a) Unity between joint tenants

There is, to use the language of Blackstone,[9] a thorough and intimate union between joint tenants. Together they form one person. This unity is fourfold, consisting of unity of title, time, interest and possession. All the titles are derived from the same grant and become vested at the same time;[10] all the interests are identical in size; and there is unity of possession, since each tenant "holds the whole yet holds nothing": *totum tenet et nihil tenet*. Each holds the whole in the sense that in conjunction with his co-tenants he is entitled to present possession and enjoyment of the whole; yet he holds nothing in the sense that he is not entitled to the exclusive possession of any individual part of the whole.[11] Unity of possession is a feature of all forms of co-ownership. For this reason one co-owner cannot, as a general rule, maintain an action of trespass against the other or others, but can do so only if the act complained of amounts either to an actual ouster, or to a destruction of the subject matter of the tenancy;[12] nor can one co-owner in sole occupation be made to pay rent to another co-owner,[13] unless he has excluded or ousted him from possession,[14] or where it is otherwise necessary in order to do equity between the parties.[15]

---

[9] Blackstone, vol. ii. p. 182.

[10] In the case of a grant to uses, the fact that the interests vested at different times did not prevent the creation of a joint tenancy, e.g. under a grant to X and Y to the use of all the sons of A born within the lifetime of the settlor, sons born after the time of the grant became joint tenants with those alive at the time of its execution.

[11] By Littleton's time the expression *totum tenet et nihil tenet* had become *per my et per tout*, which in Blackstone's view (vol. ii. p. 182) meant that each tenant was seised "by the half or moiety and by all". *My*, however, did not mean half, but was an early form of the French word *mie* (a (bread-) crumb: used figuratively to mean a fragment, or part).

[12] Blackstone, vol. ii. p. 183; *Martyn v Knowllys* (1799) 8 Term Rep 145; *Murray v Hall* (1849) 7 CB 441; *Stedman v Smith* (1857) 8 E & B 1; *Wilkinson v Haygarth* (1847) 12 QB 837.

[13] *M'Mahon v Burchell* (1846) 2 Ph 127; *Jones v Jones* [1977] 1 WLR 438. See also *Chhokar v Chhokar* [1984] FLR 313, M & B p. 157; *Wright v Johnson* [2002] 2 P & CR 15 (one co-owner led other to believe that she could reside rent-free). Rent received by one co-owner from a stranger will be shared with another co-owner.

[14] *Dennis v McDonald* [1981] 1 WLR 810 (ousted mistress); affd [1982] Fam 63 (application under LPA 1925, s. 30); p. 432, ante; *Bernard v Josephs* [1982] Ch 391; cf *Stott v Ratcliffe* (1982) 126 SJ 310; *Harvey v Harvey* [1982] Fam 83 (application under Matrimonial Causes Act 1973, s. 25); [1982] Conv 305 (J. Martin). The rule of ouster has not always been applied in matrimonial cases where application was made under the Married Women's Property Act 1882, s. 17. See *Bedson v Bedson* [1965] 2 QB 666 (rent of £1 a week ordered); *Leake v Bruzzi* [1974] 1 WLR 1528; *Suttill v Graham* [1977] 1 WLR 819; [1978] Conv 161 (F. R. Crane); (1978) 97 Law Notes 78 (A. Treleaven).

[15] *Re Pavlou (A Bankrupt)* [1993] 1 WLR 1046 at 1050, per MILLETT J (equitable accounting as between trustee in bankruptcy of co-owner not in occupation, and the other co-owner in occupation; but "if a tenant in common leaves the property voluntarily, but would be welcome back and would be in a position to enjoy his or her right to occupy, it would normally not be fair or equitable to the remaining tenant in common to charge him or her with an occupation rent which he or she never expected to pay"); *Byford v Butler* [2004] 1 FLR 56 (wife in occupation entitled against co-owner's trustee in bankruptcy to contribution to interest payments she had made on mortgage, but trustee entitled to set-off for occupation rent).

It is, however, possible for A and B to assign their legal estate to A alone. As Lord NICHOLLS OF BIRKENHEAD said:[16]

The legal concept relied upon . . . is that a joint tenant, as distinct from a tenant in common, has nothing to transfer to the other tenant, because each already owns the whole. I have to say that this esoteric concept is remote from the realities of life.

(b) Right of survivorship

The other characteristic that distinguishes a joint tenancy is the right of survivorship, or *jus accrescendi*, by which, if one joint tenant dies without having obtained a separate share in his lifetime, his interest is extinguished and accrues to the surviving tenants whose interests are correspondingly enlarged.[17] For example:

A and B may be joint tenants in fee simple, but the result of the death of B is that his interest totally disappears and A becomes owner of the land.

There are cases, however, where the right of survivorship does not benefit both tenants equally, for if there is a grant to

A and B during the life of A

and A dies first, there is nothing that can accrue to B.[18]

(2) Equity Prefers Tenancy in Common to Joint Tenancy

From early times the right of survivorship caused a divergence of views between common law and equity. Common law favoured joint tenancies because they inevitably led to the vesting of the property in one person through the operation of the doctrine of survivorship, and thus facilitated the performance of those feudal dues that were incident to the tenure of land.[19] But a tenancy in common never involved this right of survivorship, and equity, which was not over-careful of the rights of the lord, soon showed a marked inclination, in the interests of convenience and justice, to construe a joint tenancy as a tenancy in common.[20]

Equity aims at equality, a feature that is conspicuous for its absence if the survivor becomes the absolute owner of the land. This preference of equity for a tenancy in common has been shown in four cases:

(a) Where money is advanced on mortgage by two or more persons

Where two or more persons advance money, either in equal or in unequal shares, and take a mortgage of land from the borrower to themselves jointly, the rule *at law* is that they are joint tenants, so that the land and the right to the money belong absolutely to the survivor. The rule *in equity*, however, which prevails over the rule at law, is that they are tenants in

[16] *Burton v Camden LBC* [2000] 2 AC 399 at 404. Similarly, one joint tenant may release his interest to the other: ibid., at 405.

[17] Litt s. 280; Co Litt 181a; Blackstone, vol. ii. p. 183. The extinction of the deceased tenant's share and the corresponding enlargement in the other tenants' share is, however, a "disposition" of it on his death for the purposes of the charge to inheritance tax: ITA 1984, s. 3; McCutcheon, *Inheritance Tax*, para. 7–133; HM Revenue and Customs, Inheritance Tax Manual, para. IHTM15012.   [18] Co Litt 181b.

[19] Pp. 41–2, ante.   [20] Burton, *Real Property*, para. 165.

common, and that the survivor is a trustee for the personal representatives of the deceased mortgagees.[21]

This equitable rule caused difficulty in those cases where trustees advanced trust money on mortgage. In practice a conveyance of land to trustees is always made to them as joint tenants, for the very nature of their office requires that the death of one shall not disturb the administration of the trust or deprive the survivor of power to execute conveyances and to give binding receipts for money. These advantages, however, will be lost if the trustees are to be regarded as tenants in common, for in that case each of them is entitled to a separate, though at present an unidentifiable, share of the land that passes on his death to his personal representatives. To avoid this inconvenience, it soon became the practice to insert a *joint account clause* in a mortgage to trustees. This declares that upon the death of one of the mortgagees the receipt of the survivor shall be a sufficient discharge for the money, and that the survivor shall be able to re-convey the land without the concurrence of the personal representatives of the deceased trustee.

The position was made clearer by the Law of Property Act 1925,[22] which provides that where there is a mortgage for the payment of money and either the sum advanced is expressly stated to be advanced by more persons than one on a joint account, or a mortgage is made to them jointly the money lent shall, as *between the mortgagees and the mortgagor*, be deemed to belong to the mortgagees on a joint account, and the survivor shall be able to give a complete discharge for the money, notwithstanding any notice to the payer of a severance of the joint account. Trustees always advance money on a joint account, and the fact that they are trustees is never disclosed in the mortgage.[23]

It will be noticed that the Act is not confined to loans of money made by trustees, but applies generally to all joint mortgages coming within the provisions of the section; and in a case where there is no question of trustees, it is important to remember that the joint account rule just stated applies only as between the mortgagor and the mortgagees, and not even between them if a contrary intention is shown in the deeds. As between the mortgagees themselves evidence is admissible to show that, despite the presence of a joint account clause, it was intended that the money should belong to them as tenants in common.[24]

(b) Where joint purchasers of land provide purchase money in unequal shares

The invariable rule *at law* is that when purchasers take a conveyance to themselves in fee simple, they become joint tenants, and upon the death of one of them the whole estate passes to the survivor. Equity adopts the same attitude and does not treat the purchasers as being tenants in common, unless it can be inferred that they did not intend to take jointly.[25]

Thus, though this is not the only circumstance that will raise the inference, it is established that purchasers who contribute the money in unequal proportions are to be regarded as tenants in common of the land conveyed.[26]

---

[21] *Petty v Styward* (1631) 1 Eq Cas Abr 290; *Steeds v Steeds* (1889) 22 QBD 537; White and Tudor, *Leading Cases in Equity*, vol. ii. pp. 882–5.   [22] LPA 1925, s. 111, re-enacting Conveyancing Act 1881, s. 61.

[23] *Encyclopaedia of Forms and Precedents*, vol. 27, para. 71.   [24] *Re Jackson* (1887) 34 Ch D 732.

[25] *Lake v Gibson* (1729) 1 Eq Cas Abr 290; *Lake v Craddock* (1732) 3 P Wms 158; White and Tudor, *Leading Cases in Equity*, vol. ii. p. 881.

[26] *Robinson v Preston* (1858) 4 K & J 505; *Lake v Craddock*, supra; White and Tudor, vol. ii. p. 882.

(c) Where land is bought by partners

In the leading case of *Lake v Craddock*,[27] where five persons joined in buying some water-logged land with a view to its improvement by drainage, the court laid down the general rule that persons who make a joint purchase for the purposes of a joint undertaking or partnership, either in trade or in any other dealing, are to be treated in equity as tenants in common. This is, however, subject to contrary agreement by the partners:[28]

it is necessary to disentangle two separate concepts, even if they bear upon one another. One is whether the property was partnership property.[29] If it was, then there is a strong presumption that the right of survivorship was not intended to apply.[30] The maxim is *ius accrescendi inter mercatores locum non habet*,[31] or the right of survivorship has no place among merchants. The other however is whether the partners nevertheless agreed to vary the normal rule of partnership property, in favour of their own autonomous consent to their being beneficial joint tenants with the standard consequence of that arrangement.

(d) Where joint purchasers of land hold it for their individual business purposes

In *Malayan Credit Ltd v Jack Chia-MPH Ltd*, where it was held that business tenants who had paid rent and service charges in agreed proportions were tenants in common, Lord BRIGHTMAN said:[32]

Their Lordships do not accept that the cases in which joint tenants at law will be presumed to hold as tenants in common in equity are as rigidly circumscribed as the plaintiff asserts. Such are not necessarily limited to purchasers who contribute unequally, to co-mortgagees and to partners. There are other circumstances in which equity may infer that the beneficial interest is intended to be held by the grantees as tenants in common. In the opinion of their Lordships, one such case is where the grantees hold the premises for their several individual business purposes.

Despite these exceptional cases, the fundamental rule is that whenever land is granted or devised to two or more persons simply and without words of severance, the donees become joint tenants holding a single title, interest and possession, and when one dies his interest is extinguished and passes to the survivor or survivors.

(3) Determination of Joint Tenancy. Severance

Since "each joint tenant stands, in all respects, in exactly the same position as each of the others",[33] it follows that anything which creates a distinction between them severs the tenancy and converts it into a tenancy in common.[34] Stated in more detail, its determination may be effected by:

(a) alienation by one joint tenant;

---

[27] (1732) 3 P Wms 158.

[28] *Bathurst v Scarborow* [2005] 1 P & CR 4 at [44], per RIX LJ; *Barton v Morris* [1985] 1 WLR 1257.

[29] Partnership Act 1890, ss. 20, 21.   [30] *Elliot v Brown* (1791) 3 Swan 489n.   [31] Co Litt 182a.

[32] [1986] AC 549 at 560.

[33] Challis, *Law of Real Property*, p. 367. See Law Commission Working Paper No. 94 Trusts of Land (1985), paras. 16.11–16.14; p. 471, n. 114, post.

[34] Where the parties expressly create a beneficial joint tenancy, the shares of the tenants in common on severance are equal, even if they contributed unequally to the purchase price; where they do not, the beneficiaries may claim shares proportionate to their contributions: *Goodman v Gallant* [1986] Fam 106; [1986] Conv 205 (S. Juss).

(b) acquisition by one tenant of a greater interest than that held by his co-tenants;

(c) partition;

(d) sale;

(e) mutual agreement;[35]

(f) any course of dealing sufficient to intimate that the interests of all were mutually treated as constituting a tenancy in common;[36] and

(g) where one joint tenant criminally kills another joint tenant.

These methods require some discussion.

(a) Alienation by a joint tenant

Although during the continuance of the tenancy one joint tenant holds nothing separately from his fellows, there is a general rule to the effect that *alienatio rei praefertur juri accrescendi*[37]—alienation of the property takes priority over the right of survivorship—and in accordance with this doctrine it has long been the law that one joint tenant can alienate his share to a stranger. The effect of such alienation, where by way of sale or mortgage,[38] is to convert the joint tenancy into a tenancy in common, since the alienee and the remaining tenant or tenants hold by virtue of different titles and not under that one common title which is essential to the existence of a joint tenancy.

If A and B are joint tenants in fee simple and A makes a grant in fee simple to X, the result is that B and X hold the lands as tenants in common, in equal undivided shares. If A, B and C are joint tenants in fee simple and A makes a grant to X in fee simple, X is tenant in common with B and C, though as between themselves the latter continue to hold as joint tenants.[39]

Severance may also be effected by involuntary alienation, as where a joint tenant is adjudicated bankrupt and his interest vests in his trustee in bankruptcy.[40]

Owing to the doctrine of survivorship, no severance results from a disposition by will—*jus accrescendi praefertur ultimae voluntati*: the right of survivorship takes priority over the last will.[41]

---

[35] *Williams v Hensman* (1861) 1 John & H 546 at 557; *Burgess v Rawnsley* [1975] Ch 429, M & B p. 306.

[36] *Williams v Hensman*, supra, at 557, per PAGE WOOD V-C.   [37] Co LITT 185a.

[38] *Cedar Holdings Ltd v Green* [1981] Ch 129 at 138, per BUCKLEY LJ; *First National Securities Ltd v Hegerty* [1985] QB 850 (joint tenancy held to be severed where husband purported to mortgage jointly owned property by forging wife's signature); *Ahmed v Kendrick* (1987) 56 P & CR 120 (severance where husband sold jointly owned house by forging wife's signature on both contract and registered transfer); cf *Penn v Bristol and West Building Society* [1995] 2 FLR 938 (no severance where purchaser colluded in forgery by husband joint tenant of his wife's signature on the conveyance); *Monarch Aluminium v Rickman* [1989] CLY 1526 (charging order nisi held to be severance).   [39] Litt s. 292.

[40] *Re Dennis* [1996] Ch 80; [1995] All ER Rev 292 (S. M. Cretney); *Re Gorman* [1990] 1 WLR 616; *Re Pavlou* [1993] 1 WLR 1046; cf *Re Palmer* [1994] Ch 316 (insolvency administration order); [1995] Conv 68 (M. Haley); [1995] CLJ 52 (L. Tee); *Emmet on Title*, para. 11.145A.

[41] Blackstone, vol. ii. pp. 185–6. The instructions to a solicitor, during the lifetime of the joint tenants, to prepare mutual wills dealing with the property can however be sufficient then to sever the joint tenancy: *Re Woolnough* [2002] WTLR 595. And a variation of the dispositions of the deceased's property on his death, made by beneficiaries of the estate for the purposes of inheritance tax (ITA 1984, s. 142), may include the severance of a joint tenancy and the re-direction of the deceased tenant's interest so as to avoid the consequences of the doctrine of survivorship: McCutcheon, *Inheritance Tax*, para. 7–133.

(b) Acquisition of larger interest by a joint tenant

A joint tenancy is also severed if one of the joint tenants subsequently acquires an interest greater in quantum than that held by his co-tenants. This destruction of the unity of interest may result from the act of the parties or by operation of law. As an instance of the former: if A and B are joint tenants for life and A purchases the fee simple in reversion, the joint tenancy is severed: A holding an undivided half in fee simple and B an undivided half for life. When B dies, the fee simple in the entirety of the land vests in A.[42]

Again, A may release his interest to B and so terminate the tenancy by vesting the whole ownership in B.[43]

A case in which a greater interest than that held by his co-tenants is cast upon a joint tenant by operation of law occurs where the reversion in fee descends to one of the joint tenants.[44]

If the joint tenants agree deliberately to put an end to the tenancy, the two methods open to them, in addition to a mutual agreement that they shall hold as tenants in common, are (c) partition and (d) sale.

(c) Partition

Partition is a method whereby the joint *possession* is disunited, and its effect is to make each former co-tenant a separate owner of a specific portion of the land, and thus to terminate the co-ownership for ever. Instead of holding an undivided share in the whole, each person will hold a divided share in severalty. If 50 acres are held by A and B as joint tenants in fee simple, the effect of the destruction of the unities of title or interest is, as we have seen, to create a tenancy in common; but the effect of partition is that each becomes absolute owner of 25 acres.

Before 1926, partition was either voluntary or compulsory. Compulsory partition was abolished in 1925.[45] Accordingly, co-owners may agree between themselves to divide the property into separate shares to be held in individual ownership.[46] The actual amount or position of the land that is to be allotted to each party may be settled by the co-owners themselves, or by an arbitrator selected by them, or even by the drawing of lots.[47] The usual practice is first to enter into a preliminary agreement whereby the co-owners consent to the land being partitioned into allotments convenient to be held in separate ownership and as nearly as possible of equal values, provision being made for the payment of a sum of money to secure equality of partition where it is impossible to give each party land of equal value. When the division has been settled, the last step is for the co-owners to execute that form of conveyance which is appropriate to the interest involved. A deed is necessary in the case of

---

[42] Co Litt s. 182b; *Wiscot's Case* (1599) 2 Co Rep 60b.   [43] *Re Schär* [1951] Ch 280.

[44] Cruise, *Digest,* Tit. xviii. c. ii. s. 7. Contrary to the view of the majority of the Court of Appeal, it is submitted that the two methods of severance already discussed avail a husband or wife in respect of the matrimonial home: *Bedson v Bedson* [1965] 2 QB 666 at 688–91, per RUSSELL LJ, dissenting, who said that the view was "without the slightest foundation in law or equity"; (1966) 82 LQR 29 (R.E.M.). The view of RUSSELL LJ has been preferred by PLOWMAN J in *Re Draper's Conveyance* [1969] 1 Ch 486 at 494, M & B p. 303; and by LAWTON LJ in *Harris v Goddard* [1983] 1 WLR 1203 at 1208.

[45] I.e. by the repeal of the Partition Acts; LPA 1925, Sch. 7.

[46] For partition by trustees of land with the consent of the beneficiaries, see TLATA 1996, s. 7; W & H, paras. 2.56–2.67.   [47] Litt ss. 55, 243–6.

land, but joint tenants must execute a deed of release, while the proper form for tenants in common is a deed of grant.[48]

(d) Sale

The normal and the simplest method of bringing a joint tenancy to an end is by sale. If all the joint tenants agree to sell, the joint title can be passed to the purchaser and the land will vest in him as single owner.[49]

(e) Mutual agreement

The mutual agreement need not be specifically enforceable. The significance of the agreement is not that it binds the parties, but that it serves as an indication of a common intention to sever.[50]

(f) Course of dealing

A course of dealing need not amount to an agreement, express or implied, for severance. As Lord DENNING said:[51]

It is sufficient if there is a course of dealing in which one party makes clear to the other that he desires that their shares should no longer be held jointly but be held in common. I emphasise that it must be clear to the other party.

Thus, it was held that there was severance where one joint tenant negotiates with another for some rearrangement of interest, even though the negotiations break down.[52]

The onus of proving severance under this heading is on the party who desires to establish it.[53]

(g) By homicide

This occurs where one joint tenant criminally kills another joint tenant. No one may bene-fit in law from his own crime, so that there is necessarily a severance that prevents the killer from taking any beneficial interest by survivorship. In *Re K*, where a matrimonial home was owned jointly by the killer and his victim, it was held to have been rightly conceded that there was a severance of the joint tenancy, so that the beneficial interest (subject to relief

---

[48] For precedents, see *Encyclopaedia of Forms and Precedents*, vol. 29; W & H, pp. 340–1 (conveyance giving effect to partition under TLATA 1996, s. 7). In registered land the disposition giving effect to partition of the legal estate will be required to be completed by registration: LRA 2002, s. 27; and in the case of land which is not yet registered, the partition will trigger compulsory first registration: ibid., s. 4(1)(a).

[49] Prior to 1926, if one joint tenant was obstructive, the others could compel a sale by the indirect method of bringing a partition action. From 1925 the solution was to apply to the court under LPA 1925, s. 30, and (since 1997) under TLATA 1996, s. 14; p. 449, ante.

[50] *Burgess v Rawnsley* [1975] Ch 429 at 445, per Sir John PENNYCUICK; M & B p. 306; *Hunter v Babbage* (1994) 69 P & CR 548 (draft agreement); cf *Edwards v Hastings* [1996] NPC 87 (agreement to sever conditional on sale of family home).   [51] *Burgess v Rawnsley*, supra at 439.

[52] Ibid. See also *Re Draper's Conveyance* [1969] 1 Ch 486, M & B p. 303; p. 471, post; *Greenfield v Greenfield* (1979) 38 P & CR 570 (conversion of house jointly owned by brothers into two self-contained maisonettes occupied separately held not to be severance); *Barton v Morris* [1985] 1 WLR 1257 (inclusion of jointly owned property as a partnership asset in the partnership accounts for tax purposes held not to be severance); *Re Gore and Snell v Carpenter* (1990) 60 P & CR 456 (negotiations between husband and wife with a view to settling claim for ancillary relief in divorce proceedings held not to be severance in absence of a final agreement between them).   [53] *Re Denny* (1947) 177 LT 291; *McDowell v Hirschfield Lipson* [1992] 2 FLR 126.

under the Forfeiture Act 1982) vested in the deceased and the survivor as tenants in common.[54]

B Tenancy in Common

(1) Creation of Tenancy in Common

A tenancy in common arises

   (i)   where land is limited to two or more persons with words of severance showing an intention, even in the slightest degree,[55] that the donees are to take separate shares, or

   (ii)   where equity treats what is at law a joint tenancy as a tenancy in common,[56] or

   (iii)   where land was originally held by joint tenants but their joint tenancy has since been severed.[57]

The following expressions have at one time and another been construed as words of severance sufficient to create a tenancy in common:

> equally to be divided;
>
> to be divided;
>
> in equal moieties;
>
> equally;
>
> amongst;
>
> share and share alike.

So, also, if land is devised to A and B on condition that they pay in equal shares ten shillings a week to X during his life, this imposition of an equal burden on both donees shows that what would normally be a joint tenancy is to be a tenancy in common.[58]

The expression "jointly and severally", which is a contradiction in terms, has been solved by the court holding that the first word prevails in a deed (thus creating a joint tenancy), but the last in a will.[59] Similarly, the words in a deed "to hold in fee simple as beneficial joint tenants in common in equal shares" have been held to create a joint tenancy rather than a tenancy in common.[60]

(2) Differences Between Tenancy in Common and Joint Tenancy

There is a fundamental distinction between tenancy in common and joint tenancy.

[54] *Re K* [1985] Ch 85; affd [1986] Ch 180; Maudsley and Burn, *Trusts and Trustees*, pp. 263–8. There was previously no English authority on the point. See *Schobelt v Barber* (1966) 60 DLR (2d) 519 and *Re Pechar* [1969] NZLR 574, where it was held that the law imposes a constructive trust of one undivided half share for the benefit of the next of kin of the deceased other than the killer.

[55] *Robertson v Fraser* (1871) 6 Ch App 696 at 699; cf *Re Osoba* [1979] 1 WLR 247 at 260.

[56] Pp. 455–7, ante.   [57] Pp. 457–61, ante.   [58] *Re North* [1952] Ch 397.

[59] *Slingsby's Case* (1587) 5 Co Rep 18b.

[60] *Joyce v Barker Bros (Builders) Ltd* (1980) 40 P & CR 512; cf *Martin v Martin* (1987) 54 P & CR 238, where similar words in a deed were held to create a tenancy in common. The second inconsistent clause constituted a severance of the joint tenancy and the creation of a tenancy in common; [1987] Conv 405 (J. E. Adams).

(a) Unity

In the first place, that intimate union which exists between joint tenants does not necessarily exist in a tenancy in common. In a tenancy in common the one point in which the tenants are united is the right to possession.[61] They all occupy the whole, and if there are two tenants in common, A and B, A has an equal right with B to the possession of the whole land. But their union may stop at that point, for they may each hold different interests, as where one has an equitable fee simple, the other a life interest; or where one is entitled to a two-thirds share, and the other to one third; and they may each hold under different titles, as for instance where one has bought and the other has succeeded to his share.[62] Each has a *share* in the ordinary meaning of that word. His share is undivided in the sense that its boundary is not yet demarcated, but nevertheless his right to a definite share exists.

(b) Survivorship

The second characteristic, and it is really the complement of the first, is that the *jus accrescendi* has no application to tenancies in common, so that, when one tenant dies, his share passes to his personal representatives, and not to the surviving tenant.[63] In the words of Challis:

A tenancy in common, though it is an ownership only of an undivided share, is, for all practical purposes, a sole and several tenancy or ownership; and each tenant in common stands, towards his own undivided share, in the same relation that, if he were sole owner of the whole, he would bear towards the whole.[64]

(3) Determination of Tenancy in Common

The three methods by which a tenancy in common is determined and converted into separate ownership are (a) partition, (b) sale, and (c) the acquisition by one tenant, whether by grant or by operation of law, of the shares vested in his co-tenants.

C Coparcenary

Coparcenary arose at common law wherever land descended to two or more persons who together constituted the heir. This occurred if a tenant in fee simple or a tenant in tail died intestate leaving only female heirs. In each case the females succeeded jointly to the estate and were called coparceners. Coparcenary also arose under the custom of gavelkind, according to which the land descended to all the sons equally, failing them to all the daughters equally, and failing them to all the brothers equally.[65] Gavelkind, however, has been abolished; the rules regulating the disposition of a fee simple estate upon the intestacy of its owner have been altered by the Administration of Estates Act 1925;[66] and coparcenary only then arose in the case of entailed interests.

If the owner of an entailed interest (other than an interest in tail male) dies without having either barred the entail or disposed of the interest by will, and if he leaves no male heirs who are entitled to succeed, the interest passes to the female heirs of the appropriate class.[67] For instance, where the owner of an entailed interest general dies intestate leaving no sons, but

---

[61] Co Litt 189a.   [62] Blackstone, vol. ii. p. 191.   [63] Ibid., p. 194.
[64] *Law of Real Property*, p. 368.   [65] P. 26, ante.
[66] For detail of the rules of distribution on intestacy, see the 16th edn of this book, chap. 26.
[67] On entailed interests, see pp. 481 et seq, post.

three daughters, the interest descends to all the daughters jointly.[68] The daughters are called coparceners because, in the words of Littleton, "by the writ, which is called *breve de participatione facienda*, the law will constrain them that partition shall be made among them."[69]

Coparceners constitute a single heir, and they occupy a position intermediate between joint tenants and tenants in common.[70] Like joint tenants they have unity of title, interest and possession; like tenants in common their estate is unaffected by the doctrine of survivorship, and if there are three coparceners and one dies, her share passes separately to her heirs or devisee, not to the survivors, though the unity of possession continues. It follows that unity of time is not necessary to constitute coparcenary, for if a man has two daughters to whom his estate descends and one dies leaving a son, such son and the surviving daughters will be coparceners.[71]

Coparcenary is converted into separate ownership (a) by partition, or (b) by the union in one coparcener of all the shares; and it is converted into a tenancy in common if one coparcener transfers her share to a stranger.[72]

The present position with regard to coparcenary is that interests held by coparceners are necessarily equitable, since for the most part they consist of entailed interests,[73] and these arise only under a settlement or a trust for sale.[74] Therefore, it would seem that when a tenant in tail dies intestate, leaving female heirs, the legal fee simple vests in the trustees in the case of a settlement and is held by them in trust for the persons interested in the land, so as to give effect to the equitable rights of the coparceners.[75]

III The Law After 1925

The object of the legislation of 1925 was to simplify conveyances of land, and where this simplicity could not otherwise be attained, to make radical alterations in the pre-1926 law. The law relating to concurrent interests was a subject that called for considerable alteration. If conveyancing is to be a simple matter, one primary essential is that the legal estate to be acquired by a purchaser should be vested in an easily ascertainable person and not distributed among a number of persons whose titles will each require to be investigated.

A Conveyancing Difficulties Before 1926

(1) Joint tenancy

Joint tenancy does not raise difficulties in this respect, for although several persons are interested in the land, yet there is only one title to be deduced, and if the purchaser is

---

[68] Litt ss. 55, 241, 265; Blackstone, vol. ii. p. 187.

[69] Litt s. 241. As distinct from the case of joint tenancy and tenancy in common, partition may be compelled at common law, since the co-tenancy arises, not by act of parties, but by operation of law.

[70] Challis, *Law of Real Property*, p. 374.   [71] Co Litt s. 164a.   [72] Litt. s. 309

[73] If a person who was of unsound mind and already of full age (twenty-one) on 1 January 1926, and was therefore incapable of making a will, dies without having recovered his testamentary capacity, his beneficial interest in land devolves according to the old canons of descent; AEA 1925, s. 51(2). Coparcenary, therefore, could still arise under this provision in the case of a fee simple estate, althought it is now highly unlikely in practice to do so.

[74] P. 494, post. Since 1997, however, no new entails can be created: p. 500, post, making the scope for coparcenary now even more severely limited.

[75] SLA 1925, s. 36(1), (2), as amended by TLATA 1996, s. 25(1), Sch. 3, para. 2(1), (11).

satisfied as to the validity of the deed or the will under which the tenancy stands limited, he is not concerned further with the tenants except to see that they are parties to the deed of sale.

(2) Tenancy in Common

In tenancy in common, however, the case is different, for the existence of a number of persons interested in the land, each of whom, as we have seen, is entitled to a separate share, raised a serious hindrance to simplicity of transfer. An analogous difficulty occurs in the case of a strict settlement where the beneficial title is distributed among a number of persons *in succession*, but we have seen that this plurality of interests is not allowed to hinder conveyancing, since the tenant for life is treated as the fee simple owner for purposes of transmission, and the interests of the various beneficiaries are not allowed to affect a purchaser. The conveyancing problem raised by a number of successive interests is in fact comparatively simple, because the tenant for life is obviously marked out as the person to act as an intermediary for passing the legal estate.

But if land can be held by tenants in common, there is no one person in whom the legal estate can appropriately be vested, for all the tenants have the equal right to present enjoyment, so that tenancy in common is a greater hindrance to simplicity of transfer than a settlement. The complication in such a case is that the separate title of each tenant must be investigated.

Lastly, all this confusion is "worse confounded" by concurrent ownership in tenancy in common. Here is an example which recently came before me in my official capacity. A man by his will devised his freeholds to the use of his wife for life, and after her death to the use of his children in fee simple. He had ten children; one of them died during the widow's life, leaving a similar will, seven children, and a widow. This is quite a simple example; yet the result is that a house worth about £150 per annum is (the widow being dead) now vested (not merely in equity but at law) in seventeen persons in the following proportions:

Each of the nine living children of the testator or their assigns: 7/70

Each of the seven children of the deceased child, subject to the prior life interest of their mother: 1/70

Moreover, several of the parties have mortgaged their shares, and in the result when the great expense of proving the title of each of the seventeen has been paid, a very small balance will remain for distribution. Thus, tenancy in common is (having regard to the Settled Land Acts) a far greater detriment to the proper management of land than settlements (which are popularly debited with this sin), and introduces infinitely greater difficulty with regard to its sale, as not only must the parties be unanimous, but the title of each of them has to be deduced.[76]

B Scheme of the 1925 Legislation and the Trusts of Land and Appointment of Trustees Act 1996

In order to overcome such difficulties, the Law of Property Act 1925 revolutionised the law relating to tenancies in common.

---

[76] Sir Arthur Underhill in Fourth Report, 1919, p. 30.

The object was to enable land which is subject to such tenancies to be sold without casting upon the purchaser any obligation to consider the titles or the beneficial rights of the tenants.[77]

(1) Tenancies in Common

(a) Legal tenancies in common abolished

The first step in the attainment of the object of the legislation was the enactment that:

a legal estate is not capable of subsisting or of being created in an undivided share in land.[78]

What this particular enactment means is that there can never again be a legal tenancy in common, that is, a tenancy in common of a legal estate.

(b) Legal estate held on trust

It is then enacted that an undivided share in land shall not be created except behind a trust[79] of land. The effect is that the legal estate must be held by trustees holding as legal joint tenants upon trust. This may be an express trust. But if no express trust is created, then an implied trust is imposed by statute. Until 1997 the trust mechanism used was that of a trust for sale. As we have seen,[80] all concurrent interests created after 1996 come within the new scheme for the trust of land. If an express trust for sale was created before 1997, it now comes within the definition of a trust of land, still with a duty to sell but now with a mandatory power to postpone the sale;[81] and the implied trust for sale is converted into a trust of land.[82]

(c) Legal joint tenancy cannot be severed

The corner stone of this new structure is the vesting of the legal estate in joint tenants as trustees of land, and since it is essential to the success of the scheme that this legal joint tenancy should remain invulnerable until terminated by sale, the old rules as to severance[83] have been abolished for legal joint tenancies. It is enacted that:

no severance of a joint tenancy of a legal estate, so as to create a tenancy in common in land, shall be permissible.[84]

The basic effect of the scheme is that the legal estate is held by trustees of land who hold it as legal joint tenants, but who are unable to sever; and, as in the case of all settlements by way of trust, the beneficial interests exist in equity behind the trust. On the sale of the legal estate by the trustees, a purchaser is not concerned with these equitable beneficial interests and takes free from them. They are overreached, provided that the purchase money is paid to at least two trustees or to a trust corporation; the beneficiaries then have corresponding rights in the purchase money.[85]

---

[77] See City of London Building Society v Flegg [1988] AC 54 at 77, per Lord OLIVER OF AYLMERTON.
[78] LPA 1925, s. 1(6). The 1925 legislation refers to "undivided share" not to "tenancy in common".
[79] SLA 1925, s. 36(4), as amended by TLATA 1996, s. 25(1), Sch. 3, para. 2(1), (11).
[80] Pp. 438–9, ante.   [81] TLATA 1996, s. 4.   [82] Ibid., s. 5, Sch. 2, para. 3.   [83] Pp. 457–61, ante.
[84] LPA 1925, s. 36(2).   [85] Pp. 447, ante; 997, post.

(d) Effect of failure to create a trust

If the correct method of a conveyance upon trust is not adopted, the Law of Property Act 1925 contains a number of provisions designed to ensure that, no matter what form the transaction may have taken, the effect shall be exactly the same as if the tenancy in common had been properly limited behind a trust. There appear to be three normal cases, namely:

a direct conveyance of the legal estate to tenants in common;

a devise to tenants in common;

a contract to convey an undivided share.

(1) CONVEYANCE

With regard to a conveyance, section 34(2)[86] of the Law of Property Act 1925 provides that:

where [after 1925] land is expressed to be conveyed to any persons in undivided shares and those persons are of full age, the conveyance shall . . . operate as if the land had been expressed to be conveyed to the grantees, or, if there are more than four grantors, then to the first four named in the conveyance, as joint tenants in trust for the persons interested in the land.

Thus, if land is conveyed in fee simple to A, B, C, D and E in equal shares, A, B, C and D become joint tenants of the legal estate, while all five are entitled under the trust as equitable tenants in common.

(2) DEVISE

A devise to two or more persons in undivided shares operates to vest the legal estate in the personal representatives of the testator for the persons interested in the land, but in either case the land is held on trust and not as settled land.[87]

(e) Settlement

As regards settlements, section 36(4) of the Settled Land Act 1925[88] provides that a tenancy in common shall not be capable of creation except under a trust instrument or under the above provisions of the Law of Property Act 1925, and shall then take effect under a trust of land. Thus if it is desired to settle land on A and B for their lives in equal shares, with remainder to C in fee simple, the legal estate must be vested in the trustees of land.

If beneficiaries under a pre-1997 settlement become entitled in possession to the land, for example, where in a devise

to X for life, remainder to X's children equally during their lives

X dies leaving three children, the legal fee simple that was formerly held by X as tenant for life must be vested in the trustees of the settlement and held by them in trust for X's children.[89] The settlement within the meaning of the Settled Land Act 1925 comes to an end and is replaced by a trust of land.

---

[86] As amended by TLATA 1996, s. 5, Sch. 2, para. 3(1), (2), (6).

[87] LPA 1925, s. 34(3), as amended by TLATA 1996, s. 5, Sch. 2, para. 3(1), (3), (6); Sch. 4.

[88] As amended by TLATA 1996, s. 25(1), Sch. 3, para. 2(1), (11).   [89] SLA 1925, s. 36(1), (2), (3).

(f) Defect in scheme of Law of Property Act 1925

The policy of the Law of Property Act 1925 was clearly to subject all forms of co-ownership to a trust for sale, except those which are within the Settled Land Act 1925. It seems doubtful, however, whether the language of these enactments covers all cases in which a tenancy in common may arise, as for example when two persons buy land and contribute the purchase price in unequal shares.[90] This was the position in *Bull v Bull*,[91] where:

a mother and son bought a house as a dwelling place for themselves, the conveyance being made to the son only, who had provided the greater part of the purchase price. In an action in which the issue was the validity of a notice to quit served on the mother, the Court of Appeal, citing s. 36(4) of the Settled Land Act 1925, held that the parties were tenants in common in equity, and that the legal estate vested in the son upon the statutory trusts for sale.

This decision, though expedient, was difficult to fit into the words of the legislation. There was nothing that could constitute a trust instrument within the meaning of the Settled Land Act 1925; and the land was not "expressed to be conveyed" to persons in undivided shares as required by the Law of Property Act 1925. It seems, then, that the courts would readily impose a trust for sale if this fulfilled the intention of the parties.

This technical difficulty still remains after 1996, since the opportunity was not taken to amend section 34(2) in the Trust of Land and Appointment of Trustees Act 1996.

(g) Advantages of scheme

Let us examine the effect of the statutory trust of land that arises in these various cases from the point of view, first, of a purchaser of the land, secondly, of the beneficiaries.

(1) TO PURCHASER

The advantage to the purchaser is that he is no longer compelled to investigate the title of each tenant in common. He is concerned only with the legal estate held by the joint tenants upon trust, since the rights of the persons beneficially entitled exist merely as equitable interests behind the trust, and they are overreached upon a conveyance of the land by the trustees, provided that the purchase money is paid to at least two trustees or to a trust corporation. It is a matter of indifference, therefore, that some of the tenants in common are minors, or that some of them are unwilling to acquiesce in the sale. Although the trustees are required, so far as practicable, to consult, and give effect to the wishes of the beneficiaries entitled in possession, or in the case of a dispute, of the majority in terms of value, yet it is expressly enacted that it shall be no concern of a purchaser to see that this requirement has been complied with.[92]

(2) TO TENANTS IN COMMON

The advantage to the tenants in common is that, no matter how numerous they may be, a sale of the land effected is always possible without difficulty or undue expense. Neither are

---

[90] P. 456, ante.

[91] [1955] 1 QB 234, followed in *Cook v Cook* [1962] P 181; affd [1962] P 235. See too *Re Buchanan-Wollaston's Conveyance* [1939] Ch 217; affd [1939] Ch 738, where a conveyance to purchasers as joint tenants (who contributed unequally) was treated as coming within LPA 1925, s. 36(1); *Williams & Glyn's Bank Ltd v Boland* [1979] Ch 312 at 329; affd [1981] AC 487 (where a matrimonial home, to whose purchase both spouses contributed, was conveyed to one spouse only).

[92] TLATA 1996, s. 11(1), 16(1), pp. 445, 448, ante, replacing LPA 1925, s. 26(3).

they prejudiced by the loss of their rights in the land itself, for they have corresponding rights in the money arising from the sale. Thus if A is entitled under the tenancy in common to a half share in the land, and B and C are entitled to a quarter share each, the duty of the trustees is to ensure that A, B and C receive the purchase money in the same proportions. They need not sell at once, nor indeed at any time, for they may instead of selling, partition the land among the persons beneficially entitled.[93] The tenants in common can still deal with their equitable interests as freely as they could formerly have dealt with their legal interests. If A, B and C are tenants in common and C sells his equitable interest to D, the legal joint tenancy remains vested in the trustees upon the trust for A, B and D.

(2) Joint Tenancies

Certain consequential changes have also been effected in joint tenancies, and the law relating to this matter varies according as the land is, or is not, settled within the meaning of the Settled Land Act 1925.

(a) Settled land

If two or more persons are beneficially entitled for their lives under a strict settlement created before 1997, as for example where land was devised to X and Y for their lives with remainder to Z in fee simple,[94] they together constitute the tenant for life within the meaning of the Settled Land Act and there is no question of any trust for sale.[95] They are invested with the legal estate, and it is their function to make title upon a sale or other disposition of the land.

(b) Joint tenants beneficially entitled

In the second case, however, where the land is not settled, but is *beneficially* limited for a legal estate to joint tenants, for example, where a father conveys Blackacre to his two sons in fee simple without words of severance, the *legal* estate is held upon trust in like manner as if the persons beneficially entitled were tenants in common.[96] Thus if land is granted to A, B and C jointly in fee simple, A, B and C become joint tenants of the legal estate upon trust for themselves as equitable joint tenants. A legal and an equitable joint tenancy are automatically and inescapably brought into existence. A, B and C are trustees of the legal estate[97] and can therefore make title, but they are joint beneficiaries with regard to the equitable interests. They may postpone the sale of the land, indefinitely, but if there is a matter of dispute, any one of them may apply to the court under section 14 of the Trusts of Land and Appointment of Trustees Act 1996.[98]

(c) Determination of joint tenancy

This change in the law is unintelligible unless we remember that a *legal* joint tenancy can no longer be severed. It is essential to the success of the post-1925 rules for tenancies

---

[93] TLATA 1996, s. 7, replacing LPA 1925, s. 28(3), p. 470, post.

[94] See also *Re Gaul and Houlston's Contract* [1928] Ch 689; devise to X and Y in fee simple, subject to a charge, created voluntarily, of £1,000 in favour of Z. Thus, the land was settled by virtue of SLA 1925, s. 1(1)(v); p. 402, n. 18, ante.   [95] SLA 1925, s. 19(2).

[96] LPA 1925, s. 36(1), as amended by TLATA 1996, s. 5, Sch. 2, para. 4(1), (2), (4).

[97] They must not exceed four in number: TA 1925, s. 34, as amended by TLATA 1996, s. 25(1), Sch. 3, para. 3(9). See (1926) 42 LQR 478 at 480 (R. R. Formoy).   [98] P. 449, ante.

in common that the legal joint tenancy which must necessarily arise should continue undisturbed and should not be convertible into a tenancy in common by some transaction or event amounting to a severance, for otherwise the legal title would be split up into a number of separate titles and the old troubles incidental to a conveyance of the legal estate would return. Hence the new rule that a *legal* joint tenancy cannot be severed.[99] The object of the introduction of an equitable tenancy is to preserve to each tenant his right to sever his interest and thus to avoid the danger of his premature death and the consequent operation of the *jus accrescendi*.

We have already considered the methods by which a joint tenancy may be severed and converted into a tenancy in common,[100] but it is important to notice with some particularity the course open to a beneficial joint tenant who desires to prevent the survivorship of his equitable interest to the other tenants. If land has been conveyed to A and B as joint tenants, what is the effect upon A's beneficial interest if he predeceases B? The answer, of course, is that it survives absolutely to B to the detriment of A's successors. The further question then arises, what can A do in his lifetime to avoid this possible loss? In other words, how can the legal or the equitable joint tenancy, or both, be determined?

The solution is, either to determine the joint tenancy altogether, or, while retaining the legal joint tenancy, to sever it on its equitable side. Let us consider the two cases separately.

(1) LEGAL AND EQUITABLE JOINT TENANCY

A joint tenancy is determined altogether by any one of the following methods.

(i) *Sale of the legal estate*

If A and B sell in their capacity as trustees of land,[101] their conveyance passes the legal fee simple to the purchaser freed from their rights as joint tenants. The purchaser is not concerned with these rights, since they exist behind the trust and are merely equitable in nature.

A trust cannot be exercised unless there are at least two trustees, but it is enacted by the Law of Property (Amendment) Act 1926 that a surviving joint tenant, who is solely and *beneficially* entitled to the land, may deal with the legal estate as if it were not held on a trust.[102] Thus if land is devised in fee simple to a husband and wife jointly, the wife, on the death of her husband, can pass a good title to a purchaser of the legal estate without appointing another trustee in place of her husband.[103]

Such a conveyance, however, is not without its dangers, for a deceased tenant, without the knowledge of the survivor, may have severed his interest, a fact that will not appear on the vendor's abstract of title to the legal estate. It was formerly felt, therefore, that the only sure method of overreaching the equitable interest arising by virtue of the severance was for the survivor to reconstitute the trust for sale by appointing a new trustee. But this is no longer necessary. The Law of Property (Joint Tenants) Act 1964,[104] which is retrospective to

---

[99] LPA 1925, s. 36(2), p. 465, ante. [100] Pp. 457–61, ante.

[101] If any of the trustees or beneficiaries refuse to agree to a sale, the other(s) may apply to the court: TLATA 1996, s. 14; p. 449, ante. [102] Schedule amending LPA 1925, s. 36.

[103] According to *Re Cook* [1948] Ch 212, this would be the position apart from the Act of 1926, since, on the death of the husband the entire interest in the land, both legal and equitable, vests in the wife. The trust ceases, since she is now owner and cannot be trustee for herself.

[104] See Wolstenholme and Cherry, vol. 2, pp. 149–51; Barnsley, *Conveyancing Law and Practice*, pp. 315–17; (1964) 28 Conv (NS) 329; (1966) 30 Conv (NS) 27 (P. Jackson); (1980) LSG 1473, 1475 (P. H. Kenny and A. Kenny).

1 January 1926, provides that:

the survivor of two or more joint tenants shall, in favour of a purchaser of the legal estate, be deemed to be solely and beneficially interested if the conveyance includes a statement that he is so interested.[105]

This provision, however, is not to apply if a memorandum of severance has been endorsed on or annexed to the conveyance by which the legal estate was vested in the joint tenants; or if a receiving order, or a petition for such an order, has been registered under the Land Charges Act 1972.[106]

The Act only applies to unregistered land. Where title to land is registered, a joint proprietor restriction should be entered on the register.[107]

(ii) Partition

If all the joint tenants are of full age it is clear that as beneficial owners they may partition the land between themselves, whereupon the legal joint tenancy will be converted into separate ownership. Apart from this, however, section 36(1) of the Law of Property Act 1925[108] provides, as we have seen, that where a legal estate is beneficially limited to persons as joint tenants it shall be held on trust *in like manner as if the persons beneficially entitled were tenants in common*. Then, section 7 of the Trusts of Land and Appointment of Trustees Act 1996 provides that, where the beneficiaries of full age are absolutely entitled in undivided shares to land subject to the trust, the trustees may, with the consent of each of those beneficiaries, partition the land or any part of it and provide by way of mortgage or otherwise for the payment of any equality money.[109]

If the trustees or any of the beneficiaries refuse to agree to a partition, any beneficiary may apply to the court under section 14 of the Act. The court may then make such order as it thinks fit, for example an order for sale. If the beneficiaries are of full age and capacity and absolutely entitled to the land, the trustees may insist that they accept a conveyance of the land.[110]

(iii) Release

Where land is held by A and B as joint tenants it is open to either of them to release his interest to the other, whereupon the alienee will become sole and several owner.[111] An agreement for such a release must satisfy the requirements for a contract for the sale or other disposition of land.[112]

(2) DETERMINATION OF EQUITABLE JOINT TENANCY. SEVERANCE

It remains to be seen how it is possible to sever the equitable joint tenancy between A and B without disturbing the joint tenancy of the legal estate. This result is achieved if either of the tenants enters into any transaction which severs the tenancy and converts it into a tenancy in common, as for example where he alienates his share to a stranger; or if one of the tenants

---

[105] S. 1(1), as amended by LP(MP)A 1994, s. 2(2), Sch. 2.

[106] LP (Joint Tenants) A 1964, s. 1(1), proviso. Registration constitutes notice of the order or petition to the purchaser.

[107] This is not, however, necessarily as effective as the 1964 Act: [2004] Conv 41 (E. Cooke), proposing amendments to LRA 2002 to bring registered land into line with unregistered land. For restrictions generally in registered land, see pp. 440, ante; 974–5 post.

[108] As amended by TLATA 1996, s. 5, Sch. 2, para. 4(1), (3), (4).

[109] Replacing LPA 1925, s. 28(3). See *Re Gorringe and Braybon Ltd's Contract* [1934] Ch 614n; *Re Brooker* [1934] Ch 610.   [110] TLATA 1996, s. 6(2).

[111] LPA 1925, s. 36(2), as amended by TLATA 1996, s. 5, Sch. 2, para. 4(1), (3), (4).

[112] Chap. 24, post; *Cooper v Critchley* [1955] Ch 431.

acquires an interest greater in quantum than that held by the other; or by mutual agreement; or by a course of dealing.[113]

The Law of Property Act 1925 added a new and very useful method of severance.[114] Section 36(2)[115] provides that if any tenant desires to sever the joint tenancy in equity, he may give to the other joint tenants a written notice[116] of such desire, whereupon he becomes entitled to his share.[117]

Suppose, for instance, that land is limited to A, B and C as joint tenants. We know that this creates both a legal and an equitable joint tenancy. If C dies without having dealt with his interest, A and B retain the legal estate as trustees, and hold the equitable interest under the doctrine of survivorship, freed from the interest of C. But if in his lifetime C gives notice in writing of his desire to sever, his equitable joint tenancy becomes an equitable tenancy in common, and A and B hold the legal estate upon trust for themselves as equitable joint tenants and the personal representatives of C. The equitable tenancy in common will continue to exist until the sale is carried out, or the shares become vested in one person, or partition is effected.

(3) Sale by Two Trustees and by One Trustee Only

We are now in a position to summarise the difference between a sale by at least two trustees of land which is beneficially co-owned and a sale by one of them only.

(a) Sale by two trustees

Where the sale is made by at least two trustees or a trust corporation the interests of the beneficiaries are overreached, provided that the purchaser pays the purchase money to the trustees.[118] And this is so whether or not the beneficial co-owners are occupying the land.

The rule is the same for both unregistered and registered land.

(b) Sale by one trustee only

A further problem arises where the sale is made by one trustee only. The overreaching provisions do not apply. It is then necessary to consider separately the position where the land is unregistered and where it is registered.

---

[113] Pp. 457–61, ante.

[114] Law Commission Working Paper No. 94 on Trusts of Land (1985) suggested that the only means of severance should be by notice in writing (para. 6.12); and that it should be possible to sever by will (para. 16.14). As to whether beneficial joint tenancies should be abolished, see [1987] Conv 29, 225 (M. P. Thompson) in favour; 273 (A. M. Prichard) against. See also [1995] Conv 105 (L. Tee).

[115] As amended by TLATA 1996, s. 5, Sch. 2, para. 4(1), (2), (4).

[116] *Re 88 Berkeley Road, London NW9* [1971] Ch 648 (notice properly served if sent by recorded delivery, even if not received by addressee: LPA 1925, s. 196(4)); *Kinch v Bullard* [1999] 1 WLR 423 (severance although wife posted notice to husband but destroyed it before he received it); [1999] Conv 60 (M. Percival); [1998] All ER Rev 261 (P. J. Clarke).

[117] *Re Draper's Conveyance* [1969] 1 Ch 486, M & B p. 303 (issue of summons held to amount to notice in writing under s. 36(2)); (1968) 84 LQR 462 (P.V.B.). Cf *Harris v Goddard* [1983] 1 WLR 1203 (wife's prayer in a divorce petition for a property adjustment order to be made in respect of the former matrimonial home held not to be notice); [1984] Conv 148 (S. Coneys); *Grindal v Hooper* [1999] EGCS 150 (notice of severance effective, even though not endorsed on conveyance). Whether a unilateral act not amounting to notice under s. 36(2) can effect severance is a matter of dispute: *Burgess v Rawnsley* [1975] Ch 429, M & B p. 306; [1976] CLJ 20 (D. J. Hayton); (1977) 41 Conv (NS) 243 (S. M. Bandali).   [118] P. 447, ante.

(1) UNREGISTERED LAND

This was first illustrated by *Caunce v Caunce*,[119] where

a husband and wife agreed that the wife would make a capital payment towards the purchase of a house, that the husband would pay the instalments to the building society, and that the conveyance would be in their joint names. The house was, however, conveyed to the husband alone, and, without the wife's knowledge, he further charged it in favour of Lloyds Bank. On the husband's bankruptcy, one question was whether the bank took subject to, or free from, the wife's equitable interest. Stamp J held that the bank took free, as a bona fide purchaser of a legal estate for value without notice.

Thus, in that situation, whether or not a purchaser is bound by the interest of the beneficial co-owner depends upon the application of the old doctrine of the bona fide purchaser without notice. If the bank had had notice, actual or constructive, of the wife's interest, the mortgage would have been subject to it.[120]

(2) REGISTERED LAND

If the title to the land is registered, notice plays no part. If a restriction has been entered in the register, it will preclude the registration of the purchaser as proprietor if the terms of the restriction have not been complied with.[121] If no restriction has been entered, registration of the purchaser as proprietor will give him priority over the beneficiary's interest unless it takes effect as an overriding interest by virtue of the beneficiary being in discoverable actual occupation of the land.[122]

The comparable case to *Caunce v Caunce* is *Williams & Glyn's Bank Ltd v Boland*,[123] where the House of Lords held that the bank was bound by the wife's overriding interest; she had not protected it by an entry on the register, but was in actual occupation when the mortgage was executed.

IV Establishing the Beneficial Interests

A *Express, Constructive and Resulting Trusts*

We have seen that, in the modern law, the legal estate, whether registered or unregistered, can be held by a number of persons (not exceeding four); but that they must hold under a joint tenancy since legal tenancies in common have not been permitted since 1926. Establishing the legal title is therefore relatively straightforward. Establishing the beneficial interests can be more difficult. Once it is found that any number of persons concurrently own the property in equity, they may hold under either a beneficial joint tenancy or a beneficial tenancy in common. However, we must now consider how the beneficial interests are

---

[119] [1969] 1 WLR 286. The actual decision was disapproved in *Williams & Glyn's Bank Ltd v Boland* [1981] AC 487, where Lord SCARMAN said at 511 that he "was by no means certain that *Caunce v Caunce* was correctly decided." So too RUSSELL LJ in *Hodgson v Marks* [1971] Ch 892 at 924–5. It was not followed in *Kingsnorth Finance Co Ltd v Tizard* [1986] 1 WLR 783, p. 62, n. 105, ante.   [120] Pp. 58 et seq, ante.

[121] LRA 2002, s. 41(1). In the case of a sole registered proprietor the appropriate restriction is Form A: LRR 2003, r. 91, Sch. 4; the proprietor of land held on trust is required to apply for the restriction to be entered: LRR 2003, r. 94(1), (2), but the beneficiary also has a sufficient interest to make application: ibid., r. 93(a).

[122] Ibid., Sch. 3, para. 2.   [123] Supra; a decision on LRA 1925, s. 70(1)(g).

to be established. The principles discussed in this section apply generally to the establishment of concurrent interests in equity, although they are most commonly encountered in relation to interests in the family home. Later we shall consider certain rules which are peculiar to the case of the family home.[124]

If a number of persons wish to own property jointly they may do so by creating an express trust of land, under which it is conveyed to trustees (who may be themselves), who become joint tenants of the legal estate upon trust for themselves, as either equitable joint tenants or equitable tenants in common. The terms of the trust may declare not only the nature of the equitable beneficial interests, but also the quantum of the interest which each partner is to own.[125] In registered land the required forms of transfer contain provision for a declaration of trust where there is more than one transferee.[126] But in some cases it may not be so simple. The quantum may not be declared. Further, the legal estate in the property may be conveyed to *one* party, but the beneficial interest is to be shared between the couple, although there is no formal declaration of trust. The first question to decide in this type of case is whether each of the parties has an interest in equity; if so, the second question is what is the quantum of their respective interests. The approach to be adopted in this area has been developed through a series of cases,[127] but the most significant in the recent past are the decisions of the House of Lords in *Lloyds Bank plc v Rosset*,[128] and of the Court of Appeal in *Oxley v Hiscock*.[129]

(1) Finding a Trust

In *Lloyds Bank plc v Rosset* the House of Lords set out two bases on which a constructive trust could be found, where there is no declaration of trust to satisfy the formality requirements of section 53 of the Law of Property Act 1925. On either basis, the trust[130] arises from a combination of an agreement to share, coupled with reliance on that agreement by the party claiming a share.

---

[124] Pp. 476 et seq, post.

[125] Fraud or mistake apart, this is conclusive: *Pettitt v Pettitt* [1970] AC 777 at 813, per Lord UPJOHN; *Goodman v Gallant* [1986] Fam 106; cf *City of London Building Society v Flegg* [1988] AC 54. For a detailed declaration of trust (and the subsequent waiver of rights of contribution to expenses incurred in relation to the property), see *Wade v Grimwood* [2004] 2 P & CR DG20.

[126] See, e.g., LRR 2003, r. 206, Sch. 1, Form TR1, p. 964, post, where at para. 11 the transferees must choose between three possibilities: "The Transferees are to hold the Property on trust for themselves as joint tenants"; "The Transferees are to hold the Property on trust for themselves as tenants in common in equal shares"; and "The Transferees are to hold the Property [*Complete as necessary*]" . "The purpose of this is not to give the registrar notice of the trusts under which the land is held, but simply to enable us to decide whether we need to enter a form A restriction [p. 472, ante]. It also serves as a memorandum of the trusts on which the property is held, although details of the trusts will not appear on the register": Land Registry Practice Guide 24 (Private Trusts of Land), para. 5.4. For the use of this form to declare a trust as a joint tenancy, see *Bathurst v Scarborow* [2005] 1 P & CR 4 at [8]–[10], [55].

[127] Beginning with the "twin peaks of *Pettitt v Pettitt* [1970] AC 777 and *Gissing v Gissing* [1971] AC 886": *Grant v Edwards* [1986] Ch 638 at 646, per NOURSE LJ. See also *Eves v Eves* [1975] 1 WLR 1338.

[128] [1991] 1 AC 107; (1990) 106 LQR 539 (J. Davies); [1990] Conv 314 (M. P. Thompson); [1991] CLJ 38 (M. Dixon); (1991) 54 MLR 126 (S. Gardner); [1998] Conv 202 (V. Riniker); (1998) 18 LS 369 (S. Wong). See also *Ivin v Blake* (1993) 67 P & CR 263.

[129] [2005] Fam 211; (2004) 120 LQR 541 (S. Gardner); [2005] Conv 79 (M. Dixon), 496 (M. P. Thompson).

[130] Lord BRIDGE referred to this giving rise to a constructive trust *or a proprietary estoppel*: [1991] 1 AC 107 at 132. The link between constructive trust and proprietary estoppel in this context is discussed further at pp. 907–8, post.

First, the question is whether:[131]

independently of any inference to be drawn from the conduct of the parties in the course of sharing the house as their home and managing their joint affairs, there has at any time prior to acquisition, or exceptionally at some later date, been any agreement, arrangement or understanding reached between them that the property is to be shared beneficially. The finding of an agreement or arrangement to share in this sense can only, I think, be based on evidence of express discussions between the partners, however imperfectly remembered and however imprecise their terms may have been.

There need have been no discussion about the value of the respective beneficial shares; the quantification of the parties' interests can be decided as a separate matter.[132] However, an excuse as to why the property has not been put into joint names may be treated as an expression of a common intention to share.[133] But before the agreement to share gives rise to a constructive trust, the partner asserting a claim to a beneficial interest against the partner entitled to the legal estate must show that he or she has acted to his or her detriment or significantly altered his or her position in reliance on the agreement.[134] The requirement of detrimental reliance is shown by significant contributions in money or money's worth, which need not be direct,[135] but not by activities which any wife would do, such as decorating and supervising builders.[136]

Secondly, however, in the absence of any express common intention, the House of Lords suggested that a common intention could be implied from the conduct of the parties, such as the direct contributions to the purchase price (either initially or by payment of mortgage instalments) by the partner who is not the legal owner. However, it was said that it was "at least extremely doubtful whether anything less will do"[137]—although direct contributions have traditionally been regarded as giving rise to a resulting trust, rather than a constructive trust. The denial of any interest to a wife who has made substantial indirect contributions seems harsh, and not supported by authority.[138] A better analysis may be that the court can infer a common intention from both parties' conduct (including direct and indirect contributions to the purchase, although it will be a question of fact whether an indirect contribution is sufficiently referable to the acquisition to constitute evidence of such an intention). And, if there is no common intention, either express or implied, to found a constructive trust, then the court should consider whether there is a resulting trust. Asking the questions in this order makes good sense, because the parties' agreement should be given priority; but if there is no agreement, one can fall back on the resulting trust: where one partner contributes part of the purchase money, in the absence of contrary intention there is a presumption of a

---

131 [1991] 1 AC 107 at 132, per Lord BRIDGE OF HARWICH.

132 *Oxley v Hiscock* [2005] Fam 211, at [40], per CHADWICK LJ.

133 *Eves v Eves* [1975] 1 WLR 1338; *Grant v Edwards* [1986] Ch 638. However, although the fact that the property is placed in joint names will usually show that the parties intended to share the beneficial ownership, it is not necessarily conclusive: *Stack v Dowden* [2006] 1 P & CR; 15 [2005] Conv 555 (E. Cooke).

134 *Lloyds Bank plc v Rosset* [1991] 1 AC 107 at 132.

135 *Grant v Edwards* [1986] Ch 638; *Eves v Eves*, supra; *Hammond v Mitchell* [1991] 1 WLR 1127 (unpaid assistance in business); [1992] Conv 218 (A. Lawson); (1993) 56 MLR 224 (P. O'Hagan).

136 *Lloyds Bank plc v Rosset*, supra.   137 [1991] 1 AC 107 at 133.

138 See *Gissing v Gissing* [1971] AC 886 (contributions must be "referable" to the costs of acquisition). A difficulty with *Lloyds Bank plc v Rosset* is the House of Lords' failure to explain the relationship between constructive trusts based on an implied common intention, and resulting trusts. The decision in *Oxley v Hiscock*, supra, resolves this by, in effect, relegating resulting trusts to rare cases where there is no implied common intention: [2005] Conv 79 (M. Dixon); 496 (M. P. Thompson); [2004] All ER Rev 247 (P. J. Clarke).

resulting trust in equity under which the other, as purchaser, holds the property on trust for them both to the extent of their respective contributions.[139]

It should be noted, however, that for a common intention to be inferred from the parties' conduct, it must be communicated between the parties. Conduct by one party which was not known by the other cannot be evidence of their common intention.[140]

(2) Valuing the Interests under the Trust

The valuation of the parties' respective interests under the constructive trust[141] is a separate matter which has recently been examined by the Court of Appeal. If the parties, in forming their agreement to share the property, also agreed what their interests should be, that will be conclusive.[142] However, where there is no evidence of an agreement on the value of the interests, the court has a discretion. Settling a certain conflict in earlier decisions,[143] CHADWICK LJ said in *Oxley v Hiscock*:[144]

It must now be accepted that (at least in this court and below) the answer is that each is entitled to that share which the court considers fair having regard to the whole course of dealing between them in relation to the property. And, in that context, "the whole course of dealing between them in relation to the property" includes the arrangements which they make from time to time in order to meet the outgoings (for example, mortgage contributions, council tax and utilities, repairs, insurance and housekeeping) which have to be met if they are to live in the property as their home.

---

[139] See e.g. *Gissing v Gissing* [1971] AC 886. The value of the share depends on the (direct) contributions made at the time of acquisition: *Curley v Parkes* [2005] 1 P & CR DG 15; [2005] Conv 79 (M. Dixon). The presumption of the resulting trust may also be rebutted by the presumption of advancement that a beneficial gift was intended. This presumption is applicable where the *husband* provides the purchase money, and is itself rebuttable. The presumption of advancement appears to be of little weight today: *Pettitt v Pettitt* [1970] AC 777; *Falconer v Falconer* [1970] 1 WLR 1333.

[140] *Lightfoot v Lightfoot-Brown* [2005] 2 P & CR 22 (repayment of mortgage by one party, not known to the other, was not evidence of common intention). At [27], per ARDEN LJ: "Chadwick LJ [in *Oxley v Hiscock*] did not dispense with the requirement for communication of the common intention when determining whether a common intention constructive trust had arisen. Indeed, the concept of communication of common intention has much in common with the manifestation of intention. An intention to share a beneficial interest in property has to be manifested to give to a rival obligation . . . . The need for communication was only held to be unnecessary in the *Oxley* case in respect to the size of the parties' beneficial interest." Intention is tested objectively from the other party's perspective: *Gissing v Gissing* at 906.

[141] In the case of a resulting trust, the value of the parties' interests is fixed by reference to the contribution, and no separate question of valuation arises. This further explains why the constructive trust (based on the parties' agreement, both as to existence and as to valuation) should be considered ahead of the resulting trust.

[142] *Oxley v Hiscock*, [2005] Fam 211 at [69]; *Wright v Johnson* [2002] 2 P & CR 15 at [16]; *Crossley v Crossley* [2005] 1 FCR 655.

[143] Especially *Springette v Defoe* (1992) 65 P & CR 1; *Midland Bank plc v Cooke* [1995] 4 All ER 562; (1996) 112 LQR 378 (S. Gardner); (1996) 55 CLJ 194 (M. Oldham); [1997] Conv 66 (M. Dixon); (1997) 60 MLR 420 (P. O'Hagan); *Drake v Whipp* [1996] 1 FLR 826; [1997] Conv 467 (A. Dunn). See also *Stokes v Anderson* [1991] 1 FLR 391; *Huntingford v Hobbs* [1993] 1 FLR 736; *McHardy & Sons v Warren* [1994] 2 FCR 1247; *Le Foe v Le Foe* [2001] 2 FLR 970.

[144] At [69]. Applied in *Cox v Jones* [2004] 2 FLR 1010; [2005] Conv 168 (R. Probert) (25% share for partner who contributed nothing to cost of the purchase of house, and a very small amount on works done on it, but forewent income from her practice as barrister, and "her real contribution was the large amounts of time and energy she put in" during the building works: at [79]); *Stack v Dowden* [2006] 1 P & CR 15 (the same test applies, whether the property was in the name of only one or of both cohabitees: per CHADWICK LJ at [26]); *Supperstone v Hurst* [2006] 1 FCR 352 (having made statement to the husband's creditors that she and her husband were equal beneficial owners in the property, wife could not obtain a determination from the court that her interest exceeded 50%, in litigation between herself and trustee for those creditors).

This allows the court to take into account the facts at the time of the hearing in order to decide what appears to be a fair share, although the relevant facts are still those which concern the parties' "course of dealing in relation to the property". It is linked to the property itself. But the valuation is not to be imputed artificially back to the parties' intention at the moment of acquisition when the court does not think that the parties at that moment had any particular intention as to the valuation of their shares.[145]

B The Family Home

(1) Ownership

The family home occupies a most important part in family property law,[146] and in many cases it is the only substantial asset of the family. We have already noted that many of the cases discussed earlier in this section concerned the family home; and the development of the principles governing the constructive trust in this area has largely occurred in this context[147]—no doubt because of the informal arrangements commonly entered into between family members.[148] In many cases, therefore, the property rights as between spouses, civil partners or cohabiting partners can be solved simply by using the general rules already set out in this chapter. However, there are some special rules applicable to the family context, in relation to improvements to the property, on the breakdown of a marriage or civil partnership, and on death.

(a) Improvements

By statute[149] a husband or wife, or one of the two civil partners, who has made a substantial contribution in money or money's worth to the improvement of real or personal property in which either or both of them has a beneficial interest, will be treated as having a share or

---

[145] *Oxley v Hiscock* [2005] Fam 211, at [71]: "in the absence of evidence that they gave any thought to the amount of their respective shares, the necessary inference is that they must have intended that question would be answered later on the basis of what was then seen to be fair", rejecting the approach taken in *Midland Bank plc v Cooke*, supra.

[146] See generally Bromley, *Family Law*, chap. 5; Cretney, Masson and Bailey-Harris, *Principles of Family Law*, Part II.

[147] In 2002 the Law Commission published a Discussion Paper on *Sharing Homes* (Law Com No. 278); [2004] Conv 268 (C. Rotherham); (2004) 24 LS 414 (J. Mee). This examined the property rights of a broad range of those who share homes: not just "couples" (married or unmarried) but also friends, relatives and others living together for a variety of reasons, including companionship or care and support. The paper concluded that it was not possible to devise a statutory scheme for the ascertainment and quantification of beneficial interests in the shared home which could operate fairly and evenly across the diversity of domestic circumstances now being encountered. See the discussion by CARNWATH LJ (former Chairman of the Law Commission) in *Stack v Dowden* [2006] 1 P & CR 15 at [70]–[78]. The Law Commission has now moved on to a project, of different scope, on Cohabitation: Ninth Programme of Law Reform 2005 (Law Com No. 293), para. 3.3; Thirty-ninth Annual Report 2004/05 (Law Com No. 294), paras 6.19–6.22. A consultation paper is promised for 2006, and a final report (but not a draft Bill) in expected in 2007.

Constructive trusts are not restricted to the domestic context: *Banner Homes Group plc v Luff Developments Ltd* [2000] Ch 372, Maudsley and Burn, *Trusts and Trustees*, p. 289 (commercial joint venture parties; an application of the "*Pallant v Morgan* equity" [1953] Ch 43); *Lloyd v Pickering* [2004] EWHC 1513 (Ch); (2004) 154 NLJ 1014 (acquisition of share in a gym business); *Cox v Jones* [2004] 2 FLR 1010 (purchase of an investment property by one of an engaged couple as nominee for the other); [2005] Conv 168.

[148] On the wider significance of formality and informality in the creation of interests in land, see chap. 25, post.

[149] Matrimonial Proceedings and Property Act 1970, s. 37 (husband and wife); Civil Partnership Act 2004, s. 65 (civil partners).

an enlarged share in that beneficial interest.[150] This is subject to any express or implied agreement to the contrary. The contributor is entitled to any share agreed, or in default as may seem in all the circumstances just.

(b) Breakdown of relationship

A spouse or civil partner who is not a legal owner cannot claim any property interest in the matrimonial home during the marriage, unless he or she has made a contribution which entitles him or her to rely on the strict principles of trust law.[151] However, if the marriage breaks down, and there is a decree of divorce, nullity of marriage or judicial separation, the court is given the widest discretionary powers[152] under the Matrimonial Causes Act 1973[153] to order a distribution of the spouses' property, and disputes between spouses relating to property are best settled under that jurisdiction.[154] In particular, section 25(2)(f) of the Act requires the court to have regard to: "the contributions which each of the parties has made or is likely in the foreseeable future to make to the welfare of the family, including any contributions made by looking after the home or caring for the family" . First consideration must, however, be given to the welfare of any minor child of the family.[155]

Similarly, there are special statutory provisions which empower the court to make such order as it thinks fit in relation to disputes between the civil partners as to title to or possession of property.[156]

(c) Death

On the death of one spouse or civil partner, the other becomes entitled to the family home by survivorship if they were beneficial joint tenants of it. In other cases the survivor may acquire the home by will, under the intestacy laws[157] or by application under the Inheritance (Provision for Family and Dependants) Act 1975.[158]

---

[150] *Davis v Vale* [1971] 1 WLR 1022; *Kowalczuk v Kowalczuk* [1973] 1 WLR 930; *Griffiths v Griffiths* [1974] 1 WLR 1350.   [151] Pp. 472 et seq, ante.

[152] Including the power to order a sale of the matrimonial home where an order for financial relief is made on a decree of divorce, nullity or judicial separation. See s. 24A, added by Matrimonial Homes and Property Act 1981, s. 7. By s. 24A(6), a third party with a beneficial interest in the home may make representations before an order for sale is made. See [1981] Conv 404 (M. Hayes and G. Battersby). Any special rules applying to married couples, such as Matrimonial Proceedings and Property Act 1970, s. 37, apply also to property disputes between parties who have broken off their engagement to marry: Law Reform (Miscellaneous Provisions) Act 1970, s. 2(1). See *Mossop v Mossop* [1989] Fam 77.

[153] Where this Act applies, it is inappropriate to make a separate award for improvements under s. 37: *Griffiths v Griffiths*, supra. For the relationship between the two jurisdictions generally, see (1974) 118 SJ 431 (S. M. Cretney).   [154] *Williams v Williams* [1976] Ch 278 at 286.

[155] Matrimonial Causes Act 1973, s. 25(1), as substituted by the Matrimonial and Family Proceedings Act 1984, s. 3.

[156] Civil Partnership Act 2004, s. 66. which applies during the subsistence of the partnership and for three years after its dissolution or annulment: s. 68; or for three years after the termination of a civil partnership agreement: s. 74. Here too the court must give first consideration to the welfare of any minor child of the family; and must take into account the contributions which each civil partner has made or is likely in the foreseeable future to make to the welfare of the family, including any contribution by looking after the home or caring for the family: ibid., s. 72(1), Sch. 5, paras. 20, 21.

[157] Intestates Estates Act 1952, Sch. 2, as amended by Civil Partnership Act 2004, s. 71, Sch. 4, Pt 2, para. 13.

[158] See the 16th edn of this book, pp. 900–8.

(2) Occupation

Separate from any beneficial interest which a spouse or civil partner may own is the right of occupation given by the Family Law Act 1996.[159] This applies where:[160]

   (a) one spouse or civil partner ("A") is entitled to occupy a dwelling-house by virtue of—
       (i) a beneficial estate or interest or contract; or
       (ii) any enactment[161] giving A the right to remain in occupation; and

   (b) the other spouse or civil partner ("B") is not so entitled.

B then has a right of occupation of the dwelling-house. More specifically, if in occupation, B has a right not to be evicted or excluded by A without the leave of the court; if not in occupation, B has a right with the leave of the court to enter and occupy the house.[162] The right is only available to B where B is "not so entitled", or has merely an equitable interest in the dwelling-house.[163] As we have seen, such an interest may arise from B's contribution to its acquisition or improvement. The court has wide powers to prohibit, suspend or restrict the occupation rights of either party, or to require one spouse or civil partner to permit the other to occupy.[164] These powers are exercisable also in the case where the applicant has rights of occupation other than those conferred by the Act, as where they are joint owners.[165] In deciding whether and how to exercise its powers the court is to have regard to all the circumstances, including the housing needs and resources of each party and any children, the financial resources of each party, the effect of making or not making an order on the health, safety and well-being of the parties and any children, and the conduct of the parties.[166] Where B's right to occupy arises under the 1996 Act, it is a charge on A's estate, and has priority, as if it were an equitable interest, from the date of A's acquisition of his estate, or of the marriage or formation of the civil partnership, or 1 January 1968,[167] whichever is the latest.[168] It ends on the death of A or on the termination of the marriage or civil partnership, unless the court makes an order to the contrary during the marriage or civil partnership.[169]

If A is adjudged bankrupt, B's charge binds the trustee in bankruptcy. B may apply for an order under the 1996 Act to the court having bankruptcy jurisdiction. The court shall make such order under the 1996 Act as it thinks just and reasonable, having regard to various factors including the interests of A's creditors and the needs of B and any children. Where, however, the application is made more than one year after the vesting of A's estate in the trustee in bankruptcy, the court shall assume, save in exceptional circumstances, that the interests of A's creditors outweigh all other considerations.[170]

---

[159] Replacing the earlier legislation. See generally the discussion of the earlier Act by MEGARRY J in *Wroth v Tyler* [1974] Ch 30; (1968) 32 Conv (NS) 85 (F. R. Crane); Bromley, *Family Law*, pp. 199 et seq; Cretney, Masson and Bailey-Harris, *Principles of Family Law*, paras. 6.005 et seq.

[160] S. 30(1). References throughout this section to provisions of the Family Law Act 1996 are to it as amended by Civil Partnership Act 2004, s. 82, Sch. 9, Pt 1. The Act does not apply to a dwelling-house that has at no time been nor intended to be (in the cases of spouses) their matrimonial home or (in the case of civil partners) their civil partnership home: s. 30(7).   [161] E.g. Rent Act 1977; HA 1988.

[162] S. 30(2)(a), (b); *Watts v Waller* [1973] QB 153 (spouse out of occupation can register before getting leave of court to re-enter); *Barnett v Hassett* [1981] 1 WLR 1385 (spouse having no intention to occupy not permitted to register in attempt to freeze proceeds of intended sale).   [163] S. 30(9).

[164] S. 33(3).   [165] S. 33(1).

[166] S. 33(6), (7). See *Chalmers v Johns* [1999] 1 FLR 392; *B v B (Occupation order)* [1999] 1 FLR 715.

[167] The commencement date of the Matrimonial Homes Act 1967.   [168] S. 31(3).

[169] S. 31(8).

[170] Insolvency Act 1986, s. 336, amended by Civil Partnership Act 2004, s. 82, Sch. 9, Pt 2, para. 21; p. 450, ante.

The statutory right of occupation is registrable in unregistered land as a Class F land charge.[171] In the case of registered land, it may be protected by the entry of a notice;[172] it is not an overriding interest, even if B is in actual occupation.[173] If there are two or more dwelling-houses subject to right of occupation, B may register a charge, or notice, against only one at any one time.[174]

B may register the charge without notifying A of the registration, and thus cause diffi-culty where A later enters into a contract to sell the dwelling-house in ignorance of the registration. Further, B may register after A has contracted to sell and thus make it impossible for A to perform the contract, at the cost of substantial damages for its breach.[175]

Before the Family Law Act 1996, no statutory occupation rights were conferred on persons other than spouses. The 1996 Act conferred limited rights on former spouses, cohabitants and former cohabitants. As we have seen, the Civil Partnership Act 2004 extends the general statutory occupation rights to civil partners, and similarly the 2004 Act confers limited rights on former civil partners, and extended the definition of cohabi-tants.[176] These rights are not capable of protection by registration. A former spouse or civil partner with no right to occupy (or whose right derives from an equitable interest only) may apply for an occupation order in relation to the former matrimonial or civil partner-ship home for a specified period not exceeding six months (although this may be extended).[177] A cohabitant or former cohabitant may similarly apply for an occupation order in relation to the home where the parties live or lived together.[178] These provisions are without prejudice to the right of a former spouse or civil partner, cohabitant or former cohabitant who has an equitable interest to apply for an occupation order under section 33 of the 1996 Act. This section, which has already been discussed in relation to spouses and civil partners, applies also where a former spouse or civil partner, cohabitant or former cohabitant is entitled to occupy the home by reason of some beneficial interest, contract or enactment. In such a case he or she may apply for an occupation order against the other party and may, for example, secure the eviction of the other party, although such an exclu-sion order is regarded as drastic.[179]

---

[171] LCA 1972, s. 2(7). Such a registration (and its registered land equivalent) entitles the spouse or civil part-ner to be given notice of any proceedings by a mortgagee, Family Law Act 1996, s. 56. For the right to be made a party to any action to enforce the mortgage, see s. 55.   [172] Family Law Act 1996, s. 31(10).

[173] Ibid.   [174] Ibid., Sch. 4, para. 2.

[175] *Watts v Waller* [1973] QB 153; *Wroth v Tyler* [1974] Ch 30; (1974) 38 Conv (NS) 110, (1975) 39 Conv (NS) 78 (D. J. Hayton); (1974) CLP 76 (D. G. Barnsley).

[176] Civil Partnership Act 2004, s. 82, Sch. 9, Pt 1, para. 13(1), (2)(a), amending the definition of "cohabitants" in Family Law Act 1996, s. 62, to read "two persons who are neither married to each other nor civil partners of each other but are living together as husband and wife or as if they were civil partners", repealing a different form of words ("two persons who, although not married to each other, are living together as husband and wife or (if of the same sex) in an equivalent relationship") substituted by Domestic Violence, Crime and Victims Act 2004, s. 3 but never brought into force.   [177] Family Law Act 1996, s. 35.

[178] S. 36. By s. 62, "cohabitants" were then a man and woman who live together as husband and wife.

[179] *Chalmers v Johns* [1999] 1 FLR 392. S. 33 also enables an applicant with no interest in the home to obtain an order against an "associated person". This expression is defined in s. 62(3) and includes engaged couples and those who have entered into a civil partnership agreement. Orders may be made under ss. 37 and 38 in relation to a home occupied by parties neither of whom is entitled to occupy by virtue of any beneficial interest, contract or enactment.

V Party-walls

We must finally examine the effect of the legislation of 1925 upon party-walls. According to FRY J the term "party-wall" may mean:[180]

(a) a wall of which two adjoining owners are tenants in common; or

(b) a wall divided vertically into two strips, one half of the thickness belonging to each of the neighbouring owners; or

(c) a wall belonging entirely to one owner, but subject to an easement in the other to have it maintained as a dividing wall; or

(d) a wall divided vertically into two equal strips, each strip being subject to a cross-easement in favour of the owner of the other.

It may be said that *most* of the party-walls in this country come within the first class, that is, are held by the adjoining owners as tenants in common, and in view of this it is clear that the effect of the statutory alterations relating to concurrent interests would have been absurd had special provisions for party-walls not been added. The effect would have been to render the majority of such walls subject to a trust for sale!

It is therefore enacted[181] that a wall which before 1926 would have been held by tenants in common shall be regarded as severed vertically as between the respective owners, and that the owner of each part shall have such rights to support and user over the other part as he would have had qua tenant in common under the old law. In other words, most party-walls now fall within the last class enumerated by FRY J.

The Party Wall etc Act 1996[182] provides for the building of and work relating to party walls and structures close to the boundary. It gives rights to carry out work in three situations: where there is no existing party structure; where there is an existing party structure; and where excavation or construction within three metres of a neighbour's building is proposed.[183] In all three cases there is a notice and counter notice procedure, and disputes are to be settled by an agreed surveyor.

The Act extends with some modifications the scheme of the London Building Acts (Amendment) Act 1939 to the whole of England and Wales as from July 1997. It does not affect matters of ownership of a party-wall.

---

180 *Watson v Gray* (1880) 14 Ch D 192 at 194–5. See generally Rudall, *Party Walls*.
181 LPA 1925, s. 38, Sch. 1, Part V; see also s. 187(2).
182 [1996] Conv 326 (J. E. Adams); (1998) 142 SJ 772 (G. Powell); Bickford-Smith and Sydenham, *Party Walls Law and Practice* (2nd edn). On party-walls and arbitration, see (2005) 115 NLJ 866 (P. Aliker).
183 Ss. 1, 2 and 6 (which accounts for the "etc").

14

ENTAILED INTERESTS

The entailed interest was once of great significance in family settlements but the last century marked its formal decline. We shall see that before 1926 it was recognised as a legal estate; thereafter it could exist only as an equitable interest; and finally after 1996 no new entailed interests can be created. However, since existing entailed interests still continue to exist, we shall here give an account of their nature in the modern law—which, as so often, can be understood only by first understanding their historical development.

I History

A Conditional Fee

The estate known to the common law as the conditional fee was the precursor of the estate tail. About the year 1200 it was becoming a common practice to limit lands to a man and a special or restricted class of his heirs, as for instance:

to a man and "the heirs of his body"; or

to a husband and wife and the heirs springing from their marriage; or to a woman and the heirs of her body—a form of gift that was called a *maritagium*.[1]

As the object of such a gift was to provide for a man's descendants, it was understood that if the donee or one of his issue to whom the land descended died without leaving any heirs of the class specified in the instrument of creation, the estate, being no longer required for the maintenance of the family, should revert to the donor, and should not, like a fee simple, pass to the general heirs of the donee.[2] The courts, however, animated probably by a desire to render land freely alienable and to this end to prevent it from being irrevocably ear-marked for a particular family, took an entirely different view of the matter, for they held that if a grant were made to A and the heirs of his body, or to him and any similarly restricted class of heirs, A could make an out-and-out alienation of his estate, binding on his own heirs and on the donor, as soon as a child of the class indicated was born to him. They said that the effect of such a gift was to confer upon A a conditional fee, that is to say, an absolute fee simple, conditional however upon the birth of issue capable of inheriting the estate according to the terms of the original gift. When once the condition was satisfied, even though the child died the next minute, A was in as favourable a position as if the lands had originally been granted to him in fee simple, for at common law a condition once performed is utterly gone; but if the condition was not fulfilled by the birth of issue, then on A's death the estate reverted to the donor and his heirs.[3]

B Statute De Donis Conditionalibus 1285

This rule, which meant in effect that the donee could alienate the land and thus defeat both the right of his issue to succeed to the estate and the right of the donor to take the estate back if issue already born became extinct, was not popular. As early as 1258 there was an outcry against a doctrine that ran so contrary to the expressed intention of donors, and the result of this feeling was the passing in 1285 of the famous statute *De Donis Conditionalibus*.[4] This enacted that the intention of the donor according as it was manifestly expressed in the original gift, should thenceforth be observed, so that those to whom the land was given should have no power to alienate it, but that it should pass to their issue, or to the giver or his heirs if such issue failed, either by an absolute default of issue or, after the birth of issue, by its subsequent extinction.[5]

The result of this statute was the appearance of a new kind of fee or inheritable estate, called a fee tail, or in Latin *feodum talliatum*, and so called because the quantum of the estate was "cut down" in the sense that, unlike the case of the fee simple, the right to inherit was

---

[1] Holdsworth, *History of English Law*, vol. iii. pp. 74, 111; Plucknett, *Legislation of Edward I*, pp. 125–31.

[2] If the gift took the form of what was called *liberum maritagium*, the rule was that after the land had descended three times there should no longer be any reverter to the donor and his heirs. Thus, the third heir became entitled in fee simple; Plucknett, pp. 126–9.

[3] Pollock and Maitland, *History of English Law*, vol. ii. pp. 16–19; Co Litt 19a; Challis, *Law of Real Property*, pp. 263–8.

[4] "On conditional gifts": Statute of Westminster II (1285), set out in full, Digby, *History of the Law of Real Property*, p. 226.   [5] See Challis, *Law of Real Property*, p. 228.

restricted to the class of heirs specially mentioned in the gift, and was not available to the heirs-general of the donee.[6]

The land could not be disposed of by the tenant in tail, it could not be seized in satisfaction of his debts after it had come into the hands of his successors, and it was not forfeitable for treason or felony—a fact which, in those disturbed times, was regarded by the Crown as a serious defect.[7]

Special remedies were given to the issue and to the donor for the recovery of the land in case the form of the original gift was not observed.[8]

There was thus set up an entailed interest in the true sense of that term, that is to say, an interest in land that was bound to descend from one generation to another to the issue of the tenant, and which could not by any means whatsoever be removed from the family so long as any lineal heirs of the class specified were in existence. It was an unbarrable entail, since neither the right of the issue to succeed, nor the right of the donor and his heirs to take on failure of issue, could be barred or taken away.[9] This state of affairs continued for some two hundred years after the Statute *De Donis*, but the statute, instead of being a blessing calculated to ensure the stability of families, proved to be one of the most mischievous institutions in the realm. Blackstone has described some of its effects:[10]

Children grew disobedient when they knew they could not be set aside; farmers were ousted of their leases made by tenants in tail; for, if such leases had been valid, then, under colour of long leases, the issue might have been virtually disinherited; creditors were defrauded of their debts, for if tenant in tail could have charged his estate with their payment, he might also have defeated his issue, by mortgaging it for as much as it was worth; innumerable latent entails were produced to deprive purchasers of the lands they had fairly bought, of suits in consequence of which our ancient books are full; and treasons were encouraged, as estates tail were not liable to forfeiture longer than for the tenant's life. So that they were justly branded as the source of new contentions and mischiefs unknown to the common law, and almost universally considered as the common grievance of the realm. But as the nobility were always fond of this statute, because it preserved their family estates from forfeiture, there was little hope of procuring repeal by the legislature.

C Methods of Barring Fee Tail

Although the legislature did not step in to remedy a grievance that appears to have borne so heavily upon the community, the ingenuity of lawyers finally—and at least as early as 1472—contrived to discover means whereby estates tail could be barred and converted into estates in fee simple, free from the succession rights of heirs and from the rights of those persons who were entitled to take upon a failure or extinction of heirs. The actual methods invented are now a matter of history, and it must suffice here to state their names and their general effect.

[6] Litt, s. 18; Challis, p. 60.

[7] First Report of Real Property Commission, 1829, p. 22.

[8] Called respectively the *writ of formedon in the descender* and the *writ of formedon in the reverter*; Holdsworth, *History of English Law*, vol. ii. p. 350.

[9] This apparently was not the intention of the draftsman of the statute. What was intended was that the land should be inalienable only until the third heir had entered, after which it could be alienated out of the family: Plucknett, *Legislation of Edward I*, pp. 131–5.　　　　[10] *Commentaries*, vol. ii. p. 116.

(1) Common Recovery

The most usual method was *to suffer a common recovery*. In the earliest days of its history a common recovery was a collusive real action which a collaborator (called the *demandant*) brought against the tenant in tail for the recovery of the land entailed. The tenant in tail did not raise a substantial plea to the claim preferred against him, but stated, contrary to the truth, that he had obtained the land by conveyance from one X, who, at the time of the conveyance, had warranted for himself and his heirs that the title granted to the tenant in tail was a good one. X, who was an accomplice of the parties, admitted the warranty by disappearing from court. The court thereupon proceeded to deliver judgment, that on the one hand the demandant should recover the entailed lands for an estate in fee simple, and that on the other hand the tenant in tail should recover lands of equal value from X.

Now the effect of this collusive action was to defeat the rights both of the tenant's issue and of the persons entitled on failure of issue, because if lands of equal value had actually been recovered from X, which they never were, they would have replaced the original entailed estate and would have descended in the same manner. Ostensibly this was so, but none of the untrue allegations made in the course of the proceedings was traversable, and therefore all that the persons entitled after the death of the tenant acquired was a judgment enforceable against a man of straw. The court was not prepared to tolerate a plea that a judgment, solemnly pronounced, was in effect nugatory.[11]

After delivery of judgment the demandant would convey either the fee simple or its value to the former tenant in tail.

(2) Fine

The second method was to levy a fine. A "fine", which from the earliest times had been regarded as the most sacred and efficacious form of conveyance known to the law,[12] was in substance a conveyance of land but in form an action.[13] It was an amicable composition or agreement of an action, made with the leave of the court, whereby the lands in question were acknowledged to belong to one of the parties, and it derived its name from the fact that it put an end (Latin *finis*) to the action.[14] One of the purposes for which it was used was to bar an estate tail. The tenant in tail covenanted to sell the fee simple to a collaborator, and when he was sued by the latter in an action of covenant he decided to capitulate, and with the leave of the court a concord was drawn up acknowledging that the lands belonged to the plaintiff.

From one point of view the levying of a fine was not so effective as the suffering of a recovery, since it barred the rights only of the tenant's issue (thus setting up what is called a "base fee"), while a recovery barred not only the issue, but also everybody who became entitled to the estate on failure of issue. On the other hand, a fine, which was a personal action, enabled a tenant in tail who was not for the moment tenant in possession to bar his own issue

---

[11] For a full account see Blackstone, vol. ii. pp. 357 et seq; Cruise, *Digest* Tit. xxxvi; Burton, *Real Property*, paras. 682–97; Pollock, *The Land Laws*, pp. 80–9; Digby, *History of the Law of Real Property*, pp. 251–4; First Report of Real Property Commissioners, 1829, pp. 21–3; Holdsworth, *History of English Law*, vol. iii. pp. 118 et seq; Simpson, *A History of the Land Law*, pp. 126 et seq.

[12] Holdsworth, *History of English Law*, vol. iii. p. 239.

[13] Pollock and Maitland, *History of English Law*, vol. ii. p. 94.

[14] Blackstone, vol. ii. p. 349; Challis, *Law of Real Property*, p. 304.

without the necessity of obtaining the possessor's collaboration.[15] In such circumstances, a common recovery was impossible unless the aid of the tenant for life, A, was obtained, because the proceedings reproduced the stages of a genuine action, and one of the fundamental rules of procedure was that a real action could be brought only against the person actually seised of the land.

(3) Fines and Recoveries Act 1833

Recoveries and fines, which even in their origin were collusive actions, gradually became wholly fictitious. Only formal matters were transacted in court. If a tenant in tail desired to bar his entail, all that he did was to instruct his solicitor to suffer a common recovery. But the solicitor, in carrying out the instructions, did not simply frame a deed expressing the tenant's intention, but was obliged to prepare a long and complicated document that recited all the stages and events of an action which was supposed, contrary to fact, to have been litigated. Moreover, the fees that would have been payable had the action been actually brought were still payable. The result was that to convert a fee tail into a fee simple was a tedious and expensive transaction, and one which, owing to the complicated and exceedingly difficult state of the law, required an expert for its completion, and even then often failed to produce a sound title. The Real Property Commissioners, in their Report issued in 1829, stated: "there is no object, however complicated, that could not be effected by a simple instrument, expressing in clear and intelligible language the intentions of the parties". The result of their recommendations was the passing of the Fines and Recoveries Act 1833, which abolished both recoveries and fines, and introduced a simple and straightforward method by which an estate tail might be barred.[16]

II Creation of Entailed Interests

We have already seen that an entailed interest is one that is given to a person and after his death to a specified class of that person's heirs. The different classes of entailed interests depend upon the terms of the instrument of gift and vary according as the estate is descendible to the heirs of the donee by any spouse or by a particular spouse, and also according as the heirs are restricted as to sex or not.

A Classes of Entailed Interests

(1) Interests in Tail General

An interest in tail general is the widest type of entailed interest. Such an interest arises when land is limited to:

A and the heirs of his body begotten,

---

[15] For example, where there was a grant to A for life, and after his death to B in tail, B could levy a fine.
[16] P. 496, post.

without any restriction either as to the wife upon whose body the heirs are to be begotten, or as to the sex of the heirs who are to take.[17] It matters not how many times A marries, for any child by any wife is eligible to succeed. If the entailed interest is not barred by the tenant during his lifetime nor disposed of by his will it still descends even today to his lineal descendants according to the old canons of descent which were formerly applicable to all inheritable fees,[18] but which were abolished by the Administration of Estates Act 1925, so far as regards the fee simple.

So where there is an interest in tail general limited to:

A and the heirs of his body,

and A dies intestate having failed to bar the entail, his eldest son by his first wife will take first. If the eldest son has predeceased A leaving no children, the second son of A, or such son's representative if he is dead, will take, and so on through the sons in the order of their seniority. Failing sons or children of sons, the daughters of A will share equally as coparceners.[19]

(a) Curtesy

Before 1926 a husband was entitled in certain circumstances to a life interest in the whole of the land of which the wife died seised in fee simple or in tail. He became what was called a "tenant by the curtesy".[20] Curtesy has been abolished with regard to all interests except an entailed interest,[21] and therefore the subject can only now be of importance when a *female tenant in tail* dies intestate.

(b) Restriction as to sex

An interest in tail general may be restricted as to sex:

(1) IN TAIL MALE GENERAL

This arises where lands are limited to

A and the heirs *male* of his body begotten,

the factor in which this species of estate differs from an interest in tail general being that only male heirs are to succeed.[22] Sons by any wife are capable of inheriting, and so are any other male issue claiming continuously through male issue, but daughters and their issue, whether male or female, can never inherit.

(2) IN TAIL FEMALE GENERAL

This is analogous to the last interest except that the only heirs entitled to take are females. Though this is a possible form of limitation, it never arises in practice.[23]

---

[17] Litt., ss. 14, 15; Blackstone, vol. ii. p. 113.

[18] LPA 1925, s. 130(4). The canons are those that affected the descent of a fee simple before 1926 except those that relate to ancestors and collaterals; p. 89, ante.   [19] P. 462, ante.

[20] Or more particularly, by the Curtesie of England: Co Litt 35.

[21] AEA 1925, s. 45(1)(b), (2); LPA 1925, s. 130(4). But curtesy in respect of a fee simple may still, though now very rarely, arise under AEA 1925, s. 51(2). This provides that the old rules of descent shall apply to realty (excluding chattels real), to which a person of unsound mind and already of full age on 1 January 1926 dies without having recovered testamentary capacity, is entitled.

[22] Litt. s. 2; Blackstone, vol. ii. p. 114.   [23] Co Litt 25a; Hargrave's note.

(2) Interests in Tail Special

The characteristic of the remaining entailed interests is that by the words of the instrument of creation their descent is restricted to the heirs of the body of two specified persons, and not to the heirs of one, as in the cases described above. Such an estate may be limited either to one donee, for example:

to H and the heirs begotten by him on the body of W,

or to two donees, for example:

to H and W and the heirs of their two bodies begotten.[24]

In both cases it will be seen that it is not the heirs of H by any wife who are capable of inheriting the interest, but only the children and their issue who can trace their descent from the particular wife W. If the limitation is to:

H and the heirs begotten by him on the body of his wife W,

H has an interest in tail special and the wife has nothing.[25] But the effect of a limitation to H and W and the heirs of their two bodies begotten varies according to the relative positions of H and W. If W is the wife of H or a person whom he may lawfully marry, the effect is to vest a joint interest in tail special in H and W;[26] but if H and W are persons who may not lawfully intermarry, by reason, for instance, of consanguinity, the limitation makes them joint tenants for life with separate inheritances.[27] That means that if H dies first and has issue, W becomes sole tenant for life, but that on the death of W the issue of H take one half and the issue of W the other half as tenants in common in tail.[28] The result will be the same if, though capable of intermarrying, H and W do not actually intermarry.

After what has been said it will be sufficient to give the appropriate words of limitation for granting the remaining species of entailed interests:

(a) In tail male special

Grant to:

A and his heirs male which he shall beget on the body of his wife X;

or to:

A and X and the heirs male of their two bodies begotten.[29]

(b) In tail female special

This arises from the same limitation as that just described, with the substitution of female for male.[30]

---

[24] Litt s. 16; *Preston on Estates*, vol. ii. p. 413. [25] Litt s. 29. [26] Co Litt 20b, 25b.
[27] Litt s.283; *Preston on Estates*, vol. ii. p. 417. [28] Co Litt 182a. [29] Litt s. 25.
[30] For the whole of this section, see Challis, *Law of Real Property*, pp. 290–5.

(3) Interests in Tail after Possibility of Issue Extinct

An entailed interest special may by implication of law give rise to what is called an entailed interest after possibility of issue extinct. If lands are given to a man and his wife, or to the man or to the wife solely, in special tail, and one of them, or the designated spouse, dies before issue has been born, the survivor is termed a *tenant in tail after possibility*; and likewise if one dies leaving issue, but the other survives the issue.[31] In both these cases it will be seen that, owing to the premature death of one of the persons from whose body the appropriate heirs are to proceed, it is impossible that any person should become entitled to succeed to the interest in accordance with the terms of the original gift. The possibility of the right class of heirs coming into being no longer exists, and therefore the survivor is said to be a tenant after possibility. Such a person is virtually in the position of a tenant for life and he is not entitled to bar the entail.[32] He is given the statutory powers of a tenant for life by the Settled Land Act 1925.[33]

B Words of Limitation

We have now to consider what words of limitation had to be used in order to create an entailed interest. Owing to the way in which the matter was dealt with by the Law of Property Act 1925, it is unfortunately necessary to discuss the rules which obtained under the previous law. The examples that have been given above of the various classes of entailed interests indicate the general nature of the proper words of limitation, and a short treatment of the subject will suffice here.

(1) Words of Limitation before 1926

(a) Creation by deed

The first point is to ascertain the proper words of limitation necessary before 1926 for the creation of an entailed interest by *deed*.

(1) WORD "HEIRS"

The requirement of common law here was that the word *heirs* must be used and not such analogous expressions as *seed, offspring, descendants, issue* and so on.[34] The effect of a grant, for example, to "A and his issue" was to confer upon A a mere life estate.

(2) WORDS OF PROCREATION

The next requirement was that some expression denoting that the inheritance was to pass to the direct descendants of A should be used, and the surest phrase for this purpose was *of his body*. A grant to "A and the heirs of his body" always conferred an entailed interest on A, but common law, though insisting upon the use of the word *heirs*, was not so exacting with regard to this second requirement, and was satisfied with any words which

---

[31] Litt s. 32.   [32] Fines and Recoveries Act 1833, s. 18.

[33] SLA 1925, s. 20(1)(i); *Hambro v The Duke of Marlborough* [1994] Ch 158; p.415, ante; p. 499, post.

[34] Co Litt 20a, b; Blackstone, vol. ii. p. 115.

expressly or by implication showed that the heirs were to issue from the body of A. Thus such expressions as:

of his flesh,

from him proceeding, or

which he shall beget of his wife,

were sufficient for the purpose.[35]

Before 1 January 1882, if the appropriate words of limitation as set out above were not adopted in a deed, the result was to confer a life estate upon the grantee, but the Conveyancing Act of 1881[36] provided that in deeds executed after that date it should be sufficient to use the words *in tail* instead of *heirs of the body*, and the words *in tail male* or *in tail female* instead of *heirs male* or *heirs female of the body*.[37]

(b) Creation by will

Greater latitude of terminology was, however, open to testators. It is more difficult to lay down hard and fast rules as to what words would, and what words would not, have created a certain interest when they were used in a testamentary as distinct from an *inter vivos* instrument, because the general principle of construction for wills is that the intention of the testator must be ascertained and given effect to, no matter what language he may have adopted. But at any rate it is clear that less formal language would create an entailed interest in a will than in a deed, and in fact any expressions that indicated an intention to give the devisee an estate of inheritance, descendible to his lineal as distinct from his collateral heirs, conferred an entailed interest upon him.[38]

Thus devises to:

A and his seed;[39]

A and his offspring;[40]

A and his family according to seniority;[41]

A and his issue;[42]

A and his posterity;[43]

have all, at one time or another, been held capable of passing an entailed interest when such a construction was consistent with the intention of the testator.

(c) Executory instruments

The same rule of construction was applied in the case of executory instruments *inter vivos*, that is, in instruments which do not finally express the limitations in technical language, but indicate their general nature and leave the settlor's intention to be carried out by apt phraseology. What are called "marriage articles" form the commonest example of an executory instrument. They constitute a contract by which an intending husband and wife specify in

---

[35] Co Litt 20b.   [36] S. 51. LPA 1925, s. 60(4)(b), (c), repealed by TLATA 1996, s. 25(2), Sch. 4.
[37] For criticism, see Challis, *Law of Real Property*, pp. 297–8.   [38] *Jarman on Wills*, p. 1825.
[39] Co Litt 9b.   [40] *Young v Davies* (1863) 2 Drew & Sm 167.
[41] *Lucas v Goldsmid* (1861) 29 Beav 657.   [42] *Oxford University v Clifton* (1759) 1 Eden 473.
[43] *Wild's Case* (1599) 6 Co Rep 16b.

general the terms upon which they are willing to enter into a marriage settlement. Thus, if marriage articles provide for the limitation of an interest to the "issue" of the husband and wife, the presumed intention will be carried out in the formal settlement by the grant of an entailed interest to the first son of the marriage, with remainders in tail to the other children.[44]

(d) The rule in Wild's Case

A devise "to A and his children" requires particular attention because of the Rule in *Wild's Case*[45] laid down in 1599.[46] The rule was that where realty was devised to "A and his children", and A had no child *at the time of the devise*, the word children was prima facie construed as a word of limitation, with the result that A acquired an estate tail.

There was some justification for this. The testator clearly intended children to take in any event, but since they were not in existence they could take nothing except through A and he could transmit to them nothing unless he was given an estate of inheritance.[47]

The rule, however, was not inflexible and it was disregarded by the courts where it would operate to defeat the intention of the testator as gathered from other passages in the will.[48]

(2) Words of Limitation after 1925 but before 1997

(a) Formal words

We are now left with this question: what words were necessary and sufficient to create an entailed interest in the case of a deed or will that came into operation after 1925, but before 1997?[49] Section 130 (1) of the Law of Property Act 1925 enacted as follows:

An interest in tail . . . (in this Act referred to as "an entailed interest") may be created by way of trust in any property, real or personal, but only by the like expressions as those by which before [1926] a similar estate tail could have been created by deed (not being an executory instrument) in freehold land.

The result is that the law on the subject became more inflexible than it was before 1926. The strict requirements of the common law applicable to deeds were extended to wills. Thus, in both instruments the limitation must be to "A in tail", or to "A and the heirs of his body", except that in the last case any expressions will suffice that without expressly saying "of the body" indicate that the heirs are to issue from the body of A. The only exception to this rule is that a direction that personal property should be enjoyed with land in which an entailed interest had already been created was sufficient to create a corresponding entailed interest in the personal property.[50]

On the other hand, informal expressions contained in the instrument which would not have been sufficient in a deed before 1926 to create an entailed interest, though they would have been sufficient in a will or executory instrument, no longer suffice to create an entailed interest.[51] If, for instance, a testator who died after 1925 devised land to "A and his issue", an interest in tail did not pass to A.

---

[44] *A-G v Bamfield* (1703) Freem Ch 268.   [45] (1599) 6 Co Rep 16b.   [46] See p. 492, n. 61, post.

[47] *Radcliffe v Buckley* (1804) 10 Ves 195 at 202, per Sir William GRANT MR.

[48] *Byng v Byng* (1862) 10 HL Cas 171 at 178; *Grieve v Grieve* (1867) LR 4 Eq 180.

[49] LPA 1925, s. 130(1)–(3), (4) were repealed by TLATA 1996, s. 25(2), Sch. 4. Since 1996 no entailed interests can be created, p. 500, post.   [50] LPA 1925, s. 130(3).

[51] *Re Brownlie* [1938] 4 All ER 54.

(b) Informal words

The question that then arises is—what interest did pass to A when informal expressions such as "issue", "seed", "descendants" or "children" were contained in a conveyance or in a devise of land?[52] The Act purported to provide an answer in section 130(2):

Expressions contained in an instrument coming into operation after [1925], which, in a will, or executory instrument coming into operation before [1926], would have created an entailed interest in freehold land, but would not have been effectual for that purpose in a deed not being an executory instrument, shall . . . operate in equity, in regard to property real or personal, to create absolute, fee simple or other interests corresponding to those which, if the property affected had been personal estate, would have been created therein by similar expressions before [1926].

The first point to notice is that this sub-section is not concerned with those formal expressions that would have been effectual in a deed before 1926 to create an estate tail in land. A gift of personality to A and the heirs of his body or to A in tail formerly gave A the absolute ownership of the property,[53] but after 1925, by virtue of section 130(1),[54] it gave him an entailed interest. What we are concerned with here are informal expressions, and we are told that if they appear in a grant or a devise of land operating after 1925 and before 1997, the donee is to acquire in the land the interest that he would have acquired in personalty had the same expression been contained in a gift of personalty. The question then is, what interest passed under a gift of personalty, in the following typical cases:

To A and his issue;

To A for life and then to his issue;

To A and his descendants;

To A and his children.

Find this and we know what interest was taken if the same expressions were adopted in a grant or devise of land.

The primary difficulty is that, since the effect of such informal expressions has always varied according as they appear in deeds or in wills, it is not obvious whether the rules for deeds or for wills were to be adopted. Presumably the solution was that a devise containing informal expressions was to have the effect that had always been allowed to a bequest containing the like expressions, and that a grant *inter vivos* was to have the effect that had always been attributed to a corresponding gift by deed of personalty.

Let us examine only *bequests* of personalty, for it is unlikely in practice that any but formal expressions would be found in a conveyance *inter vivos* of land.[55] It must be realised at once, however, that no unqualified rule can be laid down with regard to the quantum of interest that passes under this or that expression, for since the object in each case is to ascertain and to implement the intention of the testator, what always has to be done is to construe the will as a whole. Strictly speaking, the only correct answer to make to the question, "What interest is taken under a gift of personalty to A and his issue?" is, "That interest which the

---

[52] See (1938) 6 CLJ 67 (S. J. Bailey); (1947) 9 CLJ 46 (R. E. Megarry); 185 (S. J. Bailey); 190 (J. H. C. Morris).

[53] *Chatham v Tothill* (1771) 7 Bro PC 453; *Portman v Viscount Portman* [1922] 2 AC 473; Hawkins and Ryder, *Construction of Wills*, pp. 254–5.   [54] P. 490, ante.

[55] For the effect of gifts by deed containing informal expressions, see (1938) 6 CLJ p. 81.

testator intended to give". Certain canons of construction, however, became established that covered most of the expressions found in practice.

(1) TO A AND HIS ISSUE

The primary canon of construction was that a gift of personalty *to A and his issue* showed an intention on the part of the testator that the issue alive when the will comes into operation should take the property jointly with A.[56]

Thus, if the gift be immediate, A and his issue (if any) living at the testator's death would take in joint tenancy; and if the gift be deferred, issue subsequently born before the period of distribution would be admitted along with them; and if no issue had come into existence before the period of distribution, A would take the whole.[57]

(2) TO A FOR LIFE AND THEN TO HIS ISSUE

Again, if there was a bequest to A for life and after his death to his issue, A took merely a life interest and the property was ultimately divided among the issue born during his life.[58]

Nevertheless this principle of construction which admitted issue as beneficiaries in the instances given was displaced if it appeared from the will as a whole that the testator meant to make A sole and absolute owner.

(3) TO A AND HIS DESCENDANTS

The word "issue" has consistently been held to mean prima facie descendants of every degree,[59] and it therefore seems to follow that a gift of personalty *to A and his descendants* is construed, in the absence of a contrary intention, in the same way as a gift to A and his issue.[60] The descendants alive at the death of the testator took the absolute ownership jointly with A.

(4) TO A AND HIS CHILDREN

A gift of personalty *to A and his children* was prima facie regarded as a gift to A and the children concurrently, so that A and his children alive at the testator's death took the property as joint tenants, or, if there were no children living at that time, A took the whole absolutely.[61]

(3) Rule in *Shelley's Case*

Finally, we must mention briefly the Rule in *Shelley's Case*,[62] which, though it was abolished by the Law of Property Act 1925,[63] still applies to instruments coming into operation before 1926.[64]

---

[56] *Re Hammond* [1924] 2 Ch 276.

[57] Hawkins and Ryder, *Construction of Wills*, pp. 241–2; the words quoted are those of Hawkins himself.

[58] *Knight v Ellis* (1789) 2 Bro CC 570; *Jarman on Wills* (6th edn), p. 1200.

[59] Hawkins and Ryder, p. 148.   [60] (1938) 6 CLJ p. 75.

[61] Hawkins and Ryder, pp. 260–2. The rule in *Wild's Case* as stated above, p. 490 never applied to personalty.

[62] See Challis, *Law of Real Property*, pp. 152 et seq; Cheshire, 11th edn of this book, pp. 198–202; [1981] Conv 128 (J. S. Coote).

[63] S. 131, as amended by TLATA 1996, s. 25(2), Sch. 3, para. 4(14).

[64] *Re Routledge* [1942] Ch 457 (testator died in 1874); *Re Williams* [1952] Ch 828 (testator died in 1921).

(a) Statement of the rule

This rule, which was a rule of law applicable to deeds and to wills, ordained that if in the same instrument an estate of *freehold* was limited to A, with remainder, either immediately or after the limitation of an intervening estate, *to the heirs* or *to the heirs of the body* of A, the remainder, though importing an independent gift to the heirs as original takers, conferred the fee simple in the first case, and the fee tail in the second case, upon A, the ancestor.[65] Thus the effect of a grant:

to A for life, remainder to his heirs,

was to give A the fee simple; and the effect of a grant:

to A for life, remainder to the heirs of his body,

was to give A an estate tail.

The interest which in terms was given to the heirs and which in most cases the donor, especially when he was a testator, meant the heirs to have, was in the eye of the law given to A. So A could dispose of the estate and thereby defeat his heir, who would take only if A died intestate still owning the estate.

Thus the operation of the rule was two-fold: it denied to a remainder the effect of a gift to the "heirs", and it attributed to the remainder the effect of a gift to A.[66] In fact, the legal effect of such a limitation was the direct opposite of what would naturally be expected, and it nearly always operated to defeat the intention of a testator.[67]

Another and more technical way of stating the rule is as follows: where the ancestor by any gift or conveyance takes an estate of freehold, and in the same gift or conveyance an estate is limited, either mediately or immediately to his heirs, in fee or in tail, in such cases "the heirs" are words of limitation of the estate and not words of purchase. We have already considered the distinction between words of limitation and words of purchase.[68] Thus, if land was given:

to A for life, remainder to the heirs of his body,

what the Rule in *Shelley's Case* declared was that the words "heirs of his body" were not words of purchase pointing out the heir as a person entitled to a definite interest in the land, but were words of limitation employed to mark out the extent of the interest given to A. Had the words "heirs of his body" been regarded as words of purchase, they would have indicated that the estate was given to the person who was found to be heir on the death of A. In other words, this person would have claimed the estate as having been given to him by the original conveyance. The result, in fact, was the same as if the grant had been:

to A and the heirs of his body,

but it is essential to notice that the Rule in *Shelley's Case* operated only where there were in terms two estates given, i.e. a freehold to the ancestor, A, and then a remainder to the heirs, for example:

---

[65] Hayes, *Introduction to Conveyancing*, vol. i. p. 542; *Preston on Estates*, vol. i, pp. 263–4.
[66] Ibid., p. 534.
[67] For the feudal reasons for this rule, see *Van Grutten v Foxwell* [1897] AC 658 at 668.   [68] P. 170, ante.

to A for life and after his death to the heirs of his body.

It is true that a limitation *to A and his heirs* or *to A and the heirs of his body* gives A a fee simple in the first case and a fee tail in the second case, but these results do not ensue from *Shelley's Case*. The law had been so established at a far earlier date.[69]

(b) Abolition of the rule

The Rule in *Shelley's Case* was abolished by section 131 of the Law of Property Act 1925 for all instruments coming into operation after 1925. Accordingly, where there is a limitation to:

A for life and then to his heirs; or to

A for life and then to the heirs of his body,

the effect is to restrict A's interest to a life interest, and to appropriate a definite interest to the heir or to the heir of the body of A. The heir is ascertained in accordance with the canons of descent that obtained before 1926,[70] and he takes the interest by way of purchase. What interest he takes is perhaps a little doubtful, but presumably in all cases he takes the fee simple or otherwise the whole interest which the donor had power to convey, unless a contrary intention appears in the deed or will.[71]

The result, then, of the abolition of the Rule in *Shelley's Case* upon the creation of an entailed interest after 1925 until 1996, seems to be this:

(i)   A gift to A for life, remainder to the heirs of his body would no longer vest an entailed interest in A, despite the enactment that such an interest may be created by the like expressions as those by which before 1 January 1926 a similar estate tail could have been created by deed.[72]

(ii) A gift to A for life, remainder to the heirs of his body would be effectual to vest a definite interest in the *heir*, although such would not have been the result of a similar conveyance by deed under the old law.

III Entailed Interests After 1925

After 1925 an entailed interest can no longer subsist as a legal estate. It is necessarily an equitable interest.[73] The only possible methods by which it could be created after 1925, and until the creation of new entailed interests was prohibited after 1996, were (a) a settlement by deed or will, and (b) an agreement for a settlement in which the trusts upon which the land was to be held were sufficiently declared.[74]

---

[69] If, for example, lands had been given "to W and her heirs for her and their use and benefit absolutely and for ever", the Rule in *Shelley's Case* would not have applied: *Re McElligott* [1944] Ch 216; (1938) 54 LQR 70 (A. D. Hargreaves).   [70] P. 89, ante.

[71] LPA 1925, s. 60(1); Wills Act 1837, s. 28; pp. 170–1, ante. The rule before the Wills Act 1837 was that a devise to the *heirs of the body* of a person conferred an estate tail (*Mandeville's Case* (1328) Co Litt 26b), and the question whether the fee simple could pass under s. 28 of the Wills Act does not seem to have arisen.

[72] P. 490, ante.   [73] LPA 1925, ss. 1, 130.

[74] Ibid., s. 130(6), repealed by TLATA 1996, s. 26(1), Sch. 4.

A Creation of Entailed Interests in any Form of Property

(1) Personalty

One of the radical changes introduced by the Law of Property Act 1925 was that any form of property, whether real or personal, could be limited in tail. At common law an estate tail could not be carved out of chattels or other personal property, but it appeared to the legislature that there was no reason why entailed interests should not be allowed in the case of such forms of property as stocks and shares and long leaseholds. Section 130(1), therefore, provided that:

an interest in tail or in tail male or in tail female or in tail special (in this Act referred to as "an entailed interest") may be created by way of trust in any property, real or personal, but only by the like expressions as those by which before the commencement of this Act a similar estate tail could have been created by deed (not being an executory instrument) in freehold land, and with the like results, including the right to bar the entail either absolutely or so as to create an interest equivalent to a base fee, and accordingly all statutory provisions relating to estates tail in real property shall apply to entailed interests in personal property.[75]

One important effect of this provision was that beneficial interests under a trust for sale, which, as we have seen, by the doctrine of conversion, were interests in personalty, could be entailed.[76] Further, an entail became subject to all rules, whether at common law or in equity, which governed and still govern estates tail in realty.[77]

(2) Heirlooms

Before the Act it sometimes happened that when freeholds were limited by settlement to a series of legal tenants for life and in tail, it was desired to give the persons who for the time being were entitled to the land the enjoyment of certain family heirlooms such as valuable pictures and the like. As the heirlooms, being chattels, could not be carved into estates in the same way as the land, the only mode of carrying out the intention was to vest them in trustees upon trust that they should go along with the land so far as the rules of law and equity would permit.[78] In such a case law and equity permitted any legal tenant for life of the land for the time being to have an equitable life interest in the heirlooms, but required that the absolute ownership should vest in the first person to get an estate tail in the land. The Act provided that when personal estate is directed to be held upon trusts corresponding with the trusts of land in which an entailed interest has been created, such direction should create a corresponding entailed interest in the personal property.[79]

---

[75] LPA 1925, s. 130(1); repealed by TLATA 1996, s. 25(2), Sch. 4. A will was not within this section unless it took effect after 1925: *Re Hope's Will Trust* [1929] 2 Ch 136.

[76] P. 428, ante. See Law of Property (Entailed Interests) Act 1932, s. 1.

[77] *Re Crossley's Settlement Trusts* [1955] Ch 627.   [78] See *Re Morrison's Settlement* [1974] Ch 326.

[79] LPA 1925, s. 130(3); repealed by TLATA 1996, s. 25(2), Sch. 4.

B Entailed Interests may be Barred

The Fines and Recoveries Act 1833, in a general enabling section, provides that every "actual tenant in tail", that is, the tenant of an entailed interest that has not been barred,[80] whether entitled in possession, remainder, contingency[81] or otherwise shall have full power to dispose of the land for an estate in fee simple or for any lesser estate.[82] This right of the tenant to disentail and so enlarge his equitable interest into a legal fee simple is absolute, and it could not be restricted by any device on the part of the grantor; so, for instance, a clause inserted in the instrument of creation providing that the interest shall not be barred, or that it shall pass from the owner upon disentailment, is null and void.[83] The present mode of disentailment, however, falls to be considered under two heads according as the tenant is or is not entitled to actual possession.

(1) Where Tenant in Tail is Entitled in Possession

A tenant in tail in possession and of full age may, without the concurrence of any other person, effectually bar the entailed interest and thereby enlarge it into a legal fee simple by adopting any form of conveyance which is sufficient to dispose of a fee simple estate in lands, provided, however, that in the case of an *inter vivos* disentailment the conveyance is effected by deed.[84] So the estate must be barred by a deed, called a disentailing assurance, and no disentailment can be effected by contract.[85]

The effect of a disentailing assurance which enlarges the entailed interest into a fee simple is to defeat entirely the rights both of the tenant's issue and of the persons whose estates are to take effect after the determination or in defeasance of the entailed interest. Suppose, for instance, that:

There was a grant of Blackacre to A in tail, remainder to B in tail, with a proviso that, if A becomes entitled to Whiteacre, his entailed interest in Blackacre shall cease and shall vest in C. If A, before he becomes entitled to Whiteacre, executes a disentailing deed of Blackacre for an estate in fee simple, the result is that he takes a fee simple estate which defeats:

first, his own issue;

secondly, B, who was entitled to take on the determination of the entailed interest; and

finally, C, whose estate was in defeasance of A's entailed interest.[86]

---

[80] Fines and Recoveries Act 1833, s. 1, as amended by TLATA 1996, s. 25(2), Sch. 4.

[81] See, for example, *Re St. Albans' Will Trust* [1963] Ch 365. Cf *Re Midleton's Will Trusts* [1969] 1 Ch 600. See the correspondence in the Times in 1995 (18 and 25 November, and 3 December) on the Bennet entail in Jane Austen's *Pride and Prejudice*.　　　　　　　　　　　　　　　　　　　　　　　　　　　　[82] S. 15.

[83] *Dawkins v Lord Penrhyn* (1878) 4 App Cas 51 at 64.

[84] Fines and Recoveries Act 1833, ss. 15, 40. For the liability of a solicitor who failed to advise that a tenant in tail in possession should disentail, see *Otter v Church, Adams, Tatham & Co* [1953] Ch 280.

[85] Registration of the deed is no longer required: LPA 1925, s. 133, repealed by Statute Law (Repeals) Act 1969, s. 1, Sched., Pt III.　　　　　　　　　　　　　　　　　　[86] See *Milbank v Vane* [1893] 3 Ch 79.

But, on the other hand, no disentailment can defeat interests that rank prior to the entailed interest.[87]

(2) Where Tenant in Tail is not Entitled in Possession

Under the normal strict settlement, by which land is limited to A for life and then to his sons successively in tail, the eldest son upon birth becomes entitled to an entailed interest in remainder. During the lifetime of his father he is not entitled to possession. The only method under the law prior to the Fines and Recoveries Act by which a tenant placed in this situation could effect a complete disentailment was to suffer a common recovery.[88] If he adopted this course, he obtained an absolute fee simple in remainder which defeated the rights both of his own issue and of the persons who were entitled to take on failure of issue. But the difficulty from his point of view was that a recovery could be suffered only if the collaboration of the tenant in actual possession of the land—that is, in the case of settled land, his father—were obtained. This was a beneficial rule of law, since it enabled the father to influence his son and gave him considerable power to check a disentailment that might be undesirable. The son, however, if he failed to obtain the collaboration of his father, was free to levy a fine, and though this did not, like a recovery, convert the entailed interest into an absolute fee simple, it did produce the effect of creating in its place what is called a base fee that was unassailable by the issue, but of no avail against the remainderman and reversioner if the issue became extinct. The base fee is described below.[89] When fines and recoveries were abolished in 1833, it seemed desirable to the legislature to retain in a different form this doctrine of the old law of recoveries, and thus to empower the father to check an ill-advised disentailment. To this end a new functionary called "the protector of the settlement" was instituted, in order to prevent a tenant in tail who was entitled only in remainder from effecting a complete disentailment.

The distinction between a tenant in tail *in possession* and a tenant in tail *in remainder*, therefore, is that the former can effect a complete bar without anyone's concurrence, while the latter can effect only a partial disentailment unless he obtains the consent of the protector.

The position is as follows.

(a) A tenant in tail in remainder can effect a complete bar by executing a disentailing deed with the consent of the protector

The protector of a settlement functions only where there is an entailed interest in remainder, preceded by one or more beneficial life interests. In this case, the Fines and Recoveries Act 1833 provides in effect that the protector shall be the owner of the prior life interest or of the first of several life interests, or who would have been the owner had he not disposed of his beneficial interest.[90] Until there has been a resettlement, there is usually only one life interest under a marriage settlement, namely that given to the husband:

Thus, if there is a limitation to H for life with remainder to his eldest son in tail, the father, H, is the protector, and the son will not be able to acquire a fee simple in remainder, valid against persons whose

---

[87] Fines and Recoveries Act 1833, ss. 15, 19.   [88] P. 484, ante.   [89] Pp. 498-9, post.

[90] Fines and Recoveries Act 1833, s. 22. The Act in s. 32, however, allowed a settlor to appoint any persons up to the number of three to act as protector in place of the person described in the text above. This power of nominating a special protector has been abolished as regards settlements made after 1925: LPA 1925, Sch. 7, repealing Fines and Recoveries Act 1833, s. 32. If there is no protector under s. 22, the court may be protector (s. 33), or the tenant in tail in remainder may disentail without consent: *Re Darnley's Will Trusts* [1970] 1 WLR 405.

interests are to take effect after the determination or in defeasance of the entailed interest, unless the consent of his father is expressed in the disentailing assurance itself or in a separate deed executed on or before the day on which the assurance is executed.[91]

The effect of a resettlement, however, is that life interests stand limited first to the father, then to the son, with the result that the son succeeds to the protectorship on the death of his father.

If there is no resettlement, the office of protector ceases on the death of the father, and the son, as tenant in tail in possession, can dispose of the land as his fancy dictates.

(b) A tenant in tail in remainder can effect a partial bar by executing a disentailing deed without the consent of the protector

When lands are subject to a strict settlement, family dissension may cause the eldest son to bar his entailed interest in remainder against the wishes of his father. The father may be niggardly or the son contumacious, and in that unfortunate event the probability is that the son will effect the partial disentailment that is within his power and will then dispose of the resultant base fee upon the best terms obtainable. The Fines and Recoveries Act 1833[92] specifically enacts that a tenant in tail who is not for the moment entitled to actual possession of the land may execute a disentailing deed without the consent of the protector, but that the effect of such a disentailment shall be merely to set up a base fee—that is to say, a fee simple that will defeat the tenant's own issue, but will not defeat persons who are entitled to take estates in the land upon the determination of the entailed interest by failure of issue or otherwise. Suppose, for instance, that:

Lands stand limited to A for life, remainder to A's eldest son in tail, remainder to A's second son in tail, and so on. If the eldest son of A disentails during his father's life and without his father's consent, he will acquire a fee simple which cannot be defeated by any of his own issue, but which nevertheless will go over to his brother's family if at any time in the future his own issue fails. In other words, the eldest son acquires a fee simple that will not fail, i.e. will not pass to somebody else, unless and until his descendants fail.

There may be other base fees than the one now under consideration,[93] but these are beside the present point, and as regards entailed interests section 1 of the Fines and Recoveries Act provides that:

The expression 'base fee' shall mean exclusively that estate in fee simple into which an estate tail is converted where the issue in tail are barred, but persons claiming estates by way of remainder or otherwise are not barred.

It is a less valuable fee simple than a fee simple absolute, since it will last only as long as there are in existence descendants who would have inherited the entailed interest had it never been barred; while a fee simple absolute continues as long as there exist any persons who are heirs, whether lineal or collateral, of the owner. In the example given above, if the eldest son of A, having barred the entail in his father's lifetime, conveys the interest so acquired to X and then dies without having issue, the base fee held by X ceases, and passes to the second son by way of remainder. On the other hand, had the interest conveyed to X been a fee simple absolute, the death of the eldest son without issue would have made no difference to the perpetual nature of X's interest.

---

[91] Fines and Recoveries Act 1833, ss. 34, 42.   [92] S. 34.

[93] Challis, *Law of Real Property*, pp. 325 et seq.

A base fee, however, may be converted, or will automatically become enlarged, into a fee simple absolute in any one of the following ways.

(1) UNION OF BASE FEE WITH REMAINDER OR REVERSION IN FEE

Suppose there is a limitation to:

A for life, remainder to B in tail, remainder to C in tail, remainder to B in fee simple.

B creates a base fee in himself by executing a disentailing deed during the life of A and without his consent. The remainderman C dies in the lifetime of B without having issue. The position now is that both the base fee and the fee simple absolute in remainder are united in B without there being any intermediate estate between them, and whenever this occurs the Fines and Recoveries Act enacts that the base fee shall be enlarged into as great an estate as the tenant in tail could have created had he been in possession at the time of disentailment.[94] In plain language, it is enlarged into a fee simple absolute.

(2) FRESH DISENTAILING DEED

If a tenant in tail in remainder creates a base fee, he can convert it into a fee simple absolute by executing a fresh disentailing deed with the consent of the protector.[95] But if the protector no longer exists, as for instance where the tenant for life under a strict settlement dies, the tenant can enlarge the base fee, whether he has parted with it or not, by himself executing a fresh disentailing deed.[96]

(3) LAPSE OF TIME

A base fee becomes valid against remaindermen and reversioners if any person takes possession under the disentailing assurance, and if he or any other person remains in possession by virtue of that assurance[97] for twelve years from the time when the tenant in tail would have been entitled to possession and therefore free to effect a complete bar of his own accord.[98]

(4) DEVISE

The owner of a base fee *in possession* is now permitted to enlarge the base fee into a fee simple absolute by will.[99]

(c) Unbarrable entailed interests

Two classes of tenants in tail are unable to disentail their estates, namely a tenant in tail after possibility[100] and a tenant in tail to whom or to whose ancestors an estate has been granted by Parliament as a reward for services rendered, if the statute by which the grant is made has expressly prohibited the right of disentailment. Examples are the Bolton, the Marlborough and the Wellington estates.[101]

---

[94] Fines and Recoveries Act 1833, s. 39.   [95] Ibid., s. 35.

[96] Ibid., s. 19; *Bankes v Small* (1887) 36 Ch D 716.   [97] *Mills v Capel* (1875) LR 20 Eq 692.

[98] Limitation Act 1980, s. 27. This section also applies to a disentailing assurance which, owing to some defect such as the lack of a deed, fails to bar the tenant's *issue*.

[99] LPA 1925, s. 176(1), (3); infra.   [100] Fines and Recoveries Act 1833, s. 18; p. 488, ante.

[101] Former examples were the Abergavenny, Shrewsbury and Arundel estates, but these have now been statutorily freed from restraints upon alienation. See also SLA 1925, s. 23(2); *Hambro v Duke of Marlborough* [1994] Ch 158.

C Entailed Interests may be Disposed of by Will

Prior to 1926 a tenant in tail could not devise his estate, and if he died without having disentailed, it passed by descent to the appropriate class of heirs. The Law of Property Act 1925, however, provides that in a will *executed* on or after 1 January 1926 a testator of full age may devise or bequeath all property of which he is tenant in tail *in possession* at the time of his death, and all money subject to be invested in the purchase of property, of which if it had been so invested he would have been tenant in tail in possession at his death.

The tenant has power to dispose of the estate: "in like manner as if, after barring the entail, he had been tenant in fee simple or absolute owner thereof for an equitable interest at his death",[102] and therefore the effect produced by the will is similar to that produced by a disentailing deed. But to guard against a disentailment by inadvertence, it is enacted that no will shall be sufficient to dispose of the estate unless it refers specifically either to the property entailed, or to the instrument creating the entail or to entailed property generally, and therefore a mere general devise or bequest is useless for the purpose.[103]

This power of disposition is also conferred by the Act[104] upon the owner of a base fee *in possession* provided that he is in a position to enlarge the base fee into a fee simple absolute. This position arises where a tenant in tail in remainder, having barred the entail without the consent of the tenant for life as protector, becomes entitled to possession upon the death of the tenant for life. In such a case, as we have already seen, the owner of the base fee may bar the entail and enlarge the base fee into a fee simple absolute in possession by executing a fresh disentailing assurance. The extension of this principle made by the Law of Property Act 1925 is that the owner may *devise* the base fee so as to pass a fee simple absolute to the devisee provided that the will refers specifically either to the base fee or to the instrument by which it was acquired. But he has no such testamentary power unless he is in possession of the base fee or of its rents and profits. It will thus be seen that the power to execute a fresh disentailing assurance given by the Fines and Recoveries Act is wider than the power of testamentary disposition given by the Law of Property Act, for the former can be exercised by the tenant in tail even after he has conveyed the base fee to a purchaser and has lost all right to possession of the land.[105]

IV No New Entailed Interests After 1996

The Trusts of Land and Appointment of Trustees Act 1996[106] does not affect existing entailed interests, but after 1996 any attempt to create an entailed interest operates as a declaration of trust in favour of the grantee absolutely. Thus, if X purports to grant a freehold in tail to Y, Y is entitled to a fee simple absolute in possession, and, if he is an adult, can call for a transfer of the property from the trustees.[107] Further, if X purports to grant a freehold to Y for life, remainder to Z in fee tail, a trust of land arises under which Y has a life interest and Z a fee simple absolute in remainder. Any attempt by X to declare himself a tenant in tail is ineffective.

---

[102] LPA 1925, s. 176(1).

[103] Ibid. The word *specifically* was interpreted in a liberal sense by Vaisey J in *Acheson v Russell* [1951] Ch 67. For a criticism of the decision, see (1950) 66 LQR 449 (R.E.M.).   [104] LPA 1925, s. 176(3).

[105] *Bankes v Small* (1887) 36 Ch D 716.   [106] S. 2, Sch. 1, para. 5.

[107] *Saunders v Vautier* (1841) 4 Beav 115.

15

LIFE INTERESTS

SUMMARY

I The General Nature of Life Interests

A Life Interests in the Modern Law

The modern life interest differs fundamentally from that found in the days of feudalism. In those days, when lands were granted not in return for a rent nor by way of settlement, but on the condition that the tenant should render services of a military nature to the grantor, the tenant was given an interest merely for his life, because, although he was known to the lord and was presumably a man upon whose fidelity and courage reliance might be placed, yet the character of his eldest son was an unknown factor, and it would have been folly for a grantor to have tied his hands by pledging himself in advance to accept the son as a new tenant on his father's death. So in the twelfth century the life estate was the greatest interest that anyone could have in land, and it arose when a feudal grant was made by a lord to a tenant. At first the grantee of such a feud did not possess the free power of alienation, for to have permitted this would have prejudiced the lord's right to make the new tenant on the death of the old pay a fine (or relief, as it was called) for the privilege of obtaining the feud; and again, a tenant possessed of a free power of alienation might cause irreparable injury by granting the land to a personal enemy of the lord. But the restraints on alienation gradually disappeared, and it was recognized by the Statute *Quia Emptores* 1290[1] that a feudal tenant could grant his interest to whom he pleased.[2] By degrees it was also recognised that the feud was an inheritable interest that would descend to the heirs-general of the tenant, and which therefore would endure as long as there were any such heirs in existence. An estate greater

---

[1] P. 16, ante.

[2] For the growth of the power of alienation, see Holdsworth, *History of English Law*, vol. iii. pp. 73 et seq; Plucknett, *Concise History of the Common Law*, pp. 523 et seq; Simpson, *A History of the Land Law*, pp. 51–6.

than a life estate thus became known to the law, and an interest which could endure only for life, as distinguished from a fee simple which might endure for ever, was added to the list of possible estates. In the words of Hayes:[3]

Some time elapsed after the feudal relation began to be known in Europe, before the right of inheritable succession was fully conceded. In its primitive state the possession was held at pleasure, or for a short term only: afterwards, the tenure was for life, the lord resuming the land on the death of the tenant, and granting it out anew. But at length the son of the tenant was permitted to succeed: an indulgence which was followed by the extension of the grant, first to the tenant and his issue (i.e. in fee tail) and finally to him and his heirs (i.e. in fee simple, expressed in legal phraseology by the word fee, without more), the law marking out a course of descent, which, enlarging by degrees, embraced his relations, lineal and collateral, male and female.

But though after the establishment of the fee simple it became possible and indeed common to create a life estate with peculiar incidents of its own, the object of this practice was materially different from that which underlies the life interest found in present-day conveyancing. The estate in those days was granted, generally by the rich ecclesiastical corporations, in return for an annual rent, and was the result of a purely business transaction analogous to the modern lease for a term of years. The tenant resembled the modern tenant farmer, except that he held for life instead of from year to year or for a fixed number of years, and although he was said to have a *lease*, the interest vested in him was a freehold interest and not a term of years.

In the modern law, however, the life interest serves a very different purpose, typically as part of the settlement of family interests in property—either under a strict settlement or (in the case of a life interest created after 1996[4]) under a trust of land. This aspect of the nature of a life interest became more important in the nineteenth century, when the Settled Land Act 1882 gave to a tenant for life powers which extended beyond those that he had as the owner of a mere life interest.[5] The crucial question at the present day therefore is not whether a claimant may enjoy the land for his life, but whether before 1997 he had the powers of a tenant for life under the Settled Land Act 1925, or after 1996 the powers delegated to him by the trustees of land under the Trusts of Land and Appointment of Trustees Act 1996.[6]

Another common example of a life interest today occurs where there is an intestacy, and the surviving spouse or civil partner is given a life interest in half the residuary estate of the deceased under the Intestates' Estates Act 1952.[7]

B Classes of Life Interests

A life interest is a freehold interest—generally called a *mere freehold* to distinguish it from fees simple and entails, which are estates of inheritance. After 1925 it can no longer exist as a legal estate, and is necessarily equitable.[8] It may be limited to endure for the life either of

---

[3] Hayes, *Introduction to Conveyancing*, vol. i. pp. 7–8.   [4] P. 436, ante.   [5] P. 74, ante.

[6] See the problems which arise where the court seeks to protect a contractual licensee for the remainder of his or her life; p. 401, n. 11, ante; p. 848, post.

[7] Amending AEA 1925, s. 46; further amended by Civil Partnership Act 2004, s. 71, Sch. 4, Pt 2, para. 7.

[8] LPA 1925, s. 1(3); p. 94, ante.

the tenant himself or of some other person, in which latter case it is called an interest *pur autre vie*.

(1) Estate for Life of Tenant

An interest for the life of the tenant himself, though normally created expressly by a settlement, made either by deed or by will, may also arise by implication of law in the case of the tenant in tail after possibility,[9] or by operation of law where a husband becomes tenant by the curtesy in the entailed lands of his deceased wife.[10]

(2) Estate *pur autre vie*

The interest *pur autre vie* is the lowest estate of freehold known to the law, and is not so great as an interest for the life of the tenant himself. It arises in two ways. The first is where there is an express limitation to A for the life of B. Such a limitation may be made, like an ordinary lease for years, in return for a rent, or as part of a settlement of land. A is called the tenant *pur autre vie*, and B the *cestui que vie*.[11] Secondly, if a person B, who is entitled to an estate for his own life assigns his interest to A, the effect is that A becomes the tenant *pur autre vie*.[12]

From the point of view of rights and liabilities, a tenant *pur autre vie* is in the same position as an ordinary tenant for life. Thus, at common law, he is entitled to the rents and profits of the land during the continuance of his interest and to cut timber within the limits of estovers, while on the negative side he is liable for waste to the same extent as if he were holding for his own life.[13] Unless holding merely under a lease at a rent, he may exercise any of the wide powers conferred by the Settled Land Act 1925.[14] No matter how the interest arises, he possesses an absolute power of alienation during his life,[15] and after his death his alienee is entitled to hold for the rest of the *cestui que vie*'s life.[16] In the absence of such alienation the interest passes on the death of the tenant to his devisee,[17] or, if he has made no will, to the persons who are entitled to take his property under the rules that govern intestacy.[18] Prior to the legislation of 1925 there were certain peculiar rules which governed the devolution of an interest *pur autre vie*, but these have been abolished.[19]

In view of the danger that a tenant pur autre vie may be tempted to conceal the death of the *cestui que vie*, the Cestui que Vie Act 1707 provides that a person entitled to the land upon the termination of the life interest may, after swearing an affidavit that he believes the *cestui que vie* to be dead, obtain an order from the High Court for the production of the *cestui que vie*. If the order is not complied with, the *cestui que vie* is taken to be dead and the person next entitled to possession may enter upon the lands.

---

[9] P. 488, ante.   [10] P. 486, ante.   [11] Litt s. 56; Co Litt 41b.

[12] Co Litt 41b. For example, the mortgage of an equitable life interest under a settlement; p. 732, post.

[13] P. 504, post (waste); p. 506, post (estovers).

[14] SLA 1925, s. 20(1)(v); he is not so entitled if he is the assignee of a tenant for life holding under a settlement; p. 418, ante.   [15] Co Litt 41b.

[16] *Dale's Case* (1590) Cro Eliz 182.   [17] Wills Act 1837, s. 3.   [18] AEA 1925, s. 46.

[19] Ibid., s. 45(1)(a); for the old law, see Challis, *Law of Real Property*, pp. 358 et seq.

II The Rights and Obligations of a Tenant for Life at Common Law

The rights and obligations at common law of a tenant for life entitled in possession may be summed up by saying that he may take the annual profits, but must not take or destroy anything that is a permanent part of the inheritance. He is entitled to fruits of all kinds, but must leave unimpaired the source of the fruits. He has certain positive rights, and one negative duty which is prescribed by the doctrine of *waste*. The object of these rules is to maintain a balance between the interests of the tenant for life and those in reversion or remainder.

These common law rules still apply to the tenant for life, except in so far as they are varied by the instrument creating his interest.[20]

A Emblements

There is little that need be said of his positive rights. The profits that arise from the land, whether they arise continuously, periodically or occasionally, belong to him. A particular hazard, however, that confronts him is that after he has sown crops his tenancy may end unexpectedly before they are ripe as, for instance, by the death of a *cestui que vie*. In this event, he is entitled to re-enter the land at harvest time and to reap what he has sown. This is known as the right to *emblements*.[21] It is enforceable, however, only in respect of crops such as corn, hemp, flax and potatoes, which bear an annual fruit.[22] One crop only can be taken,[23] and the right does not extend to seeds that do not produce a crop within a year of sowing, such as young fruit trees or the second crop of clover.[24]

The right can be exercised only if the estate comes to an end unexpectedly without any fault on the part of the tenant for life, and therefore, if it is forfeited in his lifetime owing to the breach of some condition, or if, being a determinable interest, it is brought to an end by the happening of the terminating event—as for instance by the re-marriage of a woman who is tenant *durante viduitate*—the crops belong to the reversioner.[25]

B Waste

The position of the tenant for life on the negative side is governed by the common law doctrine of waste as enlarged by statute and equity, a doctrine that also affects a tenant for years.[26]

---

[20] *Re Harker's Will Trusts* [1938] Ch 323; but see (1938) 2 Conv (NS) 233 (H. Potter). In the case of a tenant for life under the Settled Land Act 1925, we have seen that there are also detailed statutory provisions relating to his powers: pp. 409 et seq, ante.

[21] Co Litt 55b. The right of the tenant for years to emblements has been replaced by a statutory right; p. 240, ante.   [22] Co Litt 55b; Blackstone, vol. ii. p. 122.

[23] *Graves v Weld* (1833) 5 B & Ad 105.   [24] Ibid.

[25] Co Litt 55b; *Oland's Case* (1602) 5 Co Rep 116a.

[26] P. 239, ante. For the history of "waste", see Holdsworth, *History of English Law*, vol. ii. pp. 248–9; vol. iii. pp. 121–3; vol. vii. pp. 275–81.

(1) Definition of Waste

Waste means in general such damage to houses or land as tends to the permanent and lasting loss of the person entitled to the inheritance, and it falls into two main classes:

(a) Voluntary waste

This is a wrong of commission consisting of a positive act of injury to the inheritance. It generally takes one of the following forms:

(1) PULLING DOWN OR ALTERING HOUSES[27]

Thus if glass windows be broken or carried away, it is waste, although they may have been put in by the tenant himself, and so also in the case of benches, doors, furnaces and other things fixed to the land.

(2) OPENING PITS OR MINES[28]

It is waste to dig for gravel, lime, clay, stone and the like, unless for the reparation of buildings; also to open a new mine, but not to work one that is already open.

(3) CHANGING THE COURSE OF HUSBANDRY

To convert wood, meadow or pasture into arable land, or to turn arable or woodland into meadow or pasture, is technically waste. The old writers state that such acts are waste, not only because they change the course of husbandry, but also because they destroy the owner's evidence of title, for if an estate which had been conveyed as pasture were found on the next conveyance to be arable, it might cause confusion.[29] This, of course, is no longer in itself a reason for regarding such an act of conversion as waste. In fact it is obvious that to change the system of husbandry must often have the effect of enhancing the value of land, as, for example, where a farm situated near a large town is tilled intensively as a market garden, and though such conversion is technically waste, the rule, established since at least 1833,[30] is that it will not entitle the owner of the inheritance to recover damages unless it causes an injury to the inheritance.[31] This kind of waste is known as *ameliorating waste*.

In *Doherty v Allman*:[32] a tenant for 999 years of land and buildings was proceeding to convert some dilapidated store buildings into dwelling-houses when the lessor filed a bill for an injunction. The injunction was refused on the ground that acts which improve the inheritance cannot constitute actionable waste. A similar decision was reached where the tenant of an agricultural lease for twenty-one years converted part of the land into a market garden and erected glass-houses thereon for the cultivation of hot-house produce for the London market.[33]

---

[27] Co Litt 53a; *Marsden v Edward Heyes Ltd* [1927] 2 KB 1; *Mancetter Developments Ltd v Garmanson Ltd* [1986] QB 1212 (tenant, who failed to make good holes left behind in landlord's brickwork when removing trade fixtures, held liable in damages); p. 159, ante.   [28] Co Litt 53b, 54b.
[29] Blackstone, vol. ii. p. 282.   [30] *Doe d Grubb v Earl of Burlington* (1833) 5 B & Ad 507.
[31] *Jones v Chappell* (1875) LR 20 Eq 539 at 541.   [32] (1878) 3 App Cas 709, M & B p. 21.
[33] *Meux v Cobley* [1892] 2 Ch 253. Although this case and that referred to in the previous note concerned a tenant for years, there would be even stronger reasons for adopting the same attitude towards a tenant for life.

(4) CUTTING TIMBER

Timber trees are regarded as part of the inheritance and not part of the annual produce, and therefore it is waste to cut them, even though they are blown down by accident and have thus become what are called *windfalls*.[34] Sir George JESSEL MR defined "timber" as follows:[35]

The question of what timber is depends, first on general law, that is, the law of England; and secondly, on the special custom of a locality. By the general rule of England, oak, ash and elm are timber, provided they are of the age of 20 years and upwards, provided also they are not so old as not to have a reasonable quantity of useable wood in them, sufficient . . . to make a good post. Timber, that is, the kind of tree which may be called timber, may be varied by local custom. There is what is called the custom of the country, that is, of a particular county or division of a county, and it varies in two ways. First of all, you may have trees called timber by the custom of the country—beech in some counties, hornbeam in others, and even whitethorn and blackthorn, and many other trees, are considered timber in peculiar localities—in addition to the ordinary timber trees.[36] Then again, in certain localities, arising probably from the nature of the soil, the trees of even 20 years old are not necessarily timber, but may go to 24 years, or even to a later period, I suppose, if necessary; and in other places the test of when a tree becomes timber is not its age but its girth.[37]

A tenant, whether for years or life, may cut and keep trees that do not fall within this definition of timber, such as larch, willows and chestnut, provided that they are ripe for felling and have not been planted for ornament, shelter or shade.[38] But only in three cases may he fell timber trees:

First, where the land is a timber estate, that is, where it is cultivated merely for the produce of saleable timber and where the timber is cut periodically.[39] In such a case it is obvious that to cut the trees does not injure the inheritance, because the total value of the timber on the estate remains, roughly speaking, the same throughout, though new trees take the place of old.[40]

Secondly, where there is a local custom to cut timber periodically according to the normal and ordinary course of husbandry practised in the neighbourhood.[41]

Thirdly, every tenant for life is entitled to cut timber or other trees for three specific purposes, namely for the fuelling or repair of a house (*housebote*), for making and repairing agricultural implements (*ploughbote*) and for repairing existing walls, fences and ditches (*haybote*). These are called *estovers*.[42] He will be liable for waste, however, if he exercises these rights in an unreasonable manner, as for instance if he fells growing trees for fuel when there is dead wood sufficient for the purpose.

---

[34] *Garth v Cotton* (1753) 3 Atk 751.   [35] *Honywood v Honywood* (1874) LR 18 Eq 306 at 309.

[36] E.g. beech in Buckinghamshire: *Dashwood v Magniac* [1891] 3 Ch 306, M & B p. 20; birch in Yorkshire: *Countess of Cumberland's Case* (1610) Moore KB 812; willows in Hampshire: *Layfield v Cowper* (1694) 1 Wood 330.

[37] If timber trees are blown down, they belong to the owner of the inheritance, but if they are dotards, i.e. decayed, they may be appropriated by the tenant: Co Litt 53a; *Herlakenden's Case* (1589) 4 Co Rep 62a at 63b; *Duke of Newcastle v Vane* (undated) 2 P Wms 241.   [38] *Re Harker's Will Trusts* [1938] Ch 323.

[39] *Honywood v Honywood* (1874) LR 18 Eq 306 at 309.

[40] *Lloyd-Jones v Clark-Lloyd* [1919] 1 Ch 424 at 436.

[41] *Dashwood v Magniac* [1891] 3 Ch 306; M & B p. 20; *Re Trevor-Batye's Settlement* [1912] 2 Ch 339.

[42] Co Litt 41b.

(b) Permissive waste

Permissive waste arises from a mere act of omission, not of commission, and it is generally the result of allowing the buildings on an estate to fall into a state of decay.[43]

(2) Extent of Liability for Waste

At common law, tenants for life or years whose tenancies arose by operation of law, such as the doweress or tenant by the curtesy, were liable for waste; but no liability arose in the case of tenancies, whether for life or years, created by act of parties, for the courts were disinclined to excuse the folly of the lessor in not imposing an express restraint upon the tenant.[44] This, however, was altered by the Statute of Marlborough[45] 1267, which provided as follows:

Fermors,[46] during their terms, shall not make waste, sale, nor exile of house, woods, nor of anything belonging to the tenements that they have to ferm, without special licence had by writing of covenant, making mention that they may do it.

This reference to a "special licence" recognised, therefore, that a tenant for life might be expressly permitted to do acts that would normally constitute waste without incurring liability,[47] and from this point of view it led to the emergence of two classes of tenants for life, namely those impeachable for waste, and those unimpeachable for waste.

(a) Tenant impeachable

A tenant who is impeachable is liable for the commission of voluntary waste,[48] but is not liable for permissive waste[49] unless the settlor has imposed upon him an obligation to keep the property in repair.[50]

Where such an obligation is imposed, an action lies against the tenant or against his personal representative, on the general equitable principle that a person who accepts a benefit must also shoulder the burden.[51]

Where, however, the property which is settled upon the tenant consists of leaseholds, he is bound to perform any covenants, such as a covenant to repair, contained in the lease under which the property is held. Thus, if a house which is held by a testator on a long lease is bequeathed to A for life, A must take the burden with the benefit, and instead of throwing the financial burden upon the testator's estate must meet the cost of performing the covenants out of his own pocket.[52]

(b) Tenant unimpeachable

If, as is nearly always the case under a settlement, a tenant for life is unimpeachable, he is not liable either for voluntary or for permissive waste, and at common law may fell timber or open new mines and deal with the produce as absolute owner.[53]

---

[43] Co Litt 53a, 54b.   [44] *Countess of Shrewsbury's Case* (1600) 5 Co Rep 13b.

[45] 52 Hen. 3, c. 23. Also called Marlbridge. See *Dayani v Bromley LBC* [1999] 3 EGLR 144, p. 239, ante.

[46] "Fermor" includes everybody holding for life or years.

[47] *Woodhouse v Walker* (1880) 5 QBD 404 at 406–7, M & B p. 18.   [48] Co Litt 53a.

[49] *Re Cartwright* (1889) 41 Ch D 532; *Re Parry and Hopkin* [1900] 1 Ch 160; *Woodhouse v Walker*, supra.

[50] *Woodhouse v Walker*, supra.   [51] *Jay v Jay* [1924] 1 KB 826 at 829.

[52] *Re Betty* [1899] 1 Ch 821; *Woodhouse v Walker*, supra.

[53] *Lewis Bowles' Case* (1615) 11 Co Rep 79b; Tudor, *Leading Cases on Real Property*, p. 153.

(c) Equitable waste

Equity, however, has consistently set its face against an abuse of this immunity and the rule has long been that any tenant who commits wanton or extravagant acts of destruction, will be restrained by injunction and ordered to rehabilitate the premises. As Lord CAMPBELL said:[54] "Equitable waste is that which a prudent man would not do in the management of his own property." Examples of the application of this rule occur where the tenant dismantles a mansion or other house,[55] cuts saplings at unreasonable times,[56] or fells timber that has been planted for the ornament or shelter of the mansion-house and its grounds.[57] It is obviously difficult to decide whether timber is ornamental or not, but the question depends upon whether the person who carried out the planting intended the trees to be ornamental, and not upon the personal opinion of the court or anybody else.[58]

Wanton acts of destruction of the kinds specified are said to constitute equitable waste because prior to the Judicature Act 1873 they could be remedied only in a court of equity; but section 135 of the Law of Property Act 1925 now provides that a tenant for life has no right to commit equitable waste unless an intention to confer such right appears in the instrument of creation.

A tenant *pur autre vie* is liable for waste to the same extent as a tenant for his own life,[59] but a tenant in tail after possibility of issue extinct incurs no liability by the commission of voluntary or of permissive waste.[60]

Where an act of waste has been committed, the remainderman or reversioner may sue for an account in the Chancery Division, or bring an action in the Queen's Bench Division, either for conversion in respect of any things that may have been severed, or for money had and received as a result of their sale,[61] or for the recovery of damages; and he may sue in either Division for an injunction.

[54] *Turner v Wright* (1860) 2 De GF & J 234 at 243, M & B p. 22.
[55] *Vane v Lord Barnard* (1716) 2 Vern 738, M & B p. 22.   [56] *Brydges v Stephens* (1821) 6 Madd 279.
[57] *Downshire v Sandys* (1801) 6 Ves 107.   [58] *Weld-Blundell v Wolseley* [1903] 2 Ch 664.
[59] Co Litt 41b; *Seymor's Case* (1612) 10 Co Rep 95b, 98a.   [60] *Williams v Williams* (1810) 12 East 209.
[61] *Seagram v Knight* (1867) 2 Ch App 628 at 632. See generally Tudor, *Leading Cases on Real Property*, p. 156.

16

FUTURE INTERESTS

SUMMARY

I Future Interests[1]

A The Effect of the Legislation of 1925

The law of future interests has the reputation of being unusually complex and difficult; Blackstone indeed said that "the doctrine of estates in expectancy contains some of the nicest and most abstruse learning of the English law".[2] Fortunately, the abstruse learning related mainly to various technical rules of the common law concerning *future legal*

---

[1] For the history of this subject, see Holdsworth, *History of English Law*, vol. vii. pp. 81 et seq; Simpson, *History of the Land Law*, pp. 208–41 and generally, see Gray, *The Rule against Perpetuities*; Morris and Leach, *The Rule against Perpetuities*; Maudsley, *The Modern Law of Perpetuities*.   [2] Blackstone, vol. ii. p. 163.

estates; and, as explained above,[3] section 1 of the Law of Property Act 1925 restricted freehold legal estates[4] to the fee simple absolute in possession. There have therefore been no future legal estates for over eighty years.[5] After 1 January 1926, future interests can exist only in equity behind a trust; and a limitation which creates future interests in land will exist under either a strict settlement or a trust of land. The only substantial restriction upon the creation or existence of future (equitable) interests in land since 1925 is the rule against perpetuities, which must be examined in some detail. As we shall see later in this chapter, the perpetuity rule was changed—and relaxed—by the Perpetuities and Accumulations Act 1964,[6] and a further reform, proposed by the Law Commission in 1998 and accepted by the Government, will again reduce its scope.[7] Even when this further reform is enacted, however, the reasons behind the rule, and the details of its operation will be understood only in the light of its historical development. Before discussing the modern law in detail, therefore, a short historical explanation will serve to show how great was the change made by the 1925 legislation, and to provide the background necessary to understand why the perpetuity rule developed in the way that it did.

B The Doctrine of Estates

In accordance with the common law doctrine of estates, which developed from the feudal system, a subject of the King did not theoretically own the land; he held it as the feudal tenant of the King.[8] The tenant was said to own, not the land, but *an estate in* the land. The largest estate known to the law was the fee simple. The tenant, being entitled to a freehold estate in possession, was "seised" of the land.

The tenant could hold an estate less than the fee simple; typically, where he held an estate for his life.[9] But the whole fee simple exists somewhere. The land may have been conveyed:

to A for life and after his death to B in fee simple,

in which case A was the owner of a life estate in possession, and B the owner of a fee simple estate in remainder; or, if the grantor only conveyed the land:

to A for life,

then the grantor would retain the fee simple; but in this case there is no remainder: the land does not "stay away"[10] from the grantor on A's death; but it "reverted" to the grantor: the grantor owns a reversion.[11]

C Remainders at Common Law

A remainder is a future interest. The term "future interest", however, is confusing. For a remainder was a present existing legal estate, capable of being bought and sold, capable of

---

[3] P. 93, ante.   [4] The only other legal estate is the term of years absolute.

[5] Except for reversionary leases; p. 208, ante.   [6] Pp. 545 et seq, post.   [7] Pp.564–5, post.

[8] One holding directly of the King is called the tenant in chief.

[9] Or fee tail; chap. 14, ante. Or estate *pur autre vie*, p. 503, ante.

[10] *Remanere* meaning "to stay away" is the origin of the term remainder, in contrast to *reverti* meaning "to come back". See Pollock and Maitland, *History of English Law*, vol. ii. p. 21; (1890) 6 LQR 22 at 25 (F. W. Maitland).   [11] See Co Litt 22b.

passing by succession on death, as any other item of real property. The only element of futurity in a vested remainder is that the owner is entitled only in the future to possession. For that reason, in the illustration given above, of a conveyance of land:

to A for life and after his death to B in fee simple,

A owned a life estate in possession, B owned a fee simple in remainder. A is seised; A was responsible for the performance of feudal services to his feudal lord, and was entitled to the use of legal remedies which were based on seisin.[12] B would be entitled to seisin on A's death. Vested remainders were the first future interests recognised by the common law.

(1) Vested and Contingent

Inevitably, the question arose of the rule which the common law should apply to a remainder where the remainder was dependent on a contingency. In the above illustration, the grantor might not wish to give the remainder to B unless B attained the age of twenty-one. The grant would then be:

to A for life with remainder to B in fee simple if he attains the age of 21 years.

At first, the common law refused to recognise contingent remainders; later they were recognised,[13] and held to be capable of alienation and of transmission on death. Thus, in the illustration, B, during his minority, had a contingent remainder; it became a vested remainder on B's attaining the age of twenty-one. It is said that B's interest then "vests in interest". His estate would vest in possession on the death of A.

(2) Destructibility of Contingent Remainders

(a) Failure to vest during continuance of prior estate

A reader who has understood the crucial importance of *seisin* under the feudal system may well ask what happens if A dies before B attains the age of twenty-one. If A dies before B attains the age of twenty-one, B's estate will not vest until a future time; there would be an abeyance of seisin. An abeyance of seisin was not permitted by the common law;[14] and the rule was clear and uncompromising that, unless a contingent remainder vested (in interest) during the existence of the prior particular[15] estate, or at the same moment (*eo instanti*) as its termination, the contingent remainder was destroyed. This rule existed until the passing of the Contingent Remainders Act 1877.[16]

(b) Merger; surrender; forfeiture by tortious feoffment

These are all methods by which the tenant in possession, the owner of the prior particular estate, could, by conscious decision, destroy the contingent remainders which were dependent upon that particular estate. We have seen that a contingent remainder required a prior particular estate to support it; if the prior particular estate disappears, there is no such estate and the contingent remainder fails.

---

[12] P. 27, ante.   [13] *Sir John Melton's Case* (1535), discussed [1996] CLJ 249 (J. H. Baker).

[14] *Preston on Estates*, vol. 1, pp. 17, 249.

[15] So called because it is *particula*, or a small part, of the estate of inheritance.

[16] The situation before the Statute of Uses was much relieved in the 17th century by the device of trustees to preserve contingent remainders; Holdsworth, *History of English Law*, vol. vii. pp. 111–15.

(1) MERGER. SURRENDER

The principle of these two methods is similar. They both involve the unity of the prior particular estate with the remainder in fee. The simple case of merger is where the life tenant acquires, by conveyance or descent, the vested remainder in fee. The life estate merged with the remainder and was no longer available to support the contingent remainder. Thus:

to A for life, with remainder to such of A's children as shall attain the age of 21 for their lives with remainder to B in fee simple.

If A, having no adult children, should acquire B's remainder by conveyance, or if B should die and devise the remainder to A, A's life estate would merge with the fee simple, and the intervening contingent remainder would be destroyed.

But this doctrine of merger did not operate in all cases where the particular estate and the next vested estate in fee became united in the same person, for if it had, many settlements would have stultified themselves. To take a common illustration: if there was a devise:

to A for life, remainder in tail male to the successive sons of A, remainder to the heirs of A,

the devisee acquired, not only a life estate, but also by virtue of the Rule in *Shelley's Case*[17] the next vested estate in fee simple, so that, if the full consequences of merger were to ensue, the result, if A were childless, would be to destroy the contingent remainders in tail at the very moment at which they were created.

To obviate this, the law of merger was modified at an early date, and the rule was laid down that a merger which took place at the same instant as the creation of the particular estate should not be complete, but that the two estates thus temporarily united should reopen and let in the contingent remainders if they became vested during the lifetime of the particular tenant.[18]

(2) FORFEITURE BY TORTIOUS FEOFFMENT

The concept of the tortious feoffment has its origins in early land law, and is based on the duty of the tenant to protect the rights of the feudal lord. Any action inconsistent with this duty involved a forfeiture of the tenant's estate. A common way for this to occur was for a life tenant to purport to convey the fee to a third party; the life tenant's estate was forfeited.

In more modern times, a tortious conveyance is affected by suffering a recovery or levying a fine; these procedures were used for centuries, as we have seen, for the purpose of barring an entail.[19] They were used also when the tenant in possession decided to destroy the contingent remainders which were dependent upon his life estate. Thus, in the case of a simple limitation:

to A for life with remainder to B in fee simple contingently on attaining the age of 21 years.

A could destroy B's contingent remainder in fee simple by suffering a recovery, and, with the co-operation of a friendly third party to whom the fee was conveyed, could obtain the fee simple for himself. This made a contingent remainder a peculiarly insecure form of estate.

---

17 P. 492, ante.   18 *Lewis Bowles's Case* (1615) 11 Co Rep 79b; Challis, *Law of Real Property*, p. 137.
19 P. 483, ante.

It may be added in passing that the rule of destructibility by tortious feoffment applied to contingent remainders only,[20] and not to vested remainders, nor to executory interests.[21] This distinction is crucial, and it played a large part in the need for the development of the modern rule against perpetuities.

(c) Abolition of destructibility of contingent remainders by merger, surrender or forfeiture. Real Property Act 1845

These methods of destructibility of contingent remainders were abolished in 1845 by the Real Property Act of that year.

(3) Distinction Between Vested and Contingent Remainders

It thus became a matter of importance to determine whether a remainder was vested or contingent.[22] The distinction in general terms is obvious. A number of technicalities arose with which we are not concerned. For present purposes it is sufficient to say that a remainder is vested where:

(a) the person (or persons) entitled to take are ascertained;

(b) the interest is ready to take effect in possession forthwith, subject only to the prior interest.

Thus, we have seen that B's remainder is vested in a conveyance:[23]

to A for life with remainder to B in fee simple.

It would be contingent if the remainderman were not ascertained, as where the remainder was:

to A's eldest child living at his death; or

to the survivor of B and C; or

to B (an infant) if he attains the age of 21; or

to B if he is called to the Bar,

or any other contingency. But the prospect of a life tenant in remainder surviving a life tenant in possession is not regarded as a contingency. Thus:

to A for life with remainder to B for life with remainder to C in fee simple if he survives A.

A's death is not a contingency; it is a certainty, and B has a vested life estate in remainder. If B wishes to sell his remainder, its value will of course vary according to the statistical likelihood of his surviving A. C's remainder is contingent on his surviving A, because the limitation expressly so provides.

---

[20] Infra.   [21] *Pells v Brown* (1620) Cro Jac 590.

[22] On the distinction between vested and contingent, see Fearne, *Contingent Remainders*, pp. 65, 74, 89; Gray, *The Rule against Perpetuities*, s. 9 and chap. iii; Morris and Leach, chap. 2; *Theobald on Wills*, chap. 43. In construing limitations, the court leans in favour of vested interests, sometimes in spite of language which at first sight appears to be contingent. See *Duffield v Duffield* (1829) 3 Bli NS 260 at 331, per BEST CJ.

[23] P. 511, ante.

Viscount DILHORNE summed up the distinction between vested and contingent remainders as follows:[24]

In *Preston; Treatise on Estates*[25] an estate in possession is stated to be one which gives "a present right of present enjoyment". This was contrasted with an estate in remainder which it was said gave "a right of future enjoyment". In *Fearne on Contingent Remainders*,[26] it was said that an estate is vested when there is an immediate fixed right of present or future enjoyment; that an estate is vested in possession when there exists a right of present enjoyment; that an estate is vested in interest when there is a present fixed right of future enjoyment; and that an estate is contingent when a right of enjoyment is to accrue on an event which is dubious and uncertain.

(4) Definition of a Remainder

It will be seen that all the illustrations so far have been cases of gifts in remainder which are limited to take effect upon *the natural termination of a prior particular estate of freehold*.[27] This is the essential feature of a remainder. A remainder was the only future interest recognised by the early common law, though, as we shall see, other interests could be created behind a use,[28] and these were accepted as valid *legal estates* after execution by the Statute of Uses 1535, under the name of executory instruments. But, for the purposes of the present discussion, we are at common law, before 1535.

A remainder, then, is an interest which is limited to take effect in possession upon the natural termination of a prior particular estate. From this it follows that a future interest is not a remainder if it is designed so as to spring up in the future, as in a conveyance:

to A (an infant) for life if he attains the age of 21 years; or

at the date of the next election; or

1 year (or 1 day) from the date of this conveyance.

Such an interest, requiring an abeyance of seisin, could not exist at common law.

Nor could a limitation which purported to "shift" or transfer the estate from the tenant in possession to another on the happening of a future event. Thus, the common law did not recognise future interests in the following limitations:

to Mrs A for life but if she remarries to X;

to A in fee simple, but if he should emigrate to the Colonies, to B in fee simple.

A further rule is commonly stated, which is self-evident. There can be no remainder after a fee simple. A remainder must be limited to take effect on the failure of a prior particular estate. The fee simple is the largest estate known to the law and is not a particular estate.

D Estates in Equity. *Springing and Shifting Uses*

By and large, the Chancellor followed the law in the development of estates in equity. But where the common law, for technical reasons applicable only to the common law,

---

[24] *Pearson v IRC* [1981] AC 753 at 772.   [25] (1820) p. 89   [26] (10th edn, 1844) vol. 1. p. 2.
[27] A life estate. But it could have been a fee tail or an estate *pur autre vie*.
[28] Springing and shifting uses; infra.

frustrated the intention of the grantor, the Chancellor allowed new developments in equity.

A contingent remainder failed at common law if it failed to vest prior to or *eo instanti* with the termination of the prior particular estate. And it failed because an abeyance would otherwise be created in the seisin. The feudal system would not allow that. But, behind the use in equity, the problem disappeared, because the seisin was in the feoffees to uses. A gap in the beneficial interest behind the use created no problem in equity. Thus, contingent remainders in equity were valid whether they vested during the continuance of the prior estate, or at the moment of its termination, *or later*.

Further, the common law recognized only remainders as future interests. But no harm would be done in equity by allowing a grantor to create an equitable estate to "spring up" in the future, or to cause the equitable ownership to "shift" from the present equitable owner to another on the happening of a future event. The seisin was unaffected in either case, because the feoffees to uses remained seised throughout. Interests of this type were permitted in equity. Thus, the following gifts were valid in equity:

(i) to X, Y, Z to the use of B (an infant) when he attains the age of 21 years; or

when he is called to the Bar; or

one year from the date of this instrument.

(ii) to X, Y, Z to the use of Mrs B for life, but if she remarry to the use of C; or to the use of B in fee simple but if he ceases to reside in the City of Oxford to the use of C and his heirs.

These interests are known as (i) springing uses and (ii) shifting uses. They played a crucial part in the history of future interests, as will be seen. For the passage of the Statute of Uses in 1535 executed the uses, turned them into legal estates and forced the common law courts into making a decision as to whether they were to be accepted as valid legal estates; and, secondly, the future interests in equity arose all over again, with the development of the trust in the place of the old use. The free acceptance of springing and shifting uses in equity gave to a settlor a power to create a perpetuity. But the problem was not faced until such interests had become legal executory interests after execution by the Statute. The problem of the possibility of creating executory interests in perpetuity was faced in the seventeenth century, and the basic rule applicable throughout the English-speaking world was laid down in the *Duke of Norfolk's Case* in 1681–1685.[29]

E Executory Interests

The situation before 1535 therefore was that the only legal future interests recognised by the common law were remainders, and contingent remainders were struck down if they failed to vest prior to or *eo instanti* with the prior particular estate of freehold.[30] But in equity the situation was more liberal. The Chancellor recognised remainders, and upheld them

---

[29] (1683) 3 Cas in Ch 1; p. 519, post.
[30] Future interests in chattels (including leaseholds) could not be remainders. Such interests if valid took effect as executory interests.

whether or not they had vested at the time of the termination of the prior particular estate. He also recognised springing and shifting uses.[31]

The Statute of Uses 1535 profoundly affected this scene. It had no effect, as such, on legal remainders, but it had the effect of "executing" the uses and making legal estates out of the estates which had previously existed behind the use.[32] Thus a gift:

to X, Y, Z to the use of A for life with remainder to the use of B (an infant) if he attains the age of 21,

was no longer an equitable contingent remainder, but a legal remainder. Similarly, springing and shifting interests behind a use became legal. The common law courts had to face the questions of determining whether to apply their own rules to the contingent remainder, and whether or not to recognise the springing and shifting interests at all. The common law judges could have decided that what had been valid in equity was valid now at law. They could have decided that these were now legal estates and would be treated in exactly the same way as similar grants at law, not preceded by a grant to uses. In fact, they compromised. They accepted as valid springing and shifting interests which were created by means of a grant to uses and the execution of the uses by the Statute of Uses. These became known as *executory interests*. It should be emphasised that such an interest would only be recognised by the common law in the case of a grant *inter vivos* if it were written in the form of a grant to uses (and the use executed by the Statute). But such interests, if created by will, were recognised as creating valid future legal estates even though not in the form of a grant to uses; these were *executory devises*.

Thus far the common law courts followed the rule in equity. But when they came to decide the fate of a grant of an equitable contingent remainder which was executed and made legal by the Statute, they could not bring themselves to depart from the old contingent remainder rule with which they were so familiar. It was held in *Purefoy v Rogers*[33] that any limitation which was in its nature a remainder was subject to the common law rules of destructibility.[34] As late as 1843, Lord St Leonards saw this rule as an article of faith:

Now, if there be one rule of law more sacred than another, it is this, that no limitation shall be construed to be an executory or shifting use, which can by possibility take effect by way of remainder.[35]

And so the contingent remainder rule continued until it was abolished by the Contingent Remainders Act 1877.

F Modern Trusts. The Problem of Perpetuity

It has been seen that the use upon a use developed into, and allowed the creation of, modern trusts.[36] Trusts, like uses before them, are free of the old technicalities which burden common law future interests. As explained above,[37] future interests can, since 1925, only exist in equity behind a trust.

---

[31] It was said in the argument in *Hopkins v Hopkins* (1734) Cas temp Talb 45 at 51, that "springing uses are as old as uses themselves". For a case between 1417 and 1424 in which the aid of the Chancellor was supplicated, see (1896) 10 Selden Society, *Select Cases in Chancery*, 1364–1471, p. 114.

[32] It was held not to apply to active uses; nor to uses of leaseholds.

[33] (1671) 2 Wms Saund 380; *Goodright v Cornish* (1694) 4 Mod Rep 255; *Brackenbury v Gibbons* (1876) 2 Ch D 417 at 419; *White v Summers* [1908] 2 Ch 256. [34] P. 511, ante.

[35] *Cole v Sewell* (1843) 4 Dr & War 1 at 27. [36] P. 52, ante. [37] P. 510, ante.

The old technicalities are mere history, and will be unlikely to affect any title which comes before a modern practitioner. But the history shows that the freedom permitted to uses before 1535 created a situation in which interests in equity could be projected into the future in perpetuity, and nothing was done to control them. After the Statute of Uses and the acceptance by the common law of executory interests, the same problem presented itself, this time in the form of future legal estates. The *Duke of Norfolk's Case*[38] decided that a projection into the future was valid provided that the interest must vest, if it vest at all, within the lifetime of a living person. Later developments[39] expanded the rule into one which said that the interest was void unless it must vest, if at all, within the period of a life or lives in being plus twenty-one years. This rule governed legal executory interests and equitable interests behind a trust.[40] Legal future interests have now disappeared; and the problem of future interests, apart from questions of construction and of tax liability, essentially resolve themselves into the question of the application of the perpetuity rule to equitable interests under trusts.

II Development of the Modern Rule against Perpetuities

A *Perpetuity Problems throughout History*

The antagonism of the law to an unbarrable entail became apparent at an early date in its doctrine of the conditional fee.[41] The purpose of a grant to a man and a specified class of heirs of his body was that the land should serve the necessities of each generation and pass from heir to heir; but, as we have seen, the common law held that the grantee obtained a fee simple with an absolute power of alienation as soon as an heir of the prescribed class was born. Irritated by such a decisive defeat of their intention, the great landowners procured the passing of the Statute *De Donis* 1285, which enacted in effect that the intention of a donor was to prevail, and that an estate given to a man and the heirs of his body was perpetually to be reserved to the appropriate class of heir.[42] Thus for the moment the power to grant an inalienable interest in the shape of an unbarrable entail came within the powers of a grantor, but the right was soon lost, for at any rate by the fifteenth century the law had recognised recoveries as methods by which entails could be barred and converted into fees simple absolute by tenants in tail in possession.

When it had thus become impossible to ensure the maintenance of land in a family by the simple means of a grant to a man and the heirs of his body, settlors began to cast about for some device whereby they could attain their desire by a more indirect but equally effectual means. One plan was to insert in settlements a *clause of perpetuity*, that is, a condition to the effect that the interest of any tenant in tail who attempted to bar his entail

---

[38] (1683) 3 Cas in Ch 1.

[39] *Stephens v Stephens* (1736) Cas temp Talb 228; *Thellusson v Woodford* (1799) 4 Ves 227; affd (1805) 11 Ves 112; *Cadell v Palmer* (1833) 1 Cl & Fin 372, M & B p. 375: p. 519, post.

[40] And contingent remainders: *Re Frost* (1889) 43 Ch D 246; *Re Ashforth* [1905] 1 Ch 535; *Whitby v Von Luedecke* [1906] 1 Ch 783; Maudsley, pp. 71–2.   [41] P. 481, ante.

[42] P. 482, ante.

should be forfeited. Such conditions were, however, held void in three cases decided between 1600 and 1613.[43]

For the next series of attempts contingent remainders were pressed into service. At first, probably about 1556,[44] it became usual to prolong the period during which the land should be inalienable by making a grant to a son for life with contingent remainders to his unborn children, instead of granting him an immediate estate tail. This form of settlement, however, did not fulfil even the limited purpose for which it was designed, since, owing to the common law rules relating to seisin, it was possible for the life tenant to deal with his estate in such a way as to cause the destruction of the contingent remainder to the children before their birth.[45] Such a premature destruction was, however, prevented at a later date by the appointment of trustees to preserve contingent remainders. Another attempt took the form of the limitation of a perpetual freehold, by which successive estates for life were granted to the unborn issue of a person *ad infinitum*. A settlor, A, would limit the land to his son for life, remainder to every person that should be his heir one after the other for the life of such heir; but it was held by the courts that all the contingent remainders after the life estate to the first unborn heir (i.e. A's son) were void.[46] This particular rule was generally, though incorrectly,[47] described as the rule against double possibilities, for it was said that the law would never countenance a possibility upon a possibility,[48] and in the limitation indicated one possibility was that A would not have a son, another that the son, if born, would himself not have a son. The rule enforced by the courts was not, however, based on any such narrow ground. It was really a particular application of the parent rule that the grant of an unbarrable entail is void, and it was reaffirmed in 1890 in the case of *Whitby v Mitchell*,[49] where the Court of Appeal decided once more that where lands were limited to a living person, and then to his unborn child, and then to the child of such an unborn child, the last remainder was absolutely void. A settlor could exercise control up to a point but not beyond. He could withhold the fee simple from the grasp of his son by granting him a mere life estate, and he could, by the grant of an estate tail to his son's heir, prevent the acquisition of a fee simple until his son's son attained twenty-one; but nothing that he could do could prevent his son and grandson from collaborating to bar the entail when the grandson attained twenty-one.

Still another device adopted by settlors was to carve a species of estate tail out of a term of years by the bequest of a long term to a person and his heirs one after the other *ad infinitum*. But such a limitation after the term to the first unborn heir was held void.[50]

Pausing here for a moment we see that the attempts which were constantly being made by settlors to keep their land within the family, although they varied in details, all had one object in common, namely, by a combination of estates tail and contingent remainders or executory bequests to set up unbarrable entails, and it was this particular species of inalienable estate that was regarded by the lawyers of the seventeenth century as a perpetuity. As Lord NOTTINGHAM said:

A perpetuity is the settlement of an estate or interest in tail, with such remainders expectant upon it as are in no sort in the power of the tenant in tail inpossession to dock by any recovery or assignment.[51]

---

[43] *Corbet's Case* (1600) 1 Co Rep 83b; *Mildmay's Case* (1605) 6 Co Rep 40a; *Mary Portington's Case* (1613) 10 Co Rep 35b.   [44] (1855) 1 Jurid Soc 47 (Joshua Williams); cited Scrutton, *Land in Fetters*, pp. 116–17.
[45] P. 511, ante.   [46] Fearne, *Contingent Remainders*, p. 502.
[47] Challis, *Law of Real Property*, pp. 116–18; *Jarman on Wills*, p. 293; Holdsworth, *Historical Introduction to Land Law*, p. 222, n. 6.   [48] Co Litt 184a.
[49] (1890) 44 Ch D 85.   [50] *Sanders v Cornish* (1631) Cro Car 230; *Jarman on Wills*, p. 291.
[51] *Duke of Norfolk's Case* (1683) 3 Cas in Ch 1.

Thus at an early date contingent remainders ceased to endanger the free alienability of land, for they failed altogether unless they had vested when the particular tenant died; they were easily destructible; and, if they were nothing more than unbarrable entails in disguise, they were void on the ground that they virtually created an inalienable interest.

B Emergence of the Modern Rule Against Perpetuities

The modern rule began to emerge about 1660,[52] and it was finally completed by the House of Lords in *Cadell v Palmer* in 1833.[53] The main stages in its development may be shortly stated.[54]

In *The Duke of Norfolk's Case*, 1681–85,[55] there was a grant of a term of 200 years to trustees upon trust for the grantor's second son Henry and the heirs male of his body, but if his eldest son Thomas died without issue male *in Henry's lifetime*, then in trust for Charles, his third son. Lord NOTTINGHAM held that the last limitation was good, since the shifting to Charles must take place, if it ever took place at all, upon the dropping of a life in being, namely that of Thomas. Thus the case did not fix the maximum period during which vesting might be suspended, but decided that an interest that must vest if ever within lives in being was valid. *Stephens v Stephens*,[56] in 1736, held that an executory devise to the unborn child of a living person upon attaining twenty-one was good, and thereby in effect extended the maximum period to lives in being plus a further twenty-one years. In *Thellusson v Woodford*,[57] in 1805, Lord ELDON was of opinion that the persons whose lives were chosen need have no connection with the settled property, but might be strangers chosen at random. This opinion was endorsed by *Cadell v Palmer*,[58] which also decided that a term of twenty-one years without any reference to minorities might be added to existing lives.

In 1925 the rule in *Whitby v Mitchell* was abolished by section 161 of the Law of Property Act:

(1) The rule of law prohibiting the limitation, after a life interest to an unborn person, of an interest in land to the unborn child or other issue of an unborn person is hereby abolished, but without prejudice to any other rule relating to perpetuities.

(2) This section only applies to limitations or trusts created by an instrument coming into operation after the commencement of this Act.[59]

Thus the rule against perpetuities, fortified by the rules against accumulations of income,[60] is now the sole determinant of whether an interest is too remote. It applies both to realty and personalty out of which future contingent interests have been carved.

---

[52] *Snowe v Cuttler* (1664) 1 Lev 135; *Wood v Sanders* (1669) 1 Ch Cas 131; Holdsworth, *History of English Law*, vol. vii. pp. 222 et seq.   [53] (1833) 1 Cl & Fin 372, M & B p. 375.

[54] Pollock, *Land Laws*, Appendix Note G; Gray, *The Rule against Perpetuities*, ss. 123 et seq; Holdsworth, *Historical Introduction to Land Law*, p. 224; Morris and Leach, pp. 8–11.

[55] (1683) 3 Cas in Ch 1.   [56] (1736) Cas temp Talb 228.

[57] (1799) 4 Ves 227; on appeal (1805) 11 Ves 112.   [58] (1833) 1 Cl & Fin 372.

[59] A limitation to the unborn issue of an unborn taker is void under the modern rule, unless it is expressly confined within due limits, as in *Re Nash* [1910] 1 Ch 1. As to the meaning of "coming into operation after" the Act, see *Re Leigh's Marriage Settlement* [1952] 2 All ER 57.   [60] P. 560, post.

III The Modern Rule Against Perpetuities[61]

A *Introduction*

The rule has been summarised by *Gray on Perpetuities* as follows:[62]

No interest is good, unless it must vest, if at all, not later than 21 years after some life in being at the creation of the interest.

Four comments should be made upon this statement at the outset.

(i)   This is not a statutory provision. It is a distinguished author's formulation of the basic operation of the rule. There are, as will be seen, several areas of operation where special factors have to be taken into consideration.

(ii)   The requirement of the rule is that the interest must vest in *interest*, if at all, within the perpetuity period. The time at which it vests in possession is immaterial. The distinction between interests which are contingent, vested in interest or vested in possession has been explained above.[63]

(iii) How is it to be determined when the interest must vest, if at all, and within twenty-one years of which lives? These two basic questions on the working of the rule are not legal questions; nor are they asked because Gray's statement of the rule is obscure. The key to understanding the operation of the rule is to appreciate that what is sought is a *relationship* between the vesting and persons living. When does the interest vest? Examine the language of the instrument to find out. Is that vesting certain to occur within 21 years of the death of some living person, if it occurs at all? Examine the *relationship* between the vesting and living persons. The relationship will be either logical or biological. Thus, in a gift:

to the first child of A to attain the age of 21,

A's first child must attain that age, if at all, within 21 years of A's death. For A cannot procreate children after his death.[64] A's is the measuring life. But if the gift were:

to the first child of A to marry,

the gift would be void. There is no living person within 21 years of whose death A's child is certain to marry, if at all. Of course a living child of A must marry, if at all, within that *child's* lifetime. That is logical (and obvious). But logically also, the first child of A to marry may be a future born child of A, if A has no married child and is alive at the date of the gift. A focus on the logical and biological *relationship* between the vesting and living people is the simplest way to understand the rule. Many millions of persons are "lives" in the sense that they

---

[61] See the accounts of this difficult subject in Morris and Leach, *The Rule against Perpetuities* (2nd edn, 1962), with supplement (1964) on PAA 1964; Maudsley, *The Modern Law of Perpetuities*; *Theobald on Wills*, chap. 44. See also (1964) 80 LQR 486 (J. H. C. Morris and H. W. R. Wade); (1981) 97 LQR 593 (R. L. Deech). This account owes much to Maudsley and M & B, chap. 7. In 1998 the Law Commission published a Report on the Rules against Perpetuities and Excessive Accumulations (Law Com No. 251), p. 564, post.

[62] S. 201.   [63] Pp. 511, 513, ante.

[64] A period of gestation is allowed, if in fact gestation takes place.

are alive, but only those persons, within 21 years of whose death the interest must vest, if at all, are the measuring lives, and it is only possible to discover who they are after an examination of the *relationship* between the time of vesting and the living persons. A gift:

to the first great-great-grandchild of A to go for a walk with X

is valid. It must vest, if at all, in X's lifetime. Application of the rule has led to a number of innocent-looking limitations being held void because of the theoretical possibility of the happening of the practically impossible, such as an old lady of seventy having further children.[65] To an ordinary person such freakish possibilities would be incomprehensible. The special situations have to be learned and recognised from the cases.

(iv) Largely for the reasons given in the previous paragraph, there were strong movements for reform. We shall see that the Perpetuities and Accumulations Act 1964[66] effected major reforms, not only providing for detailed reforms in particular situations, but also introducing the principle of "wait and see". Rather than hold an interest void because it is not certain to vest, if at all, within the period, why not wait and see whether or not it does vest within the period, and hold it valid if it does, and void if it does not? That is a very attractive solution, and has been used in many jurisdictions in Australia, Canada, Northern Ireland, New Zealand, and the United States of America.[67] Manitoba has gone further in abolishing the rule and in its place widening the court's jurisdiction to vary trusts.[68] The 1964 Act creates a number of difficulties in the application of the principle.

B The Rule Applicable to Instruments Taking Effect Before 16 July 1964

(1) Applicability of the Common Law Rule

It is still necessary to understand the working of the common law rule: firstly, because the 1964 Act only applies to instruments taking effect after 15 July 1964, and questions of perpetuity

---

[65] *Jee v Audley* (1787) 1 Cox Eq Cas 324, M & B p. 382; *Re Dawson* (1888) 39 Ch D 155, M & B p. 396; *Ward v Van der Loeff* [1924] AC 653, M & B p. 382. *Re Sayer's Trusts* (1868) LR 6 Eq 319; *Re Deloitte* [1926] Ch 56; *Figg v Clarke* [1997] 1 WLR 603 (1963 settlement; capital gains; CGTA 1979, s. 54(1)); [1997] Conv 237 (I. Ferrier).

[66] Which came into operation on 16 July 1964, and gave substantial effect to the recommendations of the Law Reform Committee Fourth Report (1956) Cmnd 18; p. 545, post.

[67] In the USA, the rule against perpetuities was considered by the Commissioners on Uniform State Laws, who favoured retention of the common law (with amendments, including the introduction of wait and see) and its codification in statutory form. This led to the Uniform Statutory Rule Against Perpetuities being approved by the National Conference of Commissioners in 1986 and revised in 1990. Up to 2005 it had been implemented in twenty-eight states.

[68] Perpetuities and Accumulations Act 1983 (SM 1982–1983, c 43); Manitoba Law Reform Commission Report on the Rules against Accumulations and Perpetuities (1982 No. 49); see (1984) 4 OJLS 454 (R. Deech) for a detailed review and criticism of this legislation; M & B pp. 371, 422; (1983) Manitoba LJ 245 (A. I. McClean) "Abolition is a great step into the unknown. The Manitoba Law Reform Commission and the Manitoba Legislator are not to be numbered amongst the law's timorous souls"; (1984) 62 Can Bar Rev 618 (J. M. Glenn), criticising the legislation. Abolition has also been recommended by the Law Reform Committee of South Australia (73rd Report, *Relating to the Reform of the Law of Perpetuities* (1984)) and the Law Reform Commission of Saskatchewan (*Proposals Relating to the Rules Against Perpetuities and Accumulations* (1987)). For reforms in other jurisdictions, see Law Commission Report on the Rules against Perpetuities and Excessive Accumulations (Law Com No. 251), Appendix B.

have a habit of turning up many years after the instrument comes into effect; secondly, because the 1964 Act provides[69] that the "wait and see" principle is applicable to instruments which fail to comply with the common law rule.[70] The common law rule, therefore, applies to all dispositions; if the limitation complies with that rule, it is valid, but, if it fails to comply with the rule it may be saved by the application of the principle of "wait and see".

(2) Statement of the Rule

The inquiry, then, in cases governed by the common law rule is to determine whether the interest in question is certain to vest in interest, if it vests at all, within a life in being plus twenty-one years, plus a period of gestation if gestation in fact takes place. For the purposes of the rule, conception is treated as equivalent to birth.[71] Thus a child, whether a beneficiary or not, who is *en ventre sa mère*[72] at the time when the instrument of gift takes effect may constitute a life in being,[73] and a child *en ventre sa mère* at the end of the perpetuity period may qualify as a beneficiary under the limitation.[74]

The test for certainty of vesting is made as of the date when the instrument comes into effect, that is, if the instrument is a deed, when the deed is executed; if it is a will, when the testator dies. Or, to put the rule another way, an interest is void if it might by any possibility vest outside the period of a life in being plus twenty-one years. A number of points arising out of the rule will now be examined.

(a) Vesting

The rule is concerned with the time of vesting in interest. The rules for such vesting are explained above.[75] The rule is in no way concerned with the time at which an interest may vest *in possession*. It is necessary to examine the language of the instrument to determine the time at which the interest will vest. Further, the rule is not concerned with the duration of interests, the time for which they may continue. Thus:

> to A for life and after his death to the first of A's children to attain the age of 21 in fee simple. A is alive and has infant children.

This interest will vest in *interest* when the first of A's children attains the age of twenty-one. That interest will vest in *possession* when A dies. The fact that the interest of A's child, being a fee simple, may last forever is immaterial. That interest is alienable, and the freedom of disposition of the property is not restricted in any way.[76]

It is sometimes said also that the rule does not apply to vested gifts. This is a truism. The requirement of the rule is that the interest must vest, if at all, within the period. If the

---

[69] S. 3.   [70] For a criticism, see p. 547, post.   [71] *Re Stern* [1962] Ch 732 at 737.

[72] "In simple English, it is an unborn child inside the mother's womb": *Royal College of Nursing of the United Kingdom v Department of Health and Social Security* [1981] AC 800 at 802, per Lord DENNING MR. For the effect on the rule against perpetuities of delayed posthumous births by means of sperm banks or other devices, see (1979) 53 ALJ 311 (C. Sappideen). See also Human Fertilisation and Embryology Act 1990, as amended by Human Fertilisation and Embryology (Deceased Fathers) Act 2003; Human Fertilisation and Embryology (Disclosure of Information) Act 1992; Law Commission Consultation Paper on The Rules against Perpetuities and Excessive Accumulations 1993 (Law Com No. 133), paras. 2.16, n. 30; 2.21, n. 45; 5.79.

[73] *Long v Blackall* (1797) 7 Term Rep 100; *Re Wilmer's Trusts* [1903] 2 Ch 411.

[74] Gray, *The Rule against Perpetuities*, s. 220; Challis, *Law of Real Property*, p. 182.

[75] P. 513, ante; Gray, s. 323.   [76] P. 513, ante.

interest is vested, no question arises. The rule is concerned with interests which are contingent, not vested.

(b) Requirement of certainty. Remorseless construction

The rule requires that the interest must be absolutely certain to vest, if at all, within the perpetuity period. This does *not* mean that the interest must be certain to vest; for we are dealing with contingent interests, and there is no such thing as a contingency which is certain to occur. It is sometimes easier to look at the alternative formulation of the rule, and say that the interest is void if by any possibility it *might vest outside the period.*

The requirement of certainty of vesting, if at all, within the period means what it says. If there is any possible way, however freakish and unlikely, in which the interest might vest outside the period, the interest is void. And possibilities which are known to be not only freakish and unlikely, but also those which are physically impossible, such as that a woman over seventy may have a baby,[77] have been allowed to render gifts void. Further, the lawyers of olden days were so concerned at the possibility of the appearance of a perpetuity, that it became established that the language of the limitation must be remorselessly construed; the fact that the settlor or testator obviously did not intend the interest to fail to comply with the perpetuity rule is ignored. Lord SELBORNE LC said in 1880:[78]

You do not import the law of remoteness into the construction of the instrument, by which you investigate the expressed intention of the testator. You take his words, and endeavour to arrive at their meaning, exactly in the same manner as if there had been no such law, and as if the whole intention expressed by the words could lawfully take effect.

and Gray:[79]

Its object is to defeat intention. Therefore every provision in a will or settlement is to be construed as if the rule did not exist, and then to the provision so construed the rule is to be remorselessly applied.

The rule is applied in relation to the facts existing at the time when the instrument comes into effect. Invalidity is unaffected by the fact that, as the facts *subsequently* work out, the interest does in fact vest within the period. There is no wait and see at common law. That principle will be discussed in connection with the 1964 Act.[80]

Much of the difficulty in applying the rule stems from the fact that interests have been held void by reason of the possibility of an occurrence which would not normally be foreseen. These points will be demonstrated by a number of illustrations below. It is thought better to take the illustrations together, because more than one important point is demonstrated in each case.

(c) The perpetuity period. Measuring lives

The perpetuity period at common law was that of a life or lives in being plus twenty-one years. To be valid the interest must be certain to vest, if at all, within the period. The requirement of vesting has been explained. Once the time of vesting is ascertained, the problem is to determine whether that vesting event must occur, if at all, within the period of a life or lives in being plus twenty-one years. This is what was meant by saying, above, that it is

---

[77] *Jee v Audley* (1787) 1 Cox Eq Cas 324; *Re Dawson* (1888) 39 Ch D 155; *Ward v Van der Loeff* [1924] AC 653.
[78] *Pearks v Moseley* (1880) 5 App Cas 714 at 719.   [79] S. 629.   [80] P. 547, post.

necessary to understand the *relationship* between the lives and the vesting. Which lives? Anybody: so long as that (living) person's relationship with the vesting is such as to enable it to be known with certainty that the vesting must occur, if at all, within twenty-one years of the dropping of that life. As has been said:[81]

What one is really looking for at common law is some life in existence at the commencement of the period which shows, in the light of the circumstances existing at that date, that the interest must vest in time. In other words, one is looking for a life that will show the gift to be valid and one rejects all others as irrelevant. . . . The search, at common law, is for a life in being at the commencement of the period which is (i) certain and identifiable and (ii) so related to the vesting contingency that the gift must vest if at all within twenty-one years of its termination. A life that does not satisfy these requirements can be of no assistance in determining the validity of the gift at common law and is therefore rejected as irrelevant (or simply not considered at all).

Some simple illustrations will explain.

(1) WHEN NO LIVES HAVE BEEN EXPRESSLY SELECTED

1. *To the first child of A to attain the age of twenty-one years.* This is valid, because it is absolutely certain that A's first child will attain the age of twenty-one years, if he or she ever does, within twenty-one years of the death of A. We will see that the rule assumed that it was possible for a man or woman to have a child at any age, however advanced, but A cannot procreate children after his death.[82] A's is the measuring life. Of course, if A were dead, his living children are certain to attain the age of twenty-one, if they ever do, within their own lifetimes. Theirs would then be the measuring lives.

2. *To the first child of A to marry.* A is alive and has unmarried children. This is void.[83] It is not certain that A's first child to marry will do so within twenty-one years of the death of any person now living. The first child to marry *may* do so within twenty-one years of the death of A, or Mrs A, or A's parents or A's neighbours, but he or she may not. Of course, each of A's children living at the date of the gift must marry, if at all, within their own lifetimes, but the first child to marry may be future born, and may marry more than twenty-one years after the death of A, Mrs A, the children alive at the date of the gift, A's parents or A's neighbours. The gift is void. There is no measuring life. Of course, if A were dead at the date of the gift, the gift would be valid. Any child of A is certain to marry, if at all, during that child's lifetime. The children's would be the measuring lives.

3. *To the first of A's great-great-grandchildren to go for a walk with X.* This is valid. It must occur, if at all, in X's lifetime. X's is the measuring life. The fact that X is unlikely to live that long is not relevant. The interest must vest, if it ever does, within X's lifetime. The gift is likely to fail, not for perpetuity, but because it will probably never vest.

---

[81] (1965) 81 LQR 106 at 107 (D. E. Allan); Maudsley, pp. 94–5; M & B pp. 390–1. See also (1981) 97 LQR 593 (R. L. Deech); p. 551, n. 234, post.

[82] Human Fertilisation and Embryology Act 1990, s. 29(3B), inserted by Human Fertilisation and Embryology (Deceased Fathers) Act 2003, s 1(2) (embryo brought about by using the sperm of a man after his death, or using the sperm of a man before his death but placed in the woman after his death, can be treated as child of the man for purposes of entry in register of births, but for no other purposes).

[83] Similarly, a gift to the first child of A to attain the age of twenty-two years was void prior to 1926; the gift was saved by LPA 1925, s. 163; p. 528, post.

4. *To the first grandchild of A to attain the age of twenty-one.* A is alive, has two children and four infant grandchildren. This is void. It is not certain that the first grandchild of A to attain the age of twenty-one will do so within twenty-one years of the death of any person now living. It is possible that A, regardless of age or sex, will have a third child. All the family, except the newborn child, then die. Suppose that newborn child has a child thirty years later, and that child attains the age of twenty-one years, fifty-one years after the death of persons living at the date of the gift. The gift is void; there are no measuring lives.

The result would be different if A were dead at the date of the gift. All of A's grandchildren would necessarily be children of the children of A, alive at the date of the gift, and *their* children must attain the age of twenty-one, if at all, within twenty-one years of the death of those living children of A. A's living children are the measuring lives. Similarly if A, by his will, makes a gift to "the first of my grandchildren to attain the age of twenty-one"; A, being a testator, is necessarily dead.

Again, the gift would be valid if it had been a gift to such of A's grandchildren as shall attain the age of twenty-one, being children of a child of A alive at the date of the gift.

Now let us go back to the first paragraph of this illustration, and assume that A is an old lady of eighty. It is obvious that the settlor or testator intended the gift to be in favour of the then living children of A. The settlor would not even consider the possibility of the old lady bearing another child. But the rule requires that possibility to be taken into consideration. And the courts were not even willing to construe the limitation to accord with what would have been the obvious intention of the settlor if he had been asked.[84]

As the number of contingencies is unlimited, so could this list of illustrations be endless. What they are intended to show is that it is necessary in every case to determine *the relationship between the vesting and the lives*, in order to discover whether that relationship is such as to enable us to say that the interest must vest, if at all, within twenty-one years of the death of some life.

(2) EXPRESSLY SELECTED LIVES

Thus far, the settlor has taken no steps to select the lives to be used for the purpose. He may select the lives, and he may choose whomsoever he wishes, but it must be substantially practicable to ascertain the date of the death of the survivor. If, however, the number of the selected lives is so great as to render it impossible to ascertain the death of the survivor, as for instance where a testator defined the period as:

twenty-one years from the death of the last survivor of all persons who shall be *living at my death,*

the gift, though not infringing the rule against perpetuities, is void for uncertainty.[85] The selected lives need have no connection with the beneficial interests. Young and healthy babies would be a good selection if it is decided to extend the period as long as possible. It became the general practice in the nineteenth century to select:

the lineal descendants of Queen Victoria living at my death.

---

[84] P. 529, post.
[85] *Re Moore* [1901] 1 Ch 936. And not even valid for twenty-one years; see *Muir v IRC* [1966] 1 WLR 1269 at 1282.

There were many of them, and they were in the public eye and easily traceable. But, the fact that as a result of World War I descendants of Queen Victoria would be scattered as refugees throughout the world could not have been foreseen.

These problems were discussed in *Re Villar*:[86]

The testator died on 6 September 1926, having made his will in 1921, and confirmed it in a codicil in 1926. He provided that his estate was to be held upon certain family trusts for the duration of "the period of restriction" after the expiration of which the estate was to be finally distributed. The "period of restriction" was defined as "the period ending at the expiration of 20 years from the day of the death of the last survivor of all the lineal descendants of Her late Majesty Queen Victoria who shall be living at the time of my death".

Since there were about 120 descendants scattered among at least ten countries in Europe alone, it was obvious that the difficulty of proving the fact and date of death of each descendant might be almost insuperable. Nevertheless, the trust was held to be valid.

Assuming that the measuring lives selected by the settlor or testator comply with the rule requiring ascertainability, the application of the rule to cases where lives are expressly selected is exactly the same as that in which no mention is made of measuring lives. The question is still the same; is it certain that the interest must vest, if at all, within twenty-one years of the death of some person or persons now living?

It will be noticed that the limitation in *Re Villar* was that the estate was to be finally distributed at the end of "the period of restriction". The final vesting would necessarily take place twenty years from the death of the survivor of persons living at the death of the testator, which must necessarily be within the period. But if the testator makes a gift

to such of my lineal descendants as shall be living 20 years from the death of the survivor of my friends X, Y and Z,

then, unless the court construes the language of the gift as intending to restrict the vesting to those descendants who vest within twenty years from the death of the survivor, the gift is void. All lineal descendants could claim at any time in the future. Measuring lives are nominated. But there is no *relationship* between the lives and the vesting.

(3) HUMAN LIVES

The lives must be those of human beings, and not "of animals or trees in California".[87]

(4) NO LIVES SPECIFIED

If no lives are specified, an absolute period of twenty-one years, and no longer, is allowed.[88] In *Re Hooper*,[89] a gift:

for the upkeep of certain monuments so far as the trustees legally can do so,

was upheld for a period of twenty-one years.

---

[86] [1928] Ch 471; affd [1929] 1 Ch 243; M & B p. 379; *Re Leverhulme (No 2)* [1943] 2 All ER 274, where MORTON J added a warning against "using the formula in the case of a testator who dies in the year 1943 or at any later date". See, however, *Re Warren's Will Trusts* (1961) 105 SJ 511, where a testatrix died in 1944 and CROSS J upheld the will.   [87] *Re Kelly* [1932] IR 255, per MEREDITH J; M & B p. 380.
[88] *Palmer v Holford* (1828) 4 Russ 403.   [89] [1932] 1 Ch 38.

(3) Operation of the Rule. Remorseless Application

A number of cases will now be examined as illustrations of the perpetuity rule at work. In each case, the language of the instrument should be examined in order to see when the interest is limited to vest, and then the *relationship* between the time of vesting and the lives of living people should be examined to see if the vesting is certain to occur, if at all, within twenty-one years of the death of some person now living.

(a) Standard illustrations of void gifts

Limitations were held void where a gift was to vest:

when a candidate for the priesthood "comes forward from St Saviour's Church, St Albans;"[90]

or,

when a house ceases to be maintained as a dwelling place;[91]

or,

where an advowson was devised to the first or other son of A that should be bred a clergyman and be in Holy Orders;[92]

or,

where there was a gift by will of an annuity of £100 to be provided to the Central London Rangers on the appointment of the next lieutenant-colonel.[93]

In each of these cases it will be seen that the time of vesting is in no way related to the lives of living people. The vesting may occur on the day after the instrument came into force. But it may not. All living people may be dead before the interest vests. This is unlikely, but we are concerned with what *might* happen, not with what is likely to happen, and we do not wait at common law to see what does happen.

(b) Vesting postponed to a date later than twenty-one years

The most common cause of invalidity in the older cases was the selection of an age of vesting greater than the age of twenty-one. The child of A is certain to attain the age of twenty-one within twenty-one years of A's death. But the child of A is not certain to attain the age of

---

[90] *Re Mander* [1950] Ch 547.   [91] *Kennedy v Kennedy* [1914] AC 215.

[92] *Proctor v Bishop of Bath and Wells* (1794) 2 Hy Bl 358.

[93] *Re Lord Stratheden and Campbell* [1894] 3 Ch 265. Other illustrations are: *Edwards v Edwards* [1909] AC 275 (when the coal under certain land is exhausted); *Re Wood* [1894] 3 Ch 381 (when a gravel pit is worked out); *Re Engels* [1943] 1 All ER 506 (after termination of the present war with Germany); *Re Fry* [1945] Ch 348 at 352 (when an unborn person, ascertainable within the perpetuity period, takes the testator's surname); *Re Jones* [1950] 2 All ER 239 ("upon the realization of my foreign estate"); *Re Flavel's Will Trusts* [1969] 1 WLR 444 (fund to provide superannuation benefits for present and past employees of a company).

twenty-two (or more commonly twenty-five) within twenty-one years of the death of any living person. In order to avoid the necessity of holding such gifts void, section 163 of the Law of Property Act 1925 provided that:

Where in a will, settlement or other instrument the absolute vesting either of capital or income of property, or the ascertainment of a beneficiary or class of beneficiaries, is made to depend on the attainment by the beneficiary of members of the class of an age exceeding twenty-one years, and thereby the gift to that beneficiary or class or any member thereof, or any gift over, remainder, executory limitation, or trust arising on the total or partial failure of the original gift, is, or but for this section would be, rendered void for remoteness, the will, settlement, or other instrument shall take effect for the purposes of such gift, gift over, remainder, executory limitation, or trust as if the absolute vesting or ascertainment aforesaid had been made to depend on the beneficiary or member of the class attaining the age of twenty-one years, and that age shall be substituted for the age stated in the will, settlement, or other instrument.

It will be seen that the age was only to be reduced to twenty-one years where the gift would thereby be validated. Section 163 was repealed by the Perpetuities and Accumulations Act 1964[94] in respect of dispositions to which the Act applies.

(c) Leach's caricature cases

The trouble with the perpetuity rule was that, because of its remorseless application, it rendered void a number of perfectly reasonable dispositions, in cases in which the settlor's or testator's intention could have been achieved if the draftsman had been competent.[95] Professor Barton Leach listed and named a number of such situations.[96]

(1) THE MAGIC GRAVEL PITS

This situation may arise when a testator assumes that his estate will be administered by his personal representatives within a reasonably short time, and then his will is drafted in such a way that a contingent interest may, beyond all reasonable expectation, vest outside the perpetuity period. Thus, in Re Wood:[97]

a testator, who was a gravel contractor, directed his trustees "to carry on my said business of a gravel contractor until my gravel pits are worked out" and then to sell them and to divide the proceeds among his issue "then living". At the date of the will it was clear that the testator knew that the gravel pits would soon be worked out, and they were in fact worked out within six years of his death.

It was held that the gift was void because there was a possibility that the gravel pits might not have been worked out within the perpetuity period of twenty-one years. As has been said, "like the widow's cruse, the gravel pits might have replenished themselves for ever—or at least for more than twenty-one years".[98]

---

94 P. 555, post   95 (1952) 68 LQR 35 at 36 (W. Barton Leach); Maudsley, pp. 37–8.
96 (1938) 51 Harv L Rev 1329; (1952) 65 Harv L Rev 721; (1952) 68 LQR 35 at 44.
97 [1894] 2 Ch 310; affd [1894] 3 Ch 381, M & B p. 388. See also Re Lord Stratheden and Campbell [1894] 3 Ch 265; p. 527, ante (a perpetual lieutenant-colonel); Re Atkins' Will Trusts [1974] 1 WLR 761, M & B p. 388 (contingency was that of a bank complying with its duty to sell land within the period. Held to be valid as there was no reason to assume that the bank would commit a breach of trust).   98 Morris and Leach, p. 74.

(2) THE UNBORN WIDOW(ER)

Gifts to children may fail because of the possibility that a mother (or father) who is now married may lose her husband (or wife) by death or divorce, and then may marry again, his second wife being someone who is now unborn. Thus, in *Re Frost*[99] there was a gift to:

Emma, a spinster, for life, and after her death to any husband she may marry for his life, and then to each of their children as shall be living at the death of the survivor of Emma and such husband.

The gift to the children was void. It was contingent on the children surviving Emma and her husband. Emma was unmarried at the date of the gift, and might marry a husband who was unborn at that date. If he then survived Emma by more than twenty-one years, the interests of the children would not vest within twenty-one years of Emma's death. The result would have been the same even if Emma had been married at the date of the gift.

Re Frost must be contrasted with *Re Garnham*,[100] where there was a gift:

to Thomas, a bachelor, for life, then to any woman he may marry for life, and then to the children of Thomas at 21.

The gift was held to be valid. The interests of the children vested in *interest* on the death of Thomas, and not, as in *Re Frost*, on the death of the *survivor* of Emma and her husband.

(3) THE FERTILE OCTOGENARIAN

The common law recognised no upper (or lower) limit of age at which a living person was supposedly capable of reproduction; and this led to the necessity to hold void a number of dispositions in which there was no physical possibility of the interest vesting outside the period, and no thought or expectation that there might be a problem. The leading case is *Ward v Van der Loeff*:[101]

By his will the testator devised his residuary estate upon trust for his widow for life and then, in the events which happened, upon trust for the children of his brothers and sisters.

By a codicil he declared that his widow's life interest should be terminable on her remarriage, unless such remarriage should be with a natural born British subject; and that, on her death or remarriage, the trustees should hold the residuary estate upon trust for such of the children of his brothers and sisters as should attain the age of 21 (or, being daughters, attain that age or marry). The widow married a Dutchman.

At the date of the testator's death, his parents were both alive, aged 66. Two brothers and two sisters were alive, each of whom was over 30 and had infant children, one of whom was born after the remarriage of the widow.

The House of Lords held that the gift in the codicil was void, because a future born niece or nephew might have attained the age of twenty-one outside the period. The living nieces and nephews would attain that age, if at all, in their own lifetimes. And future born children of the testator's brothers and sisters living at the time would also attain that age, if at all, within twenty-one years of the death of their parents (the living brothers and sisters of the testator). But if the testator's parents were still alive, they might have another child, a new brother or sister to the testator. Everyone else might die, and then that child might have a child which

---

[99] (1889) 43 Ch D 246, M & B p. 387.   [100] [1916] 2 Ch 413, M & B p. 387.
[101] [1924] AC 653, M & B p. 382.

might attain the age of twenty-one more than twenty-one years after the death of any person living at the date of the testator's death. The rule relating to class gifts, as will be seen, is that the gift to the class is valid only if its exact composition must be known within the period. The result was that the gift in the codicil failed.[102]

For all its complications, this case reduces itself to an illustration of the simple proposition, discussed above, that a gift to the grandchildren of living persons is void.[103] It illustrates dramatically the application of the rule of remorseless construction. What would the testator have said if he had been asked the question: By "children of my brothers and sisters", do you mean the children of your *living* brothers and sisters,[104] or do you wish to include the children of a future brother or sister to which your sixty-six-year-old mother might give birth after your death? It will be seen that the Perpetuities and Accumulations Act 1964 has enacted the permissible periods of reproduction for males and females.[105]

(4) THE PRECOCIOUS TODDLER

Logically, the presumption of fertility attributed to the old should equally affect the young. Whether it must be presumed that no person can be too young to beget children was canvassed in *Re Gaite's Will Trusts*[106] but was not determined. On the facts of that case, the argument in favour of such a presumption rested upon the possibility that within the short space of five years after the settlor's death a child might be born to his widow, already sixty-five years old, and might then marry and have issue. The judge evaded the question of physical impossibility by holding that such a hypothetical marriage, contracted by a person under sixteen years of age contrary to the Age of Marriage Act 1929,[107] was a legal impossibility. And the court will not take into account an event which presupposes a contravention of statute or a breach of trust.[108]

(4) Gifts to a Class

(a) General

(1) MEANING OF GIFT TO A CLASS

As Lord SELBORNE said in *Pearks v Moseley*:[109]

A gift is said to be to a class of persons when it is to all those who shall come within a certain category or description defined by a general or collective formula, and who, if they take at all, are to take one divisible subject in certain proportionate shares.

There is a gift to a class if the limitation is:

to all the children of A who shall attain 21.

---

[102] But the story had a happier ending. The House of Lords further held that (i) the codicil did not revoke the gift in the will, by applying the doctrine of dependent relative revocation and (ii) the gift in the will itself was valid. That was saved by the interrelation of the class closing rules and the perpetuity rule, as a result of which the child who was born after the remarriage of the widow was excluded. See p. 532, post; Maudsley, pp. 54–6.

[103] One of the grandparents in fact died before the litigation. But that of course made no difference.

[104] In which case the gift would have been valid. In the Court of Appeal ATKIN LJ would have upheld the codicil on the ground that this was the testator's obvious intention: *Re Burnyeat* [1923] 2 Ch 52 at 70.

[105] P. 546, post.   [106] [1949] 1 All ER 459, M & B p. 377.

[107] Now the Marriage Act 1949, s. 2.   [108] *Re Atkins' Will Trusts* [1974] 1 WLR 761, M & B p. 388.

[109] (1880) 5 App Cas 714 at 723.

On the other hand, a gift of:

£2,000 to each of the daughters of B,

is not a class gift.[110]

(2) VESTING OF INTEREST OF MEMBER OF CLASS

We have seen that,[111] for the purpose of determining whether an individual member of a class has a vested interest, each member of the class obtains a vested interest on satisfying the necessary qualifications. Thus in a gift:

to A for life and after his death to such of his children as shall attain 25,

each child of A obtains a vested interest on reaching that age. The significance of this vesting is that the child's interest is then indefeasible. If his interest vests and he then dies before A, the child's estate will claim. If however he dies at the age of twenty-four, it will have no claim. The interest of a child of A who attains twenty-five is said to be vested "subject to open"; that is to say, subject to open and admit future born children of A. Thus if A has three children and all have attained 25, they all have vested interests. But if A then has three more children, the interest of the three eldest will be reduced from one third each to one sixth; and will increase again if any of the younger children dies under the age of 25.

(3) REQUIREMENT THAT INTEREST OF EACH MEMBER VEST WITHIN PERIOD

However, for the purpose of determining the validity of a gift on the ground of remoteness, the rule is that the gift to a class is only valid if the interest of every possible member of the class must vest, if at all, within the perpetuity period. If the interest of even one potential member could possibly vest outside the period, the *whole* gift fails. Those whose interests have already vested take nothing.[112] "The vice of remoteness affects the class as a whole, if it may affect an unascertained number of its members."[113] In other words, a class gift cannot be partially good, partially bad.

Suppose, for instance, that a testator leaves his residuary estate:

to such of the children of A who shall marry.

If A survives the testator, the whole gift is void. Even if, when the testator dies, A already has children who must therefore marry, if at all, within their own lifetimes, there is no certainty that all his children who marry will do so within the perpetuity period. For A may have a future born child who marries more than twenty-one years after the death of lives in being. The whole gift, however, would be valid if it were expressed to be to the *living* children of A who marry; or if, when the testator dies, A were dead and therefore unable to have further children.[114]

---

[110] *Wilkinson v Duncan* (1861) 30 Beav 111, M & B p. 404.   [111] P. 513, ante.

[112] *Leake v Robinson* (1817) 2 Mer 363.

[113] *Pearks v Moseley* (1880) 5 App Cas 714 at 723, per Lord SELBORNE.

[114] The gift would also be saved if one of the children of A were married when the testator dies. This would have the effect of bringing into operation the class-closing rules, and of artificially closing the class at

(b) Class closing rules[115]

(1) RULE IN *ANDREWS V PARTINGTON*

Rules of construction, sometimes known as the rule in *Andrews v Partington*,[116] have developed, which have the effect of determining which members of a class can take. They have the effect of artificially closing the class, and of excluding members who would otherwise have taken. They are rules of construction only, and defer to a contrary intention; and the courts in recent years, it seems, are more ready than previously to find that intention.[117]

A class is artificially closed under these rules in order to allow the trustees to make a distribution[118] when one member of the class attains a vested interest and is entitled to be paid. Let us consider the position of trustees where there is a gift "to such of the children of A who shall attain twenty-one"; and when A's eldest child, X, becomes twenty-one, there is a brother, Y, aged eleven and a sister, Z, aged one. X asks the trustees for payment; what are they to pay to him? If A is still alive, there is danger in paying to X a one-third share, because future born children of A would reduce X's entitlement. So the class closing rules, for the convenience of the administration of the trust, say that the trustees may calculate X's share by providing for only those children of A who have been born. His future born children are excluded. Y and Z can claim their shares when they attain twenty-one. This is very convenient for the trustees and for X, Y and Z; but inconvenient for any future born children of A.

The key to understanding when the class closes is to appreciate that it closes when the time for distribution arises; when, that is, the first claimant becomes entitled to be paid. Thus, in an immediate gift to a class, such as "to the children of A", that class closes to include those alive at the date of the gift. If vesting is postponed, for example, "to such of the children of A who shall attain twenty-one", the class closes when the first child of A becomes twenty-one. If it is an interest in remainder, for example, "to X for life, remainder to the children of A who shall attain twenty-one", the class closes when X has died and when the first child of A has attained twenty-one, whichever event happens last, because that is the time at which the first member of the class becomes entitled to be paid. There is an exception to these rules where there is an immediate gift and no existing claimant. Thus if there is a gift to the children of A and A has no children, the class remains open to include all A's children.[119]

the date of the gift, to include only those children of A who were alive at that time. They must marry, if at all, within their own lifetimes. For these rules and the interrelation between them and the rule against perpetuities, see infra.

115 For a full discussion of these rules see (1954) 70 LQR 61 (J. H. C. Morris); [1958] CLJ 39 (S. J. Bailey); Morris and Leach, pp. 109–25; Maudsley, pp. 17–25; *Theobald on Wills*, chap. 32.

116 (1791) 3 Bro CC 401.

117 *Re Bleckly* [1951] Ch 740; *Re Cockle's Will Trusts* [1967] Ch 690; *Re Kebty-Fletcher's Will Trusts* [1969] 1 Ch 339; *Re Harker's Will Trusts* [1969] 1 WLR 1124; *Re Henderson's Trusts* [1969] 1 WLR 651; (1970) 34 Conv (NS) 393 (J. G. Riddall); *Re Edmondson's Will Trusts* [1972] 1 WLR 183; *Re Deeley's Settlement* [1974] Ch 454; *Re Chapman's Settlement Trusts* [1977] 1 WLR 1163; [1978] Conv 73 (F. R. Crane); *Re Clifford's Settlement Trusts* [1981] Ch 63; *Re Tom's Settlement* [1987] 1 WLR 1021; *Re Drummond* [1988] 1 WLR 234; [1988] Conv 427 (P. Luxton).

118 The rules apply to all forms of property, and to settlements as well as to wills.

119 *Weld v Bradbury* (1715) 2 Vern 705; *Re Ransome* [1957] Ch 348 at 359, per Upjohn J.

(2) INTER-RELATION BETWEEN CLASS-CLOSING AND PERPETUITY RULES

We have seen that the purpose of the class-closing rules is to simplify the administration of a trust by enabling the trustees to make payment to beneficiaries as soon as they have become entitled. Essentially the rules have nothing to do with the rule against perpetuities. But it will be appreciated that there may be situations in which the rules interact, as for instance where there is a gift to a class in which the interests of some of the members must vest within the perpetuity period, but there is a possibility that those of others may vest outside it, with the result that the whole gift is void under the rule against perpetuities. But if, as it were by a fluke, the class-closing rules exclude all the members whose interests would invalidate the gift, then it will be valid. Thus if there was a gift "to the children of A who shall attain twenty-five", that was void. But, if at the date of the gift there was a child of A who was already twenty-five, the class-closing rules operate to include only those children of A who are alive at the date of the gift; and they will clearly attain twenty-five, if at all, within their own lifetimes. The gift is therefore valid.[120] Further, to return to our earlier example[121] of a gift "to such of the children of A who shall marry": we saw that this is void, if A is alive at the date of the gift. If, however, one of the children of A is then married, the gift is valid.[122]

(5) Powers of Appointment

We now deal with a number of situations in which it is necessary to apply special rules. Gray's formulation of the rule is no longer adequate. The first of these situations concerns powers of appointment.

Before stating the law on this, however, we must first explain the nature of powers of appointment.

(a) Definition and terminology

A power of appointment gives to the donee of the power the right to effect dispositions of property which he does not own, and in which he may have no interest at all.[123] Thus, property may be given by a testator on trust:

to my widow for life and after her death to such of our children and in such shares as she shall in her absolute discretion appoint.

Or the power of appointment may be given to the trustees; or to one who holds no legal or equitable interest in the property, as where the testator gives property:

to my widow for life and after her death to such of my nieces and nephews as my brother, X, in his absolute discretion shall appoint.

---

[120] *Picken v Matthews* (1878) 10 Ch D 264.   [121] P. 531, ante.

[122] See [1988] Conv 339 (P. Sparkes and R. Snape), arguing that the rules should be applied during the "wait and see" period.

[123] Powers of appointment were unknown at common law, but originated with uses in equity. See Co Litt 237a; *Gilbert on Uses*, p. xxxix, 158 n.; Hayes, *Introduction to Conveyancing*, vol. 1. p. 70. On powers generally, see *Farwell on Powers*; H & M, chap. 6; Maclean, *Trusts and Powers*; *Thomas on Powers*.

As regards terminology, when A gives X the right to exercise a power of appointment, A is called the *donor*; X the *donee* or *appointor*; the person in whose favour the appointment is made is termed the *appointee*; and when the donee exercises the power he is said to make an appointment.

(b) General and special powers

Powers of appointment may be either general, or special. If the appointor is authorised to appoint in favour of anybody in the world, including himself, without being required to obtain the consent of another person, he is said to have a *general power*, but if he may appoint only to the members of a restricted class, as for instance, "amongst the children of A", he has a *special power*, and the persons whom he may select to take the property are called the *objects* of the power.

(c) Powers and the rule against perpetuities

A power of appointment may infringe the rule against perpetuities in two respects, for either its *creation* or its *exercise* may be too remote.

To give a person a general power is in effect to give him the absolute fee, for it entitles him to vest the whole fee in any person in the world, including himself, and therefore it does not tend to the creation of remote interests: "He has an absolute disposing power over the estate, and may bring it into the market whenever his necessities or wishes may lead him to do so . . . The donee may sell the estate the next moment."[124] On the other hand, the grant of a special power has an immediate tendency to be a perpetuity, for, since the objects in whose favour it is exercisable are restricted, it imposes from the moment of its creation a fetter upon the free disposability of the land.[125] It is important to notice, however, that a general power exercisable jointly by two or more persons or by one person with the consent of another is a special power for the purposes of the rule against perpetuities, the view taken by the law being that a power which cannot be exercised without the concurrence of two minds is not equivalent to property.[126]

(1) GENERAL POWERS

(i) Validity of creation

A general power to appoint by deed, or either by deed or by will, is void unless it will become effectively exercisable, if at all, within the perpetuity period. At the date when the instrument of creation takes effect, it must be possible to say that within that period the donee will be ascertainable, the event upon which the power is to arise will have occurred and any condition precedent to the right of exercise will have been satisfied.

---

[124] Sugden, *Powers* (8th edn), pp. 395–6, cited Morris and Leach, p. 148.

[125] Co Litt 272a, Butler's note.

[126] *Re Churston Settled Estates* [1954] Ch 334; *Re Earl of Coventry's Indentures* [1974] Ch 77. This is an example of a power which is intermediate or hybrid in the sense that it conforms neither to special nor general powers. For an account, see Morris and Leach, *The Rule against Perpetuities* (2nd edn), pp. 136–8; Fourth Report of Law Reform Committee 1956 (Cmnd 18), paras. 44–6. See *Re Lawrence's Will Trusts* [1972] Ch 418, where that category is discussed by MEGARRY J.

On this basis, each of the following powers is void:

A power given to the survivor of two living persons and their children.[127]

A power to arise upon the general failure of the issue of a marriage.[128]

A power given to an unborn person upon his marriage.[129]

If a general power to appoint by deed, or either by deed or by will, is exercisable within the perpetuity period, it is not rendered objectionable by the fact that it may possibly be exercised after the period has expired, as may well happen, for instance, if it is given to the unborn child of a living person. By virtue of the power, such a donee ascertained within due limits acquires an unrestricted right of alienation, and as in the case of any absolute owner he is free to decide when he will exercise that right.[130]

On the other hand, a general testamentary power, that is, one that is exercisable only by will, though it will vest in the donee, if at all, within the perpetuity period, is void if it may be exercised beyond that period. The reason is that the property is tied up during the lifetime of the donee in the sense that he possesses no right of alienation until his death. Therefore, such a power is void if, as in the case of one given to the unborn child of a living person, it may be exercisable at too remote a time.[131]

(ii) Validity of appointment

The donee of a general power, since he can appoint to anybody in the world, including himself, has complete and absolute freedom of disposition, and therefore for the purpose of testing the validity of his appointments the perpetuity period is reckoned from the exercise of the power, not from its creation.

This rule applies whether the general power is exercisable *inter vivos*, or whether it is a general testamentary power, exercisable only by will. It is arguable that the validity of an appointment made under a general testamentary power should be subject to the restrictions imposed on special powers, discussed below, on the ground that the disposition of the property is restricted during the lifetime of the donee. However, the donee has complete power of disposition on death, and the restriction imposed during the donee's lifetime is not thought to be a substantial breach of perpetuity policy. This view is confirmed, as we shall see, by the Act of 1964.

(2) SPECIAL POWERS

(i) Validity of creation

As regards the validity of its creation, a special power is subject to the following rule:

A special power which, according to the true construction of the instrument creating it, is capable of being exercised beyond lives in being and 21 years afterwards is, by reason of the rule against perpetuities, absolutely void."[132]

---

[127] *Re Hargreaves* (1889) 43 Ch D 401.

[128] *Bristow v Boothby* (1826) 2 Sim & St 465. Prima facie, "issue" includes descendants of every degree. See *Theobald on Wills*, paras. 33–06 to 33–09.

[129] *Morgan v Gronow* (1873) LR 16 Eq 1 (in the case of the original appointment).

[130] *Re Fane* [1913] 1 Ch 404 at 413.

[131] *Wollaston v King* (1869) LR 8 Eq 165; *Morgan v Gronow*, supra.

[132] *Re De Sommery* [1912] 2 Ch 622 at 630, per PARKER J; M & B p. 402.

As in the case of a general power, a special power is too remote in its creation if the donee may not be ascertained or if the condition precedent to its exercise may not have occurred within lives in being and twenty-one years afterwards. But in the case of a special power there is the further requirement that the objects must be ascertainable within the same period. The difference in this respect between the two classes of powers may be illustrated by a power, to be exercised by deed, given to an unborn person.

A special power to this effect, as, for instance, one conferred by settlement upon the eldest son of X, a bachelor, to appoint to his children, is void *ab initio*.[133] At the time of the settlement, it can no doubt be said that the appointor will be ascertained, if at all, within twenty-one years from the death of the life in being, X; but it cannot be said that the children in whose favour alone the appointment may be made will be ascertainable, if at all, within the same period. In other words, the occasion upon which the power is to become operative may be too remote.[134]

On the other hand, as we have seen, a general power to the same effect exercisable by deed is valid. The donee, being ascertainable within the perpetuity period, has complete control over the property and, once ascertained, is in the same position as if he were already its absolute owner.[135]

Provided that a special power is so limited that it cannot be *exercised* beyond the perpetuity period, it is immaterial that under its terms an appointment may possibly be made that will be too remote, as in the case, for instance, of a devise:

to X for life, remainder to such of his issue as he shall by will appoint.[136]

At the date of such a devise, it is impossible to say whether the perpetuity rule will be transgressed or not, but this uncertainty does not invalidate the power. The appointments will fail only if in fact they are too remote.[137] The question is not what may be done, but what in fact is done. In other words this is an exceptional case at common law where it is necessary to wait and see what happens.

(ii) Validity of appointment

Presuming now that the power itself is valid in the sense that it is exercisable only within the perpetuity period, it remains to consider the test that governs the validity of appointments in fact made. It differs radically from that applicable to a general power.

In the case of a special power, the disposition of the property remains controlled by the donor; the donee has power only to appoint to a limited class. As Lord ROMER said: "It is as though the settlor had left a blank in the settlement which [the donee] fills up for him if and when the power of appointment is exercised."[138] The rule therefore is that, for the purposes of the perpetuity rule, the appointment which is in fact made must be "read back" into the instrument which created the power; and the perpetuity period is reckoned from the time when the instrument came into operation.

---

133 *Wollaston v King* (1869) LR 8 Eq 165.   134 Gray, *The Rule against Perpetuities*, ss. 475, 477.
135 *Bray v Bree* (1834) 2 Cl & Fin 453.
136 *Slark v Dakyns* (1874) 10 Ch App 35; *Re Vaux* [1939] Ch 465 at 472.
137 *Re Fane* [1913] 1 Ch 404 at 413–14.   138 *Muir (or Williams) v Muir* [1943] AC 468 at 483.

Thus, in *Whitby v Von Luedecke*:[139]

A settlement made in 1844, upon the marriage of H and W, limited land to W for life and after her death to such of her children as she should appoint. The terms of her appointment were that the income of the land should be divided equally between her two daughters, X and Y, during their respective lives, but that upon the death of one it should pass in its entirety to the survivor.

It was held that the gift to the survivor was void. It was a contingent gift, and the event upon which it was to vest—the death of one of the daughters—would not necessarily occur within twenty-one years from the deaths of H and W who constituted the sole lives in being when the special power was created in 1844.

The rule, that the appointment ultimately made must be regarded as having been made in the original instrument of creation, merely ensures that the donee of the power shall not grant interests that the donor himself could not have granted. It is permitted, however, to read and construe the appointments in the light of the circumstances existing at the time when they are intended to take effect, not at the time when the power was created.[140]

Thus in *Re Paul*,[141] a disposition was saved by the application of the rule:

A testator died in 1895, leaving a share in his residuary estate to his daughter, Mrs A, for life and after her death as she should appoint among her children. She made an appointment in 1919 to her son on attaining the age of 25 years. The son was then 18. The appointment was read back into the will as an appointment by Mrs A to her son at an age which he must attain, if at all, within 21 years of Mrs A's death. It was therefore valid.

(6) Effect of Infringement on Subsequent Interests[142]

Where one of a series of limitations is void for perpetuity, the question arises as to the effect of that void limitation upon the other limitations which are not in themselves void. The obvious solution would seem to be to ignore the void limitation, and to let the valid limitations take effect as if the void limitation never existed. But the matter is not so simple.[143]

(a) Where subsequent limitation is subject to a void contingency

Where the subsequent limitation is itself subject to a void contingency, whether the same as or different from that of the earlier void limitation, the subsequent limitation is of course void. Thus a limitation:

to A for life with remainder to such of his grandchildren as shall marry, but if no grandchildren of A shall marry, then to the children of B (who is alive) absolutely.

---

[139] [1906] 1 Ch 783; *Re Legh's Settlement Trusts* [1938] Ch 39. W, however, might have achieved her object by making the interest in the entire income vested instead of contingent. An appointment of one-half to X for life with remainder to Y for life, and of one-half to Y for life with remainder to X for life, would have been valid. The rule against perpetuities is, indeed, of a highly technical nature; see (1952) 68 LQR, pp. 47–9 (W. B. Leach). See also *Re Brown and Sibly's Contract* (1876) 3 Ch D 156, M & B p. 403.

[140] Gray, *The Rule against Perpetuities*, s. 523; *Wilkinson v Duncan* (1861) 30 Beav 111, M & B p. 404; *Von Brockdorff v Malcolm* (1885) 30 Ch D 172; *Re Thompson* [1906] 2 Ch 199; *Re Paul* [1921] 2 Ch 1, M & B p. 404.

[141] *Supra.*   [142] See (1950) 10 CLJ 392 (J. H. C. Morris); (1950) 14 Conv (NS) 148 (A. K. R. Kiralfy).

[143] Many questions of this type are settled in the United States by the application of the doctrine of "infectious invalidity". Under this doctrine, the invalidity of an important part of a limitation may cause the whole limitation to be held void. The justification is that, if the testator's plan is so changed by the invalidity of one part, then he may well prefer to rely on the intestacy provisions instead.

The gift to the children of B is void. Those who qualify may include future born children of B; and the takers will not be ascertained until it is known whether any of A's grandchildren marry, and that may not be known until a time outside the perpetuity period.

If the gift over had been to the living (or named) children of B for their lives, the gift over would be valid; for the gift over in those circumstances must vest, if at all, within the lifetime of those living children of B. The contrary was, however, held in *Re Hewett's Settlement*:[144]

In a marriage settlement, life interests were given to the husband and wife, and after their deaths the property was to be divided between such of their children as should attain the age of 25, and "if there should be no child of the marriage who should attain twenty-five" then on trust for the testator's three sisters, Helga, Hilda and Hulda.

The gift to the sisters was held to be void. Such a result could only be reached by failing to appreciate that the gift must vest in the sisters, if at all, during their own lifetimes. They were therefore the lives in being in relation to the gift to themselves; and the fact that that intermediate gift was void should have been treated as irrelevant.

(b) Intention that subsequent limitation should take effect only after termination of prior void limitation

In *Re Abbott*,[145] Stirling J said, in a famous dictum:

It is settled that any limitation depending or expectant upon a prior limitation which is void for remoteness is invalid. The reason appears to be that the persons entitled under the subsequent limitation are not intended to take unless and until the prior limitation is exhausted; and as the prior limitation which is void for remoteness can never come into operation, much less be exhausted, it is impossible to give effect to the intentions of the settlor in favour of the beneficiaries under the subsequent limitation.

There is little to be said in support of this proposition. But some cases can only be supported on this ground. In *Re Backhouse*:[146]

A picture was bequeathed for a series of life interests, some of which were void for perpetuity, with an ultimate gift to the testator's right heirs. This last gift was in favour of persons who would be ascertained at the testator's death, and would therefore vest at that time. Even so, it was held void on the ground that it was subsequent to the prior void limitations.

The modern and better view is that the subsequent limitation, valid in itself, should be accelerated so as to take effect in the place of the earlier void limitation.

(c) Later limitation not dependent

Where an interest is created which will not take effect in possession until a future date, but must vest in interest within the perpetuity period, and its possessory enjoyment is not dependent on the exhaustion of the precedent interests, it will be unaffected by remoteness in any of the antecedent interests.[147] This is illustrated by *Re Coleman*:[148]

---

[144] [1915] 1 Ch 810; *Re Thatcher's Trusts* (1859) 26 Beav 365 at 369; *Re Hubbard's Will Trusts* [1963] Ch 275, M & B p. 406; *Re Buckton's Settlement Trusts* [1964] Ch 497.   [145] [1893] 1 Ch 54 at 57.
[146] [1921] 2 Ch 51.
[147] *Re Hubbard's Will Trusts*, supra, 85–7. *Re Backhouse*, supra, however, is inconsistent with this proposition.
[148] [1936] Ch 528; followed in *Re Allan* [1958] 1 WLR 220.

A testator left his residuary estate on discretionary trusts to H for life; after H's death upon similar discretionary trusts for any widow who might survive him; and after the death of such widow upon trust (not discretionary) for the children of H at 21 in equal shares.

By virtue of the discretionary trusts, the trustees were empowered to make payments of income to H or his widow. But this trust in the widow's case was void, for H might marry a woman born after the testator's death, and if so the discretion of the trustees, which was a condition precedent to her right to an interest, might be exercisable beyond the perpetuity period. Nevertheless, it was held that the limitation to the children was valid. The interests of the children would necessarily vest, if at all, within 21 years of H's death. Their interests were not dependent on the validity of the discretionary power to pay income to the widow.

(d) Divestment on occurrence of void condition

Where a testator or settlor gives property to A either immediately or at some future date which is not too remote, but so frames his trusts that the interest of A may be displaced by the exercise of some power or discretion, the interest of A will be unaffected by any invalidity of that power or discretion on the ground of remoteness.[149]

In one case, for instance, a testator allocated a fund to be used at the discretion of trustees upon the maintenance of a mansion-house so long as any person entitled to the house under a strict settlement should be under twenty-one years of age, "and subject thereto" upon trust for A absolutely. The discretionary trust for the maintenance of the house was admittedly too remote, but it was held that the trust in favour of A was an independent limitation and was valid.[150]

The destination of the property affected by a remote limitation differs according as the disposition is made by deed or by will. In the former case it results to the settlor. In the case of a will, it goes to the residuary legatee or devisee, but to the persons entitled as on an intestacy of the testator if there is no residuary gift or if the residue itself is the subject matter of the limitation. If the void limitation is effected by the exercise of a special power of appointment, the property concerned passes to the persons entitled in default of appointment.

(7) Alternative Limitations

Where a settlor makes the vesting of a future gift dependent upon two alternative events, one of which is too remote and the other not, the gift is allowed to take effect if the event which is not too remote is the one that actually happens.[151] This doctrine provides an exception to the rule that possible, not actual, events are alone considered, for the court waits to see which of the two events in fact occurs.[152] Thus in the early case of *Longhead v Phelps*[153] a marriage settlement declared that certain trusts should arise:

if H should die without issue male *or* if such issue male should die without issue.

The latter contingency was obviously too remote, for whether H's male issue died without themselves leaving issue might not necessarily be known within twenty-one years of the

---

[149] *Re Hubbard's Will Trusts* [1963] Ch 275, at 287, per BUCKLEY J.

[150] *Re Canning's Will Trusts* [1936] Ch 309; see also *Re Abbott* [1893] 1 Ch 54. The difficulties arising from this doctrine of dependency no longer affect instruments taking effect after 15 July 1964; PAA 1964, s. 6; p. 559, post.

[151] *Longhead v Phelps* (1770) 2 Wm Bl 704; *Leake v Robinson* (1817) 2 Mer 363; *Re Curryer's Will Trusts* [1938] Ch 952; Gray, *The Rule against Perpetuities*, chap. ix.   [152] Morris and Leach, pp. 181–4.

[153] (1770) 2 Wm Bl 704.

death of any person living at the date of the testator's death, but in fact he died without male issue and it was held that the trusts were valid. In a more recent case[154] a testator created a trust to take effect:

upon the decease of my last surviving child *or* the death of the last surviving widow or widower of my children as the case may be whichever shall last happen.

Here again the last contingency was too remote, since one or more of the children might marry a person born after the testator's death, but it was held that the trust would be valid if the first contingency in fact happened, that is, if all the widows and widowers were dead when the last surviving child died.

The courts, however, have consistently held that this indulgence will not be shown to the valid gift unless the settlor has himself expressly and distinctly designated the two alternative contingencies.[155] If vesting is in terms made dependent upon a single event which in fact includes two contingencies, one too remote the other not too remote, the future gift is void, although the contingency which actually happens is the one that satisfies the perpetuity rule. The court will not split the expression used by the settlor, i.e. will not separate and state in an alternative form the two events that the expression in fact includes. By way of illustration we may refer once more to *Proctor v Bishop of Bath and Wells*.[156] In that case the fee simple was devised:

to the first or other son of A that should be bred a clergyman, and be in Holy Orders, but in case he should have no such son, then to B in fee simple.

It is clear on analysis that the event upon which the gift to B was dependent included two contingencies, namely:

(a) failure of A to leave sons;

(b) failure of any son to take Holy Orders.

A gift to B to take effect if A left no sons would obviously be valid, but though A did in fact die childless, it was held that B was not entitled to the fee simple. If the description of the event had been alternative, instead of single, in point of expression, all would have been well; that is, if the testator had expressly stated that the fee simple was to vest in B:

if A had no son *or* if he had no son who should take Holy Orders,

B's claim would have been upheld, since it was the first contingency that in fact happened. What the court refused to do was to redraft in an alternative form the single expression appearing in the will. In cases of this kind the court does not concentrate upon implementing the testator's intention, for a man who says that an estate is to go over to B if none of A's sons becomes a clergyman obviously means it to go over if A never has a son. Whether the intention will prevail is purely a question of words: "You are bound to take the expression as you find it, and if, giving the proper interpretation to that expression, the event may transgress the limit, then the gift over is void."[157]

---

154 *Re Curryer's Will Trusts* [1938] Ch 952.
155 *Re Bence* [1891] 3 Ch 242; *Miles v Harford* (1879) 12 Ch D 691 at 702, per JESSEL MR.
156 (1794) 2 Hy Bl 358; p. 527 ante.   157 *Miles v Harford* (1879) 12 Ch D 691 at 703, per JESSEL MR.

(8) Exceptions to the Rule against Perpetuities

(a) Limitations after entailed interests

A tenant in tail can bar his own and all subsequent interests. The rule, therefore, is that no limitation after an entailed interest is void for remoteness, provided that the subsequent limitation must vest, if at all, at or before the end of the perpetuity period. There is in fact no perpetuity.[158]

(b) Contracts and options[159]

"It is settled beyond argument that an agreement merely personal, not creating any interest in land, is not within the rule against perpetuities."[160] Therefore, it is not void simply because the obligation it creates may last for an indefinite time.[161] For instance, in *Walsh v Secretary of State for India*[162] the East India Company entered into a covenant in 1770 whereby they promised to pay a certain sum of money if, at any time after 1794, they should cease to have a military force in their pay and service in the East Indies. It might have been centuries before such a state of things occurred, and in point of fact it was nearly a century, but nevertheless the court upheld the validity of the obligation.

It is equally well settled at common law that even a contract which creates an interest in land remains binding upon the parties themselves, notwithstanding that it may be enforceable beyond the perpetuity period. So long as privity of contract exists, there is no room for the rule against perpetuities. Thus in *Hutton v Watling*[163] a written agreement by which X sold his business to Y stipulated that Y should have the option, exercisable at any time in the future, to purchase the premises in which the business was carried on. An action by Y for specific performance brought seven years later was met by the plea that the stipulation was void for remoteness. The plea failed. In such a case, Y is entitled not only to recover damages from X,[164] but also to a decree of specific performance if the land is still retained by X, for "specific performance is merely an equitable mode of enforcing a personal obligation with which the rule against perpetuities has nothing to do".[165]

But once the promisee seeks to enforce the promise against a third person, the position is changed. We now pass from the law of contract to the law of property, with the result that such an option as that in *Hutton v Watling* or an option given to a lessee to purchase the reversion, since it creates an executory interest in land, cannot be enforced against third persons who later acquire the promisor's land unless it is confined within the perpetuity period.[166] Thus where a railway company sold land to one Powell subject to a right of repurchase if at any time thereafter the land was required for the railway, it was held that the right was unenforceable against the appellant, to whom Powell's heir had sold the land.[167]

---

[158] *Nicolls v Sheffield* (1787) 2 Bro CC 215; *Heasman v Pearse* (1871) 7 Ch App 275.

[159] See (1954) 18 Conv (NS) 576 (J. H. C. Morris and W. B. Leach).

[160] *South Eastern Rly Co v Associated Portland Cement Manufacturers (1900) Ltd* [1910] 1 Ch 12 at 33, per Farwell J.   [161] *Witham v Vane* (1883) 32 WR 617; Challis, *Law of Real Property*, p. 440.

[162] (1863) 10 HL Cas 367.   [163] [1948] Ch 26; affd on other grounds [1948] Ch 398.

[164] *Worthing Corpn v Heather* [1906] 2 Ch 532.

[165] *Hutton v Watling* [1948] Ch 26 at 36, per Jenkins J. This rule has been reversed in the case of instruments taking effect after 15 July 1964; p. 558, post.

[166] *Woodall v Clifton* [1905] 2 Ch 257, M & B p. 409; *London and South Western Rly Co v Gomm* (1882) 20 Ch D 562, M & B p. 409; *Griffith v Pelton* [1958] Ch 205.

[167] *London and South Western Rly Co v Gomm*, supra.

JESSEL MR said:

If then the rule as to remoteness applies to a covenant of this nature, this covenant clearly is bad as extending beyond the period allowed by the rule. Whether the rule applies or not depends upon this as it appears to me—does or does not the covenant give an interest in the land? If it is a bare or mere personal contract it is of course not obnoxious to the rule, but in that case it is impossible to see how the present appellant can be bound. He did not enter into the contract, but is only a purchaser from Powell who did. If it is a mere personal contract it cannot be enforced against the assignee. Therefore the company must admit that it somehow binds the land. But if it binds the land it creates an equitable interest in the land. The right to call for a conveyance of the land is an equitable interest or equitable estate.

Thus, an option to call for a lease of land exemplifies this principle and is void if it is exercisable beyond the perpetuity period, but it has long been recognised that an option given to a tenant to *renew* his existing lease is entirely unaffected by the rule against perpetuities.[168]

(c) *Certain easements and mortgages*

A further illustration of the principles laid down by JESSEL MR is that the grant of an easement to arise *in futuro* may be void on the ground of remoteness, as for example where it entitles the grantee to use the drains and sewers "now passing *or hereafter to pass*" under a private road.[169]

The rule against perpetuities has no application to mortgages, and therefore a postponement of the right of redemption for longer than the perpetuity period is not void for remoteness,[170] though it may be void on other grounds.[171]

(d) *Certain rights of entry*

The rule affects certain rights of entry, but not others.

(1) FORFEITURE OF LEASE

The right usually reserved to a lessor to enter upon the land and to terminate the lease if the tenant commits a breach of covenant[172] is not subject to the rule.[173]

(2) ENFORCEMENT OF RENTCHARGE

There are three situations to consider in relation to the enforcement of a rentcharge.

First, the owner of a rentcharge, that is, a person, other than a reversioner, entitled to the payment of an annual sum of money out of land,[174] is empowered by the Law of Property Act 1925,[175] in the event of non-payment to enter upon the land and to recover the money due either by levying distress or by leasing the land to a trustee until all arrears have been paid. The Act puts this right of entry, together with its attendant remedies, outside the rule against perpetuities.[176]

---

[168] *Woodall v Clifton*, supra, at 265, 268; *Weg Motors Ltd v Hales* [1961] Ch 176; affd [1962] Ch 49.

[169] *Dunn v Blackdown Properties Ltd* [1961] Ch 433; (1961) 25 Conv (NS) 415 (G. Battersby); *Newham v Lawson* (1971) 22 P & CR 852. The right may however be construed as an immediate right which has not yet been exercised, and not as a future right: *SE Rly Co v Associated Portland Cement Manufacturers (1900) Ltd* [1901] 1 Ch 12; cf *Sharpe v Durant* [1911] WN 158. See Morris and Leach, pp. 228–31.

[170] *Knightsbridge Estates Trust Ltd v Byrne* [1939] Ch 441 at 463; affd [1940] AC 613.

[171] Pp. 738, post.   [172] Pp. 273, 280, ante.

[173] *Re Tyrrell's Estate* [1907] 1 IR 292 at 298, per WALKER LC.   [174] P. 712, post.   [175] S. 121.

[176] S. 121(6).

If the instrument creating the charge expressly empowers the creditor to enter the land and to determine the fee simple estate of the debtor for non-payment of rent, or to enter and enforce some covenant other than that to pay the sum due, it is doubtful whether such a power is excluded from the perpetuity rule by virtue of the Act.[177]

Secondly, a rentcharge is sometimes created merely by way of indemnity against another rentcharge.[178] If, for instance, an estate which as a whole is subject to a rentcharge is being sold off in lots, it is a common practice to throw the burden of the charge entirely upon one lot. In practice the purchaser of that lot then gives the purchasers of the other lots an indemnity rentcharge issuing out of his land, so that if they as purchasers of parts of the whole land are compelled by the rent-owner to pay the charge, they will have a right to reimburse themselves out of the lot on which it has been thrown.

The former doubt whether the law of remoteness applied to such cases was dispelled by the Law of Property Act 1925, which provides that rentcharges created only by way of indemnity against other rentcharges and powers to distrain or to take possession of land affected by such rentcharges, shall be excluded from the operation of the rule against perpetuities.[179]

Thirdly, if a fee simple is sold in return for a perpetual annual rentcharge, the right of entry or re-entry that accrues to the vendor in the event of non-payment,[180] although exercisable for an unlimited period, does not withdraw the land from commerce and therefore is unaffected by the rule against perpetuities.[181]

(3) CONDITION BROKEN

A right of entry for condition broken attached to a fee simple is void if it is exercisable beyond the perpetuity period.[182]

(e) Accumulative trust of income for the purpose of paying debts

The rule does not apply to a trust directing that income shall be accumulated with a view to the payment of the settlor's debts, or for the discharge of incumbrances charged upon the land, for such a trust, though capable of enduring for an indefinite time, may be determined at any moment either by the beneficiaries paying the debts and freeing the land, or by the creditors enforcing their claims by the seizure of the land.[183] Neither does the rule apply to a trust under which money is to be accumulated for the reduction of the National Debt.[184]

(f) Pension and superannuation funds

If there were no specific exemption for pension and superannuation funds, they would become void after the end of the perpetuity period, because interests in the fund might vest at too remote a time.[185] Under the common law rule, the trust fund would have been wholly

---

[177] See Morris and Leach, p. 218. The doubt has been removed by PAA 1964, s. 11, which, however, is not retrospective; see p. 559, post. [178] P. 706, post.

[179] LPA 1925, s. 162(1)(a). [180] P. 169, ante; p. 707, post.

[181] Compare the remarks of Lord BROUGHAM in *Keppell v Bailey* (1834) 2 My & K 517 at 528–9.

[182] *Re Hollis' Hospital Trustees and Hague's Contract* [1899] 2 Ch 540; LPA 1925, s. 4(3); p. 572, post.

[183] *Tewart v Lawson* (1874) LR 18 Eq 490; *Lord Southampton v Marquis of Hertford* (1813) 2 Ves & B 54.

[184] Superannuation and Other Trust Funds (Validation) Act 1927, s. 9.

[185] *Re Flavel's Will Trusts* [1969] 1 WLR 444; p. 527, n. 93, ante.

void unless expressly limited to the perpetuity period. In order to avoid this problem, the Pension Schemes Act 1993 makes express provision for all qualifying occupational pension schemes to be exempt from the rule.[186]

(g) Administrative powers of trustees

The former rule was that administrative powers given to trustees, such as a power to sell or lease land, or to receive remuneration for their services, were void if they were capable of being exercised at too remote a time, notwithstanding that they were attached to a trust which itself was not too remote. This may be illustrated by Re Allott:[187]

A testator left his mines to trustees upon trust to pay annuities to his daughters out of the profits. He directed that if a daughter married, and was survived by her husband, such survivor should be entitled for his life to her annuity.

After the testator's death, a deed of family arrangement was entered into which incorporated the trusts of the will and which inter alia gave the trustees powers to grant leases not exceeding 99 years.

The life interest given to any surviving husband was valid despite the fact that he might be a person not born at the date of the execution of the deed. His life interest would necessarily arise, if it ever arose at all, immediately on the death of his wife. Nevertheless, the power of leasing was void, since it might be exercised, and so create a fresh interest, more than twenty-one years after the dropping of the lives in being if the husband lived so long.

The effect of administrative powers is not to tie up the property, but to facilitate its management, and therefore the Law Reform Committee recommended that they should be excluded from the perpetuity rule provided that the trusts to which they are ancillary are valid and subsisting. This recommendation was accepted by the Perpetuities and Accumulations Act 1964, in the only section that is retrospective. It provides that:[188]

The rule against perpetuities shall not operate to invalidate a power conferred on trustees or other persons to sell, lease, exchange or otherwise dispose of property for full consideration, or to do any other act in the administration (as opposed to the distribution) of any property, and shall not prevent the payment to trustees or other persons of reasonable remuneration for their services.

It should be noticed that it is only *administrative* powers that are exempt from the rule against perpetuities. The rule applies to beneficial powers such as powers of appointment,[189] powers of distribution under a discretionary trust and powers of maintenance and advancement.[190]

(h) Certain limitations to charities

An interest given to a charity, like any other gift, is void unless it will vest within the perpetuity period.[191] On the other hand, a limitation transferring property from one charity to

[186] S. 163; Personal and Occupational Pension Schemes (Perpetuities) Regs 1990 (SI 1990 No. 1143). For a perceptive criticism, see (1995) Private Client Business, pp. 133–45, 223–32 (G. Thomas). See also *Air Jamaica Ltd v Charlton* [1999] 1 WLR 1399; [2000] Conv 170 (C. Harpum).   [187] [1924] 2 Ch 498.

[188] S. 8(1). If a power has been created before the commencement of the Act, i.e. 16 July 1964, this section is applicable, provided that the exercise is effected after that date: s. 8(2).   [189] P. 533, ante.

[190] *Pilkington v IRC* [1964] AC 612; *Re Hastings-Bass* [1975] Ch 25 (statutory power of advancement under TA 1925, s. 32).

[191] *Chamberlayne v Brockett* (1872) 8 Ch App 206; *Re Lord Stratheden and Campbell* [1894] 3 Ch 265; *Re Mander* [1950] Ch 547.

another upon a certain contingency is valid, although the contingency may not occur until some indefinite time in the future. Provided that the interest of the first charity will begin within the perpetuity period, it is immaterial that the second charity may not take until a remote date. Thus in *Re Tyler*[192], where a testator bequeathed £42,000 to the London Missionary Society with a gift over to the Blue Coat School if the Society failed to keep his family vault in repair, it was held that the gift over was valid. Had the gift over been, not to another charity, but to private persons, it would have been void.[193]

A gift to a charity is not void as a perpetuity merely because it creates an interest that may remain subject to the charitable trust for an indefinite period.[194]

C The Rule Applicable to Instruments Taking Effect After 15 July 1964[195]

The Perpetuities and Accumulations Act 1964 came into operation on 16 July 1964.[196] It can be regarded as achieving two things: first, it provided a number of specific solutions to specific problems created by the common law rule,[197] and secondly, it altered the whole basis of operation of the perpetuity rule, by introducing the principle of "wait and see". "Wait and see" is applicable, in the place of the common law rule requiring certainty of vesting, to dispositions which fail to comply with the common law rule. The draftsman expected the question of the validity of a disposition to be determined by the application first of the common law rule; if valid, all is well; if void, the disposition may be saved by the application of "wait and see". It will be seen, when section 3 is discussed, that this method has caused a number of unnecessary difficulties. It would have been preferable to abolish the common law rule, and to replace it by "wait and see". The sections of the Act will be examined in order.

(1) Section 1. The Perpetuity Period

As an alternative to the common law period during which it is permissible to suspend the vesting of interests, section 1 allows the settlor to specify a fixed period of years not exceeding eighty.[198] This provision was intended to provide a more attractive option than the royal lives clause[199] in cases where, as is usual with discretionary trusts, the settlor or testator intended to lay down the period of duration of a trust; and it has had that effect.

---

[192] [1891] 3 Ch 252; following *Christ's Hospital v Grainger* (1849) 1 Mac & G 460. For a criticism of this decision see Gray, *The Rule against Perpetuities*, 603.

[193] *Re Talbot* [1933] Ch 895; *Re Bland-Sutton's Will Trusts* [1951] Ch 485; revsd in part [1952] AC 631.

[194] *Chamberlayne v Brockett* (1872) 8 Ch App 206 at 211; *Goodman v Saltash Corpn* (1882) 7 App Cas 633 at 650, 651; *Re Bowen* [1893] 2 Ch 491 at 494.

[195] See generally Morris and Leach, Supplement; (1964) 80 LQR 486 (J. H. C. Morris and H. W. R. Wade); Wolstenholme and Cherry, *Conveyancing Statutes*, 13th edn, vol. 2, pp. 135 et seq; Maudsley, chaps. 4, 5 and 6.

[196] The Act applies where there is a disposition contained in an instrument. On disposition, see *Re Thomas Meadows & Co Ltd and Subsidiary Companies (1960) Staff Pension Scheme Rules* [1971] Ch 278; and on instrument, see *Re Holt's Settlement* [1969] 1 Ch 100 (court order approving an arrangement under the Variation of Trusts Act 1958 constitutes an instrument). [197] Ss. 1, 2, 5, 6 and 7.

[198] PAA 1964, s. 1(1); *Re Green's Will Trusts* [1985] 3 All ER 455, M & B p. 376 (period specified as "from the date of my death to the 1st day of January 2020" held valid as being "unambiguously identified" or "made clear" as a period of $43\frac{1}{2}$ years from the testator's death on 1 February 1976 to 1 January 2020). This provision does not apply to certain options to acquire an interest in land; s. 9(2), p. 551, post. [199] P. 525, ante.

It must be emphasised that this alternative period must be expressly specified in the instrument. And, in order to be valid under the common law rule, the vesting of interests under the trust must be related to the period selected. Thus, it is a valid specification of the alternative period of years if the settlor or testator provides for a "trust period" of eighty years (or smaller period) during which the trustee can exercise various discretionary powers, with a provision that the trust assets vest in identifiable beneficiaries at the conclusion of the period. The vesting is then related to the alternative perpetuity period. But a disposition would be void under the common law rule if the gift was not related to the alternative period. There is no "wait and see" period of eighty years. Thus, either of the two following dispositions would be void under the rule:

to such of the issue of X as may be living at the expiration of 80 years after X's death. The period was not specified.

to the lineal issue of X. I specify the period of 80 years as the perpetuity period applicable to this disposition. The period was specified, but the vesting was not related to the period.

In each case, the gift being void, the "wait and see" provisions of section 3 will apply. Those beneficiaries whose interests in fact vest within twenty-one years of the dropping of the survivor of the *statutory* measuring lives will take.

The donor of a special power may provide that the perpetuity period applicable to the limitations shall be a fixed number of years not exceeding eighty. Such period will, of course, begin to run from the effective creation of the power, and it cannot be extended by the donee when he makes an appointment.[200]

(2) Presumptions as to Fertility

The rule at common law that a person of whatever age must be regarded as capable of having children[201] has been abolished in the case of instruments taking effect after 15 July 1964.

Under the Act it is to be presumed in any proceedings that a male can beget a child at, but not under, the age of fourteen years; and that a female can have a child at, but not over, the age of fifty-five years.[202] In the case of a living person, however, evidence may be given to rebut these presumptions, by showing that he or she will not be able to have a child at the time in question.[203]

The Act extends these presumptions to the possibility that a person will at any time have a child by adoption, legitimation or other means.[204] If a person is adopted or legitimated, the question arises whether or not he will take as a "child" of an adopting or legitimating parent under a gift to that person's "children". The rule prior to the coming into force of the Children Act 1975 was that an adopted or legitimated child took under such a disposition if he had been adopted or legitimated *before* the instrument came into effect.[205] Under the Children Act 1975, which applies to instruments coming into effect after 1 January 1976,

---

[200] PAA 1964, s. 1(2).   [201] Pp. 529–30, ante.   [202] PAA 1964, s. 2(1)(a).   [203] Ibid., s. 2(1)(b).

[204] See also Family Law Reform Act 1969, s. 15 (reference to child or other person in dispositions made after 1969 include reference to illegitimate child, etc; there are corresponding provisions for legitimated and adopted persons: Legitimacy Act 1976, s. 5(2); Adoption Act 1976, s. 39); Family Law Reform Act 1987, s. 1(1) (in dispositions after 3 April 1988, references to any relationship between two persons is (unless contrary intention) construed on basis that it is immaterial whether or not a person's parents have or had been been married to each other at any time).   [205] Adoption Act 1958, s. 16; Legitimacy Act 1926, s. 3.

such a person can take whether the adoption or legitimation was before or after the date of the instrument.[206]

A further question arises in relation to the presumption in section 2 of the Perpetuities and Accumulations Act 1964 to the effect that a woman over the age of fifty-five is incapable of giving birth to a child. A woman over that age might, of course, adopt or legitimate a child.[207] For the purpose of the perpetuity rule, however, the presumption remains.[208] If property has been distributed on the basis of the presumption, and a woman does give birth to, or adopt, or legitimate, a child inconsistently with it, the High Court is empowered to make such order "so far as may be just", for placing the beneficiaries in the position they would have held had the presumption not been applied.[209]

(3) Uncertainty as to Remoteness. Section 3. Wait and See

It has been seen that a disposition is void under the common law rule unless it is certain to vest, if at all, within twenty-one years of the death of some person living at the date when the instrument comes into effect. The disposition is void even though it is 99 per cent certain that it will vest, if at all, within the period. And the void disposition is not helped by the fact that it *does in fact vest* within the period. We saw that a gift to the first child of A to marry is void under the common law rule. It is immaterial that, at the date of the gift, three of A's children are engaged to be married, and do in fact marry on the following Saturday.

Factors like these brought the rule into disrepute. The Law Reform Committee[210] examined the problem and accepted the very convincing argument that, instead of basing the decision on the certainty of vesting as seen from the date when the instrument came into effect, it would be very much better to wait and see whether it did in fact vest within the period. If it did vest within the period, it was valid. If it did not, it was void.

This solution is deceptively simple. Two important principles have to be observed if "wait and see" is to be made to work. The first principle is that, if "wait and see" is enacted, that is, if validity is to be determined by waiting to see whether the disposition vests within the period of a life in being plus twenty-one years—it is essential to specify which lives are to be used to measure the period of a life in being plus twenty-one years. Otherwise, it is not known how long to wait and see.[211]

The Act introduces a comprehensive list of lives to be used to measure the period of waiting and seeing. The list will be examined in detail below.[212]

The second principle is that, once "wait and see" is enacted, the common law rule becomes irrelevant, and should be abolished. The common law rule becomes irrelevant, because it is no longer relevant to know whether or not a disposition complies with the common law rule.

---

[206] Adoption Act 1976, s. 39. On legitimation, see Legitimacy Act 1976, s. 5, Schs. 1 and 2.

[207] Or even give birth to a child.

[208] PAA 1964, s. 2(4). As it does also in relation to an adoption after the date of the instrument: Adoption Act 1976, s. 42(5) and n. 205, supra. For a precedent authorising trustees to assume that no child will be born to a woman over the usual age of child-bearing, see Conv. Prec. 11-C3. [209] Ibid., s. 2(2).

[210] Fourth Report, 1956 (Cmnd 18).

[211] It seems that the Law Reform Committee did not consider this question, nor did many jurisdictions which have selected wait and see; (1965) 81 LQR 106 (D. E. Allan); Maudsley, Appendix D. But the draftsman came to the rescue. In 1987 the American Uniform Act of Perpetuities adopted a period of ninety years as the wait and see period, in preference to a life in being and twenty-one years: (1987) 21 *Real Property, Probate & Trust Journal* 569; [1987] CLJ 234 (L. W. Waggoner). [212] S. 3(5); p. 551, post.

If an interest *must* vest, if at all, within the period, then it *will* vest, if at all, within the period. To say that it *must* vest, if at all, says nothing; the trustees still have to wait until the interest vests before paying out the money to the beneficiaries. Compare two dispositions:

(a) to the first child of A to attain the age of 21. A is alive and has a child aged 16.

(b) to the first great-grandchild of A to attain the age of 21. A is alive and has a zgreat-grandchild aged 16.

The first disposition is valid under the common law rule. The trustees wait for five years to see if the child attains the age of twenty-one, and then pay out the money.

The second disposition is void under the common law rule. So, under the Act, the trustees wait and see whether the first great-grandchild attains the age of twenty-one within the period.

There is no difference between these cases in the era of "wait and see", and they should both be solved on the principle of "wait and see".

If the Act had *replaced* the common law rule by "wait and see", the whole of the learning on the common law rule would have disappeared. It is impossible, however, to ignore it, because the list of measuring lives in section 3 fails to include *all* the lives which could be used to determine validity at common law. There are situations in which the disposition may be valid at common law, using the common law lives, but not so if the measuring lives listed in section 3 are used. Illustrations are cases where the settlor or testator has selected his own lives; these are omitted from the list in section 3. There are other cases of which the following may be taken as an example:

to the first of A's lineal descendants to go for a walk with X.

This would be valid at common law. But X is not included in the statutory list. If the walk takes place more than twenty-one years after the death of the survivor of the persons in the statutory list, it will be void under the "wait and see" provision but valid under the common law.

There seems to be no point in preserving all the old learning on the common law rule to deal with situations of this type. But that is what happened. It is necessary therefore to understand both the common law and the "wait and see" principle. Simple alterations to the Act would make this unnecessary.[213]

Section 3 provides that,[214] where an interest would be void under the common law rule on the ground that it might vest outside the common law perpetuity period, the disposition shall be treated as not subject to the rule, until it becomes established that the vesting can only occur *outside* the period. Sub-section (4) provides that where the section applies, the perpetuity period shall be measured by the lives of the persons listed in sub-section (5), plus twenty-one years.[215] In other words, if the disposition is void under the common law rule, using either the common law lives plus twenty-one years or, if so specified, the specified period not exceeding eighty years, the interest will be treated as valid (unless it becomes clear that the interest will *not* vest within the period) during a period measured by the *statutory* lives plus twenty-one years. In short, if the disposition is void under the common law rule, there is "wait and see" for a period measured by the statutory lives plus twenty-one years.

---

[213] Maudsley, Appendix E.   [214] Apart from ss. 4 and 5.
[215] See ss. 1 (80-year period), p. 545, ante; 9 (2) (21-year period in connection with options to purchase).

As a result of the Act, there are no less than three perpetuity periods and two basic doctrines.[216] This reinforces the argument made above that the common law rule should have been abolished and replaced by "wait and see". There would then have been one period, one doctrine, and one set of lives.[217] Illustrations of the working of the principle of "wait and see" will be delayed until the statutory lives have been examined.

(a) Each part of limitation a separate disposition

In the application of the "wait and see" principle, each distinct part of a limitation is treated by the Act as a separate disposition. For instance:

A testator devises land to A for life, remainder to his widow for life, remainder to such of the children of A as are alive at the death of the widow; but if there be no such children, then to the first son of X to marry.

In such a case, the gift to the children of A and the gift to the first son of X to marry are distinct dispositions subject to different waiting periods.

(b) Special power of appointment

The "wait and see" principle applies equally to the validity of appointments made by the exercise of a special power:

Suppose that a testator, who dies in 1965, devises land to A, a bachelor, for life, remainder to such of his issue as he shall by will appoint. A appoints in favour of his infant daughter, X *on her marriage*. A dies in 1975.

At common law the appointment is too remote.[218] Under the Act, it is valid provided that the daughter marries within twenty-one years after A's death.

(c) Intermediate income

One problem raised by these provisions is the destination of the intermediate income during the waiting period.[219] The general rule, subject to certain exceptions, is that, although the vesting contingency may ultimately never be satisfied, a contingent gift carries the income arising from the corpus, except so far as such income has been otherwise disposed of by the donor.[220] Suppose, for example, that a testator bequeaths the residue of his estate to his grandchild, X, upon her marriage and that she is an infant and unmarried at the time of the testator's death. In these circumstances, the income is accumulated during her infancy and the trustees may use it for her maintenance and education,[221] and may make advances to her out of capital,[222] but at her majority the income becomes and remains payable to her even though she may never marry.[223]

---

[216] I.e., certainty of vesting and "wait and see".

[217] Or two, if the 80-year period were applicable for "wait and see".

[218] Compare the example, discussed, p. 536, ante.   [219] See Morris and Leach, pp. 93–5.

[220] See e.g. LPA 1925, s. 175(2).

[221] Trustee Act 1925, s. 31(1)(i); 31(2). For dispositions taking effect after 1969 the age of majority has been reduced to eighteen: Family Law Reform Act 1969, s. 1, Schs. 1, 3, para. 5.   [222] Ibid., s. 32.

[223] Ibid., s. 31(1)(ii).

The rights of the beneficiaries in such a case, however, are subject to the perpetuity rule, the effect of which varies according as the disposition falls to be determined by the common law or by the Act of 1964:

Suppose, for instance, that a will bequeaths the residue of the estate to the daughters of X when they marry, and that X is childless at the time of the testator's death.

At common law the bequest is void *ab initio*. It is impossible to say at the time when the will takes effect that, if any daughters born to X marry, they will do so within twenty-one years from her death.

But under the statutory "wait and see" provisions the gift is not void *ab initio*. It is void only if at the end of twenty-one years from the death of the last of the statutory lives none of X's daughters, if any, has married. The destination of the income of the corpus during this waiting period therefore presents a problem. If a daughter is born to X, is she to receive the benefit of the income although the bequest may ultimately become void for remoteness? The recommendation of the Law Reform Committee that such should be the rule[224] was accepted by the Act of 1964, which provides that when it becomes established that the vesting of a gift must occur, if at all, after the end of the perpetuity period, "the validity of anything previously done in relation to the interest disposed of by way of advancement, application of intermediate income or otherwise" shall not be affected.[225]

(d) General powers of appointment

A general power of appointment that may possibly be exercised beyond the perpetuity period, and which is therefore void at common law,[226] is to be treated as valid until it is established that it will not in fact be exercised at too remote a time.[227] If, for instance, it is exercisable only by will and is given to the unborn child of X, it will be valid if the donee is born and dies within twenty-one years after X's death; if it is exercisable by deed, or either by deed or by will, but only on the marriage of the unborn child, it will be valid if the marriage occurs within the same period.

(e) Any power, option or other right

In a more comprehensive section, the Act deals separately with the remote exercise of "any power, option or other right". It provides that a power, option or other right is no longer to be rendered void merely because it may possibly be exercised at too remote a time. It will be void only if it is not in fact fully exercised within the perpetuity period:[228] for instance, a special power granted by a deed of settlement to the eldest son of X, a bachelor, is void *ab initio* at common law;[229] but under the Act it is not void unless exercised beyond the perpetuity period calculated from the date of the settlement. On the other hand, if the exercise of a special power satisfies the test of remoteness prescribed by this subsection, the question whether the appointed interests are too remote is governed, as we have seen, by an earlier sub-section.[230]

The reference in this enactment to an "option" means, inter alia, that a right conferred by contract upon one person to purchase the land of another at some unspecified time in the

---

224 Para. 22 (1956 Cmnd 18).   225 PAA 1964, s. 3(1).   226 P. 534, ante.
227 PAA 1964, s. 3(2).
228 Ibid., s. 3(3). It will be noticed that a general power is caught by this sub-section as well as by sub-section (2).
229 Pp. 535–7, ante.   230 PAA 1964, s. 3(1); see the example given, p. 549, ante.

future is no longer void *ab initio*,[231] but void only if it is not in fact exercised within the perpetuity period.

But, except where the option is one that entitles a tenant to purchase his landlord's reversion, which is exercisable throughout the continuance of the lease however long this may be,[232] the only period applicable to an option to acquire for valuable consideration any interest in land is twenty-one years.[233]

(4) Duration of the Waiting Period. The Statutory Lives

(a) General

Before examining the statutory list of measuring lives, three important preliminary points need to be made. First, as explained above, there is the obvious point that it is impossible to wait and see for lives in being plus twenty-one years unless it is known whose lives are to be used for the period of waiting and seeing. Those lives need to be known exactly and precisely; otherwise difficult questions will be asked when the period comes to an end. And, for the convenience of the trustees administering the fund, it is more important to have the lives specified at the time when the intrument comes into operation. Otherwise, they will have to add new "lives" as the years go by.

The second point is that the common law lives will not do. The common law lives, as has been seen, are those within twenty-one years of whose death the interest must vest, if it vest at all. They are, in other words, the lives which validate the gift. There are no other common law lives additional to the validating lives.[234] The "wait and see" system cannot work if only the common law validating lives are used; one could only wait and see where the disposition was already valid. As Professor Allan said: "There would never be any occasion for waiting and seeing at all."[235]

Thirdly, it is necessary to consider who the measuring lives ought to be for "wait and see". The common law lives are irrelevant, and have nothing to do with the choice. The basic question under "wait and see" is to ask: if that person does in fact live to a date within twenty-one years of the actual time of vesting, would it be sensible policy that that person should be used as a life which validates the gift?

---

[231] As under the common law, *London and South Western Rly Co v Gomm* (1882) 20 Ch D 562; pp. 541–2, ante; *Dunn v Blackdown Properties Ltd* [1961] Ch 433; p. 542, ante.   [232] PAA 1964, s. 9(1); p. 559, post.

[233] Ibid., s. 9(2).

[234] P. 523, ante. A different view is expressed in many of the books, and, in most detail, in (1964) 80 LQR 496 (J. H. C. Morris and H. W. R. Wade). It is there suggested that the common law lives are persons whose lives may or may not validate the interest. It is necessary to ascertain who the lives are, and the test is said to be whether there is a causal relationship between the lives and the vesting. Some lives which are causally connected will validate the interest, but others may not. It is further suggested that this principle is the one that should have been used for the measuring lives applicable to "wait and see".

The problem is to determine who those lives are. Causal connection is too uncertain. The standard example which is usually taken is that of a gift to the grandchildren of A who is still alive. The article in 80 LQR seems to suggest that the grandparent is a measuring life because he is causally connected, and so are his living children. It is suggested however that the living grandchildren themselves are inappropriate. It is difficult to see how the grandparent is causally connected with the vesting, because the vesting might occur at any time quite independently of the life or death of the grandparent. On the other hand, the living grandchildren would appear to be measuring lives because it is the continuance of their lives which causes the vesting to occur.

For a detailed discussion of this controversy, see Maudsley pp. 87–109; (1981) 97 LQR 593 (R. L. Deech); (1986) 102 LQR 250 (J. Dukeminier).

[235] (1965) 81 LQR 109.

For example, a settlor creates a trust under which interests are given to such of the grand-children of A as shall marry. A is alive and has infant children. The gift is void at common law. If a grandchild of A should marry within 21 years of the death of A, or of Mrs A, or of any of the living children of A, or of the settlor, *should* each or any of those lives be used for the purpose of validating the gift? The statutory lives have been selected on that basis. In such a case they would indeed be A, Mrs A, A's living children and the settlor.

(b) Statutory lives

(1) DEFINITION

The statutory lives are defined in section 3(5) as follows:

(a) The person by whom the disposition is made, if made by deed, even though he himself takes no interest in the property.[236]

(b) Any of the following persons in whose favour the disposition is made, namely:

(i) In the case of a class gift, any member or potential member of the class.[237]

A person is a member of the class if he has satisfied all the conditions that entitle him to an interest; he is a potential member if he has satisfied only some of the conditions but may in time satisfy the remainder.[238] If, for instance, there is a gift by will to such of the daughters of X as may marry and if at the time of the testator's death X has an unmarried daughter, she constitutes a life. She has satisfied the condition relating to birth and there is a possibility that she may later marry.

(ii) In the case of an individual disposition to a person subject to certain conditions, any person as to whom some of the conditions are satisfied and the remainder may in time be satisfied.[239]

This would be the position, for instance, if in the last illustration the gift had been to the first granddaughter of X to marry, and if at the time of the testator's death a granddaughter had been born but was not yet married.

(iii) The above two provisions apply equally to special powers of appointment.[240] If, for instance, the power is conferred by will and is exercisable in favour of any of the issue of X, descendants of X alive at the testator's death constitute statutory lives.

(iv) The person on whom any power, option or other right is conferred.[241]

Trustees who possess a special power of appointment, for instance, fall within this category.

(c) In certain circumstances, the parents and grandparents of the designated beneficiaries also constitute persons whose lives are relevant in the present context. The Act provides in section 3(5) that:

The persons capable of ranking as "statutory lives" shall include a person having a child or grandchild who would be a life in being under the rules (b)(i) to (iv) given above; and also a person any of whose

---

[236] PAA 1964, s. 3(5)(a).   [237] Ibid., s. 3(5)(b)(i).   [238] Ibid., s. 15(3).
[239] Ibid., s. 3(5)(b)(ii).   [240] Ibid., s. 3(5)(b)(iii) and (iv).
[241] Ibid., s. 3(5)(b)(v). For a view that this relates only to the *validity* of the power, and not to appointments made under the power, see Maudsley, pp. 133–7.

children or grandchildren, if subsequently born, would by virtue of descent be a life in being under the same rules.[242]

It must be remembered that a person has two parents and four grandparents. The "in-laws" are included by this provision.

Suppose, for instance, that a bequest is made to such of X's daughters as may marry, and that at the testator's death a daughter has been born to X but has not yet married. In these circumstances, as we have seen in dealing with rule (b)(i),[243] the daughter ranks as a statutory life. So also is X, and so are Mrs X, X's parents, and the parents of Mrs X. Under the instant rule, therefore, X is equally qualified in that respect, and so also are such of X's parents and grandparents who are alive at the testator's death.[244]

Again, suppose that there is a bequest to the first granddaughter of X to marry, and that at the testator's death X has one unmarried son. In these circumstances, X, X's wife and X's unmarried son are lives in being under the instant rule, because, if a daughter is subsequently born to X's son, she would qualify under rule (b)(ii). If X's son were married after the testator's death, his wife and her parents would also qualify.

(d) Any person on the failure or determination of whose prior interest the disposition is limited to take effect constitutes a life in being.[245]

A simple illustration of this is that under a limitation to A for life, remainder to the first grandchild of X to marry, A ranks as a life in being. It would seem, however, that he will not qualify as such under a limitation to A for life, remainder to B for life, remainder to the first grandchild of X to marry, for it is on the determination of B's interest that the gift to the grandchild is to take effect.[246] Nor, it seems, would X be a statutory life in a gift:

to the first son of X that should be bred a clergyman and be in Holy Orders, but in case X should have no such son, then to B in fee simple,[247]

because the gift over is to take effect on the failure of the interest of the son, and not that of X. These omissions appear to be unintended, and to be an oversight on the part of the draftsman.

(2) IN BEING AND ASCERTAINABLE

Sub-section (4)(a) limits the statutory lives to those individuals in sub-section (5) who are "in being and ascertainable to the commencement of the perpetuity period".

The object of this provision is that the trustees are able to make their list of statutory lives when the instrument comes into operation, and will not be required to add new ones. "In being" includes children *en ventre sa mère*.[248]

(3) IMPRACTICABILITY OF ASCERTAINMENT

Following the common law rule relating to expressly selected lives,[249] the statutory list limits the lives in sub-section (4)(a) by providing that the:

---

[242] PAA 1964, s. 3(5)(c).   [243] Supra.   [244] See [1969] CLJ 284 (M. J. Prichard).
[245] PAA 1964, s. 3(5)(d); *Re Thomas Meadows & Co Ltd and Subsidiary Companies (1960) Staff Pension Scheme Rules* [1971] Ch 278.   [246] See (1964) 80 LQR, p. 505 (J. H. C. Morris and H. W. R. Wade).
[247] *Proctor v Bishop of Bath and Wells* (1794) 2 Hy & Bl 358.   [248] PAA 1964, s. 15(2).
[249] P. 525, ante.

lives of any description of persons falling within paragraph (b) or (c) of sub-section (5) shall be disregarded if the number of persons of that description is such as to render it impracticable to ascertain the date of death of the survivor.[250]

It has been assumed that this is an attempt to enact the common law rule relating to the selection of express lives.[251] Clearly, some provision of this nature is required. The problem is likely to arise in cases, which are common in modern practice, where a successful business executive sets up a trust in favour of his family, and employees and their dependants.[252] It would not be possible to ascertain each beneficiary, and the restriction in sub-section (4)(a) will come into operation. The difficulty is to know which person shall be "disregarded". It is tempting to assume that the "dependants" would be disregarded, or the "employees", but the subsection refers to the "lives of any description of persons falling within paragraph (b) or (c)" of sub-section (5). If the categories of sub-section (5) determine who shall be disregarded, the beneficiaries are all in the same category and should all be disregarded. Perhaps the statute intends their parents and grandparents to be disregarded; for that is a separate description in the Act. No doubt the courts will determine the matter in a way which makes the Act workable. It should be noted also that the subsection on its terms applies only when it is the "number of persons" that renders impracticable the ascertainment of the date of death of the survivor. This appears to be a wrong emphasis. Very large numbers can be traced in modern times through births and deaths registers. But there are many other reasons why the ascertainment of the date of death of the survivor may be impossible to determine; as in the case of the ascertainment of the grandparents of an immigrant from a third world country where no such records are kept. Again, the Act will presumably be construed in a pragmatic manner, with no undue emphasis on the word "number".

(4) NO STATUTORY LIVES

If there are no statutory lives and no specified period, a period in gross of twenty-one years is allowed.[253]

(5) Special Provisions Designed to Save Remote Interests

The Act of 1964 contains three additional provisions designed to cure the vice of remoteness, but it is essential to bear in mind that these are not to be invoked until it has become clear that the limitations in question will not be saved by the "wait and see" rule.[254] The provisions are as follows:

(a) *Provisions concerning death of surviving spouse*

This deals with the case of the possibly unborn spouse. Suppose for instance that the limitations contained in a will are:

to X, a bachelor, for life, remainder to his future wife for life, remainder to such of his children as are living at the death of the survivor of X and such wife.

---

[250] I.e., rules (b) and (c); p. 552, ante.   [251] (1964) 80 LQR 486, p. 502.

[252] *McPhail v Doulton* [1971] AC 424, Maudsley and Burn, *Trusts and Trustees*, p. 84.

[253] PAA 1964, s. 3(4)(b).

[254] Because s. 3, which introduces the "wait and see" rule is expressed to operate "apart" from ss. 4 and 5 which contain these three additional provisions.

As we have seen, the limitation to the children is void at common law.[255] It is possible that X may marry a woman not yet born, and therefore it cannot be affirmed at the time of the testator's death that the vesting contingency will necessarily occur within the perpetuity period.

If X marries a woman who is alive at the date of the will, the gift to the children will not be saved by the "wait and see" rule unless she dies not later than twenty-one years after X's death. The wife cannot qualify as a "statutory life", though possibly and most probably she is alive at the date of the testator's death, for under the Act of 1964 lives in being for the purposes of the "wait and see" rule must be ascertainable at the commencement of the perpetuity period.[256]

It is therefore provided by the Act of 1964 that a disposition such as that given above, which fails for remoteness, shall be treated for all purposes as if it had been limited to take effect immediately before the end of the perpetuity period, if to do so will save it from being void for remoteness.[257]

If, then, in the case of the above example, X marries, and his wife dies within twenty-one years of his death, the limitation to the children is saved under the "wait and see" rule. If she survives beyond that time, the "wait and see" rule is impotent, but the limitation is none the less saved, since by virtue of the above enactment it vests at the end of twenty-one years from X's death in the children then living and will take effect in possession on the death of the wife.

(b) Age reduction provisions

An interest whose vesting is postponed until the attainment by the beneficiary of an age exceeding twenty-one years is void *ab initio* at common law, but as we have already seen it was provided by section 163 of the Law of Property Act 1925 that in such a case the age of twenty-one years should be substituted for that specified by the donor.[258]

Such a disposition contained in an instrument taking effect after 15 July 1964 may well be saved by the "wait and see" provisions of the Act of 1964:

Suppose, for instance, that a gift is made by will to the first son of X, a bachelor, to attain the age of 30 years; and that X is survived by a son aged 10.

If the son satisfies the prescribed contingency, he will have done so within twenty-one years from the death of X, the life in being.

On the other hand, the "wait and see" rule may be ineffective. If, for instance, in the example just given the eldest son is only five years of age at X's death, the vesting contingency cannot be satisfied within the perpetuity period, though if section 163 were applicable the gift to him would be saved by the reduction of the vesting age from thirty to twenty-one years.

It was felt, however, that instead of mechanically reducing the age to twenty-one years in every case, it would be preferable to conform more closely with the donor's wishes and to reduce it only to whatever age would suffice to prevent the limitation from being too

---

[255] P. 529, ante.   [256] PAA 1964, s. 3(4)(a); p. 553, ante.   [257] Ibid., s. 5.   [258] P. 528, ante.

remote. The Act of 1964, therefore, repeals section 163 of the Law of Property Act 1925[259] though not retrospectively,[260] and replaces it by the following provision:

Where a disposition is limited by reference to the attainment by any person or persons of a specified age exceeding twenty-one years, and it is apparent at the time the disposition is made or becomes apparent at a subsequent time

(a) that the disposition would, apart from this section, be void for remoteness, but

(b) that it would not be so void if the specified age had been twenty-one years,

the disposition shall be treated for all purposes as if, instead of being limited by reference to the age in fact specified, it had been limited by reference to the age nearest to that age which would, if specified instead, have prevented the disposition from being so void.[261]

Suppose that in a will there is a gift to the first son of X, a bachelor, to attain the age of thirty and that, at the death of the last of the statutory lives,[262] his son is only four years old. In these circumstances it has become apparent that the "wait and see" rule cannot save the ultimate limitation. The son cannot attain the prescribed age within the perpetuity period. Hence the above section operates, and the qualifying age is reduced from thirty to twenty-five years.

If the disposition is in favour of two or more persons, as for example to the children of X at thirty years of age, and if at X's death his son is four and his daughter five years old, the reduction of the specified age to twenty-five, necessary to save the son's interest, affects the daughter also.[263]

If the disposition specifies different ages for distinct classes of beneficiaries, as for instance thirty for sons and twenty-five for daughters, the classes are segregated for the purpose of estimating the extent of the reduction. The reduction must be such as is necessary in each separate class.[264]

(c) Class exclusion provisions

We have already seen that at common law a class gift cannot be partly good, partly bad. If some members of the class may possibly fail to satisfy the vesting contingency within the perpetuity period, the whole gift fails even in respect of those members whose interests are already vested.[265]

The Act however abolishes this rule and in its place provides that the disposition shall take effect in favour of those members who acquire vested interests within the perpetuity period to the exclusion of those who fail to qualify within that time. This policy applies to two distinct cases.

First, it applies where the only cause of failure at common law is that some members of the class may not be ascertainable within the perpetuity period. In such a case, the Act provides that, unless their interests are saved by virtue of the "wait and see" provision, those members shall be excluded from the class.[266]

---

[259] PAA 1964, s. 4(6), (7) as added by Children Act 1975, s. 108, Sch. 3, para. 43. See (1965) 81 LQR 346 (J. D. Davies) which had argued that the repeal of s. 163 by s. 4(6) was defective; (1976) 120 SJ 498 (F. A. R. Bennion).   [260] Ibid., s. 15(5).

[261] Ibid., s. 4(1).   [262] X and X's parents.

[263] The reason is that there is only one "disposition", not several "dispositions" to cover all members of the class; (1964) 80 LQR p. 509 (J. H. C. Morris and H. W. R. Wade). See [1969] CLJ 284 at 286–91 (M. J. Prichard).

[264] PAA 1964, s. 4(2).   [265] Pp. 531, ante.   [266] PAA 1964, s. 4(4).

Suppose, for instance, that a disposition is made by will to X, a bachelor, for life, remainder to such of his children as may marry. Suppose further that X dies leaving a married son and an unmarried daughter.

If the daughter marries within twenty-one years after the death of the last of the statutory lives, her interest is saved by the "wait and see" provisions; if she is still a spinster at the expiry of that time, she is excluded from the class. In the latter event, the gift, which would have been wholly void at common law, takes effect in favour of the son.

  The second case is where neither the "wait and see" principle nor the age reduction provisions will save the gift, as may occur if the attainment by the members of the class of an age exceeding twenty-one is part of the vesting contingency. The following is an example of such a case:

A bequest to X, a bachelor, for life, remainder to such of his children as marry and attain the age of 25 years. X dies leaving a married daughter aged 19 and a son aged 3.

The inability of the son to reach the prescribed age within the perpetuity period which ends twenty-one years from the death of the last of the statutory lives, may no doubt be rectified under the age reduction provisions.[267] But the marriage contingency remains, for whether this is satisfied may not be established until too remote a time. If in fact he marries within twenty-one years after the death of the last of the statutory lives, the "wait and see" rule will operate to validate the whole gift. If not, then the daughter becomes the sole beneficiary, for the effect of the Act of 1964 is to exclude the son from the class of designated beneficiaries.[268]

(6) General and Special Powers of Appointment

We have already discussed the importance of the distinction between general and special powers of appointment in the context of the doctrine of remoteness.[269] We have also seen that it is sometimes difficult to determine whether a so-called "hybrid" power is to be classed as general or special.[270] This difficulty is removed by the Act of 1964 which defines what powers shall be treated as special powers for the purposes of the rule against perpetuities, but only for those purposes. By virtue of this enactment a power is to be treated as a special power, unless:

(a) in the instrument creating the power it is expressed to be exercisable by one person only, and

(b) it could, at all times during its currency when that person is of full age and capacity, be exercised by him so as immediately to transfer to himself the whole of the interest governed by the power without the consent of any other person or compliance with any other condition, not being a formal condition relating to the mode of exercise of the power.[271]

The result is that the only general power is one under which "there is a sole donee who is at all times free without the concurrence of any other person to appoint to himself".[272]

  Thus, for instance, a power is to be regarded as a special power if it is exercisable by the donee jointly with other persons or only with the consent of other persons; or exercisable in

---

[267] P. 555, ante.   [268] PAA 1964, s. 4(3).   [269] Pp. 533 et seq, ante.   [270] P. 534, n. 126, ante.
[271] PAA 1964, s. 7.   [272] Fourth Report of Law Reform Committee (1956 Cmnd 18), para. 47.

favour of any persons alive at the donee's death; or exercisable in favour of any person except the donee. On the other hand, a power to appoint to any person in the world except X should be classified as general.[273]

But the general testamentary power, that is, one unrestricted in respect of objects but exercisable only by will,[274] is treated as exceptional by the Act. Under the existing case law, such a power is regarded as special so far as the validity of its creation is concerned;[275] but as general when the question is whether an appointment is too remote.[276] The perpetuity period runs from the date of the instrument of creation in the former case, in the latter from the date of the appointment. To classify such a power as general in respect of the appointments is illogical for, unlike the case where exercise by deed is permissible, the donee is in no sense the virtual owner of the property. Any transfer of the ownership to himself is necessarily ineffective until after his death. Nevertheless, it was felt to be unwise to revise a rule that had obtained for some seventy years, and one upon which conveyancing precedents in constant use had been based. Therefore, the distinction between the validity of the power itself and the validity of appointments is retained by the Act.[277]

The expression "power of appointment" includes any discretionary power to transfer a beneficial interest in property without the furnishing of consideration.[278] It ranks as a special power.

(7) Extended Scope of the Rule

(a) Possibilities of reverter

The scope of the rule against perpetuities is enlarged in two respects by the Act of 1964. It is extended to possibilities of reverter and analogous possibilities, a matter that is dealt with in a later chapter;[279] and its effect upon certain contracts for the purchase of land is expanded.

(b) Contract for purchase of land

We have seen that at common law a contract for the purchase of land, since it creates an equitable interest in favour of the promisee, is not enforceable by or against third parties if it is too remote; but that it remains enforceable without any limit of time between the parties themselves, since the rule against perpetuities is not concerned with personal obligations.[280]

The second limb of the common law rule, however, is now abolished. The Act provides in effect that where a disposition, made *inter vivos* and creating proprietary rights capable of transfer, would be void for remoteness as between persons other than the original parties, it shall be void as between the person by whom it was made and the person in whose favour it was made or any successor of his.[281]

(8) Effect of an Infringement of the Rule upon Subsequent Interests

The Law Reform Committee, after castigating the doctrine of dependency, recommended that: "no limitation which itself complies with the rule should be invalidated solely by

---

[273] Morris and Leach, p. 137.   [274] P. 535, ante.

[275] *Wollaston v King* (1869) LR 8 Eq 165; *Morgan v Gronow* (1873) LR 16 Eq 1; p. 535, ante.

[276] *Rous v Jackson* (1885) 29 Ch D 521.   [277] PAA 1964, s. 7, proviso.   [278] Ibid., s. 15(2).

[279] P. 572, post.   [280] Pp. 541–2, ante.

[281] S. 10. See (1964) 80 LQR pp. 524–5 (J. H. C. Morris and H. W. R. Wade).

reason of being preceded by one or more invalid limitations, whether or not it expressly or by implication takes effect after or subject to, or is dependent upon, any such invalid limitations".[282]

The Act of 1964 deals with this recommendation in the following terms:

A disposition shall not be treated as void for remoteness by reason only that the interest disposed of is ulterior to and dependent upon an interest under a disposition which is so void, and the vesting of an interest shall not be prevented from being accelerated on the failure of a prior interest by reason only that the failure arises because of remoteness.[283]

Thus each limitation in a chain of limitations must be considered separately according to its own intrinsic validity and without regard to the remoteness of its predecessors. An interest which is already vested or which will necessarily vest, if at all, within the perpetuity period takes effect according to its individual terms.

It will be noticed that the concluding words of the enactment do not direct that the ulterior interest *shall* be accelerated, that is, allowed to take effect immediately upon the failure for remoteness of the prior interest, but that such failure *shall not prevent* acceleration. The reason for this negative approach is that there may be other obstacles to acceleration. If, for example, the interest that fails is followed by a contingent interest, which in turn is followed by a vested interest, the latter is not accelerated until it is established whether or not the contingent interest will take effect.[284]

(9) Exceptions to the Rule

The exceptions to the rule recognised by the common law have been affected in three respects.

(a) Administrative powers

First, as we have already seen, the administrative powers of trustees are excluded from the rule even in respect of instruments taking effect before 16 July 1964.[285]

(b) Option to purchase leasehold reversion

Secondly, an option to acquire for valuable consideration the freehold interest expectant upon a lease, is wholly exempted from the rule regardless of the length of the lease, provided that it is exercisable only by the lessee or his successors in title, and provided that it is not exercisable later than one year after the end of the lease.[286]

(c) Remedies for recovery of rentcharge

Thirdly, the former doubt as to the ambit of section 121 of the Law of Property Act 1925[287] has been removed. It is provided by the 1964 Act that the perpetuity rule shall not apply to any powers or remedies for recovering or compelling the payment of an annual sum to which that section relates, or otherwise becoming exercisable or enforceable on the breach of any condition or other requirement relating to that sum.[288]

---

[282] Para. 33 (1956 Cmnd 18).   [283] S. 6.   [284] *Re Townsend's Estate* (1886) 34 Ch D 357.
[285] PAA 1964, s. 8(1); pp. 544, ante.   [286] Ibid., s. 9(1).   [287] P. 542, ante.
[288] PAA 1964, s. 11(1).

IV The Rule Against Accumulations of Income[289]

At common law, the rule against perpetuities governs not only the right to suspend the vesting of an estate, but also the right to direct the accumulation of income arising from an estate.
Therefore, before the law was altered by statute in 1800 it was held that a direction for the
accumulation of income for a period which did not exceed the perpetuity period was valid.[290]
This was decided in the famous case of *Thellusson v Woodford*,[291] where the facts were these:

At the end of the eighteenth century a certain Peter Thellusson, a man of great wealth, took advantage
of the rule and made a will the object of which was to accumulate an enormous fortune for the benefit of certain future and unascertained members of his family. He directed that the income arising from
his land should be accumulated at compound interest during the lives of all his sons, grandsons and
great-grandsons living at his death or born in due time afterwards, and that, on the death of the survivor, the capital sum so produced should be divided amongst the male representatives of his son's
families. At the time of the controversy engendered by this will it was calculated that the accumulation
would endure for about 80 years, and produce an amount of approximately 100 million pounds.[292] It
was held that these trusts for accumulation were valid, but a statute, generally called the Thellusson
Act,[293] was subsequently passed in order to prevent further examples of what has been called posthumous avarice.

An explanation of the statutory permitted periods will follow. But it may first be useful
to put the whole question of accumulations of income in perspective. It has been customary for nearly two hundred years to concentrate upon the criticisms of Mr Thellusson's
testamentary plan; and this has brought accumulations of income into disrepute with
suggestions that accumulations are evil in themselves. The truth is that they are in some
areas encouraged. Thus, accumulation of income is permitted during the infancy of a
beneficiary, and, since 1925, trustees holding property on trust for an infant for any interest, whether vested or contingent, have power, under section 31 of the Trustee Act 1925,
provided that the gift carries the intermediate income,[294] to apply the income for the
maintenance and education of the beneficiary, and they are required to accumulate the
surplus. Again, it is common to provide for the accumulation of the income of a discretionary trust. The trustees would be under a duty to distribute the income to some member or members of the class of beneficiaries, unless power is given to them to accumulate
the income.

A social problem could arise if many testators made provision for large accumulations for
the period of perpetuity, as did Mr Thellusson. In fairness to him, however, it should be
pointed out that he made ample provision for his widow and children, and that he refrained
from giving more to the children for the very good reason that he wanted them to have to

---

[289] See Morris and Leach, pp. 266–306; *Theobald on Wills*, paras. 44–59 to 44–70; Maudsley, chap. 7; Simes,
Public Policy and the Dead Hand, chap. iv.   [290] Fearne, *Contingent Remainders*, p. 537, note.
[291] (1799) 4 Ves 227; affd (1805) 11 Ves 112, M & B p. 414.
[292] Challis, *Law of Real Property* (3rd edn), p. 201; Holdsworth, *History of English Law*, vol. vii, pp. 228 et seq;
Morris and Leach, p. 267, n. 5; (1970) NILQ 131 (G. W. Keeton); (1997) 147 NLJ 1046 (S. Hooper). "On the
death of the last surviving grandson in 1856, the estate was divided (not without more litigation) between the
two male representatives of two of Peter Thellusson's sons who had left issue. But owing to mismanagement and
costs of litigation, the estate realised a comparatively small amount": Holdsworth, at p. 230.
[293] Accumulations Act 1800.   [294] H & M, para. 20–029.

work for their living.[295] Furthermore, on the failure of the provisions in favour of those remote successors, he provided an alternative gift to the Crown to the use of the Sinking Fund.

A Statutory Periods

The Thellusson Act has been re-enacted and amended by the Law of Property Act 1925,[296] as well as by the Perpetuities and Accumulations Act 1964,[297] and the position now is that a person[298] who desires the income of his property to be accumulated is restricted to choose *one* only[299] of the following periods for the duration of the accumulation:

(1) the life of the grantor or settlor;

(2) a term of twenty-one years from the death of the grantor, settlor or testator;

(3) the minority[300] or respective minorities of any person or persons living or *en ventre sa mère* at the death of the grantor, settlor or testator;

(4) the minority or respective minorities only of any person or persons who, under the limitations of the instrument directing the accumulations, would for the time being, if of full age, be entitled to the income directed to be accumulated;[301]

(5) a term of twenty-one years from the date of the making of the disposition;

(6) the minority or respective minorities of any person or persons in being at that date.[302]

The last two periods were added by the Act of 1964 with the object of giving a wider choice to persons who make an *inter vivos* settlement. They apply only to instruments taking effect after 15 July 1964.

B Selection of Periods

The difference between the third and fourth periods is that while the third period is for the minority of a person living at the death of the settlor or testator, the fourth includes the minority of any person who may *afterwards* become entitled to an interest in the land.[303] Thus by the choice of the fourth period an accumulation may lawfully be directed for the

---

[295] "The Provision which I have made for my said three sons, and the very great success they have met with, will be sufficient to procure them comfort, and it is my earnest wish and desire, that they will avoid ostentation, vanity and pompous show; as that will be the best fortune they can possess."

[296] Ss. 164–6. The Act affects not only an express direction to accumulate income, but also a power of accumulation: *Re Robb* [1953] Ch 459; see also PAA 1964, s. 13(2). The same point was decided in Scotland under Trusts (Scotland) Act 1961, s. 5; *Baird v Lord Advocate* [1979] AC 666.

[297] See Law Reform Committee, Fourth Report, Section C (1956 Cmnd 18).

[298] A corporate settlor is not a person within the section: *Re Dodwell & Co Ltd's Trust* [1979] Ch 301.

[299] *Jagger v Jagger* (1883) 25 Ch D 729.

[300] In the case of dispositions taking effect after 1969, minority ends at the age of eighteen: Family Law Reform Act 1969, s. 1. There are transitional provisions so that the change from twenty-one to eighteen shall not invalidate any direction for accumulation in a settlement or other disposition made by a deed, will or other instrument which was made before 1970: ibid., s. 1(4), Sch. 3, para. 7.   [301] LPA 1925, s. 164(1)(a)–(d).

[302] PAA 1964, s. 13(1).   [303] Fearne, *Contingent Remainders*, p. 537, Butler's note citing Preston.

minorities of persons who are not alive at a testator's death. This is illustrated by the case of *Re Cattell*,[304] where:

a testator vested property in trustees upon trust for the children of his sons and daughters. He directed that the income of the property should be accumulated during the minorities of any of the children. The testator died in 1880. Gladys was born to one of his sons in 1885 and Frederick to another of his sons in 1912. It was argued that it was inadmissible to accumulate the income during these minorities, since the infants were not alive at the testator's death.

The Court of Appeal held that accumulation during both minorities was warranted by the statute. Lord PARKER said:

In my opinion the fourth alternative period covers not only children who are born or *en ventre sa mère* at the death of the settlor, but children who are subsequently born, and I think that the fact that the fourth alternative comes immediately after, and in contrast with, the third alternative, which refers only to born children, and children *en ventre sa mère*, at the time of the death of the settlor, points strongly to this conclusion.[305]

This interpretation necessarily admits of accumulations during successive minorities, and is open to the objection that income may be withdrawn from use for a very considerable time; but, as Challis points out,[306] this latitude of choice is set off by the fact that the minorities chosen must be those of persons who are prospectively entitled to the income.

A settlor sometimes directs an accumulation of income to be made, not for the purpose of dividing the capital among children, but for the purchase of land. It is provided by section 166 of the Law of Property Act 1925,[307] that an accumulation for this particular purpose may be made to endure only for the fourth statutory period.

C Effect of Excessive Accumulation

Where an excessive accumulation has been directed, the effect differs according as the direction violates the general perpetuity period or one of the six statutory periods. A direction for accumulation which transgresses the rule against perpetuities, by designating a period longer than a life or lives in being and twenty-one years afterwards, is void *in toto* and no income can be accumulated;[308] but a direction which, while it exceeds the statutory periods yet keeps within the general perpetuity period, is good *pro tanto*, and is void only in so far as it exceeds the appropriate statutory period.[309] The excess alone is void.[310] So if accumulation is ordered for the life of a person other than the settlor (which is not one of the statutory periods), it will be good for twenty-one years.[311]

---

[304] [1914] 1 Ch 177, M & B p. 416.   [305] Ibid., at 188.

[306] *Law of Real Property* (3rd edn), p. 202.   [307] Re-enacting Accumulations Act 1892.

[308] *Curtis v Lukin* (1842) 5 Beav 147. It seems unfortunate that PAA 1964 left the test of compliance with the perpetuity rule to be governed still by the common law rule. A provision for "wait and see" to be applied in this situation would have been welcome.

[309] What is the appropriate period raises a difficult question of construction that must be determined according to the language of the instrument and the facts of the case: *Re Watt's Will Trusts* [1936] 2 All ER 1555 at 1562, a test described by UPJOHN J as "artificial and difficult": *Re Ransome* [1957] Ch 348 at 361, M & B p. 421.

[310] For the destination of the excessive accumulation, see e.g. *Green v Gascoyne* (1864) 4 De GJ & Sm 565, M & B p. 420; *Theobald on Wills*, para. 44–68.

[311] *Longdon v Simson* (1806) 12 Ves 295; *Griffiths v Vere* (1803) 9 Ves 127. See also *Re Ransome*, supra.

If the person entitled to property under a trust is a minor, there is a statutory power given to the trustees to maintain the minor out of the income, and to accumulate any surplus income during the remainder of the minority.[312] Where, in accordance with the directions of a settlor, income has been accumulated for one of the statutory periods, and at the termination of that period the beneficiary is a minor, so that a further accumulation may be necessary, it is enacted that the two accumulations shall not be counted together and so held to amount to an infringement of the Act.[313]

D Rule in Saunders v Vautier

In the case of instruments taking effect after 15 July 1964, the presumption that no woman over fifty-five years of age can have a child, introduced by the Act of 1964,[314] applies to the right of beneficiaries to put an end to accumulations.[315] That right is defined in *Saunders v Vautier*[316] and later cases and is as follows: Where there is a gift of capital and income to a beneficiary absolutely, but subject to a trust that the income is to be accumulated beyond the time of his majority, he may, on reaching it, stop the accumulation and insist that the capital and accumulated income be paid to him forthwith. Once the property belongs to him absolutely, his free enjoyment of it cannot be fettered. This right, however, will not avail existing beneficiaries if it is possible that further beneficiaries may come into existence, and before 16 July 1964 the possibility that a woman over fifty-five years of age might have children sufficed to exclude the rule in *Saunders v Vautier*.[317]

E Exceptions to the Rule Against Accumulations

Section 164 of the Law of Property Act 1925 sets out certain exceptions to the rule against accumulations.[318] If a settlor directs income to be accumulated for any of the following purposes, the direction will be valid although it may exceed the statutory periods.

(1) Payment of Debts

Provisions for the payment of the debts of any person need not be confined within one of the six periods.[319]

(2) Raising of Portions

Provisions for raising portions for any children or remoter issue of the grantor, settlor or testator, or for any children or remoter issue of a person taking any interest under the settlement, or for a person to whom any interest is thereby limited,[320] are excepted from the Act.[321]

---

[312] Trustee Act, 1925, s. 31.   [313] LPA 1925, s. 165; *Re Maber* [1928] Ch 88.
[314] P. 546, ante.   [315] PAA 1964, s. 14.
[316] (1841) 4 Beav 115; *Wharton v Masterman* [1895] AC 186; Morris and Leach, pp. 289–95; Fourth Report of Law Reform Committee (1956 Cmnd 18) para. 14.   [317] *Re Deloitte* [1926] Ch 56.
[318] Re-enacting Accumulations Act 1800, s. 2.   [319] LPA 1925, s. 164(2)(i).
[320] I.e., the interest need not be carved out of the precise property, the income of which is to be accumulated.
[321] LPA 1925, s. 164(2)(ii).

The reason appears to be that unless such accumulations were permissible, it would be necessary for large owners to sell part of their estates in order to make provision for their younger children; but at the same time it must be recognised that this particular exception admits of a latitude that may be productive, in a great degree, of all the inconveniences that were felt or apprehended under the rules of the common law, because, by a will artfully prepared, every purpose aimed at by Mr Thellusson may be accomplished.[322]

But on the whole the courts have construed this enactment (which repeats the corresponding section of the Thellusson Act) in such a way as to render a flagrant evasion of the spirit of the statute impossible. Thus, an accumulation for the purpose of creating a fund out of which it would be possible to pay portions is not within the exception.[323] Again, an accumulation of the whole of a testator's property with a view to swelling a portions fund has been held void.[324]

As Lord CRANWORTH said, in *Edwards v Tuck*:[325]

a direction to accumulate all a person's property to be handed over to some child or children when they attain twenty-one can never be said to be a direction for raising portions for the child or children; it is not raising a portion at all, it is giving everything. "Portion" ordinarily means a part or a share, and although I do not know that a gift of a whole might not, in some circumstances, come under the term of a gift of a portion, yet I do not think it comes within the meaning of a portion in this clause of the Act which points to the raising of something out of something else for the benefit of some children or class of children . . . If every direction for accumulation for a child was a portion, the intention of the Legislature, which was to prevent accumulations, such accumulations being most frequently directed for the benefit of children, would be entirely defeated.

(3) Timber or Wood

The Act does not apply to any provision respecting the accumulation of the produce of timber or wood.[326]

The probable explanation of this exception is that timber is not usually regarded as annual income, but merely as a resource for some particular occasion, so that a direction concerning its accumulation, provided that it conforms to the rule against perpetuities,[327] does not in effect withdraw income from the owner of the estate.[328]

V Law Reform

In 1998 the Law Commission published a Report on the Rules against Perpetuities and Excessive Accumulations.[329] It recommends[330] that the application of the rule against perpetuities should be restricted to interests and rights arising under wills and trusts. The rule

[322] Fearne, *Contingent Remainders*, p. 541, note by Preston.
[323] *Re Bourne's Settlement Trusts* [1946] 1 All ER 411.　　[324] *Wildes v Davies* (1853) 1 Sm & G 475.
[325] (1853) 3 De GM & G 40 at 58.　　[326] LPA 1925, s. 164(2)(iii).
[327] *Ferrand v Wilson* (1845) 4 Hare 344.　　[328] Fearne, *Contingent Remainders*, p. 537, Butler's note.
[329] Law Com No. 251; (1988) 12 TLI 148 (P. Sparkes)
[330] Law Commission Thirty-Third Annual Report 1998 (Law Com No. 258), para. 5.9. See the Consultation Paper 1993 (Law Com No. 133); (1994) 57 MLR 602 (C. T. Emery); [1994] Conv 92 (H. W. Wilkinson); [1995] Conv 212 (P. Sparkes)

would not apply to rights over property such as options, rights of first refusal or future easements created after any legislation was brought into force. All pension schemes would be exempted from the application of the rule.[331] The circumstances in which the rule would apply would be set out in clear statutory form, and there would be one fixed perpetuity period of 125 years. A future interest or right would be void for perpetuity only when it became clear that it would not take effect within 125 years from the date on which the instrument creating it took effect. The rule against excessive accumulations would be abolished except in relation to charitable trusts.[8] The only restriction on accumulations would be the 125-year perpetuity period.

The effect of the proposals, if enacted, is that for many years to come there will co-exist three different rules against perpetuities for instruments made:

(a) prior to the coming into force of the 1964 Act;

(b) after the coming into force of that Act but before the recommended reforms are implemented; and

(c) after the coming into force of those reforms.

The Government accepted the proposals in March 2001, but they have not yet been implemented.[332]

It would have been simpler to have abolished the rule against perpetuities altogether, but it was thought that there must be a saving for vested rights; and that that saving could not be achieved simply or accomplished fairly.

---

[331] See *Air Jamaica Ltd v Charlton* [1999] 1 WLR 1399, where the Law Commission's analysis was expressly approved.

[332] The Lord Chancellor's Department issued a consultation paper in September 2002 on the partial implementation of the Report (on accumulations) by way of a Regulatory Reform Order, but no progress was made at that stage. In January 2006, however, a Legislative and Regulatory Reform Bill was introduced into Parliament which, if enacted, will replace the existing procedures for Regulatory Reform Orders under the Regulatory Reform Act 2001, and will allow a Minister to implement by Statutory Instrument recommendations of the Law Commission, with or without changes, as long as certain preconditions are met. The Law Commission Report on Rules against Perpetuities and Excessive Accumulations 1998 (Law Com No. 251) has been identified as containing recommendations which would be suitable for implementation under this procedure: Notes on the Bill, produced by the Cabinet Office.

17

DETERMINABLE INTERESTS AND INTERESTS UPON CONDITION SUBSEQUENT

SUMMARY

I Determinable Interests

A *Definition and Terminology*

A determinable interest is one that may come to an end before the completion of the maximum period designated by the grantor. For instance, the first clause in a deed of settlement, made by a man in view of his approaching marriage, would typically provide that the settlor shall hold the land in trust for himself in fee simple *until the solemnisation of the intended marriage*. In such a case the maximum interest taken by the settlor is a fee simple, but it is a modified, not an absolute fee, since it will not run its full course if the terminating event—the marriage—supervenes:

A *direct* limitation marks the duration of estate by the life of a person; by the continuance of heirs; by a space of precise and measured time; making the death of the person in the first example; the continuance of heirs in the second example; and the length of the given space in the third example, the boundary of the estate or the period of duration.

A *collateral* [i.e. determinable] limitation, at the same time that it gives an interest which may have continuance for one of the times, in a direct limitation, may, on some event which it describes, put an end to the right of enjoyment *during the continuance of that time*.[1]

---

[1] *Preston on Estates*, vol. i. p. 42, cited Challis, *Law of Real Property*, pp. 252–3.

Much confusion of terminology is apparent among the writers on this subject. Thus Preston, in the above quotation, speaks of *collateral* limitations; Littleton describes the terminating event as a *condition in law*, while most of the other early writers adopt the expression *conditional limitations*. The words *collateral* and *conditional*, however, besides being obscure, are used in many different senses, and the modern practice is to describe this particular species of modified interest as a determinable interest, and the limitation by which it is created as a determinable limitation.[2]

B Determinable Fee Simple

The older writers deal fully with determinable fees simple, and the classic example is that given by Blackstone, who states that the effect of a grant to A and his heirs, *tenants of the manor of Dale*, is to give A and his heirs a fee simple which will be defeated as soon as they cease to be tenants of that manor.

In such a case there resides in the grantor and his heirs a *possibility of reverter*,[3] since there is a possibility that the terminating event will occur and so cause the estate to revert.[4]

Another example of a determinable fee is afforded by *Re Leach*,[5] where freeholds were devised: "upon trust to pay the rents to Robert until he should assign, charge or otherwise dispose of the same, or become bankrupt". It was held that Robert took an equitable fee simple which would determine if one of the specified events occurred in his lifetime, but which would become absolute if he died without their having occurred.

Determinable fees, however, disappeared from practical conveyancing (and gave way to shifting future estates operating under the Statute of Uses) when it was once decided that the fee simple in the case of a determinable limitation could not be made to pass to a stranger on the occurrence of the terminating event. The common law has never allowed a fee to be limited after a fee simple. As was said by Lord CAIRNS in *The Buckhurst Peerage Case*:[6] "There is no instance in the books that we are aware of in which a fee simple, or a fee tail qualified in the way that I have mentioned, as by the addition of the words 'lords of the manor of Dale', is followed by a remainder to other persons upon the first takers ceasing to be lords of the manor." Thus at the present day, if it is desired to make a fee simple pass from the grantee to some other person when a given event does or does not happen, the limitation will take the form of the grant of an equitable future interest.

(1) Settled Land

The uncertain duration of a determinable fee does not impede its effective disposition. If it was created before 1997, the instrument by which it is limited constitutes a settlement for the purposes of the Settled Land Act 1925;[7] the person entitled to possession is a tenant for life, and as such he may convey the land by way of sale, mortgage or lease under his statutory powers.[8] When a person is granted a determinable fee after 1996, the land is held on trust under the Trusts of Land and Appointment of Trustees Act 1996, with the grantor as trustee.[9]

---

[2] Challis, pp. 253–4.   [3] Blackstone, vol. ii. p. 109.   [4] Co Litt 18a.   [5] [1912] 2 Ch 422.
[6] (1876) 2 App Cas 1 at 23.   [7] S.1(1)(ii)(c); p. 401, ante.   [8] Pp. 409 et seq, ante.
[9] TLATA 1996, s. 25(1), Sch. 3, para. 2(1), (2), excluding a fee simple absolute within LPA 1925, s. 7, p. 169, ante.

(2) *Rule against Perpetuities*

The matter aroused considerable controversy, but, in one case it was decided that the possibility of reverter arising on the grant of a determinable fee simple was subject to the rule against perpetuities.[10] This view was adopted by the Perpetuities and Accumulations Act 1964.[11] Thus, if the terminating event in fact occurs within the perpetuity period (i.e. twenty-one years, unless the instrument of creation refers to lives in being or specifies a fixed period of years not exceeding eighty), the reverter will take effect by virtue of the "wait and see" provisions of the Act. Otherwise, it will be void and the determinable fee will become absolute.[12]

(3) *Resulting Trust*

An interest analogous to a possibility of reverter arises where a testator gives *personalty* to trustees upon trust to pay the income to a corporation or other body until some event occurs that may not occur within the perpetuity period. In such a case, the occurrence of the event raises a resulting trust in favour of the person entitled to the undisposed residue of the testator's estate. Formerly, a resulting trust of this nature was exempt from the rule against perpetuities,[13] but it has been subjected to the rule by the Act of 1964.[14]

C *Determinable Life Interest*

There may be a limitation of a determinable *life* interest:

> If a man grant an estate to a woman *dum sola fuit*, or *durante viduitate*, or *quamdiu se bene gesserit*, or to a man and a woman during the coverture, or so long as such a grantee dwell in such a house, . . . or for any like incertaine time, which time, as Bracton saith, is *tempus indeterminatum*: in all these cases if it be of lands or tenements, the lessee hath in judgment of law an estate for life determinable.[15]

The *protective trust* is a common example of a determinable life interest. Its basis is a life interest subject to an executory gift over upon the happening of a certain event such as bankruptcy or attempted alienation. The gift over may be in favour of other members of the family, but today it is more commonly in favour of trustees to hold upon discretionary trusts for a class which includes the tenant for life and members of his family; and the latter is the basis of the protective trust adopted by section 33 of the Trustee Act 1925. It is now common practice, in drafting settlements, to give a protected life interest to a beneficiary, especially if the beneficiary is a minor, or if there is some doubt as to the beneficiary's financial stability. The protected life interest is followed by discretionary trusts stating how the trustees may deal with the income of the property if the interest of the beneficiary is determined. These trusts were formerly set out in detail, but this is no longer necessary, for section 33 enacts that a mere declaration directing income to be held on *protective trusts* shall confer certain

---

[10]   *Hopper v Liverpool Corpn* (1943) 88 SJ 213 (limitation of a house in fee simple so long as it shall be used as a news room and coffee room). On the subject generally, see Morris and Leach, *The Rule against Perpetuities*, pp. 209–18.   [11]   S. 12(1)(a).

[12]   Law Reform Committee Fourth Report 1956 (Cmnd 18), para. 39.

[13]   *Re Randell* (1888) 38 Ch D 213; *Re Blunt's Trusts* [1904] 2 Ch 767; *Re Chardon* [1928] Ch 464; *Re Chambers' Will Trusts* [1950] Ch 267.   [14]   S. 12(1)(b).

[15]   Co Litt 42a.

discretionary powers upon the trustees.[16] The statutory effect of using the expression is that the interest of the beneficiary automatically determines if he or she attempts to alienate or charge it or if he becomes bankrupt,[17] and the trustees at their discretion may apply the income during the rest of his life for the maintenance or support, or otherwise for the benefit, of any one or more of the following persons: the spouse or civil partner, and the children or remoter issue of the beneficiary, or, if there is no spouse or civil partner or issue, the persons who, if the beneficiary were dead, would be entitled to the trust property or its income.

In cases of a determinable life interest the grantee takes an interest that may endure for life, or may determine sooner by the occurrence of the terminating event. It differs from a determinable fee in that it may be followed by a gift over to a third party which may validly take effect when the event occurs.[18]

D Determinable Term of Years

Lastly, a *term of years* may be made determinable upon the happening of some uncertain event before the period of the term has expired.

As Lord TEMPLEMAN said in *Prudential Assurance Co Ltd v London Residuary Body*:[19]

A lease can be made for five years subject to the tenant's right to determine if the war ends before the expiry of five years. A lease can be made from year to year subject to a fetter on the right of the landlord to determine the lease before the expiry of five years unless the war ends. Both leases are valid because they create a determinable certain term of five years.

II Interests upon Condition Subsequent

A General Nature and Effect

(1) Definition

An interest upon condition subsequent arises where a qualification is annexed to a conveyance, whereby it is provided that, in case a particular event does or does not happen, or in case the grantor or the grantee does or omits to do a particular act, the interest shall be defeated.[20] Examples of such interests taken from the Law Reports are:

grant to trustees in fee simple on condition that, if the land granted shall ever be used for other than hospital purposes, it shall revert to the heirs of the grantor;[21]

---

[16] Amended by Civil Partnership Act 2004, s. 261(1), Sch. 27, para. 6. See generally H & M, chap. 7; Snell, paras. 20–52 to 20–55; (1957) 21 Conv (NS) 110; 323 (L. A. Sheridan).

[17] If, by virtue of a power contained in the settlement, the husband makes an advancement to an infant beneficiary, this is a disposition that will cause his life interest to be forfeited: *Re Shaw's Settlement* [1951] Ch 833.

[18] Blackstone, vol. ii. p. 155.   [19] [1992] 2 AC 386 at 395; p. 211, ante.

[20] Litt s. 325; Cruise, *Digest*, Tit. xiii. c. 1. This must be distinguished from a condition *precedent* where the qualification provides that the interest will not *commence* until the occurrence of some event, e.g., a grant to A if he becomes a barrister; p. 513, ante.

[21] *Re Hollis' Hospital Trustees and Hague's Contract* [1899] 2 Ch 540.

devise in fee simple to the council of a school on condition that the council shall publish annually a statement of payments and receipts;[22]

devise of land to J "on condition that he never sells out of the family";[23]

devise to A for life provided that he makes the mansion-house his usual common place of abode and residence;[24]

devise to A for life on condition that he assumes the name and arms of the testator within 12 months.[25]

In all cases of this type there vests in the grantor, his heirs and assignees a right of re-entry, the exercise of which determines the estate of the grantee.

In principle, therefore, a fee simple subject to a condition subsequent should be classified as an equitable interest, not as a legal estate, for since it may be defeated by a re-entry before its full course is run it can scarcely be described as "absolute". Nevertheless, for reasons already explained,[26] it has been given the status of a legal estate by the Law of Property (Amendment) Act 1926,[27] in words that are wide enough to include any right of re-entry. They state that:

a fee simple subject to a legal or equitable right of entry or re-entry is for the purposes of [the Law of Property Act 1925] a fee simple absolute.

In registered land, such a fee simple is capable of registration and the right of entry must be noted on the register.[28]

(2) Distinction between Interest upon Condition and Determinable Interest

There is a fundamental and somewhat subtle distinction[29] between limitations upon condition and determinable limitations. Some writers contend that the distinction is a mere matter of words. On this basis the effect of such expressions as *until, so long as, whilst, during,* is to create a determinable interest; while such phrases as *on condition that, provided that, if, but if it happen that,*[30] will raise an interest upon condition.

But the distinction goes deeper than this. We must differentiate between a limitation properly so called, and a condition.

A limitation is a form of words which creates an estate and denotes its extent by designating the event upon which it is to commence and the time for which it is to endure.[31] It marks the utmost time for which the estate can continue. It appears in two forms. A direct limitation marks the time by denoting the size of the estate in familiar terms, e.g. by using

---

22 *Re Da Costa* [1912] 1 Ch 337.   23 *Re Macleay* (1875) LR 20 Eq 186.

24 *Wynne v Fletcher* (1857) 24 Beav 430.   25 *Re Evans's Contract* [1920] 2 Ch 469.

26 P. 169, ante.   27 LPA 1925, s. 7(1) as amended by LP(A)A 1926, Sched.; M & B p. 7, n. 4.

28 R & R, para. 7.004; an expressly granted legal right of entry must be completed by registration: LRA 2002, s. 27(1), (2)(e), (4), Sch. 2, para. 7; an equitable right of entry will need to be protected by a notice in the register if it is to have priority over a registrable disposition made for valuable consideration: ibid., s. 29.

29 It has been referred to as "extremely artificial" by PENNYCUICK V-C in *Re Sharp's Settlement Trusts* [1973] Ch 331 at 340, M & B p. 23; and as "little short of disgraceful to our jurisprudence" by PORTER MR in *Re King's Trusts* (1892) 29 LR IR 401 at 410.

30 See Sanders, *Uses and Trusts*, vol. i. p. 156; *Sheppard's Touchstone*, 122; *Bacon's New Abridgement*, under the title Condition (A); Challis, *Law of Real Property*, p. 283.

31 *Sheppard's Touchstone*, 117; Blackstone, vol. ii. p. 155; *Preston on Estates*, vol. i. p. 40.

such expressions as "for life" or "in fee simple"; a determinable limitation gives an interest for one of the times possible in a direct limitation, but also denotes some event that may determine the estate during the continuance of that time. In the simple example of a grant to A and his heirs, tenants of the manor of Dale, the terminating event is incorporated in, and forms an essential part of, the whole limitation, and if the estate expires because the tenancy of Dale is no longer in A's family, it is none the less considered to have lasted for the period originally fixed by the limitation. So in general the province of a limitation is to fix the period for the commencement and the duration of an estate, and to mark its determinable qualities.[32]

A condition, on the other hand, specifies some event which, if it takes place during the time for which an estate has already been limited to continue, will defeat that estate: "And here is condition, because there is not a new estate limited over but the estate to which it is annexed is destroyed."[33]

In short, if the terminating event is an integral and necessary part of the formula from which the size of the interest is to be ascertained, the result is the creation of a determinable interest; but if the terminating event is external to the limitation, if it is a divided clause from the grant, the interest granted is an interest upon condition.[34]

(3) Effect of Distinction

Outwardly a condition resembles a determinable limitation, for the difference between a grant:

to a woman for life, but if she remarries then her life interest shall cease,

and a grant:

to a woman during widowhood,

is not apparent at first sight. The natural inference is that the legal effect must be the same in each case. Nevertheless, certain practical distinctions between the two limitations existed at common law and to a diminished degree still exist.[35] The present position appears to be as follows.

(a) Determination

A determinable interest comes to an end automatically upon the occurrence of the terminating event, as for example upon the remarriage of a woman to whom an estate has been granted during her widowhood. This is inevitable, for according to the limitation itself, that is, according to the words fixing the space of time for which the widow's right of enjoyment is to continue, her interest ceases with her remarriage and nothing remains to be done to defeat her right. There can, indeed, be no question of defeating what has already come to an end.[36]

[32] Fearne, *Contingent Remainders*, p. 11, Butler's note.
[33] *Serjeant Rudhall's Case* (1586) Sav 76, cited *Re Hollis' Hospital Trustees and Hague's Contract* [1899] 2 Ch 540 at 549.
[34] Fearne, p. 11, note (h); vol. ii. s. 36 (Smith, *An Original View of Executory Interests*); Challis, *Law of Real Property*, p. 260.
[35] "Although in some respects a condition and a limitation may have the same effect, yet in English law there is a great distinction between them": *Re Moore* (1888) 39 Ch D 116 at 129, per COTTON LJ.
[36] *Preston on Estates*, vol. i. p. 47; Challis, *Law of Real Property*, p. 219; *Re Evans's Contract* [1920] 2 Ch 469 at 472.

The effect of a condition operating by way of re-entry, on the other hand, is to defeat an interest *before* it has reached the end of the period for which it has been limited. The interest becomes voidable upon the breach of the condition. It does not become void unless and until the grantor, his heir or assignee re-enters upon the land.[37]

(b) Rule against perpetuities

The rule against perpetuities applies both to conditions subsequent and to a possibility of reverter arising on the grant of a determinable fee.

The position as regards common law conditions was established long before the rule came into existence, and the old authorities never doubted that a right of entry was enforceable at any distance of time by the grantor or his heirs.[38] But, after several dicta in favour of subjecting conditions to the rule,[39] the point was finally decided to that effect[40] and was later confirmed by the Law of Property Act 1925.[41]

As we have already seen, a possibility of reverter appertaining to a determinable fee simple has been subjected to the rule by the Perpetuities and Accumulations Act 1964.[42]

(c) Assignability

At common law, a right of entry affecting a fee simple was neither devisable nor alienable *inter vivos*, and availed only the grantor and his heirs.[43] This, however, is no longer the position. The Wills Act 1837 allows a testator to devise "all rights for condition broken and other rights of entry",[44] and the Law of Property Act 1925 deals with their assignment *inter vivos* by providing that: "All rights and interests in land may be disposed of, including—a right of entry into or upon land whether immediate or future, and whether vested or contingent."[45]

Whether a possibility of reverter is on the same footing in both these respects is not so clear. It has, indeed, been held that it may be disposed of by a testator since it is covered by the words of the Wills Act cited above.[46] But its assignment *inter vivos* presents some difficulty. In the view of the common law, what was left in the grantor of a determinable interest was not an estate but a possibility that he might acquire an estate at a future time. Such a *bare possibility*, as it was called, was not assignable at common law,[47] but it seems a reasonable assumption that it now falls within the wide language quoted above from the Law of Property Act 1925.

(d) Void conditions

As will be seen in the next section, a condition attached to any limitation of property may prove to be void for a variety of reasons. A condition subsequent that is thus invalidated is

---

[37] Co Litt 218a. At common law, the seisin transferred by livery cannot be divested without its actual resumption by re-entry: Co Litt 214b. [38] Challis, *Law of Real Property*, pp. 187 et seq.

[39] *Re Macleay* (1875) LR 20 Eq 186; *London and South Western Rly Co v Gomm* (1882) 20 Ch D 562 at 582; *Dunn v Flood* (1883) 25 Ch D 629.

[40] *Re Hollis' Hospital Trustees and Hague's Contract* [1899] 2 Ch 540; *Re Da Costa* [1912] 1 Ch 337. A contrary view was expressed by PALLES CB in *A-G v Cummins* [1906] 1 IR 406, and his view has prevailed in Northern Ireland: *Walsh v Wightman* [1927] NI 1. [41] S. 4(3).

[42] S. 12(1)(a); p. 558, ante. [43] Fearne, *Contingent Remainders*, Butler's note, p. 381. [44] S. 3.

[45] LPA 1925, s. 4(2)(b).

[46] *Pemberton v Barnes* [1899] 1 Ch 544, where it was held that the possibility of reverter arising upon the grant of a determinable fee in copyholds was within the Act.

[47] As to the three different meanings of the word *possibility*, see Challis, *Law of Real Property*, p. 76, note.

totally cancelled, and the limitation takes effect as if it had not been imposed;[48] but a determinable interest fails altogether if the possibility of reverter is invalidated, for to treat it as absolute would be to alter its quantum as fixed by the limitation.[49]

(e) Interest followed by remainder

At common law, a remainder might be limited to take effect after a determinable life estate, but not after a life estate that was defeasible by a condition subsequent. If, for instance, there were a feoffment:

to A during widowhood and then to B for life,

the remainder to B was valid, since by force of the limitation itself it took effect upon the natural determination of the particular estate. But had the limitation been:

to A, a widow, for life on condition that if she remarried then to B for life,

B's remainder would have come into conflict with three rules of ancient origin: a remainder was not allowed to cut short a particular estate;[50] none but the grantor and his heirs could exercise a right of re-entry; and in any event, the effect of re-entry was to defeat all the estates that depended upon the original livery of seisin.[51]

The matter has long been of only historical interest, for a settlor, minded to impose such a condition upon a widow's interest, could at an early date frame his limitation as a shifting use, and can now effect the same result by way of a future interest under a trust.

B Void Conditions

There are three types of conditions subsequent that are void when annexed to the grant of an estate or interest.

(1) Conditions Repugnant to the Interest Granted[52]

A condition that is repugnant to the interest to which it is annexed is absolutely void.[53] For instance, a condition attached to the grant of a fee simple that the grantee shall always let the land at a definite rent, or cultivate it in a certain manner or be deprived of all power of sale, is void on the ground of its incompatibility with that complete freedom of enjoyment, disposition and management that the law attributes to the ownership of such an estate.[54] It is not permissible to grant an interest and then to provide that the incidents attached to it by law shall be excluded. The most important examples of repugnant conditions that arise in practice are those designed to prohibit alienation or to exclude the operation of the bankruptcy laws.

---

[48] *Re Wilkinson* [1926] Ch 842 at 846; *Re Croxon* [1904] 1 Ch 252. If the illegal condition is *precedent*, the gift fails entirely.

[49] *Re Moore* (1888) 39 Ch D 116. If, however, a possibility of reverter or a condition subsequent is void under the rule against perpetuities, the interest of the grantee becomes absolute: PAA 1964, s. 12.

[50] P. 514, ante.

[51] Fearne, *Contingent Remainders*, pp. 261–2, 381, note; *Preston on Estates*, vol. i. pp. 50 et seq.

[52] For a trenchant criticism of this doctrine, see (1943) 59 LQR 343 (G L Williams).

[53] *Re Dugdale* (1888) 38 Ch D 176; *Bradley v Peixoto* (1797) 3 Ves 324.

[54] *Jarman on Wills* (8th edn), p. 1477.

(a) *Conditions against alienation*

(1) TOTAL RESTRAINTS

In accordance with the cardinal principle that the power of alienation is necessarily and inseparably incidental to ownership, it has been held in a long line of decisions that if an *absolute* interest is given to a donee—whether it be a fee simple, a fee tail, a life interest or any other interest, and whether it be in possession or *in futuro*—any restriction which *substantially* takes that power away is void as being repugnant to the very conception of ownership.[55] Therefore, a condition[56] that the donee:

shall not alienate at all;[57] or

shall not alienate during a particular time, such as the life of a certain person,[58] or during his own life;[59] or

shall alienate only to one particular person,[60] or to a small and diminishing class of persons, such as to one of his three brothers;[61]

or shall not adopt some particular mode of assurance such as a mortgage,[62] or shall not bar an entail,[63]

is void.

(2) PARTIAL RESTRAINTS

A restraint that is partial, however, and which therefore does not substantially deprive the owner in fee of his power of alienation, is valid. Thus it has been held that a condition is valid which restrains the owner from alienating to a specified person[64] or to anyone except a particular class of persons, provided, however, that the class is not too restricted.[65] But when does a restraint cease to be total? In the case of *Re Macleay*,[66] where there was a devise:

to my brother J on the condition that he never sells out of the family,

the condition was held by JESSEL MR to be valid, though some doubt has been thrown on the correctness of this decision by a later case.[67]

The difficulty, indeed, is to ascertain the principle upon which such restraints have been permitted, for they would seem to be just as repugnant to ownership as a total restraint.

---

⁵⁵ Cf the position of a tenant for life under SLA 1925 the exercise of whose powers cannot be prohibited or limited, s. 106; p. 417, ante. But restraints even of a general nature may be valid in the case of a determinable interest: *Re Dugdale*, supra; *Re Leach* [1912] 2 Ch 422; p. 567, ante; and this is the basis of the protected life interest under TA 1925, s. 33; p. 568, ante.

⁵⁶ But a *covenant* against alienation is not repugnant: *Caldy Manor Estate Ltd v Farrell* [1974] 1 WLR 1303.

⁵⁷ Litt, s. 360; Co Litt 206b, 223a; *Re Dugdale*, supra.   ⁵⁸ *Re Rosher* (1884) 26 Ch D 801.

⁵⁹ *Corbett v Corbett* (1888) 14 PD 7.

⁶⁰ *Muschamp v Bluet* (1617) J Bridg 132; *Re Cockerill* [1929] 2 Ch 131.

⁶¹ *Re Brown* [1954] Ch 39, M & B p. 9.   ⁶² *Ware v Cann* (1830) 10 B & C 433.

⁶³ *Mildmay's Case* (1605) 6 Co Rep 40a; *Mary Portington's Case* (1613) 10 Co Rep 35b; *Dawkins v Lord Penrhyn* (1878) 4 App Cas 51.   ⁶⁴ Co Litt 223a.

⁶⁵ *Doe d Gill v Pearson* (1805) 6 East 173 ("except to four sisters or their children"). But racial discrimination in the disposal of property is made unlawful by the Race Relations Act 1976, s. 21. See also Sex Discrimination Act 1975, s. 30; Disability Discrimination Act 1995, s. 22   ⁶⁶ (1875) LR 20 Eq 186.

⁶⁷ *Re Rosher* (1884) 26 Ch D 801. But the restriction was placed only on a sale, and it was to endure only for the life of J. See too *Re Brown* [1954] Ch 39; (1954) 70 LQR 15 (R.E.M.).

Perhaps the truth is that the courts, losing sight of the fundamental doctrine of repugnancy, have, unintentionally and unwittingly, allowed the necessities of public policy to engraft certain exceptions on the main rule.[68]

(b) Conditions excluding operation of bankruptcy laws

Just as the donee of property cannot be deprived of the normal rights of ownership, so also is it impossible to render his interest immune from involuntary alienation for insolvency or bankruptcy.[69] It is not permissible, for instance, to annex to the grant of a life interest a condition that it shall not be liable to seizure for debt. Thus in *Graves v Dolphin*:[70]

a testator directed his trustees to pay £500 a year to his son for life, and declared that it should not on any account be subject or liable to the debts, engagements, charges or incumbrances of his son, but that it should always be payable to him and to no other person. The son became bankrupt, and it was held that the annuity became the property of his creditors.

But, as we have seen in discussing the protective trust,[71] there is no objection to the grant by one person to another of an interest which is to determine upon the bankruptcy of the grantee. Lord ELDON, adverting to the distinction between a determinable limitation and a limitation upon condition, made this clear over 190 years ago:

A disposition to a man until he shall become bankrupt, and after his bankruptcy over, is quite different from an attempt to give to him for his life, with a proviso that he shall not sell or alien it. *If that condition is so expressed as to amount to a limitation*, reducing the interest short of a life interest, neither the man nor his assignees can have it beyond the period limited.[72]

The distinction at first sight seems fine and far from obvious, but in fact it is fundamental. In one case the only interest passing under the limitation is an interest *until* the donee becomes bankrupt; in the other, an absolute interest is first limited for life, and then an attempt is made to remove one of the incidents, namely liability for debts, to which all absolute interests are subject.

Thus, if husband and wife both bring property into a marriage settlement, the wife's property may be limited to the husband until he becomes bankrupt and then over to the trustees. But the husband cannot settle his own property upon himself in the same manner, for this would be a fraud on the bankruptcy laws.[73] On the other hand, it has long been recognised that a settlor may protect himself against other forms of alienation, voluntary and involuntary. Thus a man may settle his own property upon himself until he attempts to assign, charge or incumber it, or until he does something that makes it liable to be taken in execution by a particular creditor, and if so over to another person. The limitation over, once it has taken effect, is not avoided by the subsequent bankruptcy of the settlor.[74]

---

[68] *Re Rosher* (1884) 26 Ch D 801 at 813.

[69] *Re Machu* (1882) 21 Ch D 838; *Re Dugdale* (1888) 38 Ch D 176.   [70] (1826) 1 Sim 66.

[71] P. 568, ante.

[72] *Brandon v Robinson* (1811) 18 Ves 429 at 432, 433–4; *Re The Trusts of the Scientific Investment Pension Plan* [1999] Ch 53. See TA 1925, s. 33, as to these protected life interests; pp. 568–9, ante.

[73] *Mackintosh v Pogose* [1895] 1 Ch 505 at 511; *Re Brewer's Settlement* [1896] 2 Ch 503; *Re Burroughs-Fowler* [1916] 2 Ch 251. This principle is retained by TA 1925, s. 33(3).

[74] *Brooke v Pearson* (1859) 27 Beav 181; *Re Detmold* (1889) 40 Ch D 585.

(2) Conditions Contrary to Public Policy

Any condition which has a tendency to conflict with the general interest of the community, even though it will not necessarily do so, is void.[75]

The following categories include the types of condition which most frequently occur.

(a) *Conditions in restraint of marriage*

The law as to the validity of conditions in restraint of marriage differs according as the gift is of real or of personal property.

(1) PERSONALTY

The rules governing personalty have come to us from the Roman Law through the ecclesiastical courts and the Court of Chancery. They are marked by numerous and fine distinctions, and in the words of a learned judge are "proverbially difficult";[76] but it is sufficient for our purposes to say that a condition in total restraint of marriage is void, while one in partial restraint is good, provided that it is reasonable from the point of view of public policy.[77]

For instance, a condition that a person shall not marry a named person,[78] a Papist,[79] a Scotchman,[80] or a domestic servant[81] is valid, but a condition that he shall not marry at all is void. But a partial restraint is not upheld unless there is a bequest over to another person in default of compliance with the condition. In the absence of such a bequest, the condition is treated as ineffectual on the ground that it has merely been imposed *in terrorem*, that is, as an idle threat calculated to secure compliance by the donee.[82] A condition, however, is valid which restrains a *second* marriage, either of a man or of a woman.[83] Similarly, a condition requiring consent to marriage is not invalid.[84]

(2) REALTY

The rules relating to real estate, on the other hand, are both few and simple. While a condition in general restraint of marriage if attached to a gift of personalty is void *per se*, in the case of realty it is not void *per se*, but only if there is an intention to promote celibacy. Thus in *Jones v Jones*[85] a man devised land to three women during their lifetime, and added:

> provided the said Mary . . . shall remain in her present state of single woman, otherwise . . . if she shall bind herself in wedlock, she is liable to lose her share of the said property immediately, and her share to be possessed and enjoyed by the other mentioned parties, share and share alike.

---

[75] *Egerton v Earl Brownlow* (1853) 4 HL Cas 1; *Re Wallace* [1920] 2 Ch 274.

[76] *Re Hewett* [1918] 1 Ch 458 at 463, per YOUNGER J.

[77] *Re Lanyon* [1927] 2 Ch 264. A determinable gift, however, is valid: *Re Lovell* [1920] 1 Ch 122.

[78] *Re Bathe* [1925] Ch 377.   [79] *Duggan v Kelly* (1848) 10 I Eq R 473.

[80] *Perrin v Lyon* (1807) 9 East 170.

[81] *Jenner v Turner* (1880) 16 Ch D 188. It is not certain, however, whether this example and those given in the preceding two notes would nowadays be treated as void for uncertainty; see, pp. 579–80, post.

[82] *Re Whiting's Settlement* [1905] 1 Ch 96; *Re Hewett* [1918] 1 Ch 458; *Leong v Chye* [1955] AC 648.

[83] *Allen v Jackson* (1875) 1 Ch D 399.   [84] *Re Whiting's Settlement*, supra.   [85] (1876) 1 QBD 279.

It was held that the condition was valid since its object was not to prevent her from marrying but to provide for her whilst unmarried.[86]

The *in terrorem* doctrine does not apply to realty,[87] and it may be said that a condition in partial restraint of marriage attached to real estate is always good,[88] and that one in total restraint *may* be good. However, a general restraint cannot be imposed upon a tenant in tail, since it is incompatible with and repugnant to an interest that is expressly made descendible to the heirs born of the marriage of the donee.[89]

(b) Conditions encouraging separation and divorce

Similarly conditions designed to encourage the separation or divorce of a married couple are invalid as being contrary to public policy;[90] but where the parties are already separated, a limitation to a woman with a condition that the interest shall cease if she and her husband live together again, is valid as constituting a maintenance of the wife while she is unprovided for, unless there is evidence showing that the donor's object is to induce her not to return to her husband.[91]

(c) Conditions affecting parental duties

A condition designed to separate a parent from his child, even where the parents are divorced, is contrary to public policy:[92] likewise a condition designed to interfere with the performance of parental duties.[93] But the operation of this principle was restricted by the House of Lords in *Blathwayt v Lord Cawley*,[94] where a condition which divested property if a child became a Roman Catholic was argued to be void on the ground that it would hamper parental duties in religious instructions. This argument was rejected by Lord WILBERFORCE: "To say that any condition which in any way might affect or influence the way in which a child is brought up, or in which parental duties are exercised, seems to me to state far too wide a rule".

(d) Conditions restricting freedom of religion

Conditions restricting the beneficiaries' freedom of religion have frequently been encountered. Sometimes they have failed on the ground of uncertainty,[95] but they have never been held to be contrary to public policy.[96] In *Blathwayt v Baron Cawley*[97] the House of Lords held

---

[86] As to the admissibility of any evidence of the donor's intention, see *Re Johnson's Will Trusts* [1967] Ch 387.

[87] *Jenner v Turner* (1880) 16 Ch D 188 at 196, per BACON V-C.   [88] *Re Bathe* [1925] Ch 377.

[89] *Earl of Arundel's Case* (1575) 3 Dyer 342b.

[90] *Re Moore* (1888) 39 Ch D 116; distinguished *Re Thompson* [1939] 1 All ER 681; *Re Caborne* [1943] Ch 224; *Re Johnson's Will Trusts* [1967] Ch 387; *Re Hepplewhite's Will Trusts* The Times, 21 January 1977.

[91] See *Re Lovell* [1920] 1 Ch 122.

[92] *Re Sandbrook* [1912] 2 Ch 471 (condition held void which divested property if the donees "should live with or be or continue under the custody, guardianship or control of their father"). See also *Re Piper* [1946] 2 All ER 503.

[93] *Re Borwick* [1933] Ch 657 (condition held void which divested a gift if the infant donee during minority became a Roman Catholic, for this tended to influence the parent in the discharge of his duty of religious instruction). But see now *Blathwayt v Baron Cawley* [1976] AC 397.   [94] Supra.

[95] *Clayton v Ramsden* [1943] AC 320, p. 579, post. The Race Relations Act 1976 does not apply to religion as such, although the position of the Jewish religion is unclear. See Race Relations Board First Annual Report. A condition relating to Jewish parentage was considered racial in *Clayton v Ramsden*.

[96] Even in the case of charitable trusts. See *Re Lysaght* [1966] Ch 191, where discrimination against Jews and Roman Catholics was merely "undesirable".   [97] [1976] AC 397.

that a condition in a will under which a beneficiary would forfeit his interest if he should "be or become a Roman Catholic" was not invalid. Although conceptions of public policy move with the times, it is not against public policy for an adherent of one religion to distinguish in disposing of his property. To invalidate such conditions would go far beyond the mere avoidance of discrimination on religious grounds:

To do so would bring about a substantial reduction of another freedom, firmly rooted in our law, namely that of testamentary disposition. Discrimination is not the same thing as choice: it operates over a larger and less personal area, and neither by express provision nor by implication has private selection yet become a matter of public policy.[98]

(e) Conditions affecting race

The Race Relations Act 1976 has no application to conditions imposed by settlors and testators. There is little authority on the point, which has mainly arisen in connection with charitable trusts, but it appears that it is not contrary to public policy for a settlor to discriminate on these grounds.[99]

(f) Other conditions

We have seen that any condition having a tendency to conflict with the general interest of the community is void. Thus in *Egerton v Earl Brownlow*[100] lands were devised to Lord Alford for ninety-nine years if he should so long live, and then to the heirs male of his body, with a proviso that if Lord Alford should not in his lifetime acquire the dignity of Duke or Marquis of Bridgewater, the estates should pass from his heirs male immediately on his decease. After great conflict of opinion the condition was held invalid by the House of Lords as being contrary to public policy. But there were special considerations applicable to that case. For instance, since the rank to be obtained was among the highest in the peerage, and one that conferred legislative rights and imposed legislative duties upon the holder, there was a danger that efforts to obtain the qualifying position would be pushed so far as to come into conflict with the general interests of the community. These special considerations were recognised in a later case, where a limitation that property should go to a certain person provided that he acquired the title of baronet was held to be capable of taking effect upon the fulfilment of the condition.[101] Unlike a peerage, no legislative powers and duties would be involved, thus the public interest could not be affected. But conditions forbidding entry into the naval or military services could affect the public interest, and have been accordingly held void.[102]

Difficulty has been encountered in the past with "name and arms clauses", whereby settlors attempt to ensure that the beneficiary adopts the settlor's name and coat of arms. In addition to problems of certainty,[103] such clauses were at one time held to be contrary to public policy on the ground that, in the case of a married woman beneficiary, the taking of another name might lead to dissension between husband and wife. But it was held by the

---

[98] [1976] AC 397 at 426, per Lord WILBERFORCE.
[99] Underhill and Hayton, *Law relating to Trusts and Trustees*, pp. 223–4.   [100] (1853) 4 HL Cas 1.
[101] *Re Wallace* [1920] 2 Ch 274 (baronetcy is "a barren title", per WARRINGTON LJ at 289). The condition here was precedent, but a condition, if contrary to public policy, is invalid whether precedent or subsequent. The *effect* of invalidity, however, is different; pp. 580–1, post.   [102] *Re Beard* [1908] 1 Ch 383.
[103] Infra.

Court of Appeal in *Re Neeld*,[104] overruling many previous decisions, that such clauses are not contrary to public policy.

(3) Uncertain Conditions

A condition subsequent, designed to defeat a vested estate, is void if it is uncertain either in expression or in operation. It must be possible, not only to affirm with precision exactly what the words imposing the condition mean, but also to ascertain with certainty the circumstances that will cause a forfeiture.[105] In a well-known passage Lord Cranworth stated the position as follows:

I consider that, from the earliest times, one of the cardinal rules on the subject has been this: that where a vested estate is to be defeated by a condition on a contingency that is to happen afterwards, that condition must be such that the court can see from the beginning, precisely and distinctly, upon the happening of what event it was that the preceding vested estate was to determine.[106]

Several cases have been concerned with conditions designed to secure the observance by a donee of a particular religion, as for example by requiring him "to be a member of" or "to conform to"[107] the Church of England, or not to marry any person "not of Jewish parentage and of the Jewish faith".[108] Such phrases are shrouded in uncertainty and are generally held to be ineffective. Of those, for instance, who profess membership of the Church of England, many are devout observers of its practice and doctrines, but the conduct of countless others affords little evidence of any religious conviction. Faith varies infinitely in degree, and, even if it were possible to do so, a donor does not normally specify the exact degree that will satisfy his anxiety.[109] Again, whether a person "conforms to" a particular religion defies any certain answer.[110] Does, for instance, conformity to the Church of England necessitate attendance at religious services? If so, how regular must the attendance be? On the other hand, a condition for the forfeiture of an interest if the donee should "become a convert to the Roman Catholic religion" has been upheld, for such a conversion requires the performance of certain definite acts.[111] The court can, therefore, say with certainty what has to be done and whether it has in fact been done.

---

[104] [1962] Ch 643.

[105] *Re Sandbrook* [1912] 2 Ch 471 at 477, per PARKER J; *Re Murray* [1955] Ch 69 at 77–8, per Lord EVERSHED MR. A less strict test applies in the case of a condition precedent, where even conceptual uncertainty may not defeat it: *Re Allen* [1953] Ch 810. Lord DENNING MR in *Re Tuck's Settlement Trusts* [1978] Ch 49 at 60, described this distinction as a "deplorable dichotomy", serving only to defeat the settlor's intention; Maudsley and Burn, *Trusts and Trustees*, p. 726. But the distinction was acknowledged by the House of Lords in *Blathwayt v Baron Cawley* [1976] AC 397 at 425. An example is *Re Barlow's Will Trusts* [1979] 1 WLR 278, Maudsley and Burn, *Trusts and Trustees*, p. 98 (option to purchase a painting at a low price from the testatrix's estate on satisfying the description "any members of my family and any friends of mine" upheld as a valid condition precedent). See Underhill and Hayton, pp. 99–100; [1980] Conv 263 (L. McKay).

[106] *Clavering v Ellison* (1859) 7 HL Cas 707 at 725.   [107] *Re Tegg* [1936] 2 All ER 878.

[108] *Clayton v Ramsden* [1943] AC 320; *Re Moss's Trusts* [1945] 1 All ER 207; *Re Tarnpolsk* [1958] 1 WLR 1157; *Re Krawitz's Will Trusts* [1959] 1 WLR 1192. Cf *Blathwayt v Baron Cawley* [1976] AC 397; *Re Tuck's Settlement Trusts*, supra (marriage to an "approved wife" of Jewish blood and faith not uncertain as condition precedent); *Re Tepper's Will Trusts* [1987] Ch 358 (gift by a devout and practising Jewish testator to children provided that "they shall not marry outside the Jewish faith": SCOTT J was reluctant to find the condition subsequent void for uncertainty and adjourned the case for further evidence of the Jewish faith as practised by the testator and his family; [1987] All ER Rev 260 (C. H. Sherrin)).   [109] *Re Donn* [1944] Ch 8.

[110] *Re Tegg*, supra.   [111] *Re Evans* [1940] Ch 629; *Blathwayt v Baron Cawley*, supra.

Many other examples might be given of uncertain conditions. For instance, provisions that an interest should be forfeited if the donee(s) have "in any way associated, corresponded or visited with any of my present wife's nephews or nieces",[112] or "social or other relationship with" a named person,[113] have been held void, since it is impossible to say with reasonable certainty which of the many connections included in the words "association" or "relationship" offend the prohibition.

Again, a condition that property shall be enjoyed by a beneficiary "only so long as she shall continue to reside in Canada" is too vague to be enforced, for there are many forms and degrees of residence and it is impossible to say precisely which of them fall under the ban.[114] But the law does not exact too high a standard of certainty. The condition need not be clear beyond peradventure. So in one case a requirement of "taking up permanent residence in England" was held to be sufficiently certain, since the word "permanent" postulates an intention to live in a place for life as opposed to living there temporarily or for a fixed period.[115]

In several cases decided between 1945 and 1960, courts of first instance, in disregard of what had been conveyancing practice for at least a century, showed a surprising tendency to stigmatise as void for uncertainty clauses in a will or settlement providing for the forfeiture of an interest given to X upon his failure to assume the surname and arms of Y. It has been held more than once, for instance, that to decree forfeiture, if X "disuses" the surname Y, does not show with sufficient precision what degree of disuser he must avoid.[116]

The Court of Appeal, however, overruled these decisions on the ground that they imposed an unreasonably rigorous test of certainty:[117]

Each of us has a surname, and it seems to me altogether fanciful to suggest that there is any real ambiguity in a requirement that I should adopt and use a surname in place of that which I at present have: for the requirement does no more nor less than postulate that I should thereafter use the new surname, just as I at present use my existing name. Equally, as it seems to me, there is no real ambiguity in a divesting provision expressed to take effect if I should at any time "disuse" or "discontinue to use" the surname which I have adopted.[118]

(4)   Effect of Void Conditions

If realty is conveyed to a person on a condition which is void, then, in the case of a condition precedent, the conveyance is void, and the interest does not arise;[119] but where a gift is

---

[112] *Jeffreys v Jeffreys* (1901) 84 LT 417.   [113] *Re Jones* [1953] Ch 125.

[114] *Sifton v Sifton* [1938] AC 656. See also *Re Brace* [1954] 1 WLR 955, when a condition requiring the donee "to provide a home for" X was held to be so vague as to be unintelligible.

[115] *Re Gape* [1952] Ch 743. Compare *Bromley v Tryon* [1952] AC 265, when it was held that a condition for forfeiture if a beneficiary became entitled to specified settled land "or the bulk thereof" was not void for uncertainty, since "bulk" meant anything over half.   [116] *Re Bouverie* [1952] Ch 400 at 404, per VAISEY J.

[117] *Re Neeld* [1962] Ch 643. We have seen that the Court of Appeal also held that a name and arms clause is not contrary to public policy; p. 578, ante. See too *Re Neeld (No 3)* [1969] 1 WLR 988.

[118] [1962] Ch 643 at 667, per Lord EVERSHED. See also at 679, per UPJOHN LJ, and at 682, per DIPLOCK LJ, as to disuser.

[119] A bequest of *personalty* subject to an illegal condition precedent is void if the condition is *malum in se*, i.e. wrong in itself, but if the condition is only *malum prohibitum*, i.e. indifferent in itself but made unlawful by statute, the bequest takes effect unfettered by the condition: *Re Elliott* [1952] Ch 217; *Re Piper* [1946] 2 All ER 503. See (1955) 19 Conv (NS) 176 (V. T. H. Delany).

subject to several conditions, some of which are valid and others void, the valid conditions are severable from the others, which alone are to be disregarded.[120] In the case of a condition subsequent the condition alone is void, and the donee takes an absolute interest in the property free from the restrictive clause.[121]

[120] *Re Hepplewhite's Will Trusts,* The Times, 21 January 1977.
[121] Co Litt 206a; *Re Croxon* [1904] 1 Ch 252; *Re Turton* [1926] Ch 96 (impossible condition). This is also the case with personalty. But in the case of a determinable interest, we have seen that the whole interest fails if the determining event is unlawful: *Re Moore* (1888) 39 Ch D 116; p. 571, ante.

D. OTHER LEGAL AND EQUITABLE INTERESTS IN LAND

SUMMARY

We have seen in the previous sections of this Part the estates, freehold and leasehold, that are recognised in modern English land law, and the various forms of equitable beneficial interest that can exist in land. In this section our concern is with rights *in alieno solo*, that is, where one has some property right that is enforceable against the land of another: easements and profits à prendre, freehold covenants, rentcharges and mortgages. These rights may sometimes exist as legal interests in the land against which they are exercisable; sometimes they exist only as equitable interests—and, as we shall see, owing to its historical origins the restrictive covenant is capable of being enforced against third parties only in equity, and never at law. However, they merit discussion together because they are all proprietary interests in the land, conferring a lesser interest than the right to the use of the land itself.

Easements, profits, covenants, rentcharges and mortgages are all interests which are recognised and protected by the law in order to make the land more useful, whether for the benefit of the landowner against whose estate the interest is enforceable (such as a mortgage, enabling the landowner to charge his estate in order to facilitate the raising of a loan), or for the benefit of neighbours (such as freehold covenants and easements, which allow a measure of private control of the use of land[1]—the restriction of the modes of use of a plot of land, or the grant to the neighbouring owner of positive rights over it, in order to safeguard the rights of the neighbour and thereby to enhance its value—whether in financial or non-financial terms).

In the final chapter of this section we consider equities, including the equity arising under the doctrine of proprietary estoppel, which appears now to have acquired a status equivalent to an equitable interest in the land. We reserve for the final section of this Part the subject of *licences*, which might also be said to confer an interest enforceable against the land of another, but where the nature of the right is not (in general, at least) proprietary—and therefore does not generally rank as a legal or equitable interest in the land.

---

[1] Indeed, the Law Commission is working on proposals to the effect that these two areas should be formally united under the general heading of "Land Obligations": p. 701, post.

D. OTHER LEGAL AND EQUITABLE
INTERESTS IN LAND

SUMMARY

18

EASEMENTS AND PROFITS

SUMMARY

I Easements and Profits as Property Rights

In the curious language of English law, easements and profits à prendre are *incorporeal hereditaments*:[1] incorporeal, or intangible, heritable interests in land which were recognised historically by the common law. They are incorporeal in the sense that, unlike the freehold

---

[1] Pp. 154–5, ante. "An easement is . . . that familiar creature of English land law: an estate or interest carved out of a larger estate or interest, but nevertheless constituting a hereditament in its own right": *Willies-Williams v National Trust* (1993) 65 P & CR 359 at 361, per HOFFMANN LJ.

or leasehold estate, they do not constitute rights to the land itself, but only rights over or in respect of the land.[2]

Easements and profits are property rights: they attach to the land in respect of which the right is exercisable (generally referred to as the *servient tenement*) so as to burden it in the hands of successive owners.[3] However, like corporeal estates and interests, easements and profits may exist at law or in equity,[4] and therefore, as in the case of all property rights, the circumstances in which the successor is burdened by the right will vary according to whether the right is legal or equitable.[5] As we shall see,[6] a legal easement or profit must satisfy the formality requirements prescribed by the law—it must be created by deed, and in certain cases, if it exists in relation to registered land, it must also be registered; and it can exist only for the same periods as those for which a legal estate can exist. Thus a legal easement or profit may exist in fee simple, or for a term of years absolute. But an easement or profit for any other period, for example, for life, or one created otherwise than by deed, can exist only in equity.

II Easements[7]

A Nature of Easements

An easement is a privilege without a profit,[8] that is to say, it is a right attached to one particular piece of land which allows the owner of that land (the dominant owner) either to use the land of another person (the servient owner)[9] in a particular manner, as by walking over

---

[2] In this respect—as, indeed, in many respects—the law of easements and profits follows closely the Roman law of *servitudes*, which were classified as incorporeal property rights, by contrast with the corporeal property rights of the landowner: Gaius, *Institutes*, Book II, paras. 12–14; although of course all property rights, whether of ownership or less than ownership are really incorporeal rights over the corporeal property: Nicholas, *Introduction to Roman Law*, p. 107. Modern legal systems based on the civil law have retained the term "servitude": e.g. French (*servitude*), Italian (*servitù*), Spanish (*servidumbre*) and Scots law (servitude). Servitude is a word that is occasionally adopted by English judges: e.g. *Dalton v Angus & Co* (1881) 6 App Cas 740 at 796, per Lord SELBORNE; but it is not admitted as a term of art in English law, where the term "easement" was generally adopted in the common law: "Our law seems to look at these rights from the standpoint of the person who enjoys them, not from that of the person who suffers by their exercise. They are not 'servitudes', they are 'easements', 'profits', 'commodities'": Pollock and Maitland, *History of English Law* (2nd edn), vol. ii. p. 145.

[3] As we shall see, an easement must exist also for the benefit of a particular piece of land—the "dominant tenement": p. 588, post; although a profit may exist either for the benefit of a dominant tenement, or "in gross"—for the benefit of the person who holds the right, who can alienate it independently of land.

[4] Pp. 599, 648, post.   [5] Pp. 632, 651, post.   [6] Pp. 601, 649, post.

[7] See generally Gale, *Law of Easements*; Jackson, *Law of Easements and Profits*; Sara, *Boundaries and Easements*; Emmet, paras, 17.051–17.080.

[8] *Hewlins v Shippam* (1826) 5 B & C 221; Termes de la Ley, "Easement". For the nature of a profit, by contrast with an easement, see p. 598, post.

[9] English law here take the language from Roman law, which referred to the owner of the dominant land (*praedium dominans*) and of the servient land (*praedium serviens*): Buckland, *Textbook of Roman Law*, p. 259. It was Bracton in the thirteenth century who borrowed the language and some of the rules of Roman law. The lawyers did not begin to speculate on the characteristics of easements until the start of the nineteenth century. Gale, writing in 1839, started the modern law. It was the industrial revolution which caused the growth of large towns and manufacturing industries which brought into prominence such easements as ways, watercourses, light and support. So too, after the end of the Second World War, reconstruction and development have given rise to a large number of cases on the subject. For a detailed discussion of the older cases, see Gale, *A Treatise on the Law of Easements* (12th edn, 1950). See also Holdsworth, *Historical Introduction to Land Law*, pp. 101–2, 265–7.

or depositing rubbish on it, or to restrict its user by that other person to a particular extent, but which does not allow him to take any part of its natural produce or its soil.[10]

Thus an easement may be either positive or negative.[11] It is positive if it consists of a right to do something upon the land of another, as, for example, to walk or to place erections such as signboards thereon. A negative easement, on the other hand, does not permit an act, but imposes a restriction upon the use which another person may make of his land. For instance, the easement of light signifies that the servient owner must not build so as unreasonably to obstruct the flow of light; and an easement of support implies that the servient owner must not interfere with his own land or building so as to disturb that of his neighbour.

A question that not infrequently arises is whether some right exercisable over the land of another is an easement or a right of a different nature. It is a question of crucial importance, since the validity and enforceability of the right, both against the original owner of the land and against his successors in title, depends upon the proper characterisation of the right. An easement confers no right to possession of the land affected: it merely imposes a particular restriction upon the proprietary rights of the owner of the servient land; a right which entitles one person to possession of the land of another may therefore be a lease, or a licence, but it cannot be an easement. Similarly, a limited right which in other respects bears some similarity to an easement,[12] but which the law does not regard as an easement, may give its holder a mere personal right against the landowner who gave it to him—and therefore, being a purely personal or contractual right, will not benefit or bind the parties' successors. A right cannot be given the status of an easement at the free will of the parties who create it, for the rule is that no right over land will be regarded as an easement unless it possesses certain characteristics which the law has determined. This being so, the first task must be to discover what those characteristics are.

(1) Characteristics of Easements

If an interest is to be an easement it must possess the four following characteristics.[13]

(a) There must be a dominant and a servient tenement[14]

The very nature of an easement, as being a right *in alieno solo*, requires that there shall be a tenement over which it is exercisable, the *servient tenement*, but in addition to this the law requires that there shall be another tenement, the *dominant tenement*, for the benefit of which the easement exists. To adopt legal phraseology an easement must be appurtenant or attached to land. If X, the owner of Blackacre, has acquired a right of way over the adjoining tenement Whiteacre, he is entitled to an easement of way not because he is X, but because he is the fee simple owner of Blackacre. The easement exists because Blackacre exists.[15]

---

[10] *Manning v Wasdale* (1836) 5 Ad & El 758.   [11] *Dalton v Angus* (1881) 6 App Cas 740 at 821.

[12] M & B pp. 691–3.

[13] *Re Ellenborough Park* [1956] Ch 131, M & B p. 694; (1964) 28 Conv (NS) 450 (M. A. Peel).

[14] Holdsworth, *History of English Law*, vol. vii. pp. 324 et seq.

[15] *Rangeley v Midland Rly Co* (1868) 3 Ch App 306 at 311; *Ackroyd v Smith* (1850) 10 CB 164 at 188; *Hawkins v Rutter* [1892] 1 QB 668.

It follows from this that there cannot be an easement *in gross*,[16] an easement that is independent of the ownership of land by the person who claims the right. Of course a person who does not own a yard of property may be granted a privilege to pass over Whiteacre, but though this may give him a personal right it certainly does not entitle him to an easement. It amounts to a licence confined in its effect to the actual parties.[17]

(b) An easement must accommodate the dominant tenement

It is a fundamental principle that an easement must not only be appurtenant to a dominant tenement, but must also be connected with the normal enjoyment of that tenement.[18] There must be a direct *nexus* between the enjoyment of the right and the user of the dominant tenement.[19] This requirement has been stated in various ways:

An easement must be connected with the enjoyment of the dominant tenement and must be for its benefit.[20] It must have some natural connection with the estate, as being for its benefit.[21] The incident sought to be annexed, so that the assignee of the land may take advantage of it, must be beneficial to the land in respect of the ownership.[22]

To take a simple example, a right of way in order to rank as an easement need not lead right up to the dominant tenement, but it must at least have some natural connection with it.[23] You cannot, remarked BYLES J, have a right of way over land in Kent appurtenant to an estate in Northumberland,[24] for a right of way in Kent cannot possibly be advantageous to Northumberland land.[25] We may expand the statement of the principle thus: a right enjoyed by one over the land of another does not possess the status of an easement unless it accommodates and serves the dominant tenement, and is reasonably necessary for the better enjoyment of that tenement, for if it has no necessary connection therewith, although it confers an advantage upon the owner and renders his ownership of the land more valuable, it is not an easement at all, but a mere contractual right personal to and only enforceable between the two contracting parties.[26]

Whether the necessary *nexus* exists depends greatly upon the nature of the dominant tenement and the nature of the right alleged. If, for example, the dominant tenement is

[16] *Ackroyd v Smith*, supra; *Weekly v Wildman* (1698) 1 Ld Raym 405, per TREBY CJ; *London and Blenheim Estates Ltd v Ladbroke Retail Parks Ltd* [1994] 1 WLR 31 (right intended as easement and attached to servient tenement before dominant tenement identified held not to be an easement); *Voice v Bell* (1993) 68 P & CR 441. See Conv Prec 19-C20. A profit à prendre may exist *in gross*: p. 641, post. In the USA both easements and profits may be *in gross*. See American Law Institute *Restatement of the Law, Third, Property (Servitudes)* (2000), and generally (1980) 96 LQR 557 (M. F. Sturley), criticising the rule; (1982) 98 LQR at p. 305 (S. Gardner); *Jobson v Record* (1997) 75 P & CR 375 ("a right of way granted for the benefit of a defined area of land may not be used in substance for accommodating another area of land" at 378, per MORRITT LJ)   [17] Pp. 831, et seq, post.

[18] *Ackroyd v Smith* (1850) 10 CB 164.   [19] *Re Ellenborough Park* [1956] Ch 131 at 174.

[20] *Gale on Easements* (12th edn), p. 20; *Clapman v Edwards* [1938] 2 All ER 507.

[21] *Bailey v Stephens* (1862) 12 CBNS 91 at 115, per BYLES J. Cf *Stroude v Beazer Homes Ltd* [2005] 48 EG 223 (CS) (right of access under TCPA 1990, s. 106, agreement (p. 1023, post), for purposes of constructing highway capable of benefiting land even though the highway, when constructed, would be public and not private).

[22] Ibid. See also *Clos Farming Estates v Easton* [2002] NSWCA 389 at [30]–[34], per STANTOW JA (right to enter servient land to carry out viticulture work and to harvest grapes, not an easement).

[23] *Todrick v Western National Omnibus Co Ltd* [1934] Ch 561; *Birmingham, Dudley and District Banking Co v Ross* (1888) 38 Ch D 295 at 314; *Pugh v Savage* [1970] 2 QB 373 (intervening land between dominant and servient tenements).   [24] *Bailey v Stephens* (1862) CBNS 91.

[25] *Todrick v Western National Omnibus Co Ltd* [1934] Ch 561 at 580, per ROMER LJ.

[26] Cited with approval in *Re Ellenborough Park* [1956] Ch 131 at 170.

a residential house and if there is annexed to it by express grant a right to use an adjoining garden for purposes of relaxation and pleasure, this is a clear case where the right is sufficiently connected with the normal enjoyment of the house to rank as an easement.[27] The fact that the right enhances the value of the dominant tenement is a relevant, but not a decisive, consideration.[28] The principle is perhaps best illustrated by *Hill v Tupper*,[29] where the facts were as follows:

A canal company leased land adjoining the canal to Hill and gave him the "sole and exclusive right" to let out pleasure boats on the canal. Tupper, an innkeeper, disregarded this privilege by himself letting out boats for fishing purposes. Hill thereupon brought an action in his own name against Tupper, his alleged cause of action being a disturbance of his easement to put boats on the canal.

It was held that the right conferred upon Hill by the contract with the company was not an easement but a mere licence personal to himself, since it was acquired in order to exploit an independent business enterprise, not to accommodate the riparian land as such.[30] The right was not beneficial to the land as land; rather, the land was required for the exploitation of the right. However, it is clear that an easement may exist for the purpose of the business carried on on the dominant tenement. In *Moody v Steggles* FRY J said:[31]

It is said that the easement in question relates, not to the tenement, but to the business of the occupant of the tenement, and that therefore I cannot tie the easement to the house. It appears to me that that argument is of too refined a nature to prevail, and for this reason, that the house can only be used by an occupant, and that the occupant only uses the house for the business which he pursues, and therefore in some manner (direct or indirect) an easement is more or less connected with the mode in which the occupant of the house uses it.

The principle that the right must accommodate the dominant tenement applies equally to profits appurtenant,[32] and may be illustrated by the remark of COKE[33] that the right of cutting turfs for fuel cannot be claimed as appurtenant to land, but only to a house, because the use of fuel has no connection with land as such. In the leading case of *Bailey v Stephens*:[34]

A, who was seised in fee of a piece of land called Bloody Field, claimed the right to enter an adjoining close for the purpose of cutting down, carrying away and converting to his own use the trees and wood growing there. It was held that, as the wood was not employed for the beneficial enjoyment of Bloody Field, it was not connected with it and so was not a valid profit.

---

[27] *Re Ellenborough Park* [1956] Ch 131.   [28] Ibid., at 173.

[29] (1863) 2 H & C 121, M & B p. 693; cf *Moody v Steggles* (1879) 12 Ch D 261, M & B p. 699 (right to advertise public house on servient land situated in front of it held to be an easement).

[30] *Re Ellenborough Park*, supra, at 175. The alleged right was also asserted as a monopoly: ibid.; i.e., an exclusive right to use the canal for the purpose and the action was to exclude others from its use, which is not of the character of an easement. Cf the problem of exclusive user: p. 596, post. Contrast the Pennsylvanian case of *Miller v Lutheran Conference and Camp Association* 331 Pa 241 (1938), Aigler, Smith and Tefft, *Cases on Property* (1960), vol. ii. p. 212, where a somewhat similar right was treated as an easement *in gross* capable of assignment.   [31] Supra, at 266.

[32] P. 641, post.   [33] *Tyrringham's Case* (1584) 4 Co Rep 36b; p. 645, post.

[34] (1862) 12 CBNS 91.

(c) Dominant and servient owners must be different persons

If one person owns two adjoining properties which, physically speaking, are separate properties, any rights that he may have been in the habit of exercising over one or other of them, as, for example, by passing over one to reach the highway, are not easements (though they are often called "quasi-easements"), because they derive from his ownership not of the quasi-dominant land, but of the quasi-servient land itself.[35] FRY LJ in one case said:

> Of course, strictly speaking, the owner of two tenements can have no easement over one of them in respect of the other. When the owner of Whiteacre and Blackacre passes over the former to Blackacre, he is not exercising a right of way in respect of Blackacre; he is merely making use of his own land to get from one part to another.[36]

Thus, if X is the owner of two separate tenements and he lets one of them to a tenant, the latter cannot acquire by prescription an easement over the other, for his occupation is in the eyes of the law the occupation of his landlord, a person who cannot acquire an easement against himself.[37] As will be seen later, however, the right to light is exceptional in this respect.[38]

If the principle were otherwise and if rights exercised by a man over one of two properties both owned by him were to be treated as easements, they would necessarily remain vested in him after a sale of the quasi-servient tenement. They would also pass without express mention to a purchaser of the quasi-dominant tenement. But these consequences do not ensue. To quote an old case:

> J.S. had a close, and a wood adjoining to it, and time out of mind a way had been used over the close to the wood to carry and re-carry. He granted the close to one, and the wood to another. The question was, if the grantee of the wood shall have the way? And it was adjudged he should not, for the grantor by the grant of the close had excluded himself of the way, because it was not saved to him; and he himself could not use it, no more can his grantee.[39]

Therefore, when a large estate is split up and sold to different purchasers, any quasi-easements which were enjoyed by the former owner should be expressly reserved to the purchaser of the quasi-dominant tenement.[40]

(d) A right over land cannot amount to an easement unless it is capable of forming the subject-matter of a grant

As we shall see, apart from statute, every easement must originate in a grant, either express, implied or presumed. It follows from this that no right can have the status of an easement unless it is the possible subject-matter of a grant.[41] This characteristic has three aspects.

---

[35] *Bolton v Bolton* (1879) 11 Ch D 968.
[36] *Roe v Siddons* (1888) 22 QBD 224 at 236; and see *Metropolitan Rly Co v Fowler* [1892] 1 QB 165; *Derry v Sanders* [1919] 1 KB 223.
[37] *Warburton v Parke* (1857) 2 H & N 64; *Gayford v Moffatt* (1868) 4 Ch App 133. A tenant may, however, grant an easement, for a period not exceeding that of his lease, in favour of another tenant of the same landlord.
[38] P. 626, post.   [39] *Dell v Babthorpe* (1593) Cro Eliz 300.
[40] *Wheeldon v Burrows* (1879) 12 Ch D 31 at 49; pp. 610–2, post.
[41] *Potter v North* (1669) 1 Wms Saund 347, in argument; *Goodman v Saltash Corpn* (1882) 7 App Cas 633 at 654; *Dalton v Angus & Co* (1881) 6 App Cas 740 at 795; *Chastey v Ackland* (1895) 11 TLR 460; *Harris v De Pinna* (1886) 33 Ch D 238 at 262; *Bryant v Lefever* (1879) 4 CPD 172 at 178, per BRAMWELL LJ.

(1) CERTAINTY OF DESCRIPTION

The nature and extent of the right must be capable of reasonably exact description.[42] If it is so vague or so indeterminate as to defy precise definition, it cannot rank as an easement. This requirement, which is common to all forms of grant, is especially important in the present context, for a right over the land of another is allowed to ripen into an easement if it has been enjoyed for a long time without any interruption by the servient owner, but this necessarily implies that there should be something definite capable of interruption.[43]

A right to the flow of light to a particular window satisfies the test of certainty, for not only does the light pass over the servient tenement along a defined channel, but it can be interrupted by an obstruction placed across its line of approach.[44] Again, it has been held that a *jus spatiandi*, that is a right to wander at large over the servient tenement, is sufficiently determinate to constitute an easement if it is limited to a particular house or group of houses and is exercisable over an adjoining garden.[45] So also the right to a flow of air can subsist as an easement if it is claimed in respect of some definite channel, such as a ventilator in a building,[46] but not if what is claimed is that the current of air flowing indiscriminately over the entire servient tenement shall not be interrupted.[47]

In *Harris v De Pinna*,[48] where a claim to the general flow of air was made, Bowen LJ said:

It would be just like amenity of prospect,[49] a subject-matter which is incapable of definition. So the passage of undefined air gives rise to no rights and can give rise to no rights for the best of all reasons, the reason of common sense, because you cannot acquire any rights against others by a user which they cannot interrupt.

And in *Hunter v Canary Wharf Ltd*,[50] Lord Hoffmann combined the concept of certainty and propinquity. In deciding that there could not be an easement for the reception of television waves from a distant transmitter, he said:

It was well settled [in *Dalton v Angus*[51]] that one could not prescribe for a right to an uninterrupted view or to a flow of air otherwise through a defined aperture or channel. Lord Blackburn . . . said that allowing the prescription of a right to a view would impose a burden 'on a very large and indefinite area.' Rights of light, air and support were strictly a matter between immediate neighbours. The building entitled to support, the windows entitled to light and the apertures entitled to air would be plain and obvious. The restrictions on the freedom of the person erecting the building would be limited and precise.

---

[42] On whether it might be easier to satisfy the test in the case of an express grant than in a claim to an easement by prescription, see *Jackson v Mulvaney* [2003] 1 WLR 360 at [10]–[15], [23], M & B p. 699; *Batchelor v Marlow* [2003] 1 WLR 764 at [4]–[6].   [43] *Webb v Bird* (1862) 13 CBNS 841 at 843.

[44] *Harris v De Pinna* (1886) 33 Ch D 238 at 259.

[45] *Re Ellenborough Park* [1956] Ch 131, M & B p. 694 (express grant); *Jackson v Mulvaney*, supra, M & B p. 699 (implied grant or prescription).   [46] *Cable v Bryant* [1908] 1 Ch 259, M & B p. 709, n. 19.

[47] *Webb v Bird*, supra; *Bryant v Lefever* (1879) 4 CPD 172. See also *Palmer v Bowman* [2000] 1 WLR 842 (no easement of unquantified right by owner of higher land to have main water pass by natural flow onto lower neighbouring land); p. 177, n. 69, ante; (2000) 150 NLJ 311 (H. W. Wilkinson).

[48] (1886) 33 Ch D 238 at 262. This may, however, be enforceable under the doctrine of non-derogation from grant. See *Aldin v Latimer Clark, Muirhead & Co* [1894] 2 Ch 437; p. 232, ante; *Lyme Valley Squash Club Ltd v Newcastle under Lyme BC* [1985] 2 All ER 405 (easement of light); p. 607, n. 177, post.

[49] *Bland v Mosely* (1587) cited in 9 Co Rep 58a. But a right to a prospect or view over neighbouring land may be framed as a restrictive covenant enforceable under the doctrine of *Tulk v Moxhay*; p. 666, post. See *Wakeham v Wood* (1981) 43 P & CR 40; *Gilbert v Spoor* [1983] Ch 27; p. 699, n. 267, post.

[50] [1997] AC 655 at 709, M & B p. 708; (1997) 113 LQR 515 (P. Cane); [1997] CLJ 483 (J. O'Sullivan); [1997] Conv 145 (P. R. Ghandi).   [51] (1881) 6 App Cas 740 at 824.

(2) CAPABLE GRANTEE

A claimant to an easement must be a person capable of receiving a grant, that is, he must be a definite person or a definite body such as a corporation. Thus a claim put forward by a vague fluctuating body of persons, such as the inhabitants of a village, will not be sustainable as an easement.[52]

(3) CAPABLE GRANTOR

Again, the same principle demands that the servient owner should have been lawfully entitled to grant the right claimed to be an easement. Thus a claim[53] against a company incorporated by statute will fail upon proof that the grant was ultra vires.[54]

(2) Examples of Easements

(a) List of easements not closed

Such, then, are the essential characteristics of easements, and it is important that they should be borne in mind, for otherwise certain judicial statements that new kinds of rights *in rem* cannot be created at will may be misunderstood. Thus Lord BROUGHAM said:[55]

There are certain known incidents to property and its enjoyment, among others, certain burdens wherewith it may be affected, or rights which may be created and enjoyed over it by parties other than the owner.... But it must not therefore be supposed that incidents of a novel kind can be devised and attached to property at the fancy or caprice of any owner; ... great detriment would arise and much confusion of rights, if parties were allowed to invent new modes of holding and enjoying real property, and to impress upon their land and tenements a peculiar character, which should follow them into all hands, however remote.

This means not that an easement of a kind never heard of before cannot be created, but that a new species of incorporeal hereditament or a new species of burden cannot be brought into being and given the status and legal effect of an easement. In other words, if a right exhibits the four characteristics described above, it is an easement that will run with the dominant and against the servient tenement, even though its object may be to fulfil a purpose for which it has not hitherto been used; but if it lacks one or more of those characteristics, it may, indeed, be enforceable between the parties who create it, but it cannot, like an easement, be enforceable by or against third parties.[56]

One of the main purposes of law is to keep pace with the requirements of society and to adapt itself to new modes of life and new business methods, a fact that was present in the mind of Lord ST LEONARDS when he said

The category of servitudes and easements must alter and expand with the changes that take place in the circumstances of mankind.[57]

[52] But a local customary right may be established; pp. 655 et seq, post.
[53] *Paine & Co Ltd v St Neots Gas and Coke Co* [1939] 3 All ER 812.
[54] *Mulliner v Midland Rly Co* (1879) 11 Ch D 611.
[55] *Keppell v Bailey* (1834) 2 My & K 517 at 535. See also *Hill v Tupper* (1863) 2 H & C 121 at 127–8, per POLLOCK CB.　　　　　　　　　　　　　　　　　[56] *Re Ellenborough Park* [1956] Ch 131 at 140–1.
[57] *Dyce v Lady Hay* (1852) 1 Macq 305.

Thus in a case where an easement was claimed to place stores and casks upon land reclaimed from the sea, the Privy Council said: "The law must adapt itself to the conditions of modern society and trade, and there is nothing in the purposes for which the easement is claimed inconsistent in principle with a right of easement as such."[58]

(b) Examples

The following list of easements, which begins with the most important kinds and which, of course, is not exhaustive, will afford some idea of how great their variety is:

(1) WAY

Rights of way, whether for general or special purposes, and whether exercisable in all modes or limited to a carriage way, bridle way, foot way or a way for cattle.

(2) LIGHT

A right that the light flowing over adjoining land to a window shall not be unreasonably obstructed.[59]

(3) WATER AND OTHER SERVICES

Rights in connection with water, such as a right to the uninterrupted passage of water over adjoining land,[60] or a right to enter upon adjoining land to divert the course of a stream for irrigation purposes, or a right to pollute a river or to discharge water onto the land of another.[61] Similarly, rights to other services, such as gas or electricity,[62] or to allow drainage from the dominant tenement over the servient tenement.[63]

(4) SUPPORT

A right to the support of buildings by adjoining land or buildings. Though a landowner has a natural right to have his *land* supported by adjoining land, yet a right to have *buildings* supported can be claimed only if it has actually been acquired as an easement.[64]

---

[58] *A-G of Southern Nigeria v John Holt & Co* [1915] AC 599 at 617; *Simpson v Godmanchester Corpn* [1896] 1 Ch 214 at 219; *Dowty Boulton Paul Ltd v Wolverhampton Corpn (No 2)* [1976] Ch 13 at 23 ("A tendency in the past to freeze the categories of easements has been overtaken by the defrosting operation in *Re Ellenborough Park*", per RUSSELL LJ).

[59] See generally *Colls v Home and Colonial Stores Ltd* [1904] AC 179, M & B p. 775, pp. 624–6, post.

[60] *Rance v Elvin* (1985) 50 P & CR 9; p. 595, n. 82, post.

[61] A landowner may have certain natural rights in respect of water; p. 177, ante; p. 599, post.

[62] *Coopind (UK) Ltd v Walton Commercial Group Ltd* [1989] 1 EGLR 2451 ("right to receive supply of water gas electricity and heat"); *Duffy v Lamb* (1997) 75 P & CR 364 (right to uninterrupted passage of electricity held to be easement).

[63] *Atwood v Bovis Homes Ltd* [2001] Ch 379, M & B p. 771; *Green v Lord Somerleyton* [2004] 1 P & CR 33.

[64] The leading case is *Dalton v Angus & Co* (1881) 6 App Cas 740. See also *Rees v Skerrett* [2001] 1 WLR 1541 (demolition of adjoining terraced house in breach of easement exposing common wall; damage caused by wind suction within scope of the right of support, and so actionable in nuisance). For the relationship between the easement of support and the claim to protection against the effects of the weather, see *Phipps v Pears* [1965] 1 QB 76, M & B p. 706, and the discussion at p. 596, n. 85, post.

(5) FENCING

A right to have a fence maintained by an adjoining owner. This has been recognised by the Court of Appeal as "a right in the nature of an easement". As Lord DENNING said in *Crow v Wood*:[65]

It is not an easement strictly so called because it involves the servient owner in the expenditure of money. It was described by Gale as a "spurious kind of easement".[66] But it has been treated in practice by the courts as being an easement . . .[67]

It seems to me that it is now sufficiently established—or at any rate, if not established hitherto, we should now declare—that a right to have your neighbour keep up the fences is a right in the nature of an easement which is capable of being granted by law so as to run with the land and to be binding on successors. It is a right which lies in grant.[68]

(6) MISCELLANEOUS EASEMENTS

Such are the easements most commonly found in practice, but we may add examples of some variations and extensions of these interests:[69]

(i)   Right to hang clothes on a line passing over neighbouring soil.[70]

(ii)   Right to run telephone lines over neighbouring land.[71]

(iii)   Right to use a close for the purpose of mixing muck and preparing manure thereon for the use of an adjoining farm.[72]

(iv)   Right to fix a signboard to the walls of another's house.[73]

(v)   Right of a landowner to use a particular seat in a parish church.[74]

(vi)   Right to nail trees to a wall.[75]

(vii)   Right to lay stones upon adjoining land to prevent sand from being washed away by the sea.[76]

(viii) Right to store casks and trade produce on a neighbour's land.[77]

(ix)   Right to use a lavatory situated on the servient tenement.[78]

---

[65] [1971] 1 QB 77 at 84, M & B p. 710. See (1971) 87 LQR 13 (P. V. Baker).

[66] Gale, *Law of Easements* (11th edn), p. 432. See too *Lawrence v Jenkins* (1873) LR 8 QB 274 at 279, per ARCHIBALD J. Cf *Hilton v Ankesson* (1872) 27 LT 519.

[67] See *Jones v Price* [1965] 2 QB 618 at 633, per WILLMER LJ; and at 639, per DIPLOCK LJ; *Egerton v Harding* [1975] QB 62.

[68] It may also be acquired (1) as an easement by prescription: *Lawrence v Jenkins* (1873) LR 8 QB 274: *Jones v Price* [1965] 2 QB 618; (2) by custom: *Egerton v Harding*, supra.

[69] For further examples, see Gale, paras. 1-64 to 1-68.

[70] *Drewell v Towler* (1832) 3 B & Ad 735.

[71] *Lancashire and Cheshire Telephone Exchange Co v Manchester Overseers* (1884) 14 QBD 267.

[72] *Pye v Mumford* (1848) 11 QB 666.

[73] *Moody v Steggles* (1879) 12 Ch D 261, M & B p. 699; *William Hill (Southern) Ltd v Cabras Ltd* [1987] 1 EGLR 37.

[74] *Mainwaring v Giles* (1822) 5 B & Ald 356; *Brumfitt v Roberts* (1870) LR 5 CP 224; *Re St Mary's Banbury* [1986] Fam 24; affd [1987] Fam 136.   [75] *Hawkins v Wallis* (1763) 2 Wils 173.

[76] *Philpot v Bath* (1905) 21 TLR 634.

[77] *A-G of Southern Nigeria v John Holt & Co (Liverpool) Ltd* [1915] AC 599; *Smith v Gates* (1952) 160 EG 512 (right to keep chicken coops on a common).   [78] *Miller v Emcer Products Ltd* [1956] Ch 304, M & B p. 702.

(x)   Right to use a letter-box.[79]

(xi)   Right to use an airfield.[80]

(xii)   Right to park a car anywhere on the forecourt of a block of flats.[81]

(c) New easements

New easements may arise, but no right which fails to exhibit the four characteristics described above can exist as an easement. Whether or not a new right, complying with the accepted requirements of an easement, will be judicially recognised or not is difficult to forecast.

There are, however, three situations in which such recognition is unlikely to be granted.

(1) EXPENDITURE BY SERVIENT OWNER

First, where the owner of the servient tenement would be under a duty to spend money.[82] There is only one right in this category, that of fencing, where the servient owner is under a duty to take positive steps to maintain the fence, including the expenditure of money. As we have seen, its exceptional nature is recognised by the Court of Appeal.[83] There may also be cases where the parties have expressly or impliedly agreed that the servient owner shall bear the burden; as in *Liverpool City Council v Irwin*[84] where a local authority, which owned a high-rise block of flats, let them to tenants. Easements of access over the common parts of the building retained by the local authority (the servient owner) were implied in favour of the tenants. The local authority was held liable, as on an implied contract, to maintain those parts.

(2) NEGATIVITY

Secondly, where the easement is negative, in the sense that it gives the owner of the dominant tenement a right to stop his neighbour doing something on his (the neighbour's) own land. This has long been recognised in the cases of the easements of light and support. But

---

[79] *Goldberg v Edwards* [1950] Ch 247, M & B p. 726.

[80] *Dowty Boulton Paul Ltd v Wolverhampton Corpn (No 2)* [1976] Ch 13.

[81] *Newman v Jones* (22 March 1982, unreported); *London and Blenheim Estates Ltd v Ladbroke Retail Parks Ltd* [1992] 1 WLR 1278 at 1288; *Handel v St Stephens Close Ltd* [1994] 1 EGLR 70. See further p. 597, post.

[82] *Regis Property Co Ltd v Redman* [1956] 2 QB 612 (covenant to supply hot water and central heating, involving the performance of services, not an easement); *Rance v Elvin* (1983) 49 P & CR 65 (right to metered water supply paid for by servient owner held not to be an easement, even though dominant owner agreed to reimburse water charges); (1985) 50 P & CR 9 (CA held that the right was to the uninterrupted passage of water, and not to its supply; it was therefore an easement, and the servient owner was liable in restitution to reimburse); [1985] CLJ 458 (A. J. Waite); *Coopind (UK) Ltd v Walton Commercial Group Ltd* [1989] 1 EGLR 241 (right to receive a supply of gas under service roads retained by lessors held to extend to right to lay new gas main); *Cardwell v Walker* [2004] 2 P & CR 9 (control of electricity supply by recording meters changed to issue of tokens available for sale by servient owners; held unrestricted easement of passage of electricity unchanged).   [83] *Jones v Price* [1965] 2 QB 618; *Crow v Wood* [1971] 1 QB 77, M & B p. 710.

[84] *Liverpool City Council v Irwin* [1977] AC 239; *King v South Northamptonshire DC* [1992] 1 EGLR 53; [1992] Conv 347 (J. E. Martin); *Duke of Westminster v Guild* [1985] QB 688 (tenant qua dominant owner of right of drainage held to be liable for repairs). See also *Stokes v Mixconcrete (Holdings) Ltd* (1978) 38 P & CR 488; *Holden v White* [1982] QB 679 (servient owner owed no duty of care at common law to milkman injured by disintegrating manhole cover on private footpath giving access to terraced house, nor under Occupiers' Liability Act 1957. See now Occupiers' Liability Act 1984, in effect reversing the decision); *McGeown v Northern Ireland Housing Executive* [1995] 1 AC 233 (public right of way).

in *Phipps v Pears*,[85] where the premises had been exposed to damp and frost owing to the demolition of an adjacent house, the Court of Appeal held that there was no easement of protection against the weather. Lord DENNING said:[86]

A right to protection from the weather . . . is entirely negative. Seeing that it is a negative easement, it must be looked at with caution. Because the law has been very chary of creating any new negative easements . . . . If such an easement were to be permitted, it would unduly restrict your neighbour in his own enjoyment of his own land.

It is, however, possible for such rights to be framed as restrictive covenants which may be enforceable under the doctrine of *Tulk v Moxhay*.[87] And the law of tort might sometimes provide a remedy to the person whose property is damaged by exposure to the weather, even if no easement is infringed.[88]

(3) EXCLUSIVE OR JOINT USER

Finally, no right will be recognised as an easement which is in effect a claim to exclusive or joint user of the servient tenement. Thus in *Copeland v Greenhalf*,[89] it was held that

---

[85] [1965] 1 QB 76, M & B p. 706, criticised in (1964) 80 LQR 318 (R.E.M.); (1964) 27 MLR 614; (1965) 28 MLR 264 (H. W. Wilkinson), and supported (1964) 27 MLR 768 (J. F. Garner). Followed in *Marchant v Capital and Counties Property Co Ltd* (1982) 263 EG 661; (1983) 267 EG 843 (award under London Building Acts (Amendment) Act 1939). Under Building Act 1984, ss. 81, 82(1)(b), replacing Public Health Act 1961, s. 29(5), a local authority may serve a notice on anyone demolishing a building, requiring him to weatherproof any surface of adjacent buildings exposed by the demolition.

In *Sedgwick Forbes Bland Payne Group Ltd v Regional Properties Ltd* [1981] EGD 44 at 56 it was suggested that a right to protection against the weather by a *roof* might be an easement, thereby limiting *Phipps v Pears* to an easement of protection against the weather in the vertical plane. Cf *Rees v Skerrett* [2001] 1 WLR 1541 (where the adjacent buildings were not free-standing; on demolition right of support was infringed: at [15]; p. 593, n. 64, ante; and there was also a breach of the duty of care to take steps to waterproof wall after demolition: at [27]. The case would now be governed by Party Wall etc Act 1996: at [34]); [2002] Conv 237 (T. H. Wu). On party-walls, see p. 480, ante. On negative easements generally, see (1998) 18 LS 510 (I. Dawson and A. Dunn).

[86] At 83.   [87] P. 666, post.

[88] *Rees v Skerrett*, supra: at [36] LLOYD J noted that "as regards the law of negligence and nuisance developments since 1965, especially *Leakey v National Trust for Places of Historic Interest or Natural Beauty* [1980] QB 485, show that the balance between the position of those who are neighbours (both in fact and in law) is now to be drawn differently in these areas of law. Moreover, it is not a question of preventing a man from pulling down his house altogether, any more than a right of support prevents demolition. . . . Rather, it is a question of requiring him, if and when he does demolish the house, to provide substitute protection, to the extent that this can be done by works which in all the circumstances it is reasonable to expect him to undertake." Where there *is* a right of support which is infringed, damages may be claimed in tort for the consequential exposure: *Bradburn v Lindsay* [1983] 2 All ER 408; [1984] Conv 54 (P. Jackson); [1987] Conv 47 (A. J. Waite); *Brace v South East Regional Housing Association Ltd* (1984) 270 EG 1286. For the use of the tort of nuisance generally to remedy infringements of a easements, see p. 635, post.

[89] [1952] Ch 488, M & B p. 700; *Ward v Kirkland* [1967] Ch 194; cf *Wright v Macadam* [1949] 2 KB 744, M & B p. 723 (right to store domestic coal in shed held to be an easement). This case was not cited in *Copeland v Greenhalf*. See also *Grigsby v Melville* [1972] 1 WLR 1355; affd [1974] 1 WLR 80, M & B p. 702 (claim to exclusive right of storage in cellar under drawing-room floor); *Thomas W Ward Ltd v Alexander Bruce (Grays) Ltd* [1959] 2 Lloyd's Rep 472 (right to ground ships on silt in defendant's dock in course of plaintiff's business as shipbrokers held not to be an easement: "it involves an almost complete exclusion of the alleged servient owner" per HARMAN LJ at 477); *Hanina v Morland* (2000) 97 (47) LSG 41 (use of adjoining roof for entertaining, sunbathing and generally as extension of living room held to be exclusive user and therefore no easement); *P & S Platt Ltd v Crouch* [2004] 1 P & CR 18 (right to moor boats on land adjacent to Norfolk Broads capable of being an easement, and not a sufficiently substantial interference with reasonable user of land by defendants to prevent it being an easement); *Jackson v Mulvaney* [2003] 1 WLR 360 (easement of use of communal garden, but no right to maintain flowerbed in a particular position within the garden).

a wheelwright had no easement to store and repair an unlimited number of vehicles on a strip of his neighbour's land. In the words of UPJOHN J:[90]

I think that the right claimed goes wholly outside any normal idea of an easement, that is, the right of the owner or the occupier of a dominant tenement over a servient tenement. This claim really amounts to a claim to a joint user of the land by the defendant. Practically, the defendant is claiming the whole benefi-cial user of the strip of land on the south-east side of the track there; he can leave as many or as few lorries there as he likes for as long as he likes; he may enter on it by himself, his servants and agents to do repair work thereon. In my judgment, that is not a claim which can be established as an easement. It is virtually a claim to possession of the servient tenement, if necessary to the exclusion of the owner; or, at any rate, to a joint user, and no authority has been cited to me which could justify the conclusion that a right of this wide and undefined nature can be the proper subject-matter of an easement. It seems to me that to succeed, this claim must amount to a successful claim of possession by reason of long adverse possession.[91]

The question is really one of degree. As ROMER LJ said in *Miller v Emcer Products Ltd*,[92] where a right to use a lavatory situated on the servient tenement was held to be an easement:

It is true that during the times when the dominant owner exercised the right the owner of the servient tenement would be excluded, but this in greater or less degree is a common feature of many easements (for example, rights of way) and does not amount to such an ouster of the servient owner's rights as was held by UPJOHN J to be incompatible with a legal easement in *Copeland v Greenhalf*.

The problem has arisen in connection with the right to park cars. In *Newman v Jones*[93] it was held that a right for a landowner to park a car anywhere in a defined area nearby was capable of existing as an easement; and the mere risk of there being not enough space for all to park simultaneously was not a reason for denying that any rights at all exist. Nor may it be an objection that charges are made by the servient owner, whether for the parking itself or for the general upkeep of the park. As Judge Paul Baker QC said in *London and Blenheim Estates Ltd v Ladbroke Retail Parks Ltd*:[94]

The essential question is one of degree. If the right granted in relation to the area over which it is to be exer-cisable is such that it would leave the servient owner without any reasonable use of his land, whether for parking or anything else, it could not be an easement though it might be some larger or different grant.[95]

This approach has now been applied at the level of the Court of Appeal,[96] and appears in principle to be correct.[97]

---

[90] [1952] Ch 488 at 498.

[91] Chap. 6, ante. See (1968) Conv (NS) 270 (M. J. Goodman); [1994] Conv 196 (H. Wallace).

[92] [1956] Ch 304 at 316, M & B p. 702; (1956) 72 LQR 172 (R.E.M.).

[93] (High Court (Chancery Division), 22 March 1982), M & B p. 703; *Handel v St Stephens Close Ltd* [1994] 1 EGLR 70.

[94] [1992] 1 WLR 1278 at 1288; affd [1994] 1 WLR 31, M & B p. 703; [1994] CLJ 229 (S. Bridge); *Handel v St Stephens Close Ltd* [1994] 1 EGLR 70; (1994) 144 NLJ 579 (H. W. Wilkinson); [1996] 16 LS 51 (P. Luther).

[95] For example, a lease, for which exclusive possession would be necessary; p. 197, ante; or, in the case of long user rather than express grant, a claim to title by adverse possession, although the regular parking of cars with-out taking further steps (such as enclosing the parking area) is unlikely to constitute the taking of possession: *Simpson v Fergus* (1999) 79 P & CR 398; *Central Midlands Estates Ltd v Leicester Dyers Ltd* [2003] 2 P & CR DG1.

[96] *Batchelor v Marlow* [2003] 1 WLR 764 (where, however, the parties agreed on the application of Judge Baker's test; exclusive right to park six cars for nine and a half hours every working day held not capable of being an easement). In *Saeed v Plustrade Ltd* [2002] 2 EGLR 19 at [22] Sir Christopher SLADE, on the basis that there was not yet authority in the Court of Appeal, preferred to leave open the general question of whether the right to park a car could exist as a valid easement, but "without intending in any way to suggest that Judge Paul Baker QC's decision [in *London and Blenheim Estates*] was wrong".

[97] Gale, paras. 9-73 to 9-75, M & B pp. 704–6.

B Easements Distinguished from Other Rights

Having seen something of the nature of easements, we will conclude this part of the subject by adverting to other rights of a somewhat similar nature from which they must be distinguished.[98]

(1) Licences

A licence is created in favour of B if, without being given any legal estate or interest, he is permitted by A to enter A's land for an agreed purpose. It is an authority that justifies what would otherwise be a trespass.

We shall discuss in chapter 23 the categories of licence and the different rules which are applicable to each of them.[99] Here it is sufficient to note the most significant difference between a licence and an easement: the former is normally only a purely personal right, which may be revocable, and does not of itself bind a purchaser from the licensor who created the licence.[100] However, an easement is a property right, of necessity annexed to a dominant tenement, and capable of binding the successor in title of the first servient owner who granted it, and being enforced by the successor in title of the first dominant owner. Moreover, as a property right, an easement is not revocable unilaterally by the grantor or his successors.

The distinction was illustrated in *IDC Group Ltd v Clark*,[101] where an agreement, which was made by deed and described as a licence, provided for a fire escape route through a party wall between two adjoining properties; the parties to the deed were expressed to include their respective successors and assigns. The Court of Appeal held that the deed, being professionally drawn and described as a licence, created personal and not property rights, and was therefore a licence. The licensees could therefore not require the current owner, a successor in title of the original licensor, to unblock the fire escape route.

(2) Local Customary Rights

Indefinite and fluctuating classes of persons, such as the inhabitants of a village, may be entitled to exercise over another's land rights which, if the matter rested between the servient owner and a definite dominant owner, would properly be termed easements. Illustrations from the cases are:

(a) where the inhabitants of a village pass across another's land on their way to church,[102] or

(b) where the fishing inhabitants dry their nets on certain property.[103]

Such rights are not easements, for an easement lies in grant, and a vague and fluctuating body of persons such as fishing inhabitants is not a legal person, and is therefore incapable

---

[98] For the difference between an easement and a profit, see p. 642, post.

[99] For the difference between a licence and a lease, see pp. 197 et seq, ante.

[100] We shall see that certain licences are irrevocable—e.g. a contractual licence which can be enforced according to the contractual terms: p. 834, post. And certain licences might give rise to proprietary rights capable of binding third parties—e.g. through the doctrine of proprietary estoppel: p. 814, post. But the starting point for the analysis of a licence is that it is a purely personal right.   [101] [1992] 1 EGLR 187; p. 201, ante.

[102] *Brocklebank v Thompson* [1903] 2 Ch 344.   [103] *Mercer v Denne* [1905] 2 Ch 538.

of taking under a grant. If, therefore, they are to be established, some other title than grant must be shown, and this, as we shall see later, is what the law calls *custom*.[104]

(3) Natural Rights

This is an expression often used to describe a right that is one of the ordinary and inseparable incidents of ownership, though its exercise requires an adjacent owner to forbear from doing something on his own land that otherwise he would be free to do. The epithet "natural" serves to distinguish such rights from easements, which do not automatically accompany ownership but must be acquired by grant, either actual, implied or presumed.[105] Thus an owner has a natural right to so much support from his neighbour's land as will support his own land, unincumbered by buildings, at its natural level;[106] and a riparian owner is entitled to demand that other riparian owners shall not divert the natural course of the stream.[107] Such natural rights differ from easements in at least two respects—their existence does not depend upon some form of grant, and they cannot be extinguished by unity of seisin.[108]

(4) Public Rights

Public rights are rights which anyone may exercise as a member of the public. Main examples are the right to pass along a public highway,[109] or to fish in the sea or to navigate over the foreshore.[110] These rights exist by virtue of the general law and do not require a dominant tenement.

C Legal and Equitable Easements

An easement is capable of subsisting as a legal interest. It will be legal if (i) it is held for "an interest equivalent to an estate in fee simple absolute in possession or a term of years absolute",[111] and (ii) is created by statute, deed or prescription,[112] and (iii) in the case of the express[113] grant or reservation of an easement over registered land, it is completed by registration.[114] If it does not satisfy these requirements, then it may be an equitable easement: for

---

[104] Pp. 655–7, post.   [105] *Backhouse v Bonomi* (1861) 9 HL Cas 503.

[106] Ibid.; *Midland Bank plc v Bardgrove Property Services Ltd* [1991] 2 EGLR 283; *Holbeck Hall Hotel Ltd v Scarborough BC* [1997] 2 EGLR 213 (rvsd. on the question of liability in tort [2000] QB 836).

[107] Pp. 177 et seq, ante.   [108] For extinguishment of easements, see p. 636, post.

[109] *Halsbury's Laws of England* (4th edn), vol. 21 (2004), paras. 1–11 (meaning of "highway" etc), 197–9 (extent of public right of highway); Sauvain, *Highway Law*. The legislation relating to highways is consolidated in Highways Act 1980 as amended.   [110] P. 180, ante.

[111] LPA 1925, s. 1(2)(a).   [112] Pp. 600 et seq, post.

[113] The registration requirement applies only to easements created by *express* grant or reservation. This does not therefore include easements created by implied grant or reservation, or prescription (p. 613, post). For these purposes an easement created by the operation of LPA 1925, s. 62, p. 603, post, is not an express grant and therefore does not require to be registered: LRA 2002, s. 27(7).

[114] LRA 2002, s. 27(2)(d). A notice of the interest must be entered in the register of the title of the servient tenement and (if the dominant tenement is also registered) the proprietor of the dominant tenement must be entered in the register as proprietor of the easement: ibid., Sch. 2, para. 7. It should be noted that the express grant of a legal easement is a registrable disposition regardless of the duration of the grant and so even if granted for the benefit of a lease for seven years or less which is not itself required to be registered, the easement must still be registered: H & B, para. 8.14.

example, if it is for the life of the grantee (even if it is created by deed), or if it is created informally,[115] or by a contract to grant a legal easement.[116] The grant of an easement implied into a contract, rather than into a deed, under the doctrine of *Wheeldon v Burrows*,[117] must also therefore create an equitable easement.

This distinction is important in relation to the enforceability of the easement against third parties. This is discussed in detail below.[118]

D Acquisition of Easements

The basic principle is that every easement must have had its origin in grant.[119]

All the methods of acquisition except one are traceable to a grant which has been or which might have been made, and the one exception, namely statute, is not of frequent occurrence. It may facilitate exposition to set the subject out in tabular form.

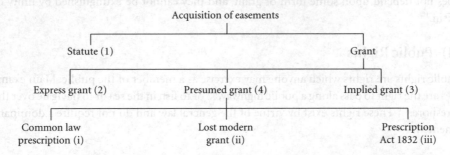

The figures in parentheses denote the order of treatment in the following pages.

(1) Acquisition by Statute

An example of statutory creation is an Inclosure Act. This is a statute that discharges land from rights of common to which it has hitherto been subject and distributes it in plots among a number of absolute owners.[120] As part of the scheme of distribution easements of way over adjoining plots are frequently reserved to the respective owners.[121] Modern examples of easements created by statute are to be found in local Acts of Parliament. Statutory rights similar to easements are also created by general Acts and are sometimes called statutory easements.[122]

A landowner may acquire an easement to enter upon his neighbour's land in order to carry out maintenance work to his own property.[123] Where an easement has not been aquired, the Access to Neighbouring Land Act 1992[124] enables him to obtain an order of the

---

[115] P. 601, post.   [116] *McManus v Cooke* (1887) 35 Ch D 681; p. 601, post.

[117] (1879) 12 Ch D 31, p. 610, post.   [118] Pp. 632 et seq, post.

[119] *Angus & Co v Dalton* (1877) 3 QBD 85 at 102, per COCKBURN CJ.   [120] P. 653, post.

[121] For example, *Adeane v Mortlock* (1839) 5 Bing NC 236.

[122] Jackson, chap. 12; (1956) 20 Conv (NS) 208 (J. F. Garner); Gale, paras. 1-10 to 1-118.

[123] *Ward v Kirkland* [1967] Ch 184, p. 232, n. 295, ante.

[124] The Act is based on the Law Commission Report on Rights of Access to Neighbouring Land 1985 (Law Com No. 151, Cmnd 9692). The Act had a chequered history: [1992] 26 EG 136 (J. Adams). It came into force on 31 January 1993. See Gale, paras. 11–41 to 11.69; Jackson, pp. 108–9. See CPR, r. 56.4(c); PD, para. 11.

court if the neighbour refuses access. An application for an access order is regarded as a pending land action.[125] In unregistered land a pending land action must be registered in the register of pending actions[126] if it is to bind a purchaser without express notice of it.[127] In registered land it must be protected by notice and cannot be an overriding interest.[128] An access order may be registered in the register of writs and orders affecting land[129] or, in the case of registered land, protected by the entry of an agreed notice against the affected title.[130] It cannot be an overriding interest.[131]

(2) Acquisition by Express Grant

(a) Creation

(1) AT COMMON LAW

An easement is an incorporeal hereditament[132] and therefore, in accordance with the historic rule of the common law, it must be granted by deed. This rule is now contained in section 52(1) of the Law of Property Act 1925:[133]

All conveyances of land or of any interest therein are void for the purpose of conveying or creating a legal estate[134] unless made by deed.

(2) IN EQUITY

At common law, a grant of an easement, made orally or by writing not executed as a deed, creates only a licence.[135] But this may create an equitable easement where equity acts on the principle that what ought to be done must be regarded as actually done—a view which has given us the doctrine of *Walsh v Lonsdale*.[136] If the grant satisfies the formalities required for a contract for the sale or other disposition of an interest in land and is for value, equity will treat this as a contract to grant a legal interest in land, and if the agreement is specifically enforceable, it will then treat the situation as if the grant by deed had already been made.[137] The leading case on the subject is *McManus v Cooke*.[138]

Between adjoining properties, belonging respectively to X and Y, there was a high party wall of unnecessary width. It was orally agreed between X and Y that in order to give more space to each owner the wall should be pulled down by X and replaced by one which was lower and thinner, the work to be at their joint expense. It was also agreed orally that each of the parties should erect a lean-to skylight, and that both of these should rest on the new wall and incline upwards and outwards to the respective houses. X duly carried out his part of the work, but Y, instead of building a lean-to

---

[125] Access to Neighbouring Land Act 1992, s. 5(6).   [126] LCA 1972, s. 1(1)(b).   [127] Ibid., s. 5(7).
[128] LRA 2002, s. 87(1), (3).   [129] LCA 1972, s. 6.   [130] LRA 2002, s. 34; LRR 2003, r. 80(c).
[131] Ibid., s. 87(1), (3); Access to Neighbouring Land Act 1992, s. 5(5), as substituted by LRA 2002, s. 133, Sch. 11, para. 26(1), (4).   [132] P. 585, ante.
[133] To be effective as a legal easement the grant must also be for an interest equivalent to a fee simple absolute or a term of years absolute; and (if granted over registered land) completed by registration: p. 599, ante.
[134] A legal easement is a "legal estate" within this definition: LPA 1925, s. 1(4).
[135] *Wood v Leadbitter* (1845) 13 M & W 838, M & B p. 597; *Fentiman v Smith* (1803) 4 East 107, pp. 832–3, post.   [136] Pp. 877 et seq, ante.
[137] *May v Belleville* [1905] 2 Ch 605.   [138] (1887) 35 Ch D 681.

skylight on his side, built one so shaped that part of it showed above the wall and in consequence obstructed the access of light to X's skylight. X sued for an injunction to restrain Y from maintaining an erection which infringed the agreement.

Kay J decided in favour of the plaintiff X on the ground that, although the parties' agreement that each should have an easement of light over the other's land was not effective at law for lack of a deed, it was effective to create an easement in equity. The case was decided in the context of the formality requirements for contracts which existed before 27 September 1989, under which an oral contract was sufficient to create an interest in land, but could not be enforced without a written memorandum or part performance by the plaintiff. Kay J found that, although there was no written memorandum of the contract to grant an easement, there was the requisite part performance. For contracts entered into after 26 September 1989 the agreement to grant an easement, if it is to have the effect of creating an equitable easement, must be in writing and signed by both dominant and servient owners, otherwise there is no contract at all.[139]

(3) IDENTIFICATION OF DOMINANT TENEMENT

If the dominant tenement has not been clearly described by the parties, the court will identify it by construing the instrument that created the easement.[140]

(b) Express reservation

If the owner of two adjoining properties desired, upon the sale of one of them, to retain rights over that one, he could do so at common law either by way of *exception* from the grant or by way of *reservation*.[141] However, the only things that could be excepted were specific parts of the land, such as timber and minerals; and the word "reservation" was only appropriate where services, such as the payment of rent, were to be rendered for the tenure of land.[142] If the vendor sought to retain an easement, therefore, it was formerly necessary either that the conveyance of the land should be executed by the *grantee* (whereupon the easement would arise by way of re-grant from him),[143] or that the conveyance should be made to him to the *use* that the vendor should enjoy the easement and subject thereto *to the use* of the purchaser in fee simple.[144]

With the repeal of the Statute of Uses the latter method is now impossible, and the former is unnecessary, for section 65(1) the Law of Property Act 1925 provides that "a reservation of a legal estate shall operate at law without any execution of the conveyance by the grantee of the legal estate out of which the reservation is made, or any regrant by him".

Such a reservation, however, still operates by way of re-grant. Thus, where an easement is reserved by a vendor of land, the terms of the reservation in cases of doubt are to be construed against the purchaser and not against the vendor.[145]

---

[139] P. 868, post.   [140] P. 629. n. 351, post.
[141] *Durham and Sunderland Rly Co v Walker* (1842) 2 QB 940.
[142] Leake, *Uses and Profits of Land*, p. 265.   [143] *Wickham v Hawker* (1840) 7M & W 63.
[144] Conveyancing Act 1881, s. 62(1).
[145] *Johnstone v Holdway* [1963] 1 QB 601; *St Edmundsbury and Ipswich Diocesan Board of Finance v Clarke (No 2)* [1975] 1 WLR 468, M & B p. 714.

It is also provided by section 65(2) that: "a conveyance of a legal estate expressed to be made subject to another legal estate not in existence immediately before the date of the conveyance shall operate as a reservation unless a contrary intention appears".[146]

(c) Section 62 of the Law of Property Act 1925

(1) THE SECTION

It is of the greatest practical importance to observe that, owing to section 62 of the Law of Property Act 1925, a grant of land may have a far-reaching, and sometimes an unexpected, effect upon the creation of easements. This section provides that unless a contrary intention is expressed in the conveyance:

A conveyance of land shall be deemed to include and shall by virtue of this Act operate to convey, with the land, all buildings, erections, fixtures, commons, hedges, ditches, fences, ways, waters, watercourses, liberties, privileges, easements, rights, and advantages whatsoever, appertaining or reputed to appertain to the land or any part thereof, or, at the time of conveyance, demised, occupied, or enjoyed with, or reputed or known as part or parcel of or appurtenant to the land or any part thereof.[147]

The object of this section is to ensure that a grantee, without inserting numerous descriptive terms, usually called *general words*, in the conveyance, shall automatically[148] acquire the benefit not only of easements and other rights appurtenant to the land in the strict sense, but also of quasi-easements and other privileges which have hitherto been enjoyed in respect of the land. It is obvious that easements already appurtenant to the land conveyed continue in favour of the grantee, but the statutory words are so sweeping and comprehensive that the conveyance, unless expressly limited in its operation, may have an effect far wider than the grantor intends. The effect indeed may be catastrophic in the sense that privileges which have hitherto been enjoyed by the permission of the grantor in respect of the land conveyed, a permission which could at any moment have been revoked, may acquire the status of permanent easements as a result of the conveyance.

Suppose, for example, that A, the owner of two adjoining closes, Blackacre and Whiteacre, leases Blackacre to X, and as a friendly act allows X to use a path over Whiteacre as a short cut to the main road and also to store his coal in a shed on Whiteacre. Later A either sells or conveys the fee simple of Blackacre to X or renews X's lease of Blackacre.

In this case at the time of the conveyance there is a "privilege . . . enjoyed with the land" conveyed. The statute therefore comes into operation, and the effect of the conveyance, unless it expresses a contrary intention, is that a right of way over Whiteacre and a right to use the shed become appurtenant to Blackacre.[149]

---

[146] *Wiles v Banks* (1983) 50 P & CR 80 (conveyance "subject to a right of way").

[147] S. 62(1), re-enacting Conveyancing Act 1881, s. 6(1).

[148] Easements created by s. 62 are commonly classified as created by express grant, rather than by implied grant, since the words are deemed by the statute to be written into the conveyance. However, such easements are not treated as expressly granted for the purpose of the registration requirement under LRA 2002, s. 27(2)(d): ibid., s. 27(7).

[149] *International Tea Stores Co v Hobbs* [1903] 2 Ch 165; *Wright v Macadam* [1949] 2 KB 744, M & B p. 723.

Again, if B, the owner of a mansion and park, allows Y, the tenant of the lodge at one of the gates, to use the main drive as a means of access to the neighbouring village, and later sells and conveys the fee simple of the lodge to him, a similar result follows. Y acquires an easement of way over the drive.[150]

The permissive nature of the privilege enjoyed prior to the conveyance is quite irrelevant in these cases. The question is not whether the grantee had an enforceable right to enjoy the privilege, but, whether it was in fact enjoyed by him as occupant of the land prior to the conveyance.[151]

(2) LIMITS OF THE SECTION

In spite of the wide wording of section 62, there are strict limits to its operation:

(i) Conveyance

The section does not operate unless there has been a "conveyance" of land, a word which by statute includes: "a mortgage, charge, lease, assent, vesting declaration, vesting instrument, disclaimer, release and every other assurance of property or of an interest therein by any instrument, except a will".[152]

This definition does not include an oral lease.[153] Nor does it include a contract for a lease or for the sale of land, since an assurance is "something which operates as a transfer of property"[154] and a mere contract has no such operation, notwithstanding that under the doctrine of *Walsh v Lonsdale*[155] it is for many purposes as effective as a lease.[156]

The right must not only be enjoyed prior to the conveyance, it must also be enjoyed with the land[157] at the time of the conveyance. As MEGARRY V-C said in *Penn v Wilkins*:[158] "Section 62 was apt for conveying existing rights, but it did not resurrect mere memories of past rights. And likewise the section is not concerned with future rights".[159]

A right which is enjoyed with only part of the land conveyed may nevertheless benefit the whole. Thus in *Graham v Philcox*[160] the purchaser of the freehold of a converted coach house was also the tenant of a first floor flat in it which had the benefit of a right of way. The Court of Appeal held that, under section 62, the benefit of the right of way enured to the whole of the building. In effect the section operated to enlarge the extent of an existing easement.

---

[150] *International Tea Stores Co v Hobbs* [1903]2 Ch 165 at 172; *Goldberg v Edwards* [1950] Ch 247, M & B p. 726.

[151] *Wright v Macadam* [1949]2 KB 744, at 750–1; *Phipps v Pears* [1965] 1 QB 76, M & B p. 728. For a critical attitude to this effect of s. 62(1), see *Wright v Macadam*, supra, at 755, per TUCKER LJ; *Green v Ashco Horticulturist Ltd* [1966] 1 WLR 889 at 896, per CROSS J; [1998] Conv 115 (L. Tee). [152] LPA 1925, s. 205(1)(ii).

[153] *Rye v Rye* [1962] AC 496, M & B p. 524.   [154] *Re Ray* [1896] 1 Ch 468 at 476.

[155] P. 877, post.   [156] *Borman v Griffith* [1930] 1 Ch 493, M & B p. 465.

[157] Enjoyment is not synonymous with user: *Re Yateley Common, Hampshire* [1977] 1 WLR 840 at 850. See *MRA Engineering Ltd v Trimster Co Ltd* (1987) 56 P & CR 1 (rights of access granted to an existing tenant held not to pass under s. 62 on sale of freehold after surrender of the lease); *Re St Clement's, Leigh-on-Sea* [1988] 1 WLR 720.

[158] (1974) 236 EG 203 (passage of sewage which ceased many years before conveyance not covered by s. 62).

[159] *Nickerson v Barraclough* [1981] Ch 426; *Payne v Inwood* (1996) 74 P & CR 42 ("section 62 cannot create new rights where there has been no actual enjoyment of a facility by the owner or occupier of the dominant tenement over the servient tenement", at 47, per ROCH LJ); [1997] Conv 453 (M. P. Thompson).

[160] [1984] QB 747, M & B p. 762, following *Wright v Macadam*, supra; [1985] Conv 60 (P. Todd); [1985] CLJ 15 (S. Tromans).

(ii) Nature of right

No right will be conveyed by virtue of the Act, however, unless it is a right known to the law.[161]

As Lord DENNING MR said in *Phipps v Pears*:[162]

A fine view, or an expanse open to the winds, may be an "advantage" to a house, but it would not pass under section 62. Whereas a right to use a coal shed or to go along a passage would pass under section 62. The reason being that these last are rights known to the law, whereas the others are not. A right to protection from the weather is not a right known to the law. It does not therefore pass under section 62.

And it must not be a right which the grantor at the time of the grant had no power to grant;[163] nor one which is merely a matter of personal contract;[164] nor one the enjoyment of which could only be expected to be temporary.[165] Further, the section only operates to pass rights which are part and parcel of the land conveyed. A conveyance of land is deemed to include all "buildings, erections and fixtures", and it has been held that a greenhouse resting on its own weight on concrete dollies was neither a fixture nor an erection within the section.[166]

(iii) Diversity of ownership or occupation

The section will not operate unless, as in the examples given above, there has been some diversity of ownership or occupation of the two closes prior to the conveyance.[167] If, for instance, the grantor, the common owner or occupier of Blackacre and Whiteacre, has been in the habit of passing over Blackacre in order to reach the highway, his conveyance of Whiteacre does not entitle the grantee to invoke the statute and to establish a right of way over Blackacre.

What the grantor was accustomed to do was attributable to his general rights as the occupying owner of both closes, not to a privilege deriving from his occupation of Whiteacre, as distinct from his occupation of Blackacre.[168] In approving what has come to be called the

---

[161] *International Tea Stores Co v Hobbs* [1903] 2 Ch 165 at 172; *Goldberg v Edwards* [1950] Ch 247; *Ward v Kirkland* [1967] Ch 194; *Green v Ashco Horticulturist Ltd* [1966] 1 WLR 889; *Phipps v Pears* [1965] 1 QB 76; *Crow v Wood* [1971] 1 QB 77, M & B p. 710.

[162] Supra, at 84, M & B p. 728.   [163] *Quicke v Chapman* [1903] 1 Ch 659.

[164] *Regis Property Co Ltd v Redman* [1956] 2 QB 612 (tenant's right to receive limited supply of hot water and central heating under contract with landlord).

[165] *Wright v Macadam* [1949] 2 KB 744 at 751, per JENKINS LJ, citing COTTON LJ in *Birmingham, Dudley and District Banking Co v Ross* (1888) 38 Ch D 295 at 307; *Green v Ashco Horticulturist Ltd*, supra, at 897; *Hair v Gillman* [2000] 3 EGLR 74 at 76, where CHADWICK LJ identified "the distinction between a right that is temporary, in the sense that it is merely precarious, so that it can be withdrawn at any time, and a right that is temporary in the sense that, to the knowledge of the parties, it will only be capable of being enjoyed for some limited period because of the nature of the property over which it is enjoyed." The former can become an easement under s. 62; the latter cannot.   [166] *H E Dibble Ltd v Moore* [1970] 2 QB 181.

[167] *Sovmots Investments Ltd v Secretary of State for the Environment* [1979] AC 144 at 169, 176, M & B p. 731, approving *Long v Gowlett* [1923] 2 Ch 177, M & B p. 729. See *Ward v Kirkland* [1967] Ch 184 at 227–31; *Wright v Macadam* [1949] 2 KB 744 at 748; *Squarey v Harris-Smith* (1981) 42 P & CR 118, per OLIVER LJ. For criticism of the rule, see Jackson, pp. 100–3; (1966) 30 Conv (NS) 342–8; [1978] Conv 449 (P. Smith); and in favour [1979] Conv 113 (C. Harpum).

[168] *Long v Gowlett*, supra, at 200–1. The right to light, however, stands on a different footing: ibid., at 202–3, citing *Broomfield v Williams* [1897] 1 Ch 602.

rule in *Long v Gowlett*, Lord WILBERFORCE said in *Sovmots Investments Ltd v Secretary of State for the Environment*:[169]

> When land is under one ownership one cannot speak in any intelligible sense of rights, or privileges, or easements being exercised over one part for the benefit of another. Whatever the owner does, he does as owner and until a separation occurs, of ownership, or at least of occupation, the condition for the existence of rights, etc., does not exist.

In order to substantiate his claim, the grantee would have to bring himself within the doctrine of an implied grant under the rule in *Wheeldon v Burrows*.[170]

In *P & S Platt Ltd v Crouch*,[171] however, the Court of Appeal has recently held that section 62 can operate to create an easement where there is no prior diversity of occupation of the dominant and servient tenements, in a case where the easement is continuous and apparent. In that case:

> the defendants owned a hotel, a house in the grounds of the hotel, and a separate plot of land adjacent to the Norfolk Broads where river moorings were used for the benefit of the hotel guests. Signs at the river side made clear that the moorings were for the use of hotel guests only, and the hotel's web site advertised the availability of the moorings. The claimant purchased the hotel, but not the other properties. It was held that it had acquired the right to the moorings, for the benefit of the hotel, as an easement by virtue of section 62.

If confirmed, this decision will be a significant exception to the rule in *Long v Gowlett*.[172]

(iv) Subject to contrary intention

Section 62 applies only if and as far as a contrary intention is not expressed in the conveyance, and has effect subject to the terms of the conveyance;[173] it is also subject to the circumstances existing at the time of the grant.[174] In determining this, however, evidence of the contractual negotiations is not normally admissible.[175]

Enough has now been said to show that a grantor, who retains property adjoining that granted, or a landlord about to renew a lease, should be extremely vigilant to ensure that any advantages or privileges hitherto enjoyed in respect of the land are either revoked or expressly excepted from the conveyance, unless he wishes them to continue.[176]

If an intention is shown in the preliminary contract of sale that a certain privilege shall not pass to the purchaser, the vendor is entitled to insert a clause in the deed of conveyance

---

169 [1979] AC 144 at 169.   170 P. 610, post.

171 [2004] 1 P & CR 18 at [47], per PETER GIBSON LJ, and [59], per LONGMORE LJ.

172 *Sovmots Investments Ltd v Secretary of State for the Environment*, supra, was not cited. It is significant in using one of the criteria for the application of the rule in *Wheeldon v Burrows* ("continuous and apparent") without the further requirement that the right be necessary for the reasonable enjoyment of the dominant tenement; p. 610, post.   173 LPA 1925. s. 62(4).

174 *Selby DC v Samuel Smith Old Brewery (Tadcaster) Ltd* [2001] 1 EGLR 71 at 75, per CHADWICK LJ.

175 *P & S Platt Ltd v Crouch*, supra, at [37]–[39], per PETER GIBSON LJ, and [52]–[56], per LONGMORE LJ.

176 See Standard Conditions of Sale, Condition 3.4.2; Wilkinson, *Standard Conditions of Sale of Land* (5th edn), pp. 29–33.

restrictive of the operation of the statute.[177] Moreover, in such a case he is entitled to have the conveyance rectified if, owing to the common mistake of the parties, it does not include a restrictive clause of this nature.[178]

(3) Acquisition by Implied Grant[179]

An owner, as we have seen, cannot have an easement over his own land.[180] Where, however, he has been accustomed to using one part in a particular manner, as for example by crossing a field to reach the highway, his practice is conveniently described as the exercise of a *quasi-easement*. If he later severs his ownership by granting part only of the land to another, such a quasi-easement is capable of ripening by implication into an easement properly so called in favour either of the land granted or the land retained.

The principle of this mode of creation is that although there has been no express mention of an easement in the grant of the land, yet it may very well be that the common intention of the parties cannot be carried out unless some particular easement is deemed to arise by implication.

The premises for the application of the doctrine are, first, that A, the owner of two separate tenements, has been in the habit of enjoying certain quasi-easements over one of them; and secondly, that the common ownership of A has been severed. Thus, if A sells the quasi-servient tenement, certain easements may be implied in his favour over the part sold (*implied reservation*); if he sells the quasi-dominant tenement, certain easements may be implied against him and in favour of the purchaser (*implied grant*); while the question of implication may also arise when he disposes of both the tenements to different persons. We shall now consider these three cases separately.

(a) Implied reservation. Common owner sells quasi-servient tenement

The law is disinclined to imply easements in favour of a grantor. The reason is not difficult to find. In the case of a grant of land the law is guided by two principles: the words of a deed must be construed as far as possible in favour of the grantee;[181] and the grantor cannot derogate from his own absolute grant by claiming rights over the thing granted.[182] If the

---

[177] *Squarey v Harris-Smith* (1981) 42 P & CR 118 (where a standard condition that the purchaser should not acquire any rights which would restrict the free use of the vendor's other land for building was held to negative the operation of s. 62); cf *Lyme Valley Squash Club Ltd v Newcastle under Lyme BC* [1985] 2 All ER 405, in which *Squarey v Harris-Smith* was not cited, and the opposite conclusion reached; [1985] Conv 243. See also *William Hill (Southern) Ltd v Cabras Ltd* [1987] 1 EGLR 37; *Pretoria Warehousing Co Ltd v Shelton* [1993] EGCS 120; [1996] Conv 238 (A. Dowling); *Millman v Ellis* (1995) 71 P & CR 158 (grant of narrower easement not necessarily a contrary intention); [1995] Conv 346 (J. West); *Selby DC v Samuel Smith Old Brewery (Tadcaster) Ltd* [2001] 1 EGLR 71.　　　　　　　　　　　　　　[178] *Clark v Barnes* [1929] 2 Ch 368.

[179] See generally Farrand, *Contract and Conveyance* (2nd edn), pp. 382–90.　　[180] P. 590, ante.

[181] *Neill v Duke of Devonshire* [1882] 8 App Cas 135 at 149, per Lord SELBORNE. Cf Lewison, *Interpretation of Contracts*, para. 7.07, noting that this *contra proferentem* rule of construction is not always applied consistently, particularly in the modern cases.

[182] *Suffield v Brown* (1864) 4 De GJ & Sm 185, per Lord WESTBURY. See generally (1964) 80 LQR 244 (D. W. Elliott). The rule may be varied by contract; see Standard Conditions of Sale (3rd edn, 1995), para. 3.4.

grantor intends to retain a right over the land, it is his duty to reserve it expressly in the grant.[183] As a general rule there will be no implication in his favour.[184]

(1) EASEMENTS OF NECESSITY

There are, no doubt, exceptions to this rule, the most obvious of which is the way of necessity. This arises where land which is entirely surrounded by other land is segregated by the common owner, and retained by him. In such a case a way is implied in favour of the grantor.[185]

The extent of the implied right is strictly limited and depends upon the mode of enjoyment of the surrounded land prevailing at the time of the grant.[186] The way may be used for any purpose which is essential to maintain that mode of enjoyment; it may not be used for other purposes. Thus where at the time of the grant the surrounded close was used only for agricultural purposes, it was held that the grantor was not entitled to carry over it timber and other materials.[187]

(2) EASEMENTS OF COMMON INTENTION[188]

Easements will also be implied in favour of the grantor as may be necessary to give effect to the common intention of grantor and grantee as for example where mutual easements of support are implied on the conveyance of one of two adjacent buildings supported by each other.[189] There may be other cases where such easements will be implied in favour of a grantor without express reservation,[190] but the scales are heavily weighted against him. The necessary inference from the circumstances must be that he was intended to retain the precise easement that he claims.[191]

(b) Implied grant. Common owner sells quasi-dominant tenement

The law is much more inclined to imply easements in favour of the grantee than in favour of the grantor.

(1) EASEMENTS OF NECESSITY

As we have seen, easements of necessity may be impliedly reserved in favour of a grantor over the quasi-servient tenement which he has granted. Consistently with the principle that

---

[183] *Wheeldon v Burrows* (1879) 12 Ch D 31 at 49, per THESIGER LJ.

[184] Ibid.; *Aldridge v Wright* [1929] 2 KB 117; *Liddiard v Waldron* [1934] 1 KB 435; *Re Webb's Lease* [1951] Ch 808, M & B p. 736.

[185] *Union Lighterage Co v London Graving Dock Co* [1902] 2 Ch 557 at 573; *Pinnington v Galland* (1853) 9 Exch 1; *Sweet v Sommer* [2004] 4 All ER 288 (retained land to be regarded as landlocked where access could be obtained only over the property granted or by destruction of a physical barrier on the retained land (a building) the continued existence of which was obviously contemplated by the parties; affd on other grounds [2005] ALL ER (D) 162(Mar).

[186] *London Corpn v Riggs* (1880) 13 Ch D 798, M & B p. 734.

[187] Ibid.; *Serff v Acton Local Board* (1886) 31 Ch D 679.

[188] This paragraph was cited with approval by CAZALET J in *Peckham v Ellison* (2000) 79 P & CR 276 at 285. Cf *Chaffe v Kingsley* [2000] 1 EGLR 104 (no easement).

[189] *Richards v Rose* (1853) 9 Exch 218; *Shubrook v Tufnell* (1882) 46 LT 886.

[190] *Re Webb's Lease* [1951] Ch 808 at 816–17, 823, M & B p. 736.

[191] Ibid., at 828 (easement not implied); *Peckham v Ellison*, supra (easement implied, having regard to length of user of path by dominant owner and disclosure of existence of right to servient owner at time of purchase); [1999] Conv 353 (L. Fox).

a grantor may not derogate from his grant, the law more readily implies easements in favour of the grantee of the quasi-dominant tenement; a fortiori an easement of necessity will be implied in his favour.[192]

In *Nickerson v Barraclough*,[193] the Court of Appeal rejected an argument that, if the implied grant of a way of necessity has been negated by an express contrary provision, such a grant may nevertheless be implied under a rule of public policy that "no transaction should, without good reason, be treated as effectual to deprive land of a suitable means of access".[194] BRIGHTMAN LJ said:[195] "The doctrine of way of necessity is not founded upon public policy at all but upon an implication from the circumstances . . . There would seem to be no particular reason to father the doctrine . . . upon public policy when implication is such an obvious and convenient candidate for paternity".

The Court of Appeal held that a way of necessity could only exist in association with a grant of land, and depended on the intention of the parties and the implication from the circumstances that, unless some way was implied, the land would be inaccessible. Public policy could not help the court to ascertain that intention;[196] it could only require the court to frustrate that intention where a contract was against public policy.

(2) EASEMENTS OF COMMON INTENTION

Similarly the law more readily implies easements of common intention in favour of the grantee. As Lord PARKER OF WADDINGTON said:[197]

The law will readily imply the grant or reservation of easements as may be necessary to give effect to the common intention of the parties to a grant of real property, with reference to the manner or purposes in and for which the land granted . . . is to be used. But it is essential for this purpose that the parties should intend that the subject of the grant . . . should be used in some definite and particular manner. It is not enough that the subject of the grant should be intended to be used in a manner which may or may not involve this definite and particular use.

In *Wong v Beaumont Property Trust Ltd*:[198]

three cellars in Exeter were let by B's predecessor in title to W's predecessor in title for the purpose of being used as a Chinese restaurant. By certain statutory regulations no premises could be used for this purpose unless they were provided with a ventilation system. In the circumstances, it was impossible to install this without affixing a duct to the outside walls of B's superjacent building.

---

[192] See *Liverpool City Council v Irwin* [1977] AC 239, p. 595, ante; cf *Manjang v Drammeh* (1990) 61 P & CR 194 (PC held no easement of necessity where available access by water across the River Gambia "albeit perhaps less convenient than access across *terra firma*"); *MRA Engineering Ltd v Trimster Co Ltd* (1987) 56 P & CR 1 (no easement of necessity because access on foot was "merely difficult and inconvenient"; land was not inaccessible or useless without right of way claimed).

[193] [1981] Ch 426 reversing MEGARRY V-C [1980] Ch 325; (1982) 98 LQR 11 (P. Jackson). For a comparative study of legal solutions on access to landlocked land, see (1982) 10 Syd LR 39 (A. J. Bradbrook).

[194] [1980] Ch 325 at 334, per MEGARRY V-C.

[195] [1981] Ch 426 at 440.

[196] EVELEIGH LJ at 383 thought that in a rare case public policy might help.

[197] *Pwllbach Colliery Co Ltd v Woodman* [1915] AC 634 at 646; cf *Stafford v Lee* (1992) 65 P & CR 172.

[198] [1965] 1 QB 173, M & B p. 720; *Stafford v Lee* (1992) 65 P & CR 172; *Mobil Oil Co Ltd v Birmingham City Council* [2002] 2 P & CR 14.

The Court of Appeal granted a declaration that W was entitled to an easement of necessity,[199] and was entitled to construct and maintain the duct.

(3) EASEMENTS WITHIN THE RULE IN *WHEELDON V BURROWS*[200]

The rule has been laid down in an obiter dictum by THESIGER LJ in *Wheeldon v Burrows*, which has been accepted as a correct statement of the law, that:

> on the grant by the owner of a tenement of part of that tenement as it is then used and enjoyed, there will pass to the grantee all those continuous and apparent easements (by which, of course, I mean quasi-easements), or, in other words, all those easements which are necessary to the reasonable enjoyment of the property granted,[201] and which have been and are at the time of the grant used by the owner of the entirety for the benefit of the part granted.

This rule is also a rule of intention, based on the proposition that a grantor may not derogate from his grant. As Lord WILBERFORCE said:[202] "He cannot grant or agree to grant land and at the same time deny to the grantee what is at the time of the grant obviously necessary for its reasonable enjoyment."

Thus, for instance, it has been law since 1663 that if one grants a house in which there are windows, he cannot build on his own adjoining land so as to obstruct the light.[203] It also follows that the rule cannot apply in the case of a compulsory purchase of land; that would mean substituting for the intention of a reasonable voluntary grantor the unilateral, opposed, intention of the acquirer.[204]

However, the implication of an easement can also be negatived by contrary intention: the rule in *Wheeldon v Burrows* only operates to the extent that it is not inconsistent with the intentions of the parties, which may be inferred from the circumstances.[205]

It will be noticed that, unlike section 62 of the Law of Property Act 1925, the rule in *Wheeldon v Burrows* is limited to continuous and apparent easements.[206] Strictly

---

[199] The court classified this as an easement of necessity, but this must be *per incuriam*. "An easement is surely not an 'easement of necessity' merely because it is necessary to give effect to the intention" (1964) 80 LQR 322 (R.E.M.). But the two headings may overlap: see *Nickerson v Barraclough* [1980] Ch 325 at 332.

[200] *Wheeldon v Burrows* (1879) 12 Ch D 31 at 49, M & B p. 718. The case itself is a decision on implied reservation.

[201] At 58 THESIGER LJ appears to treat these as two alternative requirements, and not, as here, synonymous. See *Ward v Kirkland* [1967] Ch 194 at 224, per UNGOED-THOMAS J; M & B p. 720; *Squarey v Harris-Smith* (1981) 42 P & CR 118 at 124, per OLIVER LJ (where it was held that a right of way was necessary to the reasonable enjoyment of land "having regard to the purpose for which, in the contemplation of both parties, it was sold", but any implied right was excluded by a condition of sale incorporated into the contract); (1967) 83 LQR 240 (A. W. B. Simpson); *Wheeler v J J Saunders Ltd* [1996] Ch 19 at 30, per PETER GIBSON LJ; [1995] Conv 239 (M. P. Thompson); [1995] All ER Rev 311 (P. J. Clarke).

[202] *Sovmots Investments Ltd v Secretary of State for the Environment* [1979] AC 144 at 168; (1977) 41 Conv NS 415 (C. Harpum). [203] *Palmer v Fletcher* (1663) 1 Lev 122; *Phillips v Low* [1892] 1 Ch 47.

[204] *Sovmots Investments Ltd v Secretary of State for the Environment*, supra.

[205] *Selby DC v Samuel Smith Old Brewery (Tadcaster) Ltd* [2001] 1 EGLR 71 at 74, per PETER GIBSON LJ.

[206] For an illuminating discussion of the origins of the words "continuous" and "apparent" in the French Civil Code, adopted first by Gale and then later by THESIGER LJ in *Wheeldon v Burrows*, see (1967) 83 LQR 240 (A. W. B. Simpson).

speaking a continuous easement is one, such as the right to light, the constant enjoyment of which does not, as in the case of a right of way, require the active intervention of the dominant owner. The word "continuous", however, is not in this context to be taken in its strict sense but rather in the sense of permanence. The two words "continuous" and "apparent" must be read together and understood as pointing to an easement which is accompanied by some obvious and permanent mark on the land itself, or at least by some mark which will be disclosed by a careful inspection of the premises.[207] Examples are:

(i) watercourses consisting of some actual construction such as pipes;[208]

(ii) a made road;[209]

(iii) light flowing through windows;[210]

(iv) drains which can be discovered with ordinary care.[211]

A right of way is not necessarily such a quasi-easement as will pass under the rule in *Wheeldon v Burrows*. To do so it must be apparent. There is no difficulty where there is a definite made road over the quasi-servient tenement to and for the apparent use of the quasi-dominant tenement. Such will clearly pass upon a severance of the common tenement.[212] But the existence of a formed road is not essential, and if there are other indicia which show that the road was being used at the time of the grant for the benefit of the quasi-dominant tenement and that it is necessary for the reasonable enjoyment of that tenement,[213] it will pass to a purchaser of the latter.[214] Thus:

A man built four cottages on his own land and left a strip between the rear of the cottages and the boundary of his land in order to afford a back means of access to the main highway. It was held that the quasi-easement of way was sufficiently continuous and apparent to pass under the present doctrine, for at the time of the grant the strip, though not formed into a made road, was worn and marked with rough tracks, so that no one seeing it could doubt that it was used as a way to the cottages.[215]

This doctrine of *Wheeldon v Burrows* has been shorn of much of its importance by section 62 of the Law of Property Act 1925,[216] but it still remains available in those cases where section 62 is inapplicable, either because there has been no diversity of occupation

---

[207] *Pyer v Carter* (1857) 1 H & N 916 at 922, adopting *Gale on Easements*; *Ward v Kirkland* [1967] Ch 194 (right to enter neighbour's land to repair and maintain a wall held to be not continuous and apparent; it was, however, held to be an easement created under LPA 1925, s. 62; p. 603, ante).

[208] *Watts v Kelson* (1871) 6 Ch App 166; *Schwann v Cotton* [1916] 2 Ch 120; affd [1916] 2 Ch 459.

[209] *Brown v Alabaster* (1887) 37 Ch D 490.   [210] *Allen v Taylor* (1880) 16 Ch D 355.

[211] *Pyer v Carter*, supra.

[212] *Brown v Alabaster*, supra; *Davies v Sear* (1869) LR 7 Eq 427.

[213] "Necessary" must not be confused with "necessity" (see "easements of necessity", p. 608, ante). A way of necessity is one without which the property cannot be used at all, but "necessary" in the present connection indicates that the way conduces to the reasonable enjoyment of the property. This note was cited with approval by PETER GIBSON LJ in *Wheeler v J J Saunders Ltd* [1996] Ch 19 at 31.

[214] *Hansford v Jago* [1921] 1 Ch 322; *Borman v Griffith* [1930] 1 Ch 493 at 499. This paragraph was cited with approval in *Ward v Kirkland* [1967] Ch 194 at 225.   [215] *Hansford v Jago* [1921] 1 Ch 322.

[216] Pp. 603, ante.

prior to a conveyance,[217] or because there has been no "conveyance" as defined by the Act.[218] Thus in *Borman v Griffith*:[219]

X, who owned a large park containing two houses, The Gardens and The Hall, agreed in writing to lease The Gardens to the plaintiff for seven years. A drive ran from the public road to The Hall, passing en route close to The Gardens. There was no separate drive for The Gardens, but at the time of the agreement X was constructing, and he later completed, an unmetalled way which ran from the back door of the house to the public road. The agreement reserved no right of way to the plaintiff, but he constantly used The Hall drive in preference to the unmetalled way. Later, the defendant took a lease from X of The Hall and the rest of the park, and began to obstruct the plaintiff in his use of the drive. In the ensuing action the plaintiff claimed to be entitled to a right of way over the drive.

The question, therefore, was whether the plaintiff had acquired the quasi-easement which the common owner of the whole land had exercised over the drive when passing from The Gardens to the public road. There was clearly no easement of necessity, since the unmetalled way provided a means of approach to the outside world. It was equally clear that section 62 was inapplicable to a contract for a lease. Nevertheless it was held that an easement of way had arisen by implication in favour of the plaintiff according to the doctrine of *Wheeldon v Burrows*. Thus, under that doctrine a grantee acquires those easements to which he has an implied contractual right; but under section 62 of the Law of Property Act 1925, the conveyance may vest in him an easement to which he has no contractual right whatsoever.[220]

(c) Contemporaneous sales to different persons

Where, instead of a sale of part of the land and a retention by the common owner of the other part, there have been simultaneous sales effected of separate but *contemporaneous* conveyances to different persons, all those continuous and apparent quasi-easements which were in use at the time of the sales pass by implication with the respective parts.[221] In other words, when the sales are by the same vendor and take place at one and the same time, the rights of each of the purchasers are exactly the same as if the common owner had sold the dominant part and kept the rest of the land.

Thus in *Schwann v Cotton*[222] where a testator devised Blackacre to X and Whiteacre to Y, it was held that a right to the free passage of water which flowed through an underground pipe running across Blackacre to Whiteacre passed by implication to the devisee of Whiteacre.

If the sales are not simultaneous, the later purchaser is in the same position as his vendor. So if the vendor first sells the quasi-servient tenement, he will not, in the absence of an express reservation, be entitled to easements over the part sold, except a way of necessity where one exists, nor will a subsequent purchaser from him be in any better position;[223] but

---

[217] On whether diversity of ownership or occupation is still a requirement for s. 62, see *P & S Platt Ltd v Crouch* [2004] 1 P & CR 18, p. 606, ante.

[218] P. 604, ante. Where the grant is implied into a contract, rather than a conveyance, it must necessarily create only an equitable easement: p. 601, ante. S. 62, however, is wider, in that the right need not be "continuous and apparent", nor "necessary to the reasonable enjoyment of the property granted".

[219] [1930] 1 Ch 493, M & B p. 524; *Horn v Hiscock* (1972) 223 EG 1437.

[220] (1952) 15 MLR pp. 265–6 (A. D. Hargreaves).

[221] *Allen v Taylor* (1880) 16 Ch D 355; *Swansborough v Coventry* (1832) 9 Bing 305; *Barnes v Loach* (1879) 4 QBD 494; *Schwann v Cotton* [1916] 2 Ch 120; affd 459; *Hansford v Jago* [1921] 1 Ch 322.   [222] Supra.

[223] *Murchie v Black* (1865) 19 CBNS 190.

if the vendor first sells the quasi-dominant tenement, the purchaser thereof can enforce quasi-easements against a subsequent purchaser of the quasi-servient tenement to the same extent as he could have done against the vendor.

(4) Acquisition by Presumed Grant or Prescription

Proof of the existence of an easement may be based upon a mere presumption that at some time in the past it has been granted by deed. There are three possible methods by which a claimant may avail himself of this presumption, for he may plead prescription:

(i)   at common law; or

(ii) under the doctrine of lost modern grant; or

(iii) under the Prescription Act 1832.

Each method is based upon identical reasoning. The established principle is that an easement must be created by deed of grant, since incorporeal hereditaments lie in grant.[224] On the other hand, it is obviously undesirable that one should be deprived of an easement long and continuously enjoyed merely because its formal creation by deed is incapable of proof. Therefore, in accordance with the maxim—*omnia praesumuntur rite et sollemniter esse acta*—the law is prepared to infer from this long enjoyment that all those acts were done that were necessary to create a valid title.[225] In this way, a claim, founded upon actual enjoyment without interruption by the servient owner, is referred to a lawful origin.

(a) Nature of user

Long enjoyment, however, is not in itself sufficient to raise the presumption of a grant. It must be of a particular nature, and this is so whether an easement is claimed by prescription at common law, or under the doctrine of lost modern grant or under the Prescription Act 1832. As we shall see, the user must be as of right and continuous, and only a grant in fee simple will be presumed.

All forms of prescription ultimately depend on the acquiescence of the servient owner. Why should long user confer a right protected by the courts? The answer is, that if the servient owner has allowed somebody to exercise an easement over his land for a considerable period and if he has omitted to prevent such exercise when he might very well have done so, it is only reasonable to conclude that the privilege has been rightfully enjoyed, for otherwise some attempt to interfere with it would long ago have been made by any owner who possessed even a modicum of common sense. FRY J said in *Dalton v Angus & Co*:[226]

In my opinion, the whole law of prescription and the whole law which governs the presumption or inference of a grant or covenant rest upon acquiescence. The courts and the judges have had recourse to various expedients for quieting the possession of persons in the exercise of rights which have not been resisted by the persons against whom they are exercised; but in all cases it appears to me that acquiescence and nothing else is the principle upon which these expedients rest. It becomes then of the

---

[224]   P. 601, ante.

[225]   *Philipps v Halliday* [1891] AC 228 at 231; *Foster v Warblington UDC* [1906] 1 KB 648 at 679.

[226]   (1881) 6 App Cas 740 at 773. Lord PENZANCE (at 803) was "in entire accord with" FRY J, and Lord BLACKBURN (at 823) described it as "a very able opinion". THESIGER LJ had used very similar language to that of FRY J in *Sturges v Bridgman* (1879) 11 Ch D 852 at 863.

highest importance to consider of what ingredients acquiescence consists . . . I cannot imagine any case of acquiescence in which there is not shewn to be in the servient owner:

(1) a knowledge of the acts done;

(2) a power in him to stop the acts or to sue in respect of them; and

(3) an abstinence on his part from the exercise of such power.

(1) USER AS OF RIGHT

This stress upon the element of acquiescence gives the clue to the kind of user required for a prescriptive title. In technical language, it must be *user as of right*,[227] or, to use the expression taken by COKE from Bracton,[228] *longus usus nec per vim, nec clam, nec precario*. The servient owner cannot be said to have acquiesced in an easement that has been enjoyed *vi, clam* or *precario* (by force, by stealth or by permission).

Thus, if the dominant owner has used coercion, or if his user is contentious in the sense that the servient owner continually and unmistakably protests against it, there is, clearly no acquiescence, and the user, being *vi*, that is, by force, will not avail the claimant.[229] Again, there is no acquiescence if the user has been *clam*, that is, by stealth, for a man cannot assent to something of which he is ignorant, and the law allows no prescriptive right to be acquired where there has been any concealment or where the enjoyment has not been open.[230] It must always be found that the servient owner had actual or constructive knowledge of the enjoyment upon which the claimant relies.[231] Lastly, where the user has been *precario*, that is, where it is enjoyed by the permission of the servient owner and the permission is one which he may withdraw at any moment, it cannot be said that he has acquiesced in the existence of the easement as a matter of right. To ask permission is to acknowledge that no right exists. In this case an explanation of the user is forthcoming, and an irrevocable right to the perpetual enjoyment of the easement is not consistent with the explanation. What a claimant must show is that he claims the privilege not as a thing permitted to him from time to time by the servient owner, but as a thing that he has a right to do.

For instance, a woman relied upon sixty years' user of a cartway from her stables through the yard of an adjoining inn, but on it appearing that she had paid 15*s.* each year

---

227 *Gardner v Hodgson's Kingston Brewery Co Ltd* [1903] AC 229, M & B p. 742; *Tickle v Brown* (1836) 4 Ad & El 369; *Healey v Hawkins* [1968] 1 WLR 1967, M & B p. 745.

228 Co Litt 113b. The use of the noun *precarium* was taken by Bracton from Roman law, but not in the same sense as it was used there: *R (Beresford) v Sunderland City Council* [2004] 1 AC 889 at [57]–[58], per Lord RODGER OF EARLSFERRY.

229 *Eaton v Swansea Waterworks Co* (1851) 17 QB 267; *Dalton v Angus & Co* (1881) 6 App Cas 740 at 786; *Hollins v Verney* (1884) 13 QBD 304 at 307; *Smith v Brudenell-Bruce* [2002] 2 P & CR 4 at [12], per PUMFREY J: "a user ceases to be user 'as of right' if the circumstances are such as to indicate to the dominant owner, or to a reasonable man with the dominant owner's knowledge of the circumstances, that the servient owner actually objects and continues to object and will back his objection either by physical obstruction or by legal action".

230 *Union Lighterage Co v London Graving Dock Co* [1902] 2 Ch 557, M & B p. 754, in which a dock-owner's claim to an easement of support by means of invisible rods sunk under the adjoining land was disallowed; *Dalton v Angus & Co* (1881) 6 App Cas 740 at 827; *Wilsons Brewery v West Yorkshire Metropolitan County Council* (1977) 34 P & CR 224; *Liverpool Corpn v H Coghill & Son Ltd* [1918] 1 Ch 307 (injurious substances discharged into the public sewer at night for more than twenty years); *Scott-Whitehead v National Coal Board* (1987) 53 P & CR 263; *Barney v BP Truckstops Ltd* [1995] NPC 5 (drain used for sewage).

231 *Lloyds Bank Ltd v Dalton Ltd* [1942] Ch 466; *Davies v Du Paver* [1953] 1 QB 184, M & B p. 752; cf *Dance v Triplow* [1992] 1 EGLR 190 (where "the plaintiffs failed to prove both their unwillingness to tolerate the interruption and some word or act making that clear to the defendant", per GLIDEWELL LJ); [1992] Conv 197 (J. Martin).

for this privilege, it was held by the House of Lords that the user, being *precario*, was not *as of right*.[232]

Thus a common method of preventing user from developing into a right is to exact a small periodical payment, and although in such a case there is in one sense a right to enjoy what has been paid for, yet it does not amount to a right to a permanent easement, but at the most to a right to damages for breach of contract.[233]

(2) USER MUST BE CONTINUOUS

In addition to being *as of right*, user must also be continuous, though the continuity varies according to the nature of the right in question. For instance, a right of way from the nature of the case admits only of occasional enjoyment, and therefore if it is used as and when occasion demands, the requirement of continuity is satisfied.[234] But so far as a discontinuous easement, such as a right of way, is concerned, it is impossible to define what in every case constitutes sufficient continuity of user. Every case must depend upon the exact nature of the right claimed, and all that can be said is that the user must be such as to disclose to the servient owner the fact that a continuous right to enjoyment is being asserted and that therefore it ought to be resisted if it is not to ripen into a permanent right.[235] It has been suggested that toleration by the alleged servient owner of a particular user is not to be equated to acquiescence, and therefore a prescriptive claim cannot be based on such user.[236] Toleration, however, is not inconsistent with user as of right,[237] and the question in each case is whether the use is such as "to bring home to the mind of a reasonable person that a continuous right of enjoyment is being asserted. If it is and the owner of the allegedly servient tenement knows or must be taken to know of it and does nothing about it the right is established. It is no answer for him to say, 'I "tolerated" it.' "[238]

The right which is claimed on the ground of its continuous and uninterrupted exercise for a period of time need not have been exercised by the same person throughout the whole period: it is sufficient that it has been exercised by the successive owners of the estate in the dominant tenement to which the easement is appurtenant. Nor need it continue to be exercised in precisely the same manner; thus, where the dominant and servient owners agreed upon a variation of the route of a right of way for their own convenience, it was held that the user of the substituted route was substantially an exercise of the old right.[239]

---

[232] *Gardner v Hodgson's Kingston Brewery Co Ltd* [1903] AC 229, M & B p. 742; [1998] Conv 442 at 448 (E. Simpson); *Diment v N H Foot Ltd* [1974] 1 WLR 1427 (agent's knowledge); *Patel v W H Smith (Eziot) Ltd* [1987] 1 WLR 853; *R (Beresford) v Sunderland City Council* [2004] 1 AC 889, where HL considered the meaning of *nec precario* in a claim to a town or village green within Commons Registration Act 1965, s. 22 (and in the prescription of easements generally).

[233] Ibid., at 231. For the effect of mistake on user as of right, see *Bridle v Ruby* [1989] QB 169, where CA held that a right of way was acquired under the doctrine of lost modern grant even though there was a mistaken view of both parties as to existing rights. See too *Thomas W Ward Ltd v Alexander Bruce (Grays) Ltd* [1959] 2 Lloyd's Rep 472, where HARMAN LJ also reviewed *Earl de la Warr v Miles* (1881) 17 Ch D 535 and *Chamber Colliery Co v Hopwood* (1886) 32 Ch D 549; *Hamilton v Joyce* [1984] 3 NSWLR 279; [1986] Conv 356 (A. H. Hudson). [234] *Dare v Heathcote* (1856) 25 LJ Ex 245.

[235] *Hollins v Verney* (1884) 13 QBD 304 at 315. In that case a right of way was claimed for the purpose of removing wood cut upon adjoining land, but the evidence showed that the right had been exercised only on three occasions at intervals of twelve years. The Court of Appeal held that there had not been sufficient continuity of enjoyment.   [236] *Patel v W H Smith (Eziot) Ltd* [1987] 1 WLR 853.

[237] *R v Oxfordshire County Council, ex p Sunningwell Parish Council* [2000] 1 AC 335 at 358, per Lord HOFFMANN.   [238] *Mills v Silver* [1991] Ch 271 at 288, per PARKER LJ, M & B p. 743.

[239] *Davis v Whitby* [1974] Ch 186, M & B p. 757; *Payne v Shedden* (1834) 1 Mood & R 382.

(3) USER IN FEE SIMPLE

Since the basis of a prescriptive claim is immemorial user, an easement can be prescribed for only in respect of a fee simple estate. The rule is absolute that an easement claimed either by prescription at common law, or under the doctrine of a lost grant or under the Prescription Act 1832 must be claimed in favour of the fee simple estate in the dominant tenement.[240] An easement may be granted expressly for a lesser interest than a fee simple, but it cannot arise by virtue of a presumed grant. A tenant for years, no matter what the length of his lease may be, cannot for instance acquire a right of way over the adjoining land of his lessor.[241] He may, however, acquire by prescription an easement against the land of a stranger, though if he does so it enures for the benefit of the fee simple and does not cease with the cessation of his leasehold interest.[242] Furthermore, if the servient tenement is occupied by a tenant for years[243] or a tenant for life[244] at the beginning of the period of user, there can be no claim for an easement by prescription. But if the user begins against a fee simple owner, then the fact that the servient tenement is subsequently let or settled will not prevent this claim.[245]

Owing, however, to the wording of the Prescription Act 1832, the right to light is an exception to these rules.[246]

(b) Methods of prescription

We must now discuss the three methods of prescription.

(1) PRESCRIPTION AT COMMON LAW[247]

At common law a prescriptive title to an easement may be founded upon long enjoyment. This, however, immediately raises the question—how long must the enjoyment have lasted before a grant in his favour will be presumed? The conclusion reached by the courts was that the right must have been enjoyed from *time immemorial*, that is to say, "from time whereof the memory of men runneth not to the contrary".[248]

It is obvious that this designation of what is generally termed *legal memory* is vague and unsatisfactory, and so the courts soon solved the difficulty in a rough and ready fashion by fixing some date at which the memory of man was supposed to begin. They did not choose a date at random, but took as their guide the statutes that from time to time restricted the period within which actions for the recovery of land had to be brought. At first those statutes, instead of fixing a given number of years, adopted the singular expedient of making the period of limitation run from particular dates or events as, for example, from the last return of King John into England. The last statute which adopted this plan was the Statute of Westminster in 1275, which fixed the first year of the reign of Richard I (i.e. 1189) as the period of limitation for the recovery of land by a writ of right. These statutes were, of course,

---

[240] *Bright v Walker* (1834) 1 Cr M & R 211 at 221 (prescription at common law); *Wheaton v Maple & Co* [1893] 3 Ch 48; *Kilgour v Gaddes* [1904] 1 KB 457 at 466, M & B p. 745 (Prescription Act 1832); *Simmons v Dobson* [1991] 1 WLR 720, M & B p. 747 (lost modern grant); criticised [1992] Conv 107 (P. Sparkes); [1992] CLJ 222 (C. Harpum), following (1958) 74 LQR 82 (V. T. H. Delany).

[241] *Gayford v Moffatt* (1868) 4 Ch App 133; *Kilgour v Gaddes*, supra.

[242] *Wheaton v Maple & Co*, supra, at 63; *Pugh v Savage* [1970] 2 QB 373.

[243] *Daniel v North* (1809) 11 East 372.   [244] *Roberts & Lovell v James* (1903) 89 LT 282.

[245] *Palk v Shinner* (1852) 18 QB 568; *Pugh v Savage*, supra.   [246] P. 624, post.

[247] For the history of prescription, see Holdsworth, *History of English Law*, vol. vii. pp. 343 et seq.

[248] Co Litt 170.

not concerned with prescription, but the courts, from time to time, adopted the various statutory dates as the time at which *legal memory* was to be taken as beginning. Thus, after the Statute of Westminster, a prescriptive claim to an easement had to be based on an enjoyment carried back to 1189. Unfortunately, this policy of keeping in line with successive statutes of limitation was not maintained, for when the legislature set up a different principle in 1623[249] by enacting that actions for the recovery of land must be brought within a fixed number of years (twenty years for the action of ejectment), the courts omitted to restrict *legal memory* to the same period.[250] So, absurd though it is, 1189 is at the present day still considered to be the time from which a claimant who is prescribing at common law must prove enjoyment of the easement. The result has been the adoption of what COCKBURN CJ described as a "somewhat startling rule",[251] for, in order to lighten the burden of a claimant, the courts are willing to presume that enjoyment has lasted from 1189 if proof is given of an actual enjoyment from as far back as living witnesses can speak.[252] A lifetime's enjoyment or even a shorter period raises the presumption that the enjoyment has stretched back to the reign of Richard I.[253]

This principle that the court will be satisfied with something like a lifetime's enjoyment affords some alleviation to claimants who, in strict theory of law, should stretch their enjoyment back to 1189, but in the majority of cases it is ineffectual because of another difficulty that confronts a claim based on prescription. If it can be shown that there was a time subsequent to 1189 when for some reason or other the easement could not possibly have existed, it is obvious that user enjoyed even for several centuries will be of no avail, since despite its length it must have started after the removal of the impossibility, and that was after 1189.[254] This almost precludes prescription at common law in the case of easements appurtenant to buildings, such as a right to light, for proof that the building did not exist in the time of Richard I must inevitably defeat the claim.[255]

(2) PRESCRIPTION UNDER LOST MODERN GRANT

The "lost modern grant" represents the second stage in the history of acquisition by presumed grant. If easements which were fortified by long enjoyment, but for the grant of which no deed could be produced, were to receive the protection they deserved, it was soon seen that something must be done to turn the flank of the rule that a prescriptive claim at common law failed if it was shown that the easement must have come into existence at some time later than 1189. Stimulated by a determination to support ancient user at all costs, judicial astuteness in course of time evolved the very questionable theory[256] of the lost modern grant. After actual enjoyment of an easement has been shown for a reasonable length of time, the court presumes that an actual grant was made at the time when enjoyment began, but that the deed has been lost. The justification for this attitude is that if a claimant, despite

---

[249] Following 32 Hen. 8, c. 2.

[250] See the judgment of COCKBURN CJ in *Bryant v Foot* (1867) LR 2 QB 161 at 180–1, M & B p. 739.

[251] Ibid.   [252] First Report of Real Property Commissioners (1829), p. 51.

[253] *Bailey v Appleyard* (1838) 8 Ad & El 161 at 166. See *Darling v Clue* (1864) 4 F & F 329 at 334, per WILLES J: "At common law twenty years uninterrupted user as of right will be prima facie evidence of the right liable to be rebutted." See also *Bealey v Shaw* (1805) 6 East 208 at 215, per Lord ELLENBOROUGH.

[254] *Hulbert v Dale* [1909] 2 Ch 570 at 577.

[255] *Bury v Pope* (1588) Cro Eliz 118; *Norfolk v Arbuthnot* (1880) 5 CPD 390; First Report of Real Property Commissioners, p. 51.   [256] *Bryant v Foot* (1867) LR 2 QB 161 at 181, per COCKBURN CJ.

his inability to prove enjoyment back to 1189 or to produce a deed of grant, has clearly exercised the easement for (say) the last sixty years, it is possible that at some time an actual grant was made to him or his predecessor, and that it was subsequently lost. Therefore, since long enjoyment must be upheld, the only course open to the court is to leave it to the jury to presume that the grant was in fact made.

The virtue of this theory is that it avoids the disaster which overtakes common law prescription when it is shown that the easement could not have existed (say) in 1750, for it does not matter what the state of affairs was then if you rely on a grant made some years later.

COCKBURN CJ said:[257]

Juries were first told that from user, during living memory or even during twenty years, they might presume a lost grant or deed;[258] next they were recommended to make such presumption; and lastly, as the final consummation of judicial legislation, it was held that a jury should be told, not only that they might, but also that they were bound to presume the existence of such a lost grant, although neither judge nor jury, nor anyone else, had the shadow of a belief that any such instrument had ever really existed.

So the lost grant fiction rested and still rests upon the basis of long user, and though in theory the user is merely presumptive evidence, in practice and effect it is decisive. At the present day it is the last expedient of a claimant who finds himself unable to rely upon prescription at common law or upon the provisions of the Prescription Act 1832.[259]

The general rule is that twenty years' enjoyment is enough to raise the presumption,[260] and a period of twenty-one years, eight and a half months has been held to suffice.[261]

The same kind of user must be shown as in the case of prescription at common law, so that if it is *vi, clam* or *precario* the doctrine will not be invoked by the court.[262] Again, in accordance with general principles, it must be clear that there was some person or body of persons to whom the grant might have been made;[263] that there was a fee simple owner capable of executing the grant;[264] and that the right claimed was one which might have been the subject matter of a grant.[265]

In *Tehidy Minerals Ltd v Norman*,[266] the Court of Appeal, after reviewing the difference of judicial opinion in *Angus v Dalton*,[267] decided that the presumption of a lost modern grant

257 *Bryant v Foot* (1867) LR 2 QB 161, M & B p. 739.

258 Here the courts acted by analogy to the Limitation Act 1623: *Bright v Walker* (1834) 1 Cr M & R 211 at 217, per PARKE B.

259 *Hulley v Silversprings Bleaching and Dyeing Co Ltd* [1922] 2 Ch 268; see e.g. *Hulbert v Dale* [1909] 2 Ch 570, M & B p. 748; *Healey v Hawkins* [1968] 1 WLR 1967, M & B p. 745; *Ward (Helston) Ltd v Kerrier DC* (1981) 42 P & CR 412 (easement); *Tehidy Minerals Ltd v Norman* [1971] 2 QB 528, M & B p. 749 (profit à prendre); *Mills v Silver* [1991] Ch 271, M & B p. 743; *Simmons v Dobson* [1991] 1 WLR 720, M & B p. 747; *Bowring Services Ltd v Scottish Widows' Fund & Life Assurance Society* [1995] 1 EGLR 158 (presumption failed because of custom of City of London that a man may rebuild upon ancient foundations to what height he pleases); *Smith v Brudenell-Bruce* [2002] 2 P & CR 4.

260 *Bryant v Foot* (1867) LR 2 QB 161 at 181, per COCKBURN CJ.

261 *Tehidy Minerals Ltd v Norman*, supra.

262 P. 614, ante; *Hanna v Pollock* [1900] 2 IR 664 at 671; *Partridge v Scott* (1838) 3 M & W 220; *Oakley v Boston* [1976] QB 270.   263 *Tilbury v Silva* (1890) 45 Ch D 98 at 122.

264 *Daniel v North* (1809) 11 East 372; *Oakley v Boston*, supra.

265 *Bryant v Lefever* (1879) 4 CPD 172.   266 [1971] 2 QB 528, M & B p. 749.

267 (1877) 3 QBD 85; on appeal (1878) 4 QBD 162; affd sub nom. *Dalton v Angus & Co* (1881) 6 App Cas 740. The views are summarised in *Tehidy Minerals Ltd v Norman*, supra, at 547.

cannot be rebutted by evidence that no such grant was in fact made. If for instance a claim to an easement of support in respect of a house were made, it might be a simple matter to prove that no grant had ever been executed, but it would not be a good reason for refusing to apply the doctrine. The doctrine is plainly a fiction; it is a means to an end, and the end is that some technical ground may be found for upholding a right that has been openly enjoyed.

A lost grant, however, will not be presumed if, during the period of user, there was no person capable of making the grant,[268] or if such a grant would have been in contravention of a statute.[269]

As BUCKLEY LJ said:[270]

In our judgment *Angus v Dalton* decides that, where there has been upwards of 20 years' uninterrupted enjoyment of an easement, such enjoyment having the necessary qualities to fulfil the requirements of prescription, then unless, for some reason such as incapacity on the part of the person or persons who might at sometime before the commencement of the 20-year period have made a grant, the existence of such a grant is impossible, the law will adopt a legal fiction that such a grant was made, in spite of any direct evidence that no such grant was in fact made.

If this legal fiction is not to be displaced by direct evidence that no grant was made, it would be strange if it could be displaced by circumstantial evidence leading to the same conclusion, and in our judgment it must follow that circumstantial evidence tending to negative the existence of a grant (other than evidence establishing impossibility) should not be permitted to displace the fiction.

(3) PRESCRIPTION UNDER THE PRESCRIPTION ACT 1832

The two chief objects of the Prescription Act were to shorten the time of legal memory, and to make it impossible in actions brought under the Act for a claim to be defeated by proof that at some point of time later than 1189 the easement could not have existed. For these purposes the Act separates the right to light from all other easements, and deals with each class in a different manner.

(i) *Easements other than light*

(1) TWENTY- AND FORTY-YEAR PERIODS

Section 2 enacts, in effect, that where an easement has been actually enjoyed without interruption for twenty years, it shall not be defeated by proof that it commenced later than 1189, but it may be defeated in any other way possible at common law.

Thus a claimant who relies on the Act is untroubled by the doctrine of legal memory, but he may still be met by the defences admissible in a case where common law prescription is pleaded, as for instance that the right is not the possible subject matter of a grant;[271] or that the user is not as of right, that is it has been *vi, clam* or *precario*.[272] The same section goes on

---

[268] *Oakley v Boston* [1976] QB 270 (incumbent of glebe land held to be capable grantor with consent of Ecclesiastical Commissioners).

[269] *Neaverson v Peterborough RDC* [1902] 1 Ch 557. Cf *Bakewell Management Ltd v Brandwood* [2004] 2 AC 519 (driving over common land without lawful authority under LPA 1925, s. 193(4), but user would not have been illegal if the landowner had consented: right of way could be acquired by prescription, thus rendering s. 68 of CROW 2000 otiose); [2004] Conv 517 (C. McNall); (2004) 148 SJ 455 (S. Bickford-Smith and C. Lamont); (2005) 121 LQR 200 (M. Templeman); [2004] All ER Rev 240 (P. J. Clarke).

[270] *Tehidy Minerals Ltd v Norman*, supra, at 552.

[271] *Staffordshire & Worcestershire Canal Navigation Proprietors v Birmingham Canal Navigation Proprietors* (1866) LR 1 HL 254 at 278.   [272] P. 614, ante.

to enact that an easement which has been enjoyed without interruption for forty years shall be deemed absolute and indefeasible unless it appears that it was enjoyed by some consent or agreement expressly given by deed or writing.

The advantage derived from enjoyment for the longer of these periods will be explained below.[273]

(2) NEXT BEFORE SOME SUIT OR ACTION

The two periods specified do not mean *any* period of twenty or forty years, but the period *next before some suit or action* wherein the claim is brought into question.[274] Thus, the claimant must prove uninterrupted enjoyment for the period which immediately precedes and which terminates in an action.[275] Until then the prescriptive right is said to be inchoate. For instance:

suppose that a claimant proves that he and his predecessors in title have enjoyed a right of way over adjoining lands for more than a hundred years, except for a short period of 18 months 12 years ago, when he happened to be seised in fee simple of both tenements. Although this is a case where the court will still presume a lost modern grant,[276] a claim under the Act will fail, because during part of the *last* 20 years he has enjoyed the privilege not as the owner of an easement over the land of another, but as the owner of the servient tenement.[277]

(3) WITHOUT INTERRUPTION

It is essential that the enjoyment for the period of twenty or forty years should be uninterrupted, but the Act provides that nothing is to be deemed a statutory interruption unless it has been submitted to or acquiesced in by the dominant owner for one year after he had notice of the interruption and of the person responsible therefor.[278]

"Interruption" means some overt act, such as the obstruction of a right of way, which shows that the easement is disputed.[279] Thus:

if A has regularly passed over a track on B's land for twenty-five years and is then sued in trespass by B, his user of the way for the twenty years next preceding the action will entitle him to judgment. If, however, before his right has been contested, he submits to or acquiesces in an interruption that continues for one year, his previous enjoyment for twenty-five years becomes unavailing to him and he must start it afresh in order to satisfy the statute.

The crucial question, therefore, is—what amounts to submission or acquiescence? This is a question of fact dependent upon the circumstances, but the test that should be applied seems a little obscure.

Suppose, in the case above, that B erects a fence across the track over which A has been passing for twenty-five years and that A, though he protests violently and threatens legal proceedings, lets thirteen months elapse without forcing the issue by a positive act of resistance.[280]

---

[273] P. 621, post.   [274] Prescription Act 1832, s. 4.

[275] *Jones v Price* (1836) 3 Bing NC 52; *Parker v Mitchell* (1840) 11 Ad & El 788; *Hyman v Van den Bergh* [1907] 2 Ch 516; affd [1908] 1 Ch 167, M & B p. 754; *Newnham v Willison* (1987) 56 P & CR 8 (interruption lasting more than one year before action brought); [1989] Conv 357 (J. E. Martin).

[276] Cf *Hulbert v Dale* [1909] 2 Ch 570, M & B p. 748.

[277] *Bright v Walker* (1834) 1 Cr M & R 211 at 219.   [278] S. 4.

[279] *Carr v Foster* (1842) 3 QB 581, per PARKE B.

[280] Cf *Davies v Du Paver* [1953] 1 QB 184, M & B p. 752.

Does his protest suffice to negative his submission to or acquiescence in the interruption? It has been held that he need not go so far as to remove the obstruction or to take legal proceedings. It is said to be enough that he communicate to the servient owner, with sufficient force and clarity, his opposition to the interruption.[281] This vague test is scarcely satisfactory. Strictly speaking, no doubt, submission or acquiescence is a state of mind, but if a dissident state of mind, unfortified by some positive act of resistance, is to nullify an aggressive act of interruption, what certainty will remain in the title to the servient tenement? A single protest will remain effective after the year has elapsed and the statutory rule that interruption for a year shall defeat a claimant will be deprived of its intended force. The weight of judicial opinion, however, is disinclined to regard inactivity by the dominant owner for longer than a year after the interruption and after his protest as necessarily fatal to his claim.[282]

An interruption that occurs after the enjoyment of an easement has persisted for nineteen years and a fraction of a year will not avail the servient owner, provided that the dominant owner sues to vindicate his right within a year afterwards.[283] The interruption is not yet an interruption within the meaning of the statute. Nevertheless, the acquisition of an easement requires enjoyment for the full period of twenty years immediately preceding an action, and therefore if the servient owner brings an action before the period has elapsed he will be entitled to a declaration that no easement exists, notwithstanding the deficiency of the interruption.[284]

(4) USER AS OF RIGHT

The nature of the enjoyment necessary for the statutory periods must be similar to that required at common law, that is to say, it must be *as of right*.[285] This is so even where user has been shown for the full period of forty years. The Act does not mean that easements enjoyed for forty years otherwise than by written permission are in all circumstances indefeasible, but only if their enjoyment has been open and notorious. Lord MACNAGHTEN gave a warning against reading too much into the Act:

The Act was passed, as its preamble declares, for the purpose of getting rid of the inconvenience and injustice arising from the meaning which the law of England attached to the expressions "time immemorial" and "time whereof the memory of man runneth not to the contrary". The law as it stood put an intolerable strain on the consciences of judges and jurymen. The Act was an Act "for shortening the time of prescription in certain cases". And really it did nothing more.[286]

This enables us to appreciate the significance of enjoyment for the longer period of forty years. A hasty reading of section 2 might induce the belief that a right enjoyed for forty years is indefeasible unless it can be proved that it was enjoyed by virtue of a written grant. But this is not so. In the case of enjoyment for the *shorter* period the claim cannot be met by the

---

[281] *Bennison v Cartwright* (1864) 5 B & S 1; *Glover v Coleman* (1874) LR 10 CP 108.

[282] *Davies v Du Paver*, supra (where, however, that view was not shared by SINGLETON LJ); *Ward v Kirkland* [1967] Ch 194.   [283] *Flight v Thomas* (1841) 8 Cl & Fin 231.

[284] *Reilly v Orange* [1955] 2 QB 112, M & B p. 756.

[285] *Tickle v Brown* (1836) 4 Ad & El 369 at 382; *Bright v Walker* (1834) 1 Cr M & R 211; *Lyell v Hothfield* [1914] 3 KB 911; *Smith v Brudenell-Bruce* [2002] 2 P & CR 4 (twenty years' uninterrupted enjoyment, but not as of right). The fact that the user was illegal under LPA 1925, s. 193(4), but would not have been illegal if the landowner had consented, does not prevent the user being as of right: *Bakewell Management Ltd v Brandwood* [2004] 2 AC 519; p. 619, n. 269, supra.

[286] *Gardner v Hodgson's Kingston Brewery Co Ltd* [1903] AC 229 at 236, M & B p. 752.

objection that enjoyment originated subsequently to 1189, but it can be met and defeated by any one of the common law defences, namely:

(a) that the right claimed lacks one or more of the characteristics essential to an easement;[287] or

(b) that the right in question, though enjoyed for twenty years, is prohibited by law, as for example, because a grant would have been *ultra vires* the grantor[288] or the grantee;[289] or

(c) that the user was not *as of right*,[290] i.e. that it was forcible, or secret, or enjoyed by permission *whether written or oral*.[291]

Next, a claim to an easement based upon forty years' enjoyment can likewise be defeated upon the first two grounds, and also by proof that the user was forcible or secret or enjoyed by *written* permission. What is not sufficient to nullify a user lasting for this longer period is the oral permission of the servient owner. On general principles user that is precarious in any sense cannot originate an easement, but the statute, by enacting that user for forty years is not to be considered precarious unless enjoyed by written permission, has, in the case of this longer period, given a special and restricted meaning to "precarious" if the claim is based on statutory prescription.[292] The difference, then, between the two periods is that an oral consent may defeat enjoyment for twenty years, but not enjoyment for forty years.

The circumstances when this may do so have been elucidated by the courts. It is clear that permission of any sort, whether written or oral, is fatal to a claim based upon prescription at common law, however long the enjoyment may have lasted. The case of a claim based on the statutory periods, however, depends upon whether the permission is given during or at the beginning of the period of user. If permission is given from time to time *during* the twenty or forty years, the user becomes *precario* and this is fatal to the claim.[293] On the other hand, if the permission is given at the *beginning* of the period of user and extends over the whole period[294] (i.e. a permission given more than twenty or forty years ago and not since renewed), then, if it is written, it is fatal to a claim based upon either of the statutory periods, and, if oral, it is only fatal to a claim based upon the twenty-year period.

As GOFF J said in *Healey v Hawkins*:[295]

In principle it seems to me that once permission has been given, the user must remain permissive and not be capable of ripening into a right save where the permission is oral and the user has continued for 40 . . . years, unless and until, having been given for a limited period only, it expires or, being general, it is revoked, or there is a change in circumstances from which revocation may fairly be implied. . . .

---

287 *Mounsey v Ismay* (1863) 3 H & C 486.

288 *Rochdale Canal Co v Radcliffe* (1852) 18 QB 287 at 315; *Staffordshire & Worcestershire Canal Navigation Proprietors v Birmingham Canal Navigation Proprietors* (1866) LR 1 HL 254 at 278.

289 *National Guaranteed Manure Co v Donald* (1859) 4 H & N 8.   290 Pp. 614–5, ante.

291 *Burrows v Lang* [1901] 2 Ch 502.

292 *Gardner v Hodgson's Kingston Brewery Co Ltd* [1901] 2 Ch 198 at 214; for the facts see pp. 614–5, ante. The annual payment of 15s had been orally fixed some sixty years before the action. That was held, however, to be no evidence that an oral agreement granting the easement had in fact been made.

293 *Gardner v Hodgson's Kingston Brewery Co Ltd* [1903] AC 229, M & B pp. 742, 752.

294 Whether it does so depends on the circumstances: *Gaved v Martyn* (1865) 19 CBNS 732; *Healey v Hawkins* [1968] 1 WLR 1967, M & B p. 745. See (1968) 32 Conv (NS) 40 (P. S. Langan).

295 [1968] 1 WLR 1967 at 1973.

Of course, when the user has continued for 40 . . . years a prior parol consent affords no answer, because it is excluded by the express terms of section 2 of the Prescription Act, but, even so, permission given during the period will defeat the claimant because it negatives user as of right. That is, in my judgment, the explanation of the distinction drawn by the House of Lords in *Gardner v Hodgson's Kingston Brewery* between antecedent and current parol consents.

Oral permission given within the period will also negative user *as of right*, where the user continues on a common understanding that the user is and continues to be permissive.[296]

(5) DISABILITIES

Another difference between the two statutory periods is that certain disabilities of the servient owner, which obstruct a claim based on twenty years' user, do not affect a claimant who has enjoyed an easement for forty years.

The Act provides that a right, even though enjoyed for the statutory periods, shall not ripen into a legal easement if the servient owner has been under certain disabilities. The time during which such person may have been an infant, idiot, *non compos mentis* or tenant for life,[297] or during which an action has been pending and diligently prosecuted, is excluded by section 7 from the period of twenty years, though it begins to run again *at the point where it was interrupted* as soon as the disability is removed. Suppose, for instance, that

the claimant began to exercise the right in 1972, when the servient owner was the fee simple owner. In 1977 the latter became tenant for life under a settlement, but on his death in 1989 his successor came to the estate as tenant in fee simple. The claimant has exercised the right continuously from 1972 until 2006, when the action is brought. Five of these thirty-four years preceded the disability of a tenancy for life and seventeen came afterwards. The twelve years during which the disability lasted must of course be excluded, but the question is whether the claimant may add the periods of five and seventeen years together and allege enjoyment for the statutory period; or whether he will be defeated by his inability to show enjoyment for the last twenty years.

He will not be defeated, for the rule is that a claimant must show twenty years' enjoyment either:

(i) wholly before the disability if it still exists at the time of the action, or

(ii) partly before or partly after, if the disability has ended.[298]

Except for that of a tenancy for life, these disabilities do not affect a claim based on a forty years' enjoyment;[299] this is to say, an uninterrupted user as of right for so long will confer an absolute title, no matter what the position of the servient owner may have been. Section 8, however, provides that where the servient tenement has been held during the whole or any part of the forty years for a term of life or for a term of years exceeding three years, the period

---

[296] *Jones v Price & Morgan* (1992) 64 P & CR 404.

[297] The text of s. 7 also counts a *feme couvert* (married woman) as under a similar disability, although Law Reform (Married Women and Tortfeasors) Act 1935, s. 1(a) overrode this by providing that a married woman shall be capable of acquitting, holding and disposing of any property in all respects as if she were a *feme sole*.

[298] Cf *Clayton v Corby* (1842) 2 QB 813.   [299] S. 7.

during which such term lasted shall be excluded in the computation, provided that the claim is resisted by the reversioner within three years of the determination of the term.[300]

A curious feature of these rules is that the deduction of the time during which the servient tenement has been held by a tenant for a term exceeding three years only affects the computation of the longer period of forty years. Thus an easement of way may be acquired by twenty years' user, though for the greater part of that time the servient tenement has been in the hands of a tenant.[301]

None of the disabilities applies to the easement of light.

(ii) Easement of light

As the Act treats this particular easement quite differently from all others, it is necessary to cite the section dealing with it in full:[302]

When the access and use of light to and for any dwelling house, workshop or other building[303] shall have been actually enjoyed therewith for the full period of 20 years without interruption, the right thereto shall be deemed absolute and indefeasible, any local usage or custom to the contrary notwithstanding,[304] unless it shall appear that the same was enjoyed by some consent or agreement expressly made or given for that purpose by deed or writing.

(1) USER NEED NOT BE AS OF RIGHT

We have seen that where a claim to any other easement is made under the Act, it must clearly appear that the enjoyment has been *as of right*, and the reason is that the statutory words *claiming right thereto* have been construed as equivalent to the common law expression *as of right*. Since these words, however, are omitted from the section dealing with light, it follows that in the case of this particular easement a fresh mode of creation has been statutorily introduced.[305] All that the claimant need show, if he claims not at common law but under the Act, is actual user and absence of written agreement,[306] but the user must have continued for

---

[300] The section is in words restricted to ways and watercourses, but there is reason to believe that the word "convenient" has crept into the section instead of "easement"; see *Wright v Williams* (1836) Tyr & Gr 375 at 380; *Laird v Briggs* (1880) 50 LJ Ch 260 at 261, per FRY J.

[301] *Palk v Shinner* (1852) 18 QB 568.

[302] S. 3. Bickford-Smith and Francis, *Rights of Light: The Modern Law*; Ellis, *Rights to Light*; *Colls v Home and Colonial Stores Ltd* [1904] AC 179, M & B p. 775 (where an injunction was refused); cf *Pugh v Howells* (1984) 48 P & CR 298 (where a mandatory injunction was granted); *Blue Town Investments Ltd v Higgs and Hill plc* [1990] 1 WLR 696; *Marine and General Mutual Life Assurance Society v St James' Real Estate Co Ltd* [1991] 2 EGLR 178 (measure of damages); *Voyce v Voyce* (1991) 62 P & CR 290 (right of light enforceable against equitable owner); *Deakins v Hookings* [1994] 1 EGLR 190; (1994) 144 NLJ 875 (H. W. Wilkinson); *Midtown Ltd v City of London Real Property Co Ltd* [2005] 1 EGLR 65 (injunction refused).

[303] *Clifford v Holt* [1899] 1 Ch 698 (church); *Hyman v Van den Bergh* [1908] 1 Ch 167 (cowshed); *Allen v Greenwood* [1980] Ch 119, M & B p. 778 (greenhouse). The quantity of light to which the owner of the dominant tenement is entitled is "what is required for the ordinary purposes of inhabitancy or business of the tenement according to the ordinary notions of mankind": *Colls v Home & Colonial Stores Ltd* [1904] AC 179 at 204, per Lord DAVEY; *Midtown Ltd v City of London Real Property Co Ltd*, supra (substantial diminution in amount of natural light to an office building was an interference amounting to a nuisance, even though all rooms were habitually lit by artificial light whenever used). In *Allen v Greenwood* it was held that a right to a specially high degree of light may be acquired by prescription. GOFF LJ left open the question whether a right to light would include the properties of the sun in relation to solar heating. See [1979] Conv 298 (F. R. Crane); [1984] Conv 408 (A. H. Hudson); Conv Prec 19–C17. See also *Carr-Saunders v Dick McNeil Associates Ltd* [1986] 1 WLR 922 (dominant owner's right under s. 3 is for access of light to the building as a whole and not to any particular room).

[304] *Bowring Services Ltd v Scottish Widows' Fund & Life Assurance* [1995] 1 EGLR 158 (custom of City of London).   [305] *Scott v Pape* (1886) 31 Ch D 554 at 571, per BOWEN LJ.

[306] *Truscott v Merchant Taylors' Co* (1856) 11 Exch 855; *Frewen v Philipps* (1861) 11 CBNS 449; *Colls v Home and Colonial Stores Ltd* [1904] AC 179 at 205; *Kilgour v Gaddes* [1904] 1 KB 457.

the period of twenty years next before the action in which the claim is brought into question. In other words, the right is not absolute and indefeasible after twenty years' user, but remains merely inchoate until it has been established in legal proceedings.[307] To defeat a claim to light, based upon user for the statutory period, the servient owner must produce an express agreement by deed or writing which shows that the user has been permissive during the last twenty years.[308] Thus, for instance, user of light for twenty years is not dismissed as precarious, merely because it has been enjoyed under an oral permission extending over the whole period.[309] Even the payment of rent by the dominant owner under an oral agreement will not prevent the acquisition of the easement,[310] unless some receipt or acknowledgment has been given which can be construed as a written agreement.

(2) INTERRUPTION

A right to light cannot, of course, be acquired if its enjoyment has been effectively interrupted within the meaning of the Prescription Act, that is, if there has been some adverse act by the servient owner which has lasted for at least one year.[311] In this type of easement, the adverse act must in the nature of things take the form of some physical structure, such as a hoarding, so sited as to obstruct the flow of light to the dominant tenement. An alternative to this cumbrous and unsightly method, however, was introduced by the Rights of Light Act 1959,[312] which enables the access of light to be notionally obstructed by the registration of a notice as a local land charge.

A notice in the prescribed form must be submitted to the local authority by the servient owner,[313] and it must state that its registration is intended to represent the obstruction to the access of light that would be caused by an opaque structure of certain specified dimensions, whether of unlimited height or not, erected upon the servient tenement.[314] The notice must also be accompanied by a certificate from the Lands Tribunal certifying either that adequate notice of the proposed registration has been given to all persons likely to be affected, or that the case is one of exceptional urgency and that therefore registration for a limited time is essential.[315] The notice, if not cancelled, expires one year after registration or, where accompanied by a certificate of exceptional urgency, at the end of the period specified in the certificate.[316]

For the purpose of determining whether a right to light has been acquired either at common law or under the Prescription Act, the access of light to the dominant tenement is to be

---

[307] *Hyman v Van den Bergh* [1907] 2 Ch 516; affd [1908] 1 Ch 167, M & B p. 754. The reason is that the third section, cited above, must be read in connection with the fourth section which requires the period to be *next before* some action.

[308] *Foster v Lyons & Co* [1927] 1 Ch 219; *Willoughby v Eckstein* [1937] Ch 167; *Midtown Ltd v City of London Real Property Co Ltd* [2005] 1 EGLR 65. [309] *Mallam v Rose* [1915] 2 Ch 222.

[310] *Plasterers' Co v Parish Clerks' Co* (1851) 6 Exch 630. [311] P. 620, ante.

[312] As amended by LLCA 1975, s. 17, Sch. 1. The Act embodies the recommendations of the Harman Committee on Rights of Light, 1958 (Cmnd 473); [1959] CLJ 182 (H. W. R. Wade). See *Hawker v Tomalin* (1969) 20 P & CR 550 at 551, per HARMAN J.

[313] I.e., the owner of a legal fee simple or of a term of years absolute of which at least seven years remain unexpired, or the mortgagee in possession of such a fee or term: Rights of Light Act 1959, s. 7(1).

[314] Rights of Light Act 1959, s. 2(1), (2); Lands Tribunal Rules 1996 (SI 1996 No. 1002); Lands Tribunal (Fees) Rules 1996 (SI 1996 No. 1021); LLCR 1977 (SI 1977 No. 985), r. 10.

[315] Ibid., s. 2(3). 938 definitive and 211 temporary certificates were issued between 1959 and 1980; see (1978) 122 SJ 515, 534; (1981) 259 EG 123 (W. A. Greene).

[316] Ibid., s. 3(2); *Bowring Services Ltd v Scottish Widows' Fund & Life Assurance Society* [1995] 1 EGLR 158 (calculation of date from which time runs).

treated as obstructed by a registered notice to the same extent and with the like consequences as if the structure specified in the application for registration has in fact been erected;[317] and any right of action that the dominant owner would have had in that event is available by reason of the notice.[318] In order to obviate the difficulties that may arise where the right is interrupted after it has been enjoyed for nineteen years and a fraction,[319] the Act provides in effect that the enjoyment by the dominant owner of the flow of light shall be notionally prolonged for one year if he sues for cancellation of the notice.[320]

(3) NOT LIMITED TO PRESCRIPTION IN RESPECT OF FEE SIMPLE

Owing to the wording of the Prescription Act 1832 the right to light is an exception to the rule that an easement can be prescribed for only in respect of a fee simple.[321] It is peculiar in two respects:

First, the fee simple estate of a landlord is bound by an easement of light acquired over the land while in the occupation of a tenant.[322] Suppose, for instance, that:

A, the fee simple owner of Blackacre, leases it to a tenant for 25 years. During the tenancy, X, the owner of an adjoining house, builds a window overlooking Blackacre and enjoys access of light to it for 20 years. A right to light is thereby acquired that is enforceable against A, his tenant and all successors in title of Blackacre.

Secondly, if two tenements are held by different lessees under a common landlord, and one lessee enjoys the use of light over the other tenement for the necessary period, he and his successors acquire an indefeasible right to the light not only against the other tenant, but also against the common landlord and all succeeding owners of the servient tenement.[323]

(c) Common law not displaced by Prescription Act 1832

The Act is only supplementary to the common law—it provides an additional method of claiming easements, but leaves the other two methods untouched. If, for instance, the claimant is unable to show enjoyment for the statutory period of the last twenty years, as will happen if there has been unity of possession for part of that period, he may either prescribe at common law or invoke the doctrine of a lost modern grant.[324] Normally, he will rely on the Act. Failing this, he will base his case on prescription at common law; and, failing that, he will plead a lost modern grant, but only if driven to it, for, as Lord LINDLEY said, "that doctrine only applies where the enjoyment cannot be otherwise reasonably accounted for".[325]

(d) Reform of the law on prescription

In *Tehidy Minerals Ltd v Norman* BUCKLEY LJ said:[326] "The co-existence of three separate methods of prescribing is, in our view, anomalous and undesirable, for it results in much

---

317   Rights of Light Act 1959, s. 2(1).
318   Ibid., s. 3(3).   319   P. 620, ante.   320   Rights of Light Act 1959, s. 3(4).   321   P. 616, ante.
322   *Simper v Foley* (1862) 2 John & H 555.
323   *Morgan v Fear* [1907] AC 425, M & B p. 708; *Willoughby v Eckstein* [1937] Ch 167 at 170.
324   See *Hulbert v Dale* [1909] 2 Ch 570, argument of counsel at 573.
325   *Gardner v Hodgson's Kingston Brewery Co Ltd* [1903] AC 229 at 240. The three alternative claims were pleaded together in *Bailey v Stephens* (1862) 12 CBNS 91; *Norfolk v Arbuthnot* (1880) 5 CPD 390; *Wheaton v Maple & Co* [1893] 3 Ch 48; *Roberts & Lovell v James* (1903) 89 LT 282. See too *Pugh v Savage* [1970] 2 QB 373.
326   [1971] 2 QB 528 at 543.

unnecessary complication and confusion. We hope that it may be possible for the Legislature to effect a long-overdue simplification in this branch of the law."

(1) LAW REFORM COMMITTEE REPORT ON ACQUISITION OF EASEMENTS AND PROFITS BY PRESCRIPTION

In 1966 the Law Reform Committee[327] recommended the abolition of the prescriptive acquisition of easements and of profits à prendre;[328] in the former case by a majority of eight to six, in the latter unanimously. The Committee, however, also considered the ways in which prescriptive acquisition—if it should be retained for easements—should operate, and was unanimous on the new system to be adopted.

The main recommendations, in brief outline, were:

(1) All existing methods of acquisition of easements and profits by prescription should be abolished. This recommendation includes the abolition of prescription at common law and under the doctrine of a lost modern grant, and the repeal of the Prescription Act 1832.[329]

(2) The following method should be adopted, if it were decided to substitute a new system for easements only:[330]

(a) The prescriptive period should be a period in gross of twelve years (i.e., it need not be "next before action brought").[331]

(b) There should be no "disabilities".[332]

(c) An easement should be capable of being acquired against the owner of a limited interest in the servient land so as to subsist as long as that servient owner's interest subsists.[333] Prescription by the owner of a limited interest in the dominant land should continue, as at present, in favour of the freeholder.[334] A tenant should be able to prescribe against his landlord and vice versa.[335]

(d) Enjoyment:

(i) by force should not count in favour of the dominant owner;[336]

(ii) must have been actually known to the servient owner or ought reasonably to have been known to him;[337]

---

[327] Fourteenth Report (1966) Cmnd 3100. See Jackson, chap. 15; (1967) 30 MLR 189 (H. W. Wilkinson); M & B pp. 718–19.

In 1971 the Law Commission Working Paper on Rights Appurtenant to Land (No. 36) suggested that "easements and covenants should be assimilated along lines hitherto regarded as appropriate to easements" (para. 9) and, in relation to prescription, "as at present advised we are inclined to agree in principle with the majority, but only on the basis that some alternative to prescription can be found. In the meantime it will be assumed that prescription will continue" (para. 99). It should be reformed along the lines recommended by the Law Reform Committee (Proposition 10).

For further criticism of the Prescription Act 1832, see Holdsworth, *Historical Introduction to the Land Law*, pp. 284–6; Holdsworth, *History of English Law*, vol. vii. pp. 350–62; Simpson, *A History of the Land Law*, pp. 266–9; Underhill, *Century of Law Reform*, p. 308. New Zealand's New Property Act, proposed by its Law Commission Report No. 29, provides for the creation of an easement in gross, and for the abolition of the acquisition of easements and profits by prescription: [1994] Conv 428 (H. W. Wilkinson).

[328] Ibid., paras. 32, 98. [329] Paras. 40, 98, 99(1)–(3). [330] Para. 99(6).

[331] Paras. 41–3. Prescription Act 1832, s. 4. [332] Para. 44. Prescription Act 1832, ss. 7, 8.

[333] Paras. 47–9. [334] Para. 50. [335] Para. 51. [336] Para. 57. [337] Para. 58.

(iii) must be of such a kind and frequency as would only be justified by the existence of an easement;[338]

(iv) by consent or agreement, whether written or oral, should not count. If so enjoyed for one year or more, the consent, like an interruption, would prevent earlier enjoyment being added to later enjoyment for the purpose of making up the required total of twelve years. A consent which is indefinite in duration should operate for one year.[339]

(e) Notional interruption, on the lines of the Rights of Light Act 1959, should be extended to easements generally; this should be by registration against the dominant land in the local land charges register after notice given. Interruption, notional or actual, should endure for twelve months in order to be effective.[340]

(f) An easement, acquired by prescription, should be lost by twelve years' continuous non-user.[341]

(3) The Committee was unanimous about provisions to facilitate, subject to compensation where appropriate, the acquisition of easements of support for buildings by land or for buildings by buildings.[342]

(4) Shelter of building by an adjoining building should be treated in the same way as support.[343]

(5) The Lands Tribunal should be empowered to discharge easements or substitute more convenient ones, subject to payment of compensation where appropriate.[344]

(2) LAW COMMISSION PROPOSALS IN RELATION TO REGISTERED LAND

In 1998 the Law Commission provisionally recommended[345] that the acquisition of easements or profits à prendre in registered land should only be possible under the Prescription Act 1832. To allow the doctrine of lost modern grant to continue would involve inventing a concept of "a lost modern registration",[346] and any such concept would undermine the primary objective of ensuring the registration of rights that are expressly created.

However, this proposal was abandoned by the Law Commission in its final Report,[347] and was therefore not implemented in the Land Registration Act 2002.[348]

E Extent of Easements

In ascertaining the nature and extent of an easement, the principles to be applied vary with the method of its creation.

[338] Para. 59.   [339] Paras. 61–3.   [340] As at present. Prescription Act 1832, s. 4. Paras. 64–9, 75.
[341] Para. 81.   [342] Paras. 89–95, 99(8)–(11)
[343] Paras. 96, 99(12); *Phipps v Pears* [1965] 1 QB 76, M & B p. 706, p. 596, ante.   [344] Paras. 97, 99(13).
[345] Law Com No. 254, paras. 10.79–10.94, 10.108–10.112.   [346] Ibid., para. 10.89.
[347] Land Registration for the Twenty-First Century 2001, Law Com No. 271, para. 1.19. The Law Commission decided that (1) there was not a compelling case for the reform of the law of prescription in the context of registered land alone; (2) it was already undertaking a comprehensive review of easements and land obligations (p. 701, post) which would include prescription, and it seemed better to "view prescription as a totality"; and (3) some of the conveyancing concerns that informed the earlier proposals were addressed in more direct ways in the Bill—in particular, by limiting the circumstances in which easements can be overriding interests: ibid., paras. 8.65–8.66.
[348] Bridge, *Prescriptive Acquisition of Easements: Abolition or Reform?* in Cooke (ed.) *Modern Studies in Property Law*, vol. 3, p. 3.

As WILLES J said in *Williams v James*:[349]

The distinction between a grant and prescription is obvious. In the case of proving a right by prescription the user of the right is the only evidence. In the case of a grant the language of the instrument can be referred to, and it is of course for the court to construe that language; and in the absence of any clear indication of the intention of the parties, the maxim that a grant must be construed most strongly against the grantor must be applied.[350]

(1) Express Grant

It follows that, if the easement is created by express grant, the question is one of construing the terms of the grant,[351] and, in cases of difficulty, the physical circumstances of the property must be considered. Thus, in determining whether the grant or reservation of "a right of way" is a right exercisable on foot only or with vehicles and, if so, what kind of vehicles, the condition of the way itself and the nature of the dominant tenement may be taken into account.[352] An unrestricted right of way may not be confined to the use of the dominant tenement contemplated by the parties at the time of the grant. Thus, where an unrestricted right of way was granted as appurtenant to a house, and the house was subsequently converted into an hotel, its owner became entitled to a right of way for the general purposes of the hotel.[353] But a grant of an unrestricted right of way does not authorise excessive use which would be an unreasonable interference with the rights of others entitled to use it.[354]

---

[349] (1867) LR 2 CP 577 at 581.

[350] Cf. Lewison, *Interpretation of Contracts*, para. 7.07, noting that this *contra proferentem* rule of construction is not always applied consistently, particularly in the modern cases.

[351] For the modern approach to interpretation of contracts and other written documents, see *Investors' Compensation Scheme Ltd v West Bromwich Building Society* [1998] 1 WLR 896, p. 319, ante; *Mobil Oil Co Ltd v Birmingham City Council* [2002] 2 P & CR 14 at [24] and [62]; Lewison, *Interpretation of Contracts*, chap. 2. The construction of a grant will take into account the normal customs of conveyancing; e.g. the grant of a right to light, in the absence of more specific provision, will be taken to be a grant of the degree of light that satisfies the test of Lord DAVEY in *Colls v Home & Colonial Stores Ltd* [1904] AC 179 at 204, p. 624, n. 303, ante; *Frogmore Developments Ltd v Shirayama Shokusan Co Ltd* [2000] 1 EGLR 121 at 124, per NEUBERGER J.

[352] *Cannon v Villars* (1878) 8 Ch D 415 at 420; *St Edmundsbury and Ipswich Diocesan Board of Finance v Clark (No 2)* [1975] 1 WLR 468, M & B p. 764; *United Land Co v Great Eastern Rly Co* (1875) 10 Ch App 586; *Robinson v Bailey* [1948] 2 All ER 791 (right of way to building plot held to include business user); *Jalnarne Ltd v Ridewood* (1989) 61 P & CR 143 (right of way held to permit its use by juggernaut lorries and customers in vans and cars for access to dominant tenements subsequently used for motorcar dealing, frozen food business and snooker club with bar); *Soames-Forsythe Properties Ltd v Tesco Stores Ltd* [1991] EGCS 22 ("full and free right of way on foot only" from supermarket to car park held to include right for customers to use supermarket trolleys on it); [1992] Conv 199 (J. Martin); *London and Suburban Land and Building Co (Holdings) Ltd v Carey* (1991) 62 P & CR 480 (express grant of a right of way to commercial premises did not imply a right to unload from the access way onto the dominant tenement); *CP Holdings v Dugdale Real Property* [1998] NPC 97 (unrestricted right of way over disused railway line; servient owner re-opening line held not able to lower level crossing barriers thereby causing temporary but lengthy queues).

[353] *White v Grand Hotel, Eastbourne, Ltd* [1913] 1 Ch 113, M & B p. 758; *Kain v Norfolk* [1949] Ch 163; *Bulstrode v Lambert* [1953] 1 WLR 1064; *Keefe v Amor* [1965] 1 QB 334, M & B p. 759; *McIlraith v Grady* [1968] 1 QB 468 (a right to "pass and repass over and along" included a right to vehicles to stop for a reasonable time and unload); See also *Minor v Groves* (1997) 80 P & CR 136 (dominant owner limited in user to extend with right of way; occasional technical trespasses caused by side of vehicles intruding into airspace of servient tenement did not give rise to a right over it).

[354] *Jelbert v Davis* [1968] 1 WLR 589, M & B p. 762; (1968) 112 SJ 172 (S. M. Cretney) (right to be used "in common with all other persons having the like right"); *Rosling v Pinnegar* (1986) 54 P & CR 124 (access to Hammerwood Park, near East Grinstead, built by Latrobe, American architect of the White House); cf *National Trust for Places of Historic Interest or Natural Beauty v White* [1987] 1 WLR 907 (access to Figsbury Ring, near Salisbury); *White v Richards* (1993) 68 P & CR 105; *Gardner v Davis* [1998] NPC 123 (extent of sewage easement unreasonable); *Hanover Trust Co Ltd v Eastern Counties Leather Group Ltd* (2000) 25 July, CA, unreported

And the dominant owner may not generally extend the scope of an easement, such as a right of way, by extending the dominant tenement, although it is always a matter of construction of the grant as to what constitutes the dominant tenement,[355] and a matter of interpretation of the facts as to whether the exercise of the right of way by the owner is in substance for the dominant tenement or for other land which he owns.[356]

(2) Implied Grant

If the easement is created by implied grant, we have already seen that where it is implied in favour of the grantor, an easement of necessity is strictly limited to the circumstances of the necessity prevailing at the time of the grant.[357] In the case of an easement implied in favour of the grantee, the grantee must establish that the parties intended that the subject of the grant should be used in some definite and particular manner; the law will then imply the grant of such easements as may be necessary to give effect to it.[358]

(3) Prescription

The extent of a prescriptive easement is commensurate with its user. Once the purposes for which it has been used during the period of its acquisition have been determined by evidence, the scope of the easement is defined. However, a question may arise as to whether the easement extends to a change in user of the dominant tenement. In considering such a case, the courts consider (i) whether the new user constitutes a radical change in the character or a change in the identity of the dominant tenement, as opposed to a mere change or intensification in its use; and (ii) whether the new user results in a substantial increase or alteration

(grant to purchaser of rights to be exercisable over retained land of vendor "in common with the vendor and all persons authorised by it" held expressly to contemplate that vendor might grant further rights over that land in favour of third parties).

[355] *Johnstone v Holdway* [1963] 1 QB 601, M & B p. 764 (extrinsic evidence admissible where dominant tenement not identified in deed); *Shannon Ltd v Venner Ltd* [1965] Ch 682; *Land Reclamation Co Ltd v Basildon DC* [1979] 1 WLR 106 at 110; *Scott v Martin* [1987] 1 WLR 841 (plan used to explain "private road"); *Hamble Parish Council v Haggard* [1992] 1 WLR 122 ("I have to put myself into the shoes of the notional judge visiting the site with the conveyance in one hand and gazing about him to identify on the ground those features which would enable him to ascertain the extent of the dominant land", per MILLETT J at 130); *West v Sharp* (2000) 79 P & CR 327. Cf, on the question of identification of the land benefited by a restrictive covenant, the judgment of UPJOHN J in *Newton Abbott Co-operative Society Ltd v Williamson and Treadgold Ltd* [1952] Ch 286, p. 685, post.

[356] *Harris v Flower* (1904) 74 LJ Ch 127 at 132, per ROMER LJ: "If a right of way be granted for the enjoyment of Close A, the grantee, because he owns or acquires Close B, cannot use the way in substance for passing over Close A to Close B", followed in *Bracewell v Appleby* [1975] Ch 408; cf *Nickerson v Barraclough* [1980] Ch 325 at 336 (such a right held to be usable as access where Close A is itself used as access to Close B at time of grant). See also *Jobson v Record* (1997) 75 P & CR 375; *Alvis v Harrison* (1991) 62 P & CR 10 at 15–16; *Peacock v Custins* [2002] 1 WLR 1815 (easement did not extend to access to field adjacent to dominant land); *Das v Linden Mews Ltd* [2002] 2 EGLR 76 (right of way over carriageway to dominant tenement did not extend to access to parking area not comprised within the dominant tenement); [2003] Conv 127 (E. Paton and G. Seabourne); *Massey v Boulden* [2003] 1 WLR 1792 at [38], [45] (the "critical question" is whether the use is more than merely ancillary to the use made for the benefit of the dominant tenement); *Macepark (Whittlebury) Ltd v Sargeant* [2003] 1 WLR 2284 (use more than merely ancillary to the right of access to the dominant land); [2004] All ER Rev 242 (P. J. Clarke). [357] P. 608, ante.

[358] *Milner's Safe Co Ltd v Great Northern and City Rly Co* [1907] 1 Ch 208; *Stafford v Lee* (1992) 65 P & CR 172; *Chaffe v Kingsley* [2000] 1 EGLR 104. For changes in intensity of use of the dominant tenement, see *McAdams Homes Ltd v Robinson*, [2005] 1 P & CR 30.

in the burden on the servient land.[359] The burden upon the servient tenement must not be increased by reason of a radical change in the character of the dominant tenement.[360] For example, a right of way that has been used to carry agricultural produce to a farm cannot lawfully be used to meet the requirements of a factory into which the farm is later converted.[361] But if the character or nature of the user remains constant, there is no objection to an increase in its intensity.[362] A right of way appurtenant to a golf club, for instance, is not misused merely because the membership of the club has greatly increased.[363]

F The Running of the Benefit and the Burden of an Easement

An easement will be binding on the original grantor in favour of the original grantee as a matter of contract. However, as an incorporeal hereditament,[364] a legal easement is capable of binding the owner for the time being of the servient tenement, in favour of the owner for the time being of the dominant tenement, as a matter of property. So too an equitable easement is capable of binding and benefiting the successors in title of the original parties. The circumstances in which the benefit and the burden will run vary according to whether the easement is legal or equitable, and whether the land is registered or unregistered.

(1) The Benefit

The benefit of an easement, whether legal or equitable, will pass on a conveyance of the dominant tenement by virtue of section 62 of the Law of Property Act 1925.[365] In the case of registered land, under the Land Registration Act 2002[366] first registration with absolute title vests the estate in the proprietor together with all interests subsisting for the benefit of the estate,[367] and therefore easements that benefited the land before it was registered continue

---

[359] *Atwood v Bovis Homes Ltd* [2001] Ch 379, M & B p. 771, per Neuberger J; [2000] All ER Rev 238 (P. J. Clarke); (2001) 151 NLJ 1307 (H. W. Wilkinson) (prescriptive easement to drain surface water); *McAdams Homes Ltd v Robinson* [2005] 1 P & CR 30 at [50], per Neuberger LJ (easement of drainage implied under the rule in *Wheeldon v Burrows*; there should be little difference between easements by prescription and implied easements as regards changes of user: at [22]).

[360] *Wimbledon and Putney Commons Conservators v Dixon* (1875) 1 Ch D 362; *Ward (Helston) Ltd v Kerrier DC* (1981) 42 P & CR 412.

[361] *Williams v James* (1867) LR 2 CP 577 at 582, per Willes J; *Loder v Gaden* (1999) 78 P & CR 223.

[362] *British Railways Board v Glass* [1965] Ch 538, M & B p. 766 (Lord Denning MR dissenting); (1965) 87 LQR 17 (R.E.M.); *Woodhouse & Co Ltd v Kirkland (Derby) Ltd* [1970] 1 WLR 1185 (considerable increase in number of customers using right of way held to be "mere increase in user and not a user of a different kind or for a different purpose"); *Giles v County Building Constructors (Hertford) Ltd* (1971) 22 P & CR 978 (erection of seven modern dwelling units in place of two houses held to be "evolution rather than mutation"); *Cargill v Gotts* [1981] 1 WLR 441 (drawing of extra water from neighbour's millpond for agricultural purposes held to be mere increase in user), p. 179, ante. Cf *Atwood v Bovis Homes Ltd*, supra (easement to discharge surface water not lost, where there was radical change of user of dominant tenement but no material effect on volume of water discharged).   [363] *British Railways Board v Glass* [1965] Ch 538 at 568, per Davies LJ.

[364] P. 585, ante.

[365] P. 603, ante; unless a contrary intention is expressed in the conveyance: s. 62(4). "Conveyance" is drafted sufficiently widely to include a transfer of registered land: s. 205(1)(ii); but does not include a contract to sell: p. 604, ante. The benefit of an existing easement can therefore pass on a contract only if expressly provision is made in the contract.

[366] LRA 1925, ss. 19(3), 22(3), used to provide explicitly that the general words implied by LPA 1925, s. 62, applied also to dispositions of a registered estate. The provisions of LRA 2002 have the same general effect as the 1925 Act as regards the passing of benefits appurtenant to registered titles: R & R, para. 3.008.01.

[367] LRA 2002, ss. 11(2) (freehold), 12(3) (leasehold).

to benefit it after registration. And a disposition of a registered estate takes effect with the benefit of rights that are appurtenant to that estate,[368] thus transferring those benefits that attached to the estate immediately before the transfer. However, the benefit of a legal easement will often be entered on the register of the dominant tenement. The policy of the new scheme for registration introduced by the 2002 Act is that, as far as possible,[369] the register should reflect rights such as legal easements, and there are provisions permitting entries of expressly granted legal easements to be made on first registration,[370] and requiring[371] or permitting[372] entries of such easements on their later creation.

(2) The Burden

(a) Registered land

Under the Land Registration Act 1925 easements enjoyed a privileged position. Under section 70(1)(a) all legal easements were overriding interests, and therefore bound all successors of the servient tenement without requiring to be protected by notice on the register. There was some doubt about the intended scope of that provision as regards equitable easements, but in *Celsteel Ltd v Alton House Holdings Ltd*[373] SCOTT J held that it extended to

all equitable easements other than such as by reason of some other statutory provision or applicable principle of law, could obtain protection otherwise than by notice on the register. The most obvious example would be equitable easements which qualified for protection under paragraph (g) as part of the rights of a person in actual occupation.

This gave a general protection to the beneficiary of an equitable easement who could therefore in most cases enforce his easement against a purchaser of the servient tenement, without the need to register it. This position has now been reversed, and under the Land Registration Act 2002 no new equitable easement will be an overriding interest either on first registration or on a registered disposition.[374] However, easements which were already overriding interests in relation to a registered estate immediately before the coming into force of the Act (13 October 2003[375]) retain their status as overriding interests[376] and therefore the old law on equitable easements will remain relevant for some time.[377]

Under the Land Registration Act 2002,[378] on a first registration all existing legal easements will override, thus allowing the legal easements which bound the servient tenement automatically under the system of unregistered land[379] to continue to bind the registered estate.

---

[368] R & R, para. 3.008.01.

[369] There is no requirement of entry where the easement is legal but not expressly granted (i.e., it is created by prescription, by implied grant or under LPA 1925 s. 62: LRA 2002, s. 27(7)), or is equitable.

[370] LRR 2003, r. 33(1); H & B, para. 2.34.

[371] LRA 2002, s. 27(2)(d); Sch. 2, para. 7(2)(b) (where the grant is out of a registered estate).

[372] LRR 2003, r. 73 (where the grant is over an unregistered legal estate).

[373] [1985] 1 WLR 204 at 220; [1986] Conv 31 (M. P. Thompson); [1999] Conv (J. Greed). The decision was followed in *Thatcher v Douglas* (1996) NLJ 282.

[374] LRA 2002, Sch. 1, para. 3, and Sch. 3, para. 3 respectively, which are both expressly restricted to legal easements.   [375] SI 2003 No. 1725, art. 2(1).

[376] LRA 2002, Sch. 2, para. 9.

[377] The problem should, however, recede over time: on the application to register a registrable disposition the applicant must provide information about interests (such as overriding interests) so that they can be entered onto the register: LRA 2002, s. 71(b); LRR 2003, r. 57(1); H & B, para. 11.17.

[378] On the impact of the changes made by the 2002 Act, see [2003] Conv 304 (P. Kenny); [2005] Conv 195 (G. Battersby).   [379] Infra.

However, in relation to new easements created in relation to a registered servient tenement, several distinctions are drawn. The express[380] grant or reservation of a legal easement is a disposition which is required to be completed by registration;[381] and the registration requirement for such easements is that a notice be entered in the register of the servient tenement and also, if it is a registered estate, the dominant tenement.[382] An expressly granted or reserved easement therefore does not take effect as a legal easement until these registration requirements have been met,[383] and, since there will then be an appropriate notice on the register, there is no question of it being an overriding interest: a purchaser of the servient tenement is bound by virtue of the notice on the register.

Other newly created legal easements—those created by implied[384] grant or prescription—are capable of being overriding interests and therefore of overriding a registered disposition without being protected by notice on the register. However, a further distinction is drawn according to the date of the disposition. Under transitional provisions[385] *all* legal easements will be overriding interests for a period of three years from the day on which the Act came into force—that is, for the period from 13 October 2003 to 12 October 2006. This therefore continues for this limited period the position which prevailed under the 1925 Act, giving overriding effect to legal easements as a general class. However, with effect from 13 October 2006 the only legal easements which qualify as overriding interests are set out in the Land Registration Act 2002, Schedule 3, paragraph 3:

(1) A legal easement or profit a prendre, except for an easement, or a profit a prendre which is not registered under the Commons Registration Act 1965, which at the time of the disposition—
   (a) is not within the actual knowledge of the person to whom the disposition is made, and
   (b) would not have been obvious on a reasonably careful inspection of the land over which the easement or profit is exercisable.

(2) The exception in sub-paragraph (1) does not apply if the person entitled to the easement or profit proves that it has been exercised in the period of one year ending with the day of the disposition.

The general effect[386] of this provision is that a legal easement or profit à prendre will still be an overriding interest if

(i) it is a right of common registered under the Commons Registration Act 1965;[387] or

(ii) it is within the actual knowledge of the disponee; or

(iii) it would have been obvious on a reasonably careful inspection of the servient tenement; or

(iv) the dominant owner proves that it has been exercised within one year of the disposition.

---

[380] This does not include an easement granted as a result of the operation of LPA 1925, s. 62: LRA 2002, s. 27(7).   [381] LRA 2002, s. 27(2)(e).

[382] Ibid., Sch. 2, para. 7.   [383] P. 599, ante.

[384] Including those granted as a result of the operation of LPA 1925, s. 62: n. 380, supra.

[385] LRA 2002, Sch. 12, para. 10.

[386] The reading of the provision is complicated by its negative formulation, which presumably has an effect on the burden of proof: and so, for example, it will be for the disponee to show that he did *not* have actual knowledge of the easement. The burden of proof in sub-para. (2) is explicit.

[387] P. 645, post. The registration renders it discoverable by the purchaser.

A legal easement will therefore bind a purchaser of the servient tenement, without being protected by a notice on the register of title, if it is, or ought reasonably to have been, known by him; or if it has been exercised within the last year. This has the effect of re-introducing the doctrine of notice into registered land in this context;[388] but also allows legal easements to bind a purchaser which are not patent, but are not dormant (in the sense of having fallen into more than a year's disuse), such as rights of drainage which, by being beneath the surface, are not necessarily obvious on inspection. It is a pragmatic exception to the general principle that a purchaser should be bound only by those rights which he could have discovered, and may not be a significant burden in practice, because pre-contract enquiries will generally seek to identify such rights.[389]

Moreover, as mentioned above, there is a general policy that legal easements should where possible be noted on the register so as to reduce reliance on the category of overriding interests.[390] A person applying either for first registration or to register a registrable disposition—such as the purchaser of the servient tenement—must provide information about overriding interests which affect the estate which are within his actual knowledge;[391] a legal easement which is disclosed under this provision will therefore be noted on the register and bind future purchasers accordingly.[392]

(b) Unregistered land

In unregistered land, in accordance with general principle,[393] the burden of a legal easement is enforceable against all the world, and therefore against all subsequent owners of the servient tenement, or of any interest in it, whether or not they give value for the acquisition of their interest, or have notice of the easement.

An equitable easement, however, does not bind all later owners of the servient tenement. Certain forms of equitable easement are registrable as land charges under the Land Charges Act 1972, and if not registered are void against a purchaser of the legal estate for money or money's worth.[394] This applies to equitable easements which arise under the doctrine of *Walsh v Lonsdale*[395] pursuant to a contract to create a legal easement (registrable as an estate contract[396]); and an "equitable easement",[397] which is defined as[398] "any easement, right or privilege over or affecting land created or arising on or after 1st January 1926, and being merely an equitable interest" but which is to be construed more narrowly[399] than might first appear. It has been limited to such proprietary interests in land as would before 1926 have been recognised as capable of being conveyed or created at law, but which since 1925 only take effect as equitable interests, as for instance an easement granted for the life of the grantee.[400]

---

[388] See also the similar issue which arises in relation to LRA 2002, Sch. 3, para. 2; p. 985, post.

[389] H & B, para. 11.15. For pre-contract enquiries generally, see chap. 24, post.

[390] H & B, paras. 11.18–11.22.

[391] LRA 2002, s. 71(a) (first registration), (b) (registrable disposition); LRR 2003, rr. 28 (first registration), 57 (registrable disposition).

[392] In addition, the registrar has a general power to note overriding interests that overrode first registration, and that come to his attention otherwise than through the disclosure requirement: LRA 2002, s. 37; LRR 2003, r. 89. [393] P. 56, ante.

[394] LCA 1972, s. 2(6). [395] P. 601, ante. [396] LCA 1972, s. 2(4)(iv), Class C(iv).

[397] Ibid., s. 2(5)(iii), Class D(iii). [398] Ibid.

[399] *Shiloh Spinners Ltd v Harding* [1973] AC 691, M & B p. 34; p. 941, post.

[400] *E R Ives Investment Ltd v High* [1967] 2 QB 379 at 395, per Lord DENNING; M & B p. 665; (1937) 53 LQR 259 (C. V. Davidge); (1948) 12 Conv (NS) 202 (J. F. Garner).

An equitable easement which is not capable of registration as a land charge[401] will be void against a purchaser without notice, actual, constructive or imputed, of it.[402]

G Remedies for Infringement of an Easement[403]

The dominant owner may seek one or more remedies in order to enforce his rights. Not being in possession of the servient tenement, he cannot maintain an action of trespass for infringement of the easement.[404] However, he may seek a declaration in order to establish the existence and extent of the easement; and since infringement of an easement constitutes the tort of nuisance against the dominant owner,[405] he may seek the usual remedies for nuisance: the self-help remedy of *abatement*; or an action for *damages* or an *injunction*.

(1) Abatement

The party suffering a nuisance may abate it: that is, take steps to stop the nuisance—such as by pulling down a physical obstruction to the light to his windows which the servient owner has erected on his land. However, "the abatement of a nuisance is a remedy which the law does not favour and is not usually advisable",[406] since it involves the party taking matters into his own hands rather than pursuing his remedies through legal action. The party purporting to exercise the right of abatement risks committing an actionable wrong himself if he does not act strictly within his rights under the easement and within the limits allowed to the remedy by the courts:[407] abatement is justified only in clear and simple cases, or in an emergency;[408] the action taken must be no more than necessary to stop the nuisance;[409] and notice must in many cases[410] first be given to the occupier of the servient tenement before the dominant

[401] Such as one arising under the doctrine of proprietary estoppel: *E R Ives Investment Ltd v High* [1967] 2 QB 379.

[402] LPA 1925, s. 199(1)(ii).   [403] Gale, chaps. 13 and 14.

[404] In this respect an easement differs from a profit à prendre, for which the remedy of trespass may therefore be available: p. 642, post; *Paine & Co Ltd v St Neots Gas & Coke Co* [1939] 3 All ER 812 at 823, per LUXMOORE LJ.

[405] "Nuisance is a tort against land, including interests in land such as easements and profits": *Hunter v Canary Wharf Ltd* [1997] AC 655 at 702, per Lord HOFFMANN. The action for infringement (or *disturbance*) of an easement has sometimes been distinguished from the action of nuisance: see, e.g., *Colls v Home and Colonial Stores Ltd* [1904] AC 179 at 186, per Lord MACNAGHTEN (right to light); *Aldred's Case* (1611) 9 Co Rep 57b. It requires different elements of pleading, since, not having possession of the property, the dominant owner must plead (and, if put in issue) prove his title to the easement in order to show his right to claim: *Paine & Co Ltd v St Neots Gas & Coke Co*, supra, at 823. However, in substance the same principles apply to the remedies available for nuisance and in an action for disturbance: Gale, para. 13–01. For detailed discussion of the law of nuisance, see Buckley, *The Law of Nuisance; Clerk and Lindsell on Torts*, chap. 19. An easement may in turn *negative* liability in nuisance: conduct by the dominant owner which would otherwise constitute a nuisance against a neighbour becomes lawful if it is exercised within the scope of a duly created easement: *Hunter v Canary Wharf Ltd*, supra, at 685; *Sturges v Bridgman* (1879) 11 Ch D 852.

[406] *Lagan Navigation Co v Lambeg Bleaching, Dyeing and Finishing Co Ltd* [1927] AC 226 at 244 per Lord ATKINSON.

[407] *Wheeldon v Burrows* (1879) 12 Ch D 31 (trespass committed by defendant who knocked down obstructions to light where the court held that he had no easement of light).

[408] *Burton v Winters* [1993] 1 WLR 1077 at 1082.   [409] *Greenslade v Halliday* (1830) 6 Bing 379.

[410] Notice is not required in an emergency, but is certainly required where the person in occupation did not himself create the nuisance, and may be required where he did: see the authorities cited in Gale, para. 14–07. Notice is not required where the dominant owner can abate the nuisance without entering onto the servient tenement.

owner enters to abate it. However, within these limits, in an appropriate case abatement can be a very useful and efficient remedy to stop the infringement of an easement.

(2) Injunction and/or Damages

More commonly, however, the dominant owner must bring an action[411] to enforce his rights under the easement. In such a case the claimant must establish his title to the easement, and show that the defendant's actual or threatened conduct constitutes an actionable interference with the easement.[412] Actual loss or damage need not be proved: the infringement of the easement is a sufficient violation of a legal right to found an action.[413] However, there must be a substantial interference with the reasonable use of the easement.[414]

The primary remedy for nuisance is an injunction;[415] damages may be awarded, in the court's discretion, in addition to, or in substitution for, an injunction[416] and, in particular, may be awarded where the injury to the claimant's legal rights is small, capable of being estimated in money and can be adequately compensated by a small money payment, and it would be oppressive to the defendant to grant an injunction.[417]

H Extinguishment of Easements

An easement may be extinguished by statute or by release or as the result of unity of seisin. There is no statutory procedure for their discharge or modification as there is in the case of restrictive covenants.[418]

(1) Statute

Easements may be extinguished by statute. Important examples are to be found in the Town and Country Planning Act 1990, under which acquiring authorities are enabled to extinguish "all private rights of way and rights of laying down, erecting, continuing or maintaining any apparatus on, under or over the land".[419] Further, local authorities may build or

[411] An action relating to an easement over land is a pending land action within the meaning of LCA 1972, which in registered land must be protected by notice and cannot be an overriding interest: LRA 2002, s. 87(1), (3). In unregistered land it must be registered in the register of pending actions: LCA 1972, s. 1(1)(b); if it is to bind a purchaser without express notice of it: ibid., s. 5 (7).

[412] If the defendant denies any of these elements, the claimant must therefore prove that the right he claims is in the nature of an easement (pp. 586 et seq, ante); that it has been created as an easement (pp. 600 et seq, ante); that he has the benefit of it and the defendant the burden of it (pp. 631 et seq, ante); and the extent of the easement, so as to demonstrate its infringement on the facts (pp. 628 et seq, ante).

[413] *Nicholls v Ely Beet Sugar Factory Ltd* [1936] Ch 343.

[414] *Celsteel Ltd v Alton House Holdings Ltd* [1985] 1 WLR 204 at 217 (right of way); *West v Sharp* (2000) 79 P & CR 327; *B & Q plc v Liverpool & Lancashire Properties Ltd* [2001] 1 EGLR 92 (right of way): "the test of an actionable interference is not whether the grantee is left with what is reasonable, but whether his insistence upon being able to continue the use of the whole of what he contracted for is reasonable": per BLACKBURNE J at 96; *Perlman v Rayden* [2004] 43 EG 142 (CS) (aggravated damages awarded).

[415] *Shelfer v City of London Electric Lighting Co* [1895] 1 Ch 287.

[416] SCA 1981, s. 50, replacing Chancery Amendment Act 1858, s. 2 (Lord Cairns' Act).

[417] *Shelfer v City of London Electric Lighting Co*, supra, at 322–3, per A. L. SMITH LJ (a "good working rule", which has been applied in many later cases. The elements of the "rule" are cumulative, emphasising the narrow practical scope of the remedy of damages as compared with that of injunction). See, e.g., *Midtown Ltd v City of London Real Property Ltd* [2005] 1 EGLR 65 (right to light: damages awarded); *Bracewell v Appleby* [1975] Ch 408 (no right of way to newly-built house; injunction would render house uninhabitable: damages awarded).

[418] P. 694, post.   [419] TCPA 1990, s. 236.

carry out work on land acquired for planning purposes, even though it involves interference with "any easement, liberty, privilege, right or advantage annexed to land and adversely affecting other land, including any natural right of support".[420]

(2) Release

An extinguishment may be effected by a release, either express or implied.

(a) Express release

The dominant owner is free to execute a deed of release relieving the servient tenement from the burden of any easement to which it is subject. At common law a deed is necessary,[421] but if the servient owner, in reliance on an agreement to release, has prejudiced his position to such an extent that it would be inequitable and oppressive to treat the easement as still in being, equity will disregard the absence of formalities and will hold the dominant owner to his bargain. If, for instance, a person who is entitled to an easement of light orally agrees to an alteration in the servient tenement which must necessarily obstruct the flow of light to the window, he cannot, after expense has been incurred in making the alteration, bring an action in respect of the resulting obstruction.[422]

(b) Implied release

(1) ABANDONMENT

A more important and at the same time more difficult point is whether in any given case there has been an implied release or abandonment of the easement by the dominant owner.

The onus of proving abandonment lies fairly and squarely on the person who alleges it, and the onus is a very heavy one.[423] As BUCKLEY LJ said in *Tehidy Minerals Ltd v Norman*:[424]

Abandonment of an easement or of a profit à prendre can only, we think, be treated as having taken place where the person entitled to it has demonstrated a fixed intention never at any time thereafter to assert the right himself or to attempt to transmit it to anyone else.

The general principle is that whether he intended to abandon his right depends upon the proper inference to be drawn from the circumstances.[425]

No one circumstance necessarily implies an abandonment, and thus, it has been laid down repeatedly that mere non-user is not decisive of the question.[426] If the non-user is explicable only on the assumption that the dominant owner intended to give up his right, it will amount to an abandonment, but not if there are other circumstances which go to show that he

---

[420] TCPA 1990, s. 237. See also Housing Act 1985, s. 295; New Towns Act 1981, s. 19; as amended by Telecommunications Act 1984, s. 109(1), Sch. 4, para. 79(3); *R v City of London Corpn and Royal London Mutual Insurance Society, ex p Master of Governors and Commonality of the Mystery of the Barbers of London* (1996) 73 P & CR 59; *Jones v Cleanthi* [2006] 1 All ER 1029 (freeholder's statutory obligation to carry out works in order to make property fit for multiple occupation sufficient to extinguish easement enjoyed by tenant).

[421] Co Litt 264b.

[422] *Davies v Marshall* (1861) 10 CBNS 697; *Waterlow v Bacon* (1866) LR 2 Eq 514. This is, in substance, an application of the principles of proprietary estoppel; chap. 22, post.

[423] *James v Stevenson* [1893] AC 162.   [424] [1971] 2 QB 528 at 553, M & B p. 782.

[425] *Cook v Bath Corpn* (1868) LR 6 Eq 177.

[426] *R v Chorley* (1848) 12 QB 515; *Ward v Ward* (1852) 7 Exch 838; *Crossley & Sons Ltd v Lightowler* (1867) 2 Ch App 478; *Re Yateley Common, Hampshire* [1977] 1 WLR 840 at 845; *Gotobed v Pridmore* (1970) 115 SJ 78; *Benn v Hardinge* (1992) 66 P & CR 246 (no abandonment in spite of 175 years' non-user); *Bosomworth v Faber* (1992) 69 P & CR 288; *Snell & Prideaux Ltd v Dutton Mirrors Ltd* [1995] 1 EGLR 259; [1995] Conv 291 (C. J. Davis); *CDC2020 plc v Ferreira* [2005] 3 EGLR 15; (2005) 155 SJ 969 (A. Rosenthal).

regarded the right as still alive. In other words, a cessation may show either an abandonment or a mere abeyance of an easement according to the particular circumstances of each case.

The principle was re-stated by POLLOCK MR in *Swan v Sinclair*:[427]

Non-user is not by itself conclusive evidence that a private right of easement is abandoned. The non-user must be considered with, and may be explained by, the surrounding circumstances. If those circumstances clearly indicate an intention of not resuming the user then a presumption of a release of the easement will, in general, be implied and the easement will be lost.

Thus in the leading case of *Moore v Rawson*:[428]

A plaintiff, who had some ancient windows, pulled down the wall in which they were situated and rebuilt it as a stable with no windows. Some fourteen years later the defendant erected on his adjoining land a building which would have obstructed the flow of light to the windows had they still been there. After another three years the plaintiff made a window in the stable in the exact spot where one of the old windows had been, and then proceeded to bring an action against the defendant for obstruction of light.

It was held that he could not succeed, because, in erecting a building entirely different from the old one, he had shown an intention to abandon the enjoyment of his former right. However, as was stated by HOLROYD J:[429]

If he had done some act to shew that he intended to build another in its place, then the new house, when built, would in effect have been a continuation of the old house, and the rights attached to the old house would have continued. If a man has a right of common attached to his mill, or a right of turbary attached to his house, if he pulls down the mill or the house, the right of common or of turbary will prima facie cease. If he show an intention to build another mill or another house, his right continues.

The same principle can be seen at work in the case of rights of way. So, where the exercise of a right of way had been discontinued for many years because the dominant owner had a more convenient route over his own land, it was held that the non-user was adequately explained and did not constitute an abandonment.[430]

But any non-user of a right of way caused by something which is adverse to the enjoyment of the right will be regarded as an abandonment. Thus in *Swan v Sinclair*:[431]

Certain houses were put up for sale in lots in 1871, one of the conditions being that a strip of land running at the back of the houses should be formed into a roadway, and that the purchaser of each lot should have a right of way along the road when made. At the time when the action was brought in 1923 the road had not been constructed, fences lay across its proposed site between each pair of lots, and in 1883 the then owner of lot 1 nearest the exit of the proposed road had levelled up the site, and by so doing had caused a sheer drop of 6 feet to occur between that lot and lot 2. The plaintiff was now desirous of building a garage on lot 2, and the question arose whether he was still entitled to a right of way over the strip of land at the back of lot 1.

---

[427] [1924] 1 Ch 254 at 266; affd [1925] AC 227.   [428] (1824) 3 B & C 332, M & B p. 782.
[429] Ibid., at 338.   [430] *Ward v Ward* (1852) 7 Exch 838.
[431] [1924] 1 Ch 254; affd [1925] AC 227.

The majority of the court dismissed his claim on the ground that, though as a rule mere non-user is insufficient to extinguish a right of way, yet in this case the continued existence of the dividing fences and the raising of the level of lot 1 were circumstances adverse to a right of enjoyment, sufficient to show an intention on the part of the various owners to abandon the project.

(2) ALTERATIONS TO DOMINANT TENEMENT

Alterations to the dominant tenement which make the enjoyment of an easement impossible or unnecessary may show an intention to abandon the right. For example, where a right of water is appurtenant to a mill, and the mill is demolished, without any intention of replacing it, the easement is impliedly released.[432] Furthermore, the easement may be extinguished where the dominant tenement is so altered as to throw a substantially increased burden on the servient tenement to the detriment of its owner.[433]

(3) ALTERATIONS TO SERVIENT TENEMENT

A servient owner has no right to alter the route of an easement of way unless such a right is an express or implied term of the grant of the easement or is subsequently conferred on him.[434] However, even if he has no such right, nevertheless such a realignment will not be an actionable interference with the easement if the realigned right is equally convenient, especially where there is no reasonable objection to the realignment. It has been held[435] that where the dominant owner had notice of the proposal and did not object and where the realignment achieved an object of substantial public importance, the dominant owner's remedy, if any, should be restricted to an award of damages.

(3) Frustration

In *Huckvale v Aegean Hotels Ltd*, the Court of Appeal considered a novel claim that an easement can be extinguished by its ceasing to accommodate the dominant tenement. In granting an interlocutory injunction, SLADE LJ said:[436]

In the absence of evidence of proof of abandonment, the court should be slow to hold that an easement has been extinguished by frustration, unless the evidence shows clearly that because of a change of circumstances since the date of the original grant there is no practical possibility of its ever again benefiting the dominant tenement in the manner contemplated by that grant.

(4) Unity of Seisin

Easements are also extinguished by unity of seisin, that is to say, if the fees simple of both the dominant and the servient tenements become united in the same owner, all easements

---

[432] *Liggins v Inge* (1831) 7 Bing 682 at p 693; *Ecclesiastical Comrs for England v Kino* (1880) 14 Ch D 213; *Scott v Pape* (1886) 31 Ch D 554.

[433] *Ankerson v Connelly* [1906] 2 Ch 544; affd [1907] 1 Ch 678 (easement of light); *Ray v Fairway Motors (Barnstaple) Ltd* (1968) 20 P & CR 261 (easement of support); *Lloyds Bank Ltd v Dalton* [1942] Ch 466 at 471–2, per BENNETT J; cf *Graham v Philcox* [1984] QB 747, M & B p. 762; p. 604, ante; Gale, para. 12–28. Cf *Atwood v Bovis Homes Ltd* [2001] Ch 379, M & B p. 771, p. 631, n. 359, ante, where there was a change in the *extent* of the user of the dominant tenement. [434] *Deacon v South-Eastern Railway Co* (1889) 61 LT 377.

[435] *Greenwich Healthcare National Health Service Trust v London and Quadrant Housing Trust* [1998] 1 WLR 1749 at 1754, per LIGHTMAN J, who granted such a declaration in the absence of the dominant owner.

[436] (1989) 58 P & CR 163 at 173; [1990] Conv 292 (K. Kodilinye).

properly so called come to an end, for the owner can do what he likes with his own land, and any right that formerly ranked as an easement because it was exercisable over another's land is now merely one of the ordinary incidents of his ownership.[437] An easement which has been destroyed by this union of title in one hand may, however, be re-created under the doctrine of *Wheeldon v Burrows* if the property is again severed into its original parts.[438] A complete extinguishment occurs when both the tenements become united in one person for an estate in fee simple, but if he acquires only a particular estate in one of them, as for instance a life interest or a term of years, the easement is merely suspended and will revive again if upon the determination of his particular estate the tenements are once more in different hands.[439]

Unity of seisin without unity of possession does not extinguish an easement of light, as, for example, where the owner of the servient tenement acquires the fee simple in the dominant tenement while the latter is in the possession of a tenant for years.[440] It is doubtful, however, whether this is true in the case of easements other than light.[441]

III Profits à Prendre

A *Nature of Profits à Prendre*

(1) General Nature

A profit à prendre consists of the right to enter another's land and to take something off the land.[442] It is this participation in the produce of the soil or in the soil itself that principally distinguishes a profit from an easement. A right is a profit only if the thing to be taken is something that is capable of ownership. Thus the rights to pasture cattle on another's land, or to take sand or fish from another's river, or to take soil, turf, stones or pheasants[443] from another's estate are all examples of profits, for such things are capable of ownership; but a right to collect and carry away water from a spring on another person's land, or to water cattle in another's stream, is not a profit but an easement, since water is not part of the soil like sand, nor the produce of soil like grass, and unless stored in a tank or other receptacle,[444] is not capable of private ownership.[445]

(2) Different Forms of Profit à Prendre

Profits à prendre may take the following forms:[446]

---

437 Co Litt 313a; *Lord Dynevor v Tennant* (1888) 13 App Cas 279.

438 (1879) 12 Ch D 31; p. 610, ante. But not under LPA 1925, s. 62, since there would be no diversity of occupation; p. 605, ante.   439 *Thomas v Thomas* (1835) 2 Cr M & R 34.

440 *Lord Richardson v Graham* [1908] 1 KB 39, M & B p. 783.

441 In *Buckby v Coles* (1814) 5 Taunt 311, MACDONALD CB was of opinion that a right of way was not extinguished by mere unity of seisin (at 315), but the Court of Common Pleas expressed a "decided opinion" to the opposite effect (at 315–16) and counsel abandoned the argument.

442 *Duke of Sutherland v Heathcote* [1892] 1 Ch 475 at 484.

443 On sporting rights, see *Peech v Best* [1931] 1 KB 1 at 9; *Pole v Peake* [1998] EGCS 125.

444 Such as a reservoir: *Mitchell v Potter* [2005] EWCA Civ 88, The Times, 24 January 2005.

445 Co Litt 4a; Blackstone, vol. ii. p. 18; *Mason v Hill* (1833) 5 B & Ad 1; *Race v Ward* (1855) 4 E & B 702; *Lowe v J W Ashmore Ltd* [1971] Ch 545 at 557. On the landowner's rights to water see generally pp. 177 et seq, ante.

446 A different classification, into *several profits* and *profits in common*, is discussed infra.

(a) Profit appurtenant

A profit appurtenant is one which exists for the benefit of, and is annexed to, an estate in land. In this respect, such a profit resembles an easement, since, as we have seen,[447] an easement must exist for the benefit of an estate (the dominant tenement). The following forms of profit à prendre, however, are different from easements.

(b) Profit appendant

A profit is appendant if it is annexed to the land by operation of law. If before the passing of the Statute *Quia Emptores* in 1290 the lord of a manor granted arable land to be held of him by a freehold tenant, the common law automatically appended to the grant a right in the tenant to pasture upon the waste lands of the manor such cattle as were necessary to plough and manure the arable land.[448] This right of pasture was held to be appendant, and necessarily appendant, to a grant of arable land within a manor, for the grantee obviously could not till the arable land without beasts of plough, and he would have no means of sustaining the animals unless he could pasture them on the manorial waste.[449] This right, therefore, arose from common right upon the grant of arable land within a manor, and it must be distinguished from profits appurtenant to land, which are opposed to common right and must be deliberately acquired by an actual or presumed grant.[450] Profits appendant are still possible, but they must have come into existence before 1290,[451] for the effect of *Quia Emptores* was that all sales by the lord of the manor since that date take the land out of the manor altogether,[452] so that the grantee does not hold of the manor in the waste of which he claims a right.

(c) Profit in gross

Unlike an easement,[453] a profit may be granted in gross to be held independently of the ownership of land.[454] From early times it was held that an express grant by deed to a man, his heirs and assigns of a perpetual right to a profit was a valid grant,[455] and as the possibility of a grant is the basis of all the methods whereby profits as well as easements may be acquired, it was later held that a profit in gross might be prescribed for at common law.[456] Such profits in gross are not common, but once established they may be sold or leased to a third party,[457] and they will pass under a will or intestacy.

(d) Profit pur cause de vicinage

A profit *pur cause de vicinage* is restricted to the common[458] of pasturage, and arises where adjacent commons are open and unfenced and there is a custom for the cattle to

---

[447] P. 588, ante.

[448] Co Litt 122a; Blackstone, vol. ii. p. 33; *Earl of Dunraven v Llewellyn* (1850) 15 QB 791 at 810; Holdsworth, *History of English Law*, vol. iii. pp. 147 et seq; Hall, *Law of Profits à Prendre and Rights of Common*, p. 224.

[449] Blackstone, vol. ii, p. 33.

[450] *Tyrringham's Case* (1584) 4 Co Rep 36b; *Warrick v Queen's College, Oxford* (1871) 6 Ch App 716.

[451] See *Davies v Davies* [1975] QB 172.   [452] P. 16, ante.   [453] P. 588, ante.

[454] *Lord Chesterfield v Harris* [1908] 2 Ch 397 at 421, per Buckley LJ.

[455] 1495 YB 11 Hen, fol. 8a, cited by Parke B in *Wickham v Hawker* (1840) 7 M & W 63 at 79.

[456] *Welcome v Upton* (1840) 6 M & W 536; *Johnson v Barnes* (1872) LR 7 CP 592; affd (1873) LR 8 CP 527; *Shuttleworth v Le Fleming* (1865) 19 CBNS 687; *Goodman v Saltash Corpn* (1882) 7 App Cas 633 at 658.

[457] *Goodman v Saltash Corpn*, supra.   [458] P. 643, post.

inter-common, that is, for the cattle rightfully put upon the common of one manor to stray and feed on the common of the adjoining manor without being treated as trespassers.[459]

(3) Differences Between Profits and Easements

We have already noted some of the differences between profits à prendre and easements: in particular, that a profit, unlike an easement, carries the right to remove something from the servient tenement; and that a profit can exist in gross. In the following pages we shall see other differences. For example, profits, as well as easements, may be prescribed for under the Prescription Act 1832; but the statutory periods of enjoyment are fixed at thirty and sixty years instead of twenty and forty.[460] The remedies available to the beneficiary of a profit are also more extensive than those of the beneficiary of an easement. Since a profit imports the privilege of carrying away something from the servient tenement, the dominant owner enjoys such possessory rights as will enable him to maintain trespass or nuisance at common law for an infringement of his right, but the owner of an easement is restricted to the remedies of abatement or an action of nuisance.[461]

(4) Similarities between Profits and Easements

Apart from the differences indicated, the nature of a profit is in general similar to that of an easement. Thus, for instance, it is necessary that a profit which is *appurtenant* to land should be connected with the dominant tenement in the sense of increasing its beneficial enjoyment.[462] The law does not recognise an unlimited profit appurtenant, as for instance a right to cut turf[463] or to catch salmon for sale,[464] or to dig clay wherever it is required for making bricks.[465] A profit appurtenant must be limited, and the limit is arrived at by estimating the needs of the dominant tenement.[466]

Further, a profit, like an easement, is capable of subsisting as a legal interest;[467] it may also be equitable.[468]

B *Classes of Profits à Prendre*

(1) Several Profits and Profits in Common

Profits fall into two classes, namely those enjoyed by their owner to the exclusion of everybody else, and those enjoyed by him in common with other persons including the owner of the servient tenement.

---

[459] Co Litt 122a; *Tyrringham's Case* (1584) 4 Co Rep 36b. See *Newman v Bennett* [1981] QB 726 (three straying cows in the New Forest).   [460] Prescription Act 1832, s. 1; p. 651, post.
  [461] *Fitzgerald v Firbank* [1897] 2 Ch 96; *Peech v Best* [1931] 1 KB 1; *Nicholls v Ely Beet Sugar Factory Ltd* [1936] Ch 343.
  [462] *Clayton v Corby* (1843) 5 QB 415 at 419; *Bailey v Stephens* (1862) 12 CBNS 91; cf p. 588, ante.
  [463] *Valentine v Penny* (1605) Noy 145.
  [464] *Lord Chesterfield v Harris* [1908] 2 Ch 397; affd [1911] AC 623.
  [465] *Clayton v Corby*, supra.   [466] See pp. 643–4, post, in reference to common of pasture.
  [467] LPA 1925, s. 1(2)(a).
  [468] *Mason v Clarke* [1955] AC 778; see *Lowe v J W Ashmore Ltd* [1971] Ch 545, esp. at 557–8, p. 648, post.

The first are called "several" profits à prendre, and the latter profits à prendre in "common", or rights of common, or more often simply *commons*: "A right of common may be said to exist where two or more take, in common with each other, from the soil of a third person a part of the natural profits thence produced."[469] Thus, while every common is a profit à prendre, it does not follow that all profits à prendre are commons.[470]

Profits à prendre are rights which have existed from a very early date in the history of this country, and which in their origin[471] were exercised by numbers of persons in common with each other. Moreover, that is the form in which they are most frequently found nowadays. It may of course happen that a person possesses the right to take something off the land of another without affecting the right of the owner to take similar things for his own use; or he may be entitled to the exclusive right of taking something, as often occurs in the case of pasturage rights over the Sussex Downs; but the type of profit that a practising lawyer will most likely have to consider is a right of common properly so called.

(2) Rights of Common

(a) Classification

As we have seen,[472] rights of common may be classified into rights appurtenant; rights appendant; rights in gross; and (in the case of the common of pasturage) rights *pur cause de vicinage*. Rights of common may also be classified according to their subject matter into four kinds, namely, common of pasture, of piscary, of turbary and of estovers.[473]

(1) COMMON OF PASTURE

This, the most usual common, arises when the owner of cattle is, in common with others, entitled to put his cattle to feed on the land of another.[473a] In the case of a common *appendant* the right is limited to "commonable cattle", that is, horses and oxen to plough the land and cows and sheep to manure it.[474] A common *appurtenant* is not limited in this way, but depends upon the extent of the enjoyment proved or upon the terms of the grant if there is one, and so a right may well be established to pasture such animals as hogs, goats and geese.[475] Common in gross may also be enjoyed in respect of any animal. Commons of pasture appendant and appurtenant are also restricted in another manner, as we have already had occasion to notice, for there is no right to pasture an unlimited number of commonable cattle.[476] The rule at common law is that the right is exercisable only in respect of cattle

---

[469] *Woolrych on Commons*, p. 13.

[470] Historically, profits à prendre in common came first, and several profits came second. Common predated the establishment of the system of manors under which the villager came to be regarded as having rights not over something that belonged to himself in common with others, but over the property of the lord of the manor, who could in turn appropriate the common land (by inclosure), as long as he left the tenant sufficient pasturage in waste. See the 11th edn of this book, pp. 546–9.

[471] For the history of profits, see the 11th edn of this book, pp. 547–8.   [472] P. 641, ante.

[473] Blackstone, vol. ii. p. 32; Co Litt 122a. See Williams, *Rights of Common and Other Prescriptive Rights* (1880).   [473a] *Tyrringham's Case* (1584) 4 Co Rep 36b, 37.

[474] Ibid. This pasture may be claimed for certain animals only, e.g. sheep (when it is called "sheep walk"): *Robinson v Duleep Singh* (1878) 11 Ch D 798; or swine (called common of "pannage"): *Chilton v Corpn of London* (1878) 7 Ch D 562.   [475] *Bennett v Reeve* (1740) Willes 227; *Tyrringham's Case*, supra.

[476] *Anderson v Bostock* [1976] Ch 312.

levant et couchant ("getting up and lying down"[477]) on the land, i.e. the number that the dominant tenement is capable of supporting through the winter.[478] Again a right of pasturage in gross cannot be prescribed for unless it is restricted in the same manner.[479]

This doctrine of *levancy et couchancy* was, however, abolished by the Commons Registration Act 1965,[480] which requires all rights of grazing to be registered, but limits registration to a defined number of animals.[481] In the case of a common in gross there is no objection in principle to the existence of pasture without stint, or, in other words, to a right to put an unlimited number of cattle on the servient tenement, because, as it is not appurtenant to anything, there is no dominant tenement with reference to the needs of which the content of the right must be proportioned. Thus, as was said by BUCKLEY LJ:[482] "it may well be that there can exist in law a right in gross to enter and take without limitation—without stint—the profits or proceeds of another's land commercially for the purposes of sale".

Such an unstinted right might no doubt be granted expressly by deed, but, though there is no objection to it in principle, the case of *Mellor v Spateman*[483] clearly decided that it could not be prescribed for: "And the court did not dislike any part of the plea, but only it was not said in the plea '*levant et couchant* within the town'. And KELYNGE CJ said positively that there cannot be any common in gross without number."

The old expression *common sans nombre* which is met with in earlier cases is not inconsistent with this principle, for it merely meant that the right was for beasts *levant et couchant*, the point being in such a case that the number was not positively fixed at a definite figure.

(2) COMMON OF PISCARY

A stranger may acquire a right to catch fish in inland waters, such as lakes, ponds and non-navigable rivers, belonging to private owners. This right takes two forms:

(i) A "several fishery" or a "free fishery", which is not a right of common, but is a right to take fish *in alieno solo* and to exclude the owner of the water from the right to take fish himself;[484]

(ii) A "common of fishery" which is a liberty of fishing in another man's water in common with other persons.[485]

"Common of piscary being given for the sustenance of the tenant's family"[486] must, if appurtenant to a house, be limited to the needs of that house, and the fish cannot be caught for sale.[487] It should be noted that though the fishery in arms of the sea and in tidal rivers is open to all subjects of the realm,[488] yet a prescriptive right to a several fishery or a common of fishery therein may be established.[489] The presumption, however, is in favour of the public.

[477] "The language was picturesque": *Bettison v Langton* [2002] 1 AC 27 at 31, per Lord NICHOLLS OF BIRKENHEAD.

[478] *Robertson v Hartopp* (1889) 43 Ch D 484 at 517; Holdsworth, *History of English Law*, vol. vii. p. 320 and authorities there cited; *Re Ilkley and Burley Moors* (1983) 47 P & CR 324.

[479] *Mellor v Spateman* (1669) 1 Saund 339.   [480] P. 645, post.   [481] S. 15.

[482] *Lord Chesterfield v Harris* [1908] 2 Ch 397 at 421.   [483] (1669) 1 Saund 339 at 346.

[484] *Foster v Wright* (1878) 4 CPD 438 at 449. See *Loose v Castleton* (1978) 41 P & CR 19; *Lovett v Fairclough* (1990) 61 P & CR 385 (claim to profit in gross of piscary over Jeffrey's Pool in the River Tweed failed).

[485] Blackstone, vol. ii. p. 34; *Seymour v Courtenay* (1771) 5 Burr 2814, per MANSFIELD CJ.

[486] Ibid., p. 35.   [487] *Lord Chesterfield v Harris* [1908] 2 Ch 397.

[488] *Fitzwalter's Case* (1674) 1 Mod Rep 105; *Carter v Murcot* (1768) 4 Burr 2162 at 2164.

[489] *Carter v Murcot*, supra.

(3) COMMON OF TURBARY

Common of turbary is the right of cutting turf or peat in another man's land to be expended as fuel in the house of the commoner.[490] For the last 400 years this right has always been treated as a common appurtenant, with the qualification that it must be appurtenant to an ancient house or to a new house erected in continuance of the ancient one.[491]

It cannot be appurtenant to land,[492] for, as we have seen, a thing which is appurtenant must agree in nature and quality with the thing to which it is attached, and turf is to be used only for a house on the land.

(4) COMMON OF ESTOVERS

Blackstone wrote:

Common of estovers or estouviers; that is, necessaries (from *estoffer*, to furnish), is a liberty of taking necessary wood, for the use or furniture of a house or farm, from off another's estate. The Saxon word, *bote*, is used by us as synonymous to the French *estovers*; and therefore house-bote is sufficient allowance of wood to repair or to burn in the house (which latter is sometimes called fire-bote); ploughbote and cart-bote are wood to be employed in making and repairing instruments of husbandry; and hay-bote, or hedge-bote, is wood for repairing hays, hedges or fences.[493]

This right, which very closely resembles common of turbary, is generally appurtenant to a house,[494] though it may be attached to land for the purpose of repairing fences. When it is appurtenant to a house, the wood taken must be expended on that house, and cannot be used for the reparation of new buildings which may have been erected, or as fuel in new fireplaces which have been built in the original house.[495] But when the old dominant house is demolished and replaced by another one, the right continues to exist according to its original extent: "If an ancient cottage which had common be fallen down, and another cottage be erected in the place where the old cottage stood; this is no new cottage, but it may claim common as an ancient cottage by prescription."[496]

A right similar to the common of estovers and also called estovers is given at common law to a tenant for life or years enabling him to cut timber which would otherwise be waste.[497] The only difference between the common law right and that which we have just considered is that the former arises in the tenant by virtue of the possession of the land rented and is exercisable over that land, while the latter is a profit to be taken out of somebody else's land.

(b) *Registration*

The policy of the Commons Registration Act 1965[498] was to have a once-for-all nationwide inquiry into commons, common rights and town and village greens. When the process had

[490] Blackstone, vol. ii. p. 34.
[491] *A-G v Reynolds* [1911] 2 KB 888; *Warrick v Queen's College, Oxford* (1871) 6 Ch App 716 at 730.
[492] *Tyrringham's Case* (1584) 4 Co Rep 36b.   [493] Blackstone, vol. ii. p. 35.
[494] *A-G v Reynolds* [1911] 2 KB 888.   [495] *Luttrel's Case* (1601) 4 Co Rep 86a.
[496] *Bryers v Lake*, cited Hall, *Law of Profits à Prendre and Rights of Common*, p. 322.   [497] P. 239, ante.
[498] See generally *Gadsden on Commons and Greens*; Ubhi and Denyer-Green, *Law of Commons, Town and Village Greens*; Jessel, *Law of the Manor* and *Law of the Manor: the Twenty-First Century*; Oswald, *A Practitioner's Guide to Common Land and the Commons Registration Act 1965*; Harris and Ryan, *Outline of the Law relating to Common Land and Public Access to the Countryside*; Clayden, *Our Common Land*; [1977] JPL 352 (R. Vane); Report of the Royal Commission on Common Land, 1955–1958 (Cmnd 462); (1972) 122 NLJ 1127

been completed, the register was to be conclusive.[499] The Act required the registration with county councils of common land in England and Wales[500] of persons claiming to be or found to be its owners, and of claims to rights of common over such land before August 1970.[501] The Act also applies to town or village greens, and to waste land of a manor not subject to rights of common.[502]

The expression "rights of common" includes:[503] "cattlegates or beastgates[504] and rights of sole or several vesture[505] or herbage or of sole or several pasture, but does not include rights held for a term of years or from year to year". And "town or village green" means:[506]

land which has been allotted by or under any Act for the exercise or recreation of the inhabitants of any locality; or on which the inhabitants of any locality have a customary right[507] to indulge in lawful

---

(V. Chapman). See Commons Registration (General) Regulations 1966 (SI 1966 No. 1471), as amended by SI 1968 Nos. 658, 989; SI 1980 No. 1195; SI 1982 Nos. 209, 210; SI 1989 No. 2167; SI 1990 No. 311; SI 2003 No. 2260.

   Lord DENNING MR said that the Act "is ill-drafted and has given rise to many difficulties": *Corpus Christi College, Oxford v Gloucestershire County Council* [1983] QB 360 at 370. There have been several proposals for reform. In 1978 the Department of the Environment issued a Consultative Document, and in 1986 the Countryside Commission published the Report of the Commons Land Forum. In 2000 the Department of the Environment, Transport and the Regions published a Consultation Paper; and in 2002 its successor, the Department for Environment, Food and Rural Affairs, published the Common Land Policy Statement, which set out the Government's plans for taking forward the proposals in the Consultation Paper. In June 2005 a Commons Bill was introduced into Parliament to implement key elements of the Policy Statement, including provisions to revise the system of commons registration; to allow rectification of mistakes in registration under the 1965 Act; to allow for voluntary deregistration of common land to allow development to take place, but only where equally advantageous land is given in exchange and it is in the public interest; and to prohibit the severance of rights of common from the land to which they are attached. The Bill completed its stages through the House of Lords by January 2006, and is expected to be considered by the House of Commons, and become law, during 2006.

   [499] *R v Oxfordshire County Council, ex p Sunningwell Parish Council* [2000] 1 AC 355 at 348, per Lord HOFFMANN; [2000] Conv 21 (J. G. Riddall).

   [500] There are 374,000 hectares of registered common land in England (about 3% of the total land area), and 175,000 hectares in Wales (about 8.4% of the total land area). Nearly 55% of common land is designated as a Site of Special Scientific Interest, and over half of England's common land is in Cumbria and North Yorkshire (30.7% and 21% respectively). For further statistics, see the Defra web site.

   [501] Commons Registration Act 1965, ss. 1–4 as amended by LGA 1972, s. 272(1), Sch. 30, and LGA 1985, s. 16, Sch. 8, para. 10(6). The Act does not apply to the New Forest, Epping Forest or to any land exempted by an order of the Secretary of State: s. 11; SI 1965 No. 2001.

   [502] Commons Registration Act 1965, s. 22(1); *Re Britford Common* [1977] 1 WLR 39; *Re Yateley Common, Hampshire* [1977] 1 WLR 840; *Re Chewton Common, Christchurch* [1977] 1 WLR 1242; *Baxendale v Instow Parish Council* [1982] Ch 14; *Hampshire County Council v Milburn* [1991] 1 AC 325 (waste land of a manor held by HL to mean "waste land now or formerly of a manor" or "waste land of manorial origin"); *Lewis v Mid Glamorgan County Council* [1995] 1 WLR 313; [1995] Conv 500 (H. W. Wilkinson).

   [503] Commons Registration Act 1965, s. 22(1).

   [504] Cattlegate or beastgate, sometimes called *stinted pasture*, is a right to pasture a fixed number of beasts on the land of another, generally for a part of the year only. See e.g. *Rigg v Earl of Lonsdale* (1857) 1 H & N 923; *Brackenbank Lodge Ltd v Peart* (1993) 67 P & CR 249.

   [505] The right of sole vesture, *vestura terrae*, is not merely to graze cattle, but to take away the product of the land, such as grass, corn, underwood, turf, peat, and so forth.

   [506] Commons Registration Act 1965, s. 22(1), as amended by CROW 2000, s. 98.

   [507] Unaccompanied local children, picnicking, fishing in a pond, collecting bullrushes and picking mushrooms; local children, accompanied by adults, playing, picking blackberries, and studying fish and plant life; local adults picnicking, taking dogs for walks, and fishing in the pond held to amount to pastimes indulged in as of right: *Re White Lane Pond, Four Dales and Clay Pits, Thorne and Stainforth, South Yorkshire* [1984] CLY 287; cf *Re River Don and its Banks* [1984] CLY 284, where it was held that walking with or without dogs along the

sports and pastimes;[508] or[509] on which for not less than 20 years a significant number of the inhabitants of any locality, or of any neighbourhood within a locality, have indulged in lawful sports and pastimes as of right,[510] and either (a) have continued to do so,[511] or (b) have ceased to do so for not more than such period as may be prescribed.[512]

Registration under the Act was final or provisional. It was final if no objection was lodged before August 1972;[513] and final registration is conclusive evidence of the matters registered at the date of registration.[514] If there was any such objection, the registration was provisional, and only became final if it was confirmed after a hearing before a Commons Commissioner.[515]

banks of the River was not indulging; *Re Foreshore, East Bank of River Ouse, Naburn, Selby District, North Yorkshire* [1989] CLY 276 (pastime of idling by a river held to be customary right, which may be proved by walking, fishing and picnicking on the foreshore as of right by usage); [1992] Conv 434 (A. Samuels); *R v Buckinghamshire County Council* [2004] 1 EGLR 69 (agricultural use incompatible with use as of right for recreation as a village green).

[508] *R v Oxfordshire County Council* [2000] 1 AC 355 at 356–7, per Lord HOFFMANN ("sports and pastimes" is a not two classes of activities but a single composite class which uses two words in order to avoid arguments about whether an activity is a sport or a pastime); [1999] All ER Rev 223 (P. J. Clarke).

[509] This third category of greens was newly created by the 1965 Act. For this category, registration is conclusive that the land is a town or village green, but does not in itself imply any formal legal right to its use, whether by the public in general or any particular group. "It is one thing to say that informal recreation may represent a 'sport or pastime' sufficient to procure registration. It is quite another to say that it brings with it a general right for the public at large to use the land for *any* sports or pastimes, however intrusive or mutually incompatible they may be, Parliament cannot be taken as intending to create a free-for-all (walkers, riders, cricketers, footballers, golfers, and so on) without any provision for its regulation": *Oxfordshire County Council v Oxford City Council* [2006] Ch 43 at [78], per CARNWATH LJ.

[510] *R v Oxfordshire County Council*, supra, at 355–6 ("as of right" reflects common law concept of *nec vi nec clam nec precario* and does not require subjective belief in the existence of the right; p. 614, ante); [1998] Conv 526 (T. Sutton); *R (Beresford) v Sunderland City Council* [2004] 1 AC 889 (mowing the grass and providing benches not sufficient to render use *precario* so as negative claim to user as of right: for this, landowner's permission, whether express or implied, must be shown to be temporary or revocable); *R (Cheltenham Builders Ltd) v South Gloucestershire DC* [2004] 1 EGLR 85 (reviewing the criteria for a village green).

[511] The requirement, added by CROW 2000, s. 98 in relation to all applications made on or after 30 January 2001, that the user be continuing, requires continuation until the date of registration: *Oxfordshire County Council v Oxford City Council* supra, at [9?]. This has the effect of preventing registration, since a landowner, once alerted to the application, can interrupt the user; an appeal to the House of Lords against the decision is expected to be heard during 2006. The Commons Bill 2005, p. 646, n. 498, ante, would remove the requirement that the user continue until registration, and substitute a time limit for registration to be prescribed by regulations.

[512] "There are as yet no prescribed provisions under sub-paragraph (b), which therefore has no practical effect. The Common Land Policy Statement 2002 proposed a provision enabling application for registration to be made up to two years after the user ceased and stated there would be consultation on the draft regulations: see para 48. No such draft regulations have yet made their appearance": *Oxfordshire County Council v Oxford City Council*, supra, at [17], per CARNWATH LJ.

[513] SI 1968 No. 989, as amended by SI 1970 No. 384; *Smith v East Sussex County Council* (1977) 76 LGR 332.

[514] Commons Registration Act 1965, s. 10; *New Windsor Corpn v Mellor* [1975] Ch 380 at 392, per Lord DENNING MR; *Cooke v Amey Gravel Co Ltd* [1972] 1 WLR 1310 (provisional registration is itself no evidence of the existence of the right registered); *Corpus Christi College, Oxford v Gloucestershire County Council* [1983] QB 360 (registration conclusive even where entry on register was wrong); *R v Mid-Sussex DC* [1993] EGCS 183; *R v Norfolk County Council, ex p Perry* (1996) 74 P & CR 1 (power to amend under s. 13, n. 519, infra, only exercisable if land ceased to be village green after date of registration).

[515] Commons Registration Act 1965, ss. 4–7; SI 1970 No. 1371; SI 1971 No. 1727; SI 1972 No. 437, as amended by SI 1993 No. 1771; SI 1973 No. 815. The Commissioners' office is at Golden Cross House, Duncannon Street, London. Their decisions covering the period from 1965 to 1990 are recorded in seventy-eight bound volumes, in

There was a right of appeal from his decision by a person aggrieved to the High Court on a point of law.[516]

After July 1970, no land then capable of being registered under the Act is to be deemed to be common land unless it is so registered, and no rights of common are exercisable over any such land unless they are registered either under the Act or in the register of title under the Land Registration Act 1925 or 2002.[517] Thus not only are unregistered rights existing before that date extinguished, but there can be no future acquisition of rights over registered commons. New commons may, however, arise, for example, by grant or by prescription, and be registered.[518] In this case the land does not cease to be common land nor do the rights of common cease to be exercisable, if not registered.

Provisions are also made for amendment of the register where land registered under the Act ceases to be common land or a town or village green; or any rights registered under the Act are apportioned, extinguished, released or varied;[519] or to deal with certain cases of fraud or mistake.[520]

C Legal and Equitable Profits à Prendre

A profit à prendre, like an easement,[521] is capable of subsisting as a legal interest, and will be legal if (i) it is held for an interest equivalent to an estate in fee simple absolute in possession

one volume or sometimes two volumes for each county in England and Wales. Most matters were determined by 1990, though any later decisions are all recorded: [1997] Conv 248 (A. Samuels). Decisions are reported in Campbell, *Decisions of the Commons Commissioners* (1972), in Current Law, and in the Annual Reports of the Commons, Open Spaces and Footpaths Preservation Society. See (1973) 117 SJ 537; (1974) 118 SJ 424 (I. Campbell).

The onus of establishing the validity of the registration is on the person making the registration: *Re Sutton Common, Wimborne* [1982] 1 WLR 647; *Re West Anstey Common, North Devon* [1985] Ch 329; *Re Newton Fell, Newton in Bowland* [1988] CLY 285. When deciding whether to confirm a provisional registration, the Commissioner should consider not only the situation as it was at the date of registration, but also events occurring since that date; *Re Merthyr Mawr Common* [1989] 1 WLR 1014. See also *Dynevor v Richardson* [1995] Ch 173 (provisional registration prevents time running for purposes of lost modern grant, even when registration subsequently rejected).

[516] Commons Registration Act 1965, s. 18. See *Wilkes v Gee* [1973] 1 WLR 742; *R v Chief Commons Comr* (1977) 37 P & CR 67; *Re Tillmire Common, Heslington* [1982] 2 All ER 615.

[517] Commons Registration Act 1965, s. 1(2), as amended by LRA 2002, s. 133, Sch. 11; SI 1966 No. 1470, as amended by SI 1970 No. 383. Applications for registration had to be made before 3 January 1970. *Central Electricity Generating Board v Clwyd County Council* [1976] 1 WLR 151 (right of common not registered by closing date held to be extinguished); *Re Turnworth Down, Dorset* [1978] Ch 251; *Howse v Newbury DC* (1998) 77 P & CR 231 (Greenham Common). For the liability of a solicitor who failed to search the register, see *G & K Ladenbau (UK) Ltd v Crawley and de Reya* [1978] 1 WLR 266.

[518] Commons Registration Act 1965, s. 13(b) and Commons Registration (New Land) Regulations 1969 (SI 1969 No. 1843). See *R (on the application of Whitmey) v Commons Commissioners* [2005] QB 282 (Commons Commissioners have no jurisdiction in dispute under s. 13; the fact that applicant can challenge refusal of registration authority to register land as a green only by way of judicial review does not violate ECHR, art. 6); [2005] JPL 159 (J. Hilliard).   [519] Commons Registration Act 1965, s. 13(a), (c).

[520] Commons Registration Act 1965, s. 14. In addition, the Common Land (Rectification of Registers) Act 1989 provided that land might be removed from the register if it could be shown that at all times since 5 August (i.e. twenty years before the passing of the 1965 Act) the land had included or had been ancillary to a dwelling-house; applications had to be made before 21 July 1992: Common Land (Rectification of Registers) Regulations 1990 (SI 1990 No. 311); Guidance Note (Chief Commons Commissioner) 30 September 1990 (set out in [1990] Conv 463); [1989] Conv 384 (A. Samuels). The Commons Bill 2005, p. 646, n. 498, ante, also proposes to allow for corrections to be made to the scope of registered commons.   [521] P. 599, ante.

or a term of years absolute,[522] and (ii) is created by statute, deed or prescription. In the case of the express[523] grant or reservation of a profit over registered land, other than a right of common which is capable of being registered under the Commons Registration Act 1965, the profit is not a legal interest until the registration requirements of the Land Registration Act 2002 have been satisfied.[524] A notice of the interest must be entered in the register of the title of the servient tenement and (if the dominant tenement is also registered) the proprietor of the dominant tenement must be entered in the register as proprietor of the profit.[525] However, a profit *in gross*, other than one created for a term not exceeding seven years, is an independently registrable legal interest; the grantee must be entered in the register as the proprietor of the interest, and a notice in respect of the interest created must be entered in the register of the servient tenement.[526]

A profit à prendre which does not satisfy these requirements may be an equitable profit: e.g. if it is created informally or by a contract to grant a legal profit.[527]

D Acquisition of Profits à Prendre

It will not be necessary to consider this topic at any length, for the methods by which easements may be acquired are applicable, with very few exceptions, to the acquisition of profits à prendre, whether rights of common or not. At the outset we can dismiss profits appendant because they have been impossible of acquisition since *Quia Emptores* in 1290, and a claimant will be required to prove that he holds arable land which was granted by the lord of a manor to a freehold tenant before that date.[528]

The four possible methods of acquiring easements are set out on page 600. We will take each of these and show to what extent it applies to profits:

(1) Statute

Profits may be acquired by statute, as when Inclosure Acts confer new rights upon manorial lords by way of compensation for the interest lost by them in the soil itself.

(2) Express Grant

Profits, whether appurtenant or in gross,[529] may be created by an express grant, which at common law must be made by deed.[530] The want of a deed, however, is not necessarily fatal to the grantee, for if he can prove a specifically enforceable contract for the grant of the profit,

---

[522] LPA 1925, s. 1(2)(a).

[523] A profit created by the operation of LPA 1925, s. 62, p. 650, post, is not an express grant and therefore does not require to be registered: LRA 2002, s. 27(7). [524] LRA 2002, s. 27(2)(d).

[525] Ibid., Sch. 2, para. 7.

[526] Ibid., s. 38; Sch. 2, para. 6. The substantive registration of a profit *in gross* was an innovation of LRA 2002.

[527] *Mason v Clarke* [1955] AC 778; *Lowe v J W Ashmore Ltd* [1971] Ch 545 at 557–8; p. 650, post.

[528] P. 16, ante; *Viner's Abridgment*—Common C. p. 1; *Comyns' Digest*, Tit. Covenant B.

[529] A profit à prendre (grazing) appurtenant to land, if limited to a fixed number of animals, can be severed so as to become a profit in gross: *Bettison v Langton* [2002] 1 AC 27. However, the Commons Bill 2005, p. 646, n. 498, ante. would prohibit the severance of rights of common from the land to which they are attached.

[530] Co Litt 9a, b; *Wood v Leadbitter* (1845) 13 M & W 838 at 842–3; *Mason v Clarke* [1954] 1 QB 460.

he may invoke the familiar doctrine of equity that the grantor must be regarded as having already done what he ought to have done, and thereby show the grant in *equity* of a profit.[531]

Thus, in an early case,[532] the defendant signed a written memorandum by which he agreed in return for valuable consideration that the plaintiff should have the exclusive right of sporting over and killing the game on the defendant's lands, but some years later he revoked the agreement. At the instance of the plaintiff, Wood V-C decreed specific performance by ordering the execution of a formal deed and meanwhile granting an injunction forbidding the defendant to interfere with the enjoyment of the right.

Section 62 of the Law of Property Act 1925, which, as we have already seen, provides that a conveyance of land shall operate to pass rights and advantages appertaining to the land at the time of the conveyance,[533] applies not only to easements but also to profits, such as a right of depasturing sheep on an adjoining mountain.[534]

(3) Implied Grant

The next method whereby easements may be acquired is that of an implied grant under the doctrine of *Wheeldon v Burrows*, but since this is confined to interests of a continuous and apparent nature, it can have no application to profits, which can possess neither of these characteristics.

(4) Presumed Grant or Prescription

(a) *Prescription at common law*

Profits can be acquired by prescription at common law, and when this method of claim is adopted it must conform to all those general principles which obtain in the case of easements, so that:

(i)   the possibility of a grant must be shown;

(ii) user is required to be *as of right*; and

(iii) the claim is liable to be defeated by proof of its origin since 1189.

There is this difference, however, between easements and profits, that although a person can only prescribe in a *que estate* for an easement, he may prescribe in himself and his ancestors for a profit.[535] Examples of this personal prescription are rare,[536] since profits in gross themselves are rare, and such cases as are to be found in the Law Reports refer to *several* profits and not to rights of common.[537] Where one does prescribe in the person, he must adduce evidence to show that either he and his ancestors, or some other person and *his* ancestors

---

[531]   P. 601, ante; p. 877, post.

[532]   *Frogley (Earl of) v Lovelace* (1859) John 333; *Mason v Clarke* [1955] AC 778 (part performance).

[533]   P. 603, ante.

[534]   *White v Williams* [1922] 1 KB 727; *White v Taylor (No 2)* [1969] 1 Ch 160; *Anderson v Bostock* [1976] Ch 312 (exclusive right of grazing without limit held to be unknown to the law), p. 643, ante; *Re Yateley Common, Hampshire* [1977] 1 WLR 840 at 850; *Re Broxhead Common, Whitehill, Hampshire* (1977) 33 P & CR 451.

[535]   Co Litt 122a. *Que estate* is Norman French for "whose estate"; land in which an interest, in the nature of an easement or profit à prendre, has been acquired by prescription.

[536]   *Shuttleworth v Le Fleming* (1865) 19 CBNS 687, per Montague Smith J.

[537]   *Welcome v Upton* (1840) 6 M & W 536; *Shuttleworth v Le Fleming*, supra; *Johnson v Barnes* (1873) LR 8 CP 527.

from whom the claimant acquired the title to the profit, have enjoyed the right from time immemorial.[538]

(b) Lost modern grant

Profits à prendre may be claimed by virtue of a lost modern grant, but instances are rarely found. If a claim is so made, it must conform to the rules and surmount the objections that apply where an easement is founded on a lost grant.[539] Even though the Prescription Act 1832 requires thirty years' user in respect of a claim to a profit, only twenty years' user is necessary to support a presumption of a lost grant.[540]

(c) Prescription Act 1832

The Prescription Act 1832 treats profits differently from easements in that it requires longer periods of enjoyment. The periods fixed for profits are thirty years and sixty years instead of twenty and forty. But, for the purposes of the Commons Registration Act 1965,[541] the time during which the servient tenement has been requisitioned, or a right of grazing has been prevented by reason of animal health, must be ignored in computing the period of thirty or sixty years or in determining whether there has been an interruption within the meaning of the Prescription Act.[542] Further, any objection to the registration of a right of common under the Commons Registration Act is deemed to be a suit or action within section 4 of the Prescription Act.[543] Otherwise the provisions of the Act of 1832 are exactly the same for both interests.

The Act of 1832 applies only to profits appurtenant, not to those in gross, for it requires the claimant to allege in his pleading that the right has been enjoyed "by the occupiers of the tenement in respect whereof the same is claimed. . . ."[544] As MONTAGUE SMITH J said in the leading case: "The whole principle of this pleading assumes a dominant tenement and an enjoyment of the right by the occupiers of it. The proof must of course follow and support the pleading. It is obvious that rights claimed in gross cannot be so pleaded or proved."[545]

E The Running of the Benefit and the Burden of a Profit à Prendre

A profit à prendre, as a property interest, is capable of binding the owner for the time being of the servient tenement. Whether the purchaser of the servient tenement is bound depends on whether the profit is legal or equitable,[546] and whether the land is registered or unregistered, under the same rules as apply to legal and equitable easements.[547]

The benefit of a profit appurtenant to land, whether legal or equitable, will also pass with the dominant tenement in the same manner as an easement.[548]

---

[538] *Welcome v Upton* (1839) 5 M & W 398; *Lovett v Fairclough* (1990) 61 P & CR 385.
[539] *Neaverson v Peterborough RDC* [1902] 1 Ch 557; *Mill v New Forest Comrs* (1856) 18 CB 60; *Loose v Castleton* (1978) 41 P & CR 19 (several fishery).
[540] *Tehidy Minerals Ltd v Norman* [1971] 2 QB 528.   [541] P. 645, ante.
[542] Commons Registration Act 1965, s. 16.   [543] Ibid., s. 16(2).
[544] Prescription Act 1832, s. 5.   [545] *Shuttleworth v Le Fleming* (1865) 19 CBNS 687 at 711.
[546] P. 648, ante.   [547] Pp. 632 et seq, ante.   [548] P. 631, ante.

F *Extinguishment of Profits à Prendre*

Several profits and profits in common may be extinguished by any of the following methods:

(1) Unity of Seisin

If the owner of the profit or common also becomes owner of the land over which the right is exercisable, the right is extinguished, provided that his estates in the right and in the land are similar both in quantum and in quality.[549] Thus a profit appurtenant is extinguished if one person becomes seised in fee both of the dominant and of the servient tenement, but if the owner of the profit takes a lease of the servient tenement, the result of this unity of possession, as distinguished from unity of seisin in the former case, is that the profit is only suspended and will revive again upon the expiration of the lease.[550]

(2) Release

A release of a profit in favour of the servient owner extinguishes the right in the sense that it ceases to exist as a right *in alieno solo*, since one cannot have a profit or common in one's own land.

(3) Alteration of Dominant Tenement

Although it has been said that "common is obtained by long sufferance and also it may be lost by long negligence",[551] it is not true that mere non-user of a profit will by itself produce an extinguishment of the right,[552] but if the character of the dominant tenement is so altered as to make any further appurtenancy impossible, a presumption is raised in favour of extinguishment. If, for instance, land to which a common of pasture was appurtenant entirely loses its agricultural character by conversion into a building estate, the common is destroyed, but if the conversion is not irrevocable, as where arable land is turned into an orchard, the profit is merely suspended and is capable of being resumed on the restoration of the land to its original state.[553]

(4) Approvement and Inclosure of Commons

Rights of common may be partially extinguished by the process known as approvement, or wholly extinguished by inclosure.

(a) Approvement

At common law it appears that the lord of a manor was entitled to *approve* the manorial waste upon which the freehold tenants had the right of pasturing their cattle, by appropriating part thereof to himself and holding it in separate ownership.[554] This practice was

---

[549] *Tyrringham's Case* (1584) 4 Co Rep 36b; *White v Taylor* [1969] 1 Ch 150; *Re Yateley Common, Hampshire* [1977] 1 WLR 840; Hall, *Law of Profits à Prendre and Rights of Common*, p. 335.

[550] Co Litt 313a, 114b.   [551] *Gateward's Case* (1607) 6 Co Rep 596.

[552] *Seaman v Vawdrey* (1810) 16 Ves 390; *Re Yateley Common, Hampshire*, supra.

[553] *Carr v Lambert* (1866) LR 1 Exch 168; *Tyrringham's Case* (1584) 4 Co Rep 36b.

[554] See authorities collected in Hall, *Law of Profits à Prendre and Rights of Common*, pp. 345 et seq; *Re Broxhead Common, Whitehill, Hampshire* (1977) 33 P & CR 451.

justified by the lords on the ground that the multiplicity of commoners rendered the manor unprofitable, but as it not unnaturally caused dissension it was ultimately regulated by two statutes—the Statute of Merton 1235, chapter 4, and the Statute of Westminster the Second 1285, chapter 46.[555] These expressly permitted the lord of a manor to appropriate or approve the manorial waste, subject to the condition that he left sufficient pasturage for the commoners, determined according to the aggregate number of animals which they were entitled to turn out, and not according to the number which they had for a fixed number of years been in the habit of turning out.[556]

The Commons Act 1876 requires a person seeking to approve a common to publish his intention in the local press on three successive occasions,[557] and the Law of Commons (Amendment) Act 1893 further provides that an approvement of any part of a common purporting to be made under the Commons Acts of 1236 and 1285 shall not be valid unless it is made with the consent of the Board of Agriculture (now the Secretary of State for Environment, Food and Rural Affairs).

(b) Inclosure

The other method of deliberate extinguishment is inclosure under the various Inclosure Acts. Inclosure differs in three respects from approvement:

(i)   it applies to all kinds of commonable rights, such as common of turbary and estovers, and is not restricted to pasture;

(ii) it involves the discharge of the whole of the lands from the rights of common; and

(iii) it does not depend upon the discretion of any one person, but requires for its validity the sanction of an Act of Parliament.

Inclosure is the process whereby a commoner, in place of the rights over the manorial waste which he formerly enjoyed, is granted a definite piece of land to be held in fee simple. It is now virtually a dead letter, but in the comparatively short period of a hundred years, from about 1760 to 1860, it led to the almost entire disappearance of those rights of common which from the earliest days had been such a striking feature of English landholding. To understand this sudden and rapid extinction of ancient rights, it is necessary to realise that even as late as the eighteenth century the greater part of the cultivated land of England was still farmed under the medieval village community system. That system[558] had outlived its raison d'être and had become by the eighteenth century nothing but a hindrance to proper cultivation.

At first inclosures were carried out by private Acts of Parliament[559] by which allotments of land to be held in separate ownership and discharged from commonage were awarded to the lord and the commoners. The expense of these private Acts was very great, and in 1801 the procedure was simplified by the passing of the Inclosure (Consolidation) Act, which set out a number of general provisions capable of being incorporated into private Acts.[560]

---

[555] The Statute Law Revision Act 1948 renamed these two chapters as the Commons Act 1236, and the Commons Act 1285. The former was repealed in toto by the Statute Law Revision Act 1953.

[556] Robertson v Hartopp (1889) 43 Ch D 484.   [557] S. 31.

[558] See Holdsworth, History of English Law, vol. ii. pp. 56 et seq, and the 11th edn of this book, pp. 547–8.

[559] See Law Commission Report on the Chronological Table of Private and Personal Acts 1999 (Law Com No. 256), para. 8.   [560] See e.g. Fisons Horticulture Ltd v Bunting (1976) 240 EG 625.

The Inclosure Act 1845[561] established a central body in the shape of the Inclosure Commissioners for England and Wales. The result of this Act, was that between 1845 and 1875, 590,000 acres were inclosed and divided among 25,930 persons. But during the last decade of this period it became practically impossible to obtain parliamentary sanction for inclosure awards, since, under the influence of the Commons Preservation Society, the nation became convinced that one of the most urgent national needs was the provision of open spaces. The new policy was not to parcel out common lands among private owners, but to throw them open to the public and provide for their management and regulation by public bodies. Effect was given to this by the Commons Act 1876, which, after reciting that "inclosure in severalty as opposed to regulation of commons should not be hereinafter made unless it can be proved to the satisfaction of the said Commissioners and of Parliament that such inclosure will be of benefit to the neighbourhood as well as to private interests", contained provisions designed to protect the public and to give local authorities an opportunity of acquiring land for the public. The functions of the Inclosure Commissioners are now carried out by the Secretary of State for the Environment, Food and Rural Affairs,[562] who, when making a provisional award for submission to Parliament, must now insert provisions, where applicable, for securing free access to any particular prospect, the preservation of particular trees or objects of historical interest, the reservation of the right of playing games where a recreation ground has not been set out, and so on.[563]

The procedure for an inclosure is governed by the Act of 1876, and the stages are as follows:

(a) An application supported by persons representing at least one-third of the value of the lands must first be made to the Secretary of State.

(b) The application must explain why inclosure is preferable to the regulation of the land as a public common.

(c) If the Secretary of State is of opinion that a *prima facie* case has been made out he orders a local inquiry to be made by one of his officers.

(d) The officer inspects the locality, holds a public meeting at which he hears the views of all persons who wish to be heard and makes a report to the Secretary of State.

---

[561] See Statute Law (Repeals) Act 1998, Sch. 1, Part VI (Inclosure Acts), based on Law Commission Report on Statute Law Revision: Sixteenth Report Draft Statute Law (Repeals) Bill 1996 (Law Com No. 252), Part VI.

[562] See *R (Ashbrook) v Secretary of State for the Environment, Food and Rural Affairs* [2005] 1 WLR 1764. In relation to Wales, this function is exercised by the National Assembly for Wales: SI 1999 No. 672, art. 2, Sch. 1.

[563] S. 7. For the regulation and management of commons, see also Metropolitan Commons Act 1866; Metropolitan Commons Amendment Act 1869; Commons Act 1899; Commons (Schemes) Regs 1982 (SI 1982 No. 209).

For the rights of the public over commons and waste lands, see LPA 1925, s. 193; *Mienes v Stone* (1985) CO/1217/84 noted [1985] Conv 415 (J. R. Montgomery); *R v Secretary of State for the Environment, ex p Billson* [1999] QB 374. See also National Parks and Access to the Countryside Act 1949, ss. 59–60, 64–82; Countryside Act 1968, ss. 6, 9; *R v Doncaster MBC, ex p Braim* (1989) 57 P & CR 1 (Doncaster Common "best known as the site of the St. Leger" held to be an open space within LGA 1972, s. 123(2A)); [1988] Conv 369 (J. Hill). CROW 2000, Part I, which gives to the general public a right of access on foot to open countryside for the purpose of open-air recreation (the "right to roam"); Access to the Countryside (Means of Access, Appeals) (England) Regulations 2004, SI 2004 No. 3305. As to whether this is compatible with the Human Rights Act 1998, see Rook, *Property Law and Human Rights*, pp. 211–19. An even more extensive provision has been adopted by the Scottish Parliament: Land Reform (Scotland) Act 2003.

A private right of way can be acquired by prescription over a common: *Bakewell Management Ltd v Brandwood* [2004] 2 AC 519.

(e) The Secretary of State, if satisfied that the matter ought to go further, prepares a draft provisional order which is ultimately submitted to Parliament.

So then at the present day inclosures are still possible, but owing to the very strong case which must be made out by the petitioners, and also to the important part played by local authorities, who are afforded facilities for making a portion of the land common to the public, it is unlikely that they will be continued.

(5) Commons Registration Act 1965

As we have seen, rights of common are no longer exercisable over land in England and Wales which is common land or a town or village green, unless they have been registered under the Commons Registration Act 1965 or the Land Registration Act 1925 or 2002.[564]

IV Rights in the Nature of Easements and Profits à Prendre Acquired by Fluctuating and Undefined Classes of Persons

There is no doubt that indefinite and fluctuating classes of persons, such as the inhabitants of a village, may acquire rights, analogous in nature to easements, over the land of another.[565] For example, they have succeeded in establishing rights to enter another's close and take water from a spring,[566] to dry their fishing nets on the land of a private person,[567] to hold horse races[568] or a fair[569] on such land, and to pass to church[570] or market over a man's private property.

A *Rights in the Nature of Easements*

Such rights are not easements capable of acquisition by prescription, for all forms of prescription presuppose the possibility of a grant, and no grant can be made to an indefinite body of persons. Nevertheless, the law, in its anxiety to protect the long sustained enjoyment of a privilege, has surmounted the technical difficulty incident to prescription by allowing rights of this nature to be established by *custom*. Hence the name *customary* rights. Custom is an unwritten rule of law which has applied from time immemorial in a particular locality and which displaces the common law in so far as that particular locality is concerned.[571] To quote the words of TINDAL CJ:[572]

A custom which has existed from time immemorial without interruption within a certain place, and which is certain and reasonable in itself, obtains the force of a law, and is, in effect, the common law within that place to which it extends, though contrary to the general law of the realm.

---

[564] S. 1(2); p. 645, ante.   [565] *Gateward's Case* (1607) 6 Co Rep 59b; *Race v Ward* (1855) 4 E & B 702.

[566] *Weekly v Wildman* (1698) 1 Ld Raym 405; *Race v Ward*, supra.

[567] *Mercer v Denne* [1905] 2 Ch 538.   [568] *Mounsey v Ismay* (1865) 3 H & C 486.

[569] *Tyson v Smith* (1838) 9 Ad & El 406.   [570] *Brocklebank v Thompson* [1903] 2 Ch 344.

[571] See *Termes de la Ley*, "Custom"; *Tanistry Case* (1608) Dav Ir 28; Litt, s. 169; *Hammerton v Honey* (1876) 24 WR 603.   [572] *Lockwood v Wood* (1844) 6 QB 50 at 64.

(1) Requisites for Custom

It has been said[573] that a custom must be

    (1) certain,[574]

    (2) not unreasonable,

    (3) commencing from time immemorial,

    (4) continued without interruption, and

    (5) applicable to a particular district.

The two outstanding requirements are existence from time immemorial[575] and restriction to a definite locality.[576]

Strictly speaking the first of these requirements means that the custom must have existed since 1189, but although the nature of the right precludes the court from presuming a lost modern grant if enjoyment cannot be proved for so long, yet the practice is to presume that the right originated at the proper time if it is obviously of respectable antiquity.[577] It is generally enough to show continuous enjoyment going as far back as living testimony can go.

    To quote TINDAL CJ again:

As to the proof of the custom, you cannot, indeed, reasonably expect to have it proved before you that such a custom did in fact exist before time of legal memory, that is, before the first year of the reign of Richard I; for if you did, it would in effect destroy the validity of almost all customs; but you are to require proof, as far back as living memory goes, of a continuous, peaceable, and uninterrupted user of the custom.[578]

Although the presumption in favour of enjoyment from time immemorial will readily be raised, it can undoubtedly be rebutted by positive evidence showing that it actually began at some later date.[579] The courts, however, are slow to rebut the presumption. In *Mercer v Denne* it was proved by witnesses that for as long as they could remember—a matter of seventy years—the fishing inhabitants of Walmer had used part of the defendant's beach for the purpose of drying their nets. The defendant, having proved that in 1844 a considerable portion of this part of the beach was under water, argued that the custom of using that particular portion must be disallowed as obviously having arisen since 1189.

    In rejecting this plea FARWELL J said:[580]

A defendant may no doubt defeat a custom by shewing that it could not have existed in the time of Richard I, but he must demonstrate its impossibility, and the onus is on him to do so if the existence of the custom has been proved for a long period; this was done, for instance, in *Simpson v Wells*,[581] where the claim of a custom to set up stalls at the Statute Sessions for the hiring of servants was defeated by shewing that such sessions were introduced by the Statutes of Labourers, the first of which was in the reign of Edward III. But no such impossibility is shewn in the present case. If the beach was of its

---

[573] *Mercer v Denne* [1905] 2 Ch 538; *New Windsor Corpn v Mellor* [1975] Ch 380 (right to indulge in lawful sports and pastimes).

[574] I.e., the persons entitled to the right must be certain and not, e.g., "poor householders": *Selby v Robinson* (1788) 2 Term Rep 758.   [575] Blackstone, vol. i. p. 76; *Chapman v Smith* (1754) 2 Ves Sen 506.

[576] *R v Rollett* (1875) LR 10 QB 469 at 480.

[577] *Mercer v Denne*, supra, at 556; *Wolstanton Ltd and A-G of Duchy of Lancaster v Newcastle-under-Lyme Corpn* [1940] AC 860 at 876.   [578] *Bastard v Smith* (1838) 2 Mood & R 129 at 136.

[579] *Hammerton v Honey* (1876) 24 WR 603 at 604, per JESSEL MR.   [580] [1904] 2 Ch 534 at 555.

[581] (1872) LR 7 QB 214.

present extent in 1795, why am I bound to infer that it cannot have been the same in 1189 from the mere fact that between 1795 and 1844 the extent diminished and has since again increased? The mere non-user during the period that the sea flowed over the spot is immaterial, for it was no interruption of the right but only of the possession, and an "interruption of the possession only for ten or twenty years will not destroy the custom".[582]

A customary right, once acquired, cannot be lost by mere non-user or by waiver.[583]

(2) Custom and Prescription

Enough has been said to show that custom bears a close and striking resemblance to prescription. Both methods depend on continuous and uninterrupted enjoyment which has lasted for the time whereof the memory of men runneth not to the contrary, and both are liable to be defeated in the same manner. COKE emphasised the resemblance in quaint language: "Prescription and custom are brothers, and ought to have the same age, and reason ought to be the father, and congruence the mother, and use the nurse, and time out of memory to fortify them both."[584]

But there is still an important difference between the two methods, for while prescription always connects the right with a definite person, custom connects it with some particular locality. Prescription is personal, custom is local. A right is always prescribed for in the name of a certain person and his ancestors, or of those whose estate he owns, or in the name of corporations and their predecessors.[585] But a right claimed by custom is not alleged to be vested in any definite person or body of persons, but is claimed on the ground that it is vested in the shifting class of persons connected from time to time with the definite locality to which the right is attached.[586] In custom you first prove the attachment of the right to a locality and then prove your connection with that locality; while in prescription you show the existence of the right in some person from whom your title is derived, or else you prove yourself to be the owner of a tenement to which the right is attached.

The importance of the distinction lies in the fact that persons who are quite unable to establish their claim to an easement by means of prescription, because prescription presupposes a grant to some definite person, may very well succeed under the cover of custom. A customary right is part of the general law applicable to a particular locality; and persons resident there, whether capable grantees or not, are entitled to enjoy the benefit of the law which runs throughout the locality.

B Rights in the Nature of Profits à Prendre

So far our account has been restricted to the capacity of a fluctuating and ever-changing class of persons to establish a claim to quasi-easements, and it remains to be considered whether such persons can sustain a claim to profits à prendre. It has been the law at least since 1607[587] that indefinite persons cannot acquire a profit by custom.[588] JAMES LJ, in one

---

582 Blackstone, vol. 1. p. 77; Co Litt 114b.

583 *Wyld v Silver* [1963] Ch 243; *New Windsor Corpn v Mellor* [1975] Ch 380.

584 *Rowles v Mason* (1612) 2 Brownl 192 at 198.   585 4 Co Rep 32a, per Sir Edward COKE.

586 Co Litt 113b; Blackstone, vol. ii. p. 263; *Foiston v Crachroode* (1587) 4 Co Rep 31b; *Gateward's Case* (1607) 6 Co Rep 59b.   587 *Gateward's Case* (1607) 6 Co Rep 59b.

588 *Gateward's Case*, supra; *Race v Ward* (1855) 4 E & B 702; *Chilton v London Corpn* (1878) 7 Ch D 735; *Constable v Nicholson* (1863) 14 CBNS 230.

case, said: "Of course it is settled and clear law that you cannot have any right to a profit *à prendre in alieno solo* in a shifting body like the inhabitants of a town or residents of a particular district."[589] Were the rule otherwise the result would be to exhaust and destroy the subject matter of the custom. Thus claims by inhabitants or classes of persons equally indefinite have been disallowed where the customs alleged were to enjoy common of pasture,[590] to collect dead wood for fuel,[591] to carry away sand that has drifted from the sea shore,[592] or to take minerals from the soil.[593]

But in all cases where ancient claims are in question we have to reckon with the tendency of the courts to presume everything reasonably possible in order to uphold a right of which there has been long enjoyment, and it is in furtherance of this general principle that two methods have been evolved whereby fluctuating classes can in certain circumstances maintain a claim even to profits *in alieno solo*. These may be termed (1) the "presumed Crown grant" method and (2) the "presumed charitable trust" method.

(1) Presumed Crown Grant

To take the Crown grant first, we start with this, that although a private person cannot make a grant to indefinite classes of persons, yet the Crown may do so. Lord ROMILLY said:[594]

The distinction between a grant by a private individual and a grant by the Crown is this, that as the Crown has the power to create corporations, so, if it is necessary for the purpose of establishing the validity of the grant, the grantees will be treated as a corporation *quoad* the grant, which is not the case with a grant by a private individual, because a private individual has no power of creating a corporation.

The Crown by virtue of this power may make a grant to the inhabitants of a town, with the result that they become by implication a corporation for the purposes of the grant and, as such, capable of enjoying a profit in the land of another. So in *Willingale v Maitland*,[595] where an actual Crown grant had been made in the time of Elizabeth to the inhabitants of a parish allowing a certain section of the parishioners to lop the branches of trees growing in the waste of a manor, it was held on demurrer that the grant was legal.

Cases where an actual grant can be found must be rare, and the real question is whether the court will presume a grant so as to incorporate the inhabitants and thus render them eligible to take profits. All that can be said is that such a presumption will be raised only where the circumstances that have accompanied the enjoyment go to show that the claimants have always regarded themselves as a corporation and have acted as such.

Such a grant was presumed in the *Faversham Fishery Case*;[596] but in *Lord Rivers v Adams*,[597] where it appeared that the enjoyment of an alleged right of inhabitants to carry away wood from a manorial waste was inconsistent with the fact that the tenants of the manor had openly asserted and exercised control over the wood, the court refused to raise the presumption. KELLY CB in this case said:

If the inhabitants had held meetings in reference to this right, or appointed any officer to look to the right, or done any act collectively of that description, the case would be different. We should then have

---

[589] *Sewers Comrs of the City of London v Glasse* (1872) 7 Ch App 456 at 465.
[590] *Grimstead v Marlowe* (1792) 4 Term Rep 717.
[591] *Selby v Robinson* (1788) 2 Term Rep 758.   [592] *Blewett v Tregonning* (1835) 3 Ad & El 554.
[593] *A-G v Mathias* (1858) 4 K & J 579.   [594] *Willingale v Maitland* (1866) LR 3 Eq 103 at 109.
[595] Supra.   [596] *Re Free Fishermen of Faversham* (1887) 36 Ch D 329; see especially at 343, per BOWEN LJ.
[597] (1878) 3 Ex D 361.

the inhabitants acting in a corporate capacity in reference to this right, and from their doing so, and from their existence *de facto* as a corporation, we might according to the ordinary rule find a legal origin by a grant from the Crown.[598]

(2) Presumed Charitable Trust

The second method, whereby uncertain bodies may establish a claim to profits, namely, that of a presumed charitable trust, is very similar to the one just described. It depends upon the decision of the House of Lords in *Goodman v Mayor and Free Burgesses of the Borough of Saltash*,[599] where the principle was in effect established that, where it appears that a definite body capable of taking by grant, such as the corporation of a borough, has enjoyed a profit *in alieno solo* for a great number of years, and where it also appears that an indefinite body has shared in this enjoyment, then the court presumes a lost grant in favour of the corporation, but declares that the corporation must hold the profit in trust for the indefinite body.

In *Goodman v Mayor and Free Burgesses of the Borough of Saltash*:

Two facts were clearly proved: first, that the Corporation of Saltash had from time immemorial exercised the right of dredging for oysters in the river Tamar; secondly, that the free inhabitants of ancient tenements in the borough had each year from Candlemas (22 February) to Easter Eve exercised a similar right for the previous 200 years. An action was brought by the corporation against two free inhabitants of ancient tenements for trespass committed in the Tamar and for converting to their own use quantities of oysters.

After holding that the free inhabitants could not be presumed to be separately incorporated, the House addressed itself to the task of discovering a legal origin for the right which undoubtedly had been enjoyed for a very considerable time. The majority of the House (Lord BLACKBURN dissenting) held that the fishery must have originally been granted to the corporation subject to a condition that the free inhabitants were to be allowed to fish for a certain period each year. Lord CAIRNS said:[600]

It appears to me that there is no difficulty at all in supposing such a grant, a grant to the corporation before the time of legal memory of a several fishery, a grant by the Crown, with a condition in that grant in some terms which are not before us, but which we can easily imagine—a condition that the free inhabitants of ancient tenements in the borough should enjoy this right, which as a matter of fact the case tells us they have enjoyed from time immemorial . . . . Such a condition would create that which in the very wide language of our courts is called a charitable, that is to say a public, trust or interest, for the benefit of the free inhabitants of ancient tenements.

But for this principle to apply, it must be established that the enjoyment of the profit was regarded by the indefinite body of persons as a right to which they were entitled without anybody's permission, not as a privilege of little significance that was tolerated by the indulgence or good nature of the servient owner.[601]

---

[598] *Lord Rivers v Adams* (1878) 3 Ex D 361 at 366–7. This is a most instructive case on the whole subject of claims to profits by fluctuating bodies.

[599] (1882) 7 App Cas 633; *Peggs v Lamb* [1994] Ch 172 (charitable trust for freemen and widows of freemen of the ancient borough of Huntingdon).   [600] (1882) 7 App Cas 633 at 650.

[601] *Alfred F Beckett Ltd v Lyons* [1967] Ch 449.

In conclusion, then, we may say that before a fluctuating class can sustain a claim to a profit, they must show either that a grant was probably made in such a way as to incorporate them, or that there is some definite corporation which is capable of taking a grant and of holding the right granted in trust for them.

V Law Reform

In 1999 the Law Commission reported that it would be examining easements and analogous private rights (particularly profits à prendre) with a view to their reform and rationalisation.[602] This would be done with a reconsideration of the Law Commission's earlier work on land obligations, which are discussed in chapter 19 in the context of the reform of the law of covenants.[603]

The proposals have been long delayed. The aim is to produce a more coherent scheme of easements and covenants which is compatible with both the commonhold system introduced by Part I of the Commonhold and Leasehold Reform Act 2002,[604] and the reformed system of land registration introduced by the Land Registration Act 2002. A Consultation Paper is now promised during the course of 2006.

---

[602] Law Commission Seventh Programme of Law Reform 1999 (Law Com No. 259) Item 5.

[603] Report on the Law of Positive and Restrictive Covenants 1984 (Law Com No. 127); Report on Obsolete Restrictive Covenants 1991 (Law Com No. 201); pp. 701 et seq, post.   [604] Chap. 9, ante.

19

COVENANTS[1]

SUMMARY

I Introduction

It sometimes happens that a landowner desires to impose a positive or a negative duty upon the owner of neighbouring land with the object of preserving the saleable value or the residential amenities of his own property. X, the owner of Whiteacre, for instance, who sells part of his garden (Blackacre) to Y, may wish to control the manner in which Y uses the land. Accordingly X may require Y to covenant that he will not build shops on Blackacre

---

[1] See generally Preston and Newsom, *Restrictive Covenants Affecting Freehold Land*; Scamell, *Land Covenants*; Francis, *Restrictive Covenants and Freehold Land*; Elphinstone, *Covenants Affecting Land*; Farrand, *Contract and Conveyance* (2nd edn), pp. 404–27; Maitland, *Equity*, pp. 162–78; Emmet, chap. 18; (1971) 87 LQR 539 (D. J. Hayton). For a historical account, see Simpson, *History of the Land Law*, pp. 116–18, 140–1, 256–60.

(a negative or a restrictive covenant) or that he will erect and maintain a fence between it and X's retained land (a positive covenant), for the benefit of X and his successors in title. Such a covenant remains binding in contract between X and Y personally, but does its benefit run with Whiteacre and its burden with Blackacre in the sense that it is enforceable by the successors in title of the former against the successors in title of the latter?

If the right granted by the covenant is characterised as an easement, there is generally no difficulty. As we have seen in the previous chapter, an easement, legal or equitable, is capable of binding the servient tenement Blackacre and of enuring for the benefit of the dominant tenement Whiteacre. If the covenant is contained in a lease, again there is no difficulty, for it will normally pass on an assignment of the whole or any part of the premises or of the reversion.[2] However, in other cases the question is whether a person who was not an original party to the covenant can be bound by it, or can enforce it. In the following pages we shall see that, over the years, the courts (both of law and of equity) and statute have intervened to modify the rule of privity of contract in its application to covenants relating to land. At the present day, the law of covenants remains complex and technical, full of detailed rules which are a product of its historical development. There are significant differences in the rules for the passing of the benefit and the passing of the burden of a covenant; and the rules differ between the common law and equity; and between positive covenants and negative covenants. There has, however, been some tendency in the last forty years to attempt to escape from the technicalities, and to simplify the rules or their application, particularly in relation to the enforcement of the benefit of a restrictive covenant by successors in title.[3] This policy is also a feature of proposals for the reform of covenants; and the Law Commission is working towards a general reform which would assimilate the law of covenants with the law of easements, and allow all Land Obligations, whether positive or negative, to run with the benefited and the burdened land.[4]

For the law as it presently stands, however, it is important to understand that, in order to enforce a covenant, the claimant must show that the defendant has the burden of the covenant, whether as the original covenantor or as owner of the land to which the burden of the covenant is attached; and that the claimant has the benefit of the covenant, whether as an original beneficiary of it or as a successor to the original beneficiary (either his personal successor as beneficiary of the covenant, or his successor as owner of the land to which the benefit of the covenant is attached). We shall begin with a consideration of the rules governing the passing of the burden of a covenant.

II The Defendant Must Have the Burden of the Covenant

If the defendant is the original covenantor, he has the burden of the covenant and the only question is whether the claimant has the benefit. As we shall see, there are a range of

---

[2] Pp. 294 et seq, ante.

[3] See, for example, the simplified approach of the courts to the annexation of the benefit of a covenant: *Federated Homes v Mill Lodge Properties Ltd* [1980] 1 WLR 594, p. 680, post; and the less strict approach to schemes of development: *Re Dolphin's Conveyance* [1970] Ch 654, p. 688, post. The general relaxation of the contractual rules for the enforcement of third-party rights, achieved by the Contracts (Rights of Third Parties) Act 1999, p. 676, post, also opens up a simpler mechanism for enforcement of a land covenant.

[4] For proposed reform, see pp. 701 et seq, post.

circumstances in which a successor to the original covenantee can enforce the covenant.[5] The law has however been much more cautious in allowing a successor to the covenantor to be bound by it. The general rule is that the burden of a covenant, whether positive or negative, does not run with the land at common law. However, the courts of equity devised a mechanism to allow the burden of a negative (restrictive) covenant to run.

A Burden does not Run with the Land at Common Law

In *Austerberry v Corporation of Oldham*[6] the view was expressed by two Lords Justices that the burden of a positive covenant made between a vendor and a purchaser does not run with the fee simple at common law. This view was reaffirmed by the House of Lords in *Rhone v Stephens*,[7] where:

Walford House and Walford Cottage were in common ownership until 1960 when Walford Cottage was sold. The vendor covenanted to keep the common roof which covered part of Walford Cottage in wind and water tight condition. Both properties were sold after 1960. The question arose whether the covenant was enforceable against the owners of Walford House.

In holding that the covenant was not enforceable, Lord TEMPLEMAN said:[8]

In the *Austerberry* case the owners of a site of a road covenanted that they and their successors in title would make the road and keep it in repair. The road was sold to the defendants and it was held that the repair covenant could not be enforced against them.

For over a hundred years it has been clear and accepted law that equity will enforce negative covenants against freehold land but has no power to enforce positive covenants against successors in title of the land. To enforce a positive covenant would be to enforce a personal obligation against a person who has not covenanted. To enforce negative covenants is only to treat the land as subject to a restriction.[9]

The House of Lords held further that *Austerberry v Corporation of Oldham* had not been "reversed remarkably but unremarked" by section 79 of the Law of Property Act 1925 where a covenant was made after 1925. The section provides that:

A covenant relating to any land of a covenantor or capable of being bound by him, shall, unless a contrary intention is expressed, be deemed to be made by the covenantor on behalf of himself his successors in title and the persons deriving title under him or them, and, subject as aforesaid, shall have effect as if such successors and other persons were expressed.

This is a welcome and restrictive interpretation of the section,[10] which is at variance with the wide construction of the corresponding section 78 on the running of the benefit of a covenant.[11]

---

[5] Pp. 677 et seq, post.   [6] (1885) 29 Ch D 750; *E and G C Ltd v Bate* (1935) L Jo 203.

[7] [1994] 2 AC 310, M & B p. 934; [1994] Conv 477 (J. Snape); (1994) 110 LQR 346 (N. P. Gravells); [1994] All ER Rev (P. J. Clarke); [1995] CLJ 60 (S. Gardner).   [8] At 434.

[9] Pp. 666 et seq, post.

[10] For its construction as a word-saving section, see *Tophams Ltd v Earl of Sefton* [1967] 1 AC 50 at 73, 81, per Lords UPJOHN and WILBERFORCE respectively; *Federated Homes Ltd v Mill Lodge Properties Ltd* [1980] 1 WLR 594, per BRIGHTMAN LJ; M & B, pp. 954, 959. See Emmet, para. 19.007; and the laconic "No" given as an answer by Sir Benjamin Cherry in his *Lectures on the New Property Acts* (1926), p. 131, to the question "Is the case of *Austerberry v Corporation of Oldham* overruled by s. 79 of the Law of Property Act?" See also *Morrells of Oxford Ltd v Oxford United Football Club Ltd* [2001] Ch 459 at [14], [35].   [11] See pp. 680 et seq, post.

(1) Devices to Circumvent Rule

There are, however, "a number of current techniques and devices by which lawyers attempt to surmount or circumvent the difficulties of enforcing positive covenants".[12]

(a) Lease instead of sale

The land may be leased instead of sold, and reliance placed upon the enforceability of covenants between landlord and tenant.[13]

(b) Chains of indemnity covenants

As we have seen, an original covenantor remains liable in contract even after he has parted with the land, and so he may protect himself by taking a covenant of indemnity from his purchaser. Each successive purchaser may give a similar covenant to his vendor with the result that a chain of indemnity covenants is created. In theory the original covenantee should be able to secure the indirect enforcement of the positive covenant by the current owner of the land by suing the original covenantor. "But in practice this device sooner or later becomes ineffective, either in consequence of the death or disappearance of the original covenantor, or because a break occurs in the chain of indemnities."[14]

(c) The doctrine of Halsall v Brizell[15]

"In some cases a positive covenant can be enforced in practice by the operation of the maxim '*qui sentit commodum sentire debet et onus*'. This obliges a person who wishes to take advantage of a service or facility (e.g. a road or drains) to comply with any corresponding obligation to contribute to the cost of providing or maintaining it. The maxim cannot, however, be invoked where the burdened owner does not enjoy any service or facility to which his obligations attach or has no sufficient interest in the continuance of these benefits."[16]

In *Thamesmead Town Ltd v Allotey*,[17] PETER GIBSON LJ explained the limits of the doctrine as follows:

The reasoning of Lord Templeman [in *Rhone v Stephens*] suggests that there are two requirements for the enforceability of a positive covenant against a successor in title to the covenantor. The first is that the condition of discharging the burden must be relevant to the exercise of the rights that enable

[12] Report of the Committee on Positive Covenants Affecting Land (1965), Cmnd 2719, para. 8, from which the quotations in this paragraph are taken. See also Law Commission Report on Positive and Restrictive Covenants 1984 (Law Com No. 127, HC 201), paras. 3.19–3.42; Farrand (2nd edn), pp. 422–7; (1973) 37 Conv (NS) 194 (A. M. Prichard); *McAuslan, Land, Law and Planning*, pp. 292–302.   [13] Pp. 294 et seq, ante.

[14] See *Radford v de Froberville* [1977] 1 WLR 1262; *TRW Steering Systems Ltd v North Cape Properties Ltd and Cornerstone Estates Ltd* (1993) 69 P & CR 265.

[15] [1957] Ch 169; *E R Ives Investment Ltd v High* [1967] 2 QB 379, M & B p. 665; *Four Oaks Estate Ltd v Hadley* [1986] LS Gaz R 2326 (no benefit to which burden could be attached); *Law Debenture Trust Corpn plc v Ural Caspian Oil Corpn Ltd* [1993] 1 WLR 138; *Rhone v Stephens* (1993) 67 P & CR 9 (doctrine not invoked where benefit "technical or minimal"; see also HL at [1994] 2 AC 310, infra). For a detailed discussion of the doctrine, see *Tito v Waddell (No 2)* [1977] Ch 106, 289–311, where MEGARRY V-C held at 303 that it covered not merely successors in title but also "anybody whose connection with the transaction creating the benefit and burden is sufficient to show that he has some claim to the benefit whether or not he has a valid title to it". See also (1977) 41 Conv (NS) 432–5 (F. R. Crane); [1985] Conv 12 (F. P. Aughterson); Emmet, para. 19.020.

[16] *Rhone v Stephens* [1994] 2 AC 310 at 322, where Lord TEMPLEMAN said: "The condition must be relevant to the exercise of the right. The obligation to repair the roof was an independent provision".

[17] [1998] 3 EGLR 97 at 99.

the benefit to be obtained. In *Rhone v Stephens* the mutual obligation of support was unrelated to and independent of the covenant to maintain the roof. The second is that the successors in title must have the opportunity to choose whether to take the benefit or, having taken it, to renounce it, even if only in theory, and thereby to escape the burden and that the successors in title can be deprived of the benefit if they fail to assume the burden.

(d) Enlargement of long leases into freeholds

This is an "untried and artificial" device, whereby a long lease is enlarged under section 153 of the Law of Property Act 1925, and the freehold is then subject "to all the same covenants . . . as the term would have been subject to if it had not been so enlarged".[18]

(e) Estate rentcharge

An estate rentcharge may be created to secure the payment of money or contribution to the maintenance of property.[19] The Rentcharges Act 1977 makes special provision for this type of rentcharge.[20]

(f) Right of re-entry

A right of re-entry may be reserved, exercisable on events which amount to the breach of a positive covenant. This right of re-entry runs with the land, but is subject to the rule against perpetuities.[21]

(g) Restriction under Land Registration Act

"Where the title to plots on a newly developed estate is going to be registered and the developer is interested in the continuing observance of the covenants, he can insert a covenant in the original conveyances that the plot shall not be sold without his consent. He can then enter a restriction in the register[22] to ensure compliance with the covenant and can refuse to give his consent to any sale under which the purchaser does not assume the appropriate positive obligations."

(h) Easement of fencing

A right to have a fence or wall kept in repair is a right which is capable of being enforced as an easement. The right is anomalous in the law of easements.[23]

---

[18] P. 327, ante. Restricted to those: (i) which were originally created for at least 300 years of which no less than 200 years is unexpired; (ii) in which no rent of money value is payable; (iii) which are not liable to be determined by re-entry for condition broken; (1958) 22 Conv (NS) 101 (T. P. D. Taylor). See also Leasehold Reform Act 1967, s. 8(3), p. 364, ante.

[19] *Morland v Cook* (1868) LR 6 Eq 252; *Austerberry v Oldham Corpn* (1885) 29 Ch D 750 at 782.

[20] S. 2(3)(c), (4), (5). See pp. 707–8, post.

[21] *Shiloh Spinners Ltd v Harding* [1973] AC 691. The possibility of relief against forfeiture reduces its effectiveness as a device. See (1950) 14 Conv (NS) 350 at 354–7 (S. M. Tolson). The express grant of a legal rentcharge or a legal right of entry exercisable over a legal term of years or annexed to a legal rentcharge is a registrable disposition: LRA 2002 s. 27(2)(e); Sch. 2, para. 6; H & B, paras. 8.17–8.20.

[22] LRA 2002, s. 40, replacing LRA 1925, s. 58, p. 974, post.

[23] *Jones v Price* [1965] 2 QB 618; *Crow v Wood* [1971] 1 QB 77, M & B p. 710; p. 594 ante; *Marlton v Turner* [1998] 3 EGLR 185.

(i) Commonhold

Under the Commonhold and Leasehold Reform Act 2002 the burden of a positive covenant may run by statute as between the unit-holders of commonhold land. Commonhold has already been discussed in detail in chapter 9.

(2) Law Reform

In spite of these methods of circumvention, the burden of a covenant, whether positive or negative, does not run with the servient land upon which it is imposed. As we are about to see, this rule has been radically relaxed by equity in the case of a negative covenant which restricts an owner from making certain defined uses of his land, but it still governs a positive covenant, such as one to contribute towards the cost of constructing and maintaining a private road. That such a covenant should be unenforceable against the successors in title of the covenantor is in many cases unreasonable, as, for instance, where the purchaser of a freehold flat has entered into positive covenants that are essential to the comfort of his neighbours in the same building.[24] "This rule, whose discovery has shocked more than one eminent judge unversed in the subtleties of property law"[25] was considered in 1965 by the Wilberforce Committee which recommended that, subject to certain conditions, the burden of positive covenants should run, and again in 1984 by the Law Commission on the wider topic of both Positive and Restrictive Covenants.[26]

B Burden of a Restrictive Covenant may Run with the Land in Equity

(1) General Nature of the Equitable Doctrine

In the historic case of *Tulk v Moxhay*,[27] the common law rule, that the burden of a covenant does not run with the land of the covenantor except in the case of a lease, was radically modified by equity so far as negative covenants are concerned. The general effect of the doctrine established by this case is that, subject to certain conditions to be discussed at length later, a covenant *negative in substance* entered into by the owner of Blackacre with the neighbouring owner of Whiteacre, imposes an equitable burden upon Blackacre that is enforceable to the same extent as any other equitable interest, such as a contract for a lease. The right to

---

[24] Where the freehold of flats is registered as a commonhold scheme, supra, this problem is overcome. But the difficulty of enforcing the burden of a positive covenant outside a commonhold scheme remains.

[25] *Rhone v Stephens* (1993) 67 P & CR 9, per NOURSE LJ.

[26] Report of the Committee on Positive Covenants Affecting Land 1965 (Cmnd 2719); Law Commission Report on Restrictive Covenants 1967 (Law Com No. 11); Law Commission Report on Positive and Restrictive Covenants 1984 (Law Com No. 127); p. 702, post; (1972B) 31 CLJ 157 (H. W. R. Wade). See *Rhone v Stephens* [1994] 2 AC 310 where Lord TEMPLEMAN said at 321: "Parliamentary legislation to deal with the decision in the *Austerberry* case would require careful consideration of the consequences. Moreover, experience with leasehold tenure where positive covenants are enforceable by virtue of privity of estate, has demonstrated that social injustice can be caused by logic. Parliament was obliged to intervene to prevent tenants losing their homes and being saddled with the costs of restoring to their original glory buildings which had languished through wars and economic depression for exactly 99 years." See *Thamesmead Town Ltd v Allotey* [1998] 3 EGLR 97 at 101, where PETER GIBSON LJ advocates a legislative solution.

[27] (1848) 2 Ph 774, M & B p. 942; [1981] Conv 55 (C. D. Bell); (1982) 98 LQR 279 (S. Gardner); [1983] Conv 29 (R. Griffith); 327 (C. D. Bell).

obtain an injunction[28] against a breach of the negative undertaking will pass to the subsequent owners of Whiteacre, and the duty to observe it will pass to all persons who take the burdened Blackacre, except a bona fide purchaser for value of the legal estate in it without notice, actual or constructive, of the covenant.[29] The facts of *Tulk v Moxhay* were as follows:

In 1808 the plaintiff, being then the owner in fee of the vacant piece of ground in the middle of Leicester Square, London, sold the ground to one Elms in fee, Elms covenanting for himself, his heirs and assigns that he and they would:

> keep and maintain the said piece of ground and square garden, and the iron railing round the same in its then form, and in sufficient and proper repair as a square garden and pleasure ground, in an open state, uncovered with any buildings in neat and ornamental order.

The piece of ground passed by various conveyances into the hands of the defendant Moxhay, who, although he had made no similar covenant with his immediate vendor, admitted that he took the land with notice of the original covenant. The defendant then openly proposed to erect buildings upon the square.

The plaintiff, who still remained the owner of several adjacent houses, succeeded in obtaining an injunction to stop the breach of covenant.[30]

This doctrine has been the subject of development, in the course of which the nature of the right and obligation arising from a restrictive covenant has undergone a radical change.[31] The earlier decisions, culminating in *Luker v Dennis* in 1877,[32] proceeded solely upon the fact of notice,[33] since this was the element that Lord COTTENHAM stressed in *Tulk v Moxhay* in the following words:[34]

It is said that, the covenant being one which does not run with the land, this court cannot enforce it, but the question is, not whether the covenant runs with the land, but whether a party shall be permitted to use the land in a manner inconsistent with the contract entered into by his vendor, and with notice of which he purchased.

To rest the enforcement of a contract against a third party on this basis is not without its dangers.

First, if the emphasis is laid upon whether the conscience of the third party acquiring the land of the covenantor is affected, instead of upon whether the land itself is affected, there will be certain persons, such as a squatter obtaining a title by twelve years' adverse possession,[35] who will enjoy an immunity that they do not deserve.

Secondly, if notice alone justifies the issue of an injunction, the remedy can scarcely be withheld in principle even though the contract is collateral, in the sense that its purpose is not to protect the covenantee's land against an undesirable use of the covenantor's land but to confer some personal privilege upon the covenantee.

---

[28] For remedies generally for breach of a restrictive covenant, see pp. 691, post.

[29] Since 1925, the test is not notice, but whether the burden of the covenant has been registered as a land charge (unregistered land) or protected by entry on the register (registered land): p. 673, post.

[30] For the continued enforceability of the covenant, see *R v Westminster City Council and London Electricity Board* (1989) 59 P & CR 51, where SIMON BROWN J describes Leicester Square as "one of London's ornaments".

[31] See especially Behan, *Covenants Affecting Land*, pp. 27 et seq.   [32] (1877) 7 Ch D 227.

[33] *LCC v Allen* [1914] 3 KB 642 at 658–9, 664–6.   [34] (1848) 2 Ph 774 at 777–8.   [35] P. 672, post.

Since the end of the nineteenth century the judicial approach to the matter has altered. The courts, choosing as the appropriate analogy either the negative easement, such as the right to light, or the tenant's covenant that is annexed to the land by virtue of *Spencer's Case*,[36] have required a restrictive covenant to possess what may be called a real, as distinct from a personal, flavour, before it becomes available to and enforceable against third parties. It must, as VAUGHAN WILLIAMS LJ said, "arise from the relation of two estates one to the other",[37] or, to use more familiar language, it must touch and concern the dominant tenement of the covenantee and must be intended to protect that land against certain uses of the servient tenement. But once it satisfies this requirement it creates an equitable right that will run with the dominant tenement and a corresponding equitable obligation binding on the servient tenement. Discussing the passing of both the benefit and the burden in equity, COLLINS LJ said:

When the benefit has been once clearly annexed to one piece of land, it passes by assignment of that land, and may be said to run with it . . . without proof of special bargain or representation on the assignment. In such a case it runs, not because the conscience of either party is affected, but because the purchaser has bought something which inhered in or was annexed to the land bought. That is the reason why, in dealing with the burden, the purchaser's conscience is not affected by notice of covenants which were part of the original bargain on the first sale, but were merely personal and collateral, while it is affected by notice of those which touch and concern the land. The covenant must be one that is capable of running with the land before the question of the purchaser's conscience and the equity affecting it can come into discussion.[38]

As the law now stands, certain essentials must be satisfied before the burden of a covenant can be laid upon an assignee of the servient tenement or before its benefit can be exploited by an assignee of the dominant tenement. These will now be stated.

(2) Conditions Precedent to the Running of the Burden in Equity

The burden of a restrictive covenant will bind an assignee of the servient tenement if the following essentials are satisfied.

(a) *The conditions precedent*

(1) THE COVENANT MUST BE NEGATIVE IN NATURE

It is essential that the covenant should be negative in substance, not a positive one requiring the expenditure of money for its performance.[39] This condition is satisfied if, for example, the owner of the land undertakes to use the premises for private residence only, or to keep certain windows obscured, or not to build, not to open a public house, or not to carry on a business. But in every case it is the substance and not the form of the covenant that must be regarded, for if an undertaking, though couched in affirmative terms, clearly implies a negative, it will be caught by the doctrine of *Tulk v Moxhay*. Indeed, in that case itself, the

---

[36] P. 298, ante; *London and South Western Rly Co v Gomm* (1882) 20 Ch D 562 at 583, M & B p. 946.

[37] *Formby v Barker* [1903] 2 Ch 539 at 553. No such relation existed, for instance, in *Tophams Ltd v Earl of Sefton* [1967] 1 AC 50.   [38] *Rogers v Hosegood* [1900] 2 Ch 388 at 407.

[39] *Haywood v Brunswick Permanent Benefit Building Society* (1881) 8 QBD 403. Positive and negative obligations may be set in a single covenant. "There cannot be any doctrine of contagious proximity whereby the presence of the positive inhibits the enforcement of the neighbouring negative": *Shepherd Homes Ltd v Sandham (No 2)* [1971] 1 WLR 1062, per MEGARRY J.

covenant was not in terms restrictive, but its provision that the piece of ground was to be used only as an ornamental garden implied a prohibition against building.[40] Again, a covenant to give the first refusal of land is regarded as negative in substance, since in effect it is a promise not to sell without giving the covenantee an option to buy.[41]

(2) THE COVENANTEE MUST AT THE TIME OF THE CREATION OF THE COVENANT AND AFTERWARDS OWN LAND FOR THE PROTECTION OF WHICH THE COVENANT IS MADE

A restrictive covenant taken from the purchaser of a freehold estate is a mere covenant in gross, personal to the contracting parties, unless it imposes an equitable burden upon the covenantor's land for the protection of land owned by the covenantee. Equity, acting on the analogy of a negative easement, will not regard a restrictive covenant as other than personal, unless there is the relation of dominancy and serviency between the respective properties.

It follows, therefore, that, if the covenantee retains no adjacent land or owns no land capable of being protected by the covenant, the covenant cannot be enforced against a person other than the covenantor, even if he has notice of it.[42] Thus in *London County Council v Allen*:[43]

A, a builder, in return for permission to lay out a new street on his land, entered into a covenant with LCC not to build upon a plot of land which lay across the end of the proposed street. The plot was eventually conveyed to Mrs A, who built on it and mortgaged it to B. The Court of Appeal held that the restrictive covenant was not binding on Mrs A and B, even if they had had notice of it.

BUCKLEY LJ in the course of his judgment said:[44]

In the present case we are asked to extend the doctrine of *Tulk v Moxhay* so as to affirm that a restrictive covenant can be enforced against a derivative owner taking with notice by a person who never has had or who does not retain any land to be protected by the restrictive covenant in question. In my opinion the doctrine does not extend to that case. The doctrine is that a covenant not running with the land, but being a negative covenant entered into by an owner of land with an adjoining owner, binds the land

---

[40] *Clegg v Hands* (1890) 44 Ch D 503 at 519; *Bridges v Harrow London Borough* (1981) 260 EG 284 at 288 (covenant to retain trees in hedgerow held to be probably negative in substance); *Bedwell Park Quarry Co v Hertfordshire County Council* [1993] JPL 349 ("It is hard to think of an obligation which was more positive in substance as well as in form").

[41] *Manchester Ship Canal Co v Manchester Racecourse Co* [1901] 2 Ch 37.

[42] But a lessor's interest in the reversion suffices to make a covenant touching and concerning the land enforceable against a sub-lessee: *Hall v Ewin* (1887) 37 Ch D 74; *Regent Oil Co Ltd v J A Gregory (Hatch End) Ltd* [1966] Ch 402 at 432–3; *Hemingway Securities Ltd v Dunraven Ltd* [1995] 1 EGLR 61.

For statutory exceptions to the rule, see National Trust Act 1937, s. 8; *Gee v The National Trust for Places of Historic Interest or Natural Beauty* [1966] 1 WLR 170 at 174; Green Belt (London and Home Counties) Act 1938, s. 22; Water Industry Act 1991, s. 164(3); National Parks and Access to Countryside Act 1949, s. 16(4); Forestry Act 1967, s. 5(2); Endowments and Glebe Measure 1976, s. 22; Ancient Monuments and Archaeological Areas Act 1979, s. 17(5); Wildlife and Countryside Act 1981, s. 39(3); Local Government (Miscellaneous Provisions) Act 1982, s. 33; Housing Act 1985, s. 609; Town and Country Planning Act 1990, s. 106; as amended by Planning and Compensation Act 1991, s. 12 (to be replaced by the new scheme of "planning contribution" under PCPA 2004, s. 46; p. 1023, post); *Re Martin's Application* (1988) 57 P & CR 119; and a number of local authorities have power under local Acts. See also *Peabody Donation Fund Governors v London Residuary Body* (1987) 55 P & CR 355 (Artisans and Labourers Dwellings Improvement Act 1875, s. 9; "a valuable site in Covent Garden").

[43] [1914] 3 KB 642, M & B p. 943; *Formby v Barker* [1903] 2 Ch 539, M & B p. 944.   [44] At 654.

in equity and is enforceable against a derivative owner taking with notice. The doctrine ceases to be applicable when the person seeking to enforce the covenant against the derivative owner has no land to be protected by the negative covenant. The fact of notice is in that case irrelevant.[45]

Again, once a covenantee has assigned the whole of the dominant land, he cannot enforce the covenant against the servient owner. His one remedy is to sue the covenantor personally on the contract, but even so he is entitled only to nominal damages, not to an injunction. The principle of *London County Council v Allen*[46] is that the equitable doctrine ought to be applied with the sole object of protecting the enjoyment of the land which the covenant was intended to protect. If it were possible for a covenantee to enforce a covenant, despite the fact that he never retained any land at all or that he later disposed of the land which he had retained, the result would be to place an unwarranted and useless burden upon subsequent purchasers from the covenantor.[47]

(3) THE COVENANT MUST TOUCH AND CONCERN THE DOMINANT LAND

The covenant must be capable of benefiting the dominant land in the sense that it must be one which touches and concerns that land.[48] To satisfy this condition in the case where a freehold estate is conveyed: "the covenant must either affect the land as regards mode of occupation, or it must be such as *per se*, and not merely from collateral circumstances, affects the value of the land."[49]

Whether the covenant benefits the dominant land is a question of fact to be determined on expert evidence presented to the court.[50] The onus is on the defendant to show that it does not do so, either originally or at the date of the action.[51] This means that, if there were possible opinions either way, the defendant will still fail unless he can show that the opinion that the covenant benefits the land could not reasonably be held.[52]

(4) IT MUST BE THE COMMON INTENTION OF THE PARTIES THAT THE BURDEN OF THE COVENANT SHALL RUN WITH THE LAND OF THE COVENANTOR

This intention may appear from the wording of the covenant itself, as, for instance, where the covenant is made by the covenantor for himself, his heirs and assigns. Covenants which are made after 1925 and relate to any land of the covenantor, or are capable of being bound by him,[53] are deemed by section 79 of the Law of Property Act 1925 to be made by the

---

[45] See, however, n. 42, supra, as to modern statutory powers of local authorities to enforce restrictive covenants otherwise than for the protection of land.

[46] [1914] 3 KB 642; *Formby v Barker*, supra; *Kelly v Barrett* [1924] 2 Ch 379.

[47] *Chambers v Randall* [1923] 1 Ch 149 at 157; *Re Union of London and Smith's Bank Ltd's Conveyance, Miles v Easter* [1933] Ch 611 at 632.

[48] Cf p. 295, ante; *Rogers v Hosegood* [1900] 2 Ch 388 at 395; *Kelly v Barrett* [1924] 2 Ch 379 at 395; *Marquess of Zetland v Driver* [1939] Ch 1 at 8. In *Stocks v Whitgift* [2001] EWCA Civ 1732, [2001] 49 EGCS 130 at [8] PARKER LJ preferred the expression "relates to the land" to the "old expression" of touch and concern.

[49] *Rogers v Hosegood*, supra, at 395, per FARWELL J, adopting BAYLEY J in *Congleton Corpn v Pattison* (1808) 10 East 130.

[50] *Marten v Flight Refuelling Ltd* [1962] Ch 115 at 137; *Earl of Leicester v Wells-next-the-Sea UDC* [1973] Ch 110; *Wrotham Park Estate Co Ltd v Parkside Homes Ltd* [1974] 1 WLR 798.

[51] *Wrotham Park Estate Co v Parkside Homes Ltd*, supra.   [52] [1974] JPL at 133 (G. H. Newsom).

[53] *Lynnthorpe Enterprises Ltd v Sidney Smith (Chelsea) Ltd* [1990] 1 EGLR 148, M & B p. 949 (land need not belong to covenantor at time of covenant).

covenantor on behalf of himself, his successors in title and the persons deriving title under him or them, unless a contrary intention is expressed.[54]

(b) Persons against whom burden runs

We must now examine more closely the effect of a covenant which satisfies the four conditions set out above, and in particular consider those persons against whom the covenant is enforceable.

The doctrine of *Tulk v Moxhay* stands on quite a different footing from the rules which regulate the running of covenants at law, and being of a far more elastic nature it affects a more extensive class of persons and embraces a more extensive class of covenants. The essence of the matter is that when the above conditions are satisfied a restrictive covenant becomes an equitable interest, and as such is enforceable on general principles against all persons who acquire the burdened land.[55] Moreover, the occupier of the burdened land is liable irrespectively of the character of his occupation. This is in sharp contrast with the common law and statutory rules that govern covenants contained in a lease. Under these rules, as we have seen,[56] the burden of a covenant, whether positive or negative, passes to an assignee of the tenant, and it is immaterial that the landlord retains no dominant land.[57] But no one is an assignee for this purpose unless there is privity of estate between him and the reversioner. Thus, though the burden is traditionally said to run with the land, what in fact it runs with is the estate created by the lease. Under the developed doctrine of *Tulk v Moxhay*, on the other hand, it runs with the servient land as such, and there is no question of privity of estate.

The effect of this distinction between running with the land and running with the estate may be illustrated by a reference to three classes of persons who are all caught by the doctrine of *Tulk v Moxhay*, but none of whom is liable at common law under the rules derived from *Spencer's Case*.

(1) SUB-LESSEES

A restrictive covenant imposed upon a lessee binds a sub-lessee, despite the absence of privity of estate between him and the lessor.[58]

(2) MERE OCCUPIERS

A person who is merely occupying land without having any definite estate or interest therein is bound by restrictive covenants. Thus in *Mander v Falcke*:[59]

a lessee who had covenanted not to use the demised premises for purposes which would cause annoyance or inconvenience to adjoining property owned by the lessor granted an under-lease of the premises.

---

[54] *Re Royal Victoria Pavilion (Ramsgate)* [1961] Ch 581, M & B p. 949; *Tophams Ltd v Earl of Sefton* [1967] 1 AC 50 at 81; p. 663, n. 10 ante; *Rhone v Stephens* [1994] 2 AC 310; *Morrells of Oxford Ltd v Oxford United Football Club Ltd* [2001] Ch 459 (one covenant contained no reference to successors in title, whereas another covenant did: held that the first covenant was intended to be personal: s. 79 did not apply because of contrary intention).

[55] For the requirements of registration of the covenant, in both registered and unregistered land, see p. 673, post.   [56] P. 302, ante.

[57] *Regent Oil Co Ltd v J A Gregory (Hatch End) Ltd* [1966] Ch 402.

[58] *Clements v Welles* (1865) LR 1 Eq 200; *Hall v Ewin* (1887) 37 Ch D 74; *John Bros Abergarw Brewery Co v Holmes* [1900] 1 Ch 188.   [59] [1891] 2 Ch 554.

The reversion was ultimately assigned to the plaintiff and the under-lease became vested in X. Apparently X did not occupy the premises himself, but allowed his father to have possession, and the evidence clearly showed that the latter, while purporting to keep an oyster bar, was in fact using the place as a brothel to the great scandal of the neighbourhood.

In seeking an injunction to restrain a breach of the covenant it was argued that such relief could not be granted against the father, as he had no interest whatever, either legal or equitable, in the land. This argument failed, and an injunction was granted against the father, LINDLEY LJ saying:

I treat him simply as an occupier managing the business. He may be neither an assignee nor purchaser, but he is in occupation, and that is enough to affect him, he having notice of the covenants in the lease.[60]

A restrictive covenant imposed after 1925 is enforceable against a mere occupier under section 79(2) of the Law of Property Act 1925.[61]

(3) SQUATTERS

A person who acquires a title to land through adverse possession is bound by any restrictive covenants which are annexed to the land.

In unregistered land we have seen[62] that the effect of the Limitation Act 1980 is merely to extinguish the title of the previous owner and not to transfer his identical interest to the adverse possessor. A covenant in a lease will therefore not bind a person who by long-continued possession of the premises acquires a superior right to the tenant, because he has no privity of estate with the landlord.[63] This lack of privity, however, will not free a squatter on the servient land from a restrictive covenant since it binds the land itself, and therefore (as long as any requirements for registration are satisfied[64]) the squatter. This is illustrated by *Re Nisbet and Potts' Contract*[65] where

Nisbet had purchased land in 1901 from X and Y, who had themselves purchased in 1890 from H, whose title was based upon occupation since 1878 (i.e. more than twelve years' adverse possession). Nisbet agreed to accept proof of title commencing at 1878, although he could have insisted on proof of forty years' title (i.e., commencing in 1861).[66] A restrictive covenant had been imposed on the land in 1867; Nisbet knew nothing of it but would have discovered it if he had insisted on proof of forty years' title. In 1903 Nisbet contracted to sell the land to Potts, who then discovered the covenants. The question was whether Potts, if he took a conveyance of the land, would be subject to the covenant imposed in 1867; and therefore whether the land was already subject to the covenant in the hands of the vendor, Nisbet.

It was argued that the covenant no longer bound assignees of the servient land, because H, who had seized the land in 1878, acquired a title quite independent of any prior holder's

---

[60] At 557.   [61] Pp. 298–9, ante.   [62] P. 135, ante.

[63] *Tichborne v Weir* (1892) 67 LT 735, M & B p. 946.   [64] P. 673, post.

[65] [1905] 1 Ch 391, affd [1906] 1 Ch 386, M & B p. 947.

[66] The period of title which a purchaser can require was later reduced to thirty years: LPA 1925, s. 44(1); and then fifteen years: LPA 1969, s. 23; p. 932, post.

title. But it was held that the equitable interest created by the covenant remained enforceable against X and Y, and Nisbet, unless the could satisfy the court that they had acquired the legal estate for valuable consideration without notice. It was held that they had constructive notice, because if they had insisted on proof of a good root of title at least forty years old, they would have been led back through the squatter H to the original covenantor; but if they chose to accept less than they might have done, they were bound to take the consequences.[67] They were therefore bound by the covenant.

In registered land, under the Land Registration Act 2002 the squatter does not acquire title to the land without being registered as proprietor.[68] Where he is registered, he is the successor in title to the previously registered proprietor, and is bound by any restrictive covenants affecting the registered title.[69]

(c) Registration of restrictive covenants

Even if the conditions precedent to the passing of the burden of a restrictive covenant are satisfied,[70] in many cases the covenant will bind an assignee of the servient tenement only if it has been registered. Different rules apply for unregistered and registered land.

(1) UNREGISTERED LAND

The requirements of registration in unregistered land depend on whether the covenant was created before 1926 or after 1925.

(i) Covenants created before 1926

Covenants created before 1 January 1926 bind all persons who acquire the burdened land, with the exception of a bona fide purchaser for value of the legal estate therein without notice, actual or constructive, of the covenants. Such a purchaser can, however, pass a title free from the restriction to a purchaser from him, even though the latter has actual notice of the covenant.[71]

(ii) Covenants created after 1925

Covenants created after 1925, except those made between lessor and lessee,[72] are void against a purchaser (including a mortgagee and lessee) of the *legal estate* in the burdened land *for money or money's worth*, unless they are registered as land charges in the appropriate register.[73] If not registered they are void against the purchaser for value of the legal estate even though he had express notice of them. Thus non-registration does not avail an assignee of a mere equitable interest in the burdened land, or an assignee of the legal estate who does

---

[67] After 1925 the question would be not whether the purchaser had notice, but whether the covenant was registered under LCA 1925 or 1972; infra.

[68] For the significant changes made in this respect by LRA 2002, see pp. 145 et seq, ante.

[69] LRA 2002, s. 97, Sch. 6, para. 9(2); H & B, chap. 31.   [70] P. 668, ante.

[71] *Wilkes v Spooner* [1911] 2 KB 473, M & B p. 27.

[72] *Dartstone Ltd v Cleveland Petroleum Co Ltd* [1969] 1 WLR 1807; [1956] 20 Conv (NS) 370 (R. G. Rowley); *Oceanic Village Ltd v United Attractions* [2000] Ch 234.

[73] LCA 1972, ss. 2(5), Class D(ii), 4(6), s. 17(1), p. 941, post. Positive and negative covenants entered into with a local authority, a Minister of the Crown or Government Department (otherwise than as between landlord and tenant) are registrable as local land charges: LLCA 1975, ss. 1, 2, p. 947, ante.

For the duty of a solicitor to advise a purchaser on the nature and effect of a restrictive covenant, see *Bittlestone v Keegan Williams* [1997] EGCS 8.

not give money or money's worth. The reason why a restrictive covenant between a lessor and lessee cannot be registered, is that it is a simple and normal step for an assignee to inspect the lease which contains the terms of the tenancy.

(2) REGISTERED LAND

In registered land the burden[74] of a restrictive covenant, except one made between a lessor and lessee,[75] can be protected by the entry of a notice on the register of the servient tenement.[76] According to the usual principles of protection of equitable interests in registered land,[77] if the covenant is not so protected it will not bind a person taking a registrable disposition[78] of the registered estate for valuable consideration.[79] It cannot be an overriding interest.[80]

The entry of a notice on the register only makes the covenant binding if it satisfies the other conditions necessary for the passing of the burden.[81]

III The Claimant Must Have the Benefit of the Covenant

We have seen that the courts were reluctant to allow a person to be burdened by a covenant which he had not himself undertaken. There is no such reluctance in the case of the benefit, for which a number of mechanisms have been developed, by statute, by the courts of common law, and by the courts of equity. In some cases the claimant will be able to enforce the covenant by virtue of being the original covenantee, or (if not the covenantee) being a person defined at the outset as a beneficiary of it. Failing that, he may be an assignee at common law of the benefit of the covenant, or he may acquire the right at common law to enforce it as being annexed to the land which he has acquired. Or, failing that, he may be able to use one of three mechanisms developed by the courts of equity to allow him to enforce the covenant. As we shall see, each of these sets of rules has its own limitations, and sometimes the claimant will need to show that he is within one set of rules; sometimes another.

A *Enforcing the Covenant as an Original Beneficiary*

Apart from the case where the claimant was himself the direct covenantee, there are two cases in which a person may still enforce a covenant as an original beneficiary of it.

---

[74] No provision is made by LRA 2002 for recording the benefit of a restrictive covenant on the register of the dominant tenement: H & B, para. 25.13; R & R, para. 42.019.01; nor for making entries relating to positive covenants since the burden does not run with the land: p. 663, ante; n. 81, infra. In practice, however, positive covenants are often intermixed with restrictive covenants, and where this occurs they are not edited out of the restrictive covenant entry.

[75] LRA 2002, s. 33(c). This exclusion from registration parallels the position in unregistered land, supra.

[76] Ibid., s. 32. R & R, paras. 9.018–9.021, 42.009. If the restrictive covenant was protected under LCA 1972, supra, before first registration it will become unenforceable if no notice is entered on first registration: *Freer v Unwins* [1976] Ch 288; (1976) 40 Conv (NS) 304 (F. R. Crane); [1976] CLJ 211 (D. Hayton); (1976) 92 LQR 338 (R. J. Smith); (1976) 126 NLJ 523 (S. M. Cretney). See (1984) 81 LSG 1723, where the Chief Land Registrar states that on first registration he does not normally enquire whether a covenant has become void for non-registration under LCA 1925; R & R, para. 9.020.   [77] Pp. 971 et seq, post.

[78] Including a transfer, the grant of a lease of more than seven years, and a legal charge: ibid., s. 27.

[79] LRA 2002, s. 29.   [80] *Hodges v Jones* [1935] Ch 657 at 671 (LRA 1925, s. 70).

[81] P. 668, ante; *Cator v Newton* [1940] 1 KB 415 (positive covenant not made binding by registration); LRA 2002, s. 32(3).

(1) Section 56 of the Law of Property Act 1925

Section 56 of the Law of Property Act 1925 provides that:[82]

A person may take an immediate or other interest in land or other property, or the benefit of any condition, right of entry, covenant or agreement over or respecting land or other property, although he may not be named as a party to the conveyance or other instrument.

This section reproduces and extends section 5 of the Real Property Act 1845, which abrogated the technical rule of common law that a grantee or covenantee, though named as such in an indenture under seal expressed to be made inter partes, could not take an immediate interest as grantee nor the benefit of a covenant as covenantee unless named as a party to the indenture.

It is important to notice that this section is not concerned with the *passing* of the benefit of a covenant. It is concerned with the *giving* of the benefit of a covenant, at the time when the covenant is created, to a person other than the covenantee. The section in effect makes the person claiming the benefit of the covenant an original covenantee, even though he was not named as a party to the deed in which the covenant was created. Once, however, the benefit of a covenant is given to a person by the section, the benefit can then pass to his successors in title by annexation or assignment.[83]

The application of section 56 is not confined to covenants that touch and concern the land,[84] nor is it confined to restrictive covenants in equity. Its application in the latter context may, however, enable an earlier purchaser of a plot of land on an estate, which is not subject to a scheme of development,[85] to enforce a restrictive covenant against a later purchaser of a plot from the common vendor.

The section has been restrictively interpreted in that the covenant must purport to be made with the claimant as covenantee and not be made merely for his benefit. Thus in *Amsprop Trading Ltd v Harris Distribution Ltd*,[86] where there was a covenant between a tenant and a sub-tenant that "it shall be lawful for the superior landlords . . . to enter and to repair at the cost of the sub-tenant", it was held that the covenant did not purport to be made with them, even though they were named as persons for whose benefit the covenant was made.

As NEUBERGER J said:[87]

The true aim of section 56 seems to be not to allow a third party to sue on a contract merely because it is for his benefit; the contract must purport to be made *with* him. Just as, under the first part of the section a person cannot benefit by a conveyance unless it purports to be made *to* him (as grantee), so he cannot benefit by a covenant which does not purport to be made *with* him (as covenantee).

However, in *Re Ecclesiastical Commissioners for England's Conveyance*:[88]

in 1887, the purchaser of Blackacre entered into restrictive covenants in favour of the Ecclesiastical Commissioners, the vendors. A separate covenant was also included in the conveyance, with the

---

[82] On the section generally, see Treitel, pp. 669–71; *Beswick v Beswick* [1968] AC 58, especially Lord PEARCE at 93–4 and Lord UPJOHN at 102–7; M & B p. 992; (1967) 30 MLR 687 (G. H. Treitel).   [83] Discussed infra.

[84] *Re Ecclesiastical Comrs for England's Conveyance* [1936] Ch 430 at 438; but see *Grant v Edmondson* [1931] 1 Ch 1.   [85] Pp. 677 et seq, post.

[86] [1997] 1 WLR 1025; [1997] All ER Rev 288 (P. J. Clarke).

[87] At 1032, adopting M & W (5th edn), p. 763; See also W & C, 13th edn, vol 1. p. 133: "the condition was propounded only by Lord Upjohn at 106–7, although he largely had the concurrence of Lord Pearce at 94, and can be regarded as obiter dicta (see at 102). Nevertheless, it rests on and clearly will carry, considerable authority."

[88] [1936] Ch 430, M & B p. 994. See also *Forster v Elvet Colliery Co Ltd* [1908] 1 KB 629; affd sub nom. *Dyson v Forster* [1909] AC 98.

vendors' "assigns, owners for the time being of the land adjoining or adjacent to" Blackacre to observe and perform the restrictive covenants. Prior to 1887, the Commissioners had sold various freehold plots, situated near Blackacre, to different purchasers and these had passed into other hands by the time of the action.

It was held that the successors in title of the adjacent owners were entitled to enforce the covenants although their respective predecessors in title had not joined in the conveyance of 1887. The separate covenant clearly fell within section 56; it purported to be made with the assigns of the vendor.

The section will not avail a person unless he might have been a party to the deed in question. If he is an ascertainable person at the time of the execution of the deed which purports to grant him an interest in property[89] or to make a covenant available to him, he and his successors in title are in as good a position as if he had been one of the original parties. On the other hand, a deed is inoperative in so far as it purports to extend the advantage of a covenant to an unascertainable person, such as the *future* owner of specified land.[90] It will not, therefore, enable a later purchaser to enforce a restrictive covenant against an earlier purchaser from a common vendor. In order to succeed, he must prove that the benefit of the covenant has passed to him by annexation, express assignment or under a scheme of development.

(2) Contracts (Rights of Third Parties) Act 1999

This Act applies to all contracts (including leases and land contracts) entered into on or after 11 May 2000. It was also possible for parties to contract into it during six months before that date.[91]

Under the Act a person who is not a party to the contract may enforce a term of it *in his own right*, either if the contract expressly provides that he may, or if the term purports to confer a benefit on him (unless on a proper construction of the contract it appears that the parties did not intend the term to be enforceable by the third party).[92] In either case, section 1(3) provides that: "the third party must be expressly identified in the contract by name, as a member of a class or as answering a particular description but need not be in existence when the contract is entered into".

In so far as this Act applies to the enforcement of a freehold covenant at common law, we can make three observations.[93] First, such phrases as "successors in title" bring the covenant

---

[89] *Stromdale and Ball Ltd v Burden* [1952] Ch 223; *Drive Yourself Hire Co (London) Ltd v Strutt* [1954] 1 QB 250; *Re Foster* [1938] 3 All ER 357 at 365, per CROSSMAN J; *Lyus v Prowsa Developments Ltd* [1982] 1 WLR 1044 at 1049, per DILLON J.

[90] *Kelsey v Dodd* (1881) 52 LJ Ch 34 at 39; *White v Bijou Mansions Ltd* [1937] Ch 610 at 625; affd [1938] Ch 351 at 365, M & B p. 995. See also *Pinemain Ltd v Welbeck International Ltd* (1984) 272 EG 1166 (benefit of covenant to sue surety on contract of guarantee not within s. 56, since plaintiffs were not identifiable when covenant was made); *Re Distributors and Warehousing Ltd* [1986] 1 EGLR 90, per WALTON J; cf *Wiles v Banks* (1983) 50 P & CR 80 (plaintiff identifiable).

[91] The Act was passed on 11 November 1999. On the Act generally, see Emmet, paras. 2.131–2.135, 19.003A; Blundell Lectures 25th Anniversary Series 2000: The Contracts (Rights of Third Parties) Act 1999 and Its Implications for Property Transactions (A. Burrows and C. Harpum); (1999) 143 SJ 1082 (S. Bright and P. J. G. Williams); [2001] CLJ 353 (N. Andrews); (2004) 120 LQR 292 (R. Stevens); Treitel, pp. 651–66. The parties may contract out of it. For subsequent variation or a rescission of the contract, see s. 2. On clauses to deal with aspects of the Act, see Conv. Prec. 19-B9.   [92] S. 1(1), (2).

[93] The Act does not affect the running of the burden of a covenant.

within section 1(3), enabling them to sue directly the original covenantor on the covenant. Secondly, being a contractual and not a land law right, there is no need to satisfy the common law requirement of touching and concerning the land and of a legal estate to be benefited. And, thirdly, it will only be rarely necessary to invoke the Act, since in most cases the width of section 78(1) of the Law of Property Act 1925 will suffice.

Where the Contracts (Rights of Third Parties) Act 1999 applies,[94] there are two differences from section 56 of the Law of Property Act 1925.[95] First, the contract may be so drafted as to give the third party a direct right to enforce the covenant by an express term under section 1(1)(a), or, failing that, by purporting to confer the "benefit on him" under section 1(1)(b). The test then is, whether, on a proper construction of the covenant, the parties have purported to confer a benefit on the third party and not whether they have purported to make the covenant with him. Secondly, there is no need for the third party to be in existence or identifiable at the time of the making of the contract; it is sufficient if he comes within the scope of section 1(3). Accordingly, a later purchaser may be able to enforce a restrictive covenant against an earlier purchaser, without the need for annexation, assignment or a building scheme.

B Enforcing the Covenant as a Successor at Common Law

(1) Benefit of a Covenant, Positive or Restrictive, may Run at Common Law

The rule at common law for several centuries has been that the *benefit* of covenants, whether positive or negative, which are made with a covenantee, having an interest in the land to which they relate, passes to his successors in title.[96] Thus in *Sharp v Waterhouse*[97] it was admitted that a covenant by the owner of a mill that he "his heirs executors and administrators" would supply pure water to the adjacent land of X, ran with that land and could be put in suit by X's devisee.

The covenantor is liable to the successors in title of the covenantee merely because of the covenant that he has made, not because of his relationship to any servient tenement.[98] He is liable even though he himself owns no land.[99]

Four things, however, are essential to bring this rule into operation:

(i) The covenant must "touch and concern" the land of the covenantee.[100] In general, the test for this requirement is the same as that for covenants in leases granted before 1996.[101]

(ii) There must be an intention that the benefit should run with the land owned by the covenantee at the date of the covenant.[102]

---

[94] (1999) 143 NLJ 1082 at 1083 (S. Bright and P. J. G. Williams).   [95] Supra.

[96] *The Prior's Case* (1368) YB 42 Ed. 3, Pl. 14, fol. 3A; Co Litt 385a; *Shayler v Woolf* [1946] Ch 320 (express assignment by covenantee of the benefit of the covenant); *Smith and Snipes Hall Farm Ltd v River Douglas Catchment Board* [1949] 2 KB 500; 1 *Smith's Leading Cases* (13th edn), pp. 51, 65, 73; M & B, p. 951.

[97] (1857) 7 E & B 816.   [98] *Smith and Snipes Hall Farm Ltd v River Douglas Catchment Board*, supra.

[99] Ibid.   [100] *Rogers v Hosegood* [1900] 2 Ch 388 at 395.   [101] Pp. 295–7, ante.

[102] *Rogers v Hosegood* [1900] 2 Ch 388 at 396; *Shayler v Woolf* [1946] Ch 320; *Smith and Snipes Hall Farm Ltd v River Douglas Catchment Board*, supra, at 506. This part of the test may be satisfied by the word-saving effect of LPA 1925, s. 78: infra.

(iii) The covenantee, at the time of making the covenant, must have the legal estate in the land which is to be benefited.[103]

(iv) A successor who seeks to enforce the covenant must have a legal estate in the land.

At common law, in order to satisfy part (iv) of this test, the successor had to have the same legal estate as the original covenantee, for the covenant was incident to that estate:[104] a covenant taken by an owner in fee simple did not therefore avail his lessee. However, this rule was abrogated for covenants made after 1925 by section 78 of the Law of Property Act 1925, which provides that:

A covenant relating to any land of the covenantee shall be deemed to be made with the covenantee and his successors in title and the persons deriving title under him or them, and shall have effect as if such successors and other persons were expressed.[105]

This provision will avail anyone holding a legal estate, either as a successor to the same estate as the original covenantee or as the holder of a derivative estate, such as a legal lessee or mortgagee.[106]

(2) Assignment under Section 136 of the Law of Property Act 1925

The benefit of a covenant may also be transferred by assignment as a chose in action under section 136 of the Law of Property Act 1925. To be effective at law, the assignment must be in writing, and express notice in writing given to the covenantor.[107]

C Enforcing the Covenant as a Successor in Equity

We have seen that equity, going further than the common law, allowed the burden of a covenant to run with the land, but only where the covenant is *restrictive*.[108] Equity also developed rules which are in many respects more generous than the common law for the passing of the benefit of a covenant—but, again, only if the covenant is restrictive.[109]

Suppose that on the sale of Whiteacre to X a restrictive covenant has been taken from him for the protection of Blackacre still retained by the vendor, A; and suppose further that A has subsequently sold Blackacre, the dominant land, to B. Can B enforce the covenant against X or against Y who is an assignee of X's land?

---

[103] *Webb v Russell* (1789) 3 Term Rep 393.

[104] *Smith and Snipes Hall Farm Ltd v River Douglas Catchment Board*, supra, at 516.

[105] Ibid. (where one of the plaintiffs was a yearly tenant); *Williams v Unit Construction Co Ltd* (1955) 19 Conv (NS) 262 (where the plaintiff was a weekly tenant). This wide interpretation of the section was followed in *Federated Homes Ltd v Mill Lodge Properties Ltd* [1980] 1 WLR 594, M & B p. 959, p. 680, post, where CA was considering the running of the benefit in equity. For a criticism of the CA decision in *Smith and Snipes Hall Farm Ltd v River Douglas Catchment Board*, see 18 Conv (NS) at 553–6. It would seem that the section was intended to abrogate (ii) and not (iv) and thus to be a "word-saving" section only. See also Wolstenholme and Cherry, vol. 1. pp. 162–3; (1972B) 31 CLJ, pp. 171–5 (H. W. R. Wade).

[106] Thus excluding a squatter who is not a successor in title, an equitable lessee or mortgagee who has no legal estate, and a licensee who has no estate.

[107] See Treitel, pp. 675 et seq. The statute does not say who is to give the express notice.   [108] P. 666, ante.

[109] The requirement that the covenant be restrictive under the rules of equity for the passing of the benefit is a limitation. At common law the benefit of a positive covenant can be annexed to the land: *Smith and Snipes Hall Farm Ltd v River Douglas Catchment Board* [1949] 2 KB 500, M & B p. 951, p. 677, ante.

The answer is that enforcement is not automatic merely because the dominant land has come into the hands of B. B must go further. He must prove, not only that he has acquired the land, but also that he has acquired the benefit of the covenant itself.[110]

We have already seen that the benefit of a covenant runs at common law subject to certain conditions.[111] If B can satisfy these, there is no need for him to rely on the rules evolved by equity for the running of the benefit. There are however circumstances in which the common law rules are inapplicable, and it is then that B must prove that he has satisfied the conditions which equity imposes.

The situations in which B must do this are:

(a) where B is, or A the original covenantee was, a mere equitable owner of Blackacre;[112]

(b) where B does not have the same legal estate in Blackacre as A had (this would only apply to covenants made before 1926[113]);

(c) where Whiteacre has been conveyed to Y and enforcement against Y depends upon the equitable doctrine of *Tulk v Moxhay*;[114]

(d) where B relies upon an express assignment of the benefit of the covenant from A, and the assignment does not comply with section 136 of the Law of Property Act 1925;[115]

(e) where part only of Whiteacre has been conveyed to B, for "at law, the benefit could not be assigned in pieces. It would have to be assigned as a whole or not at all";[116]

(f) where B relies upon his land being part of a scheme of development.[117]

In these situations there are only three ways[118] in which B can show that he has acquired the benefit of the covenant itself, namely by proving:

(1) that the benefit of the covenant has been effectively annexed to the dominant land, and that he had acquired the whole of that land, or the part of it to which the covenant was annexed; or,

(2) that the benefit of the covenant was separately and expressly assigned to him at the time of the sale; or,

(3) that both the dominant and servient lands are subject to a scheme of development.

Let us take these methods separately.

(1) Annexation of Covenant to Dominant Land

(a) *Intention to annex*

Whether or not the benefit of a restrictive covenant runs with the dominant land by virtue of its express annexation to that land depends on the intention of the parties to be inferred

---

[110] [1938] CLJ 339 (S. J. Bailey); [1971] 82 LQR 539 (D. J. Hayton); (1982) 2 Legal Studies 53 (D. J. Hurst); (1982) 98 LQR 279 (S. Gardner). [111] P. 677, ante.

[112] *Fairclough v Marshall* (1878) 4 Ex D 37; *Rogers v Hosegood* [1900] 2 Ch 388, M & B p. 957 (mortgagor before 1926). [113] LPA 1925, s. 78(1); p. 678, ante.

[114] *Renals v Cowlishaw* (1878) 9 Ch D 125, M & B p. 959; *Re Union of London and Smith's Bank Ltd's Conveyance, Miles v Easter* [1933] Ch 611 at 630 per ROMER LJ; M & B p. 971; *Marten v Flight Refuelling Ltd* [1962] Ch 115, M & B p. 976. [115] Pp. 111 et seq, post.

[116] *Re Union of London and Smith's Bank Ltd's Conveyance*, supra, at 630, per ROMER LJ; *Federated Homes Ltd v Mill Lodge Properties Ltd* [1980] 1 WLR 594, M & B p. 969. [117] Pp. 687 et seq, post.

[118] *Re Pinewood Estate, Farnborough* [1958] Ch 280, M & B p. 955.

from the language which they used in the deed creating the covenant. This intention to annex is commonly inferred when the covenant is made: " 'with so and so, owners or owner for the time being of whatever the land may be'. Another method is to state by means of an appropriate declaration that the covenant is taken 'for the benefit of' whatever the lands may be."[119]

Thus in *Rogers v Hosegood*[120] the following covenant was held to be annexed to the land:

with intent that the covenants might so far as possible bind the premises thereby conveyed and every part thereof and might enure to the benefit of the vendors . . . their heirs and assigns and others claiming under them to all or any of their lands adjoining or near to the said premises.

(b) Dominant land must be ascertainable

Furthermore, the exact land to which the parties intend to annex the benefit of the covenant must be ascertainable. Whether this is so depends primarily upon the construction of the deed of conveyance. A competent draftsman will describe the land in precise terms, as for instance by declaring that the covenant is taken for the benefit of "the property known as Blackacre"; or for the "land marked red on the plan drawn on these presents". If the description is more vague, as for instance "the land adjoining" the servient land, extrinsic evidence is admissible to identify the particular land that the parties had in mind.[121]

In summary, the land must be clearly,[122] or easily,[123] identified in the conveyance creating the covenant.[124] As we shall see, this is a stricter rule of identification than that which applies in the case of express assignment.[125]

(c) Law of Property Act 1925, section 78

However, the problem of determining whether the language of a conveyance is sufficient to show an intention to annex the covenant has disappeared in respect of a covenant entered into after 1925 since the decision of the Court of Appeal in *Federated Homes Ltd v Mill Lodge Properties Ltd*.[126] In that case:

A owned land for development which was subject to restrictions on the overall number of houses to be built on it. A sold three parts of the land (blue, red and green) to separate purchasers. The blue land was

---

[119] *Drake v Gray* [1936] Ch 451 at 456, per GREENE LJ.

[120] [1900] 2 Ch 388, M & B p. 957. Cf *Renals v Cowlishaw* (1878) 9 Ch D 125, M & B p. 959 (covenant with the vendors "their heirs, executors, administrators and assigns" held insufficient to annex, since no dominant land was specified). See also *J Sainsbury plc v Enfield London Borough Council* [1989] 1 WLR 590, M & B p. 959; *Re MCA East Ltd* [2003] 1 P & CR 9 (no intention to annex). [121] See Preston and Newsom, para. 2.19.

[122] *Newton Abbot Co-operative Society Ltd v Williamson and Treadgold Ltd* [1952] Ch 286 at 289, per UPJOHN J.

[123] *Marquess of Zetland v Driver* [1939] Ch 1 at 8, per FARWELL J; followed in *Crest Nicholson Residential (South) Ltd v McAllister* [2004] 1 WLR 2409 at [30]–[33], per CHADWICK LJ, noting that this has not been changed by the decision in *Federated Homes Ltd v Mill Lodge Properties Ltd*, supra, in which *Marquess of Zetland v Driver* was not cited.

[124] The relevant date for identifying the benefited land is that of transfer not registration: *Mellon v Sinclair* [1997] CLY 4258.

[125] P. 685, post. Cf, however, *Whitgift Homes Ltd v Stocks* [2001] EWCA Civ 1732; [2001] 48 EGCS 130 (language sufficient to identify land for purposes of annexation under LPA 1925, s. 78, but not sufficient to define area for scheme of development, p. 689, post).

[126] [1980] 1 WLR 594, M & B p. 959; *Robins v Berkeley Homes (Kent) Ltd* [1996] EGCS 75; *Whitgift Homes Ltd v Stocks*, supra; *Crest Nicholson Residential (South) Ltd v McAllister*, supra; [2004] Conv 507 (J. Howell); [2005] Conv 2.

sold to M who covenanted with A that "in carrying out the development the Purchaser shall not build at a greater density than a total of 300 dwellings so as not to reduce the number of units which the Vendor might eventually erect on the retained land." The conveyance contained a reference to the retained lands as "any adjoining or adjacent property retained" by A. It will be seen that the terms of the covenant were not such as, from its express language, to annex the benefit of it to A's land under the rule in *Rogers v Hosegood*.

A then sold the red and green lands to other purchasers, and eventually F became owner of both of them. In the case of the green land, there was a complete chain of assignments of the benefit of the covenant through the various purchasers to A, but not in the case of the red land.

F sought an injunction to restrain M from breaking the restrictive covenant.

In granting the injunction the Court of Appeal held that F was entitled to the benefit of the covenant in respect of the green land, by reason of the chain of assignments.[127] This was sufficient to entitle F to relief, but the Court then went on to consider whether F also had the benefit of the covenant in his capacity as owner of the red land. It was held that F had that benefit under section 78(1) of the Law of Property Act 1925.[128] The actual wording of the covenant was "sufficient to intimate that the covenant was one relating to the land of the covenantee",[129] and, therefore, the benefit was annexed to the land without the need to use appropriate language from which an intention to annex might be inferred. As BRIGHTMAN LJ said:[130]

If the condition precedent of section 78 is satisfied—that is to say, there exists a covenant which touches and concerns the land of the covenantee—that covenant runs with the land for the benefit of his successors in title, persons deriving title under him or them and other owners and occupiers.

This decision simplifies the rules as to the passing of the benefit of a restrictive covenant, but it has been criticised on the ground that a narrow construction of the section is preferable, in other words that it is merely a statutory shorthand for reducing the length of legal documents.[131] On this view the section would only operate when annexation had already been established according to the general rule. There are strong arguments in favour of the narrow view. The Law of Property Act 1925 is a consolidation statute and "if the words are

---

[127] P. 685, post.

[128] P. 678, ante. The Court of Appeal found support for this wide construction in *Smith and Snipes Hall Farm Ltd v River Douglas Catchment Board* [1949] 2 KB 500, M & B p. 951; p. 677, ante; *Williams v Unit Construction Co Ltd* (1955) 19 Conv (NS) 262, M & B p. 953. John Mills QC had decided in favour of F at first instance, but under LPA 1925, s. 62; p. 603, ante; p. 682, n. 138, post.

[129] See *Bridges v Harrow London Borough Council* (1981) 260 EG 284; [1982] Conv 313 (F. Webb).

[130] At 605.

[131] [1980] JPL 371; [1981] 97 LQR 32; [1981] JPL 295; (1982) 98 LQR 202 (G. H. Newsom); (1980) 43 MLR 445 (D. J. Hayton); 130 NLJ 531 (T. Bailey); [1985] Conv 177 (P. N. Todd). And there is no suggestion of a wide construction in Sir Benjamin Cherry's book (Wolstenholme and Cherry's *Conveyancing Statutes*, 11th edn, 1925). See also the 30th Anniversary Blundell Lecture (27 June 2005), where NEUBERGER LJ, whilst noting that the decision in *Crest Nicholson Residential (South) Ltd v McAllister* [2004] 1 WLR 2409, confirms that *Federated Homes* is authority for the wider construction, which renders the law much simpler and clearer, said that "there do seem to be pretty formidable arguments . . . for doubting the correctness of the decision in *Federated Homes*", especially the failure to repeat in s. 78 the annexation formulae in the two preceding sections, ss. 76 and 77: [1982] JPL 295; (1982) 98 LQR 202 (G. H. Newsom and E.H.B).

capable of more than one construction then the Court will give effect to the construction which does not change the law";[132] and the predecessor to section 78, section 58 of the Conveyancing Act 1881, did not have the effect of annexing the benefit of a restrictive covenant to the covenantee's land.[133] Further, if a far-reaching and substantial alteration to the law had been intended by Parliament, one would expect it to be expressed in unambiguous terms,[134] and a formula was ready to hand to do this; the repetition of the wording in the two immediately preceding sections would have given the effect of the wider construction without any ambiguity.[135] The Court of Appeal's view is also at variance with the narrow interpretation by the House of Lords of the similar but not identical section 79 in respect of the running of the burden of a covenant.[136]

The decision in *Federated Homes Ltd v Mill Lodge Properties Ltd* was further considered in *Roake v Chadha*,[137] where a covenant contained the words "so as to bind . . . the land hereby transferred into whosoever hands the same may come . . . but so that this covenant shall not enure for the benefit of any owner or subsequent purchaser of any part of the estate unless the benefit of this covenant shall be expressly assigned". It was held that the annexation of the benefit under section 78 was not automatic, notwithstanding that section 78, unlike its counterpart, section 79, does not contain the words "unless a contrary intention is expressed". Even where a covenant is deemed to be made with successors in title as section 78 requires, "one still has to construe the covenant as a whole to see whether the benefit of the covenant is annexed".[138] This was approved by the Court of Appeal in *Crest Nicholson Residential (South) Ltd v McAllister*[139] where CHADWICK LJ said that section 78 did not include the words "unless a contrary intention is expressed" because "it did not need to".[140] The effect of the section is to annex the benefit of the covenant to the land in the hands of the covenantee's "successors in title"—which are defined[141] as "the owners and occupiers for the time being of the land of the covenantee intended to be benefited".

---

[132] *Beswick v Beswick* [1968] AC 58 at 87 and 105, per Lord GUEST and Lord UPJOHN respectively. In that case the rule was used to restrict the scope of LPA 1925, s. 56; p. 675, ante.

[133] *Forster v Elvet Colliery Co Ltd* [1908] 1 KB 629 at 635, per COZENS-HARDY MR; NEUBERGER LJ, 30th Anniversary Blundell Lecture, supra; *J Sainsbury plc v Enfield London Borough Council* [1989] 1 WLR 590, M & B p. 959 (covenant made in 1894). [134] *Beswick v Beswick*, supra at 93, per Lord PEARCE.

[135] LPA 1925, ss. 76(6) (covenants for title), 77(5) (implied covenants in conveyances subject to rents). The two sub-sections have identical wording: "The benefit of a covenant implied as aforesaid shall be annexed to, and shall go with, the estate of interest of the implied covenantee, and shall be capable of being enforced by every person in whom that estate or interest is, for the whole or any part thereof, from time to time vested." See also ss. 141(1), 142(1); pp. 299, 301, ante. Similar language is also used in Rentcharges Act 1977, s. 11(3), LT(C)A 1995, s. 3(1) and LP(MP)A 1994, s. 7. [136] *Rhone v Stephens* [1994] 2 AC 310, M & B p. 948; p. 663, ante.

[137] [1984] 1 WLR 40, M & B p. 963; [1983] All ER Rev 331 (P. J. Clarke); [1984] Conv 68 (P. N. Todd). The decision was approved by CA in *Crest Nicholson Residential (South) Ltd v McAllister* [2004] 1 WLR 2409, at [37]–[42].

[138] Per Judge Paul Baker QC at 46. He also held that the benefit of the covenant did not pass under LPA 1925, s. 62; p. 603, ante. It was not a right "appertaining or reputed to appertain" to land. He also thought that the rights in s. 62 might be confined to legal rights, thereby excluding the benefit of a restrictive covenant, which is an equitable right. See also *Kumar v Dunning* [1989] QB 193, where BROWNE-WILKINSON V-C said at 198: "A right under covenant cannot appertain to the land unless the benefit is in some way annexed to the land. If the benefit of a covenant passes under s. 62 even if not annexed to the land, the whole modern law of restrictive covenants would have been established on an erroneous basis." See also *Mahon v Sims* [2005] 3 EGLR 67 (requirement that covenantor obtain consent of "the Transferor" before carrying out work; on construction, this was not personal to the original transferor, but referred to successor in title for the time being); [2004] All ER Rev 244 (P. J. Clarke).

[139] [2004] 1 WLR 2409 at [37]–[44]; [2004] All ER Rev 244 (P. J. Clarke). [140] Ibid., at [43].

[141] LPA 1925, s. 78(1), second paragraph.

In a case where the parties to the instrument make clear their intention that land retained by the covenantee at the time of the conveyance effected by the transfer is to have the benefit of the covenant only for so long as it continues to be in the ownership of the original covenantee, and not after it has been sold on by the original covenantee—unless the benefit of the covenant is expressly assigned to the new owner—*the land of the covenantee intended to be benefited* is identified by the instrument as (i) so much of the retained land as from time to time has not been sold off by the original covenantee and (ii) so much of the retained land as has been sold off with the benefit of an express assignment, but as not including (iii) so much of the land as has been sold off without the benefit of an express assignment.[142]

Finally, we should notice the proviso to section 78(1):

For the purposes of this subsection in connexion with covenants restrictive of the user of land 'successors in title' shall be deemed to include the owners and occupiers for the time being of the land of the covenantee intended to be benefited.

The effect is that in the case of restrictive covenants any owner or occupier for the time being can enforce the annexed covenant even though he may be a squatter or licensee.[143]

(d) Annexation to whole of covenantee's land

Even if the language of the covenant indicates an intention to annex the benefit of the covenant to the whole of the land of the covenantee, such annexation will not be effected unless substantially the whole of the land is capable of benefiting. Thus in *Re Ballard's Conveyance*[144] the benefit of a covenant which imposed a restriction on 18 acres was annexed by the conveyance to "the Childwickbury Estate". The area of this estate was about 1700 acres, by far the largest part of which could not possibly be directly affected by a breach of the covenant.

Although it would seem that an injury to a part of any unity is inevitably an injury to the whole, CLAUSON J held that the covenant was not enforceable by assignees of the whole of the dominant land. Moreover, he refused to sever the covenant and thus to regard it as annexed to the part of the land that was in fact touched and concerned. The decision seems to amount to this: that if a covenantee over-estimates to a moderate degree the area of the dominant land capable of deriving advantage from a restrictive covenant, his attempt to preserve the amenities of the neighbourhood and to maintain the selling value of what he retains will fail.[145] Why the well-known doctrine of severance should be excluded from this type of contract is difficult to appreciate.[146]

On the other hand, a covenant which is annexed to the whole *or any part or parts* of the dominant land is enforceable by a successor in title to any part of that land which is in fact benefited by the covenant. In *Marquess of Zetland v Driver*,[147] for instance:

The covenant was expressed to be for the benefit and protection of "such part or parts of the [dominant land] (a) as shall for the time being remain unsold or (b) as shall be sold by the vendor or his successors in title with the express benefit of this covenant." Certain parts of the unsold land were contiguous to the land of the covenantor, but other parts were more than a mile distant. The covenant, therefore, did not benefit the whole of the dominant land.

---

[142] *Crest Nicholson Residential (South) Ltd v Mc Allister* [2004] 1 WLR 2409 at [42], per CHADWICK LJ.
[143] But neither can enforce a positive covenant: p. 678, n. 106, ante   [144] [1937] Ch 473.
[145] (1941) 57 LQR pp. 210–11 (G. R. Y. Radcliffe).
[146] See Elphinstone, *Covenants Affecting Land*, p. 60, n. 10.   [147] [1939] Ch 1.

It was held that the person who succeeded to the dominant land could enforce the covenant against a purchaser of the servient land. The Court of Appeal, without expressing approbation of *Re Ballard's Conveyance*, distinguished it on the ground that: "in that case the covenant was expressed to run with the whole estate, whereas in the present case . . . the covenant is expressed to be for the benefit of the whole or any part or parts of the unsold settled property".[148]

Extrinsic evidence is admissible to show whether a covenant is capable of operating to the advantage of the dominant land;[149] and, as we have seen, the onus is on the defendant to show that it does not do so, either originally, or at the date of the action.[150]

(e) Annexation to part of covenantee's land

The benefit of a restrictive covenant, once it has been annexed to the dominant land, runs automatically with that land and is enforceable by the successors in title of the covenantee, even though they do not learn of its existence until after execution of the conveyance.[151] If a successor in title acquires the whole of the land, the benefit passes to him without question; but if he acquires only part he must show that the benefit was annexed to that particular part alone or to each portion of the whole.

For instance, A, the owner of a large property, sells part of it to Y and takes a covenant that no public house shall be opened on it. This covenant is annexed to A's land. Later A sells part of the dominant land to B. If B seeks to enforce the covenant by virtue of its annexation to A's land, he must prove that its benefit was annexed to each and every part of those lands or to the very part bought by him.

Whether or not there has been effective annexation to each and every part of the land is once again a question of construction of the language of the covenant. Thus in *Re Selwyn's Conveyance*[152] it was held that a covenant "to enure for the protection of the adjoining or neighbouring land part of, or lately part of, the Selwyn Estate" was annexed to each part of the dominant land.

Furthermore, even if the covenant has been annexed only to the whole of the dominant land, a purchaser of part of it will be able to enforce the covenant if the benefit of the covenant has been expressly assigned to him.[153]

Finally, we must notice that this problem of construction will disappear if the approach of the Court of Appeal in *Federated Homes Ltd v Mill Lodge Properties Ltd*[154] is subsequently

---

[148] *Marquess of Zetland v Driver*, [1939] Ch 1, at 10.

[149] *Marten v Flight Refuelling Ltd* [1962] Ch 115, M & B, p. 976; *Earl of Leicester v Wells-next-the-Sea UDC* [1973] Ch 110 (expert evidence admitted to show that a covenant restricting 19 acres afforded "great benefit and much needed protection to the Holkham Estate as a whole" i.e. to 32,000 acres). In *Re Ballard's Conveyance* [1937] Ch 473 no evidence was offered to show benefit to the dominant land as a whole.

[150] *Wrotham Park Estate Co v Parkside Homes Ltd* [1974] 1 WLR 798; p. 670, ante; *Cryer v Scott Bros (Sunbury) Ltd* (1986) 55 P & CR 183; [1988] Conv 172 (J. E. Adams).

[151] *Rogers v Hosegood* [1900] 2 Ch 388, M & B p. 957.

[152] [1967] Ch 674. Cf *Russell v Archdale* [1964] Ch 38, M & B p. 968; *Re Jeff's Transfer (No 2)* [1966] 1 WLR 841; *Stilwell v Blackman* [1968] Ch 508. See *Griffiths v Band* (1974) 29 P & CR 243 ("this somewhat muddy corner of legal history", per GOULDING J at 246); Law Commission Report on Restrictive Covenants 1967 (Law Com No. 11), p. 15 which recommends that the benefit of a land obligation should be annexed to each and every part unless a contrary intention is expressed. See too a valuable article in (1968) 84 LQR 22 (P. V. Baker).

[153] *Russell v Archdale*, supra (against the original covenantor who was still owner of the servient land); *Stilwell v Blackman*, supra (against a successor in title of the original covenantor).

[154] [1980] 1 WLR 594 at 606, 607, M & B p. 969. This would involve reconsideration of the decisions in n. 152, supra.

adopted. In that case the court found it difficult to understand how a covenant, which is annexed to the land as a whole, is not also annexed to the individual parts of that land. It favoured a rule that the benefit of such a covenant annexed to the whole is prima facie annexed to every part thereof, unless a contrary intention clearly appears.

(2) Express Assignment of Covenant

Failure to establish the annexation described above is not necessarily fatal to an assignee of the covenantee's land, for he will succeed in an action for an infringement of the restriction if he shows that he is not only an assignee of the land, but also the express assignee of the covenant itself.[155]

Such an express assignment will be necessary in fewer instances in the future, as a result of the decision in *Federated Homes Ltd v Mill Lodge Properties Ltd*,[156] in which, as we have seen, annexation was held to be effected under section 78 of the Law of Property Act 1925 without the need for appropriate language in the deed creating the covenant. Instances may, however, still arise, as for example where there is express provision to the effect that express assignment of the covenant shall be required,[157] or where there is no identification in the conveyance of the land to be benefited.[158]

As we have already seen, the benefit of a covenant may be transferred at law by assignment as a chose in action under section 136 of the Law of Property Act 1925.[159] "Where the defendant is liable at law (as the original covenantor or his personal representative) there is no difficulty peculiar to the case of covenants affecting land: such an action is governed by the ordinary rules as to the assignment of a chose in action. But where the defendant is sued as an assign of the land burdened by the covenant, the plaintiff can only establish the defendant's liability in equity under the rule in *Tulk v Moxhay*."[160]

The equitable rules under which an express assignment is permissible were crystallised by ROMER LJ in *Re Union of London and Smith's Bank Ltd's Conveyance, Miles v Easter*:[161]

(i) The covenant must have been taken for the benefit of the land of the covenantee and (ii) that land must be indicated with reasonable certainty. This indication need not appear in the conveyance creating the covenant. It is sufficient if in the light of the attendant circumstances the identity of the dominant land is in some other way ascertainable with reasonable certainty. (iii) It must also be retained in whole or part by the plaintiff and (iv) be capable of benefiting from the covenant. (v) The assignment of the covenant and the conveyance of the land to which it relates must be contemporaneous.

Whether the first two requirements were satisfied was neatly raised in *Newton Abbot Co-operative Society Ltd v Williamson and Treadgold Ltd*[162] on the following facts:

The owner of Devonia, in which she carried on the business of an ironmonger, sold a shop on the opposite side of the street to a purchaser who traded there as a grocer. The purchaser covenanted not

---

[155] *Reid v Bickerstaff* [1909] 2 Ch 305 at 320; *Re Union of London and Smith's Bank Ltd's Conveyance, Miles v Easter* [1933] Ch 611.   [156] [1980] 1 WLR 594, M & B p. 959; p. 680, ante.

[157] *Marquess of Zetland v Driver* [1937] Ch 651; *Roake v Chadha* [1984] 1 WLR 40, M & B p. 963; p. 682, ante.

[158] *Newton Abbot Co-operative Society Ltd v Williamson and Treadgold Ltd* [1952] Ch 286, infra. But see *Federated Homes Ltd v Mill Lodge Properties Ltd* [1980] 1 WLR 594 at 604, per BRIGHTMAN LJ.

[159] P. 678, ante.   [160] Preston and Newsom, *Restrictive Covenants* (4th edn), p. 30.

[161] [1933] Ch 611 at 631–2, M & B p. 971.

[162] [1952] Ch 286, M & B p. 972, approved by WILBERFORCE J in *Marten v Flight Refuelling Ltd* [1962] Ch 115 at 133. But see (1952) 68 LQR 353 (Sir Lancelot Elphinstone).

to trade as an ironmonger at the premises. The conveyance did not define any dominant land for the benefit of which the covenant was taken, but simply described the vendor as "of Devonia".

UPJOHN J held in the first place that the covenant was not a mere covenant in gross. Its objects were not only to protect the vendor personally against competition, but also to enhance the selling value of Devonia if sold to someone intending to trade there as an iron-monger. The learned judge further held that the identity of the dominant land was suffi-ciently clear. The only reasonable inference to draw from the surrounding circumstances, especially from the propinquity of the two shops, was that the covenant was taken for the benefit not only of the vendor's business, but also of the land that she retained.

Nevertheless, in order to appreciate the limits within which assignment is permissible it is essential to stress that the reason why equity allows a restrictive covenant to be enforced against third parties is that the land of the covenantee may be protected, and in particular, that its sale value shall not be diminished.[163] Such a covenant is not an independent entity having its own intrinsic value. It has no *raison d'être* apart from the land for whose protec-tion it was taken. Therefore, as we have already seen, even the covenantee himself cannot enforce the covenant against an assignee of the covenantor after he has disposed of the whole of his dominant land, for it is obvious that he no longer requires protection.[164] This theory, that the maintenance of the value of the covenantee's land is the sole justification for allowing restrictive covenants to run in favour of his successors in title, leads to this result, that the express assignment of the benefit of a covenant is ineffective unless it is contempo-raneous with the assignment of the land affected. The covenant has spent its force if the covenantee has not required its aid in disposing of the dominant land.[165]

But if he has been able to sell any particular part of his property without assigning to the purchaser the benefit of the covenant, there seems no reason why he should at a later date and as an independent transaction be at liberty to confer upon the purchaser such benefit. To hold that he could do so would be to treat the covenant as having been obtained, not only for the purpose of enabling the covenantee to dispose of his land to the best advantage, but also for the purpose of enabling him to dispose of the benefit of the covenant to the best advantage.[166]

Subject to these limitations, however, an express assignment of a covenant to a purchaser of the whole or part of the dominant land made at the time of the purchase is effective.

The benefit of a restrictive covenant is also capable of assignment by operation of law. Thus on the death of the covenantee it passes to his executors and is held by them as bare trustees for the devisee of the dominant land and becomes assignable to him.[167]

There remains to be noticed the question whether the express assignment of the benefit of a restrictive covenant annexes it to the dominant land, so that it will thereafter run automatically with that land without the necessity for any further express assignment. There are judicial dicta which support the view that an express assignment has this effect of

---

[163] *Chambers v Randall* [1923] 1 Ch 149; *Re Union of London and Smith's Bank Ltd's Conveyance, Miles v Easter* [1933] Ch 611 at 632.   [164] P. 669, ante.

[165] *Chambers v Randall*, supra; *Re Union of London and Smith's Bank Ltd's Conveyance, Miles v Easter* [1933] Ch 611; *Re Rutherford's Conveyance* [1938] Ch 396.

[166] *Re Union of London and Smith's Bank Ltd's Conveyance, Miles v Easter*, supra, at 632, per ROMER LJ.

[167] *Newton Abbot Co-operative Society Ltd v Williamson and Treadgold Ltd* [1952] Ch 286, M & B p. 972; *Earl of Leicester v Wells-next-the-Sea UDC* [1973] Ch 110 (special executors of settled land held to be bare trustees of benefit of restrictive covenant for beneficiary under SLA 1925, s. 7(1)).

annexation,[168] but recent cases are against it. The decision in *Re Pinewood Estate, Farnborough*[169] assumes without argument that a chain of assignments is necessary, and the decision in *Stilwell v Blackman*[170] is inconsistent with the dicta.

This problem disappears if the successor in title of the covenantee is able to enforce the restrictive covenant under the Contracts (Rights of Third Parties) Act 1999.[171] He then bypasses the land law requirements of annexation and assignment and enforces the covenant directly in his own right.

(3) Scheme of Development (or Building Scheme)[172]

The third case in which a restrictive covenant is enforceable by and against persons other than the original covenanting parties is when lands are held by their respective owners under a scheme of development.

(a) Nature of scheme

A scheme of development comes into existence where land is laid out in plots and sold to different purchasers or leased to different lessees, each of whom enters into a restrictive covenant with the common vendor or lessor agreeing that his particular plot shall not be used for certain purposes. In such a case these restrictive covenants are taken because the whole estate is being developed on a definite plan, and it is vital, if the value of each plot is not to be depreciated, that the purchasers or lessees should be prevented from dealing with their land so as to lower the tone of the neighbourhood. When the existence of a scheme of development has been established, the rule is that each purchaser and his assignees can sue or be sued by every other purchaser and his assignees for a breach of the restrictive covenants.[173] In such an action for breach it is immaterial whether the defendant acquired his title before or after the date on which the plaintiff purchased his plot. In other words, the restrictive covenants constitute a special local law for the area over which the scheme extends, and not only the plot-owners, but even the vendor himself, become subject to that law,[174] provided that the area[175] and the obligations to be imposed therein are defined. "They

168 *Renals v Cowlishaw* (1878) 9 Ch D 125 at 130–1; *Rogers v Hosegood* [1900] 2 Ch 388 at 408; *Reid v Bickerstaff* [1909] 2 Ch 305 at 320.

169 [1958] Ch 280. See the criticism in (1957) CLJ 146 (H. W. R. Wade). See also *Federated Homes Ltd v Mill Lodge Properties Ltd* [1980] 1 WLR 594 at 603, where John Mills QC said at first instance: "I am not satisfied or prepared to hold that there is any such thing as 'delayed annexation by assignment' to which the covenantor is not party or privy."   170 [1968] Ch 508; (1968) 84 LQR at 29–32 (P. V. Baker).

171 P. 676, ante, p. 883, n. 216, post.

172 "Scheme of development is the genus: building scheme a species": *Brunner v Greenslade* [1971] Ch 993 at 999, per MEGARRY J. For successful schemes, see *Baxter v Four Oaks Properties Ltd* [1965] Ch 816, M & B p. 984; *Re Dolphin's Conveyance* [1970] Ch 654, M & B p. 984; *Eagling v Gardner* [1970] 2 All ER 838; *Brunner v Greenslade*, supra; *Texaco Antilles Ltd v Kernochan* [1973] AC 609, M & B p. 1000; *Re 6, 8, 10 and 12 Elm Avenue, New Milton* [1984] 1 WLR 1398. Cf *Lund v Taylor* (1975) 31 P & CR 167, M & B p. 987, especially STAMP LJ at 176; *Kingsbury v L W Anderson Ltd* (1979) 40 P & CR 136; *Allen v Veranne Builders Ltd* [1988] NPC 11; *Emile Elias & Co Ltd v Pine Groves Ltd* [1993] 1 WLR 305. This is in marked contrast to the usual fate of schemes during the previous four decades: Preston and Newsom, paras. 2–74 to 2–75.

173 *Spicer v Martin* (1888) 14 App Cas 12; *Renals v Cowlishaw* (1878) 9 Ch D 125; affd (1879) 11 Ch D 866; M & B p. 959; *Hudson v Cripps* [1896] 1 Ch 265 (lease).

174 *Reid v Bickerstaff* [1909] 2 Ch 305 at 319; *Brunner v Greenslade*, supra at 1004. The scheme may expressly entitle the vendor to dispose of plots free from its restrictions: *Mayner v Payne* [1914] 2 Ch 555.

175 *Lund v Taylor*, supra, where there was no scheme because no area was defined. See also *Harlow v Hartog* (1977) 245 EG 140 (no scheme, due to no estate plan).

all have a common interest in maintaining the restriction. This community of interest necessarily requires and imports reciprocity of obligation."[176] There thus arises what SIMONDS J has called: "an equity which is created by circumstances and is independent of contractual obligation".[177]

(b) Essentials of scheme

Pre-eminent among the essentials for the creation of a scheme of development is proof of a common intention that the restrictive covenants have been taken for the mutual benefit of the respective purchasers.[178] This community of interest and intention may be evidenced by the existence of a deed of mutual covenant to which all the several purchasers are parties,[179] or it may be inferred on the construction of the conveyances of the several parts of the estate.[180] If, however, the necessary intention cannot be derived solely from the formal documents, but extrinsic evidence is also required, a scheme of development may nevertheless come into existence. In these circumstances the conditions formulated by PARKER J in *Elliston v Reacher*[181] must exist before the benefit and the burden of the restrictive covenants can pass to the various purchasers and their assignees:

(a) Both the plaintiff and the defendant to the action for breach of the restrictive covenant must have derived their titles to the land from a common vendor.

(b) Before the sale of the plots to the plaintiff and the defendant, the common vendor must have laid out his estate for sale in lots[182] subject to restrictions which it was intended to impose on all the lots, and which were consistent only with some general scheme of development.[183]

(c) The restrictions were intended by the common vendor to be and were for the benefit of all the lots sold.[184] This intention is gathered from all the circumstances of the case, but if the restrictions are obviously calculated to enhance the value of each lot,[185] the intention is readily inferred.

---

176 *Spicer v Martin* (1888) 14 App Cas 12 at 25, per Lord MACNAGHTEN.

177 *Lawrence v South County Freeholds Ltd* [1939] Ch 656 at 682.

178 *Nottingham Patent Brick and Tile Co v Butler* (1885) 15 QBD 261 at 268, per WILLS J; approved in *White v Bijou Mansions Ltd* [1938] Ch 351 at 361. See Preston and Newsom, paras. 2–53 et seq.

179 *Baxter v Four Oaks Properties Ltd* [1965] Ch 816 (where the common vendor had not laid out the estate in lots before the sale); *Price v Bouch* (1986) 53 P & CR 257 (co-operative scheme on part of fifty-three Victorian tradesmen in Northumberland).

180 *Re Dolphin's Conveyance* [1970] Ch 654 (where there was no common vendor and no lotted estate). See (1970) 114 SJ 798 (G. H. Newsom): (1970) 86 LQR 445 (P. V. Baker). For the modification of these covenants under LPA 1925, s. 84, see *Re Farmiloe's Application* (1983) 48 P & CR 317; p. 694, post.

181 [1908] 2 Ch 374 at 385, M & B p. 982; for a case in which all these conditions are considered, see *Eagling v Gardner* [1970] 2 All ER 838. For a succinct formulation, see *Briggs v McCusker* [1996] 2 EGLR 197 at 199C, per Judge Rich QC.   182 *Lawrence v South County Freeholds Ltd* [1939] Ch 656 at 674.

183 *Willé v St John* [1910] 1 Ch 84; affd [1910] 1 Ch 325.

184 "It is not necessary that the covenants entered into should benefit only the defined area: . . . The mere fact that the covenant is not expressly stated to be for the benefit of the plot holders is in no sense decisive . . . I do not think that it is inconsistent with the existence of a scheme of development that the vendor retains his right to exempt part of the [Wildernesse] Estate from stipulations": *Allen v Veranne Builders Ltd* [1988] NPC 11, per Sir Nicolas BROWNE-WILKINSON V-C. See also *Jamaica Mutual Life Assurance Society v Hillsborough Ltd* [1989] 1 WLR 1101 (no reciprocity: no building scheme).

185 "Enhancement in value . . . does not mean merely monetary enhancement, but also enhancement of the ambience in which the residents live": *Allen v Veranne Builders Ltd*, supra.

(d) The original purchasers must have bought their lots on the understanding that the restrictions were to enure for the benefit of the other lots.

(e) The geographical area to which the scheme extends must be ascertained with reasonably clear definitiveness.[186]

To a certain extent the first three conditions overlap, but the basic requirement is the existence of common regulations, obviously intended to govern the area that is to be developed. As GREENE MR explained:

The material thing I think is that every purchaser ... must know when he buys what are the regulations to which he is subjecting himself, and what are the regulations to which other purchasers on the estate will be called upon to subject themselves. Unless you know that, it is quite impossible in my judgment to draw the necessary inference, whether you refer to it as an agreement or as a community of interest importing reciprocity of obligation.[187]

In order to create a valid scheme, the purchasers of all the land within the area of the scheme must also know what that area is.[188]

The conditions in *Elliston v Reacher* are "a valuable, and perhaps complete guide to what has to be sought in the extrinsic evidence when such evidence is the foundation of the case".[189] This may include parol evidence from the common vendor[190] or his predecessor in title[191] and evidence of what was said and done before the contracts which preceded the conveyances.

The common vendor may reserve the power to waive or vary the restrictive covenants, especially in the case of land of which he has not yet disposed.[192] Furthermore the restrictions which he imposes may vary in detail.[193] But the variation was held to preclude a scheme where covenants imposed on some plots were expressed to be by way of indemnity only, and on others were all by way of absolute covenant.[194]

The subject-matter of a scheme generally consists of freehold land which is to be sold in plots to persons who desire to erect houses, but it may equally well comprise houses or a block of flats that have already been built,[195] and leaseholds as well as freeholds.[196] There may also be a sub-scheme within an area which is itself subject to a scheme of development.[197]

(c) Registration of building schemes

Finally we should notice that there is some controversy over the question whether the registration provisions of the Land Charges Act 1972 apply to restrictive covenants under

---

[186] *Osborne v Bradley* [1903] 2 Ch 446; *Reid v Bickerstaff* [1909] 2 Ch 305, M & B p. 983; *Torbay Hotel Ltd v Jenkins* [1927] 2 Ch 225; *Lund v Taylor* (1975) 31 P & CR 167. See *Jackson v Bishop* (1979) 48 P & CR 57 (developer held liable for breach of covenant of title and negligence where there was a double conveyance due to inaccurate plans of neighbouring plots).   [187] *White v Bijou Mansions* [1938] Ch 351 at 362.

[188] *Emile Elias & Co Ltd v Pine Groves Ltd* [1993] 1 WLR 305 at 310, per Lord BROWNE-WILKINSON; *Whitgift Homes Ltd v Stocks* [2001] EWCA Civ 1732, [2001] 48 EGCS 130 (no defined area within which scheme intended to operate).   [189] (1970) 114 SJ at 800 (G. H. Newsom).

[190] *Kelly v Battershell* [1949] 2 All ER 830 at 843.

[191] *Kingsbury v L W Anderson Ltd* (1979) 40 P & CR 136.

[192] *Elliston v Reacher* [1908] 2 Ch 665 at 672; *Pearce v Maryon-Wilson* [1935] Ch 188; *Re Wembley Park Estate Co Ltd's Transfer* [1968] Ch 491 at 497.

[193] *Collins v Castle* (1887) 36 Ch D 243 at 253; *Elliston v Reacher* [1908] 2 Ch 374 at 384.

[194] *Kingsbury v L W Anderson Ltd*, supra.   [195] See *Torbay Hotel Ltd v Jenkins*, supra, at 241.

[196] See *Spicer v Martin* (1888) 14 App Cas 12; *Hudson v Cripps* [1896] 1 Ch 265.

[197] See *Knight v Simmonds* [1896] 1 Ch 653; *King v Dickeson* (1889) 40 Ch D 596; *Lawrence v South County Freeholds Ltd* [1939] Ch 656; *Brunner v Greenslade* [1971] Ch 993.

schemes of development. The better view is that they do.[198] In registered land, similarly, the burden of a covenant under a scheme of development must be registered.[199] The Registrar will not, however, refer on the register to an arrangement as being a scheme of development unless its existence as such is demonstrated to him unequivocally.[200]

(4) Contracts (Rights of Third Parties) Act 1999

We have seen in connection with the running of the benefit of covenants at common law that a successor in title of the covenantee may enforce the benefit of a covenant in his own right under the Contracts (Rights of Third Parties) Act 1999.[201] Here too the Act may be applicable in cases such as *Tulk v Moxhay*, where the covenant is enforceable in equity against a successor in title of the covenantor. It will, however, still be necessary to prove the four requirements of equity; that the covenant is negative in nature, that it touches and concerns the dominant land, that the covenantee at the time of the creation of the covenant and afterwards owns land for the protection of which the covenant is made, and that the covenant is registered.[202] These are necessary requirements for the running of the burden of the covenant, and the Act does not affect the rules for the running of the burden in any way.

IV Remedies for Breach of Covenant

A *Positive Covenants*

The claim for breach of a positive covenant is generally[203] a claim to enforce an obligation at common law, and so is based on the same principles as are generally applicable for breach of contract.[204] As we have seen, the defendant is liable for breach (actual or threatened) of a positive covenant only if he is the original covenantor,[205] and only at the suit of the original covenantee or a person for whom the benefit of the obligation was initially created;[206] or an assignee from the original covenantee;[207] or a person holding a legal estate in the land to which the benefit of the covenant was annexed and therefore having the right as estate owner to enforce the covenant at law.[208] Thus, the claim for breach of a positive covenant will generally be for damages for breach of contract,[209] although an injunction may also be sought to restrain a threatened breach and, presumably, the remedy of specific performance is available to the court in an appropriate case.[210]

---

[198] (1928) 78 LJ 39 (J.M.L.); (1933) 77 SJ 550; (1950) 20 Conv (NS) 370 (R. G. Rowley); Emmet, para. 17–043; Farrand, *Contract and Conveyance* (2nd edn), pp. 420–1; Barnsley, *Conveyancing Law and Practice*, p. 388; Preston and Newsom, *Restrictive Covenants*, paras. 2-80 to 2-83, 3-25.   [199] P. 674, ante.

[200] R & R, para. 42.019.01.   [201] P. 676, ante.   [202] Pp. 668 et seq.

[203] Setting aside claims made under the devices to circumvent the rule against the passing of the burden at common law: pp. 664 et seq, ante.

[204] The defendant's action in breach of covenant may also give rise to other claims, e.g. in nuisance for building in breach of covenant so as to interfere with the claimant's reasonable enjoyment of his property: cf the discussion in relation to easements, pp. 635–6, ante.   [205] P. 663, ante.

[206] Contracts (Rights of Third Parties) Act 1999, p. 676, ante; LPA 1925, s. 56, p. 675, ante.

[207] LPA 1925, s. 136, p. 678, ante.   [208] P. 677, ante.

[209] *Smith and Snipes Hall Farm Ltd v River Douglas Catchment Board* [1949] 2 KB 500, M & B p. 951. For a discussion of the general principles for assessment of damages for breach of contract, see Treitel, pp. 926 et seq.

[210] The equitable remedies of injunction and specific performance are available for breach of contract: Treitel, pp. 1019 et seq. Damages are however the primary remedy. Specific performance is available only where (inter alia) damages cannot adequately compensate the breach, and may not often be awarded in a case of breach of covenant. For the refusal to award specific performance of a tenant's covenant in a lease, see *Co-operative*

B Restrictive Covenants

Where the defendant is the original covenantor, the claim for breach of a restrictive covenant may still be simply a claim for breach of contract. However, as we have seen, the great step forward taken by *Tulk v Moxhay*[211] was to allow the burden of a restrictive covenant to bind a successor of the covenantor where he had notice of it. This was an equitable rule, which related only to negative covenants, for breach or threatened breach of which the appropriate remedy was the equitable remedy of injunction. Although the jurisdictions of the common law courts and the courts of equity have now been fused for over a hundred and thirty years,[212] the claim today to enforce a restrictive covenant against a successor of the covenantor, in so far as it rests on the principles derived from *Tulk v Moxhay*, is still a claim in equity.[213] The primary remedy is therefore the injunction. However, by statute the court has a discretion to award damages in addition to, or in substitution for, an injunction.[214] Questions therefore arise as to when the court will award damages in substitution for an injunction; and the basis on which such damages will be calculated.

(1) Damages in Substitution for an Injunction[215]

The courts are reluctant to refuse an injunction and therefore to allow a defendant, who is bound by the covenant, to act in disregard of it. However, damages may be awarded in substitution for an injunction where the injury to the claimant's legal rights is small, capable of being estimated in money and can be adequately compensated by a small money payment, and it would be oppressive to the defendant to grant an injunction.[216] This test was applied in *Jaggard v Sawyer*[217] where

the plaintiff and defendants each owned one of a development of ten houses, served by a private road which was a cul de sac. All ten houses were subject to restrictive covenants against using their unbuilt land other than as a private garden, and positive covenants to keep the road in good repair. The defendants, in breach of covenant, but in the erroneous belief that the road was public and without appreciating the problem of the covenant, built an additional house on their own unbuilt land. The plaintiff complained to the defendants before the building work was started, but brought proceedings only once the building was at an advanced stage.

Insurance Society Ltd v Argyll Stores Ltd [1998] AC 1; p. 889, post. An injunction is more readily granted in the case of a breach or threatened breach of a negative (i.e. restrictive) covenant, but even there damages may be preferred: infra.

[211] (1848) 2 Ph 774, M & B p. 942; p. 666, ante.   [212] Supreme Court of Judicature Act 1873, s. 3.

[213] Ibid., s. 24, which preserved the equitable rights and remedies which existed before the fusion of the jurisdictions.

[214] SCA 1981, s. 50. This discretion was originally conferred on the courts of equity, before the fusion of the jurisdictions, by Chancery Amendment Act 1858, s. 2 (Lord Cairns' Act). See generally [1975] CLJ 224 (J. A. Jolowicz). On the jurisdiction of the Court of Chancery to award damages before the 1858 Act, see (1992) 108 LQR 652 (P. M. McDermott).

[215] Preston and Newsom, paras. 8–11 to 8–19; [1996] Conv 329 (J. Martin); Jones and Goodhart, *Specific Performance*, chap. 8.

[216] *Shelfer v City of London Electric Lighting Co* [1895] 1 Ch 287 at 322–3, per A. L. SMITH LJ. This is the general test for the application of the court's discretion under the statute, applicable also in relation to the tort of nuisance and the infringement of an easement: p. 636, ante.

[217] [1995] 1 WLR 269; [1995] Conv 141 (T. Ingram). Cf *Bracewell v Appleby* [1975] Ch 408 (no right of way to newly-built house: injunction similarly refused).

The trial judge, confirmed by the Court of Appeal, held that an injunction should be refused. Millett LJ said:[218]

The outcome of any particular case usually turns on the question: would it in all the circumstances be oppressive to the defendant to grant the injunction to which the plaintiff is prima facie entitled? Most of the cases in which the injunction has been refused are cases where the plaintiff has sought a mandatory injunction to pull down a building which infringes his right to light or which has been built in breach of a restrictive covenant.[219] In such cases the court is faced with a fait accompli. The jurisdiction to grant a mandatory injunction in those circumstances cannot be doubted, but to grant it would subject the defendant to a loss out of all proportion to that which would be suffered by the plaintiff if it were refused, and would indeed deliver him to the plaintiff bound hand and foot to be subjected to any extortionate demands the plaintiff might make.

(2) Measure of Damages

Damages awarded under the Supreme Court Act 1981[220] in substitution for, or in addition to, an injunction are measured on the same basis as damages at common law.[221] However, a number of cases have considered the particular difficulties of assessing damages for breach of a restrictive covenant. In *Jaggard v Sawyer*[222] the Court of Appeal reviewed the cases and approved the approach taken by Brightman J in *Wrotham Park Estate Co Ltd v Parkside Homes Ltd*.[223] Damages are calculated to compensate the claimant's injury, not to deprive the defendant of a gain he has made by his breach of covenant.[224] However, in calculating the claimant's loss, the defendant's profit can be a relevant consideration. The defendant might have avoided breaking the covenant by seeking from the claimant a relaxation of it—for which the claimant would have sought payment.

A just substitute for a mandatory injunction would be such a sum of money as might reasonably have been demanded by the plaintiff from [the defendant] as a quid pro quo for relaxing the covenant.[225]

---

[218] [1995] 1 WLR 269 at 288. The judge also held that the injury to the plaintiff's right was small, because the increase in traffic would be minimal, and there would be no significant increase in the cost of upkeep of the road, which the defendants had in any event agreed to pay; the value of the injury to the plaintiff's right could be estimated in money and compensated by a small money payment (see infra); and he was influenced by the conduct of the parties, including the plaintiff's failure to apply for interlocutory relief: ibid., at 275, 282–3. The plaintiff's failure or delay in applying for an interim injunction is relevant but not conclusive: *Mortimer v Bailey* [2005] 2 P & CR 9; (2004) 154 NLJ 1896 (M. Pawlowski); [2005] Conv 460 (G. Watt); distinguishing *Gafford v Graham* (1998) 77 P & CR 73.

[219] See also *Wrotham Park Estate Co Ltd v Parkside Homes Ltd* [1974] 1 WLR 798 at 811, per Brightman J: "I cannot close my eyes to the fact that the houses now exist. It would, in my opinion, be an unpardonable waste of much needed houses to direct that they now be pulled down and I have never had a moment's doubt during the hearing of this case that such an order ought to be refused."

[220] To be known as the Senior Courts Act 1981: Constitutional Reform Act 2005, Sch. 11, para. 1.

[221] *Johnson v Agnew* [1980] AC 367 at 400, per Lord Wilberforce.　　　[222] [1995] 1 WLR 269.

[223] [1974] 1 WLR 798.

[224] In recent years the courts have begun to accept that damages for breach of contract can be calculated so as to deprive the defendant of a profit, rather than to compensate the claimant for a loss: *A-G v Blake* [2001] 1 AC 268. However, such a measure is appropriate only in exceptional circumstances: ibid., at 285, per Lord Nicholls of Birkenhead; *Experience Hendrix LLC v PPX Enterprises Inc* [2003] 1 All ER (Comm) 830 (where CA applied the *Wrotham Park* measure).

[225] *Wrotham Park Estate Co Ltd v Parkside Homes Ltd* [1974] 1 WLR 798 at 815, per Brightman J.

And in calculating this sum, the amount which the defendant might have expected to make by way of profit would be relevant, because it would have been part of the (hypothetical) bargaining which would have been entered into between the parties—the bargain of which the claimant has been deprived.[226]

V Discharge and Modification of Restrictive Covenants[227]

A Position at Common Law

(1) Express or Implied Release

A covenantee (including his assignees) is deprived of his right to enforce the covenant if he has expressly released it; or if he has submitted to a long course of usage wholly inconsistent with its continuance, as where he remains inactive for a considerable time while open breaches of the covenant are taking place;[228] or if he disregards breaches in such a way as to justify a reasonable person in believing that future breaches will be disregarded.[229]

(2) Unity of Seisin

A restrictive covenant will be discharged when a person becomes entitled in the same capacity[230] to both the dominant and servient lands to which it relates.[231] This is similar to the extinguishment of an easement by the unity of ownership and possession.[232] In *Texaco*

---

[226] In *Wrotham Park* the plaintiff was awarded £2,500, being 5% of the defendant's anticipated profits, on the basis that this would have been a fair price to have agreed for the release of the covenant. In *Jaggard v Sawyer* [1995] 1 WLR 269 the plaintiff was awarded her proportionate share (as one of nine beneficiaries of the defendants' covenant) of the price (£6,250) that the judge held the defendants should have been prepared to pay for release of the covenant. See also *Gafford v Graham* (1998) 77 P & CR 73 at 86–7; *Amec Developments Ltd v Jury's Hotel Management Ltd* [2001] 1 EGLR 81; *Lane v O'Brien Homes* [2004] EWHC 303 (collateral contract; date of assessment is time at which defendants would have sought to be released from their contractual commitment). For a different approach, see *Surrey County Council v Bredero Homes Ltd* [1993] 1 WLR 1361; [1994] Conv 110 (T. Ingram) (nominal damages; disapproved in so far as it may be inconsistent with *Wrotham Park* in *A-G v Blake* [2001] 1 AC 268 at 283). See generally Treitel, pp. 928–30.

[227] See generally Preston and Newsom, *Restrictive Covenants*, chaps. 10–16; Scamell, chaps. 11–21; (1986) 49 MLR 195 (P. Polden).

[228] *Gibson v Doeg* (1857) 2 H & N 615; *Hepworth v Pickles* [1900] 1 Ch 108; *Re Summerson* [1900] 1 Ch 112n; discussed in *Lloyds Bank Ltd v Jones* [1955] 2 QB 298 at 320–2. See also *Shaw v Applegate* [1977] 1 WLR 970 (where an injunction was refused against original covenantor on grounds of acquiescence, but damages were awarded); *A-G of Hong Kong v Fairfax Ltd* [1997] 1 WLR 149 (covenant in 999-year Crown lease held to be abandoned); *Gafford v Graham*, supra.

[229] *Chatsworth Estates Co v Fewell* [1931] 1 Ch 224, M & B p. 998. This is "in many ways analogous to the doctrine of estoppel": per FARWELL J at 231.

[230] *University of East London Higher Education Corpn v Barking and Dagenham London Borough Council* [2005] Ch 354 at [57]–[60] (local authority holding dominant and servient land for different statutory purposes: covenant not extinguished, on analogy of trustee holding on different trusts).

[231] *Re Tiltwood, Sussex* [1978] Ch 269; (1980) 54 ALJ 156 (G. M. Bates); (1982) 56 ALJ 587 (A. A. Preece); *Re Victoria Recreation Ground, Portslade's Application* (1979) 41 P & CR 119.   [232] P. 640, ante.

Antilles Ltd v Kernochan,[233] however, the Privy Council held that, if there is a scheme of development, unity of seisin does not automatically discharge a covenant within the area of unity, and that on severance it revives, unless there is evidence from the circumstances surrounding the severance that the parties intended that it should not do so.

(3) Change in Circumstances relating to Covenant or in Character of Neighbourhood

A covenant may be so drafted that it ceases to apply in changed circumstances.[234] Furthermore, it will no longer be enforceable if the character of the neighbourhood in which the protected property lies is so entirely altered that it would be inequitable and senseless to insist upon the rigorous observance of a covenant that is no longer of any value.[235]

B Section 84 of the Law of Property Act 1925

(1) Power to Discharge or Modify Covenants

Section 84 of the Law of Property Act 1925[236] develops this last ground of extinction, and sets up a new method whereby restrictions may be discharged or modified.[237]

The first point to notice is that the Act mainly applies to restrictions imposed on freehold estates. It has no application to leaseholds which are subject to restrictive covenants, except

---

233   [1973] AC 609, M & B p. 1000; *Brunner v Greenslade* [1971] Ch 993.

234   *Dano Ltd v Earl Cadogan* [2004] 1 P & CR 13 (covenant for benefit of "the Cadogan Settled Estate in Chelsea" no longer binding after the Estate ceased to exist on settlement being brought to an end in 1961. However, ETHERTON J had held at first instance that restriction of use of property to the "housing of the working classes" would still be enforceable: "There is no difficulty in conferring on the restrictive covenant today a similar meaning, namely the use of the property for the housing of those who, by virtue of their low incomes, might find it difficult to purchase or rent suitable and appropriate accommodation in the private sector": [2003] 2 P & CR 10 at [99]); *Crest Nicholson Residential (South) Ltd v McAllister* [2004] 1 WLR 2409 at [36]. See also the decision at first instance in *Crest Nicholson* [2003] 1 All ER 46, where NEUBERGER J held that a covenant which imposed a restriction unless the covenantee's approval was obtained was discharged by the dissolution of the covenantor.

235   *Chatsworth Estates Co v Fewell* [1931] 1 Ch 224; *Robins v Berkeley Homes Ltd* [1996] EGCS 75 (heavy burden of proof to show change); see generally, Behan, *Covenants Affecting Land*, pp. 148 et seq; Elphinstone, *Covenants Affecting Land*, pp. 110 et seq; *Westripp v Baldock* [1938] 2 All ER 779; affd [1939] 1 All ER 279; (1966) 5 Melbourne University Law Review, pp. 209–14 (D. Mendes da Costa).

236   As amended by LPA 1969, s. 28. See Law Commission Report on Restrictive Covenants 1967 (Law Com No. 11), pp. 21–6. Applications made under the section are noted in Current Law and in the Journal of Planning and Environment Law. Some are recorded in P & CR, EGLR and the EG. Condensed reports of all applications from 1974–79 appeared in Lands Tribunal Cases, and decisions since 2000 can be found on the Lands Tribunal web site: www.landstribunal.gov.uk.

237   S. 84(1); see *Richardson v Jackson* [1954] 1 WLR 447; *Re University of Westminster* [1998] 3 All ER 1014 (ultimate discretion of tribunal); *Re Lee's Application* (1996) 72 P & CR 439 (greater presumption that restriction under building scheme will be upheld; and greater burden of proof on applicant); *Re Kentwood Properties Ltd's Application* [1987] JPL 137 (discretion to modify not exercised where there had been a flagrant, cynical and continuing breach of the covenant). For an unsuccessful application to the European Commission of Human Rights (No. 1074/84) on the ground that the Northern Ireland equivalent of s. 84 violated the ECHR, see [1986] Conv 124 (N. Dawson). As to whether s. 84 is compatible with the Human Rights Act 1998, see Rook, *Property Law and Human Rights*, pp. 208–11.

where the lease was originally made for more than forty years, and twenty-five years of this term have expired when the question of extinction arises.[238]

It is then provided that any person interested in any such freehold or leasehold land[239] affected by the restrictive covenant,[240] may apply to the Lands Tribunal to have the restriction either wholly or partially discharged, or modified.[241]

In making an order discharging or modifying a restriction the Tribunal may direct the applicant to pay to any person entitled to the benefit of the restriction such sum by way of consideration[242] as it may think it just to award.[243] This must fall under one of the following heads:

(i) a sum to make up for any loss or disadvantage suffered by that person in consequence of the discharge or modification;[244]

(ii) a sum to make up for any effect which the restriction had, at the time when it was imposed, in reducing the consideration then received for the land affected by it.[245]

Before making any order the Tribunal must be satisfied:

(a) that by reason of changes in the character of the property or the neighbourhood[246] or other circumstances of the case[247] which the Lands Tribunal may deem material, the restriction ought to be deemed obsolete; or

---

[238] S. 84(12), as amended by Landlord and Tenant Act 1954, s. 52. The twenty-five years is reckoned from the date of the lease, and not from any earlier date at which the term is expressed in the lease to begin: *Earl of Cadogan v Guinness* [1936] Ch 515.

[239] The tribunal should be more reluctant to interfere with leasehold than freehold covenants: *Ridley v Taylor* [1965] 1 WLR 611, M & B p. 1004.

[240] It may be personal only: *Shepherd Homes Ltd v Sandham (No 2)* [1971] 1 WLR 1062; *Gilbert v Spoor* [1983] Ch 27. It must be restrictive, not positive: *Blumenthal v Church Commissioners for England* [2005] 1 EGLR 78.

[241] Lands Tribunal Rules 1996 (SI 1996 No. 1002); Lands Tribunal (Fees) Rules 1996 (SI 1996 No. 1021); Lands Tribunal (Amendment) Rules 1997 (SI 1997 No. 1965); Lands Tribunal (Fees) Amendment Rules 2002 (SI 2002 No. 770); Lands Tribunal (Amendment) Rules 2003 (SI 2003 No. 2945); Scamell, chap. 21. Where proceedings are taken to enforce a restrictive covenant the defendant may apply to the court to stay the proceedings to allow an application to be made to the Lands Tribunal: s. 84(9); *Luckies v Simons* [2003] 2 P & CR 30 (court should normally order stay). See also the Practice Direction by the President of the Lands Tribunal on Procedural Guidance [2005] RVR 9; *R (Sinclair Gardens Investments (Kensington) Ltd) v Lands Tribunal* [2006] 06 EG 172 (judicial review of decision of Lands Tribunal refused).

On the Lands Tribunal generally, see Jones, *The Lands Tribunal*, and the Lands Tribunal web site, n. 236 supra. Lands Tribunal Practice Directions 2005 can be viewed on the web site.

[242] See *SJC Construction Co Ltd v Sutton London Borough Council* (1975) 29 P & CR 322, where STEPHENSON LJ said, in argument, that "consideration" was probably a misprint for "compensation": Preston and Newsom, para. 13-02.

[243] LPA 1925, s. 84(1), as amended by LPA 1969, s. 28(3). See generally [1976] JPL 18 (W. A. Leach).

[244] *SJC Construction Co Ltd v Sutton London Borough Council*, supra ("there is no method prescribed by the Act by which it is to be assessed; it is essentially a question of quantum", per Lord DENNING MR at 326). The basis of an award by the Lands Tribunal is not the same as an award of damages by the court for breach of covenant, p. 692, ante; *Stockport Metropolitan Borough Council v Alwiyah Developments* (1983) 52 P & CR 278 (loss of bargaining power not a benefit); [2005] 35 EG 107 (H. Williamson)

[245] *Re Davies' Application* [2001] 1 EGLR 111 (reduction in consideration, increased for inflation).

[246] *Keith v Texaco Ltd* (1977) 34 P & CR 249 (coming of oil industry to Aberdeenshire); *Re Bradley Clare Estates Ltd's Application* (1987) 55 P & CR 126; *Re Quaffers Ltd's Application* (1988) 56 P & CR 142 (advent of motorway network); *Re North's Application* (1997) 75 P & CR 117 (change in neighbourhood not material; house in Winkfield, Berkshire, retained attractive semi-rural character despite infilling).

[247] *Re Cox's Application* (1985) 51 P & CR 335 (covenant requiring occupiers of extension of house in East Sussex to be domestic staff employed for service in the house held obsolete); cf *Re Beechwood Homes Ltd's*

(aa) that the continued existence thereof would impede some reasonable user of the land for public or private purposes or, as the case may be, would unless modified so impede such user.[248]

Under this paragraph the Lands Tribunal must be satisfied that the restriction, in impeding the user, either:

(i) does not secure to persons entitled to the benefit of it any practical benefits of substantial value or advantage to them; or

(ii) is contrary to the public interest;

and that money will be an adequate compensation for the loss or disadvantage (if any) which any such person will suffer from the discharge or modification.[249]

(b) that the persons of full age and capacity for the time being or from time to time entitled to the benefit of the restriction, whether in respect of estates in fee simple or any lesser estates or interests in the property to which the benefit of the restriction is annexed, have agreed, either expressly or by implication,[250] by their acts or omissions, to the same being discharged or modified; or

(c) that the proposed discharge or modification will not injure the persons entitled to the benefit of the restriction.[251]

The Lands Tribunal may, however, add further restrictive provisions if it appears to it to be reasonable to do so.[252] This cannot be done unless the applicant accepts them, but, if he does not, the application may be refused.

(2) Changes Made to Section 84 by Law of Property Act 1969

The substantive change made by the Law of Property Act 1969 was to widen the scope of section 84 of the Law of Property Act 1925, and, in particular, to redraft paragraph (1)(aa),

Application [1994] 2 EGLR 178 (covenant to prevent cul-de-sac development, involving lopping of trees held not obsolete); *Re Kalsi's Application* (1993) 66 P & CR 313; *Re Wards Construction (Medway) Ltd's Application* (1994) 67 P & CR 379 (green field area now an infill site); *Re Kennet Properties' Application* [1996] 1 EGLR 163 (original purpose of unimpeded views across each neighbour's land no longer possible due to housing development); *Re Nichols' Application* [1997] 1 EGLR 144; *Re Marcello Developments Ltd's Application* [2002] RVR 146 (frontage and building line restrictions obsolete); *Re Davies' Application* [2001] 1 EGLR 111; *Re Broomhead's Application* [2003] 2 EGLR 157 (purpose of covenant to control development and extract premium on release held not to be obsolete).

[248] See *Stannard v Issa* [1987] AC 175, where PC construed a similar but not identical paragraph under the Restrictive Covenants (Discharge and Modification) Act (No. 2 of 1960) of Jamaica, s. 3(1).

[249] LPA 1925, s. 84(1A). For the formulation of the questions to be answered by the Lands Tribunal, see *Re Bass Ltd's Application* (1973) 26 P & CR 156.

[250] See *Re Memvale Securities Ltd's Application* (1974) 233 EG 689; *Re Fettishaw's Application (No 2)* (1973) 27 P & CR 292.

[251] *Re Forestmere Properties Ltd's Application* (1980) 41 P & CR 390 ("replacement of one eyesore (Odeon cinema) by another could hardly be said to be an improvement"); *Re Bailey's Application* (1981) 42 P & CR 108 ("quaint rural backwater" not to be changed into riding school with attendant manure and noise including sound of human voice); *Re Livingstones' Application* (1982) 47 P & CR 462 ("eyesore" carport); *Re Severn Trent Water Ltd's Application* (1993) 67 P & CR 236 (site for sewage disposal works to become leisure centre).

[252] *Re Patten Ltd's Application* (1975) 31 P & CR 180; *Re Dransfield's Application* (1975) 31 P & CR 192; *Re Kershaw's Application* (1975) 31 P & CR 187; *Re Banks Application* (1976) 33 P & CR 138; *Re Forestmere Properties Ltd's Application* (1980) 41 P & CR 390; *Re Austin's Application* (1980) 42 P & CR 102; *Re Shah and Shah's Application* (1991) 62 P & CR 450; *Re University of Westminster's Application* [1997] 1 EGLR 191 ("it is a matter of discretion to limit or cut down the form of relief sought").

so as to enable the Lands Tribunal "to take a broader view of whether the use of land is being unreasonably impeded; and to make clear provision for an award of monetary compensation where the Tribunal thinks that the injury which an objector would suffer by a modification or discharge can be properly compensated in that way".[253] As CARNWATH LJ has said:[254]

The general purpose is to facilitate the development and use of land in the public interest, having regard to the development plan and the pattern of permissions in the area. The section seeks to provide a fair balance between the needs of development in the area, public and private, and the protection of private contractual rights. "Reasonable user" in this context seems to me to refer naturally to a long term use of land, rather than the process of transition to such a use. The primary consideration, therefore, is the value of the covenant in providing protection from the effects of the ultimate use, rather than from the short-term disturbance which is inherent in any ordinary construction project. There may, however, be something in the form of the particular covenant, or in the facts of the particular case, which justifies giving special weight to this factor.

To enable it to take this broader view the Tribunal must take into account the development plan and any declared or ascertainable pattern for the grant or refusal of planning permissions in the relevant areas, as well as the period at which and context in which the restriction was created or imposed and any other material circumstances.[255]

The statutory provisions apply to restrictive covenants entered into either before or after the commencement of the Act, but do not apply where the restriction was imposed on the occasion of a disposition made gratuitously, or for a nominal consideration, for public purposes.[256] Any person aggrieved by the decision of the Tribunal on the ground that it is erroneous in point of law may appeal to the Court of Appeal.[257]

(a) Public interest

Since 1969 the new paragraph (1)(aa) and the power to award compensation have resulted in an increased number of cases before the Lands Tribunal.[258] Several important criteria have been established for deciding whether a covenant should be modified or discharged. In particular, where the applicant has obtained planning permission for the proposed user, the effect is very persuasive in considering whether that user is reasonable.[259] The proposition that impeding that user is contrary to the public interest may also be aided by a planning permission, but in rather a different way. The question is not whether

---

[253] Law Commission Report on Restrictive Covenants 1967 (Law Com No. 11), p. 23.

[254] *Shephard v Turner* [2006] All ER (D) 144 (Jan) at [58].

[255] LPA 1925, s. 84(1B). See *Re Collins' Application* (1974) 30 P & CR 527.   [256] LPA 1925, s. 84(7).

[257] Lands Tribunal Act 1949, s. 3(4) proviso, as amended by SI 2000 No. 941.

[258] See generally Preston and Newsom, *Restrictive Covenants*, chaps. 10–16; [1974] JPL 72, 130; [1975] JPL 644; [1976] JPL 407; [1979] JPL 64; [1981] JPL 551, 656; [1982] JPL 552; [1984] JPL 847 (G. H. Newsom); and for a useful summary of the cases (1979) 129 NLJ 523; (2000) 150 NLJ 1525, 1623 (H. W. Wilkinson); M & B pp. 1005–12.

[259] *Re Beecham Group Ltd's Application* (1980) 41 P & CR 369 (refusal to differ from very "closely reasoned decision" of Secretary of State granting planning permission on appeal from inspector); *Gilbert v Spoor* [1983] Ch 27 ("the subsection does not make planning decisions decisive", per EVELEIGH LJ at 34); *Re Martin's Application* (1988) 57 P & CR 119, M & B p. 1012; *Re Kennet Properties' Application* [1996] 1 EGLR 163 (development plan); *Re Hextall's Application* (2000) 79 P & CR 382 (planning permission strongly persuasive); *Re Diggens' Application (No 2)* [2001] 2 EGLR 163 (planning permission, but application to modify covenant refused).

the proposed user is in the public interest, but whether impeding the proposed user is contrary to it. "There is here more than a narrow nuance of difference: a planning permission only says, in effect, that a proposal will be allowed; it implies that such a proposal will not be a bad thing, but it does not necessarily imply that it will be positively a good thing."[260]

Consistently with this restrictive approach, the President of the Lands Tribunal said in 1975:[261]

For an application to succeed on the ground of public interest it must be shown that that interest is so important and immediate as to justify the serious interference with private rights and the sanctity of contract.

An acute shortage of building land in a particular locality does not establish that any restriction which prevents development of land is ipso facto contrary to the public interest;[262] nor does a housing need in the area.[263] In only two situations so far has an application succeeded on the ground of public interest. The first was where there was a scarcity of land available for building development, and, if the restriction were not modified, building work costing £47,000 would have to be demolished. That was to be avoided in "the present economic circumstances of the country".[264] The second was where modification did not involve the demolition of a building.[265] A covenant not to carry on any trade or business in a large house in Worthing was modified to permit use as a community care home for ten psychiatric patients who had been assessed as ready to live independently in the community. The restriction was contrary to the public interest, because government policy was for mental patients to be rehabilitated in the community, and there was a desperate need for such a facility in the area. The restriction did not confer any substantial benefit or advantage because there was already a home for forty-one old people which had been built next door in breach of covenant; and planning permission had already been granted.

---

[260] *Re Bass Ltd's Application* (1973) 26 P & CR 156 at 157.

[261] *Re Collins' Applications* (1974) 30 P & CR 527 per Douglas Frank QC. See also *Re Mansfield District Council's Application* (1976) 33 P & CR 141 at 143; *Re Brierfield's Application* (1976) 35 P & CR 124; *Re Solarfilms (Sales) Ltd's Application* (1993) 67 P & CR 110.

[262] *Re Beardsley's Application* (1972) 25 P & CR 233; *Re Gardner's Application* [1974] JPL 728.

[263] *Re New Ideal Homes Ltd's Application* (1978) 36 P & CR 476 (where, however, the covenant was modified on payment by consent of £51,000 compensation because it did not secure practical benefits of substantial value to objecting local authority); *Re Osborn's and Easton's Application* (1978) 38 P & CR 251; *Re Beech's Application* (1990) 59 P & CR 502 (residential enclave in predominantly commercial setting). See also *Re London Borough of Islington's Application* [1986] JPL 214 (covenant forbidding use of land in Islington "except for open space", purchased from Greater London Council who remitted half of the purchase price, discharged on repayment of that half with adjustments for inflation).

[264] *Re SJC Construction Co Ltd's Application* (1974) 28 P & CR 200; affd. by CA on method of assessing compensation sub nom. *SJC Construction Co Ltd v Sutton London Borough Council* (1975) 29 P & CR 322; *Re Fisher & Gimson (Builders) Ltd's Application* (1992) 65 P & CR 312 (risk of demolition of important housing accommodation against public interest; £6,000 compensation); *Re Bradley Clare Estates Ltd's Application* (1987) 55 P & CR 126. Cf *Re O'Reilly's Application* (1993) 66 P & CR 485; *Re Hounslow and Ealing London Borough Council's Application* (1995) 71 P & CR 100 (part of ground floor of mansion to be used as horticultural training centre); *Re Bromor Properties Ltd's Application* (1995) 70 P & CR 569; *Re Milius's Application* (1995) 70 P & CR 427 (restriction adopted by local authority pursuant to lawful policy approved by Parliament held not contrary to public interest).   [265] *Re Lloyd's and Lloyd's Application* (1993) 66 P & CR 112.

(b) Practical benefits of substantial value or advantage

Further, in considering whether the restriction secures to the persons entitled to the benefit of the covenant practical benefits of substantial[266] value or advantage,[267] the Lands Tribunal has observed that the words "value or advantage" are not intended to be assessed in terms of pecuniary value only.[268] It takes account of any matters however unusual or personal they may be.[269]

[266] On the meaning of substantial, see *Re Gaffney's Application* (1974) 35 P & CR 440; *Re Dransfield's Application* (1975) 31 P & CR 192; *Re Jillas' Application* [2000] 2 EGLR 99 (covenant modified to allow for extension of house: reduction in value of adjoining house of £10,000, about 1.5% of its value, was not substantial, so compensation ordered); (2000) 150 NLJ 1523 (H. W. Wilkinson).

[267] *Re John Twiname Ltd's Application* (1971) 23 P & CR 413 at 417–18; *Re Wards Construction (Medway) Ltd's Application* (1973) 25 P & CR 223 at 231 ("even ordinary people not infrequently value space and quiet and light"); *Re Gossip's Application* (1972) 25 P & CR 215 at 220 ("houses built on the application land would overlook the garden and the principal rooms, albeit somewhat screened by a hawthorn, a poor substitute for a covenant"); *Re Ballamy's Application* [1977] JPL 456 (enjoyment of evening sunshine in the sun-lounge); *Re Banks Application* (1976) 33 P & CR 138 ("direct view of the sea is of immense value"); *Re Bovis Homes Southern Ltd's Application* [1981] JPL 368 (beauty and aesthetic and historic interest of National Trust house and its setting); *Gilbert v Spoor* [1983] Ch 27 (magnificent view over Tyne Valley from road *adjacent* to objector's land); [1984] Conv 429 (P. Polden); *Re Burr's Application* [1987] JPL 137 (amenities of a high class development); *Stannard v Issa* [1987] AC 175 ("the privacy and quietude of an enclave of single dwellings in large gardens is going to be adversely affected by the introduction on adjoining lands of no less than 40 additional families", per Lord OLIVER OF AYLMERTON at 196); cf *Stockport Metropolitan Borough Council v Alwiyah Developments* (1983) 52 P & CR 278 (loss of bargaining power not a benefit); *Re Bennett's and Tamarlin Ltd's Applications* (1987) 54 P & CR 378 (loss of ability to extract money for agreeing to modification of restriction not a benefit); *Re Bushell's Application* (1987) 54 P & CR 386 (particularly fine landscape view at Wimbledon "very unusual so near the centre of London"); *Re Purnell's Application* (1987) 55 P & CR 133 (large garden providing privacy in Orpington, Kent). See also *Re Crest Homes plc's Application* (1983) 48 P & CR 309 (proposal to build twelve houses to replace neglected Edgware Lawn Tennis Club would cause undesirable increase in housing density and change area from semi-rural to urban); *Re Lake's Application* [1984] JPL 887 (proposal to erect split-level house in Lyme Regis would be design out of character with surroundings); *Re Williams' Application* (1987) 55 P & CR 400 (sense of spaciousness; preventing nuisance of building works); *Re Whiting's Application* (1988) 58 P & CR 321 (natural beauty of Howley, Gloucestershire); *Re Tarhale Ltd's Application* (1990) 60 P & CR 368 (preventing intolerable nuisance during construction work); *Re Sheehy's Application* (1991) 63 P & CR 95 (moral obligation undertaken by the St Aubyn Discretionary Trustees to maintain a scheme of covenants within the Devonport Estate, where cost of administration exceeded total rental income, held to be of practical benefit); *Re Beechwood Homes Ltd's Application* [1994] EGCS 57. See also *Re Edwards' Application* (1983) 47 P & CR 458 (restriction modified to enable house in Mold, North Wales, to be used as a general village store, for "groceries, sweets, tobacco, cigarettes, cigars, soft drinks, ice cream, newspapers, trinkets, haberdashery, gardening utensils and supplies, tools, nuts and bolts" subject to payment of £500 as compensation to objector for loss of amenity); *Re Shah and Shah's Application* (1991) 62 P & CR 450 (restriction impeding nursing home user so small as to warrant monetary compensation only of £23,000); *Re Hopcraft's Application* (1993) 66 P & CR 475 (pleasant open area to remain open); *Re Kalsi Application* (1993) 66 P & CR 313; *Re Hydeshire Ltds Application* (1993) 67 P & CR 93 (right to build within set limit, provided no one else had done so, not a practical benefit); *Re Cornick's Application* (1994) 68 P & CR 372 (jam factory); *Re Azfar's Application* [2002] 1 P & CR 215 (adverse impact from traffic, parking, access to neighbouring properties and unsightliness of large extension).

[268] *Re Bass Ltd's Application* (1973) 26 P & CR 156; *Re Diggens' Application (No 2)* [2001] 2 EGLR 163 (practical benefits secured by density restriction were preservation of view, privacy, seclusion and sense of spaciousness and tranquillity in semi-rural atmosphere). Loss of bargaining power is not a proper head of compensation: *Stockport Metropolitan Borough Council v Alwiyah Developments* (1983) 52 P & CR 278; *Re Bennett's and Tamarlin Ltd's Application* (1987) 54 P & CR 378 (loss of ability to extract money for agreeing to modification of restriction not a benefit); cf *Re Quaffers Ltd's Application* (1988) 56 P & CR 142 (loss of competition advantage).

[269] *Re Matcham's Application* [1981] JPL 431 (house built on tranquil site because of wife's severe migraine).

(c) Thin end of the wedge

In *McMorris v Brown* Lord COOKE OF THORNDON explained the argument of the thin end of the wedge:[270]

A familiar and at times legitimate argument in this branch of the law is known as the thin end of the wedge argument. Other expressions are sometimes coupled with it, such as "the first is the worst." . . . [Decisions in Jamaica] have accepted that cases may arise in which it is very difficult to say that the particular thing which the applicant wishes to do will of itself cause anyone any harm; but that harm may still come to the persons entitled to the benefit of the restriction if it were to become generally allowable to do similar things. Or such harm may flow from the very existence of the order making the modification through the implication that the restriction is vulnerable to the action of the Lands Tribunal in England or the Supreme Court in Jamaica . . .

Their Lordships find more recent decisions of the Lands Tribunal in England in the same line of cases collected in *Maudsley and Burn's Land Law: Cases and Materials* (7th edn, 1998), p. 926.[271]

(3) Registered Land

Where title to the servient estate is registered, any release, discharge or modification of a restrictive covenant should be noted on the register, either by the cancellation of the original notice and the entry of a fresh notice, or by a supplementary notice.[272]

(4) Declaration Whether Restriction Binding

In order to meet the case where it may be doubtful whether an effectual restrictive covenant has been imposed on land and if so what persons it now affects, the Act confers jurisdiction upon the court:[273]

(a) to declare whether or not in any particular case any freehold land is, or would in any given event be, affected by a restriction imposed by any instrument; or

(b) to declare what, upon the true construction of any instrument purporting to impose a restriction, is the nature and extent of the restriction thereby imposed and whether the same is, or would in any given event be, enforceable and if so by whom.

C Housing Act 1985

If it is proved that a house cannot readily be let as a single tenement but can readily be let if converted into two or more tenements, the Housing Act 1985 empowers the county court to

---

270 [1999] 1 AC 142 at 151.

271 See now 8th edn 2004, p. 1008. See also *Re Chapman's Application* (1980) 42 P & CR 114; *Re Farmiloe's Application* (1983) 48 P & CR 317; *Re Love's and Love's Application* (1993) 67 P & CR 101; *Re Solarfilms (Sales) Ltd's Application* (1993) 67 P & CR 110; *Re Page's Application* (1995) 71 P & CR 440; *Re Snaith and Dolding's Application* (1995) 71 P & CR 104 ("erection of this house could materially alter the context in which further applications would be considered"); *Re Churchill's Application* (1994) LP/45/94; *Re Hunt's Application* (1996) 73 P & CR 126.

272 R & R, para. 42.019.02. If the original notice was unilateral, no proof of the release, modification or discharge is required: LRA 2002, s. 35(3); but if it was an agreed notice, the Registrar must be satisfied about it: LRR 2003, r. 87(2).

273 LPA 1925, s. 84(2), as amended by LPA 1969, s. 28(4); *Re Sunnyfield* [1932] 1 Ch 79; *Re Freeman-Thomas Indenture* [1957] 1 All ER 532; *In The Girl's Day School Trust (1872) Application* [2002] 2 EGLR 89 (application by objectors; tribunal could have determined the matters itself, but had no discretion to refuse to suspend proceedings under Lands Tribunal Rules 1996 (SI 1996 No. 1002), r. 16; costs awarded against objectors whose motives were to delay development of property); *Re MCA East Ltd* [2003] 1 P & CR 9 (application by developer).

vary any provisions in a lease or any restrictive covenant affecting the lease if these impede the proposed conversion.[274] Such a variation is not permissible unless the converted tenements will be wholly contained within one house.[275]

D Town and Country Planning Act 1990

Under section 106, a local planning authority has power to regulate land use by agreement.[276] It may enter into an agreement with any person interested in land in their area for the purpose of restricting or regulating the development or use of land, either permanently or during such period as may be prescribed by the agreement. Where such an agreement has been made, the authority is said to hold the benefit of the covenant as custodian of the public interest.[277] Such an agreement may be modified or discharged under the Law of Property Act 1925, section 84.[278] Section 106 will be replaced by the new scheme of "planning contribution" under section 46 of the Planning and Compulsory Purchase Act 2004, when it is brought into force.[279]

Under section 237, a local planning authority is authorised, subject to the payment of compensation, to carry out a scheme of development, notwithstanding that it interferes with an easement or infringes a restrictive covenant.[280]

VI Law Reform

A Land Obligations

The Law Commission is currently examining easements, covenants and similar land law rights with a view to their reform and rationalisation. The aim is to produce a more coherent

---

[274] S. 610(1), (2), replacing Housing Act 1957, s. 165. See Preston and Newsom, *Restrictive Covenants*, para. 10–20.   [275] *Josephine Trust Ltd v Champagne* [1963] 2 QB 160.

[276] Replacing TCPA 1971, s. 52. Such an agreement is within LP(MP)A 1989, s. 2; p. 868, post. *Jelson Ltd v Derby City Council* [1999] 3 EGLR 91; [1999] Conv 379 (J.E.A.). See Current Law Statutes TCPA 1990, s. 106, annotated by M. Grant, paras. 8-299 to 8-302. As to the Contracts (Rights of Third Parties) Act 1999 in this context, see p. 1023, n. 75, post.

[277] *Re Abbey Homesteads (Developments) Ltd's Application* [1986] 1 EGLR 24; *Re Martin's Application* (1988) 57 P & CR 119, especially at 125, M & B p. 905, per Fox LJ; *Re Houdret & Co Ltd's Application* (1989) 58 P & CR 310; *Re Jones' and White & Co's Application* (1989) 58 P & CR 512; *Re Quartley's Application* (1989) 58 P & CR 518; *Re Beech's Application* (1990) 59 P & CR 502; [1990] Conv 455 (N. D. M. Parry); *Re Wallace & Co's Application* (1993) 66 P & CR 124; *Re Hopcraft's Application* (1993) 66 P & CR 475 (storage of touring caravans refused); *Re Bromor Properties Ltd's Application* (1995) 70 P & CR 569.

[278] For successful modifications, see *Re Cox's Application* (1985) 51 P & CR 335; *Re Towner's and Goddard's Application* (1989) 58 P & CR 316 (tennis-court with chain link fencing); *Re Barclays Bank plc's Application* (1990) 60 P & CR 354 (discharge in favour of mortgagee); *Re Poulton's Application* (1992) 65 P & CR 319 (extension of bungalow in Metropolitan Green Belt). *Re O'Reilly's Application* (1993) 66 P & CR 485 (use for car parking only modified to allow erection of six houses on payment of £11,000 compensation); *Re Williamson's Application* (1994) 68 P & CR 384 (granny annexe as a separate dwelling); *Re Bewick's Application* (1996) 73 P & CR 240; *Re Willis' Application* [1997] 2 EGLR 185 (bed and breakfast establishment wholly compatible with surrounding residential area).   [279] P. 1023, post.

[280] *Sutton London Borough Council v Bolton* (1993) 68 P & CR 166. See Local Government Act 1972, ss. 120(3), 124(2); *R v City of London Council, ex p Master Governors and Commonality of the Mystery of the Barbers of London* [1996] 2 EGLR 128; *Thames Water Utilities v Oxford City Council* (1998) 77 P & CR D16; cf Scammell, pp. 191–3; *Re Wiggins Application* [1998] JPL 599; *Re Caton's Application* [1999] 3 EGLR 121 (changes in planning policy did not render restriction obsolete).

scheme of easements and covenants which is compatible with both the commonhold system introduced by Part I of the Commonhold and Leasehold Reform Act 2002,[281] and the reformed system of land registration introduced by the Land Registration Act 2002. A Consultation Paper is promised during the course of 2006.

The Law Commission proposes to tie this work in with a reconsideration of its own earlier Report on the Law of Positive and Restrictive Covenants 1984, which recommended a comprehensive reform of the law relating to covenants affecting freehold land.[282] Until the Law Commission publishes its new proposals, it therefore remains valuable to consider the earlier proposals.

The 1984 Report took as its model the existing law of easements (paras. 4.21–4.36; 27.1(1)). The reforms proposed would enable obligations, whether restrictive or positive in nature, to run with the benefited and the burdened land so as to be directly enforceable by and against the current owners of each. They would also be such as to cater not only for the simple case of an obligation created between two neighbouring landowners, but also for the more complex needs of property developments (including those involving freehold flats). This last point has now in certain respects been dealt with by the introduction of commonhold.[283]

In outline the main recommendations were:

(1) There should be a new interest in land, to be known as a Land Obligation (paras. 5.2; 27.1(2)). The Land Obligation should be one of two types.

    (a) *The neighbour obligation* (paras. 6.2–6.16; 27.1(3)–(6)) This was to be used where the obligation is imposed on one plot for the benefit of another plot. It could take one of three forms: a restrictive obligation; a positive obligation, which requires either the carrying out of works or the provision of services for the dominant land; and a reciprocal payment obligation, which requires the making of payments for expenditure incurred by a person who carries out a positive covenant, e.g. paying half the cost when the neighbour is under a covenant to repair the boundary fence.

    (b) *The development obligation* (paras. 4.29–4.36; 27.1(7)–(11)) This was to be used where an area of land is to be divided into separately owned but inter-dependent units, such as a housing development or a block of flats. This obligation was to be of a necessarily wider scope than the neighbour obligation and it was to be capable of enforcement not only by owners of other parts of the development but also by a manager acting on their behalf, such as an estate agent, a management company or a residents' association.

(2) The development obligation could take the form of a restrictive or of a positive or of a reciprocal payment obligation. It could also require the servient land to be used in a particular way which benefits the whole or part of the development (such as to

---

[281] Chap. 9, ante.

[282] Law Com No. 127. For earlier Reports, see Wilberforce Committee on Positive Covenants 1965 (Cmnd 2719); Law Commission on Restrictive Covenants 1967 (Law Com No. 11) and its Working Paper on Rights Appurtenant to Land 1971 (No. 36); Benson Committee on Legal Services 1979 (Cmnd 7648); Second Report of the Conveyancing Committee: Conveyancing Simplifications 1985, paras. 4.52–4.57, 7.21–7.22. See also [1984] JPL 222, 317, 401, 485 (S. B. Edell); 134 NLJ 459, 481 (H. W. Wilkinson); (1984) 47 MLR 566 (P. Polden).

See A New Property Law Act, drafted by the Law Commission of New Zealand (Law Com Report No. 29) which proposes that the burden of both negative and positive covenants should run with the land if they relate to the subject matter of the land and are noted on the register; [1994] Conv 428 (H. W. Wilkinson).

[283] Chap. 9, ante.

provide shopping facilities there), and to require payment to a manager for expenditure incurred in performing his functions under the development scheme.

(3) The Land Obligation may be either legal or equitable. To be legal, it must be created by deed, and be equivalent to an estate in fee simple absolute in possession or to a term of years absolute. If created in writing or if created for any other interest, such as for life, it would be equitable.

In either case, the obligation must be stated to be a Land Obligation, in order to distinguish it from an easement or similar right. The rule against perpetuities would not apply (paras. 27.1(12)–(20)).

(4) The person who enters into the Land Obligation would cease to be subject to it when he has disposed of the land. His liability under the doctrine of privity of contract to the covenantee would end and there would thus be no point in the creation of a chain of indemnity covenants (paras. 11.32–11.34).

(5) Land Obligations, whether legal or equitable, would be registrable as a new type of Class C land charge under the Land Charges Act 1972, in the case of unregistered land. In the case of registered land, they would be noted in the dominant and servient titles, and would not be overriding interests (Part IX; paras. 27.1.(21)–(23)).

(6) The new scheme would only apply to Land Obligations created after it comes into force. There would thus be three different schemes for covenants affecting freehold land; those created before 1926; those created after 1925 and those under the new scheme (Part XXIV; paras. 27.1.(93)–(101)).

B Obsolete Restrictive Covenants

The Law Commission, in its Report on Obsolete Restrictive Covenants in 1991,[284] made proposals to phase out most existing restrictive covenants after the introduction of the Land Obligations scheme envisaged in its Report on the Law of Positive and Restrictive Covenants.

The main proposal was that all restrictive covenants should automatically lapse eighty years after they were first created, but anyone entitled to the benefit of a covenant which was not then obsolete would have the right to replace it with a Land Obligation to the like effect. It would be up to him to take positive action to replace it; failure to do so would involve the automatic lapse of the covenant. A five-year period of grace would be allowed for assessing restrictions which are already more than eighty years old.

Implementation of these proposals was not pursued, given that the Report on Positive and Restrictive Covenants was not implemented. However, the issues it raised will once more become live when the Law Commission produces its new proposals on Land Obligations.[285]

VII Covenants and Planning

Tulk v Moxhay[286] was decided in 1848 and the doctrine to which it gave rise was one of the bases for control of land use by private landowners during the suburban expansion of the nineteenth century. Together with leasehold and reciprocal positive freehold covenants, it is

284 Law Com No. 201.   285 P. 702, ante.   286 (1848) 2 Ph 774, M & B p. 942.

fundamental to all private planning. Private planning, however, co-exists side by side with the public control of the use and development of land in the hands of local planning authorities under the principal planning statute, the Town and Country Planning Act of 1990.[287]

It is important to notice that these two methods of control, private and public, are cumulative.[288] A purchaser of land must not only satisfy himself about the existence of private covenants that may bind the land which he is buying, but he must also investigate its planning aspect.

An outline of the public planning law is given in Part IV below.[289]

---

[287] See Law Commission Report on Restrictive Covenants 1967 (Law Com No. 11), paras. 16–19 and on the Law of Positive and Restrictive Covenants 1984 (Law Com No. 127, HC 201), paras. 2.5–2.7.
[288] See (1964) 28 Conv (NS) 190 (A. R. Mellows).   [289] Pp. 1011 et seq, post.

20

RENTCHARGES[1]

SUMMARY

I Nature of a Rentcharge

A Origin and History

We have already seen that a rent payable by a tenant to a landlord is called rent service because of the tenure which exists between the parties, but that it is called a rentcharge if there is no tenure between the creditor and the debtor from whose land it issues.[2] In former days this lack

---

[1] See generally Preston and Newsom, *Restrictive Covenants Affecting Freehold Land*, chap. 7; Easton, *Law of Rentcharges*; Law Commission Report on Rentcharges 1975 (Law Com No. 68) on which the Rentcharges Act 1977 is based. [2] Pp. 265–7, ante.

of tenurial interest between the parties meant that the rent owner had no automatic right at law to distrain upon the land of the debtor for the recovery of arrears, and generally speaking, rentcharges, though of considerable antiquity, were regarded as contrary to the policy of the common law, since the debtor was rendered less able to perform the military service due to his overlord, while the rent owner himself was free from all feudal obligations in respect of the land.[3] It became usual, therefore, for the parties to enter into an express agreement that the creditor should have a power of distress over the debtor's land. A rent supported in this way by a specially reserved power of distress, as distinct from a rent service where such power existed of common right, was called a rentcharge, since the land liable for payment was charged with a distress.[4] We have seen that there is no longer any necessity to charge the land expressly, for the Law of Property Act 1925, re-enacting the Landlord and Tenant Act 1730, and the Conveyancing Act 1881, confers the right of distress upon all rentcharge owners.[5]

A rentcharge is thus an annual sum of money issuing and payable out of land, the due payment of which is secured by a right of distress that is not the result of tenure between the parties but is either expressly reserved or allowed by statute.[6] It is now defined in the Rentcharges Act 1977[7] as:

any annual or other periodic sum charged on or issuing out of land, except

   (a) rent reserved by a lease or tenancy, or

   (b) any sum by way of interest.

B Legal and Equitable

A legal rentcharge is an incorporeal interest that may be limited for all the estates recognised at common law.[8]

Thus, before 1926, it could be limited to a person for an estate in fee simple, in tail, for life, for years or in remainder, but under the Law of Property Act 1925, which reduced the estates that could be created at law to the fee simple absolute in possession and the term of years absolute,[9] the interest conferred on the rent owner is a legal interest only where it is in possession and either perpetual or for a term of years absolute.[10] Thus, an annual sum of money granted to a widow for life and charged upon the settled lands by a marriage settlement confers an equitable interest. Furthermore, a rentcharge can only be legal if the proper formalities for its creation have been observed.[11]

C Rentcharge on a Rentcharge

As the essence of a rentcharge lies in the power of the owner to distrain upon lands, it follows that, strictly speaking, it can issue only out of corporeal hereditaments. A dominant owner, for instance, cannot charge a right of way to which he is entitled, since there is nothing on which the rent owner can distrain, though of course the debtor will be liable for the amount

---

[3] Cruise *Digest*, Tit. xxvii. c. i. ss. 1, 7.   [4] Co Litt 144a.   [5] LPA 1925, s. 121; p. 267, ante.

[6] See Co Litt 143b, 147b.

[7] S. 1(1). This includes an annual sum known by a name other than rentcharge, e.g. chief rent (or chief), fee farm rent and ground rent (a confusing name since it usually means rent payable under a long lease).

[8] Cruise *Digest*, Tit. xxviii. c. ii. ss. 1–3.   [9] LPA 1925, s. 1(1); p. 94, ante.

[10] S. 1(1)(b). A rentcharge, provided that it is not limited to take effect upon the determination of some other interest, is "in possession" notwithstanding that its payment is to commence at some time subsequent to its creation: Law of Property (Entailed Interests) Act 1932, s. 2.   [11] P. 896, post.

he has agreed to pay.[12] For the same reason at common law a rent cannot be reserved out of a rent,[13] and therefore if A, who is entitled to a rentcharge of £50, grants it to B, but reserves to himself thereout a rentcharge of £25, the reservation is void in the sense that the £25 does not constitute a rentcharge properly so called.

But this rule of the common law has in part been abrogated by the Law of Property Act 1925, which enacts that a rentcharge or annual sum of money (not being a rent service) may be reserved out of or charged on another rent charge in the same manner as it could have been charged on land.[14] In such a case the ordinary remedies of distress and entry upon the lands are impossible, and therefore it is provided that where the rent is in arrears for twenty-one days, the owner of the second rent (£25) shall have power to appoint a receiver of the rent (£50) on which it is charged. The receiver is then entitled to acquire the £50 by action, distress or otherwise, and out of this to pay arrears, expenses and his own remuneration.

II Examples of Rentcharges

Rentcharges have been used in three main situations:

A Sale of Land

On the sale of land a vendor, instead of receiving the purchase money in the form of a lump sum, may reserve to himself a legal rentcharge, under which a sum of money is payable annually to himself and his heirs for ever, and, in addition, receive a capital payment. The rentcharge, being legal, binds all subsequent purchasers of the land. This type of transaction occurs mainly in Manchester and other parts of the North West of England, and in the County of Avon, including Bristol, where some 80 per cent of owner-occupied residential property may be subject to rentcharges.[15]

B Secured Family Annuities

In this situation, a rentcharge is created voluntarily or in consideration of marriage or by way of family settlement for the life of any person (or for any shorter but indefinite period, such as widowhood) or for providing sums for the advancement, maintenance or benefit of any persons. In this case the rentcharge is equitable and if created before 1997 the land on which the payments are secured became settled land under the Settled Land Act 1925,[16] unless it was already settled land or was held upon trust for sale. If such a rentcharge is created after 1996 the land becomes subject to a trust of land under the Trusts of Land and Appointment of Trustees Act 1996.[17]

C Positive Covenants

Where, as a result of a property development, there is a distinct grouping of separate freehold houses or where a single building is divided into separate freehold parts,[18] a rentcharge

---

[12] Co Litt 47a.   [13] *Earl of Stafford v Buckley* (1750) 2 Ves Sen 170 at 177.

[14] LPA 1925, s. 122. This occurs very rarely in practice.   [15] Law Com No. 68, para. 16.

[16] S. 1(1)(v), p. 402, ante.   [17] S. 2, Sch. 1, para. 3; s. 25(1), Sch. 3, para. 15(1), (2).

[18] Since 27 September 2004, however, it has been possible to use a commonhold scheme under CLRA 2002 for the registered freehold owners of two or more units of land, for example, in a block of flats or offices; and positive covenants will be enforceable amongst the owners: chap. 9, ante.

is sometimes used as a conveyancing device to enable the burden of positive covenants to run against the unit holder for the time being. As we have seen, it was held in *Rhone v Stephens*[19] that the burden of positive covenants on the sale of land by a freeholder does not run at common law, and neither does it in equity under the doctrine of *Tulk v Moxhay*[20] which is confined to restrictive covenants. In *Austerberry v Corporation of Oldham* LINDLEY LJ expressly mentioned the use of the rentcharge for this purpose.[21]

One scheme in common use for smaller developments has been described as follows:[22]

a rentcharge affecting each unit will be imposed for the benefit of the other units and this rentcharge will be supported by positive covenants to repair, insure, and so on. The purpose of this scheme is not to procure the actual payment of the rentcharge—its amount may be nominal and the rent owners are unlikely to trouble very much whether it is paid or not—but to create a set of positive covenants which are actually designed to preserve the development as a whole but which are directly enforceable because they happen incidentally to support the rentcharge.

The amount of the rentcharge may, however, not be nominal, but considerable, where the object is to provide funds for a management company to look after the maintenance of a large development as a whole.

III Rentcharges Act 1977

The policy of the Rentcharges Act 1977[23] is to abolish existing rentcharges where possible and to prevent their creation in the future. The creation of a rentcharge under example (A) above is void after 21 August 1977, and an existing rentcharge will be extinguished sixty years after the date of the passing of the Act (i.e. 22 July 2037) or sixty years after the date on which it first becomes payable, whichever is the later.[24] Such a rentcharge can cause conveyancing difficulties, especially where the land sold is divided in subsequent sales; the amount of the rentcharge may be very small in relation to the property purchased, and the purchaser may feel that "a liability to pay an annual sum to a former owner who is not necessarily the vendor is repugnant to the concept of freehold ownership"[25]

Rentcharges under the above examples (B) secured family annuities and (C) positive covenants, however, are expressly preserved by the Rentcharges Act,[26] although the conveyancing device of (C) will become unnecessary if the recommendations of the Law Commission on Land Obligations, which are expected during 2006, follow its earlier report on the Law of Positive and Restrictive Covenants[27] in allowing for the enforcements of positive covenants between freeholders, and are implemented. The Act calls (C) an estate rentcharge and defines it as follows:[28]

A rentcharge created for the purpose

  (i) of making covenants to be performed by the owner of the land affected by the rentcharge enforceable by the rent owner against the owner for the time being of the land; or

---

[19] [1994] AC 310, M & B p. 934; p. 663, ante.   [20] (1848) 2 Ph 774, M & B p. 942; p. 666, ante.
[21] (1885) 29 Ch D 750 at 783.   [22] Law Com No. 68, para. 49; [1988] Conv 99 (S. Bright).
[23] See generally (1977) 127 NLJ 1042 (H. W. Wilkinson).   [24] Rentcharges Act 1977, ss. 2(1), 3.
[25] Law Com No. 68, para. 26.   [26] Rentcharges Act 1977, s. 2(3).
[27] 1984 (Law Com No. 127). See generally pp. 701–3, ante. The introduction of commonhold already enables positive covenants to be enforced between the registered freehold owners of two or more units of land held within a commonhold scheme; n. 18, supra.   [28] Rentcharges Act 1977, s. 2(4).

(ii) of meeting, or contributing towards, the cost of the performance by the rent owner of covenants for the provision of services, the carrying out of maintenance or repairs, the effecting of insurance or the making of any payment by him for the benefit of the land affected by the rentcharge or for the benefit of that and other land.

A rentcharge of more than a nominal amount is not treated as an estate rentcharge unless it represents a reasonable payment for the performance of covenants in (ii) of the definition of an estate rentcharge.[29]

Two other kinds of rentcharge are also preserved by the Act:[30]

(i) a rentcharge under any Act of Parliament providing for the creation of rentcharges in connection with the execution of works on land (whether by way of improvements, repairs or otherwise) or the commutation of any obligation to do any such work; and

(ii) a rentcharge by, or in accordance with the requirements of, any order of a court.

Since the year 2037 is sometime in the future and certain kinds of rentcharge may still exist, it is necessary to set out some details of the law apart from the Act.

IV Creation of a Rentcharge

A rentcharge may be created by instrument *inter vivos*, by will, or by statute.

A By Instrument Inter Vivos

At common law a rentcharge, if created *inter vivos*, must be granted by deed.[31] But the equitable principle underlying the doctrine of *Walsh v Lonsdale* applies here just as it does in the case of a contract to grant a term of years[32] or an easement, so that, where one person has made a contract to grant a rentcharge to another, an equitable rentcharge may be created.[33]

The quantum of the interest in a rentcharge depends upon the words of limitation which are inserted in the deed of grant, and the rule is that such words are construed in exactly the same way as in a grant of corporeal hereditaments. Thus before 1926, in order to pass a perpetual rentcharge it was necessary to convey the rent to the grantee *and his heirs*, or to the grantee *in fee simple*, but the changes which were effected by the Law of Property Act 1925 in regard to words of limitation sufficient to pass a fee simple estate in land[34] apply to rentcharges, and at the present day the effect of a grant which contains no technical words of limitation is to give the grantee a perpetual rentcharge, or if that is impossible owing to the grantor only having a smaller estate, then to give him a rentcharge for the whole interest possessed by the grantor. This rule is, however, displaced if a contrary intention is shown in the conveyance, and in such a case the size of the grantee's interest will depend upon the intention of the parties.[35]

---

[29] Rentcharges Act 1977, s. 2(5).   [30] Ibid., s. 2(3).

[31] Co Litt 169a; *Hewlins v Shippam* (1826) 5 B & C 221 at 229.   [32] Pp. 223 et seq, ante; p. 877, post.

[33] *Jackson v Lever* (1792) 3 Bro CC 605. A contract to grant a rentcharge must comply with the formalities required for the disposition of an interest in land: chap. 24, post.   [34] LPA 1925, s. 60; p. 172, ante.

[35] S. 60(1). See Megarry and Wade, *Law of Real Property* (5th edn), p. 823 for an argument that s. 60 may not apply to the creation of rentcharges by deed.

B By Will

A rentcharge may be validly created by will, and whether it is so or not depends upon the intention of the testator. If he directs that an annual sum shall be paid to a donee and uses words which show that the money is to be a charge upon the land and not upon his personal property, it is a rentcharge as distinct from an annuity, as for instance where he devises land to A:

subject to and charged and chargeable with the payment of £100 a year to B for twenty-five years.[36]

Section 28 of the Wills Act 1837[37] only applies to the transfer of an existing rentcharge; it does not apply to the creation of a new one. Thus, if a rentcharge is created by will without any words of limitation, the devisee can take it only for life.[38]

C By Statute

There are two distinct series of enactments under which an owner of land may carry out certain improvements and arrange that the cost shall be charged upon the land and reimbursed in full, together with interest, by a definite number of annual payments. The chief statute of the first class is the Improvement of Land Act 1864, which allows "landowners" (i.e. anyone except a lessee at a rack rent[39] who is in actual possession of the rents and profits) to borrow money for improvements from certain private land improvement companies.

Money may not be borrowed in this way for every improvement, but only for those specified in the Settled Land Act 1925.[40] No rentcharge can be imposed upon the land until the Secretary of State for Environment, Food and Rural Affairs[41] has, on the application of the landowner, satisfied himself that the suggested improvement will permanently increase the yearly value of the land to an extent greater than the annual rentcharge which is contemplated.[42]

If satisfied on this point the Secretary of State issues a provisional order which specifies the sum to be charged upon the land, the rate of interest and the number of years within which it must be paid off. The rate of interest is at the discretion of the Secretary of State,[43] but the period for payments must not exceed forty years.[44] After the improvements are completed the Secretary of State issues an absolute order imposing the annual sum as a rentcharge upon the fee simple, and this has priority over all existing and future incumbrances affecting the land with the certain specified exceptions.[45] The remedies for its recovery are

---

[36] *Ramsay v Thorngate* (1849) 16 Sim 575.   [37] P. 171, ante.

[38] *Nichols v Hawkes* (1853) 10 Hare 342.   [39] I.e. the full yearly value of the land.

[40] P. 413, ante. The improvements specified in the 1864 Act are all covered by those set out in SLA 1925, and the latter are expressly brought within the operation of the earlier Act.

[41] Or, in Wales, the National Assembly for Wales: SI 1999 No. 672, art. 2, Sch. 1.

[42] Improvement of Land Act 1864, s. 25. There are certain improvements which may be allowed although they will not permanently increase the yearly value of the land, i.e. construction of waterworks for the use of residents on the estate (40 & 41 Vict. c. 31, s. 5); erection of mansion house under Limited Owners Residences Acts 1870, 1871; planting, under Improvement of Land Act 1864, s. 15; erection or improvement of farmhouse or cottage for use of workers on the land, under Agricultural Credits Act 1923, s. 3(3).

[43] Agricultural Credits Act 1923, s. 3(1).   [44] Improvement of Land Act 1899, s. 1(1).

[45] Improvement of Land Act 1864, s. 59.

the same as in the case of other rentcharges,[46] except that the landowner is not personally liable.

The second class of statute is represented by the Settled Land Act 1925, which allows a limited owner to raise money for the purpose of carrying out permanent improvements on the settled land. Prior to 1 January 1926, there was an important difference between the operation of the Improvement of Land Acts and that of the Settled Land Acts in this matter, for, while under the former a tenant for life could raise new money for the purpose, all that the Settled Land Acts did was to authorise the expenditure upon improvements of capital money which happened to be in the hands of the trustees. A tenant for life could not raise new money by mortgage under the Settled Land Acts for carrying out improvements, but this power, as we have seen, was expressly conferred upon him by the Settled Land Act 1925.[47]

D Registered Land

The express grant over a registered estate of a rentcharge in possession which is either perpetual or for a term of years absolute—that is, a rentcharge that can exist at law under the Law of Property Act 1925[48]—is a registrable disposition.[49] Such a rentcharge does not therefore take effect at law, but is only equitable, until the registration requirements are met.[50] A legal rentcharge, other than one created for a term not exceeding seven years, is an independently registrable legal interest;[51] the grantee must be entered in the register as the proprietor of the interest, and a notice in respect of the interest created must be entered in the register.[52] In the case of a rentcharge for a term not exceeding seven years, a notice must be entered in the register of the estate affected.[53]

V Remedies for the Recovery of a Rentcharge

The following remedies are available to a rentcharge owner:

A Distress

A power to distrain upon the land, out of which the rent issues, is, as we have seen, an implicit incident of a rentcharge, though formerly it had to be specifically reserved. Even when the Landlord and Tenant Act 1730 had conferred the power of distress on rent owners, it was the usual practice to insert an express provision to the same effect in all instruments creating rentcharges, but this has ceased to be the practice in the case of instruments coming into effect after 31 December 1881. The Conveyancing Act of that year provides that where any rent (not incident to the relationship of landlord and tenant) is in arrears for

---

[46] Infra. [47] SLA 1925, s. 71(1)(ii); p. 413, ante. [48] S. 1(2)(b); p. 94, ante.
[49] LRA 2002, s. 27(2)(e). [50] Ibid., s. 27(1).
[51] Cf LRA 2002, s. 3(1)(b), (3) (voluntary registration of existing unregistered legal rentcharges except those for a term of which more than seven years are unexpired). See also ibid., s. 5(2)(b) (Lord Chancellor's power to make registration compulsory); p. 953, post. [52] Ibid., Sch. 2, para. 6.
[53] Ibid., Sch. 2, para. 7.

twenty-one days, the person entitled to receive it may enter into and distrain upon the land charged or any part thereof, and dispose of any distrainable objects according to the general law.[54] This remedy is now re-enacted by the Law of Property Act 1925.[55]

B Entry upon the Land Charged

The Law of Property Act 1925[56] provides that, when a rentcharge is in arrears for forty days, even though no legal demand has been made for payment, the owner may enter into possession of and hold the land charged or any part thereof and take the income thereof until all arrears and costs and expenses occasioned by the non-payment of the rent are satisfied. The Act, it will be noticed, does not give the owner of the rent a power of entry that will cause a forfeiture of the debtor's interest in the land, as is usual between landlord and tenant, but such a power may be, and generally is, reserved in the instrument of creation.

As we have seen, neither type of power, whether to hold the land until payment or to determine the debtor's interest, is subject to the rule against perpetuities.[57]

C Lease to Trustees

When a rentcharge is in arrears for forty days, the person entitled to payment, whether taking possession or not, may by deed lease the whole or part of the land to a trustee for a term of years, with or without impeachment of waste, on trust to raise and pay the rent together with all arrears, costs and expenses.[58] The trustee may adopt any reasonable means[59] to raise the money, as for instance by the mortgage, assignment or sub-lease of the term vested in him, or by appropriating the income of the land, but he cannot create a *legal* mortgage unless the rentcharge itself is held for a legal estate.

The above three remedies are not enforceable if a contrary intention is expressed in the instrument under which the annual sum arises,[60] and they are subject to the provisions of such instrument. Moreover, when a rentcharge is charged on another rentcharge, the above remedies are excluded and replaced by a right in the rent owner to appoint a receiver of the annual sum charged whenever payment is in arrears for twenty-one days.[61]

D Action for Payment

(1) Action of Debt

It is well settled that an action of debt for the recovery of arrears lies against the *terre tenant*[62] for the time being of the whole or part only of the land charged,[63] provided that he holds a

---

54 P. 267, ante.   55 S. 121(2).   56 S. 121(3).

57 LPA 1925, s. 121(6), pp. 542, 559 ante (right to enter for purpose of distraint or leasing); PAA 1964, s. 11(1), p. 542, ante (right to effect forfeiture).   58 Ibid., s. 121(4).

59 Ibid.   60 Ibid., s. 121(5).   61 Ibid., s. 122; p. 707, ante.

62 A *terre tenant* is the person who has the actual possession or occupation of land.

63 *Thomas v Sylvester* (1873) LR 8 QB 368.

freehold as distinct from a leasehold interest.[64] It is no defence that the profits of the land do not equal in amount the value of the rentcharge. Thus in *Pertwee v Townsend*:[65]

Lands were charged with the payment of a rentcharge of £80 a year. A certain portion of these lands was acquired by the defendant's predecessor in title, who released the rest of the land from the burden of the charge and imposed it upon the portion so acquired. At the time of the action for the recovery of £80, being one year's arrears, the defendant was able to show that the annual profits of the portion charged, of which he was tenant for life, amounted only to £7.5*s*, but nevertheless he was held personally liable for the whole £80.

Collins J said:[66] "The defendant holds the land subject to a charge, and he cannot keep the land and refuse to pay the charge. If he does refuse, the remedy against him is personal for the amount of the charge itself."

Although the right to sue runs with the rentcharge and the liability to be sued runs with the land, the benefit of a covenant to pay a rentcharge does not run with the rentcharge so as to entitle an assignee thereof to maintain an action *on the covenant* against the covenantor or his assignee.[67] Thus:

where A granted a fee simple to B on the terms that A his heirs and assigns should be entitled to a rent issuing out of the land, and the conveyance contained a covenant by B to pay the rent to A his heirs and assigns, it was held that X, to whom A had demised the rent for 1,000 years, could not sue B on the covenant.[68]

The technical nature of this rule was demonstrated by Lawrence LJ:

Whatever may be the foundation of the rule, and whether it rests on the broader principle that (except as between lessor and lessee) no covenant can run with an incorporeal hereditament, or whether it rests on the narrower principle that a covenant to pay a rentcharge is a collateral covenant or a covenant in gross which does not touch or concern the rentcharge, or whether it rests on no principle and is merely arbitrary, I am of opinion that it is too firmly established to be disturbed by this court.[69]

(2) Apportionment

A purchaser of any part of land which is burdened by a rentcharge is liable for the whole of the rent, unless there has been an apportionment. This may be legal where the owner of the rentcharge has formally severed the rent so as to charge part only of it on the land sold, or so as to exonerate the land from the rent. If, however, the owner of the rentcharge is not a party to the severance, the apportionment is equitable, and he is not bound by it. The person affected by the rentcharge remains liable to him for the whole of the rent, with a right of contribution from the other owners of the land.[70]

---

[64] *Re Herbage Rents, Greenwich* [1896] 2 Ch 811. Distress, however, may be levied on the premises.
[65] [1896] 2 QB 129.   [66] At 134.   [67] *Grant v Edmondson* [1931] 1 Ch 1.
[68] *Milnes v Branch* (1816) 5 M & S 411.
[69] *Grant v Edmondson* [1931] 1 Ch 1 at 26. See (1931) 47 LQR 380 (W. Strachan).
[70] For the problems which arise, see Law Com No. 68, paras. 12–15, 29–30. In 1982 a consultation paper proposed new arrangements for the apportionment and redemption of rentcharge and ground rents under which they would be primarily operated by the parties themselves: Law Commission Seventeenth Annual Report 1981–1982 (1983 Law Com No. 119), para. 2.105.

Under the Rentcharges Act 1977,[71] subject to small exceptions, a rentcharge may be legally apportioned by the Secretary of State for Environment, Food and Rural Affairs[72] on the application of any landowner whose land is affected by it. The Secretary of State may make an order, with or without conditions, apportioning the rentcharge between the rentpayer's land and the remaining land affected by the rentcharge. The order is made after a draft apportionment order is served on the person who appears to be the rent owner or his agent, and, subject to their rights of appeal to the Lands Tribunal, the order takes effect after twenty-eight days from the date on which it was made. The effect of the order is to release the applicant's land from any part of the rentcharge not apportioned to it and to release the remaining land from such part (if any) of the rentcharge as is apportioned to the applicant's land.[73]

The Law of Property Act 1925 provides[74] that, where equitable apportionment has been made in a conveyance for valuable consideration, then the apportionment, without prejudice to the rights of the rent owner, shall be binding between the grantor and the grantee under the conveyance and their respective successors in title. If the owner of part of the land fails to pay the rentcharge in accordance with the agreement or fails to perform some covenant, and the owner of the other part is in consequence obliged to pay the charges or damages, the latter may distrain upon the land of the former and may also take the income thereof until he has been satisfied.[75]

VI Extinction of a Rentcharge

There are several ways in which a rentcharge may be extinguished and the land freed from liability.

A Release

If the rent owner releases the whole of the land charged from any further liability to pay, the rent is extinguished. Indeed, on the somewhat questionable ground that a rent, being entire and issuing out of every part of the land, cannot be thrown upon one particular part not apportioned between several parts, the old rule was that a release of *part* of the land discharged the whole land and produced a total extinguishment of the rent.[76] But the Law of Property Act 1925,[77] re-enacting the Law of Property (Amendment) Act 1859, provides that the release from a rentcharge of part of the lands charged shall not extinguish the whole rentcharge, but shall only render it unenforceable against the part released. This provision, however, is not to prejudice the rights of the persons who are interested in the unreleased part of the lands unless they concur in or confirm the release. The effect of this enactment is that where the owner of land which is subject to a rentcharge sells the land in separate portions to different persons, and only one portion is released from the charge by the rent

---

71 Ss. 4–7. Application for apportionment may also be made under LTA 1927, s. 20, as amended by Rentcharges Act 1977, s. 17(1), Sch. 1, para. 3.

72 Or, in Wales, the National Assembly for Wales: SI 1999 No. 672, art. 2, Sch. 1.

73 Rentcharges Act 1977, s. 7(4).   74 S. 190.   75 S. 190(2); *Whitham v Bullock* [1939] 2 KB 81.

76 Co Litt 147b.   77 S. 70.

owner, the purchaser of the unreleased portions will be liable for the whole rent if they concur in the release, but will be liable only for an apportioned part if they do not concur.[78]

B Merger

A rentcharge may also be extinguished by merger.[79] The rigid rule of common law is that, whenever a lesser and a greater estate in the same lands become united in one person in his own right, the lesser estate is merged in the greater and extinguished without regard to the intention of the parties. As we shall see later, however, the equitable view that no merger occurs if it is contrary to the intention of the party in whom the two estates vest now obtains in all courts,[80] and it will suffice to say here that this principle applies to the merger of a rentcharge. Thus, if the absolute owner of a rentcharge also becomes absolute owner in his own right of the land charged, either by grant or by devise, there is prima facie a merger of the rent in the estate because there is no obvious advantage in keeping both the interests alive.[81] But, on the other hand, if the person who is responsible for the rent mortgages the land charged to the rent owner, there is no merger, since the two interests do not unite in one person in the same right.

C Lapse of Time

The usual provisions relating to limitation periods and adverse possession generally apply to rentcharges.[82]

In unregistered land, if a rentcharge is not paid for twelve years,[83] and no sufficient acknowledgment of the owner's title is made, the rentcharge is extinguished under the Limitation Act 1980.[84] If it is wrongly paid to a third party, after twelve years from the last receipt of rent by the rightful owner the latter's title to the rentcharge is extinguished and the third party acquires a new title to it by adverse possession.

In registered land, as in all cases of adverse possession under the new regime introduced by the Land Registration Act 2002,[85] there is no automatic extinction of the title to a rentcharge by non-payment or by wrongful payment to a third party, however long the period may be. In the case of non-payment for a period of ten years ending with the date of the application,[86] the proprietor of the land over which the rentcharge exists may apply to the registrar to close the registered title of the rentcharge; and where a third party has been in adverse possession of the rentcharge, by virtue of receipt of the rent under it, for a period of ten years he may apply to be registered as the proprietor of the registered rentcharge.[87]

---

[78] *Booth v Smith* (1884) 14 QBD 318.

[79] As to merger generally, see *Forbes v Moffatt* (1811) 8 Ves 384; Tudor, *Leading Cases on Real Property*, p. 244; chap. 28, post.   [80] P. 1006, post.

[81] *Freeman v Edwards* (1848) 2 Exch 732.

[82] Chap 6, ante. In the case of registered land, the provisions of LRA 2002, Sch. 6 are modified to apply to rentcharges by LRR 2003, r. 191, Sch. 8.

[83] Time runs from the last receipt of rent by the rightful owner: Limitation Act 1980, s. 38(8). For the implications of this, see p. 127, ante.   [84] Limitation Act 1980, ss. 15(1), 38(1); *Shaw v Crompton* [1910] 2 KB 370.

[85] P. 145 et seq, ante.

[86] The rentcharge need not have been registered throughout the whole period of adverse possession: LRA 2002, Sch. 6, para. 1(3), as substituted by LRR 2003, r. 191, Sch. 8.

[87] LRA 2002, Sch. 6, para. 1(1), as substituted by LRR 2003, r. 191, Sch. 8.

But notice is then given to the registered proprietor of the rentcharge,[88] who may resist the claim, and has two years to regularise his position. Only after that period does the claimant, if then still in adverse possession, have the right[89] to closure of the title in the case of non-payment,[90] or to registration of himself as proprietor in the case of the third party.[91]

D Statute

Lastly, under the Rentcharges Act 1977,[92] the owner of any land affected by a rentcharge may apply to the Secretary of State for Environment, Food and Rural Affairs[93] for a reduction certificate which certifies that the rentcharge has been redeemed.[94] The certificate is issued when the redemption price certified by the Secretary of State has been paid to the rent owner or into court.[95] The price is calculated in accordance with a formula based on the length of time which the rentcharge has still to run.[96] The effect of the certificate is to release the applicant's land from the rentcharge, but it does not affect the rent owner's rights and remedies to recover previous arrears.[97]

This statutory method of redemption does not apply to rentcharges which can still be created, nor to variable rentcharges.[98] It does not, therefore, apply to estate rentcharges,[99] whose attractiveness is thereby enhanced; they had been liable to redemption under the former procedure of the Law of Property Act 1925 for statutory discharge.

---

[88] LRA 2002, Sch. 6, para. 2.

[89] On making a further application: ibid., para. 6.

[90] LRR 2003, r. 192. If the registered title also comprises other rentcharges, the Registrar must cancel the particular rentcharge, rather than closing the whole title: ibid., r. 192(2).

[91] LRA 2002, Sch. 6, para. 7, as substituted by LRR 2003, r. 191, Sch. 8.

[92] Replacing the similar but not identical procedure under LPA 1925, s. 191.

[93] Or, in Wales, the National Assembly for Wales: SI 1999 No. 672, art. 2, Sch. 1.

[94] Rentcharges Act 1977, s. 8(1); Rentcharges Regulations 1978 (SI 1978 No. 16).   [95] Ibid., s. 9(5).

[96] Ibid., s. 10(1).   [97] Ibid., s. 10(3).

[98] Ibid., s. 8(4), (5); p. 708, ante. A rentcharge is variable if the amount of the rentcharge will, or may, vary in accordance with the provisions of the instrument under which it is payable: s. 8(5).   [99] P. 708, ante.

21

MORTGAGES[1]

SUMMARY

I Introduction

A mortgage is a conveyance or other disposition of an interest in property designed to secure the payment of money or the discharge of some other obligation.[2] The party who conveys the property by way of security is called the *mortgagor*, the lender who obtains an

---

[1] See generally Coote, *Law of Mortgages*; Cousins, *Law of Mortgage*; Fairest, *Mortgages*; Fisher and Lightwood, *Law of Mortgage*; Waldock, *Law of Mortgages*; Snell, Part VII; M & B chap. 11; (1978) 94 LQR 571 (P. Jackson); Council of Mortgage Lenders, *Lenders' Handbook* (2nd edn 2002, revised from time to time: the up-to-date version is available on the CML web site, www.cml.org.uk). The Code of Mortgage Lending Practice, a voluntary code followed by lenders (from 1 July 1997) and mortgage intermediaries (from 31 April 1998) in their relations with personal customers in the United Kingdom, ceased to apply from 31 October 2004, and was superseded by the Mortgages: Conduct of Business requirements published by the Financial Services Authority as statutory regulator of the mortgage industry; n. 15, infra. See also American Law Institute, *Restatement of the Law, Property 3d, Mortgages* (1997).

[2] See *Santley v Wilde* [1899] 2 Ch 474, per LINDLEY MR: "A mortgage is a conveyance of land or an assignment of chattels as a security for the payment of a debt or the discharge of some other obligation for which it is given."

interest in the property is called the *mortgagee*, and the debt for which the security is created is called the mortgage debt. The mortgagee, since he is the grantee of a proprietary interest, acquires a real, not merely a personal, security that prevails against the general body of creditors in the event of the mortgagor's bankruptcy. He is not only a creditor of the mortgagor; he is a secured creditor. As long as the mortgaged property remains worth as much as the debt, the mortgagee will receive payment in full; but if it falls in value and becomes worth less than the debt, the mortgagee will only be a secured creditor to the extent of its value, and he must prove in the mortgagor's bankruptcy with the unsecured creditors for the remainder of the debt.

A common feature of our present-day society is the purchase of a dwelling-house by an individual; and inseparable from the purchase is the mortgage of that house to a bank, building society or other lender. The political economist refers to a property-owning democracy, and, with more particularity, Lord DIPLOCK referred to:[3]

a real-property-mortgaged-to-a-building-society-owning democracy.

There may be other reasons why a loan of money is required, as, for instance, where a borrower calculates that he can make more money from the use of borrowed money than the loan will cost him in interest. His capital may be locked up in his business, and he may need a loan in order to expand it.[4] Or a house owner may wish to raise money for a particular project, such as home improvements; or to provide capital or income to spend during retirement.[5]

The mortgage industry is big business. Building societies, banks, insurance companies and local authorities are all substantial lenders of money on mortgage. Until the mid-1990s the building societies[6] were the single most significant sector providing residential mortgages,[7]

---

[3] *Pettitt v Pettitt* [1970] AC 777 at 824. In 1997 the number of dwellings in the United Kingdom rose by nearly half between 1961 and 1997 to 24.8 million: *Central Statistical Office Social Trends* (1999 edn), pp. 168–9. Between 1971 and 2002 home ownership increased from 49% to 69%, with most of the increase occurring in the 1980s: Office for National Statistics, *Living in Britain*, No. 31 (2004) p. 7; and in 2003–04 29% of households owned their property outright; 40% owned it on mortgage; 20% rented from the social sector and 11% rented privately: Office for National Statistics, *Social Trends 35* (2005), p. 139. For the idea that there should be a *Eurohypothec*—a common mortgage for Europe—see [2005] Conv 32 (S. Nasarre-Aznar).

[4] The loan is usually made to the company, but the lender may also insist on a personal guarantee from its directors secured by a charge on their own property. For problems which can arise in practice where a jointly-owned home is mortgaged to support a business loan to only one of the joint owners, see *Royal Bank of Scotland plc v Etridge (No 2)* [2002] 2 AC 773, M & B p. 827, p. 751, post.

[5] Very significant increases in property values in recent decades have made it particularly attractive for home owners to release capital in this way; several banks and building societies now offer "equity release schemes", one form of which involves the provision of a capital sum (often up to 50% of the market value of the home) or a regular income payment, secured on a "lifetime mortgage" intended to be called in only on the death of the borrower, thus giving the borrower the freedom to release some of the capital value of his major asset during his lifetime—at the expense of those who would otherwise inherit on his death. The equity release market grew by 10% in 2004, compared with exceptional growth of 70% in 2003, bringing the total number of outstanding loans by the end of 2004 to over 83,000 with a total value of just under £4 billion: CML Newsletter, 21 June 2005.

[6] Building societies have also extended the range of their own activities under reforms introduced by Building Societies Act 1986, as amended by Building Societies Act 1997. A Society may now lend for all forms of housing, rented as well as owner-occupied and, with a few exceptions, may carry on any type of business within the terms of its memorandum. See generally Wurtzburg and Mills, *Building Society Law*; Cousins, chap. 8; Fisher and Lightwood, paras. 12.73–12.79. Building Societies Act 1986 established the Building Societies Commission as the industry regulator. Financial Services and Markets Act 2000, s. 336 and SI 2001 No. 2617 substituted the Financial Services Authority as regulator.

[7] In 1990 building societies collectively took 75% of the new mortgage market, regaining a share close to that achieved in 1985, before the banks and other lenders greatly increased their capacity in the mortgage market: Annual Report of the Building Societies' Commission 1990–1991, para. 2.5; M & B (6th edn, 1992), p. 713.

but thereafter some of the largest societies converted into banks, or were taken over by banks.[8] The Bank of England publishes monthly statistics on lending; these show, for example, that the gross lending secured on dwellings during 2004 was £291,224 million, including lending of £202,756 million by banks, and £46,864 million by building societies.[9]

When a borrower falls into arrears with his payments, a bank or a building society does all it can to avoid repossession, but if it has to take action to enforce the security, difficult social questions arise.[10] The mortgagor has given as security, not an investment, but his home. And a mortgagor who has defaulted with one lender will have difficulty in borrowing money from another.

The law of mortgages which grew up in the eighteenth and nineteenth centuries has had to be adapted to meet twentieth century circumstances:

Courts of Equity have looked upon a mortgage transaction as one in which the terms were likely to be dictated by the mortgagee. In early days the mortgagor was at a disadvantage in that he was in need of money and must take it on the mortgagee's terms; it was a lender's market. And, while the law followed the maxim "caveat emptor" in the affairs of merchants and trade, equity not surprisingly took a different view in the case of mortgages. The fact that mortgagors were, in the early days, often members of great families and mortgagees were professional money lenders no doubt contributed to some extent to the development. A consideration of the changed position of borrowers and lenders in the capitalist society of the present day will suggest that the old cases should be accepted with some reserve. The cases on this subject show a continual struggle between the principle of binding precedent and the requirements of a changing society; they can only be understood with this in mind. Those which were decided about the turn of the twentieth century do not create the principle they apply. That litigation was a challenge to the validity of the principle laid down in earlier centuries, but generally it succeeded only in re-affirming the old principles; it was not until 1914[11] that substantial progress was made.[12]

The problem at the present day is the extent to which these old rules still hold good. A modern mortgage of land is very commonly, as already discussed, a transaction between a house-buyer and an institutional lender such as a bank or building society; or it may form part of a development project embarked upon by property financiers. In either case the historical concerns of the Courts of Equity hardly find a place in the modern mortgage market. Although there is some statutory protection peculiar to consumers,[13] the terms of mortgages

---

[8] Between 1995 and 1997 seven building societies converted to banks, or were taken over by banks; most significantly, in 1997 five of the eight largest societies converted, accounting for around 60% of the total assets of the sector: see the notes to FSA Building Society Statistics 2005.

[9] Bank of England Monetary and Financial Statistics, August 2005, Table A5.10, taking the four quarters of 2004 together. For a detailed breakdown of statistics relating to lending by building societies between 1995 and 2004, see FSA, Building Society Statistics 2005.

[10] As interest rates rose during the late 1980s and early 1990s, repayments became increasingly difficult, and arrears and repossessions increased. However, largely owing to lower interest rates, arrears and repossessions have fallen since then. At its peak in 1992, the number of loans in arrears by six to twelve months was 205,000. By 2002 this had fallen to 34,000, and the number of homes repossessed had fallen (from a peak of over 75,000) to 12,000: Office for National Statistics, *Social Trends 34* (2004), p. 164.

[11] *Kreglinger v New Patagonia Meat and Cold Storage Co Ltd* [1914] AC 25, M & B p. 816; p. 744, post.

[12] M & B p. 789.

[13] CCA 1974, pp. 745 et seq, post (giving protection to individuals (i) who borrow up to £25,000, but—given property prices across the UK—this has a limited scope of application; and (ii) on loans of any size, in respect of "extortionate credit bargains"); Unfair Terms in Consumer Contracts Regulations 1999, SI 1999 No. 3159, p. 748, post; AJA 1970, p. 765, post (giving the court power to restrict the mortgagee's right to possession of dwelling-house).

are generally dictated by the market, with significant competition amongst the numerous lenders who seek business from domestic or commercial borrowers.[14] The individual borrower is generally protected from unfair pressure by the high standards set by institutional lenders as well as by the regulation of the mortgage industry[15]—and by the general law of contract[16] and the criminal law,[17] which apply equally, of course, to protect commercial borrowers.

II Creation of Mortgages

A The Modern Law in Historical Perspective

If we are to understand the methods of creating mortgages in the modern law, it is first necessary to appreciate something of their history. The nature of a mortgage in the twenty-first century follows from radical changes which were made in the twentieth century to the methods of mortgaging land; and those changes can themselves be understood only by reference to the earlier law.

(1) History of Mortgages before 1926[18]

(a) Mortgages of freehold

(1) AT COMMON LAW

The developed law of mortgages is the joint product of common law, equity and statute. In the earliest days of the common law a mortgage was a mere pledge, which took one of two

---

[14] The rate of interest will be fixed by institutional lenders by reference to the prevailing financial market, and according to the other terms of the mortgage (including the length of the term, and the ratio of the loan to the value of the security). The loan may be repayment (where the capital is repaid over the life of the mortgage, along with interest on the outstanding balance) or interest-only (where the capital is paid off separately on the maturity of a separate investment contract); and the interest may be fixed (either for a particular period or, less commonly, throughout the life of the loan) or variable; Office for National Statistics, *Social Trends 34* (2004), pp. 162–3. The Bank of England produces statistics giving the average quoted household interest rates for different types of mortgage.

[15] The Financial Services Authority is the regulator responsible for the authorisation and regulation of mortgage lending and mortgage advice business in the UK under Financial Services and Markets Act 2000. A regulated mortgage contract is a loan to an individual or trustees, secured by a first legal mortgage on land of which at least 40% of that land is used, or is intended to be used, as or in connection with a dwelling by the borrower (or, in the case of credit provided to trustees) by an individual who is a beneficiary of the trust, or by a related person: Financial Services and Markets Act 2000 (Regulated Activities) Order 2001, SI 2001 No. 544, art. 61(3) as substituted by Financial Services and Markets Act 2000 (Regulated Activities) (Amendment) Order 2001, SI 2001 No. 3544, art. 8. This includes business loans to customers under a regulated mortgage contract. The detailed provisions for regulation are set out in the FSA's *Mortgages: Conduct of Business* (MCOB), which can be viewed on the FSA web site: www.fsa.gov.uk. Regulation of Financial Services (Land Transactions) Act 2005 amends Financial Services and Markets Act 2000 to bring Islamic mortgages within the regulatory framework; [2005] 34 EG 107 (M. Rutter).   [16] P. 748, post.

[17] On mortgage fraud, see Clarke, *Mortgage Fraud*; Osborn, *Mortgage Fraud*; [1993] Conv 181 (H. W. Wilkinson); Theft (Amendment) Act 1996, creating two new offences by inserting into the Theft Act 1968, ss. 15A (obtaining a money transfer by deception) and 24A (dishonestly retaining a wrongful credit), thereby reversing *R v Preddy* [1996] AC 815. See Law Commission Report Offences of Dishonesty: Money Transfers (1996) Law Com No. 243.

[18] Holdsworth, *History of English Law*, vol. iii. p. 128; Plucknett, *Concise History of the Common Law*, pp. 603–9; Simpson, *A History of the Land Law*, pp. 141–3, 242–7.

forms. It might be agreed that the lender should enter into possession of the land, and should take the rents and profits in discharge of both the principal and the interest on the loan. This was called a *vivum vadium*, or living pledge, since it automatically and by its own force discharged the entire debt. But, on the other hand, the arrangement might be that the lender should take the rents and profits of the land in discharge of the interest only, in which case the transaction was called a *mortuum vadium*, a dead pledge,[19] since it did not effect the gradual extinction of the debt.

By the time of Littleton (1402–81), however, a mortgage had become a species of estate upon condition, created by a feoffment defeasible upon condition subsequent. The land was conveyed in fee simple to the mortgagee on condition that if the loan was repaid upon the day which had been fixed by agreement, the conveyance should be defeated, and the mortgagor be free to re-enter. If repayment was not made on the exact date fixed, then the estate of the mortgagee became absolute, and the mortgagor's interest in the land was extinguished. In the words of Littleton:

If a feoffment be made upon such condition, that if the feoffor pay to the feoffee at a certain day etc. 40 pounds of money, that then the feoffor may re-enter, etc., in this case the feoffee is called tenant in mortgage, which is as much to say in French as mortgage, and in Latin *mortuum vadium*. And it seemeth that the cause why it is called mortgage is, for that it is doubtful whether the feoffor will pay at the day limited such sum or not, and if he doth not pay, then the land which is put in pledge upon condition for the payment of the money is taken from him for ever, and so dead to him upon condition etc. And if he doth pay the money, then the pledge is dead as to the tenant.[20]

That a feoffor should be bound to repay the loan on the exact day fixed or be precluded for ever from redeeming his property was a hard rule, and "what made the hardship on the debtor a glaring one was that the debt still remained unpaid and could be recovered from the feoffor notwithstanding that he had actually forfeited the land to his mortgagee".[21]

(2) IN EQUITY. EQUITY OF REDEMPTION

By the time of Charles I, equity had so fundamentally altered this strict legal view that the law of mortgages was transformed. The form as indicated by Littleton remained, but equity interfered on the general principle that relief should be granted against forfeiture for breach of a penal condition.[22] No longer was redemption to depend upon a strict compliance with the contract. In the view of equity the essential object of a mortgage is to afford security to the lender, and as long as the security remains intact there is no justification for expropriating the property of the mortgagor merely because of his failure to make prompt payment. In the words of Lord NOTTINGHAM:

In natural justice and equity the principal right of the mortgagee is to the money, and his right to the land is only as a security for the money.[23]

Hence the rule ultimately established by courts of equity was that a mortgagor must be allowed to redeem his fee simple despite his failure to make repayment on the appointed

---

[19] In French: *mort* (dead) *gage* (pledge).   [20] Litt, s. 332.

[21] *Kreglinger v New Patagonia Meat and Cold Storage Co Ltd* [1914] AC 25 at 35, per Lord HALDANE.

[22] Holdsworth, *History of English Law*, vol. v. p. 330; Turner, *The Equity of Redemption*.

[23] *Thornborough v Baker* (1675) 3 Swan 628 at 630. For Lord NOTTINGHAM's contribution to the development of mortgages, see (1961) 79 Selden Society, pp. 7 et seq (D. E. C. Yale).

day. Time was not to be of the essence of the transaction. This is still the rule, although a mortgage is no longer created by the conveyance of a fee simple estate. The position, then, is this: that upon the date fixed for repayment (which is usually six months after the creation of the mortgage, although in most cases neither mortgagor nor mortgagee intends that the loan shall be repaid on that date) the mortgagor has at common law a contractual right to redeem. If this date passes without repayment, he obtains a right to redeem in equity.

However, as Lord PARKER said:[24] "The equity to redeem, which arises on failure to exercise the contractual right of redemption, must be carefully distinguished from the equitable estate, which, from the first, remains in the mortgagor, and is sometimes referred to as an equity of redemption." This equity of redemption is an equitable interest which arises as soon as the mortgage is created, and is an equitable interest owned by the mortgagor. It is an interest in land which may be conveyed, devised or entailed, and it may descend on intestacy or pass as *bona vacantia* to the Crown.[25] It is destructible only by four events, namely, its release by the mortgagor, the lapse of time under the Limitation Act 1980,[26] the exercise by the mortgagee of his statutory power of sale,[27] and a foreclosure decree, that is, a judicial decree that the subject-matter of the mortgage shall be vested absolutely in the mortgagee free from any right of redemption.[28]

(3) POSITION PRIOR TO 1926

Up to 1 January 1926, the normal method by which a mortgage of the fee simple was created was for the mortgagor to convey the legal fee simple to the mortgagee together with a covenant to repay the loan in, say, six months' time, with a proviso, however, that if the loan were repaid at such date, the mortgagee would reconvey the legal estate. Outwardly it still seemed as if the mortgagee became absolute owner failing repayment within six months, but essentially, owing to the doctrine of the equity of redemption, the mortgagor was the true owner. Technically he was a mere equitable owner, but in the eyes of equity he was the real owner and, on his repaying the principal and interest with costs to the mortgagee, equity was prepared to grant specific performance of the proviso for reconveyance of the legal estate to him.

A still older method of creating a mortgage, used between the thirteenth and fifteenth centuries and worthy of notice because of its revival by the 1925 legislation, was for the mortgagor to lease his land to the mortgagee for a short term of years. If the debt was not repaid at the end of the lease, the right of the mortgagor was extinguished, and the term was automatically enlarged into a fee simple which vested absolutely in the mortgagee.[29] This method, however, went out of use, mainly because the law in its growing strictness could not countenance this facile mode of enlarging a term of years into a fee. An attempt to resuscitate it was made about the beginning of the nineteenth century, but owing to certain disadvantages, such as the doubt whether the mortgagee was entitled to possession of the title deeds, it failed, and the term of years was used only in family settlements where it was desired to secure money lent for the payment of portions.[30]

(b) *Mortgages of leasehold*

If the security offered by the borrower was a leasehold interest, not the fee simple, there were two methods before 1926 by which the mortgage might be created. Usually the mortgagor

---

[24] *Kreglinger v New Patagonia Meat and Cold Storage Co Ltd*, supra, at 48.

[25] *Casborne v Scarfe* (1738) 1 Atk 603; *Re Sir Thomas Spencer Wells* [1933] Ch 29, M & B p. 801; Waldock, *Law of Mortgages*, pp. 202 et seq.   [26] P. 756, post. This applies only to unregistered land.

[27] P. 770, post.   [28] P. 775, post.   [29] Holdsworth, *History of English Law*, vol. iii. p. 129.

[30] (1925) 60 LJ News 46 (J. M. Lightwood).

sub-leased his term of years to the mortgagee for a period slightly shorter than the remainder of the term. This was the most desirable method, since the sub-lease did not involve privity of estate between the mortgagee and the superior landlord, and therefore the mortgagee was immune from liability on the covenants contained in the original lease, unless they were negative covenants enforceable under the doctrine of *Tulk v Moxhay*.[31] The alternative method was for the mortgagee to take an assignment of the whole remainder of the term, but in this case he became liable to covenants and conditions under the doctrine of *Spencer's Case*.[32]

(c) Equitable mortgages

In addition to the conveyance of a legal estate, whether a fee simple or a term of years, by way of security, it has long been possible to create an equitable mortgage by the grant of an equitable interest. This is necessarily the method where the borrower himself is an equitable owner, as, for instance, where before 1926 a mortgagor created a second mortgage in the same land: the legal estate had been conveyed to the first mortgagee and what the mortgagor conveyed to the second mortgagee was his equity of redemption. A further example of an equitable mortgage, made by a borrower who is an equitable owner, is where a beneficiary under a trust of land mortgages his equitable life interest.

On the other hand, it is also possible for an equitable mortgage to be created by the owner of a legal estate, as for instance where he enters into a contract to create a legal mortgage which entitles the lender in equity to specific performance of the contract, and thereby constitutes the grant of a mortgage in equity. Indeed, without the grant even of an equitable interest, an owner may charge his land with the repayment of a loan and so entitle the lender in equity to enforce a sale of the property. These equitable mortgages are considered in more detail later.[33]

(2) Changes Made by the Law of Property Act 1925

The prevailing practice, by which the legal fee simple was conveyed to a mortgagee, presented a difficult problem to the draftsmen of the 1925 legislation. How were they to bring it into line with the principles that they intended to introduce?

The corner-stone of their policy was that the legal fee simple should always be vested in its true owner and that he should be able to convey it free from equitable interests. In the eyes of the law the true owner is the mortgagor. Yet, all that he held before 1926 was an equitable interest, and unless some alteration were made there could be no question of his ability to convey any kind of legal estate during the continuance of the mortgage.

On the other hand it was important to protect the mortgagee in the enjoyment of certain valuable advantages that he derived from his legal ownership. Pre-eminent among these was the priority which, by virtue of the legal fee simple, he obtained over other mortgages created in the same land, for these were necessarily equitable in nature. Moreover, his possession of the title deeds enabled him to control the actions of the mortgagor in his dealings with the land. He also enjoyed the right to take actual possession of the land, and therefore to grant leases; and lastly, when he exercised his power of sale on failure by the mortgagor to repay the loan, he was able to vest the legal estate in the purchaser.[34]

---

[31] Pp. 666 et seq, ante.   [32] Pp. 298 et seq, ante.   [33] P. 729, post.

[34] (1925) 60 LJ News 91 (J. M. Lightwood).

The solution contained in the Law of Property Act 1925 was to revert to the old fifteenth-century method of effecting mortgages by means of a lease for a term of years.

Mortgages by which the legal fee simple is vested in the mortgagee were prohibited, and a mortgagee who required a legal estate instead of a mere equitable interest became compelled to take either a long term of years or a newly invented interest[35] called a *charge by deed expressed to be by way of legal mortgage*. In the first case both parties have legal estates: the mortgagee has a legal term of years absolute, and the mortgagor has a reversionary and legal fee simple, subject to the mortgagee's term. In the case of a charge by way of legal mortgage, however, the mortgagee does not have a legal estate, but a legal interest in the land[36] which by statute gives him the same protection, powers and remedies as if he had taken a legal term of years.

In this way the principle that the legal fee simple should always remain vested in the true owner was maintained. The mortgagor is owner at law as well as in equity, and the mortgagee has only a right *in alieno solo*. The charge expressed to be by way of legal mortgage at last provided a method reflecting the reality of the transaction and went some way towards rebutting Maitland's description of a mortgage deed as one long *suppressio veri* and *suggestio falsi*.[37] We should also notice two important consequences of the changes made by the 1925 legislation. First, the mortgagor's retention of the legal estate means that any second and subsequent mortgages which he creates may be legal. And secondly, the rights of the parties remain unchanged, and in particular, the mortgagor's equity of redemption is still of importance. This, as before 1926, is an equitable proprietary interest and is in value equal to the value of the land less the amount of the debt secured by the mortgage. The mortgagor retains that interest and keeps a legal estate as well. On the other hand, the mortgagee retains all his remedies, and, for instance, may sell and convey the legal fee simple, if the mortgagor defaults in his obligations.[38]

(3) Changes Made by the Land Registration Act 2002

The Land Registration Act 1925 followed, for registered land, the new scheme of the Law of Property Act 1925 for mortgages; accordingly the proprietor of registered land had in general terms the same powers to mortgage the land as if the land had not been registered;[39] and so a legal mortgage of registered land could be made by a charge by way of legal mortgage, or by demise or sub-demise, although the default position, if no contrary express provision were made in the deed creating it, was that it took effect as a charge.[40] The Land Registration Act 2002, however, has taken the reforms of 1925 one step further. Now it is no longer possible for the owner of a registered estate to create a mortgage by demise or sub-demise;[41] the

---

[35] Charges over *registered* land were however introduced by Land Transfer Act 1875: Law Commission Report on Land Registration for the Twenty-First Century 2001 (Law Com No. 271), para. 7.2. The 1875 Act gave the registered proprietor of a registered charge the right to enter the land and take its rent and profits: s. 25; and the same powers of foreclosure and sale as if the land had been transferred to him by way of mortgage: s. 26. But the 1875 Act was not successful, because it provided for only a voluntary system of registration, and by 1885 only 113 titles had been registered under it: Rowton Simpson, *Land Law and Registration* (1976), p. 44. For mortgages of registered land in the modern law, see infra.   [36] LPA 1925, s. 1(2)(c).

[37] Maitland, *Equity*, p. 182. For a precedent of a legal charge, see p. 726, post.   [38] P. 769, post.

[39] LRA 1925, s. 106(1). The mortgage could therefore be equitable or (if in proper form and registered) legal: s. 106(2).   [40] Ibid., s. 27(1), (2).

[41] LRA 2002, s. 23(1)(a). Nor may the mortgagee under an existing mortgage by demise be registered as the proprietor of the lease where there is a subsisting right of redemption: ibid., s. 3(5); this latter rule was already

legal charge is therefore the only method of creating a legal mortgage over registered land—a reform made not only to simplify the law but also to reflect reality, mortgages by demise or sub-demise having been obsolete in practice for some time.[42] And the powers of the owner of a registered charge to mortgage his own interest under the charge are now limited: he may not transfer his interest by way of legal mortgage, nor create a mortgage of it by sub-demise, nor grant a legal charge of it; but is limited to charging at law with the payment of money the indebtedness being secured by the registered charge.[43]

(4) Impact of History on the Modern Law

The modern law of mortgages cannot therefore be understood without the perspective of history. The registered proprietor today has the power to make any disposition of his estate—including mortgaging it—*except* for the mortgage by demise or sub-demise.[44] To comprehend this, it is necessary to understand the general powers of mortgaging which are still contained in the Law of Property Act 1925. But the principles of mortgages contained in that Act are themselves a development of the pre-1926 law of mortgages and have to be understood in that light. Although the Land Registration Act 2002 has prohibited the creation of mortgages by demise, the form of mortgage which is retained as the universal method of mortgaging registered land—the legal charge—is itself defined in the Law of Property Act 1925, for the purposes of registered land as much as unregistered land,[45] as giving the mortgagee the same protection, powers and remedies as if it had been a mortgage by demise. The 2002 Act does not therefore break with history: the theory of a demise underpins the present day law.

B Methods of Creating Mortgages Today

(1) Legal Mortgages

(a) Unregistered land

As we have seen, the Law of Property Act 1925 provided that a legal mortgage of an estate in fee simple must be effected by either:

(1) a demise for a term of years absolute, subject to a provision (called a provision for cesser) that the term shall cease if repayment is made on a fixed day; or

(2) a charge by deed expressed to be by way of legal mortgage;[46]

and, similarly, that a legal mortgage of a term of years absolute must be effected by a demise (a sub-lease) for a term of years absolute or by a legal charge.[47] These provisions continue to

---

established in LRA 1925, s. 8(1). "It would make no sense to register a mortgage term where the estate charged was an unregistered freehold or leasehold and the mortgage might still be redeemed": Law Commission Report on Land Registration for the Twenty-First Century 2001 (Law Com No. 71), para. 3.12.

[42] H & B, para. 12.2; Law Com No. 271, para. 7.2; Emmet, para. 25.001.   [43] LRA 2002, s. 23(2).

[44] Ibid., s. 23(1).

[45] LPA 1925, s. 87(4), inserted by LRA 2002, s. 133, Sch. 11, para. 2(1), (8), reinforces this by providing that it is not affected by the removal of the registered owner's power to mortgage by demise.

[46] LPA 1925, s. 85(1).   [47] Ibid., s. 86(1).

apply to the creation of a mortgage over land which is, and is to continue for the time being, to be unregistered. In practice, this is therefore limited to the creation of a mortgage by a freeholder or leaseholder of his existing estate in unregistered land, since in the more common case of the conveyance of an estate to a purchaser who his financing the purchase by mortgage, the conveyance will generally trigger the compulsory registration of the estate and of the mortgage—which must therefore comply with the rules for the creation of a legal mortgage of registered land.[48] Moreover, even where the mortgage is of an existing unregistered estate, if it is a legal mortgage protected by the deposit of documents relating to the mortgaged estate, the mortgage triggers the compulsory registration of the title to the estate and the mortgage.[49]

Although there are no doubt mortgages still in existence at the present time that were created by demise or sub-demise, the creation of new mortgages by this method is in practice obsolete.[50] Instead, for some time it has been usual to create a legal mortgage of unregistered land using the simpler and more realistic method provided by the Law of Property Act 1925: the legal charge.

(1) PRECEDENT OF A LEGAL CHARGE

The following simple form of legal charge was provided by the Law of Property Act 1925:[51]

CHARGE BY WAY OF LEGAL MORTGAGE.

This Legal Charge is made [&c.] between A. of [&c.] of the one part and B. of [&c.] of the other part.

[*Recite the title of A. to the freeholds or leaseholds in the Schedule and agreement for the loan by B.*]

Now in consideration of the sum of . . . pounds now paid by B. to A. (the receipt &c.) this Deed witnesseth as follows:—

(1) A. hereby covenants with B. to pay [Add the requisite covenant to pay principal and interest].

(2) A. as Beneficial Owner[52] hereby charges by way of legal mortgage All and Singular the property mentioned in the Schedule hereto with the payment to B. of the principal money, interest, and other money hereby covenanted to be paid by A.

(3) [*Add covenant to insure buildings and any other provisions desired.*]

In witness [&c.] [*Add Schedule*].

This precedent gives the flavour of the simplicity of a legal charge, although in practice legal charges take a more expanded form, containing further appropriate covenants by the borrower.[53]

---

[48] LRA 2002, s. 4(1)(a); pp. 728 et seq, post.

[49] Ibid., s. 4(1)(g), (8); R & R para. 27.019. A legal mortgage over unregistered land which is *not* protected by the deposit of documents should instead be protected by the registration at the Land Charges Registry of a land charge, Class C(i): Land Charges Act 1972, s. 2(4)(i); pp. 795, 940, post.

[50] P. 725, n. 42 supra. For an account of the form of a mortgage by demise or sub-demise, and the precedent of a mortgage deed, see the 16th edition of this book, pp. 724–7.

[51] S. 206, Sch. 5, Form No. 1; this was repealed in 2004: Statute Law (Repeals) Act 2004, s. 1(1), Sch. 1, Part 12. Forms of statutory legal charge are also provided by LPA 1925, s. 117, Sch. 4, Forms 1 and 4, but these are in practice rarely used: Emmet, para. 25.006.

[52] The words "as beneficial owner" were designed to imply certain covenants; since 30 June 1995 the appropriate wording is "with full title guarantee": LP(MP)A 1994: pp. 967 et seq, post.

[53] For a fuller precedent, see *Encyclopaedia of Forms and Precedents*, vol. 28, Form 2.

(2) EFFECT OF CHARGE

The Law of Property Act 1925 does not vest a term of years in the mortgagee,[54] but it provides that he shall have "the same protection, powers and remedies" as if he had taken a lease of a fee simple or a sub-lease of demised premises.[55] In other words, he is in exactly the same position as if the relationship of landlord and tenant existed between him and the mortgagor.[56] If, for instance, A has charged his term of years in favour of B and later commits a breach of a covenant contained in the lease by reason of which his landlord starts proceedings for the enforcement of his right of re-entry under a forfeiture clause, B is entitled to claim relief under section 146 of the Law of Property Act 1925.[57]

This method of creating a mortgage steadily gained popularity since its introduction, and at the present day is adopted in preference to the long lease. Its defect is that it does not contain the provision for cesser that always figured in the mortgage by demise. This provision corresponds to the old provision for redemption, the importance of which lay in fixing the date at which the mortgagor's right to redeem and the mortgagee's right to foreclose came into being. Although the right of a legal *chargee* to foreclose probably arises by implication at the date fixed in the covenant for repayment, provided that the mortgagor makes default, it is safer to insert an express provision for redemption or discharge in addition to the covenant for repayment.[58]

(3) ADVANTAGES OF LEGAL CHARGE

There are three advantages that may be claimed for the legal charge as compared with the mortgage by demise.

First, its form is short and simple and more intelligible to a mortgagor.

Secondly, the legal charge is as appropriate for leaseholds as it is for freeholds, and therefore it provides a simple method of executing a compound mortgage which relates to both these different interests.

Thirdly, a mortgagor with a leasehold interest who holds his term on condition that he will not sub-lease without the consent of his landlord, must clearly obtain this consent if his mortgage takes the form of a sub-demise,[59] but a legal charge, since it does not create an actual legal estate, is presumably not in breach of a covenant against under-letting.[60]

(4) SUB-MORTGAGE

If the legal chargee desires to create a sub-mortgage, he cannot do so by means of a sub-lease, since he himself holds no term of years. He must, therefore, either charge his own interest under the mortgage, or assign the mortgage debt to the sub-mortgagee subject to a right of redemption.

---

[54] *Weg Motors Ltd v Hales* [1962] Ch 49; *Cumberland Court (Brighton) Ltd v Taylor* [1964] Ch 29; *Thompson v Salah* [1972] 1 All ER 530; *Edwards v Marshall-Lee* (1975) 235 EG 901.   [55] LPA 1925, s. 87(1).

[56] *Regent Oil Co Ltd v J A Gregory (Hatch End) Ltd* [1966] Ch 402 at 431, M & B p. 794; *Weg Motors Ltd v Hales*, supra, at 77, per DONOVAN LJ.

[57] *Grand Junction Co Ltd v Bates* [1954] 2 QB 160; *Church Comrs for England v Ve-Ri-Best Manufacturing Co Ltd* [1957] 1 QB 238. See also p. 287, ante.

[58] The forms of statutory legal charge provided by LPA 1925, s. 117, Sch. 4, Forms 1 and 4, n. 51, supra, contain by statute implied covenants for payment and discharge.

[59] *Matthews v Smallwood* [1910] 1 Ch 777.

[60] *Grand Junction Co Ltd v Bates* [1954] 2 QB 160 at 168, per UPJOHN J.

(b) Registered land

(1) MORTGAGES CREATED UNDER LAND REGISTRATION ACT 1925

Under the Land Registration Act 1925 a legal mortgage could be created by registered charge, a legal interest which must be created by deed and completed by the Registrar entering on the charges register the chargee as proprietor of the charge.[61] It could be made by a charge by way of legal mortgage, or it could contain, in the case of freehold land, an express demise, and, in the case of leasehold land, an express sub-demise.[62] Subject to any contrary provision in the charge, however, it would take effect as a charge by way of legal mortgage.[63]

(2) MORTGAGES CREATED UNDER LAND REGISTRATION ACT 2002

The Land Registration Act 2002 does not permit the owner of a registered estate to create a mortgage by demise or sub-demise.[64] The only method of creating a legal mortgage of registered land, whether freehold or leasehold, is now[65] therefore the charge by way of legal mortgage. As in the case of unregistered land, a legal charge must be executed as a deed,[66] but in registered land the grant of a legal charge is a registrable disposition[67] which therefore does not take effect at law until the registration requirements have been met:[68] the chargee must be entered in the register as the proprietor of the charge.[69] On completion of the registration requirements, the charge has the same effect as a charge by deed by way of legal mortgage in unregistered land, and the proprietor of the charge has, in relation to the property subject to the charge, the powers of disposition conferred by law on the owner of a legal mortgage.[70]

The mortgagor can create a second or further legal mortgages in respect of the same registered estate, following the same rules as to formality and registration as are required for a first legal mortgage. Registered charges on the same registered estate rank in the order shown on the register.[71]

(3) SUB-MORTGAGES UNDER LAND REGISTRATION ACT 2002

The proprietor of a registered charge (the mortgagee) cannot now create a legal sub-mortgage of his own interest under the mortgage by transfer or sub-demise. The only permitted method is to charge at law with the payment of money the indebtedness being secured by the registered charge.[72] The effect of a legal sub-charge is to give the sub-chargee the right to exercise the chargee's rights under the principal charge.[73]

(4) FORM OF LEGAL CHARGE

Under the Land Registration Act 2002 rules may provide requirements as to the form and content of a charge which must be satisfied before it takes effect.[74] No such mandatory rule has been made, but a form in which a legal charge may be made is provided.[75] In practice, many

---

[61] LRA 1925, s. 26(1).

[62] Ibid., s. 27(1), (2); LRR 1925, r. 139 and Schedule as substituted by LR (Charges) R 1990 (SI 1990 No. 2613), r. 2, and LRR 1997 (SI 1997 No. 3037) r. 2(1), Sch. 1, para. 32.18.   [63] LRA 1925, s. 27(1).

[64] LRA 2002, s. 23(1)(a).

[65] Existing mortgages, registered under LRA 1925, are unaffected: LRA 2002, s. 134, Sch. 12, para. 1.

[66] LPA 1925, ss. 85(1), 87.   [67] LRA 2002, s. 27(2)(f).   [68] Ibid., s, 27(1).

[69] Ibid., s. 27(4), Sch. 2, para. 8.   [70] Ibid., ss. 51, 52(1).   [71] Ibid., s. 48(1); pp. 807–8, post.

[72] Ibid., s. 23(2).   [73] H & B, paras. 7.4, 12.8.

[74] LRA 2002, s. 25. Cf LRA 1925, s. 25(2) (charge could be in any form, subject to certain provisos).

[75] LRR 2003, r. 103; Form CH1.

institutional lenders will have their own form of charge which will have been approved by the Land Registry.[76] The general form provided by the rules (form CH1[77]) is set out on page 730.

(2) Equitable Mortgages

The statutory provisions that have been noticed so far apply only to the creation of a legal mortgage, and do not affect equitable mortgages and charges. It always has been, and still is, possible to confer upon a lender an equitable right over the land by way of security, instead of passing a legal estate or interest to him.

The commonest examples of equitable mortgages before 1926 were those which followed a legal mortgage in the same land, but, as we have seen, second and subsequent mortgages may now be created so as to give each lender a legal estate or interest. The following forms of equitable mortgages, however, still remain.

(a) *Equitable mortgages under the doctrine of* Walsh v Lonsdale

(1) CONTRACT TO CREATE A LEGAL MORTGAGE

Under the doctrine of *Walsh v Lonsdale*[78] if A enters into a contract that, in consideration of money advanced, he will execute a legal mortgage in favour of B, then as long as the contract is one of which the court would be prepared to grant the equitable remedy of specific performance, it is treated in equity as creating an equitable mortgage in favour of B.[79] But such a contract does not have this effect unless the money has been actually advanced, for a contract to make a loan, whether executed as a deed or not, can never be specifically enforced by either party.[80] The only remedy is the recovery of damages.

However, it must be remembered that an agreement for the sale or other disposition in land—which includes a mortgage—is not a contract unless it is in writing, signed by both parties in compliance with section 2 of the Law of Property (Miscellaneous Provisions) Act 1989.[81]

(2) IMPERFECT LEGAL MORTGAGE

An imperfect legal mortgage may also be treated in equity as if it were a contract to create a legal mortgage, with similar consequences. This may happen, for example, where A purports to create a legal mortgage in writing without executing it as a deed. However, for the doctrine of *Walsh v Lonsdale* to apply, there must at least be sufficient formality to comply with section 2 of the Law of Property (Miscellaneous Provisions) Act 1989.

(3) DEPOSIT OF TITLE DEEDS

It used to be held, following the case of *Russel v Russel*[82] in 1783, that an equitable mortgage is created by the delivery to the lender of the title deeds relating to the borrower's land, provided that it is intended to treat the land as security. In reality this is a further example

---

[76] H & B, para. 12.14; Land Registry Practice Guide 30, *Approval of Mortgage Documentation* (March 2003).

[77] Source acknowledgement: CH1 produced by Land Registry. © Crown copyright material is reproduced with the permission of Land Registry.   [78] (1882) 21 Ch D 9; p. 877, post.

[79] *Tebb v Hodge* (1869) LR 5 CP 73.   [80] *Sichel v Mosenthal* (1862) 30 Beav 371.

[81] Pp. 868 et seq, post. See also *Kinane v Mackie-Conteh* [2005] EWCA Civ 45; [2005] 2 P & CR DG3 (agreement to create mortgage not in writing as required by LP(MP)A 1989, s. 2(1) but enforceable because constructive trust created under s. 2(5)). For contracts made before 27 September 1989, the formality requirements of LPA 1925, s. 40, apply (sufficient memorandum or part performance): pp. 864 et seq, post; *Re Leathes* (1833) 3 Deac & Ch 112.

[82] (1783) 1 Bro CC 269. The right to create this kind of equitable mortgage was saved by LPA 1925, s. 13. The mortgagee can retain the deeds until he is paid, but has no separate legal lien: *Re Molton Finance Ltd* [1968] Ch 325; see also *Capital Finance Co Ltd v Stokes* [1969] 1 Ch 261 at 278.

Legal charge of a   **Land Registry**
registered estate

This form should be accompanied by Form AP1 or Form FR1.
If you need more room than is provided for in a panel, use continuation sheet CS and attach to this form.

1. Title number(s) of the Property *Leave blank if not yet registered.*
2. Property
3. Date
4. Lender *Give full name(s) and company's registered number, if any.*
5. Borrower **for entry on the register** *Give full name(s) and company's registered number, if any. For Scottish companies use an SC prefix and for limited liability partnerships use an OC prefix before the registered number, if any. For foreign companies give territory in which incorporated.*
6. The Borrower with *(Delete as appropriate)* **[full title guarantee][limited title guarantee] charges the Property by way of legal mortgage as security for the payment of the sums detailed in panel 8**   **7.** *Place "X" in the appropriate box(es).*   ☐   The Lender is under an obligation to make further advances and applies for the obligation to be entered in the register   ☐   The Borrower applies to enter the following restriction in the proprietorship register of the registered estate
8. Additional provisions *Insert here details of the sums to be paid (amounts and dates), etc.*

9. Execution *The Borrower must execute this charge as a deed using the space below. If there is more than one Borrower, all must execute. Forms of execution are given in Schedule 9 to the Land Registration Rules 2003. If a note of an obligation to make further advances has been applied for in panel 7 this document must be signed by the Lender or its conveyancer.*

© Crown copyright (ref: LR/HQ/CD-ROM) 6/03

of the application of the doctrine of *Walsh v Lonsdale* to mortgages, since the deposit of deeds was evidence of a contract to create a mortgage, or an imperfect legal mortgage.

Before 27 September 1989 this caused no difficulty, since under the formalities then applicable to a contract for an interest in land the deposit ranked as an act of part performance,[83] and so the deposit alone, without writing, was treated as constituting a contract to execute a legal mortgage.[84] Since 26 September 1989, however, the formalities of section 2 of the Law of Property (Miscellaneous Provisions) Act 1989 have to be satisfied.[85]

This is not to suggest that mortgages have commonly been made by deposit of title deeds without any accompanying written document. In practice the borrower would sign a memorandum executed as a deed contemporaneously with the delivery of the title deeds, for such a memorandum makes the transaction a mortgage by deed within the meaning of the Law of Property Act 1925, and entitles the equitable mortgagee to exercise all the powers, including the power of sale, given by the Act.[86] And since an equitable mortgagee cannot convey the legal estate to a purchaser, it is usual to insert a power of attorney or a declaration of trust, or both, in the memorandum, so as to enable the mortgagee to deal with the legal estate.[87] But the significance of the 1989 Act goes beyond this, since it requires all the express terms of the contract to be in writing signed by or on behalf of *both* parties: a memorandum signed only by the borrower will not therefore satisfy the requirements of the Act.

It should be noted that there is now no place for mortgages by deposit in registered land. Although provision was made in the Land Registration Act 1925 for the creation of a charge by deposit of the land certificate or charge certificate,[88] this is not reproduced in the 2002 Act because of the change in formalities for contracts under the Law of Property (Miscellaneous Provisions) Act 1989, and the consequential re-assessment of the place of mortgages by deposit.[89] It is a necessary reform, however, in any event because land certificates and charge certificates have themselves now been abolished.[90]

(b) Mortgage of an equitable interest

A mortgage of an equitable interest, such as a life interest arising under a settlement, or a contract for a lease,[91] is itself necessarily equitable. The method of creation corresponds to that employed before 1926 in the case of a legal mortgage of the fee simple, namely, the entire equitable interest is assigned to the mortgagee, subject to a proviso for reassignment on redemption.[92]

---

[83]   *Bank of New South Wales v O'Connor* (1889) 14 App Cas 273 at 282.

[84]   *Carter v Wake* (1877) 4 Ch D 605 at 606, per JESSEL MR. An actual deposit, though essential, was not in itself sufficient. The depositee must go further, and prove by parol or by written evidence that the deposit was intended to be by way of security, for the mere deposit by a customer of his deeds with a bank would not, for instance, constitute the bank an equitable mortgagee in respect of an overdraft: *Dixon v Muckleston* (1872) 8 Ch App 155; *Re Wallis & Simonds (Builders) Ltd* [1974] 1 WLR 391; *Thames Guaranty Ltd v Campbell* [1985] QB 210 (deposit of land certificate to secure a debt by one joint tenant without consent of the other joint tenant not effective to create equitable charge of the jointly owned land; but it could create a charge of the equitable interest of the depositor, if the deposit amounts to an act of severance, p. 458, ante); *First National Securities Ltd v Hegerty* [1985] QB 850; p. 458, n. 38, ante.

[85]   *United Bank of Kuwait plc v Sahib* [1997] Ch 107 ("The clear intention of section 2 . . . is to introduce certainty in relation to contracts for the disposition of interests in land where uncertainty existed before", per PHILLIPS LJ at 387); Emmet, para. 25.116; (1997) 113 LQR 533 (M. Robinson). For the liability of a solicitor for failing to advise (even before *Kuwait*) that the mortgage was required to satisfy s. 2, see *Dean v Allin & Watts* [2001] 2 Lloyd's Rep 249.   [86]   Pp. 782 et seq, post.

[87]   *Encyclopaedia of Forms and Precedents*, vol. 28, Form 47 (power of attorney).   [88]   LRA 1925, s. 66.

[89]   *United Bank of Kuwait plc v Sahib*, supra; H & B, para 12.5; Law Com No. 271, para. 7.9.

[90]   H & B, ch 21; p. 109, ante. The practice of entering a notice on the register, to support a deposit of the land certificate with the lender, was however already discontinued in 1995, following the decision at first instance in *United Bank of Kuwait plc v Sahib*, supra: H & B, para. 12.86.   [91]   *Rust v Goodale* [1957] Ch 33.

[92]   Waldock, *Law of Mortgages*, pp. 136–9.

The assignment, if not made by will, must be in writing signed by the mortgagor or by his agent thereunto lawfully authorised in writing[93] and the mortgagee should protect himself by giving written notice of it to the owner of the legal estate.[94]

(c) Equitable charge

Another form of equitable security, differing in respect of the remedies it confers from the forms already described, is the equitable charge. This arises where, without any transfer of, or agreement to transfer, ownership or possession, property is appropriated to the discharge of a debt or some other obligation.[95]

In *Matthews v Goodday*[96] KINDERSLEY V-C said:

With regard to what are called equitable mortgages, my notion is this. Suppose a man signed a written contract, by which he simply agreed that he thereby charged his real estate with £500 to A, what would be the effect of it?

It would be no agreement to give a legal mortgage, but a security by which he equitably charged his lands with payment of a sum of money, and the mode of enforcing it would be by coming into a court of equity to have the money raised by sale or mortgage; that would be the effect of such a simple charge. It is the same thing as if a testator devised an estate to A charged with the payment of a sum of money to B. B's right is not to foreclose A, but to have his charge raised by sale or mortgage of the land . . . But the thing would be distinctly an equitable charge, and not a mortgage nor an agreement to give one. On the other hand the party might agree that, having borrowed a sum of money, he would give a legal mortgage whenever called upon. That agreement might be enforced according to its terms, and the court would decree a legal mortgage to be given, and would also foreclose the mortgage, unless the money was paid.

An equitable charge does not have to satisfy section 2 of the Law of Property (Miscellaneous Provisions) Act 1989, because it involves the *creation* of a security rather than an *agreement to create* a legal charge. Its validity depends on section 53(1)(a) of the Law of Property Act 1925, which requires the writing to be signed by the chargor only.[97]

The remedies of an equitable chargee will be considered later.[98]

(d) Equitable mortgages in registered land

The registered proprietor has the general power to make any disposition permitted by the general law in relation to the description of interest that he holds,[99] and so, with two exceptions, he can create an equitable mortgage or charge in the same way as the owner of unregistered land. First, no mortgage by demise or sub-demise is now permitted in registered land;[100] and so a contract to create a legal mortgage by demise cannot be recognised as creating an equitable mortgage.[101] Secondly, as we have already noted, a mortgage by deposit of title deeds cannot be created since there are no longer documents of title in registered land.[102]

---

[93] LPA 1925, s. 53(1)(c); p. 904, post.

[94] Ibid., s. 137(1).

[95] *London County and Westminster Bank Ltd v Tompkins* [1918] 1 KB 515 at 528.

[96] (1861) 31 LJ Ch 282 at 282–3; *Swiss Bank Corpn v Lloyds Bank Ltd* [1982] AC 584 at 594–5, per BUCKLEY LJ; [1982] AC 584 at 613, per Lord WILBERFORCE; *Thames Guaranty Ltd v Campbell* [1985] QB 210. A purported legal charge of jointly owned property by one co-owner without the authority of the other has the effect only of charging in equity the former's interest: *First National Securities Ltd v Hegerty* [1985] QB 850; *Edwards v Lloyds Bank plc* [2005] 1 FCR 139 (wife's signature forged).

[97] Emmet, paras 25.116–25.117.   [98] P. 783, post.   [99] LRA 2002, s. 23(1).   [100] Ibid.

[101] The doctrine of *Walsh v Lonsdale*, p. 729, ante, rests on the basis that the court would order specific performance of the contract, which it could not do in the case of a contract to create a mortgage by demise. The language of LRA 2002, s. 23(1)(a) appears in any event sufficient to deprive the registered owner of the power to create an equitable mortgage by demise or sub-demise.   [102] P. 732, ante.

It should be recalled that, until the relevant registration requirements are met,[103] a mortgage over registered land executed as a legal charge does not operate at law, but takes effect only as an equitable mortgage.[104]

If it is to bind a purchaser from the mortgagor, an equitable mortgage requires protection by notice on the register unless it is an overriding interest by virtue of the mortgagee being in discoverable actual occupation (for example, where he has taken possession).[105]

(3) Charging Orders

The court has powers under the Charging Orders Act 1979 to impose a charge on the land of a judgment debtor to secure the payment of his judgment debt. Such a charge has the same effect as an equitable charge created by the debtor by writing under his hand.[106]

The Land Charges Act 1972 and the Land Registration Act 2002 apply to charging orders as they apply to other orders or writs made for the purpose of enforcing judgments.[107] Where the interest affected by the order is a beneficial interest under a trust of land, the interest can be overreached on sale,[108] and there is no provision for registration in unregistered land;[109] in registered land the order should be protected by a restriction.[110] All other charging orders should be protected by registration under the Land Charges Act 1972[111] (in the case of unregistered land) or by a notice on the register of the debtor's title[112] (in the case of registered land).

(4) Summary of Forms of Mortgage

If we look back at the different kinds of mortgages, we see that they may be either legal or equitable, and that the same land may be subjected both to several legal and to several equitable mortgages.

For example, the fee simple owner may have entered into the mortgages in the following order:

a legal charge to A;

a contract (not completed) to enter into a legal charge in favour of B;

a written agreement charging his land in favour of C;

a legal charge to D.

---

[103] P. 728, ante.   [104] LRA 2002, s. 27(1).

[105] Ibid., s. 29; Sch. 3, para. 2. Where, however, the mortgage is constituted by the transfer by way of charge of an interest which is an overreachable interest (e.g. a beneficial interest under a trust of land) the mortgage is itself overreachable.

[106] S. 3(4); *Ladup Ltd v Williams & Glyn's Bank plc* [1985] 1 WLR 851; *Clark v Chief Land Registrar* [1994] Ch 370. See generally Walker, *Charging Orders against Land.* See CPR r. 73.2–73.10.

If a charging order is obtained over land which is subject to a trust of land, the judgment creditor may then apply to the court under TLATA 1996, s. 14, p. 449 ante, for an order for sale of the property. See *Mortgage Corpn v Shaire* [2001] Ch 743 at 756–1, per NEUBERGER J (under TLATA 1996 the interest of the chargee (unlike that of the trustee in bankruptcy) is only one factor to be taken into account in deciding whether to order sale, thus changing the position which formerly applied in cases such as *Lloyds Bank plc v Byrne & Byrne* [1993] 1 FLR 369). A sample form of order for sale following a charging order is set out in Appendix A to CPR, PD73.

[107] Charging Orders Act 1979, s. 3, amended by LRA 2002, s. 133, Sch. 11, para. 15.

[108] For overreaching, see p. 447, ante; pp. 997–1000, post.

[109] LCA 1972, s. 6(1A), inserted by TLATA 1996, s. 25(1), Sch. 3, para. 12(1), (3).

[110] LRR 2003, r. 91, Sch. 4 (Form K).

[111] S. 6 (register of writs and orders affecting land).   [112] LRA 2002, s. 32.

The mortgages in favour of A and D, so long as they satisfy the necessary formalities,[113] take effect as legal mortgages; those in favour of B and C are only equitable.[114] It can be seen that a legal mortgage may follow an equitable mortgage of the same property.

We shall see later that whether a mortgage is legal or equitable can have significance for the rights it gives to the mortgagee;[115] and for the method—principally, registration—by which it should be protected so as to give the mortgagee's security priority as against later mortgagees and third parties.[116]

III Position and Rights of the Mortgagor[117]

A The Equity of Redemption

(1) Protection of the Mortgagor

A mortgagor, as we have seen, is the owner of the equity of redemption.[118] This is fundamental to the law of mortgages. It arises in the case of every conveyance or other transaction

---

[113] Execution as a deed and, in the case of registered land, completed by registration: pp. 725 et seq, ante.

[114] Respectively, an equitable mortgage under the doctrine of *Walsh v Lonsdale*: p. 729, ante; and an equitable charge: p. 733, ante.   [115] Pp. 762 et seq, post.

[116] Pp. 784 et seq, post.

[117] For a mortgagor's action in negligence against:

    (a) his solicitor where he enters into a mortgage as a result of the solicitor's failure to give proper advice, see *Forster v Outred & Co* [1982] 1 WLR 86; *Mortgage Express Ltd v Bowerman & Partners* [1996] 2 All ER 836 (duty of solicitor acting for mortgagor and sub-purchaser to inform mortgagor of price increase) [1996] Conv 204 (M. P. Thompson); *National Home Loans Corpn plc v Giffen Couch & Archer* [1998] 1 WLR 207 (solicitor acting for both mortgagor and mortgagee under a duty to inform mortgagee of mortgagor's default in previous mortgage);

    (b) the mortgagee's surveyor on whose negligent report he relied, see *Smith v Eric S Bush* [1990] 1 AC 831; [1989] Conv 359 (C. Francis); [1989] CLJ 306 (W. V. H. Rogers); (1989) 105 LQR 511 (D. Allen); (1989) 52 MLR 841 (T. Kaye); *Midland Bank v Cox McQueen* [1999] 1 FLR 1002 (solicitor not liable for loss caused by forged signature of wife executing charge); *Nationwide Building Society v Goodwin Harte* [1999] Lloyd's Rep PN 338 (breach of contract and fiduciary duty). On the duties of a solicitor acting for both mortgagor and mortgagee, see also Solicitors' Practice Rules 1990, r. 6(3), as amended; [1999] Conv 2 (P. H. Kenny); *Beaumont v Humberts* [1990] 2 EGLR 166; *Roberts v J Hampson & Co* [1990] 1 WLR 94;

    (c) a valuer: *South Australian Asset Management Corpn v York Montague Ltd* (the *Banque Bruxelles* case) [1997] AC 191 (extent of liability of valuer who provided mortgagee with negligent over-valuation, where mortgagee would not have lent if it had received careful valuation); (1997) 113 LQR 1 (J. Stapleton); [1997] CLJ 19 (J. O'Sullivan); *Nykredit Mortgage Bank plc v Edward Erdman Group Ltd (No 2)* [1997] 1 WLR 1627; Cartwright, *Misrepresentation*, para. 5.41; *Oates v Anthony Pitman & Co* (1998) 76 P & CR 490; *Platform Home Loans Ltd v Oyston Shipways Ltd* [1996] 2 EGLR 110, per Jacob J ("valuation is an art not a science, but it is not astrology"); on appeal [2000] 2 AC 190; (1999) 115 LQR 527 (J. Stapleton) (imprudent lending policy can constitute contributory negligence when loan made in reliance on negligent valuation); *United Bank of Kuwait plc v Prudential Property Services Ltd* [1994] 30 EG 103 (criteria for valuation; contributory negligence of mortgagee in making advance); RICS Appraisal and Valuation Standards (5th edn, 2003); *Bristol and West Building Society v Mothew* [1998] Ch 1 (causation and relationship with measure of damages). On the applicability of the Unfair Contract Terms Act 1977, s. 11(3) see *Smith v Eric S Bush*, supra; *Davies v Parry* [1988] 1 EGLR 147; *Cheltenham and Gloucester Building Society v Ebbage* [1994] CLY 3292.

[118] Pp. 721, ante.

relating to property, whether styled a mortgage or not, in which the true intention of the parties is that the subject matter shall be security for a debt or other obligation. Outwardly a transaction may wear the appearance of an absolute conveyance; it may even be deliberately couched in language calculated to give that appearance, yet evidence is admissible to disclose the true intention of the parties.[119] A transaction, for instance, which takes the form of a sale by A to B, with a right in B of repurchase upon payment of a given sum on a day certain may or may not be a mortgage. It is a matter of intention. "The question always is—was the original transaction a bona fide sale with a contract for repurchase, or was it a mortgage under the form of a sale."[120] If it was the former, there is no right in B to redeem the property after the contract date.

What particularly concerns us here, however, is to notice that equity, in order to ensure that a transaction intended to be by way of mortgage shall afford nothing more than security to the lender, has laid down two important rules concerning, first, the inviolability of the right of redemption; and secondly, the limits within which collateral advantages may be reserved to a mortgagee.

It will be seen, as the cases on these two rules are discussed, that in the twentieth century there was a development from a rigid to a more flexible attitude to the relationship between mortgagor and mortgagee, and an increasing awareness that, unless there is evidence of harsh and unconscionable dealing, a bargain freely entered into between the parties must be kept.

Let us consider these rules separately.

(a) The right of redemption is inviolable

Since the object of a mortgage is merely to provide the mortgagee with a security, any provision which directly or indirectly prevents the recovery by the mortgagor of his property upon performance of the obligation for which the security was created, is repugnant to the very nature of the transaction and therefore void, for when performance is completed there is no longer any need or justification for the retention of the security. As ROMER J said:

Now there is a principle which I will accept without any qualification . . . that on a mortgage you cannot, by contract between the mortgagor and mortgagee, clog, as it is termed, the equity of redemption so as to prevent the mortgagor from redeeming on payment of principal, interest and costs.[121]

This principle is generally expressed in the aphorism, *once a mortgage always a mortgage*.[122] There are two aspects of this rule:

(1) THE RIGHT TO REDEEM MUST NOT BE EXCLUDED

The courts refuse to countenance any provision which unduly restricts, even if it does not altogether prevent, the right of redemption. Each of the following cases exemplifies an

---

[119] "No mortgage by any artificial words can be altered, unless by subsequent agreement"; *Jason v Eyres* (1681) 2 Cas in Ch 33.

[120] *Williams v Owen* (1840) 5 My & Cr 303 at 306, per Lord COTTENHAM; *Greendon Holdings Ltd v Oragwu* [1989] EGCS 100; *Lavin v Johnson* [2002] EWCA Civ 1138 at [82], per ROBERT WALKER LJ: "to say that the identification of a mortgage is a matter of substance, not form, is not to say that any transaction which is expected to produce the same economic consequences as a mortgage must be a mortgage in the eyes of the law".

[121] *Biggs v Hoddinott* [1898] 2 Ch 307 at 314.

[122] *Samuel v Jarrah Timber and Wood Paving Corpn Ltd* [1904] AC 323 at 329.

agreement that was held void as being inconsistent with or repugnant to the true nature of a mortgage transaction:

(1) An agreement that redemption should be available to the mortgagor and *the heirs of his body*, and not to anyone else.[123]

(2) An agreement which renders part of the mortgaged property absolutely irredeemable.[124]

(3) A covenant by the mortgagor that the mortgagee, if he so desired, should be entitled to a conveyance of so much of the mortgaged estate as should equal the value of the loan at twenty years' purchase.[125]

(4) A covenant that if the borrower died before his father the subject matter of the mortgage should belong absolutely to the mortgagee.[126]

In two cases at the beginning of the last century the House of Lords considered provisions in mortgages which gave to the mortgagee an option to purchase the mortgaged property. In *Samuel v Jarrah Timber and Wood Paving Corpn Ltd*,[127] the option was given at the time of the creation of the mortgage and was held to be void; for otherwise the mortgagee by exercising the option could exclude the mortgagor's right of redemption. In *Reeve v Lisle*,[128] however, an option to purchase was held to be valid, where it was given by a subsequent and independent transaction, even though the only consideration was the release of the mortgagor from his obligation to pay the original loan. Lord HALSBURY and Lord MACNAGHTEN, who delivered speeches in both cases, expressed a lack of enthusiasm for their decision in *Samuel v Jarrah*. Lord HALSBURY said:[129]

A perfectly fair bargain made between two parties to it, each of whom was quite sensible of what they were doing, is not to be performed because at the same time a mortgage arrangement was made between them. If a day had intervened between the two parts of the arrangement, the part of the bargain which the appellant claims to be performed would have been perfectly good and capable of being enforced; but a line of authorities going back for more than a century has decided that such an arrangement as that which was here arrived at is contrary to a principle of equity, the sense or reason of which I am not able to appreciate, and very reluctantly I am compelled to acquiesce in the judgments appealed from.

And Lord MACNAGHTEN said[130] of the decision:

I should not be sorry if your Lordships could see your way to modify it so as to prevent its being used as a means of evading a fair bargain come to between persons dealing at arms' length and negotiating on equal terms. The directors of a trading company in search of financial assistance are certainly in a very different position from that of an impecunious landowner in the toils of a crafty money-lender.

Samuel v Jarrah was followed in *Lewis v Frank Love Ltd*[131] where, on the transfer of a mortgage, the mortgagor gave to the transferees an option to purchase. There were separate

---

[123] *Howard v Harris* (1682) 1 Vern 33; *Salt v Marquess of Northampton* [1892] AC 1.

[124] *Davis v Symons* [1934] Ch 442.

[125] *Jennings v Ward* (1705) 2 Vern 520, as explained in *Biggs v Hoddinott* [1898] 2 Ch 307 at 315, 323.

[126] *Salt v Marquess of Northampton*, supra.

[127] [1904] AC 323, M & B p. 802. For searching criticisms of this scholastic attitude, see (1903) 18 LQR 359 (Sir Frederick Pollock); M & B p. 803; (1944) 60 LQR at 191 (G. L. Williams).

[128] [1902] AC 461, M & B p. 803. See also *Alec Lobb (Garages) Ltd v Total Oil GB Ltd* [1985] 1 WLR 173; p. 755, n. 233, post. [129] [1904] AC 323 at 325.

[130] At 327. [131] [1961] 1 WLR 261; (1961) 77 LQR 163 (P.V.B.).

documents for the transfer and the mortgage, but PLOWMAN J held that the loan and the grant of the option were all part and parcel of one transaction.

In two cases the Court of Appeal has recently applied the doctrine set out in *Samuel v Jarrah*, but has expressed some misgivings about it. In one case an option to purchase fell within the doctrine, and was therefore struck down;[132] but in the other the Court emphasised that the court should look at the substance of the transaction, to inquire as to the true nature of the bargain which the parties have made. The mere fact that, contemporaneously with the grant of a mortgage over his property, the mortgagor grants the mortgagee an option to purchase the property does no more than raise the question whether the rule against 'clogs' applies.[133] Lord PHILLIPS MR has said:[134]

The doctrine of a clog on the equity of redemption is . . . an appendix to our law that no longer serves a useful purpose;

and JONATHAN PARKER LJ has added:[135]

it has to be accepted that the "unruly dog" is still alive (although one might perhaps reasonably expect its venerable age to inhibit it from straying too far or too often from its kennel); and that however desirable an appendectomy might be thought to be, no such relieving operation has as yet been carried out.

The doctrine of *Samuel v Jarrah Timber and Wood Paving Corpn Ltd* is due for reconsideration by the House of Lords.[136]

(2) THE RIGHT TO REDEEM MAY BE POSTPONED

(i) Postponement

An important question is whether the postponement for a considerable period of the contractual right to redeem is objectionable as being an unreasonable interference with the rights of the mortgagor. If a mortgage is in essence a mere security, it is arguable that a clause which prolongs the security after the mortgagor is ready and willing to pay all that is due, is one that ought not to be upheld, even though it was accepted by him without objection at

---

[132] *Jones v Morgan* [2002] 1 EGLR 125, M & B p. 804 (variation of existing mortgage which gave mortgagee right to buy part of property comprised in original mortgage: the right to purchase was an integral part of the financing agreement; PILL LJ dissenting on construction); [2001] Conv 500 (M. P. Thompson).

[133] *Warnborough Ltd v Garmite Ltd* [2003] EWCA Civ 1544, [2004] 1 P & CR DG8 (where option to purchase is granted against the background of a sale of the property by the grantee of the option, as owner of the property, to the grantor for a price which is to be left outstanding on mortgage, there must be a very strong likelihood that, on an examination of all the circumstances, the court will conclude that the substance of the transaction is one of sale and purchase and not one of mortgage: per JONATHAN PARKER LJ at [76]: case remitted for decision on facts at trial, where judge held that the transaction was sale and purchase: [2006] 03 EG 121 (CS)).

[134] *Jones v Morgan* [2002] I EGLR 125, at 136.   [135] *Warnborough Ltd v Garmite Ltd*, supra, at [72].

[136] See also other developments in other aspects of the equity of redemption, discussed in the following sections; and especially *Knightsbridge Estates Trust Ltd v Byrne* [1939] Ch 441, infra; and *Kreglinger v New Patagonia Meat and Cold Storage Co Ltd* [1914] AC 25, p. 744, post. See also (1985) Real Property Probate and Trust Journal 821 (L. C. Prebble and D. W. Cartwright); (1986–86) 60 St John's Law Review 452 (J. L. Light).

For proposals to reform the law to abolish the equitable jurisdiction concerned with clogs and fetters on the equity of redemption, see p. 811, post. For legislation in the USA removing the mortgagee's option from the purview of the doctrine of clogs, see Uniform Land Security Interest Act 1986, para. 211; New York General Obligations Law 1986, para. 5.334; California Civil Code (1984), para. 2906; cited 60 St John's Law Review at pp. 492–7.

the time of the loan. The question was much canvassed by the Court of Appeal in *Knightsbridge Estates Trust Ltd v Byrne*,[137] where the facts were as follows:

The Knightsbridge Company had mortgaged their property, consisting of 75 houses, eight shops and a block of flats, to the Prudential Assurance Company in return for a loan of £300,000 at 6½ per cent. The loan was liable to be called in at any time, and the mortgagors, desiring to obtain a reduction in the rate of interest and also to spread the repayment of the principal sum over a long term of years, transferred the mortgage to the Royal Liver Friendly Society. This mortgage was for £310,000 at 5¼ per cent, and at the suggestion of the mortgagors it was agreed that the loan should be repaid in forty years by half-yearly instalments. The mortgagees agreed not to call the money in before the end of this period, provided that the instalments were punctually paid. A few years later, when mortgage interest rates fell again, the mortgagors sued for a declaration that they were entitled, on giving the usual six months' notice, to redeem the mortgage upon payment of principal, interest and costs.

It was argued for the mortgagors that this suspension for forty years of the contractual right to redeem their property was unreasonable and therefore void. The Court of Appeal, however, upheld the suspension and denied that reasonableness, whether in respect of time or in other respects, is the true criterion of validity in such a case.[138] A contract freely entered into after due deliberation by parties dealing with each other at arms' length is not lightly to be interfered with.

As Sir WILFRID GREENE MR said:

The resulting agreement was a commercial agreement between two important corporations experienced in such matters, and has none of the features of an oppressive bargain where the borrower is at the mercy of an unscrupulous lender.[139]

A court of equity, indeed, is vigilant in its support of the principle that "redemption is of the very nature and essence of a mortgage",[140] but none the less it does not attempt to reform mortgage transactions.

(ii) Illusory right of redemption

A provision, however, which leaves the mortgagor with nothing more than an illusory right of redemption has been held to be void. In *Fairclough v Swan Brewery Co Ltd*,[141] for instance:

the mortgagor was a tenant of a brewery in Western Australia, with an unexpired lease of seventeen and a half years. The mortgage prevented redemption until a date six weeks before the lease expired. There was no evidence of oppression.

The Privy Council held that this provision rendered the property substantially irredeemable, and therefore the mortgagor was entitled to redeem at an earlier date.

---

[137] [1939] Ch 441, M & B p. 808; on appeal, [1940] AC 613, the House of Lords decided the case on an entirely different ground, namely that the mortgage was a valid debenture under the Companies Act 1929, s. 74 (now 1985, s. 193) and expressed no opinion upon the reasoning of the Court of Appeal.

[138] See *Multiservice Bookbinding Ltd v Marden* [1979] Ch 84 at 108, p. 742, post.

[139] [1939] Ch 441 at 455.   [140] *Noakes & Co Ltd v Rice* [1902] AC 24 at 30 per Lord MACNAGHTEN.

[141] [1912] AC 565, M & B p. 807. Restraint of trade was also pleaded, at 566.

This decision of the Privy Council is in conflict with an earlier decision of the Court of Appeal, which was not cited to the Council. In *Santley v Wilde*:[142]

S was the lessee of a theatre, the lease still having ten years to run. In return for a loan for the purpose of carrying on the theatre, S mortgaged the lease to W, and covenanted that she would repay the capital by instalments and also that she would "during the residue of the term, notwithstanding that all principal moneys and interest may have been paid, pay a sum equal to one-third part of the clear net profit rent or rents to be derived" from the lease. There was a provision that the mortgage should determine on payment of the principal sum and interest and "all other the moneys hereinbefore covenanted to be paid".

As LINDLEY MR said, W's "security depended not only on the solvency of the lady but also on the success of the theatre". S claimed a declaration that she was entitled to redeem on payment of principal interest and costs and that the provision for a share of the profits was illegal and void. The Court of Appeal held that S could not redeem except by observing all the covenants for which her property was given as security, including the profit-sharing covenant. In effect the mortgage was irredeemable until the end of the lease, since only then could the net profits be earned and calculated.

Accordingly, another old rule may come under review in the future, and rather than remorselessly applying the rule in *Fairclough v Swan Brewery Co Ltd* the courts may, in the absence of fraud or oppression, hold the parties to their bargain.

(b) Collateral advantages

A collateral advantage in favour of the mortgagee means something that is granted to him in addition to the return of his loan with interest, as for instance where a mortgagor agrees that for a given number of years he will purchase beer (or oil and petrol) for sale on the premises only from the mortgagee.

The question whether the reservation of such an advantage is valid is rendered difficult by a number of apparently irreconcilable decisions stretching back for more than a century. Indeed, the case law will be unintelligible unless it is realised that the attitude of the courts towards the matter has changed materially in the course of the last century, and that reliance can no longer be placed upon many of the older decisions. Lord HALDANE, in a reference to one of the early cases of the modern era,[143] said: "In the 17th and 18th centuries a Court of Equity could hardly have so decided, and the judgment illustrates the elastic character of equity jurisdiction and the power of equity judges to mould the rules which they apply in accordance with the exigencies of the time."[144]

In early days the judges frowned upon any attempt by a mortgagee to reap some additional advantage, as is shown by a remark of TREVOR MR in 1705 that:

a man shall not have interest for his money on a mortgage, and a collateral advantage besides for the loan of it.[145]

---

142 [1899] 2 Ch 474, M & B p. 805. It was the view of Dr J. H. C. Morris that "the transaction was not in essence one of mortgage, but a partnership agreement to share in the profits of the theatre", and therefore valid on that ground: Waldock, *Law of Mortgages*, p. 187.　　143 *Biggs v Hoddinott* [1898] 2 Ch 307, M & B p. 812.

144 *Kreglinger v New Patagonia Meat and Cold Storage Co Ltd* [1914] AC 25 at 38.

145 *Jennings v Ward* (1705) 2 Vern 520.

In a time when there was statutory control of interest rates, through usury laws designed to avoid the exploitation of borrowers, it was natural that the courts should be wary of any attempt by lenders to circumvent the statute by securing an advantage that did not constitute interest. However, in modern times a more realistic and favourable note has been struck. The usury laws were repealed in 1854,[146] which therefore removed an objection to collateral advantages in a contact of loan. And the mortgagor is no longer seen as in need of such general special protection.[147] As Lord HALDANE said in 1914:[148]

The rule as to collateral advantages . . . has been much modified by the repeal of the usury laws and by the recognition of modern varieties of commercial bargaining.

In the eye of the novelist, no doubt, the mortgagor is an impoverished debtor on the brink of ruin, unable to resist the demands of the rapacious lender, and it is perhaps true that the Court of Chancery in its more paternal days tended to take a somewhat similar view of his predicament. In fact, however, the parties to a modern mortgage may be hard-headed businessmen well able to protect their own interests, and in these days, when so much stress is laid upon the sanctity of contracts, it is difficult to appreciate why one of them should be allowed to disregard a bargain freely made, simply because he happens to be a mortgagor. Such maxims as "Once a mortgage, always a mortgage" and "A mortgage cannot be made irredeemable", undoubtedly express an important principle, but to apply them in an unbending and inflexible fashion so as to upset an ordinary commercial transaction would be out of keeping with the times. As Lord PARKER OF WADDINGTON said:[149]

Such maxims, however convenient, afford little assistance where the court has to deal with a new or doubtful case. They obviously beg the question, always of great importance, whether the particular transaction which the court has to consider is, in fact, a mortgage or not, and if they be acted on without a careful consideration of the equitable considerations on which they are based, can only, like Bacon's idols of the market place, lead to misconception and error.

Despite the judicial uncertainties of the past, the modern law on the subject is clear, though its application to particular cases may be a difficult matter. As we shall see, collateral advantages are no longer struck down simply because they are collateral advantages. They are only invalidated where they are either unfair or unconscionable, or where they unfairly restrict redemption.

(1) THE COLLATERAL ADVANTAGE MUST NOT BE UNFAIR OR UNCONSCIONABLE

In certain circumstances, a contract may be set aside as an "unconscionable bargain".[150] In English law[151] this is not a principle that has been applied generally to all types of contract,

---

[146] Usury Laws Repeal Act 1854.

[147] Statutory protection against "harsh and unconscionable transactions" was introduced by Money-Lenders Act 1900; see now CCA 1974, ss. 137–40, p. 747, post. The equitable jurisdiction to relieve against unconscionable bargains, infra, was also developed after the repeal of the usury laws as a tool to control unconscionable loans: Ibbetson, *Historical Introduction to the Law of Obligations*, p. 254. But these are more flexible rules, capable of discriminating between those borrowers that need protection, and those that can look after themselves.   [148] *Kreglinger v New Patagonia Meat and Cold Storage Co Ltd* [1914] AC 25 at 38.

[149] *Kreglinger v New Patagonia Meat and Cold Storage Co Ltd*, supra, at 53, M & B p. 816.

[150] Anson, pp. 296–8; Chitty, paras. 7–111 to 7–120.

[151] Commonwealth jurisdictions and the courts in the USA have been more favourable to the development of a general doctrine of unconscionability in contract: Chitty, para. 7–121.

nor one that has been applied very often in the modern law;[152] but one area in which it has been applied, both historically[153] and in the recent cases,[154] is that of mortgages.

In order to invoke this principle, the terms of the transaction must be "not merely hard or improvident, but overreaching and oppressive".[155] The court will always be astute to invalidate a mortgage which is unfair and unconscionable. Thus, in *Cityland and Property (Holdings) Ltd v Dabrah*:[156]

the mortgagor was a tenant who was buying the freehold of his house from his landlord and was "obviously of limited means"; he undertook to pay a premium or bonus which represented either no less than 57 per cent of the amount of the loan or interest at 19 per cent.

GOFF J stressed that this was not a "bargain between two large trading concerns" and held that the mortgagor was entitled to redeem by paying the capital sum borrowed with reasonable interest fixed by the court.

In *Multiservice Bookbinding Ltd v Marden*,[157] BROWNE-WILKINSON J emphasised that the mortgagor must show that the bargain was unfair and unconscionable and not merely unreasonable and, furthermore,

a bargain cannot be unfair and unconscionable unless one of the parties to it has imposed the objectionable terms in a morally reprehensible manner, that is to say, in a way which affects his conscience.[158]

Not only, therefore, must *terms* of the transaction be unconscionable, but also the mortgage must have been obtained by unconscionable *conduct*. In that case:

the mortgagor was a small but progressive company in need of cash to enable it to expand; it had acted with independent legal advice. The mortgagee was only willing to lend money if he could be safeguarded against a decline in the purchasing power of sterling. The terms of the mortgage were that (i) interest be payable at 2 per cent above bank rate on the full capital sum for the duration of the mortgage, (ii) arrears of interest be capitalised after 21 days (thus providing for interest on interest), (iii) the loan be neither called in nor redeemed for ten years, and (iv) the value of the capital and interest be index-linked to the Swiss franc. When the mortgage became redeemable at the end of ten years in 1976, the total capital repayment had become £87,588 as against £36,000 lent, and the average rate of interest over the ten years would have been 16.01 per cent.

---

[152] More commonly claims have been brought under the equitable doctrine of undue influence, p. 749, post.

[153] *Earl of Aylesford v Morris* (1873) 8 Ch App 484; *Barrett v Hartley* (1866) LR 2 Eq 789 at 795; *James v Kerr* (1889) 40 Ch D 449; Waldock, *Law of Mortgages*, chap. 8.

[154] *Cityland and Property (Holdings) Ltd v Dabrah*, infra; *Multiservice Bookbinding Ltd v Marden*, infra; *Alec Lobb (Garages) Ltd v Total Oil (Great Britain) Ltd* [1985] 1 WLR 173; *Crédit Lyonnais Bank Nederland NV v Burch* [1997] 1 All ER 144 (transaction set aside for undue influence, but was also an unconscionable bargain: at 151, per NOURSE LJ; see also at 152–3, per MILLETT LJ). See also [1995] LMCLQ 538 (N. Bamforth).

[155] *Alec Lobb (Garages) Ltd v Total Oil (Great Britain) Ltd* [1983] 1 WLR 87 at 95, per Peter MILLETT QC. See also *Crédit Lyonnais Bank Nederland NV v Burch*, supra, at 152–3, per MILLETT LJ.

[156] [1968] Ch 166. See also CCA 1974, ss. 137–40, pp. 747–8, post. It would appear that the mortgagor would also have succeeded under these sections.

[157] [1979] Ch 84, M & B p. 820; [1978] Conv 346 (H. W. Wilkinson), 432 (D. W. Williams); and for an economist's view (1981) 131 NLJ 4 (R. A. Bowles). CCA 1974 was not applicable, since the mortgagor was a body corporate. The rate may be linked to "the base rate of X Bank plc"; see Conv Prec. 5–11.

[158] Ibid., at 110. See *Boustany v Piggott* (1995) 69 P & CR 288, where PC set aside a lease on the grounds that it was an unconscionable bargain; *Commercial Bank of Australia Ltd v Amadio* (1983) 46 ALR 402, [1996] Conv 434 (M. Pawlowski); *Jones v Morgan* [2002] 1 EGLR 125 at 129–30.

It was held that all the terms of the mortgage were valid. An index-linked money obligation was not contrary to public policy, and the bargain, though hard, was not unfair and unconscionable.[159]

(2) THE COLLATERAL ADVANTAGE MUST NOT UNFAIRLY RESTRICT REDEMPTION

We must now turn to the chequered history of collateral advantages. Most of the cases are concerned with an advantage which is to continue *after* redemption. In *Biggs v Hoddinott*,[160] however, where it was designed to cease with redemption, the Court of Appeal had no difficulty in holding it valid. In that case:

Hoddinott mortgaged his hotel to Biggs, the brewer, in return for an advance of £7,654, and agreed that during the continuance of the mortgage he would sell no other beer than that supplied by B. It was mutually agreed that the mortgage should not be redeemable, nor should the loan be repayable, for five years.

The claim of Hoddinott, made two years later, that he was entitled to be released from the solus agreement and to procure beer elsewhere upon repayment of the loan, was rejected.[161]

Where, however, the advantage was designed to continue after redemption, the House of Lords struck it down in two cases. First, in *Noakes & Co Ltd v Rice*,[162] where:

the tenant of a public-house, under a lease which had 26 years to run, mortgaged the premises as security for a loan and covenanted that for the duration of the lease, whether he had already repaid the mortgage money or not, he would not sell any malt liquors except those provided by the mortgagees. Three years later he claimed a declaration that he should be released from the covenant upon payment of all moneys due under the mortgage.

It was held by the House of Lords that he was entitled to the release he claimed. His right of redemption was hampered in the sense that after attainment of the object for which the security was created he would not be master in his own house—he would not recover his property as it was before the mortgage. "The public-house, which was free when mortgaged, would have been tied to the mortgagee when redeemed."[163]

Secondly, in *Bradley v Carritt*:[164]

the defendant, who owned shares which gave him a controlling interest in a tea company, mortgaged them to the plaintiff, a tea-broker, and in further consideration for the loan, entered into the following contract:

"I agree . . . to use my best endeavours as a shareholder to secure that you or any firm of brokers of which you for the time being shall be a partner shall *always hereafter* have the sale of the company's teas

---

[159] A building society has power to make an index-linked mortgage: *Nationwide Building Society v Registry of Friendly Societies* [1983] 1 WLR 1226 (decided under Building Societies Act 1962, ss. 1, 4). See also Building Societies Act 1986, ss. 10(10), 11(2) (repealed by Building Societies Act 1997, s. 12(1)), 9A (inserted by Building Societies Act 1997, s. 10).

[160] [1898] 2 Ch 307, M & B p. 812; approved by the House of Lords in *Noakes & Co Ltd v Rice* [1902] AC 24, M & B p. 813.

[161] There was no appeal from the decision of Romer J at first instance, that the postponement of the right to redeem for five years was valid; p. 736, ante.

[162] [1902] AC 24, M & B p. 813. See also *Morgan v Jeffreys* [1910] 1 Ch 620. The discussions in these two cases could not be justified on the ground that the tie imposed upon the publican was void as being in restraint of trade; see *Esso Petroleum Co Ltd v Harper's Garage (Stourport) Ltd* [1968] AC 269, p. 755, post.

[163] *Bradley v Carritt* [1903] AC 253 at 277–8, per Lord Lindley.

[164] [1903] AC 253, M & B p. 815.

as broker, and in the case of any of the company's teas being sold otherwise than through you or your firm, I personally agree to pay you or your firm the amount of the commission which you or your firm would have earned if the teas had been sold through you or your firm."

The plaintiff was appointed broker; but the defendant repaid the loan, redeemed his shares and transferred them to another mortgagee, X, who succeeded in ousting the plaintiff from his appointment.

The House of Lords, reversing by a majority of three to two the court of first instance and the Court of Appeal, held that the agreement set out above was void, and that the defendant was not liable for its breach. Lord LINDLEY and Lord SHAND, however, dissented. What weighed with the majority was that, after redemption, the shares would be more or less frozen assets in the hands of the mortgagor, since, unless he showed great vigilance, their sale would almost certainly result in his being liable to the plaintiff for loss of brokerage; they gave him a controlling interest in the tea company, and it was only by retaining them that he could ensure the continued employment of the plaintiff as broker.

In spite of these two decisions, the House of Lords came to a different conclusion in *Kreglinger v New Patagonia Meat and Cold Storage Co Ltd*,[165] where the facts were as follows:

A firm of woolbrokers lent £10,000 to a company which carried on business as meat preservers, the agreement being that the company might pay off the loan at any time by giving a month's notice. The loan was secured, not by an ordinary mortgage, but by an analogous security called a floating charge.[166] It was agreed that for five years from the date of the loan the company would not sell sheepskins to any person other than the lenders, so long as the latter were willing to pay the full market price. It was also agreed that the lenders would not demand repayment before five years had elapsed. The loan was repaid within two and a half years. The point that fell to be decided was whether the option on the sheepskins was enforceable by the lenders after repayment of the loan.

The House held unanimously that the lenders were entitled to an injunction restraining the company from selling skins to third parties during the remainder of the five years. While it was true that the company would not be as free in the conduct of their business after repayment of the loan as they were before the grant of the charge, the House of Lords unanimously held that the agreement should be upheld, and that it should continue to bind the mortgagor even though it was to continue after redemption. For Viscount HALDANE LC the matter was one of construction:[167]

The question in the present case is whether the right to redeem has been interfered with. And this must . . . depend on the answer to a question which is primarily one of fact. What was the true character of the transaction? Did the appellants make a bargain such that the right to redeem was cut down, or did they simply stipulate for a collateral undertaking, outside and clear of the mortgage, which would give them an exclusive option of purchase of the sheepskins of the respondents? The question is in my opinion not whether the two contracts were made at the same moment and evidenced by the same instrument, but whether they were in substance a single and undivided

---

165 [1914] AC 25, M & B p. 816.

166 This, though a charge upon the assets for the time being, does not prevent a company from dealing with its property in the ordinary course of business, but it does so when the chargee takes steps, such as by the appointment of a receiver, to crystallize the security. For the characteristics of the charge, see *Re Yorkshire Woolcombers Association Ltd* [1903] 2 Ch 284 at 295, per ROMER J; *Re Spectrum Plus Ltd* [2005] 2 AC 680; and for crystallisation of a charge, see *Re Woodroffes (Musical Instruments) Ltd* [1986] Ch 366; *Re Brightlife Ltd* [1987] Ch 200; (1976) 40 Conv (NS) 397 (J. H. Farrar); [1988] CLJ 213 (E. Ferran); *William Gaskell Group Ltd v Highley (Nos 1, 2, 3)* [1993] BCC 200. See generally [1994] CLJ 81 (S. Worthington); *Re Cosslett (Contractors) Ltd* [1998] Ch 495.

167 At 39. See *De Beers Consolidated Mines Ltd v British South Africa Co* [1912] AC 52, M & B p. 823; *Re Petrol Filling Station, Vauxhall Bridge Road, London* (1968) 20 P & CR 1, M & B p. 824.

contract or two distinct contracts . . . If your Lordships arrive at the conclusion that the agreement for an option to purchase the respondents' sheepskins was not in substance a fetter on the exercise of their right to redeem, but was in the nature of a collateral bargain the entering into which was a preliminary and separable condition of the loan, the decided cases cease to present any great difficulty.

And their Lordships so concluded. This approach provides the court with a much needed flexibility in the area of collateral advantages and enables it to adapt the earlier strict rules to modern circumstances.

Bradley v Carritt thus represents the high-water mark of the conception of a mortgage as an onerous obligation imposed upon a necessitous borrower, in whose favour the court should therefore intervene.[168] The *Kreglinger* case, on the other hand, reveals a judicial appreciation of a mortgage as a transaction freely concluded by businessmen without colour of oppression, which should therefore form no exception to the maxim *pacta sunt servanda*. This is a more realistic and reasonable approach, and one more compatible with the business conditions of the modern era.

In 1914 Lord MERSEY said in the *Kreglinger* case:[169]

The doctrine itself seems to me to be like an unruly dog, which, if not securely chained to its own kennel, is prone to wander into places where it ought not to be. Its introduction into the present case would give effect to no equity and would defeat justice.

The dog is now under control.

We must now consider further bases of protection of the mortgagor. The first two are statutory, the third equitable and the fourth common law.

(c) Consumer Credit Act 1974

(1) REGULATED AGREEMENTS

The Consumer Credit Act 1974[170] establishes a comprehensive code which regulates the supply of credit to an individual.[171] The Act includes provisions on advertising[172] and canvassing; the licensing of credit and hire businesses; all aspects of the agreement; and judicial control over its enforcement.

To come within the Act, a mortgage must constitute a regulated consumer credit agreement, that is to say, a personal credit agreement by which a creditor provides a debtor with credit not exceeding £25,000.[173] There are, however, exempt agreements,[174] of which the

---

[168] Waldock, *Law of Mortgages*, chap. viii.   [169] [1914] AC 25 at 46.

[170] See Bennion and Dobson, *Consumer Credit Control*; Lomnicka, *Encyclopaedia of Consumer Credit Law*; Goode, *Consumer Credit Law and Practice*; Cousins, chap. 11; Fisher and Lightwood, chap. 10; [1975] CLJ 79 (R. M. Goode); (1975) 39 Conv (NS) 94 (J. E. Adams). On consumer credit reform, see (2004) 154 NLJ 1294 (K. Mather). A Consumer Credit Bill, to amend CCA 1974, is expected to become law in 2006.

[171] This includes a partnership: s. 189(1).

[172] Consumer Credit (Advertisement) Regulations 2004 (SI 2004 No. 1484); (2004) 148 SJ 1298 (N. Chowdhury).

[173] S. 8. Consumer Credit (Increase of Monetary Limits) Amendment Order 1998 (SI 1998 No. 996), increasing the amount from £15,000. It was originally £5,000. The Consumer Credit Bill, n. 170, supra, would remove this limit, so that all consumer credit agreements will be regulated by the 1974 Act unless specifically exempted, regardless of the amount of the credit.

[174] S. 16, as amended by Building Societies Act 1986, Sch. 18, para. 10. Consumer Credit (Exempt Agreements) Order 1989 (SI 1989 No. 869); as amended by SI 1989 Nos 1841 and 2337; SI 1991 Nos. 1393, 1949 and 2844; SI 1993 Nos. 346 and 2922; SI 1994 Nos. 869 and 2420; SI 1996 Nos. 1445 and 3081; SI 1995 No. 2914;

most important are loans secured by a land mortgage made by a building society, bank[175] or local authority or housing authority for house purchase.

Owing to the financial limit of £25,000, only second mortgages are likely to come within the definition of a regulated consumer agreement. As the Crowther Report, on which the Act is based, said:[176]

Much of the money borrowed on second mortgage is spent on improvements of various kinds to houses that are used as security. But there is no necessary tie, in most cases, between the loan and the purpose for which it is used—indeed, many of the advertisements emphasise the borrower's freedom to spend it on anything he chooses. Undoubtedly, there are people who have been led by this sort of advertising to endanger the security of their homes for the sake of some unnecessary extravagance.

A land mortgage securing a regulated agreement is enforceable on an order of the court only.[177] And a regulated agreement which is "improperly executed" (that is, it does not comply with the formalities prescribed in Part V of the Act) can also be enforced only on an order of the court.[178]

There are other provisions which protect a debtor. These include section 93 which prohibits any term requiring the rate of interest to be increased on default; and section 94 under which the debtor has the right, on giving notice to the creditor, to repay prematurely at any time. Any provision in the agreement which limits his rights in this respect is void.[179] It would seem that if a provision to postpone the contractual right to redeem[180] were included in a regulated agreement it would be void.

(2) EXTORTIONATE CREDIT BARGAINS

The most far-reaching provision for the protection of the mortgagor is the power given to the court under sections 137–140 to "re-open" a credit agreement if the credit bargain is

---

SI 1998 No. 1944; SI 1999, No. 1956; SI 2001 Nos. 544 and 3649. The Act does not regulate a consumer credit agreement if (a) it is secured by a land mortgage; and (b) entering into that agreement as lender is a regulated activity for the purposes of the Financial Services and Markets Act 2000: s. 16(6C), inserted by SI 2001 No. 544, art. 90(2). See also CCA 1974 (Electronic Communications) Order 2004 (SI 2004 No. 3226), which makes amendments for the purpose of enabling and facilitating communications for concluding regulated agreements and when sending notices and other documents; Consumer Credit (Enforcement, Default and Termination Notices) (Amendment) Regulations 2004 (SI 2004 No. 3237) which amend the Consumer Credit (Enforcement, Default and Termination Notices) Regulations 1983 to ensure that all notices sent under the Regulations are sent in paper format.

[175] "Deposit-taker": a person with permission under Part 4 of the Financial Services and Markets Act 2000 to accept deposits: CCA 1974, s. 16(1)(h), (10), inserted by Banking Act 1987, s. 88, and substituted by SI 2001 No. 3649, art. 165(1), (2)(b), (6).   [176] (1971) Cmnd 4596, para. 2.4.52.

[177] S. 126.

[178] S. 65. The county court has exclusive jurisdiction: s. 141(1). See also s. 127 (enforcement orders); R v Modupe The Times, 27 February 1991; Nissan Finance UK v Lockhart [1993] CCLR 39; Dimond v Lovell [2002] 1 AC 384. In certain cases the court is precluded from making an enforcement order where there is improper execution: s. 127(3), (4); in which case the creditor has no claim in restitution: Wilson v First County Trust Ltd (No 2) [2004] 1 AC 816.

[179] S. 173(1).   [180] Knightsbridge Estates Trust Ltd v Byrne [1939] Ch 441; p. 739, ante.

[181] These sections replace Money-lenders Act 1900, s. 1, under which a court could re-open a transaction with a money-lender where the interest or other charges were excessive and the transaction was "harsh

extortionate.[181] This power extends to *all* credit bargains, whether regulated, exempt or above the £25,000 limit, other than those in which the debtor is a body corporate.[182]

Under section 138(1), a credit bargain is extortionate either if the payments to be made under it are "grossly exorbitant" or if it "otherwise grossly contravenes ordinary principles of fair dealing". The court is required to take into account:[183]

(i) interest rates prevailing when the bargain was made,

(ii) factors in relation to the debtor, such as his age, experience, business capacity and state of health, and the degree to which he was under financial pressure when he made the bargain,

(iii) the creditor's relationship to the debtor and the degree of risk accepted by him, having regard to the value of the security provided, and

(iv) any other relevant considerations.

The test of extortionate is similar but not identical to that of unconscionability which is the basis of the equitable protection of the mortgagor. There is overlap, and it has been said:

Under the Act the test is not whether the creditor has acted in a morally reprehensible manner, but whether one or other of the conditions of section 138(1) is fulfilled, and although it may be thought that if either condition is fulfilled there is likely to be something morally reprehensible about the creditor's conduct, the starting and ending point in determining whether a credit bargain is extortionate must be the words of section 138 (1).[184]

All these matters were considered in *A Ketley Ltd v Scott*,[185] where the court refused an application to re-open a credit agreement involving a loan of £24,500, secured by a legal

---

and unconscionable": CCA 1974, s. 192(3), Sch. 5. They "apply to agreements and transactions whenever made": s. 192 (1), Sch. 3, para. 42; [1989] Conv 164 (L. Bently and C. G. Howells). The County Court has unlimited jurisdiction, whatever the amount involved in the proceedings: s. 139(5)(b); High Court and County Court Jurisdiction Order 1991 (SI 1991 No. 724), art. 3(1)(h). The Consumer Credit Bill, n. 170, supra, would repeal the existing provisions contained in ss. 137–40, and replace them with new provisions to give the court wide powers in relation to address unfairness in credit agreements, regardless of the amount of credit given, where the relationship between the creditor and the debtor arising out of the agreement (or the agreement taken with any related agreement) is unfair to the debtor because of (a) any of the terms of the agreement or of any related agreement; or (b) the way in which the creditor has exercised or enforced any of his rights under the agreement or any related agreement; or (c) any other thing done (or not done) by, or on behalf of, the creditor (either before or after the making of the agreement or any related agreement).

[182] Where the mortgagor is a company, the court has power to set aside or vary the terms of any extortionate credit transaction entered into within three years before the day on which the company entered administration or went into liquidation: Insolvency Act 1986, s. 244, amended by Enterprise Act 2002, s. 248(3), Sch 17, paras. 9, 30.

[183] All these matters must be considered as at the date when the credit bargain is made: *Paragon Finance plc v Nash* [2002] 1 WLR 685.

[184] *Davies v Directloans Ltd* [1986] 1 WLR 823 at 831, per Edward Nugee QC. It is for the creditor to prove that a bargain is not extortionate: s. 171(7); *Coldunell Ltd v Gallon* [1986] QB 1184; *Broadwick Financial Services Ltd v Spencer* [2002] All ER (Comm) 446.

[185] [1981] ICR 241; 130 NLJ 749; (1979) 8 Anglo-Am 240; (1986) 136 NLJ 796 (H. W. Wilkinson). See also *Castle Phillips Finance Co Ltd v Khan* [1980] CCLR 1; *First National Securities v Bertrand* [1980] CCLR 5, discussed in (1982) 132 NLJ 1041 (R. G. Lawson); *Wills v Wood* The Times, 24 March 1984, where Sir John DONALDSON MR said: "The word is 'extortionate' not 'unwise'. The jurisdiction seems to me to contemplate at least a substantial imbalance in bargaining power of which one party has taken advantage";

charge on a flat, at 12 per cent for three months; this was equal to a rate of interest of 48 per cent per annum. The mortgagor had been advised by his own solicitor, and "judging by his earnings and business experience knew exactly what he was doing".[186]

(d) Unfair Terms in Consumer Contracts Regulations 1999

The Unfair Terms in Consumer Contracts Regulations 1999[187] apply to mortgages entered into by consumers[188]—that is, where the mortgagor is a natural person acting for purposes which are outside his trade, business or profession.[189] An unfair term is not binding on the consumer, but the contract continues to bind the parties if it is capable of continuing in existence without the unfair term[190]—and so the court has the power to strike out just the unfair clause. A term which has not been individually negotiated is regarded as unfair if, contrary to the requirement of good faith, it causes a significant imbalance in the parties' rights and obligations arising under the contract, to the detriment of the consumer.[191]

Woodstead Finance Ltd v Petrou [1986] NLJ Rep 188 (interest of 42.5% per annum for short term loan of £25,000 for six months held to be the normal rate, and therefore not extortionate); Shahabinia v Gyachi (1989) unreported (debtor took three loans from creditor for business purposes with flat rates of interest at 78%, 104% and 156%. CA reopened bargain and substituted flat rate of 30% on each loan. "It seems that the word 'extortionate' is to be equated with the words 'harsh and unconscionable'", per RUSSELL LJ); Castle Phillips Co Ltd v Wilkinson and Wilkinson [1992] CCLR 83 (rate of interest three and a half times rate charged by a building society; debtor was person of little financial understanding; rate of 20% substituted); Batooneh v Asombang [2003] EWHC 2111, [2004] BPIR 1 (continuing interest rate of 100% grossly exorbitant and reduced to 25%).

186 See Castle Phillips Finance Co Ltd v Williams [1986] BTCL 186, where interest was charged on a short-term loan at the rate of 48% per annum; CA, instead of staying an order for possession and remitting the case to the county court to consider whether the bargain was extortionate, referred it to the Director General of Fair Trading to consider the revocation of the lender's licence or any other action under the 1974 Act.

187 SI 1999 No. 2083 implementing Council Directive 93/13/EEC, and replacing Unfair Terms in Consumer Contracts Regulations 1994. The Law Commission has proposed the replacement of the Regulations and the Unfair Contract Terms Act 1977 with a single unified legislative regime, which would continue maintain the control on unfair contract terms in land contracts (including mortgages) in favour of a consumer: Law Com No. 292 (2005), Cm 6464, paras. 3.80, 5.76.

188 Falco Finance Ltd v Michael Gough (1999) 17 Tr LR 526 (terms providing for (i) higher interest rate payable in case of single default; (ii) flat rate of interest; and (iii) six-month deferment of redemption of mortgage all unfair within 1994 Regulations, n. 187, supra); (1999) 143 SJ 572 (C. Banks); Emmet, paras. 25.143–25.148; [1995] CLJ 235 (J. Beatson); (1995) 111 LQR 655 (S. Bright and C. Bright); (1999) 115 LQR 360 (S. Bright); (2000) 4 L & T Rev 38 (J. Holbrook). On the Regulations see generally Lawson, Exclusion Clauses and Unfair Contract Terms.

189 Unfair Terms in Consumer Contracts Regulations 1999, reg. 3(1).   190 Ibid., reg. 8.

191 Ibid., reg. 5(1). An "indicative and non-exhaustive list of terms which may be regarded as unfair" is set out in Sch. 2. The list is drafted with contracts of sale or supply of goods in mind, and is not aimed at the terms normally found in a mortgage, but includes such things as (para. 1(j), (k), (l)) the power to increase the price or change other terms unilaterally—but with specific exception (para. 2(b), (c) and (d)) for interest rate fluctuations in contracts of financial services, as long as the supplier is required to notify the consumer, and the consumer has the right to dissolve the contract; and lawful price indexation clauses, so it

(e) Undue influence. Misrepresentation

A mortgage may be set aside for duress,[192] undue influence[193] or misrepresentation,[194] not only where it is exerted by the mortgagee himself on the mortgagor, but also in some circumstances[195] where it is exerted by a third party. In a number of cases the mortgage was given to secure not the mortgagor's own borrowings or business activities but those of another family member. Sometimes the mortgagor has claimed that the mortgagee himself exerted undue influence on him,[196] but more often the claim is of undue influence or misrepresentation exerted by the third party for whose benefit the mortgage was entered into: commonly the husband, for whom the wife has agreed to mortgage her interest in the family home.

This area of the law was clarified by the House of Lords in *Royal Bank of Scotland plc v Etridge (No 2)*.[197]

(1) ESTABLISHING UNDUE INFLUENCE OR MISREPRESENTATION

Whether the claim is that it was exerted by the mortgagee or by a third party, the mortgagor must first establish the undue influence or misrepresentation. Misrepresentation must be proved on the facts.[198] The earlier cases spoke of two distinct categories of undue

appears that an index-linked mortgage (p. 743, n. 159, ante) would not normally be unfair within the meaning of the Regulations. On the application of the test (as set out in the 1994 Regulations: n. 187, supra) to an unsecured credit agreement regulated under CCA 1974, see *Director General of Fair Trading v First National Bank plc* [2002] 1 AC 481. A term of the mortgage which might appear unfair might, on proper construction, be limited: *Paragon Finance plc v Pender* [2005] 1 WLR 3412 (increase by mortgagee in rate of interest; whether breach of implied obligation not to exercise variation right improperly); leave to appeal to HL refused [2006] 1 WLR 398.

[192] On duress generally, see Anson, pp. 277–84; Chitty, paras. 7–001 to 7–046.

[193] On undue influence generally, see Anson, pp. 284–96; Chitty, paras. 7–047 to 7–110; H & M, paras. 26–007 to 26–013. On the relationship between the doctrine and unconscionability, see (1997) 113 LQR 10 (H. Tjio); [1997] CLJ 71 (E. O'Dell); (1998) 114 LQR 479 (D. Capper).

[194] On misrepresentation generally, see Anson, pp. 237–62; Chitty, chap. 6; Cartwright, *Misrepresentation*, especially chap. 3.   [195] P. 751, post.

[196] See, in particular, *Lloyds Bank Ltd v Bundy* [1975] QB 326 (undue influence presumed where assistant bank manager obtained mortgage guaranteeing £10,000 on property worth only £11,000 from client's aged father to support client's failing company, visiting him at home in presence of his family to obtain his signature on forms already filled in, without leaving them for him to consider or giving him the opportunity of taking independent advice: he "crossed the line": at 347, per Sir Eric SACHS); *National Westminster Bank plc v Morgan* [1985] AC 686 (mortgage by wife to support husband's business not entered into under undue influence, even though signed on visit by bank manager to their home, where the "atmosphere . . . was plainly tense. Mr. Morgan was in and out of the room, 'hovering around.'": at 701, per Lord SCARMAN. "A relationship of banker and customer may become one in which the banker acquires a dominating influence. If he does and a manifestly disadvantageous transaction is proved, there would then be room for the court to presume that it resulted from the exercise of undue influence": ibid., at 707. But the manger did not "cross the line", nor was the transaction unfair to the wife).

[197] [2002] 2 AC 73, M & B p. 827; [2002] Conv 174 (M. P. Thompson); [2002] CLJ 229 (M. Oldham); (2002) 65 MLR 435 (R. Bigwood); (2002) 118 LQR 337 (D. O'Sullivan); [2001] All ER Rev 254 (P. J. Clarke). The speech of Lord NICHOLLS OF BIRKENHEAD sets out the view of the House: at [3], per Lord BINGHAM OF CORNHILL. For a useful comparison between *O'Brien* and *Etridge*, see Emmet, paras. 25.040–25.040D8.

[198] For the elements of the claim to rescission for misrepresentation, see Cartwright, *Misrepresentation*, paras. 3.10 et seq.

influence:[199] "actual undue influence", which can be affirmatively proved on the evidence of
the defendant's conduct; and "presumed undue influence", which cannot be proved affirmatively but is presumed from the relationship of the parties, coupled with a consideration
of the terms of the contract.[200] The House of Lords has now made clear that there is just a
single doctrine:[201]

Whether a transaction was brought about by the exercise of undue influence is a question of fact. Here,
as elsewhere, the general principle is that he who asserts a wrong has been committed must prove it.
The burden of proving an allegation of undue influence rests upon the person who claims to have been
wronged. This is the general rule. The evidence required to discharge the burden of proof depends on
the nature of the alleged undue influence, the personality of the parties, their relationship, the extent
to which the transaction cannot readily be accounted for by the ordinary motives of ordinary persons
in that relationship, and all the circumstances of the case.

   Proof that the complainant placed trust and confidence in the other party in relation to the management of the complainant's financial affairs, coupled with a transaction which calls for explanation,
will normally be sufficient, failing satisfactory evidence to the contrary, to discharge the burden of
proof. On proof of these two matters the stage is set for the court to infer that, in the absence of a satisfactory explanation, the transaction can only have been procured by undue influence. In other
words, proof of these two facts is prima facie evidence that the defendant abused the influence he
acquired in the parties' relationship. He preferred his own interests. He did not behave fairly to the
other. So the evidential burden then shifts to him. It is for him to produce evidence to counter the
inference which otherwise should be drawn. . . .

Even if there is no evidence of actual pressure or the like, the court may therefore still be satisfied, on the balance of probabilities, that the mortgagor was subject to undue influence by
a person (either the mortgagee or a third party) in whom he placed trust and confidence, if
the terms of the transaction cannot otherwise be explained. The "presumption" of undue
influence is only a rebuttable evidential presumption.[202]

   This must, however, be distinguished from a different kind of presumption: in certain
types of relationship the law presumes, irrebuttably, that one party had influence over the
other, thus dispensing with the necessity of proving on the facts that the claimant actually
reposed trust and confidence in the other party.[203] This will not, however, apply in the situations which have commonly arisen in relation to mortgages: the relationship between bank

---

[199] "Class 1" (actual undue influence) and "Class 2" (presumed undue influence, sub-divided into 2A,
where the relationship is in an established category giving rise automatically to a presumption, and 2B, where
the relationship has to be shown on the facts to be sufficient to give rise to the presumption): *Bank of Credit
and Commerce International SA v Aboody* [1990] 1 QB 923 at 953, adopted by Lord BROWNE-WILKINSON in
Barclays Bank plc v O'Brien [1994] 1 AC 180 at 189. In the case of presumed influence, the presumption could
be rebutted by showing that the party was in fact acting independently of any influence, typically by showing
that he had advice from a fully informed independent adviser: *Inche Noriah v Shaik Allie Bin Omar* [1929]
AC 127.
   [200] *National Westminster Bank plc v Morgan*, n. 196, supra, used the language of (i) a relationship of "dominating influence" coupled with (ii) a "manifestly disadvantageous transaction". This terminology was disapproved in *Royal Bank of Scotland plc v Etridge (No 2)* [2002] 2 AC 773 at [11], [26].
   [201] *Royal Bank of Scotland plc v Etridge (No 2)*, supra, at [13]–[14], per Lord NICHOLLS OF BIRKENHEAD.
   [202] Ibid., at [16].
   [203] Ibid., at [18]. This was formerly known as "Class 2A" undue influence: n. 199, supra. Proof of such a relationship does not establish undue influence: it only establishes the relationship of confidence, or influence; there
is no presumption that the confidence has been abused: ibid., at [104], per Lord HOBHOUSE OF WOODBOROUGH.

and customer,[204] or between husband and wife,[205] are not without more presumed to be relationships of trust and confidence for this purpose.

(2) UNDUE INFLUENCE OR MISREPRESENTATION BY A THIRD PARTY

In recent years many cases[206] have arisen in which the mortgagor has sought to avoid being bound by the mortgage on the basis of undue influence or misrepresentation by a third party. Lord NICHOLLS OF BIRKENHEAD explained that this is a comparatively recent phenomenon:[207]

It arises out of the substantial growth in home ownership over the last 30 or 40 years and, as part of that development, the great increase in the number of homes owned jointly by husbands and wives. More than two-thirds of householders in the United Kingdom now own their own homes. For most home-owning couples, their homes are their most valuable asset. They must surely be free, if they so wish, to use this asset as a means of raising money, whether for the purpose of the husband's business or for any other purpose. Their home is their property. The law should not restrict them in the use they may make of it. Bank finance is in fact by far the most important source of external capital for small businesses with fewer than ten employees. These businesses comprise about 95% of all businesses in the country, responsible for nearly one-third of all employment. Finance raised by second mortgages on the principal's home is a significant source of capital for the start-up of small businesses.

If the freedom of home-owners to make economic use of their homes is not to be frustrated, a bank must be able to have confidence that a wife's signature of the necessary guarantee and charge will be as binding upon her as is the signature of anyone else on documents which he or she may sign. Otherwise banks will not be willing to lend money on the security of a jointly owned house or flat.

At the same time, the high degree of trust and confidence and emotional interdependence which normally characterises a marriage relationship provides scope for abuse. One party may take advantage of the other's vulnerability. Unhappily, such abuse does occur. Further, it is all too easy for a husband, anxious or even desperate for bank finance, to misstate the position in some particular or to mislead the wife, wittingly or unwittingly, in some other way. The law would be seriously defective if it did not recognise these realities.

The House of Lords first explored this problem in detail in *Barclay's Bank plc v O'Brien*,[208] in which the wife had joined her husband in mortgaging the matrimonial home as surety for

---

[204] Ibid., at [10]; *Lloyds Bank Ltd v Bundy* [1975] QB 326; *National Westminster Bank plc v Morgan* [1985] AC 686.

[205] Ibid., at [19]; *Leeder v Stevens* [2005] EWCA Civ 50 (where CA assumed that the presumption applies to a relationship between fiancé and fiancée and by analogy between a man and a woman who were not engaged but had talked about getting married); (2005) 121 LQR 567 (N. Enonchong). A presumption of undue influence has been considered in *Turkey v Awadh* [2005] 2 P & CR 29 (father and his daughter and son-in-law); *Watson v Huber* [2005] All ER (D) 156 (March) (half-sisters); *Hughes v Hughes* [2005] 1 FCR 679 (loving relationship between mother and son); (2005) 155 NLJ 1579.

[206] In *Royal Bank of Scotland plc v Etridge (No 2)* the House of Lords heard appeals in eight separate cases. In the earlier decision in *Barclay's Bank plc v O'Brien* [1994] 1 AC 180 at 185–6 Lord BROWNE-WILKINSON noted that there had been eleven reported decisions in such cases in the Court of Appeal in the previous eight years. For cases since *Etridge*, see *National Westminster Bank plc v Amin* [2002] 1 FLR 735; [2002] Conv 499 (M. Haley); *UCB Corporate Services Ltd v Williams* [2003] 1 P & CR 12; *Bank of Scotland v Hill* [2002] EWCA Civ 1081, [2003] 1 P & CR DG 7; *Lloyds TSB Bank plc v Holdgate* [2003] HLR 25; *First National Bank plc v Achampong* [2004] 1 FCR 18; [2003] Conv 314 (M. P. Thompson); *Chater v Mortgage Agency Services Number Two Ltd* [2004] 1 P & CR 4.   [207] *Royal Bank of Scotland plc v Etridge (No 2)* [2002] 2 AC 773 at [34]–[36].

[208] [1994] 1 AC 180; (1998)114 LQR 220 (MILLETT LJ)

debts owed to the bank by a company in which the husband, but not the wife, had an interest. The wife sought to resist the mortgagor's claim to possession on the basis of the husband's undue influence or misrepresentation in procuring her agreement to the mortgage. The House of Lords held that the wife in such a case could avoid the mortgage as against the bank if (i) the wrongdoing of the husband could be shown, and (ii) *either* the husband was acting as agent for the bank in obtaining the mortgage, *or* the bank had notice, actual or constructive, of the wrongdoing.[209]

The theory that the husband can be treated as acting as agent for the bank when procuring his wife to become surety is highly artificial. In reality the husband is acting on his own behalf and not as agent for the mortgagee. Since *O'Brien* the doctrine of notice has gained the upper hand.[210] *O'Brien* turned on the application of the doctrine of constructive notice. Lord BROWNE-WILKINSON said that, unless the creditor who is put on inquiry of the risk of the husband's undue influence or misrepresentation takes reasonable steps to satisfy himself that the wife's agreement to stand surety has been properly obtained, the creditor will have constructive notice of the wife's rights—and therefore the wife will be able to avoid the surety contract with the bank. The bank is put on inquiry by two factors:

(i) the transaction is on its face not to the financial advantage of the wife and,

(ii) there is a substantial risk in a transaction of that kind that, in procuring the wife to act as surety, the husband has committed a legal or equitable wrong that entitles the wife to set aside the transaction.[211]

His Lordship set out guidelines for the future as to what reasonable steps a bank should take in order to avoid being fixed by constructive notice:[212]

Unless there are special circumstances, a creditor will have taken reasonable steps . . . if the creditor warns the surety (at a meeting not attended by the principal debtor) of the amount of her potential liability and of the risks involved and advises the surety to take independent legal advice . . . I would not exclude exceptional cases where a creditor has knowledge of further facts which render the presence of undue influence not only possible but probable. In such cases the creditor to be safe will have to insist that the wife is separately advised.

In *O'Brien* the bank was put on inquiry, but had failed to warn and advise, and the wife was therefore entitled to avoid the mortgage as against the bank.

The basis of the decision in *O'Brien* was further reviewed by the House of Lords in *Royal Bank of Scotland plc v Etridge (No 2)*.[213] Lord NICHOLLS OF BIRKENHEAD noted that the use of the concept of constructive notice in *O'Brien* was not conventional,[214] and that the

209 [1994] 1 AC 180, at 191, per Lord BROWNE-WILKINSON.

210 *Royal Bank of Scotland plc v Etridge (No 2)*,[2002] 2 AC 773. Before *O'Brien* agency was found in *Kingsnorth Trust Ltd v Bell* [1986] 1 WLR 119; cf *Coldunell Ltd v Gallon* [1986] QB 1184; *Midland Bank plc v Perry* [1988] 1 FLR 161; *Barclays Bank plc v Kennedy* (1988) 58 P & CR 221. See also *National Westminster Bank plc v Beaton* [1997] EGCS 53 (postscript in letter from bank asking solicitor to advise wife did not make solicitor agent of bank).

211 [1994] 1 AC 180 at 196.

212 Ibid., at 199. As to past transactions it was said to depend on the facts of each case whether the bank has taken steps to bring home to the wife the risk she is taking by standing as surety and to advise her to take independent advice.   213 Supra.

214 "The traditional use of this concept concerns the circumstances in which a transferee of property who acquires a legal estate from a transferor with a defective title may nonetheless obtain a good title, that is, a better title than the transferor had. That is not the present case": at [39]. See also [1994] Conv 421 (M. Dixon and C. Harpum). On the general equitable principle of notice, see pp. 58–65, ante. The development made by

decision had made a change in the law:[215]

The traditional view of equity in this tripartite situation seems to be that a person in the position of the wife will only be relieved of her bargain if the other party to the transaction (the bank, in the present instance) was privy to the conduct which led to the wife's entry into the transaction. Knowledge is required . . . The law imposes no obligation on one party to a transaction to check whether the other party's concurrence was obtained by undue influence. But O'Brien has introduced into the law the concept that, in certain circumstances, a party to a contract may lose the benefit of his contract, entered into in good faith, if he ought to have known that the other's concurrence had been procured by the misconduct of a third party.

There is a further respect in which O'Brien departed from conventional concepts. Traditionally, a person is deemed to have notice (that is, he has "constructive" notice) of a prior right when he does not actually know of it but would have learned of it had he made the requisite inquiries. A purchaser will be treated as having constructive notice of all that a reasonably prudent purchaser would have discovered. In the present type of case, the steps a bank is required to take, lest it have constructive notice that the wife's concurrence was procured improperly by her husband, do not consist of making inquiries. Rather, O'Brien envisages that the steps taken by the bank will reduce, or even eliminate, the risk of the wife entering into the transaction under any misapprehension or as a result of undue influence by her husband. The steps are not concerned to discover whether the wife has been wronged by her husband in this way. The steps are concerned to minimise the risk that such a wrong may be committed.

These novelties do not point to the conclusion that the decision of this House in O'Brien is leading the law astray. Lord Browne-Wilkinson acknowledged he might be extending the law.[216] Some development was sorely needed. The law had to find a way of giving wives a reasonable measure of protection, without adding unreasonably to the expense involved in entering into guarantee transactions of the type under consideration. The protection had to extend also to any misrepresentations made by a husband to his wife. In a situation where there is a substantial risk the husband may exercise his influence improperly regarding the provision of security for his business debts, there is an increased risk that explanations of the transaction given by him to his wife may be misleadingly incomplete or even inaccurate.

The scope of this new application of the principle of constructive notice was also explained. It clearly applies to the case of a wife entering into a contract of surety (including a mortgage) to guarantee her husband's debts.[217] But it also applies between unmarried couples, whether heterosexual or homosexual, where the bank is aware of the relationship; and cohabitation is not essential.[218] In short, the bank is "put on inquiry" in every case where the relationship between the surety and the debtor is non-commercial.[219]

O'Brien in England also applies to Scotland: Smith v Governor & Co of Bank of Scotland [1997] NPC 94, M & B p. 846, although Lord CLYDE preferred to base it on the principle of good faith: "The law already recognises that there may arise a duty of disclosure to a potential cautioner in certain circumstances. As a part of the same good faith which lies behind that duty it seems to me reasonable to accept that there should also be a duty in particular circumstances to give the potential cautioner certain advice"; (1998) 114 LQR 17 (C. E. F. Rickett).

[215] [2002] 2 AC 773 at [40]–[42].   [216] [1994] 1 AC 180 at 197.   [217] [2002] 2 AC 773 at [48].

[218] Ibid., at [47]. See also Massey v Midland Bank plc [1995] 1 All ER 929 (long-standing emotional and sexual relationship, but not living in same house); Banco Exterior Internacional SA v Thomas [1997] 1 WLR 221 (bank "has no business inquiring into the personal relationship between those with whom it has business dealings or as to their personal motives for wanting to help one another. A bank is not to be treated as a branch of the social services agencies" per Sir Richard SCOTT V-C at 230); Barclays Bank plc v Rivett [1999] 1 FLR 730 (husband surety); Northern Rock Building Society v Archer (1999) 78 P & CR 65 (brother and sister). In Smith v Bank of Scotland [1997] NPC 94, n. 214, ante, Lord JAUNCEY OF TULLICHETTLE said: "If the creditor has no information to suggest that cautioner and principal debtor are co-habiting I do not consider that he is under any obligation to make enquiries thereanent."

[219] [2002] 2 AC 773 at [87]. See also Credit Lyonnais Bank Nederland NV v Burch [1997] 1 All ER 144 (relationship between 18-year-old employee and her 28-year-old Italian employer for whom she baby sat at his

The relationship between the mortgagor and the third party is only half the picture, however. In addition, in the formulation set out in *O'Brien*,[220] the transaction must on its face be not to the financial advantage of the wife. Where, as in *O'Brien*'s case, the wife's mortgage is to support a company in which she has no personal interest, the case is clear. In *CIBC Mortgages plc v Pitt*,[221] however, the result was different. In that case:

the bank made a loan to the husband and wife jointly. The wife established actual undue influence by the husband. The husband was not acting as agent for the bank, and there was nothing to indicate to the bank that this was anything other than a normal advance to husband and wife for their joint benefit.

What distinguishes the case of the joint advance from that of the surety is that, in the latter, there is not only the possibility of undue influence having been exercised but also the increased risk of it having in fact been exercised, because at least on its face, the guarantee by a wife of her husband's debts is not for her financial benefit. It is the combination of these two factors that puts the creditor on inquiry.[222]

(3) THE STEPS THE BANK SHOULD TAKE

In *Etridge* the House of Lords revised the guidance given in *O'Brien* as to the steps expected of a bank, once put on inquiry, to avoid being fixed with constructive notice of the husband's misrepresentation or undue influence towards the wife. Most significantly, it was made clear that Lord Browne-Wilkinson's suggestion[223] that the bank should hold a private meeting with the wife was not mandatory. It had already become clear that banks were unwilling to hold such a meeting, because they feared that it would increase their liability.[224]

The furthest a bank can be expected to go is to take reasonable steps to satisfy itself that the wife has had brought home to her, in a meaningful way, the practical implications of the proposed transaction. This does not wholly eliminate the risk of undue influence or misrepresentation. But it does mean that a wife enters into a transaction with her eyes open so far as the basic elements of the transaction are concerned.[225]

To fulfil this duty, the bank is entitled to rely on confirmation from a solicitor, acting for the wife, that he has advised the wife appropriately.[226]

---

substantial house in Gerrards Cross and who visited the family on holidays at his large villa in Italy); [1997] CLJ 60 (M. Chen-Wishart); discussed in *Etridge* [2002] 2 AC 773 at [83], [86], [89].

[220] P. 752, ante.

[221] [1994] 1 AC 200, discussed in *Etridge* at [48]. See also *Britannia Building Society v Pugh* (1996) 29 HLR 423 (wife joint borrower with husband for development intended for their joint benefit); *Barclays Bank plc v Sumner* [1996] EGCS 65 (wife had financial interest in company as great as that of her husband and nothing in her involvement with company to alert bank to make inquiries); cf *Bank of Cyprus (London) Ltd v Markou* [1999] 2 All ER 707; *Dunbar Bank plc v Nadeem* [1998] 3 All ER 876 (joint loan facility for purchase of lease in joint names). The mere fact that the wife holds shares in the company whose debts she guarantees is not conclusive: *Etridge* [2002] 2 AC 773 at [49].   [222] [1994] 1 AC 200 at 211, per Lord Browne-Wilkinson.

[223] P. 752, ante.   [224] [2002] 2 AC 773 at [51], [55].   [225] Ibid., at [54].

[226] Ibid., at [56]. If, however, the bank knows that the solicitor has not duly advised the wife, or knows facts from which it ought to have realised that the wife has not received the appropriate advice, the bank will proceed at its own risk: at [57]. For a detailed account of what the legal advice should contain in order to satisfy the test, see at [58]–[68]; and for the extent to which the solicitor must be independent of the husband and the bank, see at [69]–[74].

(4) PROCEDURE

In *Barclays Bank plc v Boulter*,[227] the House of Lords held that the wife must adequately plead and discharge the burden of proving that the bank has notice of the misrepresentation or undue influence of the husband. As Lord HOFFMANN said:[228]

In the case of undue influence exercised by a husband over a wife, the burden is prima facie very easily discharged. The wife needs to show only that the bank knew that she was a wife living with her husband and that the transaction was not on its face to her financial advantage. The burden is then on the bank to show that it took reasonable steps to satisfy itself that her consent was properly obtained.

(5) EFFECT OF UNDUE INFLUENCE OR MISREPRESENTATION

Undue influence or misrepresentation render the mortgage[229] voidable by the wife. However, the extent of the relief accorded may vary. In *TSB Bank plc v Camfield*[230]

The wife charged her interest in the matrimonial home to the bank in order to secure the business debts of her husband, who had innocently misrepresented that her liability under the charge was restricted to £15,000. The bank had constructive notice of the misrepresentation. It was held that the wife's charge should be set aside in its entirety; the bank could be in no better position than the husband.

But if the wife has herself derived some benefit from the transaction, then she can have the guarantee set aside only if she makes counter-restitution in respect of the benefit she has received.[231]

If only part of the charge is voidable for undue influence, the voidable part may be severed, leaving the rest of the charge valid.[232]

(f) *Restraint of trade*

A mortgage is subject to the common law doctrine that invalidates any contract in restraint of trade which places an unreasonable restriction upon the freedom to pursue a trade or profession.[233] This test is unreasonableness and not unconscionability; it takes into account

---

[227] [1999] 1 WLR 1919; [2000] Conv 43 (M. P. Thompson).   [228] At 1925.

[229] And any replacement mortgage, at any rate if it is taken out as a condition of discharging an earlier voidable mortgage: *Yorkshire Bank plc v Tinsley* [2004] 1 WLR 2380; [2004] Conv 399 (M. P. Thompson); [2005] CLJ 42 (N. P. Gravells); [2004] All ER Rev 250 (P. J. Clarke).

[230] [1995] 1 WLR 430; (1995) 111 LQR 555 (P. Ferguson); [1996] RLR 21 (L. Proksch).

[231] *Midland Bank plc v Greene* (1993) 27 HLR 350; *Dunbar Bank plc v Nadeem* [1998] 3 All ER 876 (wife would have had to pay half to bank, if there had been undue influence).

[232] *Barclays Bank plc v Caplan* (1997) 78 P & CR 153.

[233] *Esso Petroleum Co Ltd v Harper's Garage (Stourport) Ltd* [1968] AC 269; *Re Petrol Filling Station, Vauxhall Bridge Road, London* (1968) 20 P & CR 1, M & B p. 824; *Texaco Ltd v Mulberry Filling Station Ltd* [1972] 1 WLR 814; *Alec Lobb (Garages) Ltd v Total Oil GB Ltd* [1985] 1 WLR 173 (trading restraints in sale and 51-year leaseback of part of property entered into between mortgagor and mortgagee after date of mortgage held to be reasonable). See Anson, pp. 366 et seq; Heydon, *Restraint of Trade Doctrine* (1971), chaps. 3, 9. See also Supply of Beer (Tied Estate) Order 1989 (SI 1989 No. 2390, now revoked by SI 2002 No. 3204); *Plummer v Tibsco Ltd* [2000] ICR 509.

As to the impact of Article 85 of the Treaty of Rome (now Article 81 of the Treaty of Amsterdam), see *Delimitis v Henninger Bräu A-G* [1991] ECR I-935; *Passmore v Morland plc* [1999] 3 All ER 1005 (tie void only during period of invalidity); *Courage Ltd v Crehan* [1999] 2 EGLR 145 (void tie severable from lease); (1998) 49 NILQ 202 (N. Hopkins); *Crehan v Inntrepreneur Pub Co* [2004] 3 EGLR 128 (damages awarded to tenant).

not only the interests of the parties but also the public interest. It may happen, therefore, that a postponement of the right of redemption which is not per se oppressive may nevertheless become so if it is accompanied by an excessive restraint upon the mortgagor's business activities. Thus where a garage was mortgaged to suppliers of motor fuels, and the mortgagors covenanted that they would not exercise their right of redemption for twenty-one years and, during the same period, would not buy or sell any fuel other than that supplied by the mortgagees, it was held that the covenant was void as being in restraint of trade, and that the mortgage was redeemable.[234]

(2) Enforcement of the Equity of Redemption

(a) Loss of right of redemption by mortgagor

The right of redemption is lost in the event of (i) the release of the right by the mortgagor to the mortgagee; (ii) (in unregistered land) the lapse of time under the Limitation Act 1980; (iii) the sale of the land by the mortgagee under his statutory power; or (iv) a foreclosure decree obtained by the mortgagee.

The last two methods are discussed later.[235]

(1) RELEASE OF RIGHT OF REDEMPTION BY MORTGAGOR

Although a provision in the mortgage deed itself giving the mortgagee an option to purchase the land is void as being a clog on the equity,[236] there is nothing to prevent the mortgagor from getting rid of the debt by releasing the equity of redemption to him, provided that it is the result of an independent bargain made subsequently to the mortgage deed.

(2) LAPSE OF TIME

In relation to a mortgage of unregistered land, the Limitation Act 1980 provides that:[237]

When a mortgagee of land has been in possession of any of the mortgaged land for a period of twelve years, no action to redeem the land of which the mortgagee has been so in possession shall be brought after the end of that period by the mortgagor or any person claiming through him.

If, however, the mortgagee in possession either receives any sum in respect of principal or interest or signs an acknowledgment of the mortgagor's title, an action to redeem the land may be brought at any time before the expiration of twelve years after the last payment or acknowledgment.[238] An acknowledgment given after the mortgagee has been in possession for twelve years, without receiving a payment in respect of principal or interest, is ineffective.[239]

---

[234] *Esso Petroleum Co Ltd v Harper's Garage (Stourport) Ltd*, [1968] AC 269.

[235] P. 769, post (sale); p. 775, post (foreclosure).   [236] P. 737, ante.

[237] S. 16. Under LRA 1925, s. 75, the same principle applied to registered land, but LRA 2002, s. 96(2), disapplies LA 1980, s. 16, in relation to a registered estate in land or rentcharge. LRA 2002 did not, however, change the law in relation to the mortgagee's right to possession or foreclosure against a mortgagor in possession: H & B, paras. 29.6, 29.7.   [238] Ibid., ss. 29(4), 30.

[239] Ibid., s. 17.

When a mortgagee has obtained a title to the land free from the mortgage by remaining in possession for twelve years he may by deed enlarge the term of years into a fee simple under the Law of Property Act 1925.[240]

When, as in the ordinary case, a mortgagee does not take possession of the land, the mortgagor can redeem regardless of the lapse of time.

(b) Redemption by mortgagor

In practice, the terms on which the mortgagor may redeem are generally provided for expressly in the contract contained in the mortgage deed.[241] However, in the absence of more specific provision, the mortgagor is entitled to tender the exact amount due,[242] and to claim redemption on the date fixed for repayment. This date is not usually, however, meant to be taken seriously,[243] and if it has elapsed, the mortgagor must give either six months' notice or six months' interest before he can redeem.[244] If a notice so given is not followed by repayment upon the date notified, he must give a fresh notice of a reasonable length.[245] Where, however, the mortgage is merely temporary, as for instance in the case of an equitable mortgage by deposit of title deeds,[246] the mortgagee is not entitled to six months' notice or interest in lieu. The mortgagor must give him a reasonable time, though it may be short, to look up the deeds.[247]

(i) Form of discharge: unregistered land

Before 1926, a reconveyance by the mortgagee was necessary to revest the legal estate in the mortgagor upon redemption, but now, when redemption has been effected, there is no need for the mortgagee to execute a deed surrendering the term. A receipt written at the foot of the mortgage deed will be sufficient to extinguish the mortgage, provided that it states the name of the person who pays the money and is executed by the person in whom the mortgage is vested.[248] In the case of a mortgage by demise this receipt effects a surrender of the term and merges it in the reversion held by the mortgagor.[249] If a person, such as a second mortgagee, to whom the immediate equity of redemption does not belong, pays the money that is due, the benefit of the mortgage passes to him by virtue of the receipt,[250] and thus his incumbrance is kept alive. But of course where there are two mortgages of the same land

---

[240] LPA 1925, ss. 88(3), 153, as amended by TLATA 1996, s. 25(1), Sch. 3, para. 4(1), (16); p. 327, ante.

[241] See, e.g., *Enyclopaedia of Forms and Precedents*, vol. 28, Form 5, cl. 2.1.2. Such provision is usual in a domestic mortgage, to enable the borrower to redeem at relatively short notice if he sells the property on moving house. However, there may be enforceable contractual restrictions on the time within which redemption may take place: p. 738, ante.

[242] In an action for redemption the mortgagor must pay all that is due in respect of principal and interest, including interest which is statute-barred: *Holmes v Cowcher* [1970] 1 WLR 834. Any person entitled to redeem must pay full amount of debt and interest even if in right of only part of the property: *Carroll v Manek* (2000) 79 P & CR 173.   [243] Pp. 721–2, ante.

[244] *Cromwell Property Investment Co Ltd v Western and Toovey* [1934] Ch 322.   [245] Ibid.

[246] Which takes effect now only if accompanied by a document which satisfies the formality requirements of a valid contract to create a legal mortgage: pp. 732, ante.

[247] *Fitzgerald's Trustee v Mellersh* [1892] 1 Ch 385, per CHITTY J.

[248] See *Erewash BC v Taylor* [1979] CLY 1831 (receipt valid in spite of miscalculation of redemption figure by mortgagee).

[249] LPA 1925, s. 115(1). A building society may use either a reconveyance or a special statutory receipt: Building Societies Act 1986, s. 6C and Sch. 2A, inserted by Building Societies Act 1997, s. 7.

[250] Ibid., s. 115(2); *Cumberland Court (Brighton) Ltd v Taylor* [1964] Ch 29.

and the mortgagor pays off the first, the receipt does not transfer the first mortgage term to him so as to enable him to keep it alive against the second mortgagee.[251] Moreover, it is enacted that a mortgage term shall, after repayment of the money, become a satisfied term, and shall cease.[252]

It is the duty of a mortgagee, upon receiving repayment of the loan, to deliver the title deeds to the person who has the best right to them, that is, the mortgagor if there is only one incumbrance, or the next mortgagee if the land has been subjected to more incumbrances than one.[253] A mortgagee will not, however, incur liability to a later mortgagee for delivering the deeds to the mortgagor, unless he has actual notice of the later mortgage.[254] Mere registration of a mortgage as a land charge under the Land Charges Act 1972[255] does not in this case constitute notice, but nevertheless he is for several reasons well advised to search at the Registry before handing over the deeds to the mortgagor.[256] If the mortgagee has lost the deeds, the mortgagor has an equitable right to compensation on redemption.[257]

(ii) Form of discharge: registered land[258]

The provisions set out above do not apply to the discharge of a registered charge.[259] Instead, two methods of discharge are provided. Under the first method, the mortgagee must execute a statutory form of discharge in documentary form,[260] and the mortgagor then makes application to the Registrar to cancel the entries relating to the charge.[261] Under the second method, which is already in use but will become the usual method once electronic conveyancing has been fully introduced, the notification of discharge is made to the Registrar electronically, directly by the mortgagee.[262]

(iii) Sale in lieu of redemption

The mortgagor may commence proceedings to enforce redemption, and if he is successful, an order will be made directing the mortgagee to surrender or give a statutory receipt upon receiving payment within six months. But where such proceedings are taken, the mortgagor may have a judgment for sale instead of for redemption, and the court may, on the request either of the mortgagor or of the mortgagee, and despite the dissent of the other party, direct a sale on such terms as it thinks fit.[263]

(iv) Transfer of mortgage

Finally, upon payment of the amount due, a mortgagor is entitled to require the mortgagee to transfer the debt and the property to a third person and the mortgagee, unless he is or has

---

[251] LPA 1925, s. 115(3); *Otter v Lord Vaux* (1856) 6 De GM & G 638; *Parkash v Irani Finance Ltd* [1970] Ch 101.

[252] Ibid., s. 116; *Edwards v Marshall-Lee* (1975) 235 EG 901; (1976) 40 Conv (NS) 102.

[253] *Re Magneta Time Co Ltd* (1915) 84 LJ Ch 814.

[254] LPA 1925, s. 96(2), as amended by LP(A)A 1926, Schedule.   [255] P. 795, post.

[256] See (1926) 61 LJ News pp. 431, 471, 488, 519 (T. Cyprian Williams).

[257] *Browning v Handiland Group Ltd* (1976) 35 P & CR 345.

[258] See generally Land Registry Practice Guide: Discharge of Charges (revised 2005); H & B, paras. 12.86–12.107.   [259] LRA 1925, s. 115(10), as amended by LRA 2002, s. 133, Sch. 11, para. 2(1), (11).

[260] LRR 2003, r. 114: Form DS1 (discharge of registered charge) or DS3 (release of part of a registered estate from a registered charge). It must be executed as a deed, or authenticated in such other manner as the registrar may approve: ibid., r. 114(3), However, the Registrar has power to accept other proof of satisfaction of a charge: ibid., r. 114(4).   [261] Ibid., r. 114(5); there is a prescribed form.

[262] Ibid., r. 115.   [263] LPA 1925, s. 91; *Palk v Mortgage Services Funding plc* [1993] Ch 330, p. 774, post.

been in possession, is bound to comply.[264] This is the procedure adopted where a third person pays the amount of the loan to the mortgagee, and then himself assumes the position of mortgagee.[265]

(v) Subrogation

A person whose money has been used to discharge a mortgage may be entitled to that mortgage by way of subrogation, or substitution, even though there has been no assignment of any rights or remedies. In a classic statement of the doctrine Lord DIPLOCK said:[266]

One of the sets of circumstances in which a right of subrogation arises is when a liability of a borrower B to an existing creditor C secured on the property of B is discharged out of moneys provided by the lender L and paid to C either by L himself at B's request and on B's behalf or directly by B pursuant to his agreement with L. In these circumstances L is prima facie entitled to be treated as if he were the transferee of the benefit of C's security on the property to the extent that the moneys lent by L to B were applied to the discharge of B's liability to C. This subrogation of L to the security upon the property of B is based upon the presumed mutual intentions of L and B; in other words where a contract of loan provides that moneys lent by L to B are to be applied in discharging a liability of B to C secured on property, it is an implied term of that contract that L is to be subrogated to C's security.

Subrogation is especially relevant to a prospective mortgagee who has advanced money in order to discharge an existing mortgage but has failed to obtain a valid security for himself. Thus in *Penn v Bristol and West Building Society*[267] a mortgage advance was used to redeem the vendor's mortgage. The transfer of title to the purchaser was held to be a sham and his mortgagee therefore failed to acquire any interest on completion. It was held that the purchaser's mortgagee was entitled to the vendor's mortgage by subrogation.

(3) Effect of Death of Mortgagor

On the death of a mortgagor the equity of redemption passes through his personal representatives to the persons entitled on intestacy if he dies without leaving a will, and to his devisee if he leaves a will. Under the law as it existed prior to 1854, such an heir or devisee was entitled to have the mortgage debt paid out of the personal estate of the deceased, and to take the property free from the mortgage burden, but, in accordance with the general principle that he who has the benefit ought to have the burden, this rule was reversed by the Real Estate Charges Acts of 1854, 1867 and 1877. These statutes have now been repealed,

---

[264] LPA 1925, s. 95. The reason for the exception is that a mortgagee, having once been in possession, remains liable to account for the profits that the transferee has, or ought to have, received after the transfer. He should, therefore, never transfer the security without an order of the court: *Hall v Heward* (1886) 32 Ch D 430 at 435.   [265] For transfer of a registered charge, see H & B, paras. 12.42–12.47.

[266] *Orakpo v Manson Investments Ltd* [1978] AC 95 at 104. On subrogation generally, see Emmet, para. 25.087A; Mitchell, *Law of Subrogation* (1994). For a critical analysis of the doctrine and its relation to restitution, see *Boscawen v Bajwa* [1996] 1 WLR 328 at 334–5, 338–41, per MILLETT LJ; *Banque Financière de la Cité v Parc (Battersea) Ltd* [1998] 2 WLR 475 at 483–6, per Lord HOFFMANN; [1998] Conv 113 (D. Wright); reviewed and explained by JONATHAN PARKER LJ in *Halifax plc v Omar* [2002] 2 P & CR 26.

[267] [1995] 2 FLR 938. See also *Halifax plc v Omar*, supra; *Cheltenham & Gloucester plc v Appleyard* [2004] 13 EGCS 127 (subsequent mortgagee paid off first legal mortgage but was unable to obtain registration of its own charge, so held only an equitable mortgage: entitled to be subrogated as a legal chargee to the value of the legal mortgage at the time it was paid off).

although their general tenor is retained, and it is enacted that property, whether land or not, which at the time of the owner's death is charged with the payment of money, whether by way of legal mortgage, equitable charge or otherwise, shall, as between the different persons claiming through the deceased, be primarily liable for the payment of the charge.[268] This rule is not to apply, however, if the deceased has expressed a contrary intention by will, deed or other document, but such intention must be clear and unambiguous, and is not to be implied merely because the deceased has directed that his debts are to be paid out of his personal estate or his residuary estate.[269]

B   Rights of a Mortgagor who Remains in Possession

In the eyes of equity the mortgagor remains the true beneficial owner of the property, and as long as he remains in possession he is entitled to appropriate the rents and profits to his own use without any liability to account for them, even though he may be in default in the payment of interest. As we shall see, the mortgagee has the right to enter into possession of the land, independently of any default on the part of the mortgagor,[270] but in normal circumstances the mortgagor remains in possession. Provided that the mortgagee has not given notice of his intention to take possession or to enter into receipt of the rents and profits, the mortgagor in possession may sue in his own name for the recovery of possession and for the rents and profits. He may bring an action to prevent, or recover damages for, any trespass or other wrong done to the land.[271]

Where a mortgagor retained possession, it was formerly a common practice to include in the mortgage deed a clause by which he *attorned* to the mortgagee, that is, acknowledged that he held the land as a tenant at will or from year to year of the mortgagee. The chief advantages were that it enabled the mortgagee to pursue the remedies available to a landlord for the recovery of arrears of rent, and also to obtain a summary judgment for possession if the need arose.

These two advantages, however, no longer exist, for the mortgagee cannot distrain upon the premises for arrears unless the attornment clause has been registered as a bill of sale;[272] and a summary judgment is available to him independently of attornment.[273] Nevertheless, an attornment clause is not altogether superfluous, for it enables a covenant by a mortgagor to be enforced against his successors in title.[274]

A mortgagor, *while in actual possession*, is given the following statutory powers:

(1)   Right to Grant Valid Leases

(a)   At common law

At common law a mortgagor is entitled to grant a lease binding between him and the lessee, and his power in this respect has not been affected by statute.[275] But if granted without the

---

268   AEA 1925, s. 35(1).
269   Ibid., s. 35(1), (2): *Re Neeld* [1962] Ch 643; *Re Wakefield* [1943] 2 All ER 29.   270   P. 764, post.
271   LPA 1925, s. 98.   272   *Re Willis, ex p Kennedy* (1888) 21 QBD 384.
273   CPR, Part 24. See generally (1969) 22 CLP, pp. 143–6 (E. C. Ryder).
274   *Regent Oil Co Ltd v J A Gregory (Hatch End) Ltd* [1966] Ch 402, where the covenant was included in a charge by way of legal mortgage. For mortgages entered into before 1996, the fact that the mortgage takes effect as a lease should make the covenant run even in the absence of attornment: (1966) 82 LQR 21. However, the LT(C)A 1995, s. 28(1), excludes a mortgage term from the definition of tenancy for the purposes of the running of covenants in leases entered into after 1995.
275   *Iron Trades Employers Insurance Association Ltd v Union Land and House Investors Ltd* [1937] Ch 313.

concurrence of the mortgagee[276] it confers only a precarious title upon the lessee, since the paramount title of the mortgagee may be asserted against both him and the mortgagor.[277]

(b) By statute

The Conveyancing Act 1881 expanded the power of the mortgagor in this particular by allowing him to grant leases for limited periods which would be binding upon the mortgagee. The present position is governed by the Law of Property Act 1925, which confers upon a mortgagor *in possession* a statutory right to grant the following leases that will be binding upon all incumbrancers:

(1) Agricultural or occupation leases for any term not exceeding twenty-one years, or, if the mortgage was made after 1925, fifty years.

(2) Building leases for any term not exceeding ninety-nine years, or, in the case of a mortgage made after 1925, 999 years.[278]

Such a lease must be made to take effect in possession not later than twelve months after its date; it must reserve the best rent that can reasonably be obtained, and no fine must be taken;[279] it must contain a condition of re-entry in the event of rent being in arrears for thirty days,[280] and the mortgagor is bound to deliver to the mortgagee within one month a counterpart of the lease executed by the lessee.[281]

Thus when a mortgagor makes a lease to A for fifty years, the effect is that the mortgagee is not entitled to actual possession during the continuance of A's term; but if he is driven to pursue his remedies, he is entitled to receipt of the rent paid by A.

These statutory powers of leasing may be, and in practice frequently are, excluded or abridged by the mortgage deed,[282] but no such exclusion or abridgement is allowed in the case of a mortgage of agricultural land made after 1 March 1948, but before 1 September 1995.[283] Exclusion is permitted in the case of a mortgage made on or after that date. Thus the power to grant a farm business tenancy,[284] which can only begin on or after that date, may be validly excluded.

(c) Effect of unauthorised lease

If a mortgagor in possession grants a lease which does not satisfy the provisions of the Law of Property Act 1925 or the terms of the mortgage deed, the lease may be binding on both the

---

[276] The mortgage deed itself may confer leasing powers within defined limits upon the mortgagor: LPA 1925, s. 99(14). There is no implied term that the mortgagee should not unreasonably withhold consent: cf LTA 1927, s. 19(1) p. 257, ante: nor is the condition contrary to Article 48 of the European Treaty: *Citibank International plc v Kessler* [1999] Lloyd's Rep Bank 123. Nor is the mortgagee under a duty in equity properly to consider any request for permission: *Starling v Lloyds TSB Bank Ltd* [2000] 1 EGLR 101 (in extreme circumstances there might be scope for a complaint of bad faith).

[277] *Corbett v Plowden* (1884) 25 Ch D 678 at 681, per Lord SELBORNE LC.　　[278] LPA 1925, s. 99(1), (3).

[279] Ibid., s. 99(5), (6). See, for example, *Rust v Goodale* [1957] Ch 33 at 39, where the consideration for a sublease was an immediate payment of £2,260 and a rent of £5.

[280] Ibid., s. 99(7). It is doubtful whether this requirement must be satisfied in the case of an oral tenancy: *Pawson v Revell* [1958] 2 QB 360; *Rhodes v Dalby* [1971] 1 WLR 1325 at 1331–2.

[281] Ibid., s. 99 (11). But not in the case of an oral tenancy: *Rhodes v Dalby*, supra. A lease which fails to comply with one or more of these requirements may be validated under s. 152, if it has been made in good faith and if the lessee has entered. It then takes effect in equity as a contract for the grant of a valid lease. See e.g., *Pawson v Revell*, supra.　　[282] Ibid., s. 99(13).

[283] Ibid., s. 99(13A), inserted by Agricultural Tenancies Act 1995, s. 31. See *Pawson v Revell* [1958] 2QB 360 *Rhodes v Dalby* [1971] 1 WLR 1325.　　[284] P. 388, ante.

mortgagor and the tenant under the doctrine of estoppel.[285] Thus the mortgagor may sue or distrain for the rent.[286] The mortgagee, however, is not bound by the lease. As between the lessee and the mortgagee and his successors in title the lease granted by the mortgagor is void,[287] and the lessee is not protected against the mortgagee by the Rent Acts.[288] The mortgagee has an option. He may either treat the lessee as a trespasser or accept him as his own tenant.[289] If, for instance, he demands that the rent be paid direct to him instead of to the mortgagor, the original tenancy is destroyed and replaced by a yearly tenancy between the mortgagee and the lessee.[290] Moreover, the acceptance of rent without any such demand raises the implication of a yearly tenancy.[291] This implication, however, does not arise merely because the mortgagee, being aware of the lease, allows the tenant to remain in possession.[292]

If a mortgagee refuses to recognise an unauthorised lease, the tenant may redeem the mortgage and thus secure himself against eviction.[293]

(2) Right to Accept Surrenders of Leases

The Law of Property Act 1925, authorises a mortgagor to accept a surrender of any lease, if, and only if, his object in doing so is to grant a new lease that falls within his statutory powers.[294] Such a surrender, however, is not valid unless a new lease is granted within one month, for a period not shorter than the unexpired term of the surrendered lease, and at a rent not less than the old rent.[295] These provisions are, however, subject to the terms of the mortgage deed, or of any other written agreement between the parties.[296]

IV Rights of the Mortgagee

A Rights of Legal Mortgagee

We now come to the five remedies which are available to a legal mortgagee for enforcing the payment of what is due to him under the mortgage:[297] the action on the personal covenant

---

[285] *Cuthbertson v Irving* (1860) 6 H & N 135; *Church of England Building Society v Piskor* [1954] Ch 553; p. 217, ante.	[286] *Trent v Hunt* (1853) 9 Exch 14.

[287] *Rust v Goodale* [1957] Ch 33; cf *Lever Finance Ltd v Trustee of Property of L N and H M Needleman and Kreutzer* [1956] Ch 375 (mortgagee's assignee estopped from asserting invalidity of lease).

[288] *Dudley and District Benefit Building Society v Emerson* [1949] Ch 707; *Sadiq v Hussain* (1997) 73 P & CR D44. Section 98 of the Rent Act 1977 prohibits the court from ordering possession of a dwelling house subject to a statutory tenancy unless certain criteria are met: it does not prohibit a prior mortgagee with title paramount from recovering possession (i) from a protected contractual tenant; *Dudley and District Benefit Building Society v Emerson*, supra: (ii) from a statutory tenant; *Britannia Building Society v Earl* [1990] 1 WLR 422; [1990] Conv 450 (S. Bridge) but it does prohibit a mortgagee in all cases where the tenancy predates the mortgagee's mortgage: *Woolwich Building Society v Dickman* [1996] 3 All ER 204, [1996] All ER Rev 254 (P. J. Clarke); 279 (P. H. Pettit); cf *Barclays Bank plc v Zaroovabli* [1997] Ch 321; (tenancy predated registration but not grant of bank's charge); (1997) 113 LQR 390; (M. Robinson). See also *Quennell v Maltby* [1979] 1 WLR 318, p. 767, post, for the court's discretion in equity to protect a lessee where possession is sought, but not in good faith to protect the security.

[289] *Stroud Building Society v Delamont* [1960] 1 WLR 431 at 434; *Chatsworth Properties Ltd v Effiom* [1971] 1 WLR 144.	[290] *Taylor v Ellis* [1960] Ch 368 at 375–6.

[291] P. 214, ante.	[292] *Taylor v Ellis*, supra.	[293] *Tarn v Turner* (1888) 39 Ch D 456.

[294] LPA 1925, s. 100(1).	[295] Ibid., s. 100(5).	[296] Ibid., s. 100(7).

[297] A mortgagee may also have an action against a valuer for a negligent valuation which causes him loss: *Coris and Investments Ltd v Druce & Co* (1978) 248 EG 315, 407; *Mount Banking Corpn Ltd v Brian Cooper & Co* [1992] 2 EGLR 142. For a similar action against a surveyor, see *London and South of England Building Society v Stone* (1981) 261 EG 463; *Anglia Hastings & Thanet Building Society v House & Son* (1981) 260 EG 1128.

to repay the principal with interest; entry into possession of the mortgaged premises; the appointment of a receiver; sale and foreclosure. The first three of these remedies do not involve the realisation of the mortgaged property, but as a result of sale and foreclosure the mortgage is terminated.

These several remedies may all be pursued concurrently as soon as the mortgagor is in default, so that, for instance, the mortgagee at one and the same time may sue upon the personal covenant and begin foreclosure proceedings. They are generally also cumulative. Thus if the mortgagee exercises his power of sale and the purchase price is less than the mortgage debt, he may sue the mortgagor for the balance on the covenant to pay.[298] Foreclosure, however, puts an end to other remedies; a mortgagee who has foreclosed can only sue on the covenant to pay if he reopens the foreclosure,[299] so that the mortgagor may redeem. If, therefore, the mortgagee sells the mortgaged property after foreclosure, he has put it out of his power to reopen the foreclosure and so can no longer sue the mortgagor[300] or his guarantor[301] on the personal covenant.

(1) Action on the Personal Covenant

(a) Personal remedy

A mortgage deed contains an express covenant whereby the mortgagor covenants to repay the principal sum, and interest at a certain rate per cent. The date at which the mortgagor becomes liable to pay is a question of construction of the deed.[302] The moment that date has passed, the mortgagee can sue on this personal covenant for the recovery of the principal sum and any interest that may be in arrear, and can have the judgment satisfied out of any property belonging to the mortgagor, though it is not comprised in the mortgage. Further, the mortgagor remains liable on the covenant to the mortgagee, even though he has transferred his interest in the mortgaged property.[303] He usually takes a covenant of indemnity from the transferee.[304]

(b) Effect of lapse of time

An action to recover the principal sum is barred unless it is brought within twelve years from the date when the right to receive the money accrued.[305] This date is that which is fixed by the mortgage deed for repayment, and is not affected by the mortgagee's subsequent exercise of

---

[298] *Rudge v Richens* (1873) LR 8 CP 358; *Gordon Grant & Co Ltd v Boos* [1926] AC 781. See also *Alliance & Leicester plc v Slayford* [2001] 1 All ER (Comm) 1 (mortgagee not prevented from pursuing money judgment after failure to realise security through possession proceedings).

[299] *Perry v Barker* (1806) 13 Ves 198.

[300] *Palmer v Hendrie* (1859) 27 Beav 349. See *Kinnaird v Trollope* (1888) 39 Ch D 636 at 642, per STIRLING LJ, M & B p. 898.   [301] *Lloyds and Scottish Trust Ltd v Britten* (1982) 44 P & CR 249.

[302] *Wilkinson v West Bromwich Building Society* [2005] 1 WLR 2303; [2005] Conv 566 (T. Prime). See also *Doodes v Gotham* [2006] 1 WLR 729. Traditionally, the mortgage deed provided for the repayment of the whole of the principal sum on a specified date, and to pay interest in the mean time: p. 722, ante. However, a modern domestic mortgage may contain detailed provisions for repayment of the capital by instalments, with interest on the capital left outstanding from time to time: e.g. *Encyclopaedia of Forms and Precedents*, vol. 28, Form 5; or may provide for repayment of capital at the end of the term under an interest-only mortgage: ibid., Form 2. Such forms will generally make the whole of the principal sum repayable on demand in the event of certain specified events of default; the action on the covenant is available whenever any sum has become due under the contract and is unpaid, whether the whole or any instalment of the capital, or any arrears of interest.

[303] *Kinnaird v Trollope* (1888) 39 Ch D 636.

[304] A transferee for value is under an implied obligation to indemnify: *Bridgman v Daw* (1891) 40 WR 253.

[305] Limitation Act 1980, s. 20(1).

his power of sale;[306] but on each occasion that some part of the principal or interest is paid or a written acknowledgment of his liability to pay is given by the mortgagor, the period of twelve years begins to run afresh.[307] In the case of interest, only six years' arrears are recoverable.[308] Once the mortgagee's right to recover the principal sum is statute barred, he loses his status as a mortgagee. He can no longer sue for possession or for foreclosure, nor can he redeem a prior mortgage.[309]

(2) Entry into possession

(a) Right to take possession

A legal mortgagee has the right to enter into possession of the mortgaged property. As HARMAN J said:

The right of the mortgagee to possession in the absence of some contract has nothing to do with default on the part of the mortgagor. The mortgagee may go into possession before the ink is dry on the mortgage unless there is something in the contract, express or by implication,[310] whereby he has contracted himself out of that right. He has the right because he has a legal term of years in the property.[311]

It is not usual, however, for a mortgagee, despite his legal right, to enter into possession of the mortgaged property, unless he wishes to do so as a preliminary to exercising his statutory power of sale, when the mortgagor is in default. As HARMAN J went on to say:

An application for possession has become a very fashionable form of relief, because, owing to the conditions now prevailing, if it is desired to realize a security by sale, vacant possession is almost essential.

In other words, entry into possession is a necessary preliminary to sale. It is important for the mortgagee to enter, so that he can evict the mortgagor and offer vacant possession to a purchaser. Otherwise, the property might be difficult to sell, or, if sold, its price might be depressed, if the sale took place with the mortgagor in possession and the purchaser had to evict him after the sale.

(b) Liability of mortgagee to account strictly

It is, in theory at least, possible for a mortgagee to enter into possession to ensure the payment of interest, but a formidable deterrent to this course is the strict supervision which equity exercises over a mortgagee in possession. The rule is that he must get no advantage out of the mortgage beyond the payment of principal, interest and costs, and he is made to account not only for what he has actually received, but also for what he might have received but for his own wilful default or neglect.[312] Thus he is liable for voluntary waste, and if he

---

306 *Wilkinson v West Bromwich Building Society* [2005] 1 WLR 2303 ("It would be strange if the lender could then stop time running by his own act in exercising the power of sale. If, therefore, the cause of action when it arose was a claim to a debt secured on a mortgage, I do not think s. 20 ceases to apply when the security is subsequently realised", per Lord HOFFMANN at [10]).   307 Limitation Act 1980, ss. 29(3), (5), 30.

308 Ibid., s. 20(5)–(7); *Barclays Bank plc v Walters* The Times, 20 October 1988.

309 *Cotterell v Price* [1960] 1 WLR 1097.

310 See *Esso Petroleum Co Ltd v Alstonbridge Properties Ltd* [1975] 1 WLR 1474 at 1484; *Western Bank Ltd v Schindler* [1977] Ch 1.

311 *Four-Maids Ltd v Dudley Marshall (Properties) Ltd* [1957] Ch 317 at 320, M & B p. 855. See generally Fisher and Lightwood, chap. 19; [1979] Conv 266 (R. J. Smith); [1983] Conv 293 (A. Clarke); [1997] LS 483 (M. Haley).

312 *Chaplin v Young* (1864) 33 Beav 330; *White v City of London Brewery Co* (1889) 42 Ch D 237 at 243.

allows property to remain vacant which might have been let, he is personally liable to pay an occupation rent.[313] Thus in *White v City of London Brewery Co*[314] Mortgagees, who happened to be brewers, took possession of the mortgaged premises and leased them to a tenant, subject to a restriction that he should take his supply of beer entirely from them. It was held that they must account for the additional rent that they would have received had they let the premises as a "free" instead of a "tied" house.

(c) *Relief of mortgagor*

(1) STATUTORY

If a mortgagee seeks possession he will usually take proceedings in the county court.[315] Unless the mortgagee agrees, the court has no jurisdiction to decline the order or to adjourn the hearing. But it may adjourn the application for a short time to enable the mortgagor to pay off the whole of the mortgage debt.[316]

Where, however, a mortgagee brings an action for possession of a *dwelling-house*,[317] wide discretionary powers are given to the court by the Administration of Justice Act 1970.[318] The Act does not abrogate the common law right of the mortgage to take possession; it supplies, as a procedural measure, a judicial discretion.[319] The court may adjourn the proceedings, or

---

[313] *Gaskell v Gosling* [1896] 1 QB 669 at 691.

[314] (1889) 42 Ch D 237, M & B p. 856; see also *Hughes v Williams* (1806) 12 Ves 493; (1979) 129 NLJ 334 (H. E. Markson); [1982] Conv 345 at 346–8 (J. E. Stannard).

[315] CPR, r. 55.3. Part 55 came into force on 15 October 2001 and changed radically the traditional jurisdiction of the Chancery Division in respect of mortgages: Chancery Guide 2002, chap. 21. Only exceptional circumstances now justify starting a claim in the High Court, e.g. there are complicated disputes of fact, or points of law of general importance. The value of the property and the amount of any financial claim may be relevant circumstances, but these factors alone will not normally justify starting the claim in the High Court. If, however, the claim is brought in the High Court, it will be assigned to the Chancery Division: CPR, PD 53.3. For details which must be set out in the particulars of claim, see PD 55.4, para. 2.5. For enforcement of a judgment or order for possession, see RSC Ord 45, r. 3.
Repossession in accordance with the terms of the loan and the domestic law is necessary for the protection of the rights and freedoms of others, namely the lender, and does not contravene ECHR, art. 8. To the extent that the mortgagor is deprived of his possessions by the repossession, this deprivation is in the public interest, that is the public interest in ensuring payment of contractual debts, and is also in accordance with the rules provided for by law: *Wood v UK* (1997) 24 EHRR CD69.

[316] *Birmingham Citizens Permanent Building Society v Caunt* [1962] Ch 883. A mortgagor's counterclaim or set off against mortgagee for sum exceeding debt is not in itself a reason for an adjournment: *Samuel Keller (Holdings) Ltd v Martins Bank Ltd* [1971] 1 WLR 43; *Mobil Oil Co Ltd v Rawlinson* (1981) 43 P & CR 221, M & B p. 857; *Citibank Trust Ltd v Ayivor* [1987] 1 WLR 1157 (right to possession not affected where mortgagor's counterclaim for damages greater than arrears due under mortgage); *First National Bank plc v Syed* [1991] 2 All ER 250; (1991) 141 NLJ 793 (H. W. Wilkinson); (1994) 110 LQR 221 (N. Hickman); *National Westminster Bank plc v Skelton* [1993] 1 WLR 72n; *Ashley Guarantee plc v Zacaria* [1993] 1 WLR 62 (no distinction in principle where mortgagor is principal debtor and where he is only guarantor); [1993] All ER Rev 253 (P. J. Clarke); *Midland Bank plc v McGrath* [1996] EGCS 61. See Derham, *Set Off*, para. 4.93.

[317] The fact that part of it is used for business purposes does not prevent a house from being a dwelling-house: AJA 1970, s. 39(2). The relevant date for determining whether premises consist of a dwelling-house is the date when the mortgagee brings the action for possession: *Royal Bank of Scotland plc v Miller* [2002] QB 255.

[318] AJA 1970, s. 36.

[319] *Ropaigealach v Barclays Bank plc* [2000] QB 263; [1999] Conv 263 (A. Dunn); [1999] CLJ 281 (M. Dixon). See Law Commission Working Paper on Land Morgages 1996 (Law Com No. 99), para. 3.69. As to the compatibility of the right to peaceable re-entry and its exclusion from AJA 1970, s. 36, with ECHR, see Rook, *Property Law and Human Rights*, pp. 199–203.

suspend or postpone the possession order for such period or periods as the court thinks reasonable[320]

if it appears to the court that in the event of its exercising the power the mortgagor is likely to be able within a reasonable period[321] to pay any sums due under the mortgage or to remedy a default consisting of a breach of any other obligation arising under or by virtue of the mortgage.[322]

Where the mortgagor is entitled to pay the principal sum by instalments, or otherwise to defer the payment of it in whole or in part, the court may treat as sums due only those instalments which are actually in arrear, even if the mortgage makes the whole of the balance outstanding payable on any default by the mortgagor.[323] But the court may only exercise its discretion if the mortgagor is likely to be able within a reasonable period also to pay any further instalments then due.[324]

The period within which the arrears had to be paid used to be usually an automatic two years. However, in *Cheltenham and Gloucester Building Society v Norgan*,[325] the Court of Appeal held that the court should take the full term of the remainder of the mortgage as its starting point in deciding what period is reasonable. EVANS LJ set out a practical summary of the relevant considerations:[326]

(a) How much can the borrower reasonably afford to pay, both now and in the future? (b) If the borrower has a temporary difficulty in meeting his obligations, how long is the difficulty likely to last? (c) What was the reason for the arrears which have accumulated? (d) How much remains of the original term? (e) What are the relevant contractual terms, and what type of mortgage is it, i.e. when is the principal due to be repaid? (f) Is it a case where the court should exercise its power to

---

[320] *National & Provincial Building Society v Ahmed* [1995] 2 EGLR 127; *Cheltenham and Gloucester Building Society v Obi* (1994) 28 HLR 22 (after mortgagee has obtained possession order, court cannot suspend effect of order unless the order itself can be set aside); *Cheltenham and Gloucester Building Society v Grattidge* (1993) 25 HLR 454; *Cheltenham and Gloucester Building Society v Johnson* (1996) 73 P & CR 293 (when a mortgagee is entitled to a money judgment, this may be suspended on same terms as, and in line with, the possession order itself). For the inter-relation between s. 36(1) and LPA 1925, s. 91(2), see *Cheltenham and Gloucester plc v Krausz* [1997] 1 WLR 1558, p. 774, post.

[321] *Royal Trust Co of Canada v Markham* [1975] 1 WLR 1416 (an order for suspension must be for a fixed period).

[322] AJA 1970, s. 36(1). The section does not apply to a mortgage which is within CCA 1974: s. 38A, added by CCA 1974, s. 192, Sch. 4, para. 30.

[323] AJA 1973, s. 8(1), reversing the effect of *Halifax Building Society v Clark* [1973] Ch 307. But the grant of the statutory discretion was unnecessary: *First Middlesbrough Trading and Mortgage Co Ltd v Cunningham* (1974) 28 P & CR 69. See (1973) 37 Conv (NS) 213; (1974) 38 Conv (NS) 1.

[324] AJA 1973, s. 8(2); *Centrax Trustees Ltd v Ross* [1979] 2 All ER 952 (principal to be repaid at indeterminate future date held to be within the section); cf *Habib Bank Ltd v Tailor* [1982] 1 WLR 1218 (overdraft secured by charge to be repaid on demand in writing held to be not within the section, since there was no agreement as to deferred payment); [1983] Conv 80 (P. H. Kenny); [1982] All ER Rev 117 (P. J. Clarke); [1984] Conv 91 (S. Tromans). In instalment mortgages, the discretionary powers extend to foreclosure actions, whether or not possession is claimed in the same proceedings: s. 8(3). See *Lord Marples of Wallasey v Holmes* (1975) 31 P & CR 94.

[325] [1996] 1 WLR 343, M & B p. 868; (1996) 146 NLJ 252 (H. W. Wilkinson); [1996] Conv 118 (M. P. Thompson); (1996) 112 LQR 553 (J. Morgan); [1996] All ER Rev 260 (P. J. Clarke).

For postponement to enable sale to take place, see *National & Provincial Building Society v Lloyd* [1996] 1 All ER 630 (sale by part disposals); *Bristol & West Building Society v Ellis* (1996) 73 P & CR 158, M & B p. 870; [1998] Conv 125 (M. P. Thompson). For retention by mortgagor while mortgagee sells, see *Target Homes Loans Ltd v Clothier* [1994] 1 All ER 439 (three months' postponement; mortgagor had better prospect of achieving earlier sale if in possession); [1993] Conv 62 (J. Martin); *Cheltenham & Gloucester plc v Booker* (1996) 73 P & CR 412 at 415 per MILLETT LJ (possible if mortgagor's presence will not depress sale price, and mortgagor will complete sale and give up possession to purchaser on completion). [326] At 357.

disregard accelerated payment provisions (section 8 of the Act of 1973)? (g) Is it reasonable to expect the lender, in the circumstances of the particular case, to recoup the arrears of interest (1) over the whole of the original term, or (2) within a shorter period, or even (3) within a longer period, i.e. by extending the repayment period? Is it reasonable to expect the lender to capitalise the interest or not? (h) Are there any reasons affecting the security which should influence the length of the period for payment? In the light of the answers to the above, the court can proceed to exercise its overall discretion, taking account of any further factors which may arise in the particular case.

This statutory relief may be given to a mortgagor,[327] whether or not he is in default under the mortgage,[328] and is available in the case of both instalment and endowment mortgages.[329] Where one spouse has defaulted on the mortgage of a dwelling-house, and the mortgagee brings an action for possession, the other spouse may be entitled to be made a party to the action.[330]

(2) IN EQUITY

In addition to the statutory relief, equity may have a wide discretion to restrain any unjust use of the right to possession. In *Quennell v Maltby*:[331]

Q mortgaged his house to a bank. The mortgage deed prohibited the creation of a tenancy without the bank's consent. In breach of that covenant Q let the house to M, who became a statutory tenant protected by the Rent Act. This tenancy was binding on Q but not on the bank.[332] Q, who wanted to sell the house with vacant possession, asked the bank to bring an action for possession against M. On the bank's refusal, Q's wife then paid off the mortgage debt, took a transfer of the mortgage from the bank and claimed possession against M as mortgagee.

The Court of Appeal held that she was not entitled to possession. According to BRIDGE and TEMPLEMAN LJJ, she was to be treated as acting as agent for Q, who, as mortgagor, could not obtain possession. Lord DENNING MR however stated a wider principle:[333]

The objective is plain. It was not to enforce the security or to obtain repayment or anything of the kind. It was in order to get possession of the house and to overcome the protection of the Rent Acts . . . Equity can step in so as to prevent a mortgage, or a transferee from him, from getting possession of a house contrary to the justice of the case. A mortgagee will be restrained from getting possession except

---

[327] Mortgagor and mortgagee includes any person deriving title under the original mortgagor or mortgagee: AJA 1970, s. 39(1); *Britannia Building Society v Earl* [1990] 1 WLR 422 (statutory tenant of mortgagor whose tenancy was not binding on mortgagee, p. 762, ante, was not such a person and court had no jurisdiction to adjourn proceedings); (1990) 140 NLJ 823 (H. W. Wilkinson).

[328] *Western Bank Ltd v Schindler* [1977] Ch 1 (GOFF LJ dubitante); (1977) 40 MLR 356 (C. Harpum).

[329] *Bank of Scotland (Governor & Co) v Grimes* [1985] QB 1179, M & B p. 867. AJA 1973, s. 8 is infelicitously drafted and was interpreted "so as to give effect to the general tenor of the language in a purposive way": per Sir John ARNOLD P at 1188. See also *Royal Bank of Scotland plc v Miller* [2002] QB 255. In an endowment mortgage, an endowment assurance policy is taken out at the same time as the money is borrowed; only interest payments are made by the mortgagor during the time of the mortgage, the outstanding debt being repaid when the policy matures. Cf an instalment or repayment mortgage, where the debt is paid off by monthly instalments at a rate which covers payment of interest and repayment of capital, so that the capital is paid off over an agreed period of time, for example twenty-five years; p. 720, n. 14, supra.

[330] Family Law Act 1996, s. 56, p. 479, ante.

[331] [1979] 1 WLR 318, M & B p. 859; (1979) 129 NLJ 624 (H. W. Wilkinson); (1979) 38 CLJ 257 (R. A. Pearce).

[332] *Dudley and District Benefit Building Society v Emerson* [1949] Ch 707, p. 762, ante.

[333] [1979] 1 WLR 318 at 322; applied in *Albany Home Loan Ltd v Massey* [1997] 2 All ER 609 at 612–13; both cases were distinguished in *Abbey National v Tufts* [1999] 2 FLR 399 at 405–7.

when it is sought bona fide and reasonably for the purpose of enforcing the security, and then only subject to such conditions as the court thinks fit to impose.

It is difficult to reconcile this wider principle with previous authority, and it would render unnecessary the protection accorded to the mortgagor by the Administration of Justice Act 1970.

(3) Appointment of a Receiver

We have seen that, owing to the strict supervision that the court exercises over a mortgagee, it is undesirable for him to take possession of the land, but, on the other hand, there are cases where it is essential that he should be able to intercept the rents and the profits, and employ them in keeping down the interest. The mortgaged property may have been leased by the mortgagor to third parties under his statutory powers or the property may consist not of land but of a rentcharge, so that there is an annual sum which can be prevented from reaching the mortgagor and can be set against interest. In such cases the most effective procedure is to appoint a receiver of the income of the property.

The mortgage deed may contain special provisions with regard to this matter, and in some cases, as for instance where the property is already let to tenants, it is not uncommon to appoint a receiver from the moment when the mortgage is created. But apart from this a mortgagee has a statutory power of appointing a receiver in the case of every mortgage created by deed,[334] even though he has already gone into possession before the appointment.[335] The appointment and removal of a receiver must be effected in writing.[336]

Although this statutory power arises as soon as the mortgage money has become due, it cannot be exercised until one of those three events that qualify a mortgagee to exercise his power of sale has occurred.[337]

The advantage of such an appointment from the mortgagee's point of view is that the receiver is deemed to be the agent of the mortgagor,[338] and that the sole responsibility for his acts and defaults falls on the latter.[339] The receiver is not entitled to grant leases without the sanction of the court,[340] but he has power to recover the income of the property by action or distress or otherwise, and to give effectual receipts,[341] and he is bound to apply any money received by him in the following order:[342]

(1) In discharge of rents, taxes,[343] rates and outgoings.

(2) In keeping down payments that rank before the mortgage.

[334] LPA 1925, s. 101(1)(iii). *Shamji v Johnson Matthey Bankers Ltd* [1991] BCLC 36 (mortgagee owes no duty of care to mortgagor or guarantor in deciding whether or not to appoint a receiver).

[335] *Refuge Assurance Co Ltd v Pearlberg* [1938] Ch 687.

[336] LPA 1925, s. 109(1), (5). In registered land the power to appoint a receiver is not exercisable until the mortgage is registered: *Lever Finance Ltd v Trustee of the Property of Needleman and Kreutzer* [1956] Ch 375.

[337] LPA 1925, s. 109 (1), p. 769, post.

[338] For the peculiar incidents of this agency, see *Silven Properties Ltd v Royal Bank of Scotland plc* [2004] 1 WLR 997 at [21]–[29], per LIGHTMAN J.

[339] LPA 1925, s. 109(2). See *Chatsworth Properties Ltd v Effiom* [1971] 1 WLR 144; *Standard Chartered Bank Ltd v Walker* [1982] 1 WLR 1410; *American Express International Banking Corpn v Hurley* [1985] 3 All ER 564; p. 773, n. 376, post. See *Lever Finance Ltd v Trustee of the Property of Needleman and Kreutzer*, supra (receipt by receiver as agent of mortgagor does not create tenancy by estoppel binding on mortgagee): *Mann v Nijar* (2000) 32 HLR 223.   [340] *Re Cripps* [1946] Ch 265.

[341] LPA 1925, s. 109(3).   [342] Ibid., s. 109(8).

[343] *Sargent v Customs and Excise Comrs* [1993] EGCS 182 (VAT).

(3) In paying his own commission, fire and other insurance premiums and, if so directed in writing by the mortgagee, the cost of repairs. His commission is at a rate not exceeding five per cent on the gross sum received; if no rate is specified, then at five per cent, or at such other rate as the court thinks fit to allow.[344]

(4) In payment of the mortgage interest.

(5) In discharging the principal sum if so directed in writing by the mortgagee. A breach of this direction renders him liable to an action for an account.[345]

Any residue that remains must be paid to the mortgagor.

A receiver, when managing the mortgaged property, owes not only a duty of good faith to the mortgagor and anyone else with an interest in the equity of redemption, but also a duty to manage the property with due diligence. The extent of the duty depends on the facts and circumstances of the case.[346]

(4) Sale[347]

(a) *Power of sale*

(1) WHEN POWER ARISES

As soon as the mortgage money has become due, that is, as soon as the date fixed for repayment has passed, the legal mortgagee or chargee has a statutory power, which may be varied or extended by the parties or excluded altogether,[348] to sell the mortgage property *provided that the mortgage has been made by deed*.[349] If the money secured by the mortgage is payable by instalments, the power of sale arises as soon as an instalment is due and unpaid.[350]

(2) WHEN POWER EXERCISABLE

Although the power of sale arises as soon as the mortgage money becomes due, it nevertheless does not become exercisable until *one* of the following events has occurred:

(i) Notice requiring payment of the mortgage money has been served on the mortgagor or one of two or more mortgagors, and default has been made in payment of the mortgage money, or of part thereof, for three months after such service.[351]

This notice, which must be in writing,[352] may demand payment either immediately or at the end of three months, and if it is drafted in the latter form, the mortgagee need not wait for a further three months before selling, but can exercise his power after the lapse of three months from the service of notice.[353]

If there are more mortgages than one, the notice should also be served upon the later mortgagees.

(ii) Some interest under the mortgage is in arrear and unpaid for two months after becoming due.[354]

---

[344] *Marshall v Cottingham* [1982] Ch 82.
[345] *Leicester Permanent Building Society v Butt* [1943] Ch 308.
[346] *Medforth v Blake* [2000] Ch 86; [1999] Conv 434 (A. Kenny); [2000] CLJ 31 (L. S. Sealy).
[347] See generally Fisher and Lightwood, chap. 20; (1976) 73 LSG 92, 654; (1977) 74 LSG 493 (H. E. Markson).
[348] *Alliance Building Society v Shave* [1952] Ch 581.   [349] LPA 1925, s. 101(1)(i).
[350] *Payne v Cardiff RDC* [1932] 1 KB 241; cf *Twentieth Century Banking Corpn Ltd v Wilkinson* [1977] Ch 99.
[351] LPA 1925, s. 103(i).   [352] Ibid., s. 196.   [353] *Barker v Illingworth* [1908] 2 Ch 20.
[354] LPA 1925, s. 103(ii).

(iii) There has been a breach of some provision contained in the mortgage deed or in the Law of Property Act 1925, and on the part of the mortgagor, or of some person concurring in making the mortgage, to be observed or performed, other than and besides a covenant for payment of the mortgage money or interest thereon.[355]

For instance, if the mortgagor has broken a covenant to keep the premises in repair, the mortgagee can exercise his power of sale immediately, despite the fact that no interest is in arrear and that he has not demanded repayment of the loan.

Sections 101–7 of the Law of Property Act 1925 contain detailed provisions dealing with the power of sale.[356] The mortgagee may sell the mortgaged property, or any part thereof, either subject to prior charges or not, and either together or in lots, by public auction or by private contract. He may sell the land either with or apart from the minerals, and may impose either on the sold or on the unsold part of the mortgaged land such conditions or restrictive covenants as seem desirable.[357]

(b) Effect of Sale

If a mortgagee realises his security by exercising the statutory power of sale, the effect is to extinguish the mortgagor's equity of redemption. It is, however, the contract to sell and not the subsequent conveyance that represents the effective exercise of the mortgagee's power; and, providing that there is no impropriety in the sale, the mortgagor's equity is extinguished as soon as the contract of sale is made.[358]

(1) FEE SIMPLE

A mortgagee, although he holds only a term of years or, more commonly, a charge by way of legal mortgage, is given express statutory power to vest the fee simple in the purchaser. The conveyance may be made in the name of the mortgagor as estate owner, and it operates to pass his legal fee simple to the purchaser and to extinguish the mortgage terms vested both in the selling mortgagee and in any subsequent mortgagees.[359] If the person exercising the power of sale is not the first mortgagee, then the purchaser takes the fee simple subject to prior mortgages.

(2) LEASEHOLD

Where a term of years has been mortgaged by a sub-lease, the effect of a sale by the mortgagee is to convey to the purchaser both the mortgage sub-term and the residue of the term vested in the mortgagor.[360] The sub-term is extinguished, since it merges in the mortgagor's reversion which thus passes to the purchaser. The conveyance, however, does not have this effect if the mortgage term does not comprise the whole of the land included in the mortgagor's term, unless the rent and the covenants have been apportioned, or unless the land excluded from the mortgage term bears a rent of no money value.[361] The acquisition of the reversion by the purchaser results in his becoming liable, in his capacity as assignee, upon

---

[355] LPA 1925, s. 103(ii), s. 103(iii).   [356] See CCA 1974, s. 126; p. 778, post.

[357] LPA 1925, s. 101(2).

[358] *Lord Waring v London and Manchester Assurance Co Ltd* [1935] Ch 310, M & B p. 875; *Property and Bloodstock Ltd v Emerton* [1968] Ch 94. For the effect of a contract of sale by the mortgagor upon the powers of the mortgagee, see *Duke v Robson* [1973] 1 WLR 267.   [359] LPA 1925, ss. 88(1), 113.

[360] Ibid., s. 89(1).

[361] Ibid., s. 89(6). "Apportionment" includes an equitable apportionment, i.e. one made without the consent of the lessor: LP(A)A 1926, Schedule, amending LPA 1925, s. 89.

the covenants contained in the lease from the lessor to the mortgagor. The Act, therefore, provides that if the leave of the court is obtained the sub-term alone may be conveyed to the purchaser to the exclusion of the mortgagor's reversion.[362]

These provisions also apply where the owner of a charge over a leasehold by way of legal mortgage exercises his power of sale.

(c) Position of purchaser from mortgagee

It is clear, therefore, that there is no difficulty in transferring to a purchaser a valid legal title to the whole interest vested in the mortgagor. Such a purchaser takes the estate freed from all estates, interests and rights to which the mortgage has priority;[363] but if he buys from a second mortgagee he will take the fee simple subject to the term vested in the first mortgagee, and he will himself be deprived of the fee simple if such a first mortgagee exercises his powers of sale or foreclosure. A sale which is made in the professed exercise of the statutory power of sale (and after 1925 every sale made by a mortgagee is deemed so to have been made unless a contrary intention appears) cannot be impeached on the ground that no case has arisen to authorise the sale, or that the power has been improperly exercised. If either of these facts is proved, then the injured person has his remedy against the mortgagee who exercised the power, not against the purchaser.[364]

A purchaser is thus only concerned to see that the power of sale has arisen, and this he can discover merely by examining the mortgage deed. He need not satisfy himself that the power of sale has become exercisable or that it has been properly exercised. If, however, he "becomes aware . . . of any facts showing that the power of sale is not exercisable, or that there is some impropriety in the sale, then, in my judgment, he gets no good title on taking the conveyance".[365]

(d) Application of purchase money

The money received from a purchaser is held by the mortgagee, after any prior mortgages have been paid off, on trust:

First, to pay all expenses incidental to the sale.

Secondly, to pay to himself the principal, interest and costs due under the mortgage, and

Thirdly, to pay the surplus, if any, to the person entitled to the mortgaged property.[366]

The words "person entitled to the mortgaged property" include subsequent mortgagees, and the rule is that where there are several mortgagees interested in the same land, a prior mortgagee holds any surplus proceeds on trust for those later mortgagees of whose incumbrances he has notice.[367] In unregistered land, registration as a land charge constitutes actual

---

[362] LPA 1925, s. 89(1)(a).   [363] Ibid., s. 104(1).   [364] Ibid., s. 104(2), (3).

[365] *Lord Waring v London and Manchester Assurance Co Ltd* [1935] Ch 310 at 318, per CROSSMAN J. See *Jenkins v Jones* (1860) 2 Giff 99; *Selwyn v Garfit* (1888) 38 Ch D 273; *Bailey v Barnes* [1894] 1 Ch 25; *Price Bros (Somerford) Ltd v J Kelly Homes (Stoke-on-Trent) Ltd* [1975] 1 WLR 1512; *Northern Development (Holdings) Ltd v UDT Securities Ltd* [1976] 1 WLR 1230; *Forsyth v Blundell* (1973) 129 CLR 477; *Pasquarella v National Australia Finance Ltd* [1987] 1 NZLR 312 and generally Emmet, para. 25.048; [1988] Conv 317; [1989] Conv 412 (S. Robinson); *Corbett v Halifax Building Society* [2003] 1 WLR 964.

[366] LPA 1925, s. 105; *Weld-Blundell v Synott* [1940] 2 KB 107.

[367] *Thorne v Heard and Marsh* [1895] AC 495.

notice,[368] and therefore if he pays the surplus to the mortgagor he is liable to that extent to the next mortgagee whose mortgage has been registered.[369] In case of doubt he may pay the money into court.[370]

If, however, the right of redemption of a mortgagor and of persons claiming through him has been extinguished under the Limitation Act 1980 (by reason of the mortgagee having been in possession for twelve years without receiving any sum in respect of principal or interest and without acknowledging the title of the mortgagor[371]), a subsequent mortgagee is not a "person entitled to the mortgaged property". Since the title which he claims through the mortgagor is extinguished, his interest has ceased. Therefore, if the mortgagee sells under his statutory power, he is entitled to retain the whole proceeds, although they may exceed the amount due to him for principal and interest.[372]

(e) Duty of mortgagee exercising power of sale

A mortgagee who exercises his power of sale is not in other respects a trustee for the mortgagor. SALMON LJ in *Cuckmere Brick Co Ltd v Mutual Finance Ltd* said:[373]

It is well settled that a mortgagee is not a trustee of the power of sale for the mortgagor. Once the power has accrued, the mortgagee is entitled to exercise it for his own purposes whenever he chooses to do so.[374] It matters not that the moment may be unpropitious and that by waiting a higher price could be obtained. He has the right to realise his security by turning it into money when he likes. Nor, in my view, is there anything to prevent a mortgagee from accepting the best bid he can get at an auction, even though the auction is badly attended and the bidding exceptionally low. Provided none of those adverse factors is due to any fault of the mortgagee, he can do as he likes. If the mortgagee's interests, as he sees them, conflict with those of the mortgagor, the mortgagee can give preference to his own interests, which of course he could not do were he a trustee of the power of sale for the mortgagor.

---

[368] LPA 1925, s. 198(1) as amended by Local Land Charges Act 1975, s. 17, Sch. 1; p. 795, post.

[369] *West London Commercial Bank v Reliance Permanent Building Society* (1884) 27 Ch D 187; affd (1885) 29 Ch D 954; *Re Thomson's Mortgage Trusts* [1920] 1 Ch 508. Distinguish the mortgagee's duty with regard to delivery of the title deeds after redemption, for which purpose registration of a later mortgage does not constitute notice; p. 758, ante.   [370] TA 1925, s. 63.

[371] LA 1980, s. 16.

[372] *Re Statutory Trusts Declared by Section 105 of the Law of Property Act 1925 affecting the Proceeds of Sale of Moat House Farm, Thurlby* [1948] Ch 191; *Halifax Building Society v Thomas* [1996] Ch 217.

[373] [1971] Ch 949 at 965.

[374] *China and South Sea Bank Ltd v Tan Soon Gin* [1990] 1 AC 536 at 545: "The creditor must decide in his own interest if and when he should sell": per Lord TEMPLEMAN; *Countrywide Banking Corpn v Robinson* [1991] 1 NZLR 75; *Cuckmere Brick Co Ltd v Mutual Finance Ltd*, supra; see *Forsyth v Blundell* (1973) 129 CLR 477 at 481, 493. In *Standard Chartered Bank Ltd v Walker* [1982] 1 WLR 1410, Lord DENNING MR said at 1415: "There are several dicta to the effect that the mortgagee can choose his own time for the sale, but I do not think this means that he can sell at the worst possible time. It is at least arguable that, in choosing the time, he must exercise a reasonable degree of care." See also *Predeth v Castle Phillips Finance Co Ltd* [1986] 2 EGLR 144 (where CA accepted the judge's finding that the exercise of reasonable care required mortgagee to expose uninhabitable bungalow at Alton in Hampshire to the market for approximately three months); *Palk v Mortgage Services Funding plc* [1993] Ch 330, p. 774, post, where Sir Donald NICHOLLS V-C said at 338: "If the mortgagee sells the property, he cannot sell hastily at a knock-down price sufficient to pay off his debt"; *Downsview Nominees Ltd v First City Corpn Ltd* [1993] AC 295; [1993] Conv 401 (R. Grantham); *Meftah v Lloyds TSB Bank plc* [2001] 2 All ER (Comm) 741 (timing of sale is for mortgagee; if there is urgency "the necessity of exposure to the market must be evaluated in the light of the circumstances", per LAWRENCE COLLINS J at 745); *Silven Properties v Royal Bank of Scotland plc* [2004] 1 WLR 997, M & B p. 883 (mortgagee under no duty to postpone sale until after further pursuit of application for planning permission or grant of lease, even though outcome of either course might increase value of property). See Emmet, para. 25.043.

It has even been held that the motive of the mortgagee for selling, such as to spite the mortgagor, is immaterial.[375]

A mortgagee, however, in exercising his power of sale, owes a duty of care to the mortgagor and to any guarantor of the mortgagor's debt.[376] This duty may be excluded by an appropriate term in the mortgage.[377] The mortgagee must act not only in good faith[378] for the purpose of protecting his security,[379] but also take reasonable care to obtain the true market value of the mortgaged property at the date on which he decides to sell it.[380] Thus, where the price is lower than would have been the case due to his negligence or that of his agent, then he must account to the mortgagor for the difference between that price and the true market value.[381] There has been some debate in recent years about the source of the mortgagee's duty of care, but it is now clearly established that it does not arise out of the mortgage contract,[382] nor in the tort of negligence, but is a duty arising in equity out of the particular relationship of mortgagor and mortgagee.[383]

[375] *Nash v Eads* (1880) 25 SJ 95 (JESSEL MR); *Belton v Bass, Ratcliffe and Gretton Ltd* [1922] 2 Ch 449; *Meretz Investments NV v ACP Ltd* The Times, 27 April 2006 (*mixed* motives do not invalidate exercise of power of sale).
[376] *Standard Chartered Bank Ltd v Walker* [1982] 1 WLR 1410; (1982) 132 NLJ 884 (H. W. Wilkinson); [1982] All ER Rev 39 (D. D. Prentice). See also *American Express International Banking Corpn v Hurley* [1985] 3 All ER 564 (mortgagee responsible for what receiver does as his agent, but not responsible for what he does as mortgagor's agent, unless the mortgagee directs or interferes with receiver's activities). Where the mortgagee fails to obtain a proper price, the amount for which the guarantor of the loan is liable is pro tanto reduced: *Skipton Building Society v Stott* [2001] QB 261.
[377] In *Bishop v Bonham* [1988] 1 WLR 742. SLADE LJ said at 752: "The duty of care imposed on a selling mortgagee, by what I may call the *Cuckmere* principle, is essentially in the nature of an obligation implied by law, and as such is, in my judgment, undoubtedly capable of being excluded by agreement. The exclusion clause must be construed strictly;"; *Mercantile Credit Co Ltd v Clarke* (1995) 71 P & CR D18 (agreement of mortgagor to a lower sale price).
[378] *Kennedy v De Trafford* [1897] AC 180; *Lord Waring v London and Manchester Assurance Co Ltd* [1935] Ch 310.
[379] *Downsview Nominees Ltd v First City Corpn Ltd* [1993] AC 295 at 312, per Lord TEMPLEMAN; *Caricom Cinemas Ltd v Republic Bank Ltd* [2003] UKPC 2.
[380] *Freeguard v Royal Bank of Scotland plc* [2006] 06 EG 169 (ransom strip: price that could be obtained only from person with special interest in purchasing it).
[381] *Cuckmere Brick Co Ltd v Mutual Finance Ltd* [1971] Ch 949 (failure to mention planning permission for flats in advertisement for sale of land by auction); *Palmer v Barclays Bank Ltd* (1971) 23 P & CR 30; *Waltham Forest London Borough v Webb* (1974) 232 EG 461; *Johnson v Ribbins* (1975) 235 EG 757; *Bank of Cyprus (London) Ltd v Gill* [1980] 2 Lloyd's Rep 51; (1981) 125 NLJ 249 (H. E. Markson); *Norwich General Trust v Grierson* [1984] CLY 2306 (mortgagee held liable for diminution of purchase price due to his negligence in allowing premises to deteriorate between date of taking possession and date of sale); *Garland v Ralph Pay & Ransom* (1984) 271 EG 106, 197 (action by mortgagor against mortgagee's selling agents for negligent marketing technique and valuation); *Predeth v Castle Phillips Finance Co Ltd* [1986] 2 EGLR 144 (action by mortgagee against surveyor instructed to provide "crash-sale" valuation); [1986] Conv 442 (M. P. Thompson); *AIB Finance Ltd v Debtors* [1997] 4 All ER 677 (security included business carried on on mortgaged property; held duty on mortgagee to ensure that on sale value of the combined asset was maximised); *Struggles v Lloyds TSB plc* [2000] EGCS 17 (for a quarry to be sold for the best possible price, it should be exposed to the market for six to twelve months to enable investigations to be made of both mineral and waste-fill potential); *Skipton Building Society v Stott* [2000] 2 All ER 779 (guarantor liable for difference between amount owed under guarantee and market value of premises at date of sale); *Michael v Miller* [2004] 2 P & CR D12 ("bracket" or margin of error approach for deciding whether mortgagee in breach of duty).
[382] *Raja v Lloyds TSB Bank plc* (2001) 82 P & CR 16 (claim against mortgagee not based on specialty within LA 1980, s. 8, and so statute barred after six years).
[383] *Parker-Tweedale v Dunbar Bank plc* [1991] Ch 12 at 18, M & B p. 875; *Downsview Nominees Ltd v First City Corpn Ltd* [1993] AC 295; [1993] Conv 401 (R. Grantham); *Medforth v Blake* [2000] Ch 86, *Raju v Austin Gray* [2003] 1 EGLR 91 (no duty owed in tort by receiver's valuer: mortgagor's remedy, if at all, is against mortgagee in equity). See also *China and South Sea Bank Ltd v Tan Soon Gin* [1990] 1 AC 536, M & B p. 878 (where PC held that no duty was owed by a mortgagee to a surety to sell depreciating mortgaged property; Lord

The Court of Appeal has imposed[384] a novel and restrictive interpretation on the mortgagee's duty of care, in holding that, where the mortgagor is a trustee of the mortgaged property, the mortgagee owes no duty to a beneficiary under the trust of whose interest he has notice. The duty on sale arises solely out of the equitable relationship between mortgagor and mortgagee.

In any event, the sale must be a genuine sale. A mortgagee cannot sell to himself either alone[385] or with others, nor to a trustee for himself, nor to anyone employed by him to conduct the sale. Such a sale is no sale at all, even though the price fixed is the full value of the property.[386] There is, however, no hard and fast rule that a mortgagee may not sell to a company in which he owns shares; but the onus lies on both the mortgagee and the company to show that the sale was in good faith and that the mortgagee took reasonable precautions to obtain the best price reasonably obtainable at the time.[387]

(f) Discretion of Court to order sale at a depressed market price

In *Palk v Mortgage Services Funding plc*[388]

a house was mortgaged for £358,587, but could only be sold for £283,000. The mortgagor wished to sell the house, but the mortgagee wished to take possession and to let it on a short-term lease and to sell when the market improved.

The Court of Appeal held that it had a discretion under section 91(2) of the Law of Property Act 1925,[389] to order a sale at a depressed market price, even against the wishes of the mortgagee.[390] As Sir Donald NICHOLLS V-C said:[391] "It is just and equitable to order a sale because otherwise unfairness and injustice will follow": interest due from the mortgagor would continue to increase and thereby compound his eventual loss.

In *Cheltenham and Gloucester plc v Krausz*,[392] however, another Court of Appeal considered the inter-relationship between the circumstances in which the mortgagor is entitled to an order for sale under section 91(2) and those in which the court has jurisdiction to suspend entry into possession by the mortgagee under section 36 of the Administration of Justice Act 1970.[393] In so doing the court restricted the operation of *Palk*. It held that in cases of negative

---

TEMPLEMAN said at 543: "The Court of Appeal [of Hong Kong] sought to find such a duty in the tort of negligence but the tort of negligence has not yet subsumed all torts and does not supplant the principles of equity or contradict contractual promises or complement the remedy of judicial review or supplement statutory rights"). There are earlier dicta to the contrary in *Standard Chartered Bank Ltd v Walker* [1982] 1 WLR 1410 at 1415.

[384] *Parker-Tweedale v Dunbar Bank plc* [1991] Ch 12, M & B p. 875; [1990] Conv 431 (L. Bently); HL Appellate Committee refused leave to appeal: [1991] Ch 12 at 25.

[385] *Williams v Wellingborough BC* [1975] 1 WLR 1327 ("a see-through dress of a sale", at 1329, per RUSSELL LJ). The decision itself was reversed by HA 1980, s. 112 for the benefit of existing local authority mortgagees.

[386] *Farrar v Farrars Ltd* (1888) 40 Ch D 395 at 409, and authorities cited by LINDLEY LJ.

[387] *Tse Kwong Lam v Wong Chit Sen* [1983] 1 WLR 1349, M & B p. 881; [1984] Conv 143 (P. Jackson); [1983] All ER Rev 57 (D. D. Prentice); *Bradford & Bingley plc v Ross* The Times, 3 May 2005 (mortgagee failed to disclose to the court its sale of mortgaged property to a "closely connected company"; mortgagor entitled to retrial, but not to have judgment set aside as abuse of process).

[388] [1993] Ch 330, M & B p. 886; [1993] Conv 59 (J. Martin); (1993) 143 NLJ 448 (H. W. Wilkinson); *Polonski v Lloyds Bank Mortgages Ltd* [1998] 1 FLR 896.   [389] P. 776, post.

[390] *Woolley v Colman* (1882) 21 Ch D 169 (sale directed by FRY J who fixed a reserve price sufficient to protect mortgagee).   [391] [1993] Ch 330 at 422.

[392] [1997] 1 WLR 1558, M & B p. 887; [1998] Conv 223 (A. Kenny); [1998] LS 279 (M. Dixon); approved in *Albany Home Loans Ltd v Massey* (1997) 73 P & CR 509 at 513, per SCHLIEMANN LJ, referring to a similar requirement by Lord TEMPLEMAN in *Downsview Nominees Ltd v First City Corpn Ltd* [1993] AC 295 at 312; and to ECHR, art. 8.   [393] P. 765, ante.

equity there was no jurisdiction to suspend an order for possession, obtained by the mortgagee, so as to enable the mortgagor to make an application under section 91(2). The mortgagee is in control of the sale.

(5) Foreclosure

(a) Foreclosure action[394]

Foreclosure is a judicial procedure by which the mortgagee acquires the land for himself freed from the mortgagor's equity of redemption. We have seen that equity regards the mortgagor's right to redeem the property as inviolable, and that, despite the lapse of the contractual right to redeem, it forbids the mortgagee to appropriate the legal fee simple without making an application to the court. Until the time fixed in the deed for repayment of the loan has arrived, no question of foreclosure can arise, but as soon as that date has passed and the equitable right to redeem has superseded the contractual right, the mortgagee can bring an action in the Chancery Division[395] praying that the mortgagor shall either pay what is due or be foreclosed, that is, deprived altogether of his right to redeem.

If the mortgagor does not pay, the court issues an order for *foreclosure nisi*, the effect of which is that the mortgagor loses his property unless he pays upon a certain date (generally six months later) specified by the Master's certificate. The judgment orders that an account shall be taken of what is due to the plaintiff for principal, interest and costs, and directs that if this amount is paid within six months, the mortgage term shall be surrendered to the defendant, but that if default in payment is made, the defendant shall stand absolutely debarred and foreclosed of and from all right, title, interest and equity of redemption in and to the mortgaged premises. The mortgagee then proves in chambers what is due to him for principal, interest and costs, and the Master draws up a certificate of what is due and fixes a day and an hour for repayment (usually six months therefrom). On that day the mortgagee attends, and waits for the mortgagor, and if the latter does not appear, an affidavit is sworn in proof of non-payment either prior to or at the appointed time, and an order is made for *foreclosure absolute*.

(b) Effect of foreclosure order

The effect of the order absolute is to vest the fee simple absolute (or other whole estate of the mortgagor) in the mortgagee, and to extinguish his mortgage term and all subsequent mortgage terms or legal charges.[396] In registered land, in order to perfect his title the mortgagee will apply to be registered as proprietor of the registered estate in respect of which the charge is registered. The registrar must then cancel the registration of the charge, cancel all entries in respect of interests over which the charge has priority, and enter the applicant as proprietor of the registered estate.[397]

---

[394] See generally Fisher and Lightwood, chap. 22; (1978) 75 LSG 447; (1979) 129 NLJ 33 (H. E. Markson), 225 (C. M. Pepper); (1981) 260 EG 899 (D. Brahams). On a revival in its popularity as a remedy, see Report of Committee on Enforcement of Judgment Debts 1969 (Cmnd 1309), para. 1360; on its rarity, see *Palk v Mortgage Services Funding plc* [1993] 2 WLR 415 at 419; and on its commercial use, see *Lloyds and Scottish Trust Ltd v Britten* (1982) 44 P & CR 249.

[395] The jurisdiction of the Chancery Division in respect of foreclosure actions was not affected by the introduction of CPR, Part 55. CPR PD4 provides for the forms of order for foreclosure nisi (N299) and foreclosure absolute (N309) of a legal mortgage of land.   [396] LPA 1925, ss. 88(2), 89(2).

[397] LRR 2003, r. 112.

(1) FORECLOSE DOWN

The rights of prior mortgagees are not affected. If there are more mortgagees than one interested in the same land, an order absolute obtained by the first mortgagee forecloses all subsequent incumbrancers, while if (say) the second mortgagee obtains such an order, its effect is to foreclose the third and later mortgagees, but to leave untouched the rights of the first mortgagee. The rule is "foreclose down".[398]

Where there are in this way several mortgagees and the first brings an action for foreclosure, not only the mortgagor, but also each of the subsequent mortgagees must be given an opportunity to redeem, and the ordinary practice is to direct in the order *nisi* that any of the subsequent incumbrancers may repay the amount due to the first man on the date appointed.[399] If subsequent mortgagees are not made parties they are not foreclosed.

(2) SALE IN LIEU OF FORECLOSURE

The court has statutory jurisdiction in a foreclosure action to order a sale instead of a foreclosure on the request of the mortgagee or mortgagor, or of any person interested in the mortgage money or the equity of redemption, notwithstanding the dissent of any other person.[400]

(3) LAPSE OF TIME

An action for foreclosure is an action to recover land,[401] and must therefore be brought within twelve years from the date upon which the right of recovery accrues.[402] The right accrues at the date fixed for payment of the principal,[403] but there is a fresh accrual, and the twelve years begin to run again, from any payment of principal or interest by the mortgagor or from a written acknowledgment by him of the mortgagee's title.[404]

(c) *Revival of equity of redemption*

But it must not be thought that a foreclosure absolute irrevocably passes the mortgagor's interest to the mortgagee, although it appears on the surface to do so, for there are certain circumstances in which the foreclosure may be re-opened and the equity of redemption revived. This re-opening takes place if the mortgagee, after obtaining an order absolute, proceeds to sue on the personal covenant,[405] but in addition to this case the court has a discretion to re-open a foreclosure if such relief appears in the special circumstances of the case to be due to the mortgagor. Moreover, the foreclosure may be re-opened against one who has

---

[398] From this must be distinguished the maxim "Redeem up, foreclose down". This applies where there are several mortgagees and in a redemption action one of them seeks to redeem a prior mortgage. Thus, if there are five mortgages and the fourth seeks to redeem the second mortgage, he must redeem up i.e. redeem the third as well as the second, and foreclose down, i.e. foreclose the fifth mortgage and the mortgagor. The first mortgage is unaffected. See Waldock, *Law of Mortgages*, p. 337.

[399] If subsequent mortgagees request that they may be granted successive periods for repayment, an order to that effect is generally issued: *Platt v Mendel* (1884) 27 Ch D 246.

[400] LPA 1925, s. 91(2); *Silsby v Holliman* [1955] Ch 552; *Twentieth Century Banking Corpn Ltd v Wilkinson* [1977] Ch 99. See also *Palk v Mortgage Services Funding plc* [1993] Ch 330, p. 774, ante; *Arab Bank plc v Mercantile Holdings Ltd* [1994] Ch 71; *Halifax Building Society v Thomas* [1996] Ch 217 at 226, per PETER GIBSON LJ, noting the modern preference to order sale under s. 91(2) rather than foreclosure).

[401] Limitation Act 1980, s. 20(4).   [402] Ibid., s. 15(1).

[403] *Purnell v Roche* [1927] 2 Ch 142; *Lewis v Plunket* [1937] Ch 306.

[404] Limitation Act 1980, s. 29; *Harlock v Ashberry* (1882) 19 Ch D 539.

[405] *Perry v Barker* (1806) 13 Ves 198; p. 763, ante.

purchased the estate from the mortgagee. It is impossible to lay down a general rule as to when the relief will be granted, for everything turns upon the particular circumstances of each case, although such a re-opening of the foreclosure is very rare.

In *Campbell v Holyland*,[406] JESSEL MR enumerated those factors which might influence the court in re-opening the foreclosure: the promptness of the mortgagor's application, his failure to redeem being due to an accident which prevented him from raising the money, the difference between the value of the property and the loan,[407] and any special value which the property had to the parties. Further the court may still re-open the foreclosure, even if the mortgagee has sold the property after the foreclosure absolute; as, for example, where a purchaser bought the property within twenty-four hours after the order and with notice of the fact that it was of much greater value than the amount of the mortgage debt.[408]

(6) Restitution

The law of restitution may provide a remedy for the mortgagee. Thus in *Goss v Chilcott*,[409] the mortgagee was held to be able to recover the amount of an advance made to the defendants which was secured by a mortgage over their property. The mortgage deed was subsequently altered by a solicitor, as a result of which the defendants were discharged from liability as from the date of alteration.

As Lord GOFF OF CHIEVELEY said:[410] "The effect of the alteration was that their contractual obligation to repay the money was discharged; but they had nevertheless been enriched by the receipt of the money, and prima facie were liable in restitution to restore it."

(7) Further Rights of Legal Mortgagees

(a) *Grant and acceptance of surrender of leases*

If a mortgagee takes possession of the land with a view to utilising the profits in satisfaction of the money due to him, he is authorised by statute to grant leases, and to accept surrenders of leases, within the limits made applicable to a mortgagor who is in actual possession.[411] He is also permitted, where the mortgage is made by deed, to cut and sell timber and other trees if they are ripe for cutting and are not planted for shelter or ornament.[412]

(b) *Insurance of the mortgaged property*

Where a mortgage is made by deed, the mortgagee has statutory authority to insure the property against loss or damage by fire, and to charge the premiums on the mortgaged

---

[406] (1877) 7 Ch D 166 at 172–5, M & B p. 896.

[407] *Lancashire & Yorkshire Reversionary Interest Co Ltd v Crowe* (1970) 114 SJ 435 (foreclosure decree made absolute in respect of mortgage of reversionary interest, and re-opened after the interest fell in possession on death of the tenant for life. The sum due was £3,000, and the fund £6,100). This is a very rare case in the modern law. There appears to be no case reported in the Law Reports since the beginning of the twentieth century in which a foreclosure was re-opened, the last such case in which a claim to re-open was made being *Pennington v Cayley* [1912] 2 Ch 236.   [408] *Campbell v Holyland*, supra.

[409] [1996] AC 788, M & B p. 894.

[410] Ibid., at 792, M & B p. 809; Goff and Jones, *The Law of Restitution*, paras. 19-007 to 19-008. See also *Portman Building Society v Hamlyn Taylor Neck* [1998] 4 All ER 202 (mortgagee's loss arising from mistake induced by solicitor: no restitution because solicitor not enriched).

[411] LPA 1925, ss. 99(2), 100(2); p. 761, ante; *Berkshire Capital Funding Ltd v Street* [1999] 2 EGLR 92 (interests of prior lender unaffected by loan).   [412] Ibid., s. 101(1)(iv).

property.[413] But the amount of the insurance must not exceed the amount specified in the mortgage deed, or, if no amount is specified, must not exceed two-thirds of the sum it would take to restore the premises in the event of their total destruction. Moreover, the mortgagee does not possess this statutory right where the mortgage deed contains a declaration that no insurance is required, or where an insurance is kept up by the mortgagor according to the mortgage deed, or where that deed contains no provision and the mortgagor himself insures up to the statutory amount.[414] Insurance money, when received, may be applied at the instance of the mortgagee in the discharge of the mortgage debt.[415]

(c) Possession of the title deeds

A legal mortgagee takes a lease or, if he is a chargee, is in the same position as if he had done so, and the ordinary rule is that a leaseholder is not entitled to hold title deeds appertaining to the fee simple of the lessor. But, since the continued possession of the deeds by the mortgagor involves considerable risk to one who has advanced money on the security of the land, it is enacted that a first mortgagee shall have the same right to possession of documents as if his security included the fee simple.[416] This is relevant only to unregistered land.

At law the mortgagee becomes the absolute owner of the title deeds, and is therefore under no duty of care in respect of them. He is subject only to pay compensation in equity for their loss on redemption.[417]

(d) Rights under the Consumer Credit Act 1974

Consonant with the object of the Act,[418] the rights of the mortgagee are curtailed. A security cannot be enforced by reason of any breach of a regulated agreement by the debtor, until the creditor has served a notice under section 87. This is similar to, but not identical with, the notice required by section 146 of the Law of Property Act 1925 in the case of the forfeiture of a lease.[419] Further, a land mortgage securing a regulated agreement is enforceable by an order of the court only.[420] This is a most important provision, since a mortgagee cannot exercise his rights of taking possession and of sale without such an order. If, however, he sells without an order, it would seem that he can pass a good title to the purchaser.[421]

Finally, under section 113, a creditor shall not derive from the enforcement of the security any greater benefit than he would obtain from enforcement of a regulated agreement, if the security were not provided. This would seem to deny the mortgagee the full benefit of foreclosure.[422]

---

[413] LPA 1925, s. 101(1)(ii).

[414] Ibid., s. 108(1), (2); *Colonial Mutual General Insurance Co Ltd v ANZ Banking Group (New Zealand) Ltd* [1995] 1 WLR 1140.   [415] Ibid., s. 108(4).

[416] Ibid., ss. 85(1), 86(1).

[417] *Browning v Handiland Group Ltd and Bush Investments Trust Ltd* (1976) 35 P & CR 345.

[418] P. 745, ante.   [419] P. 281, ante.

[420] CCA 1974, s. 126. For orders which the court can make, see Part IX of the Act; *First National Bank plc v Syed* [1991] 2 All ER 250; *Cedar Holdings Ltd v Thompson* [1993] CCLR 7 (extension time). For making an order to reschedule mortgage agreements made under the Act; see ss. 129 and 136; *Southern and District Finance plc v Barnes* [1996] 1 FCR 679; [1996] Conv 209 (A. Dunn). As to the application of Limitation Act 1980, ss. 5 and 9, see *Ricketts v Hurstanger* Ltd [1997] CLY 962; *Homestead Finance Ltd v Warriner* [1997] CLY 961.

[421] S. 177(2).   [422] P. 775, ante; (1975) 39 Conv (NS) 94 at 108.

(e) Tacking of further advances

We shall see later that a mortgagee who makes a further loan to the mortgagor is allowed, in certain circumstances, to demand that both loans shall be paid out of the land in priority to loans made by other mortgagees, although the latter may have taken their securities before the date of such further loan.[423]

(f) Consolidation

Consolidation is the right[424] of a person who holds two or more mortgages granted by the same mortgagor on different properties to refuse in certain circumstances to be redeemed as to one, unless he is also redeemed as to the other or others.[425]

The mortgages in actual fact are quite separate, having been given on different properties and perhaps at different times, but none the less the mortgagee is allowed in certain cases to consolidate them and treat them as one. The right is based upon the doctrine that *he who comes to equity must do equity*; for a mortgagor who is seeking to redeem is in truth asking a favour in the sense that he is petitioning equity for the restoration of his property after the date fixed by the mortgage deed for redemption has passed, and this being so, he must himself be prepared to act equitably.

Suppose, for instance, that:

A has mortgaged Blackacre to B for £10,000 and Whiteacre to B for £10,000. If Blackacre diminishes, while Whiteacre appreciates, in value, it is unethical that A should be allowed to redeem the latter unless he is also prepared to repay the loan of £10,000 on Blackacre. In such a case B can insist that both properties shall be treated as one and redeemed together.

This example illustrates the primary meaning and the simplest application of consolidation, but the doctrine has been developed further and extended to cases where the mortgages were originally made to different mortgagees. In such a case if the mortgages ultimately become vested in one person, that is, in one mortgagee, he possesses the right of consolidation.[426] Thus, if:

A mortgages W to B,

A mortgages X and Y to C,

B and C transfer their mortgages to D,

A cannot redeem any one of the properties W, X, Y, unless, if called upon, he pays the amount due on the other two.

But consolidation extends even further than this, and applies to a case where the person who is entitled to redeem is not the original mortgagor, but a transferee of one or more of the equities. There are two different cases to be considered, since the law differs according as

---

[423] Pp. 789, 802, post.   [424] The right must be expressly reserved: p. 782, post.

[425] *Jennings v Jordan* (1881) 6 App Cas 698 at 700; White and Tudor, *Leading Cases in Equity*, vol. ii. p. 129. For a criticism of the doctrine, see Waldock, *Law of Mortgages*, pp. 293–5. As to whether the right amounts to a general equitable charge within LCA 1972, s. 2(4), Class C(iii), see (1948) 92 SJ 736; Wolstenholme and Cherry, vol. 1. p. 189. For registered land, see LRA 2002, s. 57 and LRR 2003, r. 110, under which a right of consolidation may be entered on the register.

[426] *Vint v Padget* (1858) 2 De G & J 611; *Pledge v White* [1896] AC 187, M & B p. 899.

the equities of redemption have all become united in one person, or have become separated so that the person claiming to redeem, that is, the person against whom the doctrine of consolidation is invoked, is not the owner of all the equities.

(1) WHERE ALL EQUITIES TRANSFERRED TO ONE PERSON

If a person acquires the equities on all the properties, whether as trustee in bankruptcy, purchaser or second mortgagee, the mortgages can in all cases be consolidated against him, even though the mortgage terms did not become vested in one mortgagee until after the person seeking to redeem had obtained the equities.

An illustration may elucidate this:

1999 A mortgages U and V to B.

2001 A mortgages W to C.

2002 A mortgages X, Y and Z to D.

2004 A sells the *equities* on U, V, W, X, Y and Z to F.

2006 E acquires all the mortgages from B, C and D.

Here all the mortgages are vested in one person, E, and, although he knew, when he bought out B, C and D, that the equities were not vested in the original mortgagor, he can require F to redeem all the properties or none.

As Lord DAVEY said in *Pledge v White*:[427]

It appears to me, my Lords, that an assignee of two or more equities of redemption from one mortgagor stands in a widely different position from the assignee of one equity only. He knows, or has the opportunity of knowing, what are the mortgages subject to which he has purchased the property, and he knows they may become united by transfer in one hand. If the doctrine of consolidation be once admitted it appears to me not unreasonable to hold that a person in such a position occupies the place of the mortgagor or assignor to him towards the holders of the mortgages, subject to which he has purchased.

(2) WHERE EQUITIES SEPARATED

Turning now to the case where the equities are separated and do not all pass to one person, it will be as well, before stating the general principle, to present an illustration showing how the purchaser of a single equity of redemption may find himself saddled with the burden of redeeming other mortgages of whose very existence he was unaware.

Thus:

If at different times A mortgages X, Y and Z to B, and then later transfers the fee simple of X to C, who gives full value and knows nothing of the other two properties which have been mortgaged, C, on tendering the amount of the loan due on X, may be unable under the doctrine of consolidation to redeem X unless he also pays what is due on Y and Z.

Where the mortgage transactions entered into by the original mortgagor are many, and where dealings have taken place both in the equities and in the mortgages, the question whether in any particular case consolidation is enforceable appears at first sight to be

---

both difficult and complicated. But all difficulty disappears if attention is paid to the cardinal rule. This rule covers all cases of separation of equities, and clearly defines the limits within which consolidation is applicable. Consolidation is allowed only if, at the date when redemption is sought, all the mortgages, having originally been made by one mortgagor, are vested in one mortgagee and all the equities are vested in one person, or if, *after these two things have once happened, the equities of redemption have become separated.*[428]

If all the mortgages are in one hand and all the equities in another, it is clear that the right of consolidation exists against the mortgagor. It is equally clear that, *once this right has been established in respect of all the properties*, a transferee of one or more of the equities cannot stand in a better position than the mortgagor from whom he took the transfer. The principle of law involved here is that a person who buys an equity of redemption from a mortgagor takes it subject to all liabilities to which it was subject at the time of the sale; one of these is the liability to have certain other mortgages consolidated with it, provided, however, that the consolidation was enforceable against that particular equity *at the time of the purchase*.[429] In the words of Lord SELBORNE:

The purchaser of an equity of redemption must take it as it stood at the time of his purchase, subject to all other equities which then affected it in the hands of his vendor, of which the right of the mortgagee to consolidate his charge on that particular property with other charges *then* held by him on other property at the same time redeemable under the same mortgagor was one.[430]

But on no principle of law would it be justifiable to hold the purchaser of an interest bound by equities which were not enforceable against that interest at the time of its sale. It follows from this that the assignee of an equity does not become subject to consolidation in respect of mortgages created *after* the sale to him, nor in respect of mortgages which, though created before that date, became united in one mortgagee afterwards.[431] Suppose, for instance, that the following transactions successively occur:[432]

A mortgages X to B,

A mortgages Y to B,

A sells the equity of redemption in Y to C,

A mortgages Z to B.

When C seeks to redeem his own property Y, he can be compelled by B to redeem X, because, at the time when he bought his equity, the equities on X and Y were vested in one person, and the mortgages were vested in one person. But he cannot be compelled to redeem Z, for the mortgage on it was created only after the sale of the equity on Y to C, so that the right to have Z consolidated with X and Y obviously did not exist at that time.

The holder of an equity of redemption who is compelled under the doctrine of consolidation to redeem some other mortgage steps into the shoes of the mortgagee, and can demand payment from the mortgagor in respect of the mortgage he has had to redeem.

---

[428] *Pledge v White* [1896] AC 187 at 198, per Lord DAVEY.
[429] *Cummins v Fletcher* (1880) 14 Ch D 699 at 712, M & B p. 901.
[430] *Jennings v Jordan* (1881) 6 App Cas 698 at 701. [431] *Harter v Colman* (1882) 19 Ch D 630.
[432] *Hughes v Britannia Permanent Benefit Building Society* [1906] 2 Ch 607, M & B p. 902.

(3) MORTGAGES MUST BE BY SAME PERSON

No right to consolidation arises if the mortgages were originally made *by* different mortgagors, even though the equities subsequently become united in one hand.[433]

(4) RESERVATION OF RIGHT

The right of consolidation does not exist as a matter of course, but only where it is expressly reserved in the various deeds *or in one of them*. When the right is not so reserved, it is enacted that:[434]

A mortgagor seeking to redeem any one mortgage is entitled to do so without paying any money due under any separate mortgage made by him, or by any person through whom he claims, solely on property other than that comprised in the mortgage which he seeks to redeem.

This is a re-enactment of the Conveyancing Act 1881, and it does not apply where all the mortgages were made before 1882. In mortgages made before that date the right of consolidation existed as a matter of course.

B Rights of Equitable Mortgagee

The remedies of an equitable mortgagee vary according as the security is a mortgage in the strict sense, namely a contract to create a legal mortgage or a mortgage of an equitable interest;[435] or is a charge upon property.[436] We will take these two classes separately.

(1) Equitable Mortgagee

If the mortgage falls within the first class the general principle is that the remedies available to the lender correspond as nearly as possible with those available to a legal mortgagee.

(a) Foreclosure

Thus the remedy of foreclosure applies where a deposit of title deeds with the lender has been accompanied by a contract by the borrower to give a legal mortgage if required to do so.[437] When such an equitable mortgagee takes foreclosure proceedings to enforce his security, the decree of the court declares that the deposit operated as a mortgage, that in default of payment the mortgagor is trustee of the legal estate for the mortgagee and that he must convey that estate to him.[438]

(b) Sale

The general rule is that foreclosure and not sale is the proper remedy for an equitable mortgagee.[439] But if the mortgage is made in a form which entitles him to require the execution of a mortgage containing a power of sale, he can exercise the statutory power of sale which

---

[433] *Sharp v Rickards* [1909] 1 Ch 109.   [434] LPA 1925, s. 93(1).   [435] Pp. 729, 732–3, ante.
[436] P. 733, ante.   [437] *York Union Banking Co v Artley* (1879) 11 Ch D 205.
[438] *Marshall v Shrewsbury* (1875) 10 Ch App 250 at 254.
[439] *James v James* (1873) LR 16 Eq 153. For the preference for sale over foreclosure in the modern law, however, see p. 776, n. 400, ante.

is given by the Law of Property Act 1925.[440] This statutory power, however, is exercisable only when the mortgage is made by deed, and therefore the proper course is for an equitable mortgagee not to be content with a mere contract, but to take a memorandum executed as a deed. If this is done he can sell the property subject to the conditions specified by the Act. The memorandum should also give the mortgagee a power of attorney authorising him, upon exercising the power of sale, to convey the mortgaged property in the name of the mortgagor to the purchaser.[441] This enables the mortgagee, though only an equitable incumbrancer, to convey the legal estate in the property to the purchaser.[442] The same result may be achieved by inserting in the memorandum a declaration of trust, stating that the mortgagor holds the legal estate on trust for the mortgagee and empowering him to appoint someone, including himself, as trustee in place of the mortgagor. The mortgagee can thus vest the legal estate in himself or the purchaser.

Again, the statutory power of the court to order a sale instead of foreclosure, which we have already noticed,[443] is exercisable in favour of an equitable mortgagee even though he has taken a mere contract without a deed.

(c) Appointment of receiver

If an equitable mortgage is created by deed, the statutory power of appointing a receiver is available to the mortgagee,[444] but in the absence of a deed the appointment must be made by the court.[445]

(d) Entry into possession

An equitable mortgagee is not entitled to take possession of the land unless the right to do so has been expressly reserved[446] or unless the court makes an order to that effect. Though this is the prevalent view, it has been argued with considerable force that it is justified neither on principle nor on the authorities.[447]

(e) Further rights of equitable mortgagee

An equitable mortgagee can sue the mortgagor personally for recovery of the money lent.

Finally, where, in unregistered land, an equitable mortgage is accompanied by the deposit of title deeds, the mortgagee has the right to retain the deeds under the mortgage until he is paid, but he has no separate legal lien.[448]

(2) Equitable Chargee

The second class of equitable security is the charge, which involves no transfer of a legal or equitable interest to the lender, but entitles him to have the debt discharged out of the land. His sole remedies in this respect are to have the charge satisfied by the sale of the land or by the appointment of a receiver under the direction of the court. He has no right to take possession of the land nor may he foreclose. In the words of Lord HATHERLEY: "Although some

---

[440] S. 101(1)(i), p. 769, ante.   [441] See Powers of Attorney Act 1971, ss. 4(1), 5(3).

[442] *Re White Rose Cottage* [1965] Ch 940, M & B p. 893.   [443] LPA 1925, s. 91; p. 776, ante.

[444] Ibid., s. 101(1)(ii); p. 768, ante.   [445] *Meaden v Sealey* (1849) 6 Hare 620.

[446] *Finck v Tranter* [1905] 1 KB 427 at 429; *Barclays Bank Ltd v Bird* [1954] Ch 274 at 280.

[447] (1955) 72 LQR 204 (H. W. R. Wade).

[448] *Re Molton Finance Ltd* [1968] Ch 325. See also *Capital Finance Co Ltd v Stokes* [1969] 1 Ch 261 at 278.

of the authorities appear to conflict with each other, it seems, on the whole, to be settled that if there is a charge *simpliciter*, and not a mortgage, or an agreement for a mortgage, then the right of the parties having such a charge is a sale and not foreclosure."[449] From a mere equitable charge must be distinguished the *charge by deed expressed to be by way of legal mortgage* introduced by the legislation of 1925, for as we have seen such a chargee has the same remedies as if he held a term of years absolute;[450] and a *registered charge* is the equivalent in registered land.[451]

V Priority of Mortgages[452]

If two or more mortgagees have advanced money on the security of the same land and if the land is of insufficient value when realised to satisfy the claims of all, it is vital to know in what order they are entitled to be paid out of the land. The mortgagor has, let us say, granted separate and successive mortgages on Blackacre to A, B, C and D. Owing to unforeseen circumstances Blackacre has depreciated in value and its sale will produce sufficient money to repay only one or perhaps two of the mortgagees the amount of their advances. This does not mean that mortgagees who fail to get satisfaction out of the land are remediless, for they can of course sue the mortgagor on his personal covenant, but since his other property may be of little value it will be their object to proceed against the land if the law allows them to do so. A knowledge of the former rules that governed this matter, although they are substantially affected by the legislation of 1925, is essential to an understanding of the modern law on this subject; and, as we shall see, there are situations in which they may still be applicable.[453]

The rules for the priority of mortgages, both before 1926 and after 1925, are subject to variation by the mortgagees amongst themselves without the mortgagor's consent, unless the mortgages otherwise provide.[454]

A Priority of Mortgages Before 1926

(1) The Priority of the Legal Mortgagee of Land

To understand the order in which mortgages ranked for repayment out of the land before 1926 we must recall that under the practice then prevailing it was usual in the case of a mortgage of the fee simple to convey the legal estate in fee simple to the mortgagee. There might be several mortgages of Blackacre, but there could be only one *legal* mortgage, and all the others, whether created before or after the legal mortgage, were necessarily equitable in nature.

(a) Where equities are equal the law prevails

The fundamental rule before 1926, based upon the maxim "where the equities are equal the law prevails", was that the mortgagee who held the legal estate ranked, for the purpose of obtaining satisfaction out of the land, before all other mortgagees of whose securities he had

---

[449] *Tennant v Trenchard* (1869) 4 Ch App 537 at 542; *Re Owen* [1894] 3 Ch 220. [450] P. 727, ante.
[451] P. 728, ante.
[452] See generally Fisher and Lightwood, chap. 24, and for a closely reasoned study [1940] CLJ 243 (R. E. Megarry); Waldock, *Law of Mortgages*, pp. 381–435. [453] Pp. 794 et seq, post.
[454] *Cheah Theam Swee v Equiticorp Finance Group Ltd* [1992] 1 AC 472.

no notice at the time when he made his advance.[455] Equity respected the legal title, and it was a rule without exception that a court of equity took away from a purchaser for value without notice nothing that he had honestly acquired.[456] Lord HARDWICKE said:

As courts of equity break in upon the common law, where necessity and conscience require it, still they allow superior force and strength to a legal title to estates; and therefore where there is a legal title and equity on one side, this court never thought fit that by reason of a prior equity against a man, who had a legal title, that man should be hurt, and this by reason of that force this court necessarily and rightly allows to the common law and to legal titles.[457]

If therefore a mortgagor granted an equitable mortgage to A and later conveyed the legal estate to B by way of mortgage, the latter had the better right to the land provided that, when he made his own advance, he had no notice of the earlier mortgage to A. The onus lay on him to prove this affirmatively.[458] B, the legal mortgagee, had an even stronger case against mortgagees who obtained their securities at a date *later* than his own, for not only did he alone hold the legal title, but having acquired it first in order of time he could invoke the maxim *qui prior est tempore potior est jure*: the first in time has the stronger right.

This rule giving priority to the legal mortgagee, however, applied only where the equities were equal, that is, where the legal mortgagee had as good a moral right as the equitable mortgagees, and in the following cases he was displaced in favour of equitable mortgagees.

(b) Cases where equities are not equal

(1) WHERE LEGAL MORTGAGEE HAD NOTICE OF EARLIER MORTGAGE

If, at the time when he advanced his money, the legal mortgagee had actual or constructive notice of an earlier incumbrance, he was postponed to the earlier incumbrancer. A legal mortgagee who failed to investigate his mortgagor's title according to the usual practice or who abstained from investigation altogether, was affected with notice of, and therefore postponed to, any earlier mortgage that he would have discovered had he followed the customary practice.[459]

(2) WHERE LEGAL MORTGAGEE WAS NEGLIGENT WITH REGARD TO TITLE DEEDS

The obvious duty of a person who acquired a legal estate by conveyance by way of legal mortgage before 1926 was to obtain and to keep possession of the title deeds, or, if for some reason this was impossible, to make inquiries for them. Title deeds are the symbol of ownership, and if they were not produced by a mortgagor the suspicion naturally arose that they had been utilised by him in order to vest some right in a third person, and that he was deliberately concealing this transaction from the mortgagee.

There were two indiscretions in this connection that a mortgagee could commit, namely, failure to obtain the deeds at the time of the transaction, and failure to retain deeds of which he had once had possession.

---

[455] *Plumb v Fluitt* (1791) 2 Anst 432.   [456] *Heath v Crealock* (1874) 10 Ch App 22 at 33.

[457] *Wortley v Birkhead* (1754) 2 Ves Sen 571 at 574.

[458] *A-G v Biphosphated Guano Co* (1879) 11 Ch D 327.   [459] *Berwick & Co v Price* [1905] 1 Ch 632.

(i) Postponement owing to failure to obtain deeds

It was well established before 1926 that a legal mortgagee who made no inquiries whatever for the deeds must be postponed to a prior equitable incumbrancer who had already secured them, and even to a later innocent incumbrancer who was more diligent in getting them into his custody.[460] On the other hand, if he made inquiry and yet failed to obtain them, it depended upon the circumstances whether he was postponed to an earlier equitable incumbrancer in whose possession they were. Postponement was not an automatic result of failure to obtain possession, for it was always held that in addition there must have been some degree of negligence. The cases show a growing severity against the legal mortgagee. At first it was laid down that he must not be postponed unless he had been guilty of fraud in the transaction under which he acquired the legal estate, or unless he had shown such wilful negligence as to indicate complicity in the fraud.[461] But a new rule more favourable to an earlier equitable mortgagee was pronounced by the Court of Appeal in 1899 in the case of *Oliver v Hinton*.[462] This may be stated in the words of LINDLEY LJ:

> To deprive a purchaser for value[463] without notice of a prior incumbrance of the protection of the legal estate it is not, in my opinion, essential that he should have been guilty of fraud; it is sufficient that he has been guilty of such gross negligence as would render it unjust to deprive the prior incumbrancer of his priority.[464]

The case related to a purchaser of a legal estate, but the result would have been the same had the person who acquired the legal estate been a mortgagee. The facts were as follows:

> A, the owner of the legal estate, deposited the title deeds with X as security for advances to the value of £400 made by the latter. Some two years later A conveyed the legal estate to the purchaser, P, in consideration of £320. P inquired about the deeds, but was told that they could not be delivered as they related also to some other property. This answer was accepted, and A was not even asked to produce the deeds for inspection. It was held that P, though entirely innocent of fraud or of any complicity in fraud, must be postponed to X.

Epithets such as "gross" are unreliable guides, and the rule as stated by the Court of Appeal left open in each case the question whether the requisite degree of negligence had been shown, but the expression "gross negligence" was described in a later case as meaning something more than mere carelessness. EVE J said:[465]

> It must at least be carelessness of so aggravated a nature as to amount to the neglect of precautions which the ordinary reasonable man would have observed and to indicate an attitude of mental indifference to obvious risks.

(1) POSTPONEMENT TO EARLIER INCUMBRANCERS

If, therefore, a mortgagee had inquired for the title deeds and had been given a reasonable excuse for their non-delivery, he would not be postponed to an earlier equitable mortgagee.

---

460 *Walker v Linom* [1907] 2 Ch 104, M & B p. 910.

461 *Hunt v Elmes* (1860) 2 De GF & J 578; *Ratcliffe v Barnard* (1871) 6 Ch App 652; see *Hudston v Viney* [1921] 1 Ch 98 at 103–4; *Northern Counties of England Fire Insurance Co v Whipp* (1884) 26 Ch D 482, M & B p. 907.

462 [1899] 2 Ch 264, M & B p. 906.   463 This includes a mortgagee.

464 It would have been simpler to apply the doctrine of the bona fide purchaser for value without notice and to postpone the later legal mortgagee unless he satisfies that test. See ROMER J at first instance in *Oliver v Hinton* [1899] 2 Ch 264 at 268; and PARKER J in *Walker v Linom*, supra, at 114.

465 *Hudston v Viney* [1921] 1 Ch 98 at 104.

An extreme case is, perhaps, *Hewitt v Loosemore*,[466] where the defendant, who had taken a legal mortgage of a leasehold interest from a solicitor by way of assignment, failed to obtain possession of the lease, which, as a matter of fact, had already been deposited with the plaintiff. Part of the answer made by the defendant to the bill which the plaintiff brought against him was as follows:

The defendant . . . was a farmer and unacquainted with legal forms; but upon the said indenture of assignment being handed to him as aforesaid, he inquired of [the mortgagor] whether the lease of the premises ought not to be delivered to him as well; when [the mortgagor] replied that it should, but that, as he was rather busy then, he would look for it and give it to the defendant when he next came to market.

It was held that in the circumstances the plaintiff had failed to make out a sufficient case for postponing the defendant.

(2) POSTPONEMENT TO LATER INCUMBRANCERS

Likewise failure to obtain the deeds might entail postponement of a legal mortgagee to a *later* equitable incumbrancer. Again, however, nothing short of gross negligence was sufficient to produce this result. Thus in *Grierson v National Provincial Bank of England Ltd*:[467]

A mortgagor, having already deposited the deeds with a bank as security for a loan, executed a legal mortgage in favour of the plaintiff. The plaintiff had actual notice of this earlier equitable mortgage, but he neither informed the bank of his legal mortgage, nor instructed them to deliver the deeds to him should the mortgagor repay their loan. The mortgagor later paid off the bank, obtained the deeds and deposited them with the defendant as security for an advance. The defendant was ignorant of the plaintiff's legal mortgage.

It was held that the plaintiff had not been sufficiently negligent to justify his postponement to the defendant.

(ii) Postponement due to subsequent negligence

It was also the case before 1926 that the conduct of the legal mortgagee in dealing with the title deeds *after* he had obtained them might be such as to justify his postponement to subsequent equitable mortgagees.

In the first place the principle of *Oliver v Hinton* applied, and any conduct on the part of the legal mortgagee in relation to the deeds which would have made it inequitable for him to claim priority over an earlier equitable mortgagee was sufficient to postpone him to a subsequent mortgage the creation of which was due entirely to his own conduct.[468] There need not have been fraudulent conduct, but there must have been gross negligence. Thus in a leading case[469] the priority of the legal mortgagee was not displaced where a company took a legal mortgage from its manager, and the manager, having stolen the deeds from a safe to which he had access, used them to create another mortgage in favour of an innocent

---

[466] (1851) 9 Hare 449, M & B p. 905. See also *Agra Bank Ltd v Barry* (1874) LR 7 HL 135.
[467] [1913] 2 Ch 18.
[468] *Walker v Linom* [1907] 2 Ch 104 at 114; *Northern Counties of England Fire Insurance Co v Whipp* (1884) 26 Ch D 482. Cf *Re King's Settlement* [1931] 2 Ch 294.
[469] *Northern Counties of England Fire Insurance Co v Whipp*, supra.

person. The following remarks were made by the court upon the arguments that had been advanced in favour of postponement:

The case was argued as if the legal owner of land owed a duty to all other of Her Majesty's subjects to keep his title deeds secure; as if title deeds were in the eye of the law analogous to fierce dogs or destructive elements, where from the nature of the thing the courts have implied a general duty of safe custody.[470]

In the second place a legal mortgagee was postponed if he constituted the mortgagor his agent with authority to raise more money on the security of the land. This postponement occurred for instance where the mortgagor, having been entrusted with the deeds for the purpose of obtaining a further loan of a given amount, procured one of a greater amount without disclosing to the lender the existence of the first mortgage. In such a case the legal mortgagee was postponed on the ground that, having enabled the mortgagor to represent himself as unincumbered owner, he was estopped from asserting that the actual authority had been exceeded.[471]

(2) Priority as Between Equitable Mortgagees of Land

(a) First made, first paid

Where the legal estate was outstanding and a conflict arose between incumbrancers who all held equitable mortgages, the rule was that the several mortgagees must be paid according to their priority of time, *qui prior est tempore potior est jure*.[472]

If, therefore, a mortgagor subjected his land to equitable charges first in favour of A and then in favour of B, or if, after granting a legal mortgage to X, he made subsequent equitable mortgages first to A and then to B, A had the prior right as against B to receive payment out of the land. He had a better and superior equity because it was an earlier equity. This rule was based upon the principle that: "An owner of property, dealing honestly with it, cannot confer upon another a greater interest in that property than he himself has."[473]

All that the mortgagor had to dispose of when he had once made a legal mortgage was the equitable interest, and it had long been the rule that: "Every conveyance of an equitable interest is an innocent conveyance, that is to say, the grant of a person entitled merely in equity passes only that which he is justly entitled to, and no more."[474]

(b) Exceptions

The rule that priority of time gave the better right to payment might, however, be excluded in two cases:

First, where the equities were in other respects not equal.

Secondly, where the doctrine of tacking operated.

---

[470] *Northern Counties of England Fire Insurance Co v Whipp* (1884) 26 Ch D 482 at 493.

[471] *Perry Herrick v Attwood* (1857) 2 De G & J 21, M & B p. 908; *Northern Counties of England Fire Insurance Co v Whipp*, supra, at 493; *Brocklesby v Temperance Permanent Building Society* [1895] AC 173.

[472] P. 785, ante; *Brace v Duchess of Marlborough* (1728) 2 P Wms 491 at 495; *Willoughby v Willoughby* (1756) 1 Term Rep 763.   [473] *West v Williams* [1899] 1 Ch 132 at 143, per LINDLEY MR.

[474] *Phillips v Phillips* (1861) 4 De GF & J 208 at 215, per Lord WESTBURY.

(1) WHERE EQUITIES ARE NOT EQUAL. NEGLIGENCE OF PRIOR MORTGAGEE

In a contest between equitable claimants, the court had to be satisfied that the party with the earlier equity had acted in such a way as to justify his retention of priority over the later incumbrancer.[475] Thus, he lost the protection that was normally due to him if his negligent failure to obtain or to retain the title deeds had misled the later mortgagee into believing that no earlier equity existed. The question as to what degree of negligence sufficed to produce this result scarcely admits of a dogmatic answer, for the judges expressed varying opinions, and one view was that the priority of an equitable mortgage was more easily displaced than that of a legal mortgage.[476] No decision has been found, however, in which the negligence held sufficient to postpone an equitable mortgagee would not also have defeated a legal mortgagee.[477] In the case before 1926 of a legal mortgage to A, followed by equitable mortgages to B and C, the question could arise only exceptionally, since A would normally hold the deeds, but it would arise in an acute form if the only transactions effected by the mortgagor were of an equitable nature. In this connection two rules at least were definitely established.

(i) Failure to obtain deeds

First, if an incumbrancer was entitled to have the deeds as part of his security but did not insist upon his right, he was postponed to a later equitable incumbrancer who obtained them without notice of the earlier equity. This occurred in *Farrand v Yorkshire Banking Co*,[478] where the mortgagor agreed to deposit the deeds relating to the mortgaged property with A, but the deposit was never made. A year later he handed the deeds to a bank with which he had made a similar agreement.

It was held that A must be postponed, for it was entirely due to his inactivity that the bank had been defrauded into advancing a second loan.

(ii) Failure to retain deeds

Secondly, if an equitable incumbrancer obtained the deeds but later delivered them to the mortgagor, he was postponed to a later lender to whom they had been delivered as security.[479]

It is an elementary principle that a party coming into equity in such a case is bound to show that he has not been guilty of such a degree of neglect as to enable another party so to deal with that which was the plaintiff's right, as to induce an innocent party to assume that he was dealing with his own.[480]

(2) TACKING

The general rule that equitable mortgagees ranked for payment according to the dates at which they took their mortgages was also liable to be displaced by the operation of the doctrine of tacking, or "the creditor's *tabula in naufragio*" ("the plank in the shipwreck").[481]

---

[475] *National Provincial Bank of England v Jackson* (1886) 33 Ch D 1 at 13, per COTTON LJ.
[476] *Taylor v Russell* [1891] 1 Ch 8 at 17; affd [1892] AC 244 at 262.
[477] See the discussion in Waldock, *Law of Mortgages*, pp. 397–8.   [478] (1888) 40 Ch D 182.
[479] *Waldron v Sloper* (1852) 1 Drew 193.   [480] Ibid., at 200, per KINDERSLEY V-C.
[481] *Brace v Duchess of Marlborough* (1728) 2 P Wms 491. On tacking generally see *Macmillan Inc v Bishopsgate Investment Trust plc (No 3)* [1995] 1 WLR 978 at 1002–5, per MILLETT J. The doctrine is of reduced importance after 1925. In relation to registered land, see LRA 2002, s. 49; p. 807, post.

This doctrine, which is founded on technical and justly suspected reasoning, is an example of the superiority attached by courts of law and of equity to the legal estate. Equitable owners who were equally meritorious in regard to honesty of dealing might compete for the legal estate, and the one who succeeded in obtaining it won the right to rank before an earlier equitable mortgagee despite the maxim *qui prior est tempore potior est jure*.[482] The reason was that, having obtained the legal estate, he could take advantage of that other and more potent maxim "where equities are equal, the legal title prevails".[483]

There were two distinct branches of tacking before 1926, and we must consider these separately.

(i) Where equitable mortgagee acquired legal estate

The first form consisted of joining an equitable mortgage to the legal mortgage in order to squeeze out and gain priority over an intermediate mortgage. If a legal mortgage to A was followed by equitable mortgages first to B and secondly to C, then C would gain priority of payment over B if he paid off A and took a conveyance of his legal estate. C now had the prior right to recover from the land not only the amount which A had advanced on the first mortgage, but also the amount which C himself had advanced to the mortgagor. But he could not tack his own advance to the legal estate and squeeze out B unless he had an equal equity with B; and the equities were not equal unless, *at the time when he made his advance*, he was without notice that B had made an earlier advance.

(ii) Where legal mortgagee made further advance

The second form of tacking was available only to a *legal* mortgagee who had made a further advance. It was not available to equitable mortgagees before 1926. If a legal mortgagee, subsequently to his original loan, made a further advance to the mortgagor without at that time having notice of equitable mortgages created after the legal mortgage, he could, by virtue of his ownership of the legal estate, tack the second to the first advance and recover the whole amount due to him in priority to all other incumbrancers.[484]

If, for instance:

The mortgagor made a legal mortgage to A for £2,000, a second mortgage to B, a third mortgage to C, and then a further mortgage to A for £500, A was entitled to be paid £2,500 out of the land before B and C received anything.

But this right did not avail the legal mortgagee if, at the time when he made his further advance, he knew that other persons had already lent money on the security of the land. Thus in *Freeman v Laing*:[485]

Three trustees advanced money jointly on a legal mortgage of land and subsequently made a further advance. At the time of this second advance one alone of the trustees had notice of an intermediate mortgage. It was held that the successors in title of the trustees could not tack the second loan to the first, for since each of them was individually entitled to the entire security, notice to one was notice to all.

---

482 P. 790, ante.   483 P. 784, ante; *Bailey v Barnes* [1894] 1 Ch 25 at 36, per LINDLEY LJ.
484 *Brace v Duchess of Marlborough*, supra.   485 [1899] 2 Ch 355.

An important application of this rule, that notice excluded the right to tack, occurred where land was mortgaged by way of security not only for the original loan, but also for such future advances as might be made. A mortgagee likes to know that he can have recourse to the land in respect of any money he may advance later, and when such further loans are contemplated it has always been customary to provide expressly in the deed that they, equally with the original loan, shall be secured by the land. But it was laid down in *Hopkinson v Rolt*[486] that, notwithstanding such an express provision, the right to tack was excluded by notice of other incumbrances. This principle was carried further by the case of *West v Williams*[487] and made applicable where the legal mortgagee had not (as in *Hopkinson v Rolt*) taken security merely for such further advances as he might *voluntarily* make, but had entered into a binding covenant to make further advances upon the security of the land, if called upon to do so. The fact that he was under a contractual obligation to increase his original loan did not entitle him to priority in respect of a further advance made with notice of a later incumbrance.

The doctrine of tacking was abolished in 1874 by the Vendor and Purchaser Act, but as this prejudiced the ability of mortgagors to obtain further advances from first mortgagees, it was restored by the Land Transfer Act of 1875.

(3) Priority between Assignees and Mortgagees of an Equitable Interest in Pure Personalty

(a) The Rule in Dearle v Hall

Priority between mortgagees of pure personalty has been governed since 1823 by the rule in *Dearle v Hall*.[488] This rule, which is of greater importance now than formerly because of its extension by the Law of Property Act 1925,[489] applied whenever successive mortgages or assignments were made of an equitable interest in pure personalty, as distinct from an interest, whether legal or equitable, in freeholds or leaseholds. To make the rule applicable, the mortgagor or assignor must have had an equitable interest in a debt or fund and he must have made two or more successive assignments of that subject matter in favour of different persons.[490] It is chiefly remarkable as being a departure from the fundamental principle that equities are entitled to rank according to the order of time in which they have been created.

The rule laid down that as between mortgagees or assignees of an equitable interest in pure personalty (i.e. excluding leaseholds, but including an interest under a trust for sale[491]) priority depended upon the order in which notice of the mortgages or assignments was received[492] by the legal owner of the personalty (i.e. in most cases by the trustees). However, a later mortgagee or assignee, who had actual or constructive notice of a prior mortgage or

---

486 (1861) 9 HL Cas 514.   487 [1899] 1 Ch 132.

488 (1823) 3 Russ 1, M & B p. 912. For comment on the rule (mostly adverse), see *Ward v Duncombe* [1893] AC 369; *B S Lyle Ltd v Rosher* [1959] 1 WLR 8; *E Pfeiffer Weinkellerei-Weineinkauf GmbH & Co v Arbuthnot Factors Ltd* [1988] 1 WLR 150; *Rhodes v Allied Dunbar Pension Services Ltd* [1987] 1 WLR 1703; (1989) 9 OJLS 513 (F. Oditah); *Compaq Computer Ltd v Abercorn Group Ltd* [1991] BCC 484, [1992] CLJ 19 (L. S. Sealy); *Australian Guarantee Corpn (NZ) Ltd v CFC Commercial Finance Ltd* [1995] 1 NZLR 129; (1996) 112 LQR 215 (A. J. Oakley). For an analysis of the rule, see [1999] Conv 311 (J. de Lacey).   489 P. 804, post.

490 *B S Lyle Ltd v Rosher* [1959] 1 WLR 8 at 16, 19.

491 *Lee v Howlett* (1856) 2 K & J 531; p. 794, post. For the doctrine of conversion in relation to the trust for sale before TLATA 1996, see pp. 428 et seq, ante.   492 *Calisher v Forbes* (1871) 7 Ch App 109.

assignment at the time when he lent his money, could not gain priority by giving notice first.[493] The head-note to the report of *Dearle v Hall* makes the general position clear:

A person having a beneficial interest in a sum of money invested in the names of trustees, assigns it for valuable consideration to A, but no notice of the assignment is given to the trustees; afterwards, the same person proposes to sell his interest to B, and B, having made inquiry of the trustees as to the nature of the vendor's title, and the amount of his interest, and receiving no intimation of the existence of any prior incumbrance, completes the purchase, and gives the trustees notice: B has a better equity than A to the possession of the fund, and the assignment to B, though posterior in date, is to be preferred to the assignment to A.

Thus in equitable mortgages of personalty notice to the trustees supplants order of time as the determining factor in the question of priorities.

(b) Principle of rule

Although the principle upon which *Dearle v Hall* was decided has been obscured by later cases, it would appear to be simply this, that in order to perfect his title a mortgagee of equitable personalty must do that which in equity is the nearest approach to the delivery of a personal chattel.[494] PLUMER MR explained this as follows:[495]

They say that they were not bound to give notice to the trustees, for that notice does not form part of the necessary conveyance of an equitable interest. I admit, that, if you mean to rely on contract with the individual, you do not need to give notice; from the moment of the contract, he, with whom you are dealing, is personally bound. But if you mean to go further, and to make your right attach upon the thing which is the subject of the contract, it is necessary to give notice; and, unless notice is given, you do not do that which is essential in all cases of transfer of personal property. The law of England has always been, that personal property passes by delivery of possession; and it is possession which determines the apparent ownership. If, therefore, an individual, who in the way of purchase or mortgage contracts with another for the transfer of his interest, does not divest the vendor or mortgagor of possession, but permits him to remain the ostensible owner as before, he must take the consequences which may ensue from such a mode of dealing.

(c) Rule extended by judicial interpretation

It is in fact the duty of an assignee or mortgagee to affect the conscience of the trustees, for by doing so he acquires a better equity than a prior mortgagee who has failed to act likewise, and where one of two innocent parties must suffer through the fraud of the mortgagor, it certainly should not be the one who has done all in his power to prevent any fraudulent dealing. But this consideration was lost sight of in later years, and instead of the principle being that priority should depend upon the diligence of the claimants in perfecting their title, it was gradually made dependent upon the bare fact of notice, it being held that it was immaterial whether notice was given with the deliberate intention of completing the title or whether it was purely informal or even accidental.[496] The following will serve to illustrate this fact and, at the same time, to state the main rules that have grown up in the application of *Dearle v Hall*.

---

[493] *Spencer v Clarke* (1878) 9 Ch D 137; *Re Holmes* (1885) 29 Ch D 786.
[494] *Meux v Bell* (1841) 1 Hare 73 at 85; *Foster v Cockerell* (1835) 3 Cl & Fin 456 at 476; but see Lord MACNAGHTEN in *Ward v Duncombe* [1893] AC 369 at 392–3.   [495] *Dearle v Hall* (1823) 3 Russ 1 at 22.
[496] See (1895) 11 LQR 337 (E. C. C. Firth).

(1) NOTICE MAY BE INFORMAL

It is not necessary, in order to gain priority, that a mortgagee should give express notice to the trustees with the intention of doing all that is possible to perfect his title. In fact it is not necessary that *he* should give notice at all, provided that the trustees have notice. It is enough if he can prove that the mind of the trustee has in some way been brought to an intelligent apprehension of the existence of the incumbrance, so that a reasonable man or an ordinary man of business would regulate his conduct by that knowledge in the execution of the trust.[497] Thus, notice which a trustee obtained from reading a newspaper has been held to be sufficient,[498] and in a later case it was held that where a trustee *before* his appointment acquired knowledge of an incumbrance on the trust estate in such a way that when appointed he would normally act on the information, the priority thereby attached to the incumbrance was not displaced by an express formal notice given after his appointment by another incumbrancer.[499]

(2) EFFECT OF NOTICE NOT GIVEN TO *ALL* TRUSTEES

The course which a diligent mortgagee should pursue is to give notice to each trustee, for a failure to do so may cause his postponement to a later mortgagee who has been more careful. The two principles relevant to the situation are, first, that a notice given to one alone of several trustees is effective against later mortgages created while that one trustee remains in office, but is ineffective against mortgages created after he vacates office;[500] secondly, that a notice to all existing trustees remains effective even after they have vacated office. The result may be appreciated from three examples.

(1) A, B and C are the trustees. Mortgagee, X, notifies A only. A later mortgagee, Y, notifies A, B and C. A dies.

X ranks before Y, for when Y took his mortgage X's notice to A was still effective.[501]

(2) A, B and C are the trustees. Mortgagee, X, notifies A only. A dies. A later mortgagee, Y, notifies B and C.

Y ranks before X, since the effectiveness of X's notice ceased with the death of the one person to whom he gave it.[502]

(3) A, B and C are the trustees. Mortgagee, X, notifies A, B and C. A, B and C retire in favour of D, E and F, who are not informed of X's mortgage. A later mortgagee, Y, notifies D, E and F.

X ranks before Y.[503]

(d) Limits of rule

We must finally observe that before 1926 the rule in *Dearle v Hall* was restricted to the assignment of choses in action, of which an equitable interest in pure personalty is an example, and to assignments of such interests in real estate as could reach the hands of the

---

[497] *Lloyd v Banks* (1868) 3 Ch App 488 at 490, per Lord CAIRNS.   [498] *Lloyd v Banks*, supra.
[499] *Ipswich Permanent Money Club Ltd v Arthy* [1920] 2 Ch 257.
[500] *Smith v Smith* (1833) 2 Cr & M 231.   [501] *Ward v Duncombe* [1893] AC 369.
[502] *Timson v Ramsbottom* (1837) 2 Keen 35; *Re Phillips' Trusts* [1903] 1 Ch 183.
[503] *Re Wasdale* [1899] 1 Ch 163.

assignor only in the shape of money, as for instance a beneficial interest given to him by a trust for sale.[504] The rule did not apply to mortgages or assignments of equitable interests in *land*, whether freehold or leasehold. Thus in a case where a testator, having bequeathed a leasehold interest to trustees, charged it with the payment of an annuity of £45 to his daughter, and the daughter mortgaged the annuity first to A and then to B, it was held that A had the prior claim against the land, although B alone had given notice to the trustees.[505]

Having thus reviewed the rules which obtained before the legislation of 1925, we are in a position to examine the existing law governing the priorities between mortgages in general.

B Priority of Mortgages After 1925

(1) Unregistered Land

The Law of Property Act 1925 and the Land Charges Act 1925 (now replaced by the Land Charges Act 1972) introduced a new system for the determination of priorities. The apparent design of this is to fix the priority of a mortgage according to the time of its creation, provided that the mortgagee has taken steps to render the completion of the transaction easily ascertainable by persons who later have dealings with the mortgagor.[506] There are three ways of doing this which vary with the circumstances.

First, by obtaining possession of the title deeds. This will put a later mortgagee upon inquiry and will normally affect him with notice of the earlier incumbrance.

Secondly, if possession of the deeds is unobtainable and if the property given as security is a *legal* estate, by recording the mortgage, whether legal or equitable, in a public register.

Thirdly, if the property given as security is an *equitable* interest in land or pure personalty, by notifying the mortgage to the owner of the legal interest, thereby putting it on record.

Such is the design in outline, but it is not fully worked out by the Acts and we shall see that certain doubts and complexities remain. The paucity of litigation on priorities may suggest that the new system has worked reasonably well, but that may be due more to the considerable rise in the value of land than to the merits of the system.

The modern rules vary not with the nature of the mortgage as under the pre-1926 law, but with the nature of the mortgaged property, and we must therefore consider:

first, legal and equitable mortgages of a *legal estate*; and

secondly, mortgages of an *equitable interest*, whether in land or in personalty.

(a) Priority as between legal and equitable mortgagees of a legal estate

We have seen that before 1926 a legal mortgagee who had not been guilty of gross negligence in respect of the title deeds enjoyed priority over the other mortgagees (necessarily equitable) of the same land of which he had no notice. It is obvious that the introduction of the

---

[504] *Lee v Howlett* (1856) 2 K & J 531; *Re Wasdale*, supra; *Ward v Duncombe*, supra.
[505] *Wiltshire v Rabbits* (1844) 14 Sim 76.   [506] Waldock, *Law of Mortgages*, pp. 409–10.

new method of creating mortgages, under which there may be several *legal* mortgages and not one only as before 1926,[507] precluded the retention of the old rule that the legal estate as such gave priority. Some substitute had to be found. The other rule of the pre-1926 law, that equitable mortgages ranked according to the order of their creation, could scarcely be made universally applicable, since it would render it difficult for a mortgagee to ascertain by inquiry the true state of the mortgagor's commitments. The Acts of 1925, therefore, attempted to introduce a new scheme, the motif of which apparently was that priorities should depend upon the order of registration, though whether in the actual result registration is as important as it was intended to be is, perhaps, a little doubtful.

(1) STATUTORY PROVISIONS

It is necessary to set out the relevant statutory provisions in order that the matter may be viewed in the right perspective.

(i) Law of Property Act 1925

The Law of Property Act 1925, section 97, provides in relation to mortgages of unregistered land as follows:

Every mortgage affecting a legal estate in land made after the commencement of this Act, whether legal or equitable (not being a mortgage protected by the deposit of documents relating to the legal estate affected) shall rank according to its date of registration as a land charge pursuant to the Land Charges Act, 1925.[508]

The same statute, in section 198(1),[509] provides that registration shall constitute notice:

The registration of any instrument or matter on any register kept under the Land Charges Act 1972 or any local land charges register shall be deemed to constitute actual notice of such instrument or matter, and of the fact of such registration, to all persons and for all purposes connected with the land affected, as from the date of registration or other prescribed date and so long as the registration continues in force.

(ii) Land Charges Act 1972. Registrable mortgages

The Land Charges Act 1972 contains two relevant sections. Section 2(4)[510] specifies the two kinds of mortgages that are registrable,[511] namely:

A "puisne mortgage",[512] i.e. a *legal* mortgage which is not protected by a deposit of documents relating to the legal estate affected (Class C (i)).

A "general equitable charge", i.e. any equitable charge which is not secured by a deposit of documents relating to the legal estate affected, does not arise, or affect an interest arising, under a trust of land[513] or a settlement, and is not included in any other class of land charge (Class C (iii)).

---

[507] P. 724, ante.   [508] Or LCA 1972. See LCA 1972, s. 18(6).
[509] As amended by Local Land Charges Act 1975, s. 17, Sch. 1.
[510] S. 2(4), Class C(i), (iii), replacing LCA 1925, s. 10(1).
[511] For registration of charges created by companies, see p. 948, post.
[512] "Puisne" is derived from the old French, *puis* (after) *né* (born); hence a later or subsequent mortgage.
[513] As amended by TLATA 1996, s. 25(1), Sch. 3, para. 12(1), (2).

The Land Charges Act 1972 finally states what the effect shall be of a failure to register. Section 4(5)[514] provides that a Class C land charge created or arising after 1925 shall:

be void as against a purchaser of the land charged with it, or of any interest in such land, unless the land charge is registered in the appropriate register before the completion of the purchase.

Section 17(1) defines "purchaser" as:

any person (including a mortgagee or lessee) who, for valuable consideration, takes any interest in land or in a charge on land.

A mortgagee does not pay the amount of the loan until the transaction has been completed by the execution of the deed. There is, therefore, a danger that after X, a mortgagee, has searched the register, another mortgage of the same land may have been registered in favour of Y, the effect of which will be to render X's mortgage at the moment of its completion void against Y. X is, therefore, allowed to protect himself by registering a *priority notice*, giving notice of his contemplated mortgage.[515]

(2) MORTGAGE ACCOMPANIED BY DEEDS IS NOT REGISTRABLE

One outstanding feature, then, of this legislation is that no mortgage, legal or equitable, under which the mortgagee obtains the title deeds, is capable of registration. The principal reason for this exclusion is to avoid the inconvenience that would arise if the efficacy of temporary advances that are so frequently made in unregistered land[516] against a deposit of deeds were to be affected by a failure to register. Section 2 of the Land Charges Act 1972, however, provides that an estate contract shall be registrable as a land charge Class C(iv). An estate contract is a contract by an estate owner to convey or create a legal estate.[517] The normal example is a contract for the sale of a legal fee simple or for the grant of a term of years absolute, but it also includes a contract to create a legal mortgage, that is, to grant a mortgage term. Further, it would seem to include the equitable mortgage that arises from a contract to create a legal mortgage, which is accompanied by a deposit of title deeds, for as we have already seen the deposit does not of itself create an equitable mortgage, but constitutes an implicit agreement to create a legal mortgage which has effect as an equitable mortgage under the doctrine of *Walsh v Lonsdale* only if it satisfies the formality requirements of a valid contract to create a legal mortgage.[518] It has therefore been suggested that an express contract, accompanied by the title deeds, to create a legal mortgage, and a deposit of title deeds by way of security accompanied by a written agreement between the parties which satisfies the formality requirements for a contract, are registrable as estate contracts, in spite of the fact that because accompanied by the deeds they are excluded from registration by the paragraph which deals specifically with mortgages.[519] It is submitted, however, that the correctness of this view is at least doubtful. If the sub-section which explicitly defines what

---

[514] Replacing LCA 1925, s. 13(2). See *Midland Bank Trust Co Ltd v Green* [1981] AC 513; p. 946, post.

[515] LCA 1972, s. 11; for details, see p. 944, post.

[516] Since 2002 mortgages of registered cannot be made involving the deposit of a land certificate since land certificates have been abolished: p. 732, ante.   [517] P. 940, post.

[518] Pp. 729, ante.

[519] (1940) CLJ pp. 250–1 (R. E. Megarry); (1962) 26 Conv (NS) pp. 446–9 (R. G. Rowley). Williams, *Contract of Sale of Land*, p. 247; Fairest, *Mortgages*, pp. 133–6; Fisher and Lightwood, *Law of Mortgages* (10th edn), p. 72; Waldock, pp. 425–8.

mortgages shall be registrable deliberately excludes those that are accompanied by a deposit of documents, it seems inconsistent with the policy underlying the Act to permit their registration in their other capacity as estate contracts. The result of doing so would be to render void against a subsequent incumbrancer an unregistered mortgage to which the sub-section concerned with mortgages denies the possibility of registration for the very reason that registration ought not to be necessary. To put this construction upon the statute would prejudice the commercial practice by which deeds are deposited with bankers to secure a temporary loan, for the result of invalidating against later lenders an arrangement that is often only transient would be to discourage a convenient business transaction. The question can scarcely be answered with assurance until it has come before the courts, and meanwhile the following account is based on the assumption that a mortgage, legal or equitable, accompanied by a deposit of the deeds is not registrable in unregistered land.

(3) PRIORITIES WHERE NO MORTGAGEE OBTAINS DEEDS

The question of priorities seems comparatively simple to determine against the legislative background if we confine ourselves to a series of mortgage transactions *none of which is accompanied by a delivery of the title deeds*. It depends upon a combination of section 97 of the Law of Property Act 1925 and section 4(5) of the Land Charges Act 1972, but it would appear that the latter is the dominating enactment. The decisive factor, in other words, is that a registrable mortgage is void against a later mortgage unless it is registered before completion of the latter transaction.[520] Suppose that:

A takes a mortgage without the title deeds on 1 May.

B takes a mortgage without the title deeds on 10 May.

A registers on 11 May.

B registers on 20 May.

C takes a mortgage without the deeds on 30 May and registers.

The order in which the parties rank, whether their mortgages are legal or equitable, is B-A-C, for A's mortgage, though created before B's was created and registered before B's was registered, was nevertheless not registered upon completion of the second mortgage. It is therefore void under section 4(5) as against B. It is not of course void as against C, since its registration was effected before completion of C's mortgage on 30 May. Moreover, by virtue of section 198(1) of the Law of Property Act 1925, C has, but B has not, statutory notice of A's mortgage.

(i) Priority of registration not in itself sufficient

It is arguable that in accordance with section 97 of the Law of Property Act 1925 A should rank before B since he was the first to register, but it is difficult to agree that a void charge can be revivified and given precedence over the very charge in relation to which its invalidity has been declared by statute. There can be no revival of that which is void. One of the main objects of registration is to enable a mortgagee to discover the state of the mortgagor's title, but if he is to be displaced by a registration effected after it has been certified to him by the Registrar that no prior charge stands in his way, the object will certainly be frustrated. The truth appears to be that there was a lack of co-ordination in the drafting of section 97 and

---

[520] But for another view, see (1950) 13 MLR 534–5 (A. D. Hargreaves).

section 13(2) of the Land Charges Act 1925 (now replaced by section 4(5) of the Land Charges Act 1972).[521]

(ii) Circulus inextricabilis. Subrogation

In the example given above priority is not difficult to determine, but this is by no means always true. Suppose, for instance, that

after a mortgage has been granted to X who takes possession of the title deeds, further mortgages of the same land are given in the following order:

A puisne mortgage to A on 1 May to secure £1,000.

A general equitable charge to B on 10 May to secure £1,000.

A puisne mortgage to C on 20 May to secure £2,000.

A registers on 11 May.

C registers on 20 May.

B's charge is not registered.

We know that A's mortgage is statutorily void against B, and that B's mortgage is void against C, but at first sight it seems impossible to arrange all three claimants in order of priority. An objection can be raised to every possible permutation. For instance, the order is not A-B-C, for though A ranks before C he must be postponed to B; neither is it B-A-C, for C is to be preferred to B though not to A; neither is it A-C-B, since A must rank after B. If such a case were to arise the court would presumably be driven to base its decision upon the doctrine of subrogation.[522] Subrogation is the process by which one creditor is substituted for another creditor when both have claims against the same debtor.[523] The relevant factors in its application to the present example are that:

B ranks before A,

A ranks before C, and

C ranks before B,

so that any starting point is as arbitrary as any other in this *circulus inextricabilis*. But a solution may be found by transferring to C the right of B to be paid £1,000 before A. C is subrogated to B, *but only to the extent to which B has priority over A*. The actual order of payment will therefore be as follows:

(1) C is entitled to a first payment of £1,000.

This is the £1,000 that is due to B in priority to A.

(2) A is entitled to the next payment of £1,000.

---

[521] "Technically LCA 1925 (the predecessor of LCA 1972) was a later statute than LPA 1925, and should prevail in the case of irreconcilable conflict": (Megarry and Wade, *Law of Real Property* (5th edn), p. 1000, n. 97). For a discussion of the question, see [1940] CLJ, pp. 255–6 (R. E. Megarry).

[522] *Benham v Keane* (1861) 1 John & H 685 at 710–12; *Re Wyatt* [1892] 1 Ch 188 at 208–9, M & B p. 914; cf *Re Weniger's Policy* [1910] 2 Ch 291.

[523] White and Tudor's *Leading Cases in Equity*, vol. i. pp. 147 et seq. On subrogation generally, see p. 759, ante.

Theoretically, at any rate, A suffers no injury. His claim is not sustainable until £1,000 has been paid out of the land, and it is no concern of his whether that sum is paid to B or to C.

(3) C is entitled to the next payment of £1,000.

This represents the remainder of C's advance, the whole of which is payable before that of B.

(4) B is entitled to £1,000 if the proceeds arising from the sale of the land are sufficient.

If the sums advanced were £1,000 by A, £1,000 by B and £600 by C, the order would be this:

(1) C: £600.

(2) B: £400.

(3) A: £1,000.

(4) B: £600.[524]

However, it cannot be said that the doctrine of subrogation provides more than a rough and ready method of solving the difficulty. It cannot escape the criticism of being arbitrary, for it is not obvious why the subrogation should begin with one claimant rather than with another. In the example just given the process might equally well start with B rather than with C. Neither is the justice of the solution obvious. In the first example, B gets nothing until £2,000 has been paid to C and £1,000 to A, and yet he has a prior right to A.

Where the value of the land is insufficient to satisfy all the mortgagees in full, it might be more just to admit the inextricable circle and to decree a payment *pari passu*, that is, a division of the proceeds among the various claimants in proportion to the respective amounts of their advances.

(4) PRIORITIES WHERE ONE MORTGAGE PROTECTED BY DEEDS

We must now consider the question of priorities where one of the competing mortgages is accompanied by the title deeds, which is, of course, the usual case. The chief problem here is: What is the significance of excluding such a mortgage from the list of registrable incumbrances? Is the implication that in all cases a person who obtains possession of the deeds ranks first? Presumably not, for it must never be forgotten that the governing principles which obtained under the pre-1926 law were not expressly altered by the legislation of 1925. These principles were that:

A legal was preferred to an equitable mortgage; mortgages ranked in the order of their creation, subject to the preference given to the legal mortgage; but either of these principles might be displaced by negligent conduct with reference to the deeds.

---

[524] A similar problem may arise under *Dearle v Hall* (1823) 3 Russ 1, p. 791, ante. See, for instance, the illustration given by FRY LJ in *Re Wyatt* [1892] 1 Ch 188 at 208–9, M & B p. 914. There are two trustees of a fund, X and Y. The first incumbrancer, A, notifies X only; the second incumbrancer, B, notifies X and Y; X then dies and the third incumbrancer, C, notifies the surviving trustee, Y. Here A ranks before B (*Ward v Duncombe* [1893] AC 369, p. 793, ante); B before C (ibid.); C before A, for A's notice is nullified as against incumbrances created after X's death (*Timson v Ramsbottom* (1837) 2 Keen 35, p. 793, ante). Therefore, says FRY LJ: "The fund would be distributed as follows: First, to the third incumbrancer to the extent of the claim of the first. Secondly, to the second incumbrancer. Thirdly, to the third incumbrancer to the extent to which he might remain unpaid after the money he had received whilst standing in the shoes of the first incumbrancer; see *Benham v Keane* (1861) 1 John &

The pre-1926 law, therefore, cannot be ignored altogether, though obviously its application is materially affected by the introduction of the system of registration. Another difficulty is the uncertainty of the statutory expression "protected by a deposit of documents", for a mortgagee may be entitled to this protection if he receives only some of the deeds relating to the legal estate, honestly and reasonably believing that he has received all.[525] Thus a contest may arise between two mortgagees, both of whom are protected by a deposit of documents and neither of whom, because of the deposit, has registered his incumbrance.[526]

The following account of the general question is based upon two hypothetical cases, first, that the mortgage with the deposit of deeds comes first in order of date, secondly that it comes later.[527]

(i) First mortgagee acquires deeds

Let us suppose that:

A takes a mortgage protected by the title deeds;

B takes a later mortgage, necessarily without the deeds.

We require to ascertain whether the order is A-B, but to do this it is necessary, having regard to the principles of the pre-1926 law which are still to a large extent relevant, to consider the problem according as the parties obtain legal or equitable mortgages.

(1) A'S MORTGAGE IS LEGAL, B'S IS EQUITABLE

Under the pre-1926 law, as we have seen,[528] the rule in such a case as this was that, by force of the legal estate and also by virtue of the maxim *qui prior est tempore potior est jure*, A ranked first, unless his subsequent negligence with regard to the deeds, as for instance by handing them back to the mortgagor, justified his postponement to B. These rules of the pre-1926 law, which specify the limits within which conduct with regard to deeds causes loss of priority, still hold good, for section 13 of the Law of Property Act 1925 provides that:

This Act shall not prejudicially affect the right or interest of any person arising out of or consequent on the possession by him of any documents relating to a legal estate in land, nor affect any question arising out of or consequent upon any omission to obtain or any other absence of possession by any person of any documents relating to a legal estate in land.

Presuming that this section is linked to the Land Charges Act by section 97 quoted above,[529] it seems clear that the ranking of A and B still depends upon precisely the same considerations as before 1926. A will rank first unless his fraud or subsequent negligence justifies his postponement.

(2) THE MORTGAGES BOTH OF A AND B ARE LEGAL

The position could not arise before 1926, when only one legal mortgage of the fee simple was possible. There seems no doubt, however, that A ranks first, since he has the earlier legal

---

H 685, where a similar problem was similarly solved." See also *Re Woodroffes (Musical Instruments) Ltd* [1986] Ch 366; [1986] CLJ 25 (L. S. Sealy). See generally (1968) 32 Conv (NS) 325 (W. A. Lee); 71 Yale LJ 53 (G. Gilmore).

[525] *Ratcliffe v Barnard* (1871) 6 Ch App 652; *Dixon v Muckleston* (1872) 8 Ch App 155.

[526] For a discussion of this particular case, see [1940] CLJ pp. 249–53 (R. E. Megarry).

[527] See the valuable series of articles in (1933) 76 LJ News 83–4, 95, 106–7, 122–3, 131–3 (R. L. Bignell and C. H. H. Wilss).   [528] Pp. 784 et seq, ante.

[529] P. 795, ante; but this is not certain.

estate and also possession of the deeds, though of course if he negligently parts with the deeds and thereby causes the deception of B, he may as in the last case lose his priority.

(3) A'S MORTGAGE IS EQUITABLE, B'S IS LEGAL

This position arises, for instance, where a mortgage by deposit of deeds is made to A, and later a legal charge is granted to B. Before 1926, B, as the holder of the legal estate, ranked first, unless he had failed to inquire for the deeds or had rested content with an unreasonable excuse for their non-production, or unless he had notice of A's equitable mortgage at the time when he took his own. The question now arises—what constitutes notice of A's mortgage? Certainly not registration, for a mortgagee with the deeds cannot register. The answer is contained in section 199(1)(ii) of the Law of Property Act 1925. It provides that a purchaser, including a mortgagee,[530] shall not be prejudicially affected by notice of any instrument or matter which is incapable of registration under the Land Charges Act unless:

(a) it is within his own knowledge, or would have come to his knowledge if such inquiries and inspections had been made as ought reasonably to have been made by him; or

(b) in the same transaction with respect to which a question of notice to the purchaser arises, it has come to the knowledge of his counsel, as such, or of his solicitor or other agent, as such, or would have come to the knowledge of his solicitor or other agent, as such, if such inquiries and inspections had been made as ought reasonably to have been made by the solicitor or other agent.

In other words, the old doctrine of actual or constructive notice is still in force with regard to mortgages that are incapable of registration. Again, there is nothing in the legislation of 1925 which deprives the owner of the legal estate of that pre-eminent position which he has always enjoyed.

It would seem, therefore, that in the majority of circumstances B will rank second, for he will have actual notice of A's mortgage if he inquires for the deeds, and constructive notice if he makes no inquiry. Presumably, however, a case like *Hewitt v Loosemore*[531] would still be decided as it was before 1926.

(4) THE MORTGAGES BOTH OF A AND OF B ARE EQUITABLE

In this case there has been a deposit of the deeds with A followed by a general equitable charge in favour of B. When there was a contest under the pre-1926 law between equitable incumbrancers, it was the maxim *qui prior est tempore potior est jure* that prevailed. In the circumstances that we are now considering A would have ranked first, unless, by a voluntary redelivery of the deeds to the mortgagor, he had negligently allowed a fraud to be perpetrated on B.[532] There is nothing in the modern legislation to upset the pre-1926 law, and there is little doubt that the maxim *qui prior est tempore potior est jure* is still applicable.[533]

(ii) First mortgagee does not acquire deeds

Let us suppose that the following transactions occur:

A takes a puisne mortgage.[534]

B takes a later mortgage, either legal or equitable, and also obtains possession of the deeds.

---

[530] LPA 1925, s. 205(1)(xxi).   [531] (1851) 9 Hare 449, M & B p. 905; p. 787, ante.

[532] P. 787, ante.   [533] Cf *Beddoes v Shaw* [1937] Ch 81.

[534] I.e., a puisne mortgage within the meaning of LCA 1972, s. 2(4): a legal mortgage not protected by deposit of deeds. On these facts it is not "puisne" (i.e., a later mortgage) within the literal meaning of the term: n. 512, ante.

It is clear that if A has registered his mortgage before the completion of B's, he will rank first, since section 97 of the Law of Property Act 1925 provides that his mortgage shall rank according to its date of registration, and furthermore section 198 provides that registration under the Land Charges Act shall constitute notice to all persons and for all purposes connected with the land affected. If, however, it was due to A's gross negligence that he failed to obtain the deeds, it is conceivable, but scarcely probable, that despite registration he might, by virtue of section 13 of the Law of Property Act 1925,[535] be postponed to B in accordance with the principles of the pre-1926 law.[536]

It seems equally clear that if A has failed to register his mortgage before the transaction with B is completed, he will in all circumstances be postponed to B. This follows from the enactment that a registrable mortgage shall be void against a purchaser of the land charged, unless it is registered before completion of the purchase.[537] It may be argued, however, that, if A inquired for the deeds in the first place and received a reasonable excuse for their non-delivery, his legal estate, as under the pre-1926 law, will still give him priority by virtue of section 13 of the Law of Property Act 1925.[538]

This seems doubtful. Not only is the mortgage rendered absolutely void against B, but it may also be said that A has been negligent in not taking advantage of the protection that registration would have afforded him.

If the facts are altered slightly and we suppose that:

A takes a general equitable charge, and

B takes a later mortgage, either legal or equitable, also obtaining possession of the deeds,

it would seem that the same result ensues. If the charge is registered, A ranks first, otherwise B will be preferred.

(5) TACKING

(i) Partial abolition

The doctrine of tacking was materially affected by the Law of Property Act 1925.[539] One branch of that doctrine was abolished, the other was retained. The first branch, which under the pre-1926 law[540] comprised the right of a later mortgagee to buy in the legal estate from the first incumbrancer and to squeeze out an intermediate mortgage, has been abolished.[541] The second branch has been retained, for it is important that a mortgagee should be at liberty to tack further advances to his first loan. In fact, the preservation of this right is essential where a bank takes a mortgage from a client as security for his current account, since a further advance is made whenever his cheque is honoured. It was therefore enacted in relation to unregistered land[542] that in certain cases, which will be given in a moment: a prior mortgagee shall have a right to make further advances to rank in priority to subsequent mortgages (whether legal or equitable).[543]

---

[535] P. 800, ante.   [536] [1940] CLJ 259 (R. E. Megarry).   [537] LCA 1972, s. 4(5).
[538] P. 800, ante; (1926) 61 LJ News 398 (J. M. Lightwood), cited and considered (1933) 76 LJ News at 132.
[539] S. 94. See (1958) 22 Conv (NS) 44 (R. G. Rowley).   [540] P. 790, ante.
[541] LPA 1925, s. 94(3). Tacking by purchase of the legal estate survives in other contexts: *McCarthy & Stone Ltd v Julian S Hodge & Co Ltd* [1971] 1 WLR 1547, p. 59, n. 86, ante.
[542] LPA 1925, s. 94(4), amended by LRA 2002, s. 133, Sch. 11, para. 2(1), (9).   [543] Ibid., s. 94(1).

(ii) Tacking of further advances

It will be noticed that this enactment does not confine the right to the first mortgagee or to a legal mortgagee, but grants it to any prior mortgagee, legal or equitable, against every later mortgagee. But it is only in the three following cases that the right may be exercised.

(1) WHEN LATER MORTGAGEES AGREE[544]

This is an obvious and not an unusual case. After mortgages of Blackacre have been granted to A, B and C, the mortgagor may seek a further advance from B on the same security. B will rank for payment of both his loans before C if he makes an arrangement to that effect with C before advancing further money. C is not likely to agree unless the land is sufficient cover for all the money with which it is charged.

(2) WHEN THERE IS NO NOTICE OF LATER MORTGAGES[545]

A mortgagee who has no notice of subsequent mortgages at the time when he makes his further advances may claim priority for both his loans over subsequent mortgagees. This is the same rule as applied before 1926,[546] with this important difference, however, that registration of a later mortgage as a land charge is deemed to constitute *actual* notice of that mortgage.[547] A mortgagee therefore who contemplates a further advance should not make it until he has ascertained by a search at the Land Registry that no later mortgages have been made.

There is, however, an important exception to this rule that the mere registration of a mortgage will prevent a prior mortgagee from tacking later advances. It is enacted that in the case of a mortgage made expressly for securing:

(a) a current account, or

(b) other further advances,

the mere registration of a subsequent mortgage shall not constitute notice sufficient to deprive the earlier mortgagee of his right to tack. In those two cases the rule is that:

A mortgagee shall not be deemed to have notice of a mortgage merely by reason that it was registered as a land charge, if it was not so registered at the time when the original mortgage was created or when the last search (if any) by or on behalf of the mortgagee was made, whichever last happened.[548]

Thus registration of a subsequent mortgage constitutes actual notice of that mortgage to a prior incumbrancer and necessarily displaces his right to tack, except where the prior mortgage was taken not merely as security for the original loan, but as security either for the original loan and further advances or for a current account. In either of these cases registration will be notice only if it was in being when the prior mortgage was created (which might of course be before any money was actually advanced by the prior mortgagee, as often happens where a current account is secured), or when the prior mortgagee last made a search at the Land Registry. Failing registration at one of these dates a prior mortgagee will not be deprived of the right to tack unless, at the time of the further advance, he had notice, in the old sense of actual or constructive notice, of the later mortgage.

---

[544] LPA 1925, s. 94(1)(a).   [545] Ibid., s. 94(1)(b).   [546] P. 790, ante.
[547] LPA 1925, s. 198(1), as amended by LLCA 1975, s. 17, Sch. 1.
[548] Ibid., s. 94(2), as amended by LP(A)A 1926, Schedule.

This exception to the rule that registration is equivalent to actual notice has been made in the interest of bankers, for were the rule unqualified it would be impracticable to take a mortgage as security for a current account. An illustration will make this clear. If A mortgages his land to a bank in order to secure an overdraft which at the time of the mortgage is £3,000, and if he subsequently grants a mortgage of the same land to B, notice of which is given to the bank, the rule as laid down in *Hopkinson v Rolt*[549] is that the bank obtains priority only for the amount due from the mortgagor at the time when the second mortgage to B was made. If the overdraft at that moment is £4,000, then £4,000 is the amount with which the land is charged in favour of the bank. When, moreover, A from time to time pays sums into his account, and the overdraft is thus reduced below £4,000, only the reduced amount is recoverable under the mortgage;[550] and although, after notice of the second mortgage, the actual overdraft may be increased as a result of drawings out, the payments or further advances by the bank in respect of these drawings cannot be tacked to the loan as it stood at the time when notice of the second mortgage was received.[551] To fix the mortgage at £4,000 is equitable if the bank has actual notice of the second mortgage, but it would make this side of banking business impossible if mere registration constituted notice, for it would be unsafe to honour the customer's cheques unless on each occasion a search were made at the Land Registry.

Two practical results emerge from this legislation.

First, a mortgage will generally provide expressly that the land shall be security for further advances, since this will enable a further advance to be made without a search at the Land Registry; secondly, a mortgagee who searches and discovers the existence of a prior mortgage expressly made to secure a current account or further advances will be careful to notify his mortgage to the prior mortgagee.

(3) WHEN THE MORTGAGE IMPOSES AN OBLIGATION ON THE MORTGAGEE TO MAKE FURTHER ADVANCES

When the provision in the prior mortgage is not that the land shall be security for any further advances which *may* be made, as in the case (b) just considered, but that the mortgagee shall be bound to make further advances if called upon to do so, the new rule is[552] that the doctrine of tacking shall apply to such advances notwithstanding the fact that at the time of making them the prior mortgagee had notice of a later mortgage. The law as laid down in *West v Williams*[553] is therefore reversed.

(b) Priority as between mortgagees of an equitable interest in land or personalty

(1) EXTENSION OF RULE IN *DEARLE V HALL*

We have already seen that under the law before 1926 the priority as between mortgagees of an equitable interest in pure personalty depended, in accordance with the rule in *Dearle v Hall*,

---

[549] (1861) 9 HL Cas 514; p. 791, ante.

[550] *Clayton's Case* (1816) 1 Mer 572; *Russell-Cooke Trust Co v Prentis* [2003] 1 All ER 478; [2005] CLJ 45 (M. Conaglen). 　　　　　　[551] *Deeley v Lloyds Bank Ltd* [1910] 1 Ch 648, reversed [1912] AC 756.

[552] LPA 1925, s. 94(1)(c). 　　　[553] [1899] 1 Ch 132; p. 791, ante.

upon the order in which the trustees had received notice from the mortgagees, but that this principle did not apply to mortgages of freeholds or of leaseholds.[554] The innovation made by the 1925 legislation is the extension of the rule in *Dearle v Hall* to mortgages of *all* equitable interests, realty being put on the same footing as personalty. This assimilation is accomplished by section 137(1) of the Law of Property Act 1925:

> The law applicable to dealings with equitable things in action which regulates the priority of competing interests therein, shall, as respects dealings with equitable interests in land, capital money, and securities representing capital money effected after the commencement of this Act, apply to and regulate the priority of competing interests therein.[555]

This extension of the rule to all mortgages and assignments of equitable interests in freeholds and leaseholds is of especial importance owing to the increased number of interests that are necessarily equitable since 1925. Thus, the purchaser or mortgagee of an interest arising under a strict settlement, such as a life interest, an entailed interest or any species of future interest, must protect himself by giving the necessary notice. In effect the priority of mortgages of equitable beneficial interests under strict settlements and trusts of land is now determined by the same rule.

(2) RULES REGARDING NOTICE

The rules that existed before 1926 with regard to the nature of the notice still hold good,[556] subject to one exception. This is that a notice given otherwise than in writing in respect of any dealing with an equitable interest in real or personal property shall not affect the priority of competing claims of purchasers or mortgagees.[557]

(i) Persons to whom notice must be given

The Law of Property Act 1925 contains the following rules with regard to the persons upon whom the written notice must be served.

(1) Where the equitable interest is in settled land or capital money.[558]

Where dealings take place with such an interest, notice must be given to the *trustees of the settlement*. If the interest in question has been created by a derivative settlement (i.e. one by which an interest already settled is resettled), then notice must be given to the trustees of the derivative settlement.

(2) Where the equitable interest is in land held on a trust of land.

In this case notice must be given to the *trustees* of such land.[559]

(3) Where the equitable interest is neither (1) nor (2).[560]

If, for instance, the subject of the transaction is a life annuity charged on land by a tenant in fee simple, it is provided that notice shall be given to the *estate owner*.

---

554 P. 791, ante. 555 For an analysis of the section, see [1993] Conv 22 (J. Howell).
556 Pp. 793, ante. 557 LPA 1925, s. 137(3). 558 Ibid., s. 137(2)(i).
559 Ibid., s. 137(2)(ii), as amended by TLATA 1996, s. 25(1), Sch. 3, para. 4(15).
560 Ibid., s. 137(2)(iii).

It will be remembered that certain complexities had arisen before 1926 with regard to a notice served on a single trustee.[561] The proper course, which, however, is not always adopted, is to serve the notice on each of the trustees and to take a receipt from each, and it is perhaps regrettable that the Act did not made this practice compulsory. No statutory direction has, however, been given, and it therefore appears that in this regard the old decisions continue to represent the law.[562]

(ii) Notice by way of endorsed memorandum

To meet any difficulty that may arise in identifying the appropriate person to receive notice, the Act provides that where:

(a) the trustees are not persons to whom a valid notice can be given; or

(b) there are no trustees to whom a valid notice can be given; or

(c) for any other reason a valid notice cannot be served, or cannot be served without unreasonable cost or delay,

the assignee may require that a memorandum of the transaction be endorsed on, or permanently annexed to, the instrument which creates the trust.[563] Such a memorandum, as respects priorities, operates in like manner as if a written notice had been given to trustees. Thus if the land in which the equitable interest exists is subject to a strict settlement, the memorandum will be annexed to the trust instrument; if it is land belonging to an owner who has died intestate, the memorandum will be annexed to the letters of administration. The objection to a memorandum of this nature is that trust instruments may become overladen with endorsements of charges and assignments. Therefore an alternative method of registering a notice has been provided.[564]

(iii) Notice to nominated trust corporation

It is provided that a settlor when drafting a settlement, or the court at a later date, may nominate a trust corporation to whom notice of dealings affecting real or personal property may be given. Where such a nomination has been made, notice of any dealings with the equitable interest must be given to the trust corporation, and if given to the trustees must be transmitted by them to the corporation. A notice which is not received by the corporation has no effect on priorities.

(iv) Right to production of notice

The object of the rule in Dearle v Hall is to enable a person to discover by inquiries addressed to the trustees whether the owner of an equitable interest has created any earlier incumbrances. But this object was not always attained under the law before 1926, for since, in the language of LINDLEY LJ:"it is no part of the duty of a trustee to assist his cestui que trust in selling or mortgaging his beneficial interest and in squandering or anticipating his fortune",[565] it was held that a trustee owed no greater duty to a person who was proposing to

---

561 P. 793, ante.

562 See (1925) 60 LJ News 264 (J. M. Lightwood); Wolstenholme and Cherry (13th edn), vol. 1 p. 246.

563 LPA 1925, s. 137(4).

564 Ibid., s. 138. See also Law Reform Committee 23rd Report (The powers and duties of trustees) 1982 (Cmnd 8733), paras. 2.17–2.24.   565 Low v Bouverie [1891] 3 Ch 82 at 99.

deal with a *cestui que trust*.[566] Thus a trustee might refuse to answer inquiries, and even if he gave an answer that contained wrong information, he was not liable for the consequences unless he had been guilty of fraud or had made such a clear and categorical statement that he was estopped from denying its truth.[567] A prospective assignee, however, is given at least this advantage by the Act, that he may demand production of any written notice that has been served on the trustees or their predecessors.[568]

(2) Registered Land

The rules governing the priority of mortgages over unregistered land are therefore extremely complex—for a number of reasons: the fact that in unregistered land some, but not all, mortgages are capable of protection by registration—and, in particular, that a mortgage protected by deposit of title deeds with the mortgagee is not capable of registration;[569] the different (historically grounded[570]) rules for the priority as between legal and equitable mortgages;[571] and difficulties which follow from the registration provisions of the Land Charges Act and their relationship to the equitable rules for notice.[572] These complexities are not, in general, reproduced in relation to registered land.

(a) Priority of charges

Registered charges on the same registered estate rank for priority between themselves in the order shown in the register.[573] This therefore means that in the normal course the order of priority is the order of registration, although the chargees may decide on a different order of priority and apply for the order shown on the register to be altered.[574]

The priority as between equitable charges depends on the general rules of priority of interests under the Land Registration Act 2002—that is, the order in which they are created.[575]

The priority as between a legal charge and an equitable charge also depends on the general rules of priority: and so the registration of a legal charge made for valuable consideration gives it priority over a prior equitable charge entered into before the legal charge was created that has not been protected by entry of a notice at the time of registration.[576]

(b) Tacking

Section 94 of the Law of Property Act 1925[577] does not apply to registered land.[578] The Land Registration Act 2002,[579] however, provides that the proprietor of a registered charge may

---

[566] *Burrowes v Lock* (1805) 10 Ves 470.   [567] Ibid.   [568] LPA 1925, s. 137(8).

[569] P. 732, ante.   [570] P. 784, ante.   [571] Pp. 794–808, ante.   [572] P. 801, ante.

[573] LRA 2002, s. 48(1), LRR 2003, r. 101; R & R, paras. 27.008–27.009. Certain statutory charges, such as the charge in favour of the Legal Services Commission under Access to Justice Act 1999, s. 10(7), may however take overriding priority: LRA 2002, s. 50, LRR 2003, rr. 105, 106; H & B, paras. 12.51–12.58.

[574] LRR, 2003, r. 102.

[575] LRA 2002, s. 28. Until 1987 such priorities in registered land were in some cases governed by the order in which "priority cautions" or "priority inhibitions" had been lodged in the Minor Interests Index: LRA 1925, s. 102; LRR 1925, r. 229. The Index was abolished by the Land Registration Act 1986. See H & B, para. 12.59, noting that, when electronic conveyancing is fully introduced, it will not be possible to create equitable charges without simultaneously registering them, and therefore the register will determine the priority for equitable, as well as legal, charges.   [576] Ibid., s. 29.

[577] P. 802, ante.   [578] LPA 1925, s. 94(4), amended by LRA 2002, s. 133, Sch. 11, para. 2(1), (9).

[579] S. 49. Under LRA 1925 the common law rule applied, but by s. 30, before making any entry on the register which would prejudicially affect the priority of any further advances, the Registrar had to give notice by registered

make a further advance on the security of his charge, which will rank in priority to a subsequent charge, if

(a) he has not received from the subsequent chargee notice of the creation of the subsequent charge;[580] or

(b) the further advance is made in pursuance of an obligation and at the time of the creation of the subsequent charge the obligation was entered in the register;[581] or

(c) the parties to the prior charge have agreed a maximum amount for which the charge is security and at the time of the subsquent charge the agreement was entered into the register.[582]

Apart from these situations, tacking in relation to a charge over registered land is only possible with the agreement of the subsequent chargee.[583]

VI Law Reform

A Law Commission Report on Land Mortgages 1991

In 1991 the Law Commission recommended that all existing methods of consensually mortgaging or charging interests in land should be abolished and replaced by a new form of mortgage to be used for mortgaging any interest in land whether legal or equitable.[584] "The present complex mortgage structure would be replaced by a new simplified structure." It also proposed a new class of "protected mortgages" by an individual of property which includes a dwelling-house, and wider powers of intervention against unfair mortgages. The rights, remedies and powers of a mortgagee would be exercisable only in good faith for the purpose of protecting or enforcing the security.

In 1998 the Government decided not to implement the Report due to lack of support, but invited the Law Commission to reconsider its proposals.[585] However, the Report contains a

---

post to the proprietor of the charge, who could tack any advances made by him up to the time when he received or ought to have received the notice in due course of post.

[580] S. 49(1). Notice is treated as received when, in accordance with rules, it ought to have been received: s. 49(2); LRR 2003, r. 107. [581] S. 49(3); LRR 2003, r. 108.

[582] S. 49(4); LRR 2003, r. 109. Rules may disapply this subsection in relation to particular types of charge, but no such rules have been made; H & B, para. 12.78. [583] S. 49(6).

[584] Land Mortgages 1991 (Law Com No. 204); [1992] Conv 69 (H. W. Wilkinson); (1992) 136 SJ 267, 292 (G. Frost). A summary of the recommendations is contained in Part X of the Report; M & B pp. 921–7.

In March 1989 the Law Commission's Conveyancing Standing Committee published a consultation document suggesting the use of a new form of mortgage called a flexi-mortgage as a means of avoiding chains, cutting out delays and defeating gazumping. Its unique feature is that for a limited time it gives the borrower the right to extend the period of the mortgage on a property he is buying and increase the amount he borrows to cover the cost of an overlapping sale and purchase. Payments under his old mortgage are suspended. This allows the house-owner to agree to buy a new property before selling his own by incurring only a small increase in mortgage interest and without increasing his capital repayments; (Law Com No. 190), para. 2.2.

[585] Law Commission Thirty-Third Annual Report (Law Com No. 258), para. 1.10. The invitation was to return to the topic when its then current work on land registration was finished. But there has not yet been any proposal from the Law Commission to work further on it.

useful discussion of the merits and demerits of the current law on mortgages. The main recommendations were:

(1) Creation of Mortgages

There should be only two methods of creating a mortgage: the formal and the informal land mortgage.

(a) The formal land mortgage would not be valid unless it was created by deed, whether the property mortgaged was a legal estate or an equitable interest. It would require registration under the Land Registration Act 1925 if any part of the mortgagor's title was itself registered; and in the case of unregistered land, it would be registrable as a land charge, Class C (i) under the Land Charges Act 1972.

(b) The informal land mortgage would not be valid unless it was made by deed or satisfied the requirements of section 2 of the Law of Property (Miscellaneous Provisions) Act 1989.[586] A mortgagee under an informal land mortgage would have no right to enforce the security, nor to take any other action in relation to the mortgaged property, but would have a right to have the mortgage perfected by the grant of a formal land mortgage.

(2) Overriding Provisions

Certain provisions would be overriding in that they cannot be varied or excluded. In particular:

(a) The mortgagor would have the right to possession unless the mortgagee took possession in order to sell or to prevent a fall in the value of the property.

(b) The power of sale would only be exercisable if the mortgagor was in arrears or there was an outstanding breach of covenant substantially prejudicing the mortgagee's security or an event had occurred which substantially reduced the mortgagor's ability to meet his financial obligations or which prejudiced the value of the property as security.

(c) There would be no right of consolidation.

(3) Protected Mortgages

A distinction was drawn between commercial and non-commercial mortgages.

The most important differences lie in the extent to which the law needs to interfere with the parties' freedom of contract. If all provisions have to apply equally to all types of mortgage, it is difficult to reconcile the need to allow maximum flexibility to commercial transactions entered into between parties of equal bargaining power, with the need to provide adequate protection for vulnerable mortgagors who in a wholly free market would have no real choice but to accept whatever terms lenders may choose to dictate. The obvious way of reconciling these conflicting needs is to have a protected class of mortgage (para. 4.1).

---

[586] P. 868, post.

(a) Definition

A protected mortgage would consist of all formal and informal land mortgages of any interest in land which included a dwelling-house except those where either (i) the mortgagor was a body corporate, or (ii) enforcement of the mortgage would not affect enjoyment of the dwelling-house, or (iii) the dwelling-house was occupied under a service tenancy.

(b) Protection

The main protection afforded to the mortgagor under a protected mortgage would be:

(1) POSSESSION

The mortgagee would not be entitled to take possession without serving an enforcement notice in the prescribed form on the mortgagor and obtaining a court order. The court would have power to order that interest payable under the mortgage should cease to accrue after twelve weeks of possession or such other period as the court should decide.

(2) SALE

Similarly, before exercising the power of sale under a formal land mortgage, the mortgagee must serve an enforcement notice and obtain a court order.

If the mortgagee applied to the court for possession or sale, the court would have powers equivalent to those applicable to residential mortgages under the Administration of Justice Acts 1970 and 1973 and the Consumer Credit Act 1974. In addition it would have power to order the debt to be rescheduled.

(3) FORECLOSURE

There is a general recommendation that the remedy of foreclosure should be abolished and replaced by the power of the mortgagee to sell to himself provided leave of the court is first obtained.

(4) Revision of Mortgage Terms

Credit bargains made by land mortgage would be removed from the Consumer Credit Act 1974 and instead be protected under a comprehensive code affecting all land mortgages. Under this the court should have power to set aside or vary any terms of a mortgage

with a view to doing justice between the parties if (a) principles of fair dealing were contravened when the mortgage was granted, or (b) the effect of the terms of the mortgage is that the mortgagee now has rights substantially greater than or different from those necessary to make the property adequate security for the liabilities secured by the mortgage, or (c) the mortgage requires payments to be made which are exorbitant, or (d) the mortgage includes a postponement of the right to redeem, or a provision intending to impede redemption (para. 8.5).[587]

This new jurisdiction would be in addition to the court's general powers to set aside on grounds such as fraud, mistake, rectification, estoppel, undue influence, or restraint of

---

[587] For a more limited reforms, see Consumer Credit Bill (expected to become Consumer Credit Act 2006); p. 745, n. 170, ante.

trade. The equitable jurisdiction concerned with clogs or fetters on the equity of redemption would be abolished.

B Limitation of Actions

In 2001 the Law Commission[588] recommended significant reforms to the law on limitation of actions in many areas of private law. Certain specific proposals are made in relation to land mortgages.[589] A long-stop limitation period of ten years should apply to claims to enforce a mortgage or charge over land, running from the date on which the mortgagee's or chargee's right to enforce the mortgage or charge accrues;[590] and the long-stop period should also apply to claims to enforce an obligation secured by a mortgage or charge by suing on the covenant to repay.[591] Where a prior mortgagee is in possession of the mortgaged property, the limitation period applicable to a claim by the subsequent mortgagee to recover arrears of interest (or damages in lieu) should, if necessary, be extended so that it does not end until a year after the prior mortgagee ceases to be in possession;[592] and the limitation period applying to foreclosure proceedings should be suspended during the period that the mortgagee is in possession of the mortgaged property.[593] No limitation period should apply to a claim by the mortgagor to redeem a mortgage over land;[594] and the expiry of the limitation period applying to claims to enforce a mortgage should extinguish the claimant's interest in the mortgaged property.[595]

The Government accepted the report in principle in July 2002.[596]

---

[588] Limitation of Actions, Law Com No. 270.   [589] Paras 4.158–4.196.

[590] Para. 4.166; similarly, for a mortgages over land and personal property together: para. 4.173.

[591] Para. 4.177.   [592] Para. 4.184.   [593] Para. 4.185.

[594] Para. 4.186. At present, the limitation period for unregistered land is twelve years from the date on which the mortgagee takes possession of the land: LA 1980, s. 16, but this has now been disapplied for registered land by LRA 2002, s. 96; p. 145, ante, thus implementing this proposal in Law Com No. 270.   [595] Para. 4.196.

[596] Law Commission Annual Report 2002–03 (Law Com No. 280), para. 3.14. The general regime governing limitation of actions was substantially modified in relation to registered land by LRA 2002; pp. 145 et seq., ante. There is no change to the position of *mortgagors* in possession: the mortgagee's rights to possession or foreclosure as against the mortgagor in possession remain subject to the limitation provisions of LA 1980: p. 145, n. 225, ante. The provisions of LA 1980 are however disapplied in relation to the *mortgagee* in possession: pp. 145–6, ante; n. 594, supra; Law Commission Report on Land Registration for the Twenty-First Century, 2001 (Law Com No. 271), paras. 14.12–14.18.

22

EQUITIES AND PROPRIETARY ESTOPPEL

SUMMARY

I Mere Equities

In the preceding chapters we have discussed those estates and interests in land that are recognised as subsisting at law or in equity. An equitable interest is distinguishable from an "equity" or, as it is often called for emphasis, a "mere equity".

A Nature of an Equity

The courts have never found a satisfactory definition of an equity.[1] But, it is generally taken to refer to an equitable right of a procedural nature. It includes a right to enforce an equitable remedy, such as specific performance, rescission for misrepresentation or undue influence, rectification for mistake, and the rights to consolidation or to re-open a foreclosure.[2]

The right to an equitable remedy is generally only characterised as an "equity" where it is ancillary to some right of property,[3] and where the remedy, if granted, would change the property rights. For example, where freehold property passes under a deed which could be

---

[1] *National Provincial Bank Ltd v Ainsworth* [1965] AC 1175 at 1238, per Lord UPJOHN; at 1252–3, per Lord WILBERFORCE; *Shiloh Spinners Ltd v Harding* [1973] AC 691 at 721, per Lord WILBERFORCE; (1976) 40 Conv (NS) 209 (A. R. Everton); (1955) 71 LQR 480 (R. E. Megarry); Law Commission Report on Land Registration for the Twenty-First Century (Law Com No. 271), para. 5.33.

[2] For consolidation of mortgages, and foreclosure, see chap. 21, ante.

[3] [1965] AC 1175 at 1238, per Lord UPJOHN; Snell, para. 2–01.

rescinded by the transferor for fraud,[4] or where a transfer is executed under a mistake as to the scope of the property it includes which renders it liable to rectification,[5] it is said that the party with the right to the remedy has, respectively, an "equity to rescind", or an "equity to rectify". If granted, the remedy of rescission would restore the property rights to the claimant; and the remedy of rectification would change the terms of the deed and therefore the respective property rights of the parties to the deed.

B Proprietary Characteristics of Equities

There is some controversy over the exact proprietary status of an equity,[6] but it can at least be said that "mere equities" are those rights in equity which subsist in relation to an estate or interest in property, and are recognised as having proprietary characteristics, but which have not been recognised as full equitable interests.[7] We have seen[8] that the most significant characteristic of a property right is that it is inherently capable of both benefiting and binding parties who were not involved in its original creation; and so the acquisition of the land brings with it the burden of property rights which are in law recognised as attaching to the land.

(1) Passing the Benefit of an Equity

The benefit of an equity, in relation to land, is capable of passing with the land.[9]

(2) Passing the Burden of an Equity

(a) Unregistered land

In relation to unregistered land, the courts recognised that certain equities could have the status of proprietary rights, in the sense that they could bind successors to the property against which the beneficiary of the equity had a claim to a remedy; but they placed the mere equity below equitable interests in the hierarchy of property rights in land. We have seen that, before 1925, the rule was that a legal estate or interest bound all those who acquired any interest in the property; and an equitable interest bound all except the bona fide purchaser of the legal estate without notice.[10] In the case of a mere equity, however, the rule was that it

---

[4] Cf *Phillips v Phillips* (1861) 4 De G F & J 208 at 218, per Lord WESTBURY. The same principle applies to chattels: *Car and Universal Finance Co Ltd v Caldwell* [1965] 1 QB 525.

[5] *Blacklocks v J B Developments (Godalming) Ltd* [1982] Ch 183; [1983] Conv 169, 257 (J.T.F.), 361 (D. G. Barnsley). See also *Smith v Jones* [1954] 1 WLR 1089, M & B p. 47 (equity to rectify lease). For rectification generally, see pp. 885–6, post.

[6] In particular, there is some disagreement about the nature of the rights of the party who has an equity to *rescind*—whether the right to rescind constitutes a retained (and therefore continuing) equitable interest in the property: Cartwright, *Misrepresentation*, para. 3.10.

[7] Some equitable interests have come to be recognised even though they too depend on, or originate in, the theory that a personal remedy in equity can create an interest in property which is then capable of binding a successor to the property who takes with notice of it: e.g. an estate contract, arising from a specifically enforceable contract under the doctrine of *Walsh v Lonsdale* (1882) 21 Ch D 9, M & B, p. 85, p. 877, post; the burden of a restrictive covenant, arising from an injunction under *Tulk v Moxhay* (1848) 2 Ph 774, M & B, p. 942, p. 666, ante; the equity of redemption, arising from equity's willingness to enforce the mortgagor's right to redeem in spite of his having no legal remedy: p. 721, ante. [8] Pp. 153 et seq, ante.

[9] LPA 1925, s. 63; *Boots the Chemist Ltd v Street* (1983) 268 EG 817 (rectification of conveyance); *Berkeley Leisure Group Ltd v Williamson* [1996] EGCS 18 (rectification of lease). [10] Pp. 56 et seq, ante.

was not binding on a bona fide purchaser of *an equitable interest* without notice.[11] A purchaser of an equitable interest therefore took subject to prior equitable interests, whether or not he had notice of them; but not mere equities *unless* he had notice. This not only restricts the capacity of a mere equity to bind a purchaser, but also—in those limited cases where an equity *can* bind a purchaser (that is, the purchaser of an equitable interest)—rests the actual binding force of an equity in any particular case on the application of the principles of notice. No provision was made in the 1925 legislation for the registration of equities in relation to unregistered land, and therefore their enforceability still depends on the doctrine of notice.[12] However, it can be difficult for the beneficiary of a mere equity to establish that the purchaser ought to have been aware of his interest.[13]

(b) Registered land

The position in registered land, however, is different. Even before the Land Registration Act 2002 it had been established that a mere equity was an interest subsisting in reference to the land, and therefore capable of binding a purchaser of the land;[14] and that, since the doctrine of notice has no place in registered land, the purchaser could be bound by an equity of which he did not have notice (and in respect of which there was no entry on the register) if the beneficiary was in actual occupation.[15]

This is confirmed by section 116 of the 2002 Act, which provides that:

It is hereby declared for the avoidance of doubt that, in relation to registered land . . .
(b) a mere equity
has effect from the time the equity arises as an interest capable of binding successors in title (subject to the rules about the effect of dispositions on priority).

In effect, therefore, no distinction is now made between an equitable interest and a mere equity for the purposes of registered land. A transferee of the land will be bound by it on the same basis as any other proprietary interest: that is, it will retain its priority on the disposition of the registered estate, except against a disponee of the estate for valuable consideration where the equity has not been protected at the time of the registration of the disposition—and it may be protected either by entry of a notice in the register, or as an overriding interest.[16]

II Proprietary Estoppel[17]

A particular form of "equity" is that which arises under the doctrine of proprietary estoppel. Again, we are concerned with the right of a person to seek a remedy in equity in relation to

---

[11] *Phillips v Phillips* (1861) 4 De GF & J 208 at 218.

[12] As now contained in statutory form in LPA 1925, s. 199(1)(ii); p. 60, ante.

[13] *Smith v Jones* [1954] 1 WLR 1089 at 1092, per UPJOHN J (purchaser entitled to take lease as containing correct terms, and not bound by equity to rectify it).

[14] *Blacklocks v J B Developments (Godalming) Ltd* [1982] Ch 183.

[15] LRA 1925, s. 70(1)(g); *Nurdin & Peacock plc v D B Ramsden & Co Ltd* [1999] 1 EGLR 119 at 125, per NEUBERGER J, distinguishing *Smith v Jones*, supra, on the basis that it was a case on unregistered land; [1998] Conv 421 (S. Pascoe).

[16] LRA 2002, ss. 28, 29, Sch. 3. For a detailed discussion of these provisions, see pp. 971 et seq, post. See also H & B, para. 9.17.

[17] Finn, *Essays in Equity*, pp. 59–94; Pawlowski, *The Doctrine of Proprietary Estoppel*; Wilken, *Waiver, Variation and Estoppel*; Spencer Bower and Turner, *Estoppel by Representation*, passim, and especially chap. 12;

property; and the question arises as to whether that right can bind a purchaser of the property. The doctrine of proprietary estoppel has undergone very significant development in recent years, to the point where it can be recognised as a basis for the informal creation of interests in land. It has been used in particular in order to give protection to a licensee, but it is not confined to licences. In this chapter we shall explain the background to the doctrine, its elements, and its status as a property right. In chapter 23 we shall see its operation in the context of licences; and in chapter 25 we shall see its more general significance as an informal means of creating rights in land.

A Different Forms of Estoppel

There are several varieties of "estoppel" in English law,[18] and there is some debate as to whether all (or at least some of them) are species of the same genus, or should be regarded as so different in principle as to be wholly independent.[19] But the common underlying idea behind them all can be understood by the very choice of the word "estoppel". This was explained by Lord DENNING:[20]

The word "estoppel" only means stopped. You will find it explained by Coke in his *Commentaries on Littleton*.[21] It was brought over by the Normans. They used the old French "estoupail." That meant a bung or cork by which you stopped something from coming out. It was in common use in our courts when they carried on all their proceedings in Norman-French. Littleton writes in the law-French of his day (15th century) using the words "pur ceo que le baron est estoppe a dire," meaning simply that the husband is *stopped* from saying something.

From an early date the common law recognised forms of estoppel by which a person who had made a statement of fact, on which the other had relied, was estopped from denying the truth of his statement in his dealing with that other: it was often described as a rule of evidence,[22] by which a party would not be permitted to lead evidence to contradict his own representation in an action by or against the party to whom he had made the representation and who had relied on it—had changed his position in some way, on the faith of the representation, to his detriment. *Estoppel by deed*[23] and *estoppel by representation* are ancient

---

Cooke, *The Modern Law of Estoppel*; Dawson and Pearce, pp. 29–36, 97–9, 144–5, 161–3; Snell, chap. 10; [1981] Conv 347 (P. N. Todd); [1983] CLJ 257 (M. P. Thompson); (1986) 49 MLR 741 (J. Dewar); (1984) 100 LQR 376 (S. Moriarty); (1994) 14 LS 147 (S. Baughen); (1995) 58 MLR 637 (G. Battersby); (1997) 17 LS 258 (E. Cooke); [1998] 18 LS 360 (A. Robinson); (1998) 58 MLR 637 (G. Battersby); Sir Christopher Slade, *The Informal Creation of Interests in Land* (1984) Child & Co Oxford Lecture.

[18] See Halsbury, vol. 16(2) (2003 reissue); Cooke, *The Modern Law of Estoppel*.

[19] *Crabb v Arun District Council* [1976] Ch 179 at 193, M & B p. 659, per SCARMAN LJ; *Amalgamated Investment and Property Co Ltd v Texas Commerce International Bank Ltd* [1982] QB 84 at 103, per ROBERT GOFF J; affd [1982] QB 84; (1982) 79 LSG 662 (P. Matthews); *Pacol Ltd v Trade Lines Ltd and R/I Sif IV* [1982] 1 Lloyd's Rep 456; for Australian developments, see *Waltons Stores (Interstate) Ltd v Maher* (1988) 164 CLR 387; (1988) 104 LQR 362 (A. Duthie); *Commonwealth of Australia v Verwayen* (1990) 95 ALR 321 at 331–2, per MASON CJ; at 333, per DEANE J, discussed by HOBHOUSE LJ in *Sledmore v Dalby* (1996) 72 P & CR 196 at 208, M & B p. 650.

[20] *McIlkenny v Chief Constable of the West Midlands* [1980] QB 283 at 316–17. The case itself raised a question about estoppel *per rem judicatam*.   [21] 19th edn, 1832, vol. II, s. 667, 352a.

[22] *Low v Bouverie* [1891] 3 Ch 82 at 105, 112.

[23] A statement of fact made by a party in a deed cannot be challenged by that party as against the other party to the deed. Cf a "tenancy by estoppel", where a person purports to grant a lease when he has no legal estate; once both parties have acted on the assumption that the deed created a tenancy, neither is allowed to deny to the other that their relationship has all the incidents of the lease: p. 217, ante.

forms of estoppel within this principle. However, the common law only recognised an estoppel based on a representation, or assumption,[24] of present fact, and not of intention or promise,[25] but equity has extended the principles of estoppel into a wider arena. Early authority can be found for *promissory estoppel*,[26] but it was not generally recognised until the judgment of DENNING J in the *High Trees* case in 1947.[27] However, the role played by promissory estoppel in English law is still limited: it can be used to vary an existing contract, but not to create new obligations.[28] By contrast, *proprietary estoppel* has been actively developed by the courts and is now recognised as a mechanism through which property rights can be created and enforced.

B The Development of Proprietary Estoppel

The courts of equity recognised a doctrine of "encouragement and acquiescence" which has recently been treated as a type of estoppel and is now called proprietary estoppel. The early cases dealt almost exclusively with situations in which a landlord encouraged the occupier of his land to believe that the latter held under a lease.[29] The principle was explained in a well-known and generally accepted dictum in a dissenting speech of Lord KINGSDOWN:[30]

If a man, under a verbal agreement with a landlord for a certain interest in land, or, what amounts to the same thing, under an expectation, created or encouraged by the landlord, that he shall have a certain interest, takes possession of such land, with the consent of the landlord, and upon the faith of such promise or expectation, with the knowledge of the landlord, and without objection by him, lays out money upon the land, a court of equity will compel the landlord to give effect to such promise or expectation.

In *Willmott v Barber*[31] FRY J set out the requirements in more detail:

It has been said that the acquiescence which will deprive a man of his legal rights must amount to fraud, and in my view that is an abbreviated statement of a very true proposition. A man is not to be deprived of his legal rights unless he has acted in such a way as would make it fraudulent for him to set up those rights.

What, then, are the elements or requisites necessary to constitute fraud of that description? In the first place the plaintiff must have made a mistake as to his legal rights. Secondly, the plaintiff must have expended some money or must have done some act (not necessarily upon the defendant's land) on

---

[24] *Estoppel by convention*: where parties to a transaction act on an assumed state of facts or law, the assumption being either shared by them both or made by one and acquiesced in by the other, but as long as the assumption is communicated by each party to the other, then each is estopped from denying the assumed facts or law if it would be unjust to allow him to go back on the assumption: *Republic of India v Indian Steamship Co Ltd (No 2)* [1998] AC 878 at 913. This bears a strong similarity to the equitable principles of the "common intention" constructive trust: pp. 473 et seq, ante.

[25] *Jordan v Money* (1854) 5 HL Cas 185 at 214–15, 226–7.

[26] *Hughes v Metropolitan Rly Co* (1877) 2 App Cas 439.

[27] *Central London Property Trust Ltd v High Trees House Ltd* [1947] KB 130.

[28] *Combe v Combe* [1951] 2 KB 215; *Baird Textiles Holdings Ltd v Marks and Spencer plc* [2002] 1 All ER (Comm) 737 at [55]; it can be used only as a "shield". By contrast, it has been used to found a cause of action to remedy the non-performance of a promise unsupported by consideration—as a "sword"—in the law of the United States: American Law Institute, *Restatement of the Law (2d), Contracts* (1981), para. 90; and Australia: *Waltons Stores (Interstate) Ltd v Maher* (1988) 164 CLR 387. See generally Anson, pp. 118–24.

[29] *Huning v Ferrers* (1710) Gilb Ch 85; *Stiles v Cowper* (1748) 3 Atk 692; *East India Co v Vincent* (1740) 2 Atk 83; *Jackson v Cator* (1800) 5 Ves 688.   [30] *Ramsden v Dyson and Thornton* (1866) LR 1 HL 129 at 170.

[31] (1880) 15 Ch D 96 at 105–6.

the faith of his mistaken belief. Thirdly, the defendant, the possessor of the legal right, must know of the existence of his own right which is inconsistent with the right claimed by the plaintiff. If he does not know of it he is in the same position as the plaintiff, and the doctrine of acquiescence is founded upon conduct with a knowledge of your legal rights. Fourthly, the defendant, the possessor of the legal right, must know of the plaintiff's mistaken belief of his rights. If he does not, there is nothing which calls upon him to assert his own rights. Lastly, the defendant, the possessor of the legal right, must have encouraged the plaintiff in his expenditure of money or in the other acts which he has done, either directly or by abstaining from asserting his legal right. Where all these elements exist, there is fraud of such a nature as will entitle the Court to restrain the possessor of the legal right from exercising it, but, in my judgment, nothing short of this will do.

C The Modern Law of Proprietary Estoppel

Building on these early cases, the courts have constructed a modern doctrine of proprietary estoppel. In *Crabb v Arun District Council*[32] SCARMAN LJ made clear that the issues in such a claim must be addressed systematically:

If the plaintiff has any right, it is an equity arising out of the conduct and relationship of the parties. In such a case I think it is now well settled law that the court, having analysed and assessed the conduct and relationship of the parties, has to answer three questions. First, is there an equity established? Secondly, what is the extent of the equity, if one is established? And, thirdly, what is the relief appropriate to satisfy the equity?

(1) Establishing the Equity

The first question, in a claim based on proprietary estoppel, is therefore whether the claimant can establish an equity. The general principle is that where one party (A) makes a representation or promise to another party (B) to the effect that B has or shall have an interest in, or right over, A's property, or acquiesces in B's mistaken belief that he has or shall have such an interest or right, then if A intends B to act in reliance to his detriment on the representation, promise or mistaken belief, and B does so act in reliance, equity may intervene to prevent (*estop*) A from asserting his own strict legal rights to his property.

(a) Unconscionability

In deciding whether an equity is established, the five probanda (as they have been called) set out in *Willmott v Barber* have been listed and applied in some cases[33] and ignored in others. The modern cases show a preference for a much broader approach based on the defendant's unconscionable behaviour. In *Taylors Fashions Ltd v Liverpool Victoria Trustees Co Ltd*,[34]

---

[32] [1976] Ch 179 at 193, M & B p. 659.

[33] *E and L Berg Ltd v Grey* (1979) 253 EG 473 (where the plaintiff failed because he was unable to satisfy the first and fifth requirements); *Crabb v Arun District Council* [1976] Ch 179, M & B p. 659. See also the approval of the probanda in *Kammins Ballrooms Co Ltd v Zenith Investments (Torquay) Ltd* [1971] AC 850 at 884, per Lord DIPLOCK, and their application in detail by Jonathan Parker QC in *Coombes v Smith* [1986] 1 WLR 808; *Matharu v Matharu* (1994) 68 P & CR 93 (where majority of CA somewhat liberally applied the five probanda); (1995) 58 MLR 412 (P. Milne). See also *Gloucestershire County Council v Farrow* [1983] 2 All ER 1031; *Jones v Stones* [1999] 1 WLR 1739 (no acquiescence where delay in complaining about acts of trespass in using wall to place flower pots thereon and to support an oil tank).

[34] [1982] QB 133n, M & B p. 627. OLIVER J approved at 151 the broad test (applied by CA in *Shaw v Applegate* [1977] 1 WLR 970) of "whether in the circumstances the conduct is unconscionable without the

OLIVER J held that, contrary to the requirements of FRY J, proprietary estoppel is not restricted to cases where the defendant knows his rights, and that it is not possible to formulate strict and rigid rules:[35]

The more recent cases indicate that the application of the *Ramsden v Dyson* principle—whether you call it proprietary estoppel, estoppel by acquiescence or estoppel by encouragement is really immaterial—requires a very much broader approach which is directed rather at ascertaining whether, in particular individual circumstances, it would be unconscionable for a party to be permitted to deny that which, knowingly, or unknowingly, he has allowed or encouraged another to assume to his detriment than to inquiring whether the circumstances can be fitted within the confines of some preconceived formula serving as a universal yardstick for every form of unconscionable behaviour.

The effect of this approach is that the court now regards the five probanda no longer as rigid criteria to be satisfied, but as being "guidelines which will probably prove to be the necessary and essential guidelines, to assist the court to decide the question whether it is unconscionable for the plaintiffs to assert their legal rights by taking advantage of the defendant".[36] OLIVER J suggested that the five probanda might be necessary where the defendant has done no positive act, and merely "stands by without protest".[37]

Unconscionability was the basis of the decision of the Privy Council in *Lim Teng Huan v Ang Swee Chuan*,[38] where:

A built a house on land which he jointly owned with L. A and L entered into a contract, under which L acknowledged that he had no title to the house and agreed to exchange his half share in the land for unspecified land which he expected to obtain from the Government of Brunei. The contract was void for uncertainty. L claimed that he was the sole beneficial owner of A's share.

In rejecting L's claim, the Privy Council held that L was estopped from denying A's title to the whole of the land, and that he was entitled to compensation representing a half-share in the present value of the land without the house; on payment L should convey his half-share in the land to A. Lord BROWNE-WILKINSON said:[39]

The decision in *Taylors Fashions* showed that, in order to found a proprietary estoppel, it is not essential that the representor should have been guilty of unconscionable conduct in permitting the representee to assume that he could act as he did: it is enough if, in all the circumstances, it is unconscionable for the representor to go back on the assumption which he permitted the representee to make.

---

necessity of forcing those circumstances into a Procrustean bed constructed from some unalterable criteria". The statement in the text was approved by OLIVER LJ in *Habib Bank Ltd v Habib Bank AG Zurich* [1981] 1 WLR 1265 at 1285; (1981) 97 LQR 513; *Pridean Ltd v Forest Taverns Ltd* (1998) 75 P & CR 447. See also SCARMAN LJ in *Crabb v Arun District Council* [1976] Ch 179 at 195, M & B p. 659; (2004) 20 JCL (N. Hopkins).

[35] At 151.

[36] *Swallow Securities Ltd v Isenberg* [1985] 1 EGLR 132 at 134, per CUMMING-BRUCE LJ (no evidence to induce in the defendant an expectation that she had legal rights more extensive than was in fact the case).

[37] *Taylors Fashions Ltd v Liverpool Victoria Trustees Co Ltd* [1982] QB 133n at 146.

[38] [1992] 1 WLR 113; [1993] Conv 173 (S K. Goo); M & B p. 671; *Lloyds Bank plc v Carrick* [1996] 4 All ER 630; *Elitestone Ltd v Morris* (1995) 73 P & CR 259; *Price v Hartwell* [1996] EGCS 98 (joint owner licensee permitted to remain on premises so long as she made mortgage repayments, but must refund payments made by licensor after his severance of joint tenancy).   [39] At 117.

It is clear that unconscionability is the underlying principle; the representor will be held to his representation only if it would be unconscionable for him to go back on it. However the claimant must still show the basic indicia of representation, reliance and detriment; these indicia are necessary but not sufficient. The courts have begun to refine them in an attempt to avoid the uncertainty of palm tree justice[40] and to limit the creation of undocumented rights. Not only must the three indicia be present; they must also be treated as one. To quote ROBERT WALKER LJ:[41]

It is important to note at the outset that the doctrine of proprietary estoppel cannot be treated as subdivided into three or four watertight compartments... in the course of the oral argument in this court it repeatedly became apparent that the quality of the relevant assurances may influence the issue of reliance, that reliance and detriment are often intertwined, and that whether there is a distinct need for a "mutual understanding" may depend on how the other elements are formulated and understood.[42] Moreover the fundamental principle that equity is concerned to prevent unconscionable conduct permeates all the elements of the doctrine. In the end the court must look at the matter in the round.

(b) The representation

In some cases the estoppel has been based on a representation that the the representee has an interest in land; and it is upon the belief in that *existing* right that the representee has incurred some detriment in reliance on it.[43]

The doctrine is not, however, limited to acts done in reliance on a belief relating to an existing right, but extends to acts done in reliance on a belief that future rights will be granted; as, for example, where a step-daughter acted to her detriment in reliance on her belief that she would ultimately benefit by receiving the deceased's property under his will.[44] However, not every idle statement of intention by the testator or assumed

---

[40] In *Taylor v Dickens* [1998] 1 FLR 806, Judge Weeks QC said: "There is no equitable jurisdiction to hold a person to a promise simply because the court thinks it unfair, unconscionable or morally objectionable to go back on it. If there were such a jurisdiction, one might as well forget the law of contract and issue every civil judge with a portable palm tree. The days of justice varying with the size of the Lord Chancellor's foot would have returned." See further *Jennings v Rice* [2003] 1 P & CR 8, p. 823, post.

[41] *Gillett v Holt* [2001] Ch 210 at 225, p. 820, post.

[42] See *Gillett v Holt* [1998] 3 All ER 917 at 930, per CARNWATH J: "[There has to be] a mutual understanding which may be express or inferred from conduct—between promisor and promisee, both as to the content of the promise and as to what the promisee is doing, or may be expected to do, in reliance on it."

On the content of the promise, see *Orgee v Orgee* [1997] EGCS 152 (claim to agricultural tenancy on basis of estoppel refused in the absence of details as to crucial terms on which tenancy was expected to be based, for example, provisions for repairs and rent and rent review regime); cf *JT Developments Ltd v Quinn* (1990) 62 P & CR 33; (1998) 114 LQR 351 (M. Pawlowski).

[43] *Pascoe v Turner* [1979] 1 WLR 430, M & B, p. 667 ("the house is yours and everything in it"); [1979] Conv 379 (F. R. Crane); (1979) 42 MLR 574 (B. Suffrin); p. 843, post. See also *E R Ives Investment Ltd v High* [1967] 2 QB 379, M & B p. 665 (garage built by landowner on own land but in belief (acquiesced in by neighbour) that he had a right of way over neighbour's land). Sometimes the belief can be characterised either as one of a present right, or of a future right: see, e.g., *Taylors Fashions Ltd v Liverpool Victoria Trustees Co Ltd* [1982] QB 133n (expenditure on property by tenants in the erroneous belief that an option to renew the lease was valid—or, in other words, that they *would* be entitled to renew), but nothing turns on this distinction.

[44] *Re Basham* [1986] 1 WLR 1498; [1987] Conv 211 (J. E. Martin); [1987] CLJ 215 (D. J. Hayton); [1987] All ER Rev 156 (P. J. Clarke), 260 (C. H. Sherrin); (1988) 8 LS 92 (M. Davey); *Jennings v Rice* [2003] 1 P & CR 8, M & B p. 646, p. 823, post (claimant worked for deceased from 1970 until her death in 1997, in belief that he would inherit, but without specific promise as to the property that he would receive); cf *Layton v Martin* [1986] 2 FLR 227 (offer of "financial security" too vague; but see *Gillett v Holt*, p. 820, post, at 226, doubting whether *Layton v Martin* can be reconciled with *Re Basham*).

expectation of inheritance by the beneficiary will give rise to an estoppel. In the context of wills, which by their nature are revocable at any time by the testator, ROBERT WALKER LJ said in *Gillett v Holt*:[45]

The inherent revocability of testamentary dispositions (even if well understood by the parties . . .) is irrelevant to a promise or assurance that "all this will be yours" . . . Even when the promise or assurance is in terms linked to the making of a will . . . the circumstances may make clear that the assurance is more than a mere statement of present (revocable) intention, and is tantamount to a promise. *A-G of Hong Kong v Humphreys Estate (Queen's Gardens) Ltd*[46] . . . is essentially an example of a purchaser taking the risk, with his eyes open, of going into possession and spending money while his purchase remains expressly subject to contract . . .

It is notorious that some elderly persons of means derive enjoyment from the possession of testamentary power, and from dropping hints as to their intentions, without any question of an estoppel arising. But in this case Mr Holt's assurances were repeated over a long period, usually before the assembled company on special family occasions and some of them (such as "it was all going to be ours anyway" . . .) were completely unambiguous.

The claimant must therefore have a sufficiently certain belief that he has or will have a right before it is unconscionable to deny it to him.[47]

(c) Reliance. Detriment

In *Crabb v Arun District Council*:[48]

C owned a two acre plot of land which had access in the northern part (at point A) onto a lane owned by the defendants and thence along a right of way over that lane to the highway. In 1967 C decided to sell the northern and southern parts of the plot separately. Since he had no means of access from the southern part to the highway (except over the northern part), he made an oral agreement with the defendants under which they would give to him a further point of access (point B) together with a further right of way along the lane. No formal grant of the right of access or easement was made. As a result of the agreement, the defendants erected a fence between their land and C's land, and gates at the two access points. C, relying on this agreement, sold the northern part with the point A access to X, without reserving a right of way over it in favour of the retained southern part. In 1969 the defendants removed the gate at point B, and fenced the gap, thus making C's southern plot land-locked; further, they asked C to pay "close on £4,000 in order to provide him with that which their representative had undertaken to provide".[49]

The Court of Appeal held that the defendants were estopped from denying C's right of access at point B and the right of way therefrom to the highway, and, in view of the sterilisation of his land for a considerable period, the rights would be granted without any payment

---

45 [2001] Ch 210 at 227–8, M & B p. 637; [2000] CLJ 453 (M. Dixon); [2000] All ER Rev 244 (P. J. Clarke), 370 (C. H. Sherrin); [2001] Conv 78 (M. P. Thompson). See also *Taylor v Dickens* [1998] 1 FLR 806, where the claimant failed (his wife told him not to count his chickens before they were hatched); *Murphy v Burrows* [2005] 1 P & CR DG 3 (not unconscionable for deceased to have changed will).

46 [1987] AC 114, M & B p. 75.

47 *Parker v Parker* [2003] EWHC 1846 at [213] (9th Earl of Mansfield could not establish estoppel entitling him to possession for life of Shirburn Castle, Oxfordshire, based only on a false tradition that the right to live in the castle went with the Earldom); *Keelwalk Properties Ltd v Waller* [2002] 3 EGLR 79 (long-standing practice cannot justify assumption that it will continue in perpetuity).

48 [1976] Ch 179 at 193, M & B p. 659; (1976) 40 Conv (NS) 156 (F. R. Crane); (1976) 92 LQR 174 (P. S. Atiyah); 342 (P. J. Millett); (1995) 58 MLR 637 at p. 640 (G. Battersby).

49 [1976] Ch 179 at 191, per LAWTON LJ.

by him to the defendants.[50] This case shows a shift of emphasis from the paradigm case, where the representee has spent money on the land of the representor, to one where he has suffered detriment arising from some activity or inactivity on his part. The detriment to C was that, in reliance on the agreement with the defendants that he would have an access to and a right of way over the defendants' land, he refrained from expressly reserving an easement of way over the northern plot when he sold and conveyed it to X.[51]

The doctrine was also widened in *Greasley v Cooke*[52] in connection with the burden of proof. In that case the Court of Appeal held that, once there is proof that a representation has been made that was likely to influence the representee, and made with the intention that it should influence him, the onus shifts to the representor to prove that the representee did not rely on it. It spite of this rule, however, the basic requirement of detriment remains unimpaired. As DUNN LJ said in that case:[53]

> There is no doubt that for proprietary estoppel to arise the person claiming must have incurred expenditure or otherwise have prejudiced himself or acted to his detriment.

And there must be a sufficient link between the detrimental reliance and the interest which is claimed. In *Brinnand v Ewens*,[54] NOURSE LJ said:

---

[50] See *Crabb v Arun District Council (No 2)* (1976) 121 SJ 86 where C was refused an inquiry as to damages. See also *Salvation Army Trustee Co Ltd v West Yorkshire Metropolitan County Council* (1980) 41 P & CR 179 (where proprietary estoppel was extended to the *disposal* of an interest in land where the disposal was closely linked by an arrangement that also involved the acquisition of an interest in land); discussed in *A-G of Hong Kong v Humphreys Estate (Queen's Gardens) Ltd* [1987] AC 114 at 126, 127.

[51] See also *Lloyd v Dugdale* [2002] 2 P & CR 13 at [36]–[38] (detriment consisted in lost opportunity to purchase alternative premises).

[52] [1980] 1 WLR 1306, M & B p. 643. This test was taken from the similar rule elsewhere, under which the court is entitled to infer, as a matter of *fact*, the representee's reliance from the (objective) materiality of the statement—that it was "calculated" to induce reliance; see, e.g., *Smith v Chadwick* (1882) 20 Ch D 27 at 44, per JESSEL MR (proof of reliance in the tort of deceit).

[53] At 1313. See *Dann v Spurrier* (1802) 7 Ves 231 at 235–6, per Lord ELDON LC, cited in *Taylors Fashions Ltd v Liverpool Victoria Trustees Co Ltd* [1982] QB 133n at 156; *Christian v Christian* (1981) 131 NLJ 43; *Watkins v Emslie* (1982) 261 EG 1192; *Watts v Story* [1983] CA Transcript 319, M & B p. 644, where DUNN LJ explains the observations of Lord DENNING MR in *Greasley v Cooke*; *Coombes v Smith* [1986] 1 WLR 808 (no detriment where wife left husband and went to live with lover and their child); [1986] CLJ 394 (D. J. Hayton); *Hammersmith and Fulham London Borough Council v Top Shop Centres Ltd* [1990] Ch 237 (failure to negotiate for grant of new lease or to apply for relief against forfeiture held to be detriment; reliance presumed); *Wayling v Jones* (1993) 69 P & CR 170; [1994] LS 15 (M. Halliwell) (requirement of promise and "conduct of such a nature that inducement may be inferred" per BALCOMBE LJ at 175); (1995) 111 LQR 389 (E. Cooke); [1995] Conv 409 (C. J. Davis); [1996] 16 LS 218 (A. Lawson); *Walton v Bell* [1994] NPC 55A (working long hours for low wages held to give rise to inference that it was induced by the promise being made and reliance on it); *Matharu v Matharu* (1994) 68 P & CR 93 (son's expenditure in improving property held to be detrimental reliance on part of his wife); [1995] 7 CFLQ 59 (G. Battersby); [1995] Conv 61 (M. Welstead); *Durant v Heritage* [1994] EGCS 134 (legal owner must be unable to prove that claimant, in relying on the belief, did not rely on it to his prejudice or detriment); *Gan v Wood* [1998] EGCS 77 (expenditure not amounting to more than minor detriment held not to suffice); *Century (UK) Ltd SA v Clibbery* [2004] All ER (D) 541 (Jul) (household chores of answering telephone calls and video-recording programmes not sufficient detriment).

[54] [1987] 2 EGLR 67 (expenditure incurred on work "done to make the home more comfortable"). See also *Bristol and West Building Society v Henning* [1985] 1 WLR 778, where, in a case concerning the priority between the beneficial interest of a spouse and the rights of a mortgagee, BROWNE-WILKINSON LJ said at 782, that "in the absence of express agreement, an intention or assumption [that a party other than the legal owner should have a beneficial interest in the property] must be proved in order to found the lesser interest of an irrevocable licence conferring a property interest: see *Re Sharpe* [1980] 1 WLR 219, p. 839, post". See also *Paddington*

The acting [to the detriment] must have taken place in the belief either that the claimant owned a sufficient interest in the property to justify the expenditure or that he would obtain such an interest.[55]

But it must always be remembered that the purpose of identifying the detrimental reliance by the claimant is to justify finding that it would be inequitable for the defendant to insist on his strict rights to the property and thereby to deny the claimant the right to it that he believed he had, or would obtain. As ROBERT WALKER LJ said in *Gillett v Holt*:[56]

The authorities show that detriment is not a narrow or technical concept. The detriment need not consist of the expenditure of money or other quantifiable financial detriment, so long as it is something substantial. The requirement must be approached as part of a broad inquiry as to whether repudiation of an assurance is or is not unconscionable in all the circumstances.... There must be sufficient causal link between the assurance relied on and the detriment asserted. The issue of detriment must be judged at the moment when the person who has given the assurance seeks to go back on it. Whether the detriment is sufficiently substantial is to be tested by whether it would be unjust or inequitable to allow the assurance to be disregarded—that is, again, the essential test of unconscionability. The detriment alleged must be pleaded and proved.

(2) Satisfying the Equity. The Remedy

In *Crabb v Arun District Council*[57] SCARMAN LJ's second and third questions were: what is the extent of the equity? And what is the relief appropriate to satisfy it? These two questions can be taken together, since they both concern the question of what remedy the courts should award in an established case of proprietary estoppel.

(a) *The range of available remedies*

As we shall,[58] see in the context of licences the remedies awarded by the court have ranged from simply negative protection, preventing the licensor from revoking a licence,[59] to positive protection through the transfer of the fee simple to the licensee.[60] The courts have also ordered that the party in whose favour an equity arises by estoppel be granted other interests in land, such as an easement[61] or a lease;[62] or that his expenditure be reimbursed rather than that he be given a positive interest in the land;[63] and have also on occasion held that, although the equity was established, it had either expired before the hearing or for other reasons no remedy was necessary or appropriate.[64] The range of remedies which the

---

Building Society v Mendelsohn (1985) 50 P & CR 244; [1985] CLJ 354 (M. Welstead); *Grant v Edwards* [1986] Ch 638 at 657.

[55] Adapted from *Snell's Equity* (29th edn), p. 575.

[56] [2001] Ch 210 at 232, referring to the judgment of SLADE LJ in *Jones v Watkins* (CA, 26 November 1987); and applied by Sir Christopher SLADE in *Lloyd v Dugdale* [2002] 2 P & CR 13 at [31].

[57] [1976] Ch 179.

[58] Pp. 842 et seq, post. For a useful of examples of remedies, see Snell, pp. 641–3, M & B p. 652–4.

[59] *Inwards v Baker* [1965] 2 QB 29, M & B p. 654.

[60] Either without compensation: *Pascoe v Turner* [1979] 1 WLR 431, M & B p. 667, supra; *Dillwyn v Llewelyn* (1862) 4 De GF & J 517; *Voyce v Voyce* (1991) 62 P & CR 290; or with compensation: *Lim Teng Huan v And Swee Chuan* [1992] 1 WLR 113, M & B p. 671.

[61] *Crabb v Arun District Council*, supra; *E R Ives Investment Ltd v High* [1967] 2 QB 379, M & B p. 665.

[62] *Griffiths v Williams* (1977) 248 EG 947

[63] *Dodsworth v Dodsworth* (1973) 228 EG 1115; M & B p. 671, p. 844, post.

[64] *Sledmore v Dalby* (1996) 72 P & CR 196, M & B p. 650 (equity had expired where licensee had enjoyed eighteen years' free occupation, had little need for the property and the licensor was in serious financial difficulty); *Appleby v Cowley* The Times, 14 April 1982, M & B p. 678 (by the time the claim was made, plaintiff

courts have at their disposal in the case of an established equity by estoppel is very wide, including the award of both proprietary and personal rights.[65] It is therefore important to know by what principles they will select the appropriate remedy.

(b) Selecting the appropriate remedy[66]

In selecting the remedy, the court asks what is now "the minimum equity to do justice to the plaintiff?"[67] And in doing so, the court has a discretion. But the fact that the courts have adopted a flexible approach in their selection of remedies does not mean that the discretion is not based on principle:[68] "the court must take a principled approach, and cannot exercise a completely unfettered discretion according to the individual judge's notion of what is fair in any particular case." The principles underlying the exercise of discretion, and their application in earlier cases, were reviewed by the Court of Appeal in *Jennings v Rice*.[69] In that case:

J began to work as a part-time gardner for Mrs Royle in 1970. Over the years he did more for her, including taking her shopping and running errands. In the late 1980s Mrs Royle stopped paying him, but she provided a deposit of £2000 to enable J and his wife to buy a house, and told him that "he would be alright" and she would "see to it". J believed that he was going to receive all or part of Mrs Royle's property on her death, although nothing was put in writing, and none of Mrs Royle's assurances were specific. Mrs Royle became increasingly dependent on J, and from 1994 until her death in 1997 J spent almost every night on a sofa in her sitting room, and provided personal care for her and cared for the house and garden. Mrs Royle died intestate, with an estate worth £1.285m, including her house worth £435,000.

The trial judge awarded J £200,000 out of Mrs Royle's estate, on the basis of proprietary estoppel, holding that it was it was not appropriate to award him the full value of the benefit he expected to receive (the house and its furniture) because it was disproportionate and excessive. The cost of full-time nursing care of the kind provided by J was around £200,000; and he would probably need £150,000 to buy a home. The judge concluded that[70]

I do not think that he could complain that he had been unfairly treated if he had been left £ 200,000 in Mrs Royle's will. Most people would say that she would, at least, then have performed her promise to

---

barristers had had sufficient satisfaction for their expenditure on property occupied as chambers: "it may be a nice academic point whether the result is that no case of proprietary estoppel has been established, or whether it is that such a case has been established but no remedy should be granted": per MEGARRY V-C); *Savva v Costa* [1980] CA Transcript 723, M & B p. 678 (claim based on proprietary estoppel premature because defendant was not (yet) seeking to disturb her enjoyment of the property); *Uglow v Uglow* [2004] EWCA Civ 987, [2004] All ER (D) 472 (Jul); *Horton v Brandish* [2005] All ER (D) 460 (Jul) (equity excluded by representee's failure to pay agreed rent to representor, and his exclusion of representor from the property).

   [65] [2005] CLJ 449 (S. Bright and B. McFarlane).
   [66] (1999) 115 LQR 438 (S. Gardner), M & B p. 652, setting out four hypotheses for the court's discretion, and discussed in *Jennings v Rice*, infra; (1997) 17 LS 258 (E. Cooke).
   [67] *Crabb v Arun District Council* [1976] Ch 179 at 198, per SCARMAN LJ. The court considers the facts at the date of the hearing, and does not limit its inquiry to what would have been unconscionable when the representation was made: n. 64, supra.
   [68] *Jennings v Rice* [2003] 1 P & CR 8 at [43], per ROBERT WALKER LJ, M & B p. 646; (2002) 118 LQR 319 (M. Pawlowski); [2003] Conv 255 (M. P. Thompson).   [69] [2003] 1 P & CR 8.
   [70] Quoted by ALDOUS LJ: ibid., at [15].

see him all right. The quality of her assurance affects not only questions of belief, encouragement, reliance and detriment, but also unconscionability and the extent of the equity.

This was affirmed by the Court of Appeal, which took the opportunity to review the question of when it is appropriate to award a remedy which gives the claimant the full value of his expectation, and when it is appropriate to depart from that. The starting-point is the expectation, and not simply the value of the detrimental reliance incurred by the claimant in order to establish the equity.[71] But the court will not simply order a remedy which protects the expectation; it will consider also the value of the claimant's reliance, and whether an award of the expectation would be disproportionate. As ALDOUS LJ said:[72]

reliance and detriment are two of the requirements of proprietary estoppel and that the basis of the estoppel is, as Lord Denning MR said in *Crabb*'s case, the interposition of equity: thus the requirement of unconscionability. If the conscience of the court is involved, it would be odd that the amount of the award should be set rigidly at the sum expected by the claimant.

Where the claimant's expectation is specific, the court may well order that the expectation be fulfilled.[73] But in a case where the expectation is uncertain, or disproportionate, it may well be appropriate to depart from that and to order a more limited remedy:[74]

there is a category of case in which the benefactor and the claimant have reached a mutual understanding which is in reasonably clear terms but does not amount to a contract. I have already referred to the typical case of a carer who has the expectation of coming into the benefactor's house, either outright or for life. In such a case the court's natural response is to fulfil the claimant's expectations. But if the claimant's expectations are uncertain, or extravagant, or out of all proportion to the

---

[71] [2003] 1 P & CR 8 at [30], per ALDOUS LJ and [54], per ROBERT WALKER LJ, contrasting the preference shown by the Australian courts for compensating only the reliance loss.

[72] Ibid., at [21]. See also at [49], per ROBERT WALKER LJ. *Commonwealth of Australia v Verwayen* (1990) 95 ALR 321 at 331, per MASON CJ; followed in *Sledmore v Dalby* (1996) 72 P & CR 196 at 208, M & B p. 650, per HOBHOUSE LJ (suggesting that "in many of its applications the equitable doctrine of proprietary estoppel bears a close relationship to restitutionary principles", under which the remedy is awarded to prevent unjust enrichment of the defendant at the claimant's expense).

[73] Or even exceeded: [2003] 1 P & CR 8 at [21] per ALDOUS LJ, referring to *Crabb v Arun District Council*, [1976] Ch 179 (claimant expected to receive easement in return for payment; court ordered easement without payment); but the expectation is normally the maximum extent of the equity: *Parker v Parker* [2003] NPC 94 at [210], and the claimant cannot be compensated for losses that do not flow from the reliance on the representation: *Wormall v Wormall* [2004] EWCA Civ 1643, The Times, 1 December 2004 (representation that daughter could occupy property as long as it continued to be family farm; disturbance costs of moving earlier than expected could not be compensated because the relocation "was always on the cards": at [39], per JONATHAN PARKER LJ). Where "the assurances, and the claimant's reliance on them, have a consensual character falling not far short of an enforceable contract . . . the consensual element of what has happened suggests that the claimant and the benefactor probably regarded the expected benefit and the accepted detriment as being (in a general, imprecise way) equivalent, or at any rate not obviously disproportionate": at [45], per ROBERT WALKER LJ. This is close to the principle of contract law that the courts will not investigate the adequacy of consideration as long as there is a bargain between the parties: Anson, pp. 97–8.

[74] [2003] 1 P & CR 8 at [50], per ROBERT WALKER LJ. His Lordship declined to give a comprehensive list, or hierarchy, of factors relevant to the court's discretion, but included (at [52]) the claimant's misconduct; particularly oppressive conduct on the part of the defendant; the court's recognition that it cannot compel people who have fallen out to live peaceably together, so that there may be a need for a clean break; alterations in the benefactor's assets and circumstances, especially where the benefactor's assurances have been given, and the claimant's detriment has been suffered, over a long period of years; the likely effect of taxation; and (to a limited degree) the other claims (legal or moral) on the benefactor or his or her estate. See also *Ottey v Grundy* [2003] EWCA Civ 1176, [2003] All ER (D) 05 (Aug), [2004] Conv 137 (M. P. Thompson); *Murphy v Burrows* [2005] 1 P & CR DG 3 (lack of proportionality).

detriment which the claimant has suffered, the court can and should recognise that the claimant's equity should be satisfied in another (and generally more limited) way.

D The Limits of Proprietary Estoppel

In English law the doctrine of proprietary estoppel has been limited to land. In *Western Fish Products Ltd v Penwith District Council*, MEGAW LJ said:[75]

We know of no case, and none has been cited to us, in which the principle set out in *Ramsden v Dyson*... has been applied otherwise than to rights and interests created in and over land. It may extend to other forms of property[76]... In our judgment there is no good reason for extending the principle further.

It may well be related to other doctrines of equity under which property rights are created in one who does not have legal ownership;[77] but the English courts have not absorbed it into a larger general doctrine within the law of property; nor have they absorbed it into a larger general doctrine of estoppel.[78]

E Proprietary Estoppel as an Interest in Land

We have seen that there are two stages in the doctrine of proprietary estoppel. First, the equity arises, as a result of one party's representation (or acquiescence) and the other party's reliance to his detriment; and second, the court grants a remedy to satisfy the equity.

There is controversy as to the status of the right before the court decides on the remedy and makes the order.[79] It may be either inchoate, that is to say, it is not a property right until the court makes the order, and therefore cannot bind third parties until that happens. Or it may be choate and is a property right at the earlier stage.

There is authority in favour of the second view. In *E R Ives Investment Ltd v High*:[80]

the defendant, High, built a house on his own land. His neighbour then erected a block of flats whose foundations encroached on High's land. They agreed orally that the foundations should remain and that High should have a right of way across the neighbour's yard. High, relying on this agreement, built a garage on his own land so sited that it could only be approached across the yard. The neighbour sold the block of flats to a purchaser, who resold it to the plaintiffs, expressly subject to High's right of way.

---

[75] [1981] 2 All ER 204 at 218 (no estoppel where owner spent money on his own land in the expectation encouraged by a local authority that he would acquire a planning permission); *West Middlesex Golf Club Ltd v Ealing London Borough Council* (1993) 68 P & CR 461 at 468.

[76] *Re Foster* [1938] 3 All ER 610 (life insurance policy); *Moorgate Mercantile Co Ltd v Twitchings* [1976] QB 225 at 242, per Lord DENNING MR.

[77] See esp. *Re Basham* [1986] 1 WLR 1498 at 1503–4, per Nugee QC (comparing proprietary estoppel to secret trusts and mutual wills); J. Cartwright, in Getzler (ed.) *Rationalizing Property, Equity and Trusts*, chap. 3. The relationship between proprietary estoppel and constructive trusts is considered infra.

[78] For such a development in Australia, see *Waltons Stores (Interstate) Ltd v Maher* (1988) 164 CLR 387 (assimilating proprietary and promissory estoppel, which in England are still kept separate: p. 816, n. 28, ante).

[79] (1990) 106 LQR 87 at 97; [1990] Conv 370 at 380 (D. Hayton); [1991] Conv 36 at 45; (1995) 58 MLR 637 at 642 (G. Battersby); (1992) 22 Fam Law 72 (P. Clarke); [1994] 14 LS 147 at 154 (S. Baughen); [1996] Conv 34 (J. Howell), 193 (C. Davis); [2003] CLJ 661 (B. McFarlane). On the question of whether the equity is overreachable, see p. 848, post.   [80] [1967] 2 QB 379; (1967) 31 Conv (NS) 332 (F. R. Crane).

The right of way was not a legal interest since it had not been formally created; nor had it been registered as an equitable easement under the Land Charges Act 1925.[81]

The Court of Appeal held that High had a right by estoppel, which, not being registrable as a land charge, was binding on the plaintiffs who had purchased the legal estate of the licensor with actual notice.[82]

In unregistered land the right has been held to bind a purchaser with notice,[83] or a donee whether he has notice or not.[84] In registered land under the Land Registration Act 1925 it was held to be an interest capable of being an overriding interest under section 70(1)(g) as long as the person with the benefit of the equity was in actual occupation.[85] This is confirmed by section 116 of the Land Registration Act 2002,[86] which provides that

It is hereby declared for the avoidance of doubt that, in relation to registered land, . . .

(a) an equity by estoppel . . .

has effect from the time the equity arises as an interest capable of binding successors in title (subject to the rules about the effect of dispositions on priority).

The equity, if it is to have priority over a registered disposition for valuable consideration, must therefore be protected by notice in the register[87] or, if it is not registered, it may take effect as an overriding interest if the beneficiary is in discoverable actual occupation.[88]

But what the purchaser is bound by—in the sense of the scope of the claimant's rights (if any) to the land—is not yet at that moment capable of being ascertained. The remedy might be the grant of an estate or interest in the land; but it might not be.[89] And the nature of the discretion exercised by the court in deciding on the remedy, although a principled discretion,[90] emphasises the uncertainty in the remedy until the court has considered the facts at the time of the hearing. Almost all cases which have come before the courts have involved the original parties; we therefore await further clarification of the position of the claimant as against the purchaser.[91]

---

[81] Land Charges Act 1972, s. 2(5), Class D (iii); p. 941, post.

[82] The CA also relied on the doctrine of *Halsall v Brizell* [1957] Ch 169, that he who takes the benefit must accept the burden; p. 664, ante.

[83] *Duke of Beaufort v Patrick* (1853) 17 Beav 60, 78; *Inwards v Baker* [1965] 2 QB 29, 37; *E R Ives Investment Ltd v High* [1967] 2 QB 379. In *Lloyds Bank plc v Carrick* [1996] 4 All ER 630, 642, MORRITT LJ commented that "[i]n the circumstances it is unnecessary to consider further the submission . . . to the effect that a proprietary estoppel cannot give rise to an interest in land capable of binding successors in title. This interesting argument will have to await another day, though it is hard to see how in this court it can surmount the hurdle constituted by the decision of this court in *Ives v High*".

[84] *Voyce v Voyce* (1991) 62 P & CR 290 at 296 (claimant equitable owner before the conveyance), per DILLON LJ; see also *Sen v Headley* [1991] Ch 425 at 440.

[85] *Brocket Hall (Jersey) Ltd v Clague* [1998] CLY 4367; *Habermann v Koehler (No 2)* The Times, 22 November 2000; *Lloyd v Dugdale* [2002] 2 P & CR 167; (2002) 146 SJ 90 (M. Pawlowski).

[86] See Law Commission Consultative Document: Land Registration in the Twenty-First Century (Law Com No. 254), paras. 3.33–3.36; [2003] CLJ 661 (B. McFarlane).   [87] LRA 2002, s. 29.

[88] Ibid, Sch. 3, para. 2.   [89] P. 822, ante.   [90] *Jennings v Rice* [2003] 1 P & CR 8.

[91] It is likely, however, that a court will take into account the particular circumstances of the purchaser— now the defendant in the claim—where such a case arises. It is already clear that the change in the original representor's circumstances is a relevant factor in determining the remedy to be awarded against him, and so the position of the purchaser as the present owner of the land should equally be relevant: *Sledmore v Dalby* (1996) 72 P & CR 196, M & B p. 650. For discussion of whether the original representor remains personally liable after disposal of the land, see [2005] Conv 14 (S. Bright and B. McFarlane).

It is clear, however, that an equity by estoppel is treated as having the character of an interest in property; and, at least in relation to registered land, the equity by estoppel and the "mere equity"[92] are treated identically in this respect by section 116 of the Land Registration Act 2002.[93] It may well be that an equity by estoppel is in the process of being accepted not simply as an equity—the right to an equitable remedy[94]—but as a new form of property in its own right. This, together with the conveyancing difficulties which arise from the acceptance of the proposition that an equity by estoppel can bind successors, are discussed later.[95]

---

[92] P. 814, ante.

[93] In this respect, the fact that an equity arising by estoppel can bind a purchaser is more problematic than the fact that a "mere equity" can. For in the case of a mere equity the nature of the right to which the purchaser is subject is more closely circumscribed, since an equity is generally defined by reference to the right to a particular equitable remedy (such as rescission or rectification) p. 813, ante.   [94] P. 812, ante.

[95] Pp. 846 et seq, post.

E. Licences

SUMMARY

23

LICENCES[1]

SUMMARY

As we have seen, a licence is essentially a permission to enter upon the land of another for an agreed purpose.[2] The permission justifies what would otherwise have been a trespass.[3] The main issue through the years has been first, whether the licensee is entitled to protection against eviction by the licensor, and, if so, whether that protection is effective also against third party transferees from the licensor. In both these issues, the availability of equitable remedies after the passing of the Supreme Court of Judicature Act 1875 played an important part, and developments in more recent years have revolutionised the position of the licensee. These come from the recognition, as relevant and applicable in this field, of the doctrine of proprietary estoppel, under which a licensee may be entitled, not only to protection from eviction, but also to a transfer of the interest or estate in the land which the licensor, by his acts or statements, had led the licensee to expect to receive.[4] Further, licensees have sometimes been protected by finding that a constructive trust arises in their favour, and this jurisdiction to find a constructive trust has been widened and developed in recent years.[5]

---

[1] See generally M & B, chap. 9; Dawson and Pearce, *Licences Relating to the Occupation or Use of Land*; (1954) 70 LQR 326 (Lord EVERSHED). [2] P. 598, ante.

[3] *Thomas v Sorrell* (1673) Vaugh 330 at 351, per VAUGHAN CJ. [4] Pp. 814, et seq, post.

[5] Pp. 839, et seq, post.

The facts in the cases will show the wide variety of circumstances in which questions of the protection of licensees can arise. They range from a visit to the grandstand at Doncaster race-course in 1845 to the provision of a house for a mistress in more modern times. The courts have been astute to adapt the law of licences to solve problems arising from the occupation of a quasi-matrimonial home.

I The Licensee at Common Law

Licences at common law may be divided into three categories:

A Bare or Gratuitous Licence

A bare or gratuitous licence is a mere permission for the licensee to enter upon the licensor's land, as for instance when permission is given to play cricket on a field. This permission may be withdrawn at any time by the licensor, although the licensee cannot be treated as a trespasser until a reasonable time after notice that the licence has been or will be withdrawn.[6]

B Licence Coupled with a Grant or Interest

A licence coupled with a grant or interest, on the other hand, may be irrevocable. It is said to be *coupled with a grant or interest* when the licensee, having been granted a definite proprietary interest in the land or in chattels lying on the land, is given permission to enter in order that he may enjoy or exploit the interest. Such a licence, as distinct from a *bare* licence, is of this nature if given to a man who is entitled to chattels,[7] or to growing timber[8] or to game on the land.[9] There are here two separate matters—the grant and the licence. "But a licence to hunt in a man's park and to carry away the deer killed to his own use; to cut down a tree in a man's ground and to carry it away the next day after to his own use, are licences as to the acts of hunting and cutting down the tree; but as to the carrying away of the deer killed and the tree cut they are grants."[10]

Such a licence is not effective at common law unless the grant is formally valid. Thus a grant merely by writing of a right to shoot and carry away game, coupled with a licence to enter the land, is ineffective, since a deed is necessary at common law for the grant of a profit à prendre.[11] But under the doctrine of *Walsh v Lonsdale*[12] a specifically enforceable contract to grant an interest is treated in equity as if the formalities required by law had been

---

[6] *R v Doncaster MBC ex p Braim* (1989) 57 P & CR 1 at 15–16; *E & L Berg Homes Ltd v Grey* (1979) 253 EG 473, applying to a bare licence the principles applicable in this respect to contractual licences in *Minister of Health v Bellotti* [1944] KB 298, p. 833, n. 19, post.   [7] *Wood v Manley* (1839) 11 Ad & El 34.

[8] *James Jones & Sons Ltd v Earl of Tankerville* [1909] 2 Ch 440.

[9] *Frogley v Earl of Lovelace* (1859) John 333. See also *Vaughan v Hampson* (1875) 33 LT 15 (right of solicitor to attend a creditors' meeting), described as a "curiosity" in *Hounslow LBC v Twickenham Garden Developments Ltd* [1971] Ch 233 at 254.   [10] *Thomas v Sorrell* (1673) Vaugh 330 at 551, per VAUGHAN CJ.

[11] *Wood v Leadbitter* (1845) 13 M & W 838, M & B p. 597.   [12] Pp. 877, post.

observed. Thus a contract to grant a right of shooting over land, as between the parties, is as effective as an actual grant by way of deed;[13] to be enforceable against third parties it must be protected by a notice in the register[14] or, in unregistered land, registered as an estate contract under the Land Charges Act 1972.[15] Where the licence is coupled with a grant or interest, the licensor cannot revoke it if the licensee is thereby prevented from exploiting the interest that the licensor has granted to him.[16] The revocability of the licence therefore depends upon the construction of the grant.

C Contractual Licence

A contractual licence is a licence supported by consideration, as for instance where the licensee buys a ticket for a race meeting or a theatre,[17] or where he is contractually entitled to the exclusive privilege of supplying refreshment in a theatre.[18] Even when it is revoked in accordance with the terms of the contract the licensee must be given a reasonable time to leave the premises.[19]

D Remedies for Wrongful Revocation

In considering the effect of these licences as between licensor and licensee, the common law drew a distinction between a mere licence, whether gratuitous or contractual, and a licence coupled with a grant.[20] We have seen that a licence coupled with a grant may be irrevocable. On the other hand the early cases[21] held that a mere licence may, at common law, be revoked at any moment, even where the licensee had entered by contract, and the revocation of the licence by the licensor was in breach of contract. The licence itself did not endure beyond the (wrongful) revocation: the licensee became a trespasser, and liable to be evicted. He had to be satisfied with a financial remedy for breach of contract.[22]

---

[13] *Frogley v Earl of Lovelace*, (1859) John 333.
[14] LRA 2002, s. 32. P. 973, post.   [15] LCA 1972, s. 2(4) Class C(iv); pp. 940–1, post.
[16] *Australian Blue Metal Ltd v Hughes* [1963] AC 74 at 94.
[17] *Wood v Leadbitter* (1845) 13 M & W 838; *Hurst v Picture Theatres Ltd* [1915] 1 KB 1.
[18] *Frank Warr & Co Ltd v LCC* [1904] 1 KB 713.
[19] *Minister of Health v Bellotti* [1944] KB 298; *Greater London Council v Jenkins* [1975] 1 WLR 155 at 158, per Lord Diplock; *Canadian Pacific Rly Co v R* [1931] AC 414; *Australian Blue Metal Ltd v Hughes* [1963] AC 74; *Wallshire Ltd v Advertising Sites Ltd* [1988] 2 EGLR 167; *Express Newspapers plc v Silverstone Circuits Ltd* The Times, 20 June 1989 (right to place advertisements on bridge at Woodcote Corner); *Re Hampstead Garden Suburb Institute* The Times, 13 April 1995 (nine months' notice given to school "for all purposes from four to four score" held to be inadequate by any standards of reasonableness; public nature of licensee's function, known to the licensor, taken into account); [1996] CLJ 229 (T. Kerbal). For the abandonment of a licence, see *Bone v Bone* [1992] EGCS 81 (no formalities are necessary: "it is enough that the parties have so conducted themselves that it ought to be inferred that they have mutually agreed to bring the contract to an end").
[20] For a doctrine of long standing, but little relied on, that a licence is irrevocable if it has been acted on, see *Webb v Paternoster* (1619) Palm 71; *Hounslow LBC v Twickenham Garden Developments Ltd* [1971] Ch 233 at 255; (1965) 29 Conv (NS) 19 (M. C. Cullity).
[21] *Wood v Leadbitter* (1845) 13 M & W 838; *Thompson v Park* [1944] KB 408.
[22] *Kerrison v Smith* [1897] 2 QB 445 (the first case to decide that an action will lie for damages for revoking a licence); *Tanner v Tanner* [1975] 1 WLR 1346, p. 835, post.

II Contractual Licence: the Intervention of Equity

The tide turned with the availability of equitable remedies after 1875. In *Hurst v Picture Theatres Ltd*:[23]

the plaintiff purchased a ticket[24] to attend the cinema. The proprietors, erroneously thinking that Hurst had not paid for the ticket, evicted him, using no more force than was reasonably necessary. Hurst successfully sued for damages for assault.

The matter was authoritatively settled by the House of Lords in *Winter Garden Theatre (London) Ltd v Millennium Productions Ltd*.[25] This case finally established that the rights of the parties to a contractual licence must be determined upon the proper construction of the contract. Their Lordships favoured the argument that, if on its construction a contractual licence is irrevocable, then, even though it is not coupled with a grant, its revocation in breach of the contract should be prevented where possible[26] by the grant of an injunction.[27] In other words, equity does what it can by means of a decree of injunction to preserve the sanctity of a bargain[28] and by that remedy it is prepared to restrain a revocation that would derogate from the right of occupation conferred by the contract. If the contract does not expressly state the time for which the licence is to last, a promise by the licensor must be implied that he will not revoke the permission in a manner contrary to the intention of the parties.[29] The exact scope of the implied promise, if any, must be ascertained in each case, for it will, of course, vary with the circumstances. For instance a spectator who buys a ticket for a theatre is a licensee with a right to occupy his seat until the spectacle is over;[30] a licence of the "front of the house rights" at a theatre cannot be revoked until a reasonable time has been afforded to the licensee for his withdrawal.[31] In those cases such as *Hurst v Picture*

---

23 [1915] 1 KB 1. See also *Cowell v Rosehill Racecourse Co Ltd* (1937) 56 CLR 605, M & B p. 598.

24 For 6d.

25 [1948] AC 173, M & B p. 602; for a critique of this case, see *Hounslow LBC v Twickenham Garden Developments Ltd* [1971] Ch 233 at 245 et seq; (1971) 87 LQR 309; *Mayfield Holdings Ltd v Moana Reef Ltd* [1973] 1 NZLR 309.

26 *Thompson v Park* [1944] KB 408 (where an injunction was refused to a licensee who "had been guilty at least of riot, affray, wilful damage, forcible entry and, perhaps, conspiracy", per GODDARD LJ at 409); *Brynowen Estates Ltd v Bourne* (1981) 131 NLJ 1212; cf *Williams v Staite* [1979] Ch 291 (effect of misbehaviour by estoppel licensee); *J Willis & Son v Willis* [1986] 1 EGLR 62, p. 846, post. See also *Ivory v Palmer* [1975] ICR 340 (licensee, whose occupation of premises was dependent on his employment, not protected when dismissed in breach of contract).

For a possession action under RSC Ord 113 by a licensee against a trespasser on the land which the licensee occupies, even though not in de facto occupation of it, see *Manchester Airport plc v Dutton* [2000] QB 133; [1999] Conv 535 (E. Paton and G. Seabourne); cf *Countryside Residential (North Thames) Ltd v Tugwell* [2000] 2 EGLR 59.

27 The House of Lords construed the licence as being revocable by the licensor, and so their views were obiter. The Court of Appeal, however, had construed it as irrevocable and had protected the licensee by granting an injunction against the licensor: [1946] 1 All ER 678 at 684, per Lord GREENE MR, M & B p. 603. For a full discussion of contractual licences, see MEGARRY J in *Hounslow LBC v Twickenham Garden Developments Ltd* [1971] Ch 233, where this approach was followed.

28 *Winter Garden Theatre (London) Ltd v Millennium Productions Ltd* [1948] AC 173 at 202, per Lord UTHWATT.   29 *Errington v Errington and Woods* [1952] 1 KB 290.

30 *Hurst v Picture Theatres Ltd* [1915] 1 KB 1.

31 *Winter Garden Theatre (London) Ltd v Millennium Productions Ltd* [1948] AC 173.

Theatres Ltd, where there is no time or opportunity to obtain an injunction, the court will presumably give judgment on the basis of what the rights of the parties would have been, had the grant of this remedy been practicable.

The injunction will last for the period of the contract or for such other period as the court thinks appropriate. The situation is simpler where, as in the *Winter Garden* case, there is an express contract. But the courts have, in some cases, including family or "mistress" situations, found the existence of a contractual licence where the evidence of the contract was of the flimsiest. Indeed, in *Tanner v Tanner*,[32] where the mistress had vacated the premises in obedience to an order of the lower court, and an injunction would have been sterile, Lord DENNING went so far as to say that the court should "imply a contract by him ... or if need be impose the equivalent of a contract by him".[33] Similarly, in *Hardwick v Johnson*[34] and *Chandler v Kerley*[35] contractual licences were found. In the latter case:

Mr and Mrs K jointly purchased a house intending it to be their matrimonial home, the mortgage payments being made by Mr K. On the breakdown of the marriage, Mr K left, never to return, and Mrs K remained with their two children. She became the mistress of C, who moved into the house with her. Mr K then ceased to pay the mortgage instalments, and Mrs K and he tried without success to sell the house for £14,300. Finally C purchased it from them for £10,000, out of which the mortgagee was repaid and the balance divided between Mr and Mrs K. Six weeks later C terminated the relationship with Mrs K and claimed possession of the house. Mrs K claimed that she was a licensee for life or for so long as the children remained in her custody. The Court of Appeal held that she was a contractual licensee for a period terminable on twelve months' notice.

It is possible even for the contractual licensee to obtain specific performance of the contractual licence. In *Verrall v Great Yarmouth Borough Council*:[36]

The Conservative council granted a licence to the National Front to hold its annual conference at the Wellington Pier Pavilion for £6,000. After the local government elections, the new Labour council purported to revoke the licence.

---

[32] [1975] 1 WLR 1346, M & B p. 600; cf *Horrocks v Forray* [1976] 1 WLR 230 where no contract was implied in similar circumstances (described in (1976) 40 Conv (NS) 362 (M. Richards) as "*Tanner v Tanner* in a middle class setting"); *Coombes v Smith* [1986] 1 WLR 808, p. 821, n. 53, ante (no contract implied that man would provide mistress with house for rest of her life).   [33] At 1350.

[34] [1978] 1 WLR 683, M & B p. 608 (where mother purchased house for son and his bride, who were to pay her £7 a week; on breakdown of marriage son left bride now pregnant for another woman. Mother sued for possession. Daughter-in-law held entitled to protection as contractual licensee for indefinite period on payment of £7 a week). Lord DENNING at 688 would have preferred to find a personal "equitable licence", following his own decision in *Errington v Errington and Woods* [1952] 1 KB 290, p. 837, post.

[35] [1978] 1 WLR 693, M & B p. 604. See also *Roach v Johannes* [1976] CLY 1549 (licence of "paying guest" terminable on giving reasonable notice, which in the circumstances was not less than twenty-one days); *Piquet v Tyler* [1978] CLY 119 (irrevocable licence for life of defendants, who had, by arrangement with plaintiff, surrendered protected tenancy to look after plaintiff's aged mother).

[36] [1981] QB 202, M & B p. 609. For the reasons given by the court for exercising its discretion to grant specific performance in the interests of freedom of speech, see at 216–18.

In granting specific performance of the contractual licence, Lord DENNING MR said:[37]

Since the *Winter Garden* case, it is clear that once a man has entered under his contract of licence, he cannot be turned out. An injunction can be obtained against the licensor to prevent his being turned out. On principle it is the same if it happens before he enters. If he has a contractual right to enter, and the licensor refuses to let him come in, then he can come to the court and in a proper case get an order for specific performance to allow him to come in.

III Contractual Licence and Third Parties

Once the courts had given specific protection to a contractual licensee against the licensor, the next question inevitably arose—whether that protection was good against a third party. On the one hand, protection of a licensee may be of little value if the licensor can defeat him by transfer to a third party. On the other hand, protection of the licensee against third parties goes a long way towards the recognition of a licence as an interest in land.[38]

A bare licence is revocable by the licensor at any time. It clearly, therefore, does not bind his successors in title. If, however, the licence is coupled with a grant or interest, it is irrevocable by the licensor as long as the grant or interest is irrevocable. If, therefore, the interest binds a third party, the licence will bind him also.

The main controversy has been in relation to contractual licences and third parties. On principle, a contract between A and B is not capable of imposing a burden on C.[39] Nor is it an answer to say that, on the principle of *Tulk v Moxhay*,[40] the fact that A has a right to an injunction against B to restrain revocation, gives him also a right to an injunction against C, as long as C is not a bona fide purchaser of a legal estate for value without notice. That, indeed, was the early view of *Tulk v Moxhay*, but was found to be impracticable in the real property cases,[41] and was never applied in cases relating to chattels.[42] The injunction is available against a third party only in cases where policy considerations justify it. And, while there may be certain compelling cases in the field of contractual licences, a rule that every contractual licence is binding on third parties who take with notice, would cause serious difficulties.

Authority is to the same effect. In *King v David Allen & Sons, Billposting, Ltd*:[43]

the licensor gave to the licensee an exclusive permission to affix advertisements to the walls of a cinema. Later the licensor granted a lease of the cinema to a cinema company, but the lease contained

---

[37] At 216.

[38] On the nature of an interest in land, see p. 153, ante; and (in the context of licences) *National Provincial Bank Ltd v Ainsworth* [1965] AC 1175 at 1248, per Lord WILBERFORCE (a property right must be "definable, identifiable by third parties, capable in its nature of assumption by third parties, and have some degree of permanence or stability"); p. 847, post.   [39] Treitel, pp. 638 et seq.

[40] P. 666. ante.   [41] *Formby v Barker* [1903] 2 Ch 539; *LCC v Allen* [1914] 3 KB 642, p. 669, ante.

[42] *De Mattos v Gibson* (1858) 4 De G & J 276; *Lord Strathcona Steamship Co Ltd v Dominion Coal Co Ltd* [1926] AC 108; *Port Line Ltd v Ben Line Steamers Ltd* [1958] 2 QB 146; *Law Debenture Trust Corpn plc v Ural Caspian Oil Corpn Ltd* [1993] 1 WLR 138. See, however, *Swiss Bank Corpn v Lloyds Bank Ltd* [1979] Ch 548 at 569–75; revsd on different grounds [1982] AC 584; (1982) 98 LQR 279 (S. Gardner).

[43] [1916] 2 AC 54, M & B p. 611. See also *Clore v Theatrical Properties Ltd and Westby & Co Ltd* [1936] 3 All ER 483.

no reference to the licence. When the company refused to allow the advertisements to be affixed to the building, the licensee brought an action against the licensor for breach of contract. The liability of the licensor depended on whether the lease to the company had deprived the licensee of his contractual right to affix advertisements. The House of Lords held that it had, and therefore the action for damages succeeded.

There are, however, two cases which appear to accept the proposition that contractual licences bind third parties, in one case a volunteer devisee,[44] and in the other a purchaser who took the premises "expressly subject" to the contract.[45]

In *Errington v Errington and Woods*:

A father bought a house for £750. He paid £250 in cash and borrowed £500 from a building society, the loan being secured by a mortgage of the house and repayable by instalments of fifteen shillings a week. He allowed his son and daughter-in-law to go into possession and told them that if they paid all the instalments he would convey the legal estate to them. They paid the instalments as they became due, but the payments were not all completed when the father died nine years later having devised the house to his widow. The son then left his wife, but the latter remained in occupation of the house and continued to pay the instalments.

An action brought by the widow for possession against the daughter-in-law was dismissed. The Court of Appeal held that the son and daughter-in-law were neither tenants at will nor weekly tenants, but licensees entitled to occupy the house as long as they paid the instalments. This licence was binding upon the licensor's devisee.

Substantially, the reasoning adopted by the court was that, since the son and daughter-in-law were entitled in equity to restrain the revocation of the licence contrary to the terms of the implied contract, they acquired in effect an equitable interest, or at least an equity[46] in the land that was capable of binding third parties.[47]

The reasoning must be considered afresh in the light of *National Provincial Bank Ltd v Ainsworth*,[48] in which Lord UPJOHN and Lord WILBERFORCE in the House of Lords and RUSSELL LJ in the Court of Appeal showed their reluctance to regard the contractual licensee as possessing more than a personal right. RUSSELL LJ, in particular, resisted the view that this personal right is converted into some form of equitable interest binding on third parties merely because the licensor may be restrained from revoking his permission.[49]

---

[44] *Errington v Errington and Woods* [1952] 1 KB 290.

[45] *Binions v Evans* [1972] Ch 359, M & B p. 617.   [46] P. 812, ante.

[47] This reasoning was principally that of DENNING LJ, with whom SOMERVELL LJ agreed at 294. The reasoning was defended by G. C. Cheshire in (1953) 16 MLR 1; but rejected in (1952) 68 LQR 337 (H. W. R. Wade). For an attack on the decision from a different angle, see (1953) 69 LQR 466 (A. D. Hargreaves). See also *Re Solomon* [1967] Ch 573 at 582–6, per GOFF J. The decision may be sustainable on several other grounds: *Ashburn Anstalt v Arnold* [1989] Ch 1 at 117, per Fox LJ: an estate contract, p. 940, post; or under the principles of constructive trust, p. 839, post, or estoppel, p. 841, post. See also *South Dowling Pty Ltd v Cody Outdoor Advertising Pty Ltd* [2005] NSWCA 407, discussed [2006] Conv 197 (A.Dowling).

[48] [1965] AC 1175, rejecting the so-called "deserted wife's equity", p. 847, post. The decision gave rise to the Matrimonial Homes Act 1967, now Family Law Act 1996, ss. 30–2, Sch. 4, p. 478, ante. The reasoning in *Errington* was also expressly disapproved by the Court of Appeal in *Ashburn Anstalt v Arnold*, supra; p. 838, post.   [49] [1964] Ch 665 at 698.

In *Binions v Evans*[50] a contractual licence was enforced against a purchaser who took a conveyance of land expressly subject to a licence, having in consequence paid a reduced price:

Mrs Evans was the widow of an employee of the Tredegar Estate. In 1968 the Estate entered into a written agreement with her under which she was permitted to reside in a cottage on the Estate for the remainder of her life free of rent and rates. She agreed to keep the cottage in a proper manner. In 1970 the Estate sold and conveyed it to the plantiffs expressly subject to the agreement. The plaintiffs paid a reduced price because of this. Six months later they claimed possession of the cottage.

The Court of Appeal unanimously held that Mrs Evans was protected, but differed in their reasons. MEGAW and STEPHENSON LJJ held that the agreement conferred a life interest and that Mrs Evans was a tenant for life under the Settled Land Act 1925.[51] Lord DENNING, however, held that the plaintiffs were bound by Mrs Evans's contractual licence, saying, on the one hand, that the plaintiffs, having purchased *expressly subject* to the rights of Mrs Evans, were bound by a constructive trust and so could not ignore them; and, on the other hand, on the wider ground that the contractual licence gave rise to an equitable interest which bound the plaintiffs to permit her to reside in the cottage during her life or as long as she wished. It is submitted that the former view is preferable. It is difficult to see how the wider view is consistent with earlier authority on contractual licences, and the expressions of opinion in the House of Lords in *National Provincial Bank Ltd v Ainsworth*.

Clearly these cases provide no support for the view that contractual licences generally are binding on third parties.[52] Moreover in *Ashburn Anstalt v Arnold*[53] the Court of Appeal held, obiter, that, where land was conveyed to a purchaser expressly "subject to" a contractual licence, the licence was not a property interest and therefore not enforceable against the third party. In rejecting the wide implications of *Errington v Errington and Woods* and *Binions v Evans*, Fox LJ emphasised that there was no other case in which a contractual licence had been held to bind a third party in the absence of a finding that the third party took the land as a constructive trustee:

The far-reaching statement of principle in *Errington* was not supported by authority, not necessary for the decision of the case and *per incuriam* in the sense that it was made without reference to authorities which, if they would not have compelled, would surely have persuaded the court to adopt a different

---

[50] [1972] Ch 359 (1972) 88 LQR 336 (P. V. B.); (1972) 36 Conv (NS) 266 (J. Martin), 277 (D. J. Hayton); [1973] CLJ 123 (R. J. Smith); (1973) 117 SJ 23 (B. W. Harvey); (1977) 93 LQR 561 (J. A. Hornby).

[51] Following *Bannister v Bannister* [1948] 2 All ER 133, infra. This is not without difficulty, p. 848, n. 125, post. MEGAW LJ also suggested at 371, that the plaintiffs would be guilty of the tort of interference with existing contractual rights if they were to evict the defendant; (1977) 41 Conv (NS) 318 (R. J. Smith).

The defendant in such a case might now be able to enforce the term in the contract of sale of the cottage by which the purchasers agreed to allow her to stay, as long as the parties expressly or impliedly intended her to have the right to enforce it: Contracts (Rights of Third Parties) Act 1999, s. 1. The licensee is not thereby enforcing her (existing) licence against the purchaser, but taking the benefit of the purchaser's (new) contractual undertaking.

[52] Nor does *Midland Bank Ltd v Farmpride Hatcheries Ltd* (1980) 260 EG 493, where the issue was not raised; p. 63, n. 110, ante.

[53] [1989] Ch 1, M & B p. 612. The case was decided against the purchaser on the ground that the agreement created a tenancy which was binding on him. See also *Patel v Patel* (CA, 30 June 1983), where SLADE LJ said: "A mere licence to occupy land, albeit of a contractual nature, as opposed to a lease, does not confer any interest on the licensee in the land".

ratio. Of course, the law must be free to develop. But as a response to problems which had arisen, the *Errington* rule (without more) was neither practically necessary nor theoretically convincing. By contrast, the finding on appropriate facts of a constructive trust may well be regarded as a beneficial adaptation of old rules to new situations.[54]

IV Licence Protected by Constructive Trust

We have seen that gratuitous licences and contractual licences do not of themselves constitute interests in land, and so do not bind third parties. The analysis of a person's occupation of land as constituting a gratuitous or contractual licence does not however preclude the finding that some other interest has also been created which is an interest in land and which is therefore capable of binding a third party. In particular, the courts will consider whether the person is in occupation of the land pursuant to a constructive trust or has an interest protected under the doctrine of proprietary estoppel.[55]

A few cases have been decided on the basis of a constructive trust. Such a trust arises by operation of law when the court is of the opinion that it is in the interests of justice or for the prevention of unjust enrichment that such a trust should be found.[56]

The first, *Bannister v Bannister*,[57] could more appropriately have been decided under the doctrine of proprietary estoppel;[58] but the protection of licences by proprietary estoppel had not generally been recognised in 1948. In that case:

the defendant, who owned two cottages, sold them in 1943 to her brother-in-law, the plaintiff, for £250 (which was £150 below market price). They made an oral agreement under which the brother-in-law would let her stay in one of the cottages "as long as you like, rent free". In 1945 the defendant gave up possession of the cottage except for one room. In 1947 the plaintiff claimed possession of the room on the ground that she was a tenant at will.

The defendant was unable to rely on an express trust, because that was required to be in writing.[59] The Court of Appeal, however, held that it would be a fraud to disregard the oral trust and that she was entitled under a constructive trust to a life interest determinable upon her ceasing to reside in the cottage.

Re Sharpe[60] could likewise have been decided under the doctrine of proprietary estoppel. In that case:

an elderly aunt lent money to her nephew to purchase and improve a house on the understanding that she would live there and be looked after by the nephew and his wife for the rest of her life. The aunt

---

[54] [1989] Ch 1 at 22.

[55] In *Ashburn Anstalt v Arnold* [1989] Ch 1, for example, the Court of Appeal held that the contractual licence did not create an interest in land; they went on however to consider whether the facts also gave rise to a constructive trust, which would have created such an interest. They found that, on the facts, there was no constructive trust.

[56] See generally Oakley, *Constructive Trusts*, pp. 53 et seq; H & M, chap. 12, esp. pp. 337–43; Maudsley and Burn, *Trusts and Trustees*, chap. 7; Snell, para. 24–07 (trust to prevent wrongdoing by the trustee).

[57] [1948] 2 All ER 133, M & B p. 615; *Hussey v Palmer* [1972] 1 WLR 1286.   [58] P. 841, post.

[59] LPA 1925, s. 53(1); p. 903, post.

[60] [1980] 1 WLR 219, M & B p. 681; [1980] Conv 207 (J. Martin); 96 LQR 336 (G. Woodman). In *Bristol and West Building Society v Henning* [1985] 1 WLR 778, BROWNE–WILKINSON LJ said at 783 that "nothing in this

moved in, and the nephew went bankrupt. His trustee in bankruptcy then entered into a contract to sell the house with vacant possession to a purchaser, and sought to recover possession of the house from the aunt.

In holding that the aunt was entitled under a constructive trust as against the trustee to remain in the house until she was repaid[61] the sums she advanced, BROWNE-WILKINSON J said:[62]

In my judgment, whether it be called a contractual licence or an equitable licence or an interest under a constructive trust, the aunt would be entitled as against the nephew to stay in the house ... The introduction of a constructive trust is an essential ingredient if the plaintiff has any right at all.

In *Hussey v Palmer*[63] and *Binions v Evans*[64] (where the constructive trust was relied on as a second ground) the constructive trust was described as an available remedy in the widest terms. Such a remedy is both too wide and too severe. "The dicta are ... certainly fine sounding, but one needs more guidance as to when such trusts will be implied."[65]

In *Ashburn Anstalt v Arnold*[66] the Court of Appeal took the view that the mere fact that land is expressed to be conveyed "subject to" a contract does not necessarily imply that the grantee is to be under an obligation, not otherwise existing, to give effect to the provisions of the contract:

The Court will not impose a constructive trust unless it is satisfied that the conscience of the estate owner is affected ... The words "subject to" will, of course, impose notice. But notice is not enough to impose on somebody an obligation to give effect to a contract into which he did not enter.[67]

judgment should be taken as expressing any view on the question . . . whether the decision in *Re Sharpe* was correct."

[61] The purchaser was not a party to the action, and it was left open whether he was also bound.

[62] [1980] 1 WLR 219 at 224, 225. See *Re Basham* [1986] 1 WLR 1498 at 1504, where Edward Nugee QC, in holding that a claim for proprietary estoppel succeeded, treated it "as giving rise to a species of constructive trust"; [1981] Conv 211 (J. Martin); [1987] CLJ 215 (D. Hayton). See also Sir Christopher SLADE's Child & Co Oxford Lecture 1984 on *The Informal Creation of Interests in Land* at p. 12.

[63] [1972] 1 WLR 1286 (elderly widow, invited to live with daughter and son-in-law, paid cost of extra bedroom built onto house for her accommodation; held entitled to recover money when she left). See also *DHN Food Distributors Ltd v Tower Hamlets LBC* [1976] 1 WLR 852 (irrevocable contractual licence which gave rise to constructive trust, under which DHN had "a sufficient interest in the land to qualify them for disturbance" upon compulsory purchase by local authority); (1977) 93 LQR 170 (D. Sugarman and F. Webb); (1977) 41 Conv (NS) 73; *Sparkes v Smart* [1990] 2 EGLR 245 (collusive transaction between purchaser of freehold farm and ageing tenant, purchaser's father-in-law, with object of destroying youngest son's tenancy; CA held, obiter, constructive trust in favour of the son).　　　　　　　　　　　　　　　　　　　　[64] [1972] Ch 359.

[65] [1973] CLJ p. 142 (R. J. Smith).

[66] [1989] Ch 1, M & B p. 618. The Appellate Committee dismissed a petition for leave to appeal [1989] Ch 32; [1988] CLJ 353 (A. J. Oakley); 104 LQR 175 (P. Sparkes); 51 MLR 226 (J. Hill); Conv 201 (M. P. Thompson); All ER Rev 176 (P. J. Clarke).

[67] At 25, per Fox LJ. See also *IDC Group Ltd v Clark* [1992] 1 EGLR 187, where Sir Nicolas BROWNE-WILKINSON V-C said at 189: "The Court of Appeal put what I hope is the *quietus* to the heresy that a mere licence creates an interest in land. They also put the *quietus* to the heresy that parties to a contractual licence necessarily become constructive trustees". See also *Canadian Imperial Bank of Commerce v Bello* (1991) 64 P & CR 48 at 51–2; *Lloyd v Dugdale* [2002] 2 P & CR 13 at [52], per Sir Christopher SLADE. A purchaser may, however, make a bargain with the vendor that he undertakes *de novo* to honour existing contractual obligations: *IDC Group Ltd v Clark* [1992] 1 EGLR 187 at 190, approving the analysis of DILLON J in *Lyus v Prowsa Developments Ltd* [1982] 1 WLR 1044; *Chattey v Farndale Holdings Inc* (1996) 75 P & CR 298 at 313, 317. Such a bargain may now be enforceable by the licensee *in contract* under the Contracts (Rights of Third Parties) Act 1999: see p. 838, n. 51, ante.

Binions v Evans was regarded as a legitimate application of the doctrine of constructive trusts, since the facts that the Tredegar Estate provided the purchasers with a copy of the agreement with Mrs Evans, and that the purchasers paid a reduced purchase price, indicated that the intention of the Estate and the purchasers was that the purchasers should give effect to Mrs Evans's agreement. If they had failed to do so, the Estate would have been liable in damages to Mrs Evans.[68]

The remedy of the constructive trust is also too severe. For if it creates undocumented proprietary interests in land,[69] it can cause difficulties for the conveyancing system. If the constructive trust creates an equitable fee simple, it will be one which is not registrable, though it may be overreachable;[70] and if it creates an interest for life, in the case of trusts created before 1997[71] it could bring the provisions of the Settled Land Act 1925 into operation. The problem will be discussed in more detail below,[72] where it will be seen that a similar problem arises on the application of the doctrine of proprietary estoppel.

V Licence Protected by Proprietary Estoppel

The doctrine of proprietary estoppel has undergone a remarkable development over the last fifty years; and this has occurred largely in the context of licences. We have already seen in chapter 22 the circumstances in which proprietary estoppel will arise, and the principles by which the courts will remedy it. We shall here explain something of the use which can be made of it in order to protect a licensee who is not otherwise adequately protected under a bare licence, a licence coupled with an interest, or a contractual licence.[73]

A The Doctrine in Outline

As we have seen,[74] the general principle of proprietary estoppel is that where one party (A) makes a representation or promise to another party (B) to the effect that B has or shall have an interest in, or right over, A's property, or acquiesces in B's mistaken belief that he has or shall have such an interest or right, then if A intends B to act in reliance to his detriment on the representation, promise or mistaken belief, and B does so act in reliance, equity may intervene to prevent (*estop*) A from asserting his own strict legal rights to his property. The doctrine can be traced back to older cases, in a wide range of situations.[75] But much of its revival and development during the twentieth century occurred in licence cases. We have already noted that in some cases courts strove to find other principles to protect the licensee, which might now better be decided under the developed doctrine of proprietary estoppel.[76]

---

[68] In *Ashburn Anstalt v Arnold* the purchaser had not paid a reduced price, nor would the licensor have been liable in damages to the licensee.

[69] For the view that a constructive trust in this situation creates a personal right, rather than an interest in the property, see (2004) 120 LQR 667 (B. McFarlane).   [70] See *Hodgson v Marks* [1971] Ch 892.

[71] TLATA 1996, s. 2(1).   [72] P. 848, post.

[73] On the relationship between contractual licences and proprietary estoppel, see the controversy between [1981] Conv 212; [1983] Conv 285 (A. Briggs) and [1983] Conv 50, 471 (M. P. Thompson).

[74] P. 817, ante.   [75] P. 816, ante.

[76] *Bannister v Bannister* [1948] 2 All ER 133, M & B p. 615, p. 839, ante (constructive trust); *Errington v Errington and Woods* [1952] 1 KB 290, p. 837, ante (contractual licence); *Re Sharpe* [1980] 1 WLR 219, M & B p. 681, p. 839, ante (constructive trust).

The advantage of proprietary estoppel is its great flexibility. Once it is established that an estoppel is working in favour of a licensee—that is, an equity has arisen[77]—the court will decide which of the available remedies is most appropriate.[78] As has been said many times in the cases:

The court must look at the circumstances in each case to decide in what way the equity can be satisfied.[79]

Moreover, the remedy may be negative or positive; personal to the licensee or an interest in the property which will protect him against third parties; the enforcement of the licence by means of a right of occupation, or only the right to reimbursement of expenditure incurred by the licensor. Some examples will be given here.

B Illustrations of the Remedies Available to Protect Licensee

(1) Negative Protection to Prevent Revocation of Licence

Once an equity arising by estoppel is established, the court may grant a remedy which is, essentially, negative: preventing the licensor from revoking the licence by refusing his claim for possession, or perhaps by granting to the licensor an injunction to prevent revocation. In *Inwards v Baker*:[80]

B's son wished to build a bungalow on land which he had hoped to purchase, but the project was beyond his means. B then said to his son "Why not put the bungalow on my land and make the bungalow a little bigger?" The son did so, building it mainly through his own labour and expense. He lived there continuously until B died in 1951, and then from B's death until the proceedings began in 1963. B had left the land elsewhere in a will dated 1922 to trustees on trust for sale in favour of others. When the trustees sought possession, the Court of Appeal held that the son "can remain there as long as he desires to use it as his home".[81]

In this case, therefore, the son was given a remedy which vindicated his expectation:[82] he claimed that he was given an oral licence for his lifetime, and relied to his detriment

---

[77] Pp. 817 et seq, ante.

[78] Pp. 822 et seq, ante; Pawlowski, *The Doctrine of Proprietary Estoppel*, pp. 43–71. See *Lord Cawdor v Lewis* (1835) 1 Y & C Ex 427 at 433; *Plimmer v Wellington Corpn* (1884) 9 App Cas 699 at 713, 714.

[79] *Plimmer v City of Wellington Corpn*, supra, at 713. See also, in particular, *Crabb v Arun DC* [1976] Ch 179 at 193, per SCARMAN LJ ("what is the relief appropriate to satisfy the equity?"). For the nature and scope of the court's discretion, see *Jennings v Rice* [2003] 1 P & CR 8, p. 823, ante.

[80] [1965] 2 QB 29, M & B p. 654; (1965) 81 LQR 183 (R. H. Maudsley). Cf *Sledmore v Dalby* (1996) 72 P & CR 196, M & B p. 650; [1997] CLJ 34 (P. Milne); [1997] Conv 458 (J. E. Adams), in which the trial judge held that the defendant had a personal licence to occupy; reversed by CA on the basis that the equity arising by estoppel had expired; *Parker v Parker* [2003] EWHC 1846 (9th Earl of Mansfield could not establish estoppel entitling him to possession for life of Shirburn Castle, Oxfordshire, a "sleeping beauty of a castle", but had licence terminable on two years' notice once negotiations for his long-term occupation broke down); [2004] Conv 516 (M. P. Thompson).   [81] [1965] 2 QB 29 at 37, per Lord DENNING MR.

[82] On the general question of when the courts will think it appropriate to grant a remedy to protect the representee's expectation, or only the value of his reliance, see pp. 823–5, ante. In *Inwards v Baker* the son claimed only that he had been promised a licence for life, and did not pursue a claim that he had been promised or given the fee simple: [1965] 2 QB 29 at 30–1. Contrast, however, *Dillwyn v Llewelyn* (1862) 4 De GF & J 517 where, however, the father had signed an unexecuted and gratuitous memorandum of conveyance in favour of his son, and the son had spent no less than £14,000 in building himself a home, with his father's knowledge and

accordingly; and the court used a negative remedy to give effect to that licence, by refusing to grant possession of the property to the legal owner. The court had to have recourse to the principles of equity because there was here no contract on which a remedy could be based.[83] But finding an equity, and not simply a contract, moves the protection for the licensee into the realm of property, since it can be enforced against a purchaser from the licensor. In *Inwards v Baker* itself, the licence was enforceable against the volunteer trustees who took under the licensor's will. But Lord DENNING MR made clear that the equity was also capable of binding a purchaser with notice.[84]

(2) Positive Protection by the Grant of a Property Right

In some cases the courts have gone further, and have held that the proper remedy to satisfy the equity is the grant to the licensee of a particular right in the property. Most such cases[85] have not involved simple licences: the court orders the grant of a property right because that is what the representee was led to believe—that is, the claim is not based on a licence to occupy the land, but on the representation that an interest in the property itself (beyond the licence to occupy) was granted or promised by the legal owner.

However, there are cases in which the remedy has been awarded in order to protect what might otherwise have been simply a licence to occupy. In *Pascoe v Turner*:[86]

In 1963 P, a businessman, and T, a widow with an invalidity pension and a small amount of capital, lived together in his house. In 1965 P purchased another house, into which they moved and lived as man and wife. In 1973 P started an affair with another woman. T remained in the house and was told by P that the house and everything in it was hers. In reliance on this statement, T spent, to P's knowledge, her own money on repairs and improvements, and also on furniture. P moved out in 1973 when the relationship ended, and in 1976 he gave T two months' notice to determine the licence.

In defence to P's claim for possession, T sought a declaration that the house and its contents were hers, and that P held the house on trust for her; alternatively, that P had given her a licence to occupy the house for her lifetime, and that P was estopped from denying the licence. The Court of Appeal held that there was a gift of the contents, since T was in possession of them as a bailee when P declared the gift. As far as the house was concerned, there was no valid declaration of trust,[87] but an estoppel arose in her favour. However, the court rejected a solution that would give T a licence to occupy the house for her lifetime, and ordered that the fee simple be conveyed to her. Only in this way could

---

approval. The House of Lords ordered a conveyance of the land without payment. It might be thought, in either of the cases, that a better solution, to balance the positions of the licensee and the licensor (or his successor), would have been to give the son the option of taking a conveyance of the land on payment of site value or of receiving compensation for the value of his expenditure on the land.

[83] [1965] 2 QB 29 at 37, per Lord DENNING MR.

[84] Ibid., at 37. For further discussion of the proprietary effect of proprietary estoppel, see p. 825, ante; p. 845, post. [85] See pp. 822 et seq, ante.

[86] [1979] 1 WLR 431, M & B p. 667; [1979] Conv 379 (F. R. Crane); (1979) 42 MLR 574 (B. Sufrin). Cf *Dillwyn v Llewelyn* (1862) 4 De GF & J 517, n. 82, ante; *Voyce v Voyce* (1991) 62 P & CR 290 (donee of farm and cottage from licensor ordered to convey fee simple to licensee).

[87] It was not evidenced in writing as required by LPA 1925, s. 53(1)(b), p. 903, post.

the defendant be "assured of security of tenure, quiet enjoyment, and freedom of action in respect of repairs and improvements without interference from the plaintiff."[88] Instead of granting a life interest to T, as a result of which she might have become tenant for life under the Settled Land Act 1925,[89] and leaving her to her remedies in tort against P, if necessary, the Court awarded T the fee simple of a house worth £16,000 at the time of the judgment for an outlay of less than £1,000. It may be thought that this solution was too extreme.

In *Sledmore v Dalby*,[90] by contrast, the Court of Appeal rejected a claim for the conveyance of the fee simple.

The licensee had carried out substantial works to a house, on the encouragement of the licensor, in order to improve it as a family home. He had enjoyed eighteen years' free occupation, had little need for the property, and the licensor was in serious financial difficulty; she was on income support and her mortgage interest, which was in arrears, was being paid by the Department of Social Security.

The Court held that the licensee's equity had now expired and therefore the owner was entitled to possession of the house. Hobhouse LJ[91] adopted the approach of the High Court of Australia in *Commonwealth of Australia v Verwayen* where Mason CJ said:[92]

A central element of the doctrine of estoppel is that there must be a proportionality between the remedy and the detriment which is its purpose to avoid. It would be wholly inequitable and unjust to insist upon a disproportionate making good of the relevant assumption.

(3) Licence to Occupy until Expenditure Reimbursed

In some cases the courts have held that the equity arising by estoppel can most appropriately be satisfied by ordering that the licensor repay the expenditure incurred by the licensee in reliance on the representation that he had a licence to occupy. For example, in *Dodsworth v Dodsworth*:[93]

the plaintiff lived alone in a bungalow. Her younger brother and his wife, the two defendants, returned to England from Australia and were looking for a home. The plaintiff persuaded them to

---

[88] [1979] 1 WLR 431 at 438.

[89] For the powers of a tenant for life, see p. 409, ante. And for the problem that, before 1997, a settlement might have been created by awarding a licence for life, see p. 848, post.

[90] (1996) 72 P & CR 196; [1997] CLJ 34 (P. Milne); [1997] Conv 458 (J. E. Adams).

[91] Ibid., at 208.

[92] (1990) 95 ALR 321 at 331. The English courts have now adopted this approach generally in proprietary estoppel, and therefore consider whether an award of the expectation would be disproportionate to the value of the claimant's reliance: *Jennings v Rice* [2003] 1 P & CR 8, M & B p. 646, p. 823, ante. For a creative solution to the problems of over-compensation (by ordering the fee simple) or under-compensation (by ordering only repayment of the expenditure incurred), whilst still avoiding the problems of SLA 1925, p. 848, post, see *Griffiths v Williams* (1977) 248 EG 947, M & B p. 673 (with the consent of the parties, the grant of a long, non-assignable lease, determinable on the death of the licensee, at a nominal rent).

[93] (1973) 228 EG 1115, M & B p. 671; *Burrows and Burrows v Sharpe* (1991) 23 HLR 82 (clean break only proper and fair solution in view of breakdown between parties; compensation in return for loss of accommodation); [1992] Conv 54 (J. E. Martin); *Baker v Baker* (1993) 25 HLR 408 (granny flat). Cf *Campbell v Griffin* (2001) 82 P & CR DG23 (family carer ordered to vacate property to enable it to be sold, but granted a charge

join her in her bungalow. They did so, and spent some £700 on improvements to the bungalow, in the expectation, encouraged and induced by the plaintiff, that the defendants and the survivor of them would be able to remain in the bungalow as their home for as long as they wished to do so. Nine months later, the plaintiff repented of her invitation and started proceedings for possession; she died before the hearing in the Court of Appeal.

The Court of Appeal held that the equity would best be satisfied by securing the occupation of the defendants until the expenditure had been reimbursed.[94]

C Third Parties

(1) The Burden of a Licence Protected by Proprietary Estoppel

We have already seen that, both in unregistered land and in registered land, the burden of an equity by estoppel has been recognised as being proprietary in character.[95] A licence which is protected by proprietary estoppel is therefore capable of binding the licensor's successor, and in accordance with the general principles can bind a purchaser of unregistered land if he has notice of it,[96] or a purchaser of registered land if the right is protected by a notice in the register[97] or as an overriding interest if the licensee is in discoverable actual occupation.[98]

A further question, however, arises which is critical to the analysis of the licensee's rights against the purchaser. Even if the equity by estoppel is recognised as having a sufficiently proprietary quality to bind the purchaser, can the purchaser overreach it by paying the purchase money to two trustees[99] and thereby transfer the burden of the equity to the purchase money? It has been said that the equity cannot be overreached.[100] However, in a case where the equity is to be satisfied with the grant of an interest which would itself be overreachable, it has been suggested that the equity arising by estoppel should also be overreachable.[101] This only adds to the controversy as to the nature of the equity before it is satisfied.

Once the court has awarded the remedy to give effect to the equity, however, its status is crystallised and, if a proprietary interest is awarded, its priority over future registered dispositions will depend on the nature of the interest in question.

---

over the property to secure the interest (£35,000) he was held to have by way of proprietary estoppel); [2002] Conv 519 (M. Pawkowski); [2003] Conv 157 (M. P. Thompson).

[94] A principal concern of the Court in awarding this remedy was to avoid the operation of the Settled Land Act 1925, p. 848, post, if a life interest were instead ordered.

[95] *E R Ives Investment Ltd v High* [1967] 2 QB 379 (unregistered land); LRA 2002, s. 116(a) (registered land); p. 826, ante.

[96] *E R Ives Investment Ltd v High*, supra (since the equity by estoppel cannot be registered as a land charge).

[97] LRA 2002, s. 29.   [98] Ibid., Sch. 3, para. 2.

[99] Or a trust corporation: LPA 1925, s. 2; pp. 997–1000, post.

[100] *Shiloh Spinners Ltd v Harding* [1973] AC 691 at 720–1, per Lord WILBERFORCE, approving the approach of CA in *E. R. Ives Investment Ltd v High* [1967] 2 QB 379 (unregistered land); *Sweet v Sommer* [2005] EWCA Civ 227, [2005] All ER (D) 162 (Mar) at [26], per MORRITT VC (registered land).

[101] *Birmingham Midshires Mortgage Services Ltd v Sabherwal* (2000) 80 P & CR 256 at [24], per ROBERT WALKER LJ.

(2) The Benefit of a Licence Protected by Proprietary Estoppel

There is no English authority on the transfer of the benefit of a licence protected by proprietary estoppel. In New South Wales, however, the Supreme Court held in *Hamilton v
Geraghty*[102] that the benefit of an estoppel based on passive acquiescence was assignable and
in fact had been assigned. The estoppel was not a personal right to sue which could not be
assigned, but an interest in the land itself.[103]

Whether a licence is transferable depends on the circumstances and in particular on its construction. In *Inwards v Baker*,[104] where the son's licence was to remain in the bungalow as long
as he desired to use it as his home, the right was clearly personal and not transferable. In *E R
Ives Investment Ltd v High*,[105] however, the benefit of High's licence would run with the land.

D Termination of Licence

A licence is revocable when it is not binding on the licensor or his successors in title in
accordance with the rules stated in this chapter. A question has arisen whether a licence,
irrevocable under the doctrine of proprietary estoppel, can be made revocable by the serious
misconduct of the licensee. In *Williams v Staite*,[106] where the licensee announced that the
successor in title of the licensor was in for "bloody trouble" and blocked the entrance to the
house which he had purchased, the Court of Appeal held that the licence did not thereby
become revocable. As GOFF LJ said:

Excessive user or bad behaviour towards the legal owner cannot bring the equity to an end or forfeit it.
It may give rise to an action for damages for trespass or nuisance or to injunctions to restrain such
behaviour, but I see no ground on which the equity, once established, can be forfeited.[107]

Lord DENNING MR thought that, in an extreme case, the licence might be revocable.

The effect of serious misconduct may, however, prevent an equity from arising in the first
place, for example, where a forged document is used to bolster the claim. This is a simple application of the equitable maxim that "he who comes to equity must come with clean hands".[108]

VI Conveyancing Difficulties

Sufficient has been said to demonstrate the dramatic development of the law of licences in
the past sixty years or so. *Hurst v Picture Theatres Ltd*[109] was then the only glimmer of hope
for the contractual licensee. Now, as has been seen, through the intervention of equity he not

---

[102] (1901) 1 SRNSW Eq 81; *Lands Comr v Hussein* [1968] EA 585; (1969) ASCL 354 (E. H. Burn).
[103] (1901) 1 SRNSW Eq 81 at 89, per OWEN J.   [104] [1965] 2 QB 29, M & B p. 654; p. 842, ante.
[105] [1967] 2 QB 379, M & B p. 665; p. 825, ante.   [106] [1979] Ch 291.
[107] At 300. Cf, however, (1) a contractual licence where misconduct may be a breach of an implied term in
it, and so prevent the licensee from relying on equitable relief against revocation: *Brynowen Estates Ltd v Bourne*
(1981) 131 NLJ 1212 (driving car at speed along roads of caravan park with sounding of horn at night; and
swearing at and making obscene gestures at visitors to it); and (2) an equitable interest arising under the
doctrine of *Walsh v Londsale* (1882) 21 Ch D 9, p. 877, post, which can be lost by misconduct of the beneficiary
sufficient to remove his entitlement to claim specific performance of the contract: *Coatsworth v Johnson* (1886)
55 LJQB 220, p. 225, ante.
[108] *J Willis & Son v Willis* [1986] 1 EGLR 62; *Gonthier v Orange Contract Scaffolding Ltd* [2003] All ER (D)
332 (Jun).   [109] [1915] 1 KB 1, M & B p. 597; p. 834, ante.

only has stronger protection against the licensor,[110] but his licence might even be protected in some circumstances by the mechanism of the constructive trust or proprietary estoppel so as to be recognised as having the quality of an interest in land; and property interests such as a life interest[111] and a fee simple[112] have been awarded to licensees even though they were volunteers and had no documentary title to such estate or interest. But this progress has produced a number of problems.

In the 1950s there grew up the concept of the deserted wife's licence. A husband who deserted his wife could not turn her out of the home, even though he owned it. And this protection was extended through a series of cases[113] to protect the deserted wife against third parties to whom the home might be transferred. This situation created conveyancing complications, and the doctrine was disapproved by the House of Lords in *National Provincial Bank Ltd v Ainsworth* in 1965,[114] on the ground that the wife held no proprietary interest recognised by the law. The deserted wife was thus left unprotected against third parties. The criticism which followed led to the registration of a deserted wife's "right of occupation" under the Matrimonial Homes Act 1967 (now Family Law Act 1996).[115]

The problem presented in *National Provincial Bank Ltd v Ainsworth* is a very real one in the context of the conveyancing system, and is relevant throughout the law of licences. One basic principle of the 1925 legislation was to provide for the documentation of all dealings with the legal estate and for equities and equitable interests to be either overreachable or registrable.[116] The principle is all the more obvious with registered land, when the intention is to record everything except overriding interests. From a conveyancer's point of view, these are good principles, but the system has not remained intact either in the case of unregistered land,[117] or in the case of registered land because of the wide provision for the protection of overriding interests of a person in actual occupation of the land.[118] A very significant inroad into these principles of conveyancing is found in the modern development of licences. If the licence has a sufficiently proprietary quality that it can bind a third party, then, even where only negative protection is given to

---

[110] *Winter Garden Theatre (London) Ltd v Millennium Productions Ltd* [1948] AC 173; p. 834, ante (injunction).

[111] *Inwards v Baker* [1965] 2 QB 29; p. 842, ante. See *Griffiths v Williams* (1977) 248 EG 947, M & B, p. 673; p. 844, n. 92, ante.

[112] *Pascoe v Turner* [1979] 1 WLR 431, M & B p. 667; p. 843, ante; *Voyce v Voyce* (1991) 62 P & CR 290.

[113] *Bendall v McWhirter* [1952] 2 QB 466; *Ferris v Weaven* [1952] 2 All ER 233; *Street v Denham* [1954] 1 WLR 624; *Lee v Lee* [1952] 2 QB 489n; *Jess B Woodcock & Son Ltd v Hobbs* [1955] 1 WLR 152; *Westminster Bank Ltd v Lee* [1956] Ch 7; *Miles v Bull* [1969] 1 QB 258.

[114] [1965] AC 1175, M & B p. 135. See also *Hall v King* [1987] 2 EGLR 121 where Sir John DONALDSON MR said at 122: "A wife's right to occupy the matrimonial home is of a very special nature, depending upon her status as a wife and not upon any leave or licence of her husband . . . This accords with common sense and experience. Whoever heard of a husband expressly or impliedly saying to his wife 'Do come and stay with me in the matrimonial home, dear'. "   [115] P. 478, ante.

[116] Pp. 102–3, ante.

[117] *E R Ives Investment Ltd v High* [1967] 2 QB 379, M & B p. 665 (proprietary estoppel), supra; *Poster v Slough Estates Ltd* [1969] 1 Ch 495 (right of entry to remove a fixture on termination of lease); *Caunce v Caunce* [1969] 1 WLR 286, M & B p. 311; *Kingsnorth Finance Co Ltd v Tizard* [1986] 1 WLR 783, M & B p. 156; p. 62, ante (beneficial interest of wife who had contributed towards purchase price); *Shiloh Spinners Ltd v Harding* [1973] AC 691, M & B p. 34 (equitable right of entry on breach of covenant); p. 100, ante.

[118] LRA 1925, s. 70(1)(g); *Hodgson v Marks* [1971] Ch 892; *Williams and Glyn's Bank Ltd v Boland* [1981] AC 487, M & B p. 136; p. 981, post; LRA 2002, s. 29, Sch. 3, para. 2; s. 116, supra.

the licensee,[119] a purchaser is faced with the interest of the licensee as a blot on his title. The licensee may be in possession, and the purchaser may thus have what would be considered to be constructive notice under the pre-1926 cases.[120] But these rules are now taken over by provisions for registration, and licences are not registrable under the Land Charges Act 1925. Indeed, it would be a disaster for the licensee if they were; for many of the licence situations arise in connection with personal family affairs, without legal advice, and as a matter of practice would hardly ever be registered; and, further, if they were registrable and not registered, they would in unregistered land be void even against a purchaser who actually knew of the licence.

The difficulties are even greater where the licensee receives an award of an undocumented proprietary interest or estate. Once the case has been determined, the proper documentation can be prepared, but the licensee's protection cannot depend upon the trial of the action. The protection is given in equity, and not by the court's decision; and, as we have seen,[121] it has been recognised that an equity arising by estoppel has a sufficiently proprietary quality to bind the purchaser before the court's decision if (in unregistered land) he has notice of it or (in registered land) it is protected by notice or as an overriding interest. And it is not at all clear whether the purchaser can overreach the equity.[122] Before 1997 there was a particular danger attached to the court's decision to award the licensee a life interest, since it was arguable that the licensee would thereby become a tenant for life under the Settled Land Act 1925. The point was first noticed by Scott LJ in *Bannister v Bannister*,[123] a case decided on the theory of constructive trust. The point was overlooked in many of the licence cases.[124] The view has been expressed that the Settled Land Act 1925 would not apply.[125] Russell LJ, on the other hand, noted in *Dodsworth v Dodsworth*,[126] that the award of a life interest would "lead, by virtue of the provisions of the Settled Land Act, to a greater and more extensive interest than was ever contemplated by the plaintiff and the defendants". Since the Trusts of Land and Appointment of Trustees Act 1996 came into force on 1 January 1997,[127] however, settlements can no longer be created under the Settled Land Act 1925, and so the award of a life interest no longer gives the licensee a statutory fee simple and the wide powers of a tenant for life. However, an even more serious problem arises for the purchaser where a fee simple is awarded to the licensee, as in *Pascoe v Turner*.[128] The licensor holds the legal estate, and the licensee has a equity entitling him to the fee simple: he is the equitable owner.[129] In registered land the licensee in actual occupation who had not protected his interest by a notice in the register would be held to have an overriding interest,[130] and therefore the purchaser is bound by the equity and liable to be deprived of his title—and without any way of having been able to determine with certainty at the time of his purchase what rights were held by the licensee, given the inchoate nature of the equity before the court order. In unregistered land the old principle of notice presumably

---

119 *Inwards v Baker* [1965] 2 QB 29.   120 *Hunt v Luck* [1901] 1 Ch 45; p. 63, ante.

121 P. 845, ante.   122 P. 845, ante.   123 [1948] 2 All ER 133, M & B p. 615; p. 839, ante.

124 Cf *Inwards v Baker*, supra.

125 *Binions v Evans* [1972] Ch 359 at 366, per Lord Denning MR (unintended settlement), p. 841, ante. See also *Ivory v Palmer* [1975] ICR 340 at 347, where Cairns LJ said "*Binions v Evans* stretched to the very limit the application of the Settled Land Act". See (1977) 93 LQR 561 (J. A. Hornby).

126 (1973) 228 EG 1115, M & B p. 671.   127 Chap. 13, ante.

128 [1979] 1 WLR 431, M & B p. 667.

129 *Voyce v Voyce* (1991) 62 P & CR 290 at 294, per Dillon LJ.

130 LRA 2002, s. 30, Sch. 3, para. 2, replacing LRA 1925, s. 70(1)(g); pp. 107, ante, 979, post.

applies;[131] and its application must be particularly difficult where, as in *Pascoe v Turner*, the licensee had not the slightest idea that she was entitled to a fee simple.

The question is sometimes asked as to whether these developments show that a licence should now be regarded as an interest in land. At an early stage the courts took the view that a licence coupled with a grant under seal was irrevocable;[132] from which one might conclude that if a licence was granted under seal, it must be the subject matter of a grant, and that makes it look like an interest in land. That theory, however, was largely exploded once it was decided that there could be no easement in gross; for that, at best, is what a licence granted under seal could claim to be.[133] From the 1940s, the doctrine has been accepted that a contractual licensee or licensee holding an equity by estoppel may be protected by injunction. And although the courts flirted with the idea that, in consequence of this protection in equity, the contractual licence can bind a third party,[134] this has been rejected.[135] Licences protected by estoppel have been held to be binding on third parties,[136] and the Land Registration Act 2002[137] has declared that an equity by estoppel is an interest capable of binding successors in title. But in none of these cases can it properly be said that the licence is itself an interest in land. The licence coupled with a grant is not irrevocable on its own account, but only by virtue of the irrevocability of the grant to which it was coupled. A licence protected only by contract carries only the benefits that the law of contract gives: and since contracts are personal, the contractual licence does not of itself create an interest in land. However, if the licensee is protected by constructive trust, or by proprietary estoppel, then the interest held by the licensee under the trust, or his equity by estoppel, may themselves have proprietary consequences. In ascertaining, therefore, the nature and strength of the licensee's rights, both against the licensor and against a third party, one must consider not just the licence itself—the permission to enter upon the land—but the circumstances surrounding the giving of the licence, and the continuing exercise of it by the licensor, to see whether there are factors to justify the analysis that the licensor has an interest in the land.[138]

---

[131] *E R Ives Investment Ltd v High* [1967] 2 QB 379; p. 825, ante.   [132] P. 832, ante.

[133] See *Cowell v Rosehill Racecourse Co Ltd* (1937) 56 CLR 605 at 616, M & B p. 598, per LATHAM CJ: "the right to see a spectacle cannot, in the ordinary sense of legal language, be regarded as a proprietary interest. Fifty thousand people who pay to see a football match do not obtain fifty thousand interests in the football ground".

[134] *Errington v Errington and Woods* [1952] 1 KB 290; p. 837, ante; *Binions v Evans* [1972] Ch 359, M & B p. 617; p. 840, ante.   [135] *Ashburn Anstalt v Arnold* [1989] Ch 1, M & B p. 618; p. 840, ante.

[136] Pp. 825, 845, ante.   [137] S. 116 ("for the avoidance of doubt"); p. 826, ante.

[138] See, e.g., *Re Sharpe* [1980] 1 WLR 219, where BROWNE-WILKINSON J analysed the nature of a licensee's rights on multiple bases (contractual licence, equitable licence and constructive trust) in order to find a basis on which they would bind the licensor's trustee in bankruptcy.

PART III

THE CREATION, TRANSFER AND EXTINCTION OF ESTATES AND INTERESTS IN LAND

SUMMARY

It may be said that what we have described so far is the law at rest. Our attention has been directed to the actual rights that can be enjoyed in land. We have taken each estate and interest that is capable of subsisting, either at law or in equity, and have explained what incidents are applicable to it when it exists. It now remains to treat of the law in motion, that is, to show how estates and interests may be validly created, transferred and dealt with generally, and how they may be extinguished.

24

THE CONTRACT[1]

SUMMARY

The creation or transfer of an estate or interest in land will often be preceded by a contract. A contract for the sale of land usually precedes the conveyance of the legal estate to the purchaser; and this is so whether the land is already registered[2] or is still unregistered.[3] Similarly, a contract for a lease may be made first, and then followed at a later date by a formal grant of the legal term of years absolute.[4] Moreover, the owner of an estate in land may contract to create an interest in it, such as an easement or a charge, the actual creation

---

[1] See generally Barnsley, *Conveyancing Law and Practice*; Emmet; M & B pp. 65–77, 84–96.
[2] LRA 2002, s. 23(1)(a); R & R, para. 13.004.03.
[3] Most dispositions of unregistered land will now trigger compulsory registration: p. 101, ante; p. 954, post.
[4] P. 219, ante.

of the interest to follow later. The formalities required for the creation and transfer of estates and interests in land, and certain aspects of the law and practice governing the creation and transfer, will be considered in chapters 25 and 27. In this chapter we are concerned with the contract.

I Formation of the Contract

Apart from the requirement of formality,[5] a contract for the sale or other disposition of an interest in land is created in the same way as any other contract.[6] There must be final and complete agreement between the parties on its essential terms,[7] that is to say, the parties, the property (and the interest to be granted in it[8]) and the consideration. However, certain particular issues arise in connection with the negotiation and formation of a contract relating to land, which are considered in this section. The formality requirements will be discussed in the following section.

A Pre-contract Enquiries and Disclosure

The general position taken by the English law of contract is *caveat emptor*: in a contract of sale it is for the purchaser to satisfy himself about what he is buying, and the vendor has no general duty of disclosure, not even a duty to disclose facts relating to the property which he knows the purchaser would regard as significant, nor to disabuse the purchaser of mistakes which the vendor realises he is making.[9] The vendor may be liable if he makes a misrepresentation, or if he gives a contractual undertaking (express or implied) about the property.[10] But otherwise the purchaser generally has no remedy against him. The vendor under a contract for the sale of land therefore has no general duty of disclosure, and no duty to disclose defects in the quality of the property,[11] although in the absence of express provision to the contrary he does have certain implied obligations at common law under the contract of sale relating to the proof of his title to the property.[12] There is some uncertainty about the

---

[5] Pp. 863 et seq, post.   [6] Anson, chaps. 2 and 3.

[7] *Rossiter v Miller* (1878) 3 App Cas 1124 at 1151, per Lord BLACKBURN. See *Gibson v Manchester City Council* [1979] 1 WLR 294 at 297 (bipartite contract must normally be formed by offer and acceptance); *Fletcher v Davies* (1980) 257 EG 1149 (flat in Inner Temple).

[8] In the case of a lease, this includes the commencement and the period of the tenancy: p. 219, ante.

[9] *Smith v Hughes* (1867) LR 6 QB 597 at 606–7; Cartwright, *Misrepresentation*, chap. 11.

[10] For the purchaser's remedies, see pp. 883 et seq, post.

[11] Emmet, para. 1.013; Farrand, *Contract and Conveyance* (4th edn), pp. 67–8; Barnsley, *Conveyancing Law and Practice*, pp. 178–80; Cartwright, *Misrepresentation*, para. 11.33; *Terrene Ltd v Nelson* (1937) 157 LT 254 at 256–7. In this respect the purchaser under a contract relating to land is even less protected than the purchaser under a contract for the sale or supply of goods, since by statute a business seller or supplier of goods impliedly guarantees such things as the quality of the goods and their fitness for purpose: Sale of Goods Act 1979, s. 14; Supply of Goods and Services Act 1982, ss. 4, 9, all as amended by Sale and Supply of Goods Act 1994, s. 7(1), Sch. 2. However, in a contract to build and sell a house the builder-vendor impliedly promises that the house will be constructed in a good and workmanlike manner, with good and proper materials, and will be fit for habitation: *Hancock v B W Brazier (Anerley) Ltd* [1966] 1 WLR 1317; and builders of new houses may provide guarantees under schemes run by the National House-Building Council, and may owe duties in tort under Defective Premises Act 1972.

[12] P. 932, post; Emmet, paras. 4.026–4.036; Farrand, *Contract and Conveyance* (4th edn), pp. 62–75; Barnsley, *Conveyancing Law and Practice*, p. 266. For the landlord's obligation (in the absence of contrary stipulation) to

scope of these implied obligations,[13] and therefore it is in the interests of both parties to a contract for the sale of land to make express provision. Moreover, since in general the purchaser's remedies in the event of his discovering a problem with his purchase are limited to claims for the vendor's misrepresentation or breach of contract, it became established practice for the party negotiating for the purchase of land to ask questions not only of the vendor personally but also through his solicitor or other agent; and to ask for certain matters to be covered explicitly in the terms of the contract. This practice grew over the years to the point where there were numerous so-called "standard" forms of enquiry used by purchasers' solicitors, and "standard" forms of contract terms which allocated to one or other party the risk of certain matters relating to the property.[14] In relation to residential conveyancing[15] this standard practice has been simplified and taken further in two respects in recent years, first by professional regulation and most recently by legislation.

First, in 1990 the Council of the Law Society issued the National Conveyancing Protocol[16] designed for use in domestic conveyancing of freehold and leasehold property, setting out the steps to be followed by solicitors acting for the vendor and purchaser; its aim was to provide the purchaser's solicitor with as much information as possible about the property at the outset, as well as to simplify the existing practice by providing a single standard form of pre-contract enquiries and a single standard form of contract.[17]

The Housing Act 2004[18] has now taken this further, and for sales of residential property with vacant possession places a statutory duty[19] on the seller or his estate agent to have in his possession a "home information pack",[20] a collection of documents relating to the property or the terms on which it is or may become available for sale. A copy of the home information pack must be provided to a potential buyer on request,[21] and the documents which it must

disclose information about his own title to the party negotiating to take a new lease, and the tenant's obligation to disclose information about the superior title to the assignee of his lease, see p. 934–5, post.

[13] In particular, the duty to disclose latent defects in the title, and the purchaser's remedies in the case of a defect which was not in fact known to the vendor: Cartwright, *Misrepresentation*, para. 11.43.

[14] Barnsley, *Conveyancing Law and Practice*, pp. 188–9.

[15] For non-residential conveyancing, see Standard Commercial Property Conditions of Sale (2nd edn, 2004); Silverman, *Conveyancing Handbook*, Appendix VI.14.

[16] [1990] Conv 137 (H. W. Wilkinson); Barnsley, *Conveyancing Law and Practice*, pp. 188–93; Silverman, *Conveyancing Handbook*, section A19. The Protocol is now in its fifth edition (2004) and is reproduced in Silverman, *Conveyancing Handbook*, Appendix II.1. It is specified by the Council of the Law Society as "preferred practice" for solicitors, but is not mandatory under the rules of professional conduct.

[17] The Standard Conditions of Sale: p. 858, post.

[18] Part 5. These provisions will come into force when the Secretary of State appoints (except for ss. 161–4 and 176, which themselves provide for the Secretary of State to make regulations preparatory to the operation of the provisions, and which came into force immediately on the passing of the Act): s. 270. In November 2005 the Government announced that the use of home information packs would be mandatory from 1 June 2007. It is expected that pilot schemes will be run on a voluntary basis from July 2006, before the provisions are brought fully into effect. See generally Silverman, *Conveyancing Handbook*, s. A26; (2005) 155 NLJ 5 (M. Garson), 206 (E. Orme); (2004) 148 SJ 1454 (C. Baker); [2005] 03 LSG 32 (P. Marsh); [2005] Conv 277.

[19] Housing Act 2004, s. 155. The duty is imposed only on either the seller or the estate agent, depending on which is for the time being responsible for marketing the property: ss. 151–3; and is enforceable not directly by the purchaser but through an enforcement authority which can require production of the pack and issue penalty charge notices for failure to comply: ss. 167–8; Sch. 8. The purchaser's remedy against the seller or his estate agent is only for recovery of fees paid to commission documents that should have been supplied in a home information pack: s. 170.   [20] Ibid., s. 148(2).

[21] ibid., s. 156. For circumstances where the request can properly be refused, see s. 156(4). The purchaser can insist on receiving a paper copy of the pack, rather than an electronic copy (s. 156(11)), but can be

contain are to be prescribed in regulations made by the Secretary of State,[22] but must be such as would contain information about the property, or its sale, that would be of interest to potential buyers, such as[23] the interest which is for sale and the terms on which it is proposed to sell it, the title to the property, anything relating to or affecting the property that is contained in registers or records, the physical condition of the property, its energy efficiency, any warranties or guarantees subsisting in relation to the property and any taxes, service charges or other charges payable in relation to it. The regulations may also[24] require or authorise the pack to include replies that the seller proposes to give to prescribed pre-contract enquiries, and may[25] require information relating to the physical condition of the property or its energy efficiency to be provided in a "home condition report" following an inspection by an individual who is a member of an approved certification scheme. In some respects this reform has only formalised good conveyancing practice which was already well-established under the National Conveyancing Protocol: for example, in relation to the provision of information about the property in the form of answers to standard pre-contract enquiries. However, it does go further not only in making the provision of prescribed information now mandatory, but also in extending the scope of the required information and in requiring the vendor to provide to a potential purchaser a survey of the physical characteristics of the property—a substantive change to the former practice under which it was the purchaser who was expected to commission his own survey. The introduction of home information packs has therefore eroded still further—and now as a matter of law, not simply as a matter of practice—the *caveat emptor* rule in so far as it relates to sales of vacant residential property.

However, the fact that the vendor is required to provide information about the property does not entirely reverse the *caveat emptor* rule. As already mentioned, before the Housing Act it had already become common practice for standard enquiries to be asked by purchasers in order to elicit important information about the property. Unless the vendor made a misrepresentation in his reply the purchaser still had no remedy; and the courts have construed the enquiries put by prospective purchasers strictly so as not to impose an inappropriate obligation of disclosure on vendors.

A striking example is *Sykes v Taylor-Rose*[26] in which the vendors of a house, who had recently discovered that a horrific murder been committed in the house some years earlier, answered their purchaser's question,[27] "Is there any other information which you think the buyer might have a right to know?" with a simple "No". Holding that this question required only an honest answer, and noting that the vendors had been acting on the advice of their solicitor to the effect that they had no duty of disclosure, the trial judge[28] rejected the

---

required to pay for a paper copy and to accept conditions relating to the use or disclosure of the copy (s. 157).

[22] Housing Act 2004, s. 163(1). Draft Regulations were published by the Government on 31 October 2005, inviting comments on the drafting, accuracy and practical application of the provisions, and the content of the draft forms. A detailed commentary and guidance (including a sample home condition report) was published in November 2005. Up-to-date information about the implementation is available on the ODPM web site. For discussion of the draft regulations, see [2006] 03 EG 115 (K. Fenn); [2006] 05 EG 265 (G. Murphy); (2006) 156 NLJ 213 (P. Ambrose).   [23] Housing Act 2004, s. 163(5).

[24] Ibid., s. 163(6).   [25] Ibid., s. 164.   [26] [2004] 2 P & CR 30; (2004) 148 SJ 497 (M. Pawlowski).

[27] Question 13 in the Law Society's standard form of pre-contract enquiries in use at the time within the National Conveyancing Protocol.

[28] Judge Langan QC, Leeds County Court (8 July 2003). Counsel for the claimants had argued that, although there is no general duty on a vendor to disclose defects in the quality or expected enjoyment of land which he is

purchaser's claims based on non-disclosure and misrepresentation. The Court of Appeal upheld the judge. PETER GIBSON LJ said:[29]

Because the *caveat emptor* rule can work harshly on purchasers, whose knowledge of material facts affecting the property they are purchasing is almost certain to be considerably less than that of the vendors, the practice of sending pre-contract enquiries has become standard and the scope of the enquiries has been extended over a period of time. It is for the buyer to decide what enquiries to raise and in what form. It cannot be doubted that a more specific and less subjective question going to the value of the property or to the ability of the purchaser to enjoy the property could have been asked. Unhappily, question 13 in the Law Society's form at that time (we are told that it is no longer in use) did allow the answer to be given in a way which only required, in my view, the vendor to answer the question honestly.

Similarly, the requirement now that a vendor of residential property provide a home information pack which contains answers to standard form pre-contract enquiries will only provide as much protection for the purchaser as the drafting of the questions allows—and only in so far as the vendor actually provides information. It should be noted that vendors are not under a legal obligation to answer questions set out in the property information form included in a home information pack.[30]

B Terms of the Contract. "Open Contract" and Special Conditions of Sale

If a contract for the sale of land specifies merely the names of the parties, a description of the property and a statement of the price, it is called an *open contract*. As has already been mentioned,[31] when this form of contract is made the parties are bound by certain obligations implied by the law, and it is in both parties' interest to include special stipulations in the contract to modify their implied obligations, as well as to make specific provision for matters on which the contract would otherwise be silent. The parties may incorporate into their contract such terms as they think fit, as long as they do not contravene any common law or statutory rule.[32] In practice contracts for the sale of land are generally

---

selling, or matters which may affect the value of the land, the particular facts of the case were so heinous that they could not be withheld because there is no other way by which the reasonably prudent purchaser would be able to discover them; and that the principle of *caveat emptor*, hallowed though it may have been in the past, is nearing the end of its useful life. This was firmly rejected by the Judge, and there was no appeal on this point: [2004] 2 P & CR 30 at [15].

[29] [2004] 2 P & CR 30 at [50].

[30] *Reforming the home buying and selling process in England and Wales: Contents of the home information pack* (Consultation Paper, Office of the Deputy Prime Minister, March 2003), para. 7.5 "We do not intend, however, to change the principle of *caveat emptor* (let the buyer beware). We are not suggesting that sellers should be under a legal obligation to answer questions set out in a property information form included in the home information pack."   [31] Pp. 854–5 ante.

[32] E.g. a stipulation that the conveyance to, or the registration of title of, the purchaser shall be prepared or carried out at the expense of the purchaser by a solicitor appointed by the vendor is void: LPA 1925, s. 48(1). See also s. 42, as amended by TLATA 1996, s. 25(1), Sch. 3, para. 4(1), (11). The general statutory controls on the fairness of exclusion and limitation clauses in the Unfair Contract Terms Act 1977, ss. 2–4 do not apply to a contract so far as it relates to the creation, transfer or termination of an interest in land: Sch. 1, para. 1(b). The Unfair Terms in Consumer Contracts Regulations 1999 do however apply to land contracts: *R (Khatun) v Newham LBC* [2005] QB 37. The Law Commission's proposals to replace the 1977 Act and the 1999 Regulations with a single unified legislative regime would continue to maintain the control on unfair contract terms in land

in standard form. For most residential sales and small commercial property sales the Standard Conditions of Sale[33] are usually employed; for more complex commercial sales the Standard Commercial Property Conditions are often used.[34] In both cases the parties will generally make amendments to the standard forms, or add their own particular terms.[35]

Further, if the contract is made by correspondence, the Statutory Form of Conditions of Sale 1925 applies, except in so far as there is any modification or intention to the contrary expressed in the correspondence.[36]

The terminology of "conditions" of sale can be misleading. DANCKWERTS LJ has referred to

the long-standing practice which has arisen among conveyancers of referring to the provisions in a contract for the sale of land as "conditions of sale", whether special or general (such as those provided by the common forms produced under the name of the National Conditions of Sale, or those produced by the Law Society). The word "condition" is traditional rather than appropriate, and these provisions are not so much concerned with the validity of the contract of sale as with the production of the title and the performance of the vendor's and purchaser's obligations leading up to completion by conveyance. Shortly, they are no more than the terms of the contract.[37]

C Negotiations or Agreement "Subject to Contract"

It is common practice in sales of land for the parties to agree a price "subject to contract".[38] The object of this procedure, "though it has drawbacks and is capable of being abused in certain circumstances, is based on a sound concept, namely, that the buyer should be free from binding commitment until he has had the opportunity of obtaining legal and other advice, arranging his finance and making the necessary inspections, searches and

contracts in favour of a consumer: Law Com No. 292 (2005), Cm 6464, paras. 3.80, 5.76. A contract term which excludes or restricts liability for misrepresentation is subject to Misrepresentation Act 1967, s. 3, as substituted by Unfair Contract Terms Act 1977, s. 8; there is no exclusion for contracts relating to land. See *Walker v Boyle* [1982] 1 WLR 495 at 507–8 (condition in National Conditions of Sale, 19th edn, unreasonable and therefore of no effect).

[33] The current edition is the 4th edn 2003 which came into effect with the implementation of LRA 2002. It is reproduced in *Silverman*, Conveyancing Handbook, Appendix VI, with Explanatory Notes at Appendix V.21; Emmet, vol. 3, Notes and Recommendations, pp. 501–3. Kenny, *Conveyancing Practice*, reproduces the 1st to 4th edn at B001–B030/3. See also (sometimes on earlier editions of the Conditions), Aldridge, *Companion to the Standard Conditions of Sale* (3rd edn 2003), Silverman, *Standard Conditions of Sale* (6th edn 1999), Wilkinson, *Standard Conditions of Sale of Land* (1989); [1990] Conv 179, [1992] Conv 316 (J. E. Adams).

[34] 2nd edn 2004, reproduced in Silverman, *Conveyancing Handbook*, Appendix VI.14; Kenny, *Conveyancing Practice*, B030/4–B033. [2004] 23 LSG 37 (M. Waters); [2004] Conv 260 (E. Slessenger, comparing the 1st and 2nd edns).

[35] Generally termed "special conditions", to distinguish them from the "general conditions" contained in the standard forms.

[36] LPA 1925, s. 46; SR & O 1925 No. 779; *Stearn v Twitchell* [1985] 1 All ER 631 (contract arising out of acceptance by single letter of oral offer to buy or sell land held to be contract by correspondence). See (1974) 90 LQR 55 (A. M. Prichard). This section was not repealed by the LP(MP)A 1989 p. 868 post. It may have been overlooked or left on the statute book out of an abundance of caution: *Commission for the New Towns v Cooper (Great Britain) Ltd* [1995] Ch 259 at 287, per STUART-SMITH LJ, although it may well have a reduced application now, given that an exchange of correspondence will often not fulfil the formality requirements of s. 2 LP(MP)A 1989; p. 868, post.   [37] *Property and Bloodstock Ltd v Emerton* [1968] Ch 94 at 118.

[38] See [1984] Conv 173, 251 (R. W. Clarke), comparing English and Irish law. For its continued use in contracts after 26 September 1989, see p. 874, post.

enquiries".[39] In 1975 the Law Commission recommended that there should be no change in this practice, even though one consequence is that the purchaser may be "gazumped" (that is, the vendor may withdraw from the bargain or threaten to do so, in the expectation of receiving a higher price).[40]

The effect of such phrases as "subject to contract",[41] or "subject to a formal contract to be drawn up by our solicitors" is that there is no contract, unless there are some very exceptional circumstances necessitating a different construction.[42] Either party is free to repudiate the bargain until a formal contract has been made.[43]

Thus in *Winn v Bull*:[44]

a written agreement was entered into whereby the defendant agreed to take from the plaintiff a lease of a house for a certain time at a certain rent, "subject to the preparation and approval of a formal contract". No formal or other contract was ever entered into between the parties. It was held that there was no contract.

The parties may, however, be bound at once, although they intend to make a more formal contract later on. In *Branca v Cobarro*,[45] for example,

a written agreement to sell the lease and goodwill of a mushroom farm ended as follows: "This is a provisional agreement until a fully legalised agreement, drawn up by a solicitor and embodying all the conditions herewith stated, is signed". It was held by the Court of Appeal[46] that the parties, by using the

---

[39] Law Commission Report on "Subject to Contract" Agreements (Law Com No. 65, 1975), para. 13. See *Cohen v Nessdale Ltd* [1981] 3 All ER 118 at 127–8; affd [1982] 2 All ER 97.

[40] See the Law Commission Conveyancing Standing Committee's suggestion of a standard form of Pre-Contract Deposit Agreement, which would go some way towards deterring gazumping. It was called a paper-tiger: The Times, 17 January 1987, and was abandoned: [1988] Conv 79. See also the Committee's House Selling the Scottish Way for England and Wales (1987). Both are reproduced in Emmet, vol. 3, Notes and Recommendations, pp. 311–16, 351–64. See generally Barnsley: *Conveyancing Law and Practice*, pp. 216–19. The converse of "gazumping" is "gazundering": the corresponding freedom of the *purchaser* to withdraw in order to achieve a *lower* price. The state of the sales market dictates which is the more likely practice. One of the Government's purposes in introducing home information packs, supra, is to reduce gazumping.

[41] *Tiverton Estates Ltd v Wearwell Ltd* [1975] Ch 146; *Munton v Greater London Council* [1976] 1 WLR 649; *Sherbrooke v Dipple* (1980) 41 P & CR 173, [1981] Conv 165.

[42] *Chillingworth v Esche* [1924] 1 Ch 97; *Alpenstow Ltd v Regalian Properties plc* [1985] 1 WLR 721 (words "subject to contract" meaningless); *Westway Homes Ltd v Moores* [1991] 2 EGLR 193 (notice served by grantee of option to purchase headed "subject to contract" held to be surplusage and of no effect); *Farah v Moody* [1998] EGCS 1; *Prudential Assurance Co Ltd v Mount Eden Land Ltd* [1997] 1 EGLR 37 (subject to licence).

See Wilkinson, *Standard Conditions of Sale of Land* (2nd edn 1974), chap. 5 for a useful summary of standard conditional phrases; Barnsley, *Conveyancing Law and Practice*, pp. 135–9, (1975) 39 Conv (NS) 229–36, 311–13; Emmet, paras. 2.016–2.019; Conv Prec pp. 8277–8285. See, for examples of valid phrases, *Janmohamed v Hassam* (1976) 241 EG 609 ("subject to purchaser obtaining mortgage on terms satisfactory to himself within one month"); *Meehan v Jones* (1982) 56 ALJR 813; [1984] Conv 243; cf *Lee-Parker v Izzet (No 2)* [1972] 1 WLR 775; (1976) 40 Conv (NS) 37 (B. Coote); *Ee v Kakar* (1979) 40 P & CR 223 ("subject to survey"); (1981) 131 NLJ 771 (H. W. Wilkinson); *Duttons Brewery Ltd v Leeds City Council* (1981) 43 P & CR 160 ("at a price of £15,000 subject to a contract to be approved by me"); *Heron Garage Properties Ltd v Moss* [1974] 1 WLR 148 ("conditional on purchaser obtaining detailed town planning consent"); cf *Balbosa v Ayoub Ali* [1990] 1 WLR 914 ("subject to obtaining from the Town and Country Planning Department of all the necessary approvals for the transfer of the premises"); *Graham v Pitkin* [1992] 1 WLR 403 ("subject to the purchaser obtaining a mortgage from [a building society] of $19,000 for 10 years"); [1992] Conv 318 (C. Harpum); [1995] Conv 83 (C. Harpum and G. Barnsley). See also *Provost Developments Ltd v Collingwood Towers Ltd* [1980] 2 NZLR 205 ("subject to a solicitor's approval"); [1981] Conv 90 (H. W. Wilkinson).

[43] Usually by exchange of contracts: p. 862, post.   [44] (1877) 7 Ch D 29.   [45] [1947] KB 854.

word "provisional" had intended the document to be immediately binding and to remain so until superseded by a more formal document.

Once applied, the words "subject to contract" are very difficult to displace except by the formal contract which the parties envisaged. Where the parties have started their negotiations under a "subject to contract" formula, their later negotiations, and any apparently final (but not yet formalised) agreement, will continue to be qualified by it, unless and until they agree expressly or by necessary implication that the qualification should be expunged.[47] It is even more difficult to displace a "subject to contract" qualification which the parties have expressly applied to a concluded agreement in principle. It has been said that a party might possibly be estopped from relying on a "subject to contract" clause, but that this is rarely likely to occur.[48] For an estoppel, one party must have created or encouraged the other party's belief or expectation that it would not withdraw from the agreement, and the latter party must have relied on that belief or expectation.[49] But the very purpose of having expressed the agreement to be "subject to contract" is to indicate that it is not to be binding until the exchange of formal contracts. If the parties have not agreed to lift the "subject to contract" restriction on their agreement—in which case there would be no need to rely on an estoppel—the continuing force of that restriction will normally preclude any assertion by one party that the other has encouraged him to believe that he will be bound unconditionally.[50]

It should be noted, however, that the words "subject to contract" only prevent an executory contract from coming into existence. If the parties perform the obligations contemplated by the "subject to contract" agreement, they may be held to have entered into an implied binding contract on the terms of the agreement.[51]

D Lock-out Agreement

As we have seen, a purchaser may be gazumped by a vendor (or a vendor gazundered by a purchaser) at any stage before completion. However he may seek to avoid this hazard by entering into a "lock-out" agreement with the vendor, that is, by making an agreement with him not to negotiate with any third party, which will be contractually binding provided that

---

[46] Reversing DENNING J, who construed "provisional" as equivalent to "tentative".

[47] *Tevanan v Norman Brett (Builders) Ltd* (1972) 223 EG 1945 at 1947, per BRIGHTMAN J; *Sherbrooke v Dipple* (1980) 41 P & CR 173; *Cohen v Nessdale Ltd* [1981] 3 All ER 118.

[48] *A-G of Hong Kong v Humphreys Estate (Queen's Gardens) Ltd* [1987] AC 114 at 127–8, M & B p. 75, per Lord TEMPLEMAN.　　　　　　　　　　　　　　　　　　　　　　　　　　　　　[49] Ibid., at 124.

[50] Ibid.; *James v Evans* [2000] 3 EGLR 1 at 4; *Edwin Shirley Productions Ltd v Workspace Management Ltd* [2001] 2 EGLR 16 at [50], M & B p. 75; *Secretary of State for Transport v Christos* [2004] 1 P & CR 17 at [41]–[44]; [2003] Conv 360.

[51] *Rugby Group Ltd v Proforce Recruit Ltd* [2005] EWHC 70, [2005] All ER (D) 22 (Feb) (not a contract relating to land. For the question of whether LP(MP)A 1989, s. 2 applies to an executed agreement relating to land, see p. 871, post, and for the relevance of the "subject to contract" qualification under that section, see p. 874, post); *Bryen & Langley Ltd v Boston* [2005] All ER (D) 507 (Jul) (parties proposed in letter that agreement shall be contained in later formal contract; this did not preclude conclusion that they had informally already contractually bound themselves on exactly the same terms).

it is made for good consideration and a specified period of time. As Lord Ackner said in *Walford v Miles*:[52]

I stress that this is a negative agreement—B, by agreeing not to negotiate for a fixed period, locks himself out of such negotiations. He has in no legal sense locked himself into negotiations with A. What A has achieved is an exclusive opportunity, for a fixed period, to try to come to terms with B, an opportunity for which he has, unless he makes his agreement under seal, to give good consideration.

However, the commercial usefulness of a lock-out agreement can be limited. All the lock-out does is to prohibit the vendor from negotiating with other parties during the lock-out period. He can decline to take further the negotiations with the purchaser, and simply wait until the end of the period and then re-market the property: the agreement may therefore give little comfort to the purchaser unless in addition to the lock-out it provides for reimbursement of the purchaser's expenditure, such as legal and surveying fees, should the vendor pull out of the transaction for no good reason.[53] Moreover, even if the vendor breaches the agreement, the courts will not normally enforce it by way of injunction, since damages are said to be an adequate remedy;[54] and even so the purchaser may have some difficulty in establishing the loss which flowed from the vendor's breach. In principle, the damages will cover the purchaser's loss of opportunity to purchase the property.[55] But to do this he has the burden of showing that he lost a real or substantial, not merely a speculative, chance of purchasing the property.[56] Lord WOOLF has said:[57]

Even though you can now arrange a "lock-out" if you are sufficiently knowledgeable to do so, that only provides partial compensation. Much more extensive protection is needed. It should be axiomatic that, once you have made an offer to purchase, you can be released from the transaction only in restricted circumstances; likewise if you have accepted an offer to purchase, subject to contract. If you withdraw, without cause, you should be liable to pay compensation on a basis that recognises that the loss that you have caused to the other party is not confined to financial loss.

[52] [1992] 2 AC 128 at 139. In this case the agreement was void since it did not say for how long it was to last. Cf *Pitt v PHH Asset Management Ltd* [1994] 1 WLR 327 (agreement whereby vendor agreed for valuable consideration not to negotiate with anyone else for fourteen days held valid); [1993] CLJ 392 (C. MacMillan); [1994] Conv 58 (M. P. Thompson). A lock-out agreement does not have to satisfy the formalities required by LP(MP)A 1989, p. 868, post.

[53] *Moroney v Isofam, Investments SA* [1997] EGCS 178, per J. Sher QC. For precedents, see Conv Prec pp. 10137–41 which do not, however, contain express provision for reimbursement of expenditure. On the courts' reluctance to award compensation for expenditure incurred under a "subject to contract" agreement in the absence of express contractual provision, see *Regalian Properties plc v London Docklands Development Corpn* [1995] 1 WLR 212; [1995] Conv 135 (M. P. Thompson); [1995] CLJ 243 (G. Virgo).

[54] *Tye v House* (1998) 76 P & CR 188 (purpose of lock-out is to protect purchasers against costs incurred by losing contract to another party at the last minute); [1998] PLJ 1, 21 (F. Richards).

[55] In *Walford v Miles*, supra, the trial judge made clear that the breach of a lock-out agreement would give rise to an assessment of damages for the loss of opportunity, although no assessment was in fact made because the Court of Appeal and the House of Lords held that there was no binding lock-out contract. The assessment of damages in *Pitt v PHH Asset Management Ltd*, supra, is not reported.

[56] *Dandara Holdings Ltd v Co-operative Retail Services Ltd* [2004] 2 EGLR 163 at [13]–[14] (breach of lock-out did not cause purchaser's loss, because there was a strong probability the vendor would have remarketed the property anyway); [2004] EG 151 (J. Murdoch)   [57] EG Millennium Issue, p. 70.

E Exchange of Contracts

Where a formal contract is drawn up, two identical copies[58] are usually made, and each of the parties signs one of them. In such a case there is no binding contract until the copies have been exchanged.[59] It used to be common practice for exchange to be effected in person or by post,[60] but other methods are now frequently used; in particular, where the contract is not an isolated transaction but part of a chain, as often in the case of contracts for the sale of residential property, speedier methods of exchange are necessary. The Council of the Law Society has given advice on how exchange may be effected by the parties' solicitors by telephone, telex or fax, including the method to be used in the case of a chain of transactions.[61]

When electronic contracts are introduced, the practice of exchange of physical copies of identical documents will be superseded by the (electronic) signature of a single copy by or on behalf of each party, which will take effect at such time as the parties have agreed.[62]

[58] Cf *Smith v Mansi* [1963] 1 WLR 26 (exchange unnecessary where there is only one document, signed by both parties, and the same solicitor acts for both); *Storer v Manchester City Council* [1974] 1 WLR 26 (exchange not necessary where informal agreement intended to be binding. This would not now satisfy LP(MP)A 1989, s. 2, p. 868 post). For a statement of the features of exchange of contracts, the "well-recognised concept understood by both lawyers and laymen", see *Commission for the New Towns v Cooper (Great Britain) Ltd* [1995] Ch 259 at 285, per STUART-SMITH LJ, following propositions submitted by counsel (see at 294–5, per EVANS LJ).

[59] This was already well-established conveyancing practice before 1989, being the formality contemplated by the parties as giving binding effect to their agreement "subject to contract": *Trollope & Sons v Martyn Bros* [1934] 2 KB 436 at 455; *Eccles v Bryant and Pollock* [1948] Ch 93; *Harrison v Battye* [1975] 1 WLR 58 (no exchange if documents not identical); *Longman v Viscount Chelsea* (1989) 58 P & CR 189 at 190, per NOURSE LJ. Under LP(MP)A 1989, s. 2, however, the contract cannot come into existence unless both parties sign the same document or separate, identical documents which are exchanged: pp. 871–3, post; *Commission for the New Towns v Cooper (Great Britain) Ltd* [1995] Ch 259. See generally Barnsley, *Conveyancing Law and Practice*, pp. 219–26.

[60] There is some uncertainty about the time at which the contract will be formed when exchange takes place by post. If the sending of the two copies is seen as analogous to, respectively, an offer and an acceptance, the normal rules of contract formation should apply, and so the posting of the later copy will conclude the contract if the parties so intended (expressly or impliedly): cf Anson, p. 43–6. The Standard Conditions of Sale make express provision to that effect: condition 2.1.1. However, in the absence of express provision judges have been divided over whether it should be implied that posting is sufficient to conclude the contract: *Domb v Isoz* [1980] Ch 548 at 564 per TEMPLEMAN LJ; or whether each party expects not to be bound until he has actual or constructive possession of the other party's signed copy: *Eccles v Bryant and Pollock*, [1948] Ch 93 at 108 per ASQUITH LJ; *Domb v Isoz*, at 557 per BUCKLEY LJ.

[61] Formulas A (where one solicitor already holds both signed copies), B (where each solicitor still holds his own client's signed copy) and C (chains of transactions), reproduced in Silverman, *Conveyancing Handbook*, Appendix III.2; Emmet, vol. 3, Notes and Recommendations, pp. 301–4; Kenny, *Conveyancing Practice*, paras. 4.092–4.097, C-010–011. The Law Society's guidance was issued in the light of a suggestion by Lord TEMPLEMAN in *Domb v Isoz* [1980] Ch 548 at 564; (1981) 78 LSG 961 (P. V. Baker and G. Woolf). A physical exchange of documents must follow to comply with LP(MP)A 1989, s. 2: [2005] 09 LSG 32; p. 871, post.

On the duties of solicitors, see Solicitors' Practice Rules 1990 (as amended) Rules 6 (avoiding conflicts of interest in conveyancing, property selling and mortgage related services) and 6A (seller's solicitor dealing with more than one prospective buyer), reproduced in Silverman, *Conveyancing Handbook*, Appendix I.1; Emmet, para. 1.012 and Kenny, paras. C-050–053; *Clarke Boyce v Mouat* [1994] 1 AC 428 (where solicitors wrongly acted for both sides in a property development transaction, the fact that they could not perform their duties to both sides did not mean that their duty to one client was impliedly modified or that they were exonerated from liability for breach of contract); [1994] Conv 404 (R. Tobin).

[62] LCD Consultation Paper, *Electronic Conveyancing—A draft order under s. 8 Electronic Communications Act 2000*, March 2001, paras. 53–55. LP(MP)A, s. 2, will be amended: p. 873, post.

II Formalities Required for Contracts for the Sale or Other Disposition of an Interest in Land

Unlike most other contracts,[63] contracts for the sale or other disposition of an interest in land are subject to formality requirements. A contract for the sale or other disposition of land or an interest in land made before 27 September 1989 is valid, even if not made in writing, but will only be enforceable by action if evidenced by a signed memorandum in writing which complies with section 40 of the Law of Property Act 1925 or, failing that, if there is a sufficient act of part performance by the party seeking to enforce it. After 26 September 1989 this was superseded by section 2 of the Law of Property (Miscellaneous Provisions) Act 1989, under which there can be *no* contract unless it is in writing signed by or on behalf of both parties. Although the doctrine of part performance cannot now render enforceable an agreement which fails to comply with the 1989 Act, we shall see that other doctrines might sometimes have a similar effect.

Although section 40 of the Law of Property Act 1925 was repealed in 1989,[64] we shall first consider it briefly[65] because even now a claim might still occasionally turn on the enforceability of a contract made before 27 September 1989;[66] and in any event it will assist in understanding some aspects of section 2 of the Law of Property (Miscellaneous Provisions) Act, which replaced it. However, it is important to keep the two provisions separate. There are some similarities in their wording, and it might be thought that decisions on the wording of section 40 would be relevant to the interpretation of section 2. But, in rejecting the view that the word "signed" in section 2 should be interpreted on the basis of cases concerning a sufficient signature for the purposes of section 40, PETER GIBSON LJ said:[67]

Prior to the Act of 1989 the courts viewed with some disfavour those who made oral contracts but did not abide by them. The courts were prepared to interpret the statutory requirements generously to enable contracts to be enforced and in relation to the question whether there was a sufficient memorandum evidencing an agreement extrinsic evidence was admissible....

The Act of 1989 seems to me to have a new and different philosophy from that which the Statute of Frauds 1677 and section 40 of the Act of 1925 had. Oral contracts are no longer permitted. To my mind it is clear that Parliament intended that questions as to whether there was a contract, and what were the terms of the contract, should be readily ascertained by looking at the single document said to constitute the contract.

This highlights a question of policy which, in other contexts, we have seen already and will see again:[68] where the law prescribes a particular formality for a transaction, how strict is the rule? and can ways properly be found around the formality rule, consistently with the

---

[63] Statute of Frauds 1677, s. 4, required five types of contract to be either in writing or evidenced by a written memorandum. Most of s. 4 was repealed by LR (Enforcement of Contracts) Act 1954, s. 1; the only remaining formality requirements in relation to contracts are land contracts and (under the only words of s. 4 Statute of Frauds still in force) for contracts of guarantee. On s. 4 generally, see Williams, *The Statute of Frauds: Section Four, in the Light of its Judicial Interpretation*; Law Reform Committee First Report 1953 (Cmnd 8809).

[64] LP(MP)A 1989, s. 4, Sch. 2.

[65] For a more detailed discussion, see the 16th edn of this book, pp. 116–126.

[66] See, e.g., *Inglorest Investments Ltd v Campbell* [2004] 2 P & CR D7.

[67] *Firstpost Homes Ltd v Johnson* [1995] 1 WLR 1567 at 1575–6. BALCOMBE LJ said at 1577 that there was "every reason for consigning [the old law] to the limbo where it clearly belongs". See p. 872, post.

[68] Pp. 905–9, post.

policy underlying the rule, in order to give some effect to the transaction which failed to comply with it? As we shall see, the courts have found ways around the statutory rules governing the formalities for contract for the sale or other disposition of an interest in land, but in this respect the approach taken under section 40 of the 1925 Act was different from that now taken under section 2 of the 1989 Act.

A Contracts Made Before 27 September 1989. Evidence of Contract

Section 40 of the Law of Property Act 1925[69] provided that:

> (1) No action may be brought upon any contract for the sale or other disposition of land or any interest in land, unless the agreement upon which such action is brought, or some memorandum or note thereof, is in writing, and signed by the party to be charged or by some other person thereunto by him lawfully authorised.
>
> (2) This section . . . does not affect the law relating to part performance . . .

This provision did not require writing as a condition of validity of the contract; it only provided that certain contracts relating to land should be unenforceable by either party in the absence of a sufficient written memorandum.[70] However, it expressly allowed the law relating to part performance to continue to provide an exception to the requirement of a memorandum.

(1) Contracts within Section 40

The section applied to any contract for the sale or other disposition of land or any interest in land. This covered not only a contract for the sale of freehold land, but also included a contract for the grant of a lease,[71] mortgage, easement or profit.[72] It applied to a contract for the creation of a new interest in land as well as to a contract for the disposition of an existing interest; it also applied to a concluded unilateral contract to enter into a written contract for the sale of land.[73] Land is given a very wide definition in the Law of Property Act,[74] and has been held to include an interest in the proceeds of sale under a trust for sale of land.[75]

(2) The Memorandum

The contract itself did not have to be in writing. All that was required was that, before any action could be brought,[76] there should be a written memorandum. In furtherance of the

---

[69] Replacing (in part) Statute of Frauds 1677, s. 4: LPA 1925, s. 207, Sch. 7; p. 863, n. 63, ante. Farrand, *Contract and Conveyance* (4th edn), pp. 321 et seq; Barnsley, *Conveyancing Law and Practice*, pp. 111–13. LPA 1925, s. 40 was repealed by LP(MP)A 1989, s. 4, Sch. 2.

[70] *Leroux v Brown* (1852) 12 CB 801; *Maddison v Alderson* (1883) 8 App Cas 467 at 474.

[71] Cf LPA 1925, s. 54(2) for the creation by parol of leases for a term not exceeding three years; p. 220, ante.

[72] LPA 1925, s. 205(ii).

[73] *Daulia v Four Millbank Nomiees Ltd* [1978] Ch 231. But it does not apply to compulsory purchase: *Munton v Greater London Council* [1976] 1 WLR 649.   [74] LPA 1925, s. 205(ix); p. 155, ante.

[75] *Cooper v Critchley* [1955] Ch 431; *Steadman v Steadman* [1974] QB 161, followed on this point without argument [1976] AC 536; *Thompson's Trustee in Bankruptcy v Heaton* [1974] 1 WLR 605 at 610.

[76] The memorandum could be created after the contract: *Barkworth v Young* (1856) 4 Drew 1 (more than fourteen years after the contract); and might even be made before the contract, where a written offer is accepted

policy underlying the statute, the courts gave a rather generous interpretation to the question of whether there was a sufficient memorandum.[77] The question was whether a written document, signed by or on behalf of the party against whom the contract was sought to be enforced, constituted sufficient evidence against him of the contract. This in turn required that the document relied on as a memorandum satisfy two conditions: it must contain the terms of the contract; and it must constitute an express or implied recognition that a contract[78] had been entered into.

The memorandum must contain a sufficient written statement of the terms of the contract of which it purported to be evidence: that is, as in the case of all contracts for the sale of land,[79] the parties, the property[80] (and the interest to be granted in it) and the consideration, together with any special terms regarded by the parties as essential.[81] However, the courts qualified this strict rule by holding that if a term which was not evidenced by the memorandum was exclusively for the benefit of one party, he might sometimes waive the benefit of it and sue for the enforcement of the other terms;[82] and that if an oral term not contained in the memorandum was beneficial to the defendant, the plaintiff could perform it and so cure its omission from the memorandum.[83] Where a term was required to be recorded in the memorandum, it must be mentioned with sufficient certainty to satisfy the normal rules for the formation of a contract,[84] and to do so without resorting to parol evidence on the very point on which the statute required written evidence.[85] However, as long as the memorandum contained something definite to go on, the courts have been prepared to apply the general principle *id certum est quod certum reddi potest*,[86] and admit extrinsic evidence to explain incomplete references such as the identity of the vendor[87] or the property to be sold.[88] Moreover, where all the terms of the agreement were not contained in a single document which satisfied section 40, but the signed document expressly or impliedly referred to another document which was necessary to complete the statement of terms, parol evidence could be given to identify the other

---

orally but unconditionally: *Reuss v Picksley* (1866) LR 1 Exch 342; *Parker v Clark* [1960] 1 WLR 286; *Tiverton Estates Ltd v Wearwell Ltd* [1975] Ch 146 at 166.

[77] *Firstpost Homes Ltd v Johnson* [1995] 1 WLR 1567 at 1575–6, per PETER GIBSON LJ, p. 863, supra.

[78] A document expressed to be "subject to contract" could not be a sufficient memorandum: *Tiverton Estates Ltd v Wearwell Ltd*, supra, the Court of Appeal not following the own previous decision in *Law v Jones* [1974] Ch 112 (which had held that "subject to contract" was a suspensive condition capable of subsequent oral waiver). On "subject to contract" agreements generally, see p. 858, ante.   [79] Pp. 854, 857, supra.

[80] The whole of the property must be described in the memorandum, otherwise the entire contract will be unenforceable unless it can be severed: *Ram Narayan s/o Shankar v Rishad Hussain Shah s/o Tasaduq Hussain Shah* [1979] 1 WLR 1349 (oral agreement for sale of land and chattels unenforceable where memorandum only related to land and the price was indivisible: decision on Fiji statute in identical terms to LPA 1925, s. 40).

[81] *Tiverton Estates Ltd v Wearwell* [1975] Ch 146 at 161; *Tweddell v Henderson* [1975] 1 WLR 1496.

[82] *Hawkins v Price* [1947] Ch 645 at 659, per EVERSHED J.

[83] *Martin v Pycroft* (1852) 2 De GM & G 785; *Scott v Bradley* [1971] Ch 850.

[84] Anson, pp. 60–9.

[85] E.g. if the intending vendor is not named but referred to only as "the vendor": *Potter v Duffield* (1874) LR 18 Eq 4, per JESSEL MR.

[86] *Plant v Bourne* [1897] 2 Ch 281 at 288; Lewison, *Interpretation of Contracts*, para. 11.03.

[87] *Sale v Lambert* (1874) LR 18 Eq 1 at 3, per JESSEL MR: "The question is, can you find out from the memorandum who the vendor is? The property is stated to be put up for sale 'by direction of the proprietor.' . . . What more do you want? It is said that the term 'proprietor' is not a sufficient description; I think that it is an excellent description; certainly in Acts of Parliament the proprietor or owner is frequently mentioned as the person on whom notices are to be served, and the like."   [88] *Plant v Bourne*, supra.

document and all the documents formed together a sufficient memorandum for the purposes of the statute.[89]

The memorandum need not be in any particular form: even a document that had been drawn up with the express intention of repudiating the oral agreement has been held to suffice.[90] The memorandum must, however, bear the signature of the "party to be charged"—in other words, the defendant in the action—or his agent.[91] If, therefore, in an agreement between A and B the memorandum was signed by A only, it follows that B could enforce the contract but A could not.[92] However, again, the courts have construed the statute quite liberally in its requirement as to the existence of a signature.[93] It need not be written at the foot of the agreement, but could appear anywhere, provided that it was written with the view to governing the whole instrument;[94] and it could consist merely of the defendant's intials,[95] or even of his printed name,[96] provided that the intention was clearly to authenticate the document.

(3) Part Performance

Even if there was no memorandum sufficient to satisfy section 40 of the Law of Property Act 1925, the agreement embodied in an oral contract could be enforced in equity by a party who could show a sufficient act of part performance on his own side. The policy underlying this has recently been stated by Lord BINGHAM OF CORNHILL:[97]

Section 4 of the Statute of Frauds was enacted in 1677 to address a mischief facilitated, it seems, by the procedural deficiencies of the day (*Holdsworth, A History of English Law*, vol VI, pp 388–390): the calling of perjured evidence to prove spurious agreements said to have been made orally. The solution applied to the five classes of contract specified in section 4 was to require, as a condition of enforceability, some written memorandum or note of the agreement signed by the party to be charged under the agreement or his authorised agent.

It quickly became evident that if the 17th century solution addressed one mischief it was capable of giving rise to another: that a party, making and acting on what was thought to be a binding oral agreement, would find his commercial expectations defeated when the time for enforcement came and the other party successfully relied on the lack of a written memorandum or note of the agreement.

In one of the five specified classes of agreement, relating to contracts for the sale or other disposition of land, this second mischief was mitigated by the doctrine of part performance. Implementation of an

---

[89] *Timmins v Moreland Street Property Co* Ltd [1958] Ch 110 at 130. For this difficult question see further the 16th edn of this book, pp. 120–1. The courts' generous interpretation of this rule again contrasts with the strict approach to joinder of documents under LP(MP)A 1989, s. 2, p. 872, post.

[90] *Bailey v Sweeting* (1861) 9 CBNS 843; *Dewar v Mintoft* [1912] 2 KB 373.

[91] An agent is "lawfully authorised" if his authority has been conferred in writing or orally, or if it is reasonably inferable from the attendant circumstances: *Davies v Sweet* [1962] 2 QB 300 at 305. An estate agent has no authority to contract on behalf of his client, unless he is instructed to sell at a definite price and to enter into the necessary agreement: *Keen v Mear* [1920] 2 Ch 574 at 579. In the case of a sale by auction, the auctioneer becomes the agent of both parties on the fall of the hammer, and so has the authority to sign a memorandum: *Bell v Balls* [1897] 1 Ch 663; *Chaney v Maclow* [1929] 1 Ch 461; *Phillips v Butler* [1945] Ch 358. LP(MP)A 1989, s. 2(5)(b) excludes a contract made in the course of a public auction from the requirement of a written contract, p. 869, post.   [92] *Laythoarp v Bryant* (1836) 2 Bing NC 735.

[93] *Firstpost Homes Ltd v Johnson* [1995] 1 WLR 1567 at 1575–6 (PETER GIBSON LJ), p. 863, ante, p. 872, post, contrasting the requirement of signature under LP(MP)A 1989, s. 2.

[94] *Johnson v Dodgson* (1837) 2 M & W 653 at 659; *Caton v Caton* (1867) LR 2 HL 127.

[95] *Hill v Hill* [1947] Ch 231.   [96] *Cohen v Roche* [1927] 1 KB 169; *Leeman v Stocks* [1951] Ch 941.

[97] *Actionstrength Ltd v International Glass Engineering IN.GL.EN SpA* [2003] 2 AC 541 at [1]–[3].

agreement (even if partial) could be relied on to prove its existence. This doctrine was expressly preserved by section 40(2) of the Law of Property Act 1925, when section 4 of the Statute of Frauds (in its application to real property) was effectively re-enacted in section 40(1).

It should be noticed that the act of part performance was not simply evidence of the contract in place of the written memorandum required by the statute, otherwise an act by either party should logically suffice. Rather, the doctrine of part performance was a creation of the courts of equity, which took the view that it would be fraudulent for a defendant to take advantage of the absence of a signed memorandum if he had stood by and allowed the plaintiff to alter his position for the worse by carrying out acts in performance of the contract.[98] In such a case the defendant was really "charged" upon the equities resulting from the acts done in execution of the contract, and not (within the meaning of the statute) upon the contract itself.[99]

We have seen already[100] that the general approach of the courts was to construe the statutory requirement of a written memorandum under section 40 of the Law of Property Act 1925 rather generously, so as to seek to find, if possible, a sufficient memorandum. The doctrine of part performance was developed to allow a contract to be enforced even in the absence of a written memorandum; and the courts[101] tended again to interpret, or develop, the requirements of the doctrine so as to enable the contract rather to be enforced than not. Yet, although one of the parties may have done several things towards performing his side of the agreement, it did not at all follow that they would amount to part performance. The act must of itself on a balance of probability[102] establish the existence of the oral contract, although it was sufficient that it proved *a* contract, and need not refer to the precise terms of *the* contract on which the plaintiff relied.[103] It must be an act intelligible only on the assumption that some such contract as that alleged had been made, and if it were explicable on some other equally good ground,[104] it did not satisfy the test. Further, there might be

---

[98] *Steadman v Steadman* [1976] AC 536 at 540, per Lord REID. There is a marked similarity between the doctrine of part performance and other equitable doctrines which allow statutory formalities to be avoided, see pp. 874–6 (LP(MP)A 1989, s. 2: constructive trust), 907–9 (LPA 1925, s. 53: constructive trust and proprietary estoppel), post. [99] *Maddison v Alderson* (1883) 8 App Cas 467 at 475, per Lord SELBORNE.
[100] P. 863, ante.
[101] In particular, the majority in *Steadman v Steadman* [1976] AC 536. For a more detailed discussion of that case, and examples of the operation of the doctrine of part performance, see the 16th edn of this book, pp. 122–5. [102] [1976] AC 536 at 564–5, per Lord SIMON OF GLAISDALE and at 541–2, per Lord REID.
[103] *Kingswood Estate Co Ltd v Anderson* [1963] 2 QB 169 at 189, per UPJOHN LJ, approving a statement in *Fry on Specific Performance*, 6th edn, p. 278, and modifying the earlier strict view that the act must be unequivocally referable to the particular contract. UPJOHN LJ's statement was approved unanimously by the House of Lords in *Steadman v Steadman*, supra. However, the House was divided on whether the act must refer to a contract relating to land.
[104] E.g. entry into possession by the plaintiff was very commonly the act of part performance: see, e.g., *Kingswood Estate Co Ltd v Anderson*, supra (entry into possession of flat sufficient act of part performance to enforce oral contract of tenancy). But *remaining* in possession, without additional circumstances, would not be sufficient because it was unequivocal: cf *Nunn v Fabian* (1865) 1 Ch App 35 (contract for new lease to tenant already in possession; payment of increased rent constitutes the act of part performance). Payment of money posed a particular difficulty, since it will often be equivocal; but a majority of the House of Lords in *Steadman v Steadman*, supra,decisively rejected the argument that it could never be a sufficient act of part performance. For insufficient acts of part performance, see *New Hart Builders Ltd v Brindley* [1975] Ch 342 (submission by purchasers of application for planning permission); *Re Gonin* [1979] Ch 16 (unmarried daughter's returning home after compassionate release from wartime service to look after ageing parents); *Daulia v Four Millbank Nominees Ltd* [1978] Ch 231 (purchasers' tender of draft contract together with banker's draft for deposit). For sufficient acts of part performance, see *Liddell v Hopkinson* (1974) 233 EG 513 (vacation of matrimonial home

more than one act, and the acts when joined together "may throw light on each other; and there is no reason to exclude light".[105]

(4) Remedies at Law or in Equity

If a party to a contract relating to land relied on a memorandum and proved his case, he was entitled to the usual range of remedies for enforcement of his contractual rights:[106] he would be entitled as of right to an award of damages at common law for breach of contract; and he might also be able to obtain a decree of specific performance in equity. However, if he was compelled to base his action on part performance, he was not in such a favourable position. He could not enforce the contract at law, and therefore had no entitlement to damages. His remedy was in equity, and therefore hinged in the first place on his showing that the contract was one for which the court had jurisdiction to grant specific performance. As long as this was the case—even if no damages would be available at common law, or a decree of specific performance would be refused on some discretionary ground—the court had power to award damages either in addition to, or in substitution for, specific performance.[107] Such damages are assessed in the same way as they would be at common law.[108]

B Contracts Made After 26 September 1989. Requirement of Writing

Section 2(1) of the Law of Property (Miscellaneous Provisions) Act 1989[109] provides that:

A contract for the sale or other disposition of an interest in land can only be made in writing and only by incorporating all the terms which the parties have expressly agreed in one document or, where contracts are exchanged, in each.

It follows, therefore, that if the requirements as to writing are not complied with, there is *no* contract. This is a major change from the position under section 40 of the Law of Property Act 1925 where, as we have seen, non-compliance meant that the contract was merely

by divorced wife so that husband could sell it, in return for his offer of two-thirds of proceeds of sale if she would give up her right of occupation); *Sutton v Sutton* [1984] Ch 184 (wife's consent to divorce on terms that matrimonial home be conveyed to her); *Dakin v Dakin* [1990] EGCS 45 (father's signing of draft conveyance as a result of son's deceit); *Morritt v Wonham* [1993] NPC 2 (extensive work to farm), [1994] Conv 233 (M. P. Thompson).

105 *Steadman v Steadman* [1976] AC 536 at 564, per Lord Simon of Glaisdale. The flexibility of this approach is enhanced when "even spoken words may themselves be part performance of a contract": ibid.

106 For further discussion of remedies for breach of contract, see pp. 883 et seq, post.

107 SCA 1981, s. 50. See *Lavery v Pursell* (1888) 39 Ch D 508 at 519 per Chitty J (Chancery Amendment Act 1858, s. 2, the predecessor of SCA 1981, s. 50, "did not give the old Court of Chancery a general jurisdiction to give damages whenever it thought fit, it was only in that kind of case where specific performance would have been the right decree and there were reasons why it would be better to substitute damages, but that could not apply to a case where you could not have given specific performance").

108 *Johnson v Agnew* [1980] AC 367, pp. 886–8, post.

109 Based on Law Commission Report on Formalities for Contracts of Sale etc of Land 1987 (Law Com No. 164, HC 2); [1987] Conv 313. The section does not apply to contacts made before it came into force: s. 2(7). LPA 1925, s. 40, ceased to have effect: s. 2(8). For the changes see Emmet, para. 2.037; Kenny, *Conveyancing Practice*, paras. 4.040–4.046; and generally (1989) 105 LQR 555 (R. E. Annand); [1989] Conv 431 (P. H. Pettit); (1990) LS 325 (L. Bently and P. Coughlan). See also Requirements of Writing (Scotland) Act 1995, which has not followed the English approach to formalities.

unenforceable by action.[110] Under section 2, there must of course still be an agreement between the parties which satisfies the general rules governing the formation of contracts.[111] But that agreement does not become a contract until the additional requirement of writing set out in section 2 is satisfied.

(1) Contracts within Section 2

Section 2, like section 40, applies to any contract for the sale or other disposition of an interest in land. "Interest in land" is widely defined as meaning any estate, interest or charge in or over land.[112] However, three types of contract are expressly excluded:[113] (a) a contract to grant a lease for a term not exceeding three years to which section 54(2) of the Law of Property Act 1925 applies;[114] (b) a contract made in the course of a public auction; and (c) certain contracts regulated under the Financial Services and Markets Act 2000.[115]

In interpreting section 2 the courts have noted that, although it represents a radical change in the law, the change relates to the substance of the law rather than to its scope:[116]

The expression "a contract for the sale or other disposition of an interest in land" is clearly modelled on s 40(1) of the Law of Property Act 1925, "any contract for the sale or disposition of land, or any interest in land . . .". There is nothing in the 1989 Act, or in the Law Commission report which preceded it, which suggests any intention to widen the category of transactions to which the special law was applicable.

The section therefore includes contracts to sell the freehold or to assign a lease, and other contracts relating to an existing estate or interest in land, such as a contract to surrender a lease,[117] or to grant a new lease or mortgage, easement or profit, and applies whether the title to the land in question is already registered or not.

A number of cases have arisen in which the limits of application of section 2 have been tested. The section has been held to apply to:

(a) An existing contract for sale where the vendor does not at the time of the contract have an interest in land but proposes to acquire it in order to complete the sale.[118]

---

[110] Ignorance of the change is professional negligence: *Green v Collyer-Bristow* [1999] Lloyd's Rep PN 798.

[111] Final and complete agreement on the parties, the property (and the interest to be granted in it) and the consideration, together with any special terms regarded by the parties as essential: p. 854, ante. Section 2 therefore contemplates offer and acceptance between the parties, before the agreement so formed is put into writing to form the contract: *Commission for the New Towns v Cooper (Great Britain) Ltd* [1995] Ch 259 at 293, per EVANS LJ.

[112] S. 2(6), as amended by TLATA 1996, s. 25(2), Sch. 4 (deleting the words "or in or over the proceeds of sale of land"). "Disposition" has the same meaning as in the Law of Property Act 1925: see LPA 1925, s. 205(1)(ii).

[113] S. 2(5), which also provides that nothing in the section affects the creation or operation of resulting, implied or constructive trusts: see pp. 874 et seq, post.

[114] P. 220, ante; *Parc Battersea Ltd v Hutchinson* [1999] 2 EGLR 33. Such a contract was within LPA 1925, s. 40.

[115] As amended by SI 2001 No. 3649, art. 317(1), (2). Otherwise, some forms of investment which include interests in land, such as unit trusts, would be within s. 2.

[116] *Nweze v Nwoko* [2004] 2 P & CR 33 at [34], per CARNWATH LJ. See also SEDLEY LJ at [31]: "A requirement for writing in a legal system which ordinarily recognises parol contracts as valid and enforceable is an exception to a rule and as such should be construed no more widely than is necessary." See also *Kilcarne Holdings Ltd v Targetfollow (Birmingham) Ltd* [2005] 2 P & CR 8 at [194], per LEWISON J (fixed charge over a lease is an interest in land within s. 2 because it was under the old law).

[117] *Commission for the New Towns v Cooper (Great Britain) Ltd* [1995] Ch 259 at 283.

[118] *Singh v Beggs* (1995) 71 P & CR 120.

(b) An agreement to enter into a formal legal mortgage;[119] and, likewise, an equitable charge by deposit of title deeds, since it is construed as an agreement to create a charge and therefore the deposit must be accompanied by a document which satisfies the requirements of the section.[120] However, section 2 does not apply to the *grant* of an equitable charge, because it takes immediate effect from the date of the grant.[121]

(c) The variation of a material term in an existing contract which was itself subject to the requirements of section 2.[122]

On the other hand, the section has been held *not* to apply to:

(a) The exercise of an option to purchase land.[123] If the agreement under which the option is granted itself satisfies the requirements of the section, then the notice which exercises the option need not do so.[124]

(b) A collateral contract. In *Record v Bell*:[125]

> before signed contracts were exchanged, the vendor offered to the purchaser a warranty as to the state of his title in order to induce him to exchange. This warranty was referred to in a side-letter which was attached to the contract, but which was only signed by the purchaser. It was held that the side-letter had not been incorporated into the main contract (there was no reference to it there), but that there was a collateral contract which fell outside section 2.

However:[126]

> Although it may be possible for parties to hive off parts of their arrangements into separate and distinct contracts,[127] the court should be wary of artificially dividing what is in truth a

---

[119] *Murray v Guinness* [1998] NPC 79; *Kinane v Mackie-Conteh* [2005] 6 EGCS 140 (agreement saved by constructive trust under s. 2(5)).

[120] *United Bank of Kuwait plc v Sahib* [1997] Ch 107, p. 732, ante; [1998] Conv 502 (P. Critchley).

[121] *Murray v Guinness*, supra; cf *Target Holdings Ltd v Priestley* (2000) 79 P & CR 305 (agreement to vary mortgage also held to be outside s. 2 because mortgage was a contract of disposition, not a contract for the disposition of land); [1999] Conv 414 (M. P. Thompson).

[122] *McCausland v Duncan Lawrie Ltd* [1997] 1 WLR 38, M & B, p. 68; [1996] Conv 366 (M. P. Thompson); (1992) 147 NLJ 219 (H. W. Wilkinson).

[123] *Spiro v Glencrown Properties Ltd* [1991] Ch 537, M & B, p. 89; p. 881, post ("call option", i.e., the right to call for a conveyance of the property); *Active Estates Ltd v Parness* [2002] 3 EGLR 13 at 18 ("put option", i.e. the right to require the other party to take a conveyance). For options generally, see pp. 880 et seq, post.

[124] There are practical difficulties, however, with the application of s. 2 to a right of pre-emption. Since the grant of the right of pre-emption does not itself create an interest in land, p. 882, post, the contract to purchase can arise only at a later date when the right is exercised, and commonly that is not done by a document signed by both parties: *Bircham & Co Nominees (No 2) Ltd v Worrell Holdings Ltd* (2001) 82 P & CR 34; cf *Butts Park Ventures (Coventry) Ltd v Bryant Homes Central Ltd* [2004] BCC 207 (both grant of pre-emption and exercise complied with s. 2). For the application of s. 2 to declarations relating to the disposition of land contained in two wills (which could not, because of the failure to comply with s. 2, take effect as mutual wills) see *Healey v Brown* [2002] 19 EGCS 147.

[125] [1991] 1 WLR 853; (1992) 108 LQR 217 (R. J. Smith); [1991] CLJ 399 (C. Harpum); [1991] Conv 471 (M. Harwood); [1991] All ER Rev 201 (P. J. Clarke). See also *Pitt v PHH Asset Management Ltd* [1994] 1 WLR 327; *Lotteryking Ltd v AMEC Properties Ltd* [1995] 2 EGLR 13 (collateral agreement to remedy defects outside s. 2).

[126] *Kilcarne Holdings Ltd v Targetfollow (Birmingham) Ltd* [2005] 2 P & CR 8 at [189], per LEWISON J.

[127] *Tootal Clothing Ltd v Guinea Properties Ltd Management Ltd* (1992) 64 P & CR 452.

composite transaction.[128] If part of a composite transaction is a contract for the sale or other disposition of an interest in land, then the contract as a whole must satisfy the statutory requirements.[129]

(c) An agreement, not itself a contract for the sale or other disposition of land, which is supplemental to a land contract which has been duly carried out, and is therefore no longer executory.[130]

(d) A contract to put property on the market and to sell to a third party if such a purchaser were found.[131]

(e) An agreement by which neighbours settled a boundary dispute; section 2 did not apply either (i) because the agreement was not one "for" the disposition of an interest in land, even if its effect was that land was to be conveyed in consequence of it; or (ii) because Parliament could not have intended the section to apply to demarcating agreements under which trivial transfers of land were involved.[132]

(2) The Writing Required

The writing requirements are[133] as follows:

2.—(1) A contract for the sale or other disposition of an interest in land can only be made in writing and only by incorporating all the terms which the parties have expressly agreed in one document or, where contracts are exchanged, in each.[134]

This refers only to express terms, and therefore does not extend to implied terms, such as a term that where there is a sale with vacant possession, vacant possession must be given on completion. However, *all* the expressly agreed terms must be incorporated in the document if the contract is to be valid.[135]

2.—(2) The terms may be incorporated in a document either by being set out in it or by reference to some other document.

---

[128] *Grossman v Hooper* [2001] 2 EGLR 82. See at [35]–[36], per Sir Christopher STAUGHTON, doubting *Tootal Clothing Ltd v Guinea Properties Management Ltd* on this point.

[129] *Godden v Merthyr Tydfil Housing Association* (1997) 74 P & CR D1.

[130] *Tootal Clothing Ltd v Guinea Properties & Management Ltd*, supra; [1993] Conv 89 (P. Luther); (1993) 109 LQR 191 (D. Wilde).

[131] *Nweze v Nwoko* [2004] 2 P & CR 33; [2004] Conv 323 (M. P. Thompson) distinguishing *Jelson Ltd v Derby City Council* [1999] 3 EGLR 91, in which the judge had held that a contract between A and B under which A has the right without more to call for the property to be transferred to a buyer whom he nominates on terms set out in the contract was a contract to which s. 2 applied, because it was in effect an option contract relating to the land. The further decision of the judge, to the effect that the contract failed because s. 2 required the signature of the third party, rather than just of the two contracting parties, was however not approved. See also *RG Kensington Management Co Ltd v Hutchinson IDH Ltd* [2003] 2 P & CR 13 at [57], per NEUBERGER J: closing words of s. 2(3) require the contract to be signed by "each party to the contract"; not by "each party to the prospective conveyance or transfer".

[132] *Joyce v Rigolli* [2004] 1 P & CR DG22; [2004] Conv 224 (M. P. Thompson).

[133] For a proposal to introduce electonic contracts, see p. 873, post.

[134] *Milton Keynes Development Corpn v Cooper (Great Britain) Ltd* [1993] EGCS 142 (exchange of faxes held not to be a contract or exchange of contracts). On the meaning of "exchange", see p. 862, ante; infra.

[135] *Rudra v Abbey National plc* (1998) 76 P & CR 537 (failure to state name of vendor; section not satisfied). For rectification to bring the document within s. 2, see p. 885, post.

This provision differs from that for joinder of documents under section 40, where there could be joinder if there was an express or implied reference in a signed memorandum to some other document or transaction. The rule under section 2 is narrower in that it requires reference to some other *document*. It is not clear whether that reference must be express or whether it can be implied, although it is likely that a court will take a stricter view than used to be taken under section 40.[136] If another document is incorporated by reference, it is the incorporating document that must be signed so as to satisfy section 2: it is insufficient that one party's signature appears only on the incorporated document.[137]

> 2.—(3) The document incorporating the terms or, where contracts are exchanged, one of the documents incorporating them (but not necessarily the same one) must be signed by or on behalf of each party to the contract.

There are several points to notice about this provision. First, *each* party to the contract must sign for the contract to come into existence. This is a marked change from the position under section 40, where, if there was a memorandum signed by only one party, the oral contract could be enforced but only by the *other* party. However, as under section 40, if a party does not himself sign the document, someone else may be authorised to sign on his behalf.

There is then a question about what constitutes "signature". It has been held that, for the purposes of section 2, the signer of the document must sign his own name with his own hand upon it. In *Firstpost Homes Ltd v Johnson*[138]

> X, who had orally agreed to purchase land from Mrs F prepared a typewritten letter addressed to himself by name, including the words "I now agree to sell to you the above land shown on the enclosed plan". X signed the plan but not the letter; Mrs F signed the letter and counter-signed the plan.

In holding that there was no contract satisfying the requirements of section 2, the Court of Appeal held, first, that the letter and the plan were not self-evidently a single document for the purposes of section 2(1); and, second, that the typing of X's name and address in the letter was not a signature. PETER GIBSON LJ said:[139] "it is an artificial use of language to describe the printing or the typing of the name of an addressee in the letter as the signature by the addressee when he has typed that document. Ordinary language does not, it seems to me, extend that far."

The section also provides that the parties' signatures can be on separate documents, if the contract is formed by exchange of contracts. The practice of "exchange of contracts" was well established before 1989,[140] but it has acquired a new significance as a result of section 2. It was held by the Court of Appeal in *Commission for the New Towns v Cooper (Great Britain) Ltd*[141] that "exchange of contracts", whilst not a term of art, is none the less a well-recognised

---

136 *Firstpost Homes Ltd v Johnson* [1995] 1 WLR 1567 at 1571, per PETER GIBSON LJ.

137 Ibid., at 1573, per PETER GIBSON LJ, discussing also the meaning of "document".

138 [1995] 1 WLR 1567; [1996] CLJ 192 (A. J. Oakley); [1995] Conv 319 (M. P. Thompson).

139 Ibid., at 1575, rejecting analogies from cases on LPA 1925, s. 40, p. 866, ante, and adopting a general statement of the normal meaning of "signature" from *Goodman v J Eban Ltd* [1954] 1 QB 550 at 561, per DENNING LJ. See also *Butts Park Ventures (Coventry) Ltd v Bryant Homes Central Ltd* [2004] BCC 207 (on balance of probabilities, lost document bore signatures of both parties, rather than the signature of one on a document which contained only the photocopy signature of the other).   140 P. 862, ante.

141 [1995] Ch 259, refusing to follow its own previous decision in *Hooper v Sherman* [1994] NPC 153 which had held that an exchange of letters of offer and acceptance, each signed by one party, could satisfy s. 2. The

concept that is to be construed in a technical sense. Each party, in the expectation that the other would do likewise and intending to bring about a binding contract, must sign a contractual document incorporating all the agreed terms and intended to take effect as a formal document of title, neither party being bound until each had delivered his part into the other's possession in a manner to be mutually agreed. The concluding stages of correspondence between the defendant and the plaintiff by which agreement had been reached could not therefore constitute an exchange of contracts for the purposes of section 2.

2.—(4) Where a contract for the sale or other disposition of an interest in land satisfies the conditions of this section by reason only of the rectification of one or more documents in pursuance of an order of a court, the contract shall come into being, or be deemed to have come into being, at such time as may be specified in the order.

Although the statute requires that the parties have incorporated all their expressly agreed terms in the written document, it also contemplates that the court might rectify a document which fails to comply with section 2 and thereby to bring it into compliance. The philosophy behind section 2 is that questions as to whether there is a contract, and what are the terms of the contract, should be readily ascertained by looking at the single document said to constitute the contract, without resort to parol evidence.[142] However, one general exception to the parol evidence rule is where a party seeks to show that that a written contract does not properly reflect the parties' agreement and should therefore be rectified in equity.[143] This may therefore equally apply to a written contract for the sale of land.[144]

(3) Electronic Contracts

Under the Land Registration Act 2002, electronic conveyancing is now gradually being introduced.[145] As part of this change, it is inevitable that parties will wish their contract, as well as the later disposition of the interest in land, to be effected electronically. However, the Land Registration Act did not make provision for electronic contracts, which were intended to be introduced through other provisions. In 2001 the Lord Chancellor's Department published draft proposals[146] for the introduction of electronic contracts. A new section 2A would be inserted into the Law of Property (Miscellaneous Provisions) Act 1989 to enable an "electronic contract" to be as effective for the purposes of section 2 (and any other enactment) as an equivalent paper contract if it meets certain conditions: all the terms which the parties have expressly agreed are incorporated in the electronic document (or by reference to some other document); the document makes provision for the time and date

---

actual decision in *Hooper v Sherman* was distinguishable, since the exchange of letters were no more than confirmation of an oral agreement which the parties had already reached: [1995] Ch 259 at 289, per STUART-SMITH LJ, at 295, per EVANS LJ. But the general approach of the earlier decision was rejected as being wrongly based on Law Commission Report No. 164, para. 4.15, since the drafting of s. 2 had not in this respect followed the Law Commission's proposal.

[142] *Firstpost Homes Ltd v Johnson* [1995] 1 WLR 1567 at 1576, per PETER GIBSON LJ.

[143] Treitel, p. 199; pp. 885–6, post.

[144] *Wright v Robert Leonard (Developments) Ltd* [1994] EGCS 69 (contract which referred only to land rectified to include furniture as agreed before exchange of contracts took place).

[145] See generally pp. 110–11, ante; p. 987, post.

[146] LCD Consultation Paper, *Electronic Conveyancing—A draft order under s. 8 Electronic Communications Act 2000*, CP 05/2001, March 2001. The paper also contained certain proposals relating generally to electronic conveyancing which are superseded by the provisions of LRA 2002.

when the contract takes effect; the document has the electronic signature of each person by whom it purports to be authenticated; and each electronic signature is certified.[147] It is proposed that this change be implemented through secondary legislation.[148] Electronic contracts (unlike most other provisions relating to electronic conveyancing) are intended to apply to unregistered land, as well as registered land;[149] and will obviate the need for exchange of contracts. The contract will be made on a secure electronic communications network,[150] to which only authorised persons have access; and each party (or their respective agents) will sign the contract electronically. The contract will be made at the time and date that has been agreed between the parties.

The Department for Constitutional Affairs published the results of its consultation on these draft proposals in December 2001,[151] but the proposals have not yet been take forward. Indeed, it has now even been questioned whether there is any need for such legislative change, or whether an electronic contract can already satisfy the requirements of writing and signature in section 2 of the Law of Property (Miscellaneous Provisions) Act 1989.[152] It seems, however, preferable to introduce new express provisions to deal with electronic contracts since they do not fit comfortably with the language of section 2.[153]

(4) Continued Use of "Subject to Contract"

It would seem at first sight that the practice of heading pre-contract correspondence with the phrase "subject to contract" is no longer necessary, since no contract can come into existence until a document is signed by both parties. However, it is still used in order to draw a clear distinction between the communications preparatory to the contract and the contract itself; and it also thereby makes clear that the parties do not yet intend their communications to have any binding force, not only as a contract but also outside the contract, such as through a constructive trust or estoppel.[154]

(5) Proprietary Estoppel and Constructive Trust

We saw[155] that when a signed memorandum was required by statute for the enforcement of a contract for the sale of land, the courts developed a doctrine under which the contract, although not complying with the statutory formality, could be enforced by a party who could show a sufficient act of part performance;[156] and that this doctrine was rooted in the

---

[147] References of an electronic signature and to the certification of a signature are to be read in accordance with Electronic Communications Act 2000, s. 7(2), (3). For a worked example of the operation of the proposed form of electronic contract, contrasted with the operation of the current law, see LCD Consultation Paper, supra, n. 146, paras. 53–55; Mason, *Electronic Signatures in Law*.

[148] An order to be made by the Lord Chancellor under Electronic Communications Act 2000, s. 8. Such an order can only make electronic communications or storage *possible*; to make it compulsory would require primary legislation: ibid, ş. 8(6)(a).

[149] LCD Consultation Paper, *Electronic Conveyancing*, Part II, para. 5.

[150] A land registry network, which is to be put in place for electronic conveyancing: LRA 2002, s. 92 and Sch. 5.

[151] *Electronic Conveyancing—Analysis of the responses to the Consultation Paper on a draft order under section 8 of the Electronic Communications Act 2000*, CP(R) 05/2001.

[152] *Electronic Commerce: Formal Requirements in Commercial Transactions: Advice from the Law Commission* (2001), discussed H & B, p. 329.   [153] H & B, pp. 329–30.

[154] P. 858, ante; infra.   [155] Pp. 866–8, ante.

[156] LPA 1925, s. 40, re-enacting Statute of Frauds 1677, s. 4, expressly retained the exception of part performance which had been developed by the courts: s. 40(2).

desire not to permit a defendant fraudulently to take advantage of the absence of a signed memorandum if he had stood by and let the plaintiff alter his position for the worse by carrying out acts in performance of the contract. The doctrine of part performance was therefore, at least in part, a form of estoppel.[157]

The doctrine of part performance, as such, is no longer relevant to contracts for the sale of land: under section 2 of the Law of Property (Miscellaneous Provisions) Act 1989 an agreement which does not comply with the statutory formalities does not constitute a contract which can be partly performed.[158] However, there are two bases on which it can be argued that an agreement which fails to comply with section 2 might none the less be enforced: either under the doctrine of proprietary estoppel; or under a constructive trust. The latter is expressly provided for in section 2(5) by the words "nothing in this section affects the creation or operation of resulting, implied or constructive trusts".

The policy arguments in relation to section 2 are not, of course, identical to those for the old formality rule under section 40.[159] There, the contract was not void but unenforceable; it may have seemed a smaller step to allow parol evidence to be given to prove the contract where it would otherwise be fraudulent to allow the defendant to rely on the statute. Under section 2, there is no contract if it is not in the required written form. However, in practice the courts have started to apply the doctrine of proprietary estoppel, and the saving for constructive trusts contained in section 2(5), to further the same policy as that which lay behind the doctrine of part performance; and they have recognised the similarity between them.

In *Yaxley v Gotts*:[160]

Y, a builder, agreed orally with a friend, BG, that he would carry out work on a building that BG was buying, in order to convert it into flats, and would manage the property thereafter, in return for being given the ground floor flats of the converted property. The property was in fact bought by AG, BG's son; but AG adopted the arrangement made by his father. After Y had done the building work, the parties fell out and AG excluded him from the property.

The Court of Appeal held that, although the agreement could not be enforced as a contract because it was not in writing for the purposes of section 2(1) of the Law of Property (Miscellaneous Provisions) Act 1989, Y was entitled to a rent-free 99-year lease of the

---

[157] *Actionstrength Ltd v International Glass Engineering IN.GL.EN SpA* [2003] 2 AC 541 at [22]–[23], per Lord HOFFMANN.

[158] P. 868, ante. For a suggestion that part performance has not been abolished but may survive as an equitable doctrine, see *Singh v Beggs* (1995) 71 P & CR 120 at 122, per NEILL LJ; [1997] Conv 293 (S. I. A. Swann); cf however *Yaxley v Gotts* [2000] Ch 162 at 172, per ROBERT WALKER LJ. See also New Zealand doubts on the English formalities: New Zealand Proposed Property Act [1994] Conv 428 at 430 (H. W. Wilkinson). [159] P. 863, ante.

[160] [2000] Ch 162, M & B p. 70; [2000] CLJ 23 (L. Tee); (2000) 116 LQR 11 (R. J. Smith); (2000) 63 MLR 912 (I. Moore); [2000] Conv 245 (M. P. Thompson); [2000] All ER Rev 242 (P. J. Clarke). See also *James v Evans* [2000] 3 EGLR 1 (no estoppel); [2001] Conv 86 (L. McMurtry); *Joyce v Rigolli* [2004] EWCA Civ 79 at [35]–[36], [2004] 1 P & CR DG22, per ARDEN LJ; *Kinane v Mackie-Conteh* [2005] EWCA Civ 45, [2005] 06 EGCS 140; *Cobbe v Yeomans Row Management Ltd* [2005] EWHC 266 (Ch) [2005] 2 P & CR DG1; [2005] Conv 247 (M.Dixon), 501 (B. McFarlane); *Representative Body of the Church in Wales v Newton* [2005] 16 EG 145 (CS) (no constructive trust where condition of contract (landlord's giving consent to assignment) had not been satisfied).

ground floor flats, either under the doctrine of proprietary estoppel, as held by the judge, or under a constructive trust. ROBERT WALKER LJ said:[161]

At a high level of generality, there is much common ground between the doctrines of proprietary estoppel and the constructive trust, just as there is between proprietary estoppel and part performance. All are concerned with equity's intervention to provide relief against unconscionable conduct, whether as between neighbouring landowners, or vendor and purchaser, or relatives who make informal arrangements for sharing a home, or a fiduciary and the beneficiary or client to whom he owes a fiduciary obligation.

The Court inferred from the Law Commission's report on which section 2 was based,[162] and from the express saving for constructive trusts in section 2(5), that the policy behind section 2 was not to prevent the court from giving effect in equity to the principles of proprietary estoppel and constructive trusts. As BELDAM LJ said:[163]

I cannot see that there is any reason to qualify the plain words of section 2(5). They were included to preserve the equitable remedies to which the Commission had referred. I do not think it inherent in a social policy of simplifying conveyancing by requiring the certainty of a written document that unconscionable conduct or equitable fraud should be allowed to prevail.

In my view the provision that nothing in section 2 of the Act of 1989 is to affect the creation or operation of resulting, implied or constructive trusts effectively excludes from the operation of the section cases in which an interest in land might equally well be claimed by relying on constructive trust or proprietary estoppel.

It has been emphasised that to use proprietary estoppel in this context is not simply to give effect to the contract:[164]

reliance on the unenforceable agreement only takes the claimant part of the way: he must still prove all the other components of proprietary estoppel. In particular, the requirement that the defendant encouraged or permitted the claimant in his erroneous belief is not satisfied simply by the admission of the invalid agreement in evidence. In this sort of case, the claimant has to show that the defendant represented to the claimant, by his words or conduct, including conduct in the provision or delivery of the agreement, that the agreement created an enforceable obligation. The cause of action in proprietary estoppel is thus not founded on the enforceable agreement but upon the defendant's conduct which, when viewed in all relevant respects, is unconscionable.

---

[161] [2000] Ch 162 at 176. See also at 189–90, per BELDAM LJ, drawing attention to the links between the old law of part performance and the use of estoppel and constructive trust under s. 2, by reference to Law Commission's report on which s. 2 was based; n. 162, infra. See also *Kinane v Mackie-Conteh*, supra, at [32], per ARDEN LJ: "section 2(5) plays a similar role to that of part performance, although it operates more flexibly than that doctrine".

[162] Formalities for Contracts for Sale etc of Land 1987 (Law Com No. 164, HC2), Part V, relied on by CLARKE LJ at 182, and BELDAM LJ at 188–90.

[163] [2000] Ch 162 at 193. For discussion of the relationship between proprietary estoppel and constructive trust, see ibid., at 176–7, 180, per ROBERT WALKER LJ and at 191–3, per BELDAM LJ, both relying on, inter alia, *Grant v Edwards* [1986] Ch 638 at 656, per Sir Nicolas BROWNE-WILKINSON; p. 473, ante. Whether proprietary estoppel is to be seen technically as separate from, or a particular manifestation of, constructive trust, both judges held that the saving in LP(M)A 1989, s. 2(5) was sufficient to support the judge's decision on the basis of proprietary estoppel. For further discussion of proprietary estoppel, see pp. 814–27, 841–6 ante, p. 907–9, post; and for constructive trusts, see pp. 472–6, 839–41 ante; pp. 905–6, post.

[164] *Kinane v Mackie-Conteh*, supra, at [29], per ARDEN LJ.

III Effect of Contract

A Contract Equivalent to Conveyance in Equity. The Doctrine of Walsh v Lonsdale

If the contract for the sale or other disposition of an interest in land is one of which the court would be prepared to grant the equitable remedy of specific performance, it is treated in equity as creating the equivalent interest to that which, if the contract were performed, would be created at law. Generally known as the doctrine of *Walsh v Lonsdale*,[165] after the case in which it was applied in the context of leases, this is an application of the maxim that "equity looks on that as done which ought to be done":[166] the contract to convey is treated as already having the same effect as the conveyance,[167] so far as equity can permit.[168] Thus an enforceable contract for the sale of the legal estate creates an equivalent equitable estate;[169] a contract for a legal lease creates an equivalent equitable lease;[170] a contract for a legal mortgage creates an equivalent equitable mortgage;[171] and a contract for a legal easement creates an equivalent equitable easement;[172] and similarly any contract to convey or create a legal estate in any hereditament, corporeal or incorporeal. The equitable interest so created is, however, precarious in that, since it depends on the contract being specifically enforceable, the equitable interest can be created by the contract, and will continue to subsist once created, only as long as there is no obstacle to the remedy of specific performance being available on the facts of the case.[173]

The following section will consider the particular application of this doctrine to the vendor and purchaser under a contract of sale. The application to contract for dispositions of other interests in land is considered in the relevant chapters in this book.[174]

B Contract of Sale. Vendor as Trustee for Purchaser[175]

If a contract for sale is capable of specific performance, an immediate equitable interest in the land passes to the purchaser, who retains it for as long as the contract remains enforceable.[176] The legal estate remains in the vendor until the conveyance has been executed or, in registered land, the transfer is completed by registration,[177] but meanwhile equity regards

---

[165] (1882) 21 Ch D 9, M & B p. 85; p. 223, ante.   [166] Snell, para. 5–25.

[167] I.e., the document required at law to perfect the contract, whether a conveyance of the unregistered freehold (p. 950, post), the transfer of a registered estate (p. 963, post), or any other transaction designed to create or dispose of a legal estate or interest; cf LPA 1925, ss. 52(1), 205(1)(ii).

[168] The conveyance in equity is in many circumstances not as good as the conveyance at law: see, e.g., the differences between a legal lease and an equitable lease: pp. 225–7, ante.

[169] Infra. *Industrial Properties (Barton Hill) Ltd v Associated Electrical Industries Ltd* [1977] QB 580, M & B p. 86 (double application of the doctrine of *Walsh v Londsale*).

[170] *Walsh v Lonsdale*, supra; p. 223, ante.   [171] P. 731, ante.   [172] P. 601, ante.

[173] *Coatsworth v Johnson* (1886) 55 LJQB 220, M & B p. 87; pp. 225–6, ante (contract for lease); *Warmington v Miller* [1973] QB 877 at 887, per STAMP J (contract for lease); *Sookraj v Samaroo* [2004] UKPC 50, (2004) 148 SJLB 1244 at [15] per Lord SCOTT OF FOSCOTE (contract of sale). For the remedy of specific performance in relation to land contracts, see pp. 888–91, post.

[174] Pp. 223–5, ante (leases); 601–2, ante (easements); 731–2, ante (mortgages).

[175] H & M, pp. 326–8; Farrand, *Contract and Conveyance* (4th edn), pp. 163–73; Barnsley, *Conveyancing Law and Practice*, pp. 245–50; Oakley, *Constructive Trusts*, chap. 6.

[176] *Sookraj v Samaroo* [2004] UKPC 50, (2004) 148 SJLB 1244 at [15], per Lord SCOTT OF FOSCOTE: "a fairly fundamental principle".   [177] LRA 2002, s. 27(1); p. 970, post.

the vendor as a trustee for the purchaser, and is prepared to decree specific performance at the instance of the latter.[178] In the words of JESSEL MR:[179]

The moment you have a valid contract for sale the vendor becomes in equity a trustee for the purchaser of the estate sold, and the beneficial ownership passes to the purchaser, the vendor having a right to the purchase money, a charge or lien on the estate for the security of that purchase money, and a right to retain possession of the estate until the purchase money is paid, in the absence of express contract as to the time of delivering possession.

Thus, for instance, pending completion, the purchaser may dispose of his equitable interest by sale or otherwise; he becomes owner of the rents and profits which fall due after the time fixed for completion; and he can demand an occupation rent if the vendor remains in possession after that time.

On the other hand, as from the date of the contract, unless it otherwise provides, the purchaser must bear the risk of any loss or damage suffered by the property, as, for instance, from an accidental fire or from a fall in price; and from the date fixed for completion he must meet the cost of all necessary outgoings.

(1) Vendor's Rights. Qualified Trusteeship

Pending the completion of the sale, the vendor occupies a fiduciary position, and therefore he must manage and preserve the property with the same care as a trustee must show with regard to trust property. He must, for instance, relet the premises if an existing lease runs out, but before doing so he must consult the purchaser.[180] Nevertheless, the vendor is not an ordinary trustee, since he possesses certain rights of a valuable nature in the land, which he is entitled to protect on his own behalf:

(i) he has a right to remain in possession until the purchase money is paid, and to protect that possession, if necessary, by the maintenance of an action, though while in possession he is under a duty to maintain the property in a reasonable state of preservation and so far as may be in the state in which it was when the contract was made;[181]

(ii) he is entitled to take the rents and profits of the land[182] until the time fixed for completion; and

(iii) he possesses an equitable lien on the property for the amount of the purchase money. An equitable lien is in the nature of a charge on land and entitles the person in whom it resides to apply to the court for a sale of the property in satisfaction of his claim. Unlike a common law lien, it is not dependent on possession.[183]

---

[178] *Shaw v Foster* (1872) LR 5 HL 321 at 333, 338; *Howard v Miller* [1915] AC 318 at 326. There may be a decree, even though, between contract and completion, a compulsory purchase order has been made by a local authority: *Hillingdon Estates Co v Stonefield Estates Ltd* [1952] Ch 627.

[179] *Lysaght v Edwards* (1876) 2 Ch D 499 at 506; *Lake v Bayliss* [1974] 1 WLR 1073.

[180] *Earl of Egmont v Smith* (1877) 6 Ch D 469; *Abdulla v Shah* [1959] AC 124.

[181] *Clarke v Ramuz* [1891] 2 QB 456 (removal of soil by trespasser); *Phillips v Lamdin* [1949] 2 KB 33 (removal of door); *Berkley v Poulett* (1976) 241 EG 911, 242 EG 39 (discussing the rights of a sub-purchaser); *Ware v Verderber* (1978) 247 EG 1081 (duty of vendor to take reasonable care of property); *Englewood Properties Ltd v Patel* [2005] 1 WLR 1961 (duty does not extend to dealing with vendor's adjoining or neighbouring premises). [182] Or dividends in the case of shares: *J Sainsbury plc v O'Connor* [1991] STC 318.

[183] See generally Emmet, paras. 15.021–15.023; [1994] CLJ 263 (S. Worthington); [1997] Conv 336 (D. G. Barnsley); *Barclays Bank plc v Estates and Commercial Ltd* [1997] 1 WLR 415 at 419, per MORRITT LJ; *Uziell-Hamilton v Keen* (1971) 22 P & CR 655; White and Tudor, *Leading Cases in Equity*, vol. ii. p. 857.

Although the equitable ownership has passed to the purchaser, the vendor retains a substantial interest in the land, and for that reason is generally called a qualified trustee.[184] Lord CAIRNS, dealing with a case where a valid contract had been made for the sale of a London theatre, said:[185]

There cannot be the slightest doubt of the relation subsisting in the eye of a Court of Equity between the vendor and the purchaser. The vendor was a trustee of the property for the purchaser; the purchaser was the real beneficial owner in the eye of a Court of Equity of the property, subject only to this observation, that the vendor, whom I have called the trustee, was not a mere dormant trustee, he was a trustee having a personal and substantial interest in the property, a right to protect that interest, and an active right to assert that interest if anything should be done in derogation of it. The relation, therefore, of trustee and *cestui que trust* subsisted, but subsisted subject to the paramount right of the vendor and trustee to protect his own interest as vendor of the property.

Thus, the trusteeship relates only to the property sold, which, failing express agreement, is confined to vacant possession of the land together with any physical accretions. Therefore the vendor is entitled to retain compensation money payable in respect of the requisitioning of the property and falling due between the date of the contract and the date of the conveyance.[186]

(2) Insurance by Purchaser

Likewise, if between these dates the premises are damaged by fire, the former rule was that the money paid by the insurance company in respect of the loss belonged to the vendor, not to the purchaser, for the policy of insurance was not part of the property sold.[187] This, however, was reversed by the Law of Property Act 1925, which provides[188] that where, after the date of any contract for sale or exchange of land, money becomes payable under any policy maintained by the vendor in respect of any damage to, or destruction of, property included in the contract, the money shall on completion of the contract be paid by the vendor to the purchaser. This obligation may be varied by the contract; it is subject to the liability of the purchaser to pay the premiums falling due after the date of the contract, and is also subject to any requisite consents of the insurers.[189]

(3) Standard Conditions of Sale

The Standard Conditions of Sale are usually incorporated into the contract.[190] When they were first introduced in 1990, a radical change was made in the rules for the passing of risk. Condition 5 provides[191] that the vendor retains the risk until completion, that he is

---

[184] *Rayner v Preston* (1881) 18 Ch D 1 at 6, per COTTON LJ.   [185] *Shaw v Foster* (1872) LR 5 HL 321 at 338.
[186] *Re Hamilton-Snowball's Conveyance* [1959] Ch 308.
[187] *Rayner v Preston*, supra. See also *Re Watford Corpn's and Ware's Contract* [1943] Ch 82.   [188] S. 47.
[189] This would appear to put the purchaser in a doubtful position. If the house which is the subject of the sale is burnt down, the purchaser is nevertheless obliged to pay the purchase money, and if the insurance company refuses to give the requisite consent to the transfer of the insurance money, he will be unable to obtain payment of that money under the section. On the other hand, having regard to the nature of fire insurance, it seems clear that the vendor is not entitled both to the insurance money and to the purchase money. A purchaser is well advised to insure the property himself immediately after the contract and not to rely on this section. See [1984] Conv 43 (M. P. Thompson). On the insurer's potential liability both to the assured and to a third party, see *Lonsdale & Thompson Ltd v Black Arrow Group plc* [1993] Ch 361; [1993] Conv 472 (M. Haley); [1993] CLJ 387 (A. J. Oakley).
[190] P. 858, ante. The current edition is the 4th edn, 2003.
[191] For a critical analysis of Condition 5, see [1989] Conv 1 (H. W. Wilkinson); Emmet, para. 1.082.

under no duty to the purchaser to insure the property, and that the provision for taking over the benefit of the vendor's insurance policy under section 47 is excluded. The purchaser has the right to rescind the contract if the physical state of the property has made it unusable for its purpose at the date of the contract, as a result of damage against which the vendor could not reasonably have insured or which it is not legally possible for him to make good.

In the light of this condition, the Law Commission recommended[192] that it would be inappropriate to propose any legislative change.

C *Registration of Contract*

Since the enforceable contract for the sale or other disposition of an interest in land creates an equitable interest in favour of the purchaser, the purchaser must protect his interest if it is not to be overridden by a subsequent dealing with the legal title before he acquires the legal title himself.

If the land is already registered, he should enter a notice in the register,[193] although if he is in actual occupation of the land his interest, if not protected by notice, might be protected as an overriding interest.[194] In the case of a contract for the sale of the land, it has not normally been the practice for the purchaser to enter a notice of his contract, since if he has applied for an official search of the register with priority before entering into the contract, his search gives him priority against other entries on the register for a period of thirty business days, within which period he will take the transfer and apply for its registration.[195] The Land Registration Act 2002 has now made specific provision for priority to be given by the noting of a contract for the making of a registrable disposition of a registered estate or charge, since, when electronic conveyancing is introduced, the formation of the electronic contract will necessarily be entered on the register.[196]

In unregistered land, a contract to convey or create a legal estate or interest is registrable as an estate contract under the Land Charges Act 1972.[197] If not registered it is void against later purchasers for money or money's worth of a legal estate in the land.[198]

IV Option to Purchase and Right of Pre-emption

We must now consider two special cases: an option to purchase, and a right of pre-emption.

---

[192] Report on Risk of Damage after Contract for Sale 1990 (Law Com No. 191).

[193] LRA 2002, ss. 32. P. 973, post.

[194] Ibid., s. 29(2), Sch. 3, para. 2; p. 979 post. A contract for the grant of lease or an easement will create an equitable lease or an equitable easement, but only legal leases and legal easements can take effect as overriding interests under Sch. 3, paras. 1 and 3; p. 979, post.

[195] Ibid., s. 72 and LRR 2003, rr. 148(3), 131, replacing LR (Official Searches) R 1990 (SI 1993, No. 3276); p. 954, post.

[196] Ibid., s. 72(6)(a)(ii); H & B, para. 19.5. For detail on official searches and priority protection, see generally H & B, chap. 19.

[197] LCA 1972, s. 2(4), Class C(iv). The contract must be registered against the name of the owner of the legal estate: s. 3(1); *Barrett v Hilton Developments Ltd* [1975] Ch 237.

[198] Ibid., s. 4(6); *Midland Bank Trust Co Ltd v Green* [1981] AC 513, M & B p. 40; p. 946, post.

An option to purchase[199] creates an immediate equitable interest in favour of the grantee as soon as it is granted. The grantee's right to call for a conveyance of the land is an equitable interest; as far as the grantor is concerned, "his estate or interest is taken away from him without his consent, and the right to take it away being vested in another, the covenant giving the option must give that other an interest in the land".[200] Since an option creates an equitable interest in favour of the grantee from the moment of the contract, the grantee must protect his interest by registration (unless, in the case of registered land, it is protected as an overriding interest).[201]

We have seen[202] that section 2 of the Law of Property (Miscellaneous Provisions) Act 1989 provides that a contract for the sale or other disposition of an interest in land must be made in writing which incorporates all the agreed terms and is signed by both parties. A question that has arisen is whether the contract to which section 2 applies is formed when the option is granted, or when it is exercised. In some contexts the grant of an option has been analysed as a conditional contract,[203] in which case section 2 would be satisfied as long as the grant of the option was in writing, incorporating all the terms and signed by both parties. Other authorities support the view that the grant of an option is an irrevocable offer, resulting in a contract only when accepted by the notice exercising the option.[204] If this is the proper analysis for the purposes of section 2, the section would not be satisfied unless the grantor signed the notice of exercise, which he could not be compelled to do.

In *Spiro v Glencrown Properties Ltd*:[205]

an option to purchase was granted by documents satisfying section 2 of the 1989 Act. The purchaser gave written notice to exercise it but failed to complete. When the vendor sued for damages for breach

---

[199] See generally Barnsley, *Land Options* (4th edn); (1974) 38 Conv (NS) 8 (A. Prichard); [1984] CLJ 55 (S. Tromans); (1991) Can BR (P. M. Perell); Blundell Memorial Lecture 1996 (T. Etherton and D. Beales).

[200] *London and South Western Rly Co v Gomm* (1882) 20 Ch D 562 at 581, per JESSEL MR; *Griffith v Pelton* [1958] Ch 205 at 225; *Webb v Pollmount* [1966] Ch 584 at 597; *Mountford v Scott* [1975] Ch 258; *George Wimpey & Co Ltd v IRC* [1974] 1 WLR 975 at 980; affd [1975] 1 WLR 995; *Pritchard v Briggs* [1980] Ch 338 at 418. For the application of the rule against perpetuities, see pp. 541–2, 550–1, ante. An option must be exercised strictly in accordance with its terms, and time is of the essence: *Di Luca v Juraise (Springs) Ltd* [1998] 2 EGLR 125; it does not however follow that time is of the essence for the compliance with any conditions in the option as to the manner in which the option, once exercised, is to be carried to completion: *Allardyce v Roebuck* [2004] 3 All ER 754. See also *BP Oil UK Ltd v Lloyds TSB Bank plc* [2005] 1 EGLR 61 (option for three joint assignees to require assignor to take re-assignment of lease not exercisable by only two); *Sainsbury's Supermarkets Ltd v Olympia Homes Ltd* [2006] 1 P & CR 17.

[201] P. 880, ante (protection by a notice in registered land; as a land charge, Class C(iv), in unregistered land: LCA 1972, s. 2(4) expressly includes option to purchase within the definition of estate contract). If the option is registered, there is no need to register the ensuing contract when the option is exercised: *Armstrong & Holmes Ltd v Holmes* [1993] 1 WLR 1482 (unregistered land); [1994] Conv 483 (N. P. Gravells). See *Freeguard v Royal Bank of Scotland plc* (1998) 79 P & CR 81 (unregistered option to purchase lost priority against later registered charge in "a thoroughly artificial transaction" involving a ransom strip). The benefit of an option may be assigned; for the mechanisms contemplated for the compliance of such an assignment with LPA 1925, s. 136 (legal assignment requires writing) under electronic conveyancing, see LRA 2002, s. 91; H & B, paras. 26.14–26.18.   [202] p. 868, ante.

[203] *Helby v Matthews* [1895] AC 471 at 482 (Lord MACNAGHTEN); *Re Mulholland's Will Trusts* [1949] 1 All ER 460; *Griffith v Pelton* [1958] Ch 205; *Armstrong & Holmes Ltd v Holmes* [1993] 1 WLR 1482.

[204] *Helby v Matthews*, supra, at 477 (Lord HERSCHELL) and 479–80 (Lord WATSON); *Beesly v Hallwood Estates Ltd* [1960] 1 WLR 549; affd [1961] Ch 105.

[205] [1991] Ch 537, M & B p. 89; [1991] Conv 140 (P. Smith); [1993] Conv 13 (P. Jenkins); [1990] Conv 9 (J. E. Adams); [1990] 47 EG 48 (C. Sydenham and M. Rodrigues); [1991] Conv 140 (P. F. Smith); [1991] CLJ 236 (A. J. Oakley); Emmet, para. 2.118 A.

of contract, the purchaser claimed that there was no contract because the notice of exercise, which was not signed by the vendor, did not satisfy section 2. HOFFMANN J held that the grant of the option, and not its exercise, was the contract to which section 2 applied.

Strictly speaking the grant of an option was neither a conditional contract nor an irrevocable offer, but created a relationship *sui generis*. The conditional contract was the more appropriate analogy in the context of section 2, as the purpose of an option would be destroyed if the purchaser had to obtain the vendor's signature to the notice of exercise, a result which had not been intended by the legislature. Thus the purchaser was liable to damages.

In *Pritchard v Briggs*, TEMPLEMAN LJ distinguished an option from a right of pre-emption as follows:[206]

Rights of option and rights of pre-emption share one feature in common: each prescribes circumstances in which the relationship between the owner of the property which is the subject of the right and the holder of the right will become the relationship of vendor and purchaser. In the case of an option, the evolution of the relationship of vendor and purchaser may depend on the fulfilment of certain specified conditions and will depend on the volition of the option holder. If the option applies to land, the grant of the option creates a contingent equitable interest ... In the case of a right of pre-emption, the evolution of the relationship of vendor and purchaser depends on the grantor, of his own volition, choosing to fulfil certain specified conditions[207] and thus converting the pre-emption into an option. The grant of the right of pre-emption creates a *mere spes* which the grantor of the right may either frustrate by choosing not to fulfil the necessary conditions or may convert into an option and thus into an equitable interest by fulfilling the conditions.

The Court of Appeal held unanimously that, unlike an option, a right of pre-emption did not confer an equitable interest in the land on the holder of the right.[208] One difficulty was that many statutory provisions assumed that a right of pre-emption was a proprietary interest.[209] GOFF LJ held that these provisions were framed on a mistaken view of the law and were, therefore, of no effect.[210] Thus a right of pre-emption was not a proprietary interest capable of binding a successor in title, and could never be converted to such an interest, even if registered as an estate contract.[211] TEMPLEMAN and STEPHENSON LJJ, on the other hand, held that a right of pre-emption, while not initially an interest in land, was

---

[206] [1980] Ch 338 at 418. See also *Brown v Gould* [1972] Ch 53 at 58. A right of pre-emption is sometimes referred to as a right of first refusal but "In so far as there is a distinction, the expression 'right of first refusal' is commonly used to describe the position (as in the present case) where the grantee has the first right to refuse an offer to purchase at the price at which the grantor is willing to sell; and the expression 'right of pre-emption' is commonly used to describe the position (as in *Pritchard v Briggs*) where the grantee has the right to purchase at a fixed price (or at a price which is not chosen by the grantor) before the grantor is free to sell to anyone else": *Bircham & Co Nominees (No 2) Ltd v Worrell Holdings Ltd* (2001) 82 P & CR 34 at [31], per CHADWICK LJ. See further *Speciality Shops v Yorkshire and Metropolitan Estates Ltd* [2003] 2 P & CR 31 at [25]–[29], per PARK J, identifying three forms of right of pre-emption; "more may exist".

[207] *Tuck v Baker* [1990] 32 EG 46 (pre-emption clause provided that there should be two months for acceptance of an offer of first refusal: the owner could change his mind about selling and withdraw the offer before acceptance within the two months).

[208] See also *Manchester Ship Canal Co v Manchester Racecourse Co* [1901] 2 Ch 37; *Murray v Two Strokes Ltd* [1973] 1 WLR 823; (1973) 89 LQR 462 (M. J. Albery); *First National Securities Ltd v Chiltern DC* [1975] 1 WLR 1075; cf *Birmingham Canal Co v Cartwright* (1879) 11 Ch D 421; *Bircham & Co Nominees (No 2) Ltd v Worrell Holdings Ltd* (2001) 82 P & CR 34; *Speciality Shops v Yorkshire and Metropolitan Estates Ltd*, supra; *Dear v Reeves* [2002] 1 Ch 1; *Tiffany Investments Ltd v Bircham & Co Nominees (No 2) Ltd* [2004] 2 EGLR 31.

[209] LCA 1972, s. 2(4), where it is registrable as an estate contract; LPA 1925, ss. 2(3)(iv), 186; SLA 1925, ss. 58(2), 61(2); PAA 1964, s. 9(2).   [210] [1980] Ch 338 at 399.

[211] ibid., at 396.

converted to an equitable interest as soon as the grantor fulfilled the condition on deciding
to sell. If registered as an estate contract, either before or after fulfilment of the condition,
the interest would be binding on the grantor's successors in title.[212]

Neither view is free from difficulties, and the precise effect of a right of pre-emption
remains uncertain in unregistered land.[213] In relation to registered land, however, the Land
Registration Act 2002[214] resolved the matter by providing that, subject to the rules about the
effect of dispositions on priority, a right of pre-emption has effect from the time of creation
as an interest capable of binding successors in title.

V Remedies of Parties to the Contract[215]

Various remedies are available to the parties[216] to the contract. Some relate to the formation
of the contract; others to a breach of the contract itself.

A Remedies Relating to the Formation of the Contract

Of the claims that might arise in relation to the formation of the contract, the most
common are for misrepresentation and mistake.[217] In practice, a misrepresentation might
give rise to claims for rescission *ab initio* of the contract, or for damages—most commonly,
in the case of a contract of sale, these are claims made by the purchaser against the vendor.
A mistake might give rise to a claim by either party to rectify the contract.[218]

(1) Remedies for Pre-contractual Misrepresentation[219]

(a) Rescission ab initio[220]

A party to the contract may rescind if he can show that a false representation was made to
him, by or on behalf of the other party,[221] on which he relied in entering into the contract;
and as long as there is no bar to his obtaining the remedy—such as the fact that rescission

---

[212] [1980] Ch 338 at 418, 423, followed in relation to registered land in *Kling v Keston Properties Ltd* (1983)
49 P & CR 212, M & B p. 93.   [213] (1980) 96 LQR 488 (H. W. R. W.); [1980] Conv 433 (J. Martin).

[214] S. 115(1). The section has effect only in relation to rights of pre-emption created on or after 13 October
2004: s. 115(2); SI 2003 No. 1725. What is meant, however, by a "right of pre-emption" for the purposes of s. 115
has still to be addressed; cf. *Speciality Shops v Yorkshire and Metropolitan Estates Ltd* [2003] 2 P & CR 31 at
[25]–[29], supra, n. 206.

[215] See generally Emmet, chap. 7; Annand and Cain, *Remedies under the Contract*.

[216] Under the Contracts (Rights of Third Parties) Act 1999 a third party may now sometimes be able to
enforce a term of the contract, and obtain the remedies that would have been available to him in an action for
breach of contract if he had been a party to the contract: s. 1(5). On the Act generally, see Emmet,
paras. 2.131–2.135, 19.003A; Blundell Lectures 25th Anniversary Series 2000: The Contracts (Rights of Third
Parties) Act and its Implications for Property Transactions (A. Burrows and C. Harpum); Treitel, pp. 580–1, 651–66.

[217] For rescission for undue influence which, in the context of contracts relating to land, has most commonly been claimed in the case of mortgage transactions, see pp. 749–55, ante.

[218] A contract might sometimes be void for a common (shared) mistake, but not voidable: *Great Peace Shipping
Ltd v Tsavliris Salvage (International) Ltd* [2003] QB 679. For mistake in contract generally, see Treitel, chap. 8.

[219] Cartwright, *Misrepresentation*; Treitel, chap. 9.   [220] Snell, chap. 13.

[221] A misrepresentation by a third party is normally insufficient to give rise to rescission; see, however, *Royal
Bank of Scotland v Etridge (No 2)* [2002] 2 AC 773 at [40], per Lord NICHOLLS, [144] per Lord SCOTT OF

would prejudice an innocent third party.[222] The remedy is available whether the misrepresentation was fraudulent or innocent;[223] and the fact that the contract has been completed is not a bar to rescission.[224] Rescission is available as of right, although in the case of a non-fraudulent misrepresentation the court has discretion to refuse it, to declare the contract subsisting, and to order damages in lieu of rescission.[225] If rescission is available the contract is voidable; the remedy of rescission for misrepresentation renders the contract a nullity *ab initio*, and restitution must be made between the parties in respect of any performance already made under the contract.[226]

(b) Damages

The misrepresentation may give rise to a claim for damages. An action in the tort of deceit may lie if the misrepresentation was made fraudulently;[227] and damages on the tort measure[228] may be recovered under the section 2(1) of the Misrepresentation Act 1967 for non-fraudulent misrepresentation, unless the party making the misrepresentation can prove that he had reasonable ground to believe and did believe up to the time the contract was made that the facts represented were true. The measure of damages in tort does not give recovery for loss of bargain;[229] it puts the plaintiff in the position he would have been in had the tort not been committed—typically, therefore, placing the purchaser in the financial position as if he had not entered into the contract at all in reliance on the misrepresentation. Damages may also be claimed in the tort of negligence, although the purchaser is more likely to rely on his claim under section 2(1) of the Misrepresentation Act if seeking a remedy against the vendor.[230]

FOSCOTE (actual knowledge of the third party's misrepresentation is required; but constructive notice is sufficient in a case covered by the principle of *Barclays Bank plc v O'Brien* [1994] 1 AC 181, p. 751, ante). A remedy, e.g. in the law of tort, must therefore normally be sought directly against the third party.

[222] The misrepresentation gives rise to an equity to rescind which, in the case of a contract for the sale of land, will be defeated by certain later dispositions to third parties: see infra. For other bars to rescission, see Cartwright, *Misrepresentation*, paras. 3.36–3.69.

[223] *Redgrave v Hurd* (1881) 20 Ch D 1 at 12, per JESSEL MR; *Derry v Peek* (1889) 14 App Cas 337 at 359, per Lord HERSCHELL.

[224] Misrepresentation Act 1967, s. 1(b). The Law Reform Committee, which proposed the Act, had proposed that contract for the sale or other disposition of an interest in land, apart from contracts for short leases, should not be capable of rescission after execution: Tenth Report, Innocent Misrepresentation, Cmnd 1782 (1962), paras. 6, 7. This was not, however, implemented in the Act.

[225] Misrepresentation Act 1967, s. 2(2); *William Sindall plc v Cambridgeshire CC* [1994] 1 WLR 1016.

[226] For some problems in this respect associated with rescission, see Cartwright, *Misrepresentation*, paras. 3.05–3.16.   [227] *Derry v Peek* (1889) 14 App Cas 337.

[228] Damages are assessed on the same basis as in the tort of deceit: *Royscot Trust Ltd v Rogerson* [1991] 2 QB 297; see however *Smith New Court Securities Ltd v Citibank NA* [1997] AC 254 at 267, 282–3; Treitel, p. 363.

[229] *McConnel v Wright* [1903] 1 Ch 546 at 554–5, per COLLINS MR. The loss recoverable in deceit may, however, include the lost opportunity of making profits from *other* contracts: *East v Maurer* [1991] 1 WLR 461.

[230] Under s. 2(1) the burden of proof of honest and reasonable belief in the truth of the statement lies on the defendant. The tort of negligence must be used if the claim is against a third party to the contract, because the Misrepresentation Act 1967, s. 2(1) does not cover that case: *Resolute Maritime v Nippon Kaiji Kyokai* [1983] 1 WLR 857. The tort of negligence may also be used by either party to impose liability in damages on their own advisers: *Smith v Eric S Bush* [1990] 1 AC 831 (surveyor's duty to mortgagee and also to mortgagor to whom contents of survey were communicated); *Hilton v Barker Booth and Eastwood* [2005] 1 WLR 567 (solicitor's breach of duty in acting for both parties); and sometimes even the other party's advisers: *McCullagh v Lane Fox & Partners Ltd* [1996] 1 EGLR 35 (vendor's estate agent; but no duty on facts). Under the Property Misdescriptions Act 1991 it is an offence to make false or misleading statements about property matters in the course of estate agency or property development business; Property Misdescriptions (Specified Matters) Order

(2) Rectification of the Contract

If, as the result of a mistake common to both parties, the written evidence omits some material term and therefore does not express the true bargain between the parties, the court has jurisdiction to rectify the contract.[231] In such a case it first rectifies the written contract by adding the oral omission or variation, and then decrees specific performance of the contract as rectified. At one and the same time it reforms and enforces the contract.[232] This remedy will be granted even where the mistake is embodied in the final deed of conveyance.[233]

In *Agip SpA v Navigazione Alta Italia SpA*,[234] SLADE LJ summarised the conditions which must be satisfied for rectification on the grounds of common mistake:

First, there must be a common intention in regard to the particular provisions of the agreement in question, together with some outward expression of accord. Secondly, this common intention must continue up to the time of execution of the instrument. Thirdly, there must be clear evidence that the instrument as executed does not accurately represent the true agreement of the parties at the time of its execution. Fourthly, it must be shown that the instrument, if rectified as claimed, would accurately represent the true agreement of the parties at that time . . .

The standard of proof required in an action of rectification to establish the common intention of the parties is the civil standard of balance of probability.

Unilateral mistake may also give rise to a claim for rectification if the mistaken party can show that it would be unconscionable for the other party to insist on the document as drafted. Normally this is satisfied by proof that the other party knows of the mistake, would benefit by it, and failed to draw it to the attention of the mistaken party.[235] For this purpose "knowledge" is not limited to actual knowledge, but extends to wilfully shutting one's eyes to the obvious, and wilfully and recklessly failing to make such inquiries as an honest and reasonable man would make.[236]

In *Commission for the New Towns v Cooper (GB) Ltd*, STUART-SMITH LJ said:[237]

Where A intends B to be mistaken as to the construction of the agreement, so conducts himself that he diverts B's attention from discovering the mistake by making false and misleading statements, and B in fact makes the very mistake that A intends, then notwithstanding that A does not actually know, but merely suspects that B is mistaken, and it cannot be shown that the mistake was induced by any misrepresentation, rectification may be granted. A's conduct is unconscionable and he cannot insist on performance in accordance with the strict letter of the contract; that is sufficient for rescission. But it may also not be unjust or inequitable to insist that the contract be performed according to B's understanding, where that was the meaning that A intended that B should put upon it.

1992 (SI 1992 No. 2834); *Lewin v Barratt Homes Ltd* [2000] 1 EGLR 77; *Dacre Son & Hartley Ltd v North Yorkshire Trading Standards* [2005] 1 EGLR 11 (conviction for false or misleading statement on dampness); although the contract is not void or unenforceable, and no right of civil action arises in respect of any loss, by reason only of the commission of an offence s. 1(4).

   [231] *United States of America v Motor Trucks Ltd* [1924] AC 196; *Joscelyne v Nissen* [1970] 2 QB 86.
   [232] [1924] AC 196 at 201, per Lord BIRKENHEAD.
   [233] *Craddock Bros Ltd v Hunt* [1923] 2 Ch 136. See also *Riverlate Properties Ltd v Paul* [1975] Ch 133.
   [234] [1984] 1 Lloyd's Rep 353 at 365.
   [235] *A Roberts & Co Ltd v Leicestershire County Council* [1961] Ch 555; *Thomas Bates & Son Ltd v Wyndham's (Lingerie) Ltd* [1981] 1 WLR 505; *Kemp v Neptune Concrete Ltd* [1988] 2 EGLR 87; *Huber (Investments) Ltd v Private DIY Co Ltd* (1995) 70 P & CR D33; *Coles v William Hill Organisation Ltd* [1998] EGCS 40; *Nurdin & Peacock plc v Ramsden & Co Ltd* [1999] 1 EGLR 119; *Oceanic Village Ltd v United Attractions Ltd* [2000] Ch 234 (London Aquarium); *George Wimpey UK Ltd v VI Construction Ltd* [2005] BLR 135.
   [236] *Commission for the New Towns v Cooper (GB) Ltd* [1995] Ch 259 at 280–1, per STUART-SMITH LJ.
   [237] Ibid., at 280.

Whether the mistake was common or unilateral, the fact that it arose through the negligence of the plaintiff or his legal advisers is normally no bar to rectification.[238]

The mistake must be as to the effect of the document which it is sought to rectify; a mistaken belief as to its relation to another document is not sufficient.[239]

(3) Passing of the Benefit and Burden of Equities to Rescind or Rectify

We saw in chapter 22 that the right to rescind and the right to rectify are "mere equities", which are not equitable interests in the property, but have proprietary characteristics. The benefit, in cases concerning land, is capable of passing with the land.[240] The burden is capable of binding successors to the property against which the beneficiary of the equity had a claim to a remedy. In unregistered land the equity can be defeated not only by a conveyance of the legal estate, but also by a conveyance of an equitable interest, to a bona fide purchaser without notice of the equity; in registered land, however, a mere equity is now[241] treated from the time it arises as being an interest capable of binding successors—and therefore as having the same protection as an equitable interest, as long it is either protected by notice on the register, or takes effect as an overriding interest by virtue of the claimant's discoverable actual occupation.[242]

B   *Remedies for Breach of Contract*

The remedies available for breach of the contract are damages, specific performance, rescission and vendor and purchaser summons.

(1) Damages

In the event of a breach of any contract the general rule that governs the measure of damages is that the plaintiff is to be placed, so far as money can do it, in the same situation as if the contract had been performed.[243] This is, however, subject to the rule relating to remoteness of damage, which limits the defendant's liability to such losses as he ought reasonably to have contemplated as likely to occur, having regard to the knowledge, actual or constructive, possessed by him at the time of the contract.[244] The defendant is therefore liable only for loss of a kind he could foresee might occur in the usual course of things, unless he knows of special circumstances by which it may be increased.[245]

---

[238] *Weeds v Blaney* (1977) 247 EG 211; *Central and Metropolitan Estates Ltd v Compusave* (1982) 266 EG 900; *Boots the Chemist Ltd v Street* (1983) 268 EG 817.

[239] *London Regional Transport v Wimpey Group Services Ltd* [1986] 2 EGLR 41 (rent review).

[240] LPA 1925, s. 63; *Boots the Chemist Ltd v Street* (1983) 268 EG 817; *Berkeley Leisure Group Ltd v Williamson* [1996] EGCS 18.   [241] LRA 2002, s. 116 ("declared for the avoidance of doubt").

[242] Pp. 813–4 et seq, ante.

[243] *Robinson v Harman* (1848) 1 Exch 850, 855 per PARKE B; Treitel, p. 937. For difficulties in applying this rule to a claim for breach of a restrictive covenant, see pp. 691–3 et seq, ante.

[244] *Hadley v Baxendale* (1854) 9 Exch 341; *Victoria Laundry (Windsor) Ltd v Newman Industries Ltd* [1949] 2 KB 528; *Koufos v C Czarnikow Ltd, The Heron II* [1969] 1 AC 350; Cheshire, Fifoot and Furmston, *Law of Contract*, pp. 658 et seq.

[245] *Cottrill v Steyning and Littlehampton Building Society* [1966] 1 WLR 753 (defendant knew plaintiff intended to develop the land for profit: "special circumstances" established); dist. *Diamond v Campbell-Jones* [1961] Ch 22.

(a) Damages recoverable by vendor

In the case of a contract for the sale of land this general rule applies when it is the vendor who brings the action. The loss caused to the vendor in the usual course of things by the failure of the purchaser to complete is the deprivation of the purchase price diminished by the value of the land that he still holds, and he is therefore entitled to recover by way of damages the difference, if any, between the value of the land which remains in his possession and the price he would have got had the contract been completed.[246] If he resells, he is entitled to recover both the difference in price and the expenses attending the resale.[247]

(b) Damages recoverable by purchaser

The general rule of assessment of damages now also applies where it is the purchaser who sues for breach. Until it was abolished by the Law of Property (Miscellaneous Provisions) Act 1989,[248] there was a rule[249] that the general principle—that damages are recoverable for loss of bargain—was excluded in a case where the vendor was unable to complete the conveyance owing to a defect in his title; he was instead limited to the recovery of his deposit, if any, and of the expenses he had incurred in investigating title. Now, however, a purchaser is entitled in all cases to damages for loss of bargain. If the value of the property is greater than the purchase price, the plaintiff recovers the difference, though in this case he cannot recover his conveyancing costs.[250] If the value of the property is less than the purchase price, he is entitled to a return of the deposit with interest and also to damages in respect of the cost of investigating the title.[251]

(c) Date for assessment of damages

It was at one time thought that, while the general rule at common law requires damages to be assessed as at the date of the breach of contract, that is, the date fixed for completion, a greater measure of damages, based on the value of the land at the date of the judgment, would be recoverable where the damages were awarded in substitution for specific performance under Lord Cairns' Act (Chancery Amendment Act 1858).[252] Lord Cairns' Act gave the Court of Chancery discretionary power to award damages either in addition to or in substitution for specific performance (in cases where the court had jurisdiction to award specific performance), the damages to be assessed in such manner as the court shall direct. Since the Judicature Act 1873, making the common law remedy of damages available in the Chancery

---

[246] *Laird v Pim* (1841) 7 M & W 474; *Harold Wood Brick Co Ltd v Ferris* [1935] 1 KB 613; affd [1935] 2 KB 198.

[247] *Noble v Edwardes* (1877) 5 Ch D 378; *Keck v Faber, Jellett and Keeble* (1915) 60 SJ 253.

[248] Ss. 3, 5(3), adopting the recommendations of the Law Commission Report on the Rule in *Bain v Fothergill* 1987 (Law Com No. 166, Cm 192).

[249] Known as the rule in *Bain v Fothergill* (1874) LR 7HL 158. For further details of this rule, see the 16th edn of this book, pp. 137–8.

[250] *Re Daniel* [1917] 2 Ch 405. The loss for which compensation is recoverable is the difference between the purchase price and the value of the property if it had been conveyed in accordance with the contract. But if the property had in fact been so conveyed, the conveyancing costs would have fallen on the purchaser, and therefore he cannot recover both the difference and the costs: ibid., at 412, per SARGANT J.

[251] *Wallington v Townsend* [1939] Ch 588; *Lloyd v Stanbury* [1971] 1 WLR 535.

[252] Now SCA 1981, s. 50. *Wroth v Tyler* [1974] Ch 30; *Grant v Dawkins* [1973] 1 WLR 1406; (1975) 34 CLJ 224 (J. A. Jolowicz); [1981] Conv 286 (T. Ingman and J. Wakefield); (1981) 97 LQR 445 (S. M. Waddams). On the jurisdiction of the court to award damages before Lord Cairns' Act, see (1992) 108 LQR 652 (P. M. McDermott).

Division, it is only necessary to invoke Lord Cairns' Act in a case where common law damages would not be available.[253] The position as to the time at which damages are to be assessed was clarified by the House of Lords in *Johnson v Agnew*.[254] Subject to the point that in some cases damages would be available under Lord Cairns' Act where none at all would be available at common law, the Act does not permit a departure from the common law rule on the quantum of damages. But there is no inflexible rule at common law that damages must be assessed as at the date of the breach of contract.[255] The principle is that the plaintiff should be put in the same position as if the contract had been duly performed. Where, after the breach, the innocent party has reasonably continued to try for completion, the damages, however awarded, should be assessed as at the date when the contract was lost.[256] This will normally be the date of the hearing, but an earlier date will be substituted if the plaintiff has delayed.[257]

Damages recoverable where completion is delayed, or where specific performance is ordered but enforcement subsequently proves impossible, are dealt with below.[258]

(2) Specific Performance

The most effective remedy available to either party is to sue for specific performance, that is, to demand that the contract be completed according to its terms. One of the general principles established by equity is that this relief should be given only where damages do not afford an adequate remedy. But the subject matter of a contract for the sale of land[259] is of unique value, so that specific performance of the contract is available to a purchaser as a matter of course. Furthermore, even though a vendor could be adequately compensated by damages for the failure of a purchaser to complete, yet, in pursuance of the doctrine that remedies should be mutual, equity grants specific performance to a vendor as well as to a purchaser.[260]

A full discussion of specific performance is outside the scope of this book,[261] but it may be noticed that the remedy is discretionary, though the discretion is not exercised in an arbitrary or capricious manner, but according to the rules that have been established by the judges. If the defendant can show any circumstances independent of the written contract which make it inequitable to decree specific performance, as for instance where the plaintiff has delayed, or in certain cases of mistake, misrepresentation and misdescription, or where the vendor or the purchaser has not acted fairly,[262] or where the completion of the contract

---

[253] Such as, perhaps, where the case is based on proprietary estoppel, which gives rise to no action at law: *Crabb v Arun DC (No 2)* (1976) 121 SJ 86. See also *Oakacre Ltd v Claire Cleaners (Holdings) Ltd* [1982] Ch 197 (action for damages at law not accrued at date of writ). [254] [1980] AC 367.

[255] Ibid. See also *Wroth v Tyler*, supra, at 57; *Radford v de Froberville* [1977] 1 WLR 1262; *Malhotra v Choudhury* [1980] Ch 52; *Techno Land Improvements Ltd v British Leyland (UK) Ltd* (1979) 252 EG 805; *Forster v Silvermere Golf and Equestrian Centre Ltd* (1981) 42 P & CR 255, (1979) 95 LQR 270 (D. Feldman and D. F. Libling); *Suleman v Shahsavari* [1988] 1 WLR 1181; Treitel, pp. 959 et seq.

[256] In *Johnson v Agnew*, this was the date on which the vendor's mortgagees contracted to sell the property, thus preventing completion of the vendor's contract with the plaintiff.

[257] *Radford v de Froberville*, supra; *Malhotra v Choudhury*, supra.   [258] Pp. 889 et seq, post.

[259] Specific performance may also be granted of a contractual licence to occupy land; *Verrall v Great Yarmouth BC* [1981] QB 202, M & B p. 609; pp. 835–6, ante.

[260] *Kenney v Wexham* (1822) 6 Madd 355 at 357, per LEACH V-C.

[261] See generally H & M, chap. 24; Snell, chap. 15; Jones and Goodhart, *Specific Performance*; White and Tudor, *Leading Cases in Equity*, vol. ii, pp. 372 et seq; Burrows, *Remedies for Torts and Breach of Contract*, chap. 20. On the availability of specific performance under the Contracts (Rights of Third Parties) Act 1999, see Emmet, para. 2.133.

[262] *Sang Lee Investment Co Ltd v Wing Kwai Investment Co Ltd* (1983) 127 SJ 410, per Lord BRIGHTMAN.

would cause hardship to an innocent vendor or purchaser,[263] the court will not grant the remedy.[264]

(a) Specific performance when completion delayed

Where a contract for the sale of land is not completed upon the date fixed in the contract, specific performance may still be available, even at the instance of the delaying party.[265] *At law* time was always considered to be of the essence of the contract, and a party who failed to complete upon the agreed date was remediless. Thus, if the vendor failed to complete, the purchaser could repudiate the contract and recover the deposit and the costs of investigating the title. Equity, however, taking a different view that now prevails in all courts,[266] did not regard time as necessarily of the essence, and has always been prepared to decree specific performance notwithstanding failure to observe the exact date fixed for completion, *provided that this will not cause injustice to either party*.

But it must be emphasised that, even where time is not of the essence of a contract, failure to complete on the contractual date is a breach of contract, both at law and in equity. The contractual duty of the parties is not merely to complete on that date or within a reasonable time thereafter.[267] The fact that time is not of the essence merely means that the delaying party does not lose the right to specific performance, nor will he forfeit his deposit, provided that he is ready to complete within a reasonable time. If completion does not occur on the contractual date, the delaying party will be liable to pay damages, as, for example, where the innocent party incurs hotel or storage expenses as a result of the breach.

While the general position is that the party in breach of contract remains entitled to specific performance, that remedy will not be decreed if the parties have expressly stipulated that time shall be essential, or if there is something in the nature of the property or in the surrounding circumstances which renders it inequitable to treat the appointed date as non-essential.[268]

So, if the nature of the property is such as to make its conveyance at the agreed date imperative, for example, when the contract is for the sale of licensed premises,[269] or of a shop as a going concern, specific performance, even with compensation, will not be decreed; but

---

[263] *Patel v Ali* [1984] Ch 283 (specific performance would inflict on vendor "a hardship amounting to injustice", per GOULDING J at 288); (1984) 100 LQR 337. But ECHR, art. 8 cannot be successfully prayed in aid to prevent a contractual purchaser from obtaining specific performance of a contract for the purchase of the house which is the vendor's home; art. 8 does not diminish the purchaser's rights under domestic law: *Harrow LBC v Qazi* [2004] 1 AC 983 at [136], per Lord SCOTT OF FOSCOTE.

[264] *Co-operative Insurance Society Ltd v Argyll Stores (Holdings) Ltd* [1998] AC 1 (covenant by tenant to keep a Safeway supermarket "open for retail trading during the usual hours of business" held not enforceable by specific performance). But damages are available: *Costain Property Developments Ltd v Finlay & Co Ltd* (1988) 57 P & CR 345; *Transworld Land Co Ltd v J Sainsbury plc* [1990] 2 EGLR 255 (loss caused on neighbouring property); (1998) 61 MLR 421 (A. Phang); [1998] Conv 396 (P. Luxton); [1997] CLJ 458 (G. Jones); (1997) 147 NLJ 1281 (H. W. Wilkinson).

[265] See generally Farrand, *Contract and Conveyance* (4th edn), pp. 208–10; Barnsley, *Conveyancing Law and Practice*, pp. 420–34. For the position where the plaintiff delays in enforcing the order for specific performance, see *Easton v Brown* [1981] 3 All ER 278.

[266] LPA 1925, s. 41, re-enacting Judicature Act 1873, s. 25(7). See generally (1980) 39 CLJ 58 (A. J. Oakley).

[267] *Raineri v Miles* [1981] AC 1050; *Oakacre v Claire Cleaners (Holdings) Ltd* [1982] Ch 197. See also *Inns v D Miles Griffiths, Piercy & Co Ltd* (1980) 255 EG 623.

[268] *Stickney v Keeble* [1915] AC 386 at 415–16, per Lord PARKER. See also *Rightside Properties Ltd v Gray* [1975] Ch 72; *Dean v Upton* [1990] EGCS 61; *Union Eagle Ltd v Golden Achievement Ltd* [1997] AC 514 (time of the essence: no decree where purchaser tendered purchase price ten minutes late); [1997] Conv 382 (M. P. Thompson).   [269] *Lock v Bell* [1931] 1 Ch 35.

if there is nothing special in the nature of the property or in the purposes for which it is required, the court will decree specific performance, subject to the condition that the defaulting party pay compensation for the delay. The principle in such a case is that specific performance will be awarded unless the plaintiff has delayed unreasonably. There is no statutory period of limitation barring claims to specific performance,[270] and no rule to lay down what is meant by unreasonable delay.

It used to be thought that the plaintiff must normally seek specific performance well within one year,[271] but it now seems that this approach is too strict.[272] An exceptional case where delay will not be a bar is where the plaintiff has taken possession under the contract, so that the purpose of specific performance is merely to vest the legal estate in him.[273]

A new contract cannot be made at the will of one of the parties and therefore, where time is not initially essential, one party cannot make it so of his own volition.[274] Nevertheless, there must be some limit to delaying tactics, and it is established that after the date fixed for completion has passed one party may serve a notice on the other requiring completion within a specified time.[275] The notice will be valueless unless the time allowed is reasonable,[276] but if satisfactory in this respect it will bind both parties.[277]

(b) Specific performance with abatement

There are other circumstances where the court will decree specific performance in favour of the plaintiff subject to the condition that compensation is paid in respect of some term of the contract which has not been literally fulfilled. Such cases of specific performance with an abatement of the purchase price are primarily concerned with misdescription of the property.[278] Subject to any conditions of sale applying to the contract, the general rule is that if the misdescription is substantial, the vendor cannot obtain specific performance even subject to an abatement, while the purchaser may enforce the contract if he so chooses.[279] But if the misdescription is not substantial either party may obtain specific performance subject to compensation.[280]

(c) Where defendant fails to comply with decree of specific performance

Where the plaintiff obtains a decree of specific performance, but the defendant fails to comply with it, the plaintiff may apply either to enforce[281] or to dissolve the contract. The contract still exists after the grant of specific performance and does not merge into the

---

270 Limitation Act 1980, s. 36(1).   271 See Farrand, *Contract and Conveyance* (4th edn), p. 216.

272 *Lazard Bros & Co Ltd v Fairfield Properties Co (Mayfair) Ltd* (1977) 121 SJ 793; [1978] Conv 184.

273 *Williams v Greatrex* [1957] 1 WLR 31 (delay of ten years no bar in such a case).

274 *Green v Sevin* (1879) 13 Ch D 589 at 599.

275 *Finkielkraut v Monohan* [1949] 2 All ER 234; *Dimsdale Developments (South East) Ltd v De Haan* (1983) 47 P & CR 1; [1984] Conv. 34 (M. P. Thompson).

276 *Smith v Hamilton* [1951] Ch 174; *Re Barr's Contract* [1956] Ch 551; *Ajit v Sammy* [1967] 1 AC 255.

277 *Finkielkraut v Monohan*, supra; *Quadrangle Development and Construction Co Ltd v Jenner* [1974] 1 WLR 68; *Oakdown Ltd v Bernstein & Co* (1984) 49 P & CR 282; *Behzadi v Shaftesbury Hotels Ltd* [1992] Ch 1; [1991] CLJ (C. Harpum); [1991] 107 LQR 534 (P. V. Baker).

278 See Farrand, *Contract and Conveyance* (4th edn), pp. 52–5; (1980) 40 CLJ 47 (C. Harpum).

279 *Flight v Booth* (1834) 1 Bing NC 370; *Rutherford v Acton-Adams* [1915] AC 866 at 870; *Rudd v Lascelles* [1900] 1 Ch 815. It is otherwise if the compensation cannot be assessed, or if the subject matter is entirely different from that contracted for; see p. 949, post.

280 *Jacobs v Revell* [1900] 2 Ch 858. This principle cannot be used so as to increase the price: *Re Lindsay and Forder's Contract* (1895) 72 LT 832.   281 See *Easton v Brown* [1981] 3 All ER 278, p. 889 n. 265, ante.

decree; thus the plaintiff is not precluded in such a case from seeking damages at common law.[282] But any subsequent performance of the contract is regulated by the provisions of the order of specific performance and not by those of the contract.[283] If the order for specific performance is not complied with, the plaintiff, having elected to affirm the contract, cannot then unilaterally terminate it for breach. He must apply to the court either for further enforcement measures or for a dissolution of the order and termination of the contract;[284] in which case he may claim for damages.

(3) Rescission for Breach of Contract[285]

(a) Terminology

A distinction must be drawn between rescission *ab initio*[286] and rescission in the sense of accepting the repudiation of the contract by the other party. Where rescission *ab initio* occurs, as, for example, in cases of misrepresentation, the position is that the contract is treated as if it had never existed; thus the innocent party cannot recover damages for breach of contract. Where, however, the vendor fails to show a good title[287] or to deliver the actual land or interest described in the contract, or where the vendor or purchaser fails to complete after time has been made of the essence,[288] it is commonly said that the innocent party may rescind. This is not rescission *ab initio*, but acceptance of a repudiation of the contract, discharging both parties from further performance. In such a case damages are recoverable at common law for breach of contract.[289] As discussed below, the terms of the contract may also confer a right to rescind in specified circumstances, and provide for the consequences. In the absence of any such terms, the innocent party may either accept the repudiation and proceed to claim damages (in which case he cannot later seek specific performance), or he may seek specific performance.[290] If an order for specific performance is made, but not complied with, he may apply to the court to enforce or to dissolve the order,[291] damages being recoverable in the latter case.[292]

(b) Contractual right to rescind

The right to rescind may also be conferred by the express terms of the contract.[293] There used commonly to be found in a contract of sale a condition that allows the vendor to rescind if

---

[282] *Johnson v Agnew* [1980] AC 367, confirming the views expressed in (1975) 91 LQR 337 (M. J. Albery) and (1977) 93 LQR 232 (F. Dawson) (enforcement impossible because after date of contract with purchaser, vendor's mortgagees contracted to sell the property).

[283] *Singh v Nazeer* [1979] Ch 474 (contractual completion notice served after decree of specific performance invalid); (1980) 96 LQR 403 (M. Hetherington).

[284] *GKN Distributors Ltd v Tyne Tees Fabrication Ltd* (1985) 50 P & CR 403.

[285] For solicitors' liability in negligence for failing to advise purchaser of lease of his right to rescind, see *Peyman v Lanjani* [1985] Ch 457.   [286] P. 883, ante.

[287] A purchaser can rescind as soon as he discovers that the vendor has no title, i.e. before date fixed for completion: *Pips (Leisure Productions) Ltd v Walton* (1980) 43 P & CR 415 (contract to sell leasehold which was already forfeited); *Pinekerry Ltd v Needs (Kenneth) (Contractors) Ltd* (1992) 64 P & CR 245.

[288] Time is not normally of the essence unless made so by the contract: p. 889, ante; cf *Allardyce v Roebuck* [2004] 3 All ER 754 (completion following exercise of option).

[289] *Johnson v Agnew* [1980] AC 367, overruling *Henty v Schröder* (1879) 12 Ch D 666, and many other authorities. See *Tilcon Ltd v Land and Real Estate Investments Ltd* [1987] 1 WLR 46.

[290] If he proceeds for these remedies in the alternative, he must elect at the trial: *Meng Leong Development Pte Ltd v Jip Hong Trading Co Pte Ltd* [1985] 1 AC 511.

[291] *Hillel v Christoforides* (1991) 63 P & CR 301 (where vendor has sought dissolution, purchaser cannot complete unless vendor has acted unconscionably).

[292] *Meng Leong Development Pte Ltd v Jip Hong Trading Co Pte Ltd*, supra; *GKN Distributors Ltd v Tyne Tees Fabrication Ltd* (1985) 50 P & CR 403.   [293] Emmet, paras. 7.008–7.0010.

the purchaser should insist on any requisition which the vendor is unable or unwilling to comply with.[294] But "a vendor, in seeking to rescind, must not act arbitrarily, or capriciously, or unreasonably. Much less can he act in bad faith . . . Above all, perhaps, he must not be guilty of 'recklessness' in entering into his contract."[295] Thus, in *Baines v Tweddle*,[296] a vendor was unable to exercise a contractual right to rescind because he had failed to seek the concurrence of his mortgagees before contracting to sell free from the mortgage.

(c) Forfeiture of deposit

Where the purchaser defaults, the vendor is entitled to retain any deposit that the purchaser may have paid. Thus in *Howe v Smith*,[297]

£500 was paid as deposit and part payment of the purchase money. The purchaser, who was in default in completing the contract, sued to recover the £500, but it was held that, since it was the intention of the parties that this sum should be deposited as a guarantee for the due performance of his obligations, it must be forfeited to the vendor.

Where a defaulting purchaser has not yet paid over the whole of the deposit, the whole or any unpaid part is recoverable by the vendor.[298] Similarly, where the vendor is in default, the purchaser may recover any deposit which he has paid. But whether the rule as to retention of the deposit applies or not is in each case a matter of construction, and if the terms show that the money has not been paid as a guarantee of performance, but solely by way of part payment, it is recoverable by the purchaser even though the contract is rescinded owing to his own default.[299]

A purchaser may be able to secure the return of his deposit under section 49(2) of the Law of Property Act 1925, which provides that:

where the court refuses to grant specific performance of a contract, or in any action for the return of a deposit, the court may, if it thinks fit, order the repayment of any deposit.

In considering this provision BUCKLEY LJ has said that it was designed simply to do justice between vendor and purchaser:

It confers on the judge a discretion, which is unqualified by any language of the subsection, to order or refuse repayment of the deposit, a discretion which must, of course, be exercised judicially and with

---

[294] See, e.g. Condition 4. 5. 2 of the Standard Conditions of Sale (1st edn 1990) This right to rescind is no longer contained in the Standard Conditions of Sale; there are however other express rights to rescind such as on the purchaser's or the vendor's failure to complete the contract: conditions 7.5.2, 7.6.2; Emmet, para. 7.008.

[295] *Selkirk v Romar Investments Ltd* [1963] 1 WLR 1415 at 1422, per Lord RADCLIFFE.

[296] [1959] Ch 679; *Re Des Reaux and Setchfield's Contract* [1926] Ch 178. See also, on misdescription, *Topfell Ltd v Galley Properties Ltd* [1979] 1 WLR 446.

[297] (1884) 27 Ch D 89. On deposits generally, see Farrand, *Contract and Conveyance* (4th edn), pp. 203–8; Barnsley, *Conveyancing Law and Practice*, pp. 233–43; [1994] Conv 41, 100 (A. J. Oakley). On 30 November 2005 ODPM issued a consultation paper on Tenancy Deposit Protection. For the position where an estate agent holds the pre-contract deposit of a prospective purchaser, see *Sorrell v Finch* [1977] AC 728; *Ramsden v James Bennett* [1993] NPC 91 (£6,000 deposit for option to purchase villa in Spain); cf *Ojelay v Neosale Ltd* [1987] 2 EGLR 167 and on stakeholders generally: *Sorrell v Finch*; *Tudor v Hamid* [1988] 1 EGLR 251; (1988) 138 NLJ 40 (H. W. Wilkinson); *Rockeagle Ltd v Alsop Wilkinson* [1992] Ch 47.

[298] *Dewar v Mintoft* [1912] 2 KB 373 at 387–8; *Millichamp v Jones* [1982] 1 WLR 1422 (where the authorities are fully reviewed by WARNER J); *Damon Cia Naviera SA v Hapag-Lloyd International SA* [1985] 1 WLR 435 (applied by CA in a case relating to ships); *John Willmott Homes Ltd v Read* (1985) 51 P & CR 90; cf *Lowe v Hope* [1970] Ch 94; Farrand, *Contract and Conveyance* (4th edn), p. 206.   [299] *Mayson v Clouet* [1924] AC 980.

regard to all relevant considerations, including the very important consideration of the terms of the contract into which the parties have chosen to enter... repayment must be ordered in any circumstances which make this the fairest course between the two parties.[300]

(4) Vendor and Purchaser Summons

The Vendor and Purchaser Act 1874 introduced a new method whereby parties to a contract of sale, whose disagreement upon some matter prevents the completion of the contract, may apply in a summary way to a judge in chambers, and obtain such an order as may appear just. This summary proceeding is termed a vendor and purchaser summons, and is now governed by the Law of Property Act 1925.[301] Typical questions which lead to a summons are the sufficiency of the title shown by the vendor,[302] the sufficiency of an answer made to a requisition,[303] the construction of the contract, and the question whether a vendor is entitled to rescind.

The Act expressly excludes the possibility of raising any question that affects the existence or the validity of the contract in its inception, as for instance, the question whether the formalities of the contract have been complied with.

Not only may the court decide the question submitted to it, but it may also grant consequential relief, that is, may order such things to be done as are the natural consequence of the decision. For instance, it may order rescission in favour of a purchaser, together with the return of his deposit.

---

[300] *Universal Corpn v Five Ways Properties Ltd* [1979] 1 All ER 552 at 555 (deposit of £88,500). Where the court orders the return of the deposit, the vendor is left to his remedy in damages. See also *James Macara Ltd v Barclay* [1944] 2 All ER 31 at 32; affd on other grounds [1945] KB 148; *Charles Hunt Ltd v Palmer* [1931] 2 Ch 287; *Finkielkraut v Monohan* [1949] 2 All ER 234; *Schindler v Pigault* (1975) 30 P & CR 328; *Faruqi v English Real Estates Ltd* [1979] 1 WLR 963 at 968; *Cole v Rose* [1978] 3 All ER 1121; *Maktoum v South Lodge Flats Ltd* The Times, 22 April 1980; 130 NLJ 668 (H. W. Wilkinson); *Dimsdale Developments (South East) v De Haan Ltd* (1983) 47 P & CR 1; *McGrath v Shah* (1987) 57 P & CR 452 (where no reference was made to LPA 1925, s. 49(2)). *Country and Metropolitan Homes Survey Ltd v Topclaim Ltd* [1996] Ch 307. See also Estate Agents Act 1979, ss. 12–17.

On the principles governing relief against forfeiture of deposit, see *Stockloser v Johnson* [1954] 1 QB 476; *Linggi Plantations Ltd v Jagatheesan* [1972] 1 MLJ 89; *Windsor Securities Ltd v Loreldal and Lester Ltd* The Times, 10 September 1975; *Workers Trust & Merchant Bank Ltd v Dojap Investments Ltd* [1993] AC 573 (relief possible where deposit is a penalty and not a true deposit; deposit exceeding 10% held not to be a true "reasonable" deposit); [1989] Conv 377 (H. W. Wilkinson); [1993] CLJ 389 (C. Harpum); (1993) 109 LQR 524 (H. Beale); *Safehaven Investments Inc v Springbok Ltd* (1995) 71 P & CR 59 (repayment of deposit refused where contract concerning commercial property made between capable businessmen with access to best professional advice. Purchaser was experienced property dealer well aware of the function of a deposit and the risks of losing it); *Union Eagle Ltd v Golden Achievement Ltd* [1997] AC 514 (10% deposit not a penalty), p. 889, n. 268, ante; *Omar v El-Wakil* [2002] 2 P & CR 3 at [36] ("I would start from the position that a deposit should not normally be ordered to be repaid", per ARDEN LJ). See generally Goff and Jones, *The Law of Restitution*, paras. 20-035 to 20-046; Emmet, paras. 7.026–7.029; [1994] Conv 41, 100 (A. J. Oakley).

[301] LPA 1925, s. 49(1). The county court has jurisdiction where the capital value of the land does not exceed £30,000: s. 49(4); County Courts Act 1984, s. 148(1), Sch. 2, para. 2; SI 1991 No. 724.

[302] See *MEPC Ltd v Christian-Edwards* [1981] AC 205, illustrating that such proceedings are not necessarily expeditious or cheap. [303] See *Faruqi v English Real Estate Ltd* [1979] 1 WLR 963.

25

FORMALITIES REQUIRED FOR THE CREATION AND TRANSFER OF ESTATES AND INTERESTS IN LAND

SUMMARY

I Introduction

The law prescribes formalities for certain transactions. Sometimes compliance with the formality is a condition of validity of the transaction; sometimes it is only a condition of legal enforceability.[1] But in any case in which a formality is prescribed, a question may arise as to how strict the formality rule is. One might begin by assuming that, if the formality is not complied with, the transaction is ineffective, or unenforceable, as the case may be. It is not, however, always quite so straightforward. In assessing the significance of a particular requirement of form, it is important to bear in mind the purposes for which formality may

---

[1] Under LPA 1925, s. 40, the written memorandum was a condition of enforceability of a contract relating to land; now LP(MP)A 1989, s. 2, makes a written contract a condition of validity: chap. 24, ante.

in general be required. Three aims of formalities are commonly identified:[2]

(a) *cautionary*: that is, trying to ensure that the maker does not enter into the transaction without realising what he is doing;

(b) *evidential*: providing evidence that the maker did enter into a transaction, and evidence of its terms;

(c) *labelling*: making it apparent to third parties what kind of a document it is and what its effect is to be.

The courts will sometimes look at the underlying purpose of the particular formality for the particular type of transaction that is before them, in order to decide how strictly they should interpret the statute which requires it.

In the context of land law, a number of formality requirements are laid down by statute. This is not perhaps surprising. For most individuals, land is their most significant asset—significant not only in financial terms, if they own their own home, but also in functional terms: it is their home.[3] As we have seen in chapter 24, the law now requires a contract for the sale or other disposition of an interest in land to be in writing, signed by both parties. This is the only contract in English law that must satisfy this formality requirement as a condition of validity.[4] In this chapter we shall see the formality requirements that are prescribed for the creation and transfer of estates and interests in land. But we shall also need to consider the law's response to the failure to comply with particular formality requirements. Sometimes the statute which sets out the formality required for a transaction gives an indication of the consequences of the failure to comply. But sometimes not; and cases often arise in which parties have quite innocently failed to comply with the requirements, and the courts have had to consider whether the law should assist them by admitting the creation or transfer of property rights in spite of the statute.

"Under a legal system recognizing the individualistic institution of private property and granting to the owner the power to determine his successors in ownership, the general philosophy of the courts should favor giving effect to an intentional exercise of that power."[5] The conflict between the certainty of a strict requirement of form, and the desire to do justice for individuals in particular cases, is at the heart of some significant developments in recent years in land law. As we shall see,[6] the development of proprietary estoppel and the use of constructive trusts as means of creating interests in land are the prime examples of this.

---

[2] Law Commission Working Paper on Transfer of Land: Formalities for Deeds and Escrows 1985 (No. 93), para. 3.2, discussing the aims of formalities for making a deed, but in this drawing on the analysis of the aims of formalities in general in (1941) 41 Colum L Rev 799, 800–1 (L. L. Fuller: "evidentiary", "cautionary", "channeling" functions); (1941) 51 Yale LJ 1, 3–5 (A. G. Gulliver and C. J. Tilson: "ritual", "evidentiary", protective" functions); (1975) 88 Harv L Rev 489, 492–7 (J. H. Langbein: "evidentiary", "channeling", "cautionary", "protective" functions); (1974) 43 Fordham L Rev 39 (J. M. Perillo: "magical, sacramental and psychological", "earmarking and classifying", "cautionary", "clarifying", "managerial", "publicity", "educational", "regulatory and taxation", "evidentiary" functions); [1984] CLJ 306 (T. G. Youdan).

[3] "Forms must be reserved for relatively important transactions. We must preserve a proportion between means and end; it will scarely do to require a sealed and witnessed document for the effective sale of a loaf of bread": (1941) 41 Colum L Rev 799, 805 (L. L. Fuller).

[4] A contract of guarantee must be at least evidenced in a written memorandum, signed by the guarantor or his authorised agent: Statute of Frauds 1677, s. 4. And a gratuitous promise can be made enforceable by the use of a deed: infra. But other provisions of the Statute of Frauds which required writing for particular types of transaction have been repealed.   [5] (1941) 51 Yale LJ 1, 2 (A. G. Gulliver and C. J. Tilson).

[6] P. 905 et seq, post.

II The Formalities

A *Formalities for the Creation and Transfer of Legal Estates and Interests*

(1) Necessity for a Deed

(a) *Forms of alienation before 1926*

The appropriate form at the present day for the conveyance of any interest in land is a deed of grant, but this form, though always required for the transfer of incorporeal hereditaments, was not extended to freehold estates in possession until 1845. Before that date the distinction drawn by the law was that freehold estates in possession *lay in livery*, that is, they were transferable by delivery of possession, and that incorporeal interests *lay in grant*, that is, they must be conveyed by deed of grant.[7] The Real Property Act of 1845,[8] however, provided that all corporeal hereditaments should, as regards the conveyance of the immediate freehold, be deemed to lie in grant as well as in livery. This Act did not, however, abolish the old forms of conveyance, and although it led to the general use of a deed of grant as a means of transferring all kinds of landed interests, there were still occasions upon which such forms as the feoffment and the bargain and sale[9] were used.

(b) *Forms of alienation after 1925*

The Law of Property Act 1925 simplified practice by providing that:[10]

All lands and all interests therein lie in grant and are incapable of being conveyed by livery or livery and seisin, or by feoffment, or by bargain and sale; and a conveyance of an interest in land may operate to pass the possession or right to possession thereof, without actual entry, but subject to all prior rights thereto.

This section, which shows that a grant is the usual method of conveying any interest in land, is followed by another which provides that:[11]

all conveyances of land or of any interest therein are void for the purpose of conveying or creating a legal estate unless made by deed.

This enactment, if unqualified, would cause inconvenience in certain cases, and it is therefore subject to exceptions. These are as follows:[12]

(2) Exceptions to Necessity for a Deed

(a) *Assent by personal representative*

The land of a deceased person vests in his personal representatives for the purposes of administration, and any devises he may have made are suspended until the administration is completed.[13] Upon such completion the land does not pass automatically to a devisee, but only when the assent of the personal representatives has been given. An assent to the vesting

---

[7] For the history of the forms of alienation, see Holdsworth, *History of English Law*, vol. iii, pp. 217–46; vol. vii, pp. 357–62. See p. 46, n. 25, ante.   [8] S. 2.
[9] P. 46, ante.   [10] LPA 1925, s. 51(1).   [11] Ibid., s. 52(1).   [12] Ibid., s. 52(2).
[13] Pp. 988 et seq, post.

of a legal estate must be *in writing*, signed by the personal representatives, and must name the person in whose favour it is given; it operates to vest in that person the legal estate to which it relates. An assent not in writing or not in favour of a named person is ineffectual to pass a legal estate.[14] An implied assent, that is, one inferred from conduct, may be effective to pass a title to equitable interests or to choses in action and personal chattels.[15]

(b) Disclaimer by trustee in bankruptcy

When any part of the estate of a bankrupt consists of land which is burdened with onerous covenants and is therefore unsaleable, the trustee in bankruptcy may, by writing, disclaim the property. Such a disclaimer operates to determine the rights and the liabilities of the bankrupt in respect of the property, but it does not affect the rights of third parties. The court may, on the application of any person who is interested in the disclaimed property, make an order vesting the property in him, and the effect of such an order is that the property vests in that person without any conveyance.[16]

(c) Surrender by operation of law

Surrender is not an instrument, but means that the owner of a smaller estate yields up that estate to the person who is entitled in reversion or remainder to the larger estate in the same lands as, for instance, where the tenant for life of Blackacre surrenders his life interest to the person who is entitled to the fee simple in the land. In such a case the life interest is merged in the fee simple.

Surrenders are either express or implied, and when implied they are said to arise by operation of law. An express surrender is void at law unless it is made by deed, but an implied surrender is effectual without any formality.[17]

(d) Lease for term not exceeding three years

A lease which is to take effect in possession, reserves the best rent which can be reasonably obtained without taking a fine, and is for a term not exceeding three years need not be created by deed, but can be created by writing or even orally. This has been discussed already.[18]

(e) Receipt not required to be under seal

An example of this before 1926 was where the legal estate of a mortgagee was re-vested in the mortgagor upon redemption not by a reconveyance under seal, but by an endorsed receipt.[19]

(f) Vesting order of the court

A vesting order is an order made by the court which may operate to vest, convey or create a legal estate in the same way as if a conveyance had been executed by the estate owner.[20] If, for

---

[14] AEA 1925, s. 36(1), (4); *Re King's Will Trusts* [1964] Ch 542; (1964) 28 Conv (NS) 298 (J. F. Garner); (1976) CLP 60 (E. C. Ryder); Farrand, *Contract and Conveyance* (4th edn), p. 106; Barnsley, *Conveyancing Law and Practice*, p. 321. See Law Commission Working Paper on Title on Death 1987 (No. 105), paras. 4.19–4.28; Law Commission Report on Title on Death 1989 (Law Com No. 184), paras. 1.5–1.6. *Re King's Will Trusts* was not followed in *Mohan v Roche* [1991] 1 IR 560; [1992] Conv 383 (J. A. Dowling).

[15] *Re Hodge* [1940] Ch 260; *Re Edwards' Will Trusts* [1982] Ch 30; [1982] Conv 4 (P. W. Smith).

[16] Insolvency Act 1986, s. 315; *Eyre v Hall* [1986] 2 EGLR 95.   [17] P. 325, ante.

[18] LPA 1925, s. 54(2); p. 220, ante.   [19] P. 757, ante.   [20] LPA 1925, s. 9.

instance, an equitable chargee applies for a sale of the land, the court may make an order vesting the land for a legal estate in the purchaser.[21]

(g) Conveyance taking effect by operation of law

Examples of these are grants of probate or of letters of administration and adjudications in bankruptcy.

(3) Form of Deeds, and Methods of Execution

In order to take effect as a deed, a document must comply with certain requirements as to its form and its method of execution. The requirements vary according to whether the document is to be executed by an individual or a company; but in both cases the formalities, originally prescribed by the common law, have been simplified in recent years by statute.

(a) General nature of a deed

A deed of grant is a formal written instrument which is signed and delivered by the grantor as his act, and in which he expresses an intention to pass an interest to the grantee.

The common law prescribed certain formalities for a deed:[22] "There are but three things of the essence and substance of a deed, that is to say, writing in paper or parchment, sealing and delivery." Section 1 of the Law of Property (Miscellaneous Provisions) Act 1989,[23] which applies to deeds executed on and after 31 July 1990, made the following general changes to the requirements to the form of a deed:

(1) Any rule of law which—
    (a) restricts the substances in which a deed may be written . . .
    is abolished.

(2) An instrument shall not be a deed unless—
    (a) it makes it clear on its face that it is intended to be a deed by the person making it or, as the case may be, by the parties to it (whether by describing itself as a deed or expressing itself to be executed or signed as a deed or otherwise); and
    (b) it is validly executed as a deed . . .

(1) PHYSICAL FORM OF A DEED

Before 31 July 1990 a deed had to be written on paper or parchment. Section 1(1) of the Act abolishes any rule of law which restricts the substance on which a deed may be written. Hence a deed may now be written on more durable material than paper, for example, fire- and flood-proof metal.[24]

---

[21] LPA 1925, s. 90.   [22] *Goddard's Case* (1584) 2 Co Rep 4b at 5a.

[23] This section is based on Law Commission Report on Deeds and Escrows 1987 (Law Com No. 163). It came into force on 31 July 1990 and is not retrospective: Law of Property (Miscellaneous Provisions) Act 1989 (Commencement) Order 1990 (SI 1990 No. 1175); [1990] Conv 1, 90. See Land Registration (Execution of Deeds) Rules 1990 (SI 1990 No. 1010); [1990] Conv 85 (D. N. Clarke) 321. See [1991] LMCLQ 209 (G. Virgo and C. Harpum) for a trenchant criticism of "the recent reforms which have left the law of deeds both more complex and less rational than it was hitherto". The section was further amended by Regulatory Reform (Execution of Deeds and Documents) Order 2005, SI 2005 No. 1906.   [24] Emmet, para. 20.001.2.

Section 1(2) requires, however, that in its form the deed be "clear on its face" that it is intended to be a deed. The simplest form will be the reference to "This deed ..." at the head of the document. The particular requirements of valid execution are discussed below.

(2) DELIVERY

(i) General requirement of delivery

A deed must be "delivered". This requirement was not changed by the 1989 Act. However, delivery does not mean a mere physical delivery, but a delivery accompanied by words or conduct signifying the grantor's intention to be bound by the provisions in the deed. The most apt and expressive mode of acknowledging this liability is for the grantor to hand the deed over, saying, "I deliver this as my deed", but any other words or acts that show an undoubted acknowledgment of immediate liability will suffice.[25]

(ii) Escrow

A physical delivery, however, unaccompanied by this express or implied acknowledgment, is insufficient, so that if, for instance, the grantor signs and seals the deed and then delivers it to his solicitor to be dealt with according to instructions to be given later, it does not operate as an immediate grant of the interest.

There are, therefore, two kinds of delivery recognised by the law in this connection, one absolute and the other conditional.[26] If a document is delivered, either to a party to it or to a stranger,[27] with an intimation, express or implied, that it is not to become effective until some condition has been performed, it is called an escrow (or scroll). In such a case the deed is inoperative until the condition is performed, but upon performance it takes effect as a deed without further delivery, and, if necessary, relates back to the time when it was delivered as an escrow.[28] As Lord CROSS OF CHELSEA said:[29]

On fulfilment of the condition subject to which it was delivered as an escrow, a deed is not taken to relate back to the date of its delivery for all purposes, but only for such purposes as are necessary to give efficacy to the transaction—*ut res magis valeat quam pereat*.[30] Thus the fact that the grantor has died before the condition of an escrow is fulfilled does not entail the consequence that the disposition fails.

If and when the condition is fulfilled the doctrine of relation back will save it, but notwithstanding the relation back for that limited purpose the grantee is not entitled to the rents of the property during the period of suspense or to lease it or to serve notices to quit.[31]

---

[25] *Xenos v Wickham* (1866) LR 2 HL 296 at 312. In the case of a deed executed by a company incorporated under the Companies Act, or a corporation aggregate, there is a presumption that the document is delivered upon its being executed; but this is now only a rebuttable presumption: LPA 1925, s. 74A(1) and Companies Act 1985, s. 36AA, both as inserted by SI 2005 No. 1906. The presumption for companies under the Companies Act was formerly irrebuttable: Companies Act 1985, s. 36A(6), as inserted by Companies Act 1989, s. 130, and now amended by SI 2005 No. 1906, art. 5.   [26] *Foundling Hospital v Crane* [1911] 2 KB 367 at 377.

[27] *London Freehold and Leasehold Property Co v Baron Suffield* [1897] 2 Ch 608 at 621–2.

[28] *Vincent v Premo Enterprises (Voucher Sales) Ltd* [1969] 2 QB 609; *Alan Estates Ltd v WG Stores Ltd* [1982] Ch 511; *Dyment v Boyden* [2005] 1 WLR 792 (party to lease not treated as bound from date when other party had delivered the lease in escrow where escrow conditions subsequently satisfied).

[29] *Security Trust Co v Royal Bank of Canada* [1976] AC 503 at 517; [1982] Conv 409 (P. H. Kenny).

[30] *Butler and Baker's Case* (1591) 3 Co Rep 25a.

[31] Sheppard's Touchstone (7th edn 1830), p. 60; *Thompson v McCullough* [1947] KB 447. See also *Terrapin International Ltd v IRC* [1976] 1 WLR 665; *Venetian Glass Gallery Ltd v Next Properties Ltd* [1989] 2 EGLR 42.

A delivery of a deed as an escrow is a final delivery in the sense that it cannot be withdrawn by the grantor before the grantee has had an opportunity to decide whether to fulfil the condition or not. A deed delivered subject to a condition and subject to such a right of withdrawal is not an escrow, but merely an undelivered deed.[32]

A common example of delivery as an escrow occurs where a vendor executes a deed of conveyance and gives it to his solicitor for transfer to the purchaser upon payment by the latter of the purchase money. If the sale is not completed in due course, the vendor is released, and the solicitor has no authority to hand over the conveyance.[33] Another example of delivery as an escrow occurs where a landlord executes a deed creating a lease, and the condition of the escrow is the execution of a counterpart by the tenant.[34]

(3) DEEDS POLL AND INDENTURES

Deeds are either deeds poll or indentures. A deed poll is one which is executed by a party of one part, an indenture is a deed (such as a conveyance by way of sale) to which there are parties of two or more parts.

In earlier days, when deeds were more concise than they are at present, it was usual, when they were made between two parties, to write two copies on the same parchment with some words written in the middle through which the parchment was cut in acute angles or indentations.[35] These two parts were called "counterparts", and, when put together so that the indentations fitted into each other, constituted the complete deed. Hence the name "indenture". Counterparts are not nowadays written on the same paper, but the part which is executed by the grantor of an interest is commonly called the *original*, while that which is executed by the party to whom the interest passes—for example, a lessee—is called the *counterpart*.[36] The custom of indenting deeds gradually died out, and all that the term "indenture", if it is used at all, now indicates is that the deed in question involves parties of more than one part.

A deed poll is so called because, unlike an indenture, it was formerly polled (or cut even) at the top.

(4) DESCRIPTION OF DEEDS IN THE MODERN LAW

Despite the provision of the Real Property Act 1845 that a deed should have the effect of an indenture although not actually indented, it remained customary to introduce every deed which involved more than one party by the expression "This Indenture . . ." But even this survival has now gone, for it is enacted by section 57 of the Law of Property Act 1925 that:

Any deed, whether or not being an indenture, may be described (at the commencement thereof or otherwise) as a deed simply, or as a conveyance, deed of exchange, vesting deed, trust instrument, settlement, mortgage, charge, transfer of mortgage, appointment, lease or otherwise according to the nature of the transaction intended to be effected.

---

[32] *Beesly v Hallwood Estates Ltd* [1961] Ch 105; *Windsor Refrigerator Co Ltd v Branch Nominees Ltd* [1961] Ch 88, reversed on a different point [1961] Ch 375; *D'Silva v Lister House Development Ltd* [1971] Ch 17; *Longman v Viscount Chelsea* (1989) 58 P & CR 189.

[33] *Kingston v Ambrian Investment Co Ltd* [1975] 1 WLR 161; *Glessing v Green* [1975] 1 WLR 863. As to the time limit for the performance of this condition, see [1975] 39 Conv (NS) 430 (F. R. Crane).

[34] *Beesly v Hallwood Estates Ltd*, supra; *Alan Estates Ltd v WG Stores Ltd*, supra (both lease and counterpart executed in escrow).   [35] Blackstone, vol. ii, p. 295.

[36] Elphinstone, *Introduction to Conveyancing*, p. 60.

(b) Deed executed by individual[37]

Section 1(3) of the Law of Property (Miscellaneous Provisions) Act 1989 lays down a new rule for the execution of a deed by an individual:

(3) An instrument is validly executed as a deed by an individual if, and only if—

    (a) it is signed[38]—

        (i) by him in the presence of a witness who attests the signature; or

        (ii) at his direction and in his presence and the presence of two witnesses who each attest the signature; and

    (b) it is delivered as a deed by him or a person authorised to do so on his behalf.[39]

(1) SEALING

Before 31 July 1990 a deed had to be sealed; that is to say, it had to bear wax, or a wafer, or some other indication of a seal.[40] Section 1(1) abolishes the requirement of a seal for the valid execution of a deed by an individual.

(2) ATTESTATION

Section 1 makes new and precise attestation provisions for the valid execution of a deed by an individual. The signature must be attested by a witness who is present at the time of the signature. If the deed is not signed by a party, for example, where he is physically incapable of doing so, then it must be signed at his direction and in his presence and there must be *two* witnesses who each attest the signature.

(c) Deed excuted by company[41]

In 1989 the requirements for the valid execution of a deed by companies incorporated under the Companies Act were also amended.[42] For such companies a document executed by a company which makes it clear on its face that it is intended by the person or persons making it to be a deed has effect, upon delivery,[43] as a deed. It may be executed either by affixing the common seal of the company, or by being signed by a director and the secretary or by two directors.

---

[37] See generally Barnsley, *Conveyancing Law and Practice*, pp. 446–56.

[38] Signing includes making one's mark on the instrument: s. 1(4).

[39] A solicitor who, in the course of a transaction involving the creation or disposition of an interest in land, purports to deliver a deed on behalf of a party is conclusively presumed in favour of a purchaser to be authorised to deliver the deed: s. 1(5).

[40] *Stromdale and Ball Ltd v Burden* [1952] Ch 223; *First National Securities Ltd v Jones* [1978] Ch 109 (legal charge without wax or wafer, but with attestation clause and signature across printed circle containing letters LS [locus sigilli: the "place of the seal"] held duly executed); (1980) 43 MLR 415 (D. C. Hoath). See also *Commercial Credit Services v Knowles* [1978] CLY 794; *TCB Ltd v Gray* [1986] Ch 621 (deed not sealed, but grantor estopped from denying that it was).

[41] For reforms designed to standardise in certain respects the formal requirements for companies, corporations and individuals, see Regulatory Reform (Execution of Deeds and Documents) Order 2005, SI 2005 No. 1906.

[42] Companies Act 1985, see s. 36A, as added by Companies Act 1989, s. 130. See Law Commission Report 1998 (Law Com No. 253), recommending detailed amendments: [1998] Conv 434. For execution by foreign companies, see Foreign Companies (Execution of Documents) Regulations 1994 (SI 1994 No. 950).

[43] *Bolton MBC v Torkington* [2004] Ch 66; [2004] Conv 9 (J. E. Adams).

No change was however then made to the requirements of execution by corporations sole, and by corporations aggregate which are not companies within the Companies Act 1985; sealing therefore remains a requirement.[44]

(4) Electronic Documents

The strict formalities discussed above cannot be maintained for transactions effected under electronic conveyancing.[45] The Land Registration Act 2002 has made provision for this, not by disapplying the requirement of a deed for the conveyance or creation of a legal interest in land; nor by making a general change to the requirements of a valid deed; but by providing that certain types of document in electronic form, when used to effect certain types of transaction, will be regarded for the purposes of any enactment as a deed.[46]

Where the disposition is of a registered estate or charge, or of an interest which is the subject of a notice in the register, or a disposition which triggers the requirement of registration, and if it is of a kind specified by the rules, then a document in electronic form which purports to effect the disposition is to be regarded as a deed if it makes provision for the time and date it is to take effect, has the certified electronic signature of each person by whom it purports to be authenticated, and it satisfies any other conditions as are provided by rules.[47]

(5) Registration Requirements

In the case of registered land, certain dispositions are required to be completed by registration, and do not operate at law until the relevant registration requirements are met. In the case of a registered estate, these dispositions are the following:[48]

(a) a transfer,[49]

(b) where the registered estate is an estate in land, the grant of a term of years absolute—
  (i) for a term of more than seven years from the date of the grant,
  (ii) to take effect in possession after the end of the period of three months beginning with the date of the grant,
  (iii) under which the right to possession is discontinuous,
  (iv) in pursuance of Part 5 of the Housing Act 1985 (the right to buy), or
  (v) in circumstances where section 171A of that Act applies (disposal by landlord which leads to a person no longer being a secure tenant),

---

[44] In favour of a purchaser an instrument shall be deemed to have been duly executed by a corporation aggregate if a seal purporting to be the corporation's seal purports to be affixed to the instrument in the presence of and attested by (a) two members of the board of directors, council or the governing body of the corporation, or (b) one such member and the clerk, secretary or other permanent officer of the corporation or his deputy: LPA 1925, s. 74(1) as substituted by SI 2005 No. 1906, art. 3.

[45] On electronic conveyancing generally, see pp. 110–11, ante; 987, post. On contracts in electronic conveyancing, see pp. 873–4, ante.   [46] Such an electronic document will therefore satisfy LPA 1925, s. 52(1).

[47] LRA 2002, s. 91; H & B, pp. 329–35. References to an electronic signature and to the certification of a signature are to be read in accordance with Electronic Communications Act 2000, s. 7(2), (3): LRA 2002, s. 91(10). The document is also to be regarded as in writing, and signed by each individual and sealed by each corporation whose electronic signature it has: s. 91(4).

[48] Ibid., s. 27(1). In the case of a registered charge, the dispositions required to be completed by registration are a transfer and the grant of a sub-charge: ibid., s. 27(2). These provisions apply also to dispositions by operation of law, except for a transfer on death or bankruptcy of an individual proprietor, or on dissolution of a corporate proprietor, and the creation of a local land charge: s. 27(5).

[49] For the prescribed form of transfer, see p. 964, post.

(c) where the registered estate is a franchise or manor, the grant of a lease,

(d) the express grant or reservation of an interest of a kind falling within section 1(2)(a) of the Law of Property Act 1925,[50] other than one which is capable of being registered under the Commons Registration Act 1965,

(e) the express grant or reservation of an interest of a kind falling within section 1(2)(b) or (e) of the Law of Property Act 1925,[51] and

(f) the grant of a legal charge.

Thus, for example, the transfer of a registered estate, the grant of a legal lease for more than seven years,[52] the express grant of a legal easement,[53] or the grant of a legal charge[54] cannot be effected simply by deed. The deed is necessary in order to satisfy section 52 of the Law of Property Act. But the grant takes effect only in equity[55] until it is perfected by registration.[56]

B Formalities for the Creation and Transfer of Equitable Interests

Finally we must consider the formalities necessary for the creation of a trust and for the disposition of an equitable interest. In neither case is a deed required.

(1) Creation of a Trust

There are very few rules restricting the method in which a trust must be created. The trust is the successor of the old use,[57] and for the raising of a use no formalities were necessary. Spoken words were as effectual as written instruments, and according to the preamble to the Statute of Uses bare signs and gestures seem to have been sufficient. The one guiding principle was that effect should be given to the intention of the settlor, no matter how it had been indicated by him. So in general is it with the modern trust.

A trust may be created either by an instrument inter vivos or by will. If it is created *inter vivos* and if it relates to land, it must conform to the Law of Property Act 1925.[58]

If it is created by will, then, whether it relates to real or to personal property, the instrument of creation must be made in accordance with the Wills Act 1837, which prescribes the manner in which all wills must be made.[59]

If neither the Law of Property Act 1925 nor the Wills Act 1837 applies, if, that is to say, the trust relates neither to freeholds nor to leaseholds, and if it is not contained in a will, it may be created by word of mouth or by some other indication of intention, and without any kind

---

[50] Legal easements and profits. This does not include a grant as a result of the operation of LPA 1925, s. 62; p. 603, ante.   [51] Rentcharges and rights of entry.

[52] P. 228, ante.   [53] Pp. 599, 633, ante.   [54] P. 728, ante.

[55] If it is to bind a purchaser it therefore requires protection by notice on the register unless it is an overriding interest (e.g., in the case of a lease, by virtue of the tenant being in discoverable actual occupation). Under LRA 1925, s. 123A(5), as substituted by LRA 1997, s. 1, dispositions which were subject to compulsory registration under LRA 1925, s. 123, were effective at law but became void as regards the transfer, grant or creation of legal estate if not registered within two months, and thereafter took effect as (in the case of a purported transfer) a bare trust for the transferee or (in the case of a purported grant of a legal estate or mortgage) a contract to grant the estate or mortgage.

[56] The registration requirements are set out in LRA 2002, Sch. 2.   [57] Pp. 42 at seq, ante.

[58] S. 53(1)(b), infra.   [59] See the 16th edn of this work, chap. 25.

of formality. A clear oral declaration by the owner of pure personalty that he is a trustee of that property for another person constitutes a valid trust and can be enforced by the volunteer in whose favour it was declared.[60]

But it was found in the case of land that parol declarations of trusts led to disputes and inconvenience, and therefore the Statute of Frauds in 1677[61] required for the first time that the creation of a trust of real estate should be manifested and proved by some writing signed by the settlor. This provision has now been re-enacted by section 53(1)(b) of the Law of Property Act 1925 in the following words:

A declaration of trust respecting any land or any interest therein must be manifested and proved by some writing signed by some person who is able to declare such trust or by his will.

There are several points that should be noticed about this enactment.

First, it is confined to land and does not interfere with the rule that a trust of pure personalty may be constituted by an oral declaration.

It does not require a deed, but only writing, and even so it does not require that the trust should have been declared by writing in the first place. The statute uses the words "manifested and proved", and it is sufficient if the trust can be proved by some writing signed by the settlor no matter what the date of the writing may have been.[62]

The writing is to be signed by "some person who is able to declare such trust", that is, the person who is the owner of the property in respect of which the trust is declared.[63] No provision is made for signature by an agent.

The statutory provisions apply only to express trusts, and not to the creation or operation of resulting, implied or constructive trusts.[64] This is very significant for the informal creation of interests in land, discussed later in this chapter.

(2) Disposition of Equitable Interest

Section 53(1)(c) of the Law of Property Act 1925 provides that:

a disposition of an equitable interest or trust subsisting at the time of the disposition must be in writing signed by the person disposing of the same, or by his agent thereunto lawfully authorised in writing or by will.

In this context the word "disposition" must be given the wide meaning that it bears in normal usage, and therefore, for instance, an oral direction by a beneficiary to trustees to hold an equitable interest upon new trusts is a disposition that is ineffective for want of writing.[65]

---

[60] *Jones v Lock* (1865) 1 Ch App 25; *Richards v Delbridge* (1874) LR 18 Eq 11; *Middleton v Pollock* (1876) 2 Ch D 104; *Paul v Constance* [1977] 1 WLR 527; see generally Maudsley and Burn, *Trusts and Trustees*, pp. 111 et seq.

[61] S. 7.   [62] *Rochefoucauld v Boustead* [1897] 1 Ch 196 at 206.

[63] *Tierney v Wood* (1854) 19 Beav 330.

[64] LPA 1925, s. 53(2); *Hodgson v Marks* [1971] Ch 892; *Ottaway v Norman* [1972] Ch 698, Maudsley and Burn, *Trusts and Trustees*, p. 146.

[65] *Grey v IRC* [1960] AC 1; *Oughtred v IRC* [1960] AC 206; *Neville v Wilson* [1997] Ch 144; *Bishop Square Ltd v IRC* (1997) 78 P & CR 169; *Vandervell v IRC* [1967] 2 AC 291; *Re Tyler* [1967] 1 WLR 1269; *Re Danish Bacon Co Ltd Staff Pension Fund* [1971] 1 WLR 248; *Re Vandervell's Trusts (No. 2)* [1974] Ch 269. See generally Maudsley and Burn, *Trusts and Trustees*, pp. 59 et seq; H & M, pp. 82 et seq; [1979] Conv 17 (G. Battersby). S. 53(1)(c) is not limited to equitable interests or trusts of land.

III Failure to Comply with the Required Formalities. The Informal Creation of Interests in Land

A General

We now need to consider how the law responds to cases in which one or both parties have not complied with the rules prescribed for the creation of an interest in land.[66] A strict line might be taken: the law requires a formality; and so failure to comply means that the transaction is simply not effective. However, this strict line has often not found favour with the courts, particularly where one party is acting inequitably, or "unconscionably", in resisting the enforcement of a property right on the basis that the formalities required for its creation or transfer were not properly complied with. The informal creation of interests in land is within the traditional domain of equity. For the most part, the courts have not been prepared to allow legal estates and interests to be created where the required statutory formalities have not strictly been followed.[67] But they have sometimes found that the failure to comply with legal formalities can be solved by the safety-net of equity.

B The Doctrine of Walsh v Lonsdale

The attempt to create a legal estate or interest in land, which fails for lack of formality, might sometimes be held none the less to create the equivalent equitable interest. This is generally known as the doctrine of *Walsh v Lonsdale*,[68] after the case in which it was applied in the context of leases. The doctrine does not, however, allow for the creation of an equitable interest in the absence of all formality; but it requires the formality of a *contract*, although not the deed of conveyance. If there is a valid contract for the sale or other disposition of an interest in land, of which the court would be prepared to grant the equitable remedy of specific performance, it is treated in equity as creating the equivalent interest to that which, if the contract were performed, would be created at law. This doctrine has been discussed already in the context of contracts relating to land.[69]

C Resulting or Constructive Trust

(1) Resulting and Constructive Trusts as Statutory Exceptions to the Formality Requirements

Certain statutory provisions relating to formalities contain an exception for resulting, implied or constructive trusts. In the context of contract formalities, we have already seen

---

[66] For the use of similar doctrines of equity to allow a party to enforce an *agreement* for the sale or other disposition of an interest in land which does not satisfy the formality requirements for a contract, see pp. 866–8 et seq, ante (part performance, where no sufficient written memorandum as required by LPA 1925, s. 40); pp. 874–6 (proprietary estoppel and constructive trust where no written contract as required by LP(MP)A 1989, s. 2).

[67] Cf, however, *Shah v Shah* [2002] QB 35 (deed signed and delivered, but attested by a person who was not present when party signed as required by LP(MP)A 1989, s. 1; held, party estopped from denying validity of the deed; following *Yaxley v Gotts* [2000] Ch 162, p. 875, ante).   [68] (1882) 21 Ch D 9, M & B p. 85; p. 223, ante.

[69] P. 877, ante.

that section 2 of the Law of Property (Miscellaneous Provisions) Act 1989, which requires a contract for the sale or other disposition of an interest in land to be in writing, provides[70] that the section does not affect the creation or operation of such trusts; and that in *Yaxley v Gotts*[71] this provision was applied to give effect to the parties' intentions that one should have an interest in property where their agreement did not satisfy the formality requirements for a contract. Similarly, the general requirements for formality contained in section 53 of the Law of Property Act 1925—that (a) no interest in land can be created or disposed of except by writing; (b) a declaration of trust respecting land must be proved by writing; and (c) a disposition of a subsisting equitable interest or trust must be in writing—do not apply to the creation or operation of resulting, implied or constructive trusts.[72]

This last provision has opened the way for the courts to find—and, sometimes, to impose—a solution under which one party who does not have an estate or interest in the property at law none the less has an equitable interest under a resulting or constructive trust.

(2) Co-ownership in Equity on the Basis of Resulting or Constructive Trusts

One context in which the courts have made particular use of resulting and constructive trusts is in co-ownership of property: the creation of concurrent equitable interests, often in the family home. This has already been discussed in detail in chapter 13,[73] where we saw that the courts can find a constructive trust to give effect to the parties' common intention that the one who has no legal title should share the beneficial interest in the property with the paper owner where the latter has not made an express declaration of trust to satisfy the formality requirements of section 53 of the Law of Property Act 1925, but where the party without legal title has acted to his or her detriment in reliance on the agreement. Similarly, where there is neither an express trust, nor a constructive trust based on the parties' evidenced common intentions, the court may find a resulting trust under which the paper owner holds the property on trust for the other to the extent of the latter's contribution to the purchase price.

(3) Licences Protected by Constructive Trust

In chapter 23[74] we saw another species of constructive trust, used to give protection in equity to a licensee. Where a purchaser of property has undertaken to the vendor to give effect to the licence and where, in addition,[75] the facts are such as to bind the vendor's conscience to give effect to the licence, the court may find that the purchaser is a constructive trustee for the benefit of the licensee, and therefore bound to give effect to the terms of the licence.[76]

---

[70]   S. 2(5).   [71]   [2000] Ch 162, M & B p. 70; p. 875, ante.

[72]   LPA 1925, s. 53(2); p. 904 ante. On constructive trusts, see Oakley, *Constructive Trusts*, pp. 53 et seq; H & M, chap. 12, esp. pp. 337–43; Maudsley and Burn, *Trusts and Trustees*, chap. 7; Snell, paras. 22–37 to 22–44. On resulting trusts generally, see H & M, chap. 10; Maudsley and Burn, *Trusts and Trustees*, chap. 6.

[73]   Pp. 472 et seq, ante.   [74]   Pp. 839 et seq., ante.

[75]   Notice by the purchaser, and even his undertaking to the vendor, are not of themselves sufficient to create a trust; more is necessary to affect the purchaser's conscience: *Ashburn Anstalt v Arnold* [1989] Ch 1 at 25, M & B, p. 618, p. 840, ante. A contract between the vendor and purchaser which expressly identifies the licensee and is (expressly or impliedly) intended to be enforceable by him, may now, however, be enforceable by the licensee *in contract* under the Contracts (Rights of Third Parties) Act 1999: p. 838, n. 51, ante

[76]   *Binions v Evans* [1972] Ch 359, M & B p. 617, p. 838, ante; *Bannister v Bannister* [1948] 2 All ER 133, M & B p. 615, p. 839, post; *Re Sharpe* [1980] 1 WLR 219, M & B p. 681, p. 839, ante; *Lyus v Prowsa Developments Ltd* [1982] 1 WLR 1044, M & B p. 176.

D Proprietary Estoppel

We have already seen the general principles applicable to the doctrine of proprietary estoppel,[77] and how the doctrine can be used to protect a licensee.[78] Here we shall consider its relationship to the constructive trust discussed in the previous section.

Under the doctrine of proprietary estoppel, an "equity by estoppel" arises—without any requirement of writing or other formality—in favour of the claimant, by virtue of the defendant's representation or acquiescence, combined with the claimant's detrimental reliance upon his belief that he has, or will acquire, a right in respect of the land. At a later stage, the court may order a remedy to give effect to that equity.

Even before the court order, the equity has a sufficiently proprietary character to be capable of binding a purchaser.[79] Proprietary estoppel can therefore be seen as a method of creating rights in land without complying with the formalities usually required for their creation. Much depends, however, on how we analyse the rights which arise at the two stages of the application of the doctrine. Section 53 of the Law of Property Act 1925 provides that:

(1) Subject to the provisions hereinafter contained with respect to the creation of interests in land by parol[80]—

(a) no interest in land can be created or disposed of except by writing signed by the person creating or conveying the same, or by his agent thereunto lawfully authorised in writing, or by will, or by operation of law . . .

(2) This section does not affect the creation or operation of resulting, implied or constructive trusts.

If the equity arising by estoppel is itself an interest in land, then it appears not to comply with this requirement, unless it can be brought within the exception of sub-section (2)—that is, it takes effect as a constructive trust.

The close relationship between the doctrines of proprietary estoppel and constructive trust has been discussed by judges in a number of cases;[81] and some cases arise on facts which might equally well be analysed as a constructive trust based on the common intention of the parties, or proprietary estoppel.[82] Some recent developments might appear to have brought these doctrines even closer together. We have seen that the Court of Appeal

---

[77] Pp. 814 et seq, ante.   [78] Pp. 841 et seq, ante.

[79] LRA 2002, s. 116(a) (registered land); *E R Ives Investment Ltd v High* [1967] 2 QB 379 (unregistered land). To bind a purchaser it must also be protected by notice in the register or as an overriding interest (registered land) or the purchaser must have notice of it (unregistered land); and it is not clear whether the equity can be overreached by the purchaser; see generally pp. 825–7, 845–6 et seq, ante.

[80] S. 54(2): leases in possession for a term not exceeding three years at the best rent which can reasonably be obtained without taking a fine.

[81] Sir Nicolas Browne-Wilkinson V-C in *Grant v Edwards* [1986] Ch 638 at 656–7; Lord Bridge of Harwich in *Lloyds Bank plc v Rosset* [1991] 1 AC 107 at 132; Robert Walker LJ in *Birmingham Midshires Mortgage Services Ltd v Sabherwal* (2000) 80 P & CR 256 at [24], *Yaxley v Gotts* [2000] Ch 162 at 176–7 and *Jennings v Rice* [2003] 1 P & CR 8 at [45]. See also Sir Christopher Slade, *The Informal Creation of Interests in Land* (1984) Child & Co Oxford Lecture.

[82] See, e.g., *Jennings v Rice*, supra, at [45], per Robert Walker LJ, discussing *Yaxley v Gotts*, [2000] Ch 162; *Kinane v Mackie-Conteh* [2005] EWCA Civ 45, [2005] 2 P & CR DG 3. The requirement of reliance by the claimant on the parties' common intention to share—which resonates with the language of estoppel—reinforces this analogy.

in *Oxley v Hiscock*[83] has emphasised the court's discretion in deciding the value of the parties' respective interests under a constructive trust based on their common intention to share property; and *Jennings v Rice*[84] has also emphasised the courts' discretion in deciding on the remedy to be awarded in a case of proprietary estoppel. However, this similiarity can be deceptive.[85] The court in *Oxley v Hiscock* described the discretion only in a case in which the parties had agreed to share but had not agreed on the value of their respective shares. In a case of constructive trust, the courts appear to assume that if there is an agreement as to the value, that agreement will be given effect.[86] In a case of proprietary estoppel, however, the court in *Jennings v Rice* made clear that, even it there is a clearly evidenced representation as to the interest to be conferred, the court will not necessarily order it; the remedy is still at the discretion of the court.[87] This emphasises that the nature of the claimant's right under the equity arising by estoppel is more uncertain, more precarious than that arising under a constructive trust which gives effect to the parties' common intention. It also shows that, in the case of such a constructive trust, the right is from the beginning an interest in land—a beneficial interest in the land itself, albeit to a share which the court may not yet have quantified, if the parties did not agree it. However, in the case of proprietary estoppel, the right is only an 'equity'—the right to seek a remedy; but it is not yet a full interest in the land. Indeed, it may never be, if the court does not order a property interest as the remedy.

An alternative analysis would be that the equity arising by proprietary estoppel is indeed an interest in land, but one which is not simply to be classified as a form of constructive trust, but is a new form of property in its own right. In the nineteenth century a new equitable property right—the restrictive covenant—emerged as the consequences of *Tulk v Moxhay*[88] became fully recognised. Perhaps proprietary estoppel is in a similar process of development into a new equitable property right.[89] There are certain technical difficulties presently standing in the way of this analysis: the prima facie limitation in the Law of Property Act 1925 on the creation of new equitable rights in land;[90] and the absence of any provision in that Act to exempt proprietary estoppel from the requirement of writing to create an interest in land.[91] However, the modern statutory recognition of the equity by estoppel as having effect as an interest capable of binding third parties[92] may show that the proprietary status of proprietary estoppel is now being recognised and that it should be assimilated into the list of known property rights.

A third possibility, however, is that the equity is not to be characterised as an interest in land, but more akin to a mere equity.[93] This gives certain proprietary characteristics to the

---

83   [2005] Fam 211; p. 475, ante.   84   [2003] 1 P & CR 8, M & B p. 646; p. 823, ante.

85   (2004) 120 LQR 541 at 545–6 (S. Gardner); [2004] Conv 496 (M. P. Thompson).

86   P. 475, ante.   87   P. 824, ante.   88   (1848) 2 Ph 774, M & B p. 942; p. 666, ante.

89   For the development of other equitable property rights, see p. 813, n. 7, ante.   90   LPA 1925, s. 4(1).

91   Cf LPA 1925, s. 55, which contains savings which were known to be required in 1925—including (para. (d)) the law relating to part performance. There is a close similarity between part performance and proprietary estoppel, in that both involve an equity arising outside the statutory formality relating to land, to prevent a party from relying on the absence of formality: p. 876, ante; cf *Crabb v Arun District Council* [1976] Ch 179 at 195, per SCARMAN LJ.

92   LRA 2002, s. 116 (although it is expressed to be only "for the avoidance of doubt"); p. 826, ante. However, s. 116 gives the same force to a mere equity (which is not generally recognised as an interest in land itself; infra).

93   P. 812, ante.

right;[94] but the effect of proprietary estoppel is not then to create an interest in the land itself, and so there is no conflict with the formality requirements for the creation of an interest in land. The interest in the land itself, if such is the remedy ordered by the court, is created only by the court's order,[95] or by the grant of the interest, in accordance with the proper formalities, by the defendant pursuant to the court order.

[94] LRA 2002, s. 116, supra.
[95] Even if it is a legal estate, this does not require a deed for its creation or transfer, since the court order suffices: LPA 1925, s. 52(2)(f); p. 897, ante. It will, however, require registration in registered land.

26

CAPACITY TO ACQUIRE, HOLD AND TRANSFER ESTATES AND INTERESTS IN LAND

SUMMARY

I Minors

A Terminology. "Infant" and "Minor"

In this section we are concerned with persons who are not of full age. Before 1970 it was common to describe such a person as an "infant". The Family Law Reform Act 1969,[1] however, provided that "a person who is not of full age may be described as a minor instead of as an infant".

In this chapter the term "minor" is generally used, in accordance with modern usage.

B Definition of Minority

A minor is a person, whether male or female, who has not attained full age. As from 1 January 1970, a person attains full age at the first moment of the eighteenth anniversary of his birth.[2] Hitherto the age of majority had been the first moment of the day preceding the twenty-first anniversary.[3]

C Minor May Not Hold Legal Estate

In accordance with the fundamental principle of the legislation of 1925, a minor can never hold a legal estate in land.[4] He cannot be an estate owner nor, therefore, can he be registered as proprietor.[5] This restriction, which is imposed in the interests of a simplified system of conveyancing, does not mean that he cannot hold and enjoy beneficially an equitable interest[6] and there is nothing to prevent land being transferred to him by way of gift, sale, settlement or lease. In such a case, the statutory policy before 1997 was to treat the land as settled land, and during the minority to vest the legal estate in trustees whose identity will depend upon whether the minor comes to his interest as grantee, devisee, heir on intestacy, beneficiary under a settlement, mortgagee, or trustee of the land for the benefit of another

---

[1] S. 12. Statutes passed before 1970 continue to use the old language. Cf Limitation Act 1980, s. 38(2) (although this was derived from Limitation Act 1939, s. 31(2)).

[2] Persons of eighteen or over, but under twenty-one attained full age on that date: Family Law Reform Act 1969, ss. 1(1), 9. See Report of the Committee on the Age of Majority (the Latey Report) 1967 (Cmnd 3342); (1979) 120 NLJ 144 (S. M. Cretney). S. 1(2) provides that for the "construction of 'full age', 'infant', 'infancy', 'minor', 'minority' and similar expressions" in any statutory provision, whenever passed or made, the references shall be deemed to be references to the age of majority as amended by the Act. Where, however, a statutory provision refers to a specified age, s. 1(3), Sch. 1, sets out those statutes in which references to twenty-one are changed to eighteen. S. 1(4), Sch. 2 excepted from s. 1(2) the Regency Acts 1937–1953; Representation of the People Act 1969 and tax statutes. For subsequent changes in fiscal legislation, however, see FA 1969, s. 16, and, in the age of franchise, Representation of the People Act 1983, s. 1. In the case of private transactions the Act is not retrospective, e.g. "to X on attaining his majority", if made in a will or settlement before 1970, X takes at twenty-one; if made after 1969, X takes at eighteen.

[3] See Report of the Committee on the Age of Majority (1967) Cmnd 3342, paras. 37–42; Re Shurey [1918] 1 Ch 263.   [4] LPA 1925, s. 1(6).

[5] If a minor is registered in error, the register is conclusive and therefore the legal estate is deemed to be vested in the minor, although it is liable to be rectified: LRA 2002, ss. 58(1), 65, Sch. 4. See generally R & R, para. 13.005.01.

[6] Kingston upon Thames Royal LBC v Prince [1999] 1 FLR (minor succeeds to secure tenancy held by her grandfather, holding equitable interest during her minority) (before 1997); applied in Newham LBC v R [2004] EWCA Civ 41 (after 1996).

person. The Trusts of Land and Appointment of Trustees Act 1996, in accordance with the general policy of the Act, replaced the mechanism of the strict settlement with the new trust of land. There is simplification without the introduction of any substantive changes.

We must first set out the position before the Trusts of Land and Appointment of Trustees Act 1996 came into force on 1 January 1997.

(1) Before 1997

(a) *Grant* inter vivos *to minor*

A conveyance of a legal estate in land to a minor alone, or to two or more persons jointly, both or all of whom are minors, for his or their own benefit, operated before 1997 only as an agreement for valuable consideration to execute a settlement in his or their favour.[7] This means that the grantor must as soon as possible execute a principal vesting deed and a trust instrument,[8] meanwhile holding the land in trust for the minor. In this case, however, the legal estate will be transferred by the vesting deed not to the minor as tenant for life, but to the trustees when they are appointed, who then become the statutory owners.[9]

If a legal estate was conveyed to a minor jointly with one or more other persons of full age, the person or persons of full age took the legal estate on trust for sale.[10] In this case the persons of full age held upon the statutory trusts applicable to a joint tenancy, that is, upon trust to sell the land and to hold the proceeds and the profits until sale for the benefit of themselves and the minor.[11] If, however, life interests were given, there was a settlement and the adults were tenants for life under the Settled Land Act 1925.[12]

(b) *Devise to minor*

In the case of a devise to a minor the legal estate vested at first in the personal representatives of the deceased by virtue of the Administration of Estates Act 1925, but in considering the ultimate destination of the legal estate we must distinguish between a devise of an absolute interest, and a devise by way of settlement in which trustees of the settlement have been appointed.

Where the land was devised to the minor for an estate in fee simple or for a term of years absolute, or where it was settled upon him for life and no trustees were appointed, the personal representatives could retain the land until the minor attained his majority, and until that time they possessed all the powers of a tenant for life under a settlement,[13] and also the powers of trustees for sale.[14] If, however, they did not desire to retain the land, they could appoint trustees to be trustees of the land for the purposes of the Settled Land Act and for the purposes of the statutory provisions relating to the management of land during a minority.[15]

Where the land was devised by way of settlement to a minor for a limited interest and the testator had appointed trustees of the settlement, the Settled Land Act directs that the

---

[7] LPA 1925, s. 19(1); SLA 1925, s. 27(1). This can be protected (in registered land) by a notice in the register or (in unregistered land) by registration as an estate contract under LCA 1972; p. 880, ante. On the grant of a lease to a minor, see Law Commission Report on Minors' Contracts 1984 (Law Com No. 134, 494), paras. 5.13–5.16, explaining supposed difficulties.

[8] Pp. 403 et seq, ante. Or he may execute a confirmatory conveyance to the minor after the minor attains majority: *Darvell v Basildon Development Corpn* (1969) 211 EG 33 at 37.　　　　　　[9] P. 409, ante.

[10] LPA 1925, s. 19(2).　　　[11] Ibid., s. 35.　　　[12] S. 19(3).　　　[13] SLA 1925, s. 26(1).

[14] AEA 1925, s. 39(1).　　　[15] Ibid., s. 42.

personal representatives shall, when their administration duties are completed, transfer the legal estate to the trustees if they are required to do so.[16]

(c) Descent of land to minor

(1) FEE SIMPLE

In the case of deaths occurring after 1925 it is impossible for a minor to become entitled to a fee simple estate by descent. The residuary estate of the intestate is held by the administrator upon trust to sell and to divide the proceeds among the relatives entitled under the Administration of Estates Act 1925. If a minor is the sole relative so entitled, he will become entitled absolutely to the fee simple when he either marries or forms a civil partnership or attains his majority. But as we have seen, a minor cannot hold a legal estate in land, and therefore, the land remains settled land until he attains his majority.[17]

(2) ENTAILED INTEREST

The old law of descent, however, still applies to the entailed interest, but if the heir is a minor the legal estate must be vested in the trustees of the settlement until he attains his majority. If money is required during his minority for his maintenance, education or benefit, the court if necessary may make an order under the Trustee Act 1925,[18] appointing a person to execute a disentailing assurance which will bar the issue and remaindermen as completely as if it were effected by the minor after attaining his majority.[19]

(d) Settlement of land in favour of minor

Before 1997 a person who desired to settle land in favour of a minor had an alternative, for he might create either a strict settlement under the Settled Land Act 1925 or a trust for sale.

In the case of a strict settlement, the statutory powers of a tenant for life and the trustees of a settlement, together with any additional powers that may be conferred by the settlement, become exercisable by the trustees,[20] who, in their capacity as "statutory owners",[21] are entitled to have the legal estate transferred to them by a vesting deed. If the settlor adopted the method of a trust for sale, the trustees not only obtain the legal estate but they also possess all the statutory powers under the Settled Land Act 1925, so long as the land remains unsold.[22]

If a tenant for life under an existing settlement is succeeded by a minor as tenant for life, the latter is not entitled to the legal estate until he attains his majority. In the meantime the legal estate and the statutory powers will be held by the trustees of the settlement.[23]

Where a minor becomes absolutely entitled under a settlement, as, for example, where there is a grant or a devise:

to A for life, remainder to B (a minor) in fee simple, and A dies during the minority of B,

the settlement continues until B attains his majority,[24] the legal estate in the meantime being vested in the trustees of the settlement. In a case such as this, statutory provision is made to

---

[16] SLA 1925, ss. 6, 26.
[17] AEA 1925, s. 47, as amended by Civil Partnership Act 2004, s. 71, Sch. 4, Pt 2, para. 8.
[18] TA 1925, s. 53.   [19] Re Gower's Settlement [1934] Ch 365.   [20] SLA 1925, s. 26(1)(b).
[21] Ibid., s. 117(1)(xxvi).   [22] LPA 1925, s. 28(1).   [23] SLA 1925, s. 26(1).
[24] Ibid., s. 3(b).

meet the contingency of the minor dying under age, for it is enacted that unless he marries or forms a civil partnership before reaching his majority he shall be deemed to have had a life interest at the time of his death.[25] In other words, the fee simple of B, in the above example, though potentially absolute,[26] is cut down to a life interest until he marries or forms a civil partnership or reaches 18. Therefore, if at his death he is still a minor, unmarried and has not formed a civil partnership, the estate will revert to the settlor if the settlement was by deed, or will pass to the residuary devisee in the case of a testamentary settlement. It is better that there should be this reversion to the settlor, rather than that the estate should enure for the benefit of some distant relative of the minor, which would be the result if he were to die owning an absolute interest.

(e) Mortgage to minor

Before 1997 section 19(6) of the Law of Property Act 1925 provided that a legal estate could not be conveyed to a minor by way of mortgage. A grant of a legal mortgage of land to a minor merely operated as an agreement for valuable consideration that the grantor would execute a proper conveyance when the minor attained full age, and that in the meantime he would hold the beneficial interest on trust for the minor.[27] If, however, the conveyance was made to the minor and to another person of full age, it operated as if the minor had not been named, though of course his beneficial interest was not prejudiced.[28]

(f) Conveyance to minor as trustee

A minor cannot be appointed a trustee.[29] A conveyance which purports to convey land to a minor as trustee does not transfer the legal estate, but operates as a declaration of trust in favour of the beneficiaries designated.[30] In such a case the person who is empowered by the trust instrument to appoint new trustees may make a new appointment,[31] or, if there is no such person, the court may do so.[32]

Similarly, the legal estate cannot pass to a minor who is appointed executor by the will of a testator.[33]

(2) After 1996

Under the Trusts of Land and Appointment of Trustees Act 1996 a purported conveyance after 1996 to a minor takes effect as a declaration of trust, the land being held by the relevant trustees under the new system.[34] Where the conveyance is made *inter vivos*, the grantor holds the land as a trustee for the minor. Where it is conveyed to a minor jointly with a person of full age, the person of full age holds the land on trust for himself and the

---

25 AEA 1925, s. 51(3), as amended by TLATA 1996, s. 25(1), Sch. 3, para. 6(1), (4) and Civil Partnership Act 2004, s. 71, Sch. 4, Pt 2, para. 11. Before the amendment in 1996, the minor's interest was deemed to be an entailed interest, not a life interest, and entails thus created before 1997 are unaffected: TLATA 1996, s. 25(4). The effect, however, of the death of the minor is the same since an unmarried minor cannot have heirs capable of taking an estate tail.   26 *Re Taylor* [1931] 2 Ch 242 at 246.

27 LPA 1925, s. 19(6). The minor's interest can be protected (in registered land) by a notice in the register or (in unregistered land) by registration as an estate contract under LCA 1972.   28 LPA 1925, s. 19(6).

29 Ibid., s. 20.   30 Ibid., s. 19(4).   31 TA 1925, s. 36.   32 Ibid., s. 41.

33 SCA 1981, s. 118. Nor can a minor be an administrator: *Re Manuel* (1849) 13 Jur 664.

34 TLATA 1996, s. 2(1), Sch. 1, paras. 1 and 2. Law Commission Report on Trusts of Land 1989 (Law Com No. 181), para. 5; W & H, paras. 6.31–6.33.

minor as joint tenants or as tenants in common according to the terms of the conveyance.[35] Where there is a devise to a minor, the personal representatives act as trustees for the minor.

As we have seen, section 19 of the Law of the Property Act 1925[36] made provision for conveyances on trust or by way of mortgage. Since a conveyance of a legal estate in land to a minor creates a trust in favour of the minor, these provisions are no longer necessary and are repealed.

D Acquisition and Alienation by Minor of Equitable Interests in Land

(1) Conveyance to Minor

An equitable interest, as distinct from a legal estate, may be effectively transferred to a minor, but since the ownership of an interest in land may occasionally prove to be more of a burden than a benefit, especially in the case of a leasehold containing onerous covenants, the long established rule is that the transfer is voidable at the option of the minor, either on attaining his majority or within a reasonable time thereafter.[37] In the event of his death his personal representatives may exercise the same power within a reasonable time.[38] But repudiation must not be unduly delayed. Thus where a minor bought land at a price payable by instalments, and continued to pay them for some time after he reached full age, it was held that his procrastination had defeated his right of avoidance and that he must pay the instalments which remained due.[39]

(2) Conveyance by Minor

A minor cannot make an irrevocable disposition of his interest, for the rule is that any disposition is voidable and can be repudiated by him during his minority or within a reasonable time after he attains full age.[40] So the disability is not absolute. It goes no further than is necessary for the protection of the minor. It leaves him the power to act during his minority, but in order that he may have protection, it permits him to avoid the transaction when he comes of age if he finds it right and proper to do so.[41] The tendency of the courts, however, is to regard very slight acts, such as the receipt of rent in the case of a lease, as amounting to a ratification of the conveyance.[42]

---

[35] Pp. 912, 914, ante. SLA 1925, s. 27 was ambiguous in that it did not expressly provide for the conveyance to minors as tenants in common. It is repealed by TLATA 1996, s. 25(2), Sch. 4.

[36] Repealed by TLATA 1996, s. 25(2), Sch. 4.   [37] *Ketsey's Case* (1613) Cro Jac 320.

[38] Blackstone, vol. 11, p. 292; *North Western Rly Co v M'Michael* (1850) 5 Exch 114 at 123.

[39] *Whittingham v Murdy* (1889) 60 LT 956; *Davies v Beynon-Harris* (1931) 47 TLR 424 (lease). If the minor repudiates the lease, he cannot recover rent already paid: *Valentini v Canali* (1889) 24 QBD 166.

[40] Co Litt 171b. The Infant Settlements Act 1855, which enabled a male infant over twenty and a female infant over seventeen to make a binding marriage settlement of property with the consent of the Chancery Division, was repealed by the Family Law Reform Act 1969, s. 11(a) as from 1 January 1970, "except in relation to anything done before" that date.

[41] *Burnaby v Equitable Reversionary Interest Society* (1885) 28 Ch D 416 at 424. This parallels the general (protective) approach in respect of minors' contracts: Chitty, paras. 8-002 et seq.

[42] *Slator v Brady* (1863) 14 ICLR 61.

(3) Will of Minor

A minor cannot make a will, either of real or of personal property[43]

(4) Settlement by Minor

In accordance with the principle applicable to alienation in general, a settlement made by a minor in contemplation of marriage is voidable, but it becomes binding upon him or her unless it is repudiated within a reasonable time after the attainment of majority.[44] The reasonable time is calculated from the attainment of majority, and not, as was once thought, from the moment when the property falls into possession.[45] If, for instance, a minor settles a reversionary interest, consisting of a fee simple estate which will come to him on the death of his mother, he will lose his right to repudiate unless he takes the necessary steps soon after he reaches full age, notwithstanding that it may be many years before possession of the land becomes available by the death of his mother.

His ignorance of the right of repudiation does not absolve him from the obligation to take steps within a reasonable time.[46]

E Management of Minor's Property

(1) Powers of Trustees

Land to which a minor is beneficially entitled, either absolutely or for a lesser interest (such as a life interest) must be held by trustees. Where the interest was created before 1997 and the land is deemed to be settled land, the trustees have all the ordinary powers conferred on a tenant for life and upon settlement trustees by the Settled Land Act 1925.[47] They may also enter into and continue in possession of the land on behalf of the minor, and if they do, they are directed to manage or superintend the management of the land, with full power, inter alia:

(1) to fell timber in the usual course for sale or for repairs;

(2) to erect, pull down, rebuild and repair buildings;

(3) to work mines which have usually been worked;

(4) to drain or otherwise improve the land;

(5) to deal generally with the land in a proper and due course of management.[48]

These powers are also exercisable, subject to any prior interests or charges, where a minor is contingently entitled to land.[49]

After 1996 the trustees have all the powers of an absolute owner, under section 6 of the Trusts of Land and Appointment of Trustees Act 1996, for the purpose of exercising their functions as trustees.[50]

---

[43] Wills Act 1837, s. 7. There is an exception for soldiers and airmen on active military service, and sailors at sea: Wills Act 1837, s. 11; Wills (Soldiers and Sailors) Act 1918, s. 3(1).

[44] *Edwards v Carter* [1893] AC 360.   [45] *Carnell v Harrison* [1916] 1 Ch 328.   [46] Ibid.

[47] SLA 1925, s. 26; pp. 409 et seq, ante.   [48] Ibid., s. 102.   [49] Ibid., s. 102(5).   [50] P. 440, ante.

(2) Application of Surplus Income

As regards the use which must be made of surplus income during the minority, it is provided[51] that the trustees may, at their sole discretion, apply a reasonable part of the income of the property for the maintenance, education or benefit of the minor, notwithstanding that some other fund may be applicable to those purposes, or that some other person, such as a parent, may be legally bound to provide for the minor's maintenance or education. But in deciding whether income shall be used for such purposes, the trustees must have regard to the age and requirements of the minor and to the circumstances of the case in general. In particular they must, in spite of the latitude allowed them, take into account whether some other fund may be used for the purpose.

The residue of the income is to be accumulated by way of compound interest, and the accumulations are to be paid over to the minor when he attains eighteen years or marries or forms a civil partnership under that age, provided that his interest is vested.[52] If the minor has a merely contingent interest, or if he dies under eighteen years of age and without having married or formed a civil partnership, the accumulations must be added to capital.[53] Where land to which a minor is entitled is subject to a trust of land, the trustees are empowered to use the capital to an amount not exceeding one-half of his presumptive or vested share for his advancement or benefit.[54]

II Married Women

In the twenty-first century, it seems hardly credible that a married woman should have any proprietary disability by virtue simply of her status. However, this used to be the case; and the history of this area forms an illuminating chapter in the growth of English law—and an understanding of it is necessary to be able fully to appreciate the context in which some of the older cases were decided.

A Common Law

At common law husband and wife are one person.[55] The general result of this merger of the wife's status in that of her husband was that he became absolute owner of her personal

---

[51] TA 1925, s. 31(1), amended by Civil Partnership Act 2004, s. 261(1), Sch. 27, para. 5.

[52] Reduced from twenty-one years by Family Law Reform Act 1969, s. 1, Sch. 3, para. 5, in respect of dispositions coming into effect after 1969.   [53] TA 1925, s. 31(2).

[54] Ibid., s. 32. The section does not apply to capital money arising under SLA 1925: s. 32(2) as substituted by TLATA 1996, s. 25(1), Sch. 3, para. 3(1), (8).

[55] For a history of the rule, see *Midland Bank Trust Co Ltd v Green (No 3)* [1979] Ch 496 at 512 et seq, where OLIVER J traces its origin to Genesis chapter 2, verse 24 and then refers to chapter 3, verses 12–13: "The common law was a trifle selective in its application of biblical doctrine. Adam after all was treated as a competent witness against Eve and his evidence was accepted and acted upon." For the "Green saga", see p. 947, n. 131 post. The decision was affirmed [1982] Ch 529, where Sir George BAKER refers at 542, to "the erudite and so felicitously expressed judgment of Oliver J". See also *Routhan v Arun DC* [1982] 1 QB 502 at 506–7, per Lord DENNING MR ("the doctrine of unity . . . says that in law 'husband and wife are one and the husband is that one.' I remember well that it was invoked when I used to prosecute in the magistrates' courts. A wife was travelling on the railway using her husband's ticket. When she put forward the excuse: 'We are one in the eyes of the law,' the collector replied: 'But not in the eyes of the Southern Railway'").

chattels, he might dispose of her leaseholds and take the proceeds, and he had the sole right of controlling and managing her freehold estates. If she predeceased him, he became absolutely entitled to any personal property of which she died possessed, and to a life estate by curtesy in her freehold estates of inheritance provided that a child had been born.[56] Again, a man could not make a grant to his wife directly or enter into a covenant with her, for to allow either of these things would have been to suppose her separate existence. In short, the effect of marriage at common law was to make a man complete master of his wife's property and to deprive her of contractual capacity.

B Equity

Gradually, however, and quite apart from legislation, wives were placed by the courts of equity in an even more favourable position than men or unmarried women, a result that was due to the invention by the Court of Chancery of the doctrine of equitable separate estate. If property was given to a married women by words which indicated either expressly or by implication that she was to enjoy it for her sole and separate use, equity removed that property from the control of the husband by regarding him as trustee, and conferred upon the wife full powers of enjoyment and disposition. But equity went even further than this, for, perceiving the danger that a husband might over-persuade his wife to sell her separate property and hand the proceeds to him, it permitted the insertion in marriage settlements of what was known as a restraint upon anticipation. The effect of such a restraint was that a woman, while possessing full enjoyment of the income, was prevented during her coverture[57] from alienating or charging the corpus of the property. She could devise, but could not sell or mortgage it.

C Statute

The next step in the emancipation of married women came with the enactment from 1870 onwards of various Married Women's Property Acts.[58] The principle of these was not to let the existence of separate property depend upon the intention of the donor, but to provide that in all cases property of married women should be separate property. Thus the intervention of the court of equity was no longer needed, for all property belonging to a married woman became her statutory separate property over which she had sole control and power of disposition.

The final stage in the emancipation of married women came with the Law Reform (Married Women and Tortfeasors) Act 1935. This provides that so far as concerns the acquisition, holding and disposition of any property a married woman shall be in the same position as if she were a feme sole. This Act also forbade the imposition of restraints upon anticipation after 1935, while preserving those already in existence, but in 1949 all restrictions upon anticipation or alienation, whether already imposed or not, were totally abolished.[59] Thus in future any restriction which it is proposed to place upon the enjoyment

---

[56] P. 486, ante.
[57] I.e., during the marriage, when she was under the authority and protection of her husband.
[58] See Dicey, *Law and Opinion in England* (2nd edn), pp. 371–95.
[59] Married Women (Restraint upon Anticipation) Act 1949.

of property by a married women must take the form of a protective trust, which is the only form of restriction applicable to a man or a feme sole.[60]

The position of a married woman has, indeed, been improved in a more positive sense by a statute which entitles her to a half share in any property acquired out of money given to her for household expenses.[61]

D The Modern Law

In the modern law, therefore, a married woman is under no legal disability. Moreover, the social changes which occurred in relation to property ownership during the second half of the last century have radically changed the position of the wife's rights in relation to the matrimonial home. This has already been discussed.[62] But it must be remembered that the significance of these changes have been fully recognised only relatively recently. As late as 1968 a judge could hold that a wife was not in apparent occupation or possession of the matrimonial home that she shared with her husband.[63] But this was finally rejected in 1980. As Lord WILBERFORCE then said:[64]

it was suggested that the wife's occupation was nothing but the shadow of the husband's—a version I suppose of the doctrine of unity of husband and wife. This expression and the argument flowing from it was used by Templeman J in *Bird v Syme-Thomson*,[65] a decision preceding and which he followed in the present case. The argument was also inherent in the judgment in *Caunce v Caunce*[66] which influenced the decisions of Templeman J. It somewhat faded from the arguments in the present case and appears to me to be heavily obsolete.

III Persons Lacking Mental Capacity[67]

A Jurisdiction

The law relating to mentally incompetent persons, originally styled "lunatics" by the legislature,[68] then "persons of unsound mind" and now "patients" suffering a "mental disorder", was codified and radically altered by the Mental Health Act 1959, later consolidated in the Mental Health Act 1983. Amongst other things, those Acts contained provisions relating to the management of property and affairs of patients,[69] the jurisdiction in respect

---

[60] P. 568, ante.

[61] Married Women's Property Act 1964, s. 1. See Cretney, Masson and Bailey-Harris, *Principles of Family Law*, para. 6.002. [62] Pp. 479 et seq, post.

[63] *Caunce v Caunce* [1969] 1 WLR 286 (STAMP J).

[64] *Williams & Glyn's Bank Ltd v Boland* [1981] AC 487 at 505. [65] [1979] 1 WLR 440 at 444.

[66] Supra.

[67] See generally Heywood and Massey, *Court of Protection Practice*; and on the new regime under the Mental Capacity Act 2005, Jones, *Mental Capacity Act Manual*; Bartlett, *Blackstone's Guide to the Mental Capacity Act 2005*. New Court of Protection Rules will be made to support the operation of the 2005 Act when it is brought into force: s. 51. For the rules under the old legislation, see Court of Protection Rules 2001 (SI 2001 No. 824), amended by SI 2001 No. 2977; SI 2002 No. 833; SI 2004 No. 1291; SI 2005 No. 667; Court of Protection (Enduring Powers of Attorney) Rules 2001 (SI 2001 No. 825), amended by SI 2002 No. 832; SI 2002 No. 1944; SI 2005 Nos. 668 and 3126; Enduring Powers of Attorney (Prescribed Form) Regulations 1990 (SI 1990 No. 1376), amended by SI 2005 No. 3116. [68] Prescription Act 1832, s. 7, still refers to "idiot" and "non compos mentis".

[69] Mental Health Act 1983, Part VII.

of which was vested in the Lord Chancellor and one or more judges of the Chancery Division, called "nominated judges", whose functions were usually exercised by the Master or a nominated officer of the Court of Protection or by the Public Trustee,[70] subject to an appeal to a nominated judge.[71] These provisions were repealed and replaced by the Mental Capacity Act 2005,[72] which gives a new definition of the lack of capacity, and provides a new framework within which the court itself or designated persons (either a deputy appointed by the court or an attorney appointed by the person himself under a lasting power of attorney) can take decisions on behalf of someone who lacks capacity, and a new structure for the regulation and supervision of such persons and of the operation of the Act generally by a newly constituted Court of Protection and a Public Guardian. The Court of Protection is now a superior court of record,[73] whose jurisdiction is exercisable by a judge nominated by the Lord Chancellor or a person acting on the Lord Chancellor's behalf, and which has the same authority and powers as the High Court.[74] The functions of the Public Guardian include establishing and maintaining a register of lasting powers of attorney, and supervising deputies appointed by the court.[75]

B Definition of Lack of Capacity

The lack of capacity is now defined not as a general disability, but as the inability to make a decision on a particular matter, at a particular time, because of an impairment of, or a disturbance in the functioning of, the mind or brain.[76] A person is unable to make a decision for himself if he is unable to understand the information relevant to the decision, to retain that information, to use or weigh the information, or to communicate his decision.[77]

C Decisions Taken by the Court or a Deputy Appointed by the Court

If a person lacks capacity to make a decision, the court may make it on his behalf, or may appoint a deputy to make decisions on his behalf.[78] The court's powers are to be exercised subject to overriding principles set out in the Act which are designed to protect the

---

[70] Mental Health Act 1983, s. 94, amended by Public Trustee and Administration of Funds Act 1986, s. 2.

[71] Ibid., s. 105.

[72] Law Commission Report on Mental Incapacity 1995 (Law Com No. 231). The Act is expected to be brought into force in April 2007. It does not replace other provisions of the Mental Health Act 1983, such as those relating to the compulsory admission to hospital and guardianship of patients suffering a mental disorder.

[73] The old Court of Protection was not in fact a court, but an office of the Supreme Court: Supreme Court Act 1981, ss. 88, 89(1), Sch. 2; it ceases to exist by virtue of Mental Capacity Act 2005, s. 45(6).

[74] Mental Capacity Act 2005, ss. 45–7. S. 53 provides for appeals to the Court of Appeal, or (if so provided by Court of Protection Rules) to higher judges of the Court of Protection.　　[75] Ibid., s. 58.

[76] Ibid., s. 2. A person is assumed to have capacity unless it is established on the balance of probabilities that he does not: s. 1(2), 2(4).　　[77] Ibid., s. 3(1).

[78] Ibid., s. 16. The predecessor of the deputy was the receiver: Mental Health Act 1983, s. 99. Under the general law, a disposition made during mental incapacity in voidable at the instance of the person making it, if the other party knows or ought to know of the incapacity: *Molton v Camroux* (1849) 4 Exch 17; *Beavan v M'Donnell* (1854) 9 Exch 309; *Imperial Loan Co v Stone* [1892] 1 QB 599; *Hart v O'Connor* [1985] AC 1000; [1986] Conv 178 (A. H. Hudson).

individual concerned, and must be done in his best interests,[79] and the appointment of a deputy is not to be made lightly: a decision by the court is preferable, and if a deputy is appointed, his powers must be as limited in scope and duration as is reasonably practicable.[80] Moreover, even if appointed, a deputy has no power to make a decision on behalf of a person if he knows or has reasonable grounds for believing that the person has capacity in relation to the matter,[81] not can he be given power to make a decision inconsistent with a decision made by the person's own attorney.[82]

In relation to the property and affairs of the person lacking capacity, the powers exercisable by the court (or which may be conferred on a deputy where appointed) are very wide, and extend to, amongst other things, the control and management of the person's property; the sale, exchange, charging, gift or other disposition of it; the acquisition of property in his name or on his behalf; the settlement of any of his property, whether for his benefit or for the benefit of others; and (as long as the person has reached the age of eighteen) the execution for him of a will.[83] This will apply equally to registered and unregistered land.[84]

The paramount consideration of the judge in his exercise of these powers is the interest of the patient, even though this may mean changing the nature of his property to the detriment of those who would otherwise have been entitled to it on his death. The Act, therefore, includes provisions designed to preserve the interests of such persons. It provides in effect that where any of the patient's property has been disposed of by sale, exchange, charging or other disposition or where money has been spent on the purchase of property, then the proprietary rights of the persons entitled under his will or intestacy shall attach to that property in its new form. If the property was real property, any property representing it shall so long as it remains part of his estate be treated as real property.[85]

As regards conveyances of property, it is enacted that when a legal estate in land (whether settled or not) is vested, either solely or jointly with any other person or persons, in a person lacking capacity suffering to convey or create a legal estate, a deputy or some other person authorised by the Court of Protection may make all requisite dispositions for conveying or

---

[79] Mental Capacity Act 2005, ss. 1, 4, 16(3).

[80] Ibid., s. 16(4). The deputy is treated as the person's agent: s. 16(6), and therefore has the corresponding general duties to him by virtue of his agency.

[81] Ibid., s. 20(1). Under the law before the 2005 Act, once a receiver had been appointed, the patient lost all legal capacity to exercise any powers of disposition *inter vivos* over his property: *Re Walker* [1905] 1 Ch 160; *Re Marshall* [1920] 1 Ch 284.   [82] Ibid., s. 20(4).

[83] Ibid., s. 18(1), (2); 19(8), broadly repeating the wide powers already conferred by Mental Health Act 1983, s. 96(1). Since 1969 the judge has had power to direct or authorise the execution of a will or codicil, provided that the patient is of full age and the judge has reason to believe that the patient is incapable of making a valid will himself. See *Re D (J)* [1982] Ch 237 at 243 where MEGARRY V-C set out the principles to be followed in making a will for a patient; *Re C* [1991] 3 All ER 866 (patient mentally disabled from birth who had never enjoyed a rational mind: HOFFMANN J held that "the court must assume that she would have been a normal decent person, acting in accordance with contemporary standards of morality"); [1991] All ER Rev 340 (C. H. Sherrin). See also CROSS J in *Re L (WJG)* [1966] Ch 135 at 145 (the making of a settlement). On the exercise of a power of appointment, see *Re B* [1987] 1 WLR 552.

[84] A squatter may not, however, make a valid application to be registered as proprietor during any period in which the existing registered proprietor is unable because of mental disability to make decisions about issues of the kind to which such an application would give rise, or unable to communicate such decisions because of mental disability or physical impairment; and the Registrar may include a note to that effect in the register: LRA 2002, Sch. 6, para. 8; R & R, para. 33.038. On squatters in registered land generally, see pp. 145 et seq, ante.

[85] Mental Capacity Act 2005, Sch. 2 para. 8, replacing Mental Health Act 1983, s. 101(1).

creating a legal estate in his name and on his behalf.[86] Again, if land is vested in such a person on trust, a new trustee must be appointed in his place.[87]

As regards the descent of land on intestacy, the rule under the Administration of Estates Act 1925 is that, where a person of unsound mind was living and already of full age on 1 January 1926 and was before that date entitled to a beneficial interest in freehold property, such interest shall in the event of his intestacy descend according to the old canons of descent applicable to freeholds of inheritance before 1926.[88]

D Lasting Power of Attorney

In order to avoid the subsequent necessity and expense of an application to the Court of Protection, a person may decide to grant a power of attorney to manage his affairs during mental incapacity. At common law a power of attorney is automatically revoked when the donor becomes mentally incapable. The Enduring Powers of Attorney Act 1985,[89] however, established a procedure for the creation of an "enduring power of attorney" which would continue to be effective notwithstanding the incapacity of the donor. Certain statutory conditions had to be complied with; for example, the power must be in a prescribed form, executed by both donor and donee, and be registered with the Court of Protection in the event of the actual or impending mental incapacity of the donor. Notice of the intention to register must first be given to the donor and to certain of his relatives who may then make objections.[90]

The 1985 Act was repealed by the Mental Capacity Act 2005, which replaced enduring powers with "lasting powers of attorney", following the same basic scheme: the power must be in a prescribed form, and must be registered with the Public Guardian before it confers authority to act.[91] Enduring powers of attorney which have already been executed when the new Act comes into force will be preserved and integrated into the new scheme.[92]

IV Corporations

A Nature of Corporations

One of the reasons for the existence of corporations is the principle of law that rights of property can be vested only in definite persons. It frequently occurs that a body of persons desires to hold and enjoy land, but apart from the case where a fluctuating class of persons

---

[86] LPA 1925, s. 22(1), as substituted by Mental Health Act 1959, s. 149(1), Sch. 7, Part I and amended by Mental Health Act 1983, s. 148, Sch. 4, para. 5, TLATA 1996, s. 25(1), Sch. 3, para. 4 (1), (6), and Mental Capacity Act 2005, s. 67(1), Sch. 6, para. 4(1), (2).

[87] Ibid., s. 22(2), as substituted by Mental Health Act 1959, s. 149(1), Sch. 7, Part I, and amended by TLATA 1996, s. 25(1), Sch. 3, para. 4(6), and Mental Capacity Act 2005, s. 67(1), Sch. 6, para. 4(1).

[88] AEA 1925, s. 51(2); pp. 89, 463, ante. See *Re Gates* [1930] 1 Ch 199; *Re Sirett* [1969] 1 WLR 60.

[89] Law Commission Report on The Incapacitated Principal 1983 (Law Com No. 122, Cmnd 8977); Cretney and Lush, *Enduring Powers of Attorney*.   [90] S. 4(3), Sch. 1.

[91] Mental Capacity Act 2005, ss. 9–14, Sch. 1, Pt 1 (formalities for creating the power), Pt 2 (registration). The lasting power of attorney can be wider in scope than the enduring power of attorney under the 1985 Act, because it can extend to matters about the person's personal welfare, as well as his property and affairs: s. 9(1)(a).   [92] Ibid., s. 66(3), Sch. 4.

acquires rights in the nature of easements by the method known as custom,[93] there are only two methods by which effect can be given to the desire. Either the land must be vested in trustees upon trust to hold and manage the land for the benefit of the proposed beneficiaries,[94] or else the indefinite body of persons must be turned into a definite, though artificial, person called a corporation; and this must be done by Royal Charter or by the authority of Parliament, whether in a special statute or, more commonly, by incorporation as a company under the Companies Act 1985 or, since 2001, as a limited liability partnership under the Limited Liability Partnerships Act 2000. The effect of this latter method is that the corporation becomes in the eye of the law a separate person, distinct from the member of which it is formed, and capable of acquiring, holding and alienating land.

Thus the modern limited liability company is not, like a partnership,[95] a mere collection or aggregate of the shareholders, but is a metaphysical entity, a legal persona with many of the rights and powers of a human person.

B Classification of Corporations

Corporations may be classified in several ways. The main classification is into aggregate and sole.

(a) Aggregate and sole

A corporation aggregate is a collection of several persons who are united together into one body and who are followed by a perpetual succession of members, so that the corporation is capable of existing for ever.[96] Examples are:

the head and fellows of a college,

the dean and chapter of a cathedral,

the mayor and corporation of a city,

a limited liability company incorporated under the Companies Act 1985,

national corporations, such as the BBC.

A corporation sole consists of a single person occupying a particular office and each and several of the persons in perpetuity who succeed him in that office, as, for instance, the vicar of a parish, the Secretary of State for Environment, Food and Rural Affairs, and the Public Trustee.

(b) Ecclesiastical and lay

Another division of corporations is into ecclesiastical and lay.

Ecclesiastical corporations are those which exist for upholding religion and perpetuating the rights of the Church, such as bishops, parsons, and deans and chapters, and the abbot and monks of an earlier age.

---

[93] Pp. 655 et seq, ante.

[94] On the holding of property by *unincorporated* associations, see Warburton, *Unincorporated Associations*, chap. 5; Baxendale-Walker, *Purpose Trusts*; Conv Prec, section 15; Maudsley and Burn, *Trusts and Trustees*, pp. 354–5; *Conservative and Unionist Central Office v Burrell* [1982] 1 WLR 522 at 525, per LAWTON LJ.

[95] A limited liability partnership, however, is a body corporate with legal personality separate from that of its members: Limited Liability Partnerships Act 2000, s. 1(2).   [96] Blackstone, vol. i., p. 469.

Lay corporations may be either trading or non-trading corporations.

Trading corporations are those which have been incorporated by charter, by special Act of Parliament or under the provisions of the Companies Act 1985, and whose main object is trade.

Non-trading corporations are those which have no concern with commerce, but which exist either for the better government of a town or district, such as urban district councils and municipal corporations, or for eleemosynary purposes, such as St Thomas's Hospital and the colleges of Oxford and Cambridge.

C Methods of Creation

A corporation can in general exist only if it has been formed under the authority of the State, and the two methods of creation in use at the present day are by charter from the Crown or by the authority of Parliament. If, for instance, a town wishes to become a borough, application must be made for a charter; while persons who wish to form themselves into a trading corporation must either secure the passing of a private Act of Parliament or take advantage of the Companies Act 1985, which contains provisions enabling companies to be formed without the necessity of a special statute.

But in addition to those that are incorporated by charter or by statute, corporations may also exist by common law and prescription.

Examples of common law corporations are a parson, a bishop, and the Crown. Corporations by prescription are those which have existed so long that the law presumes that they received from the Crown a grant or charter that has been lost.[97]

D Doctrine of Ultra Vires

Statutory corporations are subject to the ultra vires doctrine.[98] At common law a corporation that has been created by charter has power to deal with its property and to bind itself by contract to the same extent as a private person, and even if the charter imposes some direction which would have the effect of limiting its natural capacity, the legal power of the corporation is not affected, though the direction may be enforced by the Attorney-General.[99]

But the case of a statutory corporation is very different.[100] Such a body exists for certain purposes which are defined in the statute to which it owes its origin, and the powers of a statutory corporation are limited to those which are reasonably necessary to the realisation of the purposes for which it is incorporated. The corporation possesses its own constitution (called, in the case of a trading company, the memorandum of association), which has statutory effect. Anything that the constitution authorises, either expressly or by implication, can be done, but what is not so authorised is ultra vires and cannot be done.

The doctrine may be rendered ineffective by the drafting of the terms of the memorandum of association in very wide and general terms;[101] and as a result of substantial changes

---

[97] *Re Free Fishermen of Faversham* (1887) 36 Ch D 329; p. 655, ante.   [98] Anson, pp. 230–2.

[99] *Baroness Wenlock v River Dee Co* (1883) 36 Ch D 675n at 684, per BOWEN LJ.

[100] A limited liability partnership, however, has unlimited capacity: Limited Liability Partnerships Act 2000, s. 1(3).

[101] See *Bell Houses Ltd v City Wall Properties Ltd* [1966] 2 QB 656; *Re Introductions Ltd* [1969] 1 All ER 887, where HARMAN LJ said at 888: "The little man starting a grocery business usually combines groceries with the power to bridge the Zambezi."

made by the European Communities Act 1972,[102] and the Companies Act 1989,[103] the doctrine is now restricted to the internal management of the company. Third parties who deal with a company are no longer bound to make inquiries about its capacity or the authority of its directors; and "the validity of an act done by a company shall not be called into question on the ground of lack of capacity by reason of anything in the company's memorandum".

However, as a matter of internal management, if the directors act ultra vires, a shareholder may be able to restrain them by injunction, if he acts in time, and the company itself may have an action against the directors.

E Capacity to Deal with Land

Corporations, whether aggregate or sole, have the same capacity as natural persons to acquire, hold and dispose of land. Where land is registered the application to register a corporation as proprietor of a registered estate or charge must be supported by evidence of its status and powers in relation to the transaction.[104] If the powers of alienation are limited in a way that would affect a purchaser the corporation should apply for the entry of a restriction on the register.[105]

(1) Abolition of technicalities

The Law of Property Act 1925 has removed certain conveyancing difficulties. There were rules at common law that leaseholds could not be granted to a corporation sole in such a way as to make them vest in the successive holders of the office; and that a grant of land to a corporation sole made at a time when the office was vacant was void. If leaseholds were granted to a parson qua parson, and he died before the term had run out, his personal representatives and not his successor in the office became entitled to the residue of the lease.[106]

It is now, however, enacted[107] that where any property or any interest therein is or has been vested in a corporation sole, whether before or after 1926, it shall pass to the successors from time to time of such corporation; and that where property is granted to a corporation sole during a vacancy of the office, or to a corporation aggregate during a vacancy of the headship, the property shall, notwithstanding such vacancy, vest in the successor of the corporation sole, or in the corporation aggregate, as the case may be.

(2) Words of limitation

Again, the rule formerly was that, unless a grant was made to a corporation sole and his successors, the grant operated to confer a life estate upon the actual holder of the office in

---

[102] S. 9(1).

[103] Companies Act 1985, ss. 35, 35A and 35B; as amended and inserted by Companies Act 1989, s. 108; (1990) 140 NLJ 709 (M. Stamp). Substantial recommendations for reform were made by the Cohen Committee in 1945 (Cmnd 6659, para. 12) and by the Jenkins Committee in 1962 (Cmnd 1249, paras. 35–42); and its abolition was recommended by the Prentice Report in 1986.

[104] LRR 2003, rr. 181 (company and limited liability partnership: registered number), 182 (corporation or trustees holding on charitable, ecclesiastical or public trusts: trust document), 183 (other corporation aggregate: evidence of powers in relation to land, including the documents constituting the corporation).

[105] R & R, para. 41.006.   [106] Co Litt 46b.   [107] LPA 1925, s. 180.

his natural capacity; but now, as we have already seen, a conveyance of freehold land to a corporation sole by his corporate designation even without the word "successors" passes to the corporation the fee simple or other the whole interest which the grantor has power to convey in such land, unless a contrary intention appears in the conveyance.[108]

(3) *Dissolution of Corporation*

The rule at common law is that when a corporation is dissolved, any land which it may have held does not escheat to the Crown, but reverts to the original donor,[109] but after 1925 when a legal estate determines for this reason, the court is empowered to vest a corresponding estate in the person who would have been entitled to the estate had it not determined.[110] This power is apparently meant to be used when the corporation has been holding land as a trustee.

(4) *Repeal of Law of Mortmain*

Until 1 January 1961, when the Charities Act 1960 came into force, the long-established rule was that no land could be assured to or for the benefit of, or acquired by or on behalf of, any corporation unless the corporation was authorised, either by some statute or by a licence from the Crown, to hold land. If land was transferred by way of gift, sale, mortgage, settlement or devise to a corporation which had no such authority, the land was liable to be forfeited to the Crown.[111] The explanation of this disability lies far back in history and is to be found in the exigencies of the feudal system.[112]

With the progress of time the restrictions imposed by the Mortmain and Charitable Uses Act 1891 had become of little significance, for the vast majority of corporations were for one reason or another exempt from the necessity to obtain a licence from the Crown. The subject, however, requires no further elaboration, for the Act was repealed by the Charities Act 1960,[113] and thus the law of mortmain is now defunct.

V Charities

Before 1997 all land which was vested in trustees[114] for charitable, ecclesiastical or public purposes was deemed to be settled land under the Settled Land Act 1925, and the trustees had all the powers conferred by that Act on a tenant for life and on the trustees of the settlement, subject to obtaining any consents or orders required apart from the Act.[115] The

---

[108] P. 172, ante.

[109] Co Litt 13b; Blackstone, vol. i., pp. 484–5; *Hastings Corpn v Letton* [1908] 1 KB 378; *Re Woking UDC (Basingstoke Canal) Act 1911* [1914] 1 Ch 300 at 310.   [110] LPA 1925, s. 181.

[111] Mortmain and Charitable Uses Act 1888, s. 1.

[112] See Simpson, *A History of the Land Law*, pp. 53–6, 183–4.   [113] S. 38.

[114] The right of a charity to acquire land was severely restricted by Mortmain and Charitable Uses Acts 1888 and 1891. Subject to many exceptions, an assurance of land *inter vivos* was void unless it was irrevocable and gave the charity the right to take immediate possession; and, if not made for valuable consideration, unless it was executed at least twelve months before the death of the alienor. Charitable devises were not generally permitted before the 1891 Act, but even then the land had to be sold within one year from the testator's death unless the High Court or the Charity Commissioners decided otherwise. These restrictions, however, disappeared with the repeal of the 1888 and 1891 Acts by Charities Act 1960, s. 38.

[115] SLA 1925, s. 29, as amended by Charities Act 1960, Sch. 7.

land did not, however, become settled land for all purposes; for instance, a conveyance to a charity did not have to be made by a vesting deed and a trust instrument, and a sole trustee might receive capital money if the trust deed for the charity allows him to do so.[116]

After 1996 charity land is no longer settled land[117] but is held on a trust of land under the Trust of Land and Appointment of Trustees Act 1996. In the case of registered land,[118] the managing trustees of the charity, or, if there are no managing trustees and the land is vested in a corporation, the corporation, will be the registered proprietors, unless the legal estate is vested in the Official Custodian for Charities,[119] who will then be registered as proprietor, notwithstanding that the powers of disposition are vested in the managing trustees.

A Restrictions on Disposition

(1) Before 1993

The freedom of charities to alienate or deal with their land has long been restricted by a series of Charitable Trusts Acts and then by the Charities Act 1960. The latter, replacing the former statutes, provided that no property forming part of the permanent endowment[120] of a charity should, without an order of the court or of the Charity Commissioners, be mortgaged or charged by way of security for the repayment of money borrowed, nor, in the case of land in England or Wales, be sold, leased or otherwise disposed of.[121] Similar restrictions applied to land which was or had at any time been occupied for the purposes of a charity, even though it did not form part of the permanent endowment; but if a transaction in respect of such land was entered into without the required order, it would nevertheless be valid in favour of a person who in good faith acquired an interest in or charge on the land for money or money's worth.[122] An order, however, was not required for a charity to grant a lease for a term ending not more than twenty-two years after it was granted, provided that it was not granted wholly or partly in consideration of a fine.[123]

(2) After 1992

The Charities Act 1992 made important changes.[124] The distinction between permanent endowment property and charity occupied property has been abolished, and the trustees of a charity may sell, lease or otherwise dispose of its land without an order of the court or of the Charity Commissioners, provided that certain procedural steps are taken.

In the case of a sale or lease, the trustees must take advice from a qualified surveyor, and, having considered that advice, decide that the terms are the best that can reasonably be

---

[116] *Re Booth and Southend-on-Sea Estates Co's Contract* [1927] 1 Ch 579.

[117] TLATA, s. 2, Sch. 1, para. 4. SLA 1925, s. 29 is repealed by TLATA s. 25(2), Sch. 4.

[118] See generally Land Registry Practice Guide 14; R & R, chap. 38; H & B, paras. 13.38–13.41.

[119] A public official in whom the property of a charity may be vested as a custodian trustee: Charities Act 1993, ss. 2, 21, 22; LRR 2003, r. 178.

[120] I.e. property held subject to a restriction on the expenditure of capital: Charities Act 1960, s. 45(3).

[121] Charities Act 1960, s. 29(1); *Michael Richards Properties Ltd v Corpn of Wardens of St Saviour's Parish, Southwark* [1975] 3 All ER 416 (contract for sale of charity land made expressly subject to approval of Charity Commissioners held valid); *Haslemere Estates Ltd v Baker* [1982] 1 WLR 1109; *Hounslow LBC v Hare* (1990) 24 HLR 9; [1993] Conv 224 (J. Martin). [122] Charities Act 1960, s. 29(2).

[123] Ibid., s. 29(3)(b). [124] Repealed and consolidated in Charities Act 1993, ss. 36–40.

obtained for the charity, and normally advertise the proposed transaction.[125] In the case of a mortgage, the trustees must take advice on its necessity, its terms and the charity's ability to repay on those terms.[126] The disposition to a charity must also contain a statement in a prescribed form which will identify whether the charity is exempt.[127] If it is not exempt, in the case of registered land a restriction must be entered on the register when the title is registered.[128] Similarly, a statement in a prescribed form must be made in a disposition by a charity.[129]

A disposition not complying with these requirements is valid in favour of a purchaser in good faith.[130]

The Charity Commissioners have a general power to authorise dealings with charity property, whether or not it would otherwise be within the powers of the charity trustees.[131]

B Exempt Charities

The restrictions upon disposition do not affect exempt charities, a list of which is given in the Act.[132] The list includes, inter alia, the universities of Oxford, Cambridge, London and Durham; the colleges and halls in Oxford, Cambridge and Durham; any university or similar institution declared by an Order in Council to be an exempt charity,[133] the British Museum and the Church Commissioners.

---

[125] Advertisement is not necessary for a lease of seven years or less (other than one granted wholly or partly in consideration of a fine): ibid., s. 36(5).   [126] Charities Act 1993, s. 38.

[127] Charities Act 1993, s. 37(5); LRR 2003, r. 179.   [128] LRR 2003, r. 176(4), Sch. 4 (Form E).

[129] Ibid., r. 180.

[130] Charities Act 1993, ss. 37(4), 39(4); *Bayoumi v Women's Total Abstinence Educational Union Ltd* [2004] Ch 46.   [131] Charities Act 1993, s. 26.

[132] Ibid., ss. 3, 96, Sch. 2; Maudsley and Burn, *Trusts and Trustees*, pp. 569–70.

[133] Further universities have been added by Exempt Charities Orders. For a list, see Maudsley and Burn, *Trusts and Trustees*, p. 569, n. 15. A Charities Bill currently before Parliament will make further changes to the list of exempt charities.

27

TRANSFER OF ESTATES AND INTERESTS IN LAND[1]

SUMMARY

I Introduction

The transfer of an estate or interest in land may take place *inter vivos* or on the death of the holder. And a transfer *inter vivos* may be either by act of parties or by act of law, that is, either due to the deliberate intention of the estate owner or in spite of his intention. Moreover, "transfer" within this context has an extended meaning, for although it is usual to regard conveyancing as the transfer of rights in property from one person to another, yet frequently an instrument creates rather than transfers a right, as for instance, in the case of the creation of a trust or grant of a mortgage or a lease.

The object of this chapter is to consider the conveyancing mechanisms for such transfers, and their effect on third-party rights. However, the detail both of the mechanisms to be employed, and the effect on third parties, varies not only according to the distinctions already mentioned, but also according to the status of the estate owners: whether they are the beneficial owners; or personal representatives of the estate owner; or trustees of land; or tenants for life or statutory owners; or mortgagors or mortgagees.

---

[1] See generally Barnsley, *Conveyancing Law and Practice*; *Emmet and Farrand on Title*; Farrand, *Contract and Conveyance* (4th edn); Silverman, *Conveyancing Handbook*; Storey, *Conveyancing*.

The discussion in this chapter will focus on the voluntary transfer by beneficial owners *inter vivos*. Through this we shall see the fundamental principles governing both unregistered and registered conveyancing. We shall then notice variations from the law applicable to such a transaction that are peculiar to the other estate owners. Involuntary transfer, where the owner of an estate or interest is sued to judgment for non-payment of a debt, or made bankrupt, or dies insolvent, and the land is liable to be seized in satisfaction of the debts, will not be treated here.[2]

II Transfer by Beneficial Owners *Inter Vivos*

There are two quite separate and distinctive methods of conveyancing in operation in England and Wales at the present day; that relating to unregistered land and that relating to registered land.[3] During the twentieth century there was a transition from unregistered to registered conveyancing, from the old to the modern: compulsory registration of title was extended to the whole of England and Wales as from 1 November 1990. The former is the development of techniques which reach back to medieval times. The system in essence is one whereby the estate owner proves his title to land by showing from deeds and documents in his possession that he derives his title lawfully from some person or persons who have been in peaceful possession for a long period of time. In the nature of things, the title to his estate can never be proved absolutely, for there may have been an interference with the rights of the true owner many years back. However, with the assistance of the Limitation Acts,[4] proof of title during the last fifteen years is, for practical purposes, sufficient; and a purchaser is now required to trace the title back to a good root of title at least fifteen years old.[5] In unregistered land the deeds were handed over to the purchaser on completion of the purchase, and he then made title in a similar manner when he decided to sell. After 1990 completion of the purchase is followed by registration of the title at the Land Registry.

A much more satisfactory system of proof of title is that of registration of the title in a central registry. New countries and states commonly use such a system. The practical difficulties, however, of changing over from a system of unregistered conveyancing to one of registered conveyancing are great. The change involves the recording of all interests in land which need to be placed on the register. In England and Wales, a system of registration of title, introduced in 1862,[6] was superseded by more comprehensive legislation in the Land Registration Act 1925. It provided for registration of title following the first conveyance of land after the Act had been made applicable to the district in question; and subsequent conveyancing is based on the title so registered. The 1925 Act has now itself been superseded by the Land Registration Act 2002.

Although the unregistered system is obsolescent, it is not yet obsolete, and it will remain necessary to investigate the title to every parcel of unregistered land for at least one final time when it is next transferred, before it is placed on the register.[7] The conveyancer must

---

[2] Reference should be made to specialist works on insolvency, such as *Muir Hunter on Personal Insolvency*; Berry, Bailey and Schaw Miller, *Personal Insolvency Law and Practice*.   [3] Pp. 91–113, ante.
[4] Chap. 6, ante.   [5] LPA 1969, s. 23, p. 932, post.   [6] Land Registry Act 1862; p. 101, ante.
[7] The Land Registry has a strategic objective of creating a Land Register with comprehensive content and national coverage by 2012. By 2005 the freehold title to 48% of the area of England and Wales had been registered: Land Registry Annual Report 2004/5, pp. 8, 9.

therefore not only fully understand the system of registration of title, its limitations as well as its strengths, but must also still be able to work within the old system of unregistered land. Moreover, as we shall see, many of the rules and principles of registered conveyancing, and the form of instruments used within it, cannot be properly understood without a prior understanding of their traditional equivalents within unregistered conveyancing. We shall therefore begin by considering the principles of unregistered conveyancing, before discussing registration of title in some detail.

A Unregistered Conveyancing

(1) Investigation of Title

(a) Stages in a conveyancing transaction

A vendor and a purchaser of land generally desire that a binding contract[8] should be concluded at the earliest possible moment, subject to the purchaser's rights to rescind (in the sense of accepting repudiation[9]) if the vendor cannot show a good unincumbered title. Accordingly the purchaser usually does not investigate the vendor's title before contract.[10] Once a binding contract has been made, however, the procedure to be followed depends upon whether the contract relates to registered or unregistered land. We discuss first the position where land is unregistered.

(1) DELIVERY OF ABSTRACT

The vendor is bound to show a good title[11] to the interest that he has contracted to sell, and to this end and with a view to simplifying the purchaser's task, he must at his own expense deliver to the purchaser an abstract of title, that is, a summary of all the documents, such as wills and deeds of conveyance, that have dealt with the interest during the period for which his ownership has to be proved, and of all the events, such as deaths, that have affected the devolution of the ownership during that period. The period is either the fifteen years fixed by statute, or that which is prescribed by a special stipulation in the contract of sale, though, as we shall see, the period will be longer than the statutory fifteen years if a good root of title cannot otherwise be shown.

(2) PERUSAL OF ABSTRACT

The vendor then verifies the abstract by producing evidence of the accuracy of the statements that he has made in the course of setting out his title. After this the purchaser's solicitor, at the expense of the purchaser, peruses the abstract, requisitions (i.e. addresses inquiries to) the vendor about any defects he may observe, satisfies himself that the property described in the contract is identical with that which has been dealt with in the documents abstracted, calls for evidence (such as death certificates) of events material to the title, and finally advises the purchaser whether he can with safety accept the title offered.

---

[8] For the creation, enforceability and effect of a contract of sale, see chap. 24, ante.   [9] P. 891, ante.
[10] For enquiries which are usually made before contract, see pp. 854–7, ante.
[11] On the meaning of good marketable title, see *Barclays Bank plc v Weeks Legg & Dean* [1999] QB 309.

(3) CONVEYANCE

The vendor is then obliged to convey the property free from incumbrances, to execute a deed of conveyance and to hand over to the purchaser all the title deeds relating to the property. The expense of preparing the deed of conveyance falls upon the purchaser.

The exact obligations of a vendor may, as we have said, be either specified or unspecified. If they are unspecified, and so left to be implied by law, the vendor is said to sell under an *open contract*.[12] Although in practice contracts for the sale of land are generally made in standard form, and most of these forms contain detailed provisions which cover the matters which will be discussed in the following paragraphs, it is important first to understand the rights and duties of the parties under an open contract, so as to be able to identify whether (and, if so, to what extent) specific terms in the contract vary them.

(b) Rights and duties of parties under an open contract

The rights and the duties of the parties under an open contract are as follows:

(1) DUTY OF VENDOR TO SHOW TITLE FOR FIFTEEN YEARS[13]

Since the obligation of the vendor is to convey to the purchaser the interest that he has agreed to sell, free from incumbrances and competing interests, it follows that he must disclose and verify the state of his title to the land. Save in the rare case where he has been invested with an absolute title by Act of Parliament, he can scarcely show that he is entitled to an interest good against the whole world, for, however long he and his predecessors may have possessed and administered the land, the existence of some adverse claimant, such as a remainderman or reversioner, is always a possibility. But possession is prima facie evidence of seisin in fee[14] and if he shows that he and his predecessors have been in possession for a considerable time, the existence of an earlier and therefore better title is at least improbable. On this assumption, the practical rule was ultimately evolved that proof of the exercise of acts of ownership over the land by the vendor and his predecessors for a period of not less than sixty years was prima facie evidence of his right to convey what he had agreed to sell. "It is a technical rule among conveyancers to approve a possession of sixty years, as a good title to a fee simple."[15] This period was statutorily reduced to forty years in 1874,[16] to thirty years in 1925,[17] and to fifteen years in 1969.[18]

Enjoyment for this period, however, is not conclusive evidence of a good title, and if it appears from the information supplied by the vendor or if it can be shown from other evidence that the title falls short of what is required by the contract, the purchaser is not bound to complete. Possession by the vendor is no doubt evidence of seisin in fee, but nevertheless he must show its origin, for though it is probably attributable to his position as freehold owner, there is always the possibility that he is a tenant for life or years. As Lord ERSKINE once said:[19] "No person in his senses would take an offer of a purchase from a man, merely because he stood upon the ground." Even the rule under the Limitation Act 1980, that a person's title to unregistered land is extinguished after twelve years' adverse possession by a disseisor, does not in itself enable a disseisor to show a good title by proving possession in himself for even fifteen years, since possession for the statutory period does not bar the

---

[12] P. 857, ante.   [13] Barnsley, *Conveyancing Law and Practice*, pp. 272–4.   [14] P. 30, ante
[15] *Barnwell v Harris* (1809) 1 Taunt 430 at 432, per HEATH J.   [16] Vendor and Purchaser Act 1874, s. 1.
[17] LPA 1925, s. 44(1).   [18] LPA 1969, s. 23.   [19] *Hiern v Mill* (1806) 13 Ves 114 at 122.

rights of remaindermen and reversioners entitled to the land upon the determination of the disseisee's interest. He must go further and show what persons were entitled to the land when he took possession and prove that their claims have been barred by his continuance in possession.[20]

The usual way, therefore, in which the vendor proves his title is to produce the deeds or other documents by which the land has been disposed of in the past in order to show that the interest which he has agreed to sell has devolved upon him. Thus, in the normal case, the evidence of his title is documentary and is set out in the abstract of title that he delivers to the purchaser. This abstract must start with what is called a *good root of title*, that is, a document which deals with the legal estate in the land, which is valid without requiring a reference to any earlier document, which adequately identifies the land,[21] and which contains nothing to cast doubts on the title of the disposing party.

Thus a conveyance by way of sale or of legal mortgage[22] effected at least fifteen years ago is a perfect root of title, since it may be presumed that the purchaser or mortgagee was satisfied at that time with the state of the vendor or mortgagor's title, and if the intervening dispositions have been satisfactory, the present purchaser will obviously acquire a good title. An assent[23] can be a good root of title,[24] but a *general*, as distinct from a *specific*, devise of land is not, since it does not identify the property and therefore does not show that the will passed the ownership of the same land as the vendor has now agreed to sell.

The obligation to begin the abstract with a good root of title may, of course, necessitate going back to some document more than fifteen years old. As NORTH J said:[25]

And when I say a [15] years' title, I mean a title deduced for [15] years, and for so much longer as it is necessary to go back in order to arrive at a point at which the title can properly commence. The title cannot commence in nubibus at the exact point of time which is represented by 365 days multiplied by [15]. It must commence at or before the [15] years with something which is in itself . . . a proper root of title.

There are a few cases in which the period for which title must be shown is longer than fifteen years.[26] Thus upon the sale of a leasehold, an abstract or copy of the lease, however

---

[20] *Games v Bonnor* (1884) 54 LJ Ch 517; *Scott v Nixon* (1843) 3 Dr & War 388 (Ireland); chap. 6.

[21] See *Re Stirrup's Contract* [1961] 1 WLR 449 at 454, where WILBERFORCE J said that the vendor must be "in the position, without the possibility of dispute or litigation, to pass the fee simple to the purchaser"; *Barclays Bank plc v Weeks Legg & Dean* [1999] QB 309 at 324, per MILLETT LJ.

[22] Even though a post-1925 mortgage does not take effect as a conveyance of the fee simple; p. 724, ante; Barnsley, *Conveyancing Law and Practice*, pp. 275–7.   [23] P. 989, post.

[24] In favour of a purchaser for money or money's worth, an assent is sufficient evidence that the beneficiary is entitled to have the legal estate conveyed to him, unless notice of a previous assent or conveyance has been endorsed on the probate copy or letters of administration: AEA 1925, s. 36(7), (11). But an assent will not avail a purchaser if his investigation of title discloses that the person in whose favour it was given was not entitled to the legal estate: *Re Duce and Boots Cash Chemists (Southern) Ltd's Contract* [1937] Ch 642.

[25] *Re Cox and Neve's Contract* [1891] 2 Ch 109 at 118. NORTH J's judgment referred to forty years' title. The period was later reduced: supra.

[26] LPA 1925, s. 44(1). See Emmet, paras. 5.032–5.034. Until 1988, where an advowson (the right to present to or bestow any ecclesiastical benefice) was sold, title had to be shown for at least a hundred years with a list of presentations during that period: Benefices Act 1898, s. 1; Benefices Act 1898 (Amendment) Measure 1923; Dart, *Vendors and Purchasers of Real Estate*, vol. i, p. 292. These provisions were repealed by Patronage (Benefices) Measure 1986 under which, with effect from 1 January 1989, the right of presentation may be exercised only if it is registered in a register held by the diocese in question.

old, must be produced with proof of dealings with the lease from a disposition at least fifteen years old,[27] but the purchaser is not entitled to call for the title to the reversion;[28] if the subject-matter of the sale is a reversionary interest, an abstract of the instrument which created the interest must be produced, with proof of fifteen years' title back from the date of purchase.

(2) DUTY OF VENDOR TO ABSTRACT AND PRODUCE DOCUMENTS[29]

The vendor must at his own expense abstract and, if under his own control, produce the document which forms the root of his title, and all subsequent documents that affect the legal estate. In addition he must state and prove all facts that have affected the legal estate in the last fifteen years.

But there are certain things that must not be abstracted, and certain titles and documents that cannot be called for.

(i) Certain equitable interests not to be abstracted

Before 1926, a purchaser who took a conveyance of the legal estate was bound by any equitable interests affecting that estate of which he had notice. If, for instance, the abstract showed that the legal estate was held by the vendor as trustee, then, provided that he was an express trustee for sale, the equitable interests were *ipso facto* notified to the purchaser. It was necessary for the vendor to abstract the title to the equitable interests, and to obtain the concurrence of the beneficiaries in the conveyance.

But, as we have seen, one of the chief objects of the legislation of 1925 was to enable a purchaser to acquire the legal estate from the estate owner without being required to concern himself with equitable interests enforceable against the land. In general pursuance of this idea the Law of Property Act 1925[30] provides that in certain cases it shall not be necessary or proper to mention equitable interests in the abstract that will be overreached by the conveyance.[31] Therefore, for example, when a trustee of land contracts to sell trust land, he is not required to abstract the equitable interests of the beneficiaries. These are overreachable and are therefore of no concern to a purchaser.

(ii) Freehold title not to be abstracted on sale of leasehold

If the subject-matter of the sale is a term of years, the vendor is bound, as we have seen, to abstract and produce the lease under which he holds the land; but it is enacted that in an open contract he shall not be required to prove the title to the freehold.[32] This latter rule applies where a fee simple owner agrees to *grant* a lease.

Thus:

If A is fee simple owner of the land, and if he agrees to grant a lease to B for 99 years, B is not entitled to call for proof of A's title to the fee simple, unless he has inserted an express stipulation to that effect

---

[27] *Frend v Buckley* (1870) LR 5 QB 213; *Williams v Spargo* [1893] WN 100.

[28] LPA 1925, s. 44(2)–(4).   [29] Barnsley, *Conveyancing Law and Practice*, pp. 281–5.

[30] S. 10(1).   [31] Pp. 994–5, 997–1000, post.   [32] LPA 1925, s. 44(2).

in the contract. Again, if B agrees later to sell his lease to C, the latter is precluded from calling for the title of A.

Similar rules apply to an agreement to sell a leasehold interest that is derived out of a leasehold interest, or to an agreement to grant such a lease.[33] If, for example:

A leases to B and B under-leases to C, and C agrees to sell his underlease to D, then D is entitled to production of the under-lease,[34] but he cannot call for the lease to B.

These rules were formerly contained in the Vendor and Purchaser Act 1874, and the Conveyancing Act 1881, and it was held under those statutes that, failing their express exclusion by the contract, a lessee or a purchaser of a term of years was bound by equities affecting the legal estate that would have come to his notice had he expressly required the freehold title to be disclosed. This was decided in *Patman v Harland*:[35]

The plaintiff sold land to A subject to a restrictive covenant. A sold to B, and B leased part of the land to the defendant, who committed a breach of the covenant. The defendant had no knowledge of the existence of the restrictive covenant, and, in an action brought against her for an injunction, it was argued that, as in an open contract she was debarred by the statute from inquiring into the title to the freehold out of which her lease was derived, she had no notice, actual or constructive, of the restrictive covenant, and therefore was not liable for its breach.

This argument was rejected by the Court of Appeal.

It is now, however, provided that, in contracts made after 1925, a person who, under the above rules, is not entitled to call for the title to the freehold or the leasehold reversion shall not be deemed to be affected with notice of any matter or thing of which, if he had contracted that such a title should be furnished, he might have had notice.[36] The doctrine of *Patman v Harland* is therefore abolished in cases where a purchaser of a leasehold interest has no right to call for the freehold title, but the alteration is subject to the qualification that the lessee remains bound by any incumbrances that have been registered under the Land Charges Act 1972.[37]

There is also a more general enactment to the effect that a purchaser shall not be deemed to have notice of any matter or thing of which, if he had investigated the title prior to the beginning of the fifteen years' period, he might have had notice, unless he actually makes the investigation.[38]

---

[33] Ibid., s. 44(3), (4).

[34] *Gosling v Woolf* [1893] 1 QB 39. C is, however, entitled to call for B's lease. This is not precluded by s. 44, and, therefore, an under-lessee has constructive notice of the restrictive covenants in a lease: *Clements v Welles* (1865) LR 1 Eq 200. See Farrand, *Contract and Conveyance*, p. 131.

[35] (1881) 17 Ch D 353, M & B p. 560. See (1950) 56 LQR 361 (D. W. Logan).

[36] LPA 1925, s. 44(5).

[37] *White v Bijou Mansions Ltd* [1937] Ch 610 at 619. See *Shears v Wells* [1936] 1 All ER 832, M & B p. 559; [1956] CLJ pp. 230–4 (H. W. R. Wade). In registered land, LPA 1925, s. 44 does not apply because the register of the landlord's title is open to inspection: p. 954, post; LPA 1925, s. 44(12), inserted by Land Registration Act 2002, s. 133, Sch. 11, para. 2(1), (4).

[38] LPA 1925, s. 44(8). *Purchaser* in this connection means one who acquires an interest for money or money's worth, and includes a lessee and a mortgagee: ibid., s. 205(1)(xxi). The expression *money's worth* excludes the consideration of marriage.

(3) OBLIGATION OF PURCHASER TO BEAR THE COST OF PRODUCING CERTAIN DOCUMENTS

We have seen that one of the duties of a vendor is to produce a perfect abstract of title; it is incidental to this that he must produce at his own expense the documents which go to prove the title. If these are not in his possession, he must arrange for the production of those dated after the period of fifteen years began in so far as they are material.[39] But as regards the expense of producing documents, the rule varies according as they are in the possession of the vendor or not.

At common law a vendor was bound to bear the cost of producing documents whether in his own possession or not, but the Conveyancing Act 1881 provided that the expenses of the production and of the inspection of documents *not in the vendor's possession*, the expenses of all journeys incidental thereto, and the expenses of procuring all evidences and informa-tion not in the vendor's possession should be borne by the purchaser.[40]

It was held under this section that where the vendor had mortgaged his property, the purchaser must pay the mortgagee's solicitor a fee for producing the deeds relating to the property.[41] This was a harsh application of the rule, and therefore the Law of Property Act 1925, while re-enacting the provisions of the Conveyancing Act, expressly provides that the expense of producing deeds which are in the possession of the vendor's *mortgagee or trustee* shall fall upon the vendor.[42] If, however, the mortgagee retains possession of a document, the purchaser must pay for any copy which he desires to have.

(4) OBLIGATION OF PURCHASER TO EXAMINE THE ABSTRACT AT HIS OWN EXPENSE

The perusal of the abstract is carried out by the purchaser's solicitor, whose duty it is to advise whether the vendor has shown a good title to the exact interest that he has agreed to sell. The solicitor must satisfy himself that the abstract exhibits an ordered sequence of all the documents and events which have disposed of or affected the interest during the last fifteen years, and if he observes defects or omissions, he must requisition the vendor on the matter. He must compare the abstract with the original deeds which are produced by the vendor's solicitor, and put in requisitions on points of discrepancy.

The solicitor must, for instance, require proper evidence of facts which affect the interest, ascertain that the abstracted documents bear stamps of the proper value, and inquire concerning the existence of tenancies and easements.

(5) OBLIGATION OF PURCHASER TO SEARCH REGISTERS OF INCUMBRANCES

One of the first essentials in the investigation of an abstract of title is that a purchaser should search for incumbrances and interests which affect the land to be sold, and which may have been registered by their owners in a public register. This will be seen to be of great impor-tance when we come to examine whether the purchaser of a legal estate takes the estate free

---

[39] *Re Stamford, Spalding and Boston Banking Co and Knight's Contract* [1900] 1 Ch 287.   [40] S. 3(6).

[41] *Re Willett and Argenti* (1889) 60 LT 735.   [42] LPA 1925, s. 45(4).

from interests charged thereon. There are two main registers to be noticed, namely:

(1) a central register[43] kept by the Land Charges Department of the Land Registry at Plymouth, where searches are carried out with the aid of a computer, and

(2) the various local land charges registers kept in London by each London borough or the City of London, and elsewhere by each district council.[44]

(i) Land Charges Register

(A) REGISTRABLE INTERESTS

Under the Land Charges Act 1972, the Registrar of the Land Registry keeps five separate Registers,[45] namely:

(1) a register of pending actions;

(2) a register of annuities;

(3) a register of writs and orders affecting land;

(4) a register of deeds of arrangement affecting land; and

(5) a register of land charges.[46]

We will take these registers separately, and notice what kind of right or interest in land may be registered in each.

1. *Register of pending actions* It is obviously impossible to bring an action relating to land to a successful termination if alienation *pendente lite* is permissible, and therefore, in order that a plaintiff may not lose the fruits of his action, the law provides him with the means of protecting himself. This is afforded by the right to register a pending land action, that is, any action, information or proceeding which is pending in court, and which relates to land or to any interest in, or charge on, land.[47]

Again, if a creditor wishes to make his debtor's property available for distribution among creditors generally, he may register in the same register the petition in bankruptcy which is the first step in setting bankruptcy proceedings in motion.[48]

---

[43] In 2004–5, there were 118,298 new registrations, rectifications and renewals of land charges, and 4,876,248 searches of the Register. 69% of search requests are made by telephone, direct access and fax, and 84% of official copy applications are delivered in those ways; and since September 2004, customers have been able to request that certain land charges certificates of result of search be delivered electronically instead of as paper certificates: Land Registry Annual Report 2004–05, pp. 56, 63.

[44] LLCA 1975, s. 3(1). Such registers need not be kept in documentary form: s. 3(3), substituted by Local Government (Miscellaneous Provisions) Act 1982, s. 34(a).

[45] LCA 1972, s. 1. The historical order of the registers, as set out in LCA 1925, s. 1(1), has been followed. The new order is land charges, pending actions, writs and orders, deeds of arrangement and annuities. See generally Barnsley, *Conveyancing Law and Practice*, pp. 189–96, 333–66; Land Registry Practice Guide 63. On the history of registration, see *Ministry of Housing and Local Government v Sharp* [1970] 2 QB 223 at 280, per CROSS LJ.

[46] Ibid., s. 1(1).

[47] Ibid., s. 5(1), (4A) as added by LP (Miscellaneous Provisions) Act 1994, s. 15(3) (registration after death), s. 17(1); see *Taylor v Taylor* [1968] 1 WLR 378; *Calgary and Edmonton Land Co Ltd v Dobinson* [1974] Ch 102; *Whittingham v Whittingham* [1979] Fam 9; *Greenhi Builders Ltd v Allen* [1979] 1 WLR 156; *Selim Ltd v Bickenhall Engineering Ltd* [1981] 1 WLR 1318; *Regan & Blackburn Ltd v Rogers* [1985] 1 WLR 870; *Sowerby v Sowerby* (1982) 44 P & CR 192; *Haslemere Estates Ltd v Baker* [1982] 1 WLR 1109; [1983] Conv 69 (J. E. M.); *Perez-Adamson v Perez-Rivas* [1987] Fam 89; [1987] Conv 58 (J. E. Martin); *Kemmis v Kemmis* [1988] 1 WLR 1307; *Willies-Williams v National Trust for Places of Historic Interest or Natural Beauty* (1993) 65 P & CR 359. See generally (1986) 136 NLJ 157 (H. W. Wilkinson); [1995] Conv 309 (J. Howell).   [48] Ibid., s. 5(1).

If a pending action (i.e. either an action relating to land or a petition in bankruptcy) is registered, the registration remains effective for five years, but it may be renewed for successive periods of five years.[49] A purchaser for value (which includes a mortgagee or lessee) of any interest in the land takes free from an *unregistered* pending action unless he has express, as distinct from constructive, notice of it.[50] In the case of an unregistered bankruptcy petition, however, this protection avails him only if he is a purchaser of a *legal* estate in good faith for money or money's worth.[51]

2. *Register of annuities* Before 1926 annuities or rentcharges did not affect purchasers of the land upon which they are charged unless they were registered in the Register of Annuities. No annuity can be entered in this Register after 1925, and it will be closed as soon as the annuities registered before 1 January 1926 have been worked off.[52]

Annuities, being interests for life, are necessarily equitable in nature after 1925, and they may now be registered as *general equitable charges* in the Register of Land Charges, provided that they do not arise under a settlement or a trust of land.[53]

3. *Register of writs and orders affecting land* Any writ or order affecting land issued by a court for the purpose of enforcing a judgment or recognisance (e.g. an order of the court charging the land of a judgment debtor with payment of the money due[54]), any order which appoints a receiver[55] or sequestrator of land, any bankruptcy order, whether it is known to affect land or not, and any access order under the Access to Neighbouring Land Act 1992[56] is void against a purchaser for value of the land unless it is registered.[57] The registration remains effective for five years, but it may be renewed for successive periods of five years.[58]

The title of a trustee in bankruptcy, however, is void only against a purchaser of a legal estate in good faith, for money or money's worth unless the bankruptcy order is registered.[59]

4. *Register of deeds of arrangement affecting land* An insolvent debtor sometimes comes to an arrangement with the general body of his creditors whereby, although he does not pay his debts in full, he obtains a release from the claims of the creditors. As a rule the debtor either compounds with his creditors, or assigns his property to a trustee for distribution among the creditors.

If such an arrangement is reduced to writing, it is called a deed of arrangement whether it is made by deed or not.[60] It is enacted that such an arrangement shall be void against a purchaser for value of the debtor's land unless it is registered in the above Register. Registration ceases to have any effect after five years unless it is renewed.[61]

---

49 LCA 1972, s. 8.   50 Ibid., s. 5(7).

51 Ibid., ss. 5(8), 6(5), as amended by Insolvency Act 1985, s. 235, Sch. 8, para. 21(2) and Sch. 10.

52 Ibid., s. 1(4), Sch. 1.

53 Ibid., s. 2(4), Class C (iii), as amended by TLATA 1996, Sch. 3, para. 12(1), (2), p. 940, post.

54 Charging Orders Act 1979, s. 1; p. 734, ante. A freezing order (formerly called a Mareva injunction) prohibiting a party from disposing of his assets is not registrable: *Stockler v Fourways Estates Ltd* [1984] 1 WLR 25.

55 *Clayhope Properties Ltd v Evans* [1986] 1 WLR 1223 (receivership order made against landlord for specific performance of repairing covenants held registrable).

56 S. 5. See p. 600, ante. No will or order affecting an interest under a trust of land may be registered under s. 6(1A), inserted by TLATA 1996, s. 21(1), Sch. 3, para. 12(3).

57 LCA 1972, s. 6(1), (4), as amended by Supreme Court Act 1981, s. 152(1), Sch. 5 and County Courts Act 1984, s. 148(1), Sch. 2, para. 18.   58 Ibid., s. 8.

59 Ibid., s. 6(5) as amended by Insolvency Act 1985, s. 235, Sch. 8, para. 21(3) and Sch. 10.

60 Deeds of Arrangement Act 1914, s. 1.   61 LCA 1972, ss. 7, 8.

5. *Register of land charges* The term *land charge* is comprehensive; it includes a number of different rights and interests affecting land. The Land Charges Act 1925, which made considerable additions to this part of the law, divided land charges into five classes, denominated A, B, C, D, and E; a further Class F was added by the Matrimonial Homes Act 1967.[62] The whole has now been consolidated in the Land Charges Act 1972.[63]

CLASS A[64]

This comprises a rent or a sum of money which is charged upon land, *pursuant to the application of some person*, under the provisions of any Act of Parliament, and with the object of securing money which has been spent on the land under the provisions of such Act. It also comprises a rent or a sum of money charged upon land in accordance with certain sections in, for example:

the Land Drainage Act 1991,[65]

the Agricultural Holdings Act 1986,[66]

the Landlord and Tenant Act 1927.[67]

Thus, if a tenant for life has to pay compensation to an outgoing tenant of an agricultural holding, he may obtain an order charging the holding with the repayment of the amount, and may have the charge registered. A land charge of this class is void against a purchaser unless it is registered before the completion of the purchase.[68]

CLASS B[69]

This comprises a charge on land (not being a local land charge) of any of the kinds described in Class A, provided that it has not been created "pursuant to the application of any person", and is imposed automatically by statute. An example is a charge on property recovered or preserved for an assisted litigant arising under the Access to Justice Act 1999,[70] in respect of unpaid contributions for services received from the Criminal Defence Service.

Charges of this class, however, are not important as regards searches in the Land Registry: because they mostly arise under the Public Health Act 1936, and being in the majority of cases of a local nature (as, for instance, those arising in respect of paving expenses) they are *local land charges* and must therefore be registered locally.[71]

Failure to register such a charge (not being a local land charge) at the Land Registry renders it void as against a purchaser for valuable consideration of the land or of any interest therein:

(i) if it arises after 31 December 1925, and has not been registered;

---

[62] Now Family Law Act 1996; p. 478, ante.

[63] See Land Charges Rules 1974 (SI 1974 No. 1286); Land Charges Fees Rules 1990 (SI 1990 No. 327); Land Charges Fees (Amendment) Rules 1994 (SI 1994 No. 286); Land Charges (Amendment) Rules 1990 (SI 1990 No. 485); Land Charges (Amendment) Rules 1995 (SI 1995 No. 1355); Land Charges (Amendment) Rules 2005 (SI 2005 No. 1981).   [64] LCA 1972, s. 2(2), Class A.

[65] S. 34(2).

[66] Ss. 85(2), (3), 86. The Act does not apply to tenancies beginning on or after 1 September 1995. In the case of a farm business tenancy such sums are payable out of capital money; Agricultural Tenancies Act 1995, s. 33(3).

[67] S. 12, Sch. 1, para. 7, as amended by Landlord and Tenant Act 1954, s. 45 and Sch. 7, Pt. I. For other examples, see LCA 1972, s. 2, Sch. 2.   [68] LCA 1972, s. 4(2).

[69] Ibid., s. 2(3), Class B as amended by LLCA 1975, s. 19, Sch. 2.   [70] S. 17(3)(g).   [71] P. 947, post.

(ii) if it arose before that date and has not been registered within a year from the first conveyance of the charge made after 31 December 1925.[72]

CLASS C[73]

This class is important in that it creates a system of registration of mortgages of land, and provides for the registration of estate contracts. It comprises four different land charges (not being local land charges), namely:

(i) Puisne mortgage This is a *legal* mortgage not protected by a deposit of documents relating to the legal estate affected.[74]

(ii) Limited owner's charge This is an equitable charge acquired under any statute by a tenant for life or statutory owner by discharging inheritance tax or other liabilities, and to which special priority is given by the statute. Thus a charge may arise under the Finance Act 1986,[75] in favour of a tenant for life who pays inheritance tax in respect of the estate out of which his life interest is carved.

(iii) General equitable charge This is a comprehensive expression that includes all equitable charges that are not assigned to a class of their own (such as estate contracts), and which do not arise or affect an interest arising under a trust of land[76] or a settlement. In particular it includes an equitable mortgage of a legal estate which is not secured by a deposit of the title deeds, but it also comprises a rentcharge for life and a vendor's lien for unpaid purchase money.[77] To be registrable, the charge must be on land, and not for instance upon the purchase money that will arise from the sale of land.[78]

(iv) Estate contract This is the only item included within Class C which is not in the nature of a mortgage. It is defined as being:[79]

a contract by an estate owner or by a person entitled at the date of the contract to have a legal estate conveyed to him to convey or create a legal estate, including a contract conferring either expressly or by statutory implication a valid option to purchase, a right of pre-emption[80] or any other like right.[81]

This in practice means a contract for the sale of a legal fee simple, a contract for the grant of a term of years absolute,[82] or an option to acquire either of these interests[83] or a contract to

---

[72] LCA 1972, s. 4(5), (7).   [73] Ibid., s. 2(4), Class C, as amended by LLCA 1975, s. 17(1)(b).

[74] P. 795, ante.

[75] LCA 1972, s. 2(4), as amended by FA 1975, s. 52, Sch. 12, para. 18(2); ITA 1984, s. 276, Sch. 8, para. 3(1)(a); FA 1986, s. 100(1)(b). See ITA 1984, ss. 2(2), 237, 238.

[76] As amended by TLATA 1996, s. 25(1), Sch. 3, para. 12(2).

[77] See *Uziell-Hamilton v Keen* (1971) 22 P & CR 655; *Property Discount Corpn Ltd v Lyon Group Ltd* [1981] 1 WLR 300 at 313.

[78] *Georgiades v Edward Wolfe & Co Ltd* [1965] Ch 487. Report of Committee on Land Charges (1956 Cmnd 9825), para. 13 suggested that Class C(iii) might be abolished, except as regards mortgages.

[79] LCA 1972, s. 2(4), Class C(iv).   [80] See pp. 880 et seq, ante.

[81] *Shiloh Spinners Ltd v Harding* [1973] AC 691 at 719.

[82] *Sharp v Coates* [1949] 1 KB 285 (contract by estate owner to convey an estate greater than he was entitled to at the time of the contract). It also includes a contract by which A agrees with B to create a legal estate in favour of such third person as B may nominate: *Turley v Mackay* [1944] Ch 37; but not a contract by which A agrees that B has the power to accept offers to purchase made by third persons: *Thomas v Rose* [1968] 1 WLR 1797.

[83] *Beesly v Hallwood Estates Ltd* [1960] 1 WLR 549. The decision was affirmed on another point: [1961] Ch 105; *Taylors Fashions Ltd v Liverpool Victoria Trustees Co Ltd* [1982] QB 133n; and approved in *Phillips v Mobil Oil Co Ltd* [1989] 1 WLR 888; [1990] Conv 168, 250 (J. Howell); [1989] All ER Rev 193 (P. H. Pettit). A notice to treat served under a compulsory purchase order is not a contract, although it may lead to one, and

grant any other legal interest, such as a mortgage or easement.[84] We have already seen that the effect of such a contract is to confer an equitable interest upon the intending purchaser or tenant under the doctrine of *Walsh v Lonsdale*.[85] The effect of the Land Charges Act is to make it capable of registration.[86]

CLASS D[87]

This comprises the three following different land charges (not being local land charges):

(i) Inland revenue charge The Commissioners of Inland Revenue may register a charge on the occasion of the transfer of land which gives rise to the liability for inheritance tax under the Finance Act 1986.[88]

(ii) Restrictive covenant This has already been described,[89] and the only remark needed here is that restrictive covenants made between a lessor and a lessee are expressly excluded, and are not capable of registration.

(iii) Equitable easement This is defined as[90] "any easement right or privilege over or affecting land created or arising on or after 1 January 1926, and being merely an equitable interest". Thus, an easement held for some smaller interest than a fee simple absolute in possession or for a term of years absolute, or an easement that has been informally created, satisfies this definition and is therefore registrable.

The three charges in Class D are not registrable unless they have arisen after 1925.

CLASS E

This class comprises annuities created before 1926 and not registered in the Register of Annuities. This register, as we have seen, was closed to new entries as from 1 January 1926,[91] but annuitants who omitted to register before that date may register under Class E.

CLASS F

This is the right of occupation of a dwelling-house given to a spouse or civil partner by Part IV of the Family Law Act 1996.[92]

---

therefore is not registrable: *Capital Investments Ltd v Wednesfield UDC* [1965] Ch 774. Cf Leasehold Reform Act 1967, s. 5(5) (notice given by tenant of his desire to acquire the freehold or an extended lease registrable as estate contract); p. 364, ante.

[84] "Legal estate" in LCA 1972, as in LPA 1925, is not limited to the legal estates properly so-called, but extends to all estates, interests and charges which can be conveyed or created at law: LCA 1972, s. 17(1); LPA 1925, s. 1(4).

[85] P. 877, ante.

[86] *Universal Permanent Building Society v Cooke* [1952] Ch 95 at 104. See *Barrett v Hilton Developments Ltd* [1975] Ch 237 (registration against the name of a person who has contracted to purchase the legal estate in land is not sufficient).   [87] LCA 1972, s. 2(5), Class D as amended by LLCA 1975, s. 17(1)(b).

[88] Ibid., s. 2(5), Class D(i), as amended by FA 1975, s. 52, Sch. 12, para. 18(3) and FA 1986, s. 100(1)(b). See ITA 1984, s. 237, Sch. 8, para. 3(1)(b).   [89] Pp. 666 et seq, ante.

[90] For a discussion of this class, see *Shiloh Spinners Ltd v Harding* [1973] AC 691, M & B p. 34 (equitable right of re-entry on breach of contract not registrable as Class D(iii) land charge); (1973) 32 CLJ 218 (P. B. Fairest); p. 634, ante. Report of the Committee on Land Charges (1956 Cmnd 9826), para. 16 suggested that Class D(iii) might be abolished. Law Commission Report on Land Charges affecting Unregistered Land 1969 (Law Com No. 18), para. 65, recommended its retention. Registrations in that class were then running at an annual rate of 2,500–3,500; there were 829 registrations during the year ended 31 March 1993: Report on HM Land Registry 1992–93, p. 21.   [91] P. 938, ante.

[92] P. 478, ante; LCA 1972, s. 2(7), amended by Family Law Act 1996, s. 66(1), Sch. 8, para. 47.

(B) EFFECT OF REGISTRATION

We must now turn to the effect of registration and its mechanics. The effect is contained in section 198(1) of the Law of Property Act 1925:

> The registration of any instrument or matter in any register kept under the Land Charges Act 1972 or any local land charges register shall be deemed to constitute actual notice of such instrument or matter, and of the fact of such registration, to all persons and for all purposes connected with the land affected, as from the date of registration ... and so long as the registration continues in force.[93]

As we have seen,[94] this makes a substantial inroad on the doctrine of the bona fide purchaser for value without notice: that doctrine no longer operates in respect of land charges which are registrable.

1. *Registration against name of estate owner* It is important to notice that land charges affecting unregistered land are registered, not against the burdened *land*, as is the case with registered land, but against the *name* of the estate owner of the land at the time when the land charge was created.[95] The name of the estate owner means the name as disclosed by the conveyance.[96]

Where a person has died and a land charge created before his death would apart from his death have been registered in his name, it should be so registered notwithstanding his death.[97] If, therefore, a purchaser desires to make a complete search at the Land Registry, he will have to discover the names of every owner of a legal estate in the land since 1 January 1926.[98] Even though this may be impossible, he will nevertheless be bound by a registered land charge. This causes difficulty to a purchaser and led to statutory intervention in 1969.[99]

(a) Land charge discovered between contract and completion

As we have seen, a purchaser does not normally investigate the vendor's title before contract.[100] In *Re Forsey and Hollebone's Contract*,[101] Eve J took the view that by virtue of section 198 of the Law of Property Act 1925, a purchaser has notice at the date of the contract of land charges which are then on the register, whether he knows of them or not. The difficulty for a purchaser under an open contract is that at the pre-contract stage he will not normally know the names of all the estate owners, and so he may be compelled to take a conveyance of the land subject to land charges on the register which he cannot discover. Section 24 of the Law of Property Act 1969 amends the law so as to ensure that in respect of contracts entered into after 1 January 1970, *as against the vendor*, a purchaser will only be deemed to have

---

[93] As amended by LLCA 1975, s. 17, Sch. 1. For an exception in the case of tacking, see LPA 1925, s. 198(2), p. 802, ante. See also s. 96(2), as amended by LP(A)A 1926, Schedule; p. 758, ante.   [94] Pp. 97–8, ante.

[95] LCA 1972, ss. 3(1), 17(1). On the mechanics of the register see *Oak Co-operative Building Society v Blackburn* [1968] Ch 730 at 741, per RUSSELL LJ.

[96] *Standard Property Investment plc v British Plastics Federation* (1985) 53 P & CR 25; [1987] Conv 135 (J.E.A.). A person entitled to have the legal estate conveyed to him is not an estate owner: *Barrett v Hilton Developments Ltd* [1975] Ch 237; *Property Discount Corpn Ltd v Lyon Group Ltd* [1981] 1 WLR 300.

[97] LCA 1972, ss. 3(1A), 5(4A), 6(2A), inserted by LP(MP)A 1994, s. 15(2). See Law Commission Report: Title on Death 1989 (Law Com No. 184, Cm 777), paras. 2-2 to 2-9; [1995] Conv 476 (L. Clements).

[98] Since January 1889 in respect of Class A land charges.

[99] LPA 1969, ss. 24, 25. See generally Report of the Committee on Land Charges 1956 (Cmnd 9825); Law Commission Report on Land Charges affecting Unregistered Land 1969 (Law Com No. 18); (1970) 34 Conv (NS) 4 (F. R. Crane).   [100] P. 931, ante.

[101] [1927] 2 Ch 379.

notice of those registered land charges of which he has actual or imputed knowledge at the date of the contract.[102] Consequently, a purchaser will no longer be prevented from rescinding the contract on the ground of an undisclosed land charge merely because it has been registered. The owner of the registered land charge, however, remains protected: here registration still constitutes notice to all the world.

Section 24 does not apply to local land charges,[103] and, where they are concerned, the rule in *Forsey and Hollebone's Contract* may still apply. In this case, however, the problem for the purchaser is different. He does not need to know the names of the estate owners; the charges are registered against the land.[104] But the need to search the register before contract rather than at the same time as the other registers, that is to say, shortly before completion, is inconvenient and entails a delay which can put the contract at risk. The correctness of the rule continues to be questioned.[105]

(b) "Old land charge" discovered after completion

In this case a purchaser, who has carried out a full and proper investigation of title, may discover after completion that he is bound by land charges registered before the commencement of the vendor's title. He can, of course, stipulate for a list of all estate owners since 1 January 1926,[106] but this may be impracticable. The risk that he may be caught by an "old land charge" is increased by the reduction of the minimum period of investigation of title to fifteen years.

The Law of Property Act 1969 preserves the validity of the registered land charge against the purchaser, but provides that where he has suffered loss as a result of its existence he is entitled to compensation.[107] This is payable if (a) his purchase was completed after 1 January 1970, (b) he purchased without actual or imputed knowledge of the land charge and (c) the charge was registered against the name of a person who did not appear as an estate owner in the relevant title.[108] Relevant title means either the statutory period of fifteen years under an open contract, or the period of title in fact contracted for, whichever is the longer.[109]

(c) Land charge discovered after grant or assignment of lease

As we have seen, in the case of an open contract for the grant or assignment of a lease or underlease, the lessee or assignee is not entitled to call for the superior reversionary titles.[110] He may, however, be bound by registered land charges affecting those titles, even though he is unable to discover the names of the estate owners which are concealed in those titles.[111]

---

[102] The parties cannot contract out of the section: LPA 1969, s. 24(2).

[103] LRA 1969, s. 24(1), (3). Nor does it apply to registered land.   [104] P. 947, post.

[105] *Rignall Developments Ltd v Halil* [1987] 3 WLR 394 "This part of Eve J's judgment... was greeted at the time by conveyancers with consternation and incredulity... It has since been subjected to severe criticism by the editors of *Emmet on Title* and other eminent conveyancers": at 402, per MILLETT J; [1987] Conv 291 (C. Harpum); (1987) 137 NLJ 1178 (H. W. Wilkinson). See also *Citytowns Ltd v Bohemian Properties Ltd* [1986] 2 EGLR 258.

[106] And perhaps should where he purchases land for development. See (1969) 113 SJ 930 (S. M. Cretney).

[107] S. 25. This does not apply to local land charges.

[108] S. 25(1). It is payable by the Chief Land Registrar out of public funds.   [109] S. 25(10).

[110] P. 934, ante.

[111] See also Law Commission Report on Land Charges Affecting Unregistered Land 1969 (Law Com No. 18), para. 37.

2. *Priority notices* The fact that a charge cannot be registered until it has actually been created occasioned some difficulty after the Land Charges Act 1925 came into operation. The provision of the Act that a charge on land, such as a restrictive covenant, shall be void against a subsequent purchaser of the legal estate for money or money's worth unless it is registered before *completion* of that purchase, produces an *impasse* in certain cases, for it is sometimes impossible to effect registration before completion. A common example of this arises where:

X agrees to sell Blackacre to Y and takes a restrictive covenant from Y. Y, being unable to find the whole of the purchase money, arranges to mortgage Blackacre to Z. The conveyance from X to Y which creates the restrictive covenant, and the mortgage from Y to Z are in practice completed at the same time, so that it is practically impossible for X to register his restrictive covenant before it is rendered void under the Act by the completion of the purchase in favour of Z.

The Law of Property (Amendment) Act 1926[112] removed this difficulty by providing that any person *intending* to apply for the registration of any *contemplated* charge may register notice of his intention at the Land Registry. This notice, which is called a *priority notice*, must be given at least fifteen days before the registration is to take effect.[113] When the contemplated charge is actually created and later registered, then, provided that it is registered within thirty days after the priority notice, it takes effect as if registration had been secured at the very moment of its creation.[114]

3. *Official searches* Although a purchaser may search in a register himself, it is usual to obtain an official search. Upon receipt of such a requisition (as it is called) the registrar, after making the search, issues an official certificate, which is conclusive in favour of the purchaser.[115] If another charge is registered by a third person between the time when the certificate is issued and the time when the purchase is completed by the certificate holder, the registration does not affect the latter, provided that he completes his purchase within fifteen days of the issue of the certificate.[116]

(C) EFFECT OF FAILURE TO REGISTER

The failure to register a land charge does not affect the original parties to the transaction; as between them it remains valid. The effect as far as third parties are concerned is, however, not uniform. We have already seen the effect in connection with each register, except for land charges Classes C, D and F. These merit more detailed treatment.

---

[112] S. 4(1); now LCA 1972, s. 11(1). See (1977) 74 LSG 136 (P. Freedman).

[113] LCA 1972, s. 11(3), (6). Days when the registry is not open to the public are excluded.

[114] Ibid., s. 11(3).

[115] Ibid., s. 10(4). To be effective registration must be in the correct full name of the estate owner. If it is not, a clear certificate as a result of an official search against the correct name will not bind a purchaser. "But if there be registration in what may fairly be described as a version of the full names of the vendor, albeit not a version which is bound to be discovered on a search in the correct full names, we would not hold it a nullity against someone who does not search for all, or who (as here) searches in the wrong name": *Oak Co-operative Building Society v Blackburn* [1968] Ch 730 at 743, per RUSSELL LJ; (1968) 31 MLR 705. See too *Du Sautoy v Symes* [1967] Ch 1146; *Horrill v Cooper* (1998) 78 P & CR 336. On liability where an erroneous certificate is issued, see *Ministry of Housing and Local Government v Sharp* [1970] 2 QB 223; *Coats Patons (Retail) Ltd v Birmingham Corpn* (1971) 69 LGR 356; *Diligent Finance Co Ltd v Alleyne* (1972) 23 P & CR 346; LCA 1972, s. 10(6).

[116] Ibid., s. 11(5)(b).

The effect of a failure to register the land charges comprised in Classes C, D, and F is as follows:

(a) Puisne mortgages (C(i))

Limited owners' charges (C(ii))

General equitable charges (C(iii))

Spouse or civil partner's right of occupation (F)

are void against:

a purchaser of the land charged with it, or of any interest in such land, unless the land charge is registered in the appropriate register before the completion of the purchase.[117]

"Purchaser" is defined in the Land Charges Act 1972[118] as "Unless the context otherwise requires, ... any person (including a mortgagee or lessee) who, for valuable consideration, takes any interest in land or in a charge on land." "Valuable consideration" is widely interpreted and includes the consideration of marriage, and may be inadequate or even nominal.[119] The effect of the words "any interest" is that a purchaser even of an equitable interest in the land affected takes free from these charges if unregistered, irrespective of whether he has actual notice or not.

(b) Estate contracts (C(iv))

Restrictive covenants (D(ii))

Equitable easements (D(iii))

are void against:

a purchaser for money or money's worth ... of a legal estate in the land charged with it, unless the land charge is registered in the appropriate register before the completion of the purchase.[120]

(c) Inland Revenue Charge (D(i)) is void against:

a purchaser in good faith for consideration in money or money's worth other than a nominal consideration and includes a lessee, mortgagee or other person who for such consideration acquires an interest in the property in question.[121]

In this case a very restricted meaning of purchaser is adopted. He must be in good faith; the consideration of marriage is excluded, and so is nominal consideration.

It therefore follows that the four charges in (a) and (b), even if unregistered, bind a purchaser of an equitable interest whether he has notice or not.[122] Again, a purchaser even of a legal estate whose title is supported only by a marriage consideration, cannot rely upon the omission to register.

---

[117] LCA 1972, s. 4(5), (8).   [118] Ibid., s. 17(1).

[119] *Midland Bank Trust Co Ltd v Green* [1981] AC 513 at 532; *Nurdin & Peacock plc v D B Ramsden & Co Ltd* [1999] 1 EGLR 119.

[120] LCA 1972, s. 4(6), as amended by FA 1975, s. 52, Sch. 12, para. 18(5); ITA 1984, s. 276, Sch. 8, para. 3(2); FA 1986, s. 100(1)(b).   [121] FA 1975, s. 51(1).

[122] *McCarthy and Stone Ltd v Julian S Hodge & Co Ltd* [1971] 1 WLR 1547, M & B p. 49 (unregistered estate contract held to have priority over subsequent equitable mortgage).

Subject to these distinctions, the general effect of the non-registration of an interest that is registrable as a land charge is that it is void against a purchaser for value of any interest in the land. It is immaterial that a purchaser has actual knowledge of the unregistered interest, and this is so even if the land is conveyed to him expressly subject to it.[123] As HARMAN J said in *Hollington Bros Ltd v Rhodes*:[124]

It appears at first glance wrong that a purchaser, who knows perfectly well of rights subject to which he is expressed to take, should be able to ignore them...It seems to me, however, that this argument cannot prevail having regard to the words in section 13(2) of the Land Charges Act 1925[125]...The fact is that it was the policy of the framers of the 1925 legislation to get rid of equitable rights of this sort unless registered.[126]

The House of Lords adopted a similar approach in *Midland Bank Trust Co Ltd v Green*,[127] when considering the effect of failure to register an estate contract. Lord WILBERFORCE said:[128]

The case is plain. The Act is clear and definite. Intended as it was to provide a simple and understandable system for the protection of title to land, it should not be read down or glossed: to do so would destroy the usefulness of the Act. Any temptation to remould the Act to meet the facts of the present case on the supposition that it is a hard one and that justice requires it, is, for me at least, removed by the consideration that the Act itself provides a simple and effective protection for persons in [the son's] position—viz—by registration.

In that case:

a father granted to his son a 10-year option to purchase the farm of which the son was his tenant. The option was not registered as an estate contract. Later the father, wishing to deprive the son of his option, conveyed the farm, then worth about £40,000 to the mother for £500. When the son found this out, he registered the option and purported to exercise it.

It was held that the mother was a purchaser for money or money's worth and therefore the option was void against her.[129] It was immaterial that she had given inadequate (or even nominal) consideration and might have intended to defeat the unregistered interest. There was no requirement of good faith in the definition of a purchaser in the Land Charges Act,

---

[123] LPA 1925, s. 199(1)(i).

[124] [1951] 2 TLR 691 at 695, M & B p. 46; LPA 1925, s. 199(1)(i). An unregistered registrable interest is not always void and unenforceable owing to lack of registration (e.g. a pending land action: LCA 1972, s. 7: in such case a purchaser with express notice is bound; p. 938, ante). Such an interest may also be binding (a) by estoppel: *Taylors Fashions Ltd v Liverpool Victoria Trustees Co Ltd* [1982] QB 133n, M & B p. 627; pp. 817–8, ante; (b) by failure to plead the non-registration when sued: *Balchin v Buckle* The Times, 1 June 1982 ("One would have thought that the purchaser could waive its effect and agree to be bound by the covenant (Class D(ii)). If he chose, whether from incompetence of his own or his legal advisers or from gentlemanly consideration for the rights or convenience of others, to be bound by the covenant or not to raise the point that it was void, there was no reason why the court should raise the point for him" per STEPHENSON LJ). But he is not bound by a bare trust "which is merely an equitable consequence of a specifically enforceable contract of sale": *Lloyds Bank plc v Carrick* [1996] 4 All ER 630; (1996) 112 LQR 549 (P. Ferguson); [1996] Conv 295 (M. P. Thompson); [1997] CLJ 32 (M. Oldham); [1996] All ER Rev 257 (P. J. Clarke); (1998) 61 MLR 486 (N. Hopkins). [125] Now LCA 1972, s. 4(6).

[126] See, however, [1982] Conv 213 (M. Friend and J. Newton) at pp. 215–17, M & B p. 50.

[127] [1981] AC 513. [128] At 528. [129] *Lloyds Bank plc v Carrick* [1996] 4 All ER 630, p. 112, ante.

and, even though it existed in other definitions in the 1925 legislation,[130] it should not be imported into that Act. There was no need to psychoanalyse a purchaser.[131]

(D) SUMMARY

In unregistered conveyancing the Land Charges Act 1972 thus plays a major part in enabling a purchaser to discover whether certain rights bind the land or not. The effect of the Act is automatic: if a registrable interest is registered, it binds; if not, in general a purchaser for value of any interest in the land takes free from it. Many of the risks which arise to him from the doctrine of constructive notice have thus been mitigated, but there is still a residual category of equitable interests which are neither registrable nor overreachable and will therefore bind a purchaser unless he is a bona fide purchaser for value of the legal estate without notice,[132] for example, a restrictive covenant entered into before 1926[133] and an equity by estoppel.[134]

Further, the difficulties which are inherent in a system of registration based on a names register are themselves mitigated by the Law of Property Act 1969.

The importance of the Land Charges register is declining now that the system of registration of title under the Land Registration Acts 1925 and 2002 has been extended throughout the country. But its importance will continue for a long time to come—until the title to every parcel of land in England and Wales has been registered.

Finally we must mention two registers which are kept in addition to those at the Land Registry.[135]

(ii) Local land charges registers

These are maintained under the Local Land Charges Act 1975[136] by all district councils in England and Wales, and also by London boroughs and the Common Council of the City of London.[137] They differ from those kept at the Land Registry in that the charges are registered

---

130 LPA 1925, s. 205(1)(xxi); SLA 1925, s. 117(1)(xxi); AEA 1925, s. 55(1)(xviii); LRA 1925, s. 3(xxi).

131 The "Green saga", which "bids fair to rival in time and money the story of *Jarndyce v Jarndyce*" (see [1980] Ch 590 at 622, per Lord DENNING MR), continued. For the liability of the solicitor for failing to advise the son to register the option and for failing to register it, see *Midland Bank Trust Co Ltd v Hett, Stubbs & Kemp* [1979] Ch 384; and for conspiracy between husband and wife, see *Midland Bank Trust Co Ltd v Green (No 3)* [1982] Ch 529. For a full review of all three cases by Sir Peter OLIVER, who tried them at first instance, see *The Green Saga* (1983) Child & Co Oxford Lecture. See also [1981] CLJ 213 (C. Harpum); (1981) 97 LQR 518 (B. Green).

132 P. 58, ante.   133 P. 673, ante.   134 Pp. 825–6 et seq, ante.

135 There are other registers which a purchaser may have to search: (a) Commons and Town and Village Greens under Commons Registration Act 1965, s. 3; p. 645, ante; (b) Agricultural charges under Agricultural Credits Act 1928, s. 5 (charge created by a farmer on his farming stock and other agricultural assets as security for sums advanced to him by a bank); this register is kept at the Land Registry at Plymouth; (c) On searches for and information on contaminated land, see Tromans and Clarke, *Contaminated Land*; (2001) 145 SJ 827; Silverman, *Conveyancing Handbook*, para. 10.5.10; (d) For other registers maintained by local authorities, see Garner, *Local Land Charges*, chap. 21; p. 1015, post. On searches generally, see Silverman, *Conveyancing Searches and Enquiries*; Silverman, *Conveyancing Handbook*, section B10. For the liability of a solicitor who failed to search the Commons Register, see *G & K Ladenbau (UK) Ltd v Crawley and de Reya* [1978] 1 WLR 266.

136 LLC Rules 1977 (SI 1977 No. 985); LLC(A) Rules 1978 (SI 1978 No. 1638); 1987 (SI 1987 No. 389); 1990 (SI 1990 No. 485); 1995 (SI 1995 No. 260); LLC(A) Rules 2003 (SI 2003 No. 2502). The Act came into force on 1 August 1977 and replaces LCA 1925, s. 15 and other sections set out in LCA 1972, s. 18, Sch. 4. See Law Commission Report on Local Land Charges 1974 (Law Com No. 62, HC 71); Garner, *Local Land Charges*, which has a useful table of all local land charges arranged alphabetically (pp. 209–28). For local authority search forms, see CON 29 Parts 1 and 2; (2002) 152 NLJ 1022; Law Society Guidance Notes, printed in Silverman, *Conveyancing Handbook*, Appendix V.

137 LLCA 1975, s. 3(1). This includes the Inner Temple and the Middle Temple: s. 3(4).

against the land and not against the name of the estate owner; they relate both to registered and to unregistered land[138] and are of public rather than a private nature.[139] Local land charges are a heterogeneous collection[140] and include charges for securing money recoverable by local authorities under public health legislation, and prohibitions of or restriction on the user of land imposed by a local authority, Minister of the Crown or a Government department.

The Act made a significant change in the effect of the non-registration of a local land charge. Section 10[141] provides that failure to register such a charge in the local land charges register shall not affect the enforcement of the charge, but that a purchaser[142] shall be entitled to compensation[143] for any loss suffered by him by reason that the charge was not registered, or was not shown as registered by an official search certificate.[144] This follows a recommendation by the Law Commission which observed that the overwhelming majority of local land charges are created in the public interest, and that it is usually inappropriate that lack of registration or non-disclosure in an official certificate of search should affect their enforceability.[145]

(iii) Companies Register

This is a register maintained in Cardiff and in London under the Companies Act 1985 of land charges created by a company for securing money.[146] Registration on this register of a charge created by a company before 1970 or so created at any time as a floating charge, is sufficient in place of registration in the Land Charges Register and has the same effect. A charge created by a company on or after 1 January 1970, other than a floating charge, must be registered at the Land Charges Registry if it is to bind a purchaser.[147] If it is to bind creditors and liquidators it must also be registered in the Companies Charges Register within twenty-one days of its creation.[148] These provisions also now apply to similar charges created by a limited partnership.[149]

---

[138] Pp. 977, 978, post.

[139] For an exception, see the notice under the Rights of Light Act 1959, s. 2; p. 625, ante.

[140] LLCA 1975, ss. 1, 2. A condition or limitation subject to which planning permission is granted is excluded: s. 2(e); p. 1015, post. See the recommendation of the Second Report of the Conveyancing Committee (1985), for a more comprehensive Local Land Charges Register by consolidating the Commons Register with it.

[141] As amended by Local Government (Miscellaneous Provisions) Act 1982, s. 34.

[142] LLCA 1975, s. 10(3)(a) defines a purchaser as a person who, for valuable consideration, acquires any interest in land or the proceeds of sale of land; and this includes a lessee or mortgagee.

[143] *Pound v Ashford BC* [2004] 1 P & CR 2 (criteria for awarding compensation).

[144] Under LCA 1925, s. 15, a local land charge was void against a purchaser for money or money's worth of a legal estate in the land affected, unless registered before completion of the purchase.

[145] Law Commission Report on Local Land Charges 1974 (Law Com No. 62), para. 90. See also paras. 52–4.

[146] Records can be inspected at Crown Way, Cardiff and Companies House, Bloomsbury Street, London, although between 1999 and 2005 there was a very significant shift to electronic searches of the register (e.g. by e-mail or online viewing), and the vast majority of company searches are now made electronically: Companies House Annual Report and Accounts 2004/05, p. 34. A company must also keep a register of charges at its registered office: Companies Act 1985, ss. 406–9, and the Registrar must keep a register of charges on property of the company: s. 397(1), inserted by Companies Act 1989, s. 94. See generally McCormack, *Registration of Company Charges*; Gough, *Company Charges*; *Gore-Brown on Companies*, chap. 31.

[147] LCA 1972, s. 3(7), (8), as substituted by Companies Act 1989, s. 107, Sch. 16, para. 1. See *Property Discount Corpn Ltd v Lyon Group Ltd* [1981] 1 WLR 300 (registration in companies register held sufficient, even though it was not in name of estate owner as required by LCA 1972, s. 3(1)); p. 942, ante; [1982] Conv 43 (D. M. Hare and T. Flanagan).

[148] Companies Act 1985, ss. 395, 396, as inserted by Companies Act 1989, s. 93. See the Diamond Report *A Review of Security Interests in Property* (1989). On the registration of charges on property of overseas companies, see Companies Act 1989, s. 105, Sch. 15, inserting a new Part XIII in the 1985 Act.

[149] Limited Partnerships Regulations 2001 (SI 2001 No. 1090), reg. 4, Sch. 2, Pt I.

(6) DUTY OF VENDOR TO CONVEY THE IDENTICAL PROPERTY THAT HE HAS AGREED TO SELL

The vendor must prove that the property which he is able to convey is substantially the same in nature, situation and quantity as that which he has agreed to sell, and it is advisable, when a contract for the sale of land is drafted, to obtain a description of the land from the "parcels" clause of the last conveyance.[150]

If, in the case of an open contract, the property is not identical in quantity or quality with that agreed to be sold, the vendor cannot compel specific performance of the contract subject to compensation, unless the difference is insignificant and his conduct has been honest.[151] "If a vendor sues and is in a position to convey substantially what the purchaser has contracted to get, the court will decree specific performance with compensation for any small and immaterial deficiency, provided that the vendor has not, by misrepresentation or otherwise, disentitled himself to his remedy."[152]

Thus, if a contract for sale is made, and investigation of the title shows that the property is subject to restrictive covenants, the vendor cannot force the title on the purchaser subject to compensation,[153] but he can do so, for example, if the sole mistake is that a right of common attached to the land extends only to sheep instead of being, as represented, unlimited.[154]

A purchaser, on the other hand, is in a more favourable position, for as a general rule he is allowed to take all that he can get, and to subject the vendor to a proportionate diminution of the purchase money. But specific performance will not be decreed at the suit of the purchaser if the property which the vendor is in a position to convey is entirely different from that which he agreed to sell, or if the difference is one for which it is impossible to fix pecuniary compensation, or if the effect of decreeing specific performance would be to cause injustice to third parties.[155]

(7) DUTY OF THE PURCHASER TO COMPLETE THE CONTRACT

After the purchaser has investigated the abstract, it is his duty either to accept or to reject the title offered to him. If he takes the latter course, the parties are left to their remedies under the contract.[156] If, however, the purchaser is satisfied with the title, then the contract must be completed in accordance with its terms. Completion of a contract means that the purchaser must at his own expense prepare a proper deed of conveyance which is effectual to pass the interest to be sold and which contains the usual covenants for title by the vendor. He must also tender the price that he has agreed to pay. On the vendor's side completion involves the execution of the conveyance and the delivery of possession of the land to the purchaser.[157]

(8) DUTY OF VENDOR TO DELIVER THE TITLE DEEDS[158]

The vendor must deliver to the purchaser all title deeds which relate solely to the property sold, though he may retain such documents where he retains any part of the land to which

---

[150] Williams, *Vendor and Purchaser*, p. 36. The "parcels clause" contains the physical description of the property sold, which may be accompanied by a plan.

[151] *Cox v Coventon* (1862) 31 Beav 378; *Re Arnold* (1880) 14 Ch D 270 at 279; p. 890, ante.

[152] *Rutherford v Acton-Adams* [1915] AC 866 at 869–70, per Viscount HALDANE.

[153] Cf *Rudd v Lascelles* [1900] 1 Ch 815.   [154] *Howland v Norris* (1784) 1 Cox Eq Cas 59.

[155] *Willmott v Barber* (1880) 15 Ch D 96; *Rudd v Lascelles*, supra, at 819.   [156] Pp. 833 et seq, ante.

[157] Williams, *Vendor and Purchaser*, p. 37; [1991] Conv 15, 81, 185 (D. G. Barnsley); Silverman, *Conveyancing Handbook*, section F.

[158] As to the right to possession of title deeds, see *Clayton v Clayton* [1930] 2 Ch 12.

they relate, or where the document consists of a trust instrument creating a trust that is still subsisting.[159] Where the documents which are necessary to show a good title remain in the vendor's possession, or where their custody belongs to some person other than the vendor, it is the vendor's duty to give a written acknowledgment of the purchaser's right to their production and to delivery of copies and a written undertaking for their safe custody. The effect of such an acknowledgment is that the purchaser, or persons claiming under him, can, at their own expense, demand to see the documents, or claim to be furnished with copies.[160]

(9) DUTY TO DELIVER VACANT POSSESSION

Lastly, it is an implicit term of a contract of sale that vacant possession shall be given to the purchaser on completion.[161] Therefore a refusal by the purchaser to complete is justified if the land is subject to an unexpired tenancy, or if it has been lawfully requisitioned by a public authority.[162]

(c) Conditions of sale under contracts containing special stipulations

We have now described in outline the nature of the parties' obligations under an open contract. Land, however, is not usually sold in this manner. As we have seen,[163] in practice it is usual for the parties to regulate their rights and duties by *special conditions* in the contract of sale. A professionally drawn contract will generally incorporate the terms of Standard Conditions of Sale with variations to meet the particular case. Reference must be made to the standard textbooks on conveyancing for full treatment.[164]

Matters which are commonly the subject of special conditions are:

the root of title and the length of title (although this is less important as a result of the Law of Property Act 1969);[165]

the date upon which possession is to be given, and the consequences if default is made; interest to be payable by the purchaser on the purchase price, if the sale is not completed on the stipulated date; the restriction of the purchaser's remedies for minor misdescriptions; and planning matters.

(2) The Conveyance

(a) Necessity for a deed

We have already seen that a deed is necessary for the creation and transfer of legal estates and interests.[166] A conveyance in unregistered land must therefore be by deed.[167]

---

[159] LPA 1925, s. 45(9).   [160] Ibid., s. 64.

[161] *Cook v Taylor* [1942] Ch 349; *Sheikh v O'Connor* [1987] 2 EGLR 269. See Farrand, *Contract and Conveyance* (4th edn), pp. 174–8; [1988] Conv 324, 400 (C. Harpum).

[162] *Cook v Taylor*, supra; *James Macara Ltd v Barclay* [1945] KB 148; cf *Re Winslow Hall Estates Co and United Glass Bottle Manufacturers Ltd's Contract* [1941] Ch 503; *Hillingdon Estates Co v Stonefield Estates Ltd* [1952] Ch 627; *Topfell Ltd v Galley Properties Ltd* [1979] 1 WLR 446.   [163] P. 857, ante.

[164] See p. 858, nn. 33 and 34, ante.   [165] P. 932, ante.

[166] LPA 1925, s. 52(1); Pp. 896 et seq, ante. For the form of a deed, and its method of execution, see pp. 898 et seq, ante.

[167] In registered land, the deed is not sufficient of itself to pass the legal title, where the disposition is required to be completed by registration: p. 970, post.

(b) Conveyance by a person to himself

It is sometimes necessary that an interest shall be conveyed by the grantor to himself jointly with another person, as for instance where a surviving trustee desires to vest the legal estate in himself and a new trustee. At common law this could not be done by one deed, for the effect of a grant by A to A and B was to vest the whole estate in B. The only solution was that A should convey to X, who would then convey to A and B, though an alternative method became available, and in fact general, under the doctrine of uses, for if A conveyed to X *to the use* of himself and B, the effect of the Statute of Uses was to vest an immediate legal estate in A and B jointly. It has been possible, however, since August 1859 in the case of leaseholds, and since 1881 in the case of freeholds, for a person to convey land to himself jointly with another person by a direct deed of grant, and as the Statute of Uses has been repealed, this is now the only method.[168]

There are also occasions when it is necessary that a person should convey land to himself, as, for example, where personal representatives assent to the land vesting in themselves as trustees of land.[169] Although, in the example given, the design could be effected in a direct manner under statutory provisions, it remained generally true, prior to 1926, that a conveyance by a person to himself required a grant to uses. It is now provided, however, that "a person may convey land to or vest land in himself".[170] This, however, does not enable an owner to grant a tenancy to himself, for a lease, though it falls within the statutory definition of a "conveyance" and no doubt vests a legal estate in the lessee, is essentially a contractual transaction. At the lowest it creates a number of implied obligations and liabilities, a situation that is impossible where only one person is involved. A man cannot contract with himself.[171]

Two or more persons whether trustees or personal representatives or not may convey any property vested in themselves to any one or more of themselves, though if the conveyance amounts to a breach of trust, it is liable to be set aside.[172]

However, in spite of these limitations, a person who holds land as a nominee for his principal may grant a valid lease to that principal.[173]

(c) The form of a deed of conveyance on sale

The deed used for the conveyance on sale of freehold land has taken a traditional form, an example of which was set out and explained in some detail in the 16th edition of this book.[174] The conveyancer will need to understand such a form of conveyance when he is investigating the title to unregistered land, since the title will generally be constituted by documents which were drafted in that form. However, although the traditional form of deed of conveyance may still be used, a simpler form may now be employed. Since the conveyance on sale of

---

[168] LPA 1925, s. 72(1), (2), replacing LP(A)A 1859, s. 21, and Conveyancing Act 1881, s. 50.

[169] *Re King's Will Trusts* [1964] Ch 542.   [170] LPA 1925, s. 72(3).

[171] *Rye v Rye* [1962] AC 496, M & B p. 521; (1962) 78 LQR 175 (P. V. Baker).   [172] LPA 1925, s. 72(4).

[173] *Ingram v IRC* [2000] 1 AC 293 (as part of an inheritance avoidance scheme HL held that Lady Ingram's solicitor, as nominee for her, granted a valid lease to her. The tax advantage has been negatived by FA 1999, s. 104); (1999) 115 LQR 351 (R. Kerridge). The convincing dissenting judgment of MILLETT LJ in CA was approved: [1997] STC 1234 at 1255.

See Lord RADCLIFFE in *Rye v Rye*, supra at 511: "In effect, putting aside conveyancing forms, a man was able to convey to himself before the 1925 Act. He could, of course, put land in trust for himself by conveying it to a nominee, and, I suppose, if there was any conceivable point in the operation, he could similarly demise land to a nominee." Cf *Kildrummy (Jersey) Ltd v IRC* [1990] STC 657, where it was held by the Court of Session that land could not be demised to a nominee. *Rye v Rye* was not cited.

[174] Pp. 847–55. It is not reproduced here for lack of space. See also Silverman, *Conveyancing Handbook*, para. 1.12.

unregistered land will trigger the compulsory registration of the title, it is possible to use one of the standard Land Registry forms of transfer.[175] Where, for example, the conveyance is by the freehold owner, and of the whole of the title comprised in the previous conveyance to him, Form TR1 can be used. An example of this form,[176] together with the an explanation of some of its key provisions, and an account of the procedures which are necessary for the first registration of the title, are set out in the following section on registered conveyancing.

B Registered Conveyancing[177]

We have already considered the system of registered conveyancing in outline.[178] We must now discuss it in more detail. This chapter explains the current regime under the Land Registration Act 2002 and the Land Registration Rules 2003, which came into force on 13 October 2003, although reference will be made where appropriate to the earlier regime under the Land Registration Act 1925, either by way of comparison and contrast, or because the new regime carries over principles from the old which render decisions on the 1925 Act still relevant to the interpretation of the new Act. For a detailed discussion of the 1925 Act, however, reference must be made to the previous edition of this book.[179]

---

[175] Land Registry Practice Guide 1, section 7; Silverman, *Conveyancing Handbook*, para. 1.3.6; *Encyclopaedia of Forms and Precedents*, vol. 37, Form 10. Conveyancers are, however, reluctant to depart from the traditional forms: Emmet, para. 13.000–1.2   [176] P. 964, post.

[177] For the current regime in relation to registered land under LRA 2002, see Ruoff and Roper, *Registered Conveyancing* (2003 looseleaf edn); Harpum and Bignell, *Registered Land: The New Law* and *Registered Land: Law and Practice under the Land Registration Act 2002*; Wolstenholme and Cherry's *Annotated Land Registration Act 2002*, which contains LRA 1925 and 2002, and LRR 1925 and 2003; Wontner's *Guide to Land Registry Practice*; Abbey and Richards, *Blackstone's Guide to the Land Registration Act 2002*; Cooke, *The New Law of Land Registration*; Current Law Statutes 2002 (chap. 9) annotated by P. H. Kenny; [2002] Conv 11 (E. Cooke); [2003] Conv 136 (M. Dixon); Law Commission Consultative Document on Land Registration for the Twenty-First Century 1998 (Law Com No. 254); Law Commission Report on Land Registration for the Twenty-First Century—a Conveyancing Revolution 2001 (Law Com No. 271). The Land Registry produces Practice Guides on many aspects of its practice and procedure, and the Chief Land Registrar publishes an Annual Report; the current versions can be viewed on the Land Registry web site. For the Land Registry, see LRA 2002, Part 10 and Sch. 7; R & R, paras. 2.001–2.003; H & B, Part 8; and for the new office of Adjudicator, whose function is to determine contested applications to the registrar which cannot be disposed of by agreement between the parties, see LRA 2002, Part 11 and Sch. 9; R & R, para. 2.004; H & B, Part 7. Adverse possession under the new regime of LRA 2002 has already been discussed: pp. 145, et seq, ante.

For the law as it used to be under LRA 1925 and before LRA 2002, see Ruoff and Roper, *Law and Practice of Registered Conveyancing* (1991 looseleaf edn, updated to 2002 before its replacement by the new 2003 looseleaf edn); Ruoff and Pryer, *Concise Land Registration Handbook*; Wolstenholme and Cherry, *Conveyancing Statutes* (13th edn), vol. 6; Barnsley, *Conveyancing Law and Practice*, chaps. 2, 3, 4, 11, 15; Potter, *Principles and Practice of Conveyancing under the Land Registration 1925* (1934; 2nd edn, 1948); Brickdale and Stewart-Wallace, *The Land Registration Act 1925*. M & B chap. 2 contains extracts from both LRA 1925 and LRA 2002, and cases and other materials relating to them, for purposes of comparison.

For earlier proposals of the Law Commission on registered conveyancing, see the first report 1983 (Law Com No. 125) on Identity and Boundaries, Conversion of Title, the Treatment of Leases and the Minor Interests Index; second report 1985 on Inspection of the Register (Law Com No. 148); third report 1987 on Overriding Interests, Rectification and Indemnity and Minor Interests (Law Com No. 158); [1987] Conv 334 (R. J. Smith). The recommendations on the last three topics of the 1983 Report were implemented in LRA 1986, and the 1985 Report was implemented in LRA 1988. The fourth report 1988 (Law Com No. 173) presented a Land Registration Bill incorporating the recommendations of the third report and "is a modern, and we hope, simpler version of the 1925 Act". In advance of this, the Law Commission published in 1995 a First Report on the Implementation of its Third and Fourth Reports (Law Com No. 235); and this was implemented in LRA 1997.

[178] Pp. 100, et seq, ante.   [179] 16th edn (2000), pp. 100–8, 855–76.

(1) The Register

(a) Scope of title registration

The Land Registration Act 2002 carries over the register which has been built up under the 1925 Act,[180] although it redefines the scope of titles which may now be registered. No change is made to the principle that only legal estates and interests may be registered with an individual register. But now the list of registrable estates is:[181]

(i)   a legal estate in land (the fee simple and certain leases);

(ii) a rentcharge;[182]

(iii) a franchise;[183]

(iv) a profit à prendre in gross.[184]

Franchises and profits à prendre are now registrable for the first time with separate titles. Manors, which were registrable under the 1925 Act, are no longer registrable.[185] In the following sections we shall focus on the registration of freehold and leasehold estates in land, which form the vast majority of registered titles.

(b) Arrangement of the register

The individual register for each registered estate has a separate title number, and is divided into three parts.[186] The *property register* must contain a description of the registered estate, by reference to a plan,[187] together with certain other matters such as easements and

---

[180] LRA 2002, s. 1(1). The register may be kept in electronic and/or paper form: LRR 2003, r. 2(1); although the last uncomputerised register was converted in 2003–4, and the Land Register is now fully electronic: Land Registry Annual Report 2004–05, p. 53.

[181] Ibid., s. 2(a), 3(1); LRR 2003, r. 2(2). A legal charge over a registered estate can also be registered but not as a separate title.   [182] Chap. 21, ante.

[183] A 'royal privilege or branch of the royal prerogative subsisting in the hands of a subject by grant from the King': *Spook Erection Ltd v Secretary of State for the Environment* [1989] QB 300 at 305, per NOURSE LJ. The most important franchise is that of the market. See Land Registry Practice Guide 18; *R (Corporation of London) v Secretary of State for the Environment, Food and Rural Affairs* [2005] 1 WLR 1286 (Covent Garden market, now operated under statutory authority).   [184] I.e., a profit without a dominant tenement: p. 641, ante.

[185] LRR 1925, rr. 50, 51. A manor which was registered under LRA 1925 may now be removed from the register on the application of the proprietor: LRA 2002, s. 119. See generally Land Registry Practice Guide 22.

[186] LRR 2003, r. 4(1), (2). If an entry in the register refers to a plan or other document the registrar must keep the original or a copy: ibid., r. 4(3). The tripartite register follows the pattern set by LRA 1925; p. 104, ante. There is also (a) an index which records all registered estates and land affected by any caution against first registration: LRA 2002, s. 68; LRR 2003, r. 10; (b) an index of proprietors' names: LRR 2003, r. 11; (c) the day list showing the date and time at which every pending application was made and of every application for an official search with priority under LRR 2003, r. 147: ibid., r. 12; (d) a register of cautions against first registration: LRA 2002, s. 19.

[187] Ibid., r. 5(1)(a). No plan is required for a registered profit à prendre. See also LRA 2002, s. 60: boundary shown for purposes of the register is a general boundary and does not determine the exact line of the boundary which may, however, be fixed in accordance with s. 60(3), (4); LRR 2003, rr. 117–23; R & R, chap. 5; Law Commission Report on Registered Land for the Twenty-First Century 2001 (Law Com No. 271), paras. 9.9–9.15; *Chadwick v Abbotswood Properties Ltd* [2005] 1 P & CR 10 (reviewing the authorities). See also s. 61 (accretion and diluvion; on which, see *Southern Centre of Theosophy Inc v State of South Australia* [1982] AC 706 at 716, per Lord WILBERFORCE).

See *Alan Wibberley Building Ltd v Insley* [1999] 1 WLR 894 at 895, per Lord HOFFMANN: "boundary disputes are a particularly painful form of litigation. Feelings run high and disproportionate amounts of money are spent. Claims to small and valueless pieces of land are pressed with the zeal of Fortinbras's army".

covenants benefiting the registered estate.[188] The *proprietorship register* must state the class of title,[189] the name and address of the proprietor, and certain other matters such as restrictions affecting the disposition of the estate, a note of positive or indemnity covenants affecting the estate, and (where practicable) the price paid on the most recent change of proprietor.[190] The *charges register* must contain, where appropriate, details of leases, charges and any other interests which adversely affect the registered estate.[191]

(c) Inspection of the register

The registers of title, documents which are referred to in the registers, and the register of cautions against first registration[192] are open to the public. Any person may inspect them and make copies of them, although certain documents which contain prejudicial information may be excluded.[193] A purchaser may make an application for an official search with priority: in this case, any entry made in the register during the priority period relating to his application is postponed to any entry made in pursuance of it.[194]

(2) First Registration of Title

(a) Compulsory registration

We have seen[195] that in 1990 compulsory registration was extended to the whole of England and Wales; and that, in pursuance of the policy of eventually producing a complete register of the title to the whole of the territory, certain transactions with unregistered land have been defined by successive enactments as requiring the title to be placed on the register. Under the Land Registration Act 2002, these triggers for compulsory registration are:[196]

(a) the transfer[197] of a "qualifying estate"—that is, an unregistered legal freehold or leasehold which (at the time of the transfer, grant or creation) has more than seven years to run;[198]

(b) the transfer of an unregistered legal estate in land in circumstances where section 171A of the Housing Act 1985 applies (disposal by landlord which leads to a person no longer being a secure tenant);

---

[188] LRR 2003, r. 5(1)(b). The property register of a registered leasehold estate must contain particulars of the lease to enable it to be identified, and any registered rentcharge, franchise or profit à prendre which was created by an instrument must contain particulars to enable the instrument to be identified: rr. 6, 7.

[189] P. 956, post.

[190] LRR 2003, r. 8. The reference to the price is removed if there is a change in the register of title which the registrar considers would result in the entry being misleading: r. 8(2).   [191] Ibid., r. 9.

[192] N. 186, supra.   [193] LRA 2002, ss. 66–7; LRR 2003, rr. 133–9; Land Registry Practice Guide 11.

[194] LRA 2002, ss. 70, 72; LRR 2003, rr. 147–54. An official search may also be made without priority: r. 155. For the priority period, see r. 131 (broadly, thirty business days excluding weekends). Searches may be made by post, telephone, fax, electronically or orally at a Land Registry Customer Information Centre. See generally Land Registry Practice Guide 12.   [195] P. 101, ante.

[196] LRA 2002, s. 4(1).

[197] This includes a transfer for valuable or other consideration, by way of gift or in pursuance of an order of any court, or by means of an assent (including a vesting assent): s. 4(1); but not a transfer by operation of law: s. 4(3); nor the assignment of a mortgage term, nor the assignment or surrender of a lease to the owner of the immediate reversion where the term is to merge in that reversion: s. 4(4). On "valuable consideration", see s. 4 (6), 132(1). A transfer by way of gift includes a transfer or grant (a) constituting a trust under which the settlor does not retain the whole of the beneficial interest (thus excluding a transfer to trustees on bare trust), or (b) uniting the bare legal title and the beneficial interests under a trust which was so constituted: s. 4(7).

[198] LRA 2002, s. 4(2).

(c) the grant out of a qualifying estate of an estate in land (i) for a term of years absolute of more than seven years from the date of the grant, and (ii) for valuable or other consideration, by way of gift or in pursuance of an order of any court;[199]

(d) the grant out of a qualifying estate of an estate in land for a term of years absolute to take effect in possession after the end of the period of three months beginning with the date of the grant;

(e) the grant of a lease in pursuance of Part 5 of the Housing Act 1985 (the right to buy) out of an unregistered legal estate in land;

(f) the grant of a lease out of an unregistered legal estate in land in such circumstances as are mentioned in paragraph (b) above;

(g) the creation of a protected first legal mortgage of a qualifying estate.[200]

The Land Registry aims to create a register with comprehensive content and national coverage by 2012.[201] The operation of these triggers for compulsory registration will not alone achieve this, since there are very many estates in land which are still unregistered and which, if not registered voluntarily,[202] are unlikely to be subject to any disposition triggering compulsory registration before then—such as land held by companies or by charities.[203] To this end, the Land Registration Act[204] empowers the Lord Chancellor by order to add further events as triggers for compulsory registration.[205]

(b) Voluntary registration

Even if no event occurs in relation to an unregistered estate which triggers compulsory registration, the owner[206] of a registrable estate[207] may apply to be registered as its proprietor.[208] To encourage voluntary registration, the fees payable to the Land Registry on first registration are reduced.[209]

(c) Demesne land of the Crown. Special rules[210]

The principles of registered conveyancing apply to the registration of legal *estates* in land. It will be recalled that, under the doctrine of estates peculiar to English land law, the holder of the

---

[199] But not including the grant of an estate by way of mortgage: s. 4(5).

[200] I.e., a mortgage which takes effect on its creation as a mortgage to be protected by the deposit of documents relating to the mortgaged estate, and which ranks ahead of any other mortgages then affecting the mortgaged estate: s. 4(8).   [201] Annual Report 2004–05, p. 50.

[202] Infra.

[203] In 2004–5 the Land Registry met with a number of large landholders, including the Crown Estate, Port of London Authority, Imperial College, a number of utility companies, Peak District National Park, Highways Agency, Blenheim Estate, Christ Church Oxford, and Boots plc to encourage them to consider the benefits of voluntary registration: Annual Report 2004–05, p. 50.   [204] S. 5.

[205] The power is to be exercised by Statutory Instrument: s. 128.

[206] Or a person entitled to require the estate to be vested in him: s. 3(2)(b).

[207] The fee simple absolute or a leasehold with more than seven years still to run (and as long as the right to possession is not discontinuous); or a rentcharge, franchise or profit à prendre in gross (in each case granted for an interest equivalent to a fee simple absolute or for a term of years with more than seven years still to run).

[208] LRA 2002, s. 3.   [209] LR Fee Order 2004 (SI 2004 No. 595), art. 2.

[210] R & R, chap. 40; H & B, chap. 6; Law Commission Report on Registered Land for the Twenty-First Century 2001 (Law Com No. 271), paras. 11.2–11.38. See also LRA 2002 ss. 81 (Demesne land: cautions against

estate does not own the land as such, but holds as tenant of the Crown.[211] A corollary of this is that the Crown does not hold an estate in "demesne land"—land which it holds in its capacity as ultimate feudal overlord. Before the 2002 Act demesne land could not therefore be registered. Now, however,[212] "Her Majesty may grant an estate in fee simple absolute in possession out of demesne land to Herself" and this will then be capable of being registered.[213]

(d) Classes of title[214]

As under the Land Registration Act 1925,[215] there are four different classes of title which may be entered on the proprietorship register; absolute, qualified, possessory and good leasehold.[216]

(1) ABSOLUTE TITLE

(i) Freehold estates

In the case of a freehold estate, a person may be registered with absolute title if the registrar is of the opinion that the person's title to the estate is such as a willing buyer could properly be advised by a competent professional adviser to accept, and in applying this test the registrar may disregard the fact that the title appears to be open to objection if he is of the opinion that the defect will not cause the holding under the title to be disturbed.[217] The registrar must therefore carry out a full investigation of the title as it exists under the old system of unregistered conveyancing for one last time before it is placed on the register, since he will be acting on behalf of the State in giving the guarantee of the status of the title by accepting it for registration.

The effect of first registration with absolute title is[218] to vest the freehold estate in the proprietor together with all interests subsisting for the benefit of the estate, and subject only to the following interests affecting the estate at the time of registration:

(a) interests which are the subject of an entry in the register in relation to the estate—notices, restrictions, or registered charges. If, on investigating the title to the (unregistered) estate, the registrar discovers that there are third party interests affecting the title, he will make such entries as are appropriate to protect the interest of the third party, so that the registered title continues to reflect the state of the title as it existed before registration;[219] and

(b) unregistered interests which fall within any of the paragraphs of Schedule 1 to the Land Registration Act 2002 (unregistered interests which override first registration);[220] and

---

first registration); 82 (Escheat etc); 83 (Crown and Duchy land: representation); 84 (Disapplication of requirements relating to Duchy land); 85 (Bona vacantia).

[211] Pp. 15 et seq, ante.   [212] LRA 2002, s. 79(1).

[213] This is a form of voluntary registration, since it takes effect only if Her Majesty then applies for registration within a prescribed period (normally two months): s. 79(2)–(5). Other grants of a fee simple or of a leasehold for more than seven years out of demesne land are subject to compulsory registration: ibid., s. 80.

[214] On classes of title, see R & R, chap. 6; H & B, chap. 3; Law Commission Report on Registered Land for the Twenty-First Century 2001 (Law Com No. 271), paras. 3.42–3.52; and on the effect of registration with each class of title, see R & R, paras. 3.007–3.008; H & B, chap. 4.   [215] P. 105, ante.

[216] LRA 2002, ss. 9, 10.   [217] Ibid., s. 9(2), (3).   [218] Ibid., s. 11(2)–(4).

[219] For details of entries on the register, see p. 973, post.   [220] Pp. 976 et seq, post.

(c) interests acquired under the Limitation Act 1980[221] of which the proprietor has notice.[222]

If the proprietor is not entitled to the estate for his own benefit, or at least not solely for his own benefit—for example, if he is holds the legal estate on trust for himself and his wife[223]—then as between himself and the person(s) beneficially entitled to the estate, the estate is vested in him subject to their interests of which he has notice.[224]

(ii) Leasehold estates

In the case of a leasehold, an absolute title may be registered only if the registrar approves not only the title to the leasehold itself, but also the lessor's title to grant the lease.[225]

The effect of first registration with absolute title is[226] to vest the leasehold estate in the proprietor together with all interests subsisting for the benefit of the estate, and subject to the same interests as in the case of the registration of the freehold with absolute title, but subject also to implied and express covenants, obligations and liabilities incident to the leasehold estate.[227]

(2) GOOD LEASEHOLD TITLE

Good leasehold title is available only for leaseholds. Where a leaseholder cannot produce the title to the reversion,[228] he may be registered as the owner of a good leasehold title. The title to the leasehold interest is alone investigated and guaranteed by the Land Registry, if the registrar is of the opinion that the person's title to the estate is such as a willing buyer could properly be advised by a competent professional adviser to accept.[229]

Registration with good leasehold title has the same effect as registration with absolute title, with the important exception that registration does not affect the enforcement of any estate, right or interest affecting, or in derogation of, the title of the lessor to grant the lease.[230]

(3) QUALIFIED TITLE

Where the registrar is of the opinion that the person's title to the freehold estate can be established only for a limited period or subject to certain reservations which cannot be disregarded, he may register the person with qualified title.[231] Qualified title may also be registered in respect of a leasehold estate, when the examination of the title either of the lessor to the reversion, or of the lessee to the leasehold interest, discloses similar problems to those described above.[232]

---

[221] Chap. 6, ante.

[222] This is a significant change from LRA 1925, under which the rights of squatters bound the registered proprietor whether or not he had notice: H & B, paras. 4.5–4.6; Explanatory Notes on the Land Registration Bill, cited Wolstenholme and Cherry, *Annotated Land Registration Act 2002*, para. 3–011.

[223] It may also include a case where another party has an equity arising by proprietary estoppel: H & B, para. 4.7.

[224] LRA 2002, s. 11(5).

[225] Ibid., s. 10(2). Again, the registrar may disregard possible objections if of the opinion that the defect will not cause the holding under the title to be disturbed: s. 10(4).   [226] Ibid., s. 12(2)–(5).

[227] The details of the covenants in the lease are not entered onto the register, but the lease itself (or a copy) forms part of the register and so can be inspected.

[228] If the reversion is already registered with absolute title, this will suffice. If not, the registrar must examine the title to the reversion if absolute title is sought to the leasehold estate.

[229] LRA 2002, s. 10(3). Again, the registrar may disregard possible objections if of the opinion that the defect will not cause the holding under the title to be disturbed: s. 10(4).   [230] Ibid., s. 12(6).

[231] Ibid., s. 9(4).   [232] Ibid., s. 10(5).

Registration has the same effect as registration with absolute title, except that it does not affect the enforcement of any estate, right or interest which appears from the register to be excepted from the effect of registration.[233]

(4) POSSESSORY TITLE

Possessory titles usually arise out of claims by squatters, and also where a title is lodged which is too weak for a better kind of title but not deserving of outright rejection—for example, where the owner has lost the title deeds. Possessory titles are mainly freeholds, although possessory leaseholds do exist. In either case, a person may be registered with possessory title if the registrar is of the opinion that the person is in actual possession of the land, or in receipt of the rents and profits of the land, by virtue of the estate, and that there is no other class of title with which be may be registered.[234]

The guarantee is a limited one, as the registration, whilst in other respects having the same effect as registration with absolute title, does not affect the enforcement of any estate, right or interest adverse to, or in derogation of, the proprietor's title subsisting or capable of arising at the time of the first registration.[235] In the case of a freehold or leasehold interest registered with a possessory title the guarantee covers, therefore, only dealings which take place after the registration and does not extend to the title prior to registration.

(5) UPGRADING OF TITLES

The Land Registration Act 2002 provides for the upgrading of inferior titles to absolute or good leasehold titles, and of good leasehold to absolute.[236] If at any time the registrar is satisfied as to the title to the estate, to the same standard as he is required to be satisfied on first registration,[237] then he may enter it as the superior title. In addition, where the title to a freehold or leasehold estate has been entered as possessory for at least twelve years,[238] the registrar may enter it as absolute or good leasehold if he is satisfied that the proprietor is in possession of the land. This reflects the idea that any existing rights adverse to the proprietor will have become barred under the Limitation Act 1980 no later than twelve years from the date of registration.[239]

(e) Cautions against first registration

Any person who claims to have an interest in an unregistered legal estate[240] may apply for a caution against first registration of title to the estate.[241] The object is to ensure that on first registration his interest will be protected on the register. The caution gives the cautioner the right to be notified of the application and to object to it. It is a procedural device, and gives no substantive right.[242]

---

[233] LRA 2002, ss. 11(6) (freehold), 12(7) (leasehold).   [234] Ibid., ss. 9(5) (freehold), 10(6) (leasehold).

[235] Ibid., ss. 11(7) (freehold), 12(8) (leasehold); *Spectrum Investment Co v Holmes* [1981] 1 WLR 221, M & B p. 245; p. 144, ante.   [236] LRA 2002, s. 62. The effect of registration is not retrospective: s. 63.

[237] Ibid., s. 62(8).

[238] The Lord Chancellor has power to amend the number by Statutory Instrument: ibid., ss. 62(9), 128.

[239] Although the Limitation Act 1980 does not apply to registered land under LRA 2002, it does apply to matters excepted from the effect of registration (such as rights then existing superior to the possessory title of the registered proprietor). On adverse possession generally, see chap. 6, ante.

[240] I.e., an estate which qualifies for individual registration: an estate in land, a rentcharge, franchise, or profit à prendre in gross: LRA 2002, s. 15(2).   [241] LRA 2002, s. 15

[242] LRR 2003, rr. 39–53; R & R, chap. 11; H & B, chap. 5; Law Commission Report on Registered Land for the Twenty-First Century 2001 (Law Com No. 271), paras. 3.54–3.65. See also LRA 2002, ss. 19 (register of cautions

(f) Conclusiveness of the register

The fundamental principle of the system of registration of title is that the register is conclusive as to the legal title of the registered proprietor to the estate which is registered in his name. If the person registered as proprietor would not (apart from the registration) be the owner of the legal estate, the estate is deemed to be vested in him as a result of the registration.[243]

If, therefore, a person is registered by mistake, or if a transaction by which he claims to have acquired the estate is a nullity, the defect is cured by registration. As long as his name appears as registered proprietor, in the eyes of the law (and as far as third parties are concerned, who search the register) he is proprietor. However, this provision deals only with the legal estate, and does not determine what equitable rights the registered owner's title may be subject to.[244] Moreover, the Land Registration Act 2002 provides for the register to be altered in certain circumstances, to correct errors. To this we now turn.

(g) Alteration and rectification of the register

(1) RECTIFICATION UNDER THE 1925 ACT

The Land Registration Act 1925 made detailed provision for *rectification* of the register.[245] Under section 82 of the Land Registration Act 1925, the register could be rectified, *inter alia*, where the court so ordered upon deciding that any person was entitled to any estate, right or interest in the land,[246] where an entry had been obtained by fraud,[247] where two or more persons were by mistake registered as proprietors of the same property, where a legal estate had been registered in the name of a person who, if the land had not been registered, would

against first registration), 20, 21 (alteration of cautions register by court and by registrar). For transitional provisions, see Sch. 12, paras. 4, 14–17.

[243] LRA 2002, s. 58(1), replacing LRA 1925, s. 69(1). All the registration requirements must be met before the registration has effect; e.g. the registration of person as proprietor of a registered lease is not effective until a note has been entered also on the title to the reversion, if it is registered: s. 58(2). Until satisfaction of the registration requirements, the transaction has effect only in equity: s. 27(1); p. 970, post.

[244] In *Malory Enterprises Ltd v Cheshire Homes (UK) Ltd* [2002] Ch 216 the CA went so far as to say that transfer which is a nullity is not a "disposition" for the purposes of LRA 1925, s. 20, and therefore the registration of the transferee as proprietor, though vesting the legal estate in him under LRA 1925, s. 69 (the predecessor to LRA 2002, s. 58), only vested the *bare* legal title on trust for the person entitled. See criticism by Harpum in Getzler, *Rationalizing Property, Equity and Trusts*, chap. 9; H & B, chap. 15.

[245] See *Norwich and Peterborough Building Society v Steed* [1993] Ch 116, M & B p. 183 for a full examination of the eight statutory grounds; *Ruoff and Roper* (1991 edn), chap. 40; Farrand, *Contract and Conveyance* (2nd edn), pp. 209–20; Barnsley, *Conveyancing Law and Practice*, chap. 4. For further powers of rectification under LRR 1925, see r. 13 (clerical errors), r. 14 (registration in error of too much land), r. 131 (where power of disposing of registered land has become vested in some person other than the proprietor), r. 283 (correction of particulars of addresses), r. 284 (corrections of plans), r. 285 (alterations to resolve conflicting descriptions). See also Law Commission Report on Land Registration for the Twenty-First Century 2001 (Law Com No. 271), para. 10.1; *Malory Enterprises Ltd v Cheshire Homes (UK) Ltd*, supra, at [79] (there is no jurisdiction to order rectification with retrospective effect: per ARDEN LJ); (2004) 119 LQR 31 (D. Sheehan).

[246] *Chowood Ltd v Lyall (No 2)* [1930] 2 Ch 156; *Calgary and Edmonton Land Co Ltd v Discount Bank (Overseas) Ltd* [1971] 1 WLR 81; *Proctor v Kidman* (1986) 51 P & CR 67. See also *Spectrum Investment Co v Holmes* [1981] 1 WLR 221, M & B p. 245, p. 144, ante; *Orakpo v Manson Investments Ltd* [1977] 1 WLR 347; affd on other grounds [1978] AC 95.

[247] *Argyle Building Society v Hammond* (1984) 49 P & CR 148; (transfer void for forgery); [1985] Conv 135 (A. Sydenham); LRA 1925, s. 114; cf *Norwich and Peterborough Building Society v Steed* [1993] Ch 116 (transfer voidable for fraud); (1993) 109 LQR 187 (R. J. Smith); [1992] Conv 293 (C. Davis). See also *Re Leighton's Conveyance* [1936] 1 All ER 667; affd [1937] Ch 149 (fraudulent misrepresentation and undue influence).

not have been the estate owner,[248] or where, because of any error or omission in the register or because of any entry made under a mistake it would be deemed just to rectify it.[249] The *proprietor in possession*, however, was protected by the provision that rectification could only take place against him if:

(a) it was to give effect to an overriding interest,[250] or an order of the court,[251] or

(b) he had caused or substantially contributed to the error or omission by fraud or lack of proper care,[252] or

(c) for any other reason, it would be unjust not to rectify the register against him.[253]

The principle which emerges is that a *purchaser* who bought registered land and remained in *possession* of it was guaranteed his possession, and rectification would only be ordered against him in exceptional circumstances.

(2) ALTERATION AND RECTIFICATION UNDER THE 2002 ACT[254]

The provisions have been recast under the Land Registration Act 2002 so as to reflect the present practice in relation to rectification and amendment of the register. The essentials of the scheme of the 1925 Act are, however, maintained.

The basic concept is now *alteration* of the register; rectification is one form of alteration. The court may make an order for the alteration of the register for the purpose of correcting a mistake, bringing the register up to date, or giving effect to any estate, right or interests excepted from the effect of registration.[255] The registrar has similar powers, and may also alter the register to remove a superfluous entry.[256] It can therefore be seen that alteration of the register is a very general term which embraces both major changes and minor corrections to tidy up the register.

Rectification is defined[257] as an alteration which:

(a) involves the correction of a mistake; and

(b) prejudicially affects the title of a registered proprietor.

In such a case, the court may not order, nor may the registrar make, any alteration to the register without the proprietor's consent in relation to land in his possession unless he has by fraud or lack of proper care caused or substantially contributed to the mistake, or it

---

[248] *Chowood Ltd v Lyall (No 2)* [1930] 2 Ch 156.

[249] *Re Dances Way, West Town, Hayling Island* [1962] Ch 490 (notice of adverse easement cancelled).

[250] *Re Chowood's Registered Land* [1933] Ch 574, M & B p. 193; *Epps v Esso Petroleum Co Ltd* [1973] 1 WLR 1071, M & B p. 189.

[251] As added by AJA 1977, s. 24(a); *Hayes v Nwajiaku* [1994] EGCS 106 (proprietor means proprietor of land, not of charge).

[252] As substituted by AJA 1977, s. 24(b). The original statutory provision had produced the undesirable result of rectification being ordered against a purchaser who innocently put forward a misleading description of property when applying for first registration of his title: *Re Deptford High Street (No 139)* [1951] Ch 884. See also *Re Seaview Gardens* [1967] 1 WLR 134.

[253] *Epps v Esso Petroleum Co Ltd*, supra; *Hounslow LBC v Hare* (1990) 24 HLR 9; [1993] Conv 224 (J. Martin); *Horrill v Cooper* (1998) 78 P & CR 336.

[254] R & R, chap. 46; H & B, chap. 22; Law Commission Report on Land Registration for the Twenty-First Century 2001 (Law Com No. 271), Part X; Land Registry Practice Guide 39.

[255] LRA 2002, Sch. 4, para. 2. The effect of alteration on priorities is prospective, not retrospective: ibid., para. 8.

[256] Ibid., para. 5.   [257] Ibid., para. 1.

would for any other reason be unjust for the alteration not to be made.[258] The protection of the proprietor in possession is therefore maintained.

(3) INDEMNITY[259]

Under the 1925 Act[260] right of indemnity—payment of compensation—was available to anyone suffering loss by reason of any rectification of the register, an error or omission on the register which was not rectified, the loss or destruction of any document lodged at the registry for inspection or safe custody, or an error in any official search.

Again, the Land Registration Act 2002 maintains the essential elements of the scheme, although the provisions are recast. Schedule 8 sets out the eight grounds on which an indemnity may be paid for loss suffered by reason of:

(a) rectification of the register,

(b) a mistake whose correction would involve rectification of the register,

(c) a mistake in an official search,

(d) a mistake in an official copy,

(e) a mistake in a document kept by the registrar which is not an original and is referred to in the register,

(f) the loss or destruction of a document lodged at the registry for inspection or safe custody,

(g) a mistake in the cautions register, or

(h) failure by the registrar to perform his duty under section 50 (duty to give notice of the creation of a statutory charge).

It is important to notice that, compensation is paid when someone *suffers loss by reason of* a rectification, etc. Hence, when a purchaser bought registered land on part of which, unknown to the purchaser, a squatter had already established a title by adverse possession and rectification was ordered (because the right was an overriding interest), the purchaser was unable to obtain an indemnity under the 1925 Act because his loss was not "by reason of the rectification" but had resulted from the purchase itself,[261] that is, because he had purchased land from a vendor against whom a squatter had already obtained title so that the rectification made him no worse off than before. If someone still suffers loss, even though the register has been rectified in his favour, he can claim an indemnity.[262] If, however, a proprietor of a registered estate or charge claims in good faith under a disposition which is forged and the register is rectified against him, he is deemed to have suffered loss by reason of the rectification.[263] But no compensation is

---

[258] LRA 2002, Sch. 4, paras. 3, 6; *Sainsbury's Supermarkets Ltd v Olympia Homes Ltd* [2006] 1 p d CR 17; *James Hay Pension Trustees Ltd v Cooper Estates Ltd* [2005] All ER (D) 144 (Jan) (proprietor in possession was accidental owner of small piece of land it never intended to acquire, useful only to extract ransom payment: transfer and register rectified).

[259] R & R, chap. 47; H & B, chap. 23; Law Commission Report on Land Registration for the Twenty-First Century 2001 (Law Com No. 271), Part X; Land Registry Practice Guide 39.

[260] LRA 1925, s. 83, as substituted by Land Registration Act 1997, s. 2; (1997) 147 NLJ 925 (H. W. Wilkinson).

[261] *Re Chowood's Registered Land* [1933] Ch 574, M & B p. 193; applied in *Re Boyle's Claim* [1961] 1 WLR 339. The Limitation Act 1980 is now however disapplied in relation to registered land: LRA 2002, s. 96; p. 145, ante.

[262] LRA 2002 Sch. 8, para. 1(1)(b), (3); H & B, para. 23.4. The predecessor to this provision, LRA 1925, s. 83(1)(b), was introduced by LRA 1997 so as to avoid a potential injustice arising from *Freer v Unwins Ltd* [1976] Ch 288 (where it was held that the rectification of the register of title to servient land by the entry of a notice of restrictive covenants does not operate retrospectively so as to bind a person taking under a prior registered disposition for valuable consideration). See (1976) 40 Conv (NS) 304 (F. R. Crane); 126 NLJ 523 (S. M. Cretney).   [263] Ibid., Sch. 8, para. 1(2)(b).

payable on account of any loss suffered by a claimant wholly or partly as a result of his fraud or wholly as a result of his own lack of proper care. Where any loss is suffered by a claimant partly as a result of his own lack of proper care "any indemnity payable to him is to be reduced to such extent as is fair having regard to his share in the responsibility for the loss".[264]

Any fraud or lack of proper care on the part of a person from whom the claimant derives title (except by a disposition for valuable consideration which is registered or protected by an entry on the register) is to be treated as if it were that of the claimant. An example is a donee or a devisee under a will.[265]

For the purposes of limitation, the period under the Limitation Act 1980 is six years; the cause of action arises when the claimant knows, or but for his own default, might have known, of the existence of his claim.[266]

Finally, where indemnity has been paid in respect of any loss, the registrar is given rights to recover the amount paid from any person who caused or substantially contributed to the loss by his fraud and to enforce any right of action which the claimant would have had.[267]

A macabre example of a refusal to rectify leading to a true owner being given indemnity is provided by the case of the acid bath murderer, Haigh.[268] Haigh forged the signature of a registered proprietor, was registered in his name and then, in that name, sold to an innocent purchaser for value. Rectification was not ordered as the purchaser was in possession. But the personal representatives of the real proprietor were compensated in full.

(3) Dispositions of Registered Land

Once the title to an estate has been registered, the rules of unregistered conveyancing[269] become irrelevant, and the estate will thereafter be transferred or otherwise disposed of under the provisions of the Land Registration Act 2002.

(a) Owner's powers in relation to a registered estate

The Act provides[270] that "owner's powers" in relation to a registered estate consist of

(a) power to make a disposition of any kind permitted by the general law in relation to an interest of that description, other than a mortgage by demise or sub-demise, and

(b) power to charge the estate at law with the payment of money.

In other words, the registered proprietor has the same general powers of disposition as an unregistered estate owner—with the single exception that he cannot create a mortgage by demise.[271] The proprietor's right to exercise these powers is to be taken to be free from any limitation affecting the validity of the disposition, unless the limitation is reflected by an entry in the register or otherwise imposed by or under the Act.[272] This follows from the

---

[264] In effect, contributory negligence, similar to the test under the Law Reform (Contributory Negligence) Act 1945.   [265] LRA 2002, Sch. 8, para. 5.

[266] Ibid., para. 8.   [267] Ibid., para. 10.   [268] Recounted in Ruoff and Roper (5th edn 1986), p. 71.

[269] Pp. 931 et seq, ante.

[270] LRA 2002, s. 23(1). See also s. 23(2) (owner's powers in relation to a registered charge). The person entitled to exercise these powers is the registered proprietor or a person entitled to be registered as the proprietor of the estate: s. 24.

[271] For the abolition in registered land of the (already obsolescent) mortgage by demise, see pp. 724–5, ante.

[272] LRA 2002, s. 26. This does not affect the lawfulness of any disposition (e.g. if it is in breach of trust, the trustee may be personally liable to the beneficiaries), but has effect to prevent the title of a disponee being questioned: s. 26(3); H & B, paras. 7.7, 7.8.

fundamental basis of the registration system that those who rely on the register can assume that its contents are true.

(b) The machinery of transfer of registered land

(1) PRE-TRANSFER MACHINERY

The preliminary inquiries and the contract of sale follow the pattern of unregistered conveyancing,[273] but the investigation of the title is radically different. No longer does the vendor need to trace the history of the transactions in which the estate has been involved, for the register is conclusive on the question of ownership.

The Land Registration Act 2002 makes no specific provision about the documents that the vendor must supply to the purchaser,[274] but the standard forms of contract conditions in common use[275] require the vendor at his own expense to supply official copy entries of the individual register, title plan and any other documents referred to in the register and kept by the registrar.

Requisitions on title follow the usual form[276] but where the title is absolute or good leasehold, they are limited to overriding interests[277] and other matters in respect of which the register is not conclusive. Possessory or qualified titles will require more careful investigation. Searches must be made of local land charges registers, for local land charges are overriding interests. But it will not be necessary to search the register of land charges under the Land Charges Act 1972, as third-party rights which would appear there if the land were unregistered will appear on the register under the Land Registration Act 1925. The main search will therefore be of the register itself, through the official copy entries supplied by the vendor, or by the purchaser himself undertaking an official search with priority.[278]

(2) FORM OF TRANSFER

The Land Registration Act 2002[279] provides that a registrable disposition of a registered estate or charge only has effect if it complies with such requirements as to form and content as rules may provide. The Land Registration Rules 2003[280] prescribe a great many forms for particular purposes, including several forms for the transfer. The form to be used for the transfer of whole of a registered title is reproduced on pages 964–5;[281] the following paragraphs explain certain of its provisions.

---

[273] Pp. 854 et seq, ante. From 1 June 2007, this will include the provision by the vendor of a home information pack under Housing Act 2004; p. 855, ante.

[274] LRA 2002, Sch. 10, para. 2, provides that rules may make provision about the obligations with respect to proof of title, or perfection of title, of the seller under a contract for the transfer, or other disposition, for valuable consideration of a registered estate or charge. No such rules have, however, been made. LRA 1925, s. 110, made detailed provision about the documents that a purchaser could require the vendor to produce.

[275] Standard Conditions of Sale (4th edn), para. 4.1.2; Standard Commercial Property Conditions of Sale (2nd edn), para. 6.1.2.   [276] Silverman, *Conveyancing Handbook*, paras. D2.3; D3.

[277] P. 975, post.   [278] On the effect of the search with priority, see p. 954, ante.   [279] S. 25.

[280] Rule 206, Sch. 1. The forms are also available for downloading from the Land Registry web site. The prescribed form of wording and layout must be used, but the Regulations permit certain variations: rr. 209–11. See generally Land Registry Practice Guide 46.

[281] Source acknowledgment: TR1 produced by Land Registry. © Crown copyright material is reproduced with the permission of Land Registry.

**Transfer of whole
of registered title(s)**

Land Registry

If you need more room than is provided for in a panel, use continuation sheet CS and attach to this form.

---

1.   Stamp Duty

Place "X" in the appropriate box or boxes and complete the appropriate certificate.

☐   It is certified that this instrument falls within category ☐ in the Schedule to the Stamp Duty (Exempt Instruments) Regulations 1987

☐   It is certified that the transaction effected does not form part of a larger transaction or of a series of transactions in respect of which the amount or value or the aggregate amount or value of the consideration exceeds the sum of   £

☐   It is certified that this is an instrument on which stamp duty is not chargeable by virtue of the provisions of section 92 of the Finance Act 2001

---

2.   Title Number(s) of the Property *Leave blank if not yet registered.*

---

3.   Property

---

4.   Date

---

5.   Transferor *Give full names and company's registered number if any.*

---

6.   Transferee for entry on the register *Give full name(s)and company's registered number, if any. For Scottish companies use an SC prefix and for limited liability partnerships use an OC prefix before the registered number, if any. For foreign companies give territory in which incorporated.*

Unless otherwise arranged with Land Registry headquarters, a certified copy of the Transferee's constitution (in Englishor Welsh) will be required if it is a body corporate but is not a company registered in England and Wales or Scotland under the Companies Acts.

---

7.   Transferee's intended address(es) for service(including postcode) for entry on the register *You may give up to three addresses for service one of which must be a postal address but does not have to be within the UK. The other addresses can be any combination of a postal address, a box number at a UK document exchange or an electronic address.*

---

8.   The Transferor transfers the Property to the Transferee

---

9.   Consideration *Place "X" in the appropriate box. State clearly the currency unit if other than sterling. If none of the boxes applies, insert an appropriate memorandum in the additional provisions panel.*

☐   The Transferor has received from the Transferee for the Property the sum of *In words and figures.*

☐   *Insert other receipt as appropriate.*

☐   The transfer is not for money or anything which has a monetary value

10. The Transferor transfers with *Place "X" in the appropriate box and add any modifications.*

☐ full title guarantee   ☐ limited title guarantee

11. Declaration of trust *Where there is more than one Transferee, place "X" in the appropriate box.*

☐ The Transferees are to hold the Property on trust for themselves as joint tenants

☐ The Transferees are to hold the Property on trust for themselves as tenants in common in equal shares

☐ The Transferees are to hold the Property *Complete as necessary.*

12. Additional provisions *Insert here any required or permitted statements, certificates or applications and any agreed covenants, declarations, etc.*

13. Execution *The Transferor must execute this transfer as a deed using the space below. If there is more than one Transferor, all must execute. Forms of execution are given in Schedule 9 to the Land Registration Rules 2003. If the transfer contains Transferee's covenants or declarations or contains an application by the Transferee (e.g. for a restriction), it must also be executed by the Transferee (all of them, if there is more than one).*

© Crown copyright (ref: LR/HQ/CD-ROM) 6/03

(i) Sections 1: stamp duty; 9: consideration

The purpose of sections 1 and 9 of the form is to certify whether stamp duty land tax is payable on the transfer. This topic is outside the scope of this book,[282] but it should be noted that most transactions, for consideration in money or money's worth, relating to estates and interests in land[283] are subject to tax, payable by the purchaser. The rate of tax payable depends on the consideration for the transaction (and any linked transaction). A land transaction, or a document effecting or evidencing a land transaction, must not be registered, recorded or otherwise reflected in the land register unless the application is accompanied by a certificate about the compliance with the statutory requirements as to the tax.[284]

The statement in section 9 that the consideration has been received is also a sufficient discharge to the purchaser without any further receipt being indorsed on the deed.[285] Again, such a receipt is sufficient evidence of the payment to a subsequent purchaser, provided that he has no notice that the money was not actually paid.[286]

(ii) Section 2: title number

The title number is the unique reference number for the individual register comprising the title. A registered lease has a different title number from the registered freehold out of which the lease was granted, because they are separate registered titles.

It should be noted that the section can be left blank, if the title is not yet registered—because the transfer form TR1 may be used for the conveyance of unregistered land which will be then subject to registration, as well as for the transfer of land which is already on the register.[287]

(iii) Section 8: the transfer

This provision is deceptively simple. It is the principal provision of the form, which by its express terms transfers the title to the property to the transferee, although of course the legal title will pass only when the relevant registration requirements are satisfied.[288] However, by statute it has a larger effect.

A grant operates to pass the rights incidental to the land, such as easements and profits which have become attached to it. But since rights such as quasi-easements which have not become legally appurtenant to the land would not pass without special mention, it was usual, prior to 1882, to insert *general words*, which were framed widely enough to include all rights actually enjoyed by the vendor in respect of the land. Since 1881, however, unless a contrary intention is expressed, such *general words* are implied in every conveyance. Thus a conveyance[289] of land now operates, by virtue of the Law of Property Act 1925, to convey[290] "all buildings, erections, fixtures, commons, hedges, ditches, fences, ways, waters, watercourses, liberties, privileges, easements, rights and advantages whatsoever, appertaining or reputed to appertain to the land or any part thereof".

An equally wide implication is raised with regard to rights appertaining to buildings.[291]

---

282 See Silverman, *Conveyancing Handbook*, section A14; FA 2003, Part 4.

283 A licence to use or occupy land is not a chargeable interest for the purpose of this tax; nor (in England, Wales and Northern Ireland) is a tenancy at will: FA 2003, s. 48(2); this therefore gives a reason to prefer a licence to the grant of a lease; cf pp. 197 et seq, ante.   284 FA 2003, s. 79(1).

285 LPA 1925, s. 67.   286 Ibid., s. 68.   287 P. 952, ante.   288 P. 970, post.

289 Defined at LPA 1925, s. 205(1)(ii) in terms sufficiently wide to include a transfer by deed in registered land.

290 LPA 1925, s. 62(1); p. 603, ante.   291 Ibid., s. 62(2).

It was also usual before 1882 to add what was called an *all estate clause* with the object of ensuring that the entire interest of the grantor should be transferred. This was as a matter of fact quite ineffective to transfer anything that would not pass automatically, and it is now omitted in reliance on the enactment that, unless a contrary intention is expressed, every conveyance is effectual to pass all the estate, right, title, interest, claim, and demand which the conveying parties respectively have in, to, or on the property.[292]

(iv) Section 10: title guarantee

Section 10 calls for some explanation, and can be understood only in the light of the history of conveyancing practice.

(1) HISTORY OF COVENANTS FOR TITLE

In former days a deed of conveyance ran to considerable length since it usually contained elaborate *covenants for title*, the object of which was to render the vendor liable in covenant if a flaw were later discovered in his title. Although titles were traditionally investigated with such care that a purchaser would seldom need to enforce this contractual liability, it was usual before 1882 to set out the appropriate undertakings at length,[293] a practice which, while it militated against simplicity and brevity, increased the profits of solicitors, whose remuneration in those days depended upon the length of the documents they prepared. Since 1881, however, covenants for title need not be expressly stated, because statute provides a mechanism for covenants to be implied by the use of simple words and phrases inserted into conveyances and transfers of land.

Before 1 July 1995[294] the appropriate words to imply these covenants upon sale of land were "beneficial owner". If the conveyance was for valuable consideration, and if the vendor "conveyed and was expressed to convey as beneficial owner",[295] and if in fact he possessed that status,[296] the effect was that four covenants were implied: that the vendor had a good right to convey; that the purchaser should have quiet enjoyment; that the property was free from incumbrances; and a covenant for further assurance which obliged the vendor to execute assurances and to do everything that is right and possible in order to perfect the conveyance.[297]

(2) CURRENT LAW ON IMPLIED COVENANTS FOR TITLE

The Law of Property (Miscellaneous) Provisions Act 1994,[298] which came into force on 1 July 1995, repealed the existing law on the implied covenants for title, and the key words which trigger them (such as "beneficial owner") are no longer effective. Instead, there are two new key words; either covenants "with full title guarantee" or covenants "with limited title guarantee".

---

[292] LPA 1925, s. 63.   [293] See (1962) 26 Conv (NS) 45 (M. J. Russell).

[294] LPA 1925, s. 76, Sch. 2. The language to be used to imply the covenants, and the content of the covenants themselves, varied according as the grantor conveyed freeholds or assigned leaseholds for valuable consideration, or by way of mortgage or settlement, or as trustee, mortgagee, personal representative, etc.

[295] Ibid., s. 76(1)(A).

[296] *Fay v Miller, Wilkins & Co* [1941] Ch 360 at 362; *Pilkington v Wood* [1953] Ch 770 at 777; *Re Robertson's Application* [1969] 1 WLR 109 at 111–12.

[297] LPA 1925, Sch. 2, Part I. The covenants may be varied or extended. The benefit of the covenants implied by the Act ran with the land, so that each person in whom the land is vested is entitled to enforce them: ibid, s. 76(6). For further detail, see the 16th edn of this book, pp. 848–50; Farrand, *Contract and Conveyance* (4th edn), pp. 258 et seq; Barnsley, *Conveyancing Law and Practice*, chap. 23; (1968) 32 Conv (NS) 123; (1970) 34 Conv (NS) 178 (M. J. Russell).

[298] Based on the Law Commission Report on Implied Covenants for Title 1991 (Law Com No. 199). See generally Kenny, *Covenants for Title*; Barnsley, *Conveyancing Law and Practice*, pp. 683–6; Emmet, chap. 16. In registered land, see LRR 2003, rr. 67, 68; H & B, para. 25.3.

Use of the covenants remains a matter of contract between the parties, but depends on the new key words being expressed in the instrument.[299] Their effect can be limited or extended by it.[300]

The archaic wording of the covenants has been shortened and modernised, and some changes of substance have been made.

(3) CHANGES FROM THE PREVIOUS LAW

First, the covenants are now to be implied on the disposition of property on the part of the person making the disposition.[301] Disposition is defined so as to include the creation of a lease.[302] This is an important change; before then only the disposition of a lease had attracted the covenants. Property includes a thing in action, and any interest in real or personal property;[303] for example, sales and acquisitions of companies and sales of chattels are now included.

Second, the new covenants may be implied into a disposition, even though there is no consideration.[304] The old covenants could only be implied in a conveyance for valuable consideration.

Third, there are now only three covenants, which are common to the new types of guarantee:

(1) The right to dispose of the property.

(2) Further assurance.

(3) Freedom from charges, incumbrances and third party rights.

The old covenant that a purchaser shall have quiet enjoyment has disappeared. It has no place in freehold conveyancing, and is otiose in leasehold conveyancing, where the covenant is implied at common law.[305] The detail of the new covenants is discussed below.

Fourth, the implied covenants for right to dispose and freedom from charges, etc, do not apply to any particular matter to which the disposition is expressly made subject.[306] Under the Standard Conditions of Sale,[307] property is sold expressly subject, for example, to the covenants mentioned in the agreement, to those discoverable by inspection of the property before the contract, and to those which the vendor does not and could not reasonably know about.

Fifth, it would be unfair if the disponor were to be liable on the implied covenants if the disponee knew of the defects. Section 6(2) provides that the covenants for right to dispose and freedom from charges etc will not apply to anything (even if the disposition is not expressly made subject to it)

(a) which at the time of the disposition is within the actual knowledge, or

(b) which is a necessary consequence of facts that are then within the actual knowledge of the person to whom the disposition is made.

Knowledge does not include deemed notice by virtue of registration under the Land Charges Act 1972, although in registered land the disponor of an interest is not liable in respect of matters entered on the register of title of the interest.[308]

---

[299] These may be in Welsh: LP (MP) A 1994, s. 8(4).   [300] S. 8(1).

[301] Ss. 1(1), (4). For specified covenants implied under statutes, see s. 21, Sch. 1, amending Leasehold Reform Act 1967, Rentcharges Act 1977, HA 1985 and Leasehold Reform, Housing and Urban Development Act 1993.

[302] S. 1(1). For implied covenants in leases, see ss. 4 (validity of lease); 5 (discharge of obligations when property subject to rentcharge or leasehold land).   [303] S. 1(4).

[304] S. 1(1).

[305] P. 230, ante. The effect of this omission is that the limitation period for all implied covenants runs from the date of the conveyance.   [306] S. 6(1).

[307] 4th edn, condition 3. See also Standard Commercial Property Conditions, 2nd edn, condition 3.

[308] S. 6(4), inserted by LRA 2002, s. 133, Sch. 11, para. 31. No reference is made on the register to the implied covenants for title, unless they are limited or extended under s. 4: LRR 2003, rr. 67(5), (6), 68.

Sixth, the annexation of the benefit of the implied covenants to the estate or interest of the disponee is repeated in section 7.[309]

(4) THE IMPLIED COVENANTS

We must now consider briefly the content of the new covenants.

1. *The right to dispose of the property* Under section 2(1)(a) there is implied a covenant that the person making the disposition has the right (with the concurrence of any other person conveying the property) to dispose of the property as he purports to.

A disponor is thus liable for breach of this covenant where he has never had title to the property described in the conveyance, or where[310] he has lost it by having been dispossessed under the Limitation Act 1980.

2. *Further assurance* Under section 2(1)(b) there is also implied a covenant by the person making the disposition that he will at his own cost do all that he reasonably can to give the person to whom he disposes of the property the title he purports to give.

Section 2(2) extends this duty to ensuring that the disponee of registered land is registered with at least the class of title registered immediately before the disposition.

These two covenants are implied whether the disposition is expressed to be made with full title guarantee or with limited title guarantee. The difference between these two guarantees occurs only in the third implied covenant.

3. *Freedom from charges, incumbrances and third party rights* Under section 3, if there is a *full title guarantee*, there is also implied a covenant that the property is disposed of free:

(a) from all charges and incumbrances (whether monetary or not); and

(b) from all other rights exercisable by third parties.

This covenant is more onerous than the similar one under the old law; the disponor is now made liable for charges etc which have been created by his predecessor in title. However, the scope of the covenant is narrowed in that it does not extend to any charges etc which the disponor does not and could not reasonably be expected to know about.

If there is *limited title guarantee*, only a qualified covenant is implied and the disponee has less protection. Under section 3(3) the limitation is that the person making the disposition has not, since the last disposition for value, created or suffered any subsisting charges etc to be created and that he is not aware that anyone else has done so.

(v) Section 11: declaration of trust

If there is more than one transferee, they are required to declare the basis on which they are to hold the property: whether on trust for themselves as joint tenants or tenants in common, or otherwise.[311]

(vi) Section 13: execution

The transfer must be executed as a deed, to comply with the requirements of section 52 of the Law of Property Act 1925.[312]

---

[309] The suggestion of Lord BRIGHTMAN in HL to adopt the wording of LPA 1925, s. 78(1) was not followed in spite of its wide interpretation in *Federated Homes Ltd v Mill Lodge Properties Ltd* [1980] 1 WLR 594, p. 680, ante. See the Proceedings of the Special Standing Committee of the House of Lords (7 June 1994 HL Paper 62).   [310] In unregistered land, or in registered land before LRA 2002: Chap. 6, ante.
[311] P. 453, ante.   [312] P. 896, ante.

(3) REGISTRABLE DISPOSITIONS[313]

Certain dispositions are required by the Land Registration Act 2002 to be completed by registration. Until the relevant registration requirements are met, the disposition does not operate at law,[314] although it will still take effect between the parties within the law of contract, and may also take effect in equity as a property right capable of binding a third party who takes a subsequent registered disposition for value, if it is protected in the manner required by the Act.[315]

(i) Dispositions required to be registered

The following dispositions relating to a registered estate are required to be completed by registration:[316]

(a)   a transfer,

(b)   where the registered estate is an estate in land, the grant of a term of years absolute—
   (i)   for a term of more than seven years from the date of the grant,
   (ii)   to take effect in possession after the end of the period of three months beginning with the date of the grant,
   (iii) under which the right to possession is discontinuous,
   (iv)   in pursuance of Part 5 of the Housing Act 1985 (c 68) (the right to buy), or
   (v)   in circumstances where section 171A of that Act applies (disposal by landlord which leads to a person no longer being a secure tenant),

(c)   where the registered estate is a franchise or manor, the grant of a lease,

(d)   the express grant or reservation of an interest of a kind falling within section 1(2)(a) of the Law of Property Act 1925,[317] other than one which is capable of being registered under the Commons Registration Act 1965,

(e)   the express grant or reservation of an interest of a kind falling within section 1(2)(b) or (e) of the Law of Property Act 1925,[318] and

(f)   the grant of a legal charge.

Thus the most common transactions—the transfer of the freehold, the grant of most leases for longer than seven years, and the creation of a charge by way of legal mortgage—must be registered if they are to take effect at law.

---

[313] H & B, chap. 8.

[314] LRA 2002, s. 27(1). The importance of this provision will be diminished when electronic conveyancing is introduced, because dispositions will then occur and be registered simultaneously. Hence s. 27(1) is disapplied by s. 93(4); p. 987, post.

[315] By entry of a notice, or as an overriding interest: s. 29(2); infra. The unregistered disposition of a legal estate takes effect in equity under the doctrine of *Walsh v Lonsdale*, p. 877, ante. For the effect in equity of a transfer before registration under LRA 1925, see *Mascall v Mascall* (1984) 50 P & CR 119; *E S Schwab & Co Ltd v McCarthy* (1975) 31 P & CR 196 at 212; *Brown & Root Technology Ltd v Sun Alliance and London Assurance Co Ltd* [1996] Ch 51 (reversed on other grounds (1996) 75 P & CR 223); p. 104, n. 132, ante.

[316] LRA 2002, s. 27(2). For registrable dispositions relating to a registered charge, see s. 27(3). The section applied to dispositions by operation of law, except for a transfer on death or bankruptcy of an individual proprietor, a transfer on the dissolution of a corporate proprietor, or the creation of a local land charge: s. 27(5).

[317] I.e., an easement or profit à prendre for an interest equivalent to the fee simple or a term of years absolute. "Express grant" does not include a grant as a result of the operation of LPA 1925, s. 62: LRA 2002, s. 27(7); easements implied by s. 62 can therefore be legal and take effect as overriding interests under LRA 2002, Sch. 3, para. 3(1); pp. 632–4, ante.   [318] I.e., a legal rentcharge or right of entry.

(ii) Registration requirements

The registration requirements are set out in Schedule 2 to the Land Registration Act 2002, and vary according to the nature of the disposition. But the general principle is that, where the disposition transfers or creates a registrable estate,[319] the disponee must be entered in the individual register as the proprietor of the estate, and if the interest subsists in relation to another registered estate, a notice must be entered on the register of the latter estate. In the case of a transfer of a registered freehold estate, therefore, the transferee must be entered in the register as the proprietor;[320] and in the case of a grant of a lease the tenant must be entered in the register as the proprietor of the lease, and a notice in respect of the lease must be entered in the register of the title to the reversion.[321] If the disposition does not create an estate which is individually registrable, such as a legal easement, a notice must be entered in the register of the estate in respect of which the interest subsists (the servient tenement) and if the interest is created for the benefit of a registered estate an entry must be made in the individual register for that estate to indicate that the proprietor has the benefit.[322]

(4) The Priority of Competing Interests in Registered Land[323]

The Land Registration Act 2002 lays down a new, simple, statutory scheme of priorities for competing interests in registered land.

(a) The basic rule: date of creation

The basic rule is that the priority of any interest is determined by the date of its creation. This is the effect (although not the literal language) of section 28, which provides that:

(1) Except as provided by sections 29 and 30, the priority of an interest affecting a registered estate or charge is not affected by a disposition of the estate or charge.

(2) It makes no difference for the purposes of this section whether the interest or disposition is registered.

This is a much more straightforward rule than that which existed before the Act in registered land, or which exists in unregistered land, and applies to all interests affecting registered land, whether legal or equitable,[324] and whether (or when) registered.[325]

However, to this basic rule there are two important exceptions.

---

[319] I.e., an interest or estate which is substantively registrable with its own individual register: a legal estate in land (fee simple and certain leases), rentcharge, franchise, or profit à prendre in gross: p. 953, ante.

[320] LRA 2002, Sch. 2, para. 2(1).

[321] Ibid., para. 3. For the registration of an independently registrable rentcharge or profit à prendre, see para. 6.

[322] Ibid., para. 7. If the dominant tenement is not yet registered, there will be no individual register of title against which the benefit can be noted. In the case of a registered charge the chargee is entered as proprietor of the charge in the register of the estate which has been charged: ibid., para. 8. On transfer of charges, see para. 10; and on sub-charges, see para. 11.

[323] R & R, chap. 15; H & B, chap. 9; Law Commission Report on Land Registration for the Twenty-First Century 2001 (Law Com No. 271), Part V. For a useful example of the operation of the principal rules, see R & R, paras. 15.032–015.039; [2006] Conv III.

[324] It applies to rights of pre-emption from the time of creation: LRA 2002, s. 115; p. 883, ante; and mere equities and equities by estoppel from the time the equity arises: LRA 2002, s. 116; pp. 814, 826, ante.

[325] For criticism, of the law under LRA 1925, see Law Commission Consultative Document on Land Registration for the Twenty-First Century 1998 (Law Com No. 254), paras. 7.15–17.19; H & B, para. 9.1. For the position in unregistered land, see pp. 92–100, ante.

(b) Registered disposition for valuable consideration

The main exception is where a registrable disposition of a registered estate[326] is made for valuable consideration,[327] and is completed by registration. Registration has the effect of postponing to the interest under the disposition any interest affecting the estate immediately before the disposition whose priority is not protected at the time of registration.[328] In other words, prior interests affecting the estate continue to bind successors to the estate and others whose interests in or over the estate are created later; but a *purchaser for value* of the legal estate takes it free of prior interests whose priority is not protected *at the time of his registration as proprietor*.[329]

A prior interests will be so protected if it is:[330]

(a) a registered charge;

(b) the subject of a notice in the register;[331]

(c) an unregistered interest which overrides a registered disposition under Schedule 3;[332]

(d) an interest which appears from the register to be excepted from the effect of registration—such as a interest to which registration of the title as possessory, rather than absolute, is subject;[333] or

(e) in the case of a disposition of a leasehold estate, an interest which is incident to the estate, such as restrictive covenants in a lease which do not have to be protected by a notice on the register.

The protection of interests by means of entries on the register, and overriding interests, are considered in detail below. But it should be noted that, as in unregistered conveyancing, actual notice of what should be protected in the register, but is not so protected, is immaterial.[334]

---

[326] Or charge: LRA 2002, s. 30.

[327] "Valuable consideration" does not include marriage consideration or a nominal consideration in money: LRA 2002, s. 132 (cf LRA 1925, s. 3(xxxi), which did not exclude marriage consideration).

[328] LRA 2002, s. 29(1).

[329] The purchaser may also be protected by having made a priority search of the register which prevents his being affected by any interests entered on the register during the priority period: p. 954, ante.

[330] LRA 2002, s. 29(2) (disposition of registered estate). See also s. 30(2) (disposition of registered charge).

[331] Pp. 973 et seq, post.   [332] Pp. 975 et seq, post.   [333] P. 958, ante.

[334] See, however, two decisions at first instance under LRA 1925, where the constructive trust was used to avoid the consequences of failure to register a right as a minor interest, but which have been much criticised: (a) *Peffer v Rigg* [1977] 1 WLR 285, M & B p. 176, where GRAHAM J treated a transferee under s. 20(1) and a purchaser, defined in s. 3(xxi) as "bona fide purchaser for value", as synonymous, and held that, where an ex-wife purchased a house from her former husband, with actual knowledge that he held it on trust for himself and her brother-in-law, she was not a bona fide transferee under s. 20(1), and therefore was bound by the trust. He also held that she was a constructive trustee of the house: (1977) 41 Conv (NS) 207 (F. R. Crane); (1977) 93 LQR 341 (R. J. Smith); [1977] CLJ 227 (D. J. Hayton); (1977) 40 MLR 602 (S. Anderson); [1978] Conv 52 (J. Martin); and, after LRA 2002, (2004) 120 LQR 640 (E. Cooke and P. O'Connor). (b) *Lyus v Prowsa Developments Ltd* [1982] 1 WLR 1044, M & B p. 176, where a purchaser, who agreed to take part of a building estate expressly "subject to and with the benefit of" an existing contract for the sale of one plot, was held bound by that contract under a constructive trust, on the ground that the LRA was not to be used as an instrument of fraud; approved in *Ashburn Anstalt v Arnold* [1989] Ch 1 at 25. For criticism, see (1983) 46 MLR 96 (P. H. Kenny); [1982] All ER Rev (P. J. Clarke); [1983] CLJ 54 (C. J. Harpum); [1983] Conv 64 (P. Jackson); (1983) 133 NLJ 798 (C. T. Emery and B. Smythe); cf (1984) 47 MLR 476 (P. Bennett); [1985] CLJ 280 (M. P. Thompson). See also *Du Boulay v Raggett* (1988) 58 P & CR 138; Emmet, para. 9.020.1.

For the use of Contracts (Rights of Third Parties) Act 1999 to solve by contract the problem addressed in *Lyus v Prowsa*, see p. 838, n. 51.

(c) Inland Revenue charge

The second exception to the basic rule concerns the Inland Revenue charge for unpaid tax, which has a separate priority rule under the Inheritance Tax Act 1984.[335]

(5) Protection of Interests by Entry on the Register[336]

We have seen[337] that the Land Registration Act 1925 designated as "minor interests" those unregistrable interests which needed to be protected by entry on the register in order to give them priority against later purchasers; and that there were four categories of entry on the register: notices, restrictions, cautions and inhibitions. The scheme of the Land Registration Act 2002 is simpler. The language of "minor interests" is not used: the rules of priority of interests[338] apply generally to all interests affecting a registered estate. And there are now only two forms of entry on the register: notices and restrictions.[339]

(a) Notices[340]

(1) NATURE AND EFFECT

A notice is an entry in the register in respect of the burden of an interest affecting a registered estate or charge. The entry of a notice does not, however, mean that the interest is valid; only that, if valid, its priority is protected against a later disposition of the estate for value.[341] The registrar does not therefore enquire into the validity of the claim to the interest when the application is made to enter it on the register.

(2) INTERESTS WHICH MAY BE PROTECTED BY ENTRY OF A NOTICE

The Act requires or permits the registrar to enter a notice in certain cases where it appears to him that a registered estate is burdened by an interest.[342] But it does not define exhaustively the interests that can be protected by notice;[343] rather, it lists five interests that *cannot* be so protected. These are:[344]

   (a) an interest under—

      (i) a trust of land, or

      (ii) a settlement under the Settled Land Act 1925,

---

[335] Ss. 237, 238; LRA 2002, s. 31.

[336] R & R, chaps. 42 (notices), 43 (cautions against dealings), 44 (restrictions), 45 (matrimonial and civil partnership homes); H & B, chap. 10; Land Registry Practice Guide 19.

[337] P. 106, ante. For detail, see the 16th edn of this book, pp. 870–6.   [338] Supra.

[339] Cautions against dealings and inhibitions are abolished: the former are subsumed under notices, the latter under restrictions. Entries on the register made before LRA 2002 came into force continue to have effect: Sch. 12. For the vacation of cautions entered under LRA 1925, see p. 106, n. 152, ante.

[340] LRA 2002, ss. 32–9; LRR 2003, Part 7.   [341] Ibid., s. 32(1), (3).

[342] Ibid., ss. 37 (permissive: entry of matters which, on first registration, would constitute overriding interests, if not otherwise excluded from protection by notice; this is in furtherance of the policy of making the register as complete as possible, rather than relying on overriding interests); 38 (mandatory: entry on the register of the burdened estate where a person is registered as proprietor of a lease, easement, profit à prendre, rentcharge or right of entry).

[343] Numerous other statutes make explicit provision for notices to be (or not to be) used to protect particular interests; e.g. a spouse or civil partner's rights of occupation under Family Law Act 1996, s. 31; p. 478, ante. For a detailed list, see Wolstenholme and Cherry, *Annotated Land Registration Act 2002*, para. 3–037.

[344] LRA 2002, s. 33.

A beneficial interest under a trust of land or a strict settlement cannot be protected by entry of a notice because, as long as it is overreached[345] it is of no concern to a purchaser. The appropriate entry on the register is therefore a restriction, to ensure that the overreaching machinery is adopted on any sale.[346]

> (b) a leasehold estate in land which—
>
> > (i) is granted for a term of years of three years or less from the date of the grant, and
> >
> > (ii) is not required to be registered,

A lease granted for more than seven years must be registered;[347] the effect of this provision is therefore to permit a notice to be entered on the title to the reversion only in respect of a lease granted for more than three years but not more than seven years. The period of three years was chosen here because it was envisaged that, when electronic conveyancing is fully introduced, the seven-year period for registration of leases will be reduced to three years,[348] and therefore the periods will be brought into line.

> (c) a restrictive covenant made between a lessor and lessee, so far as relating to the demised premises,

The purchaser of land will be able to inspect the lease, and therefore discover the covenants.[349]

> (d) an interest which is capable of being registered under the Commons Registration Act 1965, and
>
> (e) an interest in any coal or coal mine, the rights attached to any such interest and the rights of any person under section 38, 49 or 51 of the Coal Industry Act 1994.[350]

(3) AGREED AND UNILATERAL NOTICES

Under the 2002 Act notices are of two kinds: agreed notices and unilateral notices.[351] An agreed notice will be entered on the application of or with the agreement of the registered proprietor of the land affected. A unilateral notice, however, may be entered without the consent of the proprietor, but the registrar must inform him of the entry so that he may exercise his right to apply for its cancellation.[352]

(b) Restrictions[353]

(1) NATURE AND EFFECT

A restriction is an entry in the register regulating the circumstances in which a disposition of a registered estate or charge may be the subject of an entry in the register. It may prohibit

---

[345] Pp. 994, 997–1000, post.   [346] Infra. This reproduces the position under LRA 1925, s. 49(2).

[347] P. 970, ante. And most leases granted for a term not exceeding seven years are overriding interests: Sch. 3, para. 1; pp. 977–8, post.   [348] H & B, para. 10.8.

[349] P. 933, ante. The burden of covenants incident to the leasehold estate have priority in any event: LRA 2002, s. 29(2)(b).

[350] Such interests are overriding interests: Sch. 1, para. 7 (first registration); Sch. 3, para. 7 (registered dispositions).

[351] LRA 2002, s. 34. These reflect the differences between notices and cautions against dealings under LRA 1925.

[352] Ibid., s. 35–6. This is more effective than the old caution since, in the absence of an objection, a unilateral notice will protect the interest in the same way as an agreed notice does. A caution only recorded the cautioner's claim, and did not give priority as such: p. 106, n. 152, ante.   [353] Ibid., ss. 40–7; LRR 2003, Part 8.

the making of an entry in respect of any particular disposition, or kind of disposition; for a defined period or indefinitely; and subject or not to particular conditions.[354] Its effect is to prevent any entry being made in the register in contravention of the terms of the restriction, unless the registrar disapplies or modifies the restriction.[355]

(2) ENTRY OF A RESTRICTION

A restriction may be entered by the registrar if it appears to him to be necessary or desirable for the purpose of:[356]

(a) preventing invalidity or unlawfulness in relation to dispositions of a registered estate or charge,

(b) securing that interests which are capable of being overreached on a disposition of a registered estate or charge are overreached, or

(c) protecting a right or claim in relation to a registered estate or charge.[357]

Restrictions can therefore be used for a variety of situations, and the Land Registration Rules 2003[358] contain numerous standard forms of restriction for particular types of case. The most common case, however, is the restriction to protect the beneficiary under a trust of land or strict settlement, to ensure that the requirements for overreaching are complied with. Where two or more persons are entered as the proprietor of a registered estate, it is mandatory for the registrar to enter an appropriate restriction.[359]

(c) Anti-abuse provision

Under section 77 of the Land Registration Act 2002, a person must not exercise the right to apply for the entry of a notice or restriction[360] without reasonable cause. This creates a statutory duty, breach of which is actionable in tort by any person who suffers damage in consequence of it.

(6) Overriding Interests[361]

Overriding interests are unregistered interests to which a registered title is subject. On first registration, certain unregistered interests will bind the registered proprietor.[362] And on a subsequent registered disposition of the registered estate for value, certain unregistered

---

[354] LRA 2002, s. 40.   [355] Ibid., s. 41.

[356] Ibid., s. 42(1). Application may be made by or with the consent of the registered proprietor, or by any person with a sufficient interest in the making of the entry: s. 43; LRR 2003, rr. 91–4. If the registrar makes an entry other than in pursuance of such an application, he must give notice to the proprietor of the registered estate or charge: s. 42(3). For entry of a restriction on the order of the court see s. 46.

[357] But not for the purpose of protecting a right of claim which is or could be the subject of a notice: ibid., s. 42(2). If priority is sought, a notice should be used.   [358] Sch. 4.

[359] LRA 2002, s. 44; p. 440, ante.

[360] Or to lodge a caution against first registration, or to object to an application to the registrar.

[361] R & R, chaps. 10, 17; H & B, chap. 11; Land Registry Practice Guide 15. "Overriding interests" was a defined term under LRA 1925, s. 3(xvi). It is no longer so used under LRA 2002, although the concept is the same, and the Land Registry still uses the old terminology: Practice Guide 15. On overriding interests under the LRA 1925, see R & R (1991 edn), chap. 6; Wolstenholme and Cherry, vol. 6, pp. 63–7; Farrand, *Contract and Conveyance* (2nd edn), pp. 184–209; Barnsley, *Conveyancing Law and Practice*, pp. 50–69; Hayton, *Registered Land*, chap. 6; M & B pp. 128–65.

[362] LRA 2002, ss. 11(4)(b) (freehold), 12(4)(c) (leasehold), Sch. 1: unregistered interests which override first registration; p. 954, ante.

interests will have priority against the disponee even though they have not been protected by the entry of a notice on the register.[363]

Overriding interests thus detract from the principle that the register should be a mirror of title. They consist of third party rights which on policy grounds should bind the registered proprietor, and a purchaser from him, even though they have not been entered on the register. The Land Registration Act 1925 listed overriding interests in section 70(1), and further additions were made by later enactments.[364] The wide scope of overriding interests was subject to criticism,[365] and the Land Registration Act 2002 reduced their number and extent in pursuance of its policy of creating as complete a register of land as possible. Some of the old categories of overriding interests are abolished; others will be phased out after ten years; others are reduced in extent or otherwise modified.[366] The basic principle is now said to be that[367] "the *only* overriding interests should be those where protection against purchasers is needed, yet it is either not reasonable to expect nor sensible to require any entry on the register".

(a) Unregistered interests which override first registration

When a person becomes proprietor of a registered estate on first registration, he takes the estate subject to those overriding interests which are set out in Schedule 1 to the 2002 Act. These are:[368]

1. A leasehold estate in land granted for a term not exceeding seven years from the date of the grant, except for a lease the grant of which falls within section 4(1) (d), (e) or (f).[369]

2. An interest belonging to a person in actual occupation, so far as relating to land of which he is in actual occupation, except for an interest under a settlement under the Settled Land Act 1925.

3. A legal easement or profit a prendre.

---

[363] LRA 2002, ss. 29(2)(a)(ii) (registered disposition of registered estate), 30(2)(a)(ii) (registered disposition of registered charge), Sch. 3: unregistered interests which override registered dispositions.

[364] LRR 1925, r. 258; Coal Act 1938, s. 41; Tithe Act 1936, s. 13(11); Leasehold Property (Temporary Provisions) Act 1951, s. 2(4); Coal Industry Act 1987, s. 1; Coal Industry Act 1994, Sch. 9, para. 1(2); Greater London Authority Act 1999, s. 219(7).

[365] See esp. Law Commission, Third Report on Land Registration 1987 (Law Com No. 158), Part II; Consultative Document on Land Registration for the Twenty-First Century 1998 (Law Com No. 254), Part IV; *Overseas Investment Services Ltd v Simcobuild Construction Ltd* [1996] 1 EGLR 49 at 51, per PETER GIBSON LJ: "As they constitute an exception [to the mirror of title principle], the court should, in my opinion, not be astute to give a wide meaning to any item constituting an overriding interest".

[366] There are transitional provisions which preserve any overriding interests acquired under the 1925 Act: LRA 2002, Sch. 12, paras. 7–13. Cases on LRA 1925, s. 70(1) may still be relevant to the interpretation of the equivalent provisions of LRA 2002.

[367] Law Commission Consultative Document on Land Registration for the Twenty-First Century 1998 (Law Com No. 254), para. 4.17, adopting Third Report on Land Registration 1987 (Law Com No. 158), para. 2.6. See also Report on Land Registration for the Twenty-First Century 2001 (Law Com No. 271), para. 8.6. An earlier rationale for overriding interests was that the system of registration of title was designed to replace the title deeds; and so it was still to be expected that a purchaser should make enquiries outside the register for those "various minor liabilities which are not usually, or at any rate not invariably, shown in title-deeds or mentioned in abstracts of title, and as to which, therefore, it is impracticable to form a trustworthy record on the register": Brickdale and Stewart Wallace, *Land Registration Act 1925*, p. 190, quoted and criticised in Law Com. No. 254, at para. 4.4.

[368] See also (i) s. 134(2), Sch. 12, para. 7, inserting para. 15 into Sch. 1, with effect only until 13 October 2006, to preserve the overriding status of rights acquired under the Limitation Act 1980 before the coming into force of the Schedule; (ii) LRA 2002, s. 90(5), adding PPP leases relating to transport in London.

[369] That is, a legal lease not exceeding seven years, which is not required to be registered with its own individual title. For LRA 2002, s. 4(1)(d), (e) and (f) see p. 955, ante.

4. A customary right.

5. A public right.[370]

6. A local land charge.[371]

7. An interest in any coal or coal mine, the rights attached to any such interest and the rights of any person under section 38, 49 or 51 of the Coal Industry Act 1994.

8. In the case of land to which title was registered before 1898, rights to mines and minerals (and incidental rights) created before 1898.

9. In the case of land to which title was registered between 1898 and 1925 inclusive, rights to mines and minerals (and incidental rights) created before the date of registration of the title.

10. A franchise.[372]

11. A manorial right.

12. A right to rent which was reserved to the Crown on the granting of any freehold estate (whether or not the right is still vested in the Crown).

13. A non-statutory right in respect of an embankment or sea or river wall.

14. A right to payment in lieu of tithe.

16. A right in respect of the repair of a church chancel.[373]

The detail of some of these categories will be explained in relation to Schedule 3 (unregistered interests which override registered dispositions), below.[374]

(b) Unregistered interests which override registered dispositions

Schedule 3 to the Land Registration Act lists the interests which will override a registered disposition of a registered estate or charge. They are:[375]

1. A leasehold estate in land granted for a term not exceeding seven years from the date of the grant, except for—

---

[370] *Secretary of State for the Environment, Transport and the Regions v Baylis* [2000] 2 EGLR 13 (dedication to the public accepted by highway authority rather than by public use); *Overseas Investment Services Ltd v Simcobuild Construction Ltd* [1996] 1 EGLR 49 (right to have road constructed under Highways Act 1980, s. 38) (LRA 1925, s. 70(1)(a)).

[371] This is a very important category of overriding interests. The Local Land Charges Act 1975 applies to both unregistered and registered land. A purchaser must therefore search in the local authority's register whether or not the land is registered.

[372] Paras. 10–14 and 16 are all repealed with effect from 13 October 2013. Those with the benefit of such rights may protect them on the register before then, without payment of fees, by a caution against first registration: LRA 2002, s. 117.

[373] Inserted by SI 2003 No. 2431, art. 2(1), to continue the position under LRA 1925, s. 70(1)(c), after decision of HL in *Aston Cantlow Parish Church Council v Wallbank* [2004] 1 AC 546 that the recovery of costs of chancel repair is not contrary to HRA 1998. Law Commission Report on Liability for Chancel Repairs 1985 (Law Com No. 152) recommended that liability should be abolished after ten years; but, if not abolished promptly, it should be registered in Local Land Charges registers, and failure to register would exonerate a purchaser of the land; (1984) 100 LQR 185 (J. H. Baker). For the liability in unregistered land, see *Hauxton Parochial Church Council v Stevens* [1929] P 240; *Chivers & Sons Ltd v Air Ministry* [1955] Ch 585.

[374] The categories of interest listed in Schs. 1 and 3 are the same, although the detail of their operation is in some respects different because first registration does not presuppose a disposition of the land—and therefore it is not necessary or appropriate for the test of overriding interests on first registration to include reference to inquiries to be made of the occupier at the time of disposition to the proprietor.

[375] See also (i) LRA 2002, Sch. 12, para. 8, inserting para. 2A into Sch. 3, to preserve the overriding status of the rights of an individual who was in receipt of rents and profits under LRA 1925, s. 70(1)(g); (ii) LRA 2002

   (a) a lease the grant of which falls within section 4(1)(d), (e) or (f);[376]

   (b) a lease the grant of which constitutes a registrable disposition.

2. An interest belonging at the time of the disposition to a person in actual occupation, so far as relating to land of which he is in actual occupation, except for—

   (a) an interest under a settlement under the Settled Land Act 1925;

   (b) an interest of a person of whom inquiry was made before the disposition and who failed to disclose the right when he could reasonably have been expected to do so;

   (c) an interest—

     (i) which belongs to a person whose occupation would not have been obvious on a reasonably careful inspection of the land at the time of the disposition, and

     (ii) of which the person to whom the disposition is made does not have actual knowledge at that time;

   (d) a leasehold estate in land granted to take effect in possession after the end of the period of three months beginning with the date of the grant and which has not taken effect in possession at the time of the disposition.

3. (1) A legal easement or profit a prendre, except[377] for an easement, or a profit a prendre which is not registered under the Commons Registration Act 1965, which at the time of the disposition—

   (a) is not within the actual knowledge of the person to whom the disposition is made, and

   (b) would not have been obvious on a reasonably careful inspection of the land over which the easement or profit is exercisable.

   (2) The exception in sub-paragraph (1) does not apply if the person entitled to the easement or profit proves that it has been exercised in the period of one year ending with the day of the disposition.

4. A customary right.

5. A public right.[378]

6. A local land charge.[379]

7. An interest in any coal or coal mine, the rights attached to any such interest and the rights of any person under section 38, 49 or 51 of the Coal Industry Act 1994.

8. In the case of land to which title was registered before 1898, rights to mines and minerals (and incidental rights) created before 1898.

9. In the case of land to which title was registered between 1898 and 1925 inclusive, rights to mines and minerals (and incidental rights) created before the date of registration of the title.

10. A franchise.[380]

11. A manorial right.

12. A right to rent which was reserved to the Crown on the granting of any freehold estate (whether or not the right is still vested in the Crown).

Sch. 12, para. 11, inserting para. 14 into Sch. 3, to preserve until 13 October 2006 the overriding status of leases that were overriding interests under LRA 1925, s. 70(i)(k) (granted for less than twenty-one years); (iii) LRA 2002, s. 90(5), adding PPP leases relating to transport in London.

[376] That is, a legal lease not exceeding seven years, which is not required to be registered with its own individual title. For LRA 2002, s. 4(1)(d), (e) and (f) see p. 955, ante.

[377] The exception is omitted until 13 October 2006: LRA 2002, Sch. 12, para. 10.

[378] See n. 370, supra.   [379] See n. 371, supra.

[380] Paras. 10–14 and 16 are all repealed with effect from 13 October 2013. Those with the benefit of such rights may protect them on the register before then, without payment of fees, by a notice: LRA 2002, s. 117.

13. A non-statutory right in respect of an embankment or sea or river wall.

14. A right to payment in lieu of tithe.

16. A right in respect of the repair of a church chancel.[381]

The first three paragraphs merit closer attention. Paragraphs 1 (legal leases) and 3 (legal easements and profits à prendre arising by implied grant or prescription) have already been discussed in detail.[382] We must now consider paragraph 2, which constitutes the most significant qualification to the general principle that the register should be a mirror of the title.

(1) THE PRINCIPLE OF PARAGRAPH 2

Paragraph 2 is the successor to section 70(1)(g) of the Land Registration Act 1925. These provisions show that the legislature has accepted a compromise in respect of its replacement of the old doctrine of notice by the system of registration. A purchaser should inspect the premises, and he should ask anyone in occupation on what grounds he is there. He will thereby be able to discover the rights and interests of persons in occupation, and it seemed right therefore to subject a purchaser to those rights and interests rather than to let him disregard them because someone had failed to enter them on the register. The paragraph thus operates as a safety-net. Some of these rights may, however, be capable of being protected by notice on the register of the title affected, and if they are, a notice should be applied for by the person entitled. Moreover, as we shall see,[383] there is a duty on the person applying for registration of an estate to disclose certain unregistered interests to the registrar so that they can be recorded on the register. In short, the general policy of the Land Registration Act 2002 is that all claims, rights and interests should be protected by entry on the register as far as possible. This special exception of paragraph 2 is made in the case of an interest belonging to a person in actual occupation. The purchaser should get to know what the rights of such a person are, and, on balance, it is better that he should take subject to them, even at the expense of the doctrine of completeness of the register.

(2) THE SCOPE OF PARAGRAPH 2

Paragraph 2 is different in character from the other paragraphs of Schedule 3. Each of the other paragraphs relates to a particular kind of interest in land: a lease, an easement, a local land charge, and so forth. Paragraph 2, however, is general. It is not limited to any particular kind of interest in land; but it covers any kind of "interest belonging at the time of the disposition to a person in actual occupation, so far as relating to land of which he is in actual occupation" with certain exceptions. We shall consider the exceptions shortly. First, we should notice the range of interests that are covered by these opening words of the paragraph.

(i) "Interest" within paragraph 2

Section 70(1)(g) of the 1925 Act referred to the "rights" of a person in actual occupation, rather than his "interest", but it appears that no change of substance is intended. Paragraph 2 is certainly not confined to an interest which confers the right to occupy, for it extends to

---

[381] Inserted by SI 2003 No. 2431, art. 2(2). See n. 373, supra.
[382] P. 227 et seq, ante (leases); pp. 632 et seq, ante (easements and profits).   [383] P. 986, post.

the *interests belonging to a person in actual occupation*. It is the interests of the occupier and not the occupation itself that are crucial. As Russell LJ put it, when discussing the 1925 Act:[384]

It seems to me that section 70 in all its parts is dealing with rights in reference to land which have the quality of being capable of enduring through different ownerships of the land, according to normal conceptions of title to real property . . . It is the rights of such a person which constitute the overriding interest and must be examined, not his occupation.

The question, therefore, is whether the person in actual occupation has a proprietary right in respect of the registered estate. Thus the deserted wife in occupation of the matrimonial home has no right affecting property entitling her to claim an overriding interest,[385] while the owner of an option to purchase a freehold contained in a lease has, since it "affects the reversion . . . and subsists in reference to the registered land".[386]

Other examples of rights which were held to be sufficient within section 70(1)(g) of the 1925 Act, and which would now constitute "interests" within paragraph 2 of Schedule 3 to the 2002 Act, are a right of pre-emption,[387] an unpaid vendor's lien where the vendor remains in occupation under a lease-back by the purchaser,[388] an equity by estoppel,[389] a right to rectify an instrument,[390] the right to seek rectification of the register,[391] and the right of a beneficiary under a bare trust to the fee simple in equity. Thus in *Hodgson v Marks*:[392]

Mrs H, an elderly widow, voluntarily transferred the registered title to her house to E, who was her lodger. She intended that the house, though it was in E's name, should remain hers, and she continued to reside there. E then sold it to M who became the registered proprietor and executed a mortgage in favour of a building society. Mrs H claimed that E held the house as a bare trustee for her, that she was

---

[384] *National Provincial Bank Ltd v Hastings Car Mart Ltd* [1964] Ch 665 at 696, a dissenting judgment which was upheld (with special reference to this passage) in the House of Lords; [1965] AC 1175 at 1226, 1228, 1240 and 1261–2.

[385] *National Provincial Bank Ltd v Ainsworth* [1965] AC 1175, M & B p. 135; p. 847, ante.

[386] *Webb v Pollmount* [1966] Ch 584 at 595–6, 597–9, per Ungoed-Thomas J; M & B p. 142. Cf *Ferrishurst Ltd v Wallcite Ltd* [1999] Ch 355, where Robert Walker LJ said at 372: "the rights of an occupier of registered land are to be distinguished from the fact of his occupation. The capacity in which a person occupies, for instance as a tenant, need not be indicative of the right which he claims, for instance an option to purchase the freehold reversion or an unpaid vendor's lien" (the effect of the actual decision is reversed by LRA 2002: n. 411, infra).

[387] *Kling v Keston Properties Ltd* (1983) 49 P & CR 212, M & B p. 93; pp. 882–3, ante. Under LRA 2002, s. 115, the right of pre-emption has effect as an interest capable of binding successors in title from the time of its creation.

[388] *London and Cheshire Insurance Co Ltd v Laplagrene Property Co Ltd* [1971] Ch 499, M & B p. 157. Cf *Nationwide Anglia Building Society v Ahmed and Balakrishnan* (1995) 70 P & CR 381 (vendor of premises who remained in possession of part under contractual licence after completion held not to have overriding interest).

[389] *Habermann v Koehler* (1996) 73 P & CR 515. Under LRA 2002, s. 116, an equity by estoppel has effect as an interest capable of binding successors in title from the time the equity arises.

[390] *Blacklocks v JB Developments (Godalming) Ltd* [1982] Ch 183. Cf *Smith v Jones* [1954] 1 WLR 1089, M & B p. 47, where Upjohn J held that a right to rectify a tenancy agreement would not be enforceable by a tenant against a purchaser of the reversion who had inspected the agreement; [1983] Conv 169, 257 (J.T.F.), 361 (D. G. Barnsley); distinguished in *Nurdin & Peacock plc v Ramsden & Co Ltd* [1999] 1 EGLR 119 as being a case on unregistered land; [1999] [Conv] 421 (S. Pascoe). Under LRA 2002, s. 116, a mere equity has effect in relation to registered land as an interest capable of binding successors in title from the time the equity arises.

[391] *Malory Enterprises Ltd v Cheshire Homes (UK) Ltd* [2002] Ch 216.

[392] [1971] Ch 892; *Collings v Lee* [2001] 2 All ER 332 (rights of beneficiary under bare trust arising as a result of transfer induced by fraudulent misrepresentation); [2001] CLJ 477 (R. Nolan); [2001] All ER Rev 253 (P. J. Clarke).

entitled to the beneficial interest in it, and that M and his mortgagee took subject to her rights "as a person in actual occupation" when M became the registered proprietor.

The Court of Appeal held that Mrs H was in actual occupation within the meaning of section 70(1)(g) of the 1925 Act and ordered rectification of the register in her favour as M had not made any enquiries of Mrs H prior to registration of the transfer to him.[393]

Further, in *Williams and Glyn's Bank Ltd v Boland*:[394]

a husband and wife each contributed to the purchase of a matrimonial home. The husband was registered under the Land Registration Act 1925 as the sole proprietor. By virtue of her contribution the wife had an equitable interest in the house; this created equitable beneficial co-ownership, and the husband held the legal title upon trust for sale for himself and his wife as equitable tenants in common.

Later the husband, without the wife's consent, created a legal charge on the house in favour of the bank. On default being made in the mortgage payments, the bank brought an action for possession of the house.

The question was whether the wife's interest was valid against the bank; it could only be so if it was an overriding interest due to her actual occupation of the house under section 70(1)(g) of the Land Registration Act 1925.

The House of Lords held that the beneficial interest of a wife as tenant in common with her husband of the matrimonial home under a statutory trust for sale[395] was an interest which subsists in reference to registered land; and that, being in actual occupation, she had an overriding interest which bound the bank to which her husband had mortgaged the house.

(ii) "belonging at the time of the disposition"

The 2002 Act appears[396] to apply the same rule as had been settled under the 1925 Act: that the date for deciding whether there is actual occupation is the date for completion of the purchase (the disposition), when the transfer is executed and exchanged for the purchase money, rather than the (later) date of registration of the transferee as proprietor.[397] This makes practical

---

[393] See (1971) 35 Conv (NS) 255, 268–276 (I. Leeming): Law Commission Working Paper No. 37 (1971), paras. 56–77.

[394] [1981] AC 487, M & B p. 136; p. 429, ante; Emmet, para. 5.141.7; [1980] Conv 361; [1981] Conv 84 (J. Martin); (1979) 95 LQR 501; (1982) 97 LQR 12 (R. J. Smith); (1980) 130 NLJ 896 (R. L. Deech); *City of London Building Society v Flegg* [1988] AC 54, M & B p. 316; p. 998, post (equitable interests of parents as tenants in common arising from contribution to purchase price of house registered in names of their daughter and son-in-law held to be overreachable by payment to two trustees, even though the parents were in actual occupation). Cf *Winkworth v Edward Baron Development Co Ltd* [1986] 1 WLR 1512. A beneficial interest under a strict settlement is not capable of being an overriding interest: LRA 2002, Sch. 3, para. 2(a), infra; p. 978, ante.

[395] Since 1997, a trust of land under TLATA 1996: pp. 436 et seq, ante.

[396] For a different view, based on the assumption that the "time of the disposition" is registration because under LRA 2002, s. 27(1), the disposition does not operate at law until registration, see Wolstenholme and Cherry, *Annotated Land Registration Act 2002*, para. 3–173A.

[397] *Abbey National Building Society v Cann* [1991] 1 AC 56, M & B p. 143; (1990) 106 LQR 32, 545 (R. J. Smith); [1990] CLJ 397 (A. J. Oakley); (1990) 87 LSG 19–24, 34–19 (M. Beaumont, junior counsel for Mrs Cann); [1991] Conv 116 (S. Baughen), 155 (P. T. Evans). The date for other overriding interests is the date of registration, except for para. 3 of Sch. 3 (legal easements and profits à prendre) where the discoverability test is applied at the time of the disposition. Under Sch. 1 (first registration), all overriding interests (including actual

sense, since it is at that date that the purchaser can make enquiries of those in occupation; he has no control over the timing of registration. The time gap between the disposition and its registration will, however, disappear once electronic conveyancing is fully introduced.[398]

If, however, there has been an overriding interest by virtue of actual occupation on the relevant date, it is not lost if its holder subsequently goes out of occupation.[399]

(iii) "in actual occupation"

Using the same language as under the Land Registration Act 1925, the paragraph protects an interest belonging to a person "in actual occupation".[400] As Lord WILBERFORCE said in *Williams and Glyn's Bank Ltd v Boland*:[401]

These words are ordinary words of plain English, and, should, in my opinion, be interpreted as such ... Given occupation, i.e. presence on the land, I do not think that the word "actual" was intended to introduce any additional qualification, certainly not to suggest that possession must be "adverse": it merely emphasises that what is required is physical presence, not some entitlement in law.

The occupation must involve some degree of permanence and continuity which would rule out mere fleeting presence. In *Abbey National Building Society v Cann*,[402] the House of Lords held that there was no actual occupation where carpets were laid out and furniture moved into a dwelling-house with the vendor's consent. As Lord OLIVER OF AYLMERTON said:[403] "These were acts of a preparatory character carried out by the courtesy of the vendor prior to completion."

Similarly, in *Epps v Esso Petroleum Co Ltd*, the parking of a car at night on an undefined strip of land did not suffice;[404] and in *Strand Securities Ltd v Caswell*,[405] it was held that the tenant of a flat was not in actual occupation, even though the tenant and members of his family used it as a London rendezvous, and he had a key to the flat which contained some of his furniture.[406]

The nature and state of the property may also be relevant. In *Lloyds Bank plc v Rosset*,[407] the Court of Appeal held that, in the case of a semi-derelict farmhouse:

there was physical presence on the property by the wife and her agent of the nature, and the extent, that one would expect of an occupier having regard to the then state of the property, namely, the

---

occupation under para. 2, and easements and profits under para. 3), are tested at the date of registration because first registration does not presuppose any disposition: p. 977, n. 374, ante.

[398] P. 987, post.

[399] *London and Cheshire Insurance Co Ltd v Laplagrene Property Co Ltd* [1971] Ch 499, M & B p. 157.

[400] LRA 1925, s. 70(1)(g) also protected a person not in actual occupation, but "in receipt of the rents and profits thereof", which meant that a landlord's rights were protected by his tenant's actual occupation. This is not reproduced in LRA 2002.

[401] [1981] AC 487 at 504–5, M & B p. 136; *Bhullar v McArdle* (2001) 82 P & CR 38 at [36] (actual occupation must be by the relevant party of the relevant land; no concept of constructive or "transferred" actual occupation).   [402] Supra.

[403] At 94.   [404] [1973] 1 WLR 1071, M & B p. 189.   [405] [1965] Ch 958, M & B p. 153.

[406] In *Chhokar v Chhokar* [1984] FLR 313, M & B p. 157, furniture was held to be relevant.

[407] [1989] Ch 350, M & B p. 150; [1988] Conv 453 (M. P. Thompson); [1989] CLJ 180 (P. G. McHugh); [1988] All ER Rev 163 (P. J. Clarke); (1988) 104 LQR 507 (R. J. Smith); [1989] Conv 342 (P. Sparkes). HL reversed CA on the ground that Mrs Rosset had no beneficial interest under a trust; no views were expressed on the question of her actual occupation: [1991] 1 AC 107. See also *Goodger v Willis* [1999] EGCS 32 (demolition of buildings and laying of concrete base held to be actual occupation); *Malory Enterprises Ltd v Cheshire*

presence involved in actively carrying out the renovation necessary to make the house fit for residential use.

A person may be in actual occupation through the agency of another, such as his caretaker or employee, but not through his gratuitous licensee acting on his own account.[408] On the other hand, it has been suggested that "physical presence" does not connote continued and uninterrupted presence: "such a notion would be absurd". Nor is the requisite presence negatived by repeated and regular absence. Thus a wife would be in actual occupation of a matrimonial home where she spent virtually some part of every day in order to discharge her duties as housewife and mother, but where she did not usually sleep.[409] However, the Court of Appeal has held that minors aged one and three, who had equitable beneficial interests under a trust for sale were not capable of being in actual occupation. "They were there because their parent is there. They have no right of occupation of their own: they are only there as shadows of their parents."[410]

(iv) "so far as relating to land of which he is in actual occupation"

This is a change from the law as it stood before the Land Registration Act 2002. Under the 1925 Act it was held[411] that a person who had an option to purchase the leasehold interest in the whole of a building comprising offices and a garage, but occupied only part of it, had an overriding interest in respect of the whole. Now, however, the overriding interest—and therefore the priority afforded by it—can exist only in relation to the part actually occupied.

(v) Exceptions from paragraph 2

We now come to the exceptions contained within paragraph 2.[412]

Homes (UK) Ltd [2002] Ch 216 (derelict block of flats only used for temporary storage; gates in fence kept locked and ground floor windows blocked up; held to be actual occupation).

[408] See *Strand Securities Ltd v Caswell*, supra; *Lloyd v Dugdale* [2002] 2 P & CR 13 (where D Ltd, rather than D, major shareholder and managing director of D Ltd, was in occupation as licensee of D, D was not in actual occupation. Nor did D's regular presence help, since he was there as managing director and not on his own account).

[409] *Kingsnorth Finance Co Ltd v Tizard* [1986] 1 WLR 783 at 788, per Judge John Finlay QC, M & B p. 156; [1987] CLJ 28 (P. C. McHugh); [1986] Conv 283 (M. P. Thompson). This was a case on unregistered land. See also *Chhokar v Chhokar*, supra (wife evicted by fraudulent purchaser of matrimonial home from husband held to be in actual occupation).

[410] *Hypo-Mortgage Services Ltd v Robinson* [1997] 2 FLR 71, per NOURSE LJ, citing *Bird v Syme Thomson* [1979] 1 WLR 440.

[411] *Ferrishurst Ltd v Wallcite Ltd* [1999] Ch 355; [1999] Conv 144 (S. Pascoe); [1999] CLJ 483 (L. Tee); (2000) 63 MLR 113 (J. Hill).

[412] In addition, certain interests are excluded by other statutes from being overriding interests under LRA 2002, Schs. 1 and 3: the spouse or civil partner's rights of occupation under Family Law Act 1996, s. 31(10)(b); the right of a tenant arising from a notice under the Leasehold Reform Act 1967 of his desire to acquire the freehold or an extended lease: Leasehold Reform Act 1967, s. 5(5); the secure tenant's "right to buy" under Part V of the Housing Act 1985: Housing Act 1985 Sch. 9A, para. 6(1), inserted by Housing and Planning Act 1986, s. 8(2), Sch. 2; the rights conferred by or under an access order under the Access to Neighbouring Land Act 1992: Access to Neighbouring Land Act 1992, s. 5; the right to an overriding lease under LT(C)A 1995, s. 20(6).

Two of them relate to particular types of interests in land. An interest under a settlement under the Settled Land Act 1925 cannot be an overriding interest, even if the beneficiary is in actual occupation.[413] Nor can[414]

a leasehold estate in land granted to take effect in possession after the end of the period of three months beginning with the date of the grant and which has not taken effect in possession at the time of the disposition.

Such leases are required to be registered.[415]

Of more general significance, however, are the other two. First, a purchaser is not bound by[416]

an interest of a person of whom inquiry was made before the disposition and who failed to disclose the right when he could reasonably have been expected to do so.

This is quite straightforward. If the purchaser has in fact asked questions of a person in actual occupation, the latter's interest is not given priority over the purchaser's disposition, once it is registered, if he failed to disclose his rights, as long as he could reasonably[417] have been expected to do so. In effect, once the question is asked, the person in actual occupation has a duty of disclosure—or, at least, he will lose his priority if he does not disclose his interest.

But we then find a final exception, new in the 2002 Act, which has the effect of re-introducing the doctrine of notice into this category of overriding interests.[418] A purchaser is not bound by[419]

an interest—

(i) which belongs to a person whose occupation would not have been obvious on a reasonably careful inspection of the land at the time of the disposition, and

(ii) of which the person to whom the disposition is made does not have actual knowledge at that time.

The question is not whether the *interest*, but the *occupation*, would have been obvious. But it makes no difference whether the purchaser did in fact make any inspections or inquiries. This exception allows a purchaser to say that, although a person who had in interest in the property was in actual occupation, he is not bound by it because (i) that occupation *would* not have been obvious[420] on a reasonably careful inspection, and (ii) he did not in fact know

---

[413] LRA 2002, Sch. 3, para. 2(a). This follows the position under LRA 1925, s. 86(2). It must therefore be protected by the entry of a restriction on the register: p. 974, ante. An interest under a trust of land should also be protected by the entry of a restriction, although if not so protected it can take effect as an overriding interest under para. 2: *Williams and Glyn's Bank Ltd v Boland*, supra.

[414] Ibid., para. 2(d). It is perhaps a rather unlikely scenario for the tenant under a lease which has not yet taken effect in possession, to be in actual occupation.   [415] Ibid., s. 4(1)(d).

[416] Ibid., Sch. 3, para. 2(b).

[417] This is in fact more favourable to the occupier than LRA 1925, s. 70(1)(g), which only excluded the overriding interest where "enquiry is made of such person . . . and the rights are not disclosed"—there was no test of reasonableness in failing to disclose.

[418] LRA 2002 also introduces the principles of notice into the category of overriding interests relating to legal easements and profits à prendre: Sch. 3, para. 3(1); p. 634, ante.   [419] LRA 2002, Sch. 3, para. 2(c).

[420] "Obviousness" may be a rather generous test in the purchaser's favour, less demanding than constructive notice of the occupation: Law Commission Report on Land Registration for the Twenty-First Century 2001 (Law Com No. 271), Explanatory Notes, para. 617.

about it. The first limb of the test is objective; the second subjective. In effect, it is a test based on (i) constructive and (ii) actual notice. But although this introduction of the doctrine of notice appears at first sight to undermine the purposes of the system of registered land, where notice is normally irrelevant,[421] it should be realised that it does not re-introduce the doctrine as it existed in unregistered land, under which the question of whether a purchaser is bound by a third party's interest depended on whether he had notice of it.[422] Instead, in registered land, in the absence of the entry of a notice on the register, it is the fact of the third party's actual occupation that renders his interest binding on the purchaser; but not if the occupation was not reasonably obvious nor in fact known by the purchaser. It is not the purchaser's notice that binds him, but his *lack* of notice that can *prevent* him being bound by the third party's right.[423]

(vi) Practical solutions to the problems of paragraph 2

The decision in *Williams and Glyn's Bank Ltd v Boland*[424] highlighted a real difficulty caused by the category of overriding interests based on actual occupation—and, in particular, a difficulty for institutional lenders, who naturally sought ways in which to avoid the consequence of being bound by such an overriding interest. They had to make more careful inquiries of the mortgagor[425] and of the property, and, if they discovered an actual occupant who had a beneficial interest in the property, they resorted to forms of consent or waiver to be signed by the occupant. But difficulties still exist. The waiver may be invalid, if there is undue influence either on the part of the lender (or of an agent acting on his behalf), or of a third party, such as the husband against the wife, and the bank has not fulfilled its duty to ensure that the wife is entering into the transaction properly informed and without undue pressure.[426]

Another possibility is to insist on the appointment of an additional trustee (there was only one trustee in *Boland*) so that the mortgage money can be paid to two trustees, thereby overreaching the beneficial interest of the occupant and attaching it to the equity of redemption in the hands of the mortgagor and the money paid to him.[427]

On the other hand, if the occupant knows that the property is being acquired by the registered proprietor with the aid of a mortgage, the occupant's interest may not bind the mortgagee, either by virtue of estoppel,[428] or by virtue of an imputed intention that his interest is subject to the rights of the mortgagee.[429]

---

[421] *Williams and Glyn's Bank Ltd v Boland* [1981] AC 487 at 503–4, per Lord WILBERFORCE: "the system is designed to free the purchaser from the hazards of notice—real or constructive... The only kind of notice recognised is by entry on the register". See however *Peffer v Rigg* [1977] 1 WLR 285, M & B p.176; *Lyus v Prowsa Developments Ltd* [1982] 1 WLR 1044, M & B p. 176; p. 972, n. 334, ante.   [422] Pp. 58 et seq, ante.

[423] It has been said, however, that whether the person is *in fact* in actual occupation is to be decided by reference to the discoverability of it: *Malory Enterprises Ltd v Cheshire Homes (UK) Ltd* [2002] Ch 216 at [81], per ARDEN LJ: "The requisite physical presence must, as it seems to me, in fairness be such as to put a person inspecting the land on notice that there was some person in occupation." This must, however, be open to question.   [424] Supra.

[425] "Reliance on the true ipse dixit of the vendor will not suffice": *Hodgson v Marks* [1971] Ch 892 at 932, per RUSSELL LJ.

[426] *Royal Bank of Scotland plc v Etridge (No 2)* [2002] 2 AC 73, M & B p. 827; pp. 749 et seq, ante.

[427] *City of London Building Society v Flegg* [1988] AC 54, p. 998, post.

[428] *Spiro v Lintern* [1973] 1 WLR 1002; Emmet, para. 12.031.

[429] *Bristol and West Building Society v Henning* [1985] 1 WLR 778; *Paddington Building Society v Mendelsohn* (1985) 50 P & CR 244; [1986] Conv 57 (M. P. Thompson); *Abbey National Building Society v Cann* [1991] 1 AC

(c) Duty to disclose overriding interests

The Land Registration Act 2002[430] introduced a new duty on the person applying for registration to provide to the registrar certain information about overriding interests affecting the estate to which the application relates. The duty arises in the case of both first registration and registration of subsequent dispositions.

There is no specific penalty for failure to disclose, but the object of the provision is to ensure that as many rights as possible are brought onto the register: the registrar may enter a notice in the register in respect of overriding interests which are disclosed.[431]

(d) Criticism of overriding interests

The effect of overriding interests is, as we have seen, to bind a transferee from a registered proprietor, whether he knows about them or not—although we have seen that the Land Registration Act 2002 has protected the transferee against certain undiscoverable interests.[432] They detract from the principle that the register should be a mirror of the title, and so it is important that they should be able to justify their existence as a separate category within the system of registered conveyancing. A balance has to be struck between the protection of the person enjoying the interest and the inconvenience to a purchaser. Sympathy for the latter leads to a plea for as complete an abolition of the category as is feasible.

Criticism of overriding interests must, however, be tempered by four considerations. First, although the range of overriding interests has been reduced by the 2002 Act,[433] the category cannot be abandoned completely, however desirable it is that the register should be a complete mirror of the title. It is impossible to enter on the register easements and profits being acquired by prescription. Secondly, as we have seen, the legislature has decided as a matter of policy that protection should be accorded to the rights of a person in actual occupation, even if he has failed to register his interest. This is most desirable in those situations where the holder of the right might not consult a solicitor and therefore

---

56 at 94; *Equity and Law Home Loans Ltd v Prestridge* [1992] 1 WLR 137 (a person who consented to a mortgage was deemed to consent to a later mortgage replacing the earlier mortgage, even if it was obtained without consent, to the extent of the amount secured by the first mortgage plus interest); *Locabail (UK) Ltd v Waldorf Investment Corpn* The Times, 31 March 1999; *Woolwich Building Society v Dickman* [1996] 3 All ER 204; [1996] All ER Rev 254 (P. J. Clarke); [1998] CLJ 328 (L. Tee). And the mortgage itself may be invalid if the registered proprietor has no power to create it.

[430] S. 71; LRR 2003, rr. 28, 57; Land Registry Practice Guide 15. There is no requirement to disclose interests that cannot be protected by notice on the register, public rights, local land charges and leases which have one year or less still to run and, in the case of first registration, interests that are apparent from the deeds and documents of title accompanying the application.

[431] LRR 2003, rr. 28(4), 57(5). Under LRA 1925 the applicant had no duty of disclosure, but the registrar has a mandatory duty to enter a notice on first registration of "any easement, right, privilege, or benefit created by an instrument" which appeared on the title and adversely affected the land: LRA 1925, s. 70(2).

[432] LRA 2002, Sch. 3, paras. 2(c) (interest belonging to person whose occupation not discoverable), 3 (easement or profit not discoverable); p. 978, ante.

[433] From 13 October 2013 the only overriding interests that will remain are: most leases granted for three years or less; interests of a person in actual occupation; legal easements and profits that have arisen by implied grant or prescription; customary and public rights; local land charges; and certain mineral rights: Abbey and Richards, *Land Registration Act 2002*, para. 12.6; nn. 372, 380, supra.

be unaware of the need for entry on the register, such as a contract for a lease. This is the opposite to the Draconian policy of the Land Charges Act 1972 for unregistered conveyancing.[434] "The rule for registered land is much more reasonable, for possession is the strongest possible title to security."[435] Thirdly, it is impracticable to require the registration of all short tenancies. Fourthly, overriding interests appear frequently on the register—and, since the introduction of the duty of disclosure under the Land Registration Act 2002,[436] more overriding interests will be entered on the register. Even before the 2002 Act the registrar had a duty to enter a note of interests on the register, and in 1969 the then Registrar was able to write:[437]

The plain fact is...that there are mandatory provisions requiring most overriding interests to be entered on the register, which operate either on first registration,[438] or on a dealing with registered land,[439] or at any time on proof of their being furnished,[440] and so ensure that, save for squatters' rights,[441] which cannot be recorded, or rights of occupiers or lessees, which are discoverable, under the rule in *Hunt v Luck*,[442] from a proper inspection and inquiry, or local land charges which obviously must be recorded locally,[443] they are all entered on the register.

(7) Electronic Conveyancing[444]

As we have seen[445] the changes made by the Land Registration Act 2002 prepare the way for the move from a paper-based system of conveyancing to one which is entirely electronic. The enabling provisions for its introduction are set out in Part 8 of the Act, and Schedule 5 sets out the details for the Land Registry network under which electronic conveyancing will take place.

When electronic conveyancing is fully introduced,[446] it will only be possible to make transfers of land and to create many rights and interests in and over land by their electronic registration. The effect will be to move from the present three-stage process, under which a document is executed in the form prescribed by the Land Registration Rules, is then lodged with the appropriate district land registry, and, after the transaction has been processed, the appropriate entry is made on the register. Under the new scheme there will be only a one-stage process by which the completion of a transaction and its registration take place simultaneously. The so-called registration gap will be eliminated.[447]

---

[434] This aspect of the LCA 1925 may have been due to an error on the part of the draftsman of the 1925 legislation: (1977) 41 Conv NS p. 419, n. 31 (C. Harpum); [1982] Conv pp. 215–17 (M. Friend and J. Newton), M & B p. 50.   [435] (1956) CLJ 228 (H. W. R. Wade).

[436] P. 986, ante.   [437] (1969) 32 MLR at 129 (T. B. F. Ruoff).   [438] LRA 1925, s. 70(2).

[439] Ibid., ss. 19(2), 22(2).   [440] Ibid., s. 70(3). This is in fact discretionary only.

[441] Ibid., s. 70(1)(f).   [442] [1902] 1 Ch 428; p. 63, ante.   [443] LRA 1925, s. 70(1)(i).

[444] R & R, chap. 19; H & B, Part 5; Land Registry Consultation on E-conveyancing (2002) and Consultation Report (2003). The current state of progress can be discovered by consulting the Land Registry web site: www.landregistry.gov.uk/e-conveyancing.   [445] P. 110–11, ante.

[446] It is being introduced incrementally; certain forms are already capable of being lodged electronically, although the full system will take some years to introduce: p. 110, ante.

[447] For an illustration of how the Law Commission thought that a typical conveyancing transaction might operate under electronic conveyancing, see Land Registration for the Twenty-First Century (Law Com No. 271), paras. 2.52–2.55; M & B pp. 200–4.

III Transfer by Other Estate Owners

A *Personal Representatives*

(1) Functions and Powers

The next class of estate owner consists of personal representatives, that is, the persons, whether executors or administrators, to whom the property of a deceased owner passes.

(a) *Executors and administrators*

An *executor* is a person who is appointed by the testator for the purpose of carrying the provisions of his will into effect: to prove the will (i.e. obtain a grant of probate), and then to administer the estate.[448] If, however, he dies intestate, or, though testate, failed to appoint an executor or his appointment of an executor fails,[449] it is necessary to make application to the court for the appointment of personal representatives. When the court does this, it is said to grant administration, or more fully, to grant letters of administration, and the personal representative to whom the grant is made is called an *administrator*.[450]

If a last surviving executor proves the will of X, and dies testate without having completed his office, then *his* executor steps into his place and becomes the executor of X.[451] But if such last surviving executor dies intestate, his administrator does not become executor of the will of X,[452] and in such a case it is necessary for the court to appoint another person to administer such property as is still unadministered. This is called administration *de bonis non*.[453]

While any legal proceeding that concerns the validity of a will is pending, the court may appoint an "administrator pending suit", who has all the powers of a general administrator except that he cannot distribute the residue among those entitled.[454]

(b) *Vesting of property in the personal representatives*

Under the Administration of Estates Act 1925, all the property of a deceased person, real as well as personal, with the exception of life interests, joint tenancies, entailed interests unless disposed of by the deceased's will and interests of a corporator sole in the corporation property, becomes vested in his personal representatives.[455] Their duties are to pay the debts

---

[448] For the rules governing testacy, and succession generally, see the 16th edn of this book, chap. 25; *Theobald on Wills*; *Williams on Wills*; Miller, *The Machinery of Succession*; Parry and Clark, *The Law of Succession*.

[449] If the deceased made a will, but it contained no appointment of executors, or if the appointment fails, for instance, by the death, renunciation, minority or lack of mental capacity of the executor, the court makes a grant of "administration with the will annexed": SCA 1981, s. 119. The order of priority of right to such a grant is based on the beneficial claims under the will, the residuary legatee or devisee having the first right: Non-Contentious Probate Rules 1987, SI 1987 No. 2024, r. 20.

[450] The Non-Contentious Probate Rules 1987, supra, set out a list of persons who are entitled to the grant, in order of priority, but the court may appoint as an administrator such a person as it thinks fit, if by reason of any special circumstances it appears to the court to be necessary or expedient: Supreme Court Act 1981, s. 116; for example, where the estate is insolvent, or where land has been settled by the intestate in his lifetime. In the latter case the grant of administration might be given to the trustees of the settlement if they were willing to act.

[451] AEA 1925, s. 7(1).   [452] Ibid., s. 7(3).

[453] Or "administration *de bonis non administratis*": a grant "concerning goods not administered".

[454] Supreme Court Act 1981, s. 117.

[455] Ss. 1(1), 3(1), (3)–(5). An executor derives his title from the will and not from the grant of probate, and therefore the general rule is that he may do all such things and perform all such duties upon the death of the

of the deceased and all expenses and dues arising on his death out of the property, and then to distribute the residue among the beneficiaries under the will or among those entitled in the case of intestacy.[456] Both at common law and by statute they have exceedingly wide powers of disposition over the property.

(c) Powers in relation to land

A conveyance by personal representatives of the legal estate may become necessary in two types of cases; where they transfer the land to a beneficiary; or where, in order to raise money for the payment of debts, they convey to a purchaser in the ordinary course of administration. Section 18 of the Trusts of Land and Appointment of Trustees Act 1996 confers on personal representatives, subject to suitable modifications, all the powers of trustees of land.[457] Three sections of the Act are excluded: section 10 on consents, section 11 on consultation with beneficiaries, and section 14 on power to apply to the court.[458]

Personal representatives have the overreaching powers of trustees of land including, if the occasion arises, overreaching by approved trustees under an *ad hoc* trust of land.[459] Thus, even equities charged on the land prior to the death of the deceased may be overreached. No approval by the court is necessary; neither is it necessary, as it is in the case of trustees of land, that there should be at least two personal representatives.[460]

(2) Transfers by Personal Representatives

(a) Land not yet registered

Where the owner of an unregistered estate dies, the personal representatives will transfer the estate either to a beneficiary or to a purchaser under the old system of unregistered conveyancing. This will, however, trigger compulsory first registration.[461]

(1) TRANSFER TO BENEFICIARY BY ASSENT

The transfer of land to a beneficiary is effected, in practice, not by a conveyance by deed, but by an *assent*, that is, a document in writing that operates to vest the estate or interest in the

deceased as fall within the province of an executor. The administrator, however, derives his title only from the grant of letters of adminstration (although once the grant is made it relates back to the date of death). The property of the deceased, both real and personal, passes to an administrator upon his appointment by the court to the same extent as it passes to an executor, but in the interval between the death of the deceased and the appointment of an administrator both the real and personal estate of the deceased vests in the Public Trustee until administration is granted: AEA 1925, s. 9, as substituted by LP (Miscellaneous Provisions) Act 1994, s. 14. Before the Act, the estate vested in the President of the Family Division of the High Court. See Law Commission Report on Title on Death 1989 (Law Com No. 184), paras. 2.24–2.26: [1990] Conv 72 (H. W. Wilkinson).

[456] For the rules for distribution of the residuary estate on intestacy, both before and under AEA 1925, see the 16th edn of this book, pp. 945–58; Sherrin and Bonehill, *Law and Practice of Intestate Succession*; Miller, *The Machinery of Succession*; Law Commission Report on Title on Death 1989 (Law Com No. 184), paras. 2.24–2.26; [1990] Conv 72 (H. W. Wilkinson). In certain limited cases the pre-1926 rules for distribution still apply: pp. 463, 486, 494, 922, ante.

[457] AEA 1925, s. 39(1)(ii), as amended by TLATA 1996, s. 25(1), Sch. 3, para. 6(1), (2); W & H, paras. 2.180–2.188.   [458] Pp. 444, 445, 449, ante.

[459] Pp. 1000, post.

[460] LPA 1925, s. 27(2), as amended by TLATA 1996, s. 25(1), Sch. 2, para. 4(8). But, if there are two or more personal representatives, a contract or conveyance of land cannot be made without the concurrence of all of them (or, in the case of executors, all the *proving* executors), or a court order: AEA 1925, s. 2(2), as amended by LP (Miscellaneous Provisions) Act 1994, s. 16(1). See Law Commission Report on Title on Death 1989 (Law Com No. 184, Cm 777), paras. 2.13–2.19.   [461] LRA 2002, s. 4(1)(a)(ii).

person entitled.[462] Prior to 1926 an assent was valid if it was oral or even if it could be inferred from conduct,[463] but, as we have already seen, this is no longer true where the interest to be transferred is a *legal estate*.[464]

The beneficiary, in order to protect himself against a later conveyance of the same land by the personal representative, usually requires that notice of the assent be endorsed on the probate copy of the will or letters of administration, i.e. on the official documents which certify that the representative is entitled to act as such.[465] Even so, a beneficiary in whose favour an assent has been made is not secure, for an unpaid creditor of the deceased may enforce payment by following the property into the hands of a devisee, except one who takes in consideration of money or marriage.[466] When this course is taken, the court, notwithstanding the assent, may declare a beneficiary to be a trustee of the land for a creditor, or may order a sale or other transaction to be carried out in order to satisfy the rights of the persons interested, or may make a vesting order with a view to the execution of a conveyance.[467]

(2) TRANSFER TO PURCHASER BY CONVEYANCE

When the personal representatives themselves convey to a purchaser, there is a danger that the legal estate may already have been passed to a beneficiary under the will. However, a written statement by a personal representative that he has not given or made an assent or conveyance in respect of a legal estate, is, in favour of a purchaser for money or money's worth, sufficient evidence that no previous assent or conveyance has been given, unless notice of such has been endorsed on the probate or administration.[468] A purchaser who obtains this written statement acquires a good title to the legal estate, subject, however, to one exception, for it is provided that the statement shall not be conclusive against an earlier purchaser for money or money's worth who has taken a conveyance either from the personal representative or from a beneficiary in whose favour an assent has been given. If, therefore, A takes a conveyance for value of a legal estate from a personal representative without having the fact endorsed on the probate, and B later takes a conveyance from the personal representative of the same estate, relying upon the written but untrue statement that no previous conveyance has been made, it would seem that B obtains no protection from the statute.

The revocation of the probate or administration after a conveyance has been made by a personal representative does not affect the title of the purchaser.[469] If, for instance, probate of a will dated 1998 is granted to an executor, A, and subsequently a different will dated 2000 is discovered, the grant of probate to A will be revoked and a new one made to the executor appointed by the 2000 will. All conveyances, however, of any interest in real or personal estate already made by A in his capacity as executor in favour of a purchaser remain valid, and therefore the registration of any estate which has been made pursuant to such a conveyance remains valid.

---

[462] AEA 1925, s. 36(1), (2). Until then the beneficiary has no more than a right to have the estate duly administered: *Passant v Jackson* [1986] STC 164 at 167.   [463] E.g. *Wise v Whitburn* [1924] 1 Ch 460.
[464] P. 896, ante.   [465] AEA 1925, s. 36(5).   [466] Ibid., s. 38(1); *Salih v Atchi* [1961] AC 778.
[467] Ibid., s. 38(2).   [468] Ibid., s. 36(6), (11).
[469] Ibid., s. 37; confirming *Hewson v Shelley* [1914] 2 Ch 13. "Purchaser" means a lessee, mortgagee or other person who in good faith acquires an interest in property for valuable consideration, and "valuable consideration" includes marriage, but does not include a nominal consideration in money: s. 55(1)(xviii).

(b) Land already registered[470]

Personal representatives of a sole registered proprietor or of the survivor of two or more joint proprietors are entitled to be registered as proprietors in place of the deceased proprietor on the production to the Registrar of the grant of probate or letters of administration.[471] There is, however, an alternative procedure which is more frequently adopted, for the personal representatives need not themselves be registered but may have the land transferred direct to the devisee, legatee or purchaser, who will be registered in place of the deceased proprietor on production of the instrument of assent or transfer together with the grant of probate or letters of administration.[472] Although this latter alternative procedure saves some trouble, it is undesirable, as, pending the lodging of the transfer or assent, the register is necessarily kept out of date, and notice served by the Land Registry on the deceased proprietor could well go astray.

Rule 162(2) of the Land Registration Rules 2003, dealing with transfer or assent by personal representatives, provides that:

The registrar shall not be under a duty to investigate the reasons a transfer of registered land by a personal representative of a deceased sole proprietor or last surviving joint proprietor is made nor to consider the contents of the will and, provided the terms of any restriction on the register are complied with, he must assume, whether he knows of the terms of the will or not, that the personal representative is acting correctly and within his powers.

This rule shows the extent to which the curtain principle applies to registered land.

B Tenants for Life and Statutory Owners

In the earlier part of the book we discussed the evolution and framework of the strict settlement.[473] On the conveyancing side three further topics require consideration: the vesting of the legal estate in each new tenant for life as and when he becomes entitled to possession; the termination of the settlement; and the statutory simplification of a conveyance of settled land.

(1) Vesting of Legal Estate

The scheme of the Act, as we have already noticed, is that the legal estate shall be vested from time to time in each new tenant for life as and when he becomes entitled to possession. In registered land, the tenant for life must therefore generally be registered as proprietor.[474] Let us take the different circumstances that may arise and observe how this procedure operates.

(a) Death of tenant for life

Let us suppose that under a settlement lands stand limited to H for life and then, after certain interests in favour of the other members of H's family, to his son, S, for life. When H dies the legal estate devolves upon his special personal representatives, i.e. the trustees of

---

[470] R & R, chap. 32; Land Registry Practice Guide 6.
[471] LRA 2002, Sch. 4, paras. 7(d), 5(b) (alteration of the register to reflect the position at law); H & B, para. 8.5.
[472] LRR 2003, r. 162; H & B, para. 13.8.   [473] Pp. 68 et seq, ante; 399 et seq., ante.
[474] LRR 2003, Sch. 7, para. 1. Although there are no doubt many settlements in existence which have not yet been registered, all settlements will in due course be registered as transfers of the legal title are effected.

the settlement, and not upon his general personal representatives whose task it is to administer his non-settled property.[475] Upon the death of H the special personal representatives come under an obligation to convey the legal estate to S.[476] In unregistered land this may be done either by a vesting deed or by a vesting assent, which contains the particulars set out above at pages 403–4. If the land is already registered, a prescribed form of transfer must be used, which contains the same particulars, and the personal representatives must apply for S to be entered in the register as proprietor.[477]

(b) Minor tenant for life reaches full age

A minor cannot be an estate owner,[478] and if he becomes entitled to a tenancy for life under a settlement the statutory powers are exercisable by the trustees, to whom, in their capacity as *statutory owners*,[479] the legal estate must be conveyed or, in registered land, in whose name it must be registered.[480] It is their duty, however, upon the attainment by the minor of his majority, to convey the legal estate to him by a vesting deed or a vesting assent[481] or, in registered land, to transfer the estate to him so that he can be entered in the register as proprietor.[482]

(c) Tenant for life deprived of statutory powers

Where, for example, there is a limitation to A for life with a limitation over to X and Y on *protective trusts* (i.e. trusts which give certain powers to X and Y if A becomes bankrupt or attempts to part with his life interest in favour of his creditors),[483] A is bound to convey (or, in registered land, transfer) the legal estate to X and Y as statutory owners upon the occurrence of an event bringing the trusts into operation.[484]

(2) Termination of Strict Settlement

A settlement comes to an end if all equitable interests have ceased and if there can be no further occasion to exercise the statutory powers, provided that the person entitled to the legal estate is of full age.[485] When this occurs it is essential that the person beneficially entitled should have a document showing his right to deal freely with the land, and it is therefore provided that he may require the trustees to execute a deed of discharge declaring that the land is free from the trusts.[486] The termination of a settlement, however, most frequently occurs on the death of a tenant for life, for example, where there is a limitation to A for life with remainder to X in fee simple and A dies. There is no room for *special* personal representatives and the legal estate must be conveyed by A's general personal representatives to X, the absolute owner.[487] In registered land, the personal representatives apply for X to be registered as proprietor, and for the restrictions relating to the settlement to be cancelled.[488]

---

[475] AEA 1925, s. 22(1). No new settlements can be created after 1996: TLATA 1996, s. 2(1).
[476] SLA 1925, s. 7(1).
[477] LRR 2003, Sch. 7, para. 12(1). The special personal representatives may themselves apply to be registered as proprietor in the mean time: ibid., para. 11.   [478] P. 911, ante.
[479] P. 403, ante.   [480] LRR 2003, Sch. 7, paras. 1, 10, 13.   [481] SLA 1925, s. 7(2), (3); s. 19(3).
[482] LRR 2003, Sch. 7, para. 9.   [483] P. 568, ante.   [484] SLA 1925, s. 7(4); LRR 2003, Sch. 7, para. 9.
[485] Ibid., s. 3; LP(A)A 1926, Schedule.   [486] Ibid., s. 17(1).
[487] Ibid., s. 7(5); *Re Bridgett and Hayes' Contract* [1928] Ch 163, M & B p. 363; *Re Bordass' Estate* [1929] P 107.
[488] LRR 2003, Sch. 7, para. 12(2). The personal representatives must show their title by the grant of probate or letters of administration, but then the registrar is under no duty to investigate why the personal representatives

(3) Simplification of Conveyancing

(a) Unregistered land

(1) POSITION OF PURCHASER

Taking the normal case, and presuming that the legal estate has been vested in the tenant for life by virtue of a vesting deed, it is worth our while to notice how the sale of the settled land to a purchaser is expedited and simplified, as compared with the practice prevailing before 1926. The main object of reducing the rights of the various beneficiaries to the status of equitable interests is to keep those rights off the title to the legal estate and to relieve a purchaser from the responsibility of seeing that they are not prejudiced by the sale. The fate of the equitable interests is to be no concern of the purchaser. His one concern is that the title to the *legal* estate shall be proved. He must investigate the title down to the first vesting deed, that is, he must require the vendor to prove that the person who purported to vest the legal estate in the estate owner by the principal vesting deed was entitled to do so, though of course if land remains settled for a generation or two the time will come when title is made by the production of a series of vesting deeds or assents. But the former practice of abstracting the beneficial limitations is forbidden. The trust instrument is not disclosed; it is not allowed to appear on the title; and with a few exceptions[489] the purchaser is not entitled to call for it or to make it the subject of interrogatories. Moreover, once satisfied that the vesting deed was executed by a party competent to execute it, "a purchaser of a legal estate in settled land" must take it at its face value and make the following assumptions:

That the estate owner named in the vesting deed is the tenant for life or statutory owner and entitled to exercise the statutory powers.

That the trustees named in the deed are the properly constituted trustees.

That the settlements contained in the deed in accordance with the requirements of the Settled Land Act 1925 are correct.

That a later deed appointing new trustees is correct.[490]

This is a distinct simplification of the practice that obtained before 1926. Before that date, as we have seen,[491] a purchaser was compelled to investigate the whole settlement, including resettlements, so as to satisfy himself that the land was settled land within the meaning of the Settled Land Act 1882, that the vendor was tenant for life within the same meaning, and that there were proper trustees of the settlement. But all these facts are now certified by the vesting deed, for this short document guarantees the fundamental matters concerning which inquiries had formerly to be made. The purchaser is secure in taking a conveyance of the legal estate from the person by whom the vesting deed asserts that this estate is held; he can presume, in reliance on the same deed, that the Settled Land Act

---

are making the transfer, and he must assume that they are acting correctly and within their powers: ibid., para. 12(3).

[489] SLA 1925, s. 110(2)(a), (b), (c), (d). For example, where a settlement *inter vivos* has not been created by the proper method or where there is a pre-1926 settlement, whether made *inter vivos* or by will. See Emmet, paras. 23.050–23.051.   [490] Ibid., s. 110(2); but the proviso to the section contains exceptions.

[491] Pp. 74–5, ante.

powers apply to the property; and, provided that he pays the purchase money to the required trustees,[492] he can ignore the equitable rights of the beneficiaries.

(2) OVERREACHABLE INTERESTS

In other words, the conveyance by the tenant for life overreaches the equitable interests of the beneficiaries and also certain other interests, that is, makes them enforceable against the money in the hands of the trustees, and no longer against the land.[493] More precisely, the position in this respect is as follows:

The conveyance by the tenant for life passes to the purchaser a title to the legal estate discharged from the following:

  (i) All legal or equitable estates, interests and charges arising *under* the settlement.[494]

  (ii) Limited owner's charges,[495] general equitable charges[496] and certain annuities.[497]

These three interests are overreached even though they have been registered as land charges and even though they were created prior to the settlement.[498] The reason is that they lose nothing in value or protection by their conversion into claims against the purchase money.

On the other hand the conveyance by the tenant for life does *not* overreach the following:

  (i) Legal estates and charges by way of legal mortgage having priority to the settlement.[499]

  (ii) Legal estates and charges by way of legal mortgage to secure money which has been actually raised before the date of the conveyance.[500] An example is a mortgage created before the conveyance by which money has been raised for the payment of portions.

  (iii) Terms of years, easements and profits granted for money or money's worth under the settlement.[501]

  (iv) Estate contracts, restrictive covenants and equitable easements created after 1925,[502] if registered as land charges.[503]

  (v) Restrictive covenants and equitable easements created before 1926, but only if the purchaser has actual or constructive notice of them.[504]

  (vi) Estate contracts created before 1926 if the purchaser has actual or constructive notice of them, or if they are capable of registration and have been registered. Such a contract becomes capable of registration upon its assignment after 1925.[505]

---

[492] P. 995, post.   [493] LPA 1925, s. 2(1)(i).   [494] SLA 1925, s. 72(2).   [495] P. 940, ante.
[496] P. 940, ante.
[497] I.e., under LCA 1972, s. 1(4), Sch. 1. "Annuity" is here limited to annuities for one or more life or lives created after 25 April 1855, and before 1 January 1926. The register in which they might formerly have been entered was closed as from 1 January 1926. All annuities created after 1925 are registrable as general equitable charges.   [498] SLA 1925, s. 72(3); see (1934) 77 LJ News 3, 21, 39, 57 (J.M.L.).
[499] SLA 1925, s. 72(2)(i).
[500] Ibid., s. 72(2)(ii). See *Re Mundy and Roper's Contract* [1899] 1 Ch 275 at 289, per CHITTY LJ.
[501] Ibid., s. 72(2)(iii)(a).   [502] Pp. 940, 941, ante.   [503] SLA 1925, s. 72(2)(iii)(a), (b).
[504] P. 947, ante.   [505] LCA 1972, s. 4(7).

For the overreaching provisions to apply, it is essential that upon a sale of the land by the tenant for life or the statutory owner, the purchase money is paid either to the trustees or into court;[506] moreover, except where the trusteeship is held by a trust corporation,[507] there must be at least two trustees to whom this payment is made.[508]

(3) FAULTY CONVEYANCES

If the machinery of the Settled Land Act 1925 is observed, then not only is conveyancing simplified in favour of a purchaser, but also adequate protection is accorded to the beneficial interests of the settlement. We have seen how the Act makes provision for failure to use the machinery at all,[509] and we must now consider some of the problems that arise where the statutory machinery is used but nevertheless mistakes occur in its use.

In the first place, section 5(3) of the Settled Land Act 1925 provides that a vesting deed shall not be invalidated by reason only of any error in any of the statements or particulars required to be contained in it. This must be read in conjunction with section 110(2) which, as we have seen,[510] provides that a purchaser of a legal estate in settled land shall not be entitled to call for the trust instrument, but, instead, must assume that certain particulars stated in the vesting deed are true. There are, however, exceptional cases in which a purchaser must examine the trust instrument and satisfy himself that the statements in the vesting deed are true. In these cases, of course, section 5(3) will not avail him.

In the second place a purchaser may take a conveyance of settled land under the mistaken impression that the vendor is still a tenant for life, whereas in fact he is no longer so. What is the position if a testator leaves Blackacre by will to W, his widow, for her life or until re-marriage, remainder to X in fee simple; W then re-marries and, as tenant for life, purports to sell Blackacre to Y who pays the purchase money to the trustees of the settlement? It is probable that Y obtains the legal estate from W, but the question then arises whether he can rely on section 110(2) and defeat a claim to the legal fee simple by

---

[506] SLA 1925, s. 18(1)(b).

[507] Ibid., s. 117(1)(xxx). "Trust corporation" means, "The Public Trustee or a corporation either appointed by the court in any particular case to be a trustee or entitled by rules made under sub-s. (3) of s. 4 of the Public Trustee Act 1906, to act as custodian trustee."

Corporations which are entitled under the Public Trustee Rules 1912 (SI 1912 No. 348), r. 30, as substituted by the Public Trustee (Custodian Trustee) Rules 1975 (SI 1975 No. 1189, as amended by SI 1976 No. 836; SI 1981 No. 358; SI 1984 No. 109; SI 1985 No. 132; SI 1987 No. 1891; SI 1994 No. 2519; SI 2002 No. 2469), include "any corporation constituted under the law of the United Kingdom . . . or of any other Member State of the European Economic Community . . . empowered by its constitution to undertake trust business [and having] one or more places of business in the United Kingdom", and being a company registered in the United Kingdom or another Member State of the European Economic Community "having a capital (in stock or shares) for the time being issued of not less than £250,000 . . . of which not less than £100,000 . . . has been paid up in cash".

The definition was extended by LP(A)A 1926, s. 3 to include the "Treasury Solicitor, the Official Solicitor, and any person holding any other official position prescribed by the Lord Chancellor, and, in relation to the property of a bankrupt and property subject to a deed of arrangement, includes the trustee in bankruptcy and the trustee under the deed respectively, and, in relation to charitable, ecclesiastical and public trusts, also includes any local or public authority so prescribed, and any other corporation constituted under the laws of the United Kingdom or any part thereof which satisfies the Lord Chancellor that it undertakes the administration of any such trusts without remuneration, or that by its constitution it is required to apply the whole of its net income after payment of outgoings for charitable, ecclesiastical or public purposes, and is prohibited from distributing, directly or indirectly, any part thereof by way of profits amongst any of its members, and is authorised by him to act in relation to such trusts as a trust corporation". See also LPA 1925, s. 205(1)(xxviii); TA 1925, s. 68(18); AEA 1925, s. 55(1)(xxvi); SCA 1981, s. 128; as amended by TLATA 1996, s. 25(2), Sch. 4.

[508] Ibid., s. 18(1)(c).   [509] P. 405, ante.   [510] P. 993, ante.

X. To do this Y must show that he is "a purchaser of a legal estate in the settled land" and he can only do this if "settled land" means "land which appears to be settled land but is not".[511]

The converse situation, where a purchaser takes a conveyance from a vendor under the mistaken impression that the vendor is an absolute owner in fee simple when he is in fact a tenant for life of settled land, however, has been the subject of two inconsistent judicial decisions at first instance. The solution to this problem depends on how far reliance can be placed on section 110(1), which reads as follows:

On a sale, exchange, lease, mortgage, charge, or other disposition, a purchaser dealing in good faith with a tenant for life or statutory owner shall, as against all parties entitled under the settlement, be conclusively taken to have given the best price, consideration, or rent, as the case may require, that could reasonably be obtained by the tenant for life or statutory owner, and to have complied with all the requisitions of this Act.

In *Weston v Henshaw* [512] X, a tenant for life, suppressed the settlement and purported to grant a legal mortgage to Y as security for advances made to him personally, professing to be absolute and beneficial owner of the fee simple. The question was whether the mortgage to Y was void against the beneficiaries under the settlement. DANCKWERTS J held that the mortgage was void because it was not a transaction authorised under section 18(1)(a).[513] He rejected an argument that Y was protected under section 110(1); admittedly Y was in good faith and had complied with all the requirements of the Act, but nevertheless the section could only be relied upon where Y knows X to be a tenant for life and deals with him on that footing.

In *Re Morgan's Lease*,[514] however, UNGOED-THOMAS J took the opposite view:

There is, in the section, no express provision limiting its benefit to a purchaser who knows that the person with whom he is dealing is a tenant for life. On its face it reads as free of limitation and as applicable to a person without such knowledge as to a person who has it. There is a limitation, namely that the purchaser must act in good faith; but that limitation reads as applicable to a purchaser with such knowledge as without. Thus my conclusion is that section 110 applies whether or not the purchaser knows that the other party to the transaction is tenant for life.[515]

This interpretation of section 110(1) seems preferable. *Weston v Henshaw* appears to be the only decision in unregistered land which is an exception to the immunity of the bona fide purchaser for value of the legal estate without notice.[516]

(b) Registered land

The position in registered land is much simpler. As in all cases of registered conveyancing, the purchaser is entitled to rely on the register to establish the vendor's title. He need not investigate the terms of the settlement, but the fact that the land is settled land appears from the fact that an appropriate restriction will be entered on the register.[517]

---

[511] For the problem and its detailed analysis, see Megarry and Wade, *Law of Real Property* (6th edn), para. 8.029, M & B p. 365; [1984] Conv 354 (P. A. Stone); [1985] Conv 377 (R. Warrington).

[512] [1950] Ch 510, M & B p. 335.   [513] *Bevan v Johnston* [1990] 2 EGLR 33; [1991] Conv 601 (J. Hill).

[514] [1972] Ch 1, M & B p. 335.   [515] At 9; *Mogridge v Clapp* [1892] 3 Ch 382.

[516] See (1971) 87 LQR 338 (D. W. Elliott); (1973) 36 MLR, p. 28 (R. H. Maudsley).

[517] In the case of a settlement under SLA 1925, the restriction will be in form G, H or I: LRR 2003, r. 91, Sch. 4; Sch. 7, paras. 2, 4(2), 5(b), 6(2), 7(1), 10(3), 12(1)(a), 13(1)(c).

The principles of overreaching, described above, apply equally in registered land. The purpose of the restriction is to ensure that no disposition of the estate is registered unless the overreaching machinery has been applied—that is, the purchase money has been paid to at least two trustees or into court.

C Trustees of Land

The definition of a trust of land and the powers of the trustees of land have already been discussed.[518] It remains to consider the investigation of title when the land is sold by the trustees, and the overreaching effect of the conveyance to the purchaser.

(1) Proof of Title

What has been said above about the proof and investigation of title in the case of a sale by a person beneficially entitled in his own right to a fee simple estate applies equally to trustees of land.[519] Failing a special stipulation, they must show by reference to a good root of title at least fifteen years old that the creator of the trust was entitled to vest the legal estate in them. In registered land, the trustees will be the registered proprietors, and therefore the purchaser is entitled to rely on the register to establish their title. There are, however, certain statutory provisions designed to protect the purchaser and to facilitate dealings with the land. We have already noticed those that relate to the limitation on the trustees' powers[520] and the requirement of consents.[521]

If the beneficiaries are all of full age and have become absolutely entitled under the limitations of the settlement, they may terminate the trust. We have already discussed the provisions for the termination of a trust of land under the Trusts of Land and Appointment of Trustees Act 1996.[522]

(2) Overreaching

(a) The principle

As we have already seen, a virtue long possessed by the trust for sale is that upon the sale of the land the equitable interests of the beneficiaries are kept off the title to the legal estate and are not disclosed to the purchaser.[523] The conveyance by the trustees overreaches the beneficial interests that arise *under* the trust.[524] The purchaser does not enjoy this immunity, however, unless he pays the purchase money to at least two trustees or to a trust corporation, if one has been appointed.[525]

In *State Bank of India v Sood*,[526] the Court of Appeal interpreted the doctrine widely, in holding that the interests of beneficiaries were overreached even when no capital money had

---

[518] Pp. 436 et seq, ante. For the trust for sale, before 1997, see pp. 426 et seq., ante.

[519] Pp. 930 et seq, ante.   [520] Pp. 447–8, ante.   [521] P. 444, ante.

[522] S. 16(4), (5), p. 448, ante.   [523] Pp. 76, ante.

[524] LPA 1925, ss. 2(1), as substituted by TLATA 1996, s. 25(1), Sch. 3, para. 4(1), (2); 27(1), as amended by TLATA 1996, s. 25(1), Sch. 3, para. 4(1), (8); TA 1925, s. 14(1), as amended by TA 2000, s. 40(1), Sch. 2, Pt II, para. 19. Although it is better to execute two deeds on the creation of a trust for sale, there is no necessity for this.

[525] LPA 1925, s. 27(2), as amended by TLATA 1996, s. 25(1), Sch. 3, para. 4(1), (8). For a definition of trust corporation see LPA 1925, s. 205(1)(xxviii), as extended by LP(A)A 1926, s. 3; p. 995, n. 507, ante.

[526] [1997] Ch 276 at 281; [1997] CLJ 494 (M. Oldham); [1997] Conv 134 (M. P. Thompson); [1997] All ER Rev 267 (P. J. Clarke).

been advanced at the time when a mortgage (which is a purchase) was created. PETER GIBSON LJ said:

The exercise intra vires of a power of disposition which does not give rise to any capital money, such as an exchange of land, overreaches just as much as a transaction which does. There is every reason to think that the draftsman of the 1925 property legislation fully appreciated the true nature of over-reaching. A principal objective of the 1925 property legislation was to simplify conveyancing and the proof of title to land. To this end equitable interests were to be kept off the title to the legal estate and could be overreached on a conveyance to a purchaser who took free of them.

(b) Bare trusts

The only change made to the doctrine by the Trusts of Land and Appointment of Trustees Act 1996 was to bring bare trusts within its scope. Before 1997 a bare trust fell outside the dual system of trust for sale and strict settlement, and, accordingly, interests under it could not be overreached. After 1996 a bare trust comes within the definition of a trust of land, and accordingly the doctrine of overreaching applies.[527]

(c) Beneficiaries in occupation

In registered land payment to at least two trustees or to a trust corporation overreaches the beneficial interests under a trust of land, even though the beneficiaries are in actual occupation.

In *City of London Building Society v Flegg*:[528]

Mr and Mrs M-B purchased Bleak House and were registered as proprietors. The house was conveyed to them upon trust for sale as beneficial joint tenants, with an express declaration that the trustees should have all the powers of mortgaging of an absolute owner. Part of the purchase price was pro-vided by Mr and Mrs F (the parents of Mrs M-B) who thereby became beneficial tenants in common in respect of their contribution; their interests were not entered on the register. Mr and Mrs M-B raised their part of the purchase price on mortgage with the consent of Mr and Mrs F. Later, without telling Mr and Mrs F, they mortgaged Bleak House by way of second and third charges, and finally they mort-gaged it to the Building Society for £37,500, again without the knowledge of Mr and Mrs F, using the proceeds to repay the three earlier loans. At all material times Mr and Mrs F were in actual occupation of the house. When Mr and Mrs M-B defaulted and were made bankrupt, the Building Society sued for possession. The House of Lords held that the society succeeded; the payment of the mortgage money had been made to two trustees, thereby overreaching the equitable interests of Mr and Mrs F, whose interests were transferred to the equity of redemption vested in Mr and Mrs M-B and to the £37,500 received by them.

Mr and Mrs F claimed that, by virtue of their actual occupation, they were entitled to an overriding interest under section 70(1)(g) of the Land Registration Act 1925[529] and that this

---

527 S. 1(2)(a), p. 439, ante. See Report on Overreaching: Beneficiaries in Occupation 1989 (Law Com No. 158), paras. 2.17, 3.10, 4.27.

528 [1988] AC 54, M & B p. 316; [1987] All ER Rev 149 (P. J. Clarke); (1988) 51 MLR 365 (S. Gardner); [1988] Conv 108 (M. P. Thompson), 141 (P. Sparkes) (2006) 69(2) MLR 214 (N. Jackson). The decision in *Flegg* is not affected by TLATA 1996: *Birmingham Midshires Mortgage Services Ltd v Sabherwal* (2000) 80 P & CR 256, M & B p. 320; (2000) 116 LQR 341 (C. Harpum); [2000] Conv 267 (M. Dixon); [2001] Conv 221 (G. Ferris and G. Battersby).   529 Now LRA 2002, Sch. 3, para. 2; p. 979, ante.

prevented the overreaching of their interests, unless they had given their consent. In rejecting this argument Lord TEMPLEMAN said:[530]

The interests of the respondents cannot at one and the same time be overreached and overridden and at the same time be overriding interests...There must be a combination of an interest which justifies continuing occupation plus actual occupation to constitute an overriding interest. Actual occupation is not an interest in itself.

And Lord OLIVER OF AYLMERTON said:[531]

Section 70(1)(g) protects only the rights in reference to the land of the occupier whatever they are at the material time—in the instant case the right to enjoy in specie the rents and profits of the land held in trust for him. Once the beneficiary's rights have been shifted from the land to capital monies in the hands of the trustees, there is no longer an interest in the land to which the occupation can be referred or which it can protect. If the trustees sell in accordance with the statutory provisions and so overreach the beneficial interests in reference to the land, nothing remains to which a right of occupation can attach and the same result must, in my judgment, follow vis-à-vis a chargee by way of legal mortgage so long as the transaction is carried out in the manner prescribed by the Law of Property Act 1925, overreaching the beneficial interests by subordinating them to the estate of the chargee which is not longer 'affected' by them so as to become subject to them on registration pursuant to section 20(1) of the Land Registration Act 1925. In the instant case, therefore, I would, for my part, hold that the charge created in favour of the appellants overreached the beneficial interests of the respondents and that there is nothing in section 70(1)(g) of the Land Registration Act 1925 or in *Boland's* case which has the effect of preserving against the appellants any rights of the respondents to occupy the land by virtue of their beneficial interests in the equity of redemption which remains vested in the trustees.

Any other decision would have undermined the main object of the doctrine of overreaching whereby a compromise is effected between on the one hand the interests of the public in securing that land held in trust is freely marketable and, on the other hand, the interests of the beneficiaries in preserving their rights under the trusts.[532]

If, however, the mortgage moneys had been paid to only *one* trustee, as in *Williams & Glyn's Bank Ltd v Boland*,[533] then the interests of Mr and Mrs F would not have been overreached, and the overriding interests geared to actual occupation would have given them an effective defence against the society's claim for possession.

It was further held that their interests were not affected by section 14 of the Law of Property Act 1925, which says:

This Part of this Act [Part I] shall not prejudicially affect the interest of any person in possession or in actual occupation of land to which he may be entitled in right of such possession or occupation.

---

530 [1988] AC 54 at 73, 74.   531 At 91.

532 Similarly in unregistered land, the possession of Mr and Mrs F would not have prevented their interests from being overreached; per Lord OLIVER OF AYLMERTON at 84. See Law Commission Report on Overreaching: Beneficiaries in Occupation 1989 (Law Com No. 188), which recommended that there should be no overreaching without the consent of every occupying beneficiary of full age irrespective of registration. This would in effect reverse the decision in *City of London Building Society v Flegg*; [1990] CLJ 277 at pp. 311–33 (C. Harpum); (1988) OJLS 367 (S. Gardner). No such change was implemented, however, by LRA 2002. See also *National Westminster Bank plc v Malhan* [2004] 2 P & CR DG9 (no decision on whether doctrine of overreaching, and especially the requirement of two trustees, is contrary to HRA 1998).

533 [1981] AC 487, M & B p. 136.

The overreaching provisions are to be found in Part I. As Lord TEMPLEMAN said:

Section 14 is not apt to confer on a tenant in common of land held on trust for sale, who happens to be in occupation, rights which are different from and superior to the rights of tenants in common, who are not in occupation on the date when the interests of all tenants in common are overreached by a sale or mortgage by trustees for sale.[534]

Finally, we must notice that the extent of overreaching in the case of a trust of land would appear to be less than that accorded to a purchaser from a tenant for life under the Settled Land Act 1925.[535] There is no power to overreach any interests which arise prior to the trust of land, apart from the creation of an ad hoc trust of land.[536]

D Approved Trustees

The overreaching effect of a conveyance either by trustees of land or by a tenant for life under a strict settlement is limited in the sense that it does not extend to equitable interests that were in existence before the creation of the trust or settlement.[537] If, for instance, a fee simple owner charges his land with the payment of a sum of money, and later subjects it to a trust, the normal rule is that a purchaser from the trustees takes the legal estate burdened by the equitable charge.

(1) *Ad hoc* Trust of Land

The Law of Property Act 1925 introduced what is variously called an *ad hoc*, or a *special* or an *approved* trust for sale which enables the trustees to overreach even prior interests.[538] Whether it is of this special nature depends entirely upon the character of the trustees. They must be either:

(a) two or more individuals approved or appointed by the court or the successors in office of the individuals so approved or appointed; or

(b) a trust corporation.[539]

(2) *Ad hoc* Strict Settlement

Before 1997, an alternative open to an estate owner whose land was already subject to an equitable interest was to create an *ad hoc* strict settlement under the Settled Land Act. If he executed a vesting deed, declaring the legal estate to be vested in him upon trust to give effect to equitable interests to which it was subject, and if at the same time he named as trustees

---

[534] At 72. See Lord OLIVER OF AYLMERTON at 80, where he says: "The ambit of section 14 is a matter which has puzzled conveyancers ever since the Law of Property Act was enacted...What section 14 does not do, on any analysis, is to enlarge or add to whatever interest it is that the occupant has in right of his occupation." He then agreed with Wolstenholme and Cherry (13th edn), vol. i. p. 63, that s. 14 was designed to preserve the principle of *Hunt v Luck* [1902] 1 Ch 428; p. 63, ante. See [1982] Conv 213 (M. Friend and J. Newton), M & B p. 50. See also *Lloyds Bank plc v Carrick* [1996] 4 All ER 630 at 642.

[535] See SLA 1925, s. 72(2), (3), p. 994, ante.

[536] As to whether ordinary trustees of land can overreach interests arising prior to the trust, see Emmet, para. 5.177; Megarry and Wade, *Law of Real Property* (5th edn), p. 404, n. 64, citing *Re Ryder and Steadman's Contract* [1927] 2 Ch 62 at 82.   [537] Except in three cases under SLA 1925, s. 72(2), (3); p. 994, ante.

[538] LPA 1925, s. 2(2).   [539] Defined p. 995, n. 507, ante.

either a trust corporation or two persons appointed or approved by the court,[540] the result was that the land became settled land and he acquired the statutory powers of a tenant for life, including the power of sale.[541] It would seem that this alternative is no longer open under the Trusts of Land and Appointment of Trustees Act 1996.

(3) Overreachable Interests

The *ad hoc* trust of land and the *ad hoc* strict settlement are similar in their effects. The land will be conveyed by the estate owner—by the trustees in the one case, by the tenant for life in the other—and, though the equitable charge will be overreached by the conveyance to the purchaser, it will be the duty of the trustees to see that it is paid out of the proceeds of sale to which it has now become attached.

Neither device, however, is of great practical use, for the number of equitable interests capable of being overreached is severely limited. It is enacted that a conveyance, whether under the trust of land or under the strict settlement, shall not affect the following interests:[542]

(i) Equitable interests protected by a deposit of documents, relating to the legal estate affected e.g., where title deeds are deposited with a bank to secure an overdraft.

(ii) Certain equitable interests that cannot be represented in terms of money, namely,

    (a) restrictive covenants;
    (b) equitable easements; and
    (c) estate contracts.[543]

These three interests, however, if created after 1925, will be void in unregistered land as against a purchaser of the legal estate for money or money's worth, unless they are registered under the Land Charges Act 1972. If they were created before 1926, they do not bind a purchaser unless he has actual or constructive notice of them.[544]

(iii) Any equitable interest that has been registered in accordance with the Land Charges Act 1972,[545] *except*

    (a) certain annuities;[546]
    (b) limited owner's charges;[547] and
    (c) general equitable charges.[548]

Registration of these three interests does not prevent them from being overreached, since they are adequately protected if enforceable against the money instead of against the land.

Thus, if land held by a beneficial owner in his own right, that is, land that is subject neither to a trust of land nor a strict settlement, is burdened with the payment of, for instance, a general equitable charge which impedes the transfer of an absolute title to a purchaser, there are four possible methods of clearing off the incumbrances, namely:

(i) The creation of an *ad hoc* trust of land.

(ii) The creation of an *ad hoc* strict settlement.

---

[540] SLA 1925, s. 21.   [541] Ibid., s. 21(1)(a).   [542] LPA 1925, s. 2(3); SLA 1925, s. 21(2).
[543] Pp. 940–1, ante.   [544] LPA 1925, s. 2(5).   [545] P. 937, ante.
[546] I.e., annuities created and registered before 1926; p. 938, ante.   [547] P. 940, ante.
[548] P. 940, ante.

(iii) A conveyance of the land to the purchaser by the beneficial owner with the concurrence of the incumbrancer.

(iv) An application for leave to pay into court a sum of money in discharge of the incumbrance.[549]

E Mortgagors and Mortgagees

It will be recalled that in a mortgage of a legal fee simple, the mortgagor remains the estate owner of the legal fee simple—or, in registered land, the registered proprietor—but nevertheless the mortgagee is entitled by virtue of his power of sale to convey it to a purchaser.[550]

The rules concerning proof of title by a beneficial owner apply to a sale by a mortgagee. He must satisfy the purchaser in the usual manner that the legal estate is vested in the mortgagor. The purchaser, however, although he must investigate the title to the legal estate, is not concerned to inquire whether a case has arisen to authorise the sale or whether notice has been given by the mortgagee to the mortgagor.[551]

IV Negligent Conveyancing

A professional adviser, such as a solicitor,[552] or a surveyor or valuer,[553] or estate agent[554] may be liable in negligence. Of the duty which a solicitor owes to his client,[555] OLIVER J said in *Midland Bank Trust Co Ltd v Hett, Stubbs & Kemp*:[556]

The test is what the reasonably competent practitioner would do having regard to the standards normally adopted in his profession.

---

[549] LPA 1925, s. 50.   [550] P. 769, ante.   [551] P. 771, ante.

[552] Emmet, paras. 1.010–1.011; Kenny, *Conveyancing Practice*, para. 1–019; (1986) 136 NLJ 1887, 911 (H. W. Wilkinson). As to the advisability of a solicitor acting for both parties in the same transaction, see pp. 862, n. 61; 884, n. 230, ante.

[553] Emmet, para. 1.065; *Perry v Sidney Phillips & Son* [1982] 1 WLR 1297; [1984] Conv 60 (K. Hodkinson); *Shankie-Williams v Heavey* [1986] 2 EGLR 139 (surveyor instructed for one flat owed no duty of care to potential purchaser of adjoining flat); *Secretary of State for the Environment v Essex, Goodman & Suggitt* [1986] 1 WLR 1432; *Smith v Eric S Bush* [1990] 1 AC 831, p. 884, n. 230, ante; *Sutcliffe v Sayer* [1987] 1 EGLR 155 (no duty on valuer to warn purchaser as to difficulties of resale); *Watts v Morrow* [1991] 1 WLR 1421(detailed examination of basis of damages); *Preston v Torfaen BC* [1993] NPC 111 (surveyor held not liable to ultimate occupier of house for negligent survey of site prepared for developer); *Patel v Hooper & Jackson* [1999] 1 WLR 1792; *Byrne v Hall Pain & Foster* [1999] 1 WLR 1849 (date of accrual of cause of action under Limitation Act 1980 is exchange not completion); [1999] Conv 341 (M.P. Thompson).

On the permissible margin of error, see *Lewisham Investment Partnership Ltd v Morgan* [1997] 2 EGLR 150; *Lion Nathan Ltd v C-C Bottlers Ltd* [1996] 1 WLR 1438; (1998) 148 NLJ 481 (H. Wilkinson); *Merivale Moore plc v Strutt & Parker* [1999] 2 EGLR 171.

[554] *Bradshaw v Press* (1982) 268 EG 565 (failure to check references of tenant; held not liable); *Computastaff Ltd v Ingledew Brown Bennison and Garrett* (1983) 268 EG 906 (estate agent acting for landlord held liable to tenant for circulating inaccurate information about property); *McCullagh v Lane Fox & Partners Ltd* [1996] 1 EGLR 35; *Letgain Ltd v Super Court Ltd* [1994] 07 EG 192.

[555] Although some professionals, such as valuers, may owe duties to parties other than their clients, a solicitor when performing duties for his client does not normally simultaneously owe a duty to third parties such as the other party in a conveyancing transaction: *Gran Gelato v Richcliff (Group) Ltd* [1992] Ch 560, although such a duty can be found where the solicitor has assumed a responsibility to the other party: *Dean v Allin & Watts* [2001] 2 Lloyd's Rep PN 249. See Cartwright, *Misrepresentation*, para. 5.32.

[556] [1979] Ch 384 at 403. The judgment contains a useful analysis of the duty.

"Further, as MEGARRY V-C said in *Ross v Caunters*:[557] "There is no longer any rule that a solicitor who is negligent in his professional work can be liable only to his clent in contract; he may be liable both to his client and to others for the tort of negligence." In that case:

solicitors who prepared a will for a testator and sent it to him for execution failed to warn him that the will should not be witnessed by the spouse of a beneficiary.[558] When the testator signed the will, one of the witnesses was the husband of the residuary beneficiary under it. It was held that the beneficiary was entitled to damages against the solicitor for negligence in respect of the loss of the benefits given to her by the will.

Solicitors were also held liable in both tort and contract in *Midland Bank Trust Co Ltd v Hett, Stubbs & Kemp*[559] for failing to advise a client to register an option to purchase as an estate contract under the Land Charges Act 1925 and for failing to register it.

The number of cases in the field of professional negligence is increasing, and reference should be made to specialist works on the subject.[560]

---

[557] [1980] Ch 297 at 322. Applied in *White v Jones* [1995] 2 AC 207 (solicitor, who failed to prepare will for client, held liable in damages to intended beneficiaries); [1995] CLJ 238 (A. Haydon); (1995) 111 LQR 357 (T. Weir); [1996] CLJ 43 (J. Murphy); [1995] All ER Rev 466 (B. W. Harvey); *Esterhuizen v Allied Dunbar Assurance plc* [1998] 2 FLR 668 (same duty owed by lay will-writer); *Carr-Glynn v Frearsons* [1999] Ch 326 (solicitor, who failed to advise 81-year-old testatrix promptly to sever joint tenancy in conjunction with execution of her will, held liable to compensate specific legatee for loss suffered thereby); (1999) 115 LQR 201; [1999] Conv 399 (R. Kerridge and A. H. R. Brierley); cf *Clarke v Bruce Lance & Co* [1988] 1 WLR 881 (solicitors who prepared will did not owe a duty of care to potential devisee when they later acted for testator in an *inter vivos* transaction which adversely affected his devise); *Hemmens v Wilson Browne* [1995] Ch 223 (solicitor who, by negligent drafting of an *inter vivos* transaction, failed to give intended beneficiary enforceable rights, held not liable to him, since it remained within power of settlor to remedy situation and the only reason he had not done so was that he had changed his mind). Cf *Walker v Geo H Medlicott & Son* [1999] 1 WLR 727 (where disappointed beneficiary sued solicitor for failing to draft will in accordance with testator's instructions by not including a specific devise to him, CA held that he should first mitigate his loss by seeking rectification under AJA 1982, s. 20, and exhausting that remedy before suing solicitor for negligence; but not if there was no prospect of any material recovery of the funds lost): *Horsfall v Haywards* [1999] 1 FLR 1182; cf *Cancer Research Campaign v Ernest Brown & Co* [1997] STC 1425 (solicitor not liable for failure to advise testator or beneficiaries on possibility of tax mitigation); (1999) 149 NLJ 931 (H. W. Wilkinson); *Worby v Rosser* [1999] Lloyd's Rep PN 972 (no duty to intended beneficiaries to ensure testator has capacity); *Gibbons v Nelsons* [2000] Lloyd's Rep PN 603 (no duty where solicitor did not know benefit the client intended to confer and the intended beneficiaries).   [558] Wills Act 1837, s. 15.

[559] [1979] Ch 384; p. 947, n. 131, post. Approved in *Henderson v Merrett Syndicates Ltd* [1995] 2 AC 145, where HL made clear that there is no obstacle to concurrent liability in contract, although the contract may modify, limit or exclude the duty that would otherwise arise in tort; *White v Jones* [1995] 2 AC 207 at 256.

[560] Jackson and Powell, *Professional Negligence*; Tottel's *Journal of Professional Negligence* (replacing, from 2004, *Tolley's Journal of Professional Negligence*); Dugdale and Stanton, *Professional Negligence*; Professional Negligence and Liability Reports (which started in 1996); Lloyd's Law Reports Professional Negligence (which started in 1999).

28

EXTINCTION OF ESTATES AND INTERESTS IN LAND

SUMMARY

A person's estate is *extinguished* where it is terminated, other than by its natural ending (such as a lease, by effluxion of time) or by its transfer (such as a transfer of the freehold or the assignment of a lease). This may happen in certain circumstances by virtue of adverse possession; or by merger.

I Extinction after a Period of Adverse Possession

We have already seen in chapter 6 that an estate in unregistered land may be extinguished[1] at the expiration of the period prescribed by the Limitation Act 1980 for the estate owner to bring a action to recover land.[2] That period is normally twelve years.[3]

In the case of registered land, the position under the Land Registration Act 1925 was not the same: the passage of the time prescribed by the Limitation Act 1980 did not extinguish the registered proprietor's legal title, but he held it on trust for the adverse possessor until the register was rectified to reflect the underlying rights which followed from the expiration of the limitation period.[4] Now, under the Land Registration Act 2002, the position is still different: again, the passage of time does not of itself affect the estate of the registered proprietor, but the adverse possessor may apply to be registered in place of the existing proprietor if he has been in possession for ten years; and although he may not often be

---

[1] There is no Parliamentary conveyance of the title of the dispossessed person to the squatter: p. 136, ante.

[2] LA 1980, s. 17; p. 135, ante. For an exception for settled land and land held on trust, see s. 18.

[3] Ibid., s. 15. For extension of the time because of disability, fraud or deliberate concealment, or mistake, see ss. 28, 32; pp. 139 et seq, ante.   [4] LRA 1925, s. 75; p. 143, ante.

entitled to be registered unless the proprietor then consents, if he retains possession for a further two years after his first application has been unsuccessful, he is then entitled as of right to be registered.[5]

The effect of both Land Registration Acts, however, is not simply to extinguish the former owner's title, but to transfer it to the adverse possessor.

II Merger

A Meaning of Merger

The term *merger* means that, where a lesser and a greater estate in the same land come together and vest, without any intermediate estate, in the same person and in the same right, the lesser is immediately annihilated by operation of law. It is said to be "merged", i.e. sunk or drowned, in the greater estate.[6]

For example:

If land is limited to A for life, remainder to B in fee simple, merger will result from any event which produces the union in one person of the life interest and the remainder in fee. Thus if A conveys his life interest to B, or if B conveys his remainder to A, there is in each case a merger. Again, a term of years may merge in a life interest, and an estate *pur autre vie* may merge in the interest held by a tenant for his own life.

B Merger at Common Law

At common law the doctrine of merger has nothing to do with the intention of the parties, and provided that certain essentials are satisfied, the effect is automatically to annihilate the smaller estate.

The essentials are that the estates shall unite in the same person without any intervening estate, and that the person in whom they unite shall hold them both in the same right.

Since 1926, the only estates that can subsist at law are the fee simple absolute in possession and the term of years absolute,[7] and so the modern application of the doctrine of merger of legal estates is limited to the case where the leasehold interest and its immediate reversion are united. This may occur where the tenant acquires the freehold from his immediate land-lord; or where a sub-tenant acquires the leasehold estate held by his landlord. But it must be remembered that the merger is not effected if the person holding the two interests does so in different capacities. For example, if an executor takes, under the Administration of Estates Act 1925, a term of years which belonged to the testator, and then purchases the reversion in fee on his own behalf, the term which the executor holds for the purposes of administration does not merge in the fee which he owns beneficially.[8]

One effect of the common law doctrine was that the merger of a term of years in the reversion destroyed the covenants contained in any sub-lease that has been carved out of the term.

---

[5] Pp. 145 et seq, ante.   [6] Blackstone, vol. 11, p. 177; Cruise, *Digest,* Tit. xxxix, s. 1.   [7] P. 94, ante.
[8] *Chambers v Kingham* (1878) 10 Ch D 743.

Suppose, for instance, that A, seised in fee, leased the land to T who sub-leased it to S. If T were to surrender his interest to A, the covenants contained in the sub-lease would become unenforceable, since the reversion to which they were formerly attached no longer existed.[9]

To remedy this, it was enacted in effect by the Real Property Act 1845,[10] in a section reproduced in the Law of Property Act 1925,[11] that where the reversion on a lease is destroyed by surrender or merger, the next vested interest in the land shall be deemed to be the reversion for the purpose of preserving the incidents and obligations of the defunct reversion. Thus, in the example given above, the covenants entered into between T and S are enforceable by and against A and S respectively.

C Merger in Equity

Equity has taken a different view of merger. At common law merger results automatically from the union of two estates in the circumstances we have mentioned, and intention does not affect the result. But equity looks to the intention and to the duties of the parties. If an intention is expressly declared to the effect that the lesser estate shall be kept alive, there is no difficulty;[12] but even in the absence of such an express declaration equity will presume an intention against merger if it is clearly advantageous to the person in whom the estates are united, or if it is consistent with his duty, that the lesser interest shall not be destroyed.[13] This view now prevails, for it was enacted by the Supreme Court of Judicature Act 1873[14] that there should be no merger by operation of law of any estate the beneficial interest in which would not be deemed to be merged or extinguished in equity.

In *Snow v Boycott*, for instance:[15]

land was limited to A for life, remainder to B for life. A, being too old to manage the property, conveyed the land to B for the rest of her life to the use that B should pay her £400 a year out of the profits. The effect of this was that an estate *pur autre vie* and an estate for his own life vested in B, so that at common law the estate *pur autre vie* was destroyed by merger. B died in the lifetime of A, and the question arose whether A's life estate had been destroyed so as to let in the estates which were limited to take effect after B's life estate. It was held that there was no merger in *equity*, and therefore no such destruction, for the parties could not have intended to create an interest *pur autre vie* in order that it should be immediately swallowed up in an existing life interest and thereby lost.

In another case:[16]

X, the first tenant for life under a settlement, agreed to let three acres of the land for 99 years to Y, the second tenant for life, at an annual ground rent of £9, in consideration that Y would erect thereon a house at a cost of £1,500. After the house had been erected, X died, with the result that at common law Y's term of years was merged in the life interest to which he now became entitled.

---

[9] *Webb v Russell* (1789) 3 Term Rep 393.
[10] S. 9; *Bromley Park Garden Estates Ltd v George* [1991] 2 EGLR 95.
[11] S. 139; *Electricity Supply Nominees Ltd v Thorn EMI Retail Ltd* [1991] 2 EGLR 46 at 48, per FOX LJ.
[12] *Golden Lion Hotel (Hunstanton) Ltd v Carter* [1965] 1 WLR 1189. See also *Belaney v Belaney* (1867) 2 Ch App 138 (no merger where conveyance contained recital that purchaser did not wish the term to merge).
[13] *Ingle v Vaughan Jenkins* [1900] 2 Ch 368; *Re Fletcher* [1917] 1 Ch 339.
[14] S. 25(4); reproduced in LPA 1925, s. 185.   [15] [1892] 3 Ch 110.
[16] *Ingle v Vaughan Jenkins* [1900] 2 Ch 368.

On the death of Y, the remainderman contended that Y's executor was prevented by this merger from claiming any further leasehold interest in the land. The contention failed. The court's one concern is the benefit of the person in whom the two interests unite, and in the instant circumstances it was obviously to the advantage of Y that the term of years should be kept separate from the life interest.

PART IV

PUBLIC CONTROL OVER THE USE OF LAND

SUMMARY

In chapter 19 we saw how the doctrine of *Tulk v Moxhay* was developed in the nineteenth century to facilitate the control by private landowners of the use of land by their neighbours. Restrictive covenants and (in so far as they are enforceable between freeholders[1]) positive covenants, and covenants in leases, are fundamental to private planning. So, too, are easements. However, these private law rules can serve only the interests of those who own land which can be benefited by the imposition of covenants, and they may even be an inadequate instrument to serve those private interests since the opportunity to impose covenants can be limited, and the enforcement of covenants requires vigilance and determination on the part of the individual landowner affected by an actual or threatened breach.

During the twentieth century, it came to be accepted that there is also a place for the *public* control of the use of land; both in the interests of the individual landowners and other occupiers of property in a neighbourhood, and in order to determine, in the public interest, the limits of the appropriate use of land and to provide public enforcement mechanisms.

In this Part we shall consider in outline the public control of the use and development of land.

---

[1] Pp. 663, ante.

29

PLANNING CONTROL[1]

SUMMARY

I The Legal Basis of Planning

A *Private and Public Planning Control*

(1) Planning Objectives

The aims of "planning control" are not identical with those of "planning". Planning control is negative: its purpose is to prevent changes on land[2] which, from the standpoint of public interest, for example, building on "greenfield sites", may be thought objectionable in particular cases. Planning is positive: its purpose is to encourage the improvement of land from the standpoint of amenity and convenience, though not necessarily of profit. These aims are all subjective, and will be tolerable only if a sufficient measure of agreement about them exists among the public at large or the people who will be affected.

The planning legislation now in force suggests that those aims remain acceptable to public opinion, though not necessarily to all individuals. Common law and equity have also developed a body of law relevant to the objectives of both "planning" and of "planning

---

[1] See generally *Butterworths Planning Law Handbook* which contains the text of the statutes and statutory instruments referred to in the following pages. See also *Encyclopedia of Planning Law and Practice*; Blackstone's *Statutes on Planning Law*; McAuslan, *Land, Law and Planning*; Telling and Duxbury, *Planning Law and Procedure*; Moore, *A Practical Approach to Planning Law; Estates Gazette Planning Reports*. On the impact of ECHR on planning law, see Rook, *Property Law and Human Rights*, section 8.10; Allen, *Property and the Human Rights Act 1998*, chap. 7; [2004] JPL Sup. (Occasional Papers No. 32), pp. 33–5 (D. Elvin).

[2] Ameliorating waste, in effect: p. 505, ante.

control". There is the positive development of land which all owners and occupiers may carry out within the framework and protection of the law—the building and engineering projects, the mining and quarrying and other forms of land exploitation, which give us our present towns and villages, farms and factories—subject to the familiar restraints on activities which unjustifiably affect other persons either directly or indirectly. There are also those obligations by which the use and development of land is regulated between private owners, or public bodies acting in the same way as private owners, namely building and letting schemes comprising restrictive and leasehold covenants.[3]

(2) Origins of Public Planning

The objectives of private planning and control by these methods are fundamentally the same as the objectives of public planning and control, but the decisions are taken largely with private ends in view, not public ones. This is very natural. The spacious squares and crescents might please the public, but these were intended primarily to please the prospective residents who would be induced to buy or rent them. Many matters of public interest might not be dealt with completely or at all: sanitation and new main roads, prevention or removal of slums, containment of industry and commerce, preservation of the countryside and open space. The conclusion drawn from this, perhaps grudgingly, was that a body of *public* land law must be brought into existence beside the already developed body of private land law concerned with these objectives, and that it could only be achieved by statute. The immense variety of private local Acts, the general Acts governing public health and housing, waterworks and tramways and innumerable other public matters affecting land, which Parliament enacted during the nineteenth century, dealt in detail with specific kinds of land use. A generalised procedure for acquiring land for these various purposes, with recourse to compulsion if necessary, was evolved at the same time. Eventually it came to be accepted that there should be a generalised public control of land use as well. The first planning statute was passed in 1909,[4] though it only applied to "town" planning, and planning on the fringes of existing towns at that. Planning control, which was still potential rather than actual, later came to be extended more generally over towns, and then over the countryside also.[5] Finally, in 1943, the general extent of control became actual instead of potential and the modern planning era opened.[6]

Private planning law is as extensive as ever it was, and the development of case law means that in theory and principle it is still growing.[7] In effect, what we now have are two

---

[3] And to a lesser extent reciprocal positive freehold covenants and also easements; pp. 585, 663, ante.

[4] Housing, Town Planning, &c Act 1909.

[5] Hence "*town and country*" planning, though it might be thought less cumbersome to speak now simply of "planning", or "land planning". Under TCPA 1932 it depended largely on the initiative of local authorities whether or not a "planning scheme" would be devised in each particular case.

[6] TCP (Interim Development) Act 1943. "Interim development" was originally development of any land begun *between* the decision to prepare a planning scheme and its coming into force; such development needed official approval if it were to rank for compensation in the event of being overridden later by the requirements of the plan. The Act of 1943 applied this control everywhere.

[7] The unwary developer who thinks that because he has a planning permission he can ignore a restrictive covenant may receive a shock. But LPA 1969, s. 28, requires the Lands Tribunal to "take into account the development plan and any declared or ascertainable pattern for the grant or refusal of planning permissions" when deciding whether a restrictive covenant should be discharged or modified; p. 697, ante. For development schemes, see p. 1014, post.

general planning systems in law: one private, one public. The latter, however, seems to have stolen much of the thunder once belonging to the former, and with it this chapter is concerned.

B The Public Planning System

(1) Administration

The system described in this chapter is that which exists in England and Wales. Parallel arrangements exist in Scotland and in Northern Ireland. The principal planning statute in England and Wales, which consolidates the previous statutes from the Town and Country Planning Act 1947 onwards, is the Town and Country Planning Act 1990.[8] There have been further refinements introduced by the Planning and Compensation Act 1991, and the Planning and Compulsory Purchase Act 2004. Many of these refinements are in the form of additional sections inserted into the Town and Country Planning Act 1990.

Planning control is administered by a system of authorities, central and local.[9] The central authority is the Secretary of State for Environment, Food and Rural Affairs, who does not usually administer planning control directly; but appeals are made to him from decisions of local planning authorities and he has the power to "call in" applications from them for decision at first instance.[10] A mass of statutory detail, including some matters of fundamental importance, is contained in subordinate legislation, the Acts having entrusted him with wide powers of making rules, orders and regulations. He also may make certain decisions on his own initiative[11] and exercises a co-ordinating function by issuing circulars which give guidance and advice to local planning authorities.

(2) Planning and Compulsory Purchase Act 2004[12]

The Act makes radical changes to the structure of planning. It also lifts Crown immunity (except in urgent cases) from planning control;[13] proposes to replace section 106 planning obligations;[14] introduces local development orders;[15] reforms the rules relating to simplified planning zones (SPZs)[16] and repeat planning applications; and reforms some of the rules of compulsory purchase and compensation.[17] Parts 1 to 3 introduce a new framework of regional and local "strategies" and local development schemes which take the place of structure and local plans.

---

[8] The 1990 Act is supplemented by the Planning (Listed Buildings and Conservation Areas) Act 1990, the Planning (Hazardous Substances) Act 1990 and the Planning (Consequential Provisions) Act 1990.

[9] For a recent report by the Audit Commission that the planning process should be reformed, by councils using private firms to take on mainstream planning work such as processing applications and appeals or even a comprehensive development control function, see their report *The Planning system: Matching expectations and capacity* 2006; [2006] 06 EG 36.   [10] See p. 1026, post.

[11] TCPA 1990, ss. 100, 104 (revocation and discontinuance).

[12] See also Current Law Statutes 2004 with annotations by M. Grant, in which paras. 5–5 to 5–11 set out the consultations which led to the Statute; [2004] JPL Sup. (Occasional Papers No. 32); [2005] 30 EG 80 (C. Dutch).   [13] P. 1028, post.

[14] P. 1023, post.   [15] P. 1021, post.   [16] P. 1021, post.   [17] Chap. 30, post.

(a) Part 1: Regional functions. Regional spatial strategy

There is to be a regional spatial strategy (the RSS) for each region which must set out the Secretary of State's policies (however expressed) in relation to the development and use of land within the region.[18]

The regions for which each RSS must be prepared are those defined by Schedule 1 of the Regional Development Agencies Act 1998, which makes provision for nine regions (RDAs) in England, including London.[19]

Each RSS supersedes existing Regional Planning Guidance. Planning Policy Statements (PPS) 1, issued by the Office of the Deputy Prime Minister, states that[20]

Spatial planning goes beyond traditional land use planning to bring together and integrate policies for the development and use of land with other policies and programmes which influence the nature of places and how they can function ... In preparing spatial plans, planning authorities should set a clear vision for the future pattern of development, with clear objectives for achieving that vision and strategies for delivery and implementation.

The system of plans introduced by the 2004 Act supersedes the structure plans and local plans of the Town and Country Planning Act 1990, introduced originally in 1968.

(b) Part 2 Local development. Survey. Development schemes

Under section 13 of the Act the local planning authority must keep under review the matters which may be expected to affect the development of their area or the planning of its development. Under section 15 the local planning authority must prepare and maintain a scheme to be known as their local development scheme. The scheme must specify the documents which are to be local development documents.

This local development framework is explained in PPS 12 as follows:[21]

The local development framework will be comprised of local development documents, which include development plan documents, that are part of the statutory development plan and supplementary planning documents which expand policies set out in a development plan document or provide additional detail. The local development framework will also include the statement of community involvement, the local development scheme and the annual monitoring report. Furthermore, local planning authorities should also include any local development orders and or simplified planning zones which have been adopted. The local development framework, together with the regional spatial strategy, provides the essential framework for planning in the local authority's area.

(c) Part 3 Development

Section 38 redefines the development plan for the purpose of planning law. It is of particular importance in relation to development control, where the legislation requires that regard

---

[18] PCPA 2004, s. 1.

[19] Ibid., s. 12, which specifies district, unitary and London Borough Councils and the City of London Corporation. For local planning authorities generally, see TCPA 1990, Part I as amended, and Greater London Authority Act 1999. There are also some specialist planning authorities.

[20] PPS1, *Delivering Sustainable Development* 2005, paras. 30, 32. The Government intends (PPS11) that structure plans will be saved for a period of three years.

The Secretary of State may give a direction recognising a body as the regional planning body for a region (RPB). The function of the RPB us to keep the RSS under review.

[21] PPS 12, *Local Development Frameworks* 2004, para. 1.4.

be had to the development plan in determining planning applications; and that it be applied in the absence of material considerations indicating to the contrary.

Section 39 introduces the concept of sustainable development. It applies to any person or body which exercises any function in relation to a regional spatial strategy, to local development documents or a local development plan, and states that the person or body must exercise the function with a view to contributing to the achievement of sustainable development.

The Government's four aims for sustainable development in planning are:[22]

(a) social progress which recognises the needs of everyone;

(b) effective protection of the environment;

(c) the prudent use of natural resources; and,

(d) the maintenance of high and stable levels of economic growth and employment.

(3) Public Interest and Public Records in Planning

A distinction is sometimes drawn between "negative" and "positive" planning, though it does not appear explicitly in the statutes. The former refers to the control exercised by planning authorities in the public interest over the development projects of others, and what is said here concerning "planning control" deals with it. The latter relates to planning authorities' own projects; and, in as much as it normally involves the acquisition of land for the carrying out of development in the public interest, it is dealt with later under "compulsory purchase in planning".[23]

A brief mention may be made here of registers which local planning authorities are required to keep for public inspection. In addition to registers of local land charges, which include various orders, agreements and notices relevant to planning and compulsory purchase,[24] there are registers kept specifically for planning. Thus there are registers of planning applications, of applications for consent to display advertisements and of caravan site licences; and there are also lists of buildings of special architectural or historic interest.[25] Prospective purchasers and their solicitors should always consult these registers and lists in appropriate circumstances, just as they normally apply for an official search of the local land charges registers.

C Planning and the Courts

(1) Planning Disputes

(a) Settlement of disputes

Planning disputes most commonly arise between local planning authorities and developers, or between acquiring authorities and owners; and the rules of planning law, like practically

---

[22] PPS1, supra, para. 4.   [23] See p. 1048, post.

[24] E.g. enforcement notices, revocation and discontinuance orders, planning agreements, tree preservation orders, lists of buildings of special interest and notices of compulsory purchase orders if general vesting declarations are to be made. See LLCA 1975; p. 947, ante.

[25] TCPA 1990, s. 69; Planning (Listed Buildings and Conservation Areas) Act 1990, ss. 1, 2; Caravan Sites and Control of Development Act 1960, s. 25; Town and Country Planning (Control of Advertisements) Regulations 1992 (SI 1992 No. 666), reg. 21.

all law, are framed with the basic purpose of giving guidance towards the settlement of disputes. If the assessment of compensation is in issue the dispute should be settled by the Lands Tribunal;[26] in other cases it is for the Secretary of State to settle the disputes (which lie between the local planning authorities and the landowners or objectors). But any dispute may have to be settled by the courts if it turns on a point of law.

(b) Law, fact and policy

The best way to understand the theory which underlies the system is to add, to the two judicial elements of law and fact, a third element, policy.[27] The Secretary of State is entitled to reach a decision on a general basis of law, fact and policy, or any of them, but his paramount concern, as the central planning authority, is with policy, so long as he ascertains the facts and complies with the law. Indeed he is normally empowered to substitute his own policy decision purely and simply for that of the local planning authority. Thus an "appeal" to the Secretary of State is to be understood in an administrative rather than a judicial sense.[28]

However, even statutory branches of law are developed by judicial interpretation, and there is a constant flow of planning cases into the law reports. These cases come before the courts whenever a dispute throws up a pure issue of law which the parties are prepared to pursue separately from disputes of fact or policy. The courts interpret the statutes, in principle and in detail, as confining them to such issues, and it is submitted that this is entirely right. The public authorities are inevitably the experts on policy, subject to Parliament and the electorate. The courts are the experts on the law.[29] Thus a court will sometimes say, for example, "the ground . . . stated by the Minister is not a valid ground at all and accordingly in my judgment this decision will have to be quashed";[30] or, "the Minister erred in law . . . In my judgment this case must go back to the Minister with the opinion of this court".[31] On the other hand the courts frequently speak in terms like these: "Having come to the conclusion that it is impossible to say that the Minister erred in law, I would dismiss the appeal".[32] But the courts must not alter a decision on policy grounds, even if they are "surprised" by a policy decision.[33]

(c) Restrictions on recourse to the courts

There are restrictions on recourse to the courts in that many, but not all, decisions of the Secretary of State (as distinct from those of other authorities) can only be challenged by application within six weeks to the High Court; and even so the court can only quash such

---

[26] See Lands Tribunal Act 1949; pp. 1040, post.

[27] Usually referred to by the courts as "discretion," to indicate that it lies outside their control so long as its exercise is intra vires.

[28] See *Stringer v Minister of Housing and Local Government* [1970] 1 WLR 1281.

[29] A quashing order (formerly known as certiorari) will lie to quash a decision of a planning authority if the grounds are ultra vires, e.g. "error of law on the face of the record": *R v Hillingdon LBC, ex p Royco Homes Ltd* [1974] QB 720.

[30] *R v Minister of Housing and Local Government, ex p Chichester RDC* [1960] 1 WLR 587 at 589, per Lord PARKER CJ. See p. 1050, n. 66, post.

[31] *Birmingham Corpn v Minister of Housing and Local Government and Habib Ullah* [1964] 1 QB 178 at 190, per Lord PARKER CJ.

[32] *Cheshire County Council v Woodward* [1962] 2 QB 126 at 135, per Lord PARKER CJ.

[33] *Bendles Motors Ltd v Bristol Corpn* [1963] 1 WLR 247 at 252, per Lord PARKER CJ. And see *London Residuary Body v Lambeth LBC* [1990] 1 WLR 744.

decisions on the ground that they are "not within the powers of [the relevant Act], or that the interests of the applicant have been substantially prejudiced" by some procedural default.[34]

This restriction on recourse to the courts applies to a dispute over the validity of a decision in detail, that is to say, which assumes that it is valid in principle. The right to challenge the existence of a decision on the ground that it is invalid in principle and so a nullity seems not to be restricted; otherwise "the court may accept and could not even inquire whether a purported determination was a forged or inaccurate order . . .", which would be absurd. "A more reasonable and logical construction is that . . . Parliament meant a real determination, not a purported determination."[35] Again, "the courts' supervisory duty is to see that [the authority] makes the authorised inquiry according to natural justice and arrives at a decision, whether right or wrong . . . they will not intervene merely because it has or may have come to the wrong answer, provided that this is an answer that lies within its jurisdiction".[36]

In a case, where it was alleged that a purported planning permission was invalid in principle, the court said, "the validity of the so-called permission being a matter completely outside the jurisdiction of the Minister, there could be no conceivable reason for the [developers] not being able, if they so desired, to proceed in the courts for a declaration as to the validity of the permission".[37] Where a statutory appeal is not available, the application would be for what is now judicial review.

(2) Legal Control of Procedure

(a) Natural justice

The reference to "natural justice" leads to the next point, that the Secretary of State's decisions, taken remotely from each locality concerned, are usually reached on the basis of first granting a hearing to objectors. Many of the statutory provisions require him to "afford . . . an opportunity of appearing before, and being heard by, a person appointed by the Secretary of State for the purpose"[38] (i.e an inspector) to objectors, appellants, claimants or "persons aggrieved". It is settled that such decisions must not be reached, and such proceedings must not be conducted in defiance of "natural justice", which comes down to two basic rules, namely that the person deciding or the person presiding must not be biased and

---

[34] See, e.g. TCPA 1990, s. 288 and ss. 284–92 generally. These provisions were considered by HL in *Griffiths v Secretary of State for the Environment* [1983] 2 AC 51. Procedural misconduct by a planning authority may however give rise to private law liability, e.g. in negligence: *Davy v Spelthorne BC* [1984] AC 262, in which a landowner was misled in respect of his statutory rights.

[35] *Anisminic Ltd v Foreign Compensation Commission* [1969] 2 AC 147 at 199, per Lord PEARCE. Contrast *R v Secretary of State for the Environment, ex p Ostler* [1977] QB 122. And see *Co-operative Retail Services Ltd v Taff Ely BC* (1979) 39 P & CR 223; p. 1024, n. 77, post.

[36] [1969] 2 AC 147, at 195. The decision questioned in this case was a determination by the Foreign Compensation Commission which, as provided by the Foreign Compensation Act 1950, s. 4(4), "shall not be called in question in any court of law". This is not a planning case, but the underlying principle is fully relevant to planning law.

[37] *Edgwarebury Park Investments Ltd v Minister of Housing and Local Government* [1963] 2 QB 408 at 417, per Lord PARKER CJ. The distinction between invalidity in detail and in principle (a "nullity") has been re-emphasised by HL in *London & Clydesdale Estates Ltd v Aberdeen DC* [1980] 1 WLR 182. The time limit for seeking judicial review is three months: *R (on the application of Burkett) v Hammersmith and Fulham LBC* [2002] 1 WLR 1593.

[38] See, e.g. TCPA 1990, ss. 77(5), (6), 79(2), (3), 98(2)–(5), 103(3)–(6), 140(3), (4).

that both sides are given a proper hearing on the points at issue.[39] A proceeding of this kind, although held as part of an *administrative* process, is often said to be "quasi-judicial" even though the rest of the process is not; so that the final decision emerging from that process can be quashed by the courts if "natural justice" is not observed. The quashing will be on an issue of law, never of fact or policy.

(b) Inquiries procedure rules

Recently some of these inquiries have been subjected to safeguards additional to the rules of "natural justice". These are planning appeal and planning enforcement appeal inquiries[40] and compulsory purchase order inquiries. The various sets of Inquiries Procedure Rules[41] governing these inquiries prescribe time limits, and what notice shall be given to the parties concerned, and above all that there shall be written submissions made in advance by the authority, stating the contentions on which they intend to rely. Another important provision is that, although the Secretary of State has full discretion to make his eventual decision, so that he may reject any or all of the recommendations made by the inspector in his report, nevertheless he must hear any further representations if he should disagree on any finding of fact (not policy) or consider any new issues or evidence of fact; and in the latter two cases he must re-open the inquiry if asked to do so.[42]

II Public Control of Land Use

A The Development Process

(1) Nature of Development

(a) General definition

The definition of "development" is the basic concept of planning law. Section 55(1) of the Town and Country Planning Act 1990 defines it as meaning "the carrying out of building,

---

[39] See *R v Bow Street Magistrate, ex p Pinochet Ugarte (No 2)* [2000] 1 AC 119; *R v Sussex Justices, ex p McCarthy* [1924] 1 KB 256, for the first rule ("justice should not only be done, but should manifestly and undoubtedly be seen to be done"); and *R v Secretary of State for Wales, ex p Emery* [1998] 4 All ER 367; *Errington v Minister of Health* [1935] 1 KB 249, for the second rule. A person affected by an official decision must be given "a fair crack of the whip": *Fairmount Investments Ltd v Secretary of State for the Environment* [1976] 1 WLR 1255 at 1266, per Lord RUSSELL OF KILLOWEN. See also *Steeples v Derbyshire County Council* [1985] 1 WLR 256. There is no such thing as a "technical" breach of natural justice: *George v Secretary of State for the Environment* (1979) 38 P & CR 609. For breach of natural justice by the chairman of a local authority planning committee, see *Ghadami v Harlow DC* [2005] 1 P & CR 19.

[40] For enforcement appeals, see under breach of planning control: p. 1030, post.

[41] TCP (Inquiries Procedure) Rules 2000 (SI 2000 No. 1624); TCP Appeals (Determination by Inspectors) (Inquiries Procedure) Rules 2000 (SI 2000 No. 1625); TCP (Hearings Procedure) Rules 2000 (SI 2000 No. 1626); TCP (Appeals) (Written Representations Procedure) Regulations 2000 (SI 2000 No. 1628).

[42] One or two requirements govern conduct of the inquiry itself, but by and large the inspector is not bound by rules of evidence and procedure which must be observed in court. Disagreement on policy is not of course disagreement on fact: see *Lord Luke of Pavenham v Minister of Housing and Local Government* [1968] 1 QB 172. Where issues wider than those of pure planning are at stake, the Secretary of State may replace an ordinary inquiry by a "planning inquiry commission", which will involve a more elaborate procedure altogether. See TCPA 1990, s. 101. See *Save Britain's Heritage v Number 1 Poultry Ltd* [1991] 1 WLR 153 (giving of reasons in compliance with Inquiries Procedure Rules).

engineering, mining[43] or other operations in, on, over or under land, or the making of any material change in the use of any buildings or other land". Thus there will be development either if an "operation" is carried out, or if a "material change of use" is brought about. Often a project involves development because there will be one or more operations and a material change of use as well.[44]

(b) Use classes

Section 55 lists specified matters which either are or are not "development". The latter include "in the case of buildings or other land which are used for a purpose of any class specified in an order made by the Minister under this section, the use thereof for any other purpose of the same class".[45] For the purposes of this provision, with effect from 1 June 1987 sixteen "use classes" were listed in the Town and Country Planning (Use Classes) Order 1987,[46] and any change within a "use class" is not development at all,[47] or in other words not "material".[48]

(2) Development in Particular Cases

(a) "Fact and degree"

Whether any work amounts to an "operation" or whether any change of use is "material" is a "question of fact and degree"[49] in the circumstances of each particular case. Building a model village as a permanent structure has been held to involve an "operation"[50] but not placing a mobile hopper and conveyor in a coal-merchant's yard.[51] Placing an egg-vending machine on the roadside of a farm has been held to involve a material change of use;[52] but

[43] The specialised nature of mining development and control involves peculiarities which, though included in TCPA 1990, cannot be discussed here for lack of space. See *Thomas David (Porthcawl) Ltd v Penybont RDC* [1972] 1 WLR 1526; *R v North Yorkshire County Council, ex p Brown* [2000] 1 AC 397.

[44] E.g. if a field used for agriculture is developed by building a house on it. For expansion of a building below ground, see TCPA 1990, s. 55(2)(a). For interpretation generally, see s. 336. Construction of a building must not be confused with its use: *Western Fish Products Ltd v Penwith DC* [1981] 2 All ER 204.

[45] TCPA 1990, s. 55(2)(f). It is not use but change of use which is in question.

[46] SI 1987 No. 764. This has been amended, and the "use classes" now number thirteen, grouped as follows: Part A, Classes A1–5; Part B, Classes B1, 2, 8; Part C, Classes C1–3; Part D, Classes D1–2.

[47] Except under a planning permission granted subject to a condition that no change of use occurs, even within the same use class: see *Kingston-upon-Thames Royal LBC v Secretary of State for the Environment* [1973] 1 WLR 1549.

[48] For the attitude of the House of Lords to this, see *Newbury DC v Secretary of State for the Environment* [1981] AC 578. Any change of use other than a change within the limits of the same use class may or may not be "development"; i.e. it is an open question to be decided by applying the principles contained in TCPA 1990, s. 55. "Material" means "relevant" to planning: *Tesco Stores Ltd v Secretary of State for the Environment* [1995] 1 WLR 759.

[49] Per GLYN-JONES J in *Marshall v Nottingham City Corpn* [1960] 1 WLR 707, quoted by Lord PARKER CJ in *East Barnet UDC v British Transport Commission* [1962] 2 QB 484 at 491. Use for agriculture or forestry of land and buildings occupied therewith is not development, despite any change in use: TCPA 1990, s. 55(2)(e). But see *Belmont Farm Ltd v Minister of Housing and Local Government* (1962) 13 P & CR 417.

[50] *Buckinghamshire County Council v Callingham* [1952] 2 QB 515.

[51] *Cheshire County Council v Woodward* [1962] 2 QB 126.

[52] *Hidderley v Warwickshire County Council* (1963) 14 P & CR 134. So has a change from bed-sitters to hotel accommodation: *Mayflower Cambridge Ltd v Secretary of State for the Environment* (1975) 30 P & CR 28. "What really has to be considered is the character of the use of the land, not the particular purpose of a particular occupier"; *Westminster City Council v Great Portland Estates plc* [1985] AC 661 at 669, per Lord SCARMAN.

not altering part of a railway station yard from a coal depot to a transit depot for crated motor vehicles.[53] In all four cases the court merely declined to invalidate a finding already made. The burden of proof, in other words, rests on that party who alleges that a finding in relation to development is ultra vires.

(b) Special aspects of development

Ownership of land, or of things placed on land, is irrelevant to planning except in special circumstances:[54] what matters is the nature of what is done on or to the land. Some ancillary questions which may be relevant are: (i) actual area involved;[55] (ii) whether there are multiple uses on a given area of land and whether these are of equal importance,[56] or are major and minor uses,[57] or are confined to separate parts of the premises,[58] or are intermittent, alternating or recurring.[59] Problems have arisen over whether demolition is an "operation", and whether the abandonment or the intensification of a use is a "material change".[60]

B Control of Development

(1) Planning Permission Generally

(a) Planning permission and development orders

Section 57 of the Town and Country Planning Act 1990 states that planning permission is "required" for carrying out development (subject to certain special exceptions).[61] Section 59 empowers the Secretary of State to make "development orders", for the purpose (among others) of actually granting permission, on a general and automatic basis, for certain forms of development. The Town and Country Planning (General Permitted Development) Order

---

[53] *East Barnet UDC v British Transport Commission* [1962] 2 QB 484. See also *West Bowers Farm Products v Essex County Council* (1985) 50 P & CR 368; construction of a private reservoir for farm irrigation was, as a matter of fact and degree, both an engineering operation (construction) and a mining operation (mineral operations).

[54] See (1960) JPL 436. Also irrelevant is the question whether a public body or a private firm is carrying out a particular use of premises: *Rael-Brook Ltd v Minister of Housing and Local Government* [1967] 2 QB 65.

[55] The relevant "planning unit" is normally the total area of land occupied, e.g. house conservatory and curtilage, not the conservatory in isolation: *Wood v Secretary of State for the Environment* [1973] 1 WLR 707. See *Jennings Motors Ltd v Secretary of State for the Environment* [1982] QB 541; *Tyack v Secretary of State for the Environment* [1989] 1 WLR 1392.   [56] *Marshall v Nottingham Corpn* [1960] 1 WLR 707.

[57] *Mansi v Elstree UDC* (1964) 16 P & CR 153; *Vickers-Armstrong Ltd v Central Land Board* (1957) 9 P & CR 33.   [58] *Hartnell v Minister of Housing and Local Government* [1965] AC 1134.

[59] *Webber v Minister of Housing and Local Government* [1968] 1 WLR 29.

[60] TCPA 1990, s. 55(1A), (2)(g), inserted by Planning and Compensation Act 1991, s. 13, which provides that demolition is now included in the definition of "development" as being within the meaning of "building operations" (a nice paradox); but the Secretary of State can give general or specific directions excluding various kinds of demolition from "development" and in addition to that has given automatic permission in most other cases by means of the GPDO: see n. 62, infra. Abandonment of any use of land is hardly likely to be held to constitute development, but resumption of use after abandonment is another matter. See *Hartley v Minister of Housing and Local Government* [1970] 1 QB 413; and *Fyson v Buckinghamshire County Council* [1958] 1 WLR 634. A planning permission, however, cannot be abandoned; see p. 1025, n. 85, post. For intensification, see *Birmingham Corpn v Minister of Housing and Local Government and Habib Ullah* [1964] 1 QB 178.

[61] Omitted here for reasons of space. They relate to temporary and intermittent uses, and lack of use, dating back to 1948, and also to resumption of uses after temporary planning permissions or enforcement notices. See *LTSS Print and Supply Services Ltd v Hackney LBC* [1976] QB 663; *Young v Secretary of State for the Environment* [1983] 2 AC 662.

1995 (the "GPDO"),[62] currently (as amended) gives such permission for thirty-three classes of development which it carefully specifies. Apart from this there are other sections in the 1990 Act under which planning permission is "deemed" to be granted.[63]

(b) Simplified planning zones

Sections 82–7 and Schedule 7 to the Town and Country Planning Act 1990[64] require local planning authorities to consider making simplified planning zone schemes, and the Secretary of State may direct them to do so. A scheme is in essence a specialised development plan: but it also resembles a development order, in that it automatically grants planning permission for specified classes of development, with or without conditions, in the whole or part of a zone.

(c) Detailed and outline applications

The Town and Country Planning (General Development Procedure) Order 1995 (the "GDPO") prescribes the procedure for making applications to the district planning authority for planning permission. If a building is to be erected, an application may be made for "outline" permission, which means for approval in principle. If this is refused no time and expense need be wasted on detailed plans. If it is granted, separate application will need to be made for details to be approved—"reserved matters".[65]

(d) Development control. Local development orders

Section 61A of the Town and Country Planning Act 1990[66] provides that

(1) A local planning authority may by order (a local development order) make provision to implement policies—
    (a) in one or more development plan documents (within the meaning of Part 2 of the Planning and Compulsory Purchase Act 2004);
    (b) in a local development plan (within the meaning of Part 6 of that Act).

(2) A local development order may grant planning permission—
    (a) for development specified in the order;
    (b) for development of any class so specified.

(3) A local development order may relate to—
    (a) all land in the area of the relevant authority;
    (b) any part of that land;
    (c) a site specified in the order.

(4) A local development order may make different provision for different descriptions of land.

---

[62] SI 1995 No. 418, as amended by SI 1996 No. 528; SI 1997 No. 366; SI 1998 No. 462; SI 1999 No. 1661; SI 2001 Nos. 2718 and 4050; SI 2005 Nos. 85 and 2935; SI 2006 No. 221. (See also the Conservation (Natural Habitats etc.) Regulations 1994, SI 1994 No. 2716; as amended by: SI 1996 No. 1243; SI 1997 No. 3055; SI 1999 No. 1820; SI 2000 No. 192). The thirty-three classes of development automatically permitted are set out in the 1995 Order, Sch. 2.   [63] See ss. 58(2), 90 and 222; pp. 1027–8, post.

[64] A simplified planning zone scheme will last for ten years. National Parks, conservation areas and other special amenity land are excluded from these provisions.

[65] GDPO (SI 1995 No. 419), arts. 3, 4. A local planning authority must abide by "outline" permission when considering the applications regarding the "reserved matters"; see *Heron Corpn Ltd v Manchester City Council* [1978] 1 WLR 937.   [66] Inserted by PCPA 2004, s. 40(1).

(5) But a development order may specify any area or class of development in respect of which a local development order must not be made.

(6) A local planning authority may revoke a local development order at any time.

Local development orders will need to accord with environment assessment principles,[67] although it is unlikely that a local planning authority would be minded to offer such significant development entitlements as would flout these principles.[68]

At any time before a local development order is adopted by a local planning authority, the Secretary of State may first direct that the order, or any part of it, be submitted to him for his approval. Sections 61(C) and (D) of the Town and Country Planning Act 1990[69] make supplementary provision for the grant of permission by a local development order for the revision of such an order.

Section 76A[70] provides that the Secretary of State may also direct that an application must be referred to him instead of being dealt with by the local planning authority if the Secretary of State thinks that the development to which the application relates is of national or regional importance.

Under section 62[71] a development order may make provision as to applications for planning permission made to a local planning authority.

(e) How to apply for planning permission

Any person may apply for planning permission; but unless no one but the applicant owns a freehold or a leasehold with at least seven years to run in the property, he must notify all who do and any farm tenants as well, either directly or, if that is not possible, by local press publicity. There are also certain classes of controversial development which must be publicised.[72] Persons notified by these methods may "make representations" which the authority (the district planning authority) must take into account.

If the proposed development comes within certain categories in accordance with EC Council Directive 85/337, as being especially likely to have harmful environmental effects, for example, pollution, planning permission must not be granted unless an "environmental statement" has been submitted in due form describing the likely significant effects on the environment, and taken into consideration.[73]

---

[67] Infra.

[68] In the case of the GPDO this is achieved by a general rule that development is not permitted by the Order if it is Schedule 1 or Schedule 2 development under TCP (Environment Impact Assessment) (England and Wales) Regulations 1999 (SI 1999 No. 293). That rule may be displaced if the local planning authority or the Secretary of State determine formally that the development is not EIA development. A local development order must be in support of policies and proposals in the DPD.   [69] Inserted by PCPA 2004, ss. 40 and 41.

[70] Inserted by PCPA 2004, s. 44.   [71] Substituted by PCPA 2004, s. 42.

[72] TCPA 1990, ss. 65–68; GPDO arts. 6–8. TCPA 1990, s. 303 authorises the Secretary of State to make regulations for the charging of fees for planning applications: see TCP (Fees for Applications and Deemed Applications) Regs. 1989 (SI 1989 No. 193), as amended. But there is no lawful authority to charge fees for the giving of advice to applicants: McCarthy & Stone (Developments) Ltd v Richmond-upon-Thames LBC [1992] 2 AC 48. But see PCPA 2004, s. 53, amending TCPA 1990, s. 303, which now provides that regulations may be made authorising "payment of a charge or fee" for the performance by the local planning authority of any function they have or anything done by them which is calculated to facilitate, or is conducive or incidental to the performance of any such function.

[73] TCP (Environmental Impact Assessment) Regs. 1999 (SI 1999 No. 293), made under European Communities Act 1972, s. 2(2); [2004] JPL Sup. (Occasional Papers No. 32), pp. 11 et seq (D. Elvin); Tromans and Fuller, Environmental Impact Assessment Law and Practice.

(f) Determinations and planning obligations

A prospective developer who needs a determination whether his project amounts to "development" may apply to the authority for a certificate of lawful proposed use or development.[74] Again, it is possible under section 106 of the Town and Country Planning Act 1990 for "a person interested in land" to make an agreement with the authority to create a planning obligation (enforceable against him or persons deriving title under him) regulating development of that land on a more general basis than for a normal planning permission.[75]

The Secretary of State is empowered by sections 46 to 48 of the Planning and Compulsory Purchase Act 2004 to make regulations which replace section 106 agreements. Section 46 provides that

(1) The Secretary of State may, by regulations, make provision for the making of a planning contribution in relation to the development or use of land in the area of a local planning authority.

(2) The contribution may be made—
   (a) by the prescribed means,
   (b) by compliance with the relevant requirements, or
   (c) by a combination of such means and compliance.

(3) The regulations may require the local planning authority to include in a development plan document (or in such other document as is prescribed)—
   (a) a statement of the developments or uses or descriptions of development or use in relation to which they will consider accepting a planning contribution;
   (b) a statement of the matters relating to development or use in relation to which they will not consider accepting a contribution by the prescribed means;
   (c) the purposes to which receipts from payments made in respect of contributions are (in whole or in part) to be put;
   (d) the criteria by reference to which the value of a contribution made by the prescribed means is to be determined.

(4) The regulations may make provision as to circumstances in which—
   (a) except in the case of a contribution to which subsection (3)(b) applies, the person making the contribution (the contributor) must state the form in which he will make the contribution;
   (b) the contribution may not be made by compliance with the relevant requirements if it is made by the prescribed means;

---

[74] TCPA 1990, s. 192, p. 1030, n. 120, post.

[75] Ibid., ss. 106–106B. These planning obligations were originally known as "planning agreements", enforceable as restrictive covenants and subject to LPA 1925, s. 84, p. 694, ante. The Planning and Compensation Act 1991, s. 12 recast s. 106. They must be entered into by deed, "by agreement or otherwise", in respect of particular land, and may be positive or negative (i.e. by requiring or restricting development or any other uses or operations). "Any person interested in land" in the area of a local planning authority may enter into a planning obligation, which also binds anyone deriving title from that person. It is enforceable by injunction and is registrable as a local land charge. If the local planning authority subsequently declines to modify or discharge a "planning obligation", appeal lies to the Secretary of State. Authorities may agree to create planning obligations irrespective of whether or not the same objectives might have been achieved by planning conditions (p. 1025, post), *Good v Epping Forest DC* [1994] 1 WLR 376. The Contracts (Rights of Third Parties) Act 1999, s. 1, enables a third party to enforce a term of a contract if the contract expressly provides that he may, or the term purports to confer a benefit on him and on construction of the contract it does not appear that the parties did not intend the term to be enforceable by the third party. The third party must be expressly identified by name, class or description. The Act however makes no express mention of planning obligations. See p. 676, ante.

(c) the contribution may not be made by the prescribed means if it is made by compliance with the relevant requirements;

(d) a contribution must not be made.

(5) The prescribed means are—

(a) the payment of a sum the amount and terms of payment of which are determined in accordance with criteria published by the local planning authority for the purposes of subsection (3)(d),

(b) the provision of a benefit in kind the value of which is so determined, or

(c) a combination of such payment and provision.

(6) The relevant requirements are such requirements relating to the development or use as are—

(a) prescribed for the purposes of this section, and

(b) included as part of the terms of the contribution,

and may include a requirement to make a payment of a sum.

(g) Grant or refusal of planning permission

On receiving an application the district planning authority must consult other authorities and government departments, as appropriate, and comply with directions given by the Secretary of State; and they must also "have regard to the provisions of the development plan", so far as material to the application and to any other material considerations.[76] Within eight weeks they must notify their decision to the applicant.[77] They may grant permission[78] unconditionally, or "subject to such conditions as they think fit", or refuse it.[79] The possibility that a project could be regulated under some other statutory procedure

---

[76] TCPA 1990, ss. 62, 70–6; GDPO, arts. 10–16. To "have regard to" the development plan does not mean that there is any duty to conform strictly with its details: *Enfield LBC v Secretary of State for the Environment* (1974) 233 EG 53; "other material considerations" (s. 70(2)) must also be taken into account: see *South Oxfordshire DC v Secretary of State for the Environment* [1981] 1 WLR 1092. But the determination shall be made in accordance with the plan, unless material conditions indicate otherwise": s. 54A.

[77] GDPO, art. 20. It must be the authority's decision, not that of an official acting on his own initiative: *Co-operative Retail Services Ltd v Taff-Ely BC* (1979) 39 P & CR 223. But they may delegate: Local Government Act 1972, s. 101.

[78] A person with the benefit of a planning permission has the choice either to make use of it or to continue as before. If he chooses the former he cannot complain of being made to forgo the latter. In *Petticoat Lane Rentals Ltd v Secretary of State for the Environment* [1971] 1 WLR 1112, permission was given, and acted on, to build upon a derelict site. An attempt to continue the previous use of the site for market trading (the new building being raised on pillars) was held to be a breach of planning control. Planning permission may be retrospective: TCPA 1990, s. 63.

[79] TCPA 1990, s. 70(1)(a), (b). Reasons must be given for refusals or conditional grants of planning permission: GDO, art. 25. Decisions will be communicated by officials, who must not exceed their authority. But they have an implied authority to allow trivial variations of permission: *Lever Finance Ltd v City of Westminster LBC* [1971] 1 QB 222. An authority may be estopped from denying a permission given in excess of an officer's powers, though not if the recipient suffers no detriment from the denial: *Norfolk County Council v Secretary of State for the Environment* [1973] 1 WLR 1400. Estoppel is not in principle to be used to hamper authorities in carrying out their functions in the public interest; see *Western Fish Products Ltd v Penwith DC* [1981] 2 All ER 204, p. 1019, n. 44, ante; but issue estoppel (*res judicata*) is relevant: see *Thrasyvoulou v Secretary of State for the Environment* [1990] 2 AC 273. See also TCPA 1990, s. 76 (provision for the disabled). Any re-application within two years of an adverse decision by the Secretary of State on a "called in" application or an appeal (p. 1026, post) need not be accepted by the local planning authority if there has been "no significant change" (s. 70A).

does not preclude a refusal of planning permission, even if that other procedure might carry with it a right to compensation.[80]

(h) Conditional planning permissions

Planning conditions are subject to a test of validity both in principle and in detail. That is to say they must "fairly and reasonably relate to the permitted development"[81] and they must be reasonable in respect of their detailed terms. A condition that cottages to be built must only be occupied by "persons whose employment or latest employment is or was employment in agriculture" seems to have satisfied both tests.[82] A condition that a project of industrial development on a site next to a dangerously congested main road must include the provision of a special access road, and that this access road should be made available to members of the public visiting adjoining premises, seems to have satisfied the first test but not the second.[83]

(i) Time limits for development

Conditions which may be valid include those which require a new use to cease after a stated time and thus give rise to temporary planning permissions;[84] but permissions are normally permanent and "enure for the benefit of the land".[85] Other time conditions, which are so frequent as to be virtually standard-form conditions, specify the time within which development must take place, or at least begin. There is a statutory three-year deadline in "outline" permissions for seeking approval for all details or "reserved matters",[86] followed by a two-year deadline for starting development after final approval; alternatively there is an overall three-year deadline for starting development,[87] as well as a three-year deadline for starting

---

[80] *Westminster Bank Ltd v Minister of Housing and Local Government* [1971] AC 508. In 1954 the Government went so far as to say that authorities choosing procedures which entitle landowners to compensation would be *penalised* for so doing; see per Viscount DILHORNE at 534. And see TCPA 1990, s. 335. A grant of permission to achieve genuine planning objective will not be vitiated merely because neighbouring owners may have to discontinue their own uses, even if the authority is saved having to subject them to a discontinuance order (p. 1027, post); *R v Exeter City Council, ex p Thomas & Co Ltd* [1991] 1 QB 471.

[81] *Pyx Granite Co Ltd v Ministry of Housing and Local Government* [1958] 1 QB 554 at 572, per Lord DENNING. This case concerned quarrying in the Malvern Hills. TCPA 1990, Sch. 5, now makes comprehensive provision for "restoration" and "aftercare" conditions to be included in planning permissions for mining operations.

An applicant may by a condition be required to do or to refrain from doing something on other land, provided that it is owned or controlled by him, not otherwise: *Pedgrift v Oxfordshire County Council* (1991) 63 P & CR 246. See TCPA 1990, s. 72(1).

[82] *Fawcett Properties Ltd v Buckingham County Council* [1961] AC 636.

[83] *Hall & Co Ltd v Shoreham-by-Sea UDC* [1964] 1 WLR 240. If an invalidated condition is trivial the planning permission will survive shorn of it, but if it is not trivial the permission falls with it: *Kent County Council v Kingsway Investments (Kent) Ltd* [1971] AC 72, per Lord MORRIS OF BORTH-Y-GEST. Yet this question would seem to be one of planning policy, not law, and should therefore be remitted to the appropriate authority to decide. Planning permissions, however conditional, ought to be regarded *as a whole*. An altered permission is a different permission, except perhaps in respect of trivial variations: see *Lever Finance Ltd v City of Westminster LBC* [1971] 1 QB 222. The court may remit a case to a planning authority; see *Birmingham Corpn v Minister of Housing and Local Government and Habib Ullah* [1964] 1 QB 178.

[84] TCPA 1990, s. 72(1)(b), (2). Planning permissions "granted for a limited period" (ibid.) are not necessarily the same as those granted subject to "limitations". See *Cynon Valley BC v Secretary of State for Wales* (1987) 53 P & CR 68.

[85] Ibid., s. 75. Therefore they cannot be abandoned: *Pioneer Aggregates (UK) Ltd v Secretary of State for the Environment* [1985] AC 132.

[86] Thus in cases of "outline" permissions applicants may submit as many detailed proposals in respect of the "reserved matters" as they wish, so long as they do so within the three-year period: *Kingsway Investments Ltd v Kent County Council* [1969] 2 QB 332 at 349, per Lord DENNING MR.   [87] TCPA 1990, s. 92.

development under ordinary as distinct from "outline" permissions.[88] The authority, however, can vary any of these periods. There is, moreover, an additional control, by "completion notice". Where any of the above deadlines applies and development has duly begun in the time specified but has not been completed in that time, the local planning authority may serve a "completion notice", subject to confirmation by the Secretary of State (with or without amendments) specifying a time, not less than a year, by which development must be complete or else the permission "will cease to have effect".[89]

(2) Planning Control in Special Cases

(a) Appeals and "called in" applications

If he so wishes, the Secretary of State may direct that a planning application be "called in" (as it is decided by the local planning authority).[90] Such cases, however, are as rare as appeals are frequent. Appeals to the Secretary of State against a refusal of permission, or a grant made subject to conditions, or a failure to give any decision within the appropriate time limit, must be made in writing within six months of the adverse decision or of the expiry of the time limit.[91] He may allow or dismiss the appeal or reverse or vary any part of the permission, and his decision is as free as if he were deciding at first instance. The procedure is now governed by statutory rules, which have already been discussed, and a hearing must be given if it is asked for.[92]

The Secretary of State's decision in such a case, or that made by an inspector on his behalf, is "final" and cannot be challenged in a court except in the circumstances described earlier.[93]

In order to facilitate the making of an appeal when an application is made to a local planning authority, a period is prescribed within which they must issue notice of their decision. That period is normally eight weeks,[94] but is sixteen weeks in cases involving Environmental Impact Assessment,[95] unless extended by written agreement.[96] If this period expires without the authority having given notice of their decision, the applicant is entitled to appeal to the Secretary of State under section 78(1) as if the application had been refused (the "deemed refusal"). The Secretary of State must draw up timetables for deciding appeals, etc.

The applicant has the choice, instead of lodging an appeal, to continue to negotiate with the local planning authority. Applicants often lodge two identical or closely similar applications ("twin-tracking"), and then, if the period expires without a decision having been given, appeal on one application while continuing to negotiate on the other.

---

[88] TCPA 1990, s. 91, as amended by PCPA 2004, s. 51(2).

[89] Ibid., s. 94, as amended by PCPA 2004, s. 51(1).

[90] Ibid., s. 77; GDPO, art. 18. The proposed development will probably be controversial.

[91] Ibid., ss. 78–9; GDPO, art. 23. The time limit of eight weeks (GDPO art. 20; see p. 1024, n. 77, ante) is merely to facilitate appeals; it is not mandatory, and a decision given later (there are many such) will not be automatically invalidated: *James v Secretary of State for Wales* [1968] AC 409.

[92] The inspector, who presides over the hearing or inquiry afforded in connection with a decision to be made by the Secretary of State, may be allowed in prescribed cases to make the decision himself instead of merely reporting back: TCPA 1990, Sch. 6. This may make for quicker results in routine cases. See p. 1018, n. 41, ante. The public are normally entitled to be present at inquiries: TCPA 1990, s. 321.

[93] See p. 1016, ante. Such challenges are in fact quite common. An instructive example is *French Kier Developments Ltd v Secretary of State for the Environment* [1977] 1 All ER 296, in which the decision was quashed for obscurity and mishandling of evidence.   [94] GDPO, art. 20.

[95] P. 1022, ante.   [96] TCP (Environmental Impact Assessment) Regulations 1999, reg. 32.

Section 78A of the Town and Country Planning Act 1990[97] allows the local planning authority an additional period for decision after the case has gone to appeal. This additional period is to be prescribed by a development order; the appeal decision must not be issued in the meantime.

(b) Revocation, modification and discontinuance orders

Planning permission can be revoked or modified.[98] The authorities which do this must pay compensation for any abortive expenditure and for any depreciation in relation to development value which, having come into existence by virtue of the permission, disappears because of the revocation or modification. Revocation or modification orders must be confirmed by the Secretary of State except in uncontested cases.[99] If permission is given automatically by the GPDO it may *in effect* be revoked or modified, if by an "article 4 direction" under the GPDO it is partly or wholly withdrawn and a specific application is then made which is refused or only granted subject to conditions.[100]

In so far as authorised development has actually taken place, even if only in part, revocation or modification orders and "article 4 directions" are ineffective.[101] To put an end to any actual development or "established use" of land (except of course where it is the necessary consequence of acting on a planning permission that this should happen) requires a discontinuance order, which must be confirmed by the Secretary of State.[102] Compensation must be paid for loss of development value and abortive expenditure and also the cost of removal or demolition.[103] As compliance involves physical action there is also an enforcement procedure in cases of recalcitrance, similar in essentials to ordinary enforcement of planning control.[104]

(c) Development involving advertisement uses

If the use of any property for the display of advertisements in accordance with advertisement regulations involves development, planning permission is deemed to be granted for it automatically.[105]

---

[97] Inserted by PCPA 2004, s. 50.

[98] TCPA 1990, s. 97. The recipient is entitled to prior notice and a hearing. For the compensation payable, see pp. 1052–3, post: ss. 107–13.

[99] Ibid., ss. 98–9. The Secretary of State may himself make an order, which will have the same consequences as if the relevant local planning authority had made it itself: s. 100.

[100] GPDO, art. 4. The Secretary of State must normally make or confirm such directions (art. 5), except for some temporary ones which the local planning authority may make: see *Thanet DC v Ninedrive Ltd* [1978] 1 All ER 703; but there is no provision for any prior notice or hearing. Or the development order itself might be partly or wholly withdrawn. For compensation, see pp. 1052–3, post; TCPA 1990, s. 108. See also GPDO art. 7 (directions restricting certain kinds of permitted mineral development).

[101] An "article 4 direction" was held to be ineffective when permitted development had already been carried out in *Cole v Somerset County Council* [1957] 1 QB 23.

[102] TCPA 1990, s. 102. See *Parkes v Secretary of State for the Environment* [1978] 1 WLR 1308. The recipient is entitled to prior notice and a hearing.

[103] Ibid., s. 115. See pp. 1052–3, post.

[104] Ibid., s. 189. For ordinary enforcement procedure, see pp. 1028–31, post.

[105] Ibid., s. 222; see pp. 1034–5, post. The special system of control for office development (TCPA 1971, ss. 73–86) was terminated by Control of Office Development (Cessation) Order 1979 (SI 1979 No. 908). The special system of control for industrial development (TCPA 1971, ss. 66–72) was repealed by the Housing and Planning Act 1986; see ss. 48(1)(b), 49(2) and Sch. 12, Part III.

(d) Land belonging to the Crown and other public authorities

Public authorities, including the Crown, are subject to planning control with certain reservations.[106]

When any project which involves expenditure requires the approval of a government department such approval may also be expressed to confer "deemed" planning permission, with or without conditions, if needed.[107] This régime applies to "statutory undertakers" as well,[108] that is, public transport, communcations or utility authorities; but with them there is also another factor, the difference between their "operational" and non-operational land (the latter being offices, houses, investment property and any other land which is not the site of their operating functions). "Operational" land has the benefit of one or two special rules in planning law, for example in regard to compensation for loss resulting from restrictions on development. As for local *planning* authorities, separate regulations are prescribed, empowering them to grant planning permissions to themselves for land in their *own areas* for their own benefit (i.e. not for subsequent owners' benefit); but in other cases the ordinary rules apply.[109]

(e) Enterprise zones

Finally, reference should be made to "enterprise zones". The Secretary of State is empowered to approve schemes designating these zones which are prepared by local authorities or new town or urban development corporations at his invitation. Planning permission is automatically granted for various kinds of development specified in each scheme; it may in some cases be "outline" permission.[110]

C Breach of Planning Control

(1) Enforcement Procedure

(a) Enforcement notices and breach of condition notices

It is not a criminal offence to develop land without planning permission. If this happens the local planning authority should first consider whether it would be "expedient" to impose sanctions, "having regard" to the development plan and to any other material considerations.[111] If so, they may issue an "enforcement notice"[112] specifying the "breach of planning control" complained of, the steps required to remedy it, the date when it is to take effect, and the time

---

[106] PCPA 2004, s. 111. On the changes made by PCPA 2004 to Crown land, see [2004] JPL Sup. (Occasional Papers No. 32), pp. 35–40 (D. Elvin).

[107] TCPA 1990, ss. 58, 90. Planning authorities can stop up highways: ibid., Part X.

[108] Ibid., ss. 262–83.

[109] Ibid., s. 316; TCP General Regulations 1992 (SI 1992 No. 1492), as amended by SI 1999 Nos. 1810 and 1892.

[110] Local Government, Planning and Land Act 1980, s. 179; TCPA 1990, ss. 88, 89. There are fiscal also benefits.

[111] TCPA s. 172(1). It would be vindictive to impose sanctions for unauthorised development if permission would have been granted in response to a proper application.

[112] Ibid., s. 172(1)–(3). Copies of it must be served (a) within twenty-eight days of issue, and (b) at least twenty-eight days before the date on which the notice states that it will take effect, on the owner and occupier of the land and on any other person whose interest in the land is in the authority's opinion "materially affected". Caravan dwellers may be "occupiers": *Stevens v Bromley LBC* [1972] Ch 400. Alternatively, the Secretary of State, after consulting the local planning authority, may himself serve an enforcement notice: TCPA 1990, s. 182. See

allowed for compliance. A "breach of condition notice" is somewhat similar to this.[113] "Breach of planning control" occurs when development takes place either without the necessary permission or in disregard of conditions or limitations contained in a permission.[114]

There is also what amounts to a limitation period, in that, if the "breach of planning control" comprises either a *change of use* to a single dwelling-house or any kind of operation, the time limit for serving an enforcement notice is restricted to four years after the breach has occurred,[115] and in other cases to ten years.

(b) *Planning contravention notices*

A local planning authority to whom "it appears...that there may have been a breach of planning control" may serve a "planning contravention notice" on the owner or occupier of the land in question, or on the person carrying out operations thereon, requiring the recipient to furnish specified information which will enable the authority to decide what action (if any) to take by way of enforcement. Failure to comply within twenty-one days is a criminal offence, punishable by a fine up to level 3 on the standard scale; the giving of false information either knowingly or recklessly is punishable by a fine up to level 5 on the standard scale.[116]

(c) *Stop notices*

The period specified in the enforcement notice before it takes effect is intended to allow for making an appeal, and the notice is "of no effect" while any appeal is going forward.[117] This may encourage a recalcitrant developer to press on with his activities in the meantime, in the hope of creating a fait accompli. Local planning authorities and the Secretary of State therefore have the additional power, during this period, to serve a "stop notice" prohibiting any activity which is "specified in the enforcement notice as an activity which the local planning authority requires to cease, and any activity carried out as part of that activity or associated with that activity".[118]

Chichester DC v First Secretary of State [2005] 1 WLR 279 (enforcement notice against gypsies not contrary to ECHR).

[113] TCPA 1990, ss. 173, 187A ("breach of condition notices" (served where planning conditions are not complied with)). If no mention is made of steps to remedy the breach, it is not an enforcement notice: *Tandridge DC v Verrechia* [2000] QB 318.

[114] Ibid., s. 171A. For the relevance of this to purchase notices, see p. 1049, n. 64, post. Breaches of planning control on Crown land by private individuals or corporations can be dealt with by a "special enforcement notice": s. 294.

[115] Ibid., s. 171B; *Sage v Secretary of State for the Environment, Transport and the Regions* [2003] 1 WLR 983.

[116] Ibid., ss. 171C, 171D.

[117] Ibid., ss. 174, 175. It may be withdrawn or varied before it "takes effect": s. 173A.

[118] Ibid., ss. 183–5. A stop notice cannot prohibit use of any building as a dwelling-house nor any use which began more than four years previously. It must take effect on a specified date three to twenty-eight days ahead. Contravention is an offence punishable by a fine up to £20,000 in summary proceedings or without a specified limit on indictment and the fine should take into account "any financial benefit which has accrued or is likely to accrue" to the offender (s. 187); but it is a defence to prove that the accused did not know or could not reasonably be expected to have known of the stop notice. But a stop notice may in effect turn out to be unjustified, and the authority will be liable then to pay compensation for loss caused thereby (s. 186). Local authorities can issue twenty-eight-day stop notices, but not in relation to residential use of buildings, under TCPA 1990, ss. 171 E–171 H, added by PCPA 2004, s. 52. See *Wilson v Wychavon DC* [2005] EWHC 2970 (Admin), The Times 18 January 2006 (exclusion of dwelling-houses from stop notices is indirectly discriminatory against gypsies, but can be objectively justified and so is not contrary to ECHR).

(2) Legal Control of Enforcement

(a) Appeals[119]

Appeals may be made against an enforcement notice by a person having an interest in the land or a relevant occupier (i.e. a licensee) within the time specified before it is to take effect. It must be made in writing to the Secretary of State, and may be on one or more of seven specified grounds:[120] (a) permission ought to be granted or a condition or limitation ought to be discharged; (b) the alleged breach did not take place; (c) the facts do not disclose any "breach of planning control"; (d) the breach occurred more than four or ten years ago, as the case may be, whichever limitation period applies; (e) copies were not served on the proper parties; (f) the specified steps for compliance are excessive; (g) the specified time for compliance is too short. The Secretary of State must arrange a hearing or inquiry before an inspector, if either side requires it; and he may uphold, vary or quash the enforcement notice and also grant planning permission if appropriate. He may correct any defect, error or misdescription in the notice, or vary its terms, if he is satisfied that the correction or variation will not cause injustice to the appellant or the local planning authority.[121] Judicial comment on all this is as follows: "an enforcement notice is no longer to be defeated on technical grounds. The Minister . . . can correct errors so long as, having regard to the merits of the case, the correction can be made without injustice. No informality, defect or error is a material one unless it is such as to produce injustice". That was said in the course of a judgment in which it was held to be at most an immaterial misrecital for an enforcement notice to allege development "without permission" when in fact a brief temporary permission existed. "The notice was plain enough and nobody was deceived by it."[122]

(b) Enforcement and the courts

A challenge to the Secretary of State's decision on an enforcement notice lies to the High Court, but only on a point of law.[123] Except by this procedure, no one may contest the

---

[119] Planning Appeal Decisions are published annually.

[120] TCPA 1990, s. 174. The burden of proof lies on the appellant: *Nelsovil Ltd v Minister of Housing and Local Government* [1962] 1 WLR 404. Ss. 191–6 enact that a conclusive presumption that there is no breach of planning control may be achieved by means of a "certificate of lawfulness of existing use or development", or a "certificate of lawfulness of proposed use or development". The certificate is obtainable from the local planning authority (penalties for supplying false information for the purpose being a fine up to the statutory maximum on summary conviction or without a specified limit on indictment, with the addition of imprisonment for up to two years for conviction on indictment). An appeal lies to the Secretary of State, whose decision is "final" (see p. 1017, n. 34, ante).

[121] TCPA 1990, ss. 175–7. Although the notice of appeal must be given within the time specified the grounds of appeal may be notified later: *Howard v Secretary of State for the Environment* [1975] QB 235. The TCP (Enforcement Notices and Appeals) Regulations 2002 (SI 2002 No. 2682) provide that the appellant must deliver a written statement specifying the grounds on which he is appealing against the notice and stating briefly the facts on which he proposes to rely in support of each of those grounds (reg. 5) within twenty-eight days of the Secretary of State requiring him to do so. See also TCP (Written Representations Procedure) Regulations 2002 (SI 2002 No. 2683); TCP (Hearings Procedure) Rules 2002 (SI 2002 No. 2684); TCP (Determination by Inspectors) (Inquiries Procedure) Rules 2002 (SI 2002 No. 2685); TCP (Inquiries Procedure) Rules 2002 (SI 2002 No. 2686). For Inquiries Procedure Rules, see p. 1018, n. 41, ante.

[122] *Miller-Mead v Minister of Housing and Local Government* [1963] 2 QB 196 at 221, per Lord DENNING. But a decision in favour of an appellant on ground (b), (c) or (d) gives rise to an estoppel *per rem judicatam* for his benefit: *Thrasyvoulou v Secretary of State for the Environment* [1990] 2 AC 273.

[123] TCPA 1990, s. 289. CPR, Sch. 1, RSC Ord. 94, r. 12, imposes a time limit of twenty-eight days. See *Button v Jenkins* [1975] 3 All ER 585.

validity of an enforcement notice in legal proceedings on any of the seven grounds specified above.[124] Conversely, a challenge on any other ground can only be made in the courts, for example, the omission of a procedural requirement, such as specifying the date on which the notice shall take effect.[125] A breach of planning control is not a criminal offence, but disregard of an enforcement notice is.[126] On prosecution for failure to carry out *works* it is specially provided that an owner who has transferred his interest to a subsequent owner can bring the latter before the court. On prosecution for failure to discontinue a *use* or to comply with any condition or limitation, the accused can in certain circumstances challenge the enforcement notice, even on the seven grounds specified above.[127]

(c) Enforcement default powers

In addition to prosecution after failure to comply with an effective enforcement notice within the time specified in it, the authority also have the power, after that time, to enter on the land and carry out the steps prescribed by the notice, other than discontinuance of any use, and recover from the owner the net cost reasonably so incurred. He may in turn recover from the true culprit, if different, his reasonable expenditure on compliance.[128]

D Amenity and Safety

(1) Meaning of Amenity and Safety

The other major aim of planning law apart from the control of development is the protection of amenity and safety. These aims are closely linked in practice; but the basic concepts are distinct. There is no statutory definition of amenity or safety; but amenity "appears to mean pleasant circumstances, features, advantages";[129] and the standpoint seems to be that of the general public rather than of particular persons.

[124] TCPA 1990, s. 285. But this is subject to the special exception mentioned below; s. 285(2); n. 127, infra. If enforcement proceedings are defied with impunity, the authority can seek an injunction; see s. 187B; *South Buckinghamshire DC v Porter (No 1)* [2003] 2 AC 558, in which HL confirmed the refusal of CA to approve the grant of injunctions on the facts of the case; *Runnymede BC v Ball* [1986] 1 WLR 353; *A-G v Bastow* [1957] 1 QB 514; *Kent County Council v Batchelor* [1979] 1 WLR 213 (tree preservation order, see p. 1032, post); *Westminster City Council v Jones* (1981) 80 LGR 241. On the general principle of injunctions to protect the public interest, see *Stoke-on-Trent City Council v B & Q (Retail) Ltd* [1984] AC 754.

[125] See *Burgess v Jarvis and Sevenoaks RDC* [1952] 2 QB 41. An omission to allege and prove the time for compliance will vitiate a subsequent prosecution: *Maltedge Ltd and Frost v Wokingham DC* (1992) 64 P & CR 487.

[126] TCPA 1990, s. 179. Landowners are expected to inform themselves of the planning situation with regard to their land; the burden does not rest on the prosecution to prove knowledge: *R v Collett* [1994] 2 All ER 372. The penalties on conviction are the same as for failure to comply with a stop notice; p. 1029, n. 118, ante. Failure to comply with a breach of condition notice (p. 1029, n. 113, ante) is an offence punishable on summary conviction by a fine up to level 3 on the standard scale: s. 187A(12). An allegation that a notice is ultra vires cannot be advanced in defence to a prosecution, as distinct from a judicial review: *R v Wicks* [1998] AC 92. Lord HOFFMANN held that a notice is intra vires if it is "formally valid" and has not been quashed: [1997] All ER Rev, p. 5 (K. Davies).

[127] Provided that no copy was served on him, his interest in the land dates back before the time for service, and he could not reasonably have known of it: TCPA 1990, s. 285(2) (as amended).

[128] TCPA 1990, s. 178. A subsequent planning permission will cause an enforcement notice to lapse; but mere compliance with the notice will not, because of the possibility that offending development may recur after compliance: ss. 180, 181.

[129] *Re Ellis and Ruislip-Northwood UDC* [1920] 1 KB 343 at 370, per SCRUTTON LJ.

The subject matter of the provisions governing amenity comprises trees, buildings of special interest, advertisements, caravan sites and unsightly land. The subject matter of the provisions concerning safety comprises advertisements and "hazardous substances".

The consolidating Acts of 1990 have distributed these provisions three ways. Trees, advertisements and unsightly land are included in the Town and Country Planning Act, Part VIII. Buildings of special interest are in a separate statute, the Planning (Listed Buildings and Conservation Areas) Act 1990. Hazardous substances are in another separate statute, the Planning (Hazardous Substances) Act 1990. Caravan sites however, remain in separate statutes, as before.

(2) Trees

To grow or cut trees is not of itself development.[130] But local planning authorities are specifically empowered, "in the interests of amenity", to make "tree preservation orders" (TPOs) for specified "trees, groups of trees or woodlands", restricting interference with the trees except with the consent of the local planning authority. Trees may, however, be cut if necessary to comply with any statutory requirements or because of nuisance or danger; and there are provisions governing replanting.[131] Unauthorised interference with any protected tree calculated to destroy it is a criminal offence.[132]

A TPO is made and confirmed by the local planning authority or the Secretary of State after considering any objections from owners and occupiers of the relevant land, though, if necessary, a provisional TPO taking immediate effect can be made for up to six months.[133] Regulations are prescribed governing the procedure for making TPOs, and their content. Standard provisions in TPOs lay down essentially the same procedure for applying for consents to interfere with protected trees as exists for making planning applications.[134]

(3) Special Buildings

(a) Conservation areas

"Amenity" is implicit, but, not expressly mentioned in relation to buildings of special interest, which are now governed by the Planning (Listed Buildings and Conservation Areas) Act 1990. Part II of that Act[135] refers to "areas of special architectural or historic interest, the

---

[130] Either might be part of a "material" change of use, and conditions in planning permissions commonly require the preservation or planting of trees. TCPA 1990, s. 197 requires "the imposition of conditions, for the preservation or planting of trees", in planning permissions, as far as is reasonably possible.

[131] TCPA 1990, ss. 198, 206. Control from the standpoint of commercial timber production is imposed by the Forestry Act 1967, as amended, together with the Forestry (Felling of Trees) Regulations 1979 (SI 1979 No. 791) and the Forestry (Exceptions for Restriction of Felling) Regulations 1979 (SI 1979 No. 792).

[132] Penalties on conviction are the same as for failure to comply with an enforcement or stop notice: nn. 118, 126, ante: TCPA 1990, s. 210. But if the offence is "otherwise" (i.e. less destructive) the maximum fine is level 4 on the standard scale: s. 210(4). "Radical" injury is equivalent to destruction: *Barnet LBC v Eastern Electricity Board* [1973] 1 WLR 430. Ignorance of the existence of the TPO is not a defence: *Maidstone BC v Mortimer* [1980] 3 All ER 552. For compensation for loss incurred because of tree preservation restrictions, see ss. 203–5; p. 1053, n. 84, post.   [133] TCPA 1990, ss. 198–202.

[134] TCP (Trees) Regulations 1999 (SI 1999 No. 1892); the Schedule contains a form of TPO.

[135] Ss. 69–80.

character or appearance of which it is desirable to preserve or enhance", and requires local planning authorities to determine where such areas exist and designate them as "Conservation Areas". When one of these areas has been designated, "special attention shall be paid to the desirability of preserving or enhancing the character or appearance of that area" by exercising appropriate powers to preserve amenities under planning legislation, and also by publicizing planning applications for development which in the authority's opinion would affect that character or appearance.[136] All trees in conservation areas are protected in the same way as if subject to a TPO.[137]

(b) Buildings of special interest

The phrase "special architectural or historic interest" applies chiefly to buildings, although trees and other objects may affect their character and appearance. The Secretary of State has the duty of compiling or approving lists of such buildings, after suitable consultations, and supplying local authorities with copies of the lists relating to their areas.[138] Such authorities must notify owners and occupiers of buildings included in (or removed from) these lists.[139] The Secretary of State may, when considering any building for inclusion in a list, take into account the relationship of its exterior with any group of buildings to which it belongs and also "the desirability of preserving . . . a man-made object or structure fixed to the building or forming part of the land and comprised within the curtilage of the building".[140] If a building is not "listed" the local planning authority may give it temporary protection by a "building preservation notice" while they try to persuade the Secretary of State to list it.[141]

(c) Control of listed buildings

Except when for the time being a "listed building" is an ecclesiastical building used for ecclesiastical purposes[142] or an ancient monument (when no doubt it will be adequately protected by either Church or State), it is a criminal offence to cause such a building to be demolished, or altered "in any manner which would affect its character as a building of special architectural or historic interest", without first obtaining and complying with a "listed building consent" from the local planning authority or the Secretary of State, unless works have to be done as a matter of urgency. A consent may be granted subject to

[136] Planning (Listed Buildings and Conservation Areas) Act 1990, ss. 69–76. Note especially s. 74, which prohibits demolition generally in a conservation area without a listed building consent granted in accordance with Part I, Chapter II of the Act; p. 1034, n. 144, post, and s. 71, which imposes on local planning authorities a duty to formulate and publicise proposals for enhancing conservation areas. As to planning applications in conservation areas, see *Bath Society v Secretary of State for the Environment* [1991] 1 WLR 1303; *South Lakeland DC v Secretary of State for the Environment* [1992] 2 AC 141.   [137] TCPA 1990, ss. 211–14.

[138] Developers can apply to the Secretary of State for a certificate that he does not intend to list a building which it is planned to alter or demolish: Planning (Listed Buildings and Conservation Areas) Act 1990, s. 6.

[139] Planning (Listed Buildings and Conservation Areas) Act 1990, s. 2. Ancient monuments, however, have a special code of protection under the Ancient Monuments and Archaeological Areas Act 1979. See *Hoveringham Gravels Ltd v Secretary of State for the Environment* [1975] QB 754, and also the National Heritage Act 1983.

[140] Ibid., s. 1.   [141] Ibid., s. 3. If they fail, they may have to pay compensation: s. 29.

[142] Ibid., s. 60. This exemption ceases to apply in cases of impending demolition; see *A-G v Howard United Reformed Church Trustees, Bedford* [1975] QB 41. The Secretary of State may make an order specifying ecclesiastical buildings in respect of which the exemption is to be restricted or excluded: s. 60(5), (6).

conditions, contravention of which is also a criminal offence;[143] and it is normally effective for five years.[144]

The procedure for applying for listed building consents, and for appeals and revocations, is laid down on lines very similar to the procedure in ordinary cases of planning permission for development; and so is the procedure for listed building enforcement notices and purchase notices.[145] Compensation is payable for depreciation or loss caused by revocation or modification of listed building consents or by the service of building preservation notices.[146] If an owner fails to keep a listed building in proper repair, a local authority or the Secretary of State may first serve a "repairs notice" and, if this is not complied with after two months, may then compulsorily purchase the property.[147] Local authorities can, on seven days' notice to the owner, carry out urgent works at his expense to preserve any unoccupied building, or part of a building, which is listed.[148]

(4) Advertisements, Caravan Sites and Unsightly Land

(a) Advertisements

Control of the display of advertisements is provided for, in the interests of amenity and safety, but not censorship.[149] The details of this control are laid down in regulations.[150] The use of any land for the display of advertisements requires in general an application to the local planning authority for consent, which in normal cases is for periods of five years. Appeal lies to the Secretary of State. There are several categories of display in which consent is "deemed" to be given, including the majority of advertisements of a routine nature and purpose; but "areas of special control" may be declared where restrictions are greater. If however the

---

[143] Planning (Listed Buildings and Conservation Areas) Act 1990, ss. 7–9, 17. The penalty on conviction for either offence is imprisonment up to six months or a fine up to £20,000, or both, in summary proceedings, and imprisonment up to two years or a fine without a specified limit, or both, on indictment; and the fine should be fixed in the light of any financial benefit enjoyed by the offender. See *R v Wells Street Metropolitan Stipendiary Magistrate, ex p Westminster City Council* [1986] 1 WLR 1046 as to the absolute nature of the offence. Acts intended to cause damage to a listed building are, unless authorised, punishable on summary conviction by a fine up to level 3 on the standard scale, with a further daily fine (up to one tenth of level 3) for failing to take steps to prevent further damage thereafter: s. 59. "Alteration" must be considered in the context of the whole, and not part only, of the structure, so that entire demolition of part may only be "alteration" of the whole: *Shimizu UK Ltd v Westminster City Council* [1997] 1 WLR 168.

[144] Ibid., s. 18. Application may be made to vary or discharge conditions: s. 19. S. 14 provides that applications for listed building consent in Greater London shall first be referred by the London boroughs concerned to the Historic Buildings and Monuments Commission for England.

[145] Ibid., ss. 10–26, 32–46. For planning compensation generally, see pp. 1052–3, post. For purchase notices, see p. 1049, post.   [146] Ibid., ss. 28–31.

[147] Ibid., ss. 47–51. If the owner does comply with the repairs notice he may apply to the magistrates to stay compulsory purchase proceedings. But if he has deliberately allowed the building to become derelict not only will the compulsory purchase take place, but he will be entitled only to "minimum compensation", excluding any element of value whatever in respect of the possibility of demolition or alteration. This procedure should be considered, as far as listed buildings are concerned, as an alternative to a dangerous structure orders under the Building Act 1984, s. 77(1)(a), or the London Buildings Act (Amendment) Act 1939, ss. 65, 69(1). For compulsory purchase of land generally, see chap. 30, post.

[148] Ibid., ss. 54, 55. The Secretary of State (to whom an appeal lies within twenty-eight days) may authorise the Historic Buildings and Monuments Commission (n. 144, supra) to carry out such works for buildings in England. In Wales, the National Assembly for Wales has the power to carry out works: SI 1999 No. 672, art. 2, Sch. 1.   [149] Ibid., s. 220.

[150] TCP (Control of Advertisements) Regulations 1992 (SI 1992 No. 666), as amended by SI 1999 No. 1810.

authority "consider it expedient to do so in the interests of amenity or public safety" they may serve a "discontinuance notice" to terminate the "deemed" consent of most kinds of advertisement enjoying such consent; but there is a right of appeal to the Secretary of State. Contravention of the regulations is a criminal offence.[151] Consent under the regulations is "deemed" to confer planning permission also, should any development be involved.[152]

(b) Caravan sites[153]

The control of caravan sites, in the context of planning law, may be regarded as a question of amenity, even though "amenity" is only referred to very incidentally in the legislation. The purpose of control is, in detail, very much a question of public health, and there is authority for the view that control for purposes of public health must not be exercised for purposes of amenity.[154] But there can be little doubt in practice that, although control is concerned with health and safety on the caravan site itself, it preserves amenity for the neighbourhood of the site.

Until 1960 disputes over the establishment of caravan sites were largely ordinary planning disputes, turning on the question of whether there was a "material" change of use in a given case, i.e. development requiring planning permission.[155] Since 1960 the question of development still arises, and planning permission must still be sought for it; but the detailed control of the use of the site is governed by a system of "site licences", obtainable from the local authority.[156] "There are two authorities which have power to control caravan sites. On the other hand, there is the planning authority . . . On the other hand, there is the site authority . . . The planning authority ought to direct their attention to matters in *outline*, leaving the site authority to deal with all matters of *detail*. Thus the planning authority should ask themselves this broad question: Ought this field to be used as a caravan site at all? If 'Yes', they should grant planning permission for it, without going into details as to number of caravans and the like, or imposing any conditions in that regard." Nevertheless—"Many considerations relate both to planning and to site . . . In all these matters there is a large overlap, where a condition can properly be based both on planning considerations and also on site considerations."[157]

It is the "occupier" of land who must apply for a site licence, which must be granted if the applicant has the benefit of a specific planning permission, and withheld if he has not; and

---

[151] Punishable summarily by a fine up to level 4 on the standard scale, while continuance after conviction is a further offence punishable by a daily fine up to one tenth of level 4 on the standard scale: TCPA 1990, s. 224, as amended by Anti-social Behaviour Act 2003, s. 53. Prima facie the owner of the land or the vendor of the goods advertised will be liable: see *John v Reveille Newspapers Ltd* (1955) 5 P & CR 95.

[152] TCPA 1990, s. 222. See also s. 223 and TCP (Control of Advertisements) Regs. 1992, reg. 17; p. 1053, n. 84, post, for compensation payable in certain special cases.

[153] Brand, *Mobile Homes and the Law*; Clayden, *Mobile Homes and Caravans*.

[154] *Pilling v Abergele UDC* [1950] 1 KB 636.

[155] "Intensification" of the use of land for caravans by means of a gradual increase in numbers was one problem: *Guildford RDC v Fortescue* [1959] 2 QB 112. Seasonal change of use is a problem which has also arisen: *Webber v Minister of Housing and Local Government* [1968] 1 WLR 29. For movement of caravans from one field to the next, see *Morel v Dudley* (1961) 178 EG 335. For the availability of an injunction as the ultimate deterrent, at the suit of the Attorney-General, see *A-G v Bastow* [1957] 1 QB 514.

[156] Caravan Sites and Control of Development Act 1960, s. 3.

[157] *Esdell Caravan Parks Ltd v Hemel Hempstead RDC* [1966] 1 QB 895 at 922, per Lord DENNING MR. It follows that a condition in a site licence based solely on planning considerations is ultra vires. See also *Wyre Forest DC v Secretary of State for the Environment* [1990] 2 AC 357 (the meaning of "caravan").

it must last as long as that permission lasts, perpetually in a normal case.[158] The practical question, therefore, is what conditions a site licence shall contain. They are "such conditions as the authority may think it necessary or desirable to impose", with particular reference to six main kinds of purpose.[159] Appeal may be made to a magistrates' court against the imposition of any conditions, or a decision or refusal to vary them at any time after imposition, on the ground that as imposed or varied they are "unduly burdensome".[160]

There are several categories of use of land for caravans which are exempted from control, and also additional powers conferred on local authorities in special cases.[161] Caravan sites for gypsies are provided by county and London borough councils.[162]

(c) Unsightly land

There is also the question of unsightly land: neglected sites, rubbish dumps and the like. Local planning authorities are empowered to deal with any land in their area the condition of which is such that "the amenity of a part of their area, or of any adjoining area, is adversely affected" thereby.[163] A notice is served on the owner and occupier specifying steps to be taken to remedy the state of the land. As with enforcement notices, two time limits must also be specified: a period (of twenty-eight days or more) before the notice takes effect, and the time for compliance.[164]

Appeal lies, at any time before the notice takes effect, to a magistrates' court on any of the following grounds: (a) the condition of the land is not injurious to amenity; (b) the condition of the land reasonably results from a use or operation not contravening planning control; (c) the specified steps for compliance are excessive; (d) the specified time for compliance is too short. The magistrates may uphold, quash or vary the notice, and "correct any informality, defect or error" if it is not material.[165]

---

[158] Caravan Sites and Control of Development Act 1960, s. 4. For the meaning of "occupier" and "caravan site", see s. 1(3), (4). A "chalet structure" falling within the definition could not therefore be made subject to an enforcement notice; p. 1028, ante; *Wyre Forest DC v Secretary of State for the Environment* [1990] 2 AC 357. Use of land as a caravan site without a site licence is an offence: s. 1(1), (2); unless the local authority have failed to grant one within two months: s. 3(4), (6). Contravention of the terms of a licence is also an offence, punishable on the third occasion by revoking the licence: s. 9. For transfer of licences to new owners, see. s. 10.

[159] Ibid., s. 5. The list of purposes is not exhaustive, but any terms unconnected with health, safety or amenity will almost certainly be ultra vires: *Chertsey UDC v Mixnam's Properties* [1965] AC 735. Agreements between owners and occupiers of such sites are now regulated by the Mobile Homes Act 1983.

[160] Ibid., ss. 7, 8.   [161] Ibid., Sch. 1, and ss. 23, 24.

[162] Ibid., s. 24(2), amended by Criminal Justice and Public Order Act 1994, s. 80(2)(a). See also HA 2004, s. 225 (local housing authorities must review the accommodation needs of gypsies and travellers in their district when carrying out reviews of housing needs); ODPM Circular 01/2006, *Planning for Gypsy and Traveller Caravan Sites*.

[163] For a site to which this control in its original form was held not to apply, see *Stephens v Cuckfield RDC* [1960] 2 QB 373; but the decision might have been different under the present form of control.

[164] TCPA 1990, s. 215. The "condition" of land is not to be regarded in isolation from its use: *Britt v Buckinghamshire County Council* [1964] 1 QB 77. Failure to comply is a summary offence punishable by a fine up to level 3 on the standard scale while continuance after conviction is a further offence punishable by a daily fine up to level 3 on the standard scale: s. 216.

[165] Ibid., s. 217. There is a further right of appeal to the Crown Court: s. 218. The notice is suspended while an appeal is going forward.

The authority may also, in default of compliance with an effective notice within the specified period, enter on the land and carry out the steps prescribed by it and recover the net cost reasonably so incurred from the owner. The owner or occupier may recover from the true culprit, if different from themselves, their reasonable expenditure on compliance: s. 219. Powers of control over dumping of refuse and abandonment of vehicles are given to local authorities by the Refuse Disposal (Amenity) Act 1978.

(5) Hazardous Substances

An additional set of controls over the use of land has been introduced into planning law in regard to the placing on any premises of substances such as dangerous chemicals. The purpose of this control is to protect safety, and to a lesser extent amenity. It is additional to existing controls upon the handling of such substances, in that its emphasis relates to the *land* as distinct from the *substances* themselves; but nevertheless it has been derived from those controls, specifically the Health and Safety at Work etc Act 1974. "Hazardous substances" are defined in the Notification of Installations Handling Hazardous Substances Regulations 1982.[166] On 1 May 1984 the Use Classes Order and the then General Development Order were amended[167] so as to withdraw generally from the scope of those orders any use of premises involving a "notifiable quantity" of any "hazardous substance", as defined in the above Regulations of 1982 (apart from certain limited types of permission preserved in the GDO).

The Planning (Hazardous Substances) Act 1990 enacts for England and Wales a new code, whereby the presence of a hazardous substance on, over or under land requires the consent of the hazardous substances authority but not if "the aggregate quantity of the substance . . . is less than the controlled quantity".[168] The Secretary of State is empowered by the Planning (Hazardous Substances) Act 1990 to define "hazardous substances" afresh by specifying them in Regulations,[169] together with "the controlled quantity of any such substance" (as distinct from the "notifiable quantity" referred to above).

Control of land, the use of which involves hazardous substances, is to be exercised whenever they are present in an appreciable amount ("controlled quantity"). The Act requires applications for "hazardous substances consents" to be made to "hazardous substances authorities" which are, by and large, the local planning authorities, including county councils where sites used for mineral workings or waste disposal are involved and in most National Parks, as well as certain urban development corporations and housing trusts. Central Government is also involved because the "appropriate ministers" are the authorities for the "operational land" of "statutory undertakers". The system of consents (with or without conditions), plus revocations, appeals, enforcement, etc., is broadly similar to planning control, and in fact was previously integrated with it; the purpose of the separation is to free this system of control from being tied to the concept of "development" as against *safety* which is the true consideration.

---

[166] SI 1982 No. 1357. Note that the Radioactive Substances Act 1960 enacts the "duty of public and local authorities not to take account of any radioactivity in performing their functions". That Act was amended by Part V of the Environmental Protection Act 1990, which empowers the Secretary of State for the Environment to appoint inspectors to enforce safety requirements.

[167] By SI 1983 Nos. 1614 and 1615 respectively. See pp. 1019, 1020–1, ante, for the Use Classes Order and the GDO (now the GPDO).

[168] Planning (Hazardous Substances) Act 1990, s. 4.

[169] The Act came into force on 1 June 1992, subject to some amendments by the Environmental Protection Act 1990. The Planning (Hazardous Substances) Regulations 1992 (SI 1992 No. 656) require "appropriate consultations" to take place with the Health and Safety Executive. DoE Circular 11/92 gives general guidance.

30

COMPULSORY PURCHASE
AND COMPENSATION[1]

SUMMARY

I The General Law of Compulsory Purchase

A Background of Compulsory Purchase

(1) Origins

(a) Early forms of compulsory purchase

Compulsory purchase of land, in effect public law conveyancing, is considerably older than planning control. In the eighteenth century it commonly took the form of inclosures, whereby various owners' rights in land were transformed compulsorily, either by redistribution or by expropriation, the compulsion being sanctioned by statute. Such statutes were private local Acts, and these specified the actual land to be dealt with in each case. Vast numbers of such Acts, at great expense, were procured between 1750 and 1850, differing (on the whole) only in respect of the particular land to which they related.

In the early nineteenth century similar local initiatives brought about the promotion, by municipal corporations or other groups of persons, of various forms of public works and

---

[1] See generally *Encyclopedia of Compulsory Purchase and Compensation*; Davies, *Compulsory Purchase and Compensation*; Denyer-Green, *Compulsory Purchase and Compensation*. On the impact of ECHR on the law relating to compulsory purchase, see Rook, *Property Law and Human Rights*, section 8.9; Allen, *Property and the Human Rights Act 1998*, chap. 6.

"improvements" such as water-works and gas-works. At the same time canal and railway undertakings were being promoted. The result was another stream of private local Acts for these purposes.

(b) Procedure standardised

Eventually the idea dawned that a general statute could be passed to standardise the repetitive grant of powers, and the Lands Clauses Consolidation Act 1845 duly provided a procedural code for compulsory purchase and compensation, though not for the actual choice of land required. It became customary for statutes to authorise compulsory purchase on the basis that particular land was to be selected when required and the necessary authorisation for its compulsory purchase given by a "provisional order", made by a Minister on the acquiring body's behalf and submitted to Parliament (with a batch of other such orders) in a Provisional Order Bill.[2] In the twentieth century the "compulsory purchase order" was devised instead, the difference being that for this submission to Parliament is not normally necessary.[3]

The development of the law governing compensation is quite recent. Until the First World War Parliament assumed that compensation was solely a question of evidence (expert or otherwise)[4] and left the courts to evolve the rules necessary to settle disputes. But eventually, in the Acquisition of Land (Assessment of Compensation) Act 1919, Parliament devised its own set of rules for assessment of the "market value" of land. Later still, the introduction of planning control gave rise to difficulties in deciding whether "market value" should comprise any "development value" over and above "existing use value" in particular cases, and the statutory rules governing "market value" had to be made more elaborate as a result.

(2) The Modern System

(a) Compulsory purchase statutes

The position now is that compulsory purchase of land normally brings into play four main sets of statutory provisions, as follows. First, there is the authorising Act. No longer is this normally a private local Act, but instead in most cases a public general Act authorising a public body or class of public bodies (for example, county councils)[5] to carry out some

---

[2] Procedure could be separately prescribed by each Act, but was later largely standardised; it is now rarely used.

[3] Compulsory purchase orders must sometimes be laid before each House of Parliament before they come into effect, though this does not involve the sequence of stages needed for legislation and is therefore not the same as "provisional order" procedure. See Statutory Orders (Special Procedure) Acts 1945 and 1965 for this "special parliamentary procedure", as it is called. The Acquisition of Land Act 1981, Part III, requires this procedure to be used when taking National Trust land, open space land or, in some cases, land held by public bodies.

[4] I.e. for juries or arbitrators. Elaborate provisions for assessment *procedure* (not valuation principles) were laid down in Lands Clauses Consolidation Act 1845, ss. 22–68.

[5] The typical acquiring authority nowadays is a local authority; but government departments, "statutory undertakers" and other public bodies are also acquiring authorities in many circumstances. As for *disposal* of land (sale, lease, exchange, appropriation to a different purpose), see Local Government Act 1972, ss. 120–3 and TCPA 1959, ss. 23, 26, both as amended by Local Government, Planning and Land Act 1980, Sch. 23. See also *London and Westcliff Properties Ltd v Minister of Housing and Local Government* [1961] 1 WLR 519; *Laverstock Property Co Ltd v Peterborough Corpn* [1972] 1 WLR 1400.

specified function; and going on to state (a) whether such a body may acquire land for the purpose, (b) whether they may buy it compulsorily, (c) whether they may obtain power to do this by compulsory purchase order (CPO) specifying the land required, and (d) if so what procedure is to be followed when making the CPO. There is now a standardised procedure laid down by the Acquisition of Land Act 1981. Secondly, therefore, is the Act of 1981, in accordance with which the CPO will be made in the majority of cases. Thirdly is the Compulsory Purchase Act 1965, which has to all intents and purposes replaced the Act of 1845 and governs the actual procedure for acquisition after the CPO has sanctioned it.[6] Fourthly is the Land Compensation Act 1961, which contains the current rules for assessing compensation in so far as it relates directly to land values.

(b) Lands Tribunal and the courts

Disputes over compulsory purchase fall broadly into two main cases, depending on whether or not they relate to the assessment of compensation. If they do (and also in one or two special cases to be mentioned below) they must be brought before the Lands Tribunal, a specialised body staffed by valuers and lawyers. Otherwise they should normally be brought before the High Court. Appeal lies to the Court of Appeal not only from the High Court but also from the Lands Tribunal (though on a point of law only, by way of case stated, and within six weeks of the Tribunal's decision).[7]

B Compulsory Purchase Procedure

(1) Compulsory Purchase Orders

Any acquiring authority, which is empowered by the appropriate authorising Act to select and acquire compulsorily the particular land they need by making a CPO, must normally do so by following the procedure laid down in the Acquisition of Land Act 1981, Parts I, II and III. This involves making the order in draft, and submitting it to a "confirming authority", which will be the appropriate Minister or Secretary of State unless of course he himself is acquiring the land. In all cases there must be prior press publicity and notification to the owners and occupiers of the land. Any objections, unless withdrawn, will be heard by an inspector from the Ministry or Department concerned, who will conduct either a public inquiry or a hearing. In the absence of objections, section 100 of the Planning and Compulsory Purchase Act 2004 amends the Acquisition of Land Act 1981 to provide that the CPO can be confirmed without more; in other cases it provides that "written representations" can be substituted if the objectors consent, except in cases where special Parliamentary procedure applies. Inquiries procedure rules for hearings and inquiries are in force, closely parallel to those discussed above in relation to planning

---

[6] In most cases the statutes which apply to the various stages of a compulsory purchase will be public general Acts, and particular land will be specified not in them but in the CPOs and other procedural instruments made under them. For a rare exception, see the Public Offices (Site) Act 1947 (a parcel of land near Westminster Abbey, specified in the Act by reference to a plan).

[7] Lands Tribunal Act 1949, s. 3(4); Lands Tribunal Rules 1996 (SI 1996 No. 1022) as amended by SI 1997 No. 1965; SI 1998 No. 22.

appeals.[8] The order, if confirmed, with or without modifications, takes effect when the acquiring authority publishes a notice in similar manner to the notice of the draft order and serves it on the owners and occupiers concerned. The order cannot be challenged (except possibly on the ground of invalidity) apart from the standard procedure for appeal to the High Court within six weeks on the ground of ultra vires or a procedural defect substantially prejudicing the appellant.[9] Broadly similar procedures apply where the acquiring authority is a Minister or Secretary of State; and they may authorise other authorities to confirm their own CPOs, if the facts justify this; for example, when the owner of the land is unknown.[10]

(2) Compulsory Purchase Conveyancing

(a) Notices to treat

The CPO will lapse, in relation to any of the land comprised in it, unless it is acted on within three years.[11] When the authority wishes to act on the order it must serve a "notice to treat" on the persons with interests in the land to be acquired, requiring them to submit details of their interests and their claims for compensation.[12] When the compensation is settled in each case, it and the notice to treat together amount to an enforceable contract for the sale of the land.[13] This is then subject to completion by the execution of a conveyance in the same way as a private land transaction.[14]

(b) General vesting declarations

There is, however, an alternative procedure at the authority's option whereby the two stages comprising respectively the notice to treat and the conveyance are telescoped into one stage. This is the "general vesting declaration". The authority must notify the owners and occupiers

---

[8] P. 1018, ante. And see *Sunley Homes v Secretary of State for the Environment* (1974) 233 EG 519 (facts distinguished from opinions). In a few cases, e.g. the New Towns Act 1981, Schs. 4 and 5, a separate procedure is laid down for the making of CPOs, which takes the place of the normal procedure under the Acquisition of Land Act 1981, though the differences are not great.

[9] 1981 Act, Part IV. On this, cf pp. 1016–7, ante. For examples of ultra vires orders, see *London and Westcliff Properties Ltd v Minister of Housing and Local Government* [1961] 1 WLR 519 (urban redevelopment), and *Webb v Minister of Housing and Local Government* [1965] 1 WLR 755 (coast protection). For a challenge which failed, see *R v Secretary of State for Transport, ex p de Rothschild* [1989] 1 All ER 933 (disagreement over alternative sites). See (1971) 35 Conv (NS) 316 (K. Davies). For prescribed forms, see Compulsory Purchase of Land (Prescribed Forms) (Ministers) Regulations 2004 (SI 2004 No. 2595).

[10] PCPA 2004, ss. 101, 102.

[11] CPA 1965, s. 4. This means that a "notice to treat" or vesting declaration must be served within that period: see *Grice v Dudley Corpn* [1958] Ch 329.

[12] Ibid., s. 5, as amended by the Planning and Compensation Act 1991, s. 67. The notice to treat will, unless superseded by a general vesting declaration, expire three years after it has been served, unless it has been acted on by (a) entry on the land, or (b) settlement of the compensation, or (c) reference of any dispute over the assessment of compensation to the Lands Tribunal. If the notice expires, the acquiring authority must notify the persons on whom it has been served and compensate them for any consequential loss. Details should be submitted, or negotiations begun, within twenty-one days, failing which, or in default of agreement, either side can apply to the Lands Tribunal: CPA 1965, s. 6.

[13] *Simpsons Motor Sales (London) Ltd v Hendon Corpn* [1964] AC 1088.

[14] Nowadays, normally by registered transfer: see *Crabb v Surrey County Council* (1982) 44 P & CR 119. The costs, including stamp duty, are borne by the acquiring authority: CPA 1965, s. 23. Local Government, Planning and Land Act 1980, Part X empowers the Secretary of State to compile a register of land acquired by public authorities which he considers to be under-used, with a view to its compulsory disposal.

concerned, in the same notice as that which states that the CPO is in force (or in a separate, later notice), that they intend to proceed in this manner by making a vesting declaration not less than two months ahead. This, when made, will by unilateral action vest the title to the land in the authority on a date not less than twenty-eight days after notification to the owners concerned; and it will by and large have the same consequences as if a notice to treat were served.[15]

(c) Interests acquired

Freeholds and leaseholds, both legal and equitable,[16] are capable of compulsory acquisition. Leaseholds with a year or less to run, including periodic tenancies, are not subject to acquisition and compensation but allowed to run out, after the due service of notice to quit if necessary, unless possession is needed in a hurry, in which case it can be taken subject to payment of compensation for the loss caused.[17] An authority cannot normally, without clear statutory authorisation, compulsorily create new leases or rights over land in the limited form of an easement or other right less than full possession (even a stratum of land or building above or beneath the surface).[18] But if they acquire a dominant tenement they acquire the easements appurtenant to it, as in private conveyancing; and if they acquire a servient tenement they either allow the easements and other servitudes over it to subsist without interference or else pay compensation for "injurious affection" to the dominant land if they do so interfere.[19]

(d) Partial acquisitions

If part only of an owner's land is to be acquired, this is "severance". The owner of "any house, building or manufactory" or of "a park or garden belonging to a house" can require the authority to take all or none; but the authority can counter this by saying that to take part

---

[15] Compulsory Purchase (Vesting Declarations) Act 1981. The notice which states that this procedure is to be used must be registered as a local land charge. The procedure will not affect leasehold tenants with a year or less to run, including periodic tenants, nor those with such longer periods to run as may be specified by the acquiring authority; though notices to treat may subsequently be served.

[16] "Land" is usually defined in the appropriate authorising Act. Equitable freeholds and leaseholds include estate contracts, under which the benefit has already passed to the purchaser: *Hillingdon Estates Co v Stonefield Estates Ltd* [1952] Ch 627. Options are included in the rule: *Oppenheimer v Minister of Transport* [1942] 1 KB 242. The same applies to equitable leases: *Blamires v Bradford Corpn* [1964] Ch 585. In this context, failure to register the estate contract as a land charge is immaterial. An authority can acquire freeholds and leave leaseholds outstanding, or even vice versa; but see *London and Westcliff Properties Ltd v Minister of Housing and Local Government* [1961] 1 WLR 519.

[17] CPA 1965, s. 20; *Newham London Borough v Benjamin* [1968] 1 WLR 694. This procedure applies whether notices to treat or general vesting declarations are being used for the interests in reversion.

[18] This was in issue when a compulsory purchase order for part of the Centre Point building in London was quashed in *Sovmots Investments Ltd v Secretary of State for the Environment* [1979] AC 144. For the taking of strata of land, see *Metropolitan Rly Co v Fowler* [1893] AC 416; *City and South London Rly Co v United Parishes of St Mary Woolnoth and St Mary Woolchurch Haw* [1905] AC 1. However, the Local Government (Miscellaneous Provisions) Act 1976, s. 13, empowers local authorities to create "new rights" compulsorily, i.e. rights "not in existence when the order specifying them is made", e.g. leases, easements, etc.

[19] This is "injurious affection arising on land not taken from the claimant": see p. 1046, post. See e.g. *Eagle v Charing Cross Rly Co* (1867) LR 2 CP 638 (easement of light) and *Re Simeon and Isle of Wight RDC* [1937] Ch 525 (restrictive covenant not to interfere with percolating water). The same principle seems to be applicable in cases of appropriation of land, as well as acquisition: *Dowty Boulton Paul Ltd v Wolverhampton Corpn (No 2)* [1976] Ch 13. But see *Earl of Leicester v Wells-next-the-Sea UDC* [1973] Ch 110.

only will not cause any "material detriment", and any such dispute is to be settled by the Lands Tribunal.[20] Similar rules apply to farms.[21]

(e) Delay and entry

Unjustifiable delay by the authority after service of a notice to treat may amount to abandonment of the acquisition.[22] As for making actual entry on the land, the authority is not normally entitled to do this until completion and the payment of compensation, unless, after service of notice to treat, they serve a "notice of entry" on both owners and occupiers; and entry before payment of compensation entitles a claimant to receive interest on the compensation to be paid.[23]

(f) Acquisition by agreement and third party rights

Many acquisitions by authorities are made by agreement.[24] Obligations owed to third parties, as in restrictive covenants, do not normally involve the expropriated owner in liability, and the third party should seek his remedy against the authority if there is any breach in such a case.[25] On the other hand an owner must not increase the authority's liability to compensation by creating new tenancies and other rights in the land or carrying out works on it after service of the notice to treat, which are "not reasonably necessary".[26]

C Compulsory Purchase Compensation

(1) Extent of Compensation

The acquiring authority must compensate the expropriated owner for the land taken, by way of purchase price, and for any depreciation of land retained by him, as well as for "all damage directly consequent on the taking".[27]

[20] CPA 1965, s. 8(1), and Land Compensation Act 1973, s. 58. The right to make the acquiring authority take all the land in such a case seems to apply even if the CPO itself relates only to the part of the land the authority require; see *Genders v LCC* [1915] 1 Ch 1. The Compulsory Purchase (Vesting Declarations) Act 1981 applies similar rules to general vesting declarations. On the meaning of "material detriment", see *Ravenseft Properties Ltd v London Borough of Hillingdon* (1968) 20 P & CR 483 (the applicant's property was "truncated").

[21] Land Compensation Act 1973, ss. 53–7. The test is whether the rest of the farm unit cannot be reasonably farmed even with any other available land.

[22] *Grice v Dudley Corpn* [1958] Ch 329. But delay was held not to amount to abandonment in *Simpsons Motor Sales (London) Ltd v Hendon Corpn* [1964] AC 1088 (the owners themselves being at least partly responsible for it). Most causes of delay will now be resolved by the expiry of the notice to treat as described on p. 1041, n. 12, ante.

[23] CPA 1965, s. 11(1). The period of notice must be at least fourteen days. For land taken "piecemeal", see *Chilton v Telford Development Corpn* [1987] 1 WLR 872. For interests conveyed by a general vesting declaration notices of entry are not needed, but interest must still be paid in respect of advance entry. For interest, the rate of which is prescribed by the Treasury from time to time and which fluctuates in accordance with interest rates generally, see Land Compensation Act 1961, s. 32.

[24] See CPA 1965, s. 3; *Munton v Greater London Council* [1976] 1 WLR 649; *Duttons Brewery Ltd v Leeds City Council* (1981) 43 P & CR 160. Authorities are usually wise to obtain a CPO first, in case negotiations break down. Agreement does not abrogate the ultra vires rule; such acquisitions are still governed by the appropriate authorising Act. The selling owner may himself be vulnerable in law, if he is in the position of a trustee, and may, therefore, apply to the Lands Tribunal to certify that a sale by agreement is "at the best price that can reasonably be obtained": Land Compensation Act 1961, s. 35.

[25] See *Baily v De Crespigny* (1869) LR 4 QB 180. But see *Matthey v Curling* [1922] 2 AC 180.

[26] Acquisition of Land Act 1981, Part V. Assignments, however, are in order: *Cardiff Corpn v Cook* [1923] 2 Ch 115.   [27] *Harvey v Crawley Development Corpn* [1957] 1 QB 485 at 492, per DENNING LJ.

(2) Purchase Price

(a) "Market value"

The basis of compensation for the taking or depreciation of land is "market value", namely "the amount which the land *if sold in the open market by a willing seller* might be expected to realise". "Special suitability or adaptability" of the land which depends solely on "a purpose to which it could be applied only in pursuance of statutory powers, or for which there is no market apart from the requirements of any authority possessing compulsory purchase powers", must be disregarded.[28] There must be no addition to nor deduction from market value purely on the ground that the purchase is compulsory, nor any addition specifically on account of the project to be carried out by the acquiring authority.[29] An increase in the value of adjoining land of the owner not taken by the authority, if it results from the compulsory acquisition, must be "set off" against compensation.[30]

If the property has been developed and used for a purpose which has no effective market value, such as a church, then the Lands Tribunal may order that compensation "be assessed on the basis of the reasonable cost of equivalent reinstatement", if "satisfied that reinstatement in some other place is bona fide intended".[31] This requires a finding that the present use of the land is for a purpose for which there is "no general demand or market".[32]

These intricate legal rules are intended for the guidance of valuers rather than lawyers. Valuers engaged in the assessment of the compensation are required, subject to such guidance, to reach a figure which will put the expropriated owner in a position as near as reasonably possible to that in which he would find himself if there had been no compulsory acquisition and he had sold his land in an ordinary private sale.[33]

---

[28] Land Compensation Act 1961, s. 5. Any restrictions burdening the land must be taken into account in the valuation: *Abbey Homesteads (Developments) Ltd v Northamptonshire County Council* (1992) 64 P & CR 377. Unauthorised uses must not: *Hughes v Doncaster MBC* [1991] 1 AC 382. For "sitting tenants", see *Lambe v Secretary of State for War* [1955] 2 QB 612. Disregard of "special suitability" used to extend to "the special needs of a particular purchaser" until the repeal of those words by the Planning and Compensation Act 1991, s. 70 and Sch. 15. Business and farm tenants are to be compensated on expropriation on the footing that the value of any statutory security of tenure is to be taken into account; and this is reflected also in their landlords' compensation: Land Compensation Act 1973, ss. 47, 48.

[29] Ibid., ss. 5, 9; *Pointe Gourde Quarrying and Transport Co Ltd v Sub-Intendent of Crown Lands* [1947] AC 565; *Wilson v Liverpool City Council* [1971] 1 WLR 302; *Jelson Ltd v Blaby DC* [1977] 1 WLR 1020; *Birmingham DC v Morris and Jacombs Ltd* (1976) 33 P & CR 27; *Melwood Units Pty Ltd v Main Roads Comr* [1979] AC 426. As to s. 9, see *English Property Corpn v Royal Borough of Kingston upon Thames* (1999) 77 P & CR 1. The so-called "Pointe Gourde rule" cannot be fully reconciled with the "willing seller" rule which is the true basis for assessing compensation, and raises doubts whether the law on compensation is fully consistent with the principle of market value.

[30] Ibid., s. 7. There must be no artificial additions to or reductions from the price of the land taken, on the assumption that it might *not* have been taken, which are attributable to the authority's development to be carried out on the rest of the land taken, if that is unlikely to have been carried out in circumstances other than those of the acquisition itself: s. 6 and Sch. 1 (as amended by New Towns Act 1966 and Local Government, Planning and Land Act 1980, s. 145 and Sch. 25). See also s. 8, and *Davy v Leeds Corpn* [1965] 1 WLR 445.

[31] Ibid., s. 5; *Birmingham Corpn v West Midland Baptist (Trust) Association (Inc)* [1970] AC 874; *Zoar Independent Church Trustees v Rochester Corpn* [1975] QB 246.

[32] In *Harrison & Hetherington Ltd v Cumbria County Council* (1985) 50 P & CR 396, HL held that these words applied to land used for a livestock market. But that is not certain.

[33] ". . . the sum to be ascertained is in essence one sum, namely, the proper price or compensation payable in all the circumstances of the case": *Horn v Sunderland Corpn* [1941] 2 KB 26 at 34, per GREENE MR. For purchases by agreement, p. 1043, ante. For particular applications of the general principle, see *Hertfordshire*

(b) Market demand and planning control

Market value, however, has in any case two distinct main elements: "existing use value" and "prospective development value".[34] Since development is not lawful without planning permission, the absence of permission will inhibit purchasers from paying any amount over and above "existing use" value, whether the land is built on or not, in its present state of development. Before the days of planning control, "prospective development value" over and above "existing use value" depended on market demand; and this is still true. "It is not planning permission by itself which increases value. It is planning permission coupled with demand."[35]

Assessing the existence of demand is essentially a question of valuers' expert evidence; the Lands Tribunal is better qualified than a court to pronounce on such evidence. Assessing the availability of planning permission, however, calls for special statutory rules, because there are many cases where planning permission is refused purely because proposed development, which is otherwise acceptable, is ruled out by the impending compulsory purchase, which in turn will often be for the purpose of a public works project with little or no market value.

(c) Planning assumptions

"Assumptions as to planning permission" are therefore, for compensation purposes *only*, authorised by statute. The most useful of these turn on the allocation or "zoning" in the current development plan of areas of land which include the owner's property for uses which command a lucrative development value: residential, commercial or industrial. There may be a range of such uses.[36] But permission can only be assumed if it is also reasonable to do so in relation to the particular physical or planning circumstances of the land itself.[37]

Whether or not the development plan happens to "zone" the land in this way the owner (or the authority) can apply to the local planning authority for a "certificate of

County Council v Ozanne [1991] 1 WLR 105 ("ransom strip"); *Stokes v Cambridge Corpn* (1961) 13 P & CR 77 (inadequate access).

[34] The latter completely excludes the cost of development, including the developer's profit; any actual development carried out will add yet another item to the eventual total cost of land. "Prospective development value" is the amount (if any) which the market adds to "existing use value" when, for example, a field is in demand as a building plot, but no steps have yet been taken to carry out building works on it, or a house is in demand for office use but has not so far been converted. It is "development potential", not actual development.

[35] *Viscount Camrose v Basingstoke Corpn* [1966] 1 WLR 1100 at 1106, per Lord DENNING MR. See also *Myers v Milton Keynes Development Corpn* [1974] 1 WLR 696. But sometimes buyers will pay "hope value".

[36] See Land Compensation Act 1961, ss. 14–16. Planning permission can be assumed (under s. 15) for the development which the acquiring authority itself intends to carry out. It can also be assumed for (a) development consisting of rebuilding works, subject to certain constraints on floor space, "so long as the cubic content of the original building is not substantially exceeded", and so long as that building existed on 1 July 1948, or, if not, "was in existence at a material date" thereafter, or was demolished between 7 January 1937 and 1 July 1948, and (b) for converting a single dwelling-house into two or more separate dwelling-houses: TCPA 1990, Sch. 3 as amended by Planning and Compensation Act 1991. But these assumptions will rarely be as beneficial to claimants as those based on "zoning"; nor will *any* assumption as to planning permission be beneficial to a claimant unless market demand for development can be proved in addition.

[37] See *Margate Corpn v Devotwill Investments Ltd* [1970] 3 All ER 864; *Provincial Properties (London) Ltd v Caterham and Warlingham UDC* [1972] 1 QB 453. If land being acquired includes a listed building, a listed building consent will be assumed for any works of alteration, but not demolition (unless in connection with development within the terms of TCPA 1990, Sch. 3; see n. 36, supra.); Planning (Listed Buildings and Conservation Areas) Act 1990, s. 49.

appropriate alternative development" in relation to the particular circumstances of the land. Appeal lies to the Secretary of State; and from him in turn lies the usual limited right of appeal within six weeks to the High Court. The cost of applying for that certificate will be included in the compensation, if the applicant is successful in claiming development value by this means.[38]

(d) Subsequent development

If, within ten years after a compulsory acquisition, any subsequent planning permission is granted which adds to the development value of the land acquired, that additional value may be claimed by the expropriated owner from the acquiring authority, calculated on the basis of values at the time of the acquisition from him.[39]

(3) Depreciation and Disturbance

(a) Severance and injurious affection

In addition to purchase price compensation there is compensation for "injurious affection" for depreciation of land retained by the claimant resulting from its "severance" from the land taken. This may refer to the pro rata reduction in value of the land retained over and above its reduction in size,[40] or to depreciation caused by what is done on the land taken, or to both.[41] The latter is closely analogous to damages in tort for private nuisance,[42] though it may well include loss not compensatable in tort.[43] But if what is done goes beyond what is authorised by the statutory powers of the acquiring authority, then it will in any case be unlawful and so compensatable (if at all) in tort and not as "injurious affection".[44]

---

[38] Land Compensation Act 1961, ss. 17–22, as amended by Local Government, Planning and Land Act 1980, s. 121 and the Planning and Compensation Act 1991, s. 65. S. 70 and Sch. 15 provide that an assumption which is upheld in a certificate of appropriate alternative development must be taken into account when considering an assumption based on the development plan even if they conflict. See *London & Clydeside Estates Ltd v Aberdeen DC* [1980] 1 WLR 182 in regard to the giving of reasons and information.

[39] Ibid., Part IV, inserted by the Planning and Compensation Act 1991, s. 66 and Sch. 14. There are various special cases specified in these provisions where this right to additional compensation is excluded. The time of the acquisition is in normal cases to be taken as the date of the notice to treat.

[40] As a result of that reduction (i.e taking part of the owner's land and leaving part). See *Holt v Gas Light and Coke Co* (1872) LR 7 QB 728; *Palmer and Harvey Ltd v Ipswich Corpn* (1953) 4 P & CR 5. CPA 1965, s. 7, speaks of "severing . . . or *otherwise* injuriously affecting . . . " the claimant's land. "Injurious affection" is in fact the Victorian term for "depreciation", whether or not arising from "severance".

[41] CPA 1965, s. 7 is the authority for "severance and injurious affection" compensation. The depreciation need not be caused *entirely* by what is done on the land taken as distinct from other land, provided that it is at least *partly* so caused: Land Compensation Act 1973, s. 44.

[42] Land "retained" by an owner may be considered for severance and injurious affection compensation even if not immediately contiguous with the land taken: *Cowper Essex v Acton Local Board* (1889) 14 App Cas 153, and even if enjoyed under a different interest, such as an option: *Oppenheimer v Minister of Transport* [1942] 1 KB 242.

[43] E.g. loss of privacy. The leading case is *Duke of Buccleuch v Metropolitan Board of Works* (1872) LR 5 HL 418. The depreciation must be compensated *in full* as a straightforward matter of valuation on a "before and after" basis, i.e. before and after severance.

[44] Including where the authority "have statutory powers which they . . . exercise in a manner hurtful to third parties" when they could have done so "in a manner innocuous to third parties", this being a perverse choice amounting to negligence: *Lagan Navigation Co v Lambeg Bleaching Dyeing and Finishing Co Ltd* [1927] AC 226, per Lord ATKINSON. Stopping up a highway does not, per se, normally give a right to compensation: see *Jolliffe v Exeter Corpn* [1967] 1 WLR 993.

(b) Injurious affection when no land is taken from the claimant

It is also possible to obtain compensation for "injurious affection" when *no* land has been acquired from the claimant. Here it is necessary to prove four things: (a) the loss is caused by activity authorised by statute, (b) it would be actionable in private law if it were not so authorised, (c) it is strictly a depreciation in land value (i.e. not business losses, nor nuisance *per se* caused by noise, dust, vibrations etc.), and (d) it arises from the carrying out of works on the compulsorily acquired land and not from its subsequent use.[45] But depreciation caused by the *use* of public works, including highways and aerodromes, is in many cases now compensatable under Part I of the Land Compensation Act 1973, if attributable to "physical factors".[46] The claim period of six years starts to run from one year after the use begins.[47]

(c) Disturbance and related matters

Another head of compensation is "disturbance", which is not strictly land value but "must . . . refer to the fact of having to vacate the premises".[48] Thus it may include the loss of business profits and goodwill, removal expenses and the cost of acquiring new premises.[49] It has been held that to claim for "disturbance" an owner must forgo "prospective development value" in his purchase price compensation; that is to say, his "true loss" is whichever is the higher: "existing use" plus "prospective development" or "existing use" plus "disturbance".[50] He must not be compensated for any item of loss twice over.

[45] *Metropolitan Board of Works v McCarthy* (1874) LR 7 HL 243. See also *Ricket v Metropolitan Rly Co* (1867) LR 2 HL 175; *Argyle Motors (Birkenhead) Ltd v Birkenhead Corpn* [1975] AC 99; *Wrotham Park Settled Estates v Hertsmere BC* [1993] RVR 56; *Re Simeon and Isle of Wight RDC* [1937] Ch 525; *Clift v Welsh Office* [1999] 1 WLR 796; *Wildtree Hotels Ltd v Harrow LBC* [2001] 2 AC 1. CPA 1965, s. 10 is the authority for this kind of compensation, in spite of its less than appropriate wording.

[46] These are: noise, vibration, smell, fumes, smoke, artificial lighting, and solid or liquid discharge. See *Hickmott v Dorset County Council* (1977) 35 P & CR 195; *Marchant v Secretary of State for Transport* [1979] RVR 113.

[47] LA 1980, s. 9; Land Compensation Act 1973, s. 3, as amended by Local Government, Planning and Land Act 1980, ss. 112, 113.

[48] *Lee v Minister of Transport* [1966] 1 QB 111 at 122, per DAVIES LJ. It is regarded as part of the price of the land, and is therefore only payable to a claimant who is *expropriated* and so entitled to a market value purchase price as well as being dispossessed. This excludes those tenants who, though dispossessed (by notice to quit or by effluxion of time), are not expropriated and landlords who, though expropriated, are not dispossessed. But expropriated landowners not in occupation can now claim *expenses* of obtaining alternative property in the UK, as if claiming disturbance compensation, provided that they do so within one year from the date of entry: Planning and Compensation Act 1991, s. 70 and Sch. 17, inserting a new s. 10A in the Land Compensation Act 1961. A dispossessed licensee as such will get nothing: *Woolfson v Strathclyde Regional Council* (1978) 38 P & CR 521 (other than a company having the same directors as a related company which *is* being expropriated: *DHN Food Distributors Ltd v Tower Hamlets LBC* [1976] 1 WLR 852). As to costs incurred in advance, see *Prasad v Wolverhampton BC* [1983] Ch 333; *Director of Buildings and Land (Hong Kong) v Shun Fung Ironworks Ltd* [1995] 2 AC 111 (PC).

[49] *Harvey v Crawley Development Corpn* [1957] 1 QB 485. The additional capital cost of buying dearer property, however, is "value for money", and not compensatable. It is not the same as compensation on the basis of "equivalent reinstatement". See the judgment of DENNING LJ. The cost of preparing the compensation claim itself may be included in the claim (*LCC v Tobin* [1959] 1 WLR 354) but as "any other matter", not "disturbance": *Lee v Minister of Transport*, supra; Land Compensation Act 1961, s. 5(6). On goodwill, see Land Compensation Act 1973, s. 46 (claimants aged over sixty) and *Bailey v Derby Corpn* [1965] 1 WLR 213. Compensation can include the cost of relocation of a business if the claimant would have used his own money for the purpose in the absence of compulsion: *Director of Buildings and Lands (Hong Kong) v Shun Fung Ironworks*, supra.

[50] *Horn v Sunderland Corpn* [1941] 2 KB 26. In a private sale to a developer a vendor would expect to sacrifice all the profits arising from the existing use in order to secure the additional value which the prospect of development would put on to the market price of the land. A vendor selling of his own free will purely at the

Since disturbance *compensation* is (illogically) supposed to be an integral part of land value[51] it is not payable where the acquiring body, having expropriated the landlord, displace a short-term tenant by *notice to quit* or by effluxion of time. In such cases the Land Compensation Act 1973[52] provides for "disturbance payments" (removal expenses, business losses) by the acquiring body to the tenant.[53]

(d) Assessment and payment of compensation

A claimant "must once for all make one claim for all damages which can be reasonably foreseen".[54] The date of the notice to treat fixes the interests which may be acquired, but not the compensation, which must be assessed[55] as at the time of making the assessment, or of taking possession (if earlier), or of the beginning of "equivalent reinstatement".[56] If compensation payments are delayed by long-drawn-out disputes, the claimants are entitled to "advance payments" on account, under the Land Compensation Act 1973[57] of up to 90 per cent of the authority's estimate with subsequent adjustment for insufficient or excessive payments. Advance payments and remaining balances alike carry interest, of which there must be yearly payments if accrued interest[58] on unpaid balances exceeds £1,000.

II Compulsory Purchase and Compensation in Planning

A Compulsory Purchase in Planning

(1) Acquisition "for Planning Purposes"

The planning statutes are themselves the authorising Acts for certain kinds of compulsory purchase of land. Thus they authorise acquisition "in connection with development and for

---

"existing use" value does not expect to get his removal expenses paid by the purchaser; so to this extent "disturbance" compensation may be a bonus. Business relocation (see n. 49, ante) involves more than removal costs.

[51] See *IRC v Glasgow and South-Western Rly Co* (1887) 12 App Cas. 315. It is therefore part of a capital sum, though some may represent lost *income* (e.g. profits). On the taxation complexities arising out of this, see *Stoke-on-Trent City Council v Wood Mitchell & Co Ltd* [1980] 1 WLR 254, and Taxation of Chargeable Gains Act 1992, s. 245. On the relevance of grants, see *Palatine Graphic Arts Co Ltd v Liverpool City Council* [1986] QB 335.

[52] Ss. 37, 38. See *R v Islington LBC, ex p Knight* [1984] 1 WLR 205. See also ss. 29–33 ("home loss payments"), ss. 34–6 ("farm loss payments") and ss. 39–43 (rehousing displaced residents). These provisions are as amended by the Planning and Compensation Act 1991, ss. 68–70 and Sch. 17. For properties in a proper state of repair or habitability, see PCPA 2004, ss. 106–9 further amending the Land Compensation Act 1973, to introduce a "basic loss" payment for freeholders or tenants of one year's standing at the time of entry, plus an "occupier's loss" payment.

[53] Farm tenants are separately catered for: ss. 59, 61. Farm and business tenants enjoying statutory security of tenure have compensation rights against their *landlords*.

[54] *Chamberlain v West End of London and Crystal Palace Rly Co* (1863) 2 B & S 617, per ERLE CJ. If a claim is not submitted within twenty-one days of service of the notice to treat (or the general vesting declaration; see pp. 1041–2, ante) the dispute is referable to the Lands Tribunal: CPA 1965, s. 6. Unreasonable delay in submitting a claim will lead to an order to pay the authority's costs incurred through the delay; and if either side refuses an unconditional offer by the other, which is then kept secret (a "sealed offer") and turns out to be more favourable than the Tribunal's award, the costs of the other side incurred through the delay thereby caused will also have to be paid: Land Compensation Act 1961, s. 4. See *Pepys v London Transport Executive* [1975] 1 WLR 234.

[55] In accordance with PCPA 2004, s. 103, confirming earlier case law.

[56] *Birmingham Corpn v West Midland Baptist (Trust) Association (Inc)* [1970] AC 874.

[57] Ss. 52 and 52A, as amended and extended by Planning and Compensation Act 1991, s. 63, and PCPA 2004, s. 104.   [58] See p. 1043, n. 23, ante.

other planning purposes".[59] This means land required "in order to secure the carrying out of one or more of the following activities, namely, development, redevelopment and improvement", or "required for a purpose which it is necessary to achieve in the interests of the proper planning of an area in which the land is situated":[60] in other words, "positive planning". Local authorities in general have this power in respect of land in their areas, subject to the standard compulsory purchase procedure. They can themselves develop land so acquired, with the Secretary of State's consent. More usually they dispose of the land with his consent in specified cases "in such manner and subject to such conditions as may appear to them to be expedient",[61] to private or public sector developers as appropriate. Section 99 of the Planning and Compulsory Purchase Act 2004[62] provides that local planning authorities can acquire land for development if they believe that development, redevelopment or improvement is likely to contribute to the achievement or promotion of the economic, social or environmental well-being of their area.

(2) Inverse Compulsory Purchase

(a) Varieties of compulsory purchase instigated by owners

Another aspect of compulsory purchase in planning is "inverse compulsory purchase", of which there are two species: purchase notices and "blight notices". The owners supply the compulsion in these cases, not the acquiring authorities.[63] A purchase notice is served in consequence of an adverse planning decision; but a blight notice is served in consequence of adverse planning proposals.

(b) Purchase notices

If planning permission is in a particular case refused, or granted subject to conditions, so that as a result "the land has become incapable of reasonably beneficial use in its existing state", then an owner may serve a purchase notice on the local borough or district council.[64] If the council are unwilling to accept it they must normally refer it to the Secretary of State who must then exercise his own judgment as to whether the notice is justifiable and ought to be

---

[59] Acquisition of land "for planning purposes" can perhaps be said to occur also under e.g. New Towns Act 1981, National Parks and Access to the Countryside Act 1949, Countryside Act 1968, Wild Life and Countryside Act 1981, Land Compensation Act 1973 Part II, Local Government, Planning and Land Act 1980, Part XVI ("urban development corporations") and Leasehold Reform, Housing and Urban Development Act 1993, Part III (Urban Regeneration Agency). Local authorities can also make grants or loans to encourage improved use of land in declining "inner city areas", with central government assistance: Inner Urban Areas Act 1978.   [60] TCPA 1990, s. 226.

[61] Ibid., ss. 232–46. This is what happens to bring about "urban renewal", meaning town-centre redevelopment in most cases. See s. 227 for acquisitions by agreement; and s. 228 for compulsory acquisition by the Secretary of State of "land necessary for the public service".   [62] Amending TCPA 1990, s. 226

[63] TCPA 1990, Part VI. No CPO is required, and an effective notice is the equivalent of a notice to treat, so that all that remains to be done is to assess the compensation by the usual procedure: ss. 139, 143 (purchase notices); 154, 160 (blight notices). Compensation for purchase notices will largely be concerned with prospective development value, for blight notices with existing use value, though not exclusively so in either case.

[64] Ibid., s. 137. The procedure can also be used in consequence of the service of revocation and discontinuance orders, etc., see p. 1027, ante. On the relevance of breaches of planning control to the meaning of "incapable of reasonable beneficial use", see *Balco Transport Services Ltd v Secretary of State for the Environment (No 2)* [1986] 1 WLR 88.

upheld.[65] He must not uphold it merely on the ground that "the land in its existing state and with its existing permissions is substantially less useful to the server", since that is true of nearly all planning refusals.[66] The land[67] must in fact be virtually useless to justify a purchase notice.

(c) Blight notices

A "blight notice" is served on the "appropriate authority", meaning a prospective acquiring authority.[68] There are four principal requirements: (1) the owner's land must be "blighted land"; (2) the server must hold a "qualifying interest"; (3) he must have made genuine but unsuccessful attempts to sell for a reasonable price on the open market; and (4) the authority must in fact intend to acquire the land.[69] Within two months the authority concerned may serve a counter-notice alleging that any of the above requirements has not been met. The claimant then has two more months in which to refer the dispute to the Lands Tribunal, before whom the burden of proof is on the authority if they deny an intention to acquire any or all of the land but on the claimant in other cases.[70]

The categories of blighted land all relate to planning proposals by public bodies which envisage compulsory acquisition by one or more public authorities. For example, land may be indicated as being required for the functions of a public[71] body in a local plan or, failing that, in a structure plan or, failing that, indicated in any development plan as required for a highway; or as land in or beside the line of a trunk or special road,[72] or sufficiently indicated in writing by the Secretary of State to the local planning authority as required for such a road, or selected for a highway by a resolution of a local highway authority; or as land covered by a CPO which has not yet been acted upon, or else subject to compulsory purchase by virtue of a special enactment.[73]

---

[65] TCPA 1990, ss. 141–3. If he considers the notice unjustified, he must reject it; if justified, confirm it. But in the latter case he has discretion to arrange for permission to be given for some alternative development, or for an alternative body to acquire the land.

[66] *R v Minister of Housing and Local Government, ex p Chichester RDC* [1960] 1 WLR 587. But see TCPA 1990, s. 142 (reversing *Adams and Wade Ltd v Minister of Housing and Local Government* (1965) 18 P & CR 60). For the meaning of "owner", see *London Corpn v Cusack-Smith* [1955] AC 337, and TCPA 1990, s. 336(1).

[67] *All* the land affected: *Smart and Courtenay Dale Ltd v Dover RDC* (1972) 23 P & CR 408.

[68] Ibid., s. 169 ("the government department, local authority or other body or person by whom . . . the land is liable to be acquired"). There may be more than one such authority: *R v Secretary of State for the Environment, ex p Bournemouth BC* [1987] 1 EGLR 198.

[69] Ibid., ss. 149–51. Land is "blighted" if it comes within any of twenty-three categories set out in Sch. 13 as amended. A "qualifying interest" is a freehold or leasehold of three years or more: s. 168(3), by virtue of which the claimant is an occupier (subject to an annual value limit for rating, if the property is not residential, of £18,000 under the TCP (Blight Provisions) Order 1990 (SI 1990 No. 465), and occupation must have lasted for six months up to the date of service of the blight notice or to an earlier date (not more than twelve months previously). If a claimant dies after service of a blight notice, it continues for the benefit of his personal representatives; and in some circumstances a mortgagee can serve a notice: TCPA 1990, ss. 161, 162.

[70] Ibid., ss. 151–3. The authority may in some cases deny that it intends to acquire the land at all and in other cases deny that it intends to acquire it during the next fifteen years: s. 151(4). See *Bolton Corpn v Owen* [1962] 1 QB 470. In *Mancini v Coventry City Council* (1982) 44 P & CR 114, CA doubted the proposition that an objection on the ground that the authority do not intend to acquire the land is "not well-founded" if undue hardship results to the claimant.

[71] Land "zoned" for housing in a development plan is *not* thereby indicated as required for the local council as housing authority, since at that stage the question is still open whether private housing development may be permitted there: *Bolton Corpn v Owen* [1962] 1 QB 470.

[72] As indicated in an operative scheme or order under the Highways Act 1980.

[73] TCPA 1990, Sch. 13. As regards the rateable value limit, see n. 69, supra; *Essex County Council v Essex Inc Congregational Church Union* [1963] AC 808. If a farm is only within the "specified descriptions" as to part of

B Betterment and Planning Compensation

(1) New and Old Meanings of Betterment

In discussing market value compensation above, "existing use value" was distinguished from "prospective development value", and the latter shown to depend on there being both market demand and planning permission for development. "Prospective development value" is synonymous with betterment in its current meaning, although formerly betterment seems to have meant the increase in the *overall* market value of land by reason of beneficial public works on other land nearby. Either way, the meaning is a purely financial one.

The switch in meaning was the result of the Uthwatt Report of 1942.[74] The new meaning has held the field since then, and with it has arisen the view that betterment, unlike existing use value or the actual cost of development, has not been earned by the owner who realises it. It may be that only the community as a whole can be said to have "earned" the prospective development value of land; but only the market can produce it, and then only if there is planning permission or the hope of planning permission ("hope value").

(2) Public Appropriation of Betterment

(a) Development charges

If betterment accrues, therefore, is the community entitled to take all or any of it? The Town and Country Planning Act 1947 went on the assumption that the community was entitled to take all of it, since it could not thenceforth come into existence without a planning permission. The Act imposed a "development charge" which appropriated to a new government body, the Central Land Board, all betterment (i.e. development value) accruing as the result of any grant of planning permission. At the same time it was decided that all owners to whom such betterment had already accrued by the time of the Act's commencement should receive once-for-all compensation for the loss of it.[75] This was to have been paid in 1953 out of a special £300 million fund; but as from 1952 development charges were abolished and the compensation proposals halted.[76] The "established claims" on the fund, however, were soon to be made use of in an unexpected manner.[77]

(b) Capital gains tax, betterment levy and development land tax

In 1965 betterment came within the scope of capital gains tax[78] at 30 per cent, after being untaxed for thirteen years. The Land Commission Act 1967 replaced this charge on betterment by a separate "betterment levy" initially set at 40 per cent,[79] and set up the Land

---

its area, the rest can be included in the blight notice provided that it is not reasonably capable of being farmed on its own or with any other available land: ibid., ss. 158, 159.

[74] Final Report of the Expert Committee on Compensation and Betterment 1942 (Cmd 6386).

[75] TCPA 1947, Part IV. The compensation was to be "once-for-all" payable on an "established claim", but development charges would be imposed every time permission was granted. Commencement occurred on 1 July 1948.   [76] TCPA 1953.

[77] This was in order to justify paying compensation for planning restrictions provided that the land affected was subject to an "unexpended balance of established development value" (UXB) derived from an "established claim". This limited entitlement to compensation survived until the Planning and Compensation Act 1991, s. 31 abolished it: p. 1052, post.   [78] Finance Act 1965.

[79] Land Commission Act 1967, ss. 27, 28; Betterment Levy (Prescribed Rate) Order 1967 (SI 1967 No. 544).

Commission to collect it. This was abolished in 1971: but betterment reverted to being taxed as a capital gain, which in 1974 became treated for tax purposes as if it were income.[80] In 1976 this "development gains tax" was superseded by "development land tax", which was set at 60 per cent (initially 80 per cent), subject to various exemptions, but was repealed by the Finance Act 1985, for disposals of land on and after 19 March 1985.[81] Betterment had thus for the third time become taxable as a capital gain.

(3) Planning Compensation

(a) Loss of development value

The converse of appropriating betterment to the community is awarding compensation to owners who are deprived of it by the community, not merely in the sense that market demand is prevented from arising for the development of particular land but in the sense also that development is prevented by planning restrictions. It might be thought that, as a principle of State policy, it would be logical to decide either that if there is 100 per cent betterment levy there should be no planning compensation, or that there should be 100 per cent compensation if there is no levy. In practice the policy applied has not been so simple, nor so logical.

The Town and Country Planning Act 1947 adopted the principle that, since betterment would be taxed at 100 per cent, there should be no compensation other than a once-for-all award to owners of land which already enjoyed development value before the "appointed day" when the Act came into force (1 July 1948). This logical but Draconian principle was jettisoned in 1952. There then followed a period of confusion in which those landowners who obtained planning permission retained the development value which then accrued, whereas those who did not were not compensated in lieu except in some limited classes of case.

These classes were abolished by section 31 of the Planning and Compensation Act 1991, subject to certain exceptions. Before section 31 came into force it was true to say that to obtain planning compensation for loss of development value caused by refusals of permission (or grants of permission subject to onerous conditions) was the exception and not the rule.[82] Thereafter such compensation ceased to be obtainable at all.[83]

(b) Entitlement to planning compensation today

Restrictions on development imposed by way of revocation, modification or discontinuance orders, since they are in effect regarded as interference with the enjoyment of development value previously conceded to an owner by the grant of planning

[80] Land Commission (Dissolution) Act 1971; Finance Act 1971, s. 55; Finance Act 1974, s. 38.

[81] Development Land Tax Act 1976, s. 1 (80%); Finance (No. 2) Act 1979, s. 24 (60%); Finance Act 1985, s. 93 (abolition).

[82] TCPA 1990, ss. 114, 119–36, repeating the substance of provisions dating back to TCPA 1954, under which compensation was payable for restrictions on development: (a) within TCPA 1990, Part II, Sch. 3, or (b) not within Sch. 3, but relating to land with a UXB; p. 1051, n. 77, ante. See *Peaktop Properties (Hampstead) Ltd v Camden LBC* (1983) 46 P & CR 177.

[83] But TCPA 1990, Sch. 3, as amended by Planning and Compensation Act 1991, Sch. 6, para. 40, retains two categories of such compensation which are obtainable in cases not of planning refusals but of compulsory purchase: p. 1045, n. 36, ante.

permission, are fully compensatable by the local planning authority.[84] This includes "article 4 directions".

Disputes are to be referred to the Lands Tribunal,[85] with the usual limited right of appeal to the Court of Appeal.[86] In addition to loss of development value, compensation may have to include abortive expenditure.[87]

III Law Reform

The current law of compulsory purchase of land is a patchwork of diverse rules, derived from a variety of statutes and cases over more than a hundred years, which are neither accessible to those affected, nor readily capable of interpretation save by specialists.[88] The case for reform has been recognised for many years.[89]

Two Consultative Reports were published by the Law Commission in 2002; the first dealt with Compensation, and the second with Procedure. The Final Reports in 2003 and 2004, entitled Towards a Compulsory Purchase Code, made recommendations for the reform of the law and, as their name implies, are not a Code but an indicative framework for one.

The Law Commissioner for Land and Trusts wrote in 2005:[90]

If the Government is serious about urban regeneration, the improvement of transport infrastructure, and the revitalisation of brownfield sites, whether it be for the Thames Gateway, for Crossrail or for the Olympic bid, an effective and efficient compulsory purchase process is essential. At the same time, clarification of the compensation principles on the basis of our compensation code will diminish the scope for argument, expedite settlement of disputes and promote greater fairness.

However, the Government does not consider that the substantial amount of additional work that would be necessary to turn the proposals into a workable code can be justified:[91]

the main value to us of the Commission's review of the law has been in confirming that there are no quick and easy solutions which could make the compulsory purchase process less daunting for both potential acquiring authorities and those whose property needs to be expropriated. The need to

---

[84] TCPA 1990, ss. 107–13, 115; p. 1027, ante. An example can be seen in *Blow v Norfolk County Council* [1967] 1 WLR 1280 (discontinuance order). For tree preservation orders and certain special cases of advertisements, see ss. 203–5, 223, and TCP (Control of Advertisements) Regs. 1992, reg. 17. See also *Bollans v Surrey County Council* (1968) 20 P & CR 745 (tree preservation). For listed buildings and building preservation notices, see Planning (Listed Buildings and Conservation Areas) Act 1990, ss. 28–31; p. 1034, ante.

[85] Ibid., ss. 118, 119. Market value is to be calculated "so far as applicable and subject to any necessary modifications" in accordance with the rules in Land Compensation Act 1961, s. 5; but it has to be assumed (irrespective of the facts) for development within Sch. 3 that there is permission which will reduce compensation, see *Canterbury City Council v Colley* [1993] AC 401.

[86] P. 1040, ante.

[87] See *Pennine Raceway Ltd v Kirklees Metropolitan BC* [1983] QB 382.

[88] Law Commission Final Report on Towards a Compulsory Purchase Code 2003 (Law Com No. 286), p. xiii.

[89] For judicial support for reform, see *Waters v Welsh Development Agency* [2004] 1 WLR 1304 at [164], per Lord Brown of Eaton-under-Heywood, and at [3], per Lord Nicholls of Birkenhead, citing *Waters v Welsh Development Agency* [2002] 4 All ER 384 at [116], per Carnwath LJ. See further *Ocean Leisure Ltd v Westminster City Council* [2004] 3 EGLR 9 at [34]–[39], per Carnwath LJ.

[90] Stuart Bridge, in The Times 1 February 2005, Law Supplement, p. 4. See also [2004] 51 EG 84 (S. Bridge).

[91] ODPM: Government Response to Law Commission Report: Towards a Compulsory Purchase Code (December 2005), para. 29.

protect the interests of the latter acts as a counterweight to attempts to make the acquisition process quicker and simpler and also explains much of the complexity of the ever-evolving statute and case law. Therefore, following the changes in the [Planning and Compulsory Purchase Act 2004], we see advantage in maintaining a period of stability where acquiring authorities can be certain of the ground rules within which they are operating. This will enable them to exercise their compulsory purchase powers to further their wider policy objectives wherever that makes sense in the public interest.

There will therefore be no reform in the foreseeable future.

SELECT BIBLIOGRAPHY

BLACKSTONE'S GUIDE TO THE LAND REGISTRATION ACT 2002, by R. Abbey and M. Richards, Oxford: Oxford University Press, 2002

AIGLER, R. W., A. F. SMITH and S. TEFFT *Cases and Materials on the Law of Property*, St Paul: West, 1960

ALDRIDGE, T. M. *Commonhold Law* (looseleaf), London: Sweet & Maxwell

ALDRIDGE, T. M. *Companion to the 4th edition of the Standard Conditions of Sale*, 3rd edn, London: Sweet & Maxwell, 2003

ALDRIDGE, T. M. *Leasehold Law* (looseleaf), London: FT Law and Tax

ALDRIDGE, T. M. *Letting Business Premises*, 8th edn, London: Sweet & Maxwell, 2004

ALDRIDGE, T. M. *Privity of Contract: Landlord and Tenant Covenants Act 1995*, London: FT Law and Tax, 1995

ALLEN, T. *Property and the Human Rights Act 1998*, Oxford: Hart Publishing, 2005

AMERICAN LAW INSTITUTE *Restatement of the Law: Property 3d: Mortgages*, Philadelphia: American Law Institute, 1997

ANDERSON, J. S. *Lawyers and the Making of English Law 1832–1940*, Oxford: Clarendon Press, 1992

ANNAND, R. and B. CAIN *Remedies under the Contract*, London: Sweet & Maxwell, 1988

ANSON'S LAW OF CONTRACT, by J. Beatson, 28th edn, Oxford: Oxford University Press, 2002

AUSTIN, J. *Lectures on Jurisprudence*, 5th edn by R. Campbell, London: John Murray, 1885

BACON, F. Reading on the Statute of Uses in *The Works of Francis Bacon*, London: J. Stephens, 1892; reprinted New York: Garland, 1979

BACON'S NEW ABRIDGEMENT OF THE LAW, 7th edn by Sir Henry Gwilliam and C. E. Dodd, London, 1832

BAKER, J. H. *An Introduction to English Legal History*, 4th edn, London: Butterworths, 2002

BARNES, D. M. W. *Leasehold Reform Act 1967*, London: Butterworths, 1968

BARNSLEY'S CONVEYANCING LAW AND PRACTICE, by M. P. Thompson, 4th edn, London: Butterworths, 1996

BARNSLEY'S LAND OPTIONS, by A. Rosenthal, M. Dray and C. Groves, 4th edn, London: Sweet & Maxwell, 2004

BARRACLOUGH, H. and P. MATTHEWS *The Trusts of Land and Appointment of Trustees Act 1996*, Sutton Coldfield: CLT Professional Publishing, 1996

BATES, J. H. *Water and Drainage Law* (looseleaf), London: Sweet & Maxwell

BAXENDALE-WALKER, P. *Purpose Trusts*, London: Butterworths, 1999

BEAN, J. M. W. *The Decline of English Feudalism*, Manchester: Manchester University Press, 1968

BEHAN, J. C. V. *The Use of Land as Affected by Covenants*, London: Sweet and Maxwell, 1924

BELL, J., S. BOYRON and S. WHITTAKER *Principles of French Law*, Oxford: Oxford University Press, 1998

BENNION, F. A. R. and P. DOBSON *Consumer Credit Control* (looseleaf), London: Longmans Professional

BERNSTEIN, R. and K. REYNOLDS *Essentials of Rent Review*, London, Sweet and Maxwell, 1995

BERRY, C., E. BAILEY and S. SCHAW MILLER *Personal Insolvency Law and Practice*, 3rd edn, London: Butterworths, 2001

BICKFORD S. and A. SYDENHAM *Party-Walls— Law and Practice*, 2nd edn, Bristol: Jordan, 2004

BICKFORD-SMITH, S. and A. FRANCIS *Rights of Light. The Modern Law*, Bristol: Jordan, 2000

BLACKSTONE, Sir William *Commentaries on the Laws of England*, 15th edn by E. Christian, London: Cadell and Davies, 1809

BLACKSTONE'S GUIDE TO COVENANTS FOR TITLE, by P. Kenny, London: Blackstone, 1995

BLACKSTONE'S GUIDE TO THE MENTAL CAPACITY ACT 2005, by P. Bartlett, Oxford: Oxford University Press, 2005

BLACKSTONE'S STATUTES ON PLANNING LAW, 3rd edn edited by V. Moore and D. Hughes, London: Blackstone, 2000

BONFIELD, L. *Marriage Settlements, 1601–1740*, Cambridge: Cambridge University Press, 1983

BRAND, C. M. *Compulsory Purchase and Compensation* (looseleaf), London: Sweet & Maxwell

BRAND, C. M. *Mobile Homes and the Law*, London: Sweet & Maxwell, 1986

BRICKDALE, C. F. and J. S. STEWART-WALLACE *The Land Registration Act 1925*, 4th edn, London: Stevens, 1939

BRIDGE, S. *Assured Tenancies*, London: Blackstone Press, 1999

BRIGHT, S. and J. DEWAR (eds.) *Land Law. Themes and Perspectives*, Oxford: Oxford University Press, 1998

BRIGHT, S. and G. GILBERT *Landlord and Tenant Law*, Oxford: Clarendon Press, 1995

BROMLEY'S FAMILY LAW, by N. V. Lowe and G. Douglas, 9th edn, London: Butterworths, 1998

BRUNYATE, J. B. *Limitation of Actions in Equity*, London: Stevens, 1932

BUCKLAND, W. W. *Textbook of Roman Law*, 3rd edn, revised by P. Stein, Cambridge: Cambridge University Press, 1963

BUCKLEY, R. A. *The Law of Nuisance*, 2nd edn, London: Butterworths, 1996

BURNETT, J. F. R. *The Elements of Conveyancing*, 8th edn, London: Sweet & Maxwell, 1952

BURROWS, A. *Remedies for Torts and Breach of Contract*, 3rd edn, Oxford: Oxford University Press, 2004

BURTON, W. H. *An Elementary Compendium of the Law of Real Property*, 8th edn by E. F. Cooper, London: Stevens & Norton, 1856

BUTTERWORTHS' PLANNING LAW HANDBOOK, 5th edn by B. Greenwood, London: Butterworths, 2000

CAFFYN, D. J. M. *The Right of Navigation on Non-Tidal Rivers*, Eastbourne: Caffyn, 2004

CARSON'S REAL PROPERTY STATUTES, edited by H. W. Law, 3rd edn, London: Sweet & Maxwell, 1927

CARTWRIGHT, J. *Misrepresentation*, London: Sweet & Maxwell, 2002

CHALLIS'S LAW OF REAL PROPERTY, 3rd edn by C. Sweet, London: Butterworths, 1911

CHERRY, Sir Benjamin *The New Property Acts. Series of Lectures with Questions and Answers*, London: Solicitors' Law Stationery Society, 1926

CHESHIRE, FIFOOT AND FURMSTON'S LAW OF CONTRACT, 14th edn by M. P. Furmston, London: Butterworths, 2001

CHITTY ON CONTRACTS, edited by H. G. Beale (general editor), 29th edn, London: Sweet & Maxwell, 2004, and supplements

CLARKE ON COMMONHOLD: LAW, PRACTICE AND PRECEDENTS, by D. Clarke, L. Crabb and N. Roberts, Bristol: Jordans, 2004

CLARKE, D. N. *Commonhold: The New Law*, Bristol: Jordans, 2002

CLARKE, M. *Mortgage Fraud*, London: Chapman & Hall, 1991

CLAYDEN, P. *Our Common Land. The Law and History of Commons and Village Greens*, 5th edn, Henley-on-Thames: Open Spaces Society, 2003

CLAYDEN, P. *The Law of Mobile Homes and Caravans*, 2nd edn, Crayford: Shaw, 2003

CLERK & LINDSELL ON TORTS, edited by A. M. Dugdale (general editor), 18th edn, London: Sweet & Maxwell, 2000, and supplements

COKE, Sir Edward *Complete Copyholder*, London, 1641

COKE, Sir Edward *Institutes of the Laws of England*, Part IV, 1644 [Co. Fourth Inst.]

COKE'S COMMENTARY UPON LITTLETON, 19th edn, with notes by F. Hargrave and C. Butler, London, 1832 [Co. Litt.]

COMYNS, SIR JOHN *A Digest of the Laws of England*, London, 1822

COOKE, E. (ed.) *Modern Studies in Property Law*, Oxford: Hart Publishing, 2001 (vol. 1), 2003 (vol. 2), 2005 (vol. 3)

COOKE, E. *The Modern Law of Estoppel*, Oxford: Oxford University Press, 2000

COOKE, E. *The New Law of Land Registration*, Oxford: Hart Publishing, 2003

COOTE'S TREATISE ON THE LAW OF MORTGAGES, 9th edn by R. L. Ramsbotham, London: Stevens, 1927

COUNCIL OF MORTGAGE LENDERS *Lenders' Handbook for England and Wales*, 2nd edn, 2002 (revised from time to time: the up-to-date version is available on the CML web site, www.cml.org.uk)

COUSINS, E. and I. CLARKE *The Law of Mortgages*, 2nd edn, London: Sweet & Maxwell, 2001

COWEN, G., J. DRISCOLL and L. TARGET *Commonhold Law and Practice*, London: Law Society, 2005

CRABB, L. *Leases Covenants and Consents*, London: Sweet & Maxwell, 1991

CRETNEY, S. M. and D. LUSH *Enduring Powers of Attorney*, 5th edn, Bristol: Jordans, 2001

CRETNEY S. M. and J. M. MASSON *Principles of Family Law*, 6th edn, London: Sweet & Maxwell, 1996

CRETNEY, S. M., J. M. MASSON and R. BAILEY-HARRIS *Principles of Family Law*, 7th edn, London: Sweet & Maxwell, 2003

CRUISE'S DIGEST OF THE LAWS OF ENGLAND, 4th edn by H. H. White, London, 1835

DARBY, J. G. N. and F. A. BOSANQUET, *A Practical Treatise on the Statutes of Limitations in England and Ireland*, 2nd edn by F. A. Bosanquet and J. R. V. Marchant, London: W. Clowes and Sons Ltd, 1893

DART'S VENDORS AND PURCHASERS OF REAL ESTATE, 8th edn by E. P. Hewitt and M. R. C. Overton, London: Stevens, 1929

DAVIES, K. *Law of Compulsory Purchase and Compensation*, 5th edn, Croydon: Tolley, 1994

DAWSON I. J. and R. A. PEARCE *Licences Relating to the Occupation or Use of Land*, London: Butterworths, 1979

DENYER-GREEN, B. *Compulsory Purchase and Compensation*, 8th edn, London: Estates Gazette, 2005

DERHAM, R. *The Law of Set-off*, 3rd edn, Oxford: Oxford University Press, 2003

DICEY, A. V. *Lectures on the Relation between Law and Public Opinion in England during the Nineteenth Century*, 2nd edn (reissued) with a preface by E. C. S. Wade, London: Macmillan, 1962

DIGBY, K. E. and W. M. HARRISON *An Introduction to the History of Law of Real Property*, 5th edn, Oxford: Clarendon Press, 1897

DIGEST OF JUSTINIAN, edited by T. Mommsen and P. Krueger and translated by A. Watson, Philadelphia: University of Pennsylvania Press, 1985

DOWDING, N. and K. REYNOLDS *Dilapidations. The Modern Law and Practice*, 3rd edn, London: Sweet & Maxwell, 2004

DUGDALE A. M. and K. M. STANTON *Professional Negligence*, 3rd edn, London: Butterworths, 1998

DUXBURY, R. M. C. *Planning Law and Procedure*, 13th edn, Oxford: Oxford University Press, 2005

EASTON, H. C. *The Law of Rentcharges (commonly called chief rents) mainly from a conveyancing standpoint*, 2nd edn, London: Sweet & Maxwell, 1931

EEKELAAR, J. and J. BELL (eds.) *Oxford Essays in Jurisprudence: Third Series*, Oxford: Clarendon Press, 1987

ELLIS, P. *Rights to Light*, London: Estates Gazette, 1989

ELPHINSTONE, Sir Lancelot *Covenants affecting Land*, London: Law Stationery Society, 1946

ELPHINSTONE, Sir Lancelot *Introduction to Conveyancing*, 7th edn by F. T. Maw, London: Sweet & Maxwell, 1918

EMMET AND FARRAND ON TITLE, by J. Farrand and A. Clarke (looseleaf), London: Longman

ENCYCLOPEDIA OF CONSUMER CREDIT LAW, edited by E. Lomnicka (looseleaf), London: Sweet & Maxwell

ENCYCLOPEDIA OF ENVIRONMENTAL LAW, edited by R. Wald (general editor) (loose-leaf), London: Sweet & Maxwell

ENCYCLOPAEDIA OF FORMS AND PRECEDENTS, 5th edn (1985) edited by Sir Raymond Walton, and since 1985 by Lord Millett, London: Butterworths

ENCYCLOPEDIA OF PLANNING LAW AND PRACTICE, edited by C. Lockhart-Mummery, J. Harper, D. Elvin and M. Grant (looseleaf), London: Sweet & Maxwell

ENCYCLOPEDIA OF THE LAW OF COMPULSORY PURCHASE AND COMPENSATION, edited by H. J. J. Brown (general editor) (looseleaf), London: Sweet & Maxwell

ENGLISH, B. and J. SAVILLE *Strict Settlement*, Hull: Hull University Press, 1985

EVANS and SMITH: *The Law of Landlord and Tenant*, 6th edn by P. F. Smith, London: Butterworths, 2002

FAIREST, P. B. *Mortgages*, 2nd edn, London: Sweet & Maxwell, 1980

FANCOURT, T. M. *Enforceability of Landlord and Tenant Covenants*, London: Sweet & Maxwell, 1997

FARRAND, J. T. *Contract and Conveyance*, 2nd edn, London: Oyez Longman, 1973; 4th edn, 1983

FARWELL ON POWERS, 3rd edn by C. J. W. Farwell and F. K. Archer, London: Stevens, 1916

FEARNE, Charles *An Essay on the Learning of Contingent Remainders and Executory Devises*, 10th edn, with notes by C. Butler, with *An Original View of Executory Interests in Real and Personal Property*, by Josiah W. Smith, London: Stevens & Norton, 1844

FETHERSTONHAUGH, G., M. SEFTON and E. PETERS *Commonhold*, Oxford: Oxford University Press, 2004

FINN, P. D. *Essays in Equity*, Sydney: Law Book Co., 1985

FISHER AND LIGHTWOOD'S LAW OF MORTGAGE, 11th edn edited by W. Clarke and others, London: Butterworths, 2001; and supplement 2003

FOA'S GENERAL LAW OF LANDLORD AND TENANT, 8th edn by H. Heathcote-Williams, Ipswich: Thames Bank Publishing Co., 1957

FRANCIS, A. *Restrictive Covenants and Freehold Land*, 2nd edn, Bristol: Jordans, 2005

FRANKS, M. J. A. *Limitation of Actions*, London: Sweet & Maxwell, 1959

FREEDMAN, E. SHAPIRO and B. SLATER *Service Charges. Law and Practice*, 3rd edn, Bristol: Jordans, 2002

FROUDE, J. A. *History of England, from the Fall of Wolsey to the Defeat of the Spanish Armada*, new edn, London: Longmans, Green and Co., 1893

FRY, Sir Charles *A Treatise on the Specific Performance of Contracts*, 6th edn by G. R. Northcote, London: Sweet & Maxwell/Ashford Press, 1921

FURBER, J., J. KARAS, J. EVANS and T. SCOTT *The Commonhold and Leasehold Reform Act 2002*, London: Butterworths, 2002

GADSDEN ON COMMONS AND GREENS, by E. Cousins and N. de Poidevin, 2nd edn, London: Sweet & Maxwell, 2005

GAIUS *The Institutes of Gaius*, Part I, translated by F. de Zulueta, Oxford: Clarendon Press, 1946

GALE ON EASEMENTS, 11th edn, edited by G. Glover, London: Sweet & Maxwell, 1932

GALE ON EASEMENTS, 12th edn, edited by D. H. McMullen, London: Sweet & Maxwell, 1950

GALE ON EASEMENTS, 17th edn, edited by J. Gaunt and P. Morgan, London: Sweet & Maxwell, 2002; and supplement, 2005

GARNER'S LOCAL LAND CHARGES, by J. E. Boothroyd, 13th edn, Crayford: Shaw, 2005

GETZLER, J. *A History of Water Rights at Common Law*, Oxford: Oxford University Press, 2004

GETZLER, J. (ed.) *Rationalizing Property, Equity and Trusts: Essays in Honour of Edward Burn*, London: LexisNexis UK, 2003

GILBERT, Sir Jeffrey *A Treatise on Rents*, London, 1758

GILBERT ON USES AND TRUSTS, 3rd edn by E. B. Sugden, London, 1811

GOFF (Lord Goff of Chieveley) and G. JONES *The Law of Restitution*, 6th edn, London: Sweet & Maxwell, 2004

GOODE, R. M. (general editor) *Consumer Credit Laws and Practice* (looseleaf), London: Butterworths

GOUGH, W. J. *Company Charges*, London: Butterworths, 1995

GRAY, C. M. *Copyhold, Equity and the Common Law*, Cambridge, Mass.: Harvard University Press, 1963

GRAY, J. C. *The Rule against Perpetuities*, 4th edn by R. Gray, Boston: Little Brown, 1942

HAGUE'S LEASEHOLD ENFRANCHISEMENT, by A. Radevsky and D. Greenish, 4th edn, London: Sweet & Maxwell, 2003; and supplement, 2005

HALEY, M. *Statutory Regulation of Business Tenancies*, Oxford: Oxford University Press, 2000

HALL, J. E. *A Treatise of the Law relating to Profits a prendre and Rights of Common*, London: Sweet, 1871

HALSBURY'S LAWS OF ENGLAND, editor in chief Lord Hailsham of St Marylebone LC, and since 1998 Lord Mackay of Clashfern LC 4th edn, London: Butterworths, 1973–98

HANBURY AND MARTIN, *Modern Equity*, 17th edn by J. E. Martin, London: Sweet & Maxwell, 2005

HARGREAVES A. D. *An Introduction to the Principles of Land Law*, 4th edn by G. A. Grove and J. F. Garner, London: Sweet & Maxwell, 1963

HARPUM, C. and J. BIGNELL *Registered Land: Law and Practice under the Land Registration Act 2002*, Bristol: Jordans, 2004

HARPUM, C. and J. BIGNELL *Registered Land: The New Law*, Bristol: Jordans, 2002

HARRIS, B. and G. RYAN *An Outline of the Law Relating to Common Land and Public Access to the Countryside*, London: Sweet & Maxwell, 1967

HARRIS, J. *Property and Justice*, Oxford: Clarendon Press, 1996

HARRIS, J. *Variation of Trusts*, London: Sweet & Maxwell, 1975

HARVEY, B. W. *Settlements of Land*, London: Sweet & Maxwell, 1973

HAWKINS AND RYDER ON THE CONSTRUCTION OF WILLS, edited by E. C. Ryder, London: Sweet & Maxwell, 1965

HAYES, William *An Introduction to Conveyancing*, 5th edn, London: Sweet, 1840

HAYTON, D. J. *Registered Land*, 3rd edn, London: Sweet & Maxwell, 1981

HEWITSON, R. *Business Tenancies*, London: Cavendish, 2005

HEYWOOD AND MASSEY: *Court of Protection Practice*, 13th edn by N. A. Heywood, A. S. Massey and D. Lush (looseleaf), London: Sweet & Maxwell, 2001

HILL, Sir George *Treasure Trove in Law and Practice from the Earliest Time to the Present Day*, Oxford: Clarendon Press, 1936

HILL AND REDMAN'S GUIDE TO LANDLORD AND TENANT LAW, edited by J. Furber (general editor), London: Butterworths, 1999

HILL AND REDMAN'S GUIDE TO RENT REVIEW, by M. Barnes, London: Butterworths, 2001

HILL AND REDMAN'S LANDLORD AND TENANT, edited by J. Furber (general editor) (looseleaf), London: Butterworths

HOLDSWORTH, Sir William *A History of English Law*, London: Methuen, 1903–1972

HOLDSWORTH, Sir William *An Historical Introduction to the Land Law*, Oxford: Clarendon Press, 1927

HOLYOAK, J. H. and D. K. ALLEN *Civil Liability for Defective Premises*, London: Butterworths, 1982

HUGHES, D. and S. LOWE *Public Sector Housing Law*, 3rd edn, London: Butterworths, 2000

IBBETSON, D. *A Historical Introduction to the Law of Obligations*, Oxford: Oxford University Press, 1999

INTERNATIONAL ENCYCLOPEDIA OF COMPARATIVE LAW, vol. VI, *Property and Trust*, edited by F. H. Lawson (general editor), Tübingen: JCB Mohr (Paul Siebeck), 1973

JACKSON AND POWELL ON PROFESSIONAL NEGLIGENCE, by J. Powell and R. Stewart, 5th edn, London: Sweet & Maxwell, 2002

JACKSON, P. *The Law of Easements and Profits*, London: Butterworths, 1978

JACKSON, P. and D. C. WILDE (eds.) *Reform of Property Law*, Aldershot: Dartmouth, 1997

JARMAN ON WILLS, 8th edn by R. W. Jennings and J. C. Harper, London: Sweet & Maxwell, 1951

JENKS, E. *Modern Land Law*, Oxford: Clarendon Press, 1899

JESSEL, C. *Law of the Manor*, Chichester: Barry Rose Law, 1998

JESSEL, C. *Law of the Manor: the Twenty-First Century*, Chichester: Barry Rose Law, 2004

JONES, G. and W. GOODHART *Specific Performance*, 2nd edn, London: Butterworths, 1996

JONES, J. H. E. *The Lands Tribunal—a Practitioner's Guide*, London: Hubert Bewlay Fund, 1932

JONES, R. *Mental Capacity Act Manual*, London: Sweet & Maxwell, 2005

JOSLING, J. F. *Periods of Limitation*, 7th edn, London: Longman, 1989

JOURDAN, S. *Adverse Possession*, London: Butterworths, 2003

KEATING ON BUILDING CONTRACTS, 7th edn by V. Ramsey and S. Furst, London: Sweet & Maxwell, 2001; and supplement, 2004

KENNY, A. *Forfeiture of Tenancies*, London: Blackstone, 1999

SWEET AND MAXWELL'S CONVEYANCING PRACTICE, by P. Kenny, J. Alexander and A. M. Kenny (looseleaf), London: Sweet & Maxwell

KENNY, P. and A. KENNY *The Trusts of Land and Appointment of Trustees Act 1996*, London: Sweet and Maxwell, 1997

LAWSON, F. H. *The Rational Strength of English Law*, London: Stevens, 1951

LAWSON, F. H. and B. RUDDEN *The Law of Property*, 3rd edn, Oxford: Clarendon Press, 2002

LAWSON, R. G. *Exclusion Clauses and Unfair Contract Terms*, 6th edn, London: Sweet & Maxwell, 2000

LEAKE, S. M. *A Digest of the Law of Uses and Profits of Land*, London: Stevens, 1888

LEWISON, K. *Drafting Business Leases*, 6th edn, London: Sweet & Maxwell, 2000

LEWISON, K. *Interpretation of Contracts*, 3rd edn, London: Sweet & Maxwell, 2004

LEWISON, K. *Lease or Licence: The Law after Street v Mountford*, London: Longman Professional, 1985

LIGHTWOOD, J. M. *A Treatise on Possession of Land*, London: Stevens, 1894

LITTLETON'S TENURES (1481). See Coke's Commentary upon Littleton (Co. Litt)

MACLEAN, D. M. *Trusts and Powers*, London: Sweet and Maxwell, 1989

MAITLAND, F. W. *Equity*, revised by John Brunyate, Cambridge: Cambridge University Press, 1936

MAITLAND F. W. *Forms of Action at Common Law*, edited by A. H. Chaytor and W. J. Whittaker, Cambridge: Cambridge University Press, 1936

MAITLAND, F. W. *The Collected Papers of Frederick William Maitland*, edited by H. A. L. Fisher, Cambridge: Cambridge University Press, 1911

MAITLAND, F. W. *The Constitutional History of England*, Cambridge: Cambridge University Press, 1908

MARKBY, W. *Elements of Law*, Oxford: Clarendon Press, 1905

MARTIN, J. E. *Residential Security*, 2nd edn, London: Sweet & Maxwell, 1995

MASON, S. *Electronic Signatures in Law*, London: LexisNexis UK, 2003

MAUDSLEY, R. H. *The Modern Law of Perpetuities*, London: Butterworths, 1979

MAUDSLEY AND BURN'S LAND LAW: *Cases and Materials*, 8th edn by E. H. Burn, Oxford: Oxford University Press, 2004

MAUDSLEY AND BURN'S TRUSTS AND TRUSTEES: *Cases and Materials*, 6th edn by E. H. Burn and G. Virgo, London: Butterworths, 2002

MCAUSLAN, P. *Land, Law and Planning: Cases, Materials and Text*, London: Weidenfeld & Nicolson, 1975

MCCORMACK, G. *Registration of Company Charges*, 2nd edn, Bristol: Jordans, 2005

McCracken, R., G. Jones, J. Pereira and S. Payne *Statutory Nuisance Law and Practice*, London: Butterworths, 2001

McCutcheon on Inheritance Tax, 4th edn by B. D. McCutcheon with Withers LLP, London: Sweet & Maxwell, 2005

McGee, A. *Limitation Periods*, 4th edn, London: Sweet & Maxwell, 2004 and supplements

McNair, Sir Arnold *The Law of the Air*, 3rd edn by M. R. E. Kerr and A. H. M. Evans, London: Stevens, 1964

Megarry, Sir Robert *The Rent Acts*, 11th edn, London: Stevens; vols. 1 and 2 by general editors J. S. Colyer and Sir Robert Megarry, 1988; vol. 3 by Sir Robert Megarry and A. Arden, 1989

Megarry, Sir Robert and H. W. R. Wade *The Law of Real Property*, 5th edn, London: Sweet & Maxwell, 1984; 6th edn, edited by C. Harpum, 1999

Miller, J. G. *The Machinery of Succession*, 2nd edn, Aldershot: Dartmouth, 1996

Moore, V. *A Practical Approach to Planning Law*, 9th edn, Oxford: Oxford University Press, 2005

Morris, J. H. C. and W. Barton Leach *The Rule against Perpetuities*, 2nd edn, London: Stevens, 1962; with supplement, 1964

Muir Hunter on Personal Insolvency by J. Briggs, C. Brougham and M. Hunter (looseleaf), London: Stevens

Muir Watt. See Watt, J. Muir

Nicholas, B. *An Introduction to Roman Law*, Oxford: Clarendon Press, 1962

Oakley, A. J. *Constructive Trusts*, 3rd edn, London: Sweet & Maxwell, 1997

Osborn, C. *Mortgage Fraud*, Birmingham: CLT Professional Publishing, 1995

Oswald, R. *A Practitioner's Guide to Common Land and Commons Registration Act 1965*, Oxford: ESC, 1989

Oughton, D. W., J. P. Lowry and R. M. Merkin, *Limitation of Actions*, London: LLP, 1998

Parry and Clark on the Law of Succession, 11th edn by R. Kerridge, London: Sweet & Maxwell, 2002

Partington, M. *Landlord and Tenant: Cases, Materials, and Text*, London: Weidenfeld & Nicolson, 1975

Pawlowski, M. *The Doctrine of Proprietary Estoppel*, London: Sweet & Maxwell, 1996

Pawlowski, M. *The Forfeiture of Leases*, London: Sweet & Maxwell, 1993

Platt, Thomas *A Practical Treatise on the Law of Covenants*, London: Saunders & Benning, 1829

Platt, Thomas *A Treatise on the Law of Leases*, London: A. Maxwell, 1847

Plucknett, T. F. T. *A Concise History of the Common Law*, 5th edn, London: Butterworths, 1956

Plucknett, T. F. T. *Legislation of Edward I*, Oxford: Clarendon Press, 1949

Pollock, Sir Frederick *The Land Laws*, 3rd edn, London: Macmillan, 1896

Pollock, Sir Frederick and F. W. Maitland *The History of English Law before the time of Edward I*, 2nd edn, Cambridge: Cambridge University Press, 1898, revised with introduction and bibliography by S. F. Milsom, 1968

Pollock, F. and R. S. Wright *An Essay on Possession in the Common Law*, Oxford: Clarendon Press, 1888

Potter, H. *Principles and Practice of Conveyancing under the Land Registration 1925*, London: Sweet & Maxwell, 1934; 2nd edn, 1948

Preston, Richard *An Elementary Treatise on Estates*, 2nd edn, London, 1820–7

Preston, Richard *An Essay in a Course of Lectures on Abstracts of Title*, 2nd edn, London, 1823

Preston and Newsom on Limitation of Actions, by G. H. Newsom and L. Abel-Smith, 3rd edn, London: Solicitors' Law Stationery Society, 1953

Preston and Newsom on Limitation of Actions, by S. Weeks, 4th edn, London: Longman, 1989

Preston and Newsom's Restrictive Covenants Affecting Freehold Land, 4th edn by G. H. Newsom, London: Sweet & Maxwell, 1967

PRESTON AND NEWSOM'S RESTRICTIVE COVENANTS AFFECTING FREEHOLD LAND, 9th edn by G. L. Newsom, London: Sweet & Maxwell, 1998

PRIME, T. and G. SCANLAN *The Modern Law of Limitation*, London: Butterworths, 1993

REDMOND-COOPER, R. *Limitation of Actions*, London: Sweet & Maxwell, 1992

REID, K. *Abolition of Feudal Tenure in Scotland*, Edinburgh: Butterworths Scotland, 2003

REYNOLDS, K. and W. CLARK *Renewal of Business Tenancies*, 2nd edn, London: Sweet & Maxwell, 2004

REYNOLDS, K. and G. FETHERSTONHAUGH *Handbook of Rent Review* (looseleaf), London: Sweet & Maxwell

ROBINSON, S. S. *Law of Game, Salmon and Freshwater Fishing in Scotland*, Edinburgh: Butterworths, 1990

RODGERS, C. P. *Agricultural Law*, 2nd edn, London: Butterworths, 1998

RODGERS, C. P. *Housing Law Residential Security and Enfranchisement*, revised edn, London: Butterworths, 2002

ROOK, D. *Distress for Rent*, London: Blackstone, 1999

ROOK, D. *Property Law and Human Rights*, London: Blackstone, 2001

ROPER, R. B., C. WEST, M. DIXON, D. FOX, S. COVENEY, S. WHEELER and P. MILNE *Registered Conveyancing* (looseleaf edn), London: Sweet & Maxwell, 2003

ROSS, Murray J. *Drafting and Negotiating Commercial Leases*, by T. Bell and others (looseleaf), 5th edn, London: Butterworths, 1988

ROUND, J. H. *Feudal England*, London: Swan Sonnenschein, 1895

ROWTON SIMPSON, S. *Land Law and Registration*, Cambridge: Cambridge University Press, 1976

RUBIN, G. R. and David SUGARMAN (eds.) *Law, Economy and Society, 1750–1914: Essays in the History of English Law*, Abingdon: Professional Books, 1984

RUDALL, A. R. *Party Walls*, 3rd edn, London: Jordan & Sons, 1922

RUOFF, T. B. F. *Rentcharges in Registered Conveyancing*, London: Sweet & Maxwell, 1961

RUOFF, T. B. F. and E. J. PRYER *Concise Land Registration Handbook Forms and Practice*, London: Sweet & Maxwell, 1990

RUOFF, T. B. F., R. B. ROPER, E. J. PRYER, C. WEST, R. FEARNELY and J. DONALDSON *The Law and Practice of Registered Conveyancing* (looseleaf edn), London: Sweet & Maxwell, 1991

SALMOND AND HEUSTON ON THE LAW OF TORTS, 21st edn by R. F. V. Heuston and R. A. Buckley, London: Sweet & Maxwell, 1996

SANDERS ON USES AND TRUSTS, 5th edn by G. W. Sanders and J. Warner, London: A. Maxwell, 1844

SARA, C. *Boundaries and Easements*, 3rd edn, London: Sweet & Maxwell, 2002; and supplement, 2004

SAUVAIN, S. *Highway Law*, 3rd edn, London: Sweet & Maxwell, 2004

SCAMELL, E. H. *Land Covenants, Restrictive and Positive, relating to Freehold Land, including Covenants for Title*, London: Butterworths, 1996

SCAMELL AND DENSHAM'S LAW OF AGRICULTURAL HOLDINGS, by H. A. C. Densham and D. Evans, 8th edn, London: Butterworths, 1997

SCOTT, Sir Leslie *The New Law of Property Explained*, with annotations by B. B. Benas, London: Sweet, 1925

SCRIVEN, J. *A Treatise on the Law of Copyholds*, 7th edn by A. Brown, London: Butterworth & Co., 1896

SCRUTTON, T. E. *Land in Fetters*, Cambridge: Cambridge University Press, 1886

SHEPPARD'S TOUCHSTONE OF COMMON ASSURANCES, 8th edn by E. G. Atherley, London, 1826

SHERRIFF, G. *Service Charges in Leases: A Practical Guide*, London: Waterlow, 1989

SHERRIN C. H. and R. C. BONEHILL *The Law and Practice of Intestate Succession*, 3rd edn, London: Sweet & Maxwell, 2004

SILVERMAN, F. *Standard Conditions of Sale*, 6th edn, Croydon: Tolley, 1999

SILVERMAN, F. *The Law Society's Conveyancing Handbook*, 12th edn, London: Law Society, 2005

SILVERMAN, F., P. WILDE and P. BUTT, *Conveyancing Searches and Enquiries*, 3rd edn, Bristol: Jordans, 2004

SIMES, Lewis M. *Public Policy and the Dead Hand*, Ann Arbor: University of Michigan Law School, 1955

SIMPSON, A. W. B. *A History of the Land Law*, 2nd edn, Oxford: Clarendon Press, 1986

SIMPSON, S. Rowton *Land Law and Registration*, Cambridge: Cambridge University Press, 1976

SLADE, Sir Christopher *The Informal Creation of Interests in Land* (public lecture given by the Rt Hon Sir Christopher Slade, Lord Justice of Appeal, on 2 March 1984, Child & Co. Oxford lecture), Oxford, 1984

SMITH, J. C. *Liability in Negligence*, London: Sweet & Maxwell, 1984

SMITH, R. J. *Plural Ownership*, Oxford: Oxford University Press, 2005

SMITH, R. J. *Property Law*, 5th edn, Harlow: Longman, 2005

SMITH'S LEADING CASES, 13th edn by Sir Thomas Chitty, A. T. Denning and C. P. Harvey, London: Sweet & Maxwell, 1929

SNELL'S EQUITY, 31st edn by J. McGhee, London: Sweet & Maxwell, 2005, and supplement

SPARKES, P. *A New Landlord and Tenant*, Oxford: Hart, 2001

SPEAIGHT A. and G. STONE *The Law of Defective Premises*, London: Pitman, 1982

SPENCER BOWER, G. and A. K. TURNER *Estoppel by Representation*, 4th edn by P. Feltham, D. Hochberg and T. Leech, London: Lexis Nexis UK, 2003

SPRING, E. *Law, Land and Family: Aristocratic Inheritance in England, 1300 to 1800*, London: Chapel Hill, 1993

STENTON, F. M. *William the Conqueror and the Rule of the Normans*, new edn, London: Putnam, 1925

STOREY'S CONVEYANCING, by I. R. Storey, S. Peaple and A. Hunjan, 5th edn, London: Butterworths, 2001

STUBBS, W. *The Constitutional History of England in its Origin and Development*, 3 vols., Oxford: Clarendon Press, 1874 (vol. i), 1875 (vol. ii), 1878 (vol. iii)

SUGDEN, Edward *A Practical Treatise of Powers*, 9th edn, London: H. Sweet, 1861

SUGDEN, Edward, *The Law of Vendors and Purchasers of Estates*, 14th edn, London: H. Sweet, 1862

SUTHERLAND, D. W. *The Assize of Novel Disseisin*, Oxford: Clarendon Press, 1973

SYDENHAM, A. and V. MAINWARING *Farm Business Tenancies—The Agricultural Tenancies Act 1995*, Bristol: Jordans, 1995

SYDENHAM A. and C. SYDENHAM *Trusts of Land—The New Law*, Bristol: Jordans, 1996

TANNEY, A. and I. TRAVERS *Distress for Rent*, Bristol: Jordans, 2000

TEE, L. *Land Law Issues, Debates, Policy*, Cullompton: Willan, 2002

THEOBALD ON WILLS, 16th edn by J. G. Ross Martyn, S. Bridge and M. Oldham, London: Sweet & Maxwell, 2001

THOMAS ON POWERS, by G. Thomas, London: Sweet & Maxwell, 1998

THOMPSON, M. P. *Co-ownership*, London: Sweet & Maxwell, 1988

TREITEL, G. H. *The Law of Contract*, 11th edn, London: Sweet & Maxwell, 2003

TROMANS, S. *Commercial Leases*, 2nd edn, London: Sweet & Maxwell, 1996

TROMANS, S. and K. FULLER *Environmental Impact Assessment Law and Practice*, London: LexisNexis UK, 2003

TROMANS, S. and R. TURRALL-CLARKE *Contaminated Land*, London: Sweet & Maxwell, 1998, and supplement

TUDOR'S LEADING CASES ON REAL PROPERTY Conveyancing, and the Construction of Wills and Deeds, 4th edn by T. H. Carson and H. B. Bompas, London, 1898

TURNER, R. W. *The Equity of Redemption*, Cambridge: Cambridge University Press, 1931

UBHI, N. and B. DENYER-GREEN *Law of Commons, Town and Village Greens*, Bristol: Jordans, 2004

UNDERHILL, A. *A Century of Law Reform*, 1911

UNDERHILL, A. *A Concise Explanation of Lord Birkenhead's Act (the Law of Property Act 1922) in Plain Language*, London: Butterworths, 1922

UNDERHILL, A. and HAYTON, D. J. *Law relating to Trusts and Trustees*, 16th edn by D. J. Hayton, London: Butterworths, 2003

VAIZEY, J. S. *A Treatise on the Law of Settlements of Property*, London: H. Sweet, 1887

VINER, Charles *A General Abridgement of Law and Equity*, 2nd edn, London: G.G.J. and J. Robinson, 1791

VINOGRADOFF, P. *Villainage in England*, Oxford: Clarendon Press, 1892

WAITE, A. and T. JEWELL *Environmental Law in Property Transactions*, 3rd edn by M. Woods, T. Jewell and A. Waite, London: LexisNexis UK, 2005

WALDOCK, C. H. M. *The Law of Mortgages*, 2nd edn, London: Stevens, 1950

WALKER, G. C. P. *Charging Orders Against Land*, 2nd edn, Chichester: Barry Rose, 2004

WARBURTON, J. *Unincorporated Associations: Law and Practice*, 2nd edn, London: Sweet & Maxwell, 1990

WATT, J. Muir and J. R. Moss *Agricultural Holdings*, 14th edn, London: Sweet & Maxwell, 1998

WEBBER, G. *Business Premises: Possession and Lease Renewal*, 3rd edn, London: Sweet & Maxwell, 2000

WEBBER, G. *Residential Possession Proceedings*, 7th edn, London: Sweet & Maxwell, 2005

WEST AND SMITH'S LAW OF DILAPIDATIONS, edited by P. F. Smith, 11th edn, London: Estates Gazette, 2001

WHITE AND TUDOR'S LEADING CASES IN EQUITY, 9th edn by E. P. Hewitt and J. B. Richardson, London: Sweet & Maxwell, 1928

WHITEHOUSE, C. and N. HASSALL *Trust of Land, Trustee Delegation and the Trustee Act 2000*, 2nd edn, London: Butterworths, 2001

WILKEN, S. *The Law of Waiver, Variation and Estoppel*, 2nd edn, Oxford: Oxford University Press, 2002

WILKINSON, H. W. *The Standard Conditions of Sale of Land*, 4th edn, London: Longman, 1990

WILLIAMS, D., C. M. BRAND and C. HUBBARD *Handbook of Business Tenancies* (looseleaf), London: Sweet & Maxwell

WILLIAMS, D., E. SHAPIRO and J. THOM *Handbook of Dilapidations* (looseleaf), London: Sweet & Maxwell

WILLIAMS, James *The Statute of Frauds: Section Four, in the Light of its Judicial Interpretation*, Cambridge: Cambridge University Press, 1932

WILLIAMS, Joshua *Principles of the Law of Real Property*, 13th edn, London: Sweet, 1880

WILLIAMS, Joshua *Rights of Common and Other Prescriptive Rights*, London: H. Sweet, 1880

WILLIAMS, T. Cyprian and J. M. LIGHTWOOD *A Treatise on the Law of Vendor and Purchaser of Real Estate and Chattels Real*, 4th edn, London: Sweet & Maxwell, 1936

WILLIAMS ON WILLS, 8th edn by C. H. Sherrin, R. F. D. Barlow, R. A. Wallington, S. L. Meadway and M. Waterworth, London: Butterworths, 2002

WOLSTENHOLME AND CHERRY'S ANNOTATED LAND REGISTRATION ACT 2002, by I. Clarke and J. Farrand, London: Sweet & Maxwell, 2004

WOLSTENHOLME AND CHERRY'S CONVEYANCING STATUTES, 11th edn by Sir Benjamin Cherry, J. Chadwick and J. R. P. Maxwell, London: Stevens, 1925–7

WOLSTENHOLME AND CHERRY'S CONVEYANCING STATUTES, 12th edn by Sir Benjamin Cherry, D. H. Parry and J. R. P. Maxwell, London: Stevens, 1932

WOLSTENHOLME AND CHERRY'S CONVEYANCING STATUTES, 13th edn by J. T. Farrand, London: Oyez, 1972

WONTNER'S GUIDE TO LAND REGISTRY PRACTICE, 21st edn by P. J. Timothy and A. Barker, London: Sweet & Maxwell, 2005

WOODFALL LANDLORD AND TENANT, edited by K. Lewison (looseleaf), London: Sweet & Maxwell

WOOLRYCH, H. W. *A Treatise on the Law of Rights of Common*, 2nd edn by H. W. Woolrych, London: Benning, 1850

WURTZBURG AND MILLS BUILDING SOCIETY LAW, 15th edn by Sir Timothy Lloyd, M. Waters and E. Ovey (looseleaf), London: Stevens

WYLIE, J. C. W. *Irish Land Law*, 3rd edn, Dublin: Butterworths, 1997

ZIMMERMANN, R., D. VISSER and K. REID (eds.) *Mixed Legal Systems in Comparative Perspective*, Oxford: Oxford University Press, 2004

INDEX

A consolidated list of terms described or defined is to be found under the entry "definitions and descriptions"